Lecture Notes in Computer Science 11239

Commenced Publication in 1973
Founding and Former Series Editors:
Gerhard Goos, Juris Hartmanis, and Jan van Leeuwen

More information about this series at http://www.springer.com/series/7410

Amos Beimel · Stefan Dziembowski (Eds.)

Theory of Cryptography

16th International Conference, TCC 2018
Panaji, India, November 11–14, 2018
Proceedings, Part I

Springer

Editors
Amos Beimel
Ben Gurion University
Beer Sheva, Israel

Stefan Dziembowski
University of Warsaw
Warsaw, Poland

ISSN 0302-9743 ISSN 1611-3349 (electronic)
Lecture Notes in Computer Science
ISBN 978-3-030-03806-9 ISBN 978-3-030-03807-6 (eBook)
https://doi.org/10.1007/978-3-030-03807-6

Library of Congress Control Number: 2018960441

LNCS Sublibrary: SL4 – Security and Cryptology

This Springer imprint is published by the registered company Springer Nature Switzerland AG
The registered company address is: Gewerbestrasse 11, 6330 Cham, Switzerland

Preface

The 16th Theory of Cryptography Conference (TCC 2018) was held during November 11–14, 2018, at the Cidade de Goa hotel, in Panaji, Goa, India. It was sponsored by the International Association for Cryptologic Research (IACR). The general chairs of the conference were Shweta Agrawal and Manoj Prabhakaran. We would like to thank them for their hard work in organizing the conference.

The conference received 168 submissions, of which the Program Committee (PC) selected 50 for presentation (with two pairs of papers sharing a single presentation slot per pair). Each submission was reviewed by at least three PC members, often more. The 30 PC members (including PC chairs), all top researchers in our field, were helped by 211 external reviewers, who were consulted when appropriate. These proceedings consist of the revised version of the 50 accepted papers. The revisions were not reviewed, and the authors bear full responsibility for the content of their papers.

As in previous years, we used Shai Halevi's excellent Web-review software, and are extremely grateful to him for writing it, and for providing fast and reliable technical support whenever we had any questions. Based on the experience from previous years, we again made use of the interaction feature supported by the review software, where PC members may anonymously interact with authors. This was used to ask specific technical questions, such as suspected bugs. We felt this approach helped us prevent potential misunderstandings and improved the quality of the review process.

This was the fifth year that TCC presented the Test of Time Award to an outstanding paper that was published at TCC at least eight years ago, making a significant contribution to the theory of cryptography, preferably with influence also in other areas of cryptography, theory, and beyond. This year the Test of Time Award Committee selected the following paper, published at TCC 2005: "Evaluating 2-DNF Formulas on Ciphertexts" by Dan Boneh, Eu-Jin Goh, and Kobbi Nissim. This paper was selected for introducing compact two-operation homomorphic encryption and developing new bilinear map techniques that led to major improvements in the design of cryptographic schemes. The authors were also invited to deliver a talk at TCC 2018. A Best Student Paper Award was given to Tianren Liu for his paper "On Basing Search SIVP on NP-Hardness."

The conference also featured two other invited talks, by Moni Naor and by Daniel Wichs.

We are greatly indebted to many people who were involved in making TCC 2018 a success. First of all, a big thanks to the most important contributors: all the authors who submitted papers to the conference. Next, we would like to thank the PC members for their hard work, dedication, and diligence in reviewing the papers, verifying the correctness, and in-depth discussion. We are also thankful to the external reviewers for their volunteered hard work and investment in reviewing papers and answering questions, often under time pressure. For running the conference itself, we are very grateful to the general chairs, Shweta Agrawal and Manoj Prabhakaran. We appreciate the sponsorship from the IACR, Microsoft Research, IBM, and Google. We also wish to thank IIT Madras and IIT Bombay for their support. Finally, we are thankful to the TCC Steering Committee as well as the entire thriving and vibrant TCC community.

November 2018

Amos Beimel
Stefan Dziembowski
TCC 2018 Program Chairs

TCC 2018

The 16th Theory of Cryptography Conference

Goa, India
November 11–14, 2018

Sponsored by the *International Association for Cryptologic Research*

General Chairs

Shweta Agrawal	Indian Institute of Technology, Madras, India
Manoj Prabhakaran	Indian Institute of Technology, Bombay, India

Program Committee

Masayuki Abe	NTT and Kyoto University, Japan
Divesh Aggarwal	National University of Singapore, Singapore
Shweta Agrawal	Indian Institute of Technology, Madras, India
Gilad Asharov	Cornell Tech, USA
Amos Beimel (Co-chair)	Ben-Gurion University, Israel
Andrej Bogdanov	The Chinese University of Hong Kong, SAR China
Zvika Brakerski	Weizmann Institute of Science, Israel
Nishanth Chandran	Microsoft Research, India
Stefan Dziembowski (Co-chair)	University of Warsaw, Poland
Sebastian Faust	TU Darmstadt, Germany
Marc Fischlin	TU Darmstadt, Germany
Iftach Haitner	Tel Aviv University, Israel
Martin Hirt	ETH Zurich, Switzerland
Pavel Hubáček	Charles University in Prague, Czech Republic
Aggelos Kiayias	University of Edinburgh, UK
Eyal Kushilevitz	Technion, Israel
Anna Lysyanskaya	Brown University, USA
Tal Malkin	Columbia University, USA
Eran Omri	Ariel University, Israel
Chris Peikert	University of Michigan – Ann Arbor, USA
Krzysztof Pietrzak	IST Austria, Austria
Antigoni Polychroniadou	Cornell University, USA
Alon Rosen	IDC Herzliya, Israel
Mike Rosulek	Oregon State University, USA
Vinod Vaikuntanathan	MIT, USA
Ivan Visconti	University of Salerno, Italy
Hoeteck Wee	CNRS and ENS, France

Mor Weiss	Northeastern University, USA
Stefan Wolf	University of Lugano, Switzerland
Vassilis Zikas	University of Edinburgh, UK

TCC Steering Committee

Ivan Damgård	Aarhus University, Denmark
Shai Halevi (Chair)	IBM Research, USA
Huijia (Rachel) Lin	UCSB, USA
Tal Malkin	Columbia University, USA
Ueli Maurer	ETH, Switzerland
Moni Naor	Weizmann Institute of Science, Israel
Manoj Prabhakaran	Indian Institute of Technology, Bombay, India

Additional Reviewers

Aydin Abadi
Shashank Agrawal
Adi Akavia
Navid Alamati
Ghada Almashaqbeh
Bar Alon
Joel Alwen
Prabhanjan Ananth
Megumi Ando
Benny Applebaum
Frederik Armknecht
Christian Badertscher
Saikrishna Badrinarayanan
Karim Baghery
Marshall Ball
Fabio Banfi
Laasya Bangalore
Carsten Baum
Aner Ben-Efraim
Fabrice Benhamouda
Nir Bitansky
Jonathan Bootle
Cecilia Boschini
Florian Bourse
Elette Boyle
Anne Broadbent
Brent Carmer
David Cash
Anrin Chakraborti
Yilei Chen
Ilaria Chillotti
Wutichai Chongchitmate
Michele Ciampi
Ran Cohen
Xavier Coiteux-Roy
Sandro Coretti
Geoffroy Couteau
Dana Dachman-Soled
Pratish Datta
Bernardo David
Jean Paul Degabriele
Akshay Degwekar
Apoorvaa Deshpande
Nico Döttling
Lisa Eckey
Naomi Ephraim
Omar Fawzi
Serge Fehr
Matthias Fitzi
Nils Fleischhacker
Georg Fuchsbauer
Eiichiro Fujisaki
Steven Galbreith
Chaya Ganesh
Adria Gascon
Romain Gay
Peter Gazi
Ran Gelles
Badih Ghazi
Satrajit Ghosh
Irene Giacomelli
Junqing Gong
Dov Gordon
Paul Grubbs
Cyprien de Saint Guilhem
Siyao Guo
Divya Gupta
Arne Hansen
Patrick Harasser
Prahladh Harsha
Julia Hesse
Minki Hhan
Ryo Hiromasa
Justin Holmgren
Kristina Hostakova
Yuval Ishai
Muhammad Ishaq
Zahra Jafargholi
Tibor Jager
Aayush Jain
Abhishek Jain
Daniel Jost
Bruce Kapron

Tomasz Kazana
Dakshita Khurana
Jiseung Kim
Sam Kim
Fuyuki Kitagawa
Susumu Kiyoshima
Karen Klein
Ilan Komargodski
Orestis Konstantinidis
Venkata Koppula
Lucas Kowalczyk
Daniel Kraschewski
Mukul Kulkarni
Ashutosh Kumar
Rajendra Kumar
Benjamin Kuykendall
Rio LaVinge
Changmin Lee
Moon Sung Lee
Nikos Leonardos
Xiao Liang
Jyun-Jie Liao
Chengyu Lin
Huijia (Rachel) Lin
Feng-Hao Liu
Qipeng Liu
Tianren Liu
Yi-Kai Liu
Chen-Da Liu Zhang
Alex Lombardi
Julian Loss
Steve Lu
Yun Lu
Vadim Lyubashevsky
Urmila Mahadev
Mohammad Mahmoody
Subhamoy Maitra
Nikolaos Makriyannis
Takahiro Matsuda
Christian Matt
Jeremias Mechler
Peihan Miao
Daniele Micciancio
Michele Minelli
Konstantinos Mitropoulos
Tarik Moataz
Fabrice Mouhartem
Tamer Mour
Pratyay Mukherjee
Priyanka Mukhopadhyay
Marta Mularczyk
Jörn Müller-Quade
Kartik Nayak
Tobias Nilges
Chinmay Nirkhe
Ryo Nishimaki
Sai Lakshmi Bhavana Obbattu
Maciej Obremski
Miyako Ohkubo
Georgios Panagiotakos
Omer Paneth
Anat Paskin-Cherniavsky
Valerio Pastro
Serdar Pehlivanoglu
Renen Perlman
Giuseppe Persiano
Thomas Peters
Christopher Portmann
Srinivasan Raghuraman
Govind Ramnarayan
Samuel Ranellucci
Michael Raskin
Michael Riabzev
João Ribeiro
Silas Richelson
Felix Rohrbach
Lior Rotem
Paul Rösler
Manuel Sabin
Katerina Samari
Alessandra Scafuro
Giannicola Scarpa
Peter Scholl
Adam Sealfon
Sruthi Sekar
Yannick Seurin
Sina Shiehian
Tom Shrimpton
Luisa Siniscalchi
Veronika Slivova
Pratik Soni
Nick Spooner
Akshayaram Srinivasan
Martjin Stam
John Steinberger
Noah Stephens-Davidowitz
Qiang Tang
Stefano Tessaro
Ni Trieu
Rotem Tsabary
Yiannis Tselekounis
Margarita Vald
Prashant Vasudevan
Muthuramakrishnan Venkitasubramaniam
Daniele Venturi
Satyanarayana Vusirikala
Hendrik Waldner
Petros Wallden
Michael Walter
Xiao Wang
Christopher Williamson
David Wu
Keita Xagawa
Yu Yu
Shota Yamada
Takashi Yamakawa
Kevin Yeo
Eylon Yogev
Thomas Zacharias
Mark Zhandry
Jiamin Zhu
Dionysis Zindros
Giorgos Zirdelis

Contents – Part I

Memory-Hard Functions and Complexity Theory

Provable Time-Memory Trade-Offs: Symmetric Cryptography Against Memory-Bounded Adversaries . . . 3
Stefano Tessaro and Aishwarya Thiruvengadam

Static-Memory-Hard Functions, and Modeling the Cost of Space vs. Time . . . 33
Thaddeus Dryja, Quanquan C. Liu, and Sunoo Park

No-signaling Linear PCPs . . . 67
Susumu Kiyoshima

On Basing Search SIVP on **NP**-Hardness . . . 98
Tianren Liu

Two-Round MPC Protocols

Two-Round MPC: Information-Theoretic and Black-Box . . . 123
Sanjam Garg, Yuval Ishai, and Akshayaram Srinivasan

Perfect Secure Computation in Two Rounds . . . 152
Benny Applebaum, Zvika Brakerski, and Rotem Tsabary

Two-Round Adaptively Secure Multiparty Computation from Standard Assumptions . . . 175
Fabrice Benhamouda, Huijia Lin, Antigoni Polychroniadou, and Muthuramakrishnan Venkitasubramaniam

Zero Knowledge

One-Message Zero Knowledge and Non-malleable Commitments . . . 209
Nir Bitansky and Huijia Lin

Smooth NIZK Arguments . . . 235
Charanjit S. Jutla and Arnab Roy

Round-Optimal Fully Black-Box Zero-Knowledge Arguments from One-Way Permutations . . . 263
Carmit Hazay and Muthuramakrishnan Venkitasubramaniam

Round Optimal Black-Box "Commit-and-Prove" . . . 286
Dakshita Khurana, Rafail Ostrovsky, and Akshayaram Srinivasan

Information-Theoretic Cryptography

On the Power of Amortization in Secret Sharing: *d*-Uniform Secret Sharing and CDS with Constant Information Rate. 317
Benny Applebaum and Barak Arkis

Information-Theoretic Secret-Key Agreement: The Asymptotically Tight Relation Between the Secret-Key Rate and the Channel Quality Ratio 345
Daniel Jost, Ueli Maurer, and João L. Ribeiro

Information-Theoretic Broadcast with Dishonest Majority for Long Messages 370
Wutichai Chongchitmate and Rafail Ostrovsky

Oblivious Transfer in Incomplete Networks 389
Varun Narayanan and Vinod M. Prabahakaran

Trapdoor Permutations and Signatures

Injective Trapdoor Functions via Derandomization: How Strong is Rudich's Black-Box Barrier?. 421
Lior Rotem and Gil Segev

Enhancements are Blackbox Non-trivial: Impossibility of Enhanced Trapdoor Permutations from Standard Trapdoor Permutations. 448
Mohammad Hajiabadi

Certifying Trapdoor Permutations, Revisited. 476
Ran Canetti and Amit Lichtenberg

On the Security Loss of Unique Signatures 507
Andrew Morgan and Rafael Pass

Coin-Tossing and Fairness

On the Complexity of Fair Coin Flipping. 539
Iftach Haitner, Nikolaos Makriyannis, and Eran Omri

Game Theoretic Notions of Fairness in Multi-party Coin Toss 563
Kai-Min Chung, Yue Guo, Wei-Kai Lin, Rafael Pass, and Elaine Shi

Achieving Fair Treatment in Algorithmic Classification 597
Andrew Morgan and Rafael Pass

Functional and Identity-Based Encryption

Upgrading to Functional Encryption 629
Saikrishna Badrinarayanan, Dakshita Khurana, Amit Sahai, and Brent Waters

Impossibility of Simulation Secure Functional Encryption Even with Random Oracles 659
Shashank Agrawal, Venkata Koppula, and Brent Waters

Registration-Based Encryption: Removing Private-Key Generator from IBE 689
Sanjam Garg, Mohammad Hajiabadi, Mohammad Mahmoody, and Ahmadreza Rahimi

Author Index 719

Contents – Part II

MPC Protocols

Topology-Hiding Computation Beyond Semi-Honest Adversaries 3
Rio LaVigne, Chen-Da Liu-Zhang, Ueli Maurer, Tal Moran, Marta Mularczyk, and Daniel Tschudi

Secure Computation Using Leaky Correlations (Asymptotically Optimal Constructions) 36
Alexander R. Block, Divya Gupta, Hemanta K. Maji, and Hai H. Nguyen

Fine-Grained Secure Computation 66
Matteo Campanelli and Rosario Gennaro

On the Structure of Unconditional UC Hybrid Protocols 98
Mike Rosulek and Morgan Shirley

Order-Revealing Encryption and Symmetric Encryption

Impossibility of Order-Revealing Encryption in Idealized Models 129
Mark Zhandry and Cong Zhang

A Ciphertext-Size Lower Bound for Order-Preserving Encryption with Limited Leakage 159
David Cash and Cong Zhang

Ciphertext Expansion in Limited-Leakage Order-Preserving Encryption: A Tight Computational Lower Bound 177
Gil Segev and Ido Shahaf

Towards Tight Security of Cascaded LRW2 192
Bart Mennink

Information-Theoretic Cryptography II and Quantum Cryptography

Continuous NMC Secure Against Permutations and Overwrites, with Applications to CCA Secure Commitments 225
Ivan Damgård, Tomasz Kazana, Maciej Obremski, Varun Raj, and Luisa Siniscalchi

Best Possible Information-Theoretic MPC 255
Shai Halevi, Yuval Ishai, Eyal Kushilevitz, and Tal Rabin

Secure Certification of Mixed Quantum States with Application to Two-Party Randomness Generation 282
Frédéric Dupuis, Serge Fehr, Philippe Lamontagne, and Louis Salvail

Classical Proofs for the Quantum Collapsing Property of Classical Hash Functions 315
Serge Fehr

LWE-Based Cryptography

Traitor-Tracing from LWE Made Simple and Attribute-Based 341
Yilei Chen, Vinod Vaikuntanathan, Brent Waters, Hoeteck Wee, and Daniel Wichs

Two-Message Statistically Sender-Private OT from LWE 370
Zvika Brakerski and Nico Döttling

Adaptively Secure Distributed PRFs from LWE 391
Benoît Libert, Damien Stehlé, and Radu Titiu

iO and Authentication

A Simple Construction of iO for Turing Machines 425
Sanjam Garg and Akshayaram Srinivasan

Succinct Garbling Schemes from Functional Encryption Through a Local Simulation Paradigm 455
Prabhanjan Ananth and Alex Lombardi

FE and iO for Turing Machines from Minimal Assumptions 473
Shweta Agrawal and Monosij Maitra

The MMap Strikes Back: Obfuscation and New Multilinear Maps Immune to CLT13 Zeroizing Attacks 513
Fermi Ma and Mark Zhandry

Return of GGH15: Provable Security Against Zeroizing Attacks 544
James Bartusek, Jiaxin Guan, Fermi Ma, and Mark Zhandry

The Security of Lazy Users in Out-of-Band Authentication 575
Moni Naor, Lior Rotem, and Gil Segev

ORAM and PRF

Is There an Oblivious RAM Lower Bound for Online Reads? 603
Mor Weiss and Daniel Wichs

Perfectly Secure Oblivious Parallel RAM 636
T.-H. Hubert Chan, Kartik Nayak, and Elaine Shi

Watermarking PRFs Under Standard Assumptions: Public Marking and Security with Extraction Queries 669
Willy Quach, Daniel Wichs, and Giorgos Zirdelis

Exploring Crypto Dark Matter: New Simple PRF Candidates and Their Applications 699
Dan Boneh, Yuval Ishai, Alain Passelègue, Amit Sahai, and David J. Wu

Author Index 731

Memory-Hard Functions and Complexity Theory

Provable Time-Memory Trade-Offs: Symmetric Cryptography Against Memory-Bounded Adversaries

Stefano Tessaro(✉) and Aishwarya Thiruvengadam

University of California, Santa Barbara, USA
{tessaro,aish}@cs.ucsb.edu

Abstract. We initiate the study of symmetric encryption in a regime where the memory of the adversary is bounded. For a block cipher with n-bit blocks, we present modes of operation for encryption and authentication that guarantee security *beyond* 2^n encrypted/authenticated messages, as long as (1) the adversary's memory is restricted to be less than 2^n bits, and (2) the key of the block cipher is long enough to mitigate memory-less key-search attacks. This is the first proposal of a setting which allows to bypass the 2^n barrier under a reasonable assumption on the adversarial resources.

Motivated by the above, we also discuss the problem of stretching the key of a block cipher in the setting where the memory of the adversary is bounded. We show a tight equivalence between the security of double encryption in the ideal-cipher model and the hardness of a special case of the element distinctness problem, which we call the *list-disjointness problem*. Our result in particular implies a conditional lower bound on time-memory trade-offs to break PRP security of double encryption, assuming optimality of the worst-case complexity of existing algorithms for list disjointness.

Keywords: Foundations · Symmetric cryptography
Randomness extraction

1 Introduction

Security proofs typically upper bound the maximal achievable advantage of an adversary in compromising a scheme as a function of its *resources*. Almost always, theoretical cryptography measures these resources in terms of *time complexity* – an adversary is considered feasible if its running time is bounded, e.g., by a polynomial, or by some conservative upper bound (e.g., 2^{100}) when the focus is on concrete parameters.

However, time alone does not determine feasibility. Another parameter is the required *memory*. For example, while the naïve birthday attack to find a collision in a hash function with n-bit outputs requires $2^{n/2}$ time *and* memory, well-known collision-finding methods based on Pollard's ρ-method [31] only require $O(n)$

A. Beimel and S. Dziembowski (Eds.): TCC 2018, LNCS 11239, pp. 3–32, 2018.
https://doi.org/10.1007/978-3-030-03807-6_1

memory. In fact, cryptanalytic attacks often achieve *time-memory* trade-offs, where time complexity increases as the memory usage decreases.

Everything else being equal, we would favor a cryptosystem that requires large memory to be compromised within feasible time over one admitting low-memory attacks. Yet, existing works on provable security that are concerned with adversarial memory costs, such as those dealing with memory-hard functions (e.g., [3,4,6]), consider a more limited scope than the security of classical cryptographic tasks like encryption and authentication. A notable exception is the recent work of Auerbach et al. [7] introducing the concept of a *memory-tight reduction*, which allows lifting conjectured lower bounds on time-memory trade-offs from the underlying assumption to the security of the overall scheme. Fortunately, many reductions are memory-tight, with the exception being mostly reductions in the random-oracle model. This approach, however, still crucially relies on a time-memory assumption for an underlying computational problem, and these are mostly problems studied in public-key cryptography.

THIS PAPER: AN OVERVIEW. This paper focuses on *symmetric cryptography* and modes of operation for block ciphers. We present the first schemes for encryption and authentication, based on a block cipher with input length n, that provably achieve security against adversaries which encrypt/authenticate more than 2^n messages, under the assumption that their memory allows storing fewer than 2^n bits. Our results only need fairly standard assumptions (i.e., strong, yet plausible, forms of PRP security) on the underlying block ciphers, and, unlike [7], we only assume hardness with respect to *time*.

Complementary to this, we will discuss how the security of key-length extension methods for block ciphers (and in particular, double encryption) improves under memory restrictions on adversaries, and show conditional results proving optimality of existing attacks against double encryption.

WHY THIS IS IMPORTANT. In provably secure symmetric cryptography, the quantity 2^n acts as a barrier on the achievable security in the analysis of schemes based on block ciphers with n-bit inputs, even if the underlying block cipher is very secure (e.g., it is a PRP against adversaries with time complexity 2^{2n}, which is plausible if the key is sufficiently long). The reason is that the core of most proofs is inherently *information-theoretic*, and analyzes the scheme after replacing the block cipher with a truly random permutation (or random function) on n-bit inputs. Here, after $\Omega(2^n)$ queries (either for encryption or verification), the underlying permutation/function is usually queried on *all* inputs – the lack of new randomness breaks down the proof, although the resulting matching attack has often doubly-exponential time complexity in n and it is only a problem because we are considering the (stronger) target of information-theoretic security. For this reason, cryptanalysis often suggests better concrete security guarantees than those given by security proofs. Of course, we have no way to directly deal with time complexity, but here we suggest that bounding the memory of the attacker to be smaller than 2^n can suffice to break this barrier.

OUR ASSUMPTIONS. The assumption that attackers have less than 2^n bits of memory is reasonable. While $n = 128$ is common, NSA's Utah data center is estimated to store 2^{67} bits of data. Moreover, accessing large memory, in practice, adds extra time complexity. Another way to view this is that high security can be achieved *even* when the block size is *smaller*. E.g., we can set $n = 80$ and $k = 128$, and still get beyond 100 bits (i.e., 2^{100} queries) of security.

Note that if we want security against time $T > 2^n$, then we need a security assumption on the block cipher which is true against time-T adversaries. If the key length is larger than $\log(T)$ bits (to thwart the naïve key-search attack), it is not unreasonable to assume that a block cipher is a PRP for T-time attackers, *even* if the block length is n.[1] This however also motivates the general question of what to do if a cipher with longer key does not exist – heuristically, one could use methods for key-length extension [15,21–24,26,28] that have been validated in the ideal cipher model, and that achieve security against time up to $T = 2^{k+n}$ when the underlying block cipher has key length k. Here, we initiate the study of key-length extension in the memory-bounded setting, and show that, under assumptions we discuss below, key-length extension can be done more efficiently.

1.1 Overview of Our Results

We give an overview of the results from this paper. We will start with the case of encryption, before moving to authentication, and our results on key-length extension.

SYMMETRIC ENCRYPTION. Consider the classical scheme which encrypts each m as $(\mathsf{iv}, \mathsf{E}_K(\mathsf{iv}) \oplus m)$ for a random n-bit iv and a block cipher E with block length n and key K. The canonical $O(2^{n/2})$-query attack against real-or-random (ROR) security waits for two encryptions of m_i and m_j with ciphertexts $c_i = (\mathsf{iv}_i, z_i)$ and $c_j = (\mathsf{iv}_j, z_j)$ such that $\mathsf{iv}_i = \mathsf{iv}_j$, and then checks whether $z_i \oplus z_j = m_i \oplus m_j$. However, if the adversary only has memory to store $O(n \cdot 2^{n/4})$ bits, the attack is not possible, as not all previous ciphertexts can be remembered. The seemingly best-possible strategy is to store $2^{n/4}$ $2n$-bit ciphertexts, and check, for each new query returning $c_i = (\mathsf{iv}_i, z_i)$, whether the iv_i value is used by any of the $2^{n/4}$ ciphertexts, and then proceed as before. This attack however requires $2^{3n/4}$ queries to succeed.

A generalization of the scheme could achieve even higher security: We now pick t random $\mathsf{iv}_1, \ldots, \mathsf{iv}_t$, and the ciphertext is[2]

$$(\mathsf{iv}_1, \ldots, \mathsf{iv}_t, \mathsf{E}_K(\mathsf{iv}_1) \oplus \cdots \oplus \mathsf{E}_K(\mathsf{iv}_t) \oplus m).$$

Of course, we need to *prove* our intuition is valid no matter what a memory-bounded attacker does. We will not be able to do so for this specific scheme, but

[1] For example, an ideal cipher with key length $\log(T)$ *is* a PRP against T-time attackers.

[2] This scheme was proposed in [13], with the different purpose of proving security beyond the birthday bound.

consider a related scheme, which we call *sample-then-extract*, using an extractor $\mathsf{Ext} : \{0,1\}^{n \cdot t} \times \{0,1\}^s \to \{0,1\}^\ell$ to encrypt an ℓ-bit message as

$$(\mathsf{iv}_1, \ldots, \mathsf{iv}_t, \mathsf{seed}, \mathsf{Ext}(\mathsf{E}_K(\mathsf{iv}_1) \| \cdots \| \mathsf{E}_K(\mathsf{iv}_t), \mathsf{seed}) \oplus m),$$

where $\mathsf{seed} \xleftarrow{\$} \{0,1\}^s$ is chosen randomly upon each encryption.

For example, assuming Ext is a sufficiently strong extractor, $\ell = n$, $t = 32n$, we will show security up to $q = 2^{1.5n}$ encryption queries for attackers with running time $T \geq q$ and memory $S \leq 2^{n(1-o(1))}$, provided E is secure against T-time attackers as a PRP.

THE CONNECTION WITH SUB-KEY PREDICTION. Our proof relies on the problem of *sub-key prediction*, which was recently revisited [11,14] in the context of big-key encryption, but which initially appeared implicitly in previous entropy preservation lemmas [5,30,36].[3] In particular, the core of the proof involves a hybrid world where the block cipher E_K is replaced by a random permutation P. For every i, we imagine an experiment where we run the attacker for the first $i-1$ queries, all answered using the encryption scheme with P in lieu of E_K, and then look at its S-bit state σ_{i-1} before it makes the i-th query. Then, we know that the average-case min-entropy of the *permutation* P given σ_{i-1} is at most S bits lower than the maximum, i.e., $\log(2^n!) \approx n \cdot 2^n$. The existing bounds on sub-key prediction give us directly a lower bound on the min-entropy of $P(\mathsf{iv}_1) \| \cdots \| P(\mathsf{iv}_t)$ conditioned on σ_{i-1}. If Ext is a suitable extractor, this makes its output random, and thus this masks the ciphertext.

The proof is perhaps obvious in retrospect, but it highlights a few interesting traits: First off, the idea of a reduction to sub-key prediction is novel. Second, handling random permutations (vs functions) comes for free by simply considering a different entropy lower bound for which the extractor needs to work.

AUTHENTICATION. The next logical step is to build a *message authentication code* (MAC) for ℓ-bit messages from an n-bit block cipher, with security for $q > 2^n$ queries for adversaries with memory $S < 2^n$. Here, $\ell > n$ in order for the question to make sense. This appears harder – as we will explain in the body in detail, if we want to go as far as building a PRF (as it is usually the case when proving security of MAC constructions), the resulting construction is likely to yield (at least when following the canonical proof approach) a PRG which is unconditionally secure for unrestricted[4] space-bounded branching programs, with much better stretch than the existing state-of-the-art [16,27], and this is currently out of reach.

We overcome this by considering a (minimally) *interactive* approach to the problem of message authentication, which we refer to as *synchronous authentication*. In this setting, we force the output of the MAC to also depend on a random

[3] In fact, the simplest lemma by Alwen, Dodis, and Wichs [5] will suffice for our purposes. One could likely obtain better concrete bounds using the techniques from [11], yet their bounds are hard to express explicitly, and we do not explore this route here.

[4] I.e., they can learn the output bits of the PRG adaptively, with no restrictions.

challenge previously sent by the other party. For example, whenever Alice sends an authenticated message to Bob, she also sends a challenge to be used by Bob to authenticate his next message to Alice. Our construction makes t calls per *bit* of the message, for a parameter t.[5] In particular, a challenge consists of t n-bit strings $\mathsf{iv}_1, \ldots, \mathsf{iv}_t$, as well as an extractor seed seed. Then, the tag of a message $M = M_1 M_2 \ldots M_\ell \in \{0,1\}^\ell$ is obtained by computing the values

$$Y_i = E_K(\langle i \rangle \| M_i \| \mathsf{iv}_1) \| \cdots \| E_K(\langle i \rangle \| M_i \| \mathsf{iv}_t),$$

where $\langle i \rangle$ is a $\log \ell$-bit encoding of i, and finally outputting the message tag $T = \bigoplus_{i=1}^{t} \mathsf{Ext}(Y_i, \mathsf{seed})$, where Ext is a randomness extractor.

We introduce a definition of synchronous message authentication and prove our scheme secure. Again, our proof will resort to a reduction to the unpredictability of the Y_i values via sub-key prediction, but an extra complication is that we need to analyze a more complex security game than in the case of encryption, where the adversary can authenticate *adaptively* chosen messages.

THE BLOCK CIPHER ASSUMPTION AND DOUBLE ENCRYPTION. If we want to prove security beyond 2^n queries, we need to use a block cipher whose PRP security holds for an attacker which runs for time $T \geq 2^n$ time and has memory $S \ll 2^n$. But: *What should we do when the key is not long enough?*

We can of course always extend the length of a key to a block cipher by using conventional key-length extension methods which are validated in the ideal-cipher model [15,21–24,26,28]. One observation however is that if we are assuming a bound on the adversary's memory, one could achieve better security and/or better efficiency (for comparable security). To this end, we initiate the study of key-length extension in the memory-bounded regime.

In particular, we look at *double encryption* (DE), i.e., given a block cipher E, we consider a new block cipher that uses two keys K_1, K_2 to map x to $\mathsf{E}_{K_1}(\mathsf{E}_{K_2}(x))$. The best known attack against DE achieves a time-memory trade-off[6] of $T^2 \cdot S = 2^{3k}$ with $T \geq 2^k$ – this was first pointed out in the work of van Oorschot and Wiener [38]. If one can show that this is indeed optimal, then we can for example hope to achieve security against time $T = 2^{1.25k}$ when $S \ll 2^{0.5k}$. In other words, in contrast to common wisdom, double encryption would increase security if memory is bounded.

Verifying this unconditionally, while possible (recall we are content with a proof in the ideal-cipher model), appears to be out of reach. However, we establish a connection between the PRP security of DE in the ICM and a problem we call *list disjointness.* In this problem, we assume we are given *two* equally long lists L_1 and L_2 as inputs, each of distinct elements, with the promise that either (1) $L_1 \cap L_2 = \emptyset$ or (2) $|L_1 \cap L_2| = 1$. An algorithm is given access to the lists as an oracle (i.e., for an i and b, it can obtain the i-th element of L_b), and the goal

[5] A higher-rate version of the scheme can be given, at the price of lower security.

[6] For comparison, the textbook meet-in-the-middle attack achieves a tradeoff of $T \cdot S = 2^{2k}$.

is to assess whether (1) or (2) holds. This problem is a special case of the well-known *element distinctness* problem [17,40], where the algorithm is given oracle access to a single list L and needs to decide whether its elements are distinct. In particular, every algorithm for distinctness yields one for list disjointness, by letting L be the concatenation of L_1 and L_2.

It is not hard to see that every algorithm for list disjointness yields a PRP distinguisher for DE with similar query and memory complexities. More interestingly, we also show that every PRP distinguisher for DE yields an algorithm (with similar query and memory complexities) that solves list disjointness in *the worst case.*

First off, there has been little progress in providing general lower bounds for query-memory trade-offs for element distinctness (existing lower bounds consider either restricted algorithms [40], and can be bypassed by more general algorithms [8], or are far from known upper bounds [2,9]). The situation does not appear easier for list disjointness. Progress on proving a tight lower bound for query-memory trade-offs for the PRP security seems therefore to necessarily involve new non-trivial insights.

Second, and perhaps more interestingly, the best algorithm for element distinctness is due to Beame, Clifford, and Machmouchi [8], and achieves a tradeoff of $T^2 \cdot S = |L|^3$. The algorithm also applies to list disjointness, and assuming it is optimal, by our reduction we get a conditional lower bound confirming the best-known time-memory trade-off for DE to be optimal.

1.2 Further Related Works

The bulk of the interest on bounded-memory algorithms stems from complexity theory. In particular, a number of works have been concerned with lower bounds for time-memory trade-offs in restricted complexity classes, such as pebbling models and branching programs. Textbooks like that of Savage [35] provide a comprehensive introduction to the topic. Particularly relevant to us is the work on building PRGs for space-bounded computation [29], which was the first to show unconditional pseudorandomness for space-bounded distinguishers.

Our work is also very related to that of Raz [32,33] on time-memory trade-offs for learning parities (and related problems). Raz shows in particular an encryption scheme with an n-bit key which unconditionally resists an attacker with memory smaller than n^2/c for a constant c when encrypting an exponential number of plaintexts. Our encryption scheme can be seen as replacing the n-bit key with a much larger random permutation table. Raz's technique is not applicable because it would require evaluating the permutation at $\Theta(2^n)$ positions upon each encryption. Time-memory trade-offs for learning lower-weight parities were also given [20], but it does not appear possible to exploit these results to obtain a cryptosystem.

Outline of this paper. Section 2 will introduce technical tools needed throughout the paper, including our model of computation, information-theoretic preliminaries, and notation for the sub-key prediction problem. Sections 3 and 4 discuss our encryption and authentication schemes. Section 5 presents our results on double encryption.

2 Preliminaries

Throughout this paper, let $N = 2^n$ for an understood $n \in \mathbb{N}$. Also, let $[i]$ denote the set $\{1, 2, \ldots, i\}$. As usual, we use the notation $|r|$ to denote the length of string r in bits. By $r \stackrel{\$}{\leftarrow} \{0,1\}^n$, we indicate that r is chosen uniformly from $\{0,1\}^n$. We let $\mathcal{F}_{m,n}$ denote the uniform distribution over functions from $\{0,1\}^m$ to $\{0,1\}^n$ and let $\mathcal{P}_n$ denote the uniform distribution over permutations on $\{0,1\}^n$. We also write $\mathcal{F}$ and $\mathcal{P}$ for $\mathcal{F}_{n,n}$ and $\mathcal{P}_n$ whenever n is clear from the context.

2.1 Information-Theoretic Preliminaries

The *min-entropy* of a random variable X (taking values from a set $\mathcal{X}$) is $\mathrm{H}_\infty(X) = -\min_{x\in\mathcal{X}} \log(\Pr[X = x])$. Moreover, for two jointly distributed random variables X, Y, and an element y such that $\Pr[Y = y] > 0$, we define $\mathrm{H}_\infty(X|Y = y) = \min_{x\in\mathcal{X}} \log\left(1/\Pr\left[X = x \,\middle|\, Y = y\right]\right)$. This is in particular the conditional min-entropy conditioned on a particular *outcome*. When conditioning on a random variable, we use the *average-case* version of min-entropy [19], i.e.,

$$\mathrm{H}_\infty(X|Y) = -\log\left(\sum_{y\in\mathcal{Y}} \max_{x\in\mathcal{X}} \Pr[X = x, Y = y]\right).$$

We will need the following simple fact about average-case min-entropies.

Lemma 1 ([19]). *Let X, Y, Z be random variables. If Y can take at most 2^λ values, then*

$$\mathrm{H}_\infty(X|YZ) \geq \mathrm{H}_\infty(XY|Z) - \lambda \geq \mathrm{H}_\infty(X|Z) - \lambda. \tag{1}$$

Extractors. Recall that a function $\mathsf{Ext} : \{0,1\}^{t\cdot n} \times \{0,1\}^s \to \{0,1\}^\ell$ is said to be a (γ, ε)-strong extractor if for every random variable X on $\{0,1\}^{t\cdot n}$ with $\mathrm{H}_\infty(X) \geq \gamma$, $(U_s, \mathsf{Ext}(X, U_s))$ is ε-close to (U_s, U_ℓ). We say that $H : \{0,1\}^k \times \{0,1\}^n \to \{0,1\}^\ell$ is 2-universal if for all n-bit $x \neq x'$, we have $\Pr[K \stackrel{\$}{\leftarrow} \{0,1\}^k : H(K, x) = H(K, x')] = 2^{-\ell}$. The following is well known.

Lemma 2 (Leftover Hash Lemma [25]**).** *If $H : \{0,1\}^k \times \{0,1\}^n \to \{0,1\}^\ell$ is 2-universal, and $\ell = \gamma - 2\log(1/\varepsilon)$, then $\mathsf{Ext}(x, K) := H(K, x)$ is a strong (γ, ε)-extractor.*

Following Dodis et al. [19], we also say that $\mathsf{Ext} : \{0,1\}^{t \cdot n} \times \{0,1\}^s \to \{0,1\}^\ell$ is an *average-case* (γ, ε)-strong extractor if for all pairs of random variables (X, I) such that X in $\{0,1\}^{t \cdot n}$ satisfies $\mathrm{H}_\infty(X|I) \geq \gamma$, $(U_s, \mathsf{Ext}(X, U_s), I)$ is ε-close to (U_s, U_ℓ, I).

In [19] the leftover hash lemma is extended to show that universal hash functions yield an average-case strong extractor with the same parameters. In general, with a slight loss in parameters, a (γ, ε)-(strong) extractor is also an average-case $(\gamma, 3\varepsilon)$-(strong) extractor as stated as shown by [37].

ENTROPY PRESERVATION. Assume we are given a vector $X \in (\{0,1\}^m)^N$, which we often will think of as the table of a function $[N] \to \{0,1\}^m$. Further, let us sample indices $i_1, \ldots, i_t$ uniformly at random from $[N]$, and consider the induced random variable

$$X[i_1, \ldots, i_t] = X_{i_1}, \ldots, X_{i_t}.$$

We are interested in the relationship between the entropy of X and that of $X[i_1, \ldots, i_t]$. The following lemma was proven by Alwen, Dodis, and Wichs [5], and considers the more general setting where we are given some auxiliary information Z, and the indices $i_1, \ldots, i_t$ are sampled independently of X and Z.[7]

Lemma 3. *Let (X, Z) be correlated random variables, where $X \in (\{0,1\}^m)^N$, and $I = (i_1, \ldots, i_t) \xleftarrow{\$} [N]^t$. Further, assume that $\mathrm{H}_\infty(X|Z) \geq N(m-1) - L$, where $L \leq (1-\delta)Nm$ for some $\delta \in [0,1]$. Then, $\mathrm{H}_\infty(X[I]|Z, I) \geq \gamma$, if*

$$\delta \geq \left[\frac{2\gamma}{t}\left(1 + \frac{n}{m}\right) + \frac{1}{m} + \frac{3\gamma + 5}{Nm}\right].$$

Note that for our application scenarios, $\left(1 + \frac{n}{m}\right) \approx 2$ and $\frac{3\gamma+5}{Nm} \to 0$, so this means in particular that we get γ bits of entropy for every $\gamma \leq t(\delta - 1/m)/4$.

2.2 Model of Computation and Cryptographic Primitives

We will consider a model of computation with space-bounded adversaries, inspired by the one from [4,6]. In particular, we consider adversaries $\mathcal{A}$ making queries to an oracle $\mathcal{O}$. This accommodates without loss of generality for the case where $\mathcal{A}$ makes queries to *multiple* oracles $\mathcal{O}_1, \mathcal{O}_2, \ldots$, which we view as one individual oracle with an appropriate addressing input. We will not specify the model of execution of $\mathcal{A}$ any further at the lowest level of detail (but we assume we fix one specific model of computation), but will introduce some convenient relaxation of memory-bounded executions that will suffice for our purposes.

More specifically, the execution of an adversary proceeds in *stages* (or *steps*), allowing one oracle query in each stage. In particular, the execution of $\mathcal{A}$ starts

[7] We note that Lemma 3 has a different expression for δ than what would be implied by the original statement [5, Lemma A.3], but this is due to a missing factor of $\frac{2\gamma}{t}$ in one of the terms (which can be inferred from their proof).

with the state $\sigma_0 = x$, where x is the input, and no previous-query answer $y_0 = \perp$. Then, in the i-th stage, the adversary computes, as a function of the state σ_{i-1} and the previous query answer y_{i-1}, a query q_i to $\mathcal{O}$, as well as the next state σ_i. Thus, formally, an adversary $\mathcal{A}$ is a randomized algorithm implementing a map $\{0,1\}^* \times \{0,1\}^* \to \{0,1\}^* \times \{0,1\}^*$. In most proofs, we will generally not need to restrict the actual space complexity of $\mathcal{A}$ itself, as long as the states σ_i are bounded in size.

We say that an adversary $\mathcal{A}$ is S-*bounded* if $|\sigma_i| \leq S$ holds for all states in the execution. We further say that an adversary $\mathcal{A}$ has time complexity (or running time) T if an execution takes overall at most T steps. We say it has *(description) size* D if the description of $\mathcal{A}$ requires at most D bits. Finally, it makes q queries if it takes q steps, resulting in q queries to $\mathcal{O}$.

BLOCK CIPHERS AND PRPS. A *block cipher* is a function $\mathsf{E} : \{0,1\}^k \times \{0,1\}^n \to \{0,1\}^n$, where $\mathsf{E}_K = \mathsf{E}(K, \cdot)$ is a permutation for all $K \in \{0,1\}^k$. Generally, we assume that E is efficiently computable *and* invertible.

We define PRP security in terms of the *PRP-CPA-advantage* of an adversary $\mathcal{A}$ against a block cipher E, which is

$$\mathsf{Adv}_{\mathsf{E}}^{\mathsf{PRP\text{-}CPA}}(\mathcal{A}) = \left| \Pr[K \xleftarrow{\$} \{0,1\}^k : \mathcal{A}^{\mathsf{E}_K} = 1] - \Pr[P \xleftarrow{\$} \mathcal{P}_n : \mathcal{A}^P = 1] \right| .$$

We also define $\mathsf{Adv}_{\mathsf{E}}^{\mathsf{PRP\text{-}CPA}}(D, T, q, S) = \max_{\mathcal{A}}\{\mathsf{Adv}_{\mathsf{E}}^{\mathsf{PRP\text{-}CPA}}(\mathcal{A})\}$, where the maximum is taken over all S-bounded adversaries $\mathcal{A}$ that run in time at most T, making q queries at most, and with size at most D.

Note that PRP security does not need to depend on the block length n if the key is long enough. Below, we repeatedly make the assumption that there exist block ciphers $\mathsf{E} : \{0,1\}^k \times \{0,1\}^n \to \{0,1\}^n$ which are secure PRPs for time complexities $T > 2^n$ (and suitably small size D) and space complexity $S < 2^n$. Note that this implicitly implies $k(n) > \log T$. This is easily seen to be satisfied by an ideal cipher, even if S is unbounded.

2.3 Sub-key Prediction

In the sub-key prediction problem [11,14], the adversary $\mathcal{A}$ is given some leakage σ on a *key*, which here we interpret as a function $F : \{0,1\}^n \to \{0,1\}^n$. The leakage is derived through some (adversarially chosen) function $\mathcal{L}$. Then, for randomly chosen indices $i_1, \ldots, i_t$, $\mathcal{A}$ tries to guess the "sub-key" $K = F(i_1) \parallel \ldots \parallel F(i_t)$, i.e., the evaluations of the function at those indices. We generalize this notion further by allowing for auxiliary information Z correlated with F. In particular, we allow both $\mathcal{L}$ and $\mathcal{A}$ to access Z. (Still, we will omit Z when not necessary.)

More formally, we consider an adversary $\mathcal{A}$ with leakage function $\mathcal{L}$ interacting in the game $G_{\mathcal{D},\mathcal{I},t}^{\mathsf{skp\text{-}aux}}(\mathcal{A}, \mathcal{L})$ described in Fig. 1. Here, we stress that both $\mathcal{A}$ and $\mathcal{L}$ are computationally unbounded with no limits on their memory–the only limitation is the size of σ. The game is parameterized by the distribution

Game $G^{\mathsf{skp\text{-}aux}}_{\mathcal{D},\mathcal{I},t}(\mathcal{A},\mathcal{L})$:
$(F,Z) \xleftarrow{\$} \mathcal{D}$; $\sigma \leftarrow \mathcal{L}(F,Z)$
$(i_1,\ldots,i_t) \xleftarrow{\$} \mathcal{I}$; $K \xleftarrow{\$} \mathcal{A}(\sigma, Z, i_1,\ldots,i_t)$
Return $(K = F(i_1)\|\ldots\|F(i_t))$

Fig. 1. Game $G^{\mathsf{skp\text{-}aux}}_{\mathcal{D},\mathcal{I},t}(\mathcal{A},\mathcal{L})$. Game defining sub-key prediction with auxiliary information. The adversary, given leakage σ and auxiliary information Z on F, wins if it guesses the output of F at indices $i_1,\ldots,i_t$.

$\mathcal{D}$ according to which (F,Z) are chosen, the distribution $\mathcal{I}$ according to which the indices are chosen, and the number of indices t.

We can then define advantage measures for an adversary in guessing the sub-key correctly in the game $G^{\mathsf{skp\text{-}aux}}_{\mathcal{D},\mathcal{I},t}(\mathcal{A},\mathcal{L})$ as follows.

Definition 1. *The advantage of an adversary $\mathcal{A}$ with leakage function $\mathcal{L}$ in the game $G^{\mathsf{skp\text{-}aux}}_{\mathcal{D},\mathcal{I},t}(\mathcal{A},\mathcal{L})$ is defined as*

$$\mathsf{Adv}^{\mathsf{skp\text{-}aux}}_{\mathcal{D},\mathcal{I},t}(\mathcal{A},\mathcal{L}) = \Pr[G^{\mathsf{skp\text{-}aux}}_{\mathcal{D},\mathcal{I},t}(\mathcal{A},\mathcal{L}) = \textit{true}].$$

Furthermore, we define

$$\mathsf{Adv}^{\mathsf{skp\text{-}aux}}_{\mathcal{D},\mathcal{I},t}(S) = \max_{\mathcal{L}:\mathcal{D}\to\{0,1\}^S} \max_{\mathcal{A}}\{\mathsf{Adv}^{\mathsf{skp\text{-}aux}}_{\mathcal{D},\mathcal{I},t}(\mathcal{A},\mathcal{L})\}.$$

Often $\mathcal{I}$ will be the uniform distribution over t-tuples of indices in $(\{0,1\}^n)^t$, for notational convenience, we drop the subscript $\mathcal{I}$ and simply refer to the advantage as $\mathsf{Adv}^{\mathsf{skp\text{-}aux}}_{\mathcal{D},t}(S)$ in such cases.

The following lemma is immediate by definition of conditional min-entropy.

Lemma 4. *If $\mathsf{Adv}^{\mathsf{skp\text{-}aux}}_{\mathcal{D},\mathcal{I},t}(S) \le 2^{-\gamma}$, then for $(F,Z) \xleftarrow{\$} \mathcal{D}$, $(\mathsf{iv}_1,\ldots,\mathsf{iv}_t) \xleftarrow{\$} \mathcal{I}$ and $\sigma \leftarrow \mathcal{L}(F,Z)$, we have*

$$\mathrm{H}_\infty(F(\mathsf{iv}_1)\|\ldots\|F(\mathsf{iv}_t)|\sigma,(\mathsf{iv}_1,\ldots\mathsf{iv}_t),Z) \ge \gamma.$$

We now derive the advantage of an adversary in the sub-key prediction game with auxiliary information when the leakage function outputs exactly S bits. In particular, the following lemma is a straightforward application of Lemmas 1 and 3.

Lemma 5 (Sub-key Prediction with Auxiliary Information). *Let correlated random variables (F,Z) be chosen according to a distribution $\mathcal{D}$ such that $F:\{0,1\}^n \to \{0,1\}^n$ and $\mathrm{H}_\infty(F|Z) \ge N(n-1) - L$.*

Let $S + L \le (1-\delta)nN$ for some $\delta \in [0,1]$. Then, $\mathsf{Adv}^{\mathsf{skp\text{-}aux}}_{\mathcal{D},t}(S) \le 2^{-\gamma}$ if $\delta \ge \left[\frac{4\gamma}{t} + \frac{1}{n} + \frac{3\gamma+5}{nN}\right]$.

In comparison to [5], the recent work by Bellare and Dai [11] provides better concrete bounds for sub-key prediction in the case where F is uniformly distributed over all functions, and with no auxiliary information (or, more generally, Z is independent of F). However, we use [5] as we need to handle both auxiliary information and the case that F is a permutation. Also, while it may be possible to extend the proofs of [11] to this more general setting, the resulting bounds are hard to express analytically. Either way, our results are generic and an improvement on sub-key prediction bounds will directly yield better bounds for our instantiations below.

3 Encryption

We give an encryption scheme for which the amount of time needed to break it increases as the memory of the adversary decreases, in particular going beyond 2^n, where n is the block length of an underlying block cipher. To this end, we first recall the standard definition of a symmetric-key encryption scheme, its security, and introduce some additional notational conventions.

ENCRYPTION SCHEME: SYNTAX. An *encryption scheme* is a tuple of algorithms $\mathcal{E} = (\mathsf{Gen}, \mathsf{Enc}, \mathsf{Dec})$ where: (1) the *key generation algorithm* Gen outputs a key K, (2) the *encryption algorithm* Enc takes as input the secret key K and a message M (from some understood message space $\mathcal{M}$), and outputs a ciphertext $c \xleftarrow{\$} \mathsf{Enc}_K(M)$, and (3) the *decryption algorithm* Dec takes as input the secret key K and a ciphertext c and outputs a message $M \leftarrow \mathsf{Dec}_K(c)$. The correctness requirement is that for any key K output by Gen, and message $M \in \mathcal{M}$, we have $\mathsf{Dec}_K(\mathsf{Enc}_K(M)) = M$ with large probability (usually one).

Occasionally, it will be convenient to think of the key K as a function $F : \{0,1\}^n \to \{0,1\}^n$ (to be instantiated for example with a block cipher), to which the scheme is given oracle access. In this case, we will simply write Enc^F and Dec^F instead of Enc_K and Dec_K. Then one can get for example $\mathsf{Enc}_K = \mathsf{Enc}^{\mathsf{E}_K}$ for the final block cipher instantiation.

SECURITY OF ENCRYPTION SCHEMES. We briefly review the notion of *real-or-random (ROR)* security [12] of an encryption scheme $\mathcal{E} = (\mathsf{Gen}, \mathsf{Enc}, \mathsf{Dec})$ with message space $\mathcal{M}$: we consider the games $\mathsf{ROR}^{\mathcal{E},b}(\mathcal{A})$ (for $b \in \{0,1\}$) for an adversary $\mathcal{A}$, as described in Fig. 2, and define

$$\mathsf{Adv}^{\mathsf{ROR}}_{\mathcal{E}}(\mathcal{A}) = \left|\mathsf{Pr}[\mathsf{ROR}^{\mathcal{E},0}(\mathcal{A}) = 1] - \mathsf{Pr}[\mathsf{ROR}^{\mathcal{E},1}(\mathcal{A}) = 1]\right|,$$

as well as $\mathsf{Adv}^{\mathsf{ROR}}_{\mathcal{E}}(D, T, q, S) = \max_{\mathcal{A}}\{\mathsf{Adv}^{\mathsf{ROR}}_{\mathcal{E}}(\mathcal{A})\}$, where the maximum is taken over all S-bounded adversaries $\mathcal{A}$ with running time at most T, making at most q queries, and have size at most D.

For our intermediate information-theoretic steps below, our statements will not depend on D and T, and we simply write $\mathsf{Adv}^{\mathsf{ROR}}_{\mathcal{E}}(q, S) = \mathsf{Adv}^{\mathsf{ROR}}_{\mathcal{E}}(\infty, \infty, q, S)$.

Game $\mathsf{ROR}^{\mathcal{E},b}(\mathcal{A})$:	Oracle $\mathcal{E}'(M,b)$:
$K \xleftarrow{\$} \mathsf{Gen}$ $b' \xleftarrow{\$} \mathcal{A}^{\mathcal{E}'(\cdot,b)}$ Return b'	If $b = 0$ then return $c \xleftarrow{\$} \mathsf{Enc}_K(M)$ If $b = 1$ then choose $M' \xleftarrow{\$} \mathcal{M}$ such that $\lvert M'\rvert = \lvert M\rvert$ Return $c \xleftarrow{\$} \mathsf{Enc}_K(M')$.

Fig. 2. Game $\mathsf{ROR}^{\mathcal{E},b}(\mathcal{A})$. Game defining the real-or-random security of the encryption scheme $\mathcal{E}$, where $b \in \{0,1\}$.

3.1 The Sample-Then-Extract Scheme

The scheme is best described using a distribution $\mathcal{D}$ on functions from n bits to n bits as a parameter. In addition, let $\mathsf{Ext} : \{0,1\}^{tn} \times \{0,1\}^s \to \{0,1\}^\ell$, and let $\mathcal{I}$ be the uniform distribution over $\{0,1\}^{tn}$. The encryption scheme $\mathsf{StE}[\mathcal{D}, t, \mathsf{Ext}] = (\mathsf{Gen}, \mathsf{Enc}, \mathsf{Dec})$ for messages in $\mathcal{M} = \{0,1\}^\ell$ is then defined as follows:

Scheme $\mathsf{StE}[\mathcal{D}, t, \mathsf{Ext}]$:

- **Key generation.** The key generation algorithm Gen outputs $F \xleftarrow{\$} \mathcal{D}$, where $F : \{0,1\}^n \to \{0,1\}^n$.
- **Encryption.** On input $M \in \mathcal{M}$, Enc^F does the following:
  1. $\mathsf{seed} \xleftarrow{\$} \{0,1\}^s$.
  2. $\mathsf{iv} = (\mathsf{iv}_1, \ldots, \mathsf{iv}_t) \xleftarrow{\$} \mathcal{I}$.
  3. $c \leftarrow \mathsf{Ext}(F(\mathsf{iv}_1)\| \ldots \|F(\mathsf{iv}_t), \mathsf{seed}) \oplus M$
  4. Return $(c, \mathsf{seed}, \mathsf{iv}_1, \ldots, \mathsf{iv}_t)$.
- **Decryption.** On input $(c, \mathsf{seed}, \mathsf{iv}_1, \ldots, \mathsf{iv}_t)$, Dec computes $M \leftarrow (\mathsf{Ext}(F(\mathsf{iv}_1)\| \ldots \|F(\mathsf{iv}_t), \mathsf{seed})) \oplus c$, and returns M.

We will then instantiate our scheme with a block cipher E, and in this case we refer to the scheme as $\mathsf{StE}[\mathsf{E}, t, \mathsf{Ext}]$. This is the special case of the above scheme when the distribution $\mathcal{D}$ samples the function $\mathsf{E}_K(\cdot)$ for $K \xleftarrow{\$} \{0,1\}^k$ where k is the key-length of E.

3.2 Security of StE

We now prove the security of StE. Our main theorem is in the information-theoretic setting, where we reduce security to the sub-key prediction problem for the distribution $\mathcal{D}$. Then, below, we instantiate the scheme with a block cipher E, assumed to be a PRP, and use the theorem to give corresponding security statements for this instantiation, showing in particular we can attain security beyond 2^n queries.

Theorem 1 (Information-theoretic security of StE). *Assume that*

$$\mathsf{Adv}^{\mathsf{skp\text{-}aux}}_{\mathcal{D},t}(S + s + \ell + tn) \leq 2^{-\gamma}$$

and that $\mathsf{Ext} : \{0,1\}^{tn} \times \{0,1\}^s \to \{0,1\}^\ell$ *is an average-case* (γ, ε)*-strong extractor. Then,*

$$\mathsf{Adv}^{\mathsf{ROR}}_{\mathsf{StE}[\mathcal{D},t,\mathsf{Ext}]}(q, S) \leq q\varepsilon.$$

Proof. The proof proceeds in two parts. In the first part, we consider a variant of the sub-key prediction problem where the adversary, instead of trying to predict the sub-key at the given indices predicts, whether it has received the output of an extractor applied to the sub-key or a uniform random string. More precisely, consider a pair of adversaries $\mathcal{A}' = (\mathcal{A}'_1, \mathcal{A}'_2)$ where $\mathcal{A}'_1$ outputs $S + s + \ell + tn$ bits, and define the game $G^b(\mathcal{A}')$ as follows:

- $F \xleftarrow{\$} \mathcal{D}$; $\sigma \leftarrow \mathcal{A}'_1(F)$; $\mathsf{iv} = (\mathsf{iv}_1, \ldots, \mathsf{iv}_t) \xleftarrow{\$} \{0,1\}^{tn}$; $\mathsf{seed} \xleftarrow{\$} \{0,1\}^s$
- If $b = 0$ then $c \leftarrow \mathsf{Ext}(F(\mathsf{iv}_1)\| \ldots \|F(\mathsf{iv}_t), \mathsf{seed})$
- If $b = 1$ then $c \xleftarrow{\$} \{0,1\}^\ell$
- $b' \leftarrow \mathcal{A}'_2(\sigma, c, \mathsf{seed}, \mathsf{iv}_1, \ldots, \mathsf{iv}_t)$
- Return b'

The following lemma bounds is a simple corollary of Lemma 4 and the fact that Ext is an average-case (γ, ε)-strong extractor.

Lemma 6. *If* $\mathsf{Adv}^{\mathsf{skp\text{-}aux}}_{\mathcal{D},t}(S + \ell + s + tn) \leq 2^{-\gamma}$ *and* $\mathsf{Ext} : \{0,1\}^{tn} \times \{0,1\}^s \to \{0,1\}^\ell$ *is an average-case* (γ, ε)*-strong extractor, then*

$$\left|\mathsf{Pr}[G^0(\mathcal{A}') = 1] - \mathsf{Pr}[G^1(\mathcal{A}') = 1]\right| \leq \varepsilon.$$

We now introduce hybrids H_i for $i = 0, \ldots, q$ such that in hybrid experiment i-th hybrid, the adversary $\mathcal{A}$ interacts with the oracle $\mathcal{E}'(M, 0)$ for the first i queries and with $\mathcal{E}'(M, 1)$ for the remaining queries. Formally, for $i = 1, \ldots, q$, we define the following hybrid experiment $H_i^{\mathsf{StE}}(\mathcal{A})$ for an adversary $\mathcal{A}$:

$$F \xleftarrow{\$} \mathsf{Gen};\, b' \leftarrow \mathcal{A}^{\mathcal{E}'(\cdot, i)};\ \text{Return } b'$$

where $\mathcal{E}'(M, i)$ responds to the j-th query as follows:

- If $j \leq i$, return $c \xleftarrow{\$} \mathsf{Enc}^F(M)$.
- Else, choose $M' \xleftarrow{\$} \mathcal{M}$ such that $|M'| = |M|$ and return $c \xleftarrow{\$} \mathsf{Enc}^F(M')$.

Then, by definition of the advantage $\mathsf{Adv}^{\mathsf{ROR}}_{\mathcal{E}}(\mathcal{A})$, we have

$$\mathsf{Adv}^{\mathsf{ROR}}_{\mathcal{E}}(\mathcal{A}) = \left|\mathsf{Pr}[H_q^{\mathsf{StE}}(\mathcal{A}) = 1] - \mathsf{Pr}[H_0^{\mathsf{StE}}(\mathcal{A}) = 1]\right|. \quad (2)$$

We now prove the following central lemma.

Lemma 7. $|\mathsf{Pr}[H_i^{\mathsf{StE}}(\mathcal{A}) = 1] - \mathsf{Pr}[H_{i-1}^{\mathsf{StE}}(\mathcal{A}) = 1]| \leq \varepsilon.$

Proof. We now construct an adversary $\mathcal{A}' = (\mathcal{A}'_1, \mathcal{A}'_2)$ for the game $G^b(\mathcal{A}')$ introduced earlier. On input F, $\mathcal{A}'_1$ proceeds as follows:

– $(\sigma_0, y_0) \leftarrow \perp$
– for $j = 1$ to $i-1$
  • $(M_j, \sigma_j) \leftarrow \mathcal{A}(\sigma_{j-1}, y_{j-1})$
  • $y_j \leftarrow \mathsf{Enc}^F(M_j)$
– Return (σ_{i-1}, y_{i-1})

Note that the output length of $\mathcal{A}_1'$ is at most S plus the length of a ciphertext, i.e., $S + s + \ell + n \cdot t$.

Now, the adversary $\mathcal{A}_2'$, is given (σ_{i-1}, y_{i-1}) from $\mathcal{A}_1'(F)$, and moreover, it receives $(u, \mathsf{seed}, \mathsf{iv}_1, \ldots, \mathsf{iv}_t)$ as its challenge from the game. It then proceeds as follows: it continues the execution of $\mathcal{A}$ with input (σ_{i-1}, y_{i-1}) and when $\mathcal{A}$ makes its i-th query by requesting the encryption of a message M, the adversary $\mathcal{A}_2'$ answers this query to $\mathcal{A}$ with the ciphertext $(u \oplus M, \mathsf{seed}, \mathsf{iv}_1, \ldots, \mathsf{iv}_t)$. It then continues the execution of $\mathcal{A}$, but answers all future encryption queries with truly random ciphertexts.

By construction, we now have

$$|\mathsf{Pr}[\overline{H}_i^{\mathsf{StE}}(\mathcal{A}) = 1] - \mathsf{Pr}[\overline{H}_{i-1}^{\mathsf{StE}}(\mathcal{A}) = 1]| = |\mathsf{Pr}[G^0(\mathcal{A}') = 1] - \mathsf{Pr}[G^1(\mathcal{A}') = 1]|$$

Applying Lemma 6 then concludes the proof of the lemma. □

Thus, Eq. 2 and Lemma 7 yield

$$\mathsf{Adv}_{\mathcal{E}}^{\mathsf{ROR}}(\mathcal{A}) \le \sum_{i=1}^{q} \left|\mathsf{Pr}[H_i^{\mathsf{StE}}(\mathcal{A}) = 1] - \mathsf{Pr}[H_{i-1}^{\mathsf{StE}}(\mathcal{A}) = 1]\right| \le q \cdot \varepsilon,$$

which gives us the theorem. □

Instantiation. We now derive a corollary stating the security of the encryption scheme with a block cipher $\mathsf{E} : \{0,1\}^k \times \{0,1\}^n \to \{0,1\}^n$ assumed to be a good pseudorandom permutation (PRP). We instantiate the extractor in the encryption scheme using the leftover hash lemma (cf. Lemma 2). The following lemma follows by replacing the block cipher with a randomly chosen permutation F (at the cost of the PRP advantage), and then using the fact that F has min-entropy $\log(N!)$.

Corollary 1 (Instantiation of StE). *Let* $\mathsf{E} : \{0,1\}^k \times \{0,1\}^n \to \{0,1\}^n$ *be a block cipher. Let* $\mathcal{H} : \{0,1\}^{tn} \times \{0,1\}^{tn} \to \{0,1\}^{\ell}$ *be a 2-universal family of hash functions. Let* $S \le (1-\delta)nN$ *for some* $\delta \in [0,1]$*. Then, if* $\delta \ge \left[\frac{4(\ell - 2\log\varepsilon)}{t} + \frac{1}{n} + \frac{4\ell - 6\log\varepsilon + 2tn + 5}{nN}\right]$ *for some* $\varepsilon > 0$*, then for all* D*,* T*, there exists* $D' \approx D$ *and* $T' \approx T$ *such that*

$$\mathsf{Adv}_{\mathsf{StE}[\mathsf{E},t,\mathcal{H}]}^{\mathsf{ROR}}(D, T, q, S) \le q\varepsilon + \mathsf{Adv}_{\mathsf{E}}^{\mathsf{PRP\text{-}CPA}}(D', T', tq, S + 2n(t-1)).$$

Beyond 2^n-security. We plug in concrete values in Corollary 1 to demonstrate that our encryption scheme can tolerate $q \gg 2^n$ queries by the adversary, as long as memory is bounded.

With $N = 2^n$, let $q \leq N^{1.5}$ and we want ε to be 2^{-3n} such that in particular $q\varepsilon \leq 2^{-1.5n}$ for an S-bounded adversary where $S \leq N^{1-\alpha}$ with $0 < \alpha \ll 1$. If $\ell = n$ and $t = an$ where $n \geq 20$ and $a \geq 32$, we have

$$\mathsf{Adv}^{\mathsf{ROR}}_{\mathsf{StE}[\mathsf{E},t,\mathcal{H}]}(D, T, q, S) \leq 2^{-1.5n} + \mathsf{Adv}^{\mathsf{PRP\text{-}CPA}}_{\mathsf{E}}(D', T', tq, S + 2n(t-1)).$$

As for the PRP-advantage term, it is reasonable to assume for a good block cipher, the advantage is small even if $T' \gg 2^n$. At the very least, this implies that key-length k of the block cipher E satisfies $k > \log q$. (This is not sufficient of course!) Also we remind here that D' is the description size.

We stress here that we are not focusing on optimizing parameters – and there is a lot of potential for this, by using either better extractors (with shorter seeds) and better sub-key prediction bounds.

Game $\mathsf{sAUTH}^{\mathcal{AS}}(\mathcal{A})$:	Oracle $\mathcal{O}_{\mathsf{Step}}(M, \mathsf{c}', (M', T'))$:

$K \xleftarrow{\$} \mathsf{Gen}$
$\mathsf{c}_0 \xleftarrow{\$} \mathsf{Ch}$
$f_0, f_1 \leftarrow \mathsf{false}$
$i \leftarrow 0$
$\mathsf{Win} \leftarrow \mathsf{false}$
Run $\mathcal{A}^{\mathcal{O}_{\mathsf{Step}}}(\mathsf{c}_0)$
Return Win
	$i \leftarrow i + 1$
	$\mathsf{c}_i \xleftarrow{\$} \mathsf{Ch}$
	$M_i \leftarrow M$
	If $i = 1$ then
	    $T_1 \leftarrow \mathsf{Tag}(K, \mathsf{c}', M)$; return (c_1, T_1)
	Else
	    If $\mathsf{Vfy}(K, \mathsf{c}_{i-2}, M', T') \wedge (\neg f_{i \bmod 2})$ then
	        If $M' \neq M_{i-1} \vee f_{i-1 \bmod 2}$ then
	            $\mathsf{Win} \leftarrow \mathsf{true}$
	        $T_i \leftarrow \mathsf{Tag}(K, \mathsf{c}', M)$; return (c_i, T_i)
	    Else $f_{i \bmod 2} \leftarrow \mathsf{true}$; return $(\perp, \perp)$

Fig. 3. Security game sAUTH. Game defining the security of two-party synchronized authentication. The oracle $\mathcal{O}_{\mathsf{Step}}$ corresponds to each party authenticating chosen messages, in an alternating fashion. Each party will stop answering subsequent queries as soon as a verification query fails. The adversary wins if it delivers a message to a party with a valid tag which was not authenticated by the other party immediately before.

4 Message Authentication

4.1 Synchronous Authentication: Definitions and Settings

We consider the interactive setting of message authentication. Here, two parties alternate communication through an insecure channel (under control of a man-in-the-middle adversary), and want to send authenticated messages to each other. We consider protocols that are *synchronous*, in the sense that at each round one party asks for a challenge c, and the next message M it receives from the other party is authenticated with a tag which depends on *both* c and M (in addition to the secret key). We are not aware of this notion having been extensively studied, but as we will point out below in Sect. 4.4, considering this setting is somewhat necessary, as building PRFs/MACs secure against memory-bounded adversaries appears out of reach without bypassing existing technical barriers in computational complexity.

SYNCHRONOUS AUTHENTICATION SCHEMES: SYNTAX. A *synchronous authentication scheme* is a 4-tuple $\mathcal{AS} = (\mathsf{Gen}, \mathsf{Ch}, \mathsf{Tag}, \mathsf{Vfy})$ of algorithms, which take the following roles:

- The *key generation algorithm* Gen generates a secret key K.
- The *challenge generation algorithm* Ch returns a challenge c.
- The *tagging algorithm* Tag takes as input the secret key K, a message to be authenticated $M \in \mathcal{M}$, and a challenge c, and returns a tag T.
- The *verification algorithm* Vfy takes as input a key K, a challenge c, a message M, and a tag T, and returns a boolean value in $\{\mathtt{true}, \mathtt{false}\}$.

We say that the scheme is ν-correct if for all $M \in \mathcal{M}$,

$$\mathsf{Pr}\left[K \stackrel{\$}{\leftarrow} \mathsf{Gen},\ \mathsf{c} \stackrel{\$}{\leftarrow} \mathsf{Ch},\ T \stackrel{\$}{\leftarrow} \mathsf{Tag}_K(\mathsf{c}, M)\ :\ \mathsf{Vfy}_K(\mathsf{c}, M, T) \neq \mathtt{true}\right] \leq \nu.$$

As in the case of encryption, it will be convenient to introduce a notation where we view a function F as the key K. In this case, we write Tag^F and Vfy^F instead of Tag_K and Vfy_K.

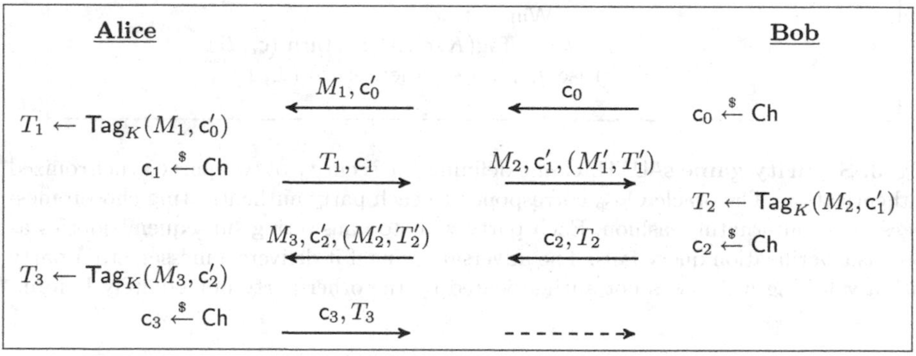

Fig. 4. Synchronous authentication security game. This illustrates the flow of the execution of the synchronous authentication game. We omit verification from the figure. At each step, if (M'_i, T'_i) does not verify with respect to c_{i-1}, a pair $(\mathsf{c}_i, T_i) = (\bot, \bot)$ is returned and the corresponding party stops accepting any future messages.

SECURITY OF AUTHENTICATION SCHEMES. We introduce a security game that captures the security of a synchronous authentication scheme as described above. The game, found in Fig. 3, considers an adversary $\mathcal{A}$ interacting with an oracle $\mathcal{O}_{\mathsf{Step}}$, which responds (in an alternating way) as Alice and Bob, each time authenticating a message *chosen* by the adversary. For ease of explanation, a more detailed depiction of the execution flow in the game is given in Fig. 4. Then, the advantage of an adversary $\mathcal{A}$ against the authentication scheme $\mathcal{AS}$ is defined as

$$\mathsf{Adv}^{\mathsf{AUTH}}_{\mathcal{AS}}(\mathcal{A}) = \Pr\left[\mathsf{sAUTH}^{\mathcal{AS}}(\mathcal{A}) = \mathtt{true}\right].$$

Further, $\mathsf{Adv}^{\mathsf{AUTH}}_{\mathcal{AS}}(D, T, q, S) = \max_{\mathcal{A}}\{\mathsf{Adv}^{\mathsf{AUTH}}_{\mathcal{AS}}(\mathcal{A})\}$, where the maximum is taken over all S-bounded adversaries $\mathcal{A}$ with running time at most T that makes at most q queries and have size at most D.

As in the case of encryption, in the information-theoretic setting, we drop T and D from the notation and denote the security of the scheme by simply $\mathsf{Adv}^{\mathsf{AUTH}}_{\mathcal{AS}}(q, S) = \mathsf{Adv}^{\mathsf{AUTH}}_{\mathcal{AS}}(\infty, \infty, q, S)$.

4.2 The Challenge-then-Verify Scheme

We give a construction of a synchronous authentication scheme for ℓ-bit messages. The scheme relies on a single function $F : \{0,1\}^n \to \{0,1\}^n$, which we think of being instantiated from a block cipher or a keyed function, but that in the general description we assume comes from a distribution $\mathcal{D}$.

We let t be a parameter, and let $\mathsf{Ext} : \{0,1\}^{t \cdot n} \times \{0,1\}^s \to \{0,1\}^m$ be a function, which should be thought of as an *extractor* later on, and we consequently refer to s as the *seed length*. Also, let $d = \lceil \log(\ell) + 1 \rceil$. We let $\mathcal{I}$ be the uniform distribution over t-tuples of indices $(\mathsf{iv}_1, \ldots, \mathsf{iv}_t) \in \left(\{0,1\}^{n-d-1}\right)^t$. Let $\langle i \rangle$ be the d-bit encoding of $i \in \{1, \ldots, \ell\}$. Generally, we will be interested in the case where $\ell > n$, and s will only depend on n and a desirable security level.

We now describe the algorithms that constitute our authentication scheme *Challenge-then-Verify* $\mathsf{CtV}[\ell, \mathcal{D}, t, \mathsf{Ext}]$. In particular:

Scheme $\mathsf{CtV}[\ell, \mathcal{D}, t, \mathsf{Ext}]$:

- **Key generation.** The key generation algorithm Gen samples F according to distribution $\mathcal{D}$ and outputs F.
- **Challenge generation.** The challenge generation algorithm Ch samples a tuple $(\mathsf{iv}_1, \ldots, \mathsf{iv}_t) \stackrel{\$}{\leftarrow} \mathcal{I}$, as well as a random seed $\mathsf{seed} \stackrel{\$}{\leftarrow} \{0,1\}^s$, and outputs $\mathsf{c} = (\mathsf{iv}_1, \ldots, \mathsf{iv}_t, \mathsf{seed})$.
- **Authentication.** To authenticate a message $M \in \{0,1\}^\ell$ for challenge $\mathsf{c} = (\mathsf{iv}_1, \ldots, \mathsf{iv}_t, \mathsf{seed})$, the tagging algorithm outputs

$$\mathsf{Tag}^F(M = M_1, \ldots, M_\ell, \mathsf{c}) = \bigoplus_{i=1}^{\ell} \mathsf{Ext}(Y_i, \mathsf{seed}),$$

where

$$Y_i = F(\langle i \rangle \parallel M_i \parallel \mathsf{iv}_1) \parallel \cdots \parallel F(\langle i \rangle \parallel M_i \parallel \mathsf{iv}_t).$$

- **Verification.** Verification is straightforward, by simply re-computing the tag and checking equality.

When we let $\mathcal{D}$ be the distribution that samples a key K for a block cipher E, and then outputs the function E_K, as above, we denote the resulting scheme simply by $\mathsf{CtV}[\ell, \mathsf{E}, t, \mathsf{Ext}]$.

We will next move to the analysis of the scheme. After that, in Sect. 4.4, we give some further background about the scheme and possible extensions.

4.3 Security Proof

We first establish the security of the CtV scheme in the information-theoretic setting, where we let the scheme depend on an oracle sampled from a distribution $\mathcal{D}$ on functions from n bits to n bits. To formulate our main theorem, we need to define a derived distribution $\mathcal{D}_{j,b}$ over pairs (F', Z) consisting of a function F' with corresponding auxiliary information Z. To this end, we sample the function $F : \{0,1\}^n \to \{0,1\}^n$ randomly from $\mathcal{D}$, and then set

$$F' = F_{j,b}\ , \quad Z = \{F_{j',b'}\}_{(j',b') \neq (j,b)}$$

where $F_{j',b'} = F(\langle j' \rangle \parallel b' \parallel \cdot)$, which is a function $\{0,1\}^{n-d-1} \to \{0,1\}^n$.

This allows us to formulate the following technical theorem. While this is not yet usable to derive bounds with respect to concrete distribution $\mathcal{D}$, as this will require analyzing $\mathcal{D}_{j,b}$, we will give concrete parameter instantiations below.

Theorem 2 (Security of CtV). *For every distribution $\mathcal{D}$ over functions $\{0,1\}^n \to \{0,1\}^n$, if*

$$\max_{j,b} \mathsf{Adv}^{\mathsf{skp\text{-}aux}}_{\mathcal{D}_{j,b},t}(S + \ell + m) \leq 2^{-\gamma}$$

and Ext *is an average-case (γ, ε)-strong extractor, then*

$$\mathsf{Adv}^{\mathsf{AUTH}}_{\mathsf{CtV}[\ell,\mathcal{D},t,\mathsf{Ext}]}(q, S) \leq 4\ell q \left(\frac{1}{2^m} + \varepsilon \right).$$

Proof. Let $\mathcal{A}$ be an S-bounded, q-query adversary for the game $\mathsf{sAUTH}^{\mathsf{CtV}}(\mathcal{A})$, where for simplicity we denote $\mathsf{CtV} = \mathsf{CtV}[\ell, \mathcal{D}, t, \mathsf{Ext}]$. We consider in particular an execution of the S-bounded adversary $\mathcal{A}$, interacting with the oracle $\mathcal{O}_{\mathsf{Step}}$. Following the notation from Fig. 4, this interaction defines a sequence of queries consisting of message-challenge pairs

$$(M_1, \mathsf{c}'_0), (M_2, \mathsf{c}'_1), \ldots, (M_q, \mathsf{c}'_{q-1}),$$

as well as forgery attempts

$$(M'_2, T'_2), \ldots, (M'_q, T'_q).$$

These come with corresponding query answers $(\mathsf{c}_1, T_1), \ldots, (\mathsf{c}_q, T_q)$, where recall that $(\mathsf{c}_i, T_i) = (\perp, \perp)$ if $\mathcal{O}_{\mathsf{Step}}$ fails to return an answer. Further, for any i and j, we denote by $M_{i,j}$ and $M'_{i,j}$, respectively, the j-th bit of M_i and M'_i. Also, we let

$\sigma_0, \sigma_1, \ldots, \sigma_q$ be the sequence of states of $\mathcal{A}$ during this execution. We can assume without loss of generality that $\mathcal{A}$ is deterministic, by hard-coding the optimal randomness in the description of $\mathcal{A}$, as our arguments will be independent of the *size* of $\mathcal{A}$. (Thus, the length of the fixed randomness does not count towards the memory resources of $\mathcal{A}$.)

We define the family of events $\mathsf{Win}_{i,j,b,d}$ where $i \in [q] \setminus \{1\}$, $j \in [\ell]$, $d, b \in \{0,1\}$. Here, $\mathsf{Win}_{i,j,b,d}$ is the event that the following conditions are simultaneously true:

(1) The adversary $\mathcal{A}$ provokes $\mathsf{Win} \leftarrow \mathtt{true}$ in the i-th query (and thus Win was $\mathtt{false}$ up to that point);
(2) $b = M'_{i,j}$
(3) If $d = 1$, the $(i-1)$-th query did not return $(\bot, \bot)$. Further, $M_{i-1,j} = 1 - b$, and $M_{i-1,j'} = M'_{i,j'}$ for all $j' < j$. That is M'_i and M_{i-1} differ in the j-th bit, which takes value b and $1-b$ respectively, and M'_i and M_{i-1} are identical on the first $j-1$ bits.
(4) If $d = 0$, the $(i-1)$-th query returned $(\bot, \bot)$.

Then, we clearly have[8]

$$\mathsf{Adv}^{\mathsf{AUTH}}_{\mathsf{CtV}}(\mathcal{A}) = \sum_{i=2}^{q} \sum_{j=1}^{\ell} \sum_{b,d \in \{0,1\}} \Pr\left[\mathsf{Win}_{i,j,b,d}\right]. \tag{3}$$

We are going to now upper bound each individual probability $\Pr\left[\mathsf{Win}_{i,j,b,d}\right]$ in terms of the sub-key prediction advantage.

Reduction to sub-key prediction. Fix i, j, b, d. We first consider a variant of the sub-key prediction game where the goal is to predict the value of Ext applied to the sub-key, rather than predicting the sub-key itself. The game involves an adversary $\mathcal{B}$ and a leakage function $\mathcal{L}$, which we specify below, and the distribution $\mathcal{D}_{j,b}$ is as defined above:

- $(F_{j,b}, Z) \xleftarrow{\$} \mathcal{D}_{j,b}$
- $\sigma \leftarrow \mathcal{L}(F_{j,b}, Z)$
- $(\mathsf{iv}_1, \ldots, \mathsf{iv}_t) \xleftarrow{\$} \mathcal{I}$
- $\mathsf{seed} \xleftarrow{\$} \{0,1\}^s$
- $T \leftarrow \mathcal{B}(\sigma, Z, i_1, \ldots, i_t, \mathsf{seed})$
- Return $(T = \mathsf{Ext}(F_{j,b}(\mathsf{iv}_1) \| \ldots \| F_{j,b}(\mathsf{iv}_t), \mathsf{seed}))$

We stress that the game returns true if and only if T equals the extractor output. It is convenient to denote by $p_{\mathcal{B},\mathcal{L}}$ the probability that this is indeed the case. We now give $\mathcal{B}$ and $\mathcal{L}$ such that

$$\Pr\left[\mathsf{Win}_{i,j,b,d}\right] \le p_{\mathcal{B},\mathcal{L}}. \tag{4}$$

[8] Note that the fact that we have equality is not really important here, but the events indeed happen to be disjoint.

Concretely, leakage function $\mathcal{L}$ is given access to the description of 2ℓ functions $F_{1,1}, F_{0,1}, \ldots, F_{\ell,0}, F_{\ell,1}$ through $(F_{j,b}, Z = \{F'_{j',b'}\}_{(j',b')\neq(j,b)})$. It simulates correctly the execution of $\mathcal{A}$ in Game $\mathsf{sAUTH}^{\mathsf{CtV}}(\mathcal{A})$ for the first $i-2$ queries to $\mathcal{O}_{\mathsf{Step}}$, using the 2ℓ functions. The $(i-2)$-th query returns in particular a tag T_{i-2} for the message M_{i-2} and challenge c'_{i-3} – here we ignore the associated challenge c_{i-2} (with some foresight, we will simulate it from $\mathcal{B}$'s input) – and note that $T_{i-2} = \perp$ is possible. The leakage function then outputs $(\sigma_{i-2}, M_{i-2}, T_{i-2})$, where σ_{i-2} is $\mathcal{A}$'s state when making the $(i-2)$-th query.
Then, the adversary $\mathcal{B}$ is now given the leakage $(\sigma_{i-2}, M_{i-2}, T_{i-2})$, the auxiliary information $Z = \{F'_{j',b'}\}_{(j',b')\neq(j,b)}$, as well as a fresh $(\mathsf{iv}_1, \ldots, \mathsf{iv}_t)$ and seed. The only thing $\mathcal{B}$ does not know is $F_{j,b}$. Then, $\mathcal{B}$ proceeds through the following steps:

1. $\mathcal{B}$ resumes the execution of $\mathcal{A}$ with input σ_{i-2}, M_{i-2}, T_{i-2}, and $\mathsf{c}_{i-2} = (i_1, \ldots, i_t, \mathsf{seed})$ (if $T_{i-2} \neq \perp$) or $\mathsf{c}_{i-2} = \perp$ (if $T_{i-2} = \perp$).
2. When $\mathcal{A}$ asks the $(i-1)$-th query to $\mathcal{O}_{\mathsf{Step}}$ with the format $(M_{i-1}, \mathsf{c}'_{i-2}, (M'_{i-1}, T'_{i-1}))$, we distinguish between two cases.
   (a) First, if $d = 0$, $\mathcal{B}$ returns $(\perp, \perp)$ to the simulated $\mathcal{A}$.
   (b) If $d = 1$, $\mathcal{B}$ stops outputting a random m-bit guess if $M_{i-1,j} \neq 1 - b$. Otherwise, it computes $T_{i-1} \leftarrow \mathsf{Tag}^F(M_{i-1}, \mathsf{c}'_{i-2})$. Note that because $M_{i-1,j} = 1 - b$, this can be done with the available functions within Z, since $F_{j,b}$ is not involved in the computation. It then returns $(T_{i-1}, \mathsf{c}_{i-1})$ to $\mathcal{A}$.
3. Finally, $\mathcal{A}$ outputs its i-th query $(M_i, \mathsf{c}'_{i-1}, (M'_i, T'_i))$. Now, if $M'_{i,j} \neq b$, $\mathcal{B}$ stops with a random m-bit guess. Otherwise, we compute, for all $j' \neq j$,
$$Y_{j'} = F_{j',M'_{i,j'}}(\mathsf{iv}_1) \| \cdots \| F_{j',M'_{i,j'}}(\mathsf{iv}_t),$$
and finally output the guess
$$T = T'_i \oplus \bigoplus_{j'\neq j} \mathsf{Ext}(Y_{j'}, \mathsf{seed}).$$

It now clear that by construction Eq. 4 is always satisfied. This is because provided $\mathsf{Win}_{i,j,b,d}$ occurs, we can map an execution from $\mathsf{sAUTH}^{\mathsf{CtV}}(\mathcal{A})$ into one where $\mathcal{L}$ and $\mathcal{B}$ correctly guess Ext's output.

To conclude the proof, we note that $\mathcal{L}$'s output has length $S + \ell + m$ bits, and therefore, because $\mathsf{Adv}^{\mathsf{skp\text{-}aux}}_{\mathcal{D}_{j,b,t}}(S + \ell + m) \leq 2^{-\gamma}$, by Lemma 4,
$$\mathrm{H}_\infty(F_{j,b}(\mathsf{iv}_1)\| \ldots \|F_{j,b}(\mathsf{iv}_t)|\sigma_{i-2}, (\mathsf{iv}_1, \ldots \mathsf{iv}_t)) \geq \gamma.$$
But because Ext is a (γ, ε)-strong extractor, this also implies that
$$(\mathsf{Ext}(F_{j,b}(\mathsf{iv}_1)\| \ldots \|F_{j,b}(\mathsf{iv}_t), \mathsf{seed}), \sigma_{i-2}, (\mathsf{iv}_1, \ldots \mathsf{iv}_t), \mathsf{seed})$$
and
$$(Z, \sigma_{i-2}, (\mathsf{iv}_1, \ldots \mathsf{iv}_t), \mathsf{seed})$$

for uniformly distributed $Z \xleftarrow{\$} \{0,1\}^m$, have statistical distance at most ε. Therefore,

$$\Pr\left[\mathsf{Win}_{i,j,b,d}\right] \leq p_{\mathcal{B},\mathcal{L}} \leq \varepsilon + \frac{1}{2^m}.$$

This also concludes the proof, by plugging this into Eq. 3. □

INSTANTIATIONS. With the goal of providing a block-cipher based instantiation of the construction, we consider the case where $\mathcal{D}$ is the uniform distribution over all n-bit permutations. Then, note that $F_{j,b}$, given $F_{j',b'}$ for (j', b'), is still uniformly distributed over a set of $2^{n-d-1}!$ possible functions.

Corollary 2. *Let* $\mathsf{E} : \{0,1\}^k \times \{0,1\}^n \to \{0,1\}^n$ *be a block cipher. Let* $\mathcal{H} : \{0,1\}^{tn} \times \{0,1\}^{tn} \to \{0,1\}^m$ *be a 2-universal family of hash functions. Let* $S + \ell + m \leq N + \frac{N(n-\log(16\ell))}{8\ell} - \delta n N$ *for some* $\delta \in [0,1]$.

Then, if $\delta \geq \left[\frac{4(m-2\log\varepsilon)}{t} + \frac{1}{n} + \frac{3(m-2\log\varepsilon)+5}{nN}\right]$ *for some* $\varepsilon > 0$*, then for all* D, T*, there exists* $D' \approx D$ *and* $T' \approx T$ *such that*

$$\mathsf{Adv}^{\mathsf{AUTH}}_{\mathsf{CtV}[\ell,\mathcal{I},t,\mathcal{H},\mathsf{E}]}(D,T,q,S) \leq 4\ell q\left(\frac{1}{2^m} + \varepsilon\right) + \mathsf{Adv}^{\mathsf{PRP-CPA}}_{\mathsf{E}}(D',T',t\ell q,S').$$

where $S' = S + 2tn + 2\ell + m$.

BEYOND 2^n-SECURITY. Again, to demonstrate that our authentication scheme can tolerate queries beyond $q = 2^n$ by the adversary and still have meaningful security, we plug in concrete values in Corollary 2. Let $q \leq 2^{1.5n}$ and $\ell = 2n$. Let the output of the extractor be of length $m = 3n$. Say we want ε to be 2^{-3n} such that $4\ell q\left(\frac{1}{2^m} + \varepsilon\right) \leq 8n2^{-1.5n}$ when an S-bounded adversary is such that $S \leq N^{2/3}$. Then, by plugging in the desired parameters, we can see that for $n \geq 10$, we achieve the preferred security bound at $t \geq 300n^2$.

4.4 Remarks and Extensions

We give here a few remarks about our construction above. We will first discuss why a stronger result (dispensing with challenges) appears hard. We then discuss briefly how to extend the domain of authenticated messages, and the combination of encryption and authentication.

BUILDING PRFS: WHY IS IT HARD? An excellent question is whether we can build an actual PRF (and consequently a MAC), thus dispensing with the need for a challenge. The natural approach is to extend the domain of a random function[9] $R : \{0,1\}^n \to \{0,1\}^n$ to a function $\mathsf{F}^R : \{0,1\}^m \to \{0,1\}^n$ where $m > n$, which is indistinguishable from a truly random function for $q \gg 2^n$ queries, provided the distinguisher's memory is bounded by $S < 2^n$. This appears

[9] Or a permutation, but we restrict ourselves to functions as this only makes the problem easier, and our point stronger.

well beyond reach of current techniques, and would require overcoming barriers in the design of PRGs against space-bounded computation.

Specifically, consider a function $G : \{0,1\}^k \to \{0,1\}^\ell$ where $k > \ell$, and we now look at a model where, for a random $x \xleftarrow{\$} \{0,1\}^k$, a distinguisher is given oracle access to either the ℓ individual bits $y_1 \ldots y_\ell = G(x)$ or to independent random bits $y_1, \ldots, y_\ell$. The function G is an ε-PRG for S-bounded distinguishers if every space-S distinguisher can only succeed in distinguishing the two cases with advantage ε. Clearly, $S < k$ must hold, and the state of the art constructions [16,27] achieve $\ell = O(k)$, even if we only demand $\varepsilon = 1/\omega(\log(k))$.[10]

A domain extender F described above would in particular define an ε-PRG $G = G^{\mathsf{F}}$ for S-bounded computation with $k = n \cdot 2^n$ and $\ell = q \cdot n$ and $\varepsilon = n^{-\omega(1)}$. The PRG would just interpret its seed x as a function $f : \{0,1\}^n \to \{0,1\}^n$, and output a sequence of bits obtained by evaluating F^f at q distinct inputs. If $q \geq 2^{n(1+\delta)}$ for a constant $\delta > 0$, then we have $\ell \approx k^{1+\delta}$. Also, because F can only make a small number $t = \mathsf{poly}(n)$ of calls to f, the resulting PRG G is *local*, in the sense that every output bit only depends on $O(\log(k))$ bits of the seed. Existing constructions [16,27] have only linear stretch and are inherently non-local.

HIGHER EFFICIENCY. There is nothing really special about the scheme processing the message one bit at a time. The analysis can easily be generalized so that the scheme processes a large number of bits per call. That is, we would have for each $i \in [\ell]$, where now ℓ is the number of b-bit blocks, and the i-th block M_i,

$$Y_i = F(\langle i \rangle \parallel M_i \parallel \mathsf{iv}_1) \parallel \cdots \parallel F(\langle i \rangle \parallel M_i \parallel \mathsf{iv}_t).$$

We would lose in security, as the iv-values are now shorter, i.e., $n - b - d$, but this gives acceptable compromises. The analysis is a straightforward adaptation of the one we have given above.

EXTENDING THE DOMAIN. Our scheme above authenticates messages of fixed length ℓ. It can however straightforwardly be extended to authenticate arbitrarily long messages if we assume a collision resistant hash function family producing ℓ-bit hashes, for a sufficiently long ℓ, which is more secure than the underlying PRP E. For example, if the key length is k bits, one could assume $\ell = 2k$ and that collisions can only be found in time 2^k.

AUTHENTICATED ENCRYPTION. We will not discuss this in detail here, but clearly encryption and authentication can be combined to obtain a resulting notion of (synchronous) authenticated encryption. The messages to be authenticated would be ciphertexts produced with the encryption scheme from Sect. 3, and both schemes would use two independent keys.

[10] We note that much better constructions exist if one imposes restrictions on the distinguisher's queries, e.g., the bits are read once from y_1 to y_ℓ.

5 Key-Length Extension in the Memory-Bounded Setting

5.1 Problem Formulation

The results from the previous sections require a block cipher with security beyond 2^n queries. This in particular requires a long key, and we may not have it (e.g., in AES-128, the key length equals the block length). The classical problem of key-length extension addresses exactly this – several solutions have been validated in the ideal-cipher model [15,21–24,26,28],[11] and are commonly assumed to work with a good block cipher. Such results however assume no bounds on the adversary's memory, and thus, if we assume the adversary can store fewer than 2^n bits, they may be overly pessimistic. To this end, here, we analyze the security of double encryption in the ideal cipher model when the memory of the adversary is bounded. Double encryption is particularly interesting, because it is known *not* to amplify security when the memory of the adversary is unbounded. We will see that when the memory of the attacker does not exceed 2^k, for a k-bit key, things are substantially different, at least under reasonable assumptions.

DEFINITIONS. Let $\mathsf{E} : \{0,1\}^k \times \{0,1\}^n \to \{0,1\}^n$ be a block cipher. Then, the double encryption scheme $\mathsf{DE} = \mathsf{DE}[\mathsf{E}]$ is the block cipher such that

$$\mathsf{DE}_{K_1,K_2}(x) = \mathsf{E}_{K_2}(\mathsf{E}_{K_1}(x)) \tag{5}$$

where $K_1, K_2 \in \{0,1\}^k$. Clearly, $\mathsf{DE}^{-1}_{K_1,K_2}(y) = \mathsf{E}^{-1}_{K_1}(\mathsf{E}^{-1}_{K_2}(y))$.

The security notion considered for the double encryption scheme is that of *strong* PRP-security, where the attacker can make both forward and backwards queries. We will consider it in particular in the ideal-cipher model – to this end, let $\mathcal{BC}_{k,n}$ be the set of all block ciphers with key length k and block length n. The adversary has access to two pairs of oracles:

1. An ideal cipher oracle $\mathsf{E} \xleftarrow{\$} \mathcal{BC}_{k,n}$ and its inverse E^{-1} s.t. $\mathsf{E}^{-1}(K', y) = \mathsf{E}^{-1}_{K'}(y)$.
2. An oracle $\mathcal{O}$ and its inverse $\mathcal{O}^{-1}$, where $\mathcal{O}/\mathcal{O}^{-1} : \{0,1\}^n \to \{0,1\}^n$. The oracle $\mathcal{O}$ is either the double encryption scheme $\mathsf{DE}_{K_1,K_2}(\cdot) = \mathsf{E}_{K_2}(\mathsf{E}_{K_1}(\cdot))$ with uniform, independent, keys K_1 and K_2 (in the real world) or a random permutation $P \xleftarrow{\$} \mathcal{P}_n$ (in the ideal world).

At the end of q steps, the adversary tries to guess if the oracle $\mathcal{O}$ it has been interacting with is DE_{K_1,K_2} or P.

More explicitly, the advantage of an adversary $\mathcal{A}$ against the double encryption scheme $\mathsf{DE}[\mathsf{E}]$ is defined as

$$\begin{aligned}\mathsf{Adv}^{\mathsf{PRP}}_{\mathsf{DE}[\mathsf{E}]}(\mathcal{A}) = |\Pr[K_1, K_2 \xleftarrow{\$} \{0,1\}^k, \mathsf{E} \xleftarrow{\$} \mathcal{BC}_{k,n} \,:\, \mathcal{A}^{\mathsf{DE}_{K_1,K_2}, \mathsf{DE}^{-1}_{K_1,K_2}, \mathsf{E}, \mathsf{E}^{-1}} = 1] \\ - \Pr[P \xleftarrow{\$} \mathcal{P}_n \,:\, \mathcal{A}^{P, P^{-1}, \mathsf{E}, \mathsf{E}^{-1}} = 1]|.\end{aligned}$$

[11] We note that the use of the ideal-cipher model is somehow necessary, as we are achieving effectively true hardness amplification.

5.2 Double Encryption and List Disjointness

We study the security of the double encryption scheme in our model by relating it to a problem that we introduce, called the *list disjointness* problem – this is a special case of the element distinctness problem studied in the literature. We show that any algorithm solving this problem immediately implies an attacker against double encryption (with the same complexity). More importantly, as our main result, we show that any attacker against double encryption also implies an algorithm solving list disjointness.

THE LIST DISJOINTNESS PROBLEM. The setting for the $\mathrm{LD}_{\kappa,k}$ problem is as follows: An algorithm is given oracle access to two lists L_1 and L_2, each containing $\kappa/2$ distinct k-bit elements, i.e., the algorithm can learn the j-th element of L_i by making a query $L_i[j]$ for $i \in \{1,2\}$ and $j \in \{1,\ldots,\ell\}$. The lists are such that they have at most one element in common, i.e., we have the promise that $|L_1 \cap L_2| = 1$ or $|L_1 \cap L_2| = 0$. The aim of the algorithm is to distinguish the two cases given oracle access to the two lists. The list disjointness problem is a special case of the element distinctness problem where given oracle access to a list, an algorithm tries to determine whether all elements in the list are distinct. The following definition formalizes this as a distinguishing problem.

Definition 2 (List Disjointness Problem). *An algorithm* Alg *with binary output is said to solve the* list disjointness *problem* $LD_{\kappa,k}$ *with advantage* ε *if it is given oracle access to two lists* L_1, L_2 *of* $\kappa/2$ k*-bit elements (which we can think of as functions* $L_1, L_2 : [\kappa/2] \to \{0,1\}^k$*) such that* $|L_1 \cap L_2| \leq 1$*, and, moreover, for any such* L_1, L_2*, the difference between the probabilities that* Alg *outputs* 1 *when* $|L_1 \cap L_2| = 1$ *and when* $L_1 \cap L_2 = \emptyset$ *is* at least ε.

We note that advantage above can be amplified via sequential repetition – this requires minimal memory overhead to estimate the number of repetitions outputting one. We omit the details.

LIST DISJOINTNESS TO DE. We first observe that an algorithm Alg that solves the list disjointness problem immediately implies a distinguisher against the PRP-security of the double encryption scheme with similar memory and time complexities, and advantage. This can be seen as follows. The distinguisher runs Alg and provides oracle access to two lists L_1 and L_2 where the lists are each of size 2^k, and each index j in L_i is associated with a unique k-bit string $K^j \in \{0,1\}^k$. The distinguisher makes a constant c number of queries to its permutation oracle (that is either DE_{K_1,K_2} or P) to obtain plaintext/ciphertext pairs $(x_1,y_1),\ldots,(x_c,y_c)$. (The constant c is related to the ratio between key length and block length of the block cipher E.) Now, when Alg queries the list L_i at index j, the distinguisher answers this query using its $\mathsf{E}/\mathsf{E}^{-1}$ oracle as follows:

- if $i = 1$, return $\mathsf{E}_{K^j}(x_1)\|\ldots\|\mathsf{E}_{K^j}(x_c)$ as the element $L_1[j]$ and
- if $i = 2$, return $\mathsf{E}^{-1}_{K^j}(y_1)\|\ldots\|\mathsf{E}^{-1}_{K^j}(y_c)$ as the element $L_2[j]$.

When the permutation oracle of the distinguisher is the double encryption oracle, L_1 and L_2 share exactly an element, while if it were a random permutation, an element is shared only with probability negligible in k.

DE TO LIST DISJOINTNESS. The reduction for transforming an adversary against the double encryption scheme to an algorithm for list disjointness is more involved. In fact, our algorithm in the list disjointness problem will require access to additional oracles that can be queried for free (i.e., such queries do not count towards the query complexity). Specifically, it will use:

- A permutation $\rho : [\kappa] \to [\kappa]$ chosen uniformly from the set of all permutations over $[\kappa]$. On input K, the output $\rho(K)$ is interpreted as $\rho(K) = (i, j)$ where $i \in \{1, 2\}$ and $j \in [\kappa/2]$.
- A permutation $\pi : \{0,1\}^n \to \{0,1\}^n$ chosen uniformly from the set of all permutations over $\{0,1\}^n$, and its inverse π^{-1}.
- An ideal cipher $F : \{0,1\}^k \times \{0,1\}^n \to \{0,1\}^n$.

We stress that these oracles do not depend on the lists L_1 and L_2. (In a heuristic implementation they could be realized e.g., from a block cipher.)

Given an adversary $\mathcal{A}$ against double encryption achieving advantage ε, we show how to solve the list disjointness problem with advantage $\varepsilon - 2^k$, given access to F, ρ, and π as defined above.

Theorem 3. *Let $\mathcal{A}$ be an S-bounded attacker making at most q ideal-cipher queries (and any number of queries to its $\mathcal{O}$ / $\mathcal{O}^{-1}$ oracle) such that*

$$\mathsf{Adv}^{\mathsf{PRP}}_{\mathsf{DE[E]}}(\mathcal{A}) \geq \varepsilon,$$

where the underlying ideal cipher has key length k and block length n. Then, there exists an S-bounded algorithm Alg *that makes q queries to the given lists, uses the oracles ρ, F, π defined above, and solves the list disjointness problem $LD_{\kappa=2^k,k}$ with advantage $\varepsilon - 2^{-k}$.*

Proof (Sketch). Fix an adversary $\mathcal{A}$ against the double encryption scheme DE such that it has the maximum advantage. We assume without loss of generality that the probability it outputs 1 in the real world is at least ε higher than in the ideal world. Recall that the algorithm Alg has access to oracles L_1, L_2, ρ, π, F as mentioned in Definition 2. The algorithm proceeds by running $\mathcal{A}$, and thus it is required to simulate the ideal cipher and permutation oracles that $\mathcal{A}$ expects access to. This is done in the following manner. If $\mathcal{A}$ queries the permutation oracle $\mathcal{O}$ or $\mathcal{O}^{-1}$, the algorithm Alg just returns the answer by querying its random permutation oracle π or its inverse π^{-1}. A query $(K, \cdot)$ to the ideal cipher oracle on key K is answered as follows: We interpret $\rho(K)$ as (i, j) where $i \in \{1, 2\}$ and $j \in [\kappa/2]$. Then, if $i = 1$:

- a forward query (K, x) is answered as $\mathsf{E}'_K(x) \leftarrow F_{L_1[j]}(x)$,
- an inverse query (K, y) is answered as $\mathsf{E}'^{-1}_K(y) \leftarrow F^{-1}_{L_1[j]}(y)$.

If $i = 2$:

- a forward query (K, x) is answered as $\mathsf{E}'_K(x) \leftarrow \pi(F^{-1}_{L_2[j]}(x))$,
- an inverse query (K, y) is answered as $\mathsf{E}'^{-1}_K(y) \leftarrow F_{L_2[j]}(\pi^{-1}(y))$.

At the end, Alg outputs $\mathcal{A}$'s output bit.

We now note the following, omitting a formal argument:

- If the lists L_1 and L_2 do not intersect, then the keys on which F is called for the cases $i = 1$ and $i = 2$ are distinct, and thus we are perfectly simulating the ideal world, since composing π with F in the $i = 2$ case does not change the distribution of the query answers.
- If the lists L_1 and L_2 intersect exactly at one point, then there are two distinct keys K_1 and K_2 such that $\rho(K_1) = (1, j_1)$, $\rho(K_2) = (2, j_2)$, and $L_1[j_1] = L_2[j_2]$. This ensures that $\mathsf{E}_{K_1}(\mathsf{E}_{K_2}(x)) = \pi(x)$. Moreover, because ρ is a random permutation, K_1 and K_2 are uniformly distributed, conditioned on $K_1 \neq K_2$. Thus, we are simulating the real world *conditioned* on $K_1 \neq K_2$.

Therefore, as claimed, Alg solves the list disjointness problem with advantage at least $\varepsilon - 2^{-k}$. □

STATE-OF-THE-ART FOR LIST DISJOINTNESS. Now that we have shown that an attacker against double encryption leads to an algorithm solving list disjointness with similar complexity, we state the best existing algorithm for list disjointness and conjecture that this is the best possible.

To this end, we first state the following result by Beame, Clifford, and Machmouchi [8] that gives an algorithm for computing element distinctness. In the following statement ED_n refers to the decision problem where given n elements belonging to some domain we need to determine if the n elements are distinct or not. Again, the advantage will measure the difference between the probability of a positive answer when the elements are distinct and when they are not. As a corollary of this result, we can derive a time-space upper bound for the list disjointness problem mentioned above.

Theorem 4 ([8]). *For any $\varepsilon > 0$, and any S with $c \log n \leq S \leq n/32$ for some constant $c > 0$, there is an S-bounded algorithm solving ED_n with advantage ε making $q = O\left(\frac{n^{3/2}}{S^{1/2}} \log^{5/2} n \log(1/(1-\varepsilon))\right)$ queries to the given list.*

This theorem immediately gives us the following corollary as list disjointness can be seen as a special case of the element distinctness problem where the elements under consideration are those belonging to the two lists.

Corollary 3. *For any $\varepsilon > 0$, and any S with $c \log \kappa \leq S \leq \kappa/32$ for some constant $c > 0$, there is an S-bounded algorithm solving $LD_{\kappa,k}$ with advantage ε, and making*

$$q = O\left(\frac{\kappa^{3/2}}{S^{1/2}} \log^{5/2}(\kappa) \log(1/(1-\varepsilon))\right)$$

queries.

We have been somewhat informal here, as the algorithm of [8] actually requires access to a random hash function. This can be implemented from the oracles made available in our extended setting of $LD_{\kappa,k}$.

We note that finding good lower bounds for the element distinctness problem has been a major open problem in complexity theory for the past three decades and progress has been slow on that front. The best known lower bound is due to Beame et al. [10] that showed $T \in \Omega\left(n\sqrt{\log(n/S)/\log\log(n/S)}\right)$. A better lower bound of $T \in \Omega\left(n^{2-o(1)}/S\right)$ was given by Yao [39] in the restricted setting of *comparison branching programs* (where access to the input is limited to pairwise comparison). Until the result stated in Theorem 4, it was not known whether the lower bound in the general setting matches the restricted setting given by Yao [39].

A CONDITIONAL LOWER BOUND. Given the current state-of-the-art, we conjecture that the result by Beame et al. [8] does in fact provide the best algorithm for computing element distinctness and hence assume that it gives a lower bound on the time-space tradeoff for the element distinctness problem. We state that following (slightly more conservative) conjecture (note that we have implicitly used that $\log(1/(1-\varepsilon)) = \Omega(\varepsilon)$ here).

Conjecture 1. There are constants c_1, c_2, such that for any $\varepsilon > 0$ and any S with $c_1 \log \kappa \leq S \leq \kappa/c_2$, every S-bounded algorithm to solve the list disjointness problem $LD_{\kappa,k}$

with advantage at least ε requires querying the lists

$$q = \Omega\left(\frac{\kappa^{3/2}}{S^{1/2}}\varepsilon\right)$$

times.

Therefore, under Conjecture 1, Theorem 3 directly yields a lower bound, and in particular for any S-bounded attacker $\mathcal{A}$ that queries the ideal cipher at most $q = O\left(\frac{2^{3k/2}}{S^{1/2}}(\varepsilon - 2^{-k})\right)$ times, the advantage is at most ε, or equivalently, for any S-bounded $\mathcal{A}$ making at most q queries to the ideal cipher,

$$\mathsf{Adv}^{\mathsf{PRP}}_{\mathsf{DE[E]}}(\mathcal{A}) = O\left(\sqrt{\frac{Sq^2}{2^{3k}}}\right) + \frac{1}{2^k}.$$

We stress that the bound is independent of the number of queries to the $\mathcal{O}$ / $\mathcal{O}^{-1}$ oracle. Note that if $S = 2^k$, we recover the traditional bound of $q/2^k$, which is tight by the meet-in-the-middle attack. (It is worth noting that Aiello et al. [1] show the slightly superior bound of $(q/2^k)^2$ here.) However, if for example $S = 2^{k/2}$, then we get security up to $q = 2^{1.25k}$ queries.

Acknowledgments. Stefano Tessaro's work was partially supported by NSF grants CNS-1553758 (CAREER), CNS-1423566, CNS-1719146, CNS-1528178, and IIS-1528041, and by a Sloan Research Fellowship. Aishwarya Thiruvengadam's work was partially supported by the Defense Advanced Research Projects Agency (DARPA) and Army Research Office (ARO) under Contract No. W911NF-15-C-0236, and a subcontract No. 2017-002 through Galois.

References

1. Aiello, W., Bellare, M., Di Crescenzo, G., Venkatesan, R.: Security amplification by composition: the case of doubly-iterated, ideal ciphers. In: Krawczyk, H. (ed.) CRYPTO 1998. LNCS, vol. 1462, pp. 390–407. Springer, Heidelberg (1998). https://doi.org/10.1007/BFb0055743
2. Ajtai, M.: A non-linear time lower bound for boolean branching programs. Theory Comput. **1**(8), 149–176 (2005)
3. Alwen, J., Blocki, J., Pietrzak, K.: Depth-robust graphs and their cumulative memory complexity. In: Coron and Nielsen [18], pp. 3–32 (2017)
4. Alwen, J., Chen, B., Pietrzak, K., Reyzin, L., Tessaro, S.: Scrypt is maximally memory-hard. In: Coron and Nielsen [18], pp. 33–62 (2017)
5. Alwen, J., Dodis, Y., Wichs, D.: Leakage-resilient public-key cryptography in the bounded-retrieval model. In: Halevi, S. (ed.) CRYPTO 2009. LNCS, vol. 5677, pp. 36–54. Springer, Heidelberg (2009). https://doi.org/10.1007/978-3-642-03356-8_3
6. Alwen, J., Serbinenko, V.: High parallel complexity graphs and memory-hard functions. In: Servedio, R.A., Rubinfeld, R. (eds.) 47th ACM STOC, Portland, OR, USA, 14–17 June 2015, pp. 595–603. ACM Press (2015)
7. Auerbach, B., Cash, D., Fersch, M., Kiltz, E.: Memory-tight reductions. In: Katz, J., Shacham, H. (eds.) CRYPTO 2017. LNCS, vol. 10401, pp. 101–132. Springer, Cham (2017). https://doi.org/10.1007/978-3-319-63688-7_4
8. Beame, P., Clifford, R., Machmouchi, W.: Element distinctness, frequency moments, and sliding windows. In: 54th FOCS, Berkeley, CA, USA, 26–29 October 2013, pp. 290–299. IEEE Computer Society Press (2013)
9. Beame, P., Saks, M., Sun, X., Vee, E.: Time-space trade-off lower bounds for randomized computation of decision problems. J. ACM **50**(2), 154–195 (2003)
10. Beame, P., Saks, M.E., Sun, X., Vee, E.: Time-space trade-off lower bounds for randomized computation of decision problems. J. ACM **50**(2), 154–195 (2003)
11. Bellare, M., Dai, W.: Defending against key exfiltration: efficiency improvements for big-key cryptography via large-alphabet subkey prediction. In: Thuraisingham, B.M., Evans, D., Malkin, T., Xu, D. (eds.), ACM CCS 17, Dallas, TX, USA, 31 October - 2 November 2017, pp. 923–940. ACM Press (2017)
12. Bellare, M., Desai, A., Jokipii, E., Rogaway, P.: A concrete security treatment of symmetric encryption. In: 38th FOCS, Miami Beach, Florida, 19–22 October 1997, pp. 394–403. IEEE Computer Society Press (1997)
13. Bellare, M., Goldreich, O., Krawczyk, H.: Stateless evaluation of pseudorandom functions: security beyond the birthday barrier. In: Wiener, M. (ed.) CRYPTO 1999. LNCS, vol. 1666, pp. 270–287. Springer, Heidelberg (1999). https://doi.org/10.1007/3-540-48405-1_17
14. Bellare, M., Kane, D., Rogaway, P.: Big-key symmetric encryption: resisting key exfiltration. In: Robshaw, M., Katz, J. (eds.) CRYPTO 2016. LNCS, vol. 9814, pp. 373–402. Springer, Heidelberg (2016). https://doi.org/10.1007/978-3-662-53018-4_14
15. Bellare, M., Rogaway, P.: The security of triple encryption and a framework for code-based game-playing proofs. In: Vaudenay, S. (ed.) EUROCRYPT 2006. LNCS, vol. 4004, pp. 409–426. Springer, Heidelberg (2006). https://doi.org/10.1007/11761679_25
16. Bogdanov, A., Papakonstantinou, P.A., Wan, A.: Pseudorandomness for linear length branching programs and stack machines. In: Gupta, A., Jansen, K., Rolim, J., Servedio, R. (eds.) APPROX/RANDOM -2012. LNCS, vol. 7408, pp. 447–458. Springer, Heidelberg (2012). https://doi.org/10.1007/978-3-642-32512-0_38

17. Borodin, A., Fischer, M.J., Kirkpatrick, D.G., Lynch, N.A., Tompa, M.: A time-space tradeoff for sorting on non-oblivious machines. J. Comput. Syst. Sci. **22**(3), 351–364 (1981)
18. Coron, J.-S., Nielsen, J.B. (eds.): EUROCRYPT 2017. LNCS, vol. 10211. Springer, Heidelberg (2017)
19. Dodis, Y., Ostrovsky, R., Reyzin, L., Smith, A.D.: Fuzzy extractors: how to generate strong keys from biometrics and other noisy data. SIAM J. Comput. **38**(1), 97–139 (2008)
20. Garg, S., Raz, R., Tal, A.: Extractor-based time-space lower bounds for learning. CoRR, abs/1708.02639 (2017)
21. Gaži, P.: Plain versus randomized cascading-based key-length extension for block ciphers. In: Canetti, R., Garay, J.A. (eds.) CRYPTO 2013. LNCS, vol. 8042, pp. 551–570. Springer, Heidelberg (2013). https://doi.org/10.1007/978-3-642-40041-4_30
22. Gaži, P., Lee, J., Seurin, Y., Steinberger, J., Tessaro, S.: Relaxing full-codebook security: a refined analysis of key-length extension schemes. In: Leander, G. (ed.) FSE 2015. LNCS, vol. 9054, pp. 319–341. Springer, Heidelberg (2015). https://doi.org/10.1007/978-3-662-48116-5_16
23. Gaži, P., Maurer, U.: Cascade encryption revisited. In: Matsui, M. (ed.) ASIACRYPT 2009. LNCS, vol. 5912, pp. 37–51. Springer, Heidelberg (2009). https://doi.org/10.1007/978-3-642-10366-7_3
24. Gaži, P., Tessaro, S.: Efficient and optimally secure key-length extension for block ciphers via randomized cascading. In: Pointcheval, D., Johansson, T. (eds.) EUROCRYPT 2012. LNCS, vol. 7237, pp. 63–80. Springer, Heidelberg (2012). https://doi.org/10.1007/978-3-642-29011-4_6
25. Håstad, J., Impagliazzo, R., Levin, L.A., Luby, M.: A pseudorandom generator from any one-way function. SIAM J. Comput. **28**(4), 1364–1396 (1999)
26. Hoang, V.T., Tessaro, S.: Key-alternating ciphers and key-length extension: exact bounds and multi-user security. In: Robshaw and Katz [34], pp. 3–32 (2016)
27. Impagliazzo, R., Meka, R., Zuckerman, D.: Pseudorandomness from shrinkage. In: 53rd FOCS, New Brunswick, NJ, USA, 20–23 October 2012, pp. 111–119. IEEE Computer Society Press (2012)
28. Lee, J.: Towards key-length extension with optimal security: cascade encryption and Xor-cascade encryption. In: Johansson, T., Nguyen, P.Q. (eds.) EUROCRYPT 2013. LNCS, vol. 7881, pp. 405–425. Springer, Heidelberg (2013). https://doi.org/10.1007/978-3-642-38348-9_25
29. Nisan, N.: Pseudorandom generators for space-bounded computation. Combinatorica **12**(4), 449–461 (1992)
30. Nisan, N., Zuckerman, D.: Randomness is linear in space. J. Comput. Syst. Sci. **52**(1), 43–52 (1996)
31. Pollard, J.M.: A monte carlo method for factorization. BIT Numer. Math. **15**(3), 331–334 (1975)
32. Raz, R.: Fast learning requires good memory: a time-space lower bound for parity learning. In: Dinur, I. (ed.), 57th FOCS, New Brunswick, NJ, USA, 9–11 October 2016, pp. 266–275. IEEE Computer Society Press (2016)
33. Raz, R.: A time-space lower bound for a large class of learning problems. In: 58th FOCS, pp. 732–742. IEEE Computer Society Press (2017)
34. Robshaw, M., Katz, J. (eds.): Advances in Cryptology – CRYPTO 2016, Part I. LNCS, vol. 9814. Springer, Heidelberg (2016). https://doi.org/10.1007/978-3-662-53018-4

35. Savage, J.E.: Models of Computation: Exploring the Power of Computing, 1st edn. Addison-Wesley Longman Publishing Co. Inc., Boston (1997)
36. Vadhan, S.P.: Constructing locally computable extractors and cryptosystems in the bounded-storage model. J. Cryptol. **17**(1), 43–77 (2004)
37. Vadhan, S.P.: Pseudorandomness. Found. Trends Theoret. Comput. Sci. **7**(1–3), 1–336 (2012)
38. van Oorschot, P.C., Wiener, M.J.: Parallel collision search with cryptanalytic applications. J. Cryptol. **12**(1), 1–28 (1999)
39. Yao, A.C.: Near-optimal time-space tradeoff for element distinctness. In: 29th FOCS, White Plains, New York, 24–26 October 1988, pp. 91–97. IEEE Computer Society Press (1988)
40. Yao, A.C.: Near-optimal time-space tradeoff for element distinctness. SIAM J. Comput. **23**(5), 966–975 (1994)

Static-Memory-Hard Functions, and Modeling the Cost of Space vs. Time

Thaddeus Dryja[1(✉)], Quanquan C. Liu[2], and Sunoo Park[2]

[1] MIT Media Lab, 75 Amherst St, Cambridge, MA, USA
tdryja@MIT.EDU
[2] MIT CSAIL, 32 Vassar St, Cambridge, MA, USA
{quanquan,sunoo}@mit.edu

Abstract. A series of recent research starting with (Alwen and Serbinenko, STOC 2015) has deepened our understanding of the notion of *memory-hardness* in cryptography—a useful property of hash functions for deterring large-scale password-cracking attacks—and has shown memory-hardness to have intricate connections with the theory of graph pebbling. Definitions of memory-hardness are not yet unified in the somewhat nascent field of memory-hardness, however, and the guarantees proven to date are with respect to a range of proposed definitions. In this paper, we observe *two* significant and practical considerations that are not analyzed by existing models of memory-hardness, and propose new models to capture them, accompanied by constructions based on new hard-to-pebble graphs. Our contribution is two-fold, as follows. First, existing measures of memory-hardness only account for *dynamic* memory usage (i.e., memory read/written at runtime), and do not consider *static* memory usage (e.g., memory on disk). Among other things, this means that memory requirements considered by prior models are inherently upper-bounded by a hash function's runtime; in contrast, counting static memory would potentially allow quantification of much larger memory requirements, decoupled from runtime. We propose a new definition of *static-memory-hard* function (SHF) which takes static memory into account: we model static memory usage by oracle access to a large preprocessed string, which may be considered part of the hash function description. Static memory requirements are *complementary* to dynamic memory requirements: neither can replace the other, and to deter large-scale password-cracking attacks, a hash function will benefit from being *both* dynamic-memory-hard and static-memory-hard. We give two SHF constructions based on pebbling. To prove static-memory-hardness, we define a new pebble game ("*black-magic pebble game*"), and new graph constructions with optimal complexity under our proposed measure. Moreover, we provide a prototype implementation of our first SHF construction (which is based on pebbling of a simple "cylinder" graph), providing an initial demonstration of practical feasibility for a limited range of parameter settings. Secondly, existing memory-hardness models implicitly assume that the cost of space and time are more or less on par: they consider only *linear* ratios between the costs of time and space. We propose a new model to capture *nonlinear* time-space

A. Beimel and S. Dziembowski (Eds.): TCC 2018, LNCS 11239, pp. 33–66, 2018.
https://doi.org/10.1007/978-3-030-03807-6_2

trade-offs: e.g., how is the adversary impacted when space is quadratically more expensive than time? We prove that nonlinear tradeoffs can in fact cause adversaries to employ different strategies from linear trade-offs.

Please refer to the full version of our paper for all results, proofs, appendices, and implementation details [DLP18].

1 Introduction

Pebble games were originally formulated to model time-space tradeoffs by a game played on DAGs. Generally, a DAG can be thought to represent a computation graph where each node is associated with some computation and a pebble placed on a node represents saving the result of its computation in memory. Thus, the number of pebbles represents the amount of memory necessary to perform some set of computations. The natural complexity measures to optimize in this game is the minimum number of pebbles used, as well as the minimum amount of time it takes to finish pebbling all the nodes; these goals correspond with minimizing the amount of memory and time of computation.

Pebble games were first introduced to study programming languages and compiler construction [PH70] but have since then been used to study a much broader range of tasks such as register allocation [Set75], proof complexity [AdRNV17,Nor12], time-space tradeoffs in Turing machine computation [Coo73,HPV77], reversible computation [Ben89], circuit complexity [Pot17], and time-space tradeoffs in various algorithms such as FFT [Tom81], linear recursion [Cha73,SS79b], matrix multiplication [Tom81], and integer multiplication [SS79a] in the RAM as well as the external memory model [JWK81]. To see a more comprehensive survey of the results in pebbling up to the last couple of years, see [Pip82] up to the 1980 s and [Nor15] up to 2015.

The relationship between pebbling and cryptography has been a subject of research interest for decades, which has enjoyed renewed activity in the last few years. A series of recent works [AB16,ABH17,ABP17a,ABP17b,AS15,AT17, ACP+16,AAC+17,BZ16,BZ17] has deepened our understanding of the notion of *memory-hardness* in cryptography, and has shown memory-hardness to have intricate connections with the theory of graph pebbling.

Memory-hard functions (MHFs) have garnered substantial recent interest as a security measure against adversaries trying to perform attacks at scale, particularly in the ubiquitous context of password hashing. Consider the following scenario: hashes of user passwords are stored in a database, and when a user enters a password p to log in, her computer sends $H(p)$ to the database server, and the server compares the received hash to its stored hash for that user's account. For a normal user, it would be no problem if hash evaluation were to take, say, one second. An attacker trying to guess the password by brute-force search, on the other hand, would try orders of magnitude more passwords, so a one-second hash evaluation could be prohibitively expensive for the attacker.

The evolution of password hashing functions has been something of an arms race for decades, starting with the ability to increase the number of rounds in the DES-based unix `crypt` function to increase its computation time—a feature that was used for exactly the above purpose of deterring large-scale password-cracking. Attackers responded by building special-purpose circuits for more efficient evaluation of `crypt`, resulting in a gap between the evaluation cost for an attacker and the cost for an honest user.

A promising approach to mitigating this asymmetry in cost between hash evaluation on general- and special-purpose hardware is to increase the use of *memory* in the password hashing function. Memory is implemented in standardized ways which have been highly optimized, and memory chips are widely regarded to be an interchangeable commodity. Commonly used forms of memory—whether on-die SRAM cache, DRAM, or hard disks—are already optimized for the purpose of data I/O operations; and while there is active research in improving memory access times and costs, progress is and has been relatively incremental. This state of affairs sets up a relatively "even playing field," as the normal user and the attacker are likely to be using memory chips of similar memory access speed. While an attacker may choose to buy more memory, the cost of doing so scales linearly with the amount purchased.

The designs of several MHFs proposed to date (e.g., [Per09, AS15, AB16, ACP+16, ABP17a]) have proven memory-hardness guarantees by basing their hash function constructions on DAGs, and using space complexity bounds from graph pebbling. Definitions of memory-hardness are not yet unified in this somewhat nascent field, however—the first MHF candidate was proposed only in 2009 [Per09]—and the guarantees proven are with respect to a range of definitions. The "cumulative complexity"-based definitions of [AS15] have enjoyed notable popularity, but some of their shortcomings have been pointed out by subsequent work proposing alternative more expressive measures, in particular, [ABP17b, AT17].

Our Contribution. We observe *two* significant and practical considerations not analyzed by existing models of memory-hardness, and propose new models to capture them, accompanied by constructions based on new hard-to-pebble graphs. Our main contribution is two-fold, as described in (1) and (2) below. We also provide an additional contribution of separate interest, described in (3).

1. ***Static-memory-hardness.*** Existing measures of memory-hardness only account for *dynamic* memory usage (i.e., memory read/written at runtime), and do not consider *static* memory usage (e.g., memory on disk). Among other things, this means that memory requirements considered by prior models are inherently upper-bounded by a hash function's runtime; in contrast, counting static memory would potentially allow quantification of much larger memory requirements, decoupled from the honest evaluator's runtime.
   We propose a new definition of *static-memory-hard* function (SHF) (Definition 24), and present two SHF constructions based on pebbling. To prove static-memory-hardness, we define a new pebble game called the *black-magic pebble game* (Definition 2), and prove properties of the space complexity of this game for new graphs (Graph Constructions 2 and 8). Graph Construction 8 gives rise to an SHF with a better asymptotic guarantee (same space

usage but sustained over more time), whereas Graph Construction 2 yields an SHF with the advantage of simplicity in practice. Informal theorems stating the constructions' static-memory-hardness guarantees are given in Sect. 1.2 and formal theorems are in Sect. 5. In our full version [DLP18], we discuss our prototype implementation based on Graph Construction 2. We emphasize that static memory requirements are *complementary* to dynamic memory requirements: neither can replace the other, and to deter large-scale password-cracking attacks, a hash function will benefit from being *both* dynamic-memory-hard and static-memory-hard.

2. ***Modeling nonlinear cost of space vs. time.*** Existing measures of memory-hardness implicitly assume a linear trade-off between the costs of space and time. This model precludes situations where the relative costs of space and time might be more unbalanced (e.g., quadratic or cubic). We demonstrate that this modeling limitation is significant, by giving an example where adversaries facing asymptotically different space-time cost tradeoffs would in fact employ *different strategies*. Then, to remedy this shortcoming, we define *graph-optimal* variants of memory-hardness measures (in Sect. 2) that *explicitly* model the relative cost of space and time. These can be seen as extending the main memory-hardness measures in the literature (namely, *cumulative complexity* and *sustained memory complexity*). We prove bounds on the new measure as elaborated in Sect. 1.2.
3. We give the first graph construction that is tight, up to $\log\log n$-factors, to the optimal cumulative complexity that can be achieved for any graph (upper bound due to [ABP17a, ABP17b]).
   Informal version of Theorem 6.23 in [DLP18]. There exists a family of graphs where the cumulative complexity of any constant in-degree graph with n nodes in the family is $\Theta\left(\frac{n^2\log\log n}{\log n}\right)$ which is asymptotically tight to the upper bound of $\Theta\left(\frac{n^2\log\log n}{\log n}\right)$ given in [ABP17a, ABP17b] in the sequential pebbling model.

The full version [DLP18] gives a brief background on graph pebbling, Sect. 1.1 gives discussion on memory-hardness measures and related work, and Sect. 1.2 give more detailed high-level overviews of our SHF contribution and nonlinear space-time tradeoff model (items (1) and (2) above), respectively.

Graph Pebbling and Memory-Hardness. Graph pebbling algorithms can be used to construct hash functions in the (parallel) random oracle model. This paradigm has been used by prior constructions of memory-hard hashing [AS15] as well as other prior works [DKW11].

Informally, the idea to "convert" a graph into a hash function is to associate with each node v a string called a *label*, which is defined to be $\mathcal{O}(v, \mathsf{pred}(v))$ where $\mathcal{O}$ is a random oracle and $\mathsf{pred}(v)$ is the list of labels of predecessors of v. For source nodes, the label is instead defined to be $\mathcal{O}(v, \zeta)$ for a string ζ which is an input to the hash function. The output of the hash function is defined to be the list of labels of target nodes. Intuitively, since the label of a node cannot be computed without the "random" labels of all its predecessors, any algorithm computing this hash function must move through the nodes of the graph according to rules very similar to those prescribed by the pebbling game; and therefore, the memory requirement of computing the hash function roughly corresponds to the pebble requirement of the graph. Thus, proving lower bounds on the pebbling complexity of graph families has useful implications for constructing provably memory-hard functions.

In our setting, in contrast to previous work, we employ a variant of the above technique: the string ζ is a fixed parameter of our hash function, and the input to the hash function instead specifies the indices of the target nodes whose labels are to be outputted.

1.1 Discussion on Memory-Hardness Measures and Related Work

The original paper proposing memory-hard functions [Per09] suggested a very simple measure: the minimum amount of memory necessary to compute the hash function. It was subsequently observed that a major drawback of this measure is that it does not distinguish between functions f and g with the same peak memory usage, even if the peak memory lasts a long time in evaluating f and is just fleeting in evaluating g (Fig. 1a). This is significant as the latter type of function is much better for a password-cracking adversary. In particular, pipelining the evaluation of the latter type of function would allow reuse of the same memory for many function evaluations at once, effectively reducing the adversary's amortized memory requirement by a factor of the number of concurrent executions (Fig. 1b).

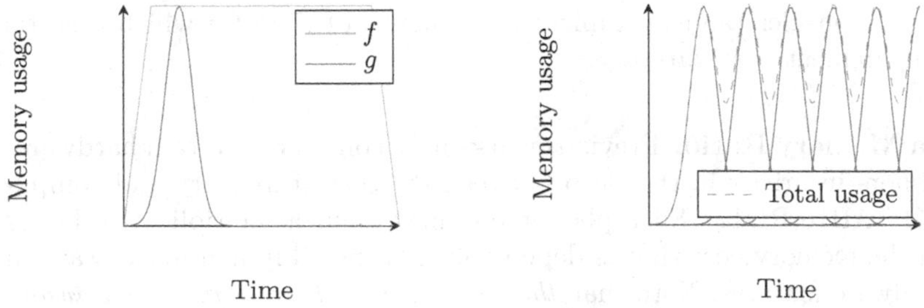

(a) Functions with the same peak memory usage

(b) Pipelined evaluations of g (reusing memory)

Fig. 1. Limitations of peak memory usage as a memory-hardness measure

Cumulative complexity [AS15] put forward the notion of *cumulative complexity* (CC), a complexity measure on graphs. CC was adopted by several subsequent works as a canonical measure of memory-hardness. CC measures the *cumulative* memory usage of a graph pebbling function evaluation: that is, the sum of memory usage over all time-steps of computation. In other words, this is the area under a graph of memory usage against time. CC is designed to be very robust against amortization, and in particular, scales linearly when computing many copies of a function on different inputs. This is a great advantage compared to the simpler measure of [Per09], which does not account well for an amortizing adversary (as shown in Fig. 1).

Depth-Robust Graphs. More recently, [AB16, ABP17a] proved bounds on optimal CC of certain graph families. They showed that a particular graph property called *depth-robustness* suffices to attain optimal CC (up to polylog factors–the CC of any graph with bounded in-degree is upper bounded by $O\left(\frac{n^2 \log\log n}{\log n}\right)$ [AB16, ABP17b]). An (r, s)-depth-robust graph is one where there exists a path of length s even when any r vertices are removed. Intuitively, this captures the notion that storing any r vertices of the graph will not shortcut the pebbling in a significant way. It turns out that depth-robustness will again be a useful property in our new model of memory-hardness with preprocessing.

Sustained Memory Complexity. Very recently, Alwen, Blocki, and Pietrzak [ABP17a] proposed a new measure of memory complexity, which captures not only the cumulative memory usage over time (as does CC), but goes further and captures the amount of time for which a particular level of memory usage is sustained. Our SHF definition also captures *sustained* memory usage: we propose a definition of capturing the duration for which a given amount of memory is required, designed to capture static as well as dynamic memory requirements. By the nature of static memory, it is especially appropriate in our setting to consider (and maximize) the amount of time for which a static memory requirement is *sustained.*

Core-area Memory Ratio. Previous works have considered certain hardware-dependent non-linearities in the ratio between the cost of memory and computation [BK15, AB16, RD17]. Such phenomena may incur a multiplicative factor increase in the memory cost that is dependent, in a possibly non-linear way, on specific hardware features. Note that *the non-linearity here is in the hardware-dependence*, rather than the space-time tradeoff itself. In contrast, our new models are more expressive, in that they make configurable the asymptotic tradeoff between space and time (by a parameter α which is in the exponent, as detailed in Definition 16) in an application-dependent way. This versatility of configuration targets applications where the trade-off may realistically depend on arbitrary and possibly exogenous space/time costs, and thus contrasts with metrics tailored for a specific hardware feature, such as core-memory ratio.

Towards a General Theory of Moderately Hard Functions. Most recently, Alwen and Tackmann [AT17] proposed a more general (though not comprehensive) framework for defining desirable guarantees of "moderately hard functions," i.e., functions that are efficient to compute but somewhat hard to invert. Their work points out a number of drawbacks of prior measures such as those described above. Notably, many of the prior measures characterized the hardness of *computing* the function with an implicit assumption that this hardness would translate to the hardness of *inverting* the function (as it would indeed in the case of a brute-force approach to inversion). In other words, these measures implicitly assume that the hash function in question "behaves like a random oracle" in the sense that brute-force inversion is the optimal approach.

1.2 Our Contributions in More Detail

To prove static-memory-hardness, we define a new pebble game called the *black-magic pebble game* (Definition 2), and prove properties of the space complexity of this game for new graphs (Graph Constructions 2 and 8).

The black-magic pebble game may additionally be of independent interest for the pebbling literature. Indeed, a pebble game used to analyze security of *proofs of space* [DFKP15] can be viewed as a non-adaptive version of the black-magic pebble game in which the target node set is sampled from a distribution by a challenger.

Based on our new graph constructions, we construct SHFs with provable guarantees on sustained memory usage, as follows. Graph Construction 8 gives a better asymptotic guarantee (same space usage but sustained over more time), whereas Graph Construction 2 has the advantage of simplicity in practice. In our full version [DLP18], we discuss our prototype implementation based on Graph Construction 2.

Static-Memory-Hard Functions (SHFs). Prior memory-hardness measures make a modeling assumption: namely, that the memory usage of interest is solely that of memory dynamically generated at run-time. However, static memory can be costly for the adversary too, and yet it is not taken into account by existing measures such as CC. Intuitively, it can be beneficial to design a function whose evaluation requires keeping a large amount of static memory on disk (which may be thought to be produced in a one-time initial setup phase). While not all the static memory might be accessed in any given evaluation, the "necessity" to maintain the data on disk can arise from the idea that an adversary attempting to evaluate the function on an arbitrary input while having stored a lesser amount of data would be forced to *dynamically* generate comparable amounts of memory. Note that the resulting *dynamic* memory requirements could be orders of magnitude larger (say, gigabytes) than the memory requirements of existing memory-hard function proposals, because unlike in prior memory-hardness models, here we have decoupled the memory requirement from the memory requirements of the honest evaluator.

We propose a new model and definitions for *static-memory-hard functions* (SHFs), in which we model static memory usage by oracle access to a large preprocessed string, which may be considered part of the hash function description. In particular, the preprocessed string can be public and known to the adversary—the important guarantee is that without storing (almost) all of it statically, the adversary will incur huge online memory requirements.

Definition (informal). We model a *static-memory-hard function family* as a two-part algorithm $\mathcal{H} = (\mathcal{H}_1, \mathcal{H}_2)$ in the parallel random oracle model, where $\mathcal{H}_1(1^\kappa)$ outputs a "large" string to which $\mathcal{H}_2$ has oracle access, and $\mathcal{H}_2$ receives an input x and outputs a hash function output y. Informally, our hardness requirement is that with high probability, any *two-part* adversary $\mathcal{A} = (\mathcal{A}_1, \mathcal{A}_2)$ must *either* have $\mathcal{A}_1$ output a large state (comparable to the output size of $\mathcal{H}_1$), *or* have $\mathcal{A}_2$ use large (dynamic) space.

We then give two constructions of SHFs based on graph pebbling. To prove static-memory-hardness, we define a new pebble game called the *black-magic pebble game* of which we give an overview in Sect. 1.2. Our simpler SHF construction is based on a family of tree-like "cylinder" graphs, which achieves memory usage proportional to the square root of the number of nodes, sustained over time proportional to the square root of the number of nodes. Furthermore, we give a better construction based on pebbling of a new graph family, that achieves better parameters: the same (square root) memory usage, but sustained over time proportional to the number of nodes.

Informal Version of Theorem 13. The "cylinder graph" (Graph Construction 2) can be used to construct an SHF with static memory requirement $\Lambda \in \Theta(\sqrt{n}/(\kappa - \xi \log(\kappa))$ where n is the number of nodes in the graph, κ is a security parameter, and $\xi \in \omega(1)$, such that any adversary using non-trivially less *static* memory than Λ must incur at least Λ *dynamic* memory usage for at least $\Theta(\sqrt{n})$ steps.

Informal Version of Theorem 14. Graph Construction 8 can be used to construct an SHF with static memory requirement $\Lambda \in \Theta(\sqrt{n})/(\kappa - \xi \log(\kappa))$ where n, κ, and ξ are as described above, such that any adversary using non-trivially less *static* memory than Λ must incur at least Λ *dynamic* memory usage for at least $\Theta(n)$ steps.

Static memory requirements are *complementary* to dynamic memory requirements: neither can replace the other, and to deter large-scale password-cracking attacks, a hash function will benefit from being *both* dynamic-memory-hard and static-memory-hard. In Sect. 4.1, we give a discussion of how, given a static-memory-hard function and a (dynamic-)memory-hard function, they can be concatenated to yield a "dynamic SHF" that inherits both the static memory requirement of the former and the dynamic memory requirement of the latter.

Black-Magic Pebble Game. We introduce a new pebble game called the *black-magic pebble game*. This game bears some similarity to the standard (black) pebble game, with the main difference that the player has access to an additional set of pebbles called *magic pebbles*. Magic pebbles are subject to different rules from standard pebbles: they may be placed anywhere at any time, but cannot be removed once placed, and may be limited in supply. The pebbling space cost of this game is defined as the maximum number of standard pebbles on the graph at any time-step plus the total number of magic pebbles used throughout the computation. Observe that while the most time-efficient strategy in the black-magic pebble game is always to pebble all the target nodes with magic pebbles in the first step, the most space-efficient strategy is much less clear.

Lower-bounds on space usage can be non-trivially different between the standard and magic pebbling games. For example, if a graph has a constant number of targets, then magic pebbling space usage will never exceed a constant number of pebbles, whereas the standard pebbling space usage can be super-constant. In particular, it is unclear, in the new setting of magic pebbling, whether known lower-bounds on pebbling space usage in the standard pebble game are transferable to the magic pebble game. We prove in Sect. 5 that for layered graphs, the best possible lower-bound for the magic pebbling game is $\Theta(\sqrt{n})$.

We leave determining the lower bound for magic pebbling space usage in general graphs as an open question. An answer to this open question would be useful towards constructing better static-memory-hard functions using the paradigm presented herein.

Our proof techniques rely on a close relationship between black-magic pebbling complexity and a new graph property which we define, called *local hardness.* Local hardness considers black-magic pebbling complexity in a variant model where *subsets* of target nodes are required to be pebbled (rather than *all* target nodes, as in the traditional pebbling game), and moreover, a "preprocessing phase" is allowed, wherein magic pebbles may be placed on the graph in advance of knowing which target nodes are to be produced. This "preprocessing" aspect bears some resemblance to the *black-white pebbling game* [CS74], a variant of the standard pebbling game in which some limited number of *white* pebbles can be placed "for free," and the black pebbles must be placed according the standard rules. However, our setting differs from the black-white pebbling game: while preprocessing and storing magic pebbles in advance can be viewed as analogous to placing white pebbles for free, the black-white pebbling game imposes restrictions on the *removal* of white pebbles from the graph, which are not present in our setting.

Capturing Relative Cost of Memory vs. Time. Existing measures such as CC and sustained memory complexity trade off space against time at a linear ratio. In particular, CC measures the minimal area under a graph of memory usage against time, over all possible algorithms that evaluate a function.

However, different applications may have different relative cost of space and time. We propose and define a variant of CC called α-CC, parametrized by α which determines the relative cost of space and time, and observe that α-CC may be meaningfully different from CC and more suitable for certain application scenarios. For example, when memory is "quadratically" more expensive than time, the measure of interest to an adversary may be the area under a graph of memory squared against time, as demonstrated by the following theorem.

Informal Version of Theorem 6.8 in [DLP18]**.** There exist graphs for which an adversary facing a linear space-time cost trade-off would in fact employ a *different pebbling strategy* from one facing a cubic trade-off.

It follows that when the costs of space and time are not linearly related, the CC measure may be measuring the complexity of *the wrong algorithm*, i.e., not the algorithm that an adversary would in fact favor. We thus see that our α-CC measure is more appropriate in settings where space may be substantially more costly than time (or vice versa).

Moreover, our parametrized approach generalizes naturally to sustained memory complexity. We show that our graph constructions are invariant across different values of α, a potentially desirable property for hash functions so that they are robust against different types of adversaries.

Informal Version of Theorem 6.13 in [DLP18]**.** Given any graph construction $G = (V, E)$, there exists a pebbling strategy that is less expensive asymptotically than any strategy using a number of pebbles asymptotically equal to the number of nodes in the graph for any time-space tradeoff.

Please refer to the full version of our paper for all results, proofs, appendices, and implementation details [DLP18].

2 Pebbling Definitions

A *pebbling game* is a one-player game played on a DAG where the goal of the player is to place pebbles on a set of one or more *target nodes* in the DAG.

In Sect. 2.1, we formally define two variations of the sequential and parallel pebble games: the *standard (black) pebble game* and the *black-magic pebble game*, the latter of which we introduce in this work. We also give the definitions of valid strategies and moves in these games. Then in Sect. 2.2, we define measures for evaluating the sequential and parallel pebbling complexity on families of graphs.

2.1 Standard and Magic Pebbling Definitions

Definition 1 (Standard (black) pebble game).

- ***Input:*** *A DAG,* $G = (V, E)$*, and a* target set $T \subseteq V$*. Define* $\mathsf{pred}(v) = \{u \in V : (u, v) \in E\}$*, and let* $S \subseteq V$ *be the set of sources of* G*.*
- ***Rules at move*** i***:*** *At the start of the game, no node of* G *contains a pebble. The player has access to a supply of* black pebbles. *Game-play proceeds in discrete moves, and* P_i *(called a "pebble configuration") is defined as the set of nodes containing pebbles after the ith move.* $P_0 = \varnothing$ *represents the initial configuration where no pebbles have been placed. Each move may consist of multiple actions adhering to the following rules.*
  1. *A pebble can be placed on any source,* $s \in S$*.*
  2. *A pebble can be removed from any vertex.*
  3. *A pebble can be placed on a non-source vertex,* v*, if and only if its direct predecessors were pebbled at time* $i - 1$ *(i.e.,* $\mathsf{pred}(v) \in P_{i-1}$*).*

    4. *A pebble can be moved from vertex v to vertex w if and only if $(v, w) \in E$ and $\mathsf{pred}(w) \in P_{i-1}$.*
- ***Goal:*** *Pebble all nodes in T at least once (i.e., $T \subseteq \bigcup_{i=0}^{t} P_i$).*

Remark 1. At first glance, it may seem that rule 4 in Definition 1 is redundant as a similar effect can be achieved by a combination of the other rules. However, the application of rule 4 can allow the usage of fewer pebbles. For example, a simple two-layer binary tree (with three nodes) could be pebbled with two pebbles using rule 4, but would require three pebbles otherwise. Nordstrom [Nor15] showed that in sequential strategies, it is always possible to use one fewer pebble by using rule 4.

We note for completeness that while rule 4 is standard in the pebbling literature, not all the papers in the MHF literature include rule 4.

Next, we define the *black-magic pebble game* which we will use to prove security properties of our static-memory-hard functions.

Definition 2 (Black-magic pebble game).

- ***Input:*** *A DAG $G = (V, E)$, a target set $T \subseteq V$, and* magic pebble bound $\mathfrak{M} \in \mathbb{N} \cup \{\infty\}$.
- ***Rules:*** *At the start of the game, no node of G contains a pebble. The player has access to two types of pebbles:* black pebbles *and up to $\mathfrak{M}$* magic pebbles. *Game-play proceeds in discrete moves, and $P_i = (M_i, B_i)$ is the pebble configuration after the ith move, where M_i, B_i are the sets of nodes containing magic and black pebbles after the ith move, respectively. $P_0 = (\varnothing, \varnothing)$ represents the initial configuration where no black pebbles or magic pebbles have been placed. Each move may consist of multiple actions adhering to the following rules.*
    1. *Black pebbles can be placed and removed according to the rules of the standard pebble game which are defined in the full version.*
    2. *A magic pebble can be placed on and removed from any node, subject to the constraint that at most $\mathfrak{M}$ magic pebbles are used throughout the game.*
    3. *Each magic pebble can be placed at most once: after a magic pebble is removed from a node, it disappears and can never be used again.*
- ***Goal:*** *Pebble all nodes in T at least once (i.e., $T \subseteq \bigcup_{i=0}^{t} (M_i \cup B_i)$).*

Remark 2. In the black-magic pebble game, unlike in the standard pebble game, there is always the simple strategy of placing magic pebbles directly on all the target nodes. At first glance, this may seem to trivialize the black-magic game. When optimizing for space usage, however, this simple strategy may not be favorable for the player: by employing a different strategy, the player might be able to use much fewer than T pebbles overall.

Next, we define valid sequential and parallel strategies in these games.

Definition 3 (Pebbling strategy). *Let G be a graph and T be a target set. A* standard (resp., black-magic) pebbling strategy *for (G, T) is defined as a sequence of pebble configurations, $\mathcal{P} = \{P_0, \ldots, P_t\}$, satisfying conditions 1 and 2 below. $\mathcal{P}$ is moreover* valid *if it satisfies condition 3, and* sequential *if it satisfies condition 4.*

1. *$P_0 = \varnothing$.*
2. *For each $i \in [t]$, P_i can be obtained from P_{i-1} by a legal move in the standard (resp., black-magic) pebble game.*
3. *$\mathcal{P}$ successfully pebbles all targets, i.e., $T \subseteq \bigcup_{i=0}^{t} P_i$.*
4. *For each $i \in [t]$, P_i contains at most one vertex not contained in P_{i-1} (i.e., $|P_i \setminus P_{i-1}| \leq 1$).*

A black-magic pebbling strategy must satisfy one additional condition to be considered valid*:*

5. *At most $\mathfrak{M}$ magic pebbles are used throughout the strategy, i.e., $|\bigcup_{i\in[t]} M_i| \leq \mathfrak{M}$ where M_i is the ith configuration of magic pebbles.*

2.2 Cost of Pebbling

In this subsection, we give definitions of several cost measures of graph pebbling, applicable to the standard and black-magic pebbling games. While these definitions assume parallel strategies, we note that the sequential versions of the definitions are entirely analogous.

Space Complexity in Standard Pebbling. We give a brief informal summary of the definitions in this subsection, before proceeding to the formal definitions.

Pebbling Complexity Measures. We informally overview the pebbling complexity definitions, some of which are new to this work.

The *time complexity* of a pebbling strategy $\mathcal{P}$ is the number of steps, i.e., $\mathsf{Time}(\mathcal{P}) = |\mathcal{P}|$. The *time complexity* of a graph $G = (V, E)$ given that at most S pebbles can be used is $\mathsf{Time}(G, S) = \min_{\mathcal{P} \in \mathbb{P}_{G,T,S}} (\mathsf{Time}(\mathcal{P}))$. Next, we overview variants of space complexity.

1. **Space complexity** of a *pebbling strategy* $\mathcal{P}$ on a graph G, denoted by $\mathbf{P}_{\mathrm{s}}(\mathcal{P})$, is the minimum number of pebbles required to execute $\mathcal{P}$. Space complexity of the *graph* G with target set T, written $\mathbf{P}_{\mathrm{s}}(G, T)$, is the minimum space complexity of any valid pebbling strategy for G.
2. **Λ-sustained space complexity** [ABP17a] of a *pebbling strategy* $\mathcal{P}$ on a graph G, denoted by $\mathbf{P}_{\mathrm{ss}}(\mathcal{P}, \Lambda)$, is the number of time-steps during the execution of $\mathcal{P}$, in which at least Λ pebbles are used. Λ-sustained space complexity of the *graph* G with target set T, written $\mathbf{P}_{\mathrm{ss}}(G, \Lambda, T)$ is the minimum Λ-sustained space complexity of all valid pebbling strategies for G.

3. **Graph-optimal sustained complexity** of a *pebbling strategy* $\mathcal{P}$, denoted by $\mathbf{P}_{\text{opt-ss}}(\mathcal{P})$, is the number of time-steps during the execution of $\mathcal{P}$, in which the number of pebbles in use is equal to the space complexity of G. Graph-optimal sustained complexity of the *graph* G with target set T, written $\mathbf{P}_{\text{opt-ss}}(G,T)$ is the minimum graph-optimal sustained complexity of all valid pebbling strategies for G.
4. **Δ-suboptimal sustained complexity** of a *pebbling strategy* $\mathcal{P}$ is the number of time-steps, during the execution of $\mathcal{P}$, in which the number of pebbles in use is at least the space complexity of G *minus* Δ. Δ-suboptimal sustained complexity of the *graph* G is the minimum Δ-suboptimal sustained complexity of all valid pebbling strategies for G.

A couple of remarks are in order.

Remark 3. The third and fourth definitions are new to this paper. They can be seen as special variants of Λ-sustained space complexity, i.e., with a special setting of Λ dependent on the specific graph family in question. They are useful to define in their own right, as unlike plain Λ-sustained space complexity, these measures express complexity for a given graph family relative to the best possible value of Λ at which sustained space usage could be hoped for. In the rest of this paper, we prove guarantees on *graph-optimal sustained complexity* of our constructions, which have high sustained space usage at the optimal Λ-value. However, we also define *Δ-suboptimal sustained complexity* here for completeness, since it is more general and preferable to graph-optimal complexity when evaluating graph families where the maximal space usage may not be sustained for very long.

Remark 4. We have found the term "Λ-sustained space complexity" can be slightly confusing, in that it measures a number of time-steps rather than an amount of space. We retain the original terminology as it was introduced, but include this remark to clarify this point.

We now present the formal definitions of the complexity measures for the standard pebbling game. In all of the below definitions, $G = (V, E)$ is a graph, $T \subseteq V$ is a target set, $\mathcal{P} = (P_1, \ldots, P_t)$ is a standard pebbling strategy on (G, T), and $\mathbb{P}_{G,T}$ denotes the set of all valid standard pebbling strategies on (G, T).

Definition 4. *The* space complexity of pebbling strategy $\mathcal{P}$ *is:* $\mathbf{P}_{\mathrm{s}}(\mathcal{P}) = \max_{P_i \in \mathcal{P}} (|P_i|)$. *The* space complexity of G *is the minimal space complexity of any valid pebbling strategy that pebbles the target set* $T \subset V$*:* $\mathbf{P}_{\mathrm{s}}(G,T) = \min_{\mathcal{P}' \in \mathbb{P}_{G,T}} (\mathbf{P}_{\mathrm{s}}(\mathcal{P}'))$.

Definition 5. *The* Λ-sustained space complexity of $\mathcal{P}$ *is:* $\mathbf{P}_{\mathrm{ss}}(\mathcal{P}, \Lambda) = |\{P_i : |P_i| \geq \Lambda\}|$. *The* Λ-sustained space complexity of G *is the minimal Λ-sustained space complexity of any valid pebbling strategy that pebbles the target set* $T \subseteq V$*:* $\mathbf{P}_{\mathrm{ss}}(G, \Lambda, T) = \min_{\mathcal{P}' \in \mathbb{P}_{G,T}} (\mathbf{P}_{\mathrm{ss}}(\mathcal{P}', \Lambda))$.

Definition 6. *The* graph-optimal sustained complexity of $\mathcal{P}$ *is:* $\mathbf{P}_{\text{opt-ss}}(\mathcal{P}) = \mathbf{P}_{\text{ss}}(\mathcal{P}, \mathbf{P}_{\text{s}}(G,T))$. *The* graph-optimal sustained complexity of *G is the minimal graph-optimal sustained complexity of any valid pebbling strategy that pebbles the target set $T \subseteq V$:* $\mathbf{P}_{\text{opt-ss}}(G,T) = \min_{\mathcal{P}' \in \mathbb{P}_{G,T}} (\mathbf{P}_{\text{opt-ss}}(\mathcal{P}'))$.

Definition 7. *The* Δ-suboptimal sustained complexity of $\mathcal{P}$ *is:*

$$\mathbf{P}_{\text{opt-ss}}(\mathcal{P}, \Delta) = \mathbf{P}_{\text{ss}}(\mathcal{P}, \mathbf{P}_{\text{s}}(G,T) - \Delta).$$

The Δ-suboptimal sustained complexity of G *is the minimal graph-optimal sustained complexity of any valid pebbling strategy that pebbles the target set $T \subseteq V$:* $\mathbf{P}_{\text{opt-ss}}(G, \Delta, T) = \min_{\mathcal{P}' \in \mathbb{P}_{G,T}} (\mathbf{P}_{\text{opt-ss}}(\mathcal{P}', \Delta))$.

Time Complexity in Standard Pebbling. We present the following formal definitions for measuring the time complexity of strategies in the standard pebble game. In all the below definitions, $G = (V,E)$ is a graph, $T \subseteq V$ is a target set, $\mathcal{P} = (P_1, \ldots, P_t)$ is a standard pebbling strategy on (G,T) where $\mathbb{P}_{G,T,S}$ denotes the set of all valid pebbling strategies on (G,T) that use at most S pebbles.

Definition 8. *The* time complexity *of a pebbling strategy $\mathcal{P}$ is* $\mathsf{Time}(\mathcal{P}) = |\mathcal{P}|$. *The* time complexity *of a graph $G = (V,E)$ given that at most S pebbles can be used is* $\mathsf{Time}(G,S) = \min_{\mathcal{P} \in \mathbb{P}_{G,T,S}} (\mathsf{Time}(\mathcal{P}))$.

Space Complexity in Black-Magic Pebbling. Next, we define the corresponding complexity notions for the black-magic pebbling game. As above, $G = (V,E)$ is a graph, $T \subseteq V$ is a target set, and $\mathfrak{M}$ is a magic pebble bound. In this subsection, $\mathcal{P} = (P_1, \ldots, P_t) = ((M_1, B_1), \ldots, (M_t, B_t))$ denotes a black-magic pebbling strategy on (G,T). Moreover, $\mathbb{M}_{G,T,\mathfrak{M}}$ denotes the set of all valid magic pebbling strategies on (G,T), and $m(\mathcal{P})$ denotes the total number of magic pebbles used in the execution of $\mathcal{P}$.

Definition 9. *The* (magic) space complexity *of $\mathcal{P}$ is:* $\mathbf{P}_{\text{s}}(\mathcal{P}) = \max(m(\mathcal{P}), \max_{P_i \in \mathcal{P}} (|P_i|))$. *The* (magic) space complexity of *G w.r.t. $\mathfrak{M}$ is the minimal space complexity of any valid magic pebbling strategy that pebbles the target set $T \subseteq V$:* $\mathbf{P}_{\text{s}}(G, \mathfrak{M}, T) = \min_{\mathcal{P} \in \mathbb{P}_{G,T,\mathfrak{M}}} (\mathbf{P}_{\text{s}}(\mathcal{P}))$.

Remark 5. We briefly provide some intuition for the complexity measure defined above in Definition 9. If we consider all magic pebbles to be static memory objects that were saved from a previous evaluation of the hash function, then the total number of magic pebbles is the amount of memory that was used to save the results of a previous evaluation of the hash function. Because of this, it is natural to take the maximum of the memory used to store results from a previous evaluation of the function and the current memory that is used by our current pebbling strategy since that would represent how much memory was used to compute the results of hash function during the current evaluation.

Definition 10. *The* (magic) Λ-sustained space complexity *of* $\mathcal{P}$ *is:* $\mathbf{P}_{\mathrm{ss}}(\mathcal{P}, \Lambda) = |\{P_i : |P_i| \geq \Lambda\}|$. *The* Λ-sustained space complexity of G w.r.t. $\mathfrak{M}$ and $T \subseteq V$ *is:* $\mathbf{P}_{\mathrm{ss}}(G, \Lambda, \mathfrak{M}, T) = \min_{\mathcal{P} \in \mathbb{P}_{G,T,\mathfrak{M}}} (\mathbf{P}_{\text{opt-ss}}(\mathcal{P}, \Lambda))$.

Definition 11. *The* (magic) graph-optimal sustained complexity *of* $\mathcal{P}$ *is:* $\mathbf{P}_{\text{opt-ss}}(\mathcal{P}) = \mathbf{P}_{\mathrm{ss}}(\mathcal{P}, \mathbf{P}_{\mathrm{s}}(G, T))$. *The* graph-optimal sustained complexity of G *w.r.t.* $\mathfrak{M}$ *and* $T \subseteq V$ *is:* $\mathbf{P}_{\text{opt-ss}}(G, \mathfrak{M}, T) = \min_{\mathcal{P} \in \mathbb{P}_{G,T,\mathfrak{M}}} (\mathbf{P}_{\text{opt-ss}}(\mathcal{P}))$.

Definition 12. *The* (magic) Δ-suboptimal sustained complexity *of* $\mathcal{P}$ *is:* $\mathbf{P}_{\text{opt-ss}}(\mathcal{P}, \Delta) = \mathbf{P}_{\mathrm{ss}}(\mathcal{P}, \mathbf{P}_{\mathrm{s}}(G, T) - \Delta)$. *The* Δ-suboptimal sustained complexity of G w.r.t. $\mathfrak{M}$ and $T \subseteq V$ *is:*

$$\mathbf{P}_{\text{opt-ss}}(G, \Delta, \mathfrak{M}, T) = \min_{\mathcal{P} \in \mathbb{P}_{G,T,\mathfrak{M}}} (\mathbf{P}_{\text{opt-ss}}(\mathcal{P}, \Delta)).$$

2.3 Incrementally Hard Graphs

We introduce the following definition for our notion of graphs which require $|T|$ pebbles to pebble regardless of the number of targets that are asked, given a constraint on the number of magic pebbles that can be used. This concept has not been previously analyzed in the pebbling literature; traditional pebbling complexity usually treats graphs with fixed target sets.

Definition 13 (Incremental Hardness). *Given at most* $\mathfrak{M}$ *magic pebbles, for any subset of targets* $C \subseteq T$ *where* $|C| > \mathfrak{M}$*, the number of pebbles (magic and black pebbles) necessary in the black-magic pebble game to pebble* C *is at least* $|T|$ *where the number of magic pebbles used in this game is upper bounded by* $\mathfrak{M}$*:* $\mathbf{P}_{\mathrm{s}}(G, |C| - 1, C) \geq |T|$.

α-tradeoff Cumulative Complexity. *α-tradeoff cumulative complexity*, or CC^{α}, is a new measure introduced in this paper, which accounts for situations where space and time do not trade off linearly. Similar notions to this have been explored before e.g. [FLW13], [BK15, AB16, RD17]. A discuss of the *core-area memory ratio* [BK15, AB16, RD17] can be found in Sect. 1.1. They considered the notion of λ-memory-hardness where intuitively $S \cdot T = \Omega\left(G^{\lambda+1}\right)$ where the space-time cost is some exponential of the size of the stored graph [FLW13]. We note that this notion is very different from our notion of α-tradeoff complexity since they only consider the space-time cost (not cumulative complexity) and do not consider nonlinear tradeoffs between space and time (one can just consider $G^{\lambda+1}$ to a constant in the tradeoff curve).

Here, we see the usefulness of defining sustained complexities in terms of the minimum required space (as opposed to being parametrized by Λ) since we can always obtain an upper bound on CC^{α}, for *any* α, of a graph directly from our proofs of the space complexity and sustained time complexity of a DAG.

Definition 14 (Standard pebbling α-space cumulative complexity). *Given a valid parallel standard pebbling strategy, $\mathcal{P}$, for pebbling a graph $G = (V, E)$, the* standard pebbling α *-space cumulative complexity is the following:*

$$\mathsf{p\text{-}cc}_\alpha(G, \mathcal{P}) = \sum_{P_i \in \mathcal{P}} |P_i|^\alpha.$$

Definition 15 (Black-magic pebbling α-space cumulative complexity). *Given a valid parallel black-magic pebbling strategy, $\mathcal{P}$, for pebbling a graph $G = (V, E)$, the* black-magic pebbling α *-space cumulative complexity is the following:*

$$\mathsf{p\text{-}cc}_\alpha^M(G, \mathcal{P}) = \max\left(m(\mathcal{P})^\alpha, \sum_{P_i \in \mathcal{P}} |P_i|^\alpha\right) = \max\left(m(\mathcal{P})^\alpha, \sum_{P_i \in \mathcal{P}} |B_i \cup M_i|^\alpha\right)$$

where $m(\mathcal{P})$ denotes the total number of magic pebbles used in the magic pebbling strategy $\mathcal{P}$.

The following definition, CC^α, is an analogous definition to CC as defined by [AS15] (specifically, CC^α when $\alpha = 1$ is equivalent to CC) to account for varying costs of memory usage vs. time.

Definition 16 ($\mathbf{CC}^\alpha$). *Given a graph, $G \in \mathbb{G}$, and a valid standard/magic pebbling strategy, $\mathcal{P}$, we define the $CC^\alpha(G)$ to be*

$$CC^\alpha(\mathcal{P}) = (\mathsf{p\text{-}cc}_\alpha(G, \mathcal{P})).$$

Given a graph, $G \in \mathbb{G}$, and a family of valid standard pebbling strategies, $\mathbb{P}$, we define the $CC^\alpha(G)$ to be

$$CC^\alpha(G) = \min_{\mathcal{P} \in \mathbb{P}} (\mathsf{p\text{-}cc}_\alpha(G, \mathcal{P})),$$

and, given a family $\mathbb{P}^M$ of valid black-magic pebbling strategies, we define $CC^\alpha(G)$ to be

$$CC^\alpha(G) = \min_{\mathcal{P}^M \in \mathbb{P}^M} \left(\mathsf{p\text{-}cc}_\alpha^M(G, \mathcal{P}^M)\right).$$

3 Parallel Random Oracle Model (PROM)

In this paper, we consider two broad categories of computations: *pebbling strategies* and *PROM algorithms*. Specifically, we discussed above the pebbling models and pebble games we use to construct our static memory-hard functions. Now, we define our PROM algorithms.

Prior work has observed the close connections between these two types of computations as applied to DAGs, and our work brings out yet more connections between the two models. In this section, we give an overview of how PROM computations work and define the complexity measures that we apply to PROM algorithms. Some of the complexity measures were introduced by prior work, and others are new in this work.

3.1 Overview of PROM Computation

The random oracle model was introduced by [BR93]. When we say random oracle, we always mean a *parallel* random oracle unless otherwise specified.

An *algorithm* in the PROM is a probabilistic algorithm $\mathcal{B}$ which has parallel access to a stateless oracle $\mathcal{O}$: that is, $\mathcal{B}$ may submit many queries in parallel to $\mathcal{O}$. We assume $\mathcal{O}$ is sampled uniformly from an oracle set $\mathbb{O}$ and that $\mathcal{B}$ may depend on $\mathbb{O}$ but not $\mathcal{O}$.

The algorithm proceeds in discrete time-steps called *iterations*, and may be thought to consist of a series of algorithms $(\mathcal{B}_i)_{i\in\mathbb{N}}$, indexed by the iteration i, where each $\mathcal{B}_i$ passes a *state* $\sigma_i \in \{0,1\}^*$ to its successor $\mathcal{B}_{i+1}$. σ_0 is defined to contain the input to the algorithm. We write $|\sigma_i|$ to denote the size, in bits, of σ_i. We write $[\![\sigma_i]\!]$ to denote $\frac{|\sigma_i|}{w}$, where w is the output length of the oracle $\mathcal{O}$. In other words, $[\![\sigma_i]\!]$ is the size of σ_i when counting in words of size w. In each iteration, the algorithm $\mathcal{B}_i$ may make a *batch* $\mathbf{q}_i = (q_{i,1}, \ldots, q_{i,|\mathbf{q}_i|})$ of queries, consisting of $|\mathbf{q}_i|$ individual queries to $\mathcal{O}$, and instantly receive back from the oracle the evaluations of $\mathcal{O}$ on the individual queries, i.e., $(\mathcal{O}(q_{i,1}), \ldots, \mathcal{O}(q_{i,|\mathbf{q}_i|}))$.

At the end of any iteration, $\mathcal{B}$ can append values to a special output register, and it can end the computation by appending a special terminate symbol $\perp$ on that register. When this happens, the contents y of the output register, excluding the trailing $\perp$, is considered to be the output of the computation. To denote the process of sampling an output, y, provided input x, we write $y \leftarrow \mathcal{B}^{\mathcal{O}}(x)$.

Definition 17 (Oracle functions). *An* oracle function *is a collection* $\mathfrak{f} = \{f^{\mathcal{O}} : D \to R\}_{\mathcal{O}\in\mathbb{O}}$ *of functions with domain D and outputs in R indexed by oracles $\mathcal{O} \in \mathbb{O}$.*

A family of oracle functions *is a set* $\mathcal{F} = \{\mathfrak{f}_\kappa : D_\kappa \to R_\kappa\}_{\kappa\in\mathbb{N}}$ *where each* $\mathfrak{f}_\kappa$ *is indexed by oracles from an oracle set* $\mathbb{O}_\kappa : \{0,1\}^\kappa \to \{0,1\}^\kappa$ *indexed by a security parameter κ.*

Definition 18 (Memory complexity of PROM algorithms). *The* memory complexity of $\mathcal{B}(x;\rho)$ *(i.e., the memory complexity of $\mathcal{B}$ on input x and randomness ρ) is defined as:*

$$\mathsf{mem}_{\mathbb{O}}(\mathcal{B}, x, \rho) = \max_{i\in\mathbb{N}} \{[\![\sigma_i]\!]\} . \tag{1}$$

Definition 19 (Λ-sustained memory complexity of PROM algorithms). *The* Λ-sustained memory complexity of $\mathcal{B}(x;\rho)$ *is defined as:*

$$\mathsf{s\text{-}mem}_{\mathbb{O}}(\Lambda, \mathcal{B}, x, \rho) = |\{i \in \mathbb{N} : |\sigma_i| \geq \Lambda\}| . \tag{2}$$

Note that (1) and (2) are distributions over the choice of $\mathcal{O} \leftarrow \mathbb{O}$.

3.2 Functions Defined by DAGs

We now describe how to translate a graph construction into a function family, whose evaluation involves a series of oracle calls in the PROM. Any family of

DAGs induces a family of *oracle functions* in the PROM, whose complexity is related to the pebbling complexity of the DAG. We first define the syntax of *labeling* of DAG nodes, then define a *graph function family.*

Definition 20 (Labeling). *Let $G = (V, E)$ be a DAG with maximum in-degree δ, let $\mathfrak{L}$ be an arbitrary "label set," and define $\mathbb{O}(\delta, \mathfrak{L}) = \left(V \times \bigcup_{\delta'=1}^{\delta} \mathfrak{L}^{\delta'} \to \mathfrak{L}\right)$. For any function $\mathcal{O} \in \mathbb{O}(\delta, \mathfrak{L})$ and any label $\zeta \in \mathfrak{L}$, the $(\mathcal{O}, \zeta)$-labeling of G is a mapping $\mathsf{label}_{\mathcal{O},\zeta} : V \to \mathfrak{L}$ defined recursively as follows.*

$$\mathsf{label}_{\mathcal{O},\zeta}(v) = \begin{cases} \mathcal{O}(v, \zeta) & \text{if } \mathsf{indeg}(v) = 0 \\ \mathcal{O}(v, \mathsf{label}_{\mathcal{O},\zeta}(\mathsf{pred}(v))) & \text{if } \mathsf{indeg}(v) > 0 \end{cases}.$$

Definition 21 (Graph function family). *Let $n = n(\kappa)$ and let $\mathbb{G}_\delta = \{G_{n,\delta} = (V_n, E_n)\}_{\kappa \in \mathbb{N}}$ be a graph family. We write $\mathbb{O}_{\delta,\kappa}$ to denote the set $\mathbb{O}(\delta, \{0,1\}^\kappa)$ as defined in Definition 20. The* graph function family *of $\mathbb{G}$ is the family of oracle functions $\mathcal{F}_{\mathbb{G}} = \{\mathfrak{f}_G\}_{\kappa \in \mathbb{N}}$ where $\mathfrak{f}_G = \{f_G^{\mathcal{O}} : \{0,1\}^\kappa \to (\{0,1\}^\kappa)^z\}_{\mathcal{O} \in \mathbb{O}_{\delta,\kappa}}$ and $z = z(\kappa)$ is the number of sink nodes in G. The output of $f_G^{\mathcal{O}}$ on input label $\zeta \in \{0,1\}^\kappa$ is defined to be*

$$f_G^{\mathcal{O}}(\zeta) = \mathsf{label}_{\mathcal{O},\zeta}(\mathsf{sink}(G)),$$

where $\mathsf{sink}(G)$ is the set of sink nodes of G.

3.3 Relating Complexity of PROM Algorithms and Pebbling Strategies

Any PROM algorithm $\mathcal{B}$ and input x induce a black-magic pebbling strategy, $\mathsf{epf\text{-}magic}_\zeta(\mathcal{B}, \mathcal{O}, x, \$)$, called an *ex-post-facto black-magic pebbling strategy.* The way in which this strategy is induced is similar to *ex-post-facto pebbling* as originally defined by [AS15] in the context of the standard pebble game. We adapt their technique for the black-magic game.

Definition 22 (Ex-post-facto black-magic pebbling). *Let $n = n(\kappa)$ and let $\mathbb{G}_\delta = \{G_{n,\delta} = (V_n, E_n)\}_{\kappa \in \mathbb{N}}$ be a graph family. Let $\zeta = \zeta(\kappa) \in \{0,1\}^\kappa$ be an arbitrary input label for the graph function family $\mathcal{F}_{\mathbb{G}}$. For any $v \in V_n$, define*

$$\mathsf{pre\text{-}lab}_{\mathcal{O},\zeta}(v) = (v, \mathsf{label}_{\mathcal{O},\zeta}(\mathsf{pred}(v))).$$

Let $\mathcal{B}$ be a non-uniform PROM algorithm. Fix an implicit security parameter κ. Let x be an input to $\mathcal{B}$. We now define a magic pebbling strategy induced by any given execution of $\mathcal{B}^{\mathcal{O}}(x; \$)$, where \$ denotes the random coins of $\mathcal{B}$. Such an execution makes a sequence of batches of random oracle calls (as defined in Sect. 3.1), which we denote by

$$\mathbf{q}(\mathcal{B}, \mathcal{O}, x, \$) = (\mathbf{q}_1, \ldots, \mathbf{q}_t).$$

The induced black-magic pebbling strategy,

$$\mathsf{epf\text{-}magic}_\zeta(\mathcal{B}, \mathcal{O}, x, \$) = ((B_0, M_0), \ldots, (B_t, M_t)), \tag{3}$$

is called an ex-post-facto black-magic pebbling, *and is defined by the following procedure.*

1. $B_0 = M_0 = \varnothing$.
2. *For* $i = 1, \ldots, t$:
   (a) $B_i = B_{i-1}$.
   (b) $M_i = M_{i-1}$.
   (c) *For each individual query* $q \in \mathbf{q}_i$, *if there is some* $v \in V_n$ *such that* $q = \textsf{pre-lab}_{\mathcal{O},\varsigma}(v)$ *and* $v \notin P_i$, *then "pebble* v*" by performing the following steps:*
      i. *If* $\textsf{pred}(v) \subseteq M_i \cup B_i$:
         – $B_i = B_i \cup \{v\}$.
      ii. *Else:*
         – $V = \{v\}$.
         – *Let* V^* *be the transitive closure of* V *under the following operation:* $V = V \cup \left(\bigcup_{v' \in V} \textsf{pred}(v') \cap (M_i \cup B_i)\right)$.
         – $M_i = M_i \cup V^*$.
3. *For* $i = 1, \ldots, t$:
   (a) *A node* $v \in M_i \cup B_i$ *is said to be* necessary at time i *if*

$$\exists j \in [t], q \in \mathbf{q}_j, v' \in V_n \ s.t. \quad j > i \wedge v \in \textsf{pred}(v') \wedge q = \textsf{pre-lab}_{\mathcal{O},\varsigma}(v') \\ \wedge \left(\nexists k \in [t], q' \in \mathbf{q}_k \ s.t. \ i < k < j \wedge q' = \textsf{pre-lab}_{\mathcal{O},\varsigma}(v)\right).$$

   In other words, a node is necessary if its label will be required in a future oracle call, but its label will not be obtained by any oracle query between now and that future oracle call.
   Remove from B_i *and* M_i *all nodes that are not necessary at time* i.

3.4 Legality and Space Usage of Ex-post-facto Black-Magic Pebbling

The following theorems establish that the space usage of PROM algorithms is closely related to the space usage of the induced pebbling.

We will use the following supporting lemma, also used in prior work such as [AS15, DKW11] (see, e.g., [DKW10] for a proof).

Lemma 1. *Let* $B = b_1, \ldots, b_u$ *be a sequence of random bits and let* $\mathbb{H}$ *be a set. Let* $\mathcal{P}$ *be a randomized procedure that gets a hint* $h \in \mathbb{H}$, *and can adaptively query any of the bits of* B *by submitting an index* i *and receiving* b_i *as a response. At the end of its execution,* $\mathcal{P}$ *outputs a subset* $S \subseteq \{1, \ldots, u\}$ *of* $|S| = \varphi$ *indices which were not previously queried, along with guesses for the values of the bits* $\{b_i : i \in S\}$. *Then the probability (over the choice of* B *and the randomness of* $\mathcal{P}$*) that there exists some* $h \in \mathbb{H}$ *such that* $\mathcal{P}(h)$ *outputs* all *correct guesses is at most* $|\mathbb{H}|/2^{\varphi}$.

Lemma 2 (Legality and magic pebble usage of ex-post-facto black-magic pebbling). *Let $n = n(\kappa)$ and let $\mathbb{G}_\delta = \{G_{n,\delta} = (V_n, E_n)\}_{\kappa\in\mathbb{N}}$ be a graph family. Let $\zeta \in \{0,1\}^\kappa$ be an arbitrary input label for $\mathbb{G}_\delta$. Fix any efficient PROM algorithm $\mathcal{B}$ and input x. With overwhelming probability over the choice of random oracle $\mathcal{O} \leftarrow \mathbb{O}$ and the random coins \$ of $\mathcal{B}$, it holds that the ex-post-facto magic pebbling* $\mathsf{epf\text{-}magic}_\zeta(\mathcal{B}, \mathcal{O}, x, \$)$ *consists of valid magic-pebbling moves, and uses fewer than $\chi = \left\lfloor \frac{|x|}{\kappa - \log(q)} + 1 \right\rfloor$ magic pebbles (i.e., for all i, $|M_i| \leq \chi$), where q is the number of oracle queries made by $\mathcal{B}(x)$.*

Lemma 3 (Space usage of ex-post-facto black-magic pebbling). *Let $n, \mathbb{G}_\delta, \zeta$ be as in Lemma 2. Fix any PROM algorithm $\mathcal{B}$ and input x. Fix any $i \in [t]$, $\lambda \geq 0$, and define*

$$\mathsf{epf\text{-}magic}_\zeta(\mathcal{B}, \mathcal{O}, x, \$) = (P_1^\mathcal{O}, \ldots, P_t^\mathcal{O}) = ((B_1^\mathcal{O}, M_1^\mathcal{O}), \ldots, (B_t^\mathcal{O}, M_t^\mathcal{O}))$$

for oracle $\mathcal{O}$. We may omit the superscript $\mathcal{O}$ for notational simplicity. It holds for all large enough κ that the following probability is overwhelming:

$$\Pr\left[\forall i \in [t],\ |P_i| \leq \chi'\right],$$

where $\chi' = \left\lfloor \frac{|\sigma_i|}{\kappa - \log(q)} + 1 \right\rfloor$, q is the number of oracle queries made by $\mathcal{B}$, and the probability is taken over $\mathcal{O} \leftarrow \mathbb{O}$ and the coins of $\mathcal{B}$.

4 Static-Memory-Hard Functions

We now define *static-memory-hard functions.* As mentioned above, prior notions of memory-hardness consider only dynamic memory usage. To model static memory usage, we consider a hash function with two parts $(\mathcal{H}_1, \mathcal{H}_2)$ where $\mathcal{H}_2(x)$ computes the output of the hash function $h(x)$ given oracle access to the output of $\mathcal{H}_1$. This design can be seen to reduce honest party computation time by limiting the hard work to one-off preprocessing phase, while maintaining a large space requirement for password-cracking adversaries. Informally, our guarantee says that unless the adversary stores a specified amount of *static* memory, he must use an equivalent amount of *dynamic* memory to compute h correctly on many outputs. Definition 23 is syntactic and Definition 24 formalizes the memory-hardness guarantee.

Notation. PPT stands for "probabilistic polynomial time." For $\boldsymbol{b} \in \{0,1\}^*$, define $\mathsf{Seek}_{\boldsymbol{b}} : \{1, \ldots, |\boldsymbol{b}|\} \to \{0,1\}$ to be an oracle that on input ι returns the ιth bit of $\boldsymbol{b}$.

Definition 23 (Static-memory hash function family (SHF)). *A static-memory hash function family $\mathcal{H}^\mathcal{O} = \{h_\kappa^\mathcal{O} : \{0,1\}^{w'} \to \{0,1\}^w\}_{\kappa\in\mathbb{N}}$ mapping $w' = w'(\kappa)$ bits to $w = w(\kappa)$ bits is described by a pair of deterministic oracle algorithms $(\mathcal{H}_1, \mathcal{H}_2)$ such that for all $\kappa \in \mathbb{N}$ and $x \in \{0,1\}^n$,*

$$\mathcal{H}_2^{\mathsf{Seek}_R}(1^\kappa, x) = h_\kappa(x), \text{ where } R = \mathcal{H}_1(1^\kappa).$$

(The superscript $\mathcal{O}$ is left implicit.)

The next definition presents a parametrized notion of $(\Lambda, \Delta, \tau, q)$-hardness of an SHF. Before delving into the formal definition, we give a brief intuition of the guarantee provided by Definition 24: any adversary who produces at least q correct input-output pairs of the hash function must *either* have used $\Lambda - \Delta$ static memory *or* incur a requirement of Λ dynamic memory *sustained over* τ time-steps at runtime.

The Role of q. The parameter q in Definition 24 serves to capture the intuitive idea that an adversary that uses a certain amount of space could always use that space to directly store output values of h_κ. Clearly, an adversary with an arbitrary input R could very easily output up to $[\![|R|]\!]$ correct output values. Our goal is to lower bound the amount of space needed by an adversary who outputs nontrivially more correct values than that—and q, which is a function of $|R|$, captures how many more.

Definition 24 (**$(\Lambda, \Delta, \tau, q)$-hardness of SHF**). *Let $\mathcal{H} = \{h_\kappa\}_{\kappa \in \mathbb{N}}$ be a static-memory hash function family described by algorithms $(\mathcal{H}_1, \mathcal{H}_2)$, mapping w' to w bits. $\mathcal{H}$ is (Λ, Δ, τ)-hard if for any large enough $\kappa \in \mathbb{N}$, any string $R \in \{0,1\}^{\Lambda - \Delta}$, and any PPT algorithm $\mathcal{A}$, for any set $X = \{x_1, \ldots, x_q\} \subseteq \{0,1\}^{w'}$, there is a negligible ε such that*

$$\Pr_{\mathcal{O},\rho}\left[\{(x_1, h_\kappa(x_1)), \ldots, (x_q, h_\kappa(x_q))\} = \mathcal{A}(1^\kappa, R; \rho) \wedge \mathsf{s\text{-}mem}_{\mathcal{O}}(\Lambda, \mathcal{A}, R, \rho) < \tau\right] < \varepsilon.$$

For simplicity, we henceforth assume $w' = w = \kappa$ (i.e., the oracle's input and output sizes are equal to the security parameter) unless otherwise stated.

4.1 Dynamic SHFs

As discussed in detail in the introduction, static memory requirements are orthogonal and complementary to dynamic memory requirements of MHFs as formalized by [AS15]. Given a pebbling-based SHF and a pebbling-based MHF, they can be combined by simple concatenation into a "dynamic SHF," a function that inherits both the static memory requirement of the former and the dynamic memory requirement of the latter, as outlined (informally) next.

Let $\mathcal{H}^{\mathcal{O}}_{\mathsf{dyn}}$ be a dynamic MHF and $(\mathcal{H}^{\mathcal{O}}_1, \mathcal{H}^{\mathcal{O}}_2)$ be a SHF family, and the computation of both of these correspond to computing labels of nodes in a DAG as a function of a pebbling algorithm and a random oracle $\mathcal{O}$. We construct a dynamic SHF $\mathcal{H}^{\mathcal{O}}$ that is defined as follows: on input $(1^\kappa, x)$, output $\mathcal{H}_2^{\mathcal{O}(0,\cdot)}(1^\kappa, x) || \mathcal{H}_{\mathsf{dyn}}^{\mathcal{O}(1,\cdot)}(1^\kappa, x)$. The resulting $\mathcal{H}^{\mathcal{O}}$ inherits both the MHF guarantees of $\mathcal{H}_{\mathsf{dyn}}$ and the SHF guarantees of $(\mathcal{H}_1, \mathcal{H}_2)$. Note that importantly, the labels of the nodes in the graphs corresponding to the MHF $\mathcal{H}_{\mathsf{dyn}}^{\mathcal{O}(0,\cdot)}$ and the SHF $(\mathcal{H}_1^{\mathcal{O}(1,\cdot)}, \mathcal{H}_2^{\mathcal{O}(1,\cdot)})$ are independent as the MHF and the SHF use disjoint partitions of the random oracle domain.

Using this method, our SHF constructions can be combined with existing MHF constructions such as [AS15, ABP17a, ABP17b], yielding a "best of both worlds" dynamic SHF that enjoys both types of memory-hardness.

5 SHF Constructions

A First Attempt. What if we pebble a hard-to-pebble graph, and then let $R_{k,i} = H(P(k), i)$ where $P(k)$ is the entire pebbling of the graph (on input k and iteration i is the i-th call to the hash function H)? This would in fact work in the random oracle model where the random oracle takes arbitrary-length input. However, in practice, hash functions do not take arbitrary-length input. While constructions like Merkle-Damgård [Mer79] and sponge [BDPA08] can transform a fixed-input-length hash function into one that takes arbitrary-length inputs, the resulting function does *not* behave like a random oracle even if the fixed-length hash function does. Moreover, the computation graphs of known length-expanding transformations such as Merkle-Damgård and sponge functions require very little space to compute. For instance, the computation graph of the Merkle-Damgård construction is a binary tree and the computation graph of the sponge function is a caterpillar graph both of which take logarithmic and constant space, respectively, to compute. Thus, we have to use special constructions to achieve the local-hardness properties we need.

Recall from Definition 13 that the property we want is this "locally hard to access" notion, meaning that if an adversarial party chooses to not store the static part of our hash function which they obtain from performing the "preprocessing" computation associated with $\mathcal{H}_1$, then they must use the same memory and sustained time to recompute the function when our static-memory-hard function is called on *any subset of inputs* larger than the memory used to store the preprocessed computation. We achieve this desired property in our $\mathcal{H}_1$ functions using two novel DAG constructions, one of which is optimal for a specific graph class and the other we conjecture to be optimal for all general graph classes.

5.1 $\mathcal{H}_1$ Constructions

We first note the differences between the graph constructions we present here and the constructions presented in previous literature [AS15, ACK+16, ABP17a, DFKP15]. Firstly, many of the constructions presented in previous work feature a single target node. This is reasonable in the context of memory-hard functions since both the honest party and the adversary must compute the hash function dynamically (obtaining a single label as the output of the function) on each input. However, in our context of static-memory-hard functions, single-target-node constructions do not make sense. Secondly, our constructions differ from even the multiple target node constructions presented in the literature (specifically, the constructions of [DFKP15]) since prior constructions mainly focused on finding graphs that have large memory vs. time tradeoffs.

Our constructions are designed with the goal that any adversary that does not store almost all the target labels must dynamically use *the same amount of space as needed to store all the labels* to compute the hash function (while *still incurring a cost in runtime*). Moreover, our constructions based on local hardness ensure a stronger guarantee than the constructions in [DFKP15]; in our case, one must use at least S space (for some definition of S) to compute *any* given subset of targets larger than one's current memory usage, whereas in their case, they use S space to compute some subset of targets chosen uniformly at random. Therefore, our specifications are stronger in that we provide a space bound as well as a time bound for adversaries; and moreover, for *honest* parties, the time cost is only a one-time setup cost. We prove our pebbling costs in terms of the black-magic pebble game (defined in Sect. 2) as opposed to the standard pebble game used in previous works. Most notably, this means that in all of our constructions, the pebbling number is upper bounded by the number of targets (since one can always just pebble the targets with magic pebbles).

We begin with some simple and clean constructions of $\mathcal{H}_1$ based on pebbling constructions that exist in the literature. We first prove a lemma regarding the minimum number of pebbles used in the PROM model and the minimum number of pebbles used in the sequential memory model. This is useful in more than one way: (1) it tells us that parallelization does not save the adversary in space so honest parties (who can only compute a constant number of labels at a time) and adversaries (who can compute an arbitrary number of labels at the same time) operate under the same space constraints and (2) it allows us to directly compare sustained time complexities between adversaries and honest parties with respect to space usage.

Lemma 4 (Standard Pebbling Sequential/Parallel Equivalence). *Given a DAG $G = (V, E)$, $\mathbf{P}_\mathrm{s}(G, T) = \mathbf{P}_\mathrm{s}^{||}(G, T)$ where $\mathbf{P}_\mathrm{s}(G, T)$ is defined to be the minimum standard pebbling space complexity in the sequential model, and we define $\mathbf{P}_\mathrm{s}^{||}(G, T)$ to be the minimum standard pebbling space complexity in the parallel model.*

We use Lemma 4 to prove an equivalent lemma for the black-magic pebble game below.

Lemma 5 (Black-Magic Pebbling Sequential/Parallel Equivalence). *Given a DAG $G = (V, E)$, $\mathbf{P}_\mathrm{s}(G, |T|, T) = \mathbf{P}_\mathrm{s}{}^{||}(G, |T|, T)$ where $\mathbf{P}_\mathrm{s}(G, |T|, T)$ was defined to be the minimum black-magic pebbling space complexity in the sequential model, and we define $\mathbf{P}_\mathrm{s}{}^{||}(G, |T|, T)$ to be the minimum black-magic pebbling space complexity in the parallel model.*

Now, we jump into our constructions. We first provide a simple construction and show why this construction is not optimal. In addition, we define some subgraph components in the pebbling literature that are important subcomponents of our constructions.

A Failed Attempt at $\mathcal{H}_1$. We first provide a failed attempt at constructing $\mathcal{H}_1$ due to the large amount of time that is needed to compute the function (for the sequential honest party) with respect to the amount of memory needed to store the output of the function. In other words, this construction is problematic in the sense that an exponential number of steps is necessary to compute the stored results of the function from scratch for the honest party but the adversary with parallel processing time can compute the function from scratch in linear time. Although the honest party could obtain the results of the preprocessing (i.e. the static part of the hash function) from elsewhere, we must ensure that they can still feasibly compute $\mathcal{H}_1$ themselves in the event that they do not trust any of the sources from which they can obtain the static data.

Intuitively, our failed attempt at constructing $\mathcal{H}_1$ is a series of binary search trees. From here onwards, we describe all constructions of $\mathcal{H}_1$ as a directed acyclic graph with n nodes and later use our theorems above to prove static memory hardness from our constructed DAGs.

Graph Construction 1 (Composite Binary Tree DAG). *Let B_h^C be a composite binary tree DAG with height h constructed in the following way where T is the number of targets of our DAG. Let $s = |T|$. In our intended construction $h = s$.*

1. *Let the set of nodes be V. Let the set of edges be E.*
2. *Create $(s+1)2^{h-1} + s$ nodes.*
3. *Create $s+1$ binary search trees using $(s+1)2^{h-1}$ nodes in total where edges are directed from children to parents in each binary tree. Let r_i for $i \in [1, s+1]$ be the roots of these binary search trees.*
4. *Order the remaining nodes in some arbitrary order, let s_j be the jth node in this order for $j \in [1, s]$.*
5. *Create directed edges (r_i, s_i) and $(r_{i+1 \bmod s}, s_i)$ for all $i \in [1, s]$.*

Given any binary search tree with height h, the minimum number of pebbles necessary to pebble the tree is h (assuming a 'tree' with one node has height 1) using the rules of the standard pebble game. Therefore, to ensure that the apex of the tree is pebbled and that both the honest party and the adversary both use h space to pebble the apex, the number of leaves necessary at the base of the tree is 2^{h-1}. If we suppose that the computationally weak honest party (who does not build special circuits) can only evaluate a constant number of random oracle calls at a time (place a constant number of pebbles), the number of sequential evaluations necessary for the honest party is $\geq \Omega(2^h)$ which is infeasible to accomplish. In constrast, the adversary only has to make $O(h)$ parallel random oracle calls, an exponential factor difference between the honest party and the adversary! Such a construction fails since it is clearly infeasible for the honest party since they would never be able to compute all target values of $\mathcal{H}_1$ from scratch (since this computation requires exponential time for the honest party). Thus, we would like a construction that has the same minimum space requirement but also small sequential evaluation time. We prove a better (but also simply defined) construction below.

Cylinder Construction. We make use of what is defined in the pebbling literature as a *pyramid graph* [GLT80] in constructing our *cylinder graph*. The key characteristic of the pyramid graph we use is that the number of pebbles that is required to pebble the apex of the pyramid is equal to the height of the pyramid [GLT80] using the rules of the standard pebble game. Note that a pyramid by itself is not useful for our purposes since the black-magic pebbling space complexity of a pyramid with one apex is 1. Therefore, we need to be able to use the pyramid in a different construction that uses superconstant number of pebbles in the magic pebble game in order to successfully pebble all target nodes.

Graph Construction 2 (Illustrated in Fig. 2). *Let Π_h^C be a* cylinder *graph with height h. We define Π_h^C as follows:*

1. *Create $2h^2$ nodes. Let this set of $2h^2$ nodes be V.*
2. *Arrange the nodes in V into $2h$ levels of h nodes each, ranging from level 0 to level $2h-1$. Let the j-th node in level i be v_i^j. Create directed edges $(v_i^{j \bmod h}, v_{i+1}^{j \bmod h})$ and $(v_i^{j \bmod h}, v_{i+1}^{(j+1) \bmod h})$ for all $i \in [0, 2h-2]$. Let this set of edges be E.*

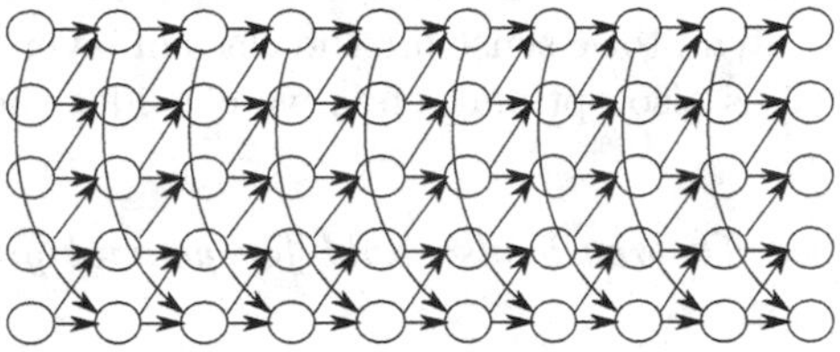

Fig. 2. Cylinder construction (Definition 2) for $h = 5$.

Lemma 6. *Given a cylinder graph with height h, Π_h^C, $\mathbf{P}_{\mathrm{s}}(\Pi_h^C, T) \geq h$.*

Lemma 7. $\mathbf{P}_{\text{opt-ss}}(\Pi_h^C, T) \geq 2h$.

Theorem 3. *Using the rules of the standard pebble game, h pebbles are necessary for at least h parallel steps to pebble* any *target of a height $2h$ cylinder graph, Π_h^C.*

Theorem 4. $\mathbf{P}_{\mathrm{s}}(\Pi_h^C, |T|, T) \geq h$ *where Π_h^C is defined as in Definition 2 where $|S| = |T| = h$.*

As a simple extension of our theorem and proof above, we get Corollary 1. Moreover, as an extension of the proof given for Theorem 4 that all magic pebbles are placed on targets and from Theorem 3, we obtain Corollary 2.

Corollary 1. *Given a cylinder $G = (V, E)$ as constructed in Graph Construction 2, G is incrementally hard: $\mathbf{P}_{\mathrm{s}}(G, |C|-1, C) \geq |T|$ for any subset $C \subseteq T$.*

Corollary 2. *Given a cylinder $G = (V, E)$ as constructed in Graph Construction 2, $\mathbf{P}_{\text{opt-ss}}(G, |C|-1, C) = \Theta(|T|)$ for all subsets of $C \subseteq T$.*

A logical question to ask after constructing our very simple hash function based on a cylinder graph is whether such a construction is optimal in terms of graph-optimal sustained complexity *and* follows our requirements for a static-memory-hard hash function. As it turns out, the graph-optimal sustained complexity of a cylinder graph is optimal in the class of layered graphs. In other words, if we choose to use layered graphs in our constructions, then we cannot hope to get a better memory and time guarantee. From an implementation and practical standpoint, layered graphs are easier to implement and hence this result has potential practical applications (as more complicated constructions need to consider memory allocation factors in the real-life implementation, not considered in the theoretical model).

Theorem 5. *Given a* layered graph, $G = (V, E)$, *if the number of target nodes is* $|T| = s$ *and* $\mathbf{P}_s(G, s, T) \geq s$, *then* $|V| = \Omega(s^2)$. *A* layered graph *is one such that the vertices can be partitioned into layers and edges only go between vertices in consecutive layers.*

Thus, our construction of the cylinder graph is optimal in terms of amount of memory used in the asymptotic sense for the class of layered graphs. An open question is whether this is also optimal when we consider the larger class of all DAGs.

Open Question. *Does Theorem 5 also hold for general graphs with bounded in-degree 2?*

Given the impossibility of providing a better space guarantee for layered graphs, we provide a general (non-layered) construction that transforms a graph from a certain class into another graph with the same space guarantee as in Theorem 5. Furthermore, we provide an example below that has the same space guarantees but a better time guarantee.

Layering *Shortcut-Free* Graphs. We now show how to convert any *shortcut-free* DAG, $G = (V, E)$, with $\mathbf{P}_s(G, T) = s$ and one target node (i.e. $|T| = 1$) into a DAG, $G' = (V', E')$, with $|T'| = s$ targets and $\mathbf{P}_s(G', s, |T'|) = s$.

Definition 25 (Shortcut-Free Graphs). *Let* $G = (V, E)$ *be a DAG where* $\mathbf{P}_s(G, T) \geq s$. *Let* $t_s^{\mathcal{P}}$ *be the last time step that exactly s pebbles must be on G during any normal and regular pebbling strategy,* $\mathcal{P}$, *(see our full version [DLP18] and [GLT80, DL17]) that uses s pebbles. More specifically, let Let X be the union of the set of nodes that are pebbled at* $t_s^{\mathcal{P}}$ *for all normal and regular strategies* $\mathcal{P}$: $X = \bigcup_{\mathcal{P} \in \mathbb{P}} P_{t_s^{\mathcal{P}}}$. *Let D be the set of descendants of nodes of X. A DAG is* shortcut-free *if* $|X| \leq s$ *and given* $s_1 < s$ *pebbles placed on any subset* $X_1 \subset X$, *no normal and regular strategy uses less than* $s - s_1$ *pebbles to pebble* $D \cup (X \setminus X_1)$.

Graph Construction 6. *Given a shortcut-free DAG,* $G = (V, E)$, *with* $\mathbf{P}_s(G, T) = s$ *and* $|T| = 1$, *we create a DAG,* $G' = (V', E')$, *with the following vertices and edges and with the set of targets* T' *where* $|T'| = s$. *Let X be defined as in Definition 25.*

1. *V' is composed of the nodes in V and $s-1$ copies of $X \cup D$. Let the i-th copy of X be X_i (the original is X_0) and let the i-th copy of $x \in X_i$ be x_i.*
2. *E' is composed of the edges in E and the following directed edges. If $(v, w) \in E$ and $v, w \in X$, then create edges $(v_i, w_i) \in E'$ for all $i \in [1, s-1]$. Create edges $(u, v_i) \in E'$ if $(u, v) \in E$ and $u \in V \backslash X, D$.*
3. *The set of targets T' is the union of the set of targets of the different copies: $T' = \bigcup_{i=0}^{s-1} T_i$.*

Using the above construction, we have created a graph $G' = (V', E')$ where $|V'| = |V| + (s-1)(|D| + |X|)$ and $|T'| = s$.

Theorem 7. *Given a shortcut-free DAG $G = (V, E)$ with $\mathbf{P}_s(G,T) = s$ and $|T| = 1$, the construction produced by Graph Construction 6 produces a DAG $G' = (V', E')$ such that $\mathbf{P}_s(G', s, |T|) = s$.*

If $D = \Theta(s)$ and $s = O(\sqrt{|V|})$, then $|V'| = \Theta(s^2 + |V|)$ which has a better sustained time guarantee than our cylinder construction.

We first note that the sustained memory graphs presented in [ABP17a] *do not* achieve optimal local memory hardness because $X \cup D$ (as defined in Definition 6) is $\Theta(n)$ (since the sources are the ones that remain pebbled in their construction). Thus, we would like to provide a construction of a shortcut-free DAG where $|X \cup D| = \Theta(s)$. Note that the size of $X \cup D$ will always be $\Omega(s)$, trivially. We now provide a definition of a shortcut-free graph class G that can be transformed using Definition 6.

Graph Construction 8 (Illustrated in Fig. 3). *Let $G = (V, E)$ be a graph defined by parameter s and in-degree 2 with the following set of vertices and edges:*

1. *Create a height s pyramid. Let r_i be the root of a* subpyramid *(i.e. a pyramid that lies in the original height s pyramid) with height $i \in [2, s]$. One can pick any set of these subpyramids.*
2. *Topologically sort the vertices in each level and create a path through the vertices in each level (see Fig. 3). Replace any in-degree-3 nodes with a pyramid of height 3, with a 6-factor increase in the number of vertices.*
3. *Create $c_1 s$ additional nodes for some constant $c_1 \geq 2$ (in Fig. 3, $c_1 = 6$). Label these nodes v_j for all $j \in [1, c_1 s]$.*
4. *Create directed edges (r_s, v_1) and $(r_i, v_{k(i-1)})$ for all $k \in [1, s]$.*
5. *Create $s-1$ additional nodes. Let these nodes be w_l for all $l \in [1, s-1]$.*
6. *Create directed edges $(v_{c_1 s}, w_1)$ and (r_i, w_{i-1}) for all $i \in [2, s]$.*
7. *The target node is w_{s-1}.*

Lemma 8. *Given a DAG $G = (V, E)$ and a parameter s where G is defined by Definition 8, $\mathbf{P}_s(G, T) = s$.*

Before we prove that $G = (V, E)$ created by Definition 8 with parameter s is shortcut-free, we first prove the following stronger lemma which will help us prove that G is shortcut-free.

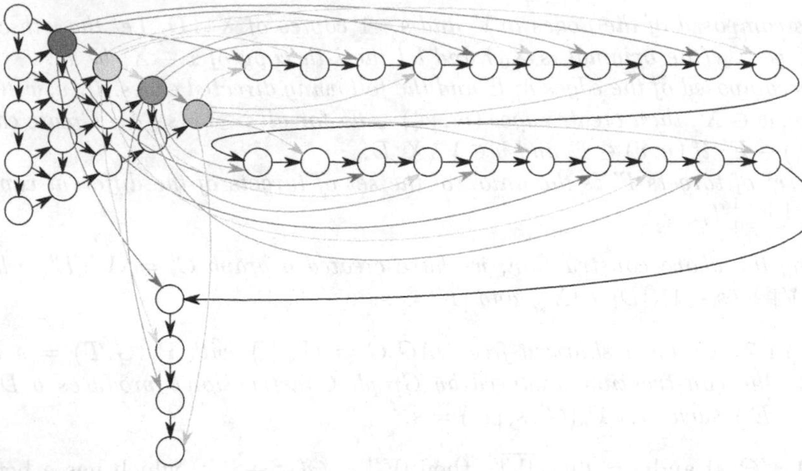

Fig. 3. Example of a time optimal graph family construction as defined in Definition 8. Here, $s = 5$.

Lemma 9. *Let $G = (V, E)$ be a graph created using Definition 8 with parameter s. Given a normal strategy $\mathcal{P}$ to pebble G, when v_q for $q \in [1, c_1 s]$ is pebbled at some time step, black pebbles are present on all nodes in $[r_i, r_s]$ where $i = (q \bmod s-1)+1$ from the time when v_1 is pebbled to when v_q is pebbled.*

Lemma 10. *Given a DAG $G = (V, E)$ and a parameter s where G is defined by Definition 8, G is shortcut-free.*

Theorem 9. *s pebbles are necessary for at least $\Theta(s^2)$ parallel steps to pebble any target of G'.*

We create $G' = (V', E')$ from G (as constructed using Definition 8) using Definition 6 , resulting in a graph with $\Theta(s^2)$ total nodes.

Theorem 10. $\mathbf{P}_{\mathrm{s}}(G', s, T) = s$.

By the proof that G' is shortcut-free, we obtain the following corollary that G' is also incrementally hard. Moreover, Corollary 4 follows directly from the proof of Theorem 7.

Corollary 3. *Given a graph $G = (V, E)$ as constructed in Graph Construction 8, G is incrementally hard: $\mathbf{P}_{\mathrm{s}}(G, |C| - 1, C) \geq |T|$ for any subset $C \subseteq T$.*

The following corollary about the graph-optimal sustained time complexity is proven directly from the proof of Lemma 9 and Theorem 9 that if less than $\frac{s}{2}$ magic pebbles are on the pyramid, then half the pyramid must be rebuilt resulting in $\Theta(s^2)$ time-steps in which s pebbles are on the graph; thus proving for the cases when $|C| - 1 < \frac{s}{2}$. We now prove the case when $|C| - 1 \geq \frac{s}{2}$.

Corollary 4. *Given a graph $G = (V, E)$ as constructed in Graph Construction 8, $\mathbf{P}_{\text{opt-ss}}(G, |C| - 1, C) = \Theta(|V|)$ for all subsets of $C \subseteq T$.*

5.2 $\mathcal{H}_2$ Construction

Our construction of $\mathcal{H}_2$ is presented in Algorithm 1.

Algorithm 1. $\mathcal{H}_2$

On input $(1^\kappa, x)$ and given oracle access to Seek_R (where R is the string outputted by $\mathcal{H}_1$):

1. Let $[\![R]\!] = |R|/w$ be the length of R in words.
1. Query the random oracle to obtain $\rho_0 = \mathcal{O}(x)$ and $\rho_1 = \mathcal{O}(x+1)$.
2. Use ρ_0 to sample a random $\iota \in [[\![R]\!]]$.
3. Query the Seek_R oracle to obtain $y' = \mathsf{Seek}_R(\iota)$.
4. Output $y' \oplus \rho_1$.

Lemma 11. *For any R, the output distribution of $\mathcal{H}_2$ is uniform over the choice of random oracle $\mathcal{O} \leftarrow \mathbb{O}$.*

Remark 6. Lemma 11 is important as an indication that our SHF construction "behaves like a random oracle." The memory-hardness guarantee alone does not assure that the hash function is suitable for cryptographic hashing: e.g., a modified version of $\mathcal{H}_2$ which directly outputted y' instead of $y' \oplus \rho_1$ would still satisfy memory-hardness, but would be an awful hash function (with polynomial size codomain). The inadequacy of existing memory-hardness definitions for assuring that a function "behaves like a hash function" is discussed by [AT17].

5.3 Proofs of Hardness of SHF Constructions

We now prove the hardness of our graph constructions given earlier in Sect. 5.

We begin by stating two supporting lemmata. The first is due to Erdős and Rényi [ER61], on the topic of the Coupon Collector's Problem.

Lemma 12 ([ER61]). *Let Z_n be a random variable denoting the number of samples required, when drawing uniformly from a set of n distinct objects with replacement, to draw each object at least once. Then for any c, $\lim_{n\to\infty} \Pr[Z_n < n\log n + cn] = e^{-e^{-c}}$.*

Corollary 5. *Let $Z_{n,k}$ be a random variable denoting the number of samples required, when drawing uniformly from a set of n distinct objects with replacement, to have drawn at least $k \in [n]$ distinct objects. Let $q \in \omega(k \log k)$. Then $\Pr[Z_{n,k} < q]$ is overwhelming (in k).*

Theorems 11–14 state the static-memory-hardness of our SHF constructions based on Graph Constructions 2 and 8.

Theorem 11. *Define a static-memory hash function family $(\mathcal{H}_1, \mathcal{H}_2)$ as follows: let $\mathcal{H}_1$ be the graph function family $\mathcal{F}_{\Pi_h^C}$ (Graph Construction 2), and let $\mathcal{H}_2$ be as defined in Algorithm 1. Let $\mathcal{H} = \{h_\kappa\}_{\kappa \in \mathbb{N}}$ be the static-memory hash function family described by $(\mathcal{H}_1, \mathcal{H}_2)$. Let $\hat{\kappa} = \kappa - \xi \log(\kappa)$ for any $\xi \in \omega(1)$, let $\hat{\Lambda}, \tau \in \Theta(\sqrt{n})$, and let $q \in \omega(\Lambda \log \Lambda)$. Then $(\mathcal{H}_1, \mathcal{H}_2)$ is $(\hat{\kappa}\hat{\Lambda}, \hat{\kappa}, \tau, q)$-hard.*

Theorem 12. *Define a static-memory hash function family $(\mathcal{H}_1, \mathcal{H}_2)$ as follows: let $\mathcal{H}_1$ be the graph function family $\mathcal{F}_G$ (Graph Construction 8), and let $\mathcal{H}_2$ be as defined in Algorithm 1. Let $\hat{\kappa} = \kappa - \xi \log(\kappa)$ for any $\xi \in \omega(1)$, let $\hat{\Lambda} \in \Theta(\sqrt{n})$, let $\tau \in \Theta(n)$, and let $q \in \omega(\Lambda \log \Lambda)$. Then $(\mathcal{H}_1, \mathcal{H}_2)$ is $(\hat{\kappa}\hat{\Lambda}, \hat{\kappa}, \tau, q)$-hard.*

The parameter q is suboptimal in Theorems 11 and 12. We can achieve optimality (i.e., $q = [\![|R|]\!]$) by the following alternative construction of $\mathcal{H}_2$: make $q' = \omega(\log(\kappa))$ random calls instead of just one call to the Seek oracle in Step 4. To preserve the output size of h_κ, it may be useful to reduce the size of node labels by a corresponding factor of q'. This can be achieved by truncating the random oracle outputs used to compute labels in Definition 20. The description of this altered $\mathcal{H}_2^{q'}$ and the definition of graph function family $\mathcal{F}q'_G$ with shorter labels are given in our full version [DLP18].

Theorem 13. *Define a static-memory hash function family $(\mathcal{H}_1, \mathcal{H}_2)$ as follows: let $\mathcal{H}_1$ be the graph function family $\mathcal{F}_{\Pi_h^C}^{\kappa/q'}$ (Graph Construction 2), and let $\mathcal{H}_2$ be $\mathcal{H}_2^{q'}$ as defined in our full version [DLP18] for some $q' \in \omega(\log \Lambda)$. Let $\hat{\kappa} = \kappa - \xi \log(\kappa)$ for any $\xi \in \omega(1)$, let $\hat{\Lambda}, \tau \in \Theta(\sqrt{n})$, and let $q = \Lambda$. Then $(\mathcal{H}_1, \mathcal{H}_2)$ is $(\hat{\kappa}\hat{\Lambda}, \hat{\kappa}, \tau, q)$-hard.*

Theorem 14. *Define a static-memory hash function family $(\mathcal{H}_1, \mathcal{H}_2)$ as follows: let $\mathcal{H}_1$ be the graph function family $\mathcal{F}_G^{\kappa/q'}$ (Graph Construction 8), and let $\mathcal{H}_2$ be $\mathcal{H}_2^{q'}$ as defined in our full version [DLP18] for some $q' \in \omega(\log \Lambda)$. Let $\hat{\kappa} = \kappa - \xi \log(\kappa)$ for any $\xi \in \omega(1)$, let $\hat{\Lambda} \in \Theta(\sqrt{n})$, let $\tau \in \Theta(n)$, and let $q = \Lambda$. Then $(\mathcal{H}_1, \mathcal{H}_2)$ is $(\hat{\kappa}\hat{\Lambda}, \hat{\kappa}, \tau, q)$-hard.*

Acknowledgements. We are grateful to Jeremiah Blocki, Krzysztof Pietrzak, and Joël Alwen for valuable feedback on earlier versions of this paper. We thank Ling Ren for helpful technical discussions. We also thank Erik D. Demaine and Shafi Goldwasser for their advice on this paper. Finally, we thank our anonymous reviewers for insightful comments.

Sunoo's research is supported by NSF MACS (CNS-1413920), DARPA IBM (W911NF-15-C-0236), SIMONS Investigator Award Agreement Dated June 5th, 2012, and the Center for Science of Information (CSoI), an NSF Science and Technology Center, under grant agreement CCF-0939370.

References

[AAC+17] Abusalah, H., Alwen, J., Cohen, B., Khilko, D., Pietrzak, K., Reyzin, L.: Beyond Hellman's time-memory trade-offs with applications to proofs of space. **10625**, 357–379 (2017)

[AB16] Alwen, J., Blocki, J.: Efficiently computing data-independent memory-hard functions. In: Robshaw, M., Katz, J. (eds.) CRYPTO 2016. LNCS, vol. 9815, pp. 241–271. Springer, Heidelberg (2016). https://doi.org/10.1007/978-3-662-53008-5_9

[ABH17] Alwen, J., Blocki, J., Harsha, B.: Practical graphs for optimal side-channel resistant memory-hard functions. In: CCS, pp. 1001–1017. ACM (2017)

[ABP17a] Alwen, J., Blocki, J., Pietrzak, K.: Depth-robust graphs and their cumulative memory complexity. In: Coron, J.-S., Nielsen, J.B. (eds.) EUROCRYPT 2017. LNCS, vol. 10212, pp. 3–32. Springer, Cham (2017). https://doi.org/10.1007/978-3-319-56617-7_1

[ABP17b] Alwen, J., Blocki, J., Pietrzak, K.: Sustained space complexity. CoRR, abs/1705.05313 (2017)

[ACK+16] Alwen, J., Chen, B., Kamath, C., Kolmogorov, V., Pietrzak, K., Tessaro, S.: On the complexity of scrypt and proofs of space in the parallel random oracle model. In: Fischlin, M., Coron, J.-S. (eds.) EUROCRYPT 2016. LNCS, vol. 9666, pp. 358–387. Springer, Heidelberg (2016). https://doi.org/10.1007/978-3-662-49896-5_13

[ACP+16] Alwen, J., Chen, B., Pietrzak, K., Reyzin, L., Tessaro, S.: Scrypt is maximally memory-hard. IACR Cryptology ePrint Archive 2016:989 (2016)

[ADN+10] Alwen, J., Dodis, Y., Naor, M., Segev, G., Walfish, S., Wichs, D.: Public-key encryption in the bounded-retrieval model. In: Gilbert, H. (ed.) EUROCRYPT 2010. LNCS, vol. 6110, pp. 113–134. Springer, Heidelberg (2010). https://doi.org/10.1007/978-3-642-13190-5_6

[AdRNV17] Alwen, J., de Rezende, S.F., Nordström, J., Vinyals, M.: Cumulative space in black-white pebbling and resolution. In: ITCS, LIPIcs, vol. 67, pp. 38:1–38:21. Schloss Dagstuhl - Leibniz-Zentrum fuer Informatik (2017)

[ADW09] Alwen, J., Dodis, Y., Wichs, D.: Survey: leakage resilience and the bounded retrieval model. In: Kurosawa, K. (ed.) ICITS 2009. LNCS, vol. 5973, pp. 1–18. Springer, Heidelberg (2010). https://doi.org/10.1007/978-3-642-14496-7_1

[AS15] Alwen, J., Serbinenko, V.: High parallel complexity graphs and memory-hard functions. In: Servedio, R.A., Rubinfeld, R. (eds.) Proceedings of the Forty-Seventh Annual ACM on Symposium on Theory of Computing, STOC 2015, Portland, OR, USA, 14–17 June 2015, pp. 595–603. ACM (2015)

[AT17] Alwen, J., Tackmann, B.: Moderately hard functions: definition, instantiations, and applications. In: Kalai, Y., Reyzin, L. (eds.) TCC 2017. LNCS, vol. 10677, pp. 493–526. Springer, Cham (2017). https://doi.org/10.1007/978-3-319-70500-2_17

[BDPA08] Bertoni, G., Daemen, J., Peeters, M., Van Assche, G.: On the indifferentiability of the sponge construction. In: Smart, N. (ed.) EUROCRYPT 2008. LNCS, vol. 4965, pp. 181–197. Springer, Heidelberg (2008). https://doi.org/10.1007/978-3-540-78967-3_11

[Ben89] Bennett, C.H.: Time/space trade-offs for reversible computation. SIAM J. Comput. **18**(4), 766–776 (1989)

[BK15] Biryukov, A., Khovratovich, D.: Tradeoff cryptanalysis of memory-hard functions. In: Iwata, T., Cheon, J.H. (eds.) ASIACRYPT 2015. LNCS, vol. 9453, pp. 633–657. Springer, Heidelberg (2015). https://doi.org/10.1007/978-3-662-48800-3_26

[BKR16] Bellare, M., Kane, D., Rogaway, P.: Big-key symmetric encryption: resisting key exfiltration. In: Robshaw, M., Katz, J. (eds.) CRYPTO 2016. LNCS, vol. 9814, pp. 373–402. Springer, Heidelberg (2016). https://doi.org/10.1007/978-3-662-53018-4_14

[BR93] Bellare, M., Rogaway, P.: Random oracles are practical: a paradigm for designing efficient protocols. In: Denning, D.E., Pyle, R., Ganesan, R., Sandhu, R.S., Ashby, V. (eds.) CCS 1993, Proceedings of the 1st ACM Conference on Computer and Communications Security, Fairfax, Virginia, USA, 3–5 November 1993, pp. 62–73. ACM (1993)

[BZ16] Blocki, J., Zhou, S.: On the computational complexity of minimal cumulative cost graph pebbling. CoRR, abs/1609.04449 (2016)

[BZ17] Blocki, J., Zhou, S.: On the depth-robustness and cumulative pebbling cost of Argon2i. In: Kalai, Y., Reyzin, L. (eds.) TCC 2017. LNCS, vol. 10677, pp. 445–465. Springer, Cham (2017). https://doi.org/10.1007/978-3-319-70500-2_15

[CDD+07] Cash, D., Ding, Y.Z., Dodis, Y., Lee, W., Lipton, R., Walfish, S.: Intrusion-resilient key exchange in the bounded retrieval model. In: Vadhan, S.P. (ed.) TCC 2007. LNCS, vol. 4392, pp. 479–498. Springer, Heidelberg (2007). https://doi.org/10.1007/978-3-540-70936-7_26

[Cha73] Chandra, A.K.: Efficient compilation of linear recursive programs. In: SWAT (FOCS), pp. 16–25. IEEE Computer Society (1973)

[CLW06] Di Crescenzo, G., Lipton, R.J., Walfish, S.: Perfectly secure password protocols in the bounded retrieval model. In: Halevi and Rabin [HR06], pp. 225–244

[Coo73] Cook, S.A.: An observation on time-storage trade off. In: Proceedings of the Fifth Annual ACM Symposium on Theory of Computing, STOC 1973, pp. 29–33. ACM, New York (1973)

[CS74] Cook, S., Sethi, R.: Storage requirements for deterministic/polynomial time recognizable languages. In: Proceedings of the Sixth Annual ACM Symposium on Theory of Computing, STOC 1974, pp. 33–39. ACM, New York (1974)

[DFKP15] Dziembowski, S., Faust, S., Kolmogorov, V., Pietrzak, K.: Proofs of space. In: Gennaro, R., Robshaw, M. (eds.) CRYPTO 2015. LNCS, vol. 9216, pp. 585–605. Springer, Heidelberg (2015). https://doi.org/10.1007/978-3-662-48000-7_29

[DKW10] Dziembowski, S., Kazana, T., Wichs, D.: One-time computable and uncomputable functions. IACR Cryptology ePrint Archive 2010:541 (2010)

[DKW11] Dziembowski, S., Kazana, T., Wichs, D.: One-time computable self-erasing functions. In: Ishai, Y. (ed.) TCC 2011. LNCS, vol. 6597, pp. 125–143. Springer, Heidelberg (2011). https://doi.org/10.1007/978-3-642-19571-6_9

[DL17] Demaine, E.D., Liu, Q.C.: Inapproximability of the standard pebble game and hard to pebble graphs. Algorithms and Data Structures. LNCS, vol. 10389, pp. 313–324. Springer, Cham (2017). https://doi.org/10.1007/978-3-319-62127-2_27

[DLP18] Dryja, T., Liu, Q.C., Park, S.: Static-memory-hard functions and nonlinear space-time tradeoffs via pebbling. IACR Cryptology ePrint Archive 2018:205 (2018)

[Dzi06] Dziembowski, S.: Intrusion-resilience via the bounded-storage model. In: Halevi and Rabin [HR06], pp. 207–224

[ER61] Erdős, P., Rényi, A.: On a classical problem of probability theory. Magyar Tudományos Akadémia Matematikai Kutató Intézetének Közleményei **6**, 215–220 (1961)

[FLW13] Forler, C., Lucks, S., Wenzel, J.: Catena: a memory-consuming password scrambler. IACR Cryptology ePrint Archive 2013:525 (2013)

[GLT80] Gilbert, J.R., Lengauer, T., Tarjan, R.E.: The pebbling problem is complete in polynomial space. **9**, 513–524 (1980)

[HPV77] Hopcroft, J., Paul, W., Valiant, L.: On time versus space. J. ACM **24**(2), 332–337 (1977)

[HR06] Halevi, S., Rabin, T. (eds.): TCC 2006. LNCS, vol. 3876. Springer, Heidelberg (2006)

[JWK81] Jia-Wei, H., Kung, H.T.: I/o complexity: the red-blue pebble game. In: Proceedings of the 13th Annual ACM Symposium on Theory of Computing, STOC 1981, pp. 326–333 (1981)

[LT82] Lengauer, T., Tarjan, R.E.: Asymptotically tight bounds on time-space trade-offs in a pebble game. J. ACM **29**(4), 1087–1130 (1982)

[Mer79] Merkle, R.C.: Secrecy, authentication, and public key systems. Ph.D. thesis, Stanford, CA, USA (1979). AAI8001972

[Nor12] Nordström, J.: On the relative strength of pebbling and resolution. ACM Trans. Comput. Log. **13**(2), 16:1–16:43 (2012)

[Nor15] Nordstrom, J.: New wine into old wineskins: a survey of some pebbling classics with supplemental results (2015)

[Per09] Percival, C.: Stronger key derivation via sequential memory-hard functions. Presented at BSDCan 2009 (2009). http://www.tarsnap.com/scrypt/scrypt.pdf

[PH70] Paterson, M.S., Hewitt, C.E.: Comparative Schematology. In: Record of the Project MAC Conference on Concurrent Systems and Parallel Computation, pp. 119–127. ACM, New York (1970)

[Pip82] Pippenger, N.: Advances in pebbling. In: Nielsen, M., Schmidt, E.M. (eds.) ICALP 1982. LNCS, vol. 140, pp. 407–417. Springer, Heidelberg (1982). https://doi.org/10.1007/BFb0012787

[Pot17] Potechin, A.: Bounds on monotone switching networks for directed connectivity. J. ACM **64**(4), 29:1–29:48 (2017)

[RD17] Ren, L., Devadas, S.: Bandwidth hard functions for ASIC resistance. In: Kalai, Y., Reyzin, L. (eds.) TCC 2017. LNCS, vol. 10677, pp. 466–492. Springer, Cham (2017). https://doi.org/10.1007/978-3-319-70500-2_16

[Set75] Sethi, R.: Complete register allocation problems. SIAM J. Comput. **4**(3), 226–248 (1975)

[SS79a] Savage, J.E., Swamy, S.: Space-time tradeoffs for oblivious integer multiplication. In: Maurer, H.A. (ed.) ICALP 1979. LNCS, vol. 71, pp. 498–504. Springer, Heidelberg (1979). https://doi.org/10.1007/3-540-09510-1_40

[SS79b] Swamy, S., Savage, J.E.: Space-time tradeoffs for linear recursion. In: Proceedings of the 6th ACM SIGACT-SIGPLAN Symposium on Principles of Programming Languages, POPL 1979, pp. 135–142. ACM, New York (1979)

[Tom81] Tompa, M.: Corrigendum: time-space tradeoffs for computing functions, using connectivity properties of their circuits. J. Comput. Syst. Sci. **23**(1), 106 (1981)

[Val77] Valiant, L.G.: Graph-theoretic arguments in low-level complexity. In: Proceedings of 6th Symposium on Mathematical Foundations of Computer Science 1977, Tatranska Lomnica, Czechoslovakia, 5–9 September 1977, pp. 162–176 (1977)

No-signaling Linear PCPs

Susumu Kiyoshima[(✉)]

NTT Secure Platform Laboratories, Tokyo, Japan
kiyoshima.susumu@lab.ntt.co.jp

Abstract. In this paper, we give a *no-signaling linear probabilistically checkable proof (PCP) system* for polynomial-time deterministic computation, i.e., a PCP system for $\mathcal{P}$ such that (1) the PCP oracle is a linear function and (2) the soundness holds against any (computational) no-signaling cheating prover, who is allowed to answer each query according to a distribution that depends on the entire query set in a certain way. To the best of our knowledge, our construction is the first PCP system that satisfies these two properties simultaneously.

As an application of our PCP system, we obtain a 2-message scheme for delegating computation by using a known transformation. Compared with existing 2-message delegation schemes based on standard cryptographic assumptions, our scheme requires preprocessing but has a simpler structure and makes use of different (possibly cheaper) standard cryptographic primitives, namely additive/multiplicative homomorphic encryption schemes.

1 Introduction

Linear PCP. *Probabilistically checkable proofs*, or PCPs, are proof systems with which one can probabilistically verify the correctness of statements with bounded soundness error by reading only a few bits of proof strings. A central result about PCPs are the *PCP theorem* [4,5], which states that every $\mathcal{NP}$ statement has a PCP system such that the proof string is polynomially long and the verification requires only a constant number of bits of the proof string (the soundness error is a small constant and can be reduced by repetition).

An important application of PCPs to Cryptography is *succinct argument systems*, i.e., argument systems that have very small communication complexity and fast verification time. A famous example of such argument systems is that of Kilian [41], which proves an $\mathcal{NP}$ statement by using PCPs as follows.

1. The prover first generates a polynomially long PCP proof for the statement (this is possible thanks to the PCP theorem) and succinctly commits to it by using Merkle's tree-hashing technique.
2. The verifier queries a few bits of the PCP proof just like the PCP verifier.
3. The prover reveals the queried bits by appropriately opening the commitment using the local opening property of Merkle's tree-hashing.

A. Beimel and S. Dziembowski (Eds.): TCC 2018, LNCS 11239, pp. 67–97, 2018.
https://doi.org/10.1007/978-3-030-03807-6_3

This argument system of Kilian has communication complexity and verification time that depend on the classical $\mathcal{NP}$ verification time only logarithmically; that is, a proof for the membership of an instance x in an $\mathcal{NP}$ language L has communication complexity and verification time $\mathsf{poly}(\lambda + |x| + \log t)$, where λ is the security parameter, t is the time to evaluate the $\mathcal{NP}$ relation of L on x, and poly is a polynomial that is independent of L. Kilian's technique was later extended to obtain succinct non-interactive argument systems (SNARGs) for $\mathcal{NP}$ in the random oracle model [46] as well as in the standard model with non-falsifiable assumptions (such as the existence of extractable hash functions), e.g., [13,28].[1]

Recently, the studies of succinct argument systems have been boosted by the use of a specific type of PCPs called *linear PCPs*, which are PCPs such that the honest proofs are linear functions (i.e., the honest proof strings are the truth tables of linear functions).[2] (The proof strings of linear PCPs are exponentially long in general, but each bit of the proof strings can be computed efficiently by evaluating the underlying linear functions). A nice property of linear PCPs is that they often have much simpler structures than the polynomially long PCPs; as a result, the use of linear PCPs often lead to simpler constructions of succinct argument systems. The use of linear PCPs in the context of succinct argument systems was initiated by Ishai, Kushilevitz, and Ostrovsky [37], who used them for constructing an argument system for $\mathcal{NP}$ with a laconic prover (i.e., a prover that sends to the verifier only short messages). Subsequently, several works obtain practical implementations of the argument system of Ishai et al. [49–53], whereas others extended the technique of Ishai et al. for the use for SNARGs and obtained practical implementations of *preprocessing SNARGs* (i.e., SNARGs that require expensive (but reusable) preprocessing setups) [9,11,16].

No-signaling PCP. Very recently, Kalai, Raz, and Rothblum [39,40] found that PCPs with a stronger soundness guarantee, called *soundness against no-signaling provers*, are useful for constructing 2-message succinct argument systems under standard assumptions. Concretely, Kalai et al. [39,40] first constructed *no-signaling PCPs* (i.e., PCPs that are sound against no-signaling provers) for deterministic computation, and next showed that their no-signaling PCPs can be used to obtain 2-message succinct argument systems for deterministic computation under the assumptions of the existence of quasi-polynomially secure fully homomorphic encryption schemes or (2-message, polylogarithmic-communication, single-server) private information retrieval schemes. The succinct argument systems of Kalai et al. differ from prior ones in that they can handle only deterministic computation but require just two messages and is proven secure under standard assumptions. (In contrast, the argument system of

[1] Actually, SNARGs in the standard model require the existence of common reference strings, and some constructions of them further require that the verifier has some private information about the common reference strings.

[2] In general, soundness is required to hold against any (possibly non-linear) functions; linear PCPs with this notion of soundness is sometimes called "strong linear PCPs" [16].

Kilian and prior SNARG systems can handle non-deterministic computation but the former requires four messages and the latter are proven secure only in ideal models such as the random oracle model or under non-falsifiable knowledge-type assumptions).

As observed by Kalai et al. [39,40], 2-message succinct argument systems have a direct application in *delegating computation* [32] (or *verifiable computation* [30]). Specifically, consider a setting where there exist a computationally weak client and a computationally powerful server, and the client wants to delegate a heavy computation to the server. Given a 2-message succinct argument system, the client can delegate the computation to the server in such a way that it can verify the correctness of the server's computation very efficiently (i.e., much faster than doing the computation from scratch).

After the results of Kalai et al. [39,40], no-signaling PCPs and their applications to delegation schemes have been extensively studied. Kalai and Paneth [38] extend the results of Kalai et al. [40] and obtain a delegation scheme for deterministic RAM computation, and Brakerski, Holmgren, and Kalai [20] further extend it so that the scheme is adaptively sound (i.e., sound even when the statement is chosen after the verifier's message) and in addition can be based on polynomially hard standard cryptographic assumptions. Paneth and Rothblum [47] give an adaptively sound delegation scheme for deterministic RAM computation with public verifiability (i.e., with a property that not only the verifier but also anyone can verify proofs) albeit with the use of a new cryptographic assumption. Badrinarayanan, Kalai, Khurana, Sahai, and Wichs [7] give an adaptively sound delegation scheme for low-space non-deterministic computation (i.e., non-deterministic computation whose space complexity is much smaller than time complexity) under sub-exponentially hard cryptographic assumptions.

Kalai et al. [39,40] and the abovementioned subsequent works on delegation schemes use no-signaling PCPs with polynomial length. As a result, compared with the delegation schemes that can be obtained from, e.g., the preprocessing SNARGs based on linear PCPs [9,11,16], their delegation schemes have complex structures.

1.1 Our Results

In this paper, we study the problem of constructing *no-signaling linear PCPs*, i.e., linear PCPs that are sound against no-signaling provers. Our main motivation is to obtain a PCP that inherits good properties from both of linear PCPs and no-signaling PCPs. Thus, our goal is to obtain a no-signaling linear PCP that can be used to obtain a 2-message delegation scheme that is secure under standard cryptographic assumptions (like those that are based on no-signaling PCPs) and has a simple structure (like those that are based on linear PCPs).

Main Result: No-signaling Linear PCP for $\mathcal{P}$. The main result of this paper is an unconditional construction of no-signaling linear PCPs for polynomial-time deterministic computation. We focus our attention on PCPs that proves correctness of arithmetic circuit computation, so our construction handles statements of the form $(C, \boldsymbol{x}, \boldsymbol{y})$, where C is a polynomial-size arithmetic circuit and the statement to be proven is "$C(\boldsymbol{x}) = \boldsymbol{y}$ holds."

Theorem ***(informal).*** *There exists a no-signaling linear PCP for the correctness of polynomial-size arithmetic circuit computation. The proof generation algorithm runs in time* $\mathsf{poly}(|C|)$*, the verifier query algorithm runs in time* $\mathsf{poly}(\lambda + |C|)$*, and the verifier decision algorithm runs in time* $\mathsf{poly}(\lambda + |\boldsymbol{x}| + |\boldsymbol{y}|)$.

A formal statement of this theorem is given as Theorem 1 in Sect. 4. To the best of our knowledge, our construction is the first linear PCP that is sound against no-signaling provers. (See Sect. 1.3 for concurrent independent works).

Our no-signaling linear PCP inherits simplicity from existing linear PCPs. Indeed, the proof string of our PCP is identical with that of the well-known linear PCP of Arora, Lund, Motwani, Sudan, and Szegedy [4]. Regarding the verifier, we added slight modifications to that of Arora et al. to simplify the analysis; however, we do not think that these modifications are fundamental.

The analysis of our PCP is, at a very high level, a combination of the analysis of the linear PCP of Arora et al. [4] and that of the no-signaling PCP of Kalai et al. [40]. A difficulty comes from the fact that the analysis of the no-signaling PCP of Kalai et al. partly rely on the specific construction of their PCP (which is based on the PCP of Babai, Fortnow, Levin, and Szegedy [6]), and we overcome this difficulty by modifying the analysis of the no-signaling PCP of Kalai et al. appropriately by borrowing techniques from the analysis of the linear PCP of Arora et al. Along the way, we also modify the analysis of Kalai et al. so that, unlike the analysis of Kalai et al., our analysis does not require that the statement is represented by an "augmented layered circuit" and only requires that it is represented by a layered circuit,[3] so our PCP can work on smaller and simpler circuits; we think that this modification may be of independent interest. (The downside of this modification is that the analysis of no-signaling soundness becomes a little more complex. Specifically, we cannot use the notion of *local-assignment generators* [47] to analyze no-signaling soundness in a modular way). A more detailed overview of our analysis is given in Sect. 3.

Application: Delegation Scheme for $\mathcal{P}$ in the Preprocessing Model. As an application of our no-signaling linear PCP, we construct a 2-message delegation scheme for polynomial-time deterministic computation under standard cryptographic assumptions. Just like previous linear-PCP–based delegation schemes and succinct arguments (such as that of Bitansky et al. [16]), our delegation scheme works in the *preprocessing model*, so our scheme uses expensive offline setups that can be used for proving multiple statements. When the statement is $(C, \boldsymbol{x}, \boldsymbol{y})$, the running time of the client is $\mathsf{poly}(\lambda + |C|)$ in the offline phase and is $\mathsf{poly}(\lambda + |\boldsymbol{x}| + |\boldsymbol{y}|)$ in the online phase. Our delegation scheme is adaptively secure in the sense that the input $\boldsymbol{x}$ can be chosen in the online phase, and is "designated-verifier type" in the sense that the verification requires a secret key.

3 Our analysis does not require the space complexity of the computation to be bounded either.

We obtain our delegation scheme by applying the transformation of Kalai et al. [39,40] on our no-signaling liner PCP. (The transformation of Kalai et al., which is closely related to those of Biehl, Meyer, and Wetzel [12] and Aiello, Bhatt, Ostrovsky, and Rajagopalan [1], transforms a no-signaling PCP to a 2-message delegation scheme).

Compared with the existing 2-message delegation schemes based on polynomially long no-signaling PCPs (such as that of Kalai et al. [40]), our scheme requires preprocessing, but has a simple structure and uses different (possibly cheaper) tools thanks to the use of linear PCPs. Concretely, thanks to the use of linear PCPs, we can avoid the use of fully homomorphic encryption schemes or 2-message private information retrieval schemes, and can instead use additive homomorphic encryption schemes over prime-order fields (such as that of Goldwasser and Micali [33]) or multiplicative homomorphic encryption schemes over prime-order bilinear groups (such as the DLIN-based linear encryption scheme of Boneh, Boyen, and Shacham [18]).

1.2 Prior Works

Delegation Scheme. Delegation schemes (and verifiable computation schemes) have been extensively studied in literature. Other than those that we mentioned above, existing results that are related to ours are the following. (We focus our attention on non-interactive or 2-message delegation schemes for all deterministic or non-deterministic polynomial-time computation).

DELEGATION SCHEMES FOR NON-DETERMINISTIC COMPUTATION. The existing constructions of (preprocessing) SNARGs, such as [13–16,19,28,29,31,34,35,44, 45], can be directly used to obtain delegation schemes for $\mathcal{NP}$, and some of them can be used even to obtain publicly verifiable ones. Additionally, it was shown recently that an interactive variant of PCPs, called *interactive oracle proofs*, can also be used to obtain delegation schemes for $\mathcal{NP}$ [10]. The security of these delegation schemes holds under non-standard assumptions (e.g., knowledge assumptions) or in ideal models (e.g., the generic group model and the random oracle model). Compared with these schemes, our scheme works only for $\mathcal{P}$ and requires preprocessing, but can be proven secure in the standard model under a standard assumption (namely the existence of homomorphic encryption schemes).

DELEGATION SCHEMES FOR DETERMINISTIC COMPUTATION. Other than the abovementioned recent works that obtain delegation schemes for $\mathcal{P}$ without preprocessing by using no-signaling PCPs (i.e., Kalai et al. [39,40] and the subsequent works), there are plenty of works that obtain delegation schemes for $\mathcal{P}$ without using PCPs. Specifically, some works obtain schemes with preprocessing by using fully homomorphic encryption or attribute-based encryption schemes [27,30,48], and others obtain schemes without preprocessing by using multilinear maps or indistinguishability obfuscators (e.g., [2,17,21–24,43]). Compared with these schemes, our scheme requires preprocessing but only uses relatively simple building blocks (namely a linear PCP and a homomorphic encryption scheme).

1.3 Concurrent Works

In independent concurrent works, Holmgren and Rothblum [36] and Chiesa, Manohar, and Shinkar [25] also observe that one can obtain no-signaling PCPs for $\mathcal{P}$ without relying on the "augmented circuit" technique of Kalai et al. [40]. The technique by Holmgren and Rothblum works when the underlying PCP is that of Babai et al. [6] (as in the work of Kalai et al. [40]) and the one by Chiesa et al. works when the underlying PCP is that of Arora et al. [4] (as in this paper).

The work of Chiesa et al. [25] actually has many other similarities with our work, and in particular their work also shows that the linear PCP of Arora et al. [4] is sound against no-signaling cheating provers. We remark however that there are also a few differences between their work and our work, such as:

- Chiesa et al. achieve constant soundness error with constant query complexity while we focus on achieving negligible soundness error and did not try to optimize the query complexity (currently, our analysis requires polynomial query complexity[4]).
- Chiesa et al. prove soundness against cheating provers that are no-signaling in a strong sense (namely, "perfect no-signaling") while we prove soundness even against those that are no-signaling in a weak sense (namely, "computational no-signaling").
- The analysis of Chiesa et al. uses the equivalence between no-signaling functions and *quasi-distributions*[5] over functions while ours does not use this equivalence. (The equivalence between no-signaling functions and quasi-distributions was shown by Chiesa, Manohar, and Shinkar [26] relying on Fourier analytic techniques).

Remark 1. Chiesa et al. [25] use the term "no-signaling linear PCPs" in a different meaning from us. Specifically, Chiesa et al. use it to refer to PCPs such that honest proofs are linear functions and the soundness holds against no-signaling cheating provers that are equivalent with quasi-distributions over linear functions, while we use it to refer to PCPs such that honest proofs are linear functions and the soundness holds against any no-signaling cheating provers (which are not necessarily equivalent with quasi-distributions over linear functions).

1.4 Outline

We introduce notations and definitions in Sect. 2, give an overview of our no-signaling linear PCP in Sect. 3, describe our no-signaling linear PCP in Sect. 4,

[4] It is likely that the query complexity of our PCP can be reduced to polylogarithmic, but we have not verified it formally.

[5] Quasi-distributions are a generalized notion of probability distributions and allow negative probabilities.

and describe the application to delegation schemes in Sect. 5. Due to space limitations, we omit the formal security analyses of our schemes and refer the readers to the full version of this paper [42].

2 Preliminaries

2.1 Basic Notations

We denote the security parameter by λ. Let $\mathbb{N}$ be the set of all natural numbers. For any $k \in \mathbb{N}$, let $[k] \stackrel{\text{def}}{=} \{1, \ldots, k\}$.

We denote a vector in a bold shape (e.g., $\boldsymbol{v}$). For a vector $\boldsymbol{v} = (v_1, \ldots, v_\lambda)$ and a set $S \subseteq [\lambda]$, let $\boldsymbol{v}|_S \stackrel{\text{def}}{=} \{v_i\}_{i \in S}$. Similarly, for a function $f : D \to R$ and a set $S \subseteq D$, let $f|_S \stackrel{\text{def}}{=} \{f(i)\}_{i \in S}$. For two vectors $\boldsymbol{u} = (u_1, \ldots, u_\lambda)$, $\boldsymbol{v} = (v_1, \ldots, v_\lambda)$ of the same length (where each element is a field element), let $\langle \boldsymbol{u}, \boldsymbol{v} \rangle \stackrel{\text{def}}{=} \sum_{i \in [\lambda]} u_i v_i$ denote their inner product and $\boldsymbol{u} \otimes \boldsymbol{v} \stackrel{\text{def}}{=} (u_i v_j)_{i,j \in [\lambda]}$ denote their tensor product.[6]

For a set S, we denote by $s \leftarrow S$ a process of obtaining an element $s \in S$ by a uniform sampling from S. Similarly, for any probabilistic algorithm Algo, we denote by $y \leftarrow \mathsf{Algo}$ a process of obtaining an output y by an execution of Algo with uniform randomness. For an event E and a probabilistic process P, we denote $\Pr[E \mid P]$ the probability of E occuring over the randomness of P.

2.2 Circuits

All circuits in this paper are arithmetic circuits over finite fields of prime orders, and they have addition and multiplication gates with fan-in 2. We assume without loss of generality that they are "layered," i.e., the gates in a circuit can be partitioned into layers such that (1) the first layer consists of the input gates and the last layer consists of the output gates, and (2) the gates in the i-th layer have children in the $(i-1)$-th layer.

Given a circuit C, we use $\mathbb{F}$ to denote the underlying finite field, N to denote the number of the wires,[7] n to denote the number of the input gates, and m to denote the number of the output gates. We assume that the first n wires of C are those that takes the values of the input gates and the last m ones are those that takes the value of the output gates. (Formally, $\mathbb{F}, N, n, m$ should be written as, e.g., $\mathbb{F}_C, N_C, n_C, m_C$ since they depend on the circuit C. However, to simplify the notations, we avoid expressing this dependence). When we consider a circuit family $\{C_\lambda\}_{\lambda \in \mathbb{N}}$, it is implicitly assumed that the size of each C_λ is bounded by $\mathsf{poly}(\lambda)$.

---

[6] In this paper, the tensor product of two vectors are viewed as a vector (with an appropriate ordering of the elements) rather than a matrix.

[7] We assume that for any gate with fan-out more than one, all the output wires from that gate share the same index $i \in [N]$.

2.3 Probabilistically Checkable Proofs (PCPs)

Roughly speaking, probabilistically checkable proofs (PCPs) are proof systems with which one can probabilistically verify the correctness of statements by reading only a few bits of the proof strings. A formal definition is given below.

Remark 2 (On the definition that we use). For convenience, we give a definition that is tailored to our purpose. Specifically, our definition differs from the standard one in the following way.

1. We require that the soundness error is negligible in the security parameter.
2. We only consider proofs for the correctness of deterministic arithmetic circuit computation, i.e., membership proofs for the following language.
$$\{(C, \boldsymbol{x}, \boldsymbol{y}) \mid C \text{ is an arithmetic circuit s.t. } C(\boldsymbol{x}) = \boldsymbol{y}\}.$$
3. We implicitly require that PCP systems satisfy two auxiliary properties (which almost all existing constructions satisfy), namely *relatively efficient oracle construction* and *non-adaptive verifier* [8].
4. We assume that the verifier's queries depend only on the circuit C and do not depend on the input $\boldsymbol{x}$ and the output $\boldsymbol{y}$. (This assumption will be useful later when we define adaptive soundness against no-signaling cheating provers). ◊

Definition 1 (PCPs for correctness of arithmetic circuit computation). A probabilistically checkable proof (PCP) system for the correctness of arithmetic circuit computation *consists of a pair of* PPT *Turing machines* $V = (V_0, V_1)$ *(called* verifier*) and a* PPT *Turing machine* P *(called* prover*) that satisfy the following.*

- ***Syntax.*** *For every arithmetic circuit* C*, there exist*
  - *finite sets* D_C *and* Σ_C *(called* proof domain *and* proof alphabet*) and*
  - *a polynomial* κ_V *(called* query complexity *of* V*)*

  such that for every input $\boldsymbol{x}$ *of* C*, the output* $\boldsymbol{y} := C(\boldsymbol{x})$*, and every security parameter* $\lambda \in \mathbb{N}$*,*
  - $P(C, \boldsymbol{x})$ *outputs a function* $\pi : D_C \to \Sigma_C$ *(called* proof*),*
  - $V_0(1^\lambda, C)$ *outputs a string* $\mathsf{st}_V \in \{0,1\}^*$ *(called* state*) and a set* $Q \subset D_C$ *of size* $\kappa_V(\lambda)$ *(called* queries*), and*
  - $V_1(\mathsf{st}_V, \boldsymbol{x}, \boldsymbol{y}, \pi|_Q)$ *outputs a bit* $b \in \{0,1\}$*.*
- ***Completeness.*** *For every arithmetic circuit* C*, every input* $\boldsymbol{x}$ *of* C*, the output* $\boldsymbol{y} := C(\boldsymbol{x})$*, and every security parameter* $\lambda \in \mathbb{N}$*,*
$$\Pr\left[V_1(\mathsf{st}_V, \boldsymbol{x}, \boldsymbol{y}, \pi|_Q) = 1 \;\middle|\; \begin{array}{l} \pi \leftarrow P(C, \boldsymbol{x}) \\ (Q, \mathsf{st}_V) \leftarrow V_0(1^\lambda, C) \end{array}\right] = 1.$$
- ***Soundness.*** *For any circuit family* $\{C_\lambda\}_{\lambda\in\mathbb{N}}$ *and any probabilistic Turing machine* P^* *(called cheating prover), there exists a negligible function* negl *such that for every security parameter* $\lambda \in \mathbb{N}$*,*
$$\Pr\left[V_1(\mathsf{st}_V, \boldsymbol{x}, \boldsymbol{y}, \pi^*|_Q) = 1 \wedge C_\lambda(\boldsymbol{x}) \neq \boldsymbol{y} \;\middle|\; \begin{array}{l} (Q, \mathsf{st}_V) \leftarrow V_0(1^\lambda, C_\lambda) \\ (\boldsymbol{x}, \boldsymbol{y}, \pi^*) \leftarrow P^*(1^\lambda, C_\lambda) \end{array}\right] \leq \mathsf{negl}(\lambda).$$

◇

A PCP system is said to be linear if it satisfies an additional property that the proof is a linear function.

Definition 2 (Linear PCPs). *Let (P, V) be any PCP system and $\{D_C\}_C$ be its proof domains. Then, (P, V) is said to be* linear *if for every arithmetic circuit C and input $\boldsymbol{x}$ of C,*

$$\Pr\left[\bigwedge_{u,v \in D_C} \pi(u) + \pi(v) = \pi(u+v) \;\middle|\; \pi \leftarrow P(C, \boldsymbol{x})\right] = 1.$$

2.4 No-signaling PCPs

No-signaling PCPs [39,40] are PCP systems that guarantee soundness against a stronger class of cheating provers called no-signaling cheating provers. The main difference between no-signaling cheating provers and normal cheating provers in that, while a normal cheating prover is required to output a PCP proof π^* before seeing queries Q, a no-signaling cheating prover is allowed to output π^* after seeing Q. There is however a restriction on the distribution of π^*; roughly speaking, it is required that for any (not too large) sets Q, Q' such that $Q' \subset Q$, the distribution of $\pi^*|_{Q'}$ when the queries are Q should be indistinguishable from the distribution of it when the queries are Q'. The formal definition is given below. (The following definition is the "computational" variant of the definition, which is given by Brakerski et al. [20]).

Definition 3 (No-signaling cheating prover). *Let (P, V) be any PCP system, $\{D_C\}_C$ and $\{\Sigma_C\}_C$ be the proof domains and proof alphabets of (P, V), $\{C_\lambda\}_{\lambda \in \mathbb{N}}$ be any circuit family, and P^* be any probabilistic Turing machine with the following syntax.*

- *Given the security parameter $\lambda \in \mathbb{N}$, the circuit C_λ, and a set of queries $Q \subset D_{C_\lambda}$ as input, P^* outputs an input $\boldsymbol{x}$ of C_λ, an output $\boldsymbol{y}$ of C_λ, and a partial function $\pi^* : Q \to \Sigma_{C_\lambda}$. (Note that π^* can be viewed as a PCP proof whose domain is restricted to Q).*

Then, for any polynomial $\kappa_{\max}$, P^* is said to be a $\kappa_{\max}$-wise (computational) no-signaling cheating prover *if for any* PPT *Turing machine $\mathcal{D}$, there exists a negligible function* negl *such that for every $\lambda \in \mathbb{N}$, every $Q, Q' \subset D_{C_\lambda}$ such that $Q' \subset Q$ and $|Q| \leq \kappa_{\max}(\lambda)$, and every $z \in \{0,1\}^{\mathsf{poly}(\lambda)}$,*

$$\left|\begin{array}{l}\Pr\left[\mathcal{D}(C_\lambda, \boldsymbol{x}, \boldsymbol{y}, \pi^*|_{Q'}, z) = 1 \;\middle|\; (\boldsymbol{x}, \boldsymbol{y}, \pi^*) \leftarrow P^*(1^\lambda, C_\lambda, Q)\right] \\ \quad - \Pr\left[\mathcal{D}(C_\lambda, \boldsymbol{x}, \boldsymbol{y}, \pi^*, z) = 1 \;\middle|\; (\boldsymbol{x}, \boldsymbol{y}, \pi^*) \leftarrow P^*(1^\lambda, C_\lambda, Q')\right]\end{array}\right| \leq \mathsf{negl}(\lambda).$$

◇

Now, we define no-signaling PCPs as the PCP systems that satisfy soundness according to the following definition.

Definition 4 (Soundness against no-signaling cheating provers). *Let (P, V) be any PCP system and $\kappa_{\max}$ be any polynomial. Then, (P, V) is said to be* sound against $\kappa_{\max}$-wise (computational) no-signaling cheating provers *if for any circuit family $\{C_\lambda\}_{\lambda\in\mathbb{N}}$ and $\kappa_{\max}$-wise no-signaling cheating prover P^*, there exists a negligible function* negl *such that for every $\lambda \in \mathbb{N}$,*

$$\Pr\left[V_1(st_V, \boldsymbol{x}, \boldsymbol{y}, \pi^*) = 1 \wedge C_\lambda(\boldsymbol{x}) \neq \boldsymbol{y} \;\middle|\; \begin{array}{l}(Q, st_V) \leftarrow V_0(1^\lambda, C_\lambda) \\ (\boldsymbol{x}, \boldsymbol{y}, \pi^*) \leftarrow P^*(1^\lambda, C_\lambda, Q)\end{array}\right] \leq \mathsf{negl}(\lambda).$$

◇

3 Technical Overview

In this section, we give an overview of our no-signaling linear PCP system. Recall that our focus is on PCP systems for the correctness of arithmetic computation, which are PCP systems that take as input a tuple $(C, \boldsymbol{x}, \boldsymbol{y})$ and prove that $C(\boldsymbol{x}) = \boldsymbol{y}$ holds. We focus on arithmetic circuits over prime-order fields. Given a circuit C, we use $\mathbb{F}$ to denote the underlying finite field, N to denote the number of the wires,[8] n to denote the number of the input gates, and m to denote the number of the output gates. We assume that the first n wires are the wires that takes the values of the input gates and the last m ones are those that takes the value of the output gates. In this overview we focus on circuits with output length 1 (i.e., $m = 1$).

3.1 Preliminary: Linear PCP of Arora et al. [4]

The construction and analysis of our PCP system is based on the linear PCP system of Arora et al. [4] (ALMSS linear PCP in short), so let us start by recalling it. We describe only the construction of ALMSS linear PCP below; good explanations of the analysis of ALMSS linear PCP can be found in, e.g., the textbook by Arora and Barak [3, Chap. 11.5].

Main Tool: Walsh–Hadamard Code. The main tool of ALMSS linear PCP system is Walsh–Hadamard code. Recall that Walsh–Hadamard code maps a string $\boldsymbol{v} \in \mathbb{F}^\ell$ to the linear function $\mathsf{WH}_{\boldsymbol{v}} : \boldsymbol{x} \mapsto \langle \boldsymbol{v}, \boldsymbol{x}\rangle$. A useful property of Walsh–Hadamard code is that errors on codewords can be easily "self-corrected." In particular, if a function f is $(1-\delta)$-*close* to a linear function $\hat{f}$ (i.e., if there exists a linear function $\hat{f}$ such that $\Pr[f(\boldsymbol{r}) = \hat{f}(\boldsymbol{r}) \mid \boldsymbol{r} \leftarrow \mathbb{F}^\ell] \geq 1-\delta$), we can evaluate $\hat{f}$ on any point $\boldsymbol{x} \in \mathbb{F}^\ell$ with error probability 2δ though the following simple probabilistic procedure.

Algorithm $\mathsf{Self\text{-}Correct}^f(\boldsymbol{x})$:
Choose random $\boldsymbol{r} \in \mathbb{F}^\ell$ and output $f(\boldsymbol{x} + \boldsymbol{r}) - f(\boldsymbol{r})$.

[8] We assume that for any gate with fan-out more than one, all the output wires from that gate share the same index $i \in [N]$.

Construction of ALMSS Linear PCP. On input $(C, \boldsymbol{x})$, the prover P computes the PCP proof as follows. First, P computes $y := C(\boldsymbol{x})$ and then obtains the following system of quadratic equations over $\mathbb{F}$, which is designed so that it is satisfiable if and only if $C(\boldsymbol{x}) = y$. Intuitively, the system has variables that represent the wire values of C, and the equations in the system guarantee that (1) the correct input values $\boldsymbol{x} = (x_1, \ldots, x_n)$ are assigned on the input gates, (2) each gate is correctly computed, and (3) the claimed output value y is assigned on the output gate. Formally, the system of equations is defined as follows.

- The variables are $\boldsymbol{z} = (z_1, \ldots, z_N)$.
- For each $i \in \{1, \ldots, n\}$, the system has the equation $z_i = x_i$.
- For each $i, j, k \in [N]$, the system has $z_i + z_j - z_k = 0$ if C has an addition gate with input wire i, j and output wire k, and has $z_i \cdot z_j - z_k = 0$ if C has a multiplication gate with input wire i, j and output wire k.
- The system has the equation $z_N = y$.

Let us denote this system of quadratic equations by $\Psi = \{\Psi_i(\boldsymbol{z}) = c_i\}_{i \in [M]}$, where M is the number of the equations. Then, P obtains the satisfying assignment $\boldsymbol{w} = (w_1, \ldots, w_N)$ of Ψ through the wire values of C on $\boldsymbol{x}$, and outputs the two linear functions $\pi_f(\boldsymbol{v}) := \langle \boldsymbol{v}, \boldsymbol{w} \rangle$ and $\pi_g(\boldsymbol{v}') := \langle \boldsymbol{v}', \boldsymbol{w} \otimes \boldsymbol{w} \rangle$ as the PCP proof.[9] (In short, the PCP proof is Walsh–Hadamard encodings of $\boldsymbol{w}$ and $\boldsymbol{w} \otimes \boldsymbol{w}$).

Next, on input $(C, \boldsymbol{x}, y)$, the verifier V verifies the PCP proof as follows. First, V obtains the system of equations $\Psi = \{\Psi_i(\boldsymbol{z}) = c_i\}_{i \in [M]}$. Then, V applies the following three tests on the PCP proof λ times in parallel.

1. **(Linearity Test).** Choose random points $\boldsymbol{r}_1, \boldsymbol{r}_2 \in \mathbb{F}^N$ and $\boldsymbol{r}'_1, \boldsymbol{r}'_2 \in \mathbb{F}^{N^2}$ and check $\pi_f(\boldsymbol{r}_1) + \pi_f(\boldsymbol{r}_2) \stackrel{?}{=} \pi_f(\boldsymbol{r}_1 + \boldsymbol{r}_2)$ and $\pi_g(\boldsymbol{r}'_1) + \pi_g(\boldsymbol{r}'_2) \stackrel{?}{=} \pi_g(\boldsymbol{r}'_1 + \boldsymbol{r}'_2)$.
2. **(Tensor-Product Test).** Choose two random points $\boldsymbol{r}_1, \boldsymbol{r}_2 \in \mathbb{F}^N$, run $a_{\boldsymbol{r}_1} \leftarrow \mathsf{Self\text{-}Correct}^{\pi_f}(\boldsymbol{r}_1)$, $a_{\boldsymbol{r}_2} \leftarrow \mathsf{Self\text{-}Correct}^{\pi_f}(\boldsymbol{r}_2)$, $a_{\boldsymbol{r}_1 \otimes \boldsymbol{r}_2} \leftarrow \mathsf{Self\text{-}Correct}^{\pi_g}(\boldsymbol{r}_1 \otimes \boldsymbol{r}_2)$, and check $a_{\boldsymbol{r}_1} a_{\boldsymbol{r}_2} \stackrel{?}{=} a_{\boldsymbol{r}_1 \otimes \boldsymbol{r}_2}$.
3. **(SAT Test).** Choose a random point $\boldsymbol{\sigma} = (\sigma_1, \ldots, \sigma_M) \in \mathbb{F}^M$, compute a quadratic function $\Psi_{\boldsymbol{\sigma}}(\boldsymbol{z}) := \sum_{i=1}^{M} \sigma_i \Psi_i(\boldsymbol{z})$, run $a_{\boldsymbol{\psi}_\sigma} \leftarrow \mathsf{Self\text{-}Correct}^{\pi_f}(\boldsymbol{\psi}_\sigma)$, $a_{\boldsymbol{\psi}'_\sigma} \leftarrow \mathsf{Self\text{-}Correct}^{\pi_g}(\boldsymbol{\psi}'_\sigma)$ for the coefficient vectors $\boldsymbol{\psi}_\sigma, \boldsymbol{\psi}'_\sigma$ such that $\langle \boldsymbol{\psi}_\sigma, \boldsymbol{z} \rangle + \langle \boldsymbol{\psi}'_\sigma, \boldsymbol{z} \otimes \boldsymbol{z} \rangle = \Psi_{\boldsymbol{\sigma}}(\boldsymbol{z})$, and check $a_{\boldsymbol{\psi}_\sigma} + a_{\boldsymbol{\psi}'_\sigma} \stackrel{?}{=} c_{\boldsymbol{\sigma}}$, where $c_{\boldsymbol{\sigma}} := \sum_{i=1}^{M} \sigma_i c_i$.

COMMENT: *Roughly speaking, Linearity Test guarantees that π_f, π_g are close to some linear functions $\hat{f}, \hat{g}$, Tensor-Product Test guarantees that $\hat{f}, \hat{g}$ are Welsh–Hadamard encodings of $\tilde{\boldsymbol{w}}, \tilde{\boldsymbol{w}} \otimes \tilde{\boldsymbol{w}}$ for some $\tilde{\boldsymbol{w}} \in \mathbb{F}^N$, and SAT Test guarantees that $\tilde{\boldsymbol{w}}$ is the satisfying assignment of Ψ, which implies that Ψ is satisfiable and thus the statement is true. (In Tensor-Product Test and SAT Test,* Self-Correct *is used so that, if π_f, π_g are indeed*

[9] Formally, P outputs a single linear function (with which the verifier can evaluate both π_f and π_g) as the PCP proof, but in this overview we simply think that the prover outputs two linear function as the PCP proof.

close to some linear functions $\hat{f}, \hat{g}$, the verifier can evaluate $\hat{f}, \hat{g}$ through π_f, π_g with high probability). We refer the readers to [3, Chap. 11.5] *for details of the analysis of ALMSS linear PCP.*

V accepts the proof if it passes these three tests in all the λ parallel trials. It can be verified by inspection that, as required in Definition 1, the verifier can be decomposed into V_0 and V_1, where V_0 samples queries to the tests and V_1 verifies the answers from the PCP proof. (Note that V_0 can sample all queries before knowing $\boldsymbol{x}$ and y since the coefficient vectors $\boldsymbol{\psi}_\sigma, \boldsymbol{\psi}'_\sigma$ in SAT Test can be computed from C).

3.2 Construction of Our No-signaling Linear PCP

The construction of our PCP system, (P, V), is essentially identical with that of ALMSS linear PCP. There is a slight difference in the verifier algorithm (in our PCP system, Self-Correct samples many candidates of the self-corrected values and takes the majority), but we ignore this difference in this overview. It can be verified by inspection that the running time of P is $\mathsf{poly}(|C|)$, the running time of V_0 is $\mathsf{poly}(\lambda + |C|)$, and the running time of V_1 is $\mathsf{poly}(\lambda + |\boldsymbol{x}| + |\boldsymbol{y}|)$.

3.3 Analysis of Our PCP

Our goal is to show that our PCP system (P, V) is sound against $\kappa_{\max}$-wise no-signaling cheating provers for sufficiently large polynomial $\kappa_{\max}$. That is, our goal is to show that for every circuit family $\{C_\lambda\}_{\lambda \in \mathbb{N}}$ and every $\kappa_{\max}$-wise no-signaling cheating prover P^*, we have

$$\Pr\left[\begin{array}{l} V_1(\mathsf{st}_V, \boldsymbol{x}, y, \pi^*) = 1 \\ \wedge\ C_\lambda(\boldsymbol{x}) \neq y \end{array} \middle| \begin{array}{l} (Q, \mathsf{st}_V) \leftarrow V_0(1^\lambda, C_\lambda) \\ (\boldsymbol{x}, y, \pi^*) \leftarrow P^*(1^\lambda, C_\lambda, Q) \end{array}\right] \leq \mathsf{negl}(\lambda) \tag{1}$$

for every $\lambda \in \mathbb{N}$.

Toward this goal, for any sufficiently large $\kappa_{\max}$ and any $\kappa_{\max}$-wise no-signaling cheating prover P^*, we assume that we have

$$\Pr\left[V_1(\mathsf{st}_V, \boldsymbol{x}, y, \pi^*) = 1 \middle| \begin{array}{l} (Q, \mathsf{st}_V) \leftarrow V_0(1^\lambda, C_\lambda) \\ (\boldsymbol{x}, y, \pi^*) \leftarrow P^*(1^\lambda, C_\lambda, Q) \end{array}\right] \geq \frac{1}{\mathsf{poly}(\lambda)} \tag{2}$$

for infinitely many $\lambda \in \mathbb{N}$ (let Λ be the set of those λ's) and show that we have

$$\Pr\left[C_\lambda(\boldsymbol{x}) \neq y \middle| \begin{array}{l} (Q, \mathsf{st}_V) \leftarrow V_0(1^\lambda, C_\lambda) \\ (\boldsymbol{x}, y, \pi^*) \leftarrow P^*(1^\lambda, C_\lambda, Q) \end{array}\right] \leq \mathsf{negl}(\lambda) \tag{3}$$

for every sufficiently large $\lambda \in \Lambda$. Clearly, showing Eq. (3) while assuming Eq. (2) is sufficient for showing Eq. (1) (this is because it implies that for every polynomial poly, either we have $V_1(\mathsf{st}_V, \boldsymbol{x}, y, \pi^*) = 1$ with probability at most $1/\mathsf{poly}(\lambda)$ or we have $C_\lambda(\boldsymbol{x}) \neq y$ with probability at most $1/\mathsf{poly}(\lambda)$ for each sufficiently large $\lambda \in \mathbb{N}$).

To explain the overall structure of our analysis, we first show Eq. (3) while assuming the following (very strong) simplifying assumptions instead of Eq. (2).

Simplifying Assumption 1. P^* convinces the verifier V with overwhelming probability. That is, we have

$$\Pr\left[V_1(\mathsf{st}_V, \boldsymbol{x}, y, \pi^*) = 1 \,\middle|\, \begin{array}{l}(Q, \mathsf{st}_V) \leftarrow V_0(1^\lambda, C_\lambda) \\ (\boldsymbol{x}, y, \pi^*) \leftarrow P^*(1^\lambda, C_\lambda, Q)\end{array}\right] \geq 1 - \mathsf{negl}(\lambda) \quad (4)$$

for infinitely many $\lambda \in \mathbb{N}$. (In what follows, we override the definition of Λ and let it be the set of these λ's). ◇

Simplifying Assumption 2. P^* creates a proof that passes each of Linearity Test, Tensor-Product Test, and SAT Test *on any points* with overwhelming probability. That is, for every sufficiently large $\lambda \in \Lambda$, we have the following. (We assume without loss of generality that P^* always outputs a PCP proof $\pi^* = (\pi_f^*, \pi_g^*)$ that consists of two functions π_f^* and π_g^*).

– **(Linearity of π_f^*).** For every $\boldsymbol{u}, \boldsymbol{v} \in \mathbb{F}^N$,

$$\Pr\left[\begin{array}{l}\pi_f^*(\boldsymbol{u}) + \pi_f^*(\boldsymbol{v}) \\ = \pi_f^*(\boldsymbol{u} + \boldsymbol{v})\end{array} \,\middle|\, (\boldsymbol{x}, y, \pi^*) \leftarrow P^*(1^\lambda, C_\lambda, \{\boldsymbol{u}, \boldsymbol{v}, \boldsymbol{u} + \boldsymbol{v}\})\right] \geq 1 - \mathsf{negl}(\lambda), \quad (5)$$

– **(Linearity of π_g^*).** For every $\boldsymbol{u}, \boldsymbol{v} \in \mathbb{F}^{N^2}$,

$$\Pr\left[\begin{array}{l}\pi_g^*(\boldsymbol{u}) + \pi_g^*(\boldsymbol{v}) \\ = \pi_g^*(\boldsymbol{u} + \boldsymbol{v})\end{array} \,\middle|\, (\boldsymbol{x}, y, \pi^*) \leftarrow P^*(1^\lambda, C_\lambda, \{\boldsymbol{u}, \boldsymbol{v}, \boldsymbol{u} + \boldsymbol{v}\})\right] \geq 1 - \mathsf{negl}(\lambda), \quad (6)$$

– **(Tensor-Product Consistency of π_f^*, π_g^*).** For every $\boldsymbol{u}, \boldsymbol{v} \in \mathbb{F}^N$,

$$\Pr\left[\begin{array}{l}\pi_f^*(\boldsymbol{u})\pi_f^*(\boldsymbol{v}) \\ = \pi_g^*(\boldsymbol{u} \otimes \boldsymbol{v})\end{array} \,\middle|\, (\boldsymbol{x}, y, \pi^*) \leftarrow P^*(1^\lambda, C_\lambda, \{\boldsymbol{u}, \boldsymbol{v}, \boldsymbol{u} \otimes \boldsymbol{v}\})\right] \geq 1 - \mathsf{negl}(\lambda), \quad (7)$$

– **(SAT Consistency of π_f^*, π_g^*).** For every $\boldsymbol{\sigma} \in \mathbb{F}^M$,

$$\Pr\left[\begin{array}{l}\pi_f^*(\boldsymbol{\psi}_\sigma) + \pi_g^*(\boldsymbol{\psi}'_\sigma) \\ = c_\sigma\end{array} \,\middle|\, (\boldsymbol{x}, y, \pi^*) \leftarrow P^*(1^\lambda, C_\lambda, \{\boldsymbol{\psi}_\sigma, \boldsymbol{\psi}'_\sigma\})\right] \geq 1 - \mathsf{negl}(\lambda). \quad (8)$$

◇

At the end of this subsection, we explain how we remove these simplifying assumptions in the actual analysis.

Under the above two simplifying assumptions, we obtain Eq. (3) as follows. Notice that if the statement is true and the PCP proof is correctly generated, then the first part of PCP proof, $\pi_f(\boldsymbol{v}) = \langle \boldsymbol{v}, \boldsymbol{w} \rangle$, is the linear function whose coefficient vector is the satisfying assignment $\boldsymbol{w}$ of the system of equations $\Psi = \{\Psi_i(\boldsymbol{z}) = c_i\}_{i \in [M]}$, so we can recover the satisfying assignment on any variable z_i by appropriately evaluating π_f. (Concretely, given π_f, we can obtain the satisfying assignment on z_i by evaluating π_f on $\boldsymbol{e}_i = (0, \ldots, 0, 1, 0, \ldots, 0) \in \mathbb{F}^N$, where only the i-th element of $\boldsymbol{e}_i$ is 1). Now, we first observe that we can obtain Eq. (3) by showing that the "cheating assignment" that we recover from the cheating prover P^* is "correct" in the following two ways.

1. The assignment on z_N (which represents the value of the output gate) is equal to the claimed output value. That is, for every sufficiently large $\lambda \in \Lambda$,

$$\Pr\left[\pi_f^*(\boldsymbol{e}_N) = y \mid (\boldsymbol{x}, y, \pi^*) \leftarrow P^*(1^\lambda, C_\lambda, \{\boldsymbol{e}_N\})\right] \geq 1 - \mathsf{negl}(\lambda). \quad (9)$$

2. The assignment on z_N is equal to the actual output value. That is, for every sufficiently large $\lambda \in \Lambda$,

$$\Pr\left[\pi_f^*(\boldsymbol{e}_N) = C_\lambda(\boldsymbol{x}) \mid (\boldsymbol{x}, y, \pi^*) \leftarrow P^*(1^\lambda, C_\lambda, \{\boldsymbol{e}_N\})\right] \geq 1 - \mathsf{negl}(\lambda). \ (10)$$

Indeed, given Eqs. (9) and (10), we can easily obtain Eq. (3) as follows: first, we obtain

$$\Pr\left[C_\lambda(\boldsymbol{x}) = y \mid (\boldsymbol{x}, y, \pi^*) \leftarrow P^*(1^\lambda, C_\lambda, \{\boldsymbol{e}_N\})\right] \geq 1 - \mathsf{negl}(\lambda)$$

by applying the union bound on Eqs. (9) and (10); then, we obtain Eq. (3) by using the no-signaling property of P^* to argue that the probability of $C_\lambda(\boldsymbol{x}) = y$ holding decreases only negligibly when the queries to P^* are changed from $\{\boldsymbol{e}_N\}$ to $\{\boldsymbol{e}_N\} \cup Q$ and from $\{\boldsymbol{e}_N\} \cup Q$ to Q.[10] (Notice that the distinguisher in the no-signaling game can check $C_\lambda(\boldsymbol{x}) \stackrel{?}{=} y$ efficiently). Therefore, to conclude the analysis (under the simplifying assumptions), it remains to prove Eqs. (9) and (10).

Step 1. Showing Consistency with the Claimed Computation. First, we explain how we obtain Eq. (9) under the simplifying assumptions on P^*.

To obtain Eq. (9), we prove a stronger claim on the cheating assignment. Recall that from the construction of $\Psi = \{\Psi_i(\boldsymbol{z}) = c_i\}_{i\in[M]}$, each equation of Ψ is defined with at most three variables, and in particular each equation $\Psi_i(\boldsymbol{z}) = c_i$ can be written as $\sum_{j\in\{\alpha,\beta,\gamma\}} d_j z_j + \sum_{j,k\in\{\alpha,\beta,\gamma\}} d_{j,k} z_j z_k = c_i$ for some $\alpha, \beta, \gamma \in [N]$ $(\alpha < \beta < \gamma)$, $d_j \in \{-1, 0, 1\}$ $(j \in \{\alpha, \beta, \gamma\})$, and $d_{j,k} \in \{-1, 0, 1\}$ $(j, k \in \{\alpha, \beta, \gamma\})$. Then, we consider the following claim.

1′. **(Consistency with Claimed Computation)** For any equation $\Psi_i(\boldsymbol{z}) = c_i$ of Ψ, which can be written as

$$\sum_{j\in\{\alpha,\beta,\gamma\}} d_j z_j + \sum_{j,k\in\{\alpha,\beta,\gamma\}} d_{j,k} z_j z_k = c_i,$$

the cheating assignment on $z_\alpha, z_\beta, z_\gamma$ is a satisfying assignment of this equation. That is, for every sufficiently large $\lambda \in \Lambda$ and every $i \in [M]$, we have

$$\Pr\left[\mathsf{Consist}_i(C_\lambda, \boldsymbol{x}, y, \pi^*) \mid (\boldsymbol{x}, y, \pi^*) \leftarrow P^*(1^\lambda, C_\lambda, \{\boldsymbol{e}_\alpha, \boldsymbol{e}_\beta, \boldsymbol{e}_\gamma\})\right]$$
$$\geq 1 - \mathsf{negl}(\lambda), \quad (11)$$

where $\mathsf{Consist}_i(C_\lambda, \boldsymbol{x}, y, \pi^*)$ is the event that we have

$$\sum_{j\in\{\alpha,\beta,\gamma\}} d_j \pi_f^*(\boldsymbol{e}_j) + \sum_{j,k\in\{\alpha,\beta,\gamma\}} d_{j,k} \pi_f^*(\boldsymbol{e}_j) \pi_f^*(\boldsymbol{e}_k) = c_i.$$

[10] We assume $\kappa_{\max}(\lambda) \geq \kappa_V(\lambda) + 1$, where κ_V is the query complexity of V.

Clearly, this claim implies Eq. (9) since Ψ has the equation $z_N = y$.

Hence, we focus on showing the stronger claim that Eq. (11) holds. Fix any sufficiently large $\lambda \in \Lambda$ and any $i \in [M]$. First, since the cheating PCP proof passes SAT Test on any points (Eq. (8) of Simplifying Assumption 2), we have

$$\Pr\left[\pi_f^*(\boldsymbol{\psi}_{\boldsymbol{e}_i}) + \pi_g^*(\boldsymbol{\psi}'_{\boldsymbol{e}_i}) = c_{\boldsymbol{e}_i} \;\middle|\; (\boldsymbol{x}, y, \pi^*) \leftarrow P^*(1^\lambda, C_\lambda, \{\boldsymbol{\psi}_{\boldsymbol{e}_i}, \boldsymbol{\psi}'_{\boldsymbol{e}_i}\})\right]$$
$$\geq 1 - \mathsf{negl}(\lambda), \tag{12}$$

where $\boldsymbol{e}_i = (0, \ldots, 0, 1, 0, \ldots, 0) \in \mathbb{F}^M$. Second, since we have $\boldsymbol{\psi}_{\boldsymbol{e}_i} = \sum_{j \in \{\alpha,\beta,\gamma\}} d_j \boldsymbol{e}_j$, $\boldsymbol{\psi}'_{\boldsymbol{e}_i} = \sum_{j,k \in \{\alpha,\beta,\gamma\}} d_{j,k} \boldsymbol{e}_j \otimes \boldsymbol{e}_k$, and $c_{\boldsymbol{e}_i} = c_i$ from the definitions, Eq. (12) implies Eq. (11) if we have the following three items with overwhelming probability.[11]

- $\pi_f^*(\sum_{j \in \{\alpha,\beta,\gamma\}} d_j \boldsymbol{e}_j) = \sum_{j \in \{\alpha,\beta,\gamma\}} d_j \pi_f^*(\boldsymbol{e}_j)$.
- $\pi_g^*(\sum_{j,k \in \{\alpha,\beta,\gamma\}} d_{j,k} \boldsymbol{e}_j \otimes \boldsymbol{e}_k) = \sum_{j,k \in \{\alpha,\beta,\gamma\}} d_{j,k} \pi_g^*(\boldsymbol{e}_j \otimes \boldsymbol{e}_k)$.
- $\pi_g^*(\boldsymbol{e}_j \otimes \boldsymbol{e}_k) = \pi_f^*(\boldsymbol{e}_j) \pi_f^*(\boldsymbol{e}_k)$ for every $j, k \in \{\alpha, \beta, \gamma\}$.

Now, we obtain Eq. (11) since these three items indeed hold with overwhelming probability due to Simplifying Assumption 2. (We use generalized versions of Eqs. (5) and (6) for the first two, and use Eq. (7) for the third one).

Step 2. Showing Consistency with the Actual Computation. Next, we explain how we obtain Eq. (10) under the simplifying assumptions on P^*.

Without loss of generality, we assume that arithmetic circuits are "layered," i.e., the gates in a circuit can be partitioned into layers such that (1) the first layer consists of the input gates and the last layer consists of the output gate, and (2) the gates in the i-th layer have children in the $(i-1)$-th layer.

The overall strategy is to prove Eq. (10) by induction on the layers. For any circuit C_λ, let us use the following notations.

- $\ell_{\max}$ is the number of the layers, and N_i is the number of the wires in layer i (i.e., the number of the wires from the gates in layer i). We assume that the numbering of the wires are consistent with the numbering of the layers, i.e., the first N_1 wires are those that are in the first layer, the next N_2 wires are those that are in the second layer, etc.
- $D_1, \ldots, D_{\ell_{\max}}$ are subset of $\mathbb{F}^N$ such that for every $\ell \in [\ell_{\max}]$,

$$D_\ell := \{\boldsymbol{v} = (v_1, \ldots, v_N) \mid v_i = 0 \text{ for } \forall i \notin \{N_{\leq \ell-1} + 1, \ldots, N_{\leq \ell-1} + N_\ell\}\},$$

  where $N_{\leq \ell-1} := \sum_{i \in [\ell-1]} N_i$. Notice that when the first part of the correct PCP proof, $\pi_f(\boldsymbol{v}) = \langle \boldsymbol{v}, \boldsymbol{w} \rangle$, is evaluated on $v_\ell \in D_\ell$, it returns a linear combination of the correct wire values of layer ℓ.

[11] Formally, to use the union bound, we need to argue that every probability that we consider in this proof does not change non-negligibly when we obtain π^* by querying $\{\boldsymbol{e}_\alpha, \boldsymbol{e}_\beta, \boldsymbol{e}_\gamma\} \cup \{\boldsymbol{e}_j \otimes \boldsymbol{e}_k\}_{j,k \in \{\alpha,\beta,\gamma\}} \cup \{\boldsymbol{\psi}_{\boldsymbol{e}_i}, \boldsymbol{\psi}'_{\boldsymbol{e}_i}\}$ to P^*. Fortunately, every probability indeed does not change non-negligibly because of the no-signaling property of P^*.

Now, to prove Eq. (10), we show that the following three claims holds for every sufficiently large $\lambda \in \Lambda$.

1. The cheating PCP proof is equal to the correct PCP proof on random λ points in D_1. That is,

$$\Pr_{U_1,\pi^*}\left[\bigwedge_{\boldsymbol{u}\in U_1} \pi_f^*(\boldsymbol{u}) = \pi_f(\boldsymbol{u})\right] \geq 1 - \mathsf{negl}(\lambda), \tag{13}$$

   where the probability is taken over $\boldsymbol{u}_{1,i} \leftarrow D_1$ ($i \in [\lambda]$), $U_1 := \{\boldsymbol{u}_{1,i}\}_{i\in[\lambda]}$, and $(\boldsymbol{x}, y, \pi^*) \leftarrow P^*(1^\lambda, C_\lambda, U_1)$, and π_f is the correct PCP proof that is generated by $\pi := P(C_\lambda, \boldsymbol{x})$.
2. For every $\ell \in [\ell_{\max}]$, if the cheating PCP proof is equal to the correct PCP proof on random λ points in D_ℓ, they are also equal on *any* point in D_ℓ. That is, for any $\boldsymbol{v} \in D_\ell$,

$$\Pr_{U_\ell,\pi^*}\left[\pi_f^*(\boldsymbol{v}) = \pi_f(\boldsymbol{v}) \;\middle|\; \bigwedge_{\boldsymbol{u}\in U_\ell} \pi_f^*(\boldsymbol{u}) = \pi_f(\boldsymbol{u})\right] \geq 1 - \mathsf{negl}(\lambda), \tag{14}$$

   where the probability is taken over $\boldsymbol{u}_{\ell,i} \leftarrow D_\ell$ ($i \in [\lambda]$), $U_\ell := \{\boldsymbol{u}_{\ell,i}\}_{i\in[\lambda]}$, and $(\boldsymbol{x}, y, \pi^*) \leftarrow P^*(1^\lambda, C_\lambda, \{\boldsymbol{v}\} \cup U_\ell)$.
3. For every $\ell \in [\ell_{\max} - 1]$, if the cheating PCP proof is equal to the correct PCP proof on random λ points in D_ℓ, they are also equal on random λ points in $D_{\ell+1}$. That is,

$$\Pr_{U_\ell,U_{\ell+1},\pi^*}\left[\bigwedge_{\boldsymbol{u}\in U_{\ell+1}} \pi_f^*(\boldsymbol{u}) = \pi_f(\boldsymbol{u}) \;\middle|\; \bigwedge_{\boldsymbol{u}\in U_\ell} \pi_f^*(\boldsymbol{u}) = \pi_f(\boldsymbol{u})\right] \geq 1 - \mathsf{negl}(\lambda), \tag{15}$$

   where the probability is taken over $\boldsymbol{u}_{\ell,i} \leftarrow D_\ell$ ($i \in [\lambda]$), $\boldsymbol{u}_{\ell+1,i} \leftarrow D_{\ell+1}$ ($i \in [\lambda]$), $U_\ell := \{\boldsymbol{u}_{\ell,i}\}_{i\in[\lambda]}$, $U_{\ell+1} := \{\boldsymbol{u}_{\ell+1,i}\}_{i\in[\lambda]}$, and $(\boldsymbol{x}, y, \pi^*) \leftarrow P^*(1^\lambda, C_\lambda, U_\ell \cup U_{\ell+1})$.

Observe that we can indeed obtain Eq. (10) from the above three claims since Eq. (14) implies that we can obtain Eq. (10) by just showing

$$\Pr_{U_{\ell_{\max}},\pi^*}\left[\bigwedge_{\boldsymbol{u}\in U_{\ell_{\max}}} \pi_f^*(\boldsymbol{u}) = \pi_f(\boldsymbol{u})\right] \geq 1 - \mathsf{negl}(\lambda)$$

(this is because we have $\pi_f(\boldsymbol{e}_N) = w_N = C_\lambda(\boldsymbol{x})$ from the construction of our PCP), and we can obtain this inequation by repeatedly using Eq. (15) on top of Eq. (13).[12] Thus, what remain to prove are Eqs. (13), (14), (15).

[12] Formally, we need to argue that the probabilities in these inequations do not change non-negligibly when we change the queries to P^*, which we can show by relying on the no-signaling property of P^*. A key point is that the number of the queries to P^* can be bounded by a fixed polynomial in λ.

1. To obtain Eq. (13), we first use the linearity of the cheating PCP proof (Eq. (5) of Simplifying Assumption 2) to argue that, since any $v \in D_1$ can be written as a linear combination of $\boldsymbol{e}_1, \ldots, \boldsymbol{e}_n \in \mathbb{F}^N$ (recall that we have $N_1 = n$), we can obtain Eq. (13) by just showing that for every $i \in [n]$ we have $\pi_f^*(\boldsymbol{e}_i) = \pi_f(\boldsymbol{e}_i)$ with overwhelming probability. Then, we observe that, since we have $\pi_f(\boldsymbol{e}_i) = w_i = x_i$ for every $i \in [n]$ from the construction of our PCP, it suffices to show that for every $i \in [n]$ we have $\pi_f^*(\boldsymbol{e}_i) = x_i$ with overwhelming probability, which we already showed as the consistency with the claimed computation (Eq. (11) in Step 1).
2. To obtain Eq. (14), we consider a mental experiment where $U_\ell = \{\boldsymbol{u}_{\ell,i}\}_{i\in[\lambda]}$ is sampled as follows: for each $i \in [\lambda]$, choose random $\boldsymbol{r}_i \in D_\ell$ and $b_i \in \{0, 1\}$ and then define $\boldsymbol{u}_{\ell,i}$ by $\boldsymbol{u}_{\ell,i} := \boldsymbol{r}_i$ if $b_i = 0$ and by $\boldsymbol{u}_{\ell,i} := \boldsymbol{v} + \boldsymbol{r}_i$ if $b_i = 1$. Since each $\boldsymbol{u}_{\ell,i}$ is still uniformly distributed, it suffices to show Eq. (14) w.r.t. this mental experiment; in addition, due to the no-signaling property of P^*, we can further change the experiment so that π^* is obtained by $(\boldsymbol{x}, y, \pi^*) \leftarrow P^*(1^\lambda, C_\lambda, \{v\} \cup \{\boldsymbol{r}_i, \boldsymbol{v} + \boldsymbol{r}_{\ell,i}\}_{i\in[\lambda]})$. Now, we obtain Eq. (14) by observing the following.
   (a) Equation (14) is implied by
$$\Pr_{U_\ell,\pi^*}\left[\pi_f^*(\boldsymbol{v}) \neq \pi_f(\boldsymbol{v}) \wedge \left(\bigwedge_{\boldsymbol{u}\in U_\ell} \pi_f^*(\boldsymbol{u}) = \pi_f(\boldsymbol{u})\right)\right] \leq \mathsf{negl}(\lambda). \quad (16)$$
   (We assume that $\wedge_{\boldsymbol{u}\in U_\ell}\pi_f^*(\boldsymbol{u}) = \pi_f(\boldsymbol{u})$ holds with high probability, which is indeed the case in our situation).
   (b) We can obtain Eq. (16) by combining the following two observations. First, we have $\pi_f^*(\boldsymbol{v}) \neq \pi_f(\boldsymbol{v})$ only when we have $\pi_f^*(\boldsymbol{v}+\boldsymbol{r}_i) \neq \pi_f(\boldsymbol{v}+\boldsymbol{r}_i)$ or $\pi_f^*(\boldsymbol{r}_i) \neq \pi_f(\boldsymbol{r}_i)$ for every $i \in [\lambda]$ (this is because we have $\pi_f^*(\boldsymbol{v}) = \pi_f^*(\boldsymbol{v} + \boldsymbol{r}_i) - \pi_f^*(\boldsymbol{r}_i)$ for every $i \in [\lambda]$ from the linearity of the cheating PCP proof[13] (Eq. (5) of Simplifying Assumption 2)). Second, when we have $\pi_f^*(\boldsymbol{v} + \boldsymbol{r}_i) \neq \pi_f(\boldsymbol{v} + \boldsymbol{r}_i)$ or $\pi_f^*(\boldsymbol{r}_i) \neq \pi_f(\boldsymbol{r}_i)$ for every $i \in [\lambda]$, we have $\wedge_{\boldsymbol{u}\in U_\ell}\pi_f^*(\boldsymbol{u}) = \pi_f(\boldsymbol{u})$ with probability at most $2^{-\lambda}$ since each $\boldsymbol{u}_{\ell,i}$ is defined by taking either $\boldsymbol{r}_i$ or $\boldsymbol{v} + \boldsymbol{r}_i$ randomly.
3. To obtain Eq. (15), we first use the linearity of the cheating PCP proof (Eq. (5) of Simplifying Assumption 2) and the union bound to argue, just like when we show Eq. (13), that we can obtain Eq. (15) by just showing that for every $k \in \{N_{\leq\ell} + 1, \ldots, N_{\leq\ell} + N_{\ell+1}\}$ we have $\pi_f^*(\boldsymbol{e}_k) = \pi_f(\boldsymbol{e}_k)$ with overwhelming probability (where the probability is conditioned on $\bigwedge_{\boldsymbol{u}\in U_\ell}\pi_f^*(\boldsymbol{u}) = \pi_f(\boldsymbol{u})$). Let us focus, for simplicity, on the case that k is the output wire of a multiplication gate in the $(\ell + 1)$-th layer, where the input wires are i and j in the ℓ-th layer. Then, we observe that we have $\pi_f^*(\boldsymbol{e}_k) = \pi_f(\boldsymbol{e}_k)$ if we have
$$\pi_f^*(\boldsymbol{e}_k) = \pi_f^*(\boldsymbol{e}_i)\pi_f^*(\boldsymbol{e}_j) \qquad \text{and} \qquad \pi_f^*(\boldsymbol{e}_i) = \pi_f(\boldsymbol{e}_i) \wedge \pi_f^*(\boldsymbol{e}_j) = \pi_f(\boldsymbol{e}_j)$$

[13] Indeed, if we have $\pi_f^*(\boldsymbol{v} + \boldsymbol{r}_i) = \pi_f(\boldsymbol{v} + \boldsymbol{r}_i)$ and $\pi_f^*(\boldsymbol{r}_i) = \pi_f(\boldsymbol{r}_i)$ for any $i \in [\lambda]$, we have $\pi_f^*(\boldsymbol{v}) = \pi_f^*(\boldsymbol{v} + \boldsymbol{r}_i) - \pi_f^*(\boldsymbol{r}_i) = \pi_f(\boldsymbol{v} + \boldsymbol{r}_i) - \pi_f(\boldsymbol{r}_i) = \pi_f(\boldsymbol{v})$.

(this is because these two items imply that $\pi_f^*(e_k) = \pi_f^*(e_i)\pi_f^*(e_j) = \pi_f(e_i)\pi_f(e_j) = \pi_f(e_k)$, where the last equality holds since $\pi_f(e_i), \pi_f(e_j), \pi_f(e_k)$ are the satisfying assignment on z_i, z_j, z_k of Ψ, which has the equation $z_i z_j - z_k = 0$). Finally, we observe that the first item holds with overwhelming probability since the cheating proof is consistent with the claimed computation (Eq. (11) in Step 1) and that the second item holds with overwhelming probability due to Eq. (14) and the union bound (both probabilities are conditioned on $\bigwedge_{u \in U_\ell} \pi_f^*(u) = \pi_f(u)$).

How to Remove the Simplifying Assumptions. In the actual analysis, we remove Simplifying Assumption 1 in the same way as previous works (such as [20, 40]), namely by considering a "relaxed verifier" that accepts a PCP proof even when the proof fails to pass a small number of the tests. (Concretely, we consider a verifier that accepts a proof as long as the proof passes the three tests in at least $\lambda - \mu$ trials, where $\mu = \Theta(\log^2 \lambda)$). We use the same argument as the previous works to show that if a cheating prover fools the original verifier with non-negligible probability, there exists another cheating prover that fools the relaxed verifier with overwhelming probability.

As for Simplifying Assumption 2, we remove it by considering the self-corrected version of the cheating proof, i.e., the proof that is obtained by applying Self-Correct on the cheating proof π^*. Our key observation is that an existing analysis of Linearity Test can be naturally extended so that it works even in the no-signaling PCP setting as long as we change the goal to showing that the self-corrected cheating proof passes Linearity Test on any points. (In the standard PCP setting, the goal of Linearity Test is to guarantee that the cheating proof is close to a linear function). Once we show that the self-corrected cheating proof passes Linearity Test on any points, it is relatively easy to show that it also passes Tensor-Product Test and SAT Test on any points.

3.4 Comparison with Previous Analysis

The high level structure of our analysis (under the abovementioned simplifying assumptions) is the same as the analysis of previous non-linear no-signaling PCPs, namely those of Kalai et al. [40] and the subsequent works. Specifically, like these works, we show $C_\lambda(\boldsymbol{x}) = y$ by showing that we have $\pi^*(e_N) = y$ and $\pi^*(e_N) = C_\lambda(\boldsymbol{x})$ simultaneously, and show $\pi^*(e_N) = C_\lambda(\boldsymbol{x})$ by induction on layers of C_λ. (In the latter part, we in particular follow the presentation by Paneth and Rothblum [47]).

A notable difference between our analysis and the previous one (other than the differences due to the use of linear PCPs rather than polynomially long PCP) is that our analysis does not require that the statement is represented as an "augmented layered circuit," and only requires that it is represented as a layered circuit. More concretely, while the previous analysis requires that each layer of the circuit is augmented with an additional circuit that computes a low-degree extension of the wire values of the layer and then applies low-degree tests on the low-degree extension, our analysis does not require such augmentation and only requires that the circuit is layered. At a high level, we do not require this augmentation since in the induction for showing $\pi^*(\boldsymbol{e}_N) = C_\lambda(\boldsymbol{x})$ (Step 2 in the previous subsection), we show that the cheating PCP proof is equal to the correct proof rather than just showing that the wire values that are recovered from the cheating PCP proof are equal to the correct ones. (That is, we do not require the augmentation of the circuit since we consider a stronger claim in the induction, which allows us to use a stronger assumption in the inductive step).

4 Construction of Our No-signaling Linear PCP for $\mathcal{P}$

In this section, we describe our no-signaling linear PCP system (P, V) for the correctness of arithmetic-circuit computation. Let $C : \mathbb{F}^n \to \mathbb{F}^m$ be an arithmetic circuit over a finite field $\mathbb{F}$ of prime order, and $\boldsymbol{x} = (x_1, \dots, x_n) \in \mathbb{F}^n$ be an input to C. Recall that we use N to denote the number of wires in C and assume that the first n wires are the those that takes the values of the input gates and the last m ones are those that takes the value of the output gates.

4.1 PCP Prover P

Given $(C, \boldsymbol{x})$ as input, the PCP prover P first computes $\boldsymbol{y} := C(\boldsymbol{x})$ and then obtains the following system of quadratic equations over $\mathbb{F}$, which is designed so that it is satisfiable if and only if $C(\boldsymbol{x}) = \boldsymbol{y}$. Intuitively, the system has variables that represent the wire values of C, and the equations in the system guarantee that (1) the correct input values $\boldsymbol{x} = (x_1, \dots, x_n)$ are assigned on the input gates, (2) each gate is correctly computed, and (3) the claimed output values $\boldsymbol{y} = (y_1, \dots, y_m)$ are assigned on the output gates. Formally, the system of equations is defined as follows.

- The variables are $\boldsymbol{z} = (z_1, \dots, z_N)$.
- For each $i \in \{1, \dots, n\}$, the system has the equation $z_i = x_i$.
- For each $i, j, k \in [N]$, the system has $z_i + z_j - z_k = 0$ if the circuit C has an addition gate with input wire i, j and output wire k, and has $z_i z_j - z_k = 0$ if C has a multiplication gate with input wire i, j and output wire k.
- For each $i \in \{1, \dots, m\}$, the system has the equation $z_{N-m+i} = y_i$.

Let M denote the number of the equations in the system Ψ. Let the system be denoted by

$$\Psi = \begin{cases} \Psi_1(\boldsymbol{z}) = c_1 \\ \quad\vdots \\ \Psi_M(\boldsymbol{z}) = c_M \end{cases},$$

where each c_i is an element in $\mathbb{F}$. For each $i \in [M]$, let $\boldsymbol{\psi}_i \in \mathbb{F}^N$ and ${\boldsymbol{\psi}'}_i \in \mathbb{F}^{N^2}$ be the coefficient vectors such that

$$\Psi_i(\boldsymbol{z}) = \langle \boldsymbol{\psi}_i, \boldsymbol{z} \rangle + \langle {\boldsymbol{\psi}'}_i, \boldsymbol{z} \otimes \boldsymbol{z} \rangle. \tag{17}$$

Let $\boldsymbol{w} = (w_1, \ldots, w_N)$ be the satisfying assignment of Ψ. Let $f : \mathbb{F}^N \to \mathbb{F}$ and $g : \mathbb{F}^{N^2} \to \mathbb{F}$ be the linear functions that are defined by $f(\boldsymbol{v}) := \langle \boldsymbol{v}, \boldsymbol{w} \rangle$ and $g(\boldsymbol{v}') := \langle \boldsymbol{v}', \boldsymbol{w} \otimes \boldsymbol{w} \rangle$. Then, the PCP prover P outputs the following linear function $\pi : \mathbb{F}^{N+N^2} \to \mathbb{F}$ as the PCP proof.

$$\pi(\boldsymbol{v}) := f(\boldsymbol{v_1}) + g(\boldsymbol{v_2}) \text{ for } \forall \boldsymbol{v} = (\boldsymbol{v_1}, \boldsymbol{v_2}) \in \mathbb{F}^{N+N^2}, \text{ where } \boldsymbol{v_1} \in \mathbb{F}^N, \boldsymbol{v_2} \in \mathbb{F}^{N^2}.$$

Remark 3. For simplicity, in what follows we usually think that P outputs two linear functions $\pi_f := f$ and $\pi_g := g$ as the PCP proof. This is without loss of generality since the verifier can evaluate f and g given access to π. ◊

4.2 PCP Verifier V

Given $(C, \boldsymbol{x}, \boldsymbol{y})$ as input, the PCP verifier V first computes the system Ψ in the same way as the PCP prover P. Next, given oracle access to the PCP proof π_f and π_g, the PCP verifier does the following tests λ times in parallel, and accepts the proof if all the tests in all the λ trials are accepted.

- **Linearity Test.** Choose random points $\boldsymbol{r}_1, \boldsymbol{r}_2 \in \mathbb{F}^N$ and $\boldsymbol{r}'_1, \boldsymbol{r}'_2 \in \mathbb{F}^{N^2}$, and check the following.

$$\pi_f(\boldsymbol{r}_1) + \pi_f(\boldsymbol{r}_2) \stackrel{?}{=} \pi_f(\boldsymbol{r}_1 + \boldsymbol{r}_2) \quad \text{and} \quad \pi_g(\boldsymbol{r}'_1) + \pi_g(\boldsymbol{r}'_2) \stackrel{?}{=} \pi_g(\boldsymbol{r}'_1 + \boldsymbol{r}'_2).$$

- **Tensor-Product Test.** Let $\mathsf{Self\text{-}Correct}^\pi$ be the following algorithm.

  Algorithm $\mathsf{Self\text{-}Correct}^\pi(\boldsymbol{v} \in \mathbb{F}^N \cup \mathbb{F}^{N^2})$.

  1. Choose λ random points $\boldsymbol{r}_{\boldsymbol{v},1}, \ldots, \boldsymbol{r}_{\boldsymbol{v},\lambda}$ from $\mathbb{F}^N$ if $\boldsymbol{v} \in \mathbb{F}^N$ and choose them from $\mathbb{F}^{N^2}$ if $\boldsymbol{v} \in \mathbb{F}^{N^2}$.
  2. For each $i \in [\lambda]$, let

  $$a_{\boldsymbol{v}}^{(i)} := \begin{cases} \pi_f(\boldsymbol{v} + \boldsymbol{r}_{\boldsymbol{v},i}) - \pi_f(\boldsymbol{r}_{\boldsymbol{v},i}) & \text{if } \boldsymbol{v} \in \mathbb{F}^N \\ \pi_g(\boldsymbol{v} + \boldsymbol{r}_{\boldsymbol{v},i}) - \pi_g(\boldsymbol{r}_{\boldsymbol{v},i}) & \text{if } \boldsymbol{v} \in \mathbb{F}^{N^2} \end{cases}.$$

  3. Let

  $$a_{\boldsymbol{v}} := \text{majority}\left(a_{\boldsymbol{v}}^{(1)}, \ldots, a_{\boldsymbol{v}}^{(\lambda)}\right).$$

  4. Output $a_{\boldsymbol{v}}$.

  Then, in Tensor-Product Test, choose two random points $\boldsymbol{r}_1, \boldsymbol{r}_2 \in \mathbb{F}^N$, run

  $$a_{\boldsymbol{r}_1} \leftarrow \mathsf{Self\text{-}Correct}^\pi(\boldsymbol{r}_1),$$
  $$a_{\boldsymbol{r}_2} \leftarrow \mathsf{Self\text{-}Correct}^\pi(\boldsymbol{r}_2),$$
  $$a_{\boldsymbol{r}_1 \otimes \boldsymbol{r}_2} \leftarrow \mathsf{Self\text{-}Correct}^\pi(\boldsymbol{r}_1 \otimes \boldsymbol{r}_2),$$

  and check the following.

  $$a_{\boldsymbol{r}_1} a_{\boldsymbol{r}_2} \stackrel{?}{=} a_{\boldsymbol{r}_1 \otimes \boldsymbol{r}_2}.$$

– **SAT Test.** Choose a random point $\boldsymbol{\sigma} = (\sigma_1, \ldots, \sigma_M) \in \mathbb{F}^M$ and define a quadratic function $\Psi_{\boldsymbol{\sigma}} : \mathbb{F}^N \to \mathbb{F}$ as

$$\Psi_{\boldsymbol{\sigma}}(\boldsymbol{z}) := \sum_{i=1}^{M} \sigma_i \Psi_i(\boldsymbol{z}).$$

Let $\boldsymbol{\psi}_{\boldsymbol{\sigma}} \in \mathbb{F}^N$ and $\boldsymbol{\psi}'_{\boldsymbol{\sigma}} \in \mathbb{F}^{N^2}$ be the coefficient vectors such that

$$\Psi_{\boldsymbol{\sigma}}(\boldsymbol{z}) = \langle \boldsymbol{\psi}_{\boldsymbol{\sigma}}, \boldsymbol{z} \rangle + \langle \boldsymbol{\psi}'_{\boldsymbol{\sigma}}, \boldsymbol{z} \otimes \boldsymbol{z} \rangle. \tag{18}$$

Let $c_{\boldsymbol{\sigma}} := \sum_{i=1}^{M} \sigma_i c_i$.
Then, in SAT Test, run

$$a_{\psi_{\sigma}} \leftarrow \mathsf{Self\text{-}Correct}^{\pi}(\boldsymbol{\psi}_{\boldsymbol{\sigma}}),$$
$$a_{\psi'_{\sigma}} \leftarrow \mathsf{Self\text{-}Correct}^{\pi}(\boldsymbol{\psi}'_{\boldsymbol{\sigma}})$$

and check the following.

$$a_{\psi_{\sigma}} + a_{\psi'_{\sigma}} \stackrel{?}{=} c_{\boldsymbol{\sigma}}.$$

We remark that, formally, $V = (V_0, V_1)$ is a pair of two algorithms as required by Definition 1, where $V_0(1^\lambda, C)$ outputs a set of queries Q for the above tests along with its internal state st_V, and $V_1(\mathsf{st}_V, \boldsymbol{x}, \boldsymbol{y}, \pi|_Q)$ performs the above tests given the answers $\pi|_Q$ from the PCP proof. The internal state st_V that V_0 outputs is $(\boldsymbol{\sigma}_{\text{in}}, \boldsymbol{\sigma}_{\text{out}})$, where

$$\boldsymbol{\sigma}_{\text{in}} := (\sigma_1, \ldots, \sigma_n) \in \mathbb{F}^n \quad \text{and} \quad \boldsymbol{\sigma}_{\text{out}} := (\sigma_{M-m+1}, \ldots, \sigma_M) \in \mathbb{F}^m,$$

where it is assumed that the first n equations in Ψ (i.e., the equations $\{\Psi_i(\boldsymbol{z}) = c_i\}_{i\in[n]}$) are those that are associated with the input gates (i.e., $\{z_i = x_i\}_{i\in[n]}$) and the last m equations in Ψ (i.e. the equations $\{\Psi_{M-m+i}(\boldsymbol{z}) = c_{M-m+i}\}_{i\in[m]}$) are those that are associated with the output gates (i.e., $\{z_{M-m+i} = y_i\}_{i\in[n]}$). Note that $V_0(1^\lambda, C)$ can indeed choose all the queries in parallel (without knowing the input $\boldsymbol{x}$ and the output $\boldsymbol{y}$) since each of the queries is chosen independently of the results of other queries and in addition the coefficient vectors of the equations of Ψ (i.e., $\{\boldsymbol{\psi}_i, {\boldsymbol{\psi}'}_i\}_{i\in M}$) can be computed from the circuit C in SAT Test. Also, note that $V_1(\mathsf{st}_V, \boldsymbol{x}, \boldsymbol{y}, \pi|_Q)$ can indeed perform the test (without knowing the circuit C) since $c_{\boldsymbol{\sigma}} = \langle \boldsymbol{\sigma}_{\text{in}}, \boldsymbol{x} \rangle + \langle \boldsymbol{\sigma}_{\text{out}}, \boldsymbol{y} \rangle$ can be computed from st_V in SAT Test.

Remark 4 (Query Complexity). By inspection, one can see that that the query complexity of V is $\kappa_V(\lambda) \stackrel{\text{def}}{=} \lambda(10\lambda + 6)$. ◇

Remark 5 (Efficiency). By inspection, one can see that the running time of P is $\mathsf{poly}(|C|)$, the running time of V_0 is $\mathsf{poly}(\lambda + |C|)$, and the running time of V_1 is $\mathsf{poly}(\lambda + |\boldsymbol{x}| + |\boldsymbol{y}|)$. ◇

4.3 Security

In the full version of this paper [42], we prove the following theorem, which states the no-signaling soundness of our PCP system.

Theorem 1 (No-signaling Soundness of (P, V)). *Let (P, V) be the PCP system in Sects. 4.1 and 4.2, $\{C_\lambda\}_{\lambda\in\mathbb{N}}$ be any circuit family, and $\kappa_{\max}$ be any polynomial such that $\kappa_{\max}(\lambda) \geq 2\lambda \cdot \max(8\lambda + 3, m_\lambda) + \kappa_V(\lambda)$, where m_λ is the output length of C_λ and κ_V is the query complexity of (P, V). Then, for any $\kappa_{\max}$-wise (computational) no-signaling cheating prover P^*, there exists a negligible function* negl *such that for every $\lambda \in \mathbb{N}$,*

$$\Pr\left[V_1(st_V, \boldsymbol{x}, \boldsymbol{y}, \pi^*) = 1 \wedge C_\lambda(\boldsymbol{x}) \neq \boldsymbol{y} \;\middle|\; \begin{array}{l}(Q, st_V) \leftarrow V(1^\lambda, C_\lambda)\\ (\boldsymbol{x}, \boldsymbol{y}, \pi^*) \leftarrow P^*(1^\lambda, C_\lambda, Q)\end{array}\right] \leq \mathsf{negl}(\lambda).$$

5 Application: Delegating Computation in Preprocessing Model

In this section, we give an application of our no-signaling linear PCP system to a 2-message delegation scheme for $\mathcal{P}$ in the preprecessing model. As mentioned in Introduction, we obtain our delegation scheme by applying the transformation of Kalai et al. [39,40] on our no-signaling linear PCP system.

We remark that our delegation scheme is actually non-interactive in the sense that, after the verifier's message is computed and published in the (expensive) offline phase, anyone can prove a statement to the verifier in the online phase by sending a single message, and the same offline verifier message can be used for proving multiple statements in the online phase. Formally, this property is guaranteed due to the adaptive soundness of our delegation scheme, which guarantees that the soundness holds even when the statement to be proven is chosen after the verifier's message.

5.1 Technical Overview

In this subsection, we give an overview of our delegation scheme. Those who are familiar with the transformation of Kalai et al. [39,40] can skip this subsection.

Recall that in the setting of delegating computation, a computationally weak client asks a powerful server to perform a heavy computation, and the server returns the computation result to the client with a proof that the result is correct. Our focus is delegation schemes for arithmetic-circuit computation, so the statement to be proven by the server is of the form $(C, \boldsymbol{x}, \boldsymbol{y})$, which states that an arithmetic circuit C outputs $\boldsymbol{y}$ on input $\boldsymbol{x}$. For simplicity, in this overview, we consider a static soundness setting where the statement is fixed before the verifier's message is generated.

In our delegation scheme, we use the following two building blocks.

- Our no-signaling linear PCP system for deterministic arithmetic-circuit computation (Sect. 4).

- An additive homomorphic encryption scheme HE, which is an encryption scheme such that the message space is a finite group and that anyone can efficiently compute a ciphertext of $m_0 + m_1$ from ciphertexts of any two messages m_0, m_1.

We assume that the message space of HE is a finite field $\mathbb{F}$ of prime order, and consider delegation scheme for arithmetic circuits over this finite field $\mathbb{F}$.

The high-level structure of our delegation scheme is quite simple. When the statement is $(C, \boldsymbol{x}, \boldsymbol{y})$, our scheme roughly proceeds as follows.

1. In the offline phase, the client firsts samples PCP queries Q of our PCP system, where $Q = \{\boldsymbol{q}_i\}_{i \in [\kappa_V]}$ and $\boldsymbol{q}_i = (q_{i,1}, \ldots, q_{i,N'}) \in \mathbb{F}^{N'}$, where $N' := N + N^2$. Next, the client encrypts those queries by HE, where each query $\boldsymbol{q}_i$ is encrypted under a fresh key. (That is, for each $i \in [\kappa_V]$, the client samples a key pair $(\mathsf{pk}_i, \mathsf{sk}_i)$ of HE and encrypts each $q_{i,j} \in \mathbb{F}$ $(j \in [N'])$ under the public-key pk_i). Finally, the verifier sends the resultant ciphertexts $\{(\mathsf{ct}_{i,1}, \ldots, \mathsf{ct}_{i,N'})\}_{i \in [\kappa_V]}$ to the server.
2. Given the ciphertexts of the PCP queries $\{(\mathsf{ct}_{i,1}, \ldots, \mathsf{ct}_{i,N'})\}_{i \in [\kappa_V]}$, the server obtain ciphertexts of the PCP answers by homomorphically evaluate the PCP oracle $\pi : \mathbb{F}^{N'} \to \mathbb{F}$ under the ciphertexts (since π is a linear function, additive homomorphism of HE suffices for evaluating π[14]), and then returns the resultant ciphertexts $\{\tilde{\mathsf{ct}}_i\}_{i \in [\kappa_V]}$ to the client.
3. Given the ciphertexts of the PCP answers $\{\tilde{\mathsf{ct}}_i\}_{i \in [\kappa_V]}$, the client obtains the PCP answers by decrypting $\{\tilde{\mathsf{ct}}_i\}_{i \in [\kappa_V]}$ and then verifies the PCP answers by using the PCP decision algorithm.

The offline phase of our delegation scheme is expensive since the verifier query algorithm of our PCP system runs in time $\mathsf{poly}(\lambda + |C|)$, while the online phase is efficient since the verifier decision algorithm of our PCP system runs in time $\mathsf{poly}(\lambda + |\boldsymbol{x}| + |\boldsymbol{y}|)$. Very roughly speaking, the soundness of our scheme holds since, somewhat surprisingly, the semantic security of HE directly guarantees that the server can answer to the PCP queries under the ciphertexts of HE only in a no-signaling way. (Formally, in order to guarantee that the server is $\kappa_{\max}$-wise no-signaling for sufficiently large $\kappa_{\max}$, we need to change the above delegation scheme and add "dummy" queries to the PCP queries).

Using Multiplicative Homomorphic Encryption Rather Than Additive One. We can replace the additive homomorphic encryption scheme in the above scheme with a multiplicative one over prime-order bilinear group as follows: we replace the scheme so that, instead of encrypting the PCP queries $\{(q_{i,1}, \ldots, q_{i,N})\}_{i \in [\kappa_V]}$ directly, the client encrypts $\{g^{q_{i,1}}, \ldots, g^{q_{i,N}}\}$, where g is a generator of the bilinear group, and the server homomorphically evaluates the PCP oracle in the exponent of g using the multiplicative homomorphic property of HE. Since the PCP verification algorithm only involves quadratic tests on the

[14] Since $\mathbb{F}$ is of prime order, it is possible to compute $\mathsf{Enc}(\mathsf{pk}, v \cdot m)$ from $\mathsf{Enc}(\mathsf{pk}, m)$ for any $v, m \in \mathbb{F}$.

PCP answers, the client can verify the PCP answers even when the PCP answers are encoded in the exponent of g. (Unfortunately, the security analysis cannot be straightforwardly modified to work for this modified scheme).

5.2 Preliminaries

In this subsection, we first give the definition of delegation scheme and next give the definition of homomorphic encryption schemes.

Preprocessing Non-interactive Delegation Scheme. For concreteness, we focus our attention on 2-message delegation schemes with adaptive soundness, or in other words, non-interactive delegation schemes in the preprocessing model where the preprocess consists of a single message from the verifier. We remark that the following definition is essentially identical with the definition of preprocessing SNARGs (e.g., [16]) as well as the definition of adaptively sound 2-message delegation schemes of [7,20]. The difference is that the following definition is tailored for deterministic arithmetic circuit computation.

A *preprocessing non-interactive delegation scheme* consists of three polynomial-time algorithms (Gen, Prove, Verify) with the following syntax.

- Gen is a probabilistic algorithm such that on input the security parameter 1^λ and an arithmetic circuit C, it outputs a public-key pk and a secret key sk.
- Prove is a deterministic algorithm such that on input the public-key pk, the circuit C, and an input $\boldsymbol{x}$ of C, it outputs a proof pr.
- Verify is a deterministic algorithm such that on input the secret key sk, the input $\boldsymbol{x}$, the output $\boldsymbol{y}$, and the proof pr, it outputs a bit $b \in \{0,1\}$.

The execution of preprocessing non-interactive delegation schemes is separated into two phases, the *offline phase* and the *online phase*.

- **Offline phase:** First, the verifier obtains an arithmetic circuit C that it wants to let the prover compute. Next, the verifier obtains (pk, sk) by running Gen on C and sends pk to the prover. After executing Gen, the prover can erase the circuit C.
- **Online phase:** The prover, on input $\boldsymbol{x}$ (which is obtained either from the verifier or from any other process), computes the output $\boldsymbol{y} = C(\boldsymbol{x})$ and the proof $\mathsf{pr} = \mathsf{Prove}(\mathsf{pk}, C, \boldsymbol{x})$ and then sends $(\boldsymbol{x}, \boldsymbol{y}, \mathsf{pr})$ to the verifier. Given $(\boldsymbol{x}, \boldsymbol{y}, \mathsf{pr})$, the verifier verifies the proof by running $\mathsf{Verify}(\mathsf{sk}, \boldsymbol{x}, \boldsymbol{y}, \mathsf{pr})$. The online phase can be repeated multiple times on the same public key and secret key (see Remark 6 below).

Note that delegation scheme is meaningful only when the running time of Verify is much smaller than the time that is needed for computing $C(\boldsymbol{x})$.

The security requirements of preprocessing non-interactive delegation schemes are the following.

Correctness. For every security parameter $\lambda \in \mathbb{N}$, arithmetic circuit C, input $\boldsymbol{x}$ of C, and the output $\boldsymbol{y} := C(\boldsymbol{x})$,

$$\Pr\left[\mathsf{Verify}(\mathsf{sk}, \boldsymbol{x}, \boldsymbol{y}, \mathsf{pr}) = 1 \;\middle|\; \begin{array}{l} (\mathsf{pk}, \mathsf{sk}) \leftarrow \mathsf{Gen}(1^\lambda, C) \\ \mathsf{pr} := \mathsf{Prove}(\mathsf{pk}, C, \boldsymbol{x}) \end{array}\right] = 1.$$

Soundness. For every circuit family $\{C_\lambda\}_{\lambda \in \mathbb{N}}$ and PPT adversary $\mathcal{A}$, there exists a negligible function negl such that for every $\lambda \in \mathbb{N}$,

$$\Pr\left[\mathsf{Verify}(\mathsf{sk}, \boldsymbol{x}, \boldsymbol{y}, \mathsf{pr}) = 1 \wedge C_\lambda(\boldsymbol{x}) \neq \boldsymbol{y} \;\middle|\; \begin{array}{l} (\mathsf{pk}, \mathsf{sk}) \leftarrow \mathsf{Gen}(1^\lambda, C_\lambda) \\ (\boldsymbol{x}, \boldsymbol{y}, \mathsf{pr}) \leftarrow \mathcal{A}(1^\lambda, C_\lambda, \mathsf{pk}) \end{array}\right] \leq \mathsf{negl}(\lambda).$$

Remark 6. It is easy to see that if a delegation scheme is sound w.r.t. the above definition, it remains sound even when the same $(\mathsf{pk}, \mathsf{sk})$ is used for generating multiple proofs as long as the results of the verification are kept secret against the cheating provers (or, equivalently, as long as a new public-key–secret-key pair is generated when the verification of a proof is rejected).[15] ◇

Homomorphic Encryption. A *public-key encryption scheme* consists of three polynomial-time algorithms $(\mathsf{Gen}, \mathsf{Enc}, \mathsf{Dec})$ with the following syntax.

- Gen is a probabilistic algorithm such that on input the security parameter 1^λ, it outputs a public-key pk and a secret key sk.
- Enc is a probabilistic algorithm such that on input the public-key pk and a message $m \in \mathbb{F}$, it outputs a ciphertext ct. (It is assumed that pk contains the information of a finite field $\mathbb{F}$, which works as the message space).
- Dec is a deterministic algorithm such that on input the secret-key sk and the ciphertext ct, it outputs the plaintext m.

For any vector $\boldsymbol{v}$, we denote by $\mathsf{Enc}(\boldsymbol{v})$ the element-wise encryption of $\boldsymbol{v}$.

The following security notion of public-key encryption schemes is used in this paper (it is easy to see that the following security notion is implied by the standard CPA-security through a simple hybrid argument).

Definition 5 ((multi-key multi-message) CPA-security). *For every polynomial p and* PPT *adversary $\mathcal{A} = (\mathcal{A}_0, \mathcal{A}_1, \mathcal{A}_2)$, there exists a negligible function* negl *such that for every security parameter $\lambda \in \mathbb{N}$ and every $z \in \{0,1\}^{\mathsf{poly}(\lambda)}$,*

$$\Pr\left[b = \tilde{b} \;\middle|\; \begin{array}{l} (\ell, \mathsf{st}_0) \leftarrow \mathcal{A}_0(1^\lambda, z), \ \ \textit{where } \ell \leq p(\lambda) \\ (\mathsf{pk}_i, \mathsf{sk}_i) \leftarrow \mathsf{Gen}(1^\lambda) \textit{ for every } i \in [\ell] \\ (\{m_{0,i}\}_{i \in [\ell]}, \{m_{1,i}\}_{i \in [\ell]}, \mathsf{st}_1) \leftarrow \mathcal{A}_1(\mathsf{st}_0, \{\mathsf{pk}_i\}_{i \in [\ell]}) \\ b \leftarrow \{0,1\} \\ \mathsf{ct}_i^* \leftarrow \mathsf{Enc}(\mathsf{pk}_i, m_{b,i}) \textit{ for every } i \in [\ell] \\ \tilde{b} \leftarrow \mathcal{A}_2(\mathsf{st}_1, \{\mathsf{ct}_i^*\}_{i \in [\ell]}) \end{array}\right] \leq \frac{1}{2} + \mathsf{negl}(\lambda).$$

◇

[15] Previous designated-verifier delegation schemes (such as the schemes of [20] and subsequent works) also have this restriction.

A public-key encryption scheme (Gen, Enc, Dec) is *additive homomorphic* if it has an additional PPT algorithm Eval^+ such that, on input $\mathsf{ct}_1 \leftarrow \mathsf{Enc}(m_1), \ldots, \mathsf{ct}_{p(\lambda)} \leftarrow \mathsf{Enc}(m_{p(\lambda)})$ for any $m_1, \ldots, m_{p(\lambda)} \in \mathbb{F}$ (where p is a polynomial), it outputs $\mathsf{Enc}(\sum_{i=1}^{p(\lambda)} m_i)$. Formally, Eval^+ is required to satisfy the following property.

Homomorphic Evaluation. For every polynomial p, every PPT adversary $\mathcal{A}$, and every $\lambda \in \mathbb{N}$,

$$\Pr\left[\tilde{m} = \sum_{i=1}^{p(\lambda)} m_i \;\middle|\; \begin{array}{l} (\mathsf{pk}, \mathsf{sk}) \leftarrow \mathsf{Gen}(1^\lambda) \\ \{m_i\}_{i \in [p(\lambda)]} \leftarrow \mathcal{A}(\mathsf{pk}, \mathsf{sk}), \text{ where } m_1, \ldots, m_{p(\lambda)} \in \mathbb{F} \\ \mathsf{ct}_b \leftarrow \mathsf{Enc}(\mathsf{pk}, m_i) \text{ for every } i \in [p(\lambda)] \\ \mathsf{ct} \leftarrow \mathsf{Eval}^+(\mathsf{pk}, \{\mathsf{ct}_i\}_{i \in [p(\lambda)]}) \\ \tilde{m} := \mathsf{Dec}(\mathsf{sk}, \mathsf{ct}) \end{array}\right] = 1.$$

To simplify the exposition, for any two ciphertext $\mathsf{ct}_0, \mathsf{ct}_1$ under a public-key pk, we use $\mathsf{ct}_0 + \mathsf{ct}_1$ as a shorthand of $\mathsf{Eval}^+(\mathsf{pk}, \mathsf{ct}_0, \mathsf{ct}_1)$. Similarly, for any ciphertext ct and a scalar $k \in \mathbb{N}$, we use $k \cdot \mathsf{ct}$ as a shorthand of $\underbrace{\mathsf{ct} + \cdots + \mathsf{ct}}_{k}$.

A public-key encryption scheme is *multiplicative homomorphic* if it has a PPT algorithm Eval^* that satisfies the above property w.r.t. multiplication over $\mathbb{F}$.

5.3 Our Result

Theorem 2. *Assume the existence of an additive homomorphic encryption scheme over fields of prime order (i.e., over the additive group of the fields) or a multiplicative homomorphic encryption scheme over bilinear groups with prime order. Then, there exists a preprocessing non-interactive delegation scheme for polynomial-time arithmetic-circuit computation with the following efficiency.*

- *The running time of Gen is* $\mathsf{poly}(\lambda + |C|)$.
- *The running time of Prove is* $\mathsf{poly}(\lambda + |C|)$.
- *The running tine of Verify is* $\mathsf{poly}(\lambda + |\boldsymbol{x}| + |\boldsymbol{y}|)$.

Due to space limitations, we only give the description of our delegation scheme based on additive homomorphic encryption below, and refer the readers to the full version of this paper [42] for the proof of Theorem 2.

Let (HE.Gen, HE.Enc, HE.Dec) be the additive homomorphic encryption scheme and (PCP.P, PCP.V) be the PCP prover and verifiers of our PCP system (Sect. 4). Recall that our PCP system satisfies the following properties.

- It can handle arithmetic circuits over any prime-order fields. Furthermore, there exists a polynomial $\kappa_{\max}$ such that the soundness holds against any $\kappa_{\max}$-wise no-signaling adversaries.[16]

[16] Formally, $\kappa_{\max}$ depends on m, which is an upper bound of the output length of the circuits to be considered.

- For an arithmetic circuit C over a finite filed $\mathbb{F}$, $\mathsf{PCP.P}$ outputs a linear function $\pi : \mathbb{F}^{N+N^2} \to \mathbb{F}$ as the PCP proof, where N is the number of wires in C. (To simplify the notations, we let $N' := N + N^2$ in what follows). Since π is linear, there exists $d_1, \ldots, d_{N'} \in \mathbb{F}$ such that $\pi(\boldsymbol{z}) = \sum_{i \in [N']} d_i z_i$.
- For an arithmetic circuit C over a finite filed $\mathbb{F}$, $\mathsf{PCP.V}_0$ outputs a set of queries $Q = \{q_i\}_{i \in [\kappa_V(\lambda)]} \subset \mathbb{F}^{N'}$ and a state $\mathsf{st}_V \in \mathbb{F}^{n+m}$, where κ_V is a polynomial (which is independent of C) and n, m are the input and output length of C.

We assume that for every security parameter λ, the arithmetic circuit C to be delegated is defined over a finite field $\mathbb{F}$ that is also the message space of HE.

Construction. The three algorithms $(\mathsf{Gen}, \mathsf{Prove}, \mathsf{Verify})$ are defined as follows.

- **Algorithm** $\mathsf{Gen}(1^\lambda, C)$
  1. Run $(Q, \mathsf{st}_V) \leftarrow \mathsf{PCP.V}_0(1^\lambda, C)$.
     Then, parse Q as $\{\boldsymbol{q}_i\}_{i \in [\kappa_V(\lambda)]}$, where $\boldsymbol{q}_i = (q_{i,1}, \ldots, q_{i,N'}) \in \mathbb{F}^{N'}$.
  2. Define $\mathsf{ct}_1, \ldots, \mathsf{ct}_{\kappa_{\max}(\lambda)}$ as follows.
     (a) Choose a random injective function $\tau : [\kappa_V(\lambda)] \to [\kappa_{\max}(\lambda)]$.
     (b) Define ct_i for each $i \in [\kappa_{\max}(\lambda)]$ by
     $$\mathsf{ct}_i \leftarrow \begin{cases} \mathsf{HE.Enc}(\mathsf{HE.pk}_i, \boldsymbol{q}_{\tau^{-1}(i)}) & (\text{if } \exists i' \in [\kappa_V(\lambda)] \text{ s.t. } \tau(i') = i) \\ \mathsf{HE.Enc}(\mathsf{HE.pk}_i, \boldsymbol{0}) & (\text{otherwise}) \end{cases},$$
     where $(\mathsf{HE.pk}_i, \mathsf{HE.sk}_i) \leftarrow \mathsf{HE.Gen}(1^\lambda)$ and $\boldsymbol{0} := (0, \ldots, 0) \in \mathbb{F}^{N'}$.
  3. Output $\mathsf{pk} := (\mathsf{ct}_1, \ldots, \mathsf{ct}_{\kappa_{\max}(\lambda)})$ and $\mathsf{sk} := (\mathsf{st}_V, \tau, \{\mathsf{HE.sk}_i\}_{i \in [\kappa_{\max}(\lambda)]})$.
- **Algorithm** $\mathsf{Prove}(\mathsf{pk}, C, \boldsymbol{x})$
  1. Run $\pi \leftarrow \mathsf{PCP.P}(C, \boldsymbol{x})$.
     Let $d_1, \ldots, d_{N'} \in \mathbb{F}$ be such that $\pi(\boldsymbol{z}) = \sum_{i \in [N']} d_i z_i$.
  2. Parse pk as $(\mathsf{ct}_1, \ldots, \mathsf{ct}_{\kappa_{\max}(\lambda)})$, where $\mathsf{ct}_i = (\mathsf{ct}_{i,1}, \ldots, \mathsf{ct}_{i,N'})$.
     Then, perform homomorphic operation to obtain
     $$\tilde{\mathsf{ct}}_i := \pi(\mathsf{ct}_i) = \sum_{j \in [N']} d_j \mathsf{ct}_{i,j}$$
     for every $i \in [\kappa_{\max}(\lambda)]$.
  3. Output $\mathsf{pr} := (\tilde{\mathsf{ct}}_1, \ldots, \tilde{\mathsf{ct}}_{\kappa_{\max}(\lambda)})$.
- **Algorithm** $\mathsf{Verify}(\mathsf{sk}, \boldsymbol{x}, \boldsymbol{y}, \mathsf{pr})$
  1. Parse sk as $(\mathsf{st}_V, \tau, \{\mathsf{HE.sk}_i\}_{i \in [\kappa_{\max}(\lambda)]})$, and pr as $(\tilde{\mathsf{ct}}_1, \ldots, \tilde{\mathsf{ct}}_{\kappa_{\max}(\lambda)})$.
     Then, run $a_i := \mathsf{HE.Dec}(\mathsf{HE.sk}_{\tau(i)}, \tilde{\mathsf{ct}}_{\tau(i)})$ for every $i \in [\kappa_V(\lambda)]$.
  2. Output $b := \mathsf{PCP.V}_1(\mathsf{st}_V, \boldsymbol{x}, \boldsymbol{y}, \{a_i\}_{i \in [\kappa_V(\lambda)]})$.

Efficiency. By inspection, it can be verified that our delegation scheme indeed has the following efficiency.

- The running time of Gen is $\mathsf{poly}(\lambda + |C|)$.
- The running time of Prove is $\mathsf{poly}(\lambda + |C|)$.
- The running tine of Verify is $\mathsf{poly}(\lambda + |\boldsymbol{x}| + |\boldsymbol{y}|)$.

References

1. Aiello, W., Bhatt, S., Ostrovsky, R., Rajagopalan, S.R.: Fast verification of any remote procedure call: short witness-indistinguishable one-round proofs for NP. In: Montanari, U., Rolim, J.D.P., Welzl, E. (eds.) ICALP 2000. LNCS, vol. 1853, pp. 463–474. Springer, Heidelberg (2000). https://doi.org/10.1007/3-540-45022-X_39
2. Ananth, P., Chen, Y.-C., Chung, K.-M., Lin, H., Lin, W.-K.: Delegating RAM computations with adaptive soundness and privacy. In: Hirt, M., Smith, A. (eds.) TCC 2016. LNCS, vol. 9986, pp. 3–30. Springer, Heidelberg (2016). https://doi.org/10.1007/978-3-662-53644-5_1
3. Arora, S., Barak, B.: Computational Complexity: A Modern Approach. Cambridge University Press, Cambridge (2009). http://theory.cs.princeton.edu/complexity/book.pdf
4. Arora, S., Lund, C., Motwani, R., Sudan, M., Szegedy, M.: Proof verification and the hardness of approximation problems. J. ACM **45**(3), 501–555 (1998)
5. Arora, S., Safra, S.: Probabilistic checking of proofs: a new characterization of NP. J. ACM **45**(1), 70–122 (1998)
6. Babai, L., Fortnow, L., Levin, L.A., Szegedy, M.: Checking computations in polylogarithmic time. In: 23rd ACM STOC, pp. 21–31. ACM Press, May 1991
7. Badrinarayanan, S., Kalai, Y.T., Khurana, D., Sahai, A., Wichs, D.: Succinct delegation for low-space non-deterministic computation. In: Diakonikolas, I., Kempe, D., Henzinger, M. (eds.) 50th ACM STOC, pp. 709–721. ACM Press, June 2018
8. Barak, B., Goldreich, O.: Universal arguments and their applications. SIAM J. Comput. **38**(5), 1661–1694 (2009)
9. Ben-Sasson, E., Chiesa, A., Genkin, D., Tromer, E., Virza, M.: SNARKs for C: verifying program executions succinctly and in zero knowledge. In: Canetti, R., Garay, J.A. (eds.) CRYPTO 2013. LNCS, vol. 8043, pp. 90–108. Springer, Heidelberg (2013). https://doi.org/10.1007/978-3-642-40084-1_6
10. Ben-Sasson, E., Chiesa, A., Spooner, N.: Interactive oracle proofs. In: Hirt, M., Smith, A. (eds.) TCC 2016. LNCS, vol. 9986, pp. 31–60. Springer, Heidelberg (2016). https://doi.org/10.1007/978-3-662-53644-5_2
11. Ben-Sasson, E., Chiesa, A., Tromer, E., Virza, M.: Succinct non-interactive zero knowledge for a von Neumann architecture. In: Proceedings of the 23rd USENIX Security Symposium, San Diego, CA, USA, 20–22 August 2014, pp. 781–796 (2014)
12. Biehl, I., Meyer, B., Wetzel, S.: Ensuring the integrity of agent-based computations by short proofs. In: Rothermel, K., Hohl, F. (eds.) MA 1998. LNCS, vol. 1477, pp. 183–194. Springer, Heidelberg (1998). https://doi.org/10.1007/BFb0057658
13. Bitansky, N., et al.: The hunting of the SNARK. J. Cryptol. **30**(4), 989–1066 (2017)
14. Bitansky, N., Canetti, R., Chiesa, A., Tromer, E.: Recursive composition and bootstrapping for SNARKS and proof-carrying data. In: Boneh, D., Roughgarden, T., Feigenbaum, J. (eds.) 45th ACM STOC, pp. 111–120. ACM Press, June 2013
15. Bitansky, N., Chiesa, A.: Succinct arguments from multi-prover interactive proofs and their efficiency benefits. In: Safavi-Naini, R., Canetti, R. (eds.) CRYPTO 2012. LNCS, vol. 7417, pp. 255–272. Springer, Heidelberg (2012). https://doi.org/10.1007/978-3-642-32009-5_16
16. Bitansky, N., Chiesa, A., Ishai, Y., Paneth, O., Ostrovsky, R.: Succinct non-interactive arguments via linear interactive proofs. In: Sahai, A. (ed.) TCC 2013. LNCS, vol. 7785, pp. 315–333. Springer, Heidelberg (2013). https://doi.org/10.1007/978-3-642-36594-2_18

17. Bitansky, N., Garg, S., Lin, H., Pass, R., Telang, S.: Succinct randomized encodings and their applications. In: Servedio, R.A., Rubinfeld, R. (eds.) 47th ACM STOC, pp. 439–448. ACM Press, June 2015
18. Boneh, D., Boyen, X., Shacham, H.: Short group signatures. In: Franklin, M. (ed.) CRYPTO 2004. LNCS, vol. 3152, pp. 41–55. Springer, Heidelberg (2004). https://doi.org/10.1007/978-3-540-28628-8_3
19. Boneh, D., Ishai, Y., Sahai, A., Wu, D.J.: Lattice-based SNARGs and their application to more efficient obfuscation. In: Coron, J.-S., Nielsen, J.B. (eds.) EUROCRYPT 2017. LNCS, vol. 10212, pp. 247–277. Springer, Cham (2017). https://doi.org/10.1007/978-3-319-56617-7_9
20. Brakerski, Z., Holmgren, J., Kalai, Y.T.: Non-interactive delegation and batch NP verification from standard computational assumptions. In: Hatami, H., McKenzie, P., King, V. (eds.) 49th ACM STOC, pp. 474–482. ACM Press, June 2017
21. Canetti, R., Chen, Y., Holmgren, J., Raykova, M.: Adaptive succinct garbled RAM or: how to delegate your database. In: Hirt, M., Smith, A. (eds.) TCC 2016. LNCS, vol. 9986, pp. 61–90. Springer, Heidelberg (2016). https://doi.org/10.1007/978-3-662-53644-5_3
22. Canetti, R., Holmgren, J.: Fully succinct garbled RAM. In: Sudan, M. (ed.) ITCS 2016, pp. 169–178. ACM, January 2016
23. Canetti, R., Holmgren, J., Jain, A., Vaikuntanathan, V.: Succinct garbling and indistinguishability obfuscation for RAM programs. In: Servedio, R.A., Rubinfeld, R. (eds.) 47th ACM STOC, pp. 429–437. ACM Press, June 2015
24. Chen, Y.C., Chow, S.S.M., Chung, K.M., Lai, R.W.F., Lin, W.K., Zhou, H.S.: Cryptography for parallel RAM from indistinguishability obfuscation. In: Sudan, M. (ed.) ITCS 2016, pp. 179–190. ACM, January 2016
25. Chiesa, A., Manohar, P., Shinkar, I.: Probabilistic checking against non-signaling strategies from linearity testing. Electronic Colloquium on Computational Complexity (ECCC), TR18-123 (2018). https://eccc.weizmann.ac.il/report/2018/123/
26. Chiesa, A., Manohar, P., Shinkar, I.: Testing linearity against non-signaling strategies. In: 33rd Computational Complexity Conference, CCC 2018, San Diego, California, USA, 22–24 June 2018, pp. 17:1–17:37 (2018)
27. Chung, K.-M., Kalai, Y., Vadhan, S.: Improved delegation of computation using fully homomorphic encryption. In: Rabin, T. (ed.) CRYPTO 2010. LNCS, vol. 6223, pp. 483–501. Springer, Heidelberg (2010). https://doi.org/10.1007/978-3-642-14623-7_26
28. Damgård, I., Faust, S., Hazay, C.: Secure two-party computation with low communication. In: Cramer, R. (ed.) TCC 2012. LNCS, vol. 7194, pp. 54–74. Springer, Heidelberg (2012). https://doi.org/10.1007/978-3-642-28914-9_4
29. Danezis, G., Fournet, C., Groth, J., Kohlweiss, M.: Square span programs with applications to succinct NIZK arguments. In: Sarkar, P., Iwata, T. (eds.) ASIACRYPT 2014. LNCS, vol. 8873, pp. 532–550. Springer, Heidelberg (2014). https://doi.org/10.1007/978-3-662-45611-8_28
30. Gennaro, R., Gentry, C., Parno, B.: Non-interactive verifiable computing: outsourcing computation to untrusted workers. In: Rabin, T. (ed.) CRYPTO 2010. LNCS, vol. 6223, pp. 465–482. Springer, Heidelberg (2010). https://doi.org/10.1007/978-3-642-14623-7_25
31. Gennaro, R., Gentry, C., Parno, B., Raykova, M.: Quadratic span programs and succinct NIZKs without PCPs. In: Johansson, T., Nguyen, P.Q. (eds.) EUROCRYPT 2013. LNCS, vol. 7881, pp. 626–645. Springer, Heidelberg (2013). https://doi.org/10.1007/978-3-642-38348-9_37

32. Goldwasser, S., Kalai, Y.T., Rothblum, G.N.: Delegating computation: interactive proofs for muggles. In: Ladner, R.E., Dwork, C. (eds.) 40th ACM STOC, pp. 113–122. ACM Press, May 2008
33. Goldwasser, S., Micali, S.: Probabilistic encryption. J. Comput. Syst. Sci. **28**(2), 270–299 (1984)
34. Groth, J.: Short pairing-based non-interactive zero-knowledge arguments. In: Abe, M. (ed.) ASIACRYPT 2010. LNCS, vol. 6477, pp. 321–340. Springer, Heidelberg (2010). https://doi.org/10.1007/978-3-642-17373-8_19
35. Groth, J.: On the size of pairing-based non-interactive arguments. In: Fischlin, M., Coron, J.-S. (eds.) EUROCRYPT 2016. LNCS, vol. 9666, pp. 305–326. Springer, Heidelberg (2016). https://doi.org/10.1007/978-3-662-49896-5_11
36. Holmgren, J., Rothblum, R.: Delegating computations with (almost) minimal time and space overhead. Electronic Colloquium on Computational Complexity (ECCC), TR18-161 (2018). https://eccc.weizmann.ac.il/report/2018/161/. To appear at FOCS 2018
37. Ishai, Y., Kushilevitz, E., Ostrovsky, R.: Efficient arguments without short PCPs. In: 22nd Annual IEEE Conference on Computational Complexity, CCC 2007, San Diego, California, USA, 13–16 June 2007, pp. 278–291 (2007)
38. Kalai, Y., Paneth, O.: Delegating RAM computations. In: Hirt, M., Smith, A. (eds.) TCC 2016. LNCS, vol. 9986, pp. 91–118. Springer, Heidelberg (2016). https://doi.org/10.1007/978-3-662-53644-5_4
39. Kalai, Y.T., Raz, R., Rothblum, R.D.: Delegation for bounded space. In: Boneh, D., Roughgarden, T., Feigenbaum, J. (eds.) 45th ACM STOC, pp. 565–574. ACM Press, June 2013
40. Kalai, Y.T., Raz, R., Rothblum, R.D.: How to delegate computations: the power of no-signaling proofs. In: Shmoys, D.B. (ed.) 46th ACM STOC, pp. 485–494. ACM Press, May/Jun 2014
41. Kilian, J.: A note on efficient zero-knowledge proofs and arguments (extended abstract). In: 24th ACM STOC, pp. 723–732. ACM Press, May 1992
42. Kiyoshima, S.: No-signaling linear PCPs. Cryptology ePrint Archive, Report 2018/649 (2018). https://eprint.iacr.org/2018/649
43. Koppula, V., Lewko, A.B., Waters, B.: Indistinguishability obfuscation for Turing machines with unbounded memory. In: Servedio, R.A., Rubinfeld, R. (eds.) 47th ACM STOC, pp. 419–428. ACM Press, June 2015
44. Lipmaa, H.: Progression-free sets and sublinear pairing-based non-interactive zero-knowledge arguments. In: Cramer, R. (ed.) TCC 2012. LNCS, vol. 7194, pp. 169–189. Springer, Heidelberg (2012). https://doi.org/10.1007/978-3-642-28914-9_10
45. Lipmaa, H.: Succinct non-interactive zero knowledge arguments from span programs and linear error-correcting codes. In: Sako, K., Sarkar, P. (eds.) ASIACRYPT 2013. LNCS, vol. 8269, pp. 41–60. Springer, Heidelberg (2013). https://doi.org/10.1007/978-3-642-42033-7_3
46. Micali, S.: Computationally sound proofs. SIAM J. Comput. **30**(4), 1253–1298 (2000)
47. Paneth, O., Rothblum, G.N.: On zero-testable homomorphic encryption and publicly verifiable non-interactive arguments. In: Kalai, Y., Reyzin, L. (eds.) TCC 2017. LNCS, vol. 10678, pp. 283–315. Springer, Cham (2017). https://doi.org/10.1007/978-3-319-70503-3_9
48. Parno, B., Raykova, M., Vaikuntanathan, V.: How to delegate and verify in public: verifiable computation from attribute-based encryption. In: Cramer, R. (ed.) TCC 2012. LNCS, vol. 7194, pp. 422–439. Springer, Heidelberg (2012). https://doi.org/10.1007/978-3-642-28914-9_24

49. Setty, S., Blumberg, A.J., Walfish, M.: Toward practical and unconditional verification of remote computations. In: Workshop on Hot Topics in Operating Systems (HotOS). USENIX - Advanced Computing Systems Association (2011)
50. Setty, S., Braun, B., Vu, V., Blumberg, A.J., Parno, B., Walfish, M.: Resolving the conflict between generality and plausibility in verified computation. In: Proceedings of the ACM European Conference on Computer Systems (EuroSys). ACM, April 2013
51. Setty, S.T.V., McPherson, R., Blumberg, A.J., Walfish, M.: Making argument systems for outsourced computation practical (sometimes). In: NDSS 2012. The Internet Society, February 2012
52. Setty, S.T.V., Vu, V., Panpalia, N., Braun, B., Blumberg, A.J., Walfish, M.: Taking proof-based verified computation a few steps closer to practicality. In: Proceedings of the 21th USENIX Security Symposium, Bellevue, WA, USA, 8–10 August 2012, pp. 253–268 (2012)
53. Vu, V., Setty, S.T.V., Blumberg, A.J., Walfish, M.: A hybrid architecture for interactive verifiable computation. In: 2013 IEEE Symposium on Security and Privacy, pp. 223–237. IEEE Computer Society Press, May 2013

On Basing Search SIVP on NP-Hardness

Tianren Liu(✉)

MIT, Cambridge, USA
liutr@mit.edu

Abstract. The possibility of basing cryptography on the minimal assumption $\mathbf{NP} \not\subseteq \mathbf{BPP}$ is at the very heart of complexity-theoretic cryptography. The closest we have gotten so far is lattice-based cryptography whose average-case security is based on the worst-case hardness of approximate shortest vector problems on integer lattices. The state-of-the-art is the construction of a one-way function (and collision-resistant hash function) based on the hardness of the $\tilde{O}(n)$-approximate shortest independent vector problem $\mathsf{SIVP}_{\tilde{O}(n)}$.

Although SIVP is **NP**-hard in its exact version, Guruswami et al. (CCC 2004) showed that $\mathsf{gapSIVP}_{\sqrt{n/\log n}}$ is in $\mathbf{NP} \cap \mathbf{coAM}$ and thus unlikely to be **NP**-hard. Indeed, any language that can be reduced to $\mathsf{gapSIVP}_{\tilde{O}(\sqrt{n})}$ (under general probabilistic polynomial-time adaptive reductions) is in $\mathbf{AM} \cap \mathbf{coAM}$ by the results of Peikert and Vaikuntanathan (CRYPTO 2008) and Mahmoody and Xiao (CCC 2010). However, none of these results apply to reductions to *search problems*, still leaving open a ray of hope: *can* **NP** *be reduced to solving search SIVP with approximation factor* $\tilde{O}(n)$?

We eliminate such possibility, by showing that any language that can be reduced to solving search SIVP with any approximation factor $\lambda(n) = \omega(n \log n)$ lies in **AM** intersect **coAM**.

1 Introduction

It is a long-standing open question whether cryptography can be based on the minimal assumption that $\mathbf{NP} \not\subseteq \mathbf{BPP}$. More precisely, one would hope to construct cryptographic primitives such that given a polynomial-time algorithm breaking the security of the primitive, one can efficiently solve SAT.

The closest we have gotten so far is lattice cryptography. This approach was born out of the breakthrough result of Ajtai [Ajt96], which constructs a one-way function family based on the *worst-case* hardness of certain lattice problems such as the γ-approximate shortest independent vectors problem (SIVP_γ), which can be stated as follows: given an n-dimensional lattice, find a set of n linearly independent vectors whose length[1] is at most $\gamma(n)$ (polynomial in n) times the length of the shortest such vector set. Since the work of Ajtai, the state of the

Research supported in part by NSF Grants CNS-1350619 and CNS-1414119.

[1] The length of a vector set is defined as the length of the longest vector in the set.

A. Beimel and S. Dziembowski (Eds.): TCC 2018, LNCS 11239, pp. 98–119, 2018.
https://doi.org/10.1007/978-3-030-03807-6_4

art is a construction of a family of collision resistant hash functions (CRHF) based on the hardness of the shortest independent vectors problem with an approximation factor $\tilde{O}(n)$ [MR04]. One would hope that this approach is viable for constructing cryptography based on **NP**-hardness since Blömer and Seifert showed that SIVP_γ is **NP**-hard for any constant factor [BS99]. Presumably, if one could construct cryptographic primitives based on the hardness of $\mathsf{SIVP}_{O(1)}$, we would be golden. Alternatively, if one could extend the result of Blömer and Seifert to show the **NP**-hardness of SIVP_γ for larger $\gamma(n)$, we would be closer to the goal of basing cryptography on **NP**-hardness.

However, there are some negative results when one considers the corresponding gap version of the same lattice problem. The gap problem, denoted by $\mathsf{gapSIVP}_\gamma$, is to estimate the length of the short independent vector set within a factor of $\gamma(n)$. Peikert and Vaikuntanathan show that $\mathsf{gapSIVP}_{\omega(\sqrt{n \log n})}$ is in **SZK** [PV08]. Thus there is no Cook reduction from SAT to $\mathsf{gapSIVP}_{\tilde{O}(\sqrt{n})}$ unless the polynomial hierarchy collapses (as $\mathbf{BPP}^{\mathbf{SZK}} \subseteq \mathbf{AM} \cap \mathbf{coAM}$ [MX10]).

Fortunately, the hardness of SIVP is not contradicted by the fact that the gap problem with the same approximation factor is easy. For instance, if one considers any ideal lattice in the field $\mathbb{Z}[x]/\langle x^{2^k}+1\rangle$, its successive minima satisfy $\lambda_1 = \ldots = \lambda_n$, thus $\mathsf{gapSIVP}_{\sqrt{n}}$ can be trivially solved using Minkowski's inequality. However, finding a set of short independent vectors in such ideal lattices is still believed to be hard. As none of these negative results apply to reductions to search SIVP, there is still a ray of hope: *can* **NP** *be reduced to solving search* SIVP *with approximation* $\tilde{O}(n)$?

Thus, in order to really understand the viability of the approach begun by the work of Ajtai, it seems one must study the search versions of lattice problems. In this work, we relate the hardness of the search version SIVP_γ, to the gap version gapSIVP. Informally, we show that if $\mathsf{gapSIVP}_\gamma$ is not hard, neither is $\mathsf{SIVP}_{\sqrt{n}\cdot\gamma}$.

Main Theorem 1. *If* $\mathsf{gapSIVP}_\gamma \in \mathbf{SZK}$ *and there exists a probabilistic polynomial-time adaptive reduction from a language* L *to* $\mathsf{SIVP}_{\sqrt{n \log n}\cdot\gamma}$, *then* $\mathsf{L} \in \mathbf{AM} \cap \mathbf{coAM}$.

As a quick corollary, combining our result with $\mathsf{gapSIVP}_{\omega(\sqrt{n \log n})} \in \mathbf{SZK}$ [PV08], any language that can be reduced to $\mathsf{SIVP}_{\omega(n \log n)}$ lies in **AM** intersect **coAM** and thus it is not **NP**-hard unless the polynomial hierarchy collapses.

Corollary 1.1. *If there exists a probabilistic polynomial-time adaptive reduction from a language* L *to* SIVP_γ *for any* $\gamma(n) = \omega(n \log n)$, *then* $\mathsf{L} \in \mathbf{AM} \cap \mathbf{coAM}$.

1.1 Proof Overview

The first step is to shift from a search problem to a sampling problem. Our goal is to obtain a black-box separation between SIVP_γ and **NP**-hardness by showing that any language L that can be reduced to SIVP_γ is in **AM** intersect **coAM**. Let $\mathcal{R}$ be the reduction from L to SIVP_γ. We will construct an **AM** protocol for L using reduction $\mathcal{R}$. For a first attempt, the naïve verifier samples a random tape and sends it to the prover. The prover simulates the reduction $\mathcal{R}$ and resolves any query to SIVP_γ using its unbounded computational power. The simulation, including the answers to the reduction's query to SIVP_γ, is sent to the naïve verifier, so that the verifier can check its correctness. But SIVP_γ is a search problem and there is no unique right answer. The prover has the freedom to decide which answer is chosen upon each query. This freedom allows a malicious prover to fool the naïve verifier. Similar difficulty were faced by Bogdanov and Brzuska, which is resolved by inherently shifting to sampling problems. In order to separate size-verifiable one-way functions from **NP**-Hardness [BB15], they force the prover to sample a random answer uniformly among all correct ones. Thus the correct answer distribution for each query is unique.

Inspired by the work of Bogdanov and Brzuska, we consider a sampling problem related to SIVP_γ, called the discrete Gaussian distribution. A discrete Gaussian over a lattice is a distribution such that the probability of any vertex $\mathbf{v}$ is proportional to $e^{-\pi\|\mathbf{v}-\mathbf{c}\|^2/s^2}$, where $\mathbf{c}$ is its "center" and parameter s is its "width". Lemma 4.3 shows that discrete Gaussian sampling is as hard as SIVP_γ in the sense that there is a black-box reduction from SIVP_γ to discrete Gaussian sampling with "width" $\gamma(n)/\sqrt{n}$. Therefore, if language L can be reduced to SIVP_γ, then it can also be reduced to discrete Gaussian sampling on lattices with "width" $s \leq \lambda_n/\sqrt{n}$.

Lemma 4.3 (Informal). *SIVP_γ can be efficiently reduced to discrete Gaussian sampling on lattices with "width" $\sigma = \frac{\gamma}{\sqrt{n}}\lambda_n$.*

Lemma 4.3 is a generalization of [Reg09, Lemma 3.17]. Its proof is quite intuitive. Repeatedly sample from the discrete Gaussian over the same lattice centered at $\mathbf{0}$. With good probability, the newly sampled vertex is short and is linearly independent from previously sampled verteces.

The next natural question is, *which property separates a sampling problem from* **NP***-hardness?* Here we introduce the notion of "probability-verifiability". Informally, a distribution family is *probability-verifiable* if for any distribution $\mathcal{D}$ in this family and for any possible value v, $\Pr[v \leftarrow \mathcal{D}]$, the probability that v is sampled from $\mathcal{D}$, can be lower bounded within an arbitrarily good precision in **AM**.

Lemma 4.4 (Informal). *If a language L can be reduced to a probability-verifiable sampling problem S, then $\mathsf{L} \in \mathbf{AM} \cap \mathbf{coAM}$.*

Lemma 4.4 is a generalization of [BB15]. Assume language L can be reduced to sampling problem S. The input of S is interpreted as the description of a distribution, let $\mathcal{P}_{\mathsf{pd}}$ denote the distribution specified by input pd.

Let $\mathcal{R}$ be the reduction from L to sampling problem S. On each input x, an execution $\mathcal{R}^{\mathsf{S}}(x)$ is determined by the random tape of reduction $\mathcal{R}$, denoted by r, and the answers to the reduction's queries to S. The *transcript* is defined as $\sigma = (r, \mathsf{pd}_1, v_1, \ldots, \mathsf{pd}_T, v_T)$ where pd_t is the t-th query to S and v_t is the corresponding response. Note that $r, v_1, \ldots, v_T$ determine the execution, since pd_t is determined by $r, v_1, \ldots, v_{t-1}$. Then

$$\Pr[\mathcal{R}^{\mathsf{S}}(x) \text{ accepts}] = \sum_{\substack{\sigma:\text{accepting transcript}\\ \text{of } \mathcal{R}^{\mathsf{S}}(x)}} \Pr[\sigma] = \sum_{\substack{\sigma:\text{accepting transcript}\\ \text{of } \mathcal{R}^{\mathsf{S}}(x)}} \Pr[r] \cdot \mathcal{P}_{\mathsf{pd}_1}(v_1) \cdot \ldots \cdot \mathcal{P}_{\mathsf{pd}_T}(v_T). \tag{1}$$

For simplicity, assume for now that there is an efficient algorithm that computes the probability $\mathcal{P}_{\mathsf{pd}}(v)$ given pd and value v. This property is stronger than probability-verifiability. Then the probability that $\mathcal{R}^{\mathsf{S}}(x)$ accepts, which equals a sum (Eq. (1)) where each term can be efficient computed, can be lower bounded using the set lower bound protocol of Goldwasser and Sipser [GS86], so $\mathsf{L} \in \mathbf{AM}$. Symmetrically, $\mathsf{L} \in \mathbf{coAM}$. The proof of Lemma 4.4 shows the same result from the weaker condition that S is probability-verifiable.

There is one last step missing between Lemmas 4.3 and 4.4: *Is discrete Gaussian sampling probability-verifiable? What is the smallest factor γ such that discrete Gaussian sampling with "width" $\leq \gamma\lambda_n$ is probability-verifiable?* Lemma 4.5 answers this question, and it connects the hardness of discrete Gaussian sampling with the hardness of gapSIVP.

Lemma 4.5 (Informal). *Assume* $\mathsf{gapSIVP}_\gamma$ *is in* **SZK**. *There exists a real valued function $s(\mathbf{B}) \in [\lambda_n, \tilde{O}(\gamma) \cdot \lambda_n]$ such that given a lattice basis $\mathbf{B}$, discrete Gaussian sampling over lattice $\mathcal{L}(\mathbf{B})$ with "width" $s(\mathbf{B})$ is probability-verifiable.*

Lemma 4.5 has an easier proof assuming the stronger condition that $\mathsf{gapSIVP}_\gamma$ is in **P**. If there were some deterministic polynomial time algorithm solving $\mathsf{gapSIVP}_\gamma$, there would exist $s(\mathbf{B}) \in [\lambda_n(\mathbf{B}), \gamma\lambda_n(\mathbf{B})]$ that can be efficiently computed by binary search. As $s(\mathbf{B}) \geq \lambda_n(\mathbf{B})$, the verifier can ask the prover to provide a set of n linearly independent vectors $\mathbf{w}_1, \ldots, \mathbf{w}_n$ whose length is no longer than $s(\mathbf{B})$. Given the lattice basis $\mathbf{B}$ and a set of short linearly independent vectors, there exists an efficient algorithm that samples from the discrete Gaussian with the desired parameter [BLP+13]. When the verifier can sample from a distribution, he can lower bound the probability of each value using the set lower bound protocol [GS86].

This informal proof assumes $\mathsf{gapSIVP}_\gamma \in \mathbf{P}$ in order to compute a function $s(\mathbf{B})$ that $s(\mathbf{B}) \approx \lambda_n(\mathbf{B})$. As the verifier only needs to compute such a function $s(\mathbf{B})$ in an **AM** protocol, this assumption can be weakened to $\mathsf{gapSIVP}_\gamma \in \mathbf{SZK}$, by combining with Lemma 3.1.

Lemma 3.1 (Informal). *Assume* $\mathsf{gapSIVP}_\gamma$ *is in* **SZK**. *There exists a real valued function $s(\mathbf{B}) \in [\lambda_n, \tilde{O}(\gamma) \cdot \lambda_n]$ that can be efficiently computed in Arthur-Merlin protocol.*

The proof technique of Lemma 3.1 crucially relies on the fact that $\mathsf{gapSIVP}_\gamma \in \mathbf{SZK}$. As a result, we can hardly make use of previous results such as $\mathsf{gapSIVP}_{\sqrt{n/\log n}} \in \mathbf{NP} \cap \mathbf{coAM}$ [GMR04].

1.2 Related Works

Prior work exploring the problem of basing cryptography on worst-case **NP**-hardness has obtained several negative results for black-box reduction. Brassard [Bra79] first showed that one-way permutations cannot be based on **NP**-hardness. Goldreich and Goldwasser [GG98] showed that public-key encryption schemes satisfying certain very specific properties cannot be based on **NP**-hardness. The required properties include the ability to certify an invalid key.

Work of Akavia, Goldreich, Goldwasser and Moshkovitz [AGGM06] and Bogdanov and Brzuska [BB15] showed that a special class of one-way functions called *size-verifiable one-way functions* cannot be based on **NP**-hardness. A size-verifiable one-way function is one in which the size of the set of pre-images can be efficiently approximated via an **AM** protocol.

Bogdanov and Lee [BL13] showed that homomorphic encryption schemes satisfying a special property cannot be based on **NP**-hardness. The required property is that the homomorphic evaluation produces a ciphertext whose distribution is statistically close to that of a fresh encrypted ciphertext.

Recently, Liu and Vaikuntanathan [LV16] showed that single-server private information retrieval (PIR) schemes cannot be based on **NP**-hardness.

Several works have also obtained a separation results for restricted types of reductions, most notably non-adaptive reductions which make all oracle queries simultaneously. The work of Feigenbaum and Fortnow [FF91], subsequently strengthened by Bogdanov and Trevisan [BT06], showed that there cannot be a *non-adaptive* reduction from SAT to the average-case hardness of any problem in **NP**, unless the polynomial hierarchy collapses.

On basing lattice problems on **NP**-hardness, the work of Goldreich and Goldwasser [GG00], subsequently strengthened by Micciancio and Vadhan [MV03], showed that $\mathsf{gapSVP}_{\sqrt{n/\log n}}$ and $\mathsf{gapCVP}_{\sqrt{n/\log n}}$ are both contained in $\mathbf{NP} \cap \mathbf{SZK}$. The shortest vector problem (SVP) and the closest vector problem (CVP), roughly speaking, is the problem of finding the shortest non-zero vector in a lattice or finding the lattice vector that is closest to a given point. The corresponding gap problem $\mathsf{gapSVP}_\gamma, \mathsf{gapCVP}_\gamma$ is to estimate within a factor of $\gamma(n)$ the length of the shortest non-zero vector or the distance to the closest lattice vector from a given point. The problem gapSVP is connected to gapSIVP via so-called "transference theorems" for lattices [Ban93]. Aharonov and Regev [AR04] explored a slightly looser approximation factor and showed that $\mathsf{gapSVP}_{\sqrt{n}}$ and $\mathsf{gapCVP}_{\sqrt{n}}$ are both contained in $\mathbf{NP} \cap \mathbf{coNP}$.

In prior work on the gap version of the SIVP problem, Guruswami, Micciancio and Regev [GMR04] showed that $\mathsf{gapSIVP}_{\sqrt{n/\log n}} \in \mathbf{NP} \cap \mathbf{coAM}$. Peikert and Vaikuntanathan [PV08] showed that $\mathsf{gapSIVP}_\gamma \in \mathbf{SZK}$ for any $\gamma(n) = \omega(\sqrt{n \log n})$. In contrast to these results for promise problems, our work explores the approximate SIVP problem. With an approximation factor $\gamma(n) = \tilde{O}(n)$, this search problem is the basis of lattice-based collision resistant hash function (CRHF) constructions [Ajt96, MR04]. In particular, Micciancio and Regev constructed CRHF from the worst-case hardness of $\mathsf{SIVP}_{\gamma(n)}$ for any $\gamma(n) = \omega(n \log n)$ [MR04]. We separate SIVP_γ from **NP**-hardness for the same approximation factor.

2 Preliminaries

Lattice A lattice in $\mathbb{R}^n$ is an additive subgroup of $\mathbb{R}^n$

$$\left\{\sum_{i=1}^{n} x_i \mathbf{b}_i : x_i \in \mathbb{Z} \text{ for } 1 \le i \le n\right\}$$

generated by n linearly independent vectors $\mathbf{b}_1, \dots, \mathbf{b}_n \in \mathbb{R}^n$. The set of vectors $\mathbf{b}_1, \dots, \mathbf{b}_n$ is called a *basis* for the lattice. A basis can be represented by matrix $\mathbf{B} \in \mathbb{R}^{n \times n}$ whose columns are the basis vectors. The lattice generated by the columns of $\mathbf{B}$ is denoted by $\mathcal{L}(\mathbf{B})$.

$$\mathcal{L}(\mathbf{B}) = \{\mathbf{Bx} : \mathbf{x} \in \mathbb{N}^n\}.$$

The *i-th successive minimum* of a lattice $\mathcal{L}$, denoted by $\lambda_i(\mathcal{L})$, is defined as the minimum length that $\mathcal{L}$ contains i linearly independent vectors of length at most $\lambda_i(\mathcal{L})$. Formally,

$$\lambda_i(\mathcal{L}) := \min\{r : \dim(\mathcal{L} \cap r\mathcal{B}) \ge i\},$$

where $r\mathcal{B}$ is the radius r ball centered at the origin defined as $r\mathcal{B} := \{\mathbf{x} \in \mathbb{R}^n : \|\mathbf{x}\|_2 \le r\}$. We abuse notations and write $\lambda_i(\mathbf{B})$ instead of $\lambda_i(\mathcal{L}(\mathbf{B}))$.

Shortest Independent Vectors Problem (SIVP). SIVP is a computational problem. Given a basis $\mathbf{B}$ of an n-dimensional lattice, find a set of n linearly independent vectors $\mathbf{v}_1, \dots, \mathbf{v}_n \in \mathcal{L}(\mathbf{B})$ such that $\max_i \|\mathbf{v}_i\|$ is minimized, i.e., $\|\mathbf{v}_i\| \le \lambda_n(\mathbf{B})$ for all $1 \le i \le n$.

SIVP_γ is the approximation version of SIVP with factor λ. Given a basis $\mathbf{B}$ of an n-dimensional lattice, find a set of n linearly independent vectors $\mathbf{v}_1, \dots, \mathbf{v}_n \in \mathcal{L}(\mathbf{B})$ such that $\|\mathbf{v}_i\| \le \gamma(n) \cdot \lambda_n(\mathbf{B})$ for all $1 \le i \le n$. The approximation factor γ is typical a polynomial in n.

$\mathsf{gapSIVP}_\gamma$ is the decision version of SIVP_γ. An input to $\mathsf{gapSIVP}_\gamma$ is a basis $\mathbf{B}$ of a n-dimensional lattice and a scalar s. It is a YES instance if $\lambda_n(\mathbf{B}) \le s$, and is a NO instance if $\lambda_n(\mathbf{B}) \ge \gamma(n) \cdot s$.

Discrete Gaussian. For any vector $\mathbf{c}$ and any $s > 0$, let

$$\rho_{\mathbf{c},s}(\mathbf{v}) = e^{-\pi\|\mathbf{v}-\mathbf{c}\|_2^2/s^2}$$

be a Gaussian function with mean $\mathbf{c}$ and width s. Functions are extends to sets in usual way, $\rho_{\mathbf{c},s}(\mathcal{L}) = \sum_{\mathbf{v} \in \mathcal{L}} \rho_{\mathbf{c},s}(\mathbf{v})$. The discrete Gaussian distribution over lattice $\mathcal{L}$ with mean $\mathbf{c}$ and width s, denoted by $\mathcal{N}_{\mathcal{L},\mathbf{c},s}$, is defined by

$$\forall \mathbf{v} \in \mathcal{L},\ \mathcal{N}_{\mathcal{L},\mathbf{c},s}(\mathbf{v}) = \frac{\rho_{\mathbf{c},s}(\mathbf{v})}{\rho_{\mathbf{c},s}(\mathcal{L})}.$$

In this work, most discrete Gaussian distributions considered are centered at the origin. Let $\rho_s, \mathcal{N}_{\mathcal{L},s}$ denote $\rho_{\mathbf{0},s}, \mathcal{N}_{\mathcal{L},\mathbf{0},s}$ respectively.

Lemma 2.1 (Lemma 1.4 in [Ban93]). *For each $a \geq 1$, for any n-dimensional lattice $\mathcal{L}$, $\rho_{as}(\mathcal{L}) \leq a^n \rho_s(\mathcal{L})$*

Lemma 2.2 (Lemma 1.5 in [Ban93]). *For any $c > 1/\sqrt{2\pi}$, n-dimensional lattice $\mathcal{L}$*

$$\rho_s(\mathcal{L} \setminus cs\sqrt{n}\mathcal{B}) < C^n \cdot \rho_s(\mathcal{L}) \tag{2}$$

where $C = c\sqrt{2\pi e} \cdot e^{-\pi c^2}$.

Sampling Problems. Besides computational problems and decision problems, we define *sampling problems.* The input of a sampling problem specifies a distribution, let $\mathcal{P}_{\mathsf{pd}}$ denote the distribution specified by input pd. The goal is to sample from the distribution $\mathcal{P}_{\mathsf{pd}}$. A probabilistic polynomial-time algorithm $\mathcal{S}$ perfectly solves the sampling problem if for any input pd

$$\forall v, \Pr[\mathcal{S}(\mathsf{pd}) \to v] = \mathcal{P}_{\mathsf{pd}}(v).$$

The probability is over the random input tape of $\mathcal{S}$. In a more practical definition, $\mathcal{S}$ solves the sampling problem if the output distribution of $\mathcal{S}(\mathsf{pd})$ is close to $\mathcal{P}_{\mathsf{pd}}$, i.e.

$$\Delta_{\mathsf{sd}}(\mathcal{S}(\mathsf{pd}, 1^\ell), \mathcal{P}_{\mathsf{pd}}) \leq \frac{1}{\ell}$$

where Δ_{sd} denotes the statistical distance.

For example, in this work, discrete Gaussian is considered as a sampling problem. For any function $s(\cdot)$ mapping lattice bases to positive real numbers, define sampling problem DGS_s. The input of DGS_s is a lattice basis $\mathbf{B}$. The target output distribution $\mathcal{P}_{\mathbf{B}}$ is the discrete Gaussian distribution $\mathcal{N}_{\mathcal{L}(\mathbf{B}),s(\mathbf{B})}$, where each vector $v \in \mathcal{L}(\mathbf{B})$ is sampled with probability

$$\mathcal{P}_{\mathbf{B}}(\mathbf{v}) = \mathcal{N}_{\mathcal{L}(\mathbf{B}),s(\mathbf{B})}(\mathbf{v}) = \frac{\rho_{s(\mathbf{B})}(\mathbf{v})}{\rho_{s(\mathbf{B})}(\mathcal{L}(\mathbf{B}))}.$$

Probability-Verifiable. A sampling problem is *probability-verifiable* if there exists an **AM** protocol to lower bound $\mathcal{P}_{\mathsf{pd}}(v)$ for any pd and v. More precisely, there exists a family of error function $\{\eta_{\mathsf{pd},m}\}$ such that for any pd, m, the error function $\eta_{\mathsf{pd},m} : \{0,1\}^* \to [0, +\infty)$ satisfies $\sum_v \eta_{\mathsf{pd},m}(v) \leq \frac{1}{m}$, and the promise problem

- YES instance: $(\mathsf{pd}, v, \hat{p}, 1^m)$ such that $\hat{p} = \mathcal{P}_{\mathsf{pd}}(v)$
- NO instance: $(\mathsf{pd}, v, \hat{p}, 1^m)$ such that $\hat{p} \geq \mathcal{P}_{\mathsf{pd}}(v) + \eta_{\mathsf{pd},m}(v)$

is in **AM**.

Sampling Oracles. In order to formalize the (probabilistic) Turing reduction to a sampling problem, we also define *sampling oracles*, which is a generalization of traditional oracles studied by complexity theorists. Let $\mathcal{S}$ be a sampling oracle for a fixed sampling problem. $\mathcal{S}$ can be queried on any valid pd; upon query pd, sampling oracle $\mathcal{S}(\mathsf{pd})$ would always output a fresh sample from distribution $\mathcal{P}_{\mathsf{pd}}$. E.g. if the sampling oracle $\mathcal{S}$ is queried for the same pd multiple times, it would output i.i.d. samples from distribution $\mathcal{P}_{\mathsf{pd}}$.

A probabilistic Turing reduction from a language L to a sampling problem S is a probabilistic poly-time oracle Turing machine $\mathcal{R}$, such that $\mathcal{R}$ can solve L given a sampling oracle of S in the sense that

$$x \in \mathsf{L} \implies \mathcal{R}^{\mathcal{S}}(x) \to 1 \text{ w.p. } \geq 2/3,$$
$$x \notin \mathsf{L} \implies \mathcal{R}^{\mathcal{S}}(x) \to 1 \text{ w.p. } \leq 1/3.$$

If such a reduction exists, we say L can be reduced to sampling problem S, denoted by $\mathsf{L} \in \mathbf{BPP}^{\mathsf{S}}$.

Similarly, a computational problem or a search problem can be reduced to a sampling problem S if they can be efficiently solved given the sampling oracle of S.

$\mathbb{R}$-TFAM *and* **$\mathbb{R}_\eta$-TFAM** The complexity class $\mathbb{R}$-**TFAM** is introduced by Mahmoody and Xiao [MX10]. Informally, it's consist of real-valued functions that can be efficiently computed in **AM**. A function $f : \{0,1\}^* \to \mathbb{R}$ is in $\mathbb{R}$-**TFAM** if the following promise problem is in **AM**:

- YES instance: $(x, f(x), 1^m)$.
- NO instance: $(x, y, 1^m)$ such that $|y - f(x)| > \frac{1}{m}$.

The definition of $\mathbb{R}$-**TFAM** emphasize on the absolute error. The complexity class $\mathbb{R}_\eta$-**TFAM** is defined to capture those functions that can be efficiently computed in **AM** with small relative error. A function $g : \{0,1\}^* \to \mathbb{R}^+$ is in $\mathbb{R}_\eta$-**TFAM** if the following promise problem is in **AM**:

- YES instance: $(x, g(x), 1^m)$.
- NO instance: $(x, y, 1^m)$ such that $|y - g(x)| > \frac{1}{m} \cdot g(x)$.

It follows directly from the definitions that $g \in \mathbb{R}_\eta - \mathbf{TFAM}$ if and only if $\log g \in \mathbb{R} - \mathbf{TFAM}$ for any function $g : \{0,1\}^* \to \mathbb{R}^+$.

Statistical Zero Knowledge. Statistical zero knowledge (**SZK**) is the class of decision problems that can be verified by a statistical zero-knowledge proof protocol. *Entropy Difference* (ED) is a complete problem for **SZK** [GV99], which is defined as the following: Given two polynomial-size circuits, C and D, let $\mathcal{C}$ and $\mathcal{D}$ be the distributions of their respective outputs when C, D are fed with uniform random inputs. The problem is to distinguish between

- YES instance: (C, D) such that $H(\mathcal{C}) - H(\mathcal{D}) \geq 1$;
- NO instance: (C, D) such that $H(\mathcal{C}) - H(\mathcal{D}) \leq -1$.

Where H is the Shannon entropy. Moreover, the mapping $H : C \mapsto H(\mathcal{C})$ is in $\mathbb{R}$-**TFAM**.

3 Gap Problems

The lattice problem gapSIVP is essentially estimating $\lambda_n(\mathbf{B})$ given a lattice basis $\mathbf{B}$. This definition can be generalized to any real valued functions. Define the gap problem of function $f : \{0,1\}^* \to \mathbb{R}^+$ with gap $\gamma : \{0,1\}^* \to [1, +\infty)$, denoted by $\mathsf{gap}f_\gamma$, as the promise problem

- YES instance: (x, y) such that $y \leq f(x)$;
- NO instance: (x, y) such that $y > \gamma(x) \cdot f(x)$.

In this work, estimating $\lambda_n(\mathbf{B})$ is of critical importance. Its gap problem, $\mathsf{gapSIVP}_\gamma$, alone is not sufficient for the proof. Instead, a stronger form of approximation is defined. Say $g : \{0,1\}^* \to \mathbb{R}^+$ is an approximation of function f within factor γ if $f(x) \leq g(x) \leq \gamma(x) \cdot f(x)$ for all x. Clearly, computing g is a harder problem than $\mathsf{gap}f_\gamma$, in the sense that there is a trivial reduction from $\mathsf{gap}f_\gamma$ to computing g.

The following Lemma shows a reduction in the other direction: if $\mathsf{gap}f_\gamma$ is in **SZK**, then there exists an approximation of f within almost the same factor, which can be computed in **AM**.

Lemma 3.1. *For any real valued function $f : \{0,1\}^* \to \mathbb{R}^+$ and any gap $\gamma : \{0,1\}^* \to [1, +\infty)$ that $\log \gamma(x) \leq \mathrm{poly}(|x|)$, if $\mathsf{gap}f_\gamma \in \mathbf{SZK}$, then for any constant $\mu > 1$, there exists $g : \{0,1\}^* \to \mathbb{R}^+$ such that $\forall x, g(x) \in [f(x), \mu\gamma(x)f(x)]$ and g is in $\mathbb{R}_\eta$-***TFAM***.*

Lemma 3.1 can be combined with previous results about gapSIVP. Peikert and Vaikuntanathan [PV08] showed that $\mathsf{gapSIVP}_\gamma \in \mathbf{NISZK} \subseteq \mathbf{SZK}$ for any $\gamma = \omega(\sqrt{n \log n})$. Thus there exists an approximation of λ_n within a factor $\tilde{O}(\sqrt{n})$ that can be computed in **AM**.

Corollary 3.2. *For any $\gamma(n) = \omega(\sqrt{n \log n})$, there exists a function g maps lattice bases to real numbers such that $g \in \mathbb{R}_\eta - \mathbf{TFAM}$ and $\lambda_n(\mathbf{B}) \leq g(\mathbf{B}) < \gamma(n) \cdot \lambda_n(\mathbf{B})$.*

Proof (Lemma 3.1). Entropy Difference (ED) is a complete problem for **SZK**, so $\mathsf{gap}f_\gamma \in \mathbf{SZK}$ implies the existence of a reduction $(x, y) \mapsto (C_{x,y}, D_{x,y})$ that maps input x together with a real number y to random circuits $C_{x,y}, D_{x,y}$. Let $\mathcal{C}_{x,y}$ and $\mathcal{D}_{x,y}$ be the output distributions of $C_{x,y}, D_{x,y}$. The reduction from $\mathsf{gap}f_\gamma$ to ED satisfies the following properties:

- There is an efficient deterministic algorithm computing $C_{x,y}, D_{x,y}$ given input (x, y).
- $H(\mathcal{C}_{x,y}) - H(\mathcal{D}_{x,y}) > 2$ for any x, y that $y \leq f(x)$.
- $H(\mathcal{C}_{x,y}) - H(\mathcal{D}_{x,y}) < -1$ for any x, y that $y > \gamma(x) \cdot f(x)$.

Define the clamp function

$$\mathrm{clamp}(y) := \begin{cases} 1, & \text{if } y \geq 1; \\ y, & \text{if } y \in (0,1); \\ 0, & \text{if } y \leq 0. \end{cases}$$

For any fixed constant $\mu > 1$, define

$$g(x) = \exp\left(\ln\mu \cdot \sum_{i=0}^{+\infty} \mathrm{clamp}(H(\mathcal{C}_{x,\mu^i}) - H(\mathcal{D}_{x,\mu^i})) + \ln\mu \cdot \sum_{i=1}^{+\infty}\left(\mathrm{clamp}(H(\mathcal{C}_{x,\mu^{-i}}) - H(\mathcal{D}_{x,\mu^{-i}})) - 1\right)\right).$$

As $\mathrm{clamp}(H(\mathcal{C}_{x,y}) - H(\mathcal{D}_{x,y})) = 1$ for $y \leq f(x)$,

$$g(x) \geq \exp\left(\ln\mu \cdot \lceil \log_\mu(f(x)) \rceil\right) \geq f(x).$$

As $\mathrm{clamp}(H(\mathcal{C}_{x,y}) - H(\mathcal{D}_{x,y})) = 0$ for $y > \gamma(x) \cdot f(x)$,

$$g(x) \leq \exp\left(\ln\mu \cdot \lceil \log_\mu(\gamma(x) \cdot f(x)) \rceil\right) \leq \mu\gamma(x) \cdot f(x).$$

In order to complete the proof, we show that g is in $\mathbb{R}_\eta$-**TFAM**. For any input $x, \hat{g}$, the prover can prove $\hat{g} \approx g(x)$ if $\hat{g} = g(x)$.

Consider the following protocol, $\varepsilon = 1/\mathrm{poly}(m, \ln\gamma)$ will be fixed later.

On any input x, define $d_i = H(\mathcal{C}_{x,\mu^i}) - H(\mathcal{D}_{x,\mu^i})$. And the honest prover should send $\hat{d}_i = d_i$. The prover have to prove that $d_i - \varepsilon < \hat{d}_i < d_i + \varepsilon$. For $\mu^i \leq f(x)$, $\hat{d}_i \geq d_i - \varepsilon \geq 1$, then $\mathrm{clamp}(\hat{d}_i) = 1 = \mathrm{clamp}(d_i)$. For $\mu^i \geq \mu\gamma(x)f(x)$, $\hat{d}_i \leq d_i + \varepsilon \leq 0$, then $\mathrm{clamp}(\hat{d}_i) = 0 = \mathrm{clamp}(d_i)$. For $f(x) < \mu^i < \mu\gamma(x)f(x)$, $|\mathrm{clamp}(\hat{d}_i) - \mathrm{clamp}(d_i)| \leq |\hat{d}_i - d_i| < \varepsilon$.

AM "protocol" on input $(x, \hat{g})$

P: Send $\ldots, \hat{d}_{-1}, \hat{d}_0, \hat{d}_1, \hat{d}_2, \ldots$ such that $\log_\mu \hat{g} = \sum_{i=0}^{\infty} \mathrm{clamp}(\hat{d}_i) + \sum_{i=1}^{\infty}(\mathrm{clamp}(\hat{d}_{-i}) - 1)$
P,V: For each $i \in \mathbb{Z}$, convince the verifier that $\hat{d}_i - \varepsilon < H(\mathcal{C}_{x,\mu^i}) - H(\mathcal{D}_{x,\mu^i}) < \hat{d}_i + \varepsilon$

Thus

$$\begin{aligned}
\left|\frac{\ln\hat{g} - \ln g(x)}{\ln\mu}\right| &\leq \sum_{i\in\mathbb{Z}} \left|\mathrm{clamp}(\hat{d}_i) - \mathrm{clamp}(d_i)\right| \\
&= \sum_{f(x)<\mu^i<\mu\gamma(x)f(x)} \left|\mathrm{clamp}(\hat{d}_i) - \mathrm{clamp}(d_i)\right| \\
&< \lceil \log_\mu(\mu\gamma(x)) \rceil \varepsilon \\
&< \frac{\ln\gamma(x) + 2}{\ln\mu}\varepsilon.
\end{aligned}$$

If ε is sufficiently small, $\hat{g}$ would be close to $g(x)$. To ensure $|\hat{g} - g(x)| \leq \frac{1}{m}g(x)$, it is sufficient to set $\varepsilon = O(\frac{1}{m(\ln\gamma(x)+2)})$.

The above "protocol" is not a real protocol, as it requires the prover to send an infinite sequence to the verifier. To compress the proof, the prover need a succinct interactive proof that $d_j > 1$ for all $j \leq i_L$ and $d_j < 0$ for all $j \geq i_H$.

For an index i, if the prover can convince the verifier that $d_i = H(\mathcal{C}_{x,\mu^i}) - H(\mathcal{D}_{x,\mu^i}) < 2$, the verifier also learns that $\mu^i > g(x)$, thus for any $j \geq i +$

$\lceil \log_\mu \gamma(x) \rceil$, $\mu^j > \gamma(x)g(x)$ and $d_j \le -1$. Similarly, if the prover can convince the verifier that $d_i = H(\mathcal{C}_{x,\mu^i}) - H(\mathcal{D}_{x,\mu^i}) > -1$, the verifier also knows that $d_j \ge 2$ for any $j \le i - \lceil \log_\mu \gamma(x) \rceil$.

Thus the real **AM** protocol that proves $\hat{g} \in (g(x) - \frac{1}{m}, g(x) + \frac{1}{m})$ is the following: □

AM protocol on input $(x, \hat{g}, 1^m)$

P: Send $\hat{d}_{i_L}, \hat{d}_{i_L+1}, \ldots, \hat{d}_{i_H-1}, \hat{d}_{i_H}$ such that
- $\log_\mu \hat{g} = i_L + \sum_{i=i_L}^{i_H} \text{clamp}(\hat{d}_i)$
- $i_H = i_L + 2\lceil \log_\mu \gamma(x) \rceil$
- $\hat{d}_{i_L + \lceil \log_\mu \gamma(x) \rceil} > 0$
- $\hat{d}_{i_L + \lceil \log_\mu \gamma(x) \rceil + 1} < 1$

P,V: For each $i \in \mathbb{Z}$, convince the verifier that $\hat{d}_i - \varepsilon < H(\mathcal{C}_{x,\mu^i}) - H(\mathcal{D}_{x,\mu^i}) < \hat{d}_i + \varepsilon$ for $\varepsilon = O(\frac{1}{m(\ln \gamma(x) + 2)})$.

---

4 Search SIVP and NP-Hardness

Theorem 4.1. *For any factor $\gamma : \mathbb{N} \to \mathbb{R}$, if $\mathsf{gapSIVP}_\gamma \in$ **SZK** and there exists a probabilistic polynomial-time adaptive reduction from a language L to $\mathsf{SIVP}_{\sqrt{n \ln n} \cdot \gamma}$, then $\mathsf{L} \in$ **AM** $\cap$ **coAM**.*

The smallest factor γ we knows that makes problem $\mathsf{gapSIVP}_\gamma$ be in **SZK** comes from [PV08]: for any factor $\gamma(n) = \omega(\sqrt{n \log n})$, problem $\mathsf{gapSIVP}_\gamma$ is in **SZK**.

Corollary 4.2. *For any factor $\gamma(n) = \omega(n \log n)$, if there exists a probabilistic polynomial-time adaptive reduction from a language L to SIVP_γ, then $\mathsf{L} \in$ **AM** $\cap$ **coAM**.*

The proof of Theorem 4.1 is the combination of Lemmas 4.3, 4.4 and 4.5. Problem $\mathsf{gapSIVP}_\gamma$ is in **SZK** and there is a reduction from language L to search problem $\mathsf{SIVP}_{\sqrt{n \ln n} \cdot \gamma}$. Lemma 4.3 shows that there is another reduction from L to sampling problem DGS_s for any s satisfying

$$s(\mathbf{B}) \in [\lambda_n(\mathbf{B}), \sqrt{\ln n} \cdot \gamma \lambda_n(\mathbf{B})]. \tag{3}$$

Lemma 4.5 shows that there exists a function s satisfying (3) such that the sampling problem DGS_s is probability-verifiable. Therefore, there exists a reduction from L to a probability-verifiable sampling problem. Finally, Lemma 4.4 shows that such a language L must live in **AM** $\cap$ **coAM**.

Lemma 4.3. *Let $s(\cdot)$ be a function mapping lattice bases to real numbers, such that $\forall \mathbf{B}, \lambda_n(\mathbf{B}) \leq s(\mathbf{B}) \leq \frac{\gamma}{\sqrt{n}}\lambda_n(\mathbf{B})$. Then there exists a probabilistic Turing reduction from* SIVP_γ *to* DGS_s.

Lemma 4.4. *If there exists a probabilistic Turing reduction from a promise problem* $\mathsf{L} = (\mathsf{L}_Y, \mathsf{L}_N)$ *to probability-verifiable sampling problems, then* $\mathsf{L} \in$ **AM** $\cap$ **coAM**.

Lemma 4.5. *For any factor $\gamma : \mathbb{N} \to \mathbb{R}$, if* $\mathsf{gapSIVP}_{\gamma(n)/\sqrt{\ln n}} \in$ **SZK**, *then there exists a function $s(\cdot)$ mapping lattice bases to real numbers, such that $\forall \mathbf{B}, s(\mathbf{B}) \in [\lambda_n(\mathbf{B}), \gamma(n) \cdot \lambda_n(\mathbf{B})]$ and* DGS_s *is probability-verifiable.*

By combining Lemmas 4.4, 4.5 and [PV08], we can also show that discrete Gaussian sampling with width $\tilde{O}(\sqrt{n}) \cdot \lambda_n$ is not **NP**-hard unless the polynomial hierarchy collapses.

Theorem 4.6. *If there exists a probabilistic Turing reduction from a promise problem* L *to* DGS_s *for $s(\mathbf{B}) = \omega(\sqrt{n}\log n) \cdot \lambda_n(\mathbf{B})$, then* $\mathsf{L} \in$ **AM** $\cap$ **coAM**.

4.1 From Search SIVP to Discrete Gaussian Sampling

This section proves Lemma 4.3, which is essentially Lemma 3.17 in Regev's work [Reg09]. Informally speaking, Regev shows a reduction from SIVP_γ to $\mathsf{DGS}_{\gamma/\sqrt{n}}$ for $\gamma = \Omega(\sqrt{n \log n})$; Lemma 4.3 uses similar technique to construct a reduction from SIVP_γ to $\mathsf{DGS}_{\gamma/\sqrt{n}}$ for $\gamma = \Omega(\sqrt{n})$.

The reduction from SIVP_γ to discrete Gaussian sampling is straightforward: Sample n^2 times from discrete Gaussian distribution of width $s \in [\lambda_n, \frac{\gamma}{\sqrt{n}}\lambda_n]$. The sampled vectors contain n short, linearly independent vectors with probability exponentially close to 1.

In order to prove Lemma 4.3, we shows that if n^2 vectors are sampled from discrete Gaussian $\mathcal{N}_{\mathcal{L}(\mathbf{B}),s(\mathbf{B})}$, the following two "bad events" occurs with probability exponentially small.

- One of the sampled vectors is too long, its Euclidean norm is larger than $\gamma\lambda_n(\mathbf{B})$.
- The sampled vectors are not full rank.

Lemma 2.2 bounds the probability that an overlong vector is sampled from a discrete Gaussian distribution. Let the constant c in formula (2) equals 1,

$$\Pr_{\mathbf{v} \leftarrow \mathcal{N}_{\mathcal{L}(\mathbf{B}),s(\mathbf{B})}}\left[\|\mathbf{v}\| > \sqrt{n} \cdot s(\mathbf{B})\right] = \frac{\rho_s(\mathcal{L}(\mathbf{B}) \setminus s\sqrt{n}\mathcal{B})}{\rho_s(\mathcal{L}(\mathbf{B}))} < \left(\sqrt{2\pi e} \cdot e^{-\pi}\right)^n < 0.2^n.$$

As $\gamma(n) \cdot \lambda_n(\mathbf{B}) \geq \sqrt{n} \cdot s(\mathbf{B})$,

$$\Pr_{\mathbf{v} \leftarrow \mathcal{N}_{\mathcal{L}(\mathbf{B}),s(\mathbf{B})}}\left[\|\mathbf{v}\| > \gamma\lambda_n(\mathbf{B})\right] \leq \Pr_{\mathbf{v} \leftarrow \mathcal{N}_{\mathcal{L}(\mathbf{B}),s(\mathbf{B})}}\left[\|\mathbf{v}\| > \sqrt{n} \cdot s(\mathbf{B})\right] < 0.2^n,$$

which is exponentially small.

To prove that the n^2 sampled vectors span the whole space, we need a lower bound on the probability a newly sampled vector is linear independent from the previous ones. Lemma 4.7 shows such a lower bound, improves [Reg09, Lemma 3.15] by a factor of $\sqrt{\ln n}$ (the so-called smoothing parameter).

Lemma 4.7. *For any n-dimensional lattice $\mathcal{L}$, real number $s \geq \lambda_n(\mathcal{L})$ and for any proper linear subspace $\mathcal{V} \subsetneq \mathbb{R}^n$, the probability $\Pr_{\mathbf{v} \leftarrow \mathcal{N}_{\mathcal{L},s}}[\mathbf{v} \notin \mathcal{V}]$ is at least $1/20$.*

Proof. By the definition of successive minimum, there exists $\mathbf{u} \in \mathcal{L} \setminus \mathcal{V}$ such that $\|\mathbf{u}\| \leq \lambda_n(\mathcal{L})$. Let $\mathcal{L}'$ denote $\mathcal{L} \cap \mathcal{V}$. As $\mathcal{L}$ is closed under addition, $\mathcal{L}' + \mathbf{u}, \mathcal{L}' - \mathbf{u}$ are subsets of $\mathcal{L}$. Moreover, as $\mathcal{V}$ is closed under addition and $\mathbf{u} \notin \mathcal{V}$, the sets $\mathcal{L}' + \mathbf{u}, \mathcal{L}', \mathcal{L}' - \mathbf{u}$ are disjointed.

$$\begin{aligned}\Pr_{\mathbf{v} \leftarrow \mathcal{N}_{\mathcal{L},s}}[\mathbf{v} \in \mathcal{V}] &= \frac{\rho_s(\mathcal{L}')}{\rho_s(\mathcal{L})} \\ &\leq \frac{\rho_s(\mathcal{L}')}{\rho_s(\mathcal{L}' - \mathbf{u}) + \rho_s(\mathcal{L}') + \rho_s(\mathcal{L}' + \mathbf{u})} = \frac{\sum_{\mathbf{v} \in \mathcal{L}'} \rho_s(\mathbf{v})}{\sum_{\mathbf{v} \in \mathcal{L}'} (\rho_s(\mathbf{v} - \mathbf{u}) + \rho_s(\mathbf{v}) + \rho_s(\mathbf{v} + \mathbf{u}))}\end{aligned}$$

As $\|\mathbf{u}\| \leq \lambda_n(\mathcal{L}) \leq s$, for any vector $\mathbf{v}$

$$\begin{aligned}\rho_s(\mathbf{v} - \mathbf{u}) + \rho_s(\mathbf{v} + \mathbf{u}) &= e^{-\pi\|\mathbf{v}-\mathbf{u}\|^2/s^2} + e^{-\pi\|\mathbf{v}-\mathbf{u}\|^2/s^2} \\ &= (e^{-2\pi\langle \mathbf{u},\mathbf{v}\rangle/s^2} + e^{2\pi\langle \mathbf{u},\mathbf{v}\rangle/s^2}) e^{-\pi\|\mathbf{u}\|^2/s^2} e^{-\pi\|\mathbf{v}\|^2/s^2} \leq 2e^{-\pi}\rho_s(\mathbf{v})\end{aligned}$$

Thus

$$\Pr_{\mathbf{v} \leftarrow \mathcal{N}_{\mathcal{L},s}}[\mathbf{v} \in \mathcal{V}] \leq \frac{\sum_{\mathbf{v} \in \mathcal{L}'} \rho_s(\mathbf{v})}{\sum_{\mathbf{v} \in \mathcal{L}'} (1 + 2e^{-\pi/2^2})\rho_s(\mathbf{v})} = \frac{1}{1 + 2e^{-\pi}} \approx 0.92.$$

□

Assume k vectors has been sampled from $\mathcal{N}_{\mathcal{L}(\mathbf{B}),s(\mathbf{B})}$ and their dimension is strictly less than n. By Lemma 4.7, the next n sampled vectors contain a vector linearly independent from the first k with probability exponentially close to 1. By union bound, n^2 samples from $\mathcal{N}_{\mathcal{L}(\mathbf{B}),s(\mathbf{B})}$ contains n linearly independent vectors with probability exponentially close to 1.

4.2 Probability-Verifiable Sampling Problem and NP-hardness

This section proves Lemma 4.4, which is a generalization of [BB15], the proof techniques are similar.

Let $\mathcal{M}$ be the reduction from a promise problem $\mathsf{L} = (\mathsf{L}_Y, \mathsf{L}_N)$ to $\mathcal{S}$. For a given input x, we want to distinguish between $\Pr[\mathcal{M}^{\mathcal{S}}(x) \to 1] \geq 8/9$ and $\Pr[\mathcal{M}^{\mathcal{S}}(x) \to 1] \leq 1/9$ in **AM**. Notice that the randomness includes the random tape of $\mathcal{M}$ and the randomness $\mathcal{S}$ used to answer each query.

A transcript of an execution of $\mathcal{M}^{\mathcal{S}}(x)$ is an tuple $(r, \mathsf{pd}_1, v_1, \mathsf{pd}_2, v_2, \ldots, \mathsf{pd}_T, v_T)$ consists of the random tape of $\mathcal{M}$, all queries to $\mathcal{S}$ and the correlated answers. The transcript fully determined the execution $\mathcal{M}^{\mathcal{S}}(x)$, and

$$\Pr[\mathcal{M}^{\mathcal{S}}(x) \to 1] = \sum_{\substack{\text{transcript } (r,\mathsf{pd}_1,v_1,\mathsf{pd}_2,v_2,\ldots,\mathsf{pd}_T,v_T) \\ \text{determines a execution where } \mathcal{M}^{\mathcal{S}}(x)\to 1}} \Pr[(r, \mathsf{pd}_1, v_1, \mathsf{pd}_2, v_2, \ldots, \mathsf{pd}_T, v_T)]$$

$$= \sum_{\substack{\text{transcript } (r,\mathsf{pd}_1,v_1,\mathsf{pd}_2,v_2,\ldots,\mathsf{pd}_T,v_T) \\ \text{determines a execution where } \mathcal{M}^{\mathcal{S}}(x)\to 1}} \Pr[r] \prod_{t=1}^{T} \mathcal{P}_{\mathsf{pd}_t}(v_t).$$

In the proof, we construct an **AM** protocol that estimates this sum.

Proof of Lemma 4.4. It's sufficient to show that $\mathsf{L} = (\mathsf{L}_Y, \mathsf{L}_N) \in \mathbf{AM}$. Then the same argument would shows $\bar{\mathsf{L}} = (\mathsf{L}_N, \mathsf{L}_Y) \in \mathbf{AM}$, which implies $\mathsf{L} \in \mathbf{coAM}$.

L can be efficiently reduced to a probability-verifiable sampling problem. Let $\mathcal{S}$ denote a correlated sampling oracle. The reduction is a probability polynomial-time oracle algorithm $\mathcal{M}$ such that

$$\begin{aligned} x \in \mathsf{L}_Y &\implies \Pr[\mathcal{M}^{\mathcal{S}}(x) \to 1] \geq \frac{8}{9}, \\ x \in \mathsf{L}_N &\implies \Pr[\mathcal{M}^{\mathcal{S}}(x) \to 1] \leq \frac{1}{9}. \end{aligned} \tag{4}$$

The probability is over the random tape of $\mathcal{M}$ and the randomness used by $\mathcal{S}$. Without loss of generality, assume there exists $T = \mathrm{poly}(n)$ that $\mathcal{M}$ uses T bits of randomness and makes T queries on any input $x \in \{0,1\}^n$.

Define a *transcript* of an execution $\mathcal{M}^{\mathcal{S}}(x)$ as a tuple $(r, \mathsf{pd}_1, v_1, \mathsf{pd}_2, v_2, \ldots, \mathsf{pd}_T, v_T)$ where $r \in \{0,1\}^T$ is the random tape of $\mathcal{M}$, pd_t is the t-th query to sampling oracle $\mathcal{S}$ and v_t is the t-th sample returned by $\mathcal{S}$. The length of v_t is bounded by some polynomial of n, let $\ell(n)$ be a polynomial that upper bound $|v_t|$.

Note that the input, the random tape and oracle's answers fully determine the reduction. Given the input and random tape, the reduction's first query is predictable; given the input, random tape and the oracle's previous answers, the reduction's next query is predictable. Therefore, we define a transcript $\sigma = (r, \mathsf{pd}_1, v_1, \mathsf{pd}_2, v_2, \ldots, \mathsf{pd}_T, v_T)$ to be *valid*, if it's potentially a transcript of an execution $\mathcal{M}^{\mathcal{S}}(x)$, i.e. if for all $1 \leq t \leq T$, pd_t would the t-th query in execution $\mathcal{M}^{\mathcal{S}}(x)$ when r is the random tape and $v_1, \ldots, v_{t-1}$ is the oracle's previous answers. By this definition, σ is a valid transcript doesn't implies v_t has non-zero probability under distribution pd_t. Let $C(x)$ denote the set of all valid transcripts of $\mathcal{M}^{\mathcal{S}}(x)$.

The transcript also determines the output of the reduction. Define a transcript σ to be *accepting*, if σ is valid and the corresponding execution $\mathcal{M}^{\mathcal{S}}(x)$ output 1. Let $C_1(x)$ denote the set of all accepting transcripts of $\mathcal{M}^{\mathcal{S}}(x)$.

Let $P_x(\sigma)$ denote the probability that σ is the transcript of $\mathcal{M}^{\mathcal{S}}(x)$ when the random tape is uniformly chosen and $\mathcal{S}$ is an ideal sampling oracle. Then by chain rule,

$$P_x(\sigma) = \frac{1}{2^T} \prod_{t=1}^{T} \mathcal{P}_{\mathsf{pd}_t}(v_t)$$

for any valid transcript $\sigma = (r, \mathsf{pd}_1, v_1, \mathsf{pd}_2, v_2, \ldots, \mathsf{pd}_T, v_T)$. For any input x, we know $C_1(x) \subseteq C(x)$,

$$\sum_{\sigma \in C(x)} P_x(\sigma) = 1, \qquad \sum_{\sigma \in C_1(x)} P_x(\sigma) = \Pr[\mathcal{M}^{\mathcal{S}}(x) \to 1]$$

by the definition of valid/accepting transcripts. Thus, by condition (4), to distinguish between $x \in \mathsf{L}_Y$ and $x \in \mathsf{L}_N$, it's sufficient to distinguish between $\sum_{\sigma \in C_1(x)} P_x(\sigma) \geq 8/9$ and $\sum_{\sigma \in C_1(x)} P_x(\sigma) \leq 1/9$.

Define $D(x)$ as the set of all tuple (σ, k) such that $\sigma = (r, \mathsf{pd}_1, v_1, \mathsf{pd}_2, v_2, \ldots, \mathsf{pd}_T, v_T) \in C_1(x)$, and k is an integer that

$$1 \leq k \leq K \cdot P_x(\sigma) = K \cdot \frac{1}{2^T} \prod_{t=1}^{T} \mathcal{P}_{\mathsf{pd}_t}(v_t)$$

where $K = 10 \cdot 2^T \cdot 2^{T(\ell+1)}$. Then the size of $D(x)$ is roughly $K \cdot \Pr[\mathcal{M}^{\mathcal{S}}(x) \to 1]$ if K is sufficiently large.

The sampling problem is probability-verifiable. By definition, there exists a family of error function $\{\eta_{\mathsf{pd},m}\}$ such that for any pd, m, the error function $\eta_{\mathsf{pd},m} : \{0,1\}^* \to [0, +\infty)$ satisfies $\sum_v \eta_{\mathsf{pd},m}(v) \leq 1$, and the promise problem

- YES instances: $(\mathsf{pd}, v, \hat{p}, 1^m)$ such that $\hat{p} = \mathcal{P}_{\mathsf{pd}}(v)$
- NO instances: $(\mathsf{pd}, v, \hat{p}, 1^m)$ such that $\hat{p} \geq \mathcal{P}_{\mathsf{pd}}(v) + \frac{1}{m}\eta_{\mathsf{pd},m}(v)$

is in **AM**. Let ProbLowerBound be the corresponding **AM** protocol.

Let set $D'(x)$ consist of all tuple (σ, k) such that $\sigma = (r, \mathsf{pd}_1, v_1, \mathsf{pd}_2, v_2, \ldots, \mathsf{pd}_T, v_T) \in C_1(x)$, and k is an integer that

$$1 \leq k \leq K \cdot \frac{1}{2^T} \prod_{t=1}^{T} \Big(\mathcal{P}_{\mathsf{pd}_t}(v_t) + \frac{1}{T} \eta_{\mathsf{pd}_t, T}(v_t) \Big).$$

Here $K = 10 \cdot 2^T \cdot 2^{T(\ell+1)}$ as in the definition of $D(x)$. By definition, $D(x) \subseteq D'(x)$.

Claim. The promise problem

- YES instances: (x, σ, k) such that $(\sigma, k) \in D(x)$
- NO instances: (x, σ, k) such that $(\sigma, k) \notin D'(x)$

is in **AM**.

Proof. TranscriptChecking is an **AM** protocol that solves this promise problem.

AM protocol TranscriptChecking on input $(x, \sigma = (r, \mathsf{pd}_1, v_1, \mathsf{pd}_2, v_2, \ldots, \mathsf{pd}_T, v_T), k)$

V: Check whether σ is a valid accepting transcript of $\mathcal{M}^{\mathcal{S}}(x)$; Reject if not
P: Send $\hat{p}_1, \ldots, \hat{p}_T$, an honest prover should send $\hat{p}_t = \mathcal{P}_{\mathsf{pd}_t}(v_t)$
P,V: Run protocol ProbLowerBound$(\mathsf{pd}_t, v_t, 1^{10T})$ for all $1 \leq t \leq T$, repeat polynomial many times in parallel and take majority so that the total error probability is exponentially small; Reject if either of these protocols reject.
V: Check whether $1 \leq k \leq K \cdot \frac{1}{2^T} \prod_{i=1}^{q} \hat{p}_i$; Reject if not

---

For $(\sigma, k) \in D(x)$, an honest prover could convince the verifier that to accept (x, σ, k).

Any prover, even if it's malicious, should send $\hat{p}_t$ such that $\hat{p}_t \leq \mathcal{P}_{\mathsf{pd}_t}(v_t) + \frac{1}{10T}\eta_{\mathsf{pd}_t, 10T}(v_t)$. Otherwise the prover will be caught in ProbLowerBound protocol with overwhelming probability. Thus no prover can make the verifier accept (x, σ, k) with high probability if $(\sigma, k) \notin D'(x)$. □

Claim. The size of $D(x)$ is at least $\frac{2}{3}K$ if $x \in \mathsf{L}_Y$.

Proof. $x \in \mathsf{L}_Y$ implies that $\Pr[\mathcal{M}^{\mathcal{S}}(x) \rightarrow 1] \geq \frac{8}{9}$. Thus

$$\begin{aligned} |D(x)| &= \sum_{\sigma \in C_1(x)} \lfloor K \cdot P_x(\sigma) \rfloor \\ &\geq \sum_{\sigma \in C_1(x)} (K \cdot P_x(\sigma) - 1) \\ &= K \cdot \sum_{\sigma \in C_1(x)} P_x(\sigma) - |C_1(x)| \\ &\geq K \cdot \Pr[\mathcal{M}^{\mathcal{S}}(x) \rightarrow 1] - |C(x)| \\ &\geq \frac{8}{9}K - 2^T \cdot 2^{T(\ell+1)} \\ &= \frac{8}{9}K - \frac{1}{10}K \\ &\geq \frac{2}{3}K \end{aligned}$$

□

Claim. $D'(x)$ has size at most $\frac{1}{3}K$ if $x \in \mathsf{L}_N$.

Proof. $x \in \mathsf{L}_N$ implies that $\Pr[\mathcal{M}^{\mathcal{S}}(x) \to 1] \leq \frac{1}{9}$.

$$
\begin{aligned}
|D'(x)| &= \sum_{\sigma=(r,\mathsf{pd}_1,v_1,\mathsf{pd}_2,v_2,\ldots,\mathsf{pd}_T,v_T)\in C_1(x)} \left\lfloor K \cdot \frac{1}{2^T} \prod_{t=1}^{T} \Big(\mathcal{P}_{\mathsf{pd}_t}(v_t) + \frac{1}{10T}\eta_{\mathsf{pd}_t,10T}(v_t)\Big)\right\rfloor \\
&\leq K \cdot \sum_{\sigma=(r,\mathsf{pd}_1,v_1,\mathsf{pd}_2,v_2,\ldots,\mathsf{pd}_T,v_T)\in C_1(x)} \frac{1}{2^T} \prod_{t=1}^{T} \Big(\mathcal{P}_{\mathsf{pd}_t}(v_t) + \frac{1}{10T}\eta_{\mathsf{pd}_t,10T}(v_t)\Big) \\
&= K \cdot \sum_{\sigma=(r,\mathsf{pd}_1,\ldots,v_T)\in C_1(x)} \left(\frac{1}{2^T} \prod_{t=1}^{T} \Big(\mathcal{P}_{\mathsf{pd}_t}(v_t) + \frac{1}{10T}\eta_{\mathsf{pd}_t,10T}(v_t)\Big) - \frac{1}{2^T}\prod_{t=1}^{T}\mathcal{P}_{\mathsf{pd}_t}(v_t)\right) \\
&\quad + K \cdot \sum_{\sigma=(r,\mathsf{pd}_1,v_1,\mathsf{pd}_2,v_2,\ldots,\mathsf{pd}_T,v_T)\in C_1(x)} \frac{1}{2^T}\prod_{t=1}^{T}\mathcal{P}_{\mathsf{pd}_t}(v_t) \\
&\leq K \cdot \sum_{\sigma=(r,\mathsf{pd}_1,\ldots,v_T)\in C(x)} \left(\frac{1}{2^T} \prod_{t=1}^{T} \Big(\mathcal{P}_{\mathsf{pd}_t}(v_t) + \frac{1}{10T}\eta_{\mathsf{pd}_t,10T}(v_t)\Big) - \frac{1}{2^T}\prod_{t=1}^{T}\mathcal{P}_{\mathsf{pd}_t}(v_t)\right) \\
&\quad + K \cdot \Pr[\mathcal{M}^{\mathcal{S}}(x) \to 1] \\
&\leq (e^{1/10} - 1)K + \frac{1}{9}K \\
&\leq \frac{1}{3}K.
\end{aligned}
$$

The second to last inequality symbol relies on the following inequality,

$$
\begin{aligned}
&\sum_{\sigma=(r,\mathsf{pd}_1,v_1,\ldots,\mathsf{pd}_T,v_T)\in C(x)} \left(\frac{1}{2^T} \prod_{t=1}^{T} \Big(\mathcal{P}_{\mathsf{pd}_t}(v_t) + \frac{1}{10T}\eta_{\mathsf{pd}_t,10T}(v_t)\Big)\right) \\
&= \sum_{\substack{(r,\mathsf{pd}_1,v_1,\ldots,\mathsf{pd}_{T-1},v_{T-1},\mathsf{pd}_T) \\ \exists v_T\ (r,\mathsf{pd}_1,v_1,\ldots,\mathsf{pd}_T,v_T)\in C(x)}} \left(\frac{1}{2^T} \prod_{t=1}^{T-1} \Big(\mathcal{P}_{\mathsf{pd}_t}(v_t) + \frac{1}{10T}\eta_{\mathsf{pd}_t,10T}(v_t)\Big) \cdot \right. \\
&\qquad\qquad \left. \sum_{v} \Big(\mathcal{P}_{\mathsf{pd}_T}(v) + \frac{1}{10T}\eta_{\mathsf{pd}_T,10T}(v)\Big)\right) \\
&\leq \sum_{\substack{(r,\mathsf{pd}_1,v_1,\ldots,\mathsf{pd}_{T-1},v_{T-1}) \\ \exists \mathsf{pd}_T,v_T\ (r,\mathsf{pd}_1,\ldots,v_T)\in C(x)}} \left(\frac{1}{2^T} \prod_{t=1}^{T-1} \Big(\mathcal{P}_{\mathsf{pd}_t}(v_t) + \frac{1}{10T}\eta_{\mathsf{pd}_t,10T}(v_t)\Big)\Big(1 + \frac{1}{10T}\Big)\right) \\
&\ \ \vdots \\
&\leq \sum_{r\in\{0,1\}^T} \frac{1}{2^T}\Big(1 + \frac{1}{10T}\Big)^T \\
&\leq \Big(1 + \frac{1}{10T}\Big)^T \\
&\leq e^{1/10}.
\end{aligned}
$$

□

Combining the claims above, L can be reduced to the following promise problem

- YES instances: x such that $|D'(x)| \geq |D(x)| \geq \frac{2}{3}K$;
- NO instances: x such that $|D(x)| \leq |D'(x)| \leq \frac{1}{3}K$.

This promise problem can be solved in AM using the set lower bound protocol of Goldwasser and Sipser [GS86]. Thus $\mathsf{L} \in \mathbf{AM}$.

4.3 DGS_s is Probability-Verifiable

By Lemma 3.1, for any approximation factor γ, if $\mathsf{gapSIVP}_{\gamma/\mu} \in \mathbf{SZK}$ for any constant $\mu > 1$, there exists a function g maps lattice bases to real numbers such that g is in $\mathbb{R}_\eta$-**TFAM** and $\lambda_n(\mathbf{B}) \leq g(\mathbf{B}) < \gamma(n)\lambda_n(\mathbf{B})$.

For any basis $\mathbf{B}$ and lattice point $\mathbf{v} \in \mathcal{L}(\mathbf{B})$, as $g \in \mathbb{R}_\eta - \mathbf{TFAM}$, the verifier can force the prover to provide a sufficiently accurate estimation of $g(\mathbf{B})$, denoted by $\hat{g}$. As $\hat{g} \approx g(\mathbf{B}) \geq \lambda_n(\mathbf{B})$, the verifier can ask the prover to provide a set of linearly independent vectors $\mathbf{W} = (\mathbf{w}_1, \ldots, \mathbf{w}_n)$ such that $\|\mathbf{W}\| \leq \hat{g}$. Here the length of a vector set, e.g. $\|\mathbf{W}\|$, is defined as the length of the longest vector in the set.

Given such a short independent vector set $\mathbf{W}$, there exists an efficient algorithm that samples from discrete Gaussian distribution $\mathcal{N}_{\mathcal{L}(\mathbf{B}),\hat{s}}$ such that $\hat{s} = \Theta(\sqrt{\log n}) \cdot \hat{g}$ [BLP+13, GPV08]. Moreover, the verifier can estimate the probability that $\mathbf{v}$ is sampled from $\mathcal{N}_{\mathcal{L}(\mathbf{B}),\hat{s}}$ using the set lower bound protocol.

Let $s(\mathbf{B}) = \Theta(\sqrt{\log n}) \cdot g(\mathbf{B})$, then $\hat{s}$ is a good estimation of $s(\mathbf{B})$. If the bias between $\hat{s}$ and $s(\mathbf{B})$ is sufficiently small, one could expect $\Pr[\mathbf{v} \leftarrow \mathcal{N}_{\mathcal{L}(\mathbf{B}),\hat{s}}] \approx \Pr[\mathbf{v} \leftarrow \mathcal{N}_{\mathcal{L}(\mathbf{B}),s(\mathbf{B})}]$.

Proof (Lemma 4.5). By Lemma 3.1, for sufficiently large n, $\mathsf{gapSIVP}_{\gamma(n)/\sqrt{\ln n}} \in$ **SZK** implies the existence of a function g maps lattice bases to real numbers such that g is in $\mathbb{R}_\eta$-**TFAM** and $g(\mathbf{B}) \in [\lambda_n(\mathbf{B}), \gamma(n)/\sqrt{\ln(2n+4)/\pi} \cdot \lambda_n(\mathbf{B})]$. Here $n \geq 2$ is sufficiently large, as it implies $\frac{\gamma(n)/\sqrt{\ln(2n+4)/\pi}}{\gamma(n)/\sqrt{\ln n}} \geq 1.01$.

Define $s(\mathbf{B}) = \sqrt{\ln(2n+4)/\pi} \cdot g(\mathbf{B})$, thus for sufficiently large n

$$\lambda_n(\mathbf{B}) \leq \sqrt{\ln(2n+4)/\pi} \cdot \lambda_n(\mathbf{B}) \leq s(\mathbf{B}) < \gamma(n)\lambda_n(\mathbf{B}).$$

Given any basis $\mathbf{B}$, vector $\mathbf{v} \in \mathcal{L}(\mathbf{B})$ and precision parameter m, the verifier can learn a good estimation on $g(\mathbf{B})$, denoted by $\hat{g}$. As $g(\mathbf{B}) \geq \lambda_n(\mathbf{B})$, the verifier could ask the prover to provide a set of linearly independent vectors of $\mathcal{L}(\mathbf{B})$, denoted by $\mathbf{W}$, such that $\|\mathbf{W}\| \leq \hat{g}$.

Given a set of linearly independent vectors $\mathbf{W}$ that $\|\mathbf{W}\| \leq \hat{g}$, there is an efficient algorithm which samples from discrete Gaussian $\mathcal{N}_{\mathcal{L}(\mathbf{B}),\sqrt{\ln(2n+4)/\pi}\cdot\hat{g}}$ [BLP+13]. Let $\mathcal{S}$ denote this sampling algorithm. Let $\hat{s} = \sqrt{\ln(2n+4)/\pi}\cdot\hat{g}$, then $\hat{s}$ is a good approximation of $s(\mathbf{B})$. Let r be the random tape in the sampling algorithm $\mathcal{S}$, then

$$\Pr[\mathbf{v} \leftarrow \mathcal{N}_{\mathcal{L}(\mathbf{B}),\hat{s}}] = \frac{\{r : \mathcal{S}(B', \hat{s}) \text{ outputs } \mathbf{v} \text{ when } r \text{ is the random input tape}\}}{2^{|r|}}.$$

We could use the set lower bound protocol to lower bound this probability $\Pr[\mathbf{v} \leftarrow \mathcal{N}_{\mathcal{L}(\mathbf{B}),\hat{s}}]$. Thus the promise problem

- YES instances: $(\mathbf{W}, \mathbf{v}, \hat{s}, \hat{p}, 1^m)$ such that $\mathbf{v} \in \mathcal{L}$, $\|\tilde{\mathbf{W}}\| \leq \frac{\hat{s}}{\sqrt{\ln(2n+4)/\pi}}$, $\hat{p} = \Pr[\mathbf{v} \leftarrow \mathcal{N}_{\mathcal{L}(\mathbf{B}),\hat{s}}]$
- NO instances: $(\mathbf{W}, \mathbf{v}, \hat{s}, \hat{p}, 1^m)$ such that $\hat{p} \geq (1 + \frac{1}{m}) \Pr[\mathbf{v} \leftarrow \mathcal{N}_{\mathcal{L}(\mathbf{B}),\hat{s}}]$

is in **AM**, as it can be solved by protocol ProbLowerBound.

AM protocol ProbLowerBound on input $(\mathbf{B}, \mathbf{v}, \hat{p}, 1^m)$

P: Send $\hat{g}$, an honest prover should send $\hat{g} = g(\mathbf{B})$
P,V: Convince the verifier that $|\hat{g} - g(\mathbf{B})| \leq c\delta \cdot g(\mathbf{B})$,
where $\delta = \frac{1}{nm^2}$, c is a sufficiently small constant
P: Send $\mathbf{W} = (\mathbf{x}_1, \ldots, \mathbf{x}_n)$
V: Check if $\mathbf{W}$ is a basis of $\mathcal{L}(\mathbf{B})$ and $\|\tilde{\mathbf{W}}\| \leq \hat{g}$
P,V: Run the set lower bound protocol to convince the verifier that $\hat{p} \leq (1 + \frac{1}{2m}) \Pr[\mathbf{v} \leftarrow \mathcal{N}_{\mathcal{L}(\mathbf{B}),\hat{s}}]$, where $\hat{s} = \sqrt{\ln(2n+4)/\pi} \cdot \hat{g}$

To prove DGS_s is probability-verifiable, it is sufficient to show that ProbLowerBound is an **AM** protocol that estimates the probability $\Pr[\mathbf{v} \leftarrow \mathcal{N}_{\mathcal{L}(\mathbf{B}),\hat{s}}]$ with high accuracy. The estimation error of ProbLowerBound has two sources: (a) the inaccuracy of the set lower bound protocol, which introduce an $O(\frac{1}{m})$ multiplicative error; and (b) the inaccuracy when estimating $s(\mathbf{B})$. Let $\eta_{\mathbf{B}}(\mathbf{v})$ be the estimation error, the error term satisfies

$$\mathcal{N}_{\mathbf{B},s(\mathbf{B})}(\mathbf{v}) + \eta_{\mathbf{B}}(\mathbf{v}) \leq \left(1 + \frac{1}{2m}\right) \max_{|\hat{s} - s(\mathbf{B})| \leq \delta \cdot s(\mathbf{B})} \mathcal{N}_{\mathbf{B},\hat{s}}(\mathbf{v}) \tag{5}$$

To complete the proof, it is sufficient to show that $\sum_{\mathbf{v} \in \mathcal{L}(\mathbf{B})} \eta_{\mathbf{B}}(\mathbf{v}) = O(\frac{1}{m})$. By summing (5) over $\mathbf{v} \in \mathcal{L}(\mathbf{B})$,

$$1 + \sum_{\mathbf{v} \in \mathcal{L}(\mathbf{B})} \eta_{\mathbf{B}}(\mathbf{v}) \leq \left(1 + \frac{1}{2m}\right) \sum_{\mathbf{v} \in \mathcal{L}(\mathbf{B})} \max_{|\hat{s} - s(\mathbf{B})| \leq \delta \cdot s(\mathbf{B})} \mathcal{N}_{\mathbf{B},\hat{s}}(\mathbf{v}).$$

Thus it is sufficient to show

$$\sum_{\mathbf{v} \in \mathcal{L}(\mathbf{B})} \max_{|\hat{s} - s(\mathbf{B})| \leq \delta \cdot s(\mathbf{B})} \mathcal{N}_{\mathbf{B},\hat{s}}(\mathbf{v}) \leq 1 + O(\frac{1}{m}). \tag{6}$$

Which is proved as

$$\begin{aligned}\sum_{\mathbf{v}\in\mathcal{L}(\mathbf{B})} \max_{|\hat{s}-s(\mathbf{B})|\le\delta\cdot s(\mathbf{B})} \mathcal{N}_{\mathbf{B},\hat{s}}(\mathbf{v}) &= \sum_{\mathbf{v}\in\mathcal{L}(\mathbf{B})} \max_{|\hat{s}-s(\mathbf{B})|\le\delta\cdot s(\mathbf{B})} \frac{\rho_{\hat{s}}(\mathbf{v})}{\rho_{\hat{s}}(\mathcal{L}(\mathbf{B}))} \\ &\le \sum_{\mathbf{v}\in\mathcal{L}(\mathbf{B})} \frac{\max_{|\hat{s}-s(\mathbf{B})|\le\delta\cdot s(\mathbf{B})} \rho_{\hat{s}}(\mathbf{v})}{\min_{|\hat{s}-s(\mathbf{B})|\le\delta\cdot s(\mathbf{B})} \rho_{\hat{s}}(\mathcal{L}(\mathbf{B}))} \\ &\le \frac{\rho_{(1+\delta)s}(\mathcal{L}(\mathbf{B}))}{\rho_{(1-\delta)s}(\mathcal{L}(\mathbf{B}))} \\ &\le (\frac{1+\delta}{1-\delta})^n \\ &= O(\frac{1}{mn})\end{aligned} \tag{7}$$

The last inequality is due to Lemma 2.1. □

Acknowledgments. I am grateful to my advisor, Vinod Vaikuntanathan, for getting me started on the topic of NP-hardness and separations. I am indebted to Adam Sealfon, Prashant Nalini Vasudevan, Srinivasan Raghuraman and Akshay Degwekar for their extensive help with the writing of this article. I would like to thank the anonymous reviewers for their careful reading and insightful comments.

References

[AGGM06] Akavia, A., Goldreich, O., Goldwasser, S., Moshkovitz, D.: On basing one-way functions on NP-hardness. In: Kleinberg, J.M. (ed.) Proceedings of the 38th Annual ACM Symposium on Theory of Computing, 21–23 May 2006, Seattle, WA, USA, pp. 701–710. ACM (2006)

[Ajt96] Ajtai, M.: Generating hard instances of lattice problems (extended abstract). In: Miller, G.L. (ed.) Proceedings of the Twenty-Eighth Annual ACM Symposium on the Theory of Computing, 22–24 May 1996, Philadelphia, Pennsylvania, USA, pp. 99–108. ACM (1996)

[AR04] Aharonov, D., Regev, O.: Lattice problems in NP ∩ coNP. In: Proceedings of 45th Symposium on Foundations of Computer Science, FOCS 2004, 17–19 October 2004, Rome, Italy [DBL04], pp. 362–371 (2004)

[Ban93] Banaszczyk, W.: New bounds in some transference theorems in the geometry of numbers. Math. Ann. **296**(1), 625–635 (1993)

[BB15] Bogdanov, A., Brzuska, C.: On basing size-verifiable one-way functions on NP-hardness. In: Dodis, Y., Nielsen, J.B. (eds.) TCC 2015. LNCS, vol. 9014, pp. 1–6. Springer, Heidelberg (2015). https://doi.org/10.1007/978-3-662-46494-6_1

[BL13] Bogdanov, A., Lee, C.H.: Limits of provable security for homomorphic encryption. In: Canetti, R., Garay, J.A. (eds.) CRYPTO 2013. LNCS, vol. 8042, pp. 111–128. Springer, Heidelberg (2013). https://doi.org/10.1007/978-3-642-40041-4_7

[BLP+13] Brakerski, Z., Langlois, A., Peikert, C., Regev, O., Stehlé, D.: Classical hardness of learning with errors. In: Boneh, D., Roughgarden, T., Feigenbaum, J. (eds.) Symposium on Theory of Computing Conference, STOC 2013, 1–4 June 2013, Palo Alto, CA, USA, pp. 575–584. ACM (2013)

[Bra79] Brassard, G.: Relativized cryptography. In: 20th Annual Symposium on Foundations of Computer Science, 29–31 October 1979, San Juan, Puerto Rico, pp. 383–391. IEEE Computer Society (1979)

[BS99] Blömer, J., Seifert, J.P.: On the complexity of computing short linearly independent vectors and short bases in a lattice. In: Vitter, J.S., Larmore, L.L., Leighton, F.T (eds.) Proceedings of the Thirty-First Annual ACM Symposium on Theory of Computing, 1–4 May 1999, Atlanta, Georgia, USA, pp. 711–720. ACM (1999)

[BT06] Bogdanov, A., Trevisan, L.: On worst-case to average-case reductions for NP problems. SIAM J. Comput. **36**(4), 1119–1159 (2006)

[DBL04] In: Proceedings of 45th Symposium on Foundations of Computer Science, FOCS 2004, 17–19 October 2004, Rome, Italy. IEEE Computer Society (2004)

[FF91] Feigenbaum, J., Fortnow, L.: On the random-self-reducibility of complete sets. In: Proceedings of the Sixth Annual Structure in Complexity Theory Conference, 30 June–3 July 1991, Chicago, Illinois, USA, pp. 124–132. IEEE Computer Society (1991)

[GG98] Goldreich, O., Goldwasser, S.: On the possibility of basing cryptography on the assumption that $P \neq NP$. IACR Cryptol. Eprint Arch. **1998**, 5 (1998)

[GG00] Goldreich, O., Goldwasser, S.: On the limits of nonapproximability of lattice problems. J. Comput. Syst. Sci. **60**(3), 540–563 (2000)

[GMR04] Guruswami, V., Micciancio, D., Regev, O.: The complexity of the covering radius problem on lattices and codes. In: 19th Annual IEEE Conference on Computational Complexity, CCC 2004, 21–24 June 2004, Amherst, MA, USA, pp. 161–173. IEEE Computer Society (2004)

[GPV08] Gentry, C., Peikert, C., Vaikuntanathan, V.: Trapdoors for hard lattices and new cryptographic constructions. In: Dwork, C. (ed.) Proceedings of the 40th Annual ACM Symposium on Theory of Computing, 17–20 May 2008, Victoria, British Columbia, Canada, pp. 197–206. ACM (2008)

[GS86] Goldwasser, S., Sipser, M.: Private coins versus public coins in interactive proof systems. In: Proceedings of the Eighteenth Annual ACM Symposium on Theory of Computing, pp. 59–68. ACM (1986)

[GV99] Goldreich, O., Vadhan, S.: Comparing entropies in statistical zero knowledge with applications to the structure of SZK. In: Proceedings of Fourteenth Annual IEEE Conference on Computational Complexity, pp. 54–73. IEEE (1999)

[LV16] Liu, T., Vaikuntanathan, V.: On basing private information retrieval on NP-hardness. In: Kushilevitz, E., Malkin, T. (eds.) TCC 2016. LNCS, vol. 9562, pp. 372–386. Springer, Heidelberg (2016). https://doi.org/10.1007/978-3-662-49096-9_16

[MR04] Micciancio, D., Regev, O.: Worst-case to average-case reductions based on Gaussian measures. In: Proceedings of 45th Symposium on Foundations of Computer Science, FOCS 2004, 17–19 October 2004, Rome, Italy [DBL04], pp. 372–381 (2014)

[MV03] Micciancio, D., Vadhan, S.P.: Statistical Zero-knowledge proofs with efficient provers: lattice problems and more. In: Boneh, D. (ed.) CRYPTO 2003. LNCS, vol. 2729, pp. 282–298. Springer, Heidelberg (2003). https://doi.org/10.1007/978-3-540-45146-4_17

[MX10] Mahmoody, M., Xiao, D.: On the power of randomized reductions and the checkability of SAT. In: 2010 IEEE 25th Annual Conference on Computational Complexity (CCC), pp. 64–75. IEEE (2010)

[PV08] Peikert, C., Vaikuntanathan, V.: Noninteractive statistical zero-knowledge proofs for lattice problems. In: Wagner, D. (ed.) CRYPTO 2008. LNCS, vol. 5157, pp. 536–553. Springer, Heidelberg (2008). https://doi.org/10.1007/978-3-540-85174-5_30

[Reg09] Regev, O.: On lattices, learning with errors, random linear codes, and cryptography. J. ACM **56**(6), 34:1–34:40 (2009)

Two-Round MPC Protocols

Two-Round MPC: Information-Theoretic and Black-Box

Sanjam Garg[1(✉)], Yuval Ishai[2], and Akshayaram Srinivasan[1]

[1] University of California, Berkeley, Berkeley, USA
sanjamg@berkeley.edu
[2] Technion, Haifa, Israel

Abstract. We continue the study of protocols for secure multiparty computation (MPC) that require only two rounds of interaction. The recent works of Garg and Srinivasan (Eurocrypt 2018) and Benhamouda and Lin (Eurocrypt 2018) essentially settle the question by showing that such protocols are implied by the minimal assumption that a two-round oblivious transfer (OT) protocol exists. However, these protocols inherently make a non-black-box use of the underlying OT protocol, which results in poor concrete efficiency. Moreover, no analogous result was known in the information-theoretic setting, or alternatively based on one-way functions, given an OT correlations setup or an honest majority.

Motivated by these limitations, we study the possibility of obtaining information-theoretic and "black-box" implementations of two-round MPC protocols. We obtain the following results:

- **Two-round MPC from OT correlations.** Given an OT correlations setup, we get protocols that make a black-box use of a pseudorandom generator (PRG) and are secure against a malicious adversary corrupting an arbitrary number of parties. For a semi-honest adversary, we get similar information-theoretic protocols for branching programs.
- **New NIOT constructions.** Towards realizing OT correlations, we extend the DDH-based *non-interactive OT* (NIOT) protocol of Bellare and Micali (Crypto'89) to the malicious security model, and present new NIOT constructions from the Quadratic Residuosity Assumption (QRA) and the Learning With Errors (LWE) assumption.
- **Two-round black-box MPC with strong PKI setup.** Combining the two previous results, we get two-round MPC protocols that make a *black-box* use of any DDH-hard or QRA-hard group.

S. Garg—Research supported in part from 2017 AFOSR YIP Award, DARPA/ARL SAFEWARE Award W911NF15C0210, AFOSR Award FA9550-15-1-0274, and research grants by the Okawa Foundation, Visa Inc., and Center for Long-Term Cybersecurity (CLTC, UC Berkeley). The views expressed are those of the author and do not reflect the official policy or position of the funding agencies.
Y. Ishai—Supported by ERC grant 742754 (project NTSC), ISF grant 1709/14, NSF-BSF grant 2015782, and a grant from the Ministry of Science and Technology, Israel and Department of Science and Technology, Government of India.

A. Beimel and S. Dziembowski (Eds.): TCC 2018, LNCS 11239, pp. 123–151, 2018.
https://doi.org/10.1007/978-3-030-03807-6_5

The protocols can offer security against a malicious adversary, and require a PKI setup that depends on the number of parties and the size of computation, but not on the inputs or the identities of the participating parties.
- **Two-round honest-majority MPC from secure channels.** Given secure point-to-point channels, we get protocols that make a black-box use of a pseudorandom generator (PRG), as well as information-theoretic protocols for branching programs. These protocols can tolerate a semi-honest adversary corrupting a strict minority of the parties, where in the information-theoretic case the complexity is exponential in the number of parties.

1 Introduction

There is an enormous body of work on the round complexity of protocols for secure multiparty computation (MPC). While the feasibility of *constant-round* MPC has been established a long time ago [Yao86,BB89,BMR90], some of the most basic questions about the *exact* number of rounds required for MPC remained wide open until recently.

A single round of interaction is clearly insufficient to realize the standard notion of MPC. The focus of this work is on MPC protocols that require only two rounds. Two-round MPC protocols are not only interesting because of the quantitative aspect of minimizing the number of rounds, but also because of the following qualitative advantage. In a two-round MPC protocol, a party can send its first round messages and then go offline until all second-round messages are received and the output can be computed. (In fact, for two-round protocols over insecure channels, the first round messages can be publicly posted.) Moreover, the first round messages can be potentially reused for several computations in which the receiver's input remains the same. Indeed, in the two-party setting, such two-round protocols are sometimes referred to as "non-interactive secure computation" [IKO+11].

The state of the art on two-round MPC can be briefly summarized as follows. Unless otherwise specified, we restrict our attention to *semi-honest* adversaries, who may non-adaptively corrupt an arbitrary subset of parties, and allow the protocols to use a common *random* string.

In the information-theoretic setting, 2-round protocols over secure point-to-point channels are known to exist with $t < n/3$ corrupted parties [IK00], leaving open the existence of similar protocols with an optimal threshold of $t < n/2$. These information-theoretic protocols, like all current general constant-round protocols in the information-theoretic setting, have complexity that grows polynomially with n and with the *branching program* size of the function being computed, and thus can only efficiently apply to rich but limited function classes such as NC^1, NL, or other log-space classes.

Settling for computational security, the above information-theoretic protocols imply (via the multi-party garbling technique of [BMR90]) similar protocols for *circuits*, capturing all polynomial-time computable functions, where the protocols only require a black-box use of any pseudorandom generator (PRG), or equivalently a one-way function. In this setting too, it was open whether the optimal[1] threshold of $t < n/2$ can be achieved.

Under stronger cryptographic assumptions, a lot of recent progress has been made on two-round MPC protocols that tolerate an arbitrary number of corrupted parties. The first such protocols required a public-key infrastructure (PKI) setup, where each party can post a public key before its input is known, and were based on the Learning With Errors (LWE) assumption via threshold fully homomorphic encryption [AJW11]. This was followed by protocols without PKI setup, first under indistinguishability obfuscation [GGHR14] or witness encryption [GLS15], and later under LWE via multi-key fully homomorphic encryption [MW16] or spooky encryption [DHRW16]. Using PKI setup, two-round protocols could also be constructed under the Decisional Diffie-Hellman (DDH) assumption via homomorphic secret sharing [BGI17,BGI+18].

In recent works, a new general technique for collapsing rounds via "protocol garbling" [GS17] has been used by Garg and Srinivasan [GS18] and Benhamouda and Lin [BL18] to settle the minimal assumptions required for two-round MPC. These works show that general two-round MPC can be based on any two-round protocol for *oblivious transfer* (OT) [Rab81,EGL85], namely a protocol allowing a receiver to obtain only one of two bits held by a sender without revealing the identity of the chosen bit. This assumption is clearly necessary, since two-round OT is an instance of two-round general MPC.

Remaining Challenges. Despite apparently settling the problem of two-round MPC, many challenges still remain. First and foremost, the recent OT-based protocols from [GS18,BL18] inherently make a *non-black-box* use of the underlying OT protocol. This results in poor concrete efficiency, which is unfortunate given the appealing features of two-round MPC discussed above. Second, the recent results leave open the possibility of obtaining information-theoretic security, or alternatively, computational security using symmetric cryptography, in other natural settings. These include protocols for the case of an *honest majority* ($t < n/2$) using secure point-to-point channels,[2] or alternatively protocols for dishonest majority based on an ideal OT oracle. Finally, the two-round MPC protocols from [GS18,BL18] did not seem to apply to the more general *client-server*

[1] Protocols that offer security with no honest majority imply oblivious transfer. Thus, they provably do not admit a *black-box* reduction to a PRG [IR89], and a non-black-box reduction would be considered a major breakthrough in cryptography.

[2] A recent work of Ananth, Choudhuri, Goel, and Jain [ACGJ18] obtains honest-majority, two-round MPC protocols from one-way functions satisfying the notion of security with abort against malicious adversaries. Our work was done in part following a public announcement of this result.

setting, where only clients hold inputs and receive outputs, and communication only involves messages from clients to servers and from servers to clients.[3]

1.1 Our Contribution

In this work we address the above challenges, focusing mainly on the goal of constructing information-theoretic and "black-box" implementations of two-round MPC protocols. We obtain the following results:

Two-Round MPC from OT Correlations. We start by studying two-round MPC using an *OT correlations setup*, which can be viewed as a minimal[4] setup for MPC with no honest majority under assumptions that are weaker than OT. An OT correlation setup allows each pair of parties to share many independent instances of correlated randomness where party P_i gets a pair of random bits (or strings) (s_0, s_1) and party P_j gets a random bit b and the bit s_b. Using such an OT correlations setup, we get protocols that make a black-box use of a PRG and are secure against either a semi-honest[5] or malicious adversary corrupting an arbitrary number of parties. For a semi-honest adversary, we get similar *information-theoretic* protocols for branching programs.

This OT correlation setup can be implemented with good concrete efficiency via OT extension [IKNP03], requiring roughly 128 bits of communication per string-OT. Alternatively, the communication complexity of the setup can be made independent of the circuit size (at a much higher computational cost) by using homomorphic secret sharing based on LWE, DDH, or DCRA [BGI16,DHRW16,FGJI17,BCG+17]. Finally, a fully non-interactive option for implementing the OT correlation setup is discussed next.

New NIOT Constructions. An appealing method of realizing the OT correlation setup is via *non-interactive OT* (NIOT) [BM90]. An NIOT protocol is the OT analogue of non-interactive key exchange: it allows two parties to obtain a joint OT correlation via a simultaneous message exchange. We present several new constructions of NIOT. First, we extend the DDH-based construction

---

3 An additional disadvantage of the protocols from [GS18,BL18] compared to most earlier protocols is that their communication complexity is always bigger than the circuit size of the function being computed. However, breaking this circuit size barrier under general assumptions such as OT would require a major breakthrough, regardless of round complexity.

4 Two-round MPC was previously known to follow from a *global* correlated randomness setup that includes garbled circuits [CEMY09,IMO18] or truth-tables [IKM+13] whose keys are secret-shared between all parties. Our setup assumption is weaker in that it only involves a simple *pairwise* correlation.

5 Our protocol for semi-honest adversaries is expensive but not prohibitively so. With some simple optimizations, the online communication consists of roughly $1750 \cdot n^3$ standard garbled circuits, which is about 135 times the cost of the BMR protocol [BMR90], and the total number of OTs required by the setup is less than 7% of the communication.

from [BM90] to the malicious security model, improving over an earlier construction based on bilinear maps from [GS17]. Second, we present new NIOT constructions from the Quadratic Residuosity Assumption (QRA) and from LWE.

Two-Round Black-Box MPC with Strong PKI Setup. Combining the protocols based on OT correlations and the NIOT constructions, we get two-round MPC protocols that make a *black-box* use of any DDH-hard or QRA-hard group. The protocols can offer security against a malicious adversary, and require a strong PKI setup that depends on the number of parties and the size of computation, but not on the inputs or the identity of the participating parties. This is arguably the first "black box" two-round MPC protocol that does not rely on an honest majority or a correlated randomness setup. Our DDH-based protocol can be compared with previous DDH-based two-round MPC protocols from [BGI+18] that require a weaker PKI setup and have better asymptotic communication complexity, but make a non-black-box use of the underlying group except when there are n clients and 2 servers.

Two-Round Honest-Majority MPC from Secure Channels. Given secure point-to-point channels, we get protocols that make a black-box use of a PRG, as well as information-theoretic protocols for branching programs. These protocols can tolerate a semi-honest adversary corrupting a strict minority of the parties, where in the information-theoretic case the complexity of the protocol grows exponentially with the number of parties. Our work leaves open the question of eliminating this slightly super-polynomial dependence as well as the question of obtaining similar results for malicious adversaries. This question has been resolved in the concurrent and independent work of Applebaum, Brakerski and Tsabary [ABT18].

From Standard MPC to Client-Server MPC. Finally, we present a general (non-black-box) transformation that allows converting previous two-round MPC protocols (including the recent OT-based protocols from [GS18,BL18]) to the stronger client-server model. Concretely, we use a PRG to transform any n-party, two-round, MPC protocol with security against semi-honest adversaries corrupting an arbitrary subset of parties to a similar protocol with n clients and m servers, where in the first round each client sends a message to each server and in the second round each server sends a message to each client. The resulting protocol is secure against a semi-honest adversary that corrupts an arbitrary subset of clients and a strict subset of the servers. This setting is particularly appealing when clients would like to be offline except when their input changes or they would like to receive an output.

1.2 Overview of Techniques

In this subsection, we describe the main techniques used to obtain our results.

1. We start with a high-level overview of the OT correlations model and describe the technical challenges in constructing a non-interactive OT protocol.
2. Later, we will show how to use OT correlations to make the compiler of Garg and Srinivasan [GS18] information theoretic. This gives efficient, two-round protocols in the OT correlations model with information theoretic security for branching programs and computational security for circuits making black-box use of a pseudorandom generator.
3. We then explain the main ideas in constructing a two-round, protocol in the honest majority setting with secure point-to-point channels.

OT Correlations Model. The OT correlation is modeled by a two-party ideal functionality. When this functionality is invoked by a (sender, receiver) pair, it samples three bits (s_0, s_1) and b uniformly at random and provides (s_0, s_1) to the sender and (b, s_b) to the receiver. For simplicity, we focus only for the case where sender's output (s_0, s_1) are bits as there are perfect, round-preserving reductions from bit OT correlations to string OT correlations (refer [BCS96, BCW03]). Given such OT correlations, there is an information theoretic, two-round OT protocol as follows. In the first round, the receiver sends $u = b \oplus c$ to the sender where c is the choice bit and in the second round, the sender computes $(x_0, x_1) = (m_0 \oplus s_u, m_1 \oplus s_{1 \oplus u})$ and sends them to the receiver. The receiver outputs $x_c \oplus r_b$.

Bellare-Micali Non-interactive Oblivious Transfer. Bellare and Micali [BM90] gave an efficient, single-round protocol based on Decisional Diffie-Hellman (DDH) assumption [DH76] for computing OT correlations when the adversary corrupting either of the two parties is semi-honest. The protocol is in the common reference string model and is as follows. Let us assume that $\mathbb{G}$ is a DDH hard group and g is a generator. The CRS is an uniform group element X. The sender chooses $a \leftarrow \mathbb{Z}_p^*$ and sends $A = g^a$ to the receiver. The receiver chooses a random $b \leftarrow \mathbb{Z}_p^*$ and sends $(B_0, B_1) = (g^b, X/g^b)$ in a randomly permuted order. The sender computes (B_0^a, B_1^a) and outputs it and the receiver computes A^b and outputs it. The receiver's choice bit b is statistically hidden from an adversarial sender and the string s_{1-b} is computationally hidden from the receiver based on the DDH assumption. However, this protocol only works in the semi-honest model as there is no efficient way to extract the receiver's choice bit or the sender's correlations. In [GS17], Garg and Srinivasan additionally used Groth-Sahai proofs [GS08] to enable efficient extraction of the correlations from a malicious adversary but this construction relies on bilinear maps.

Our Construction of Non-interactive Oblivious Transfer. Our approach of constructing non-interactive oblivious transfer is via a generalization of the dual-mode framework introduced in the work of Peikert, Vaikuntanathan and Waters [PVW08]. In the dual mode framework, the common reference string can be in one of two indistinguishable modes: namely, the receiver extraction mode or the sender extraction mode. In the receiver extraction mode, the CRS trapdoor enables the simulator to extract the receiver's correlation b and in the sender extraction mode, the it enables the simulator to extract the sender's correlation (s_0, s_1) from the malicious party. In either of the two modes, the secrets of the honest party are statistically hidden. We give efficient instantiations of this framework from DDH, Quadratic Residuocity assumption [GM82] and the Learning with Errors assumption [Reg05]. Our DDH and QR based constructions make black-box use of the underlying group. We stress that constructions of dual-mode cryptosystem in [PVW08] do not yield non-interactive oblivious transfer and we need to come up with new constructions. We refer the reader to Sect. 3.1 for the details.

Round-Collapsing Compiler in the OT Correlations Model. Independent works by Benhemouda and Lin [BL18] and Garg and Srinivasan [GS18] gave a "round-collapsing" compiler that takes an arbitrary multi-round MPC protocol and collapses it to two-rounds assuming the existence of a two-round oblivious transfer and garbled circuits. The compiler makes use of the code of the underlying protocol and thus, if the underlying protocol performs cryptographic operations then the resultant two-round protocol makes non-black box use of cryptography. In this work, we will use OT correlations to modify the compiler of [GS18] so that the resulting protocol makes black-box use of cryptography even if the underlying protocol performs cryptographic operations. Let us see how this is done.

We start by observing that OT correlations allow for perfect (resp., statistical) information-theoretic protocols in the presence of an arbitrary number of semi-honest (resp., malicious) corrupted parties. Hence, we will round-collapse, perfectly/statistically secure protocols that are in the OT-hybrid model (e.g., [GMW87,Kil88,IPS08]). We first give a reduction from perfectly/statistically secure protocols in the OT-hybrid model to a perfectly/statistically secure protocols in the OT correlations model. This reduction has a property that all the OT correlations are generated before the actual execution of the protocol and the operations performed in the protocol are information theoretic. Another useful property is that number of OT correlations needed depends only the number of parties and the size of the computation to be performed and in particular, is independent of the actual inputs. At a high level, this reduction relies on the fact that OT correlations can be used to perform information theoretic OTs. Now, given such a protocol in the OT correlations model, we modify the compiler of Garg and Srinivasan to have a pre-processing phase where all the OT correlations needed for the underlying protocol and those consumed by the round-collapsing compiler are generated. Later, these OT correlations are used to perform information theoretic OTs both in the underlying protocol and the round-collapsing compiler. Additionally, we also replace the garbled circuits used in the round-collapsing compiler with a perfectly secure analogue, namely a so-called "decomposable randomized encodings" for low-depth circuits [IK00,AIK04]. With these changes to the [GS18] compiler, we get a perfectly secure two-round protocol in the OT correlations model for constant size functions. Later, we use a result from [BGI+18] to bootstrap this to a perfectly secure, two-round protocol in the OT correlations model for NC^0 circuits. Two immediate corollaries of this result are a perfectly secure, two-round protocol in the OT correlations model for polynomial sized branching programs and a computationally secure, two-round protocol in the OT correlations model for arbitrary circuits making black-box use of a pseudorandom generator.

Two-Round Protocol in the Honest Majority Setting. To construct a two-round protocol in the plain model (with secure point-to-point channels) when the adversary corrupts a strict minority of the parties, we use the same high level idea of the [GS18] compiler. That is, we take a larger round protocol secure with honest majority and round-collapse it to two-rounds. Two immediate issues arise: (1) The first issue is that the round-collapsing compiler requires the existence of two-round oblivious transfer, (2) the second issue is that round-collapsing compiler could only compress protocols in the presence of a broadcast channels and fails for protocols with secure channels. To address the first issue, we construct a perfectly secure, two-round OT protocol in the presence of honest majority (building on the work of [IKP10]) and to address the second issue, we give a generalization of the [GS18] compiler to compress protocols that may require secure channels. We then use this OT protocol in parallel with the round-collapsing compiler of [GS18] (enhanced to work for protocols with secure channels) to obtain a two-round protocol in the honest majority setting. However, the resulting communication complexity of the protocol grows super-polynomially with the number of parties n. Still, for constant n, the protocol is efficient.

1.3 Organization

In Sect. 2, we will recall some standard definitions about secure computation and tools such as garbled circuits and decomposable randomized encoding. In Sect. 3, we define the OT correlations functionality and give various methods to realize it. In Sect. 4 we give the construction of 2-round semi-honest MPC in the OT correlations hybrid model. We point the reader to the full version of our paper for the other results.

2 Preliminaries

We recall some standard cryptographic definitions in this section. Let λ denote the security parameter. A function $\mu(\cdot) : \mathbb{N} \to \mathbb{R}^+$ is said to be negligible if for any polynomial $\mathsf{poly}(\cdot)$ there exists λ_0 such that for all $\lambda > \lambda_0$ we have $\mu(\lambda) < \frac{1}{\mathsf{poly}(\lambda)}$. We will use $\mathsf{negl}(\cdot)$ to denote an unspecified negligible function and $\mathsf{poly}(\cdot)$ to denote an unspecified polynomial function.

For a probabilistic algorithm A, we denote $A(x;r)$ to be the output of A on input x with the content of the random tape being r. When r is omitted, $A(x)$

denotes a distribution. For a finite set S, we denote $x \leftarrow S$ as the process of sampling x uniformly from the set S. We will use PPT to denote Probabilistic Polynomial Time algorithm.

2.1 Decomposable Randomized Encoding

We recall the definitions of randomized encoding [Yao86, IK00, AIK04].

Definition 1 (Randomized Encoding). *Let $f : \{0,1\}^n \rightarrow \{0,1\}^m$ be some function. We say that a function $\widehat{f} : \{0,1\}^n \times \{0,1\}^\rho \rightarrow \{0,1\}^m$ is a perfect randomized encoding of f if for every input $x \in \{0,1\}$, the distribution $\widehat{f}(x;r)$ induced by an uniform choice of $r \xleftarrow{\$} \{0,1\}^\rho$, encodes the string $f(x)$ in the following sense:*

- ***Correctness.*** *There exists a decoding algorithm* Dec *such that for every $x \in \{0,1\}^n$, it holds that:*

$$\Pr_{r \xleftarrow{\$} \{0,1\}^\rho} [\mathsf{Dec}(\widehat{f}(x;r)) = f(x)] = 1$$

- ***Privacy:*** *There exists a randomized algorithm S such that for every $x \in \{0,1\}^n$ and uniformly chosen $r \xleftarrow{\$} \{0,1\}^\rho$ it holds that*

$$S(f(x)) \text{ is distributed identically to } \widehat{f}(x;r).$$

Definition 2 (Decomposable Randomized Encoding). *We say that $\widehat{f}(x;r)$ is decomposable if $\widehat{f}$ can be written as $\widehat{f}(x;r) = (\widehat{f}_0(r), \widehat{f}_1(x_1;r), \dots, \widehat{f}_n(x_n;r))$ where $\widehat{f}_i$ is chooses between two vectors based on x_i, i.e., it can be written as $\mathbf{a}_{i,x_i}$ and $(\mathbf{a}_{i,0}, \mathbf{a}_{i,1})$ arbitrarily depend on the randomness r. We will use $\widehat{f}(;r)$ to denote $(\widehat{f}_0(r), (\mathbf{a}_{1,0}, \mathbf{a}_{1,1}), \dots, (\mathbf{a}_{n,0}, \mathbf{a}_{n,1}))$.*

We will recall the following two constructions of randomized encoding.

Lemma 1 ([Kil88, IK00]). *Let $f : \{0,1\}^n \rightarrow \{0,1\}^m$ be a function computable in NC^0. Then f has a perfectly secure decomposable randomized encoding $\widehat{f}$ where the size of the encoding is $2^{O(d)}(n+m)$ where d is the depth of the circuit.*

Lemma 2 ([Yao86]). *Let $f : \{0,1\}^n \rightarrow \{0,1\}^m$ be a function computable by an arbitrary circuit. Assuming the existence of one-way functions, f has a computationally secure randomized encoding $\widehat{f}$.*

2.2 Universal Composability Framework

We work in the Universal Composition (UC) framework [Can01] to formalize and analyze the security of our protocols. (Our protocols can also be analyzed in the stand-alone setting, using the composability framework of [Can00], or in other UC-like frameworks, like that of [PW00].) We give the details in the full version. We only focus on static (non-adaptive) adversaries but we note that our perfectly secure protocols are also secure against adaptive adversaries.

3 OT Correlations Functionality

In this section, we define the $\mathcal{F}_{\text{OTCor}}$ functionality in Fig. 1. Intuitively, the $\mathcal{F}_{\text{OTCor}}$ functionality obtains a bit b from the receiver and samples two bits (s_0, s_1) randomly from $\{0,1\}$ and outputs (s_0, s_1) to the sender and s_b to the receiver.[6] In the definition, we focus on the case where the sender's output are just two bits (s_0, s_1) instead of two strings as there are efficient reductions from 1-out-of-2 string OTs to 1-out-of-2 bit OTs using self-intersecting codes or randomness extractors [BCS96, BCW03]. By abusing notation, we will interchangeably use the same functionality to sample two strings instead of two bits.

Parametrized with parties $P_1, \ldots, P_n$ and an adversary $\mathcal{S}$ controlling a subset of the parties. Let H be the set of parties not controlled by the adversary.

On receiving $(sid, \textbf{receiver}, pid, b)$ (where $b \in \{0,1\}$) or $(sid, \textbf{sender}, pid)$ from a party with id pid, store this message.

On receiving (sid, pid_1, pid_2) from a party with id pid_1, check if $(sid, \textbf{receiver}, pid_2, b)$ and $(sid, \textbf{sender}, pid_1)$ are stored. If not stored, then do nothing. Else, do the following:

- If both $pid_1, pid_2 \in H$, sample $(s_0, s_1) \xleftarrow{\$} \{0,1\}$, send (s_0, s_1) to the party pid_1 and s_b to the party pid_2.
- If $pid_1 \notin H$ but $pid_2 \in H$ then send the message $(\textbf{sender}, pid_1)$ to S and receive (s_0, s_1) from S. Send s_b to the party pid_2.
- If $pid_1 \in H$ but $pid_2 \notin H$, send the message $(\textbf{receiver}, pid_2)$ to S and receive s_b from S. Sample $s_{1-b} \xleftarrow{\$} \{0,1\}$ and send (s_0, s_1) to the party pid_1.
- If both $pid_1, pid_2 \notin H$, ignore the message.

Fig. 1. OT Correlations Functionality $\mathcal{F}_{\text{OTCor}}$.

We first discuss two generic ways from literature for realizing $\mathcal{F}_{\text{OTCor}}$ functionality and then give two new ways for realizing it.

OT Extension. We first note that any OT protocol can be used to realize $\mathcal{F}_{\text{OTCor}}$ functionality. A more efficient way would be to use an oblivious transfer extension protocol [Bea96, IKNP03, ALSZ13, ALSZ15, KOS15]. Any OT extension protocol with security against semi-honest/malicious adversaries can be used to realize the $\mathcal{F}_{\text{OTCor}}$ functionality against semi-honest/malicious adversaries. The only downside of this approach is that it involves multiple rounds of interaction (which is inherent if we want to make black-box use of cryptography [GMMM18]).

[6] Here, we let the receiver to choose the bit b and provide as input to the functionality. We can also work with a weaker formulation wherein the functionality can sample a random bit b. However, we chose this formulation as it will lead to concrete improvements in the cost of our two-round MPC protocols.

Homomorphic Secret Sharing/Threshold FHE. A reusable and a non-interactive approach to realize the weaker formulation wherein the receiver's choice bit is sampled randomly by the functionality is to use Homomorphic Secret Sharing (HSS) [BGI16,BGI17,BGI+18,BCG+17]. Using Homomorphic Secret Sharing, each party can generate a HSS encoding of a randomly chosen PRG seed and broadcasts this encoding to all other parties. When an OT correlation is to be generated, the parties (using the encodings) locally compute a functionality that expands the receiver's and the sender's PRG seed to the required length and samples the prescribed OT correlation from the expanded seeds. At the end of this local computation, the parties hold an additive secret sharing of the OT correlation and the actual correlation can be obtained non-interactively by sending these additive shares to the receiver. This approach is reusable as the encodings just needs to be sent once and can be resused to generate fresh correlations each time.[7] We also note that we can replace the above homomorphic secret sharing with any threshold FHE construction [MW16,DHRW16,BGG+18]. The downsides of using HSS or threshold FHE is that they make non-black box use of one-way functions in expanding the short seed to a pseudorandom string and they are computationally expensive when compared to the OT extension. Additionally, HSS requires the use of secure channels between every pairs of parties.

In Sect. 3.1, we describe a non-interactive approach to realize $\mathcal{F}_{\mathrm{OTCor}}$. The advantage of this approach over HSS/threshold-FHE is that it makes black-box use of a groups where either DDH or QR is hard (we also provide an efficient construction from the LWE assumption). However, unlike HSS/threshold-FHE they are not reusable.

3.1 Realizing $\mathcal{F}_{\mathrm{OTCor}}$: Non-interactive Oblivious Transfer

In this subsection, we define a Non-interactive Oblivious Transfer (NIOT) and show how to realize $\mathcal{F}_{\mathrm{OTCor}}$ functionality from NIOT.

Definition. A Non-interactive Oblivious Transfer (NIOT) is a tuple of algorithms $(\mathsf{K}_{\mathrm{R}}, \mathsf{K}_{\mathrm{S}}, \mathsf{Sen}, \mathsf{Rec}, \mathsf{out}_{\mathrm{S}}, \mathsf{out}_{\mathrm{R}})$ having the following syntax, correctness and security guarantees.

- K_{R} and K_{S} are randomized algorithms that take as input the security parameter (encoded in unary) and output a common random string σ along with some trapdoor information τ.
- Sen is a randomized algorithm that takes σ as input and outputs $\mathsf{msg}_{\mathrm{S}}$ along with secret randomness ω.
- Rec is a randomized algorithm that takes σ and a bit b as input and outputs $\mathsf{msg}_{\mathrm{R}}$ along with secret randomness ρ_b.

[7] The HSS constructions in [BGI16,BGI17,BGI+18,BCG+17] have a polynomial error probability and this might leak information about the correlations to an adversary. [BCG+17] mentions two ways to prevent such leakages: either bootstrap random pads or use a punctured OT [BGI17]. We refer the reader to [BCG+17] for the details.

- $\mathsf{out_S}$ is a deterministic algorithm that takes as input σ, $\mathsf{msg_R}$ and the secret randomness ω and outputs two bits k_0, k_1.
- $\mathsf{out_R}$ is a deterministic algorithm that takes as σ, $\mathsf{msg_S}$ and the secret randomness ρ_b and outputs a bit k'_b.

Correctness. We require that for all $b \in \{0,1\}$,

$$\Pr\left[k'_b = k_b : (\sigma,\tau) \leftarrow \mathsf{K_R}(1^\lambda), (\mathsf{msg_S},\omega) \leftarrow \mathsf{Sen}(\sigma), (\mathsf{msg_R},\rho_b) \leftarrow \mathsf{Rec}(\sigma,b),\right.$$
$$\left.(k_0,k_1) \leftarrow \mathsf{out_S}(\sigma,\omega,\mathsf{msg_R}), k'_b \leftarrow \mathsf{out_R}(\sigma,\rho_b,\mathsf{msg_S})\right] \geq 1 - \mathsf{negl}(\lambda)$$

Security. We require the following security properties to hold.

- **CRS Indistinguishability.** We require that

$$\{\sigma : (\sigma,\tau) \leftarrow \mathsf{K_R}(1^\lambda)\} \stackrel{c}{\approx} \{\sigma : (\sigma,\tau) \leftarrow \mathsf{K_S}(1^\lambda)\}$$

- **Sender Security.** We require that there exists a PPT a lgorithm $\mathsf{Ext_R}$ such that for all non-uniform PPT adversarial Rec^* the following two distributions are statistically close.

$$\left\{\begin{array}{l}(\sigma,\tau) \leftarrow \mathsf{K_R}(1^\lambda),\\ (\mathsf{msg_S},\omega) \leftarrow \mathsf{Sen}(\sigma),\\ \mathsf{msg_R} \leftarrow \mathsf{Rec}^*(\sigma,\mathsf{msg_S})\\ (k_0,k_1) \leftarrow \mathsf{out_S}(\sigma,\omega,\mathsf{msg_R}):\\ \text{Output }(\mathsf{msg_S},\mathsf{msg_R},k_0,k_1)\end{array}\right\} \stackrel{s}{\approx} \left\{\begin{array}{l}(\sigma,\tau) \leftarrow \mathsf{K_R}(1^\lambda),\\ (\mathsf{msg_S},\omega) \leftarrow \mathsf{Sen}(\sigma),\\ \mathsf{msg_R} \leftarrow \mathsf{Rec}^*(\sigma,\mathsf{msg_S})\\ b' \leftarrow \mathsf{Ext_R}(\sigma,\mathsf{msg_R},\tau):\\ (k_0,k_1) \leftarrow \mathsf{out_S}(\sigma,\omega,\mathsf{msg_R}),\\ \ell_{b'} := k_{b'}, \ell_{1-b'} \leftarrow \{0,1\}:\\ \text{Output }(\mathsf{msg_S},\mathsf{msg_R},\ell_0,\ell_1).\end{array}\right\}$$

- **Receiver Security.** We require that there exists a PPT algrithm $\mathsf{Ext_S}$ such that for all non-uniform PPT adversarial Sen^* and for all $b \in \{0,1\}$, the following two distributions are statistically close.

$$\left\{\begin{array}{l}(\sigma,\tau) \leftarrow \mathsf{K_S}(1^\lambda),\\ (\mathsf{msg_R},\rho_b) \leftarrow \mathsf{Rec}(\sigma,b),\\ \mathsf{msg_S} \leftarrow \mathsf{Sen}^*(\sigma,\mathsf{msg_R}),\\ k'_b \leftarrow \mathsf{out_R}(\sigma,\rho_b,\mathsf{msg_S}):\\ \text{Output }(\mathsf{msg_S},\mathsf{msg_R},k'_b)\end{array}\right\} \stackrel{s}{\approx} \left\{\begin{array}{l}(\sigma,\tau) \leftarrow \mathsf{K_S}(1^\lambda),\\ (\mathsf{msg_R},\rho_0,\rho_1) \leftarrow \mathsf{Ext_S}(\sigma,\tau),\\ \mathsf{msg_S} \leftarrow \mathsf{Sen}^*(\sigma,\mathsf{msg_R}),\\ k'_b \leftarrow \mathsf{out_R}(\sigma,\rho_b,\mathsf{msg_S}):\\ \text{Output }(\mathsf{msg_S},\mathsf{msg_R},k'_b)\end{array}\right\}$$

NIOT $\Rightarrow \mathcal{F}_{\text{OTCor}}$. In this subsection, we give a realization of the $\mathcal{F}_{\text{OTCor}}$ functionality from any non-interactive oblivious transfer.

Theorem 1. *Assuming the existence of non-interactive oblivious transfer, there is a single round protocol for realizing $\mathcal{F}_{\text{OTCor}}$ against malicious adversaries in the common reference string model.*

Construction. We give a construction realizing the $\mathcal{F}_{\text{OTCor}}$ functionality in Fig. 2.

Let $(\mathsf{K_R}, \mathsf{K_S}, \mathsf{Sen}, \mathsf{Rec}, \mathsf{out_S}, \mathsf{out_R})$ be a non-interactive oblivious transfer.

Inputs: Party P_i for $i \in [n]$, receives a session id *sid*.

Common Reference String: For every $i, j \in [n]$, sample $(\sigma_{i,j}, \tau_{i,j}) \leftarrow \mathsf{K_R}(1^\lambda)$. Publish $\{\sigma_{i,j}\}_{i,j\in[n]}$ as the common reference string.

Let us assume that P_i is the sender and P_j is the receiver.

Message sent by $P_i \to P_j$: Compute $(\mathsf{msg_S}, \omega) \leftarrow \mathsf{Sen}(\sigma_{i,j})$ and send $\mathsf{msg_S}$ to P_j.

Message sent by $P_j \to P_i$: On input $b \in \{0,1\}$, compute $(\mathsf{msg_R}, \rho_b) \leftarrow \mathsf{Rec}(\sigma_{i,j}, b)$. Send $\mathsf{msg_R}$ to P_i.

Computation: P_i sets $(s_0, s_1) := \mathsf{out_S}(\sigma_{i,j}, \omega, \mathsf{msg_R})$. P_j sets $s_b := \mathsf{out_R}(\sigma_{i,j}, \rho_b, \mathsf{msg_S})$.

Fig. 2. Realizing the $\mathcal{F}_{\mathrm{OTCor}}$ functionality

Description of the Simulator. We assume that $\mathcal{A}$ is static and hence the set of honest parties H is known before the execution of the protocol. Recall the properties of $\mathsf{Ext_R}$ and $\mathsf{Ext_S}$ from the definition of non-interactive oblivious transfer.

Simulating the CRS. For every $i \in [n]$,

- If $P_i \in H$, sample $(\sigma_{i,j}, \tau_{i,j}) \leftarrow \mathsf{K_R}(1^\lambda)$ for every $j \in [n] \setminus \{i\}$.
- If $P_i \notin H$, sample $(\sigma_{i,j}, \tau_{i,j}) \leftarrow \mathsf{K_S}(1^\lambda)$ for every $j \in [n] \setminus \{i\}$.

Publish $\{\sigma_{i,j}\}_{i,j\in[n]}$ as the common reference string.

Simulating the Interaction with $\mathcal{Z}$. For every input value for the set of corrupted parties that S receives from $\mathcal{Z}$, S writes that value to $\mathcal{A}$'s input tape. Similarly, the output of $\mathcal{A}$ is written as the output on S's output tape.

Simulating the Interaction with $\mathcal{A}$. For every concurrent interaction with the session identifier *sid* that $\mathcal{A}$ may start and for every choice of sender P_i and the receiver P_j, the simulator does the following:

- **Both $P_i, P_j \in H$:**
  1. Compute $(\mathsf{msg_S}, \omega) \leftarrow \mathsf{Sen}(\sigma_{i,j})$ on behalf of P_i and send $\mathsf{msg_S}$ to P_j.
  2. Sample $b \leftarrow \{0,1\}$ and compute $(\mathsf{msg_R}, \rho_b) \leftarrow \mathsf{Rec}(\sigma_{i,j}, b)$ on behalf of P_j. Send $\mathsf{msg_R}$ to P_i.
- **$P_i \in H$ and $P_j \notin H$:**
  1. Compute $(\mathsf{msg_S}, \omega) \leftarrow \mathsf{Sen}(\sigma_{i,j})$ on behalf of P_i and send $\mathsf{msg_S}$ to $\mathcal{A}$.
  2. $\mathcal{A}$ outputs $\mathsf{msg_R}$.

3. Run $b' \leftarrow \mathsf{Ext}_\mathrm{R}(\sigma_{i,j}, \tau_{i,j}, \mathsf{msg}_\mathrm{R})$.
4. Compute $(s_0, s_1) := \mathsf{out}_\mathrm{S}(\sigma_{i,j}, \omega, \mathsf{msg}_\mathrm{R})$.
5. Send $s_{b'}$ to the $\mathcal{F}_{\mathrm{OTCor}}$ functionality and output whatever $\mathcal{A}$ outputs.

– $P_i \notin H$ **and** $P_j \in H$:
1. Compute $(\mathsf{msg}_\mathrm{R}, \rho_0, \rho_1) \leftarrow \mathrm{S}(\sigma_{i,j}, \tau_{i,j})$ and send msg_R to $\mathcal{A}$.
2. $\mathcal{A}$ outputs msg_S.
3. Compute $s_b := \mathsf{out}_\mathrm{R}(\sigma_{i,j}, \rho_b, \mathsf{msg}_\mathrm{S})$ for all $b \in \{0,1\}$.
4. Send (s_0, s_1) to the $\mathcal{F}_{\mathrm{OTCor}}$ functionality and output whatever $\mathcal{A}$ outputs.

Lemma 3. *Assuming the security of non-interactive oblivious transfer, for every $\mathcal{Z}$ that obeys the rules of interaction for UC security we have* $\mathrm{EXEC}_{\mathcal{F},\mathcal{S},\mathcal{Z}} \overset{c}{\approx} \mathrm{EXEC}_{\pi,\mathcal{A},\mathcal{Z}}$.

We prove this lemma in the full version.

NIOT from Quadratic Residuocity. In this section we present a construction of non-interactive oblivious transfer from the quadratic residuocity (QR) assumption. We will begin by reviewing the assumption, then describe the construction, and finally prove its correctness and security.

Notations. For a positive integer N, we use $\mathcal{J}(N)$ to denote the set $\{x \in \mathbb{Z}/N\mathbb{Z} : \left(\frac{x}{N}\right) = 1\}$, where $\left(\frac{x}{N}\right)$ is the Jacobi symbol of x in $\mathbb{Z}/N\mathbb{Z}$. We use $\mathcal{QR}(N)$ to denote the set of quadratic residues in $\mathcal{J}(N)$. The security of our scheme is based on the following computational assumption.

Definition 3 (Quadratic Residuocity (QR) Assumption [GM82]**).** *Let* $\mathsf{QRgen}(\cdot)$ *be a PPT algorithm that generates two equal size primes p, q and $N = pq$. The following two distributions are computationally indistinguishable:*

$$\left\{(p,q,N) \leftarrow \mathsf{QRgen}(1^\lambda); V \leftarrow \mathcal{QR}(N) : (N,V)\right\} \overset{c}{\approx}$$
$$\left\{(p,q,N) \leftarrow \mathsf{QRgen}(1^\lambda); V \leftarrow \mathcal{J}(N) \setminus \mathcal{QR}(N) : (N,V)\right\}$$

In the construction and the proof of security, we make use of the notion IBE compatible algorithm proved in [BGH07].

Definition 4 ([BGH07]). *Let $\mathcal{Q}$ be a deterministic algorithm that takes as input (N, S, R) where $N \in \mathbb{Z}^+$ and $R, S \in \mathbb{Z}/N\mathbb{Z}$. The algorithm outputs two polynomials $f, g \in \mathbb{Z}/N\mathbb{Z}[x]$. We say that $\mathcal{Q}$ is IBE-compatible if the following two conditions hold:*

1. *(Condition 1) If S and R are quadratic residues then $f(s)g(r)$ is a quadratic residue for all square roots r of R and s of S.*
2. *(Condition 2) If S is a quadratic residue then $f(s)f(-s)R$ is a quadratic residue for all square roots s of S.*

Boneh et al. [BGH07] showed a concrete instantiation of such an IBE-compatible algorithm.

Theorem 2. *Assuming the Quadratic Residuocity assumption, there exists a construction of non-interactive oblivious transfer.*

The Construction. We give the construction of non-interactive oblivious transfer in Fig. 3.

- $\mathsf{K_R}(1^\lambda)$:
  1. $(p, q, N) \leftarrow \mathsf{QRgen}(1^\lambda)$..
  2. Sample a random $u \leftarrow \mathcal{J}(N) \setminus \mathcal{QR}(N)$.
  3. Output $\sigma := (N, u), \tau := (p, q)$.
- $\mathsf{K_S}(1^\lambda)$:
  1. $(p, q) \leftarrow \mathsf{QRgen}(1^\lambda)$.
  2. Sample a random $u \leftarrow \mathcal{QR}(N)$.
  3. Output $\sigma := (N, u), \tau := (p, q)$.
- $\mathsf{Sen}(\sigma)$:
  1. Pick a random $s \in \mathbb{Z}/N\mathbb{Z}$.
  2. $S := s^2$.
  3. Output $\mathsf{msg_S} := S, \omega := s$.
- $\mathsf{Rec}(\sigma, b)$:
  1. Pick a random $r \in \mathbb{Z}/N\mathbb{Z}$.
  2. If $b = 0$, let $\mathsf{msg_R} := r^2$, otherwise let $\mathsf{msg_R} := r^2 u$.
  3. Output $\mathsf{msg_R}$ and $\rho_b := (r, b, \mathsf{msg_R})$.
- $\mathsf{out_S}(\sigma, \omega, \mathsf{msg_R})$:
  1. Parse ω as s, and let $S := s^2$.
  2. $(f, g) \leftarrow \mathcal{Q}(N, S, \mathsf{msg_R})$, $(\bar{f}, \bar{g}) \leftarrow \mathcal{Q}(N, S, u \cdot \mathsf{msg_R})$.
  3. Output $k_0 := \left(\frac{f(s)}{N}\right), k_1 := \left(\frac{\bar{f}(s)}{N}\right)$.
- $\mathsf{out_R}(\sigma, \rho_b, \mathsf{msg_S})$:
  1. Parse ρ_b as $(r, b, \mathsf{msg_R})$; parse $\mathsf{msg_S}$ as S.
  2. If $b = 0$, let $(f, g) \leftarrow \mathcal{Q}(N, S, r^2)$ and $k'_b := \left(\frac{g(r)}{N}\right)$; otherwise let $(\bar{f}, \bar{g}) \leftarrow \mathcal{Q}(N, S, (ru)^2)$ and $k'_b := \left(\frac{\bar{g}(ru)}{N}\right)$.
  3. Output k'_b.

Fig. 3. Non-interactive oblivious transfer from QR

Correctness. We start with the correctness proof. Notice that if $b = 0$ then msg_R is a quadratic residue and otherwise, $u \cdot \mathsf{msg}_R$ is a quadratic residue. Let us first consider the case where msg_R is a quadratic residue. In that case, Condition 1 in Lemma 4 implies that $\left(\frac{f(s)}{N}\right) = \left(\frac{g(r)}{N}\right)$. Hence, $k'_0 = k_0$. A similar argument can be used to show that if $u \cdot \mathsf{msg}_R$ is a quadratic residue then $k'_1 = k_1$.

CRS Indistinguishability. The CRS indistinguishability property follows directly from quadratic residuocity assumption.

Sender Security. We first give the description of the extractor $\mathsf{Ext}_{\mathsf{R}}$. On input msg_R, the extractor uses the trapdoor $\tau = (p, q)$ to check if msg_R is a quadratic residue. It outputs $b' = 0$ if it is the case and 1 otherwise. We now need to show that $k_{1-b'}$ is statistically indistinguishable to random and this follows directly from the following lemma given in [BGH07].[8]

Lemma 4 ([BGH07]). *Let $N = pq$ be a QR modulus, $X \in \mathcal{QR}(N)$ and $R \notin \mathcal{QR}(N)$. Let x be a random variable uniformly chosen among the four square roots of X. Let f be a polynomial such that $f(x)f(-x)R$ is a quadratic residue for all four values of x. Then, $\left(\frac{f(x)}{N}\right)$ is uniformly distributed in $\{\pm 1\}$.*

Proof. Some parts of the proof are taken verbatim from [BGH07]. Let x, x' be two square-roots of X such that $x = x' \mod p$ and $x = -x' \mod q$. Then, the four square roots of X are $\{\pm x, \pm x'\}$. By definition, we have that $\left(\frac{f(x)}{p}\right) = \left(\frac{f(x')}{p}\right)$ and $\left(\frac{f(x')}{q}\right) = \left(\frac{f(-x)}{q}\right)$. Also, from the fact that $f(x)f(-x)R$ is a quadratic residue, we have that $\left(\frac{f(x)}{p}\right)\left(\frac{f(-x)}{p}\right)\left(\frac{R}{p}\right) = 1$ and $\left(\frac{f(x)}{q}\right)\left(\frac{f(-x)}{q}\right)\left(\frac{R}{q}\right) = 1$. Since $R \notin \mathcal{QR}(N)$ either $\left(\frac{R}{p}\right) = -1$ or $\left(\frac{R}{q}\right) = -1$. We consider two cases:

- **Case-1:** $\left(\frac{R}{q}\right) = -1$. In this case, $\left(\frac{f(x)}{q}\right) = -\left(\frac{f(-x)}{q}\right) = -\left(\frac{f(x')}{q}\right)$. Thus, $\left(\frac{f(x)}{N}\right) = -\left(\frac{f(x')}{N}\right)$. Similarly, one can show that $\left(\frac{f(-x)}{N}\right) = -1\left(\frac{f(-x')}{N}\right)$. Thus, among $f(x), f(x'), f(-x), f(-x')$, the first two have different Jacobi symbols and the last two have different Jacobi symbols modulo N. Thus, $\left(\frac{f(x)}{N}\right)$ is uniformly distributed over $\{\pm 1\}$.
- **Case-2:** $\left(\frac{R}{p}\right) = -1$. In this case, $\left(\frac{f(x)}{p}\right) = -\left(\frac{f(-x)}{p}\right) = -\left(\frac{f(-x')}{p}\right)$. Thus, $\left(\frac{f(x)}{N}\right) = -\left(\frac{f(-x')}{N}\right)$. Similarly, one can show that $\left(\frac{f(x')}{N}\right) = -\left(\frac{f(-x)}{N}\right)$. Thus, among $f(x), f(-x'), f(-x), f(x')$, the first two have different Jacobi symbols and the last two have different Jacobi symbols modulo N. Thus, $\left(\frac{f(x)}{N}\right)$ is uniformly distributed over $\{\pm 1\}$.

Receiver Security. We first give the description of the extractor $\mathsf{Ext}_{\mathsf{S}}$. On input σ, τ, it uses τ to find the square root u' of u. It samples a random r and sets $\mathsf{msg}_R = r^2 u$, $\rho_0 = ru'$ and $\rho_1 = r$. It is easy to see that this extractor satisfies the receiver security definition.

4 Two-Round Semi-Honest MPC in the $\mathcal{F}_{\mathrm{OTCor}}$ Model

In this section, we give our construction of two-round MPC against semi-honest adversaries in the $\mathcal{F}_{\mathrm{OTCor}}$ model when the adversary is allowed to corrupt an

[8] The lemma in [BGH07] was shown only for $R \in \mathcal{J}(N)$. We extend it to arbitrary $R \notin \mathcal{QR}(N)$.

arbitrary subset of the parties. The results we obtain against semi-honest adversaries are as follows (all our results are in the $\mathcal{F}_{\text{OTCor}}$ model):

1. We first give a perfectly secure, two-round protocol for constant-size functionalities.
2. Next, using s result in [BGI+18] and the protocol from Step 1, we will give a protocol with perfectly (resp. statistical) secure, two-round protocol for functionalities with perfect (resp. statistical) randomized encodings with constant degree. Following [AIK04], we will denote the class of functions with perfectly (resp. statistically) secure constant degree randomized encodings as PREN (resp. SREN). Applebaum et al. [AIK04] showed that some of the natural complexity classes such as NC^1 and mod-2 branching programs $\oplus L/\mathsf{poly}$ are contained in PREN. A complexity class that is in SREN but not known to be in PREN is NL.
3. Next, using the result in [BMR90] and the protocol from Step 1, we will give a protocol for all circuits making black-box use of a pseudorandom generator.

4.1 Protocols for Constant-Size Functionalities

For a constant n, let $f : \{0,1\}^n \rightarrow \{0,1\}$ be a function with constant circuit size.[9] For each $i \in [n]$, the party P_i has input bit x_i and the parties want to securely compute $f(x_1, \ldots, x_n)$.[10] We give perfectly secure, two-round protocols for computing f both in the dishonest majority setting in the $\mathcal{F}_{\text{OTCor}}$ hybrid model.

To construct a two-round protocol in the dishonest majority setting, we will use the same high level idea of Garg and Srinivasan [GS18]. To be more precise, we will take an arbitrary round protocol that securely computes the function f and compress it to two-rounds. However, to construct a perfectly secure protocol we will make the following changes to the round-collapsing compiler of [GS18],

1. All the executions of two-round oblivious transfer used by the round-collapsing compiler in [GS18] are replaced with perfectly secure, two-round oblivious transfer from OT correlations.
2. The garbled circuits used in [GS18] compiler are replaced with perfectly secure, decomposable randomized encodings for NC^0 circuits (cf. Definition 2).
3. The underlying multi-round protocol that we want to round-compress might use cryptographic operations (which is necessary in the dishonest majority setting) and this creates the following two problems: (i) we can no longer argue perfect/statistical security, (ii) a subtle but a more important problem is that the compiler in [GS18] makes use of the code of the

9 For simplicity, we restrict ourselves to functions that output a single bit. We note that all our results can be generalized to functions with multiple bits with efficiency growing linearly with this number. We also assume that all the parties get the output of this functionality. We can also generalize our result for the case where some specific parties get the output.

10 Again, for simplicity we restrict ourselves to parties with a single input bit and our results naturally generalize to parties with multiple bits as input.

underlying protocol and hence if the underlying protocol involves cryptographic operations then the resultant two-round protocol makes non-black box use of cryptographic primitives. To solve the first problem, we will only round-compress perfect/statistical protocols in the OT-hybrid model (e.g., [GMW87,Kil88,IPS08]). Notice that any protocol in the OT-hybrid model can be reduced information theoretically to a protocol in the $\mathcal{F}_{\mathrm{OTCor}}$ functionality. To make the operations performed by all the parties information theoretic, we will generate OT correlations and make these correlations as part of the party's input. For example, consider two parties P_1 and P_2 who wish to do an OT in some round of the underlying protocol. Now, P_1 and P_2 will use the OT correlations from their input to perform an information theoretic OT.

The rest of the subsection is organized as follows. We will first recall the notion of conforming protocols from [GS18]. Intuitively, conforming protocols are MPC protocols with some additional structure. [GS18] showed that any MPC protocol can be transformed to a conforming protocol (with some efficiency loss). We give a generalization of the notion of conforming protocols to work in $\mathcal{F}_{\mathrm{OTCor}}$ model. Then, we will describe our construction of two-round MPC in the $\mathcal{F}_{\mathrm{OTCor}}$ hybrid model.

Conforming Protocol. We will now recall the notion of conforming protocols from [GS18]. We introduce an additional parameter s such that in each round of the conforming protocol, a single party computes s NAND gates and broadcasts the output of these NAND gates to every party. We note that in the formulation of [GS18], the parameter s was set to 1. We introduce this parameter for better concrete efficiency.

Consider a n-party deterministic[11] MPC protocol Φ between parties $P_1, \ldots, P_n$ with inputs $x_1, \ldots, x_n$, respectively. For each $i \in [n]$, we let $x_i \in \{0,1\}^m$ denote the input of party P_i (x_i's also include the randomness used in the protocol and hence they are m bits long). A conforming protocol Φ in the $\mathcal{F}_{\mathrm{OTCor}}$ is defined by functions pre, post, and a OT correlations generation phase and computations steps or what we call *actions* $\phi_1, \cdots \phi_T$. The protocol Φ proceeds in four stages: the OT correlations generation phase, the pre-processing stage, the computation stage and the output stage.

- **OT correlations generator:** For every instance of the OT to be performed in the protocol, interact with the $\mathcal{F}_{\mathrm{OTCor}}$ functionality to generate OT correlations.
- **Pre-processing phase**: For each $i \in [n]$, party P_i computes

$$(z_i, v_i) \leftarrow \mathsf{pre}(i, x_i)$$

where pre is a randomized algorithm and the input x_i is now augmented with the OT correlations generated in the previous step. The algorithm pre takes

[11] Randomized protocols can be handled by including the randomness used by a party as part of its input.

as input the index i of the party, its input x_i and outputs $z_i \in \{0,1\}^{\ell/n}$ and $v_i \in \{0,1\}^{\ell}$ (where ℓ is a parameter of the protocol). Finally, P_i retains v_i as the secret information and broadcasts z_i to every other party. We require that $v_{i,k} = 0$ for all $k \in [\ell] \setminus \{(i-1)\ell/n + 1, \ldots, i\ell/n\}$.

- **Computation phase**: For each $i \in [n]$, party P_i sets

$$\mathsf{st}_i := (z_1 \| \cdots \| z_n).$$

Next, for each $t \in \{1 \cdots T\}$ parties proceed as follows:

1. Parse action ϕ_t as $(i, (a_1, b_1, c_1), \ldots, (a_s, b_s, c_s))$ where $i \in [n]$ and $a_j, b_j, c_j \in [\ell]$ for all $j \in [s]$.
2. Party P_i computes s NAND gates as

$$\mathsf{st}_{i,c_j} = \mathsf{NAND}(\mathsf{st}_{i,a_j} \oplus v_{i,a_j}, \mathsf{st}_{i,b_j} \oplus v_{i,b_j}) \oplus v_{i,c_j}$$

for all $j \in [s]$ and broadcasts $\{\mathsf{st}_{i,c_j}\}_{j \in [s]}$ to every other party.
3. Every party P_k for $k \neq i$ updates st_{k,c_j} for all $j \in [s]$ to the bits received from P_i.

We require that for all $t, t' \in [T]$ such that $t \neq t'$, if $\phi_t = (\cdot, (\cdot, \cdot, c_1), \ldots, (\cdot, \cdot, c_s))$ and $\phi_{t'} = (\cdot, (\cdot, \cdot, c'_1), \ldots, (\cdot, \cdot, c'_s))$ then $\{c_j\} \cap \{c'_j\} = \varnothing$. We use $A_i \subset [T]$ to denote the set of rounds in which the party P_i sends a message. Namely, $A_i = \{t \in T \mid \phi_t = (i, (\cdot, \cdot, \cdot), \ldots, (\cdot, \cdot, \cdot))\}$.

- **Output phase**: For each $i \in [n]$, party P_i outputs $\mathsf{post}(i, \mathsf{st}_i, v_i)$.

We now show the following lemma which is a generalization of the lemma proved in [GS18].

Lemma 5. *For $s = 1$, any MPC protocol Π in the OT hybrid model can be transformed into a conforming protocol Φ in the $\mathcal{F}_{\mathrm{OTCor}}$ model while inheriting the correctness and the security of the original protocol. Furthermore, there exists a choice of s such that the number of rounds of the resulting conforming protocol is $O(n \cdot d_{\max} \cdot r)$ where $d_{\max}$ is the maximum depth of the boolean circuit computing the next message function of any party and r is the number of rounds of the original protocol Π.*

We prove the lemma in the full version.

Remark 1. We note that if the i-th party's output is public then the algorithm post need not take v_i as input.

Compiled Protocol. We describe the compiled protocol in Fig. 4 and give an informal overview below.

Overview. Our construction involves a pre-preprocessing phase followed by the two-rounds of interaction (described in Fig. 4) and a local evaluation phase (described below). In the pre-processing phase, the parties interact with the $\mathcal{F}_{\mathrm{OTCor}}$ functionality to generate two sets of OT correlations. The first set of OT correlations are generated to execute the two-round oblivious transfer used in the compiler of Garg and Srinivasan [GS18]. The second set of OT correlations are to be hardwired as part of the input in the conforming protocols so that the operations done by each party in the conforming protocol are information theoretic. To obtain perfect security, we also use a decomposable randomized encoding in place of garbled circuits. Apart from these changes, our two-round protocol is exactly same as in [GS18].

Evaluation. To compute the output of the protocol, each party P_i does the following:

1. For each $k \in [n]$, let $\widehat{x}^{k,1}$ be the input encoding received from P_k at the end of round 2.
2. **for** each t from 1 to T do:
   (a) Parse ϕ_t as $(i^*, (a_1, b_1, c_1), \ldots, (a_s, b_s, c_s))$.
   (b) Compute $(\{(\xi_j, \omega_j)\}_{j\in[s]}, \widehat{x}^{i^*,t+1}) := \mathsf{Dec}(\widetilde{f}^{i,t}, \widehat{x}^{i,t})$.
   (c) Set $\mathsf{st}_{i,c_j} := \xi_j$.
   (d) **for** each $k \neq i^*$ do:
      i. Compute $(\{\mathsf{ots}_j^2\}_{j\in[s]}, \{\widehat{x}_h^{k,t+1}\}_{h\in[\ell]\setminus\{c_j\}_{j\in[s]}}) := \mathsf{Dec}(\widetilde{f}^{i,t}, \widehat{x}^{i,t})$.
      ii. For every $j \in [s]$:
         A. Parse ots_j^2 as (Y_0, Y_1) and ω_j as $\{\gamma_j^k\}_{k\in[n]\setminus\{i^*\}}$.
         B. Recover $\widehat{x}_{c_j}^{k,t+1} := Y_{\xi_j} \oplus \gamma_j^k$.
      iii. Set $\widehat{x}^{k,t+1} := \{\widehat{x}_h^{k,t+1}\}_{h\in[\ell]}$.
3. Compute the output as $\mathsf{post}(i, \mathsf{st}_i, v_i)$.

Asymptotic Cost. Since the function f is constant size, the number of rounds of the underlying protocol and the maximum depth of the next message functions are constant (e.g., if we use [GMW87] as the underlying protocol). As a result of Lemma 5, the number of rounds of the conforming protocol is also a constant since k is a constant. Hence, the asymptotic cost of our protocol is a constant (though concretely it grows as $2^{O(T)}$ where T is the number of rounds of the conforming protocol).

Security. The only changes that we make when compared to the protocol in [GS18] is that we use information theoretic, two-round oblivious transfer (based on OT correlations) and perfectly secure DRE in place of garbled circuits. We prove the security in the full version.

Theorem 3. *For every constant size function f, the protocol in Fig. 4 perfectly computes f against a semi-honest adversaries who might corrupt an arbitrary subset of the parties.*

Let Φ be an n-party conforming semi-honest MPC protocol (with T rounds in the computation phase) and $\widehat{f}$ be a DRE (See Definition 2).

Pre-processing Phase: On input the number of parties n, the number of functions s, the size of each of these functions and the size of each party's input m, the party P_i does the following:

1. For each $j \in [s]$ and $\alpha, \beta \in \{0,1\}$:
   (a) For each $t \in A_i$ (recall the definition of A_i from the description of conforming protocol), send $((t,j,\alpha,\beta), \mathbf{receiver}, i, r_{t,j,\alpha,\beta})$ (where $r_{t,j,\alpha,\beta}$ is chosen randomly) and for each $t \in [T] \setminus A_i$, send $((t,j,\alpha,\beta), \mathbf{sender}, i)$ to $\mathcal{F}_{\mathrm{OTCor}}$ functionality.
   (b) Receive $\omega_{t,j,\alpha,\beta} = \{\gamma^k_{t,j,\alpha,\beta}\}_{k\in[n]\setminus\{i\}}$ for each $t \in A_i$ and $(\gamma^0_{t,j,\alpha,\beta}, \gamma^1_{t,j,\alpha,\beta})$ if $t \in [T] \setminus A_i$ from $\mathcal{F}_{\mathrm{OTCor}}$.
2. Execute the OT correlations generation phase of the conforming protocol Φ.

Round-1: Each party P_i does the following:

1. Compute $(z_i, v_i) \leftarrow \mathsf{pre}(i, x_i)$.
2. For each $t \in A_i$, for each $j \in [s]$ and $\alpha, \beta \in \{0,1\}$, compute

$$\mathsf{ots}^1_{t,j,\alpha,\beta} \leftarrow \left(v_{i,c_j} \oplus \mathsf{NAND}(v_{i,a_j} \oplus \alpha, v_{i,b_j} \oplus \beta)\right) \oplus r_{t,j,\alpha,\beta},$$

   where $\phi_t = (i, (a_1, b_1, c_1), \ldots, (a_s, b_s, c_s))$.
3. Send $\left(z_i, \{\mathsf{ots}^1_{t,j,\alpha,\beta}\}_{t\in A_i, j\in[s], \alpha,\beta\in\{0,1\}}\right)$ to every other party.

Round-2: In the second round, each party P_i does the following:

1. Set $\mathsf{st}_i := (z_1 \| \ldots \| z_i \| \ldots \| z_n)$.
2. Set $\mathbf{a}^{i,T+1}_{k,0} = \mathbf{a}^{i,T+1}_{k,1} = \bot$ for all $k \in [\ell]$.
3. **for** each t from T down to 1,
   (a) Parse ϕ_t as $(i^*, (a_1, b_1, c_1), \ldots, (a_s, b_s, c_s))$.
   (b) If $i = i^*$ then
      i. Let $f^{i,t}$ be a NC^0 function that takes st as input, updates st_{c_j} as per the action for every $j \in [s]$ and outputs $\omega_{t,j,\mathsf{st}_{a_j},\mathsf{st}_{b_j}}$ for every $j \in [s]$ along with $\mathbf{a}^{i,t+1}_{k,\mathsf{st}_k}$ for every $k \in [\ell]$.
   (c) If $i \neq i^*$ then for every $\alpha, \beta \in \{0,1\}$,
      i. Compute $\mathsf{ots}^2_{t,j,\alpha,\beta} := (\mathbf{a}^{i,t+1}_{c_j,0} \oplus X_0, \mathbf{a}^{i,t+1}_{c_j,1} \oplus X_1)$ where $X_b = \gamma^{b\oplus \mathsf{ots}^1_{t,j,\alpha,\beta}}_{t,j,\alpha,\beta}$ for every $j \in [s]$.
      ii. Let $f^{i,t}$ be a NC^0 function that takes st as input and outputs $\mathbf{a}^{i,t+1}_{k,\mathsf{st}_k}$ for all $k \in [\ell] \setminus \{c_j\}$ and $\mathsf{ots}^2_{t,j,\mathsf{st}_{a_j},\mathsf{st}_{b_j}}$ for every $j \in [s]$.
   (d) Compute $(\widehat{f}^{i,t}, \{(\mathbf{a}^{i,t}_{k,0}, \mathbf{a}^{i,t}_{k,1})\}_{k\in[\ell]}) \leftarrow \widehat{f}^{i,t}(;r)$.
4. Send $\left(\{\widehat{f}^{i,t}\}_{t\in[T]}, \{\mathbf{a}^{i,1}_{k,\mathsf{st}_k}\}_{k\in[\ell]}\right)$ to every other party.

Fig. 4. Two-round MPC for constant size functions in the $\mathcal{F}_{\mathrm{OTCor}}$ hybrid model

Extensions. We will now describe two-extensions to the protocol in Fig. 4.

- f **need not be known until the second round.** We will now describe how to augment the protocol so that the function f to be computed need not be known until the beginning of the second round and only the size of these functions need to be known before the first round. Let us assume for simplicity that, $|f| = m'$. We define a $(k + m'k)$-party functionality C that takes x_i from party P_i for every $i \in [k]$ and takes a bit $y_{i\ell}$ from party $P_{i\ell}$ for each $i \in [k]$ and $\ell \in [m']$ and does the following: it checks if for each $i, i' \in [n]$ and $\ell \in [m']$, $y_{i,\ell} \stackrel{?}{=} y_{i',\ell}$; if yes, it interprets $y_{1,1}, \ldots, y_{1,m'}$ as the function f and computes an universal circuit $U(x_1, \ldots, x_k, f)$ that outputs $f(x_1, \ldots, x_k)$. With this functionality, let us now see how to change the two-round protocol so that the parties need not know f until the beginning of the second-round. We will use an underlying conforming protocol that securely computes the constant size circuit C. In the compiled protocol, we will let each party P_i to additionally emulate the parties $\{P_{i\ell}\}_{\ell \in [m']}$. To be more precise, in the first round of the protocol, for each $\ell \in [m']$, the party P_i sends two first round messages on behalf of party $P_{i\ell}$; the first message assuming the bit $y_{i\ell} = 0$ and the second message assuming the bit $y_{i\ell'} = 1$. In the beginning of the second round, all the parties know the description of the functions f and hence can choose the first round message corresponding to the correct value of $y_{i\ell}$ and ignore the other message. Based on the chosen messages, the parties generate the second round message in the compiled protocol.
- **Extension to the Client-Server setting.** We now describe an extension of our two-round protocol to the client-server setting. In the client server setting, there are n-input clients who holds the inputs, m servers who do not have any input and one output client. The input clients send a single message to each of the m servers and the servers send a single message to the output client and the output client learns the output of the function based on the server's message. We will assume that any number of clients can be corrupted but there is at least one server who is uncorrupted. We will transform our 2-round protocol in the $\mathcal{F}_{\text{OTCor}}$ model to one in the client-server model. In the full version, we give a general transformation from any two-round MPC protocol with security against semi-honest adversaries who might corrupt an arbitrary subset of the parties to a protocol in the client-server model. However, this general transformation might make non-black-box use of cryptography but the transformation we give here is specific to protocol in Fig. 4 and is information theoretic.
  1. The i-th input client computes the first round message $(z_i, \{\mathsf{ots}^1_{t,j,\alpha,\beta}\}_{t \in A_i, j \in [s], \alpha, \beta \in \{0,1\}})$ of our two-round protocol and sends it to each of the servers.
  2. In addition to the protocols first round message, the client will generate a randomized encoding of NC^0 circuits $\overline{f}^{i,t}$ for every $t \in [T]$, and sends these randomized encodings along with an additive secret share of the input encoding $(\mathbf{a}_0^{i,1}, \mathbf{a}_1^{i,1})$ to the servers. Let us now describe the functionality computed by $\overline{f}^{i,t}$. The functionality takes in the first round messages of all parties and reconstructs st_i. If $t \in A_i$, then it computes the same

function as that of $f_{i,t}$ (described in Fig. 4). If $t \notin A_i$, it will use $\mathsf{ots}^1_{t,j,\alpha,\beta}$ (obtained from the first round messages of the parties) and will generate $\mathsf{ots}^2_{t,j,\alpha,\beta}$ exactly as described in the protocol. Then, it computes the same functionality as that of $f^{i,t}$.

3. The servers on receiving the first round messages from all the input clients, choose the secret share of the input encodings corresponding to the first round messages from all the clients and sends the chosen secret shares to the output client.
4. The output client reconstructs the input encodings from the shares and decodes the randomized encodings exactly as given the evaluation procedure of our two-round protocol to obtain the output.

4.2 Protocols for PREN and SREN

In this subsection, we will use the protocols described in Sect. 4.1 to construct protocols for functions in PREN and SREN. We first define the dMULTPlus function below.

$$\mathsf{dMULTPlus}((x_1, z_1), \ldots, (x_d, z_d)) = x_1 \cdot \ldots \cdot x_d + \sum_{i=1}^{d} z_i.$$

We recall the following lemma from [BGI+18].

Lemma 6 ([BGI+18]). *Let $g : \{0,1\}^n \to \{0,1\}$ be a constant degree function i.e., there exists a constant d such that $g(x_1, \ldots, x_n) = \sum a^{\ell}_{i_1 \ldots i_d} x_{i_1} x_{i_2} \ldots x_{i_d}$. There exists a perfectly secure, two-round protocol in the presence of secure channels between every pair of parties for computing g against semi-honest adversary (corrupting an arbitrary subset of parties) in the $\mathcal{F}_{\mathsf{dMULTPlus}}$ hybrid model. The efficiency of the protocol is $O(m + n^2)$ where m is the number of monomials in g.*

We obtain the following corollary of our Theorem 3.

Corollary 1. *There exists a perfectly secure, two-round protocol for realizing $\mathcal{F}_{\mathsf{dMULTPlus}}$ functionality against semi-honest adversary (corrupting an arbitrary subset of parties) in the $\mathcal{F}_{\mathrm{OTCor}}$ hybrid model. The efficiency of the protocol is $2^{\mathsf{poly}(d)}$.*

Combining Lemma 6 and Corollary 1 and the observation that $\mathcal{F}_{\mathrm{OTCor}}$ implies secure channels, we get the following lemma.

Lemma 7. *Let $g : \{0,1\}^n \to \{0,1\}$ be a constant degree function i.e., there exists a constant d such that $g(x_1, \ldots, x_n) = \sum a^{\ell}_{i_1 \ldots i_d} x_{i_1} x_{i_2} \ldots x_{i_d}$. There exists a perfectly secure, two-round protocol for computing g against semi-honest adversary (corrupting an arbitrary subset of parties) in the $\mathcal{F}_{\mathrm{OTCor}}$ hybrid model. The efficiency of the protocol is $O(m + n^2)$ where m is the number of monomials in g.*

We now show our main theorem regarding securely computing functions in PREN and SREN.

Theorem 4. *Every* $f : \{0,1\}^n \to \{0,1\}$ *in* PREN *(resp.* SREN*) has an efficient, perfectly secure (resp., statistically secure) two-round protocol in the* $\mathcal{F}_{\mathrm{OTCor}}$ *model against a semi-honest adversary corrupting an arbitrary subset of parties. The computational cost incurred by each party is* $O(m+n^2)$ *where* m *is the size of the randomized encoding for* f.

Proof. Let $\widehat{f} : \{0,1\}^n \times \{0,1\}^\rho \to \{0,1\}$ be the randomized encoding of the function f. Each party P_i chooses r_i uniformly at random from $\{0,1\}^\rho$ and the parties wish to securely compute the functionality $\widehat{f}(x_1,\ldots,x_n; r_1 \oplus r_2 \ldots \oplus r_n)$ (i.e., the input of party P_i is set as (x_i, r_i)).

Let $\widehat{f}(x_1,\ldots,x_n; r_1 \oplus r_2 \ldots \oplus r_n) = \sum a^\ell_{i_1 i_2 \ldots i_d} v_{i_1} v_{i_2} \ldots v_{i_d}$ where each v_{i_d} is either some input bit x_j or a bit of some random string r_j. We will use the protocol from Lemma 7 to securely compute $\widehat{f}$.

It now follows from the privacy of randomized encodings and the security of the protocol for computing $\widehat{f}$ the above protocol securely computes f against semi-honest corruptions.

Remark 2. For simplicity, in Theorem 4, we considered a setting where each party holds a single bit as input and the output of the function f is also a single bit. This can be naturally generalized to a setting wherein each party holds a string as input and the number of outputs of the functions is greater than 1.

We obtain the following corollary from Theorem 4.

Corollary 2. *There is a perfectly (resp. statistical) secure two-round protocol for branching programs (resp. non-deterministic branching programs) in the* $\mathcal{F}_{\mathrm{OTCor}}$ *model against a semi-honest adversary corrupting an arbitrary subset of parties.*

4.3 Protocols for Circuits

In this subsection, we will use the protocols described in Sect. 4.1 and make black-box use of a PRG to obtain secure protocols for computing circuits. Without loss of generality, we will restrict ourselves to circuits with fan-in 2 NAND gates. The high level idea is to use the protocol in Sect. 4.1 to compute the BMR garbling of a gate [BMR90]. To obtain the labels for executing the BMR garbled circuit, we run the BMR online phase in parallel.

BMR Garbling. We will now recall the semantics of a BMR garbled gate. The BMR garbling for a NAND gate g that takes wires a and b as input and the output wire is c is a set of values $\{\widetilde{G}^i_{r_1,r_2}\}_{r_1,r_2 \in \{0,1\}, i \in [n]}$, where

$$\widetilde{G}^j_{r_1,r_2} = \left(\bigoplus_{i=1}^{n} F_{k^i_{a,r_1}}(g,j,r_1,r_2) \oplus F_{k^i_{b,r_2}}(g,j,r_1,r_2) \right) \oplus k^j_{c,0} \oplus (\chi_{r_1,r_2} \wedge (k^j_{c,1} \oplus k^j_{c,0}))$$

where $\chi_{r_1,r_2} = ((\bigoplus_{i=1}^n \lambda_{i,a} \oplus r_1) \cdot (\bigoplus_{i=1}^n \lambda_{i,b} \oplus r_2) \oplus 1) \oplus (\bigoplus_{i=1}^n \lambda_{i,c})$. Here, F is a PRF, $k_{x,r}^i$ where $x \in \{a, b, c,\}$ and $r \in \{0, 1\}$ is a PRF key, $\lambda_{i,x}$ for $x \in \{a, b, c,\}$ are bits.[12] The PRF keys $k_{x,r}^i$ and the bits $\lambda_{i,x}$ are chosen by each party before the first round of the protocol.

We notice that each output bit of $\{\widetilde{G}_{r_1,r_2}^i\}_{r_1,r_2 \in \{0,1\}, i \in [n]}$ is a constant degree (precisely, a degree 3 functionality). We will use the protocol in Lemma 7 to securely compute each output bit of $\{\widetilde{G}_{r_1,r_2}^i\}_{r_1,r_2 \in \{0,1\}, i \in [n]}$.[13]

Online Phase of BMR. We now describe the two-round BMR online phase.

1. For every wire w, which is the input wire of a party P_i, the other parties P_j will set $\lambda_{j,w} = 0$. The party P_i will compute $\alpha_w = \lambda_{i,w} \oplus x_w$ and broadcast it to all other parties.
2. For every α_w obtained, the party P_i will broadcast k_{w,α_w}^i to every other party.

Asymptotic Cost. The cost of computing every bit of $\widetilde{G}_{r_1,r_2}^i$ is $O(n^2)$ since the number of monomials in $\widetilde{G}_{r_1,r_2}^i$ is $O(n^2)$. So the overall complexity of our protocol is $O(n^3|C|\lambda)$. This gives a factor of n improvement over the cost in [GS18].

Using the above protocol for computing the BMR garbled gate in parallel with the online phase, we obtain the following theorem:

Theorem 5. *There is a computationally secure two-round protocol for any circuit C in the $\mathcal{F}_{\text{OTCor}}$ model against a semi-honest adversary corrupting an arbitrary subset of parties, where the protocol makes a black-box use of a PRG. The computational cost incurred by each party is dominated by $O(n^3|C|)$ invocations of a length-doubling PRG.*

We the following two corollaries by realizing $\mathcal{F}_{\text{OTCor}}$ under DDH/QR or LWE in the strong-PKI model.

Corollary 3 (DDH/QR). *There is a computationally secure, two-round protocol for any circuit C in the strong-PKI model against a semi-honest adversary corrupting an arbitrary subset of parties, where the protocol makes a black-box use of a PRG and black-box use of a DDH/QR hard group.*

Corollary 4 (LWE). *Under the LWE assumption, there is a computationally secure, two-round protocol for any circuit C in the strong-PKI model against a semi-honest adversary corrupting an arbitrary subset of parties, where the protocol makes a black-box use of a PRG.*

---

[12] For simplicity we consider a PRF. But all our results also work with a length doubling pseudorandom generator.

[13] Here, the parties will compute the PRF outputs locally and give these as inputs to the protocol.

References

[ABT18] Applebaum, B., Brakerski, Z., Tsabary, R.: Perfect secure computation in two rounds. To appear in TCC (2018). https://eprint.iacr.org/2018/894

[ACGJ18] Ananth, P., Choudhuri, A.R., Goel, A., Jain, A.: Round-optimal secure multiparty computation with honest majority. In: Shacham, H., Boldyreva, A. (eds.) CRYPTO 2018. LNCS, vol. 10992, pp. 395–424. Springer, Cham (2018). https://doi.org/10.1007/978-3-319-96881-0_14

[AIK04] Applebaum, B., Ishai, Y., Kushilevitz, E.: Cryptography in NC^0. In: 45th FOCS, Rome, Italy, 17–19 October 2004, pp. 166–175. IEEE Computer Society Press (2004)

[AJW11] Asharov, G., Jain, A., Wichs, D.: Multiparty computation with low communication, computation and interaction via threshold FHE. IACR Cryptology ePrint Archive, p. 613 (2011)

[ALSZ13] Asharov, G., Lindell, Y., Schneider, T., Zohner, M.: More efficient oblivious transfer and extensions for faster secure computation. In: Sadeghi, A.-R., Gligor, V.D., Yung, M. (eds.) ACM CCS 13, Berlin, Germany, 4–8 November 2013, pp. 535–548. ACM Press (2013)

[ALSZ15] Asharov, G., Lindell, Y., Schneider, T., Zohner, M.: More efficient oblivious transfer extensions with security for malicious adversaries. In: Oswald, E., Fischlin, M. (eds.) EUROCRYPT 2015. LNCS, vol. 9056, pp. 673–701. Springer, Heidelberg (2015). https://doi.org/10.1007/978-3-662-46800-5_26

[BB89] Bar-Ilan, J., Beaver, D.: Non-cryptographic fault-tolerant computing in constant number of rounds of interaction. In: Proceedings of the Eighth Annual ACM Symposium on Principles of Distributed Computing, Edmonton, Alberta, Canada, 14–16 August 1989, pp. 201–209 (1989)

[BCG+17] Boyle, E., Couteau, G., Gilboa, N., Ishai, Y., Orrù, M.: Homomorphic secret sharing: Optimizations and applications. In: Thuraisingham, B.M., Evans, D., Malkin, T., Xu, D. (eds.) ACM CCS 17, Dallas, TX, USA, 31 October–2 November 2017, pp. 2105–2122. ACM Press (2017)

[BCS96] Brassard, G., Crépeau, C., Santha, M.: Oblivious transfers and intersecting codes. IEEE Trans. Inf. Theory **42**(6), 1769–1780 (1996)

[BCW03] Brassard, G., Crépeau, C., Wolf, S.: Oblivious transfers and privacy amplification. J. Cryptol. **16**(4), 219–237 (2003)

[Bea96] Beaver, D.: Correlated pseudorandomness and the complexity of private computations. In: Proceedings of the Twenty-Eighth Annual ACM Symposium on the Theory of Computing, Philadelphia, Pennsylvania, USA, 22–24 May 1996, pp. 479–488 (1996)

[BGG+18] Boneh, D., et al.: Threshold cryptosystems from threshold fully homomorphic encryption. To appear in Crypto (2018). https://eprint.iacr.org/2017/956

[BGH07] Boneh, D., Gentry, C., Hamburg, M.: Space-efficient identity based encryption without pairings. In: 48th FOCS, Providence, RI, USA, 20–23 October, pp. 647–657. IEEE Computer Society Press (2007)

[BGI16] Boyle, E., Gilboa, N., Ishai, Y.: Breaking the circuit size barrier for secure computation under DDH. In: Robshaw, M., Katz, J. (eds.) CRYPTO 2016. LNCS, vol. 9814, pp. 509–539. Springer, Heidelberg (2016). https://doi.org/10.1007/978-3-662-53018-4_19

[BGI17] Boyle, E., Gilboa, N., Ishai, Y.: Group-based secure computation: optimizing rounds, communication, and computation. In: Coron, J.-S., Nielsen, J.B. (eds.) EUROCRYPT 2017. LNCS, vol. 10211, pp. 163–193. Springer, Cham (2017). https://doi.org/10.1007/978-3-319-56614-6_6

[BGI+18] Boyle, E., Gilboa, N., Ishai, Y., Lin, H., Tessaro, S.: Foundations of homomorphic secret sharing. In: ITCS 2018, pp. 21:1–21:21, January 2018

[BL18] Benhamouda, F., Lin, H.: k-round multiparty computation from k-round oblivious transfer via garbled interactive circuits. In: Nielsen, J.B., Rijmen, V. (eds.) EUROCRYPT 2018. LNCS, vol. 10821, pp. 500–532. Springer, Cham (2018). https://doi.org/10.1007/978-3-319-78375-8_17

[BM90] Bellare, M., Micali, S.: Non-interactive oblivious transfer and applications. In: Brassard, G. (ed.) CRYPTO 1989. LNCS, vol. 435, pp. 547–557. Springer, New York (1990). https://doi.org/10.1007/0-387-34805-0_48

[BMR90] Beaver, D., Micali, S., Rogaway, P.: The round complexity of secure protocols (extended abstract). In: 22nd ACM STOC, Baltimore, MD, USA, 14–16 May, pp. 503–513. ACM Press (1990)

[Can00] Canetti, R.: Security and composition of multiparty cryptographic protocols. J. Cryptol. **13**(1), 143–202 (2000)

[Can01] Canetti, R.: Universally composable security: a new paradigm for cryptographic protocols. In: 42nd FOCS, Las Vegas, NV, USA, 14–17 October 2001, pp. 136–145. IEEE Computer Society Press (2001)

[CEMY09] Choi, S.G., Elbaz, A., Malkin, T., Yung, M.: Secure multi-party computation minimizing online rounds. In: Matsui, M. (ed.) ASIACRYPT 2009. LNCS, vol. 5912, pp. 268–286. Springer, Heidelberg (2009). https://doi.org/10.1007/978-3-642-10366-7_16

[DH76] Diffie, W., Hellman, M.E.: New directions in cryptography. IEEE Trans. Inf. Theory **22**(6), 644–654 (1976)

[DHRW16] Dodis, Y., Halevi, S., Rothblum, R.D., Wichs, D.: Spooky encryption and its applications. In: Robshaw, M., Katz, J. (eds.) CRYPTO 2016. LNCS, vol. 9816, pp. 93–122. Springer, Heidelberg (2016). https://doi.org/10.1007/978-3-662-53015-3_4

[EGL85] Even, S., Goldreich, O., Lempel, A.: A randomized protocol for signing contracts. Commun. ACM **28**(6), 637–647 (1985)

[FGJI17] Fazio, N., Gennaro, R., Jafarikhah, T., Skeith, W.E.: Homomorphic secret sharing from paillier encryption. In: Okamoto, T., Yu, Y., Au, M.H., Li, Y. (eds.) ProvSec 2017. LNCS, vol. 10592, pp. 381–399. Springer, Cham (2017). https://doi.org/10.1007/978-3-319-68637-0_23

[GGHR14] Garg, S., Gentry, C., Halevi, S., Raykova, M.: Two-round secure MPC from indistinguishability obfuscation. In: Lindell, Y. (ed.) TCC 2014. LNCS, vol. 8349, pp. 74–94. Springer, Heidelberg (2014). https://doi.org/10.1007/978-3-642-54242-8_4

[GLS15] Dov Gordon, S., Liu, F.-H., Shi, E.: Constant-round MPC with fairness and guarantee of output delivery. In: Gennaro, R., Robshaw, M. (eds.) CRYPTO 2015. LNCS, vol. 9216, pp. 63–82. Springer, Heidelberg (2015). https://doi.org/10.1007/978-3-662-48000-7_4

[GM82] Goldwasser, S., Micali, S.: Probabilistic encryption and how to play mental poker keeping secret all partial information. In: 14th ACM STOC, San Francisco, CA, USA, 5–7 May 1982, pp. 365–377. ACM Press (1982)

[GMMM18] Garg, S., Mahmoody, M., Masny, D., Meckler, I.: On the round complexity of OT extension. In: Shacham, H., Boldyreva, A. (eds.) CRYPTO 2018. LNCS, vol. 10993, pp. 545–574. Springer, Cham (2018). https://doi.org/10.1007/978-3-319-96878-0_19

[GMW87] Goldreich, O., Micali, S., Wigderson, A.: How to play any mental game or a completeness theorem for protocols with honest majority. In: Aho, A. (ed.) 19th ACM STOC, New York City, NY, USA, 25–27 May 1987, pp. 218–229. ACM Press (1987)

[GS08] Groth, J., Sahai, A.: Efficient non-interactive proof systems for bilinear groups. In: Smart, N. (ed.) EUROCRYPT 2008. LNCS, vol. 4965, pp. 415–432. Springer, Heidelberg (2008). https://doi.org/10.1007/978-3-540-78967-3_24

[GS17] Garg, S., Srinivasan, A.: Garbled protocols and two-round MPC from bilinear maps. In: 58th FOCS, pp. 588–599. IEEE Computer Society Press (2017)

[GS18] Garg, S., Srinivasan, A.: Two-round multiparty secure computation from minimal assumptions. In: Nielsen, J.B., Rijmen, V. (eds.) EUROCRYPT 2018. LNCS, vol. 10821, pp. 468–499. Springer, Cham (2018). https://doi.org/10.1007/978-3-319-78375-8_16

[IK00] Ishai, Y., Kushilevitz, E.: Randomizing polynomials: a new representation with applications to round-efficient secure computation. In: 41st FOCS, Redondo Beach, CA, USA, 12–14 November 2000, pp. 294–304. IEEE Computer Society Press (2000)

[IKM+13] Ishai, Y., Kushilevitz, E., Meldgaard, S., Orlandi, C., Paskin-Cherniavsky, A.: On the power of correlated randomness in secure computation. In: Sahai, A. (ed.) TCC 2013. LNCS, vol. 7785, pp. 600–620. Springer, Heidelberg (2013). https://doi.org/10.1007/978-3-642-36594-2_34

[IKNP03] Ishai, Y., Kilian, J., Nissim, K., Petrank, E.: Extending oblivious transfers efficiently. In: Boneh, D. (ed.) CRYPTO 2003. LNCS, vol. 2729, pp. 145–161. Springer, Heidelberg (2003). https://doi.org/10.1007/978-3-540-45146-4_9

[IKO+11] Ishai, Y., Kushilevitz, E., Ostrovsky, R., Prabhakaran, M., Sahai, A.: Efficient non-interactive secure computation. In: Paterson, K.G. (ed.) EUROCRYPT 2011. LNCS, vol. 6632, pp. 406–425. Springer, Heidelberg (2011). https://doi.org/10.1007/978-3-642-20465-4_23

[IKP10] Ishai, Y., Kushilevitz, E., Paskin, A.: Secure multiparty computation with minimal interaction. In: Rabin, T. (ed.) CRYPTO 2010. LNCS, vol. 6223, pp. 577–594. Springer, Heidelberg (2010). https://doi.org/10.1007/978-3-642-14623-7_31

[IMO18] Ishai, Y., Mittal, M., Ostrovsky, R.: On the message complexity of secure multiparty computation. In: Abdalla, M., Dahab, R. (eds.) PKC 2018. LNCS, vol. 10769, pp. 698–711. Springer, Cham (2018). https://doi.org/10.1007/978-3-319-76578-5_24

[IPS08] Ishai, Y., Prabhakaran, M., Sahai, A.: Founding cryptography on oblivious transfer – efficiently. In: Wagner, D. (ed.) CRYPTO 2008. LNCS, vol. 5157, pp. 572–591. Springer, Heidelberg (2008). https://doi.org/10.1007/978-3-540-85174-5_32

[IR89] Impagliazzo, R., Rudich, S.: Limits on the provable consequences of one-way permutations. In: Proceedings of the 21st Annual ACM Symposium on Theory of Computing, Seattle, Washigton, USA, 14–17 May 1989, pp. 44–61 (1989)

[Kil88] Kilian, J.: Founding cryptography on oblivious transfer. In: 20th ACM STOC, Chicago, IL, USA, 2–4 May 1988, pp. 20–31. ACM Press (1988)

[KOS15] Keller, M., Orsini, E., Scholl, P.: Actively secure OT extension with optimal overhead. In: Gennaro, R., Robshaw, M. (eds.) CRYPTO 2015. LNCS, vol. 9215, pp. 724–741. Springer, Heidelberg (2015). https://doi.org/10.1007/978-3-662-47989-6_35

[MW16] Mukherjee, P., Wichs, D.: Two round multiparty computation via multi-key FHE. In: Fischlin, M., Coron, J.-S. (eds.) EUROCRYPT 2016. LNCS, vol. 9666, pp. 735–763. Springer, Heidelberg (2016). https://doi.org/10.1007/978-3-662-49896-5_26

[PVW08] Peikert, C., Vaikuntanathan, V., Waters, B.: A framework for efficient and composable oblivious transfer. In: Wagner, D. (ed.) CRYPTO 2008. LNCS, vol. 5157, pp. 554–571. Springer, Heidelberg (2008). https://doi.org/10.1007/978-3-540-85174-5_31

[PW00] Pfitzmann, B., Waidner, M.: Composition and integrity preservation of secure reactive systems. In: Jajodia, S., Samarati, P. (eds.) ACM CCS 2000, Athens, Greece, 1–4 November 2000, pp. 245–254. ACM Press (2000)

[Rab81] Rabin, M.: How to exchange secrets by oblivious transfer. Technical report TR-81, Harvard Aiken Computation Laboratory (1981)

[Reg05] Regev, O.: On lattices, learning with errors, random linear codes, and cryptography. In: Gabow, H.N., Fagin, R. (eds.) 37th ACM STOC, Baltimore, MA, USA, 22–24 May 2005, pp. 84–93. ACM Press (2005)

[Yao86] Yao, A.C.-C.: How to generate and exchange secrets (extended abstract). In: 27th FOCS, Toronto, Ontario, Canada, 27–29 October 1986, pp. 162–167. IEEE Computer Society Press (1986)

Perfect Secure Computation in Two Rounds

Benny Applebaum[1(✉)], Zvika Brakerski[2], and Rotem Tsabary[2]

[1] Tel-Aviv University, Tel Aviv, Israel
bennyap@post.tau.ac.il
[2] Weizmann Institute of Science, Rehovot, Israel
{zvika.brakerski,rotem.tsabary}@weizmann.ac.il

Abstract. We show that any multi-party functionality can be evaluated using a two-round protocol with perfect correctness and perfect semi-honest security, provided that the majority of parties are honest. This settles the round complexity of information-theoretic semi-honest MPC, resolving a longstanding open question (cf. Ishai and Kushilevitz, FOCS 2000). The protocol is efficient for NC^1 functionalities. Furthermore, given black-box access to a one-way function, the protocol can be made efficient for any polynomial functionality, at the cost of only guaranteeing computational security.

Technically, we extend and relax the notion of randomized encoding to specifically address *multi-party functionalities*. The property of a multi-party randomized encoding (MPRE) is that if the functionality g is an encoding of the functionality f, then for any (permitted) coalition of players, their respective outputs and inputs in g allow them to simulate their respective inputs and outputs in f, without learning anything else, including the other outputs of f.

1 Introduction

Secure multi-party computation (MPC) is perhaps the most generic cryptographic task. A collection of n parties, each with its own input x_i, wish to jointly compute function of all of their inputs $(y_1, \ldots, y_n) = f(x_1, \ldots, x_n)$ so that each party learns its y_i and nothing else, and even a coalition of adversarial players should not learn more than the collection of outputs of its members. Throughout this work, we will be concerned with the most basic variant of this problem, denoted as *private computation*, where even adversarial parties are

The full version of this paper is available at https://eprint.iacr.org/2018/894.
B. Applebaum—Supported by the European Union's Horizon 2020 Programme (ERC-StG-2014-2020) under grant agreement no. 639813 ERC-CLC, and the Check Point Institute for Information Security.
Z. Brakerski and R. Tsabary—Supported by the Israel Science Foundation (Grant No. 468/14), Binational Science Foundation (Grants No. 2016726, 2014276), and by the European Union Horizon 2020 Research and Innovation Program via ERC Project REACT (Grant 756482) and via Project PROMETHEUS (Grant 780701).

A. Beimel and S. Dziembowski (Eds.): TCC 2018, LNCS 11239, pp. 152–174, 2018.
https://doi.org/10.1007/978-3-030-03807-6_6

assumed to follow the protocol but try to learn as much as they can from their view (a.k.a semi-honest adversaries). Unless stated otherwise, we further assume that the adversary is computationally unbounded, and correspondingly, require information-theoretic (perfect) privacy.

The seminal works of Ben-Or, Goldwasser and Wigderson [7] and Chaum, Crépeau and Damgård [11] established that in this setting security for non-trivial functions can only be achieved if the adversarial coalition includes strictly less than half of the total number of parties (a.k.a honest majority). They showed that in the presence of honest majority, any function f can be privately computed, thus existentially resolving the problem.

However, as with all computational tasks, one wishes to minimize the resources required to carry out an MPC protocols. A resource that received much attention is the round complexity: the number of rounds of communication required to carry out the protocol. We consider the standard simultaneous communication model where at each round each party can send a message to any other party, but these messages can only depend on information received in previous rounds. The aforementioned [7,11] solutions depend on the (multiplicative) depth of (the arithmetic representation of) the function f. For depth d, they require d rounds of communication (and the communication and computational complexity are polynomial in the number of parties n and the circuit size of f). In terms of lower bound, it is not hard to show that most functions cannot be privately computed with less than two rounds, but no better lower bound is known.

Constant-round information-theoretic protocols were first constructed by Bar-Ilan and Beaver [5] and were later extended in several works (cf. [13]). Ishai and Kushilevitz [21,22] approached the 2-round lower bound: They presented a 3-round protocol, and in fact showed that a 2-round protocol is possible if instead of honest majority one requires that more than two-thirds of the parties are honest. Ishai and Kushilevitz note that their methods fall short of achieving the ultimate result and leave it as an open problem to resolve whether it is possible to achieve 2-round honest-majority protocol for all functions [21, Sect. 6]:

> *"An open question of a somewhat different flavor is that of finding the exact number of rounds required for privately evaluating an arbitrary (i.e., a worst-case) function f with an optimal privacy threshold. Using randomizing polynomials, an upper bound of 3 was obtained. If this bound is tight (i.e., 2 rounds are not enough) then, in a very crude sense, the randomizing polynomials approach is non-restrictive."*

In this work, we resolve the aforementioned open question. We show that indeed any functionality can be privately computed in a 2-round protocol that only requires honest majority. The communication and computational complexity are asymptotically comparable to previous solutions.

Theorem 1 (2-round unconditional MPC). *At the presence of honest majority, privately computing any functionality with perfect correctness and perfect privacy reduces non-interactively to the task of privately computing a degree-2 functionality. Consequently, in this setting, any function f can be privately* *computed in two rounds with polynomial efficiency in the number of parties and in the size of the formula (or even branching program) that computes f.*[1]

Furthermore, under the assumption that one-way functions exist, it is possible to improve the computational and communication complexity to polynomial in the size of the circuit computing f (rather than its formula size or exponential in the circuit depth), at the cost of only achieving computational security. Note that the honest majority condition cannot be lifted in this setting (unless one-way functions imply oblivious transfer).

Theorem 2 (2-round MPC in minicrypt). *Assume the existence of one-way functions. Then, privately computing any polynomial-time functionality with computational privacy and honest majority reduces non-interactively to the task of privately computing a polynomial-time computable degree-2 functionality. Consequently, in this setting, any function f can be privately computed in two rounds with polynomial efficiency in the number of parties and the circuit size of f. The protocol makes only a black-box use of the one-way function.*

Prior to this work, Beaver, Micali and Rogaway [6,24] (henceforth BMR) constructed the first constant-round computationally private MPC assuming honest majority and one-way functions. A careful analysis of their construction leads to 3 rounds.[2]

See Sect. 1.3 below for comparison with recent related results such as [1,14].

The Client-Server Setting. Our results extend to the so-called client-server setting [12], which considers a communication graph of the following form: A set of *clients* that have inputs send messages (in a single round) to a set of *servers*, the servers perform local computation and send messages (in a single round) back to the clients, who can then recover their outputs. Our methods show how to achieve security in the semi-honest setting so long as there is an honest majority among clients and an honest majority among servers. We note that ideally we would like to only require honest majority among servers, our methods provide a path towards this goal but falls short of achieving it. (This point will be further discussed towards the end of Sect. 1.1.)

1.1 Our Techniques

Ishai and Kushilevitz introduced the notion of randomizing polynomials, which was since generalized to the notion of randomized encoding (RE) [3]. A function f is encoded by a function g if the output of g allows to reconstruct the output of f and nothing else. The [21] result essentially shows that any function f can be

[1] Branching programs (BP) are believed to be more powerful than formulas since the BP complexity of any function is at most polynomial in its formula size, whereas the converse is believed to be false.

[2] Throughout the paper, we refer to the simplified version of the BMR protocol that appears in Rogaway's thesis [24].

encoded by a function g of multiplicative degree 3 (over the binary field). Thus, instead of applying the [7,11] protocol to compute the function f directly, it is possible to apply it to compute g (the encoding of f). Since degree 3 functions can be computed in 3 rounds with honest majority, or in 2 rounds if more than two-thirds of the parties are honest, the encoding of [21,22] implies MPC protocols with these properties for all functions. We note that the computational complexity and output length of the encoding g may be significantly larger than those of f and indeed scale (roughly) polynomially with its formula size. An additional minor caveat is that the encoding g is a randomized function, even if f was deterministic. This is resolved using the standard technique of secret sharing the random tape between all users, i.e. each user holds private randomness and the function g is computed with a random tape that is the XOR of all private tapes. This transformation does not effect the multiplicative degree and therefore does not change the round complexity of the resulting protocol (though it incurs a poly(n) factor in computational and communication complexity).

It is evident from the above outline that if one could find a RE with multiplicative degree 2, the round complexity of MPC will be resolved. However, it was shown in [21] that such randomized encodings do not exist, at least if perfect correctness and security are sought (we recall that our solution achieves perfect correctness and security). The quotation above therefore suggests that the resolution of the round complexity of MPC will also resolve the question of optimality of the RE approach to the problem.

In this work, we show that indeed RE is too restrictive to resolve the round complexity problem. We present a natural generalization that we call multi-party randomized encoding (MPRE). This object allows to analyze randomized encodings in the specific context of MPC, and naturally translate it to protocols similarly to RE. While RE encodes a *computation* and ignores the partitioning of inputs between the parties, an MPRE takes into account the way that inputs and outputs are distributed among parties. Correspondingly, this notion of encoding allows to encode a *multiparty functionality* by another *multiparty functionality* (in contrast to the RE notion which allows to encode a function by another function). In this sense MPRE is much closer in spirit to MPC protocols, and one can easily go from protocols to MPREs and back. Being a *multiparty functionality*, in MPRE inputs are split between different parties who may also employ private local randomness (which does not make sense in the context of standard RE). The round complexity of the protocol induced by the MPRE depends on the *effective degree*, which allows preprocessing of local randomness. Theorem 1 follows by showing that any functionality has MPRE with effective degree 2 which is private against adversarial minority.

Multi-party Randomized Encoding (MPRE). The definition of MPRE is inspired by that of RE, but with the emphasis that inputs and outputs can belong to different players. If we consider a multi-party functionality $f(x_1, \ldots, x_n) = (y_1, \ldots, y_n)$, then an MPRE of f would be a randomized functionality

$$g((x_1, r_1), \ldots, (x_n, r_n); s) = (z_1, \ldots, z_n),$$

where s is a global random string (which, we bear in mind, will be shared among users when a protocol is to be derived) and r_i is the local random string of player i. Decoding requires that for each i, y_i can be recovered from z_i. The privacy requirement is that for any "legitimate" adversarial coalition $A \subseteq [n]$, the r and z values of all players in A can be simulated given their x and y values. In the context of honest majority we can consider protecting against all A of cardinality strictly less than $n/2$, but the MPRE notion is more general and allows some function classes to be encoded while allowing *any* adversarial $A \subseteq [n]$ (indeed we show such an encoding for a useful class). It is possible to show the expected composition theorem, arguing that if g is MPRE of f which is private against some class of adversarial coalitions $\mathcal{A}_1 \subseteq 2^{[n]}$, and there is a protocol that privately computes g against some class of adversarial coalitions $\mathcal{A}_2 \subseteq 2^{[n]}$, then the same protocol (augmented with local decoding) can be used to compute f, and is private against $\mathcal{A}_1 \cap \mathcal{A}_2$. It thus follows that if g is MPRE of f which is private against all adversarial minorities, and if g has effective degree 2 (allowing preprocessing of local randomness), then f has a 2-round protocol which is private against any adversarial minority.[3] Showing that all functions have such encoding will be our goal towards proving Theorem 1. For formal definitions of MPRE, composition and relation to other notions see Sect. 3.

How to Encode any Function. As explained above, our goal is to show that any functionality $f(x_1, \ldots, x_n) = (y_1, \ldots, y_n)$ has an encoding that is both secure against all adversarial minorities and has effective degree 2. We do this in a sequence of steps. The first step is noticing that we can get a "friendly" MPRE from *any* protocol for computing f, even one with many rounds. We stress that this will not be our final MPRE. The definition of this MPRE g is straightforward: the output of party i is simply its view in the protocol, augmented with all the intermediate values computed locally by i. Note that this new functionality now requires local randomness of the parties. The fact that these views were generated by a protocol will be of particular use to us since the outputs of g can be viewed as wires of a boolean circuit, where each wire belongs to a different party in the computation. The view of each party in the protocol (i.e. its output in the functionality g) consists of values that it received from other parties, and values that it computed locally. We can thus envision a circuit whose gates are "owned" by players, and there are additional syntactic "transmission gates" that represent a message passing from one player to the other. Transmission gates do not have any functionality but rather represent change of ownership, still they will be useful for our next step. We call such an MPRE "protocol compatible" and describe their properties formally in Sect. 4. Specifically, we will consider the MPRE induced (essentially) by the 3-round protocol that is based on [7,22].

---

[3] In fact, we show that the computation of f privately reduces to g via a non-interactive reduction that makes a single call to g.

By employing a composition theorem for MPRE, it suffices to encode the functionality g by an MPRE h of effective degree 2. Indeed, we show that any *protocol-compatible functionality* g (i.e. one whose outputs can be represented as local views of parties in a multi-party protocol, or equivalently as wires of a circuit of the structure described above), can be encoded with effective degree-2 and privacy against *any* adversarial coalition. The MPRE takes great resemblance to the well known RE scheme that is based on information-theoretic garbled circuit [22]. (Specifically, it is based on the point-and-permute variant of Yao's garbled circuit [6,24,26].) This randomized encoding scheme takes a circuit, and for each wire it samples two wire keys and a permutation bit, and its output is a list of "garbled tables" together with the permutation bits of the output wires. Expressing this in algebraic form leads to degree 3 randomized encoding. More generally, the degree of each garbled gate G is $\deg(G) + 1$.

In our MPRE, the wire keys will be sampled using the global randomness (which down the line is shared between all parties). Crucially, the permutation bits will be generated using the local randomness of the party that "owns" this wire, as per the protocol compatible functionality. One can verify that this description results in an encoding with effective degree 2. Indeed, the encoding consists of two type of gates: local-computation gates and transmission gates. In local-computation gates G, the input and output wires of the gate are owned by the same party, thus this party can preprocess the permutation bits and reduce the degree to 2. In the case of transmission gates, the fan-in is 1, and so the degree is only 2. The same proof as in [4,6,22,24] can be used to show MPRE privacy. The construction is described in detail in Sect. 5.

Putting the two components together results in an MPRE h for every f which is secure against all adversarial minorities and has effective degree 2, giving rise to our final 2-round protocol. The computational and communication complexity are analyzed in the respective sections. Section 6 contains the proof of Theorem 1, putting together all relevant components.

The Computational Setting. To prove Theorem 2, we start with the standard observation that for shallow circuits the computational and communication complexity of the information theoretic protocol are polynomial. We again use standard properties of the [6] protocol, to obtain an MPRE that can be written as an evaluation of a shallow circuit over values that are computed locally by the players with a black-box access to a pseudorandom generator. This allows us to apply Theorem 1 towards proving Theorem 2. See Sect. 6 for details.

The Client-Server Setting and an Open Problem. MPREs are applicable to the client-server setting in an immediate manner. Let g be an MPRE of f which is secure against some class of adversarial coalitions $\mathcal{A}$. Assume that g can be computed in the client-server setting with security against a class $\mathcal{A}$ of client coalitions and a class $\mathcal{B}$ of server coalitions. Then f is computable in the client-server setting with security against $\mathcal{A}$ client coalitions and $\mathcal{B}$ server coalitions.

In our setting, we show that all functions f have g with effective degree 2 and security against dishonest minority. One can verify that the protocols of [7,11], when applied to degree 2 functions, imply client-server protocols with security against arbitrary client collusion and dishonest server minority. The conclusion is that security is achieved if there is honest majority of both clients and servers.

This application constitutes an additional motivation to investigate whether every function f has an MPRE g with effective degree 2 and security against arbitrary collusion. We are not aware of any impossibility result for such encoding (in particular, honest majority will still be needed for our MPC application in order to compute g). Its existence, however, will allow to remove the requirement for honest majority of clients in the client-server setting and is expected to have other interesting consequences.

1.2 Broader Perspective: Degree vs. Round Complexity

Since the pioneering constructions of perfect MPC [7,11], there appears to be a tight relation between the round complexity of privately computing a functionality f at the presence of honest majority to its algebraic degree. This relation was refined by [21], who showed that instead of considering the degree of f, one should focus on the degree of a RE $\hat{f}$ of f. Our work further replaces the notion of RE-degree with the *effective degree* of an MPRE $\hat{f}$ of f. As a result, we finally prove the conjectured *equivalence* between round complexity and (the "right" notion of) degree.

It is instructive to take a closer look at the notion of effective degree and see how it relates to existing notions. Recall that effective degree essentially allows the parties to apply arbitrary local-preprocessing of their private randomness (and inputs) "for free", without charging it towards the degree. This relaxation is crucial for our results. Indeed, it can be shown that degree-d MPRE directly imply degree-d RE (see full version). Also observe that the notion of effective degree inherently requires to treat the encoding $\hat{f}$ as a *multiparty functionality*, and therefore effective degree becomes meaningless in the case of RE. In this sense, MPRE is a convenient intermediate point between a protocol to RE; It takes into account the views of different players (which is crucial for defining effective degree) while being a non-interactive (and therefore easy to manipulate) object.

Let us further note that the methodology of degree-reduction via local preprocessing is not new. In particular, it is crucially employed in classical constant-round MPC protocols including Yao's two-party protocol [26] and its multiparty variant [6,24]. Using our terminology, these protocols implicitly yield computational MPRE of constant effective degree. In particular, assuming one-way functions, Yao's protocol yields a computational MPRE of effective degree 2 for any efficiently computable 2-party functionality, and the BMR protocol yields a computational MPRE of effective degree 3 for any efficiently computable n-party functionality. Indeed, an important part of our conceptual contribution is to provide a formal, easy-to-handle, framework that captures this use of degree-reduction via preprocessing.

1.3 Other Related Works

Benhamouda and Lin [8] and Garg and Srinivasan [16] have recently constructed 2-round computationally-private protocols for arbitrary (efficiently computable) functions. This result is incomparable to Theorem 2: It does not require honest majority (i.e., privacy holds against arbitrary coalitions), but relies on a stronger computational assumption (the existence of (two-round) Oblivious Transfer which is minimal in this setting). We further note that our high level approach shares some similarities with these works. Indeed, our notion of MPRE abstracts and generalizes the notion of *garbled protocols*, introduced by Garg and Srinivasan [15], which plays a key role in both [8] and [16].

Independently of our work, two recent papers study the notion of minimal round complexity for MPC in the honest majority setting. Ananth et al. [1] focus on secure computation in the presence of certain types of active (malicious) adversaries, and present protocols under the assumption of honest majority in addition to some computational and/or setup assumptions. Most relevant to our work is a consequence of one of their result showing that based on one-way functions there is a 2-round protocol against semi-honest adversarial minority (in fact, they achieve a stronger notion called "security with abort"). Contrary to our work, the [1] protocol is not applicable in the information theoretic setting, and therefore does not have bearing on the question of MPC with perfect security. Furthermore, our approach shows a reduction from the computation of general functionalities to the computation of degree-2 functionalities, which is not achieved by [1] (even implicitly, as far as we can tell).

Garg, Ishai and Srinivasan [14] study the construction of information theoretic security for semi-honest MPC in various settings. Most relevant to this work is their construction of a 2-round protocol with perfect security for formulas. However, in their protocol, unlike ours, communication complexity grows super-polynomially with the number of players. One can again attribute this to falling short of reducing the general MPC task to the task of computing degree-2 functionalities.

1.4 Paper Organization

We begin with some general background on multiparty functionalities and secure multiparty computation in Sect. 2. In Sect. 3, we introduce the notion of multipatry randomized encoding, and discuss its properties. In Sect. 4 we show how to use MPC protocols (in particular [7]) to obtain "protocol-compatible" MPRE, and in Sect. 5 show how to transform such an encoding into a degree-2 MPRE based on information-theoretic garbled circuits. Section 6 uses these tools to prove our main theorems. Some of the proofs are omitted from this version and can be found in the full version (available on eprint).

2 Preliminaries

This section defines multiparty functionalities and provides some basic background on secure computation. It will convenient to use a somewhat non-standard notation for functionalities, and so even an expert reader may want to read this part carefully. (In contrast, the MPC subsection can be safely skipped.)

2.1 Multi-party Functionalities

An n-party functionality is a function that maps the inputs of n parties to a vector of outputs that are distributed among the parties. Without loss of generality, we assume that the inputs of each party are taken from some fixed input domain X (e.g., bit strings of fixed length). It will be convenient to represent a functionality by a pair $f : X^n \to \{0,1\}^m$ and $P : [m] \to 2^{[n]}$. The function f maps the joint inputs of all parties $x = (x_1, \ldots, x_n)$ to an output vector $y = (y_1, \ldots, y_m)$, and the mapping $P : [m] \to 2^{[n]}$ determines the distribution of outputs between the parties, i.e., the i-th output y_i should be delivered to the parties in the set $P(i)$. By default (and without loss of generality), we assume that $P(i)$ is always a singleton and therefore think of P as a mapping from $[m]$ to $[n]$. Sometimes the output partition function P will be implicit, and refer to f as a functionality. We further use the convention that, for a string $y = f(x)$ and a subset of parties $T \subseteq [n]$, the restriction of y to the coordinates held by the parties is denoted by $y[T] = (y_j)_{j:P(j)\in T}$. When $T = \{i\}$ is a singleton, we simply write $y[i]$.

We will also make use of *randomized functionalities.* In this case, we let f take an additional random input r_0 and view r_0 as an internal source of randomness that does not belong to any party. We typically write $f(x_1, \ldots, x_n; r_0)$ and use semicolon to separate the inputs of the parties from the internal randomness of the functionality.

Finally, a central notion in this work is that of *effective degree* of a functionality, which generalizes the standard notion of degree. A multi-output functionality f has degree D if each of its outputs can be written as an $\mathbb{F}_2$-polynomial of degree D over the deterministic and random inputs. Intuitively, the effective degree is the degree of the functionality if the parties are allowed arbitrary local preprocessing. A formal definition follows.

Definition 1 (Effective degree). *A (possibly randomized) n-party functionality $f : X^n \times R' \to \{0,1\}^m$ has* effective degree *d if there exists a tuple of local preprocessing functions $(h_1, \ldots, h_n)$ and a degree-d function h such that*

$$h(h_1(x_1), \ldots, h_n(x_n); r') = f(x_1, \ldots, x_n; r'), \quad (1)$$

for every $x_1, \ldots, x_n$ and internal randomness r'.

2.2 Standard Background on Secure Computation

Through the paper, we assume a fully-connected network with point-to-point private channels. We focus on semi-honest (aka passive) secure computation hereafter referred to as *private* computation. (See, e.g., [9,10,17], for more detailed and concrete definitions.)

Definition 2 (Private computation). *Let $f(x_1, \ldots, x_n)$ be a (possibly randomized) n-party functionality. Let π be an n-party protocol. We say that the protocol* τ-privately computes f with perfect privacy *if there exists an efficient randomized simulator* Sim *for which the following holds. For any subset of corrupted parties $T \subseteq [n]$ of size at most τ, and every tuple of inputs $x = (x_1, \ldots, x_n)$ the joint distribution of the simulated view of the corrupted parties together with output of the honest parties in an ideal implementation of f,*

$$\mathsf{Sim}(T, x[T], y[T]), \quad y[\bar{T}], \qquad \text{where } y = f(x) \text{ and } \bar{T} = [n] \setminus T,$$

is identically distributed to

$$\mathsf{View}_{\pi,T}(x), \quad \mathsf{Output}_{\pi,\bar{T}}(x),$$

where $\mathsf{View}_{\pi,T}(x)$ and $\mathsf{Output}_{\pi,\bar{T}}(x)$ are defined by executing π on x with fresh randomness and concatenating the joint view of the parties in T (i.e., their inputs, their random coin tosses, and all the incoming messages), with the output that the protocol delivers to the honest parties in $\bar{T}$. The computational variant of the definition is obtained by settling for computational indistinguishability with respect to non-uniform polynomial-time adversaries.

Secure Reductions. To define secure reductions, consider the following *hybrid* model. An n-party protocol augmented with an oracle to the n-party functionality g is a standard protocol in which the parties are allowed to invoke g, i.e., a trusted party to which they can securely send inputs and receive the corresponding outputs. The notion of τ-security generalizes to protocols augmented with an oracle in the natural way.

Definition 3. *Let f and g be n-party functionalities. A τ* perfectly-private *reduction from f to g is an n-party protocol that given an oracle access to the functionality g, τ-privately realizes the functionality f with perfect security. We say that the reduction is* non-interactive *if it involves a single call to f (and possibly local computations on inputs and outputs), but no further communication. The notions of τ* computationally-private *reduction is defined analogously.*

Appropriate composition theorems, e.g. [17, Theorems 7.3.3, 7.4.3] and [9], guarantee that the call to g can be replaced by any protocol that τ-privately realize g, without violating the security of the high-level protocol for f.

3 Multi-party Randomized Encodings

In this section we formally present the notion of *multi-party randomized encodings* (Sect. 3.2), relate it to MPC protocols (Sect. 3.3), and study its properties (Sect. 3.4). As discussed in the introduction, this new notion can be viewed as a relaxation of the more standard notion of randomized encoding of functions. (See Sect. 3.1).

3.1 Randomized Encoding of Functions

We begin with the standard notion of randomized encoding (RE) [3,21]. In the following let X, Y, Z, and R be finite sets.

Definition 4 (Randomized Encoding [3,4]**).** *Let $f : X \to Y$ be a function. We say that a function $\hat{f} : X \times R \to Z$ is a δ-correct, (t, ϵ)-private* randomized encoding *of f if the following hold:*

- *δ-**Correctness:** There exist a deterministic decoder Dec such that for any input $x \in X$,*

$$\Pr_{r \xleftarrow{\$} R}[\mathsf{Dec}(\hat{f}(x;r)) \neq f(x)] \leq \delta.$$

- *(t, ϵ)-**Privacy:** There exists a randomized simulator Sim such that for any $x \in X$ and any circuit Adv of size t*

$$\left| \Pr[\mathsf{Adv}(\mathsf{Sim}(f(x))) = 1] - \Pr_{r \xleftarrow{\$} R}[\mathsf{Adv}(\hat{f}(x;r)) = 1] \right| \leq \epsilon.$$

We refer to the second input of $\hat{f}$ as its random input, *and a use semicolon (;) to separate deterministic inputs from random inputs.*

An encoding $\hat{f}$ is useful if it is simpler in some sense than the original function f. In the context of MPC the main notion of simplicity is the degree of the encoding, where the each output of $\hat{f}$ is viewed as a polynomial over (x, r). Other notions of simplicity have been used in other contexts. (See [2,20] for surveys on REs.)

3.2 MPRE Definition

Inspired by the notion of randomized encoding of functions [3,21], we define the notion of multiparty randomized encoding (MPRE). Syntactically, we encode a *functionality* $f(x_1, \ldots, x_n)$ by a randomized functionality

$$\hat{f}((x_1, r_1), \ldots, (x_n, r_n); r_0)$$

that employs internal randomness $r_0 \in R$ and augments the input of each party by an additional random input $r_i \in R$, for some fixed domain R (by default bit-string of fixed length). Roughly speaking, the view of the encoding $\hat{f}((x_1, r_1), \ldots, (x_n, r_n); r_0)$ that is available to a subset T of parties (i.e., the parties inputs, randomness and outputs) should contain the same information that is revealed to the subset T by the functionality $f(x)$ (i.e., the inputs and outputs).

The following heavily relies on our (somewhat non-standard) formalization of multi-party functionalities, see Sect. 2.1.

Definition 5 (Multi-Party Randomized Encoding (MPRE). *Let* $f : X^n \to \{0,1\}^m$ *be an* n*-party deterministic functionality with an output partition* $P : [m] \to [n]$. *We say that an* n*-party randomized functionality* $\hat{f} : (X \times R)^n \times R \to \{0,1\}^s$ *with output partition* Q *is a multi-party randomized encoding of* f *with privacy threshold of* τ *if the following hold:*

- ***Perfect Correctness:*** *There exists a deterministic decoder* Dec *such that for every party* $i \in [n]$, *and every tuple of input-randomness pairs*

$$((x_1, r_1), \dots, (x_n, r_n)) \in (X \times R)^n$$

and every internal randomness $r_0 \in R$ *it holds that*

$$\mathsf{Dec}(i, \hat{y}[i], x_i, r_i) = y[i],$$

where $y = f(x_1, \dots, x_n)$, $\hat{y} = \hat{f}((x_1, r_1), \dots, (x_n, r_n); r_0)$, *and, recall that* $\hat{y}[i]$ *is the restriction of* $\hat{y}$ *to the coordinates delivered to party* i *by* $(\hat{f}, Q)$, *and* $y[i]$ *is the restriction of* y *to the coordinates delivered to party* i *by* (f, P).[4]
- (τ, t, ϵ)*-**Privacy:*** *There exists a randomized simulator* Sim *such that for every set* $T \subseteq [n]$ *of parties of size at most* τ *and every set of inputs* $x = (x_1, \dots, x_n)$ *it holds that the random variable*

$$\mathsf{Sim}(T, x[T], y[T]), \qquad \text{where } y = f(x_1, \dots, x_n)$$

and the random variable

$$(x[T], r[T], \hat{y}[T]),$$

where

$$\hat{y} = \hat{f}((x_1, r_1), \dots, (x_n, r_n); r_0), \text{ and } (r_0, r_1, \dots, r_n) \xleftarrow{\$} R^{n+1},$$

cannot be distinguished by a t*-size circuit with advantage better than* ϵ.

We say that privacy is perfect *if* (τ, t, ϵ)*-privacy holds for any* t *and* $\epsilon = 0$. *We always represent an MPRE* $\hat{f}$ *by a Boolean circuit that computes* $\hat{f}$, *and define the* size *and* depth *of* $\hat{f}$ *to be the size and depth of the corresponding circuit. We refer to the randomness* r_0 *as the* internal randomness *of the encoding. When such randomness is not used, we refer to* $\hat{f}$ *as an MPRE with no internal randomness.*

Observe that any functionality trivially encodes itself. Indeed, MPRE $\hat{f}$ becomes useful only if it is simpler in some sense than f. Jumping ahead, our main notion of simplicity will be effective degree.

[4] As in the case of RE, one can relax correctness and allow a small decoding error. Since all our constructions natively achieve perfect correctness, we do not define this variant.

Remark 1 (Perfect and Computational encodings of infinite functionalities). Definition 5 naturally extends to an infinite sequence of functionalities $f = \{f_\lambda\}_{\lambda\in\mathbb{N}}$ where f_λ is an $n(\lambda)$-party functionality whose domain, range, and complexity may grow polynomially with λ. We say that a sequence of $n(\lambda)$-party functionalities $\hat{f} = \{\hat{f}_\lambda\}_{\lambda\in\mathbb{N}}$ is a perfectly correct $(\tau(\lambda), t(\lambda), \epsilon(\lambda))$-private MPRE of f if there exists an efficient algorithm (compiler) which gets as an input 1^λ and outputs (in time polynomial in λ) three circuits $(\hat{f}_\lambda, \mathsf{Dec}_\lambda, \mathsf{Sim}_\lambda)$ which form a perfectly correct $(\tau(\lambda), t(\lambda), \epsilon(\lambda))$-private MPRE of f_λ. We refer to an MPRE as *perfect* if the above holds for any function $t(\cdot)$ and for $\epsilon = 0$, and refer to it as being *computational* if the above holds for $t(\lambda) = \lambda^{\omega(1)}$ and $\epsilon(\lambda) = 1/\lambda^{\omega(1)}$. Similar extensions applies to REs (as was done in previous works).

Remark 2. The parameter λ is being used to quantify both the complexity of f (circuit size and input length) and the security level (computational privacy). When describing some of our constructions, it will be convenient to separate between these two different roles and treat λ solely as a security parameter (independently from the complexity of f). Computational privacy will be guaranteed (in the sense of the above definition) as long as λ is set to be polynomial in the complexity of f.

3.3 From MPRE to MPC Protocol

The main motivation for studying MPRE's is the following simple observation.

Proposition 1. *Let f be an n-party functionality. Let g be a perfect (resp., computational) MPRE of f with privacy threshold of τ. Then, the task of τ-privately computing f with perfect privacy (resp., computational privacy) reduces non-interactively to the task of τ-privately computing g with perfect privacy (resp., computational privacy).*

In particular, by using standard composition theorems any protocol π that τ-privately computes g with perfect (resp., computational) privacy can be turned into a protocol π' with the same complexity and round complexity that τ-privately computes f with perfect (resp., computational) privacy.

The proof of Proposition 1 appears in the full version.

3.4 Manipulating MPRE

One can always get rid of the internal randomness r_0 of an MPRE

$$\hat{f}((x_1, r_1), \ldots, (x_n, r_n); r_0)$$

by extending the randomness of each party with an additional random string r'_i and applying the functionality $\hat{f}$ with r_0 set to $\sum_i r'_i$. Here, we assume that the randomness domain R is a set of fixed length strings and so addition stands for bit-wise XOR. (More generally, this transformation works as long as "addition" forms a group operation over the randomness space R.) Formally, the following holds.

Proposition 2 (Removing internal randomness). *Suppose that the functionality* $\hat{f}((x_1,r_1),\ldots,(x_n,r_n);r_0)$ *is a perfectly correct* (τ,t,ϵ)*-private MPRE of* (f,P)*. Then the functionality*

$$g((x_1,r_1,r'_1),\ldots,(x_n,r_n,r'_n)) := \hat{f}((x_1,r_1),\ldots,(x_n,r_n);\sum_i r'_i)$$

is a perfectly correct (τ,t,ϵ)*-private MPRE of* (f,P)*.*

Note that g has the same algebraic degree and the same effective degree as $\hat{f}$ over $\mathbb{F}_2$. (A multi-output functionality f has degree D if each of its outputs can be written as an $\mathbb{F}_2$-polynomial of degree D over the deterministic and random inputs. For effective degree see Definition)

Composition (Re-Encoding MPRE). The composition property of REs ([3,4]) asserts that if we take an encoding $g(x;r)$ of $f(x)$, view it as a deterministic function $g'(x,r)$ over x and r, and re-encode this function by a another RE $h(x,r;r')$, then the function $h'(x;(r,r'))$ is an encoding of f. We prove a similar statement regarding MPRE's.

Lemma 1 (Composition). *Let* $(f(x_1,\ldots,x_n),P)$ *be an* n*-party functionality and assume that the functionality* $(g((x_1,r_1)\ldots,(x_n,r_n)),Q)$ *perfectly encodes* f *with threshold* τ_1 *and no internal randomness. Further assume that the functionality* $(h(((x_1,r_1),r'_1)\ldots,((x_n,r_n),r'_n);r'_0),M)$ *perfectly encodes the functionality* (g,Q) *(viewed as a deterministic functionality over the domain* $(X')^n$ *where* $X'=(X\times R)$ *with threshold* τ_2*). Then, the functionality* (h',M)*, where*

$$h'((x_1,(r_1,r'_1)),\ldots,(x_n,(r_n,r'_n));r'_0) := h(((x_1,r_1),r'_1)\ldots,((x_n,r_n),r'_n)),$$

is a perfect MPRE of f *with threshold* $\min(\tau_1,\tau_2)$*.*

(Observe that h' is defined identically to h except each party i treats x_i as its deterministic input of i and (r_i,r'_i) as its randomness.)
A similar lemma holds in the computational setting as well.

Lemma 2 (Composition (Computational version)). *Let* $f=\{f_\lambda\}$ *be an infinite family of* $n(\lambda)$*-party functionalities which is computationally encoded by the families of functionalities* $g=\{g_\lambda\}$ *with privacy threshold* $\tau(\lambda)$ *and with no internal randomness. Suppose that* $h=\{h_\lambda\}$ *computationally encode* g *with privacy threshold of* $\tau'(\lambda)$*. Then,* (h',P)*, defined as in Lemma 1, forms a computational encoding of* f *with privacy threshold of* $\min(\tau,\tau')$*.*

4 Encoding via Protocol-Compatible Functionalities

In this section we show that any functionality f can be encoded by a so-called *protocol compatible* functionality g that enjoys "nice" syntactic properties.

4.1 From MPC Protocol to MPRE

We begin by noting that any protocol naturally induces an MPRE as shown below.

Definition 6 (The view functionality). *Let π be an n-party protocol in which the i-th party holds a deterministic input x_i and private randomness r_i. The n-party* view functionality *g_π is defined as follows:*

- *The input of the i-th party is (x_i, r_i).*
- *The output of the i-th party consists of all the messages that are sent to her in an execution of π (on the inputs $(x_1, r_1), \ldots, (x_n, r_n)$).*

We also consider the extended view functionality *in which, in addition to the above, g_π delivers to each party i all intermediate values that are computed locally by i, where the local computation of every party is viewed as a Boolean circuit.*

Note that the view and extended view can deterministically be derived from each other.

Proposition 3. *Let π be a protocol that implements the n-party functionality $f(x_1, \ldots, x_n)$ with perfect correctness and perfect (resp., computational) privacy against a passive adversary that may corrupt up to τ players. Then the view functionality and the extended view functionality of π encode the functionality f with perfect correctness and perfect (resp., computational) privacy threshold τ.*

Proof. The proposition follows immediately from the fact that π privately implements f as per Definition 2. The correctness of π translates into correctness of g_π and the τ-privacy of the protocol immediately translates into τ-privacy of the MPRE.

An extended view functionality g_π has several useful syntactic properties. These are captured by the following notion of *protocol compatible* functionality.

Definition 7. *A* protocol compatible *functionality (f, P) is a functionality with no internal randomness that can be represented by a Boolean circuit C as follows.*

- *The circuit C takes the same inputs as f. The outputs $y = (y_1, \ldots, y_m)$ of $f(x)$ consist of the values of all the wires in the circuit (including internal wires and input wires) sorted under some topological order (inputs are first).*
- *The computation in C is performed via two types of gates.*
  - *A* transmission gate *delivers a value from one party to another, i.e. it maps a single input y_a to a single output y_b such that $y_a = y_b$ and possibly $P(a) \neq P(b)$.*
  - *A* local computation gate *(wlog, NAND gate) maps two inputs (y_a, y_b) to a single output y_c, where $P(a) = P(b) = P(c)$.*

Proposition 4. *Let π be an n-party protocol and let g_π be its extended view functionality. Then, g_π is protocol compatible.*

Proof. By definition, every output bit of g_π is either an input bit, the result of some local computation, or some incoming message.

Remark 3 (Extended view in a hybrid model). Consider a protocol π operates in a h-hybrid model where h is some n-party functionality. (Recall that this means that the parties can invoke a call to an ideal version of h.) In this case, the view functionality and the extended view functionality (which are still well defined) still form an MPRE of f just like in Proposition 3. However it will not satisfy the syntax of Definition 7.

4.2 BGW-Based MPRE

The extended view functionality of the semi-honest protocol from [7], henceforth denoted BGW, gives rise to the following MPRE.

Theorem 3 (BGW-based protocol-compatible encoding). *Every n-party functionality f can be perfectly encoded with threshold privacy of $\tau = \lfloor \frac{n-1}{2} \rfloor$ by a protocol-compatible MPRE g of size $O(S \cdot \mathrm{poly}(n))$ and depth $O(D \cdot \log n)$ where S denotes the circuit size of f and D denotes the multiplicative depth of f.*

Jumping ahead, we mention that in order to derive our main theorem with complexity which grows polynomially in the number of parties, it is crucial to make sure that the depth of g is at most logarithmic in n.

Proof. We consider the BGW protocol π for computing f against a passive adversary that corrupts up to τ parties. By Propositions 3 and 4, it suffices to show that π can be implemented so that its extended-view functionality g_π is of size $O(S \cdot \mathrm{poly}(n))$ and depth $O(D \cdot \log n)$.

Recall that π interprets f as an arithmetic circuit over a sufficiently large field $\mathbb{F}$ of size $|\mathbb{F}| > n$ and that each party i is associated with a fixed public field element $\alpha_i \in \mathbb{F}$ (as a property of the protocol and independently of the input). Thus the first n powers of each α_i are to be treated as pre-computed constants. The local computation L of every party for each multiplication gate (and for the input gates) can be implemented by a $\mathrm{poly}(n)$-size arithmetic circuit of constant depth whose addition gates have unbounded fan-in and the multiplication gates have fan-in 2. (Indeed, all local computation can be written as matrix-vector multiplications.) This gives rise to an arithmetic circuit with bounded fan-in gates, $\mathrm{poly}(n)$ size, $O(\log n)$ depth and *constant* multiplicative depth.

We continue by showing that such an arithmetic circuit L can be realized by a Boolean NC^1 circuit (of size $\mathrm{poly}(n)$, depth $O(\log n)$ and bounded-fan gates). Indeed, letting $\mathbb{F} = \mathrm{GF}[2^{O(\log n)}]$ be a binary extension field, we can trivially implement field addition by a Boolean circuit of constant depth and $O(\log n)$ size (and bounded-fan gates). Field multiplication can be implemented by an $\mathrm{AC}^0[\oplus]$ circuit of size $\mathrm{polylog}(n)$ [19], and therefore by a Boolean circuit of size $\mathrm{polylog}(n)$, depth $\log(\mathrm{polylog}(n))$ and bounded-fan gates. It follows that L is in NC^1.

Finally, we note that in BGW addition gates require only local computation. This local computation consists of $O(n)$ parallel fan-in-2 additions of field elements. Since $\mathbb{F}$ is a binary extension field this can be implemented by a constant depth (NC^0) circuit of size $O(n \log n)$. We conclude that the extended view functionality g_π has the desired complexity.

5 Degree-2 Encodings for Protocol-Compatible Functionalities

In this section we show that any protocol-compatible functionality f can be encoded by a functionality $\hat{f}$ with *effective degree* 2. That is, each output of $\hat{f}$ can be computed as a degree-2 function over n values that can be computed by the parties locally (see Definition 1).
The following theorem will be proved in Sect. 5.1.

Theorem 4. *Let (f, P) be a protocol-compatible n-party functionality of depth d and output length m. Then, f has a perfect n-private MPRE $\hat{f}$ of effective-degree 2 and total complexity* $\text{poly}(2^d, m)$.[5]

Remark 4 (Other properties of the MPRE). The encoding $\hat{f}$ constructed in Theorem 4 satisfies several additional properties that will not be used in our work, but may be useful elsewhere.

1. The encoding $\hat{f}$ is fully-decomposable and affine in x, that is for any fixing of the private randomness the residual functionality $\hat{f}(x)$ is a degree-1 function in x and each output bit of $\hat{f}$ depends on at most a single bit of the input x.
2. The preprocessing functions $(h_1, \ldots, h_n)$ that achieve effective degree of 2 only manipulate the private randomness. That is, we construct $h_i(x_i, r_i)$ s.t. $h_i(x_i, r_i) = (x_i, h'_i(r_i))$, where h'_i is a degree-2 function.

5.1 Proof of Theorem 4

Let $f : X^n \to \{0,1\}^m$ be a protocol-compatible functionality of depth d. We now show how to encode f via a functionality

$$\hat{f} : (X \times R)^n \times R' \to Y'$$

with effective degree of 2. In addition to the private randomness r_i of each party, the functionality $\hat{f}$ uses internal randomness r'. (The latter can be removed via Proposition 2 while keeping an effective degree of 2.)

[5] Note that the circuit size of f does not appear explicitly in this statement, however for protocol-induced functionalities, the circuit size of f is equal to the output length m.

Notation. Let C be the Boolean circuit that represents f (as per Definition 7). Recall that the circuit C has m wires and it contains gates of two types: local computation gates and transmission (identity) gates. We prove the theorem with respect to circuits C in which the fan-out of transmission gates is one and the fan-out of local computation gates is two. This is without loss of generality, since any circuit C can be transformed to satisfy these restrictions while preserving the size (up to a constant factor), and at the expense of increasing the depth to $d' = d \log m$; we may ignore this overhead since $\mathrm{poly}(2^{d'}, m) = \mathrm{poly}(2^d, m)$. For every $i \in [m]$, let $P(i) \in [n]$ denote the party that holds the value of the ith wire in C.

Randomness. Our MPRE employs the following random bits. For every wire $i \in [m]$, the party $P(i)$ samples a random masking bit α_i. In addition, for every wire i, the functionality uses the internal randomness to sample a pair of random strings (keys) s_i^0, s_i^1 of length ω_i. The length ω_i of an "output wire" (i.e., a wire that does not enter any gate) is set to zero and the length of all other keys will be defined recursively (from top-to bottom) later. We assume that both strings, s_i^0, s_i^1, are partitioned to two equal-size blocks, and index these blocks by a bit $b \in \{0,1\}$, where $s_i^{a,b}$ denotes the bth block of s_i^a.

The outputs of the MPRE. We traverse the circuit C gate-by-gate in reverse topological order (from the output gates to the input wires), and let the functionality $\hat{f}$ deliver the following outputs to *all* parties.

- For every **local computation gate** g with incoming wires i, j and outgoing wires k, ℓ, we output four values (known as the gate table) defined as follows. For every $\beta_i, \beta_j \in \{0,1\}$, set

$$\gamma = G(\alpha_i \oplus \beta_i, \alpha_j \oplus \beta_j), \tag{2}$$

  where $G(\cdot,\cdot)$ is the function computed by the gate, and output the value

$$\begin{aligned} Q_g^{\beta_i,\beta_j} := &((s_k^\gamma \| \gamma \oplus \alpha_k) \| (s_\ell^\gamma \| \gamma \oplus \alpha_\ell)) \\ &\oplus\ s_i^{\alpha_i \oplus \beta_i, \beta_j}\ \oplus\ s_j^{\alpha_j \oplus \beta_j, \beta_i}. \end{aligned} \tag{3}$$

  One should view $Q_g^{\beta_i,\beta_j}$ as a ciphertext where the message is associated with the outgoing wires (first line of Eq. 3) is encrypted using a one-time pad under the combination of the keys associated with the incoming wires (second line of Eq. 3). Correspondingly, we set the length ω_i (resp., ω_j) of the keys s_i^0, s_i^1 (resp., s_j^0, s_j^1) to be $2(\omega_k + 1 + \omega_\ell + 1)$.
- **Transmission gates** are treated analogously. That is, for every transmission (identity) gate g with incoming wire i and outgoing wire k, we output the following two values. For every $\beta_i \in \{0,1\}$, set $\gamma = \beta_i \oplus \alpha_i$ and output the value

$$Q_g^{\beta_i} := (s_k^\gamma \| \gamma \oplus \alpha_k)\ \oplus\ s_i^{\alpha_i \oplus \beta_i}.$$

  Correspondingly, we set the length ω_i of the keys s_i^0, s_i^1 to be $\omega_k + 1$.

- For every **input wire** i, output the *masked value* $x_i \oplus \alpha_i$ and the *active key* $s_i^{x_i}$.

Effective Degree and Complexity. Observe that a term of the form s^a can be written as a degree-2 function of a and s (i.e., $a \cdot s^1 + (1-a) \cdot s^0$). Hence, all the outputs of the encoding are of degree 2 except for ciphertexts that correspond to local computation gates as in Eq. (3) in which the selection bit γ itself is a degree-2 function (and so the overall degree of $Q_g^{\beta_i,\beta_j}$ increases to 3). However, since the party $p = P(i) = P(j)$ knows both α_i and α_j, the value γ can be locally pre-computed and so the effective degree of the encoding is 2.

The complexity of the encoding is polynomial in the circuit size and the size of the largest key. A proof by induction shows that the length ω_i of the ith key is at most $O(4^{h_i})$ where h_i is the height of the ith wire (i.e., the length of the longest path from i to an "output wire" that does not enter any gate). Following this analysis, the complexity of $\hat{f}$ is bounded by $\text{poly}(2^d, m)$.

Correctness. Fix some input $x = (x_1, \ldots x_n) \in X^n$ and let y_i denote the value induced by x on the ith wire. We show that the party $P(i)$ can recover y_i from the encoding $\hat{y}$ and its private randomness. Since the ith mask α_i is given to $P(i)$ as part of its private randomness, it suffices to show that $P(i)$ can recover the *masked value* $\hat{y}_i := y_i \oplus \alpha_i$. Indeed, as in standard garbled circuits, every party can recover the masked bit $\hat{y}_k := y_k \oplus \alpha_k$ together with the *active key* $s_k^{y_k}$, for every wire k. This is done by traversing the circuit from the inputs to the outputs as follows. For input wires the pair $\hat{y}_k, s_k^{y_k}$ is given explicitly as part of the encoding. For an internal wire k, that leaves a local computation gate g with incoming wires i, j this is done by using the masked bits $\hat{y}_i, \hat{y}_j$ of the input wires to select the ciphertext $Q_k^{\hat{y}_i,\hat{y}_j}$ and then decrypting (i.e., XOR-ing) it with $s_i^{y_i,\hat{y}_j} \oplus s_j^{y_j,\hat{y}_i}$ that can be computed based on the active keys of the incoming wires. One can verify that this procedure recovers the desired values correctly. The case of transmission gates is treated similarly.

Privacy. We first claim that an external observer (that does not see the private randomness) can perfectly simulate the encoding given the list of masked values $(\hat{y}_k)_{k \in [m]}$.

Claim 1. *There exists a simulator* Sim' *that takes as an input an* m*-bit vector* $\hat{y} = (\hat{y}_i)_{i \in [m]}$*, runs in time* $\text{poly}(m, 2^d)$ *and satisfies the following guarantee. For every input* x *and every fixing of* $\alpha = (\alpha_i)_{i \in [m]}$*, the random variable*

$$\mathsf{Sim}'(y_1 \oplus \alpha_1, \ldots, y_m \oplus \alpha_m),$$

where y_i *is the value induced by* x *on the* i*th wire, is distributed identically to the encoding* $\hat{f}(x)$ *conditioned on the above fixing of* α.

The claim is implicit in the standard proof of information-theoretic garbled circuit (cf. [22]); it is proved in the full version.

Based on Claim 1, we define a perfect simulator Sim for the MPRE. Fix an arbitrary coalition $T \subseteq [n]$ and let I be the set of wires owned by parties in T, i.e., $I = \{i : P(i) \in T\}$. Given the inputs $x[T]$ of T, and a vector of output values $(y_i)_{i\in I}$, the simulator does the following. For $i \in I$, sample uniformly the local randomness α_i and set $\hat{y}_i = y_i \oplus \alpha_i$. For $i \notin I$ sample $\hat{y}_i$ uniformly at random. Next invoke the simulator Sim' on $\hat{y} = (\hat{y}_i)_{i\in[m]}$ and output the result.

We prove that the simulation is perfect. Fix some input x, some $\alpha_I = (\alpha_i)_{i\in I}$, and let $y = f(x)$ and $y_I = (y_i)_{i\in I}$. We claim that the distribution sampled by $\mathsf{Sim}(T, x[T], \alpha_I, y_I)$ is identical to the joint distribution of the encoding $\hat{f}(x)$ induced by the choice of $\alpha_{[m]\setminus I}, (s_i^0, s_i^1)_{i\in[m]}$ (and conditioned on the above fixing of α_I). Indeed, since the marginal distribution of the vector of masked bits $(\hat{y}_1, \ldots, \hat{y}_m)$ is perfectly simulated, this follows from Claim 1.

6 Putting It All Together

In this section we prove the following theorems using the tools we developed in previous sections.

Theorem 5. *Every n-party functionality f can be encoded by a perfect MPRE g with privacy threshold of $\tau = \lfloor \frac{n-1}{2} \rfloor$, effective degree 2 and complexity polynomial in n and S where S is the size of the branching program that computes f.*

Theorem 6. *Every n-party functionality f can be encoded by a computational MPRE g with privacy threshold of $\tau = \lfloor \frac{n-1}{2} \rfloor$, effective degree 2 and complexity polynomial in n and S where S is the size of the circuit that computes f. Moreover, the MPRE makes use of one-way functions in a balck-box way only as part of the local preprocessing step.*

Theorems 5 and 6 (whose proof is deferred to Sects. 6.1 and 6.2) can be used to derive our main results (Theorems 1 and 2).

Proof (Proof of Theorems 1 *and* 2*).* We prove Theorem 1 (resp., Theorem 2): Given an n-party functionality f that is computable by a branching program of size S (resp., computable by a Boolean circuit of size S), construct the perfect MPRE g promised by Theorem 5 (resp., the computational MPRE g promised by Theorem 6). By Proposition 1, f non-interactively $\lfloor \frac{n-1}{2} \rfloor$-reduces to g with perfect privacy (resp., computational privacy). Since g has an effective degree 2, the functionality g itself n-privately reduces to a degree-2 functionality g' (in a trivial way). A composition of these reductions yields the desired reduction.

To prove the second ("Consequently") part of the theorem, we employ the BGW protocol $\pi_{g'}$ to privately compute g' in 2 rounds (since its degree is 2) and complexity of $\text{poly}(n, S)$ at the presence of honest majority. Plugging this protocol into the above reduction and using standard composition theorems (cf. [9]), we get a 2-round protocol for f with similar complexity and perfect (resp., computational) privacy.

6.1 Perfect MPRE for Branching Programs (Proof of Theorem 5)

Let f be an n-party functionality that is computable by a branching program of size S. By [21], such a function has degree-3 perfect randomized encoding $g_1(x;r)$ of poly(S) size. Recall that such an RE yields an n-private MPRE, and let us get rid of the private randomness by applying Proposition 2. This gives us a degree-3 MPRE g_2 of f whose complexity is poly(S) with privacy threshold of n. Next, we encode g_2 by the BGW-based protocol-compatible encoding (Theorem 3) and get a protocol-compatible perfect MPRE g_3 of size $O(S \cdot \text{poly}(n))$, depth $O(\log n)$ and privacy threshold of $\tau = \lfloor \frac{n-1}{2} \rfloor$. Using our information-theoretic encoding from Theorem 4 (based on garbled circuits), we get a τ-private perfect MPRE g_4 of g_3 with complexity poly(n, S) and effective degree 2. By the composition lemma (Lemma 1), the MPRE g_4 perfectly encode f with privacy threshold of τ. □

6.2 Computational MPRE for Circuits (Proof of Theorem 6)

To prove the theorem we make use of the following MPRE that is based on the BMR protocol [6].

Claim 2. *Let f be an n-party functionality that is computable by an S-size circuit. Then f has a computational MPRC g that does not use internal randomness and has privacy threshold of $n-1$ and polynomial complexity in n and S. Most importantly, the function g can be written as*

$$A(B_1(x_1, r_1), \ldots, B_n(x_n, r_n)),$$

where the combining function A can be computed by a circuit of size poly(n, S) *and depth $O(\log(nS))$, and each of the functions B_i (that correspond to local computations) make a black-box use of a PRG.*

The proof of the Claim appears in the full version. The proof of Theorem 6 proceeds as follows. It suffices to prove the theorem with respect to PRG, since the latter reduce to OWF via a black-box reduction [18].

Let f be an n-party functionality with complexity S and let g denote the computational MPRE

$$g(x, r) = A(B_1(x_1, r_1), \ldots, B_n(x_n, r_n)),$$

promised in Claim 2.

Since A can be computed by a circuit of size poly(n, S) and depth $O(\log(nS))$ it can also be computed by a branching program of size $S' = \text{poly}(n, S)$. Therefore, by Theorem 5, the function A admits a perfect MPRE

$$\hat{A}((y_1, r'_1), \ldots, (y_n, r'_n))$$

with privacy threshold of $\tau = \lfloor \frac{n-1}{2} \rfloor$, effective degree 2 and complexity poly(n, S') = poly(n, S). Consider the functionality $\hat{g}$ obtained by substituting y_i with $B_i(x_i, r_i)$, i.e.,

$$\hat{g}\left((x_1, (r_1, r'_1)), \ldots, (x_n, (r_n, r'_n))\right) := \hat{A}\left((B_1(x_1, r_1), r'_1), \ldots, (B_n(x_n, r_n), r'_n)\right).$$

Observe that $\hat{g}$ has an effective degree 2 and complexity of poly(n, S). Moreover, since $\hat{A}$ perfectly encodes A with τ-privacy, $\hat{g}$ also perfectly encodes g with τ-privacy. (Indeed, one can verify that this form of local substitution preserves privacy and correctness.) By the composition property of MPRE (Lemma 2), this means that $\hat{g}$ is a computational τ-private MPRE of f as required. □

Acknowledgements. We are grateful to Yuval Ishai, Akshayaram Srinivasan, Muthuramakrishnan Venkitasubramaniam, and Hoteck Wee for valuable discussions and to the anonymous referees of TCC 2018 for carefully reading this paper and for providing us with helpful feedback.

References

1. Ananth, P., Choudhuri, A.R., Goel, A., Jain, A.: Round-optimal secure multiparty computation with honest majority. In: Shacham, H., Boldyreva, A. (eds.) CRYPTO 2018. LNCS, vol. 10992, pp. 395–424. Springer, Cham (2018). https://doi.org/10.1007/978-3-319-96881-0_14
2. Applebaum, B.: Garbled circuits as randomized encodings of functions: a primer. Tutorials on the Foundations of Cryptography. ISC, pp. 1–44. Springer, Cham (2017). https://doi.org/10.1007/978-3-319-57048-8_1
3. Applebaum, B., Ishai, Y., Kushilevitz, E.: Cryptography in NC^0. In: Proceedings of 45th Symposium on Foundations of Computer Science (FOCS 2004), 17–19 October 2004, Rome, Italy, pp. 166–175. IEEE Computer Society (2004)
4. Applebaum, B., Ishai, Y., Kushilevitz, E.: Computationally private randomizing polynomials and their applications. Comput. Complex. **15**(2), 115–162 (2006)
5. Bar-Ilan, J., Beaver, D.: Non-cryptographic fault-tolerant computing in constant number of rounds of interaction. In: Rudnicki, P. (ed.) Proceedings of the Eighth Annual ACM Symposium on Principles of Distributed Computing, Edmonton, Alberta, Canada, 14–16 August 1989, pp. 201–209. ACM (1989)
6. Beaver, D., Micali, S., Rogaway, P.: The round complexity of secure protocols (extended abstract). In: Ortiz, H. (ed.) Proceedings of the 22nd Annual ACM Symposium on Theory of Computing, 13–17 May 1990, Baltimore, Maryland, USA, pp. 503–513. ACM (1990)
7. Ben-Or, M., Goldwasser, S., Wigderson, A.: Completeness theorems for non-cryptographic fault-tolerant distributed computation (extended abstract). In: Simon [25], pp. 1–10 (1988)
8. Benhamouda, F., Lin, H.: k-round multiparty computation from k-round oblivious transfer via garbled interactive circuits. In: Nielsen and Rijmen [23], pp. 500–532 (2018). https://doi.org/10.1007/978-3-319-78375-8_17
9. Canetti, R.: Security and composition of multiparty cryptographic protocols. J. Cryptol. **13**(1), 143–202 (2000)
10. Canetti, R.: Universally composable security: a new paradigm for cryptographic protocols. In: 42nd Annual Symposium on Foundations of Computer Science, FOCS 2001, 14–17 October 2001, Las Vegas, Nevada, USA, pp. 136–145. IEEE Computer Society (2001)
11. Chaum, D., Crépeau, C., Damgård, I.: Multiparty unconditionally secure protocols (extended abstract). In: Simon [25], pp. 11–19 (1988)
12. Damgård, I., Ishai, Y.: Constant-round multiparty computation using a black-box pseudorandom generator. In: Shoup, V. (ed.) CRYPTO 2005. LNCS, vol. 3621, pp. 378–394. Springer, Heidelberg (2005). https://doi.org/10.1007/11535218_23

13. Feige, U., Kilian, J., Naor, M.: A minimal model for secure computation (extended abstract). In: Leighton, F.T., Goodrich, M.T. (eds.) Proceedings of the Twenty-Sixth Annual ACM Symposium on Theory of Computing, 23–25 May 1994, Montréal, Québec, Canada, pp. 554–563. ACM (1994)
14. Garg, S., Ishai, Y., Srinivasan, A.: Two-round MPC: information-theoretic and black-box. (2018, to appear in TCC)
15. Garg, S., Srinivasan, A.: Garbled protocols and two-round MPC from bilinear maps. In: Umans, C., (ed.) 58th IEEE Annual Symposium on Foundations of Computer Science, FOCS 2017, 15–17 October 2017 Berkeley, CA, USA, pp. 588–599. IEEE Computer Society (2017)
16. Garg, S., Srinivasan, A.: Two-round multiparty secure computation from minimal assumptions. In: Nielsen and Rijmen [23], pp. 468–499 (2018). https://doi.org/10.1007/978-3-319-78375-8_16
17. Goldreich, O.: The Foundations of Cryptography - Volume 2, Basic Applications. Cambridge University Press, Cambridge (2004)
18. Håstad, J., Impagliazzo, R., Levin, L.A., Luby, M.: A pseudorandom generator from any one-way function. SIAM J. Comput. **28**(4), 1364–1396 (1999)
19. Healy, A., Viola, E.: Constant-depth circuits for arithmetic in finite fields of characteristic two. In: Durand, B., Thomas, W. (eds.) STACS 2006. LNCS, vol. 3884, pp. 672–683. Springer, Heidelberg (2006). https://doi.org/10.1007/11672142_55
20. Ishai, Y.: Randomization techniques for secure computation. In: Prabhakaran, M., Sahai, A. (eds.) Secure Multi-Party Computation. Cryptology and Information Security Series, vol. 10, pp. 222–248. IOS Press, Amsterdam (2013)
21. Ishai, Y., Kushilevitz, E.: Randomizing polynomials: a new representation with applications to round-efficient secure computation. In: 41st Annual Symposium on Foundations of Computer Science, FOCS 2000, 12–14 November 2000, Redondo Beach, California, USA, pp. 294–304. IEEE Computer Society (2000)
22. Ishai, Y., Kushilevitz, E.: Perfect constant-round secure computation via perfect randomizing polynomials. In: Widmayer, P., Eidenbenz, S., Triguero, F., Morales, R., Conejo, R., Hennessy, M. (eds.) ICALP 2002. LNCS, vol. 2380, pp. 244–256. Springer, Heidelberg (2002). https://doi.org/10.1007/3-540-45465-9_22
23. Nielsen, J.B., Rijmen, V. (eds.) Advances in Cryptology - EUROCRYPT 2018 - 37th Annual International Conference on the Theory and Applications of Cryptographic Techniques, Proceedings, Part II, 29 April–3 May 2018, Tel Aviv, Israel. LNCS, vol. 10821. Springer, Heidelberg (2018). https://doi.org/10.1007/978-3-319-78375-8
24. Rogaway, P.: The round-complexity of secure protocols. Ph.D. thesis, MIT (1991)
25. Simon, J. (ed.) Proceedings of the 20th Annual ACM Symposium on Theory of Computing, 2–4 May 1988, Chicago, Illinois, USA. ACM (1988)
26. Yao, A.C.-C.: How to generate and exchange secrets (extended abstract). In: FOCS, pp. 162–167 (1986)

Two-Round Adaptively Secure Multiparty Computation from Standard Assumptions

Fabrice Benhamouda[1(✉)], Huijia Lin[2], Antigoni Polychroniadou[3], and Muthuramakrishnan Venkitasubramaniam[4]

[1] IBM Research, Yorktown Heights, NY, USA
fabrice.benhamouda@normalesup.org
[2] University of California, Santa Barbara, CA, USA
[3] Cornell Tech, New York, NY, USA
[4] University of Rochester, Rochester, NY, USA

Abstract. We present the first *two-round* multiparty computation (MPC) protocols secure against malicious *adaptive* corruption in the common reference string (CRS) model, based on DDH, LWE, or QR. Prior two-round adaptively secure protocols were known only in the two-party setting against semi-honest adversaries, or in the general multiparty setting assuming the existence of indistinguishability obfuscation (iO).

Our protocols are constructed in two steps. First, we construct two-round oblivious transfer (OT) protocols secure against malicious adaptive corruption in the CRS model based on DDH, LWE, or QR. We achieve this by generically transforming any two-round OT that is only secure against static corruption but has certain oblivious sampleability properties, into a two-round adaptively secure OT. Prior constructions were only secure against semi-honest adversaries or based on iO.

Second, building upon recent constructions of two-round MPC from two-round OT in the weaker *static* corruption setting [Garg and Srinivasan, Benhamouda and Lin, Eurocrypt'18] and using equivocal garbled circuits from [Canetti, Poburinnaya and Venkitasubramaniam, STOC'17], we show how to construct two-round *adaptively* secure MPC from two-round *adaptively* secure OT and constant-round *adaptively* secure MPC, with respect to both malicious and semi-honest adversaries. As a corollary, we also obtain the first 2-round MPC secure against semi-honest adaptive corruption in the plain model based on augmented non-committing encryption (NCE), which can be based on a variety of assumptions, CDH, RSA, DDH, LWE, or factoring Blum integers. Finally, we mention that our OT and MPC protocols in the CRS model are, in fact, adaptively secure in the Universal Composability framework.

1 Introduction

The notion of secure multi-party computation (MPC) allows N mutually distrustful parties $P_1, \ldots, P_N$ to securely compute a functionality $f(\bar{x}) =$

A. Beimel and S. Dziembowski (Eds.): TCC 2018, LNCS 11239, pp. 175–205, 2018.
https://doi.org/10.1007/978-3-030-03807-6_7

$f_1(\bar{x}), \ldots, f_N(\bar{x})$ of their corresponding private inputs $\bar{x} = x_1, \ldots, x_N$, such that party P_i receives the value $f_i(\bar{x})$. Loosely speaking, the security requirements are that the parties learn nothing more from the protocol than their prescribed output, and that the output of each party is distributed according to the prescribed functionality. This should hold even in the case that a malicious adversary seizes control of an arbitrary subset of the parties and make them arbitrarily deviate from the protocol. A major achievement in the 80's is demonstrating that any function that can be efficiently computed, can be efficiently computed securely [3,29,38]. Since then, the round complexity of computing general functionalities has been a central question in the area of MPC.

Answering this question depends on what powers the adversaries have. In the *static corruption* model, the adversary may seize control, or *corrupt*, a subset of parties *before* the protocol begins, and dictate their behavior throughout the protocol execution. A stronger and more realistic model is the *adaptive corruption* model, where the adversary can decide to corrupt more parties at any time *during* the execution of the protocol. The adaptive corruption model captures "hacking attacks" where an adversary has the capability to seize control of parties' machines at any time, through for instance known vulnerabilities or backdoor; in an extreme, the adversary may eventually corrupt all parties. Protecting against such attacks provides stronger security guarantees. Moreover, security against adaptive corruption is instrumental for achieving everlasting security and leakage resilience.

In the static corruption model, a long line of research on two-round protocols [2,6–9,14,20,25–27,31,34,36] that culminated in two recent works by Benhamouda and Lin [5] and Garg and Srinivasan [28] has completely resolved the round complexity of MPC from minimal assumptions. The works of [5] and [28] constructed two-round MPC protocols from any two-round oblivious transfer protocols, in the Common Reference String (CRS) model.[1] Moreover, in the semi-honest setting, these works provide two-round protocols in the plain model (i.e., without CRS).

In contrast, the round-complexity of MPC in the adaptive corruption model is far from being resolved. Prior works [14,16,22,26] constructed 2-round MPC protocols secure against adaptive corruption, based on the strong assumption of Indistinguishability Obfuscation (iO) for polynomial-sized circuits, and other standard assumptions. However, the security of current indistinguishability obfuscation schemes is not well understood. When restricting to using only standard assumptions, Damgård et al. [23] construct 3-round protocols based on LWE for all-but-one corruptions and Canetti et al. [17] construct a constant round protocol based on simulatable public key encryption for arbitrary corruptions. Only in the most restricted case of 2-Party Computation (2PC) in the presence of semi-honest adversaries, they gave a *two-round* protocol based on

[1] Actually, the protocol of [5] additionally relies on Non-Interactive Zero-Knowledge (NIZK) proofs in the CRS model. But as observed in [28] and this work, the use of NIZK can be removed.

the minimal assumptions. The state-of-affairs leaves the following basic questions open:

Can we have the following based on standard assumptions?
- *Two-round MPC secure against adaptive corruption by semi-honest adversaries in the plain model.*
- *Two-round MPC secure against adaptive corruption by malicious adversaries in the CRS model.*

In fact, the second question remains open even for the special case of 2PC protocols computing the Oblivious Transfer (OT) functionality. In the literature, there are 2-round OT protocols secure against either static corruption by malicious adversaries, *or* adaptive corruption by semi-honest adversaries, from various assumptions [18,19,37]. However, when considering adaptive corruption by malicious adversaries, the best protocols based on standard assumptions have 3 rounds whether assuming erasures [19] or not [1].[2] Therefore, another basic question that remains open so far is,

Can we achieve a two-round OT protocol that is secure against adaptive corruption by malicious adversaries in the CRS model from standard assumptions?

In this work, we answer all above questions affirmatively, obtaining two-round MPC protocols secure against adaptive corruption by semi-honest adversaries in the plain model from minimal assumptions, and 2-round protocols secure against malicious adversaries in the CRS model from any of the following assumptions: Decisional Diffie-Hellman (DDH), Quadratic Residuosity (QR), or Learning with Error (LWE). Our constructions satisfy the stronger UC-security notion [10].

Our Results

We present our results in the *local* CRS model where every session of protocol execution has a local independently sampled CRS. We believe that our protocol constructions and security proofs can be easily adapted to the *single* CRS model where all sessions share a single CRS as in [15]; see Sect. 2.4 for more discussion.

Towards constructing 2-round MPC protocols secure against adaptive corruption, or adaptive-MPC for short, we first show that this task can be reduced to constructing a 2-round OT protocol secure against adaptive corruption, or adaptive-OT for short, at the presence of either semi-honest or malicious adversaries. More precisely,

Theorem 1.1 (Informal). *Assuming the existence of a two-round oblivious transfer protocol and a constant-round MPC protocol secure against adaptive*

[2] Abdalla et al. [1] constructed a two-round OT protocol secure against the weaker semi-adaptive corruption model where the adversary corrupts one of the two parties at the beginning of the execution and the other party adaptively during or after the execution. It is known that such a protocol can be generically converted to become secure against adaptive corruption using NCE. However, the resulting protocol would be 3-round.

corruption by malicious adversaries in the CRS model (resp. semi-honest adversaries in the plain model), there exists a 2-round MPC protocol for any functionality f that is UC-secure against adaptive corruption of any subset of the parties by malicious adversaries, in the CRS model (resp. or semi-honest adversaries in the plain model).

At a high-level, our construction follows the blueprint of the recent constructions of 2-round MPC from 2-round OT in the static corruption model [5,28]. Their key idea is collapsing the number of rounds of arbitrary multi-round MPC protocols into just 2, using just garbled circuits and 2-round OT. Following the same technique, we show that adaptive security follows naturally, when the underlying garbled circuits and OT are also adaptively secure. The work by Canetti et al. [17] constructs adaptively secure garbled circuits, called *equivocal garbling scheme*, from the minimal assumption of one-way functions. However, using equivocal garbled circuits directly only allows us to collape rounds of *constant-round* MPC protocols; otherwise, the resulting 2-round protocol would become inefficient (see Sect. 2.3 for more discussion). The work of Canetti et al. [17] also constructs constant-round adaptive-MPC protocols based on simulatable PKE. Thus, it boils down to construct 2-round adaptive-OT.

When the adversaries are semi-honest, two-round adaptive-OT can be based on augmented Non-Committing Encryption (NCE) [15], which in turn can be based on CDH, RSA, DDH, LWE or factoring Blum-integers [18]. Furthermore, constant-round MPC secure against adaptive corruption can be be constructed from NCE (which is implied by augmented NCE) and semi-honest two-round adaptive-OT [17]. Thus, we obtain the following corollary.

Corollary 1.2. *Assuming augmented non-committing encryption, there exists a 2-round MPC protocol for any functionality f that is UC-secure against adaptive corruption of any subset of the parties by semi-honest adversaries.*

However, there are no known constructions of 2-round adaptive OT protocols against malicious adversaries even in the (local) CRS model. The natural approach of using non-interactive zero-knowledge proofs to convert a *semi-honest* adaptive-OT protocol, say the one in [15], into a *malicious* adaptive-OT protocol require additional rounds, specifically, to incorporate a coin-tossing protocol. The work of [1] comes close by achieving a weaker notion of semi-adaptivity in two rounds based on DDH. Our main technical contribution is constructing two-round adaptive-OT against malicious adversaries from various assumptions. More precisely,

Theorem 1.3 (Informal). *Assuming DDH, QR, or LWE, there exists a 2-round OT protocol that is UC-secure against adaptive corruption by malicious adversaries in the CRS model.*

Combined with previous theorem and the construction of constant-round adaptive-MPC in [17] (which can be constructed from simulatable PKE, which can itself be build from DDH, QR, or LWE too [18]) we obtain as a corollary 2-round adaptive-MPC against malicious adversaries from the same assumptions:

Corollary 1.4. *Assuming DDH, QR, or LWE, there exists a 2-round MPC protocol for any functionality f that is UC-secure against adaptive corruption of any subset of the parties by malicious adversaries in the CRS model.*

To achieve the above theorem, we provide a generic framework that compiles any OT protocol secure against static corruption, or static-OT for short, with appropriate "oblivious sampleability" properties, to a full-fledged adaptive-OT protocol, in just 2-rounds. Roughly speaking, oblivious sampleability refers to the following properties: *(i) Receiver-oblivious-sampleability*:one can obliviously sample the OT receiver's message, and claim that an honestly generated receiver's message *was* obliviously sampled, and similarly *(ii) Sender oblivious sampleability*: one can obliviously sample the sender's message, and claim that an honestly generated sender's message for *random* input strings was obliviously sampled. Then, we show that static-OT with such oblivious sampleability can be instantiated from various concrete assumptions, including DDH, or LWE, or QR.

2 Technical Overview

We start with an overview of our construction of 2-round adaptive-OT and then move to 2-round adaptive MPC in the local CRS model. In the end, we briefly discuss future work on extending our results to the single CRS model.

2.1 2-Round Adaptive-OT

To construct a 2-round adaptive-OT Π_3, we start with a basic 2-round static-OT[3] Π with the special property of sender and receiver *oblivious sampleability*, and transform it in three steps to gradually achieve security against different adaptive corruption scenarios:

- *Sender semi-adaptive corruption* refers to the case where the receiver is corrupted at the beginning of the protocol execution and the sender is corrupted after the execution, i.e. post-execution.
- *Receiver semi-adaptive corruption* refers to the symmetric case where the sender is corrupted from the beginning and the receiver is corrupted post-execution.
- *Semi-adaptive corruption* refers to either of the above two scenarios. In comparison, full fledged *adaptive corruption* considers the additional scenario where neither sender nor receiver is corrupted during execution, and both corrupted post-execution in an arbitrary order; we refer to the latter *semi-honest post-execution corruption.*

Starting with a static-OT Π with sender and receiver oblivious sampleability,

[3] In fact, it suffices if the OT protocol Π is secure against semi-honest senders, and malicious receivers.

- *In Transformation 1,* we transform Π into Π_1 that achieves security against sender-semi-adaptive corruption (and preserves security in static corruption scenarios). This step crucially relies on the sender oblivious sampleability of Π, and preserves receiver oblivious sampleability.
- *In Transformation 2,* we rely on receiver oblivious sampleability to transform Π_1 into Π_2 to achieve security under receiver-semi-adaptive corruption, while preserving security under sender-semi-adaptive corruption. Π_2 is now secure under semi-adaptive corruption.
- *In Transformation 3,* finally, we transform the semi-adaptive-OT Π_2 into an adaptive-OT Π_3, using additionally augmented NCE.

Below, we describe ideas in these three transformation, starting with the third transformation.

Transformation 3: Semi-Adaptive-OT to Adaptive-OT. Consider a semi-adaptive OT Π_2, whose algorithms for generating the CRS, the sender, and receiver messages are denoted as Setup, S_2, R_2. The only corruption scenario that Π_2 does not handle is *semi-honest post-execution corruption* (i.e., neither sender nor receiver is corrupted during execution, but both corrupted post-execution in an arbitrary order). It is known that semi-adaptive OT can be transformed into adaptive-OT by sending messages of the former using private channels implemented by Non-Committing Encryption (NCE) [24], which, however, produces a three-round protocol. In two rounds, the above corruption case *alone* can be handled using *augmented* NCE as done in the construction of semi-honest adaptive-OT by Canetti, Lindell, Ostrovsky, and Sahai (CLOS) [15]. Below, we use their protocol to lift the security of Π_2.

Augmented NCE. NCE is a public key encryption with the special property of *equivocality*: one can simulate a pair of pubic key and ciphertext (pk, c) and later "open" them to any plaintext m, by efficiently finding randomness ρ and τ that "explains" the public key and ciphertext consistently w.r.t. m (meaning $\tilde{c} = \mathsf{NEnc}(\tilde{\mathrm{pk}}, m; \rho)$, $(\tilde{\mathrm{pk}}, \tilde{\mathrm{sk}}) = \mathsf{NGen}(1^\lambda; \tau)$, $m = \mathsf{NDec}(\tilde{\mathrm{sk}}, \tilde{c})$).

A NCE is "augmented" if it has *i) oblivious key sampleability*: one can obliviously sample a public key pk' without knowing any corresponding secret key, and *ii) inverse key sampleability*: one can claim that an honestly generated or simulated public key pk was sampled obliviously by efficiently finding randomness that would make the oblivious key sampling algorithm produce pk.

"Patch" Semi-Adaptive-OT Π_2 Using Augmented NCE. To handle semi-honest post-execution corruption, we run Π_2 with the CLOS semi-honest adaptive-OT from augmented NCE in parallel as depicted below. The instance of Π_2 is generated using the receiver's choice bit σ and the sender's messages padded with two random strings $(m_0 \oplus r_0, m_1 \oplus r_1)$. In the instance of CLOS, the receiver samples one public key pk_σ honestly with sk_σ, and another $\mathrm{pk}_{1-\sigma}$ obliviously, followed by the sender encrypting the two random pads r_0, r_1 using respectively these two keys.

$S(m_0, m_1)$ $\xleftarrow{\text{ot1}(\sigma)}$ $\xleftarrow{\text{pk}_0,\ \text{pk}_1}$ $R(\sigma)$

$\xrightarrow{\text{ot2}(m_0 \oplus r_0, m_1 \oplus r_1)}$ $\xrightarrow{c_0 \leftarrow \mathsf{NEnc}(\text{pk}_0, r_0),\ c_1 \leftarrow \mathsf{NEnc}(\text{pk}_1, r_1)}$

To handle semi-honest post-execution, the trick is simulating the instance (ot1, ot2) of Π_2 using its simulator Sim_2 *for the case where the sender is statically corrupted* (recall that Π_2 is secure under semi-adaptive corruption). This can be done as the simulator can generate ot2 honestly using just random messages r'_0, r'_1: effectively, the sender of Π_2 is "corrupted" and instructed to act honestly with input r'_0, r'_1. Thus, Sim_2 can be used to simulate and equivocate the receiver's messages. The keys and ciphertexts in the instance of CLOS is simulated relying on properties of augmented NCE. Later, for instance, when the sender is corrupted first post-execution, the simulator, learning (m_0, m_1), finds the right "pads" $r_0 = m_0 \oplus r'_0$, $r_1 = m_1 \oplus r'_1$, and uses the equivocality of NCE to "explain" that the keys and ciphertexts are consistent with r_0, r_1. In the other case, when the receiver is corrupted first post-execution, the simulator, learning σ, m_σ, can explain pk_σ consistently with r_σ, and claim that $\text{pk}_{1-\sigma}$ were obliviously sampled using the inverse oblivious sampleability property.

It might seem that the above transformation can use any semi-honest adaptive OT. This is indeed the case only if semi-honest post-execution corruption was concerned. But, we also want the transformation to preserve security under semi-adaptive corruption (when Π_2 has this property). For that, we rely on special properties of the CLOS protocol; in particular, it is already secure against *malicious* sender, and simulated public keys from the receiver can be easily equivocated. See Sect. 5.5 for more details.

Transformation 2: Handling Receiver-Semi-Adaptive Corruption. We now move to handling the first scenario in semi-adaptive corruption, i.e. receiver semi-adaptive corruption. When the sender is maliciously corrupted from the beginning and the receiver is corrupted post-execution, the simulator needs to *(i)* simulate the receiver's message $\widetilde{\text{ot1}}$ without knowing the choice bit, *(ii)* extract both sender's messages m_0, m_1, *(iii)* and later equivocate $\widetilde{\text{ot1}}$ to any choice bit σ. A common approach in the literature for enabling equivocation is relying on appropriate oblivious sampleability property. We follow this approach and formalize the following receiver oblivious sampleability property.

Receiver Oblivious Sampleability: A two-round OT protocol (in the CRS model) has receiver oblivious sampleability if *(1)* one can obliviously sample receiver's message $\widetilde{\text{ot1}}$, and *(2)* can claim that an honestly generated receiver's message ot1 for any choice bit σ was obliviously sampled, by efficiently finding consistent randomness ρ that would make the oblivious sampling algorithm produce ot1. Furthermore, messages and randomness produced in these two ways are indistinguishable

$$(\text{crs}, \widetilde{\text{ot1}}, \widetilde{\rho}) \approx (\text{crs}, \text{ot1}, \rho).$$

A Naive Idea and its Problem. Given Π_1 with receiver oblivious sampleability, the basic idea is to let the receiver of Π_2 send two messages, where $\mathrm{ot1}_\sigma$ is generated honestly using the choice bit σ while $\widetilde{\mathrm{ot1}}_{1-\sigma}$ is sampled obliviously. The sender then replies $\mathrm{ot2}_0, \mathrm{ot2}_1$ respectively, where $\mathrm{ot2}_b$ is generated honestly w.r.t. $\mathrm{ot1}_b$ using message m_b at slot b and random message r_b at slot $1-b$. See the depiction below on the left.

$S(m_0, m_1)$		$R(\sigma)$	A		Sim
	$\mathrm{ot1}_0(0), \widetilde{\mathrm{ot1}}_1$ if $\sigma = 0$ $\widetilde{\mathrm{ot1}}_0, \mathrm{ot1}_1(1)$ if $\sigma = 1$ $\longleftarrow$			$\mathrm{ot1}_0(0), \mathrm{ot1}_1(1)$ $\longleftarrow$	
	$\mathrm{ot2}_0(m_0, r_0), \mathrm{ot2}_1(r_1, m_1)$ $\longrightarrow$			$\mathrm{ot2}_0, \mathrm{ot2}_1$ $\longrightarrow$	
	Left: Naive Protocol			*Right: Simulation*	

For the above protocol, simulation under receiver-semi-adaptive corruption can be done as follows: *(i)* the simulator can "plant" honestly generated receiver's messages $\mathrm{ot1}_0, \mathrm{ot1}_1$ for both choice bit 0 and 1. *(ii)* Upon receiving sender's messages $\mathrm{ot2}_0, \mathrm{ot2}_1$, it uses the OT output strings as the extracted sender's messages. Finally, *(iii)* the simulator equivocates the receiver's messages w.r.t. a choice bit by revealing the randomness ρ_σ used for generating $\mathrm{ot1}_\sigma$ honestly, and reverse sampling randomness $\widetilde{\rho}_{1-\sigma}$ for claiming that $\mathrm{ot1}_{1-\sigma}$ were obliviously sampled.

Though receiver-semi-adaptive corruption is resolved, unfortunately, the above protocol is not secure against malicious receivers (even though Π_1 is), as a cheating receiver can use the same strategy the simulator uses and violate sender's privacy.

Fixing the Problem. To overcome this, the simulator needs to have some unique advantage that malicious receivers do not have. Our idea is using an equivocal commitment ECom (in CRS model). More specifically, the receiver should send a ECom commitment c to its choice bit σ, so that, only the simulator can generate a simulated commitment $\tilde{c}$ and open it to both 0 and 1, but not cheating receivers. To incorporate this, the rest of the protocol needs to be modified accordingly: The two instances of OT Π_1 are replaced with two instances of 2 Party Computation (2PC): the b'th instance reveals to the receiver the message m_b conditioned on the receiver having a valid opening of c to b.

$S(m_0, m_1)$		$R(\sigma)$
	$\{\mathrm{ot1}_{0,k}(\tau_k)\}_k, \quad \{\widetilde{\mathrm{ot1}}_{1,k}\}_k$ if $\sigma = 0$	
	$c = \mathsf{ECom}(\sigma; \tau), \quad \{\widetilde{\mathrm{ot1}}_{0,k}\}_k, \quad \{\mathrm{ot1}_{1,k}(\tau_k)\}_k$ if $\sigma = 1$ $\longleftarrow$	
	$\left(\{\mathrm{ot2}_{0,k}(\ell^0_{k,0}, \ell^0_{k,1})\}_k, \mathrm{GC}_0\right), \left(\{\mathrm{ot2}_{1,k}(\ell^1_{k,0}, \ell^1_{k,1})\}_k, \mathrm{GC}_1\right)$ $\longrightarrow$	

Simulation in the receiver-semi-adaptive corruption scenario uses similar ideas as described above w.r.t. the naive protocol. Again, the simulator "plants" valid receiver's messages for both choice bit 0 and 1. In particular, it generates a simulated ECom commitment $\tilde{c}$ and two sets of ot1 messages corresponding to both opening τ^0, τ^1 of $\tilde{c}$ to 0 and 1, $\{\mathrm{ot1}_{0,k}(\tau_k^0)\}_k$, $\{\mathrm{ot1}_{1,k}(\tau_k^1)\}_k$. To equivocate to any choice bit σ, the simulator can again reveal the randomness used for generating the set $\{\mathrm{ot1}_{\sigma,k}\}$ of messages corresponding to τ_σ, and claim that the other set $\{\mathrm{ot1}_{1-\sigma,k}\}$ was sampled obliviously. The advantage of this protocol is that now malicious receiver cannot copy the simulator's strategy, as it cannot find opening of a ECom commitment to both 0 and 1.

Preserving Security under Sender-Semi-Adaptive Corruption. Furthermore, we show that if Π_1 is secure under sender-semi-adaptive corruption (i.e. where the receiver is maliciously corrupted from the beginning and the sender is corrupted post-execution), the above transformation preserves it. To this end, we need the second message of 2PC to be equivocal. This can be achieved by implementing 2PC using Π_1 and *equivocal garbled circuits* constructed by [17] from one-way functions.

In summary, our transformation 2 produces a semi-adaptive OT, starting from one that is only secure under sender-semi-adaptive corruption (and static corruption of the sender by a semi-honest adversary). We remark that our transformation is quite similar to the transformation presented in the recent work of [28] for achieving some equivocal property of receiver's message. However, their notion of equivocality is tailored for simulation in static corruption cases, and only need to provide *partial* randomness consistent with a choice bit σ. In adaptive corruption, equivocation requires providing *complete* randomness for generating the receiver's message. Thus, the two transformation differ in details; in particular, we crucially rely on receiver oblivious sampleability which is not needed in [28].

Transformation 1: Handling Sender-Semi-Adaptive Corruption. When the receiver is maliciously corrupted from the beginning and the sender is corrupted post-execution, the simulator needs to *(i)* extract the choice bit σ from the receiver's message ot1, and then obtain the output message m_σ, *(ii)* next simulate the sender's message $\widetilde{\mathrm{ot2}}$ knowing only m_σ, *(iii)* and finally be able to equivocate $\widetilde{\mathrm{ot2}}$ w.r.t. arbitrary $m_{1-\sigma}$. To enable equivocation, we again formulate an oblivious sampleability property now w.r.t. sender's messages.

> *Sender Oblivious Sampleability (Overly Simplified):* Roughly speaking, we want the property that *(1)* one can obliviously sample a sender's message $\widetilde{\mathrm{ot2}}$ (w.r.t. a crs and receiver's message ot1), and *(2)* can claim that an honestly generated sender's message ot2 for *random* messages r_0, r_1 was obliviously sampled, by efficiently finding randomness ρ that would make the oblivious sampling algorithm output ot2. Moreover, messages and randomness generated in these two ways are indistinguishable:

$$(\mathrm{crs}, \mathrm{ot1}, \widetilde{\mathrm{ot2}}, \widetilde{\rho}) \approx (\mathrm{crs}, \mathrm{ot1}, \mathrm{ot2}, \rho).$$

We remark that unfortunately the above description is overly simplified; for the proof to go through, the actual sender oblivious sampleability is more complex.

However, for simplicity of exposition, we use the above simple version in this high-level overview.

Staring from a static-OT Π with sender oblivious sampleability, we construct a bit-OT Π_1 with security under sender semi-adaptive corruption. (Note that constructing bit-OT is without loss of generality, as it implies string-OT with the same security in different corruption scenarios.) The basic idea is again to let sender of Π_1 send multiple messages of Π. This redundancy allows simulation to "plant" honestly generated sender's messages for both input bit 0 and 1, at either slot. Then, later to equivocate to $m_{1-\sigma}$, the simulator can correctly open the message generated with value $m_{1-\sigma}$, and claim that the other message was sampled obliviously.

$S(m_0, m_1)$ $\qquad\qquad\qquad\qquad$ $R(\sigma)$

$$\xleftarrow{\quad \mathrm{ot1}(\sigma) \quad}$$

$$\xrightarrow[\text{ot2 messages are ordered by index in subscript}]{r_{00}, r_{11},\ \ \mathrm{ot2}_{0,m_0}(r_{00}, r_{01}),\ \widetilde{\mathrm{ot2}}_{0,1-m_0},\ \mathrm{ot2}_{1,m_1}(r_{10}, r_{11}),\ \widetilde{\mathrm{ot2}}_{1,1-m_1}}$$

More specifically, Π_1 (depicted above) works as follows. Upon receiving a single receiver's message ot1 of Π, the sender replies two pairs of sender's messages of Π: The b'th pair contains $\mathrm{ot2}_{b,m_b}, \widetilde{\mathrm{ot2}}_{b,1-m_b}$, where the former is honestly generated for random messages (r_{b0}, r_{b1}), and the latter obliviously sampled. The 4 ot2 messages are ordered according to their index. In addition, the sender reveals in the clear r_{00} and r_{11}. It is easy to see that an honest receiver with a choice bit σ will recover exactly the string $r_{\sigma\sigma}$ from message $\mathrm{ot2}_{\sigma,m_\sigma}$, and from the order of $\mathrm{ot2}_{\sigma,m_\sigma}$ in the 4 ot2 messages, it learns m_σ.

Sender Semi-Adaptive Corruption. Simulation in the sender-semi-adaptive corruption scenario can now be achieved as follows. *(i)* The simulator can extract the receiver's choice bit σ using the simulator of Π for the case with a (statically corrupted) malicious receiver, and then learns the output string m_σ. *(ii)* To simulate sender's message, it generates the σ'th pair $(\mathrm{ot2}_{\sigma,m_\sigma}, \widetilde{\mathrm{ot2}}_{\sigma,1-m_\sigma})$ honestly as Π_1 specifies, and simulates the $1-\sigma$'th pair by generating both $\mathrm{ot2}_{1-\sigma,0}, \mathrm{ot2}_{1-\sigma,1}$ honestly, using the same message $r_{1-\sigma,1-\sigma}$ at slot $1-\sigma$ and *different* random strings at slot σ; in addition r_{00}, r_{11} are revealed in the clear.

Sim $\qquad\qquad\qquad\qquad$ A

$$\xleftarrow{\quad \mathrm{ot1}(\sigma) \quad}$$

$$\xrightarrow[\mathrm{ot2}_{1-\sigma,0}(r_{1-\sigma,1-\sigma}, r_{1-\sigma,\sigma}),\ \mathrm{ot2}_{1-\sigma,1}(r_{1-\sigma,1-\sigma}, r'_{1-\sigma,\sigma})]{r_{00}, r_{11},\ \ \mathrm{ot2}_{\sigma,m_\sigma}(r_{\sigma,0}, r_{\sigma,1}),\ \widetilde{\mathrm{ot2}}_{\sigma,1-m_\sigma}}$$

Both input messages to ot2*, and* ot2 *messages themselves are ordered by index.*

(iii) Finally, to equivocate to sender's true inputs (m_0, m_1), the simulator can reveal the randomness used for generating the σ'th pair $(\mathrm{ot2}_{\sigma,m_\sigma}, \widetilde{\mathrm{ot2}}_{\sigma,1-m_\sigma})$, which were generated correctly using m_σ. For the $1-\sigma$'th pair $\mathrm{ot2}_{1-\sigma,0}, \mathrm{ot2}_{1-\sigma,1}$,

the simulator needs to "explain" w.r.t. $m_{1-\sigma}$. This can simply be done by revealing the randomness used for generating $\mathrm{ot2}_{1-\sigma,m_{1-\sigma}}$ honestly, and claim that $\mathrm{ot2}_{1-\sigma,1-m_{1-\sigma}}$ were sampled obliviously.

Making the above idea work turns out to require a more complex formulation of the sender oblivious sampleability property. Roughly speaking, the complexity stems from the fact that when reducing to sender oblivious sampleability, to simulate the adversary's view, the reduction needs to obtain the choice bit σ of the corrupted receiver (as simulation of sender's message depends on σ). This means sender oblivious sampleability needs to hold against adversaries (the reduction) who receive help in "breaking" a receiver's message of its choice. We omit the complexity here and refer the reader to Sect. 5.3 for more detail.

Fortunately, we can achieve such strong sender oblivious sampleability, as well as receiver oblivious sampleability, from various concrete assumptions, including DDH, QR, and LWE.

2.2 Instantiation of Static-OT with Oblivious Sampleability

We now briefly summarize ideas behind our instantiation from concrete assumptions. To construct the static-OT with oblivious sampleability, we start from a variant of the OT construction based on Smooth Projective Hash Functions (SPHFs) from Halevi and Kalai [32] which generalizes the construction from Naor and Pinkas [35]. In our setting, the SPHF we consider is a primitive which allows some party to generate a hash value H of a pair (ct, σ') of a ciphertext ct and a value σ', together with what is called a projection key hp so that: if ct is indeed a ciphertext of σ', it is possible to compute H from hp and the random coins used to generated ct. But if ct is not a ciphertext of σ', H looks completely random even knowing hp.

The construction works as follows. The CRS contains a public key of an encryption scheme. The receiver's message is a ciphertext ct of the selection bit σ. The sender then uses the SPHF to mask its inputs x_0 and x_1, so that only the one corresponding to the plaintext of ct can be unmasked. More precisely, the sender's message consists of two projection keys hp_0 and hp_1 for the ciphertext ct and the values 0 and 1 respectively, as well as the values $\mathsf{H}_0 \oplus x_0$ and $\mathsf{H}_1 \oplus x_1$ where H_0 and H_1 are the two hash values corresponding to hp_0 and hp_1. Using the random coins used to generate ct, the receiver, can recover H_σ and then x_σ. But the value $x_{1-\sigma}$ will remain completely hidden, masked by $\mathsf{H}_{1-\sigma}$ which looks random to the receiver.

To achieve oblivious sampleability, we just need ciphertexts of the encryption scheme and projection keys of the SPHF to be obliviously sampleable. We can instantiate them using the ElGamal encryption scheme and the associated SPHF from [21], which already satisfies the oblivious sampleability requirements. This directly gives a static-OT with oblivious sampleability under the Decisional Diffie-Hellman (DDH) assumption.

To instantiate the scheme under the Quadratic Residuosity assumption (QR), we start from the Goldwasser-Micali [30] encryption scheme and the SPHF from [21]. While the Goldwasser-Micali encryption scheme satisfies ciphertext oblivious sampleability, we do not know how to obliviously sample the projection keys of the associated SPHF. The issue is that projection keys are quadratic residues which we do not know how to sample obliviously. To solve this issue, we slightly change the SPHF to use the group of signed quadratic residues instead [33].

Finally, we show how to achieve a slightly weaker variant of 2-round static-OT, called *half-OT*, with oblivious sampleability under LWE. Roughly speaking, in a half-OT, the sender has a bit b and a single message m, and the receiver with choice bit σ only receives m if $b = \sigma$. We show that this weaker variant of *half-OT*, is already sufficient for our transformation to obtain adaptive-OT. We then instantiate half-OT essentially using the IND-CPA encryption scheme and the SPHF from [4] based on LWE. At a very high-level, the encryption scheme can be seen as the dual-Regev encryption scheme where decryption is done using a full trapdoor for the lattice, to ensure that incorrect ciphertexts are far away from the lattice in all directions (otherwise, we do not know how to prove smoothness of the associated SPHF).

Please see Sect. 5.6 for more details of our instantiation.

2.3 From Adaptive-OT to Adaptive-MPC

Two recent works [5,28] constructed 2-round static-MPC in the CRS model from 2-round static-OT. Actually, the protocol presented in [5] additionally relies on NIZK; but as implicitly observed in [28] and in this paper the use of NIZK can be removed. Moving to the adaptive setting, the natural approach is replacing static-OT with adaptive-OT and ask whether the resulting MPC protocols become adaptively secure. We give affirmative answer. At a very high-level, the proof follows similar ideas as in [5,28]. Still, the formal proof requires carefully examination of all adaptive corruption scenarios and new analysis. In particular, the garbled circuits used in the protocols need to be equivocal for adaptive security to hold.

A subtle issue arises when using equivocal garble circuits: If using them modularly as black-box, we can only collapse rounds of *constant*-round MPC protocols, as opposed to any polynomial-round protocols as in [5,28]. The overall approach of [5,28], followed by this work, is using garbled circuits and OT to collapse rounds of a multi-round MPC protocol. The resulting protocol generates chains of garbled circuits, where each circuit in a chain corresponds to one round in the original MPC protocol, has the lables of the next garble circuit in the chain hardcoded inside. Equivocating a chain entails recursively equivocating the garbled circuits in it. Due to the complexity requirement of equivocal garbling scheme, the size of the equivocal garbled circuits grows exponentially with the length of the chain. As a result, we can only collapse rounds of constant-round MPC protocols. (Note that this issue does not exist in the static setting, simulating a chain of standard garbled circuits does not lead to exponential size-growth.) We can alternatively address the issue of exponential size-growth by applying the techniques of [17] for constructing equivocal garbling scheme (instead of using equivocal garbled circuits as black-boxe).[4] For simplicity and modularity, we take the first approach and collapse rounds of the constant-round MPC protocols from [17] using the equivocal garbling scheme in the same work. See Sect. 6 for the new protocol and analysis.

In terms of writing, we follow the protocol of [5], but for convenience, we present directly the entire protocol without using their intermediate abstraction (namely witness selectors and garbled interactive circuits); this avoids re-defining every intermediate notion in the adaptive setting, which would add unnecessary complexity.

2.4 Future Work: Moving to the Single CRS Model

Our constructions are in the local CRS model, where every session of protocol execution has its "local" independently sampled CRS. A more stringent model is the single CRS model as formalized in [15], where all sessions share a single CRS.[5] We believe that our construction of 2-round adaptive-OT can be adapted to the single CRS model, and when plugging such an OT in our construction of MPC, the resulting 2-round adaptive MPC protocols also work with single CRS. Recall that we gradually transform a static-OT with sender and receiver oblivious sampleability into an adaptive-OT in three steps. We believe that these transformation also works in the single CRS model. Thus it boils down to instantiate static-OT with oblivious sampleability in the single CRS model from concrete assumptions. The main difference from our current instantiation in the local CRS model is that in the single CRS model, the protocols must satisfy certain non-malleability or simulation-extractability property. But, they can be easily achieved using CCA encryption, which is implied by DDH, QR, and LWE. We leave the formal proof as future work.

3 Preliminaries

3.1 Notation

Throughout the paper $\lambda \in \mathbb{N}$ will denote the security parameter. We say that a function $f : \mathbb{N} \rightarrow \mathbb{R}$ is negligible if $\forall c\ \exists\ n_c$ such that if $n > n_c$ then $f(n) < n^{-c}$. We will use $\mathrm{negl}(\cdot)$ to denote an unspecified negligible function. We often use $[n]$ to denote the set $\{1, ..., n\}$. The concatenation of a with b is denoted by $a||b$. Moreover, we use $d \leftarrow \mathcal{D}$ to denote the process of sampling d from the

[4] For example, the complexity of all equivocal garbled circuits can simply be proportional to the entropy of the secrets that need to be equivocated, which in the case of MPC are the inputs and randomness of the uncorrupted parties.

[5] We emphasize that the CLOS model of single CRS should be differentiated from the global CRS model formalized in [11]. The key difference lies in that the latter allows the environment to access the global CRS (and hence the CRS cannot be programmed), whereas in the former all protocol execution can access the same CRS but not the environment.

distribution $\mathcal{D}$ or, if $\mathcal{D}$ is a set, a uniform choice from it. If $\mathcal{D}_1$ and $\mathcal{D}_2$ are two distributions, then we denote that they are statistically close by $\mathcal{D}_1 \approx_s \mathcal{D}_2$; we denote that they are computationally indistinguishable by $\mathcal{D}_1 \approx_c \mathcal{D}_2$; and we denote that they are identical by $\mathcal{D}_1 \equiv \mathcal{D}_2$.

For the sake of simplicity, we suppose that all circuits in a circuit class have the same input and output lengths. This can be achieved without loss of generality using appropriate padding. We recall that for any T-size circuit class $\mathcal{C} = \{\mathcal{C}_\lambda\}_{\lambda \in \mathbb{N}}$, there exists a universal poly(T)-size circuit family $\{U_\lambda\}_{\lambda \in \mathbb{N}}$ such that for any $\lambda \in \mathbb{N}$, any circuit $C \in \mathcal{C}_\lambda$ with input and output lengths n, l, and any input $x \in \{0,1\}^n$, $U_\lambda(C, x) = C(x)$.

3.2 Equivocal Garbling Scheme

Definition 3.1 (Equivocal Garbling Scheme [17]**).** Let $\mathcal{C} = \{\mathcal{C}_\lambda\}_{\lambda \in \mathbb{N}}$ be a poly-size circuit class with input and output lengths n and l. A *garbled circuit* scheme GC for $\mathcal{C}$ is a tuple of four polynomial-time algorithms GC = (GC.Gen, GC.Garble, GC.Eval, GC.Sim):

Input Labels Generation: $\mathbf{keys} \leftarrow \mathsf{GC.Gen}(1^\lambda)$ generates input labels $\mathbf{keys} = \{\mathsf{keys}_i\}_{i \in [n]}$ (with $\mathsf{keys}_i[b] \in \{0,1\}^\kappa$ being the input label corresponding to the value b of the i-th input wire) for the security parameter λ, input length n, and input label length κ;
Circuit Garbling: $\widehat{C} \leftarrow \mathsf{GC.Garble}(\mathbf{keys}, C; \sigma)$ garbles the circuit $C \in \mathcal{C}_\lambda$ into $\widehat{C}$;
Evaluation: $y = \mathsf{GC.Eval}(\widehat{C}, \{\mathsf{keys}_i[x_i]\}_{i \in [n]})$ evaluates the garbled circuit $\widehat{C}$ using input labels $\mathsf{keys}_i[x_i]$ for input some input $x = (x_1, \ldots, x_n)$ and returns the output $y \in \{0,1\}^l$;
Simulation: $(\widetilde{\mathsf{keys}}, \widetilde{C}, \mathsf{st}) \leftarrow \mathsf{GC.Sim}(1^\lambda, y)$ simulates input labels $\widetilde{\mathsf{keys}}$, a garbled circuit $\widetilde{C}$ and state st for the security parameter λ on the output $y \in \{0,1\}^l$;
Equivocation: $(\mathsf{keys}', \sigma) \leftarrow \mathsf{GC.Equiv}(C, x, \mathsf{st})$ such that given C and x, the simulator generates (inactive) labels and fake randomness σ of the garbling that makes $\widetilde{C}, \mathsf{keys}'$ look like a real garbling of C, x.

satisfying the following security properties:

Correctness: For any security parameter $\lambda \in \mathbb{N}$, for any circuit $C \in \mathcal{C}_\lambda$, for any input $x \in \{0,1\}^n$, for any **keys** in the image of $\mathsf{GC.Gen}(1^\lambda)$ and any $\widehat{C}$ in the image of $\mathsf{GC.Garble}(\mathbf{keys}, C)$:

$$\mathsf{GC.Eval}(\widehat{C}, \{\mathsf{keys}_i[x_i]\}_{i \in [n]}) = C(x).$$

Security: There exists a pair of PPT algorithm (S_1, S_2), such that any PPT adversary A wins the following game with at most negligible advantage:
1. A gives a circuit C and an input x to the challenger;
2. The challenger flips a bit b.

If $b = 0$:

- It chooses random garbling key $\mathsf{keys} \leftarrow \mathsf{GC.Gen}(1^\lambda)$;
- It sets $(\widetilde{C} \leftarrow \mathsf{GC.Garble}(\mathsf{keys}, C; \sigma), \widetilde{x}_i = \mathsf{keys}_i[x_i](i \in [n])$;
- It sends $\widetilde{C}, \widetilde{x}, \mathsf{keys}, \sigma$ to the adversary.

If $b = 1$:
- It sets $y = C(x)$;
- It runs the simulator $(\widetilde{C}, \widetilde{x}, \mathsf{st}) \leftarrow S_1(C, y)$
- It runs the simulator $(\mathsf{keys}, \sigma) \leftarrow S_2(\mathsf{st}, x)$
- It sends $\widetilde{C}, \widetilde{x}, \mathsf{keys}, \sigma$ to the adversary.

3. The adversary outputs a bit b'.

The adversary wins if $b = b'$.

We recall that (equivocal) garbled circuit schemes can be constructed from one-way functions.

Terminology of Input Labels. We note that, labels in boldface **keys** refer to all labels corresponding to all input wires. keys_i refers to the two input labels of the i-th wire and $\mathsf{keys}_i[b]$ refers to exactly one of them for $b \in \{0, 1\}$.

3.3 Equivocal Commitments

We define (adaptive) equivocal commitments (in the local CRS model).

Definition 3.2 (Non-interactive Equivocal Commitment). A *non-interactive equivocal commitment* scheme C is a tuple of five polynomial-time algorithms $\mathsf{C} = (\mathsf{C.Setup}, \mathsf{C.Setup_{equiv}}, \mathsf{C.Com}, \mathsf{C.Sim}, \mathsf{C.Equiv})$

Setup: $\mathrm{ck} \leftarrow \mathsf{C.Setup}(1^\lambda)$ expects as input the unary representation of the security parameter λ and outputs a public parameter ck.

Equivocal Setup: $(\mathrm{ck}, \mathsf{trap_q}) \leftarrow \mathsf{C.Setup_{equiv}}(1^\lambda)$ outputs a public parameter ck together with a trapdoor $\mathsf{trap_q}$ (used for equivocation).

Commitment: $\mathsf{com} = \mathsf{C.Com}(\mathrm{ck}, x; r)$ generates a commitment com of $x \in \{0,1\}^{\mathrm{poly}(\lambda)}$ using random tape $x \in \{0,1\}^{\mathrm{poly}(\lambda)}$;

Simulation: $(\mathsf{com}, \mathsf{st^c}) = \mathsf{C.Sim}(\mathrm{ck}, \mathsf{trap_q})$ outputs a simulated commitment and a state used to equivocate the commitment;

Equivocation: $\tilde{r} = \mathsf{C.Equiv}(\mathrm{ck}, \mathsf{trap_q}, \mathsf{com}, \mathsf{st^c}, x)$ equivocates the commitment com to open to x;

satisfying the following properties:

Equivocality: For any polynomial-time circuit family $A = \{A_\lambda\}_{\lambda \in \mathbb{N}}$, there exists a negligible function negl, such that for any $\lambda \in N$:

$$\left| \Pr\left[A_\lambda(\mathsf{st}, \mathsf{com}, r) = 1 : \begin{array}{l} (\mathrm{ck}, \mathsf{trap_q}) \leftarrow \mathsf{C.Setup_{equiv}}(1^\lambda); \\ (x, \mathsf{st}) \leftarrow A(\mathrm{ck}); \\ \mathsf{com} \leftarrow \mathsf{C.Com}(1^\lambda, x; r) \end{array} \right] \right.$$
$$\left. - \Pr\left[A_\lambda(\mathsf{st}, \mathsf{com}, \tilde{r}) = 1 : \begin{array}{l} (\mathrm{ck}, \mathsf{trap_q}) \leftarrow \mathsf{C.Setup_{equiv}}(1^\lambda); \\ (x, \mathsf{st}) \leftarrow A(\mathrm{ck}); \\ (\mathsf{com}, \mathsf{st^c}) \leftarrow \mathsf{C.Sim}(\mathrm{ck}, \mathsf{trap_e}); \\ \tilde{r} \leftarrow \mathsf{C.Equiv}(\mathrm{ck}, \mathsf{trap_e}, \mathsf{com}, \mathsf{st^c}, x) \end{array} \right] \right| \leq \mathrm{negl}(\lambda).$$

Binding: For any polynomial-time circuit family $A = \{A_\lambda\}_{\lambda \in \mathbb{N}}$, there exists a negligible function negl, such that for any $\lambda \in \mathbb{N}$:

$$\Pr\left[\begin{array}{l}\mathsf{C.Com}(x_0; r_0) = \mathsf{C.Com}(x_1; r_1) \\ \text{and } x_0 \neq x_1\end{array} : \begin{array}{l}\mathsf{ck} \leftarrow \mathsf{C.Setup}(1^\lambda); \\ (x_0, r_0, x_1, r_1) \leftarrow A_\lambda(\mathsf{ck})\end{array}\right] \leq \mathrm{negl}(\lambda).$$

Indistinguishability of Public Parameters: We require that the two following distributions are computationally indistinguishable:

$$\{\mathsf{ck} : \mathsf{ck} \leftarrow \mathsf{C.Setup}(1^\lambda)\}, \qquad \{\mathsf{ck} : (\mathsf{ck}, \mathsf{trap_q}) \leftarrow \mathsf{C.Setup_{equiv}}(1^\lambda)\}.$$

Claim. Assuming the existence one-way functions, there exist equivocal commitments.

Proof. We can use the construction that is implicit in Appendix B of the full version of [28], using a pseudorandom generator G from $\{0,1\}^\lambda$ to $\{0,1\}^{3\lambda}$:

Setup: $\mathsf{ck} \leftarrow \mathsf{C.Setup}(1^\lambda)$ outputs a uniform string $\mathsf{ck} \in \{0,1\}^{3\lambda}$.

Equivocal Setup: $(\mathsf{ck}, \mathsf{trap_q}) \leftarrow \mathsf{C.Setup_{equiv}}(1^\lambda)$ generates a pair of uniform strings $\mathsf{trap_q} = (\mathsf{trap_{q0}}, \mathsf{trap_{q1}}) \in \{0,1\}^{2\lambda}$ and sets $\mathsf{ck} = G(\mathsf{trap_{q0}}) \oplus G(\mathsf{trap_{q1}})$.

Commitment: $\mathsf{com} = \mathsf{C.Com}(\mathsf{ck}, x; r)$ with $r \in \{0,1\}^\lambda$, sets $\mathsf{com} = G(r)$ if $x = 0$ and $\mathsf{com} = G(r) \oplus \mathsf{ck}$ if $x = 1$ (assuming messages x are bits, extension to strings is straightforward by parallel repetition).

Simulation: $(\mathsf{com}, \mathsf{st^c}) = \mathsf{C.Sim}(\mathsf{ck}, \mathsf{trap_q})$ sets $\mathsf{com} = G(\mathsf{trap_{q0}})$ and $\mathsf{st^c} = \perp$.

Equivocation: $\tilde{r} = \mathsf{C.Equiv}(\mathsf{ck}, \mathsf{trap_q}, \mathsf{com}, \mathsf{st^c}, x)$ returns $\tilde{r} = \mathsf{trap_{q0}}$ if $x = 0$ and $\tilde{r} = \mathsf{trap_{q1}}$ if $x = 1$.

Binding comes from the fact that with overwhelming probability over $\mathsf{ck} \in \{0,1\}^{3\lambda}$, there does not exist r_0 and r_1 such that $G(r_0) \oplus G(r_1) = \mathsf{ck}$. Indistinguishability of public parameters and equivocality follows from the security of the pseudorandom generator G. ■

3.4 (Augmented) Non-committing Encryption

Let us now recall the definitions of non-committing encryption (NCE) and augmented NCE from [12,15].

Definition 3.3 (Non-committing encryption). A non-committing (bit) encryption scheme (NCE) consists of a tuple (NC.Gen, NC.Enc, NC.Dec, NC.Sim) where (NC.Gen, NC.Enc, NC.Dec) is an encryption scheme and NC.Sim is the simulation satisfying the following property: for $b \in \{0,1\}$ the following distributions are computationally indistinguishable:

$$\{(\mathrm{pk}, c, \rho_G, \rho_E) : (\mathrm{pk}, \mathrm{sk}) \leftarrow \mathsf{NC.Gen}(1^\lambda; \rho_G), c = \mathsf{NC.Enc_{pk}}(b; \rho_E)\}_{\lambda, b},$$
$$\{(\mathrm{pk}, c, \rho_G^b, \rho_E^b) : (\mathrm{pk}, c, \rho_G^0, \rho_E^0, \rho_G^1, \rho_E^1) \leftarrow \mathsf{NC.Sim}(1^\lambda)\}_{\lambda, b}.$$

Definition 3.4 (Augmented non-committing encryption). An augmented non-committing encryption scheme (NCE) consists of a tuple (NC.Gen, NC.Enc, NC.Dec, NC.Sim, $\mathsf{NC.Gen_{Obl}}$, $\mathsf{NC.Gen_{Inv}}$) where (NC.Gen, NC.Enc, NC.Dec, NC.Sim) is an NCE and:

Oblivious Sampling: $\mathsf{NC.Gen_{Obl}}(1^\lambda)$ obliviously generates a public key pk (without knowing the associated secret key sk.

Inverse Key Sampling: $\mathsf{NC.Gen_{Inv}}(\mathrm{pk})$ explains the randomness for the key pk.

satisfying the following property:

Obliviousness: The following distributions are indistinguishable:

$$\{(\mathrm{pk}, \rho) : \mathrm{pk} \leftarrow \mathsf{NC.Gen_{Obl}}(1^\lambda; \rho)\}_\lambda,$$
$$\{(\mathrm{pk}, \tilde{\rho}) : (\mathrm{pk}, \mathrm{sk}) \leftarrow \mathsf{NC.Gen}(1^\lambda);\ \tilde{\rho} \leftarrow \mathsf{NC.Gen_{Inv}}(\mathrm{pk})\}_\lambda.$$

4 Definitions of UC Adaptive MPC

4.1 General Definition of Universal Composability

We refer the reader to the full version and to [10] for the general definitions for UC security.

General Functionality. We consider the general-UC N-party functionality $\mathcal{F}$, which securely evaluates any polynomial-time (possibly randomize) function $f : (\{0,1\}^{\ell_{in}})^N \rightarrow (\{0,1\}^{\ell_{out}})^N$. The functionality $\mathcal{F}_f$ is parameterized with a function f.

From Deterministic to Randomized Functionalities. Our multi-party Protocol 1 UC-securely realizes the general functionality $\mathcal{F}_f$ when the function f is restricted to be any deterministic poly-time function with N inputs and single output. This functionality is defined in Fig. 1. Standard techniques allow to obtain a protocol that UC-securely realizes the general functionality $\mathcal{F}_f$ for any function f. See details in the full version.

Adversarial Model. A *static* adversary $\mathcal{A}$ chooses the set of corrupted parties before the protocol starts, as opposed to an *adaptive* adversary that can corrupt the players during the protocol. We say that the adversary is *semi-honest* if $\mathcal{A}$ follows the protocol but tries to extract some information about the other parties' inputs from his view of the protocol. We say that the adversary is *malicious* if $\mathcal{A}$ is allowed to deviate arbitrarily from the protocol specifications. We will say that a protocol is *semi-honest-secure* if it is secure against a semi-honest adversary and *malicious-secure* if it is secure against a malicious adversary. In this work, we consider malicious security against an adaptive adversary.

Communication Channel. In our results we consider a secure simultaneous message exchange channel in which all parties can simultaneously send messages over the channel at the same communication round in the presence of a *rushing* adversary. In every communication round, a rushing adversary sees the messages from the honest parties and only then chooses the messages on behalf of the malicious parties. For simplicity, we assume that the parties can broadcast messages and have authenticated channels. This can be achieved using standard methods.

Functionality $\mathcal{F}_f$

$\mathcal{F}_f$ parameterized by an N-ary deterministic single output function f, running with parties $\mathcal{P} = \{P_1, \ldots P_N\}$ (of which some may be corrupted) and an adversary $\mathcal{S}$, proceeds as follows:

1. Each party P_i (and $\mathcal{S}$ on behalf of P_i if P_i is corrupted) sends $(\mathsf{input}, \mathsf{sid}, \mathcal{P}, P_i, x_i)$ to the functionality. Upon receiving $(\mathsf{input}, \mathsf{sid}, \mathcal{P}, P_i, x_i)$, record the tuple (P_i, x_i), send the message $(\mathsf{input}, \mathsf{sid}, \mathcal{P}, P_i)$ to the adversary $\mathcal{S}$, and ignore subsequent such messages for the same P_i.
2. Upon receiving the inputs from all parties, evaluate $y \leftarrow f(x_1, \ldots, x_N)$. Send the message $(\mathsf{output}, \mathsf{sid}, \mathcal{P}, y)$ to the adversary $\mathcal{S}$ if at least one party is corrupted, and the message $(\mathsf{output}, \mathsf{sid}, \mathcal{P})$ if no party is corrupted.
3. On receiving $(\mathsf{deliver}, \mathsf{sid}, \mathcal{P}, P_i)$ from $\mathcal{S}$, output $(\mathsf{output}, \mathsf{sid}, \mathcal{P}, y)$ to P_i. (And ignore the message if inputs from all parties in $\mathcal{P}$ have not been received or if such a message has already been received for this party P_i.)

Fig. 1. General functionality for deterministic single output functionalities.

4.2 The Local CRS Model

In the common reference string (CRS) model [13,15], all parties in the system obtain from a trusted party a reference string, which is sampled according to a pre-specified distribution D. The reference string is referred to as the *CRS*. In the UC framework, this is modeled by an ideal functionality $\mathcal{F}^D_{CRS}$ that samples a string ρ from a pre-specified distribution D and sets ρ as the CRS. $\mathcal{F}^D_{CRS}$ is described in Fig. 2.

Functionality $\mathcal{F}^{\mathbf{D}}_{\mathbf{CRS}}$

1. Upon activation with session id *sid* proceed as follows. Sample $\rho = D(r)$, where r denotes uniform random coins, and send $(\mathtt{crs}, sid, \rho)$ to the adversary.
2. On receiving $(\mathtt{crs}, sid)$ from some party send $(\mathtt{crs}, sid, \rho)$ to that party.

Fig. 2. The common reference string functionality.

5 Two-Round UC Adaptive-OT

5.1 Definition of Oblivious Transfer

(Two-out-of-one) oblivious transfer is a two-party functionality, involving a sender S with input x_0, x_1, and a receiver R with input $\sigma \in \{0, 1\}$. R learns x_σ (or $\perp$ if the protocol fails) and nothing else. S learns nothing about σ. The definition of the ideal oblivious transfer functionality, denoted by $\mathcal{F}_{\mathsf{OT}}$, appears in Fig. 3.

Functionality $\mathcal{F}_{\mathsf{OT}}$

$\mathcal{F}_{\mathsf{OT}}$ running with an oblivious transfer sender S, a receiver R and an adversary $\mathcal{S}$ proceeds as follows:

1. Upon receiving a message $(\mathsf{sender}, \mathsf{sid}, x_0, x_1)$ from S, where each $x_i \in \{0,1\}^\lambda$, record the tuple (x_0, x_1), send the message $(\mathsf{sender}, \mathsf{sid})$ to the adversary $\mathcal{S}$, and ignore subsequent such messages.
2. Upon receiving a message $(\mathsf{receiver}, \mathsf{sid}, \mathsf{R}, \sigma)$ from R, where $\sigma \in \{0,1\}$, check if a $(\mathsf{sender}, \mathsf{sid}, x_0, x_1)$ message was previously received. If no such message was received, do nothing. Otherwise, send $(\mathsf{output}, \mathsf{sid})$ to the adversary $\mathcal{S}$ if the receiver R is not corrupted, and send $(\mathsf{output}, \mathsf{sid}, x_\sigma)$ to the adversary $\mathcal{S}$.
3. Upon receiving $(\mathsf{deliver}, \mathsf{sid}, \mathsf{R})$ from $\mathcal{S}$, output (sid, x_σ) to R. (And ignore the message if inputs from all parties have not been received or if such a message has already been received.)
4. Upon receiving $(\mathsf{deliver}, \mathsf{sid}, \mathsf{S})$ from $\mathcal{S}$, output (sid) to S. (And ignore the message if inputs from all parties have not been received or if such a message has already been received.)

Fig. 3. Oblivious transfer functionality.

Adversarial Model. Our construction of 2-round OT secure against adaptive corruption will start with 2-round OT that is only secure against static corruption and has certain special properties, and gradually transform this property to handle different adaptive corruption scenario. We list all the corruption scenarios we consider below.

1. *Static corruption* where the adversary chooses the corrupted parties at the beginning of the protocol execution.
2. *Sender-semi-adaptive corruption* where the adversary statically corrupts the receiver from the beginning and adaptively chooses whether and when to corrupt the *sender* during the execution of the protocol.
3. *Receiver-semi-adaptive corruption* where the adversary statically corrupts the sender from the beginning and adaptively chooses whether and when to corrupt the *receiver* during the execution of the protocol.
4. *Semi-adaptive corruption* where the adversary either performs sender-semi-adaptive corruption or receiver-semi-adaptive corruption. In other words, the adversary always corrupts one party from the beginning and adaptively chooses whether and when to corrupt the other party during the execution.
5. *Adaptive corruption* where the adversary adaptively chooses whether and when to corrupt any party during the execution. Note that adaptive corruption covers semi-adaptive corruption, as well as the scenarios where the receiver and/or sender are corrupted after the entire execution is complete.

Two-Round Oblivious Transfer Protocols. In this work, we consider 2-round oblivious transfer protocols, denoted as $\Pi = \langle \mathsf{S}, \mathsf{R} \rangle$. For convenience, we often use S and R to refer to the sender and the receiver. We also use them to denote the sender and receiver algorithms, where the sender's algorithm $\mathsf{S}(\mathsf{sid}, x_0, x_1)$ takes input a session id and two input strings, and receiver's algorithm $\mathsf{R}(\mathsf{sid}, \sigma)$ takes input a session id and a selection bit. Below, for convenience of notation, in context where the session id is clear, or can be arbitrary, we suppress sid from the algorithms. For the cases where we consider 2-round oblivious transfer in the CRS-hybrid model, we denote by K the CRS algorithm generation. We denote by $\mathcal{S}_\mathsf{R}$ ($\mathcal{S}_\mathsf{S}$) the ideal world simulator for $\mathcal{F}_{\mathsf{OT}}$ simulating the view of an adversarial receiver (sender).

5.2 Oblivious Sampling

Definition 5.1 (Receiver-oblivious-sampleability). A 2-round oblivious transfer protocol with receiver oblivious sampleability is a 2-round oblivious OT protocol ($\Pi = \langle \mathsf{S}, \mathsf{R} \rangle, \mathsf{K}$) with the additional algorithms ($R_{\mathsf{Obl}}, R_{\mathsf{Inv}}$), such that for any bit $\sigma \in \{0,1\}$, the following two distributions are computationally indistinguishable:

$$\{(\text{crs}, \tilde{\mu}, \tilde{\rho}) \ : \ \text{crs} \leftarrow \mathsf{K}(1^\lambda);\ \tilde{\rho} \leftarrow \{0,1\}^\lambda;\ \tilde{\mu} \leftarrow \mathsf{R}_{\mathsf{Obl}}(\text{crs}; \tilde{\rho})\},$$
$$\{(\text{crs}, \mu, \rho) \ : \ \text{crs} \leftarrow \mathsf{K}(1^\lambda);\ \mu = \mathsf{R}(\text{crs}, \sigma); \rho \leftarrow \mathsf{R}_{\mathsf{Inv}}(\text{crs}, \mu)\}.$$

Definition 5.2 [Sender-oblivious-sampleability]. A 2-round oblivious transfer protocol with sender oblivious sampleability is a 2-round oblivious OT protocol ($\Pi = \langle \mathsf{S}, \mathsf{R} \rangle, \mathsf{K}$) with the additional algorithms ($\mathsf{S}_{\mathsf{Obl}}, \mathsf{S}_{\mathsf{Inv}}$) such that, for any message $x_0, x_1 \in \{0,1\}^\lambda$, no PPT adversary $\mathcal{A}$ (acting as a malicious receiver), can distinguish the following two experiments:

Real-world experiment:

1. A challenger $\mathcal{C}$ runs the simulator $\mathcal{S}_\mathsf{R}$ of Π, which interacts with $\mathcal{A}$ in a straight-line: (i) $\mathcal{S}_\mathsf{R}$ simulates the CRS crs for $\mathcal{A}$; (ii) when $\mathcal{A}$ sends a first OT message μ, $\mathcal{S}_\mathsf{R}$ extracts from μ a selection bit σ.
2. $\mathcal{C}$ runs S to obtain an obliviously sampled OT second message $\nu \leftarrow \mathsf{S}_{\mathsf{Obl}}(\text{crs}, \mu; \tilde{\rho})$, picks a random string $t \leftarrow \{0,1\}^\lambda$, and sends to $\mathcal{A}$ the selection bit σ, the message ν, and the string t.
3. $\mathcal{C}$ sends $\tilde{\rho}$ to $\mathcal{A}$.

Simulated-world experiment:

1. A challenger $\mathcal{C}$ runs the simulator $\mathcal{S}_\mathsf{R}$ of Π, which interacts with $\mathcal{A}$ in a straight-line: (i) $\mathcal{S}_\mathsf{R}$ simulates the CRS crs for $\mathcal{A}$; (ii) when $\mathcal{A}$ sends a first OT message μ, $\mathcal{S}_\mathsf{R}$ extracts from μ a selection bit σ.
2. $\mathcal{C}$ runs S to obtain an honestly generated OT second message $\nu \leftarrow \mathsf{S}(\text{crs}, \mu, t_0, t_1)$ for $t_0, t_1 \leftarrow \{0,1\}^\lambda$ and sends to $\mathcal{A}$ the selection bit σ, the message ν, and the string $t_{1-\sigma}$.
3. $\mathcal{C}$ computes $\rho \leftarrow \mathsf{S}_{\mathsf{Inv}}(\text{crs}, \nu)$ and sends ρ to $\mathcal{A}$.

5.3 Transformation 1: Achieving Sender Equivocality

Proposition 5.3. *Assume the existence of two-round oblivious transfer with the following properties:*

- *UC-Security against static receiver corruption by a malicious adversary.*
- *UC-Security against static sender corruption by a semi-honest adversary.*
- *Sender oblivious sampleability.*

Then, there exists a two-round oblivious transfer protocol in the CRS-hybrid model with the following properties:

- *UC-Security against static receiver corruption and post-execution sender corruption (or UC-Security against sender-semi-adaptive corruption for short) by a malicious adversary.*

Additionally, the compilation preserves (1) receiver-oblivious-sampleability and (2) UC-Security against static sender corruption by a semi-honest adversary, if the original protocol satisfies either of the properties.

Our Protocol. In this section we will present our UC oblivious transfer protocol Π_{OT} secure against sender-semi-adaptive corruption, described in Fig. 4. For simplicity of exposition, in the sequel, we will assume that random coins are an implicit input to the sender and receiver algorithms, unless specified explicitly. The security proof is provided in the full version.

Protocol Π_{OT}

Let $(\Pi = \langle \mathsf{S}, \mathsf{R} \rangle, \mathsf{K}, \mathsf{S}_{\mathsf{Obl}})$ be an oblivious transfer protocol with an oblivious sender algorithm $\mathsf{S}_{\mathsf{Obl}}$.

COMMON REFERENCE STRING: Generate $\mathrm{crs} \leftarrow \mathsf{K}(1^\lambda)$.
INPUTS: Sender holds two strings $x_0, x_1 \in \{0,1\}$ and receiver holds a bit σ.

1. Given input $(\mathsf{receiver}, \mathsf{sid}, \sigma)$, receiver R_{OT} runs S on input $(\mathsf{receiver}, \mathsf{sid}, \sigma)$ to obtain the message (sid, μ) which R_{OT} sends to S_{OT}.
2. Given input $(\mathsf{sender}, \mathsf{sid}, x_0, x_1)$ and message (sid, μ), sender S_{OT} generates random strings $r_0, r_1, s_0, s_1 \in \{0,1\}^\lambda$ and generates the following:
$$\nu_{0,x_0} = \mathsf{S}(\mathrm{crs}, \mu, r_0, s_0) \qquad \nu_{0,1-x_0} = \mathsf{S}_{\mathsf{Obl}}(\mathrm{crs}, \mu)$$
$$\nu_{1,x_1} = \mathsf{S}(\mathrm{crs}, \mu, s_1, r_1) \qquad \nu_{1,1-x_1} = \mathsf{S}_{\mathsf{Obl}}(\mathrm{crs}, \mu)$$
and sends $(\mathsf{sid}, r_0, r_1, \nu_{0,0}, \nu_{0,1}, \nu_{1,0}, \nu_{1,1})$ to R_{OT}.
3. Upon receiving the message $(\mathsf{sid}, r_0, r_1, \nu_{0,0}, \nu_{0,1}, \nu_{1,0}, \nu_{1,1})$, R_{OT} feeds R with $(\mathsf{sid}, \nu_{\sigma,0})$ and $(\mathsf{sid}, \nu_{\sigma,1})$ in two parallel invocations to obtain y and y'. If $y = r_\sigma$, it outputs $(\mathsf{sid}, 0)$, and if $y' = r_\sigma$ it outputs $(\mathsf{sid}, 1)$.

Fig. 4. Sender-semi-adaptive oblivious transfer $\Pi_{\mathsf{OT}} = \langle \mathsf{S}_{\mathsf{OT}}, \mathsf{R}_{\mathsf{OT}} \rangle$ protocol.

5.4 Transformation 2: Achieving Receiver Equivocality Against Malicious Sender

Proposition 5.4. *Assume the existence of two-round oblivious transfer with the following properties:*

- *UC-Security against static sender corruption by a semi-honest adversary.*
- *UC-Security against a static receiver corruption and post-execution sender corruption (or UC-Security against sender-semi-adaptive corruption for short) by a malicious adversary.*
- *Receiver-Oblivious-sampleability.*

Then there exists a two-round oblivious transfer protocol in the CRS-hybrid model with the following properties:

- *UC-Security against semi-adaptive corruption by a malicious adversary.*

Our Protocol. In this section we will present our UC oblivious transfer protocol Π_{OT} secure against semi-adaptive corruption, described in Fig. 5. The security proof is provided in the full version.

5.5 Transformation 3: From Semi-Adaptive-OT to Adaptive-OT

Proposition 5.5. *Assume the existence of augmented non-committing encryption and two-round oblivious transfer with the following property:*

- *UC-Security against semi-adaptive corruption by a malicious adversary.*

Then there exists a two-round oblivious transfer protocol with the following property:

- *UC-Security against adaptive corruption.*

Our Protocol. In this section we will present our UC oblivious transfer protocol Π_{OT} secure against adaptive corruptions, described in Fig. 6. For simplicity of exposition, in the sequel, we will assume that random coins are an implicit input to the sender and receiver algorithms, unless specified explicitly. Furthermore, to simplify notation, we suppose that the sender's inputs are bits. Extension to strings is straightforward: it just requires to use string NCE instead of bit NCE (which can be constructed by parallel repetition of bit NCE). The security proof is provided in the full version.

5.6 Instantiation of Static-OT with Oblivious Sampleability

In the full version, we show instantiations of static-OT with oblivious sampleability from the DDH and the QR assumptions. We also construct a slightly weaker variant of 2-round static-OT (called *half-OT*) with oblivious sampleability from LWE using a variant of the previous generic construction. Finally, we provide a variant of Transformation 1 (Sect. 5.3) that starts from a half-OT instead of a static-OT.

Protocol Π_{OT}

Let ($\Pi = \langle \mathsf{S}, \mathsf{R} \rangle, \mathsf{K}, \mathsf{R}_{\mathsf{Obl}}$) be a UC static receiver corruption and sender-semi-adaptive corruption oblivious transfer protocol with an oblivious receiver algorithm $\mathsf{R}_{\mathsf{Obl}}$, let ($\mathsf{NC.Gen}, \mathsf{NC.Enc}, \mathsf{NC.Dec}, \mathsf{NC.Sim}$) be a somewhat NCE scheme, let $\mathsf{GC} = (\mathsf{GC.Gen}, \mathsf{GC.Garble}, \mathsf{GC.Eval})$ be an equivocal garbling scheme and let $\mathsf{C} = (\mathsf{C.Setup}, \mathsf{C.Com})$ be a non-interactive equivocal commitment scheme.

Common Reference String: Generate $\mathrm{crs}' \leftarrow \mathsf{K}(1^\lambda)$, $\mathrm{ck} \leftarrow \mathsf{C.Setup}(1^\lambda)$ and set $\mathrm{crs} = (\mathrm{crs}', \mathrm{ck})$.

Inputs: Sender holds two strings $x_0, x_1 \in \{0,1\}$ and receiver holds a bit σ.

1. Given input $(\mathsf{receiver}, \mathsf{sid}, \sigma)$, receiver R_{OT} generates commitment $\mathsf{com} = \mathsf{C.Com}\big(\sigma; (r_1 \| r_2 \| ... \| r_T)\big)$ where $r_i \in \{0,1\}$ and an NCE key pair $(\mathrm{pk}, \mathrm{sk}) \leftarrow \mathsf{NC.Gen}(1^\lambda)$. Send pk and for all $i \in [\kappa]$, R_{OT} invokes R to generate and send to S_{OT} the following:
$$\mu_{\delta,i} = \begin{cases} \mathsf{R}(\mathrm{crs}, r_i) & \text{if } \delta = \sigma \\ \mathsf{R}_{\mathsf{Obl}}(\mathrm{crs}) & \text{otherwise} \end{cases}$$
2. Given input $(\mathsf{sender}, \mathsf{sid}, x_0, x_1)$ and messages $(\mathsf{sid}, \{\mu_{\delta,i}\})$, sender S_{OT} proceeds as follows:
   (a) For $\delta \in \{0,1\}$ generate circuit C_δ as follows:
   $$C_\delta(r_1 \| r_2 \| ... \| r_T) = \Big\{ \text{output } x_\delta \text{ if } \mathsf{com} = \mathsf{C.Com}\big(\delta; (r_1 \| r_2 \| ... \| r_T)\big) \Big\}$$
   (b) Generate the garble circuit $\widehat{\mathrm{C}}_\delta$, with input labels $\mathbf{keys}^\delta \leftarrow \mathsf{GC.Gen}(1^\lambda)$:
   $$\widehat{\mathrm{C}}_\delta \leftarrow \mathsf{GC.Garble}(\mathbf{keys}^\delta, C_\delta)$$
   (c) For $\delta \in \{0,1\}$ and $i \in [T]$ generate $\nu_{\delta,i} = \mathsf{S}(\mathrm{crs}, \mu_{\delta,i}, \mathsf{keys}_i^\delta)$;

   and sends $\big(\mathsf{sid}, \mathsf{ct} \leftarrow \mathsf{NC.Enc}(\mathrm{pk}, \{\widehat{\mathrm{C}}_\delta, \nu_{\delta,i}\}_{\delta \in \{0,1\}, i \in [T]})\big)$ to R_{OT}.
3. Upon receiving the message $(\mathsf{sid}, \mathsf{ct})$ compute $\{\widehat{\mathrm{C}}_\delta, \nu_{\delta,i}\}_{\delta \in \{0,1\}, i \in [T]} = \mathsf{NC.Dec}(\mathrm{sk}, \mathrm{ct})$, R_{OT} feeds R with $(\mathsf{sid}, \nu_{\delta,i})$ for all $i \in [T]$ to obtain the labels $\{\mathsf{keys}_i^\delta[r_i]\}$ corresponding to r_i. Next, it evaluates the garbled circuits to get $x_\delta = \mathsf{GC.Eval}(\widehat{C}_\delta, \mathsf{keys}_i^\delta[r_i])$. If $x_\delta \neq \perp$ for at least one $\delta \in \{0,1\}$ then output (sid, x_δ) else output $\perp$.

Fig. 5. Semi-adaptive oblivious transfer $\Pi_{\mathsf{OT}} = \langle \mathsf{S}_{\mathsf{OT}}, \mathsf{R}_{\mathsf{OT}} \rangle$ protocol.

6 Two-Round UC Adaptive-MPC

In this section we upgrade the static construction of [5] to the adaptive setting. The changes we make to the construction of [5] is to lift the security of the garble circuit and oblivious transfer schemes to the adaptive setting. Unlike [5], we also obtain security against adaptive malicious adversaries without NIZK.

Protocol Π_{OT}

Let $(\Pi = \langle \mathsf{S}, \mathsf{R} \rangle, \mathsf{K})$ be a UC-secure semi-adaptive oblivious transfer protocol. Let $(\mathsf{NC.Gen}, \mathsf{NC.Enc}, \mathsf{NC.Dec}, \mathsf{NC.Sim}, \mathsf{NC.Gen_{Obl}}, \mathsf{NC.Gen_{Inv}})$ be an augmented NCE scheme.

COMMON REFERENCE STRING: Generate $\mathsf{crs} \leftarrow \mathsf{K}(1^\lambda)$.
INPUTS: Sender holds two bits $x_0, x_1 \in \{0,1\}$ and receiver holds a bit σ.

1. Given input $(\mathsf{receiver}, \mathsf{sid}, \sigma)$, receiver $\mathsf{R_{OT}}$ does the following:
   (a) run R on input $(\mathsf{receiver}, \mathsf{sid}, \sigma)$ to obtain the message (sid, μ).
   (b) generate an NCE key pair $(\mathrm{pk}_\sigma, \mathrm{sk}_\sigma) \leftarrow \mathsf{NC.Gen}(1^\lambda)$.
   (c) obliviously sample an NCE public key $\mathrm{pk}_{1-\sigma} \leftarrow \mathsf{NC.Gen_{Obl}}(1^\lambda)$.
   (d) send $(\mathsf{sid}, \mu, \mathrm{pk}_0, \mathrm{pk}_1)$ to the sender $\mathsf{S_{OT}}$.
2. Given input $(\mathsf{sender}, \mathsf{sid}, x_0, x_1)$ and message (sid, μ), sender $\mathsf{S_{OT}}$ does the following:
   (a) pick two random strings $r_0, r_1 \leftarrow \{0,1\}^\lambda$
   (b) run S on input $(\mathsf{sender}, \mathsf{sid}, r_0 \oplus x_0, r_1 \oplus x_1)$ to obtain the message (sid, ν).
   (c) encrypts x_0 and x_1 under pk_0 and pk_1 respectively: $\mathrm{ct}_0 \leftarrow \mathsf{NC.Enc}(\mathrm{pk}_0, x_0)$ and $\mathrm{ct}_1 \leftarrow \mathsf{NC.Enc}(\mathrm{pk}_1, x_1)$.
   (d) send $(\mathsf{sid}, \nu, \mathrm{ct}_0, \mathrm{ct}_1)$ to the receiver $\mathsf{R_{OT}}$.
3. Upon receiving the message $(\mathsf{sid}, \nu, \mathrm{ct}_0, \mathrm{ct}_1)$, $\mathsf{R_{OT}}$ feeds R with (sid, ν) to obtain y. It also decrypts ct_σ into r: $r = \mathsf{NC.Dec}(\mathrm{sk}_\sigma, \mathrm{ct}_\sigma)$ and output $y \oplus r$.

Fig. 6. Adaptive oblivious transfer $\Pi_{\mathsf{OT}} = \langle \mathsf{S_{OT}}, \mathsf{R_{OT}} \rangle$ protocol.

Protocol Π_{MPC}. We provide an intuitive description of the protocol. A formal description appears in Protocol 1. The main idea is to collapse a constant L-round adaptive N-party protocol π secure against malicious adversaries into a two-round protocol based on equivocal garbled circuits and adaptive oblivious transfer. The first round of the protocol acts as a catalyst for a virtual execution of π via equivocal garbled circuits sent by all the parties in the second round. In particular, each party P_i garbles their next-step circuit $\mathsf{Nextmsg}_i(x_i, r_i, \star)$ in an execution of the inner protocol π computing the desired functionality f. The next-step circuit contains hardcoded the input and randomness (x_i, r_i) of party P_i and produces P_i's next message m_i^ℓ for round ℓ on input the messages received from all parties in all previous rounds $M^{<\ell} = \{m_j^{\ell'}\}_{j\in[N],\ell'<\ell}$. We denote these circuits by $\widehat{\mathrm{F}}_i^\ell$. These garbled circuits expect as input messages from other parties as well as output messages for other garbled circuits. There are certain barrier to put this idea into practice. First of all, parties can perform residual attacks on the honest parties inputs. To overcome this barrier, we use the first round to "bind" the parties to their inputs via an oblivious transfer protocol. Next, each party in the second round needs to generate verification circuits $\widehat{\mathrm{V}}_{i,j}$ that take as input a proof for each other party's input message and verify that the message is honestly generated from the inputs and random tapes committed in the first round. This ensures that only the unique sequence of honestly generated messages is accepted by honest parties' $\widehat{\mathrm{F}}_i^\ell$ garbled circuits. Our protocol below describes how to combine the above ideas.

6.1 The Protocol

In this section we present our adaptively secure two-round MPC protocol secure against malicious adversaries, described in Protocol 1.

Protocol 1 (Adaptive malicious protocol Π_{MPC}). Let f be an arbitrary N-party functionality. Protocol Π_{MPC} relies on the following components:

- An adaptive malicious constant L-round N-party protocol $\pi = (\mathsf{Setup}_\pi, \mathsf{Nextmsg}, \mathsf{Output})$ for f. Setup_π generates the CRS crs_π which is an implicit input of $\mathsf{Nextmsg}$ and Output. Without loss of generality, we will assume that in each round ℓ of π, each party P_i broadcasts a single message that depends on its input x_i, randomness r_i and on the messages $M^{<\ell} = \{m_j^{\ell'}\}_{j\in[N],\ell'<\ell}$ that it received from all parties in all previous rounds such that $m_j^\ell = \mathsf{Nextmsg}_j(x_j, r_j, M^{<\ell})$. $\mathsf{Nextmsg}_j$ is the next message function that computes the message broadcast by P_j. In the last round L of π each party P_i locally computes the output $y_i = \mathsf{Output}_i(x_i, r_i, M)$ after receiving all the messages $M = \{m_j^\ell\}_{j\in[N],\ell\in[L]}$.
- A malicious adaptive OT protocol $(\Pi = \langle S, R\rangle, \mathsf{K})$ where K is the OT setup algorithm.
- An equivocal garbling scheme $\mathsf{GC} = (\mathsf{GC.Gen}, \mathsf{GC.Garble}, \mathsf{GC.Eval}, \mathsf{GC.Sim})$.

Common Reference String: Generate $\mathrm{crs}_{\mathrm{OT}} \leftarrow \mathsf{K}(1^\lambda)$ and $\mathrm{crs}_\pi \leftarrow \mathsf{Setup}_\pi(1^\lambda, 1^N)$.[6] Set the CRS to be $\mathrm{crs} = (\mathrm{crs}_{\mathrm{OT}}, \mathrm{crs}_\pi)$.
Input: Parties $P_1, \ldots, P_N$ are given input $(x_1, \ldots, x_N)$, respectively.

- Round 1: For ℓ from L to 1 each party $P_{i^\star}$ proceeds as follows:
  1. Generate input labels $\mathbf{cKeys}_{i^\star}^\ell \leftarrow \mathsf{GC.Gen}(1^\lambda)$.
  2. Garble a *commitment* circuit $C_{i^\star}^\ell = U_\lambda(\star, (x_{i^\star}, r_{i^\star}))$, which is the universal circuit (with input size T) partially evaluated on $(x_{i^\star}, r_{i^\star})$: $\widehat{C}_{i^\star}^\ell \leftarrow \mathsf{GC.Garble}(\mathbf{cKeys}_{i^\star}^\ell, C_{i^\star}^\ell)$ where $r_{i^\star}$ is the random tape for running protocol π.
  3. For each $k \in [|\widehat{C}_{i^\star}^\ell|]$, generate OT receiver messages for the k-th bit of $\widehat{C}_{i^\star}^\ell$, denoted $|\widehat{C}_{i^\star}^\ell|_k$:
$$\overline{\mu}_{i^\star,k}^\ell = \mathsf{R}(\mathrm{crs}_{\mathrm{OT}}, |C_{i^\star}^{\prime\ell}|_k; \overline{\rho}_{i^\star,k}^\ell)$$
  4. For each $t \in [T]$, for each bit $b \in \{0,1\}$, generate OT receiver messages
$$\mu_{i^\star,t,b}^\ell = \mathsf{R}(\mathrm{crs}_{\mathrm{OT}}, \mathsf{cKeys}_{i^\star,t}^\ell[b]; \rho_{i^\star,t,b}^\ell)$$

[6] Formally, we need a CRS $\mathrm{crs}_{\mathrm{OT}}$ for each instantiation of the OT protocol. For the sake of simplicity, we assume that there is a single CRS.

Output $c_{i^*}^\ell = (\{\overline{\mu}_{i^*,k}^\ell\}, \{\mu_{i^*,t,b}^\ell\})$

- Round 2: For ℓ from L to 1 each party P_{i^*} garbles the *evaluation* circuits $\mathrm{F}_{i^*} = \{\mathrm{F}_{i^*}^\ell\}_{\ell \in [L]}$, defined in Fig. 7, as follows:
  1. Generate input labels
  $$\{\mathbf{cirKeys}_{i^*,j}^\ell\}_{j \in [N]}, \mathbf{stateKeys}_{i^*}^\ell, \{\mathbf{dataKeys}_{i^*,j}^\ell\}_{j \in [N]} \leftarrow \mathsf{GC.Gen}(1^\lambda).$$
  2. Garble the *evaluation* circuit $\mathrm{F}_{i^*}^\ell$ and broadcast $\widehat{\mathrm{F}}_{i^*} = \{\widehat{\mathrm{F}}_{i^*}^\ell\}_{\ell \in [L]}$:
  $$\widehat{\mathrm{F}}_{i^*}^\ell \leftarrow \mathsf{GC.Garble}(\{\mathbf{cirKeys}_{i^*,j}^\ell\}_j, \mathbf{stateKeys}_{i^*}^\ell, \{\mathbf{dataKeys}_{i^*,j}^\ell\}_j, \mathrm{F}_{i^*}^\ell).$$
  3. Generate OT sender messages on the received messages $\{\overline{\mu}_{j,k}^\ell\}_{j,k}$:
  $$\overline{\nu}_{i^*,j,k}^\ell = \mathsf{S}(\mathsf{crs}_{\mathsf{OT}}, \overline{\mu}_{j,k}^\ell, \mathsf{cirKeys}_{i^*,j,k}^\ell[0], \mathsf{cirKeys}_{i^*,j,k}^\ell[1]).$$
  4. For each $k \in [|\widehat{C}_{i^*}^\ell|]$ output the randomness $\overline{\rho}_{i^*,k}^\ell$ used to generate $\overline{\mu}_{i^*,k}^\ell$.
- Output phase: Each party evaluates the *evaluation* garbled circuits. In particular P_{i^*} proceeds as follows in L iterations ($\ell \in [L]$):
  1. For all $i \in [N]$, $j \in [N]$, and $k \in [|\widehat{C}_j^\ell|]$, given $\overline{\rho}_{j,k}^\ell$ recover the labels $\mathsf{cirKeys}_{i,j,k}^\ell[b]$ corresponding to the bit $b = |\widehat{C}_j^\ell|_k$. For all $i \in [N]$, denote all the $[|\widehat{C}_j^\ell|]$ garble labels $\mathsf{cirKeys}_{i,j,k}^\ell[b]$ by $\gamma_{i,j}^\ell$.
  2. If $\ell = 1$, for $i \in [N]$, evaluate the *evaluation* garble circuit $\mathsf{GC.Eval}(\widehat{\mathrm{F}}_i^1, \{\gamma_{i,j}^1\}_j)$ to obtain $(\mathsf{stateKeys}_i^2, \{\widehat{\mathrm{V}}_{i,j}^1, \nu_{i,j,t}^1, d_{i,t}^1\}_{j,t}, m_i^1)$ for all $j \in [N]$ and $t \in [T]$. Note that for $\ell = 1$, $\mathsf{stateKeys}_i^1$ and $\{\mathsf{dataKeys}_{i,j}^1\}_j$ are the empty set.
  3. For every $1 < \ell \leq L$, for $i \in [N]$ and for each $j \in [N]$ proceed as follows. For all $t \in [T]$ set $g_{j,t}^{\ell-1} = |G_j^{\ell-1}|_t$ as the t-th bit of the circuit $G_j^{\ell-1}$. For simplicity of exposition, denote by $\alpha_{j,t}^{\ell-1} = \mathsf{cKeys}_{j,t}^{\ell-1}[b]$ the garble label of the *commitment* circuit corresponding to the bit $b = g_{j,t}^{\ell-1}$ and proceed as follows:
     (a) Given the randomness $d_{j,t}^{\ell-1}$, used to generate the Π_{OT} message $\nu_{i,j,t}^{\ell-1}$, recover the κ garble labels $\{\mathsf{vKeys}_{i,j,t'}^{\ell-1}[\alpha_{j,t}^{\ell-1}]\}_{t'}$ of the *verification* circuit where $(t-1) \cdot \kappa < t' \leq t \cdot \kappa$. Denote all of the $\kappa \cdot T$ labels by $\beta_{i,j}^\ell$.
     (b) Evaluate the *verification* circuit $\mathsf{GC.Eval}(\widehat{\mathrm{V}}_{i,j}^{\ell-1}, \beta_{i,j}^\ell)$ to receiver the garble labels corresponding to the message $m_j^{\ell-1}$ of the *evaluation* circuit i.e. $\mathsf{dataKeys}_{i,j}^\ell[m_j^{\ell-1}]$.
     (c) Evaluate the *evaluation* circuit $\mathsf{GC.Eval}(\widehat{\mathrm{F}}_i^\ell, \{\gamma_{i,j}^\ell\}_j, \mathsf{stateKeys}_i^\ell[M^{<\ell-1}], \{\mathsf{dataKeys}_{i,j}^\ell[m_j^{\ell-1}]\}_j)$ to obtain the values $(\mathsf{stateKeys}_i^{\ell+1}[M^{<\ell}], \{\widehat{\mathrm{V}}_{i,j}^\ell, \nu_{i,j,k}^\ell, d_{i,t}^\ell\}_{j,t}, m_j^\ell)$ for the next round $\ell+1$.

(d) For the case where $\ell = L$, the evaluation circuit outputs the empty set for the values $\mathsf{stateKeys}_i^{\ell+1}[M^{<\ell}]$ and $\{\widehat{\mathrm{V}}_{i,j}^{\ell}, \nu_{i,j,t}^{\ell}\}_j$.

4. After all L iterations, $P_{i^\star}$ obtains the set of all messages M, and computes the output $y_{i^\star} = \mathsf{Output}_{i^\star}(x_{i^\star}, r_{i^\star}, M)$.

Circuit F_i^{ℓ}

Hardwired Values: 1^λ, crs, ℓ, i, x_i, r_i, $\{\mu_{j,t,b}^{\ell}\}$, $\mathbf{stateKeys}_i^{\ell+1}$, $\{\mathbf{dataKeys}_{i,j}^{\ell+1}\}_{j\in[N]}$, $\{\rho_{i,t,b}^{\ell}\}_{t\in[T],b\in\{0,1\}}$.

Inputs: $(\{\widehat{C}_j^{\ell}\}_j, M^{<\ell-1}, \bar{m}^{\ell-1})$ where for $\ell > 1$:

- Garble labels corresponding to the circuits $\widehat{C}_j^{\ell}$ are denoted by $\mathbf{cirKeys}_{i,j}^{\ell}$.
- The input messages $M^{<\ell-1}$ are the messages of protocol π of the first $\ell-2$ rounds. Garble labels corresponding to this input are denoted by $\mathbf{stateKeys}_i^{\ell}$.
- The input messages $\bar{m}^{\ell-1} := \{m_j^{\ell-1}\}_{j\in[N]}$ are the $\ell-1$ round messages of protocol π. Garble labels corresponding to this input are denoted by $\mathbf{dataKeys}_{i,j}^{\ell}$.

Procedure:

1. Define the circuit G_j^{ℓ} as $G_j^{\ell}(\star,\star) = \mathsf{Nextmsg}_j(\star,\star,M^{<\ell-1},\bar{m}^{\ell-1})$, for $j \in [N]$ and set $g_{j,t} = |G_j^{\ell}|_t$ as the t-th bit of G_j^{ℓ}.
2. Compute the ℓ-th round message of P_i of the inner protocol π: $m_i^{\ell} = \mathsf{Nextmsg}_i\left(x_i, r_i, (M^{<\ell-1}, \bar{m}^{\ell-1})\right)$.
3. Set $d_{i,t}^{\ell} = \rho_{i,t,b}^{\ell}$ as the randomness used to generate P_i's Π_{OT} messages (acting as the receiver) corresponding to the bit $b = g_{i,t}$.
4. Generate the verification circuits $\mathrm{V}_{i,j}^{\ell}$ for all $j \in [N], t \in [T]$:
$$\mathrm{V}_{i,j}^{\ell}(\alpha_{j,t}) = \begin{cases} m_j^{\ell} = \mathsf{GC.Eval}(\widehat{\mathrm{C}}_j^{\ell}, \alpha_{j,t}) \\ \text{output } \mathsf{dataKeys}_{i,j}^{\ell+1}[m_j^{\ell}] \end{cases}$$
5. Generate input labels $\mathbf{vKeys}_{i,j}^{\ell} \leftarrow \mathsf{GC.Gen}(1^\lambda)$ and garble the circuit $\widehat{\mathrm{V}}_{i,j}^{\ell} \leftarrow \mathsf{GC.Garble}(\{\mathbf{vKeys}_{i,j}^{\ell}\}_j, \mathrm{V}_{i,j}^{\ell})$ for $j \in [N]$.
6. Generate P_i's Π_{OT} message (acting as the sender) corresponding to the Π_{OT} message of P_j (acting as the receiver) corresponding to the bit $b = g_{j,t}$ for all $j \in [N], t \in [T]$:
$$\nu_{i,j,t}^{\ell} = \mathsf{S}(\mathsf{crs}_{\mathrm{OT}}, \mu_{j,t,b}^{\ell}, \{\mathsf{vKeys}_{i,j,t'}^{\ell}\}_{t'})$$
Since the input $\alpha_{j,t}$ to the *verification* circuit $\mathrm{V}_{i,j}$ is a κ-bit garbled label for the *commitment* garble circuit $\widehat{\mathrm{C}}_j$, each OT sender message $\nu_{i,j,t}$ includes κ pairs of labels vKeys. That said, $(t-1)\cdot\kappa < t' \leq t\cdot\kappa$.
7. Select the input labels $\mathsf{stateKeys}_i^{\ell+1}[M^{<\ell-1}, \bar{m}^{\ell-1}]$ for the next round $(\ell+1)$, corresponding to the messages $M^{<\ell-1}, \bar{m}^{\ell-1}$.

Output: $(\mathsf{stateKeys}_i^{\ell+1}[M^{<\ell-1}, \bar{m}^{\ell-1}], \{\widehat{\mathrm{V}}_{i,j}^{\ell}, \nu_{i,j,k}^{\ell}, d_{i,k}^{\ell}\}_{j,k}, m_i^{\ell})$.

Fig. 7. Pseudocode of circuit F_i^{ℓ}

6.2 Security Proof

Theorem 6.1. *Let f be an arbitrary N-party functionality. Assume the existence of two-round adaptively secure malicious oblivious transfer protocol Π_{OT} in the $\mathcal{F}_{\mathsf{CRS}}$-hybrid model and an N-party malicious constant-round adaptively secure computation protocol π for f in $\mathcal{F}_{\mathsf{CRS}}$. Then the two-round protocol Π_{MPC}, presented in Protocol 1, UC-securely realizes the ideal functionality $\mathcal{F}_f$ in the $\mathcal{F}_{\mathsf{CRS}}$-hybrid model against adaptive corruption of any subset of the parties by a malicious adversary.*

The protocol π can be instantiated based on simulatable PKE [17] in the CRS model. In the semi-honest setting, no CRS is required and the protocol π can be instantiated based on augmented NCE [17]. See the full version for details.

The security proof is provided in the full version.

Acknowledgments. We thank the anonymous reviewers of TCC 2018 for their insightful comments. Huijia Lin was supported by NSF grants CNS-1528178, CNS-1514526, CNS-1652849 (CAREER), a Hellman Fellowship, the Defense Advanced Research Projects Agency (DARPA) and Army Research Office (ARO) under Contract No. W911NF-15-C-0236, and a subcontract No. 2017-002 through Galois. Antigoni Polychroniadou was supported by the Junior Simons Fellowship awarded by the Simons Society of Fellows. Muthuramakrishnan Venkitasubramaniam was supported by Google Faculty Research Grant and NSF Award CNS-1526377 and this work was partly carried out during a visit to DIMACS supported by the National Science Foundation under grant number CNS-1523467. The views expressed are those of the authors and do not reflect the official policy or position of the Department of Defense, the National Science Foundation, or the U.S. Government.

References

1. Abdalla, M., Benhamouda, F., Pointcheval, D.: Removing erasures with explainable hash proof systems. In: Fehr, S. (ed.) PKC 2017, Part I. LNCS, vol. 10174, pp. 151–174. Springer, Heidelberg (2017). https://doi.org/10.1007/978-3-662-54365-8_7
2. Asharov, G., Jain, A., López-Alt, A., Tromer, E., Vaikuntanathan, V., Wichs, D.: Multiparty computation with low communication, computation and interaction via threshold FHE. In: Pointcheval, D., Johansson, T. (eds.) EUROCRYPT 2012. LNCS, vol. 7237, pp. 483–501. Springer, Heidelberg (2012). https://doi.org/10.1007/978-3-642-29011-4_29
3. Ben-Or, M., Goldwasser, S., Wigderson, A.: Completeness theorems for non-cryptographic fault-tolerant distributed computation (extended abstract). In: 20th ACM STOC, pp. 1–10. ACM Press, May 1988
4. Benhamouda, F., Blazy, O., Ducas, L., Quach, W.: Hash proof systems over lattices revisited. In: Abdalla, M., Dahab, R. (eds.) PKC 2018. LNCS, vol. 10770, pp. 644–674. Springer, Cham (2018). https://doi.org/10.1007/978-3-319-76581-5_22
5. Benhamouda, F., Lin, H.: k-round multiparty computation from k-round oblivious transfer via garbled interactive circuits. In: Nielsen, J.B., Rijmen, V. (eds.) EUROCRYPT 2018, Part II. LNCS, vol. 10821, pp. 500–532. Springer, Cham (2018). https://doi.org/10.1007/978-3-319-78375-8_17

6. Boyle, E., Gilboa, N., Ishai, Y.: Function secret sharing: improvements and extensions. In: Weippl, E.R., Katzenbeisser, S., Kruegel, C., Myers, A.C., Halevi, S. (eds.) ACM CCS 16, pp. 1292–1303. ACM Press, October 2016
7. Boyle, E., Gilboa, N., Ishai, Y.: Group-based secure computation: optimizing rounds, communication, and computation. In: Coron, J.-S., Nielsen, J.B. (eds.) EUROCRYPT 2017, Part II. LNCS, vol. 10211, pp. 163–193. Springer, Cham (2017). https://doi.org/10.1007/978-3-319-56614-6_6
8. Boyle, E., Gilboa, N., Ishai, Y., Lin, H., Tessaro, S.: Foundations of homomorphic secret sharing. In: ITCS (2018, to appear)
9. Brakerski, Z., Perlman, R.: Lattice-based fully dynamic multi-key FHE with short ciphertexts. In: Robshaw, M., Katz, J. (eds.) CRYPTO 2016, Part I. LNCS, vol. 9814, pp. 190–213. Springer, Heidelberg (2016). https://doi.org/10.1007/978-3-662-53018-4_8
10. Canetti, R.: Universally composable security: a new paradigm for cryptographic protocols. In: 42nd FOCS, pp. 136–145. IEEE Computer Society Press, October 2001
11. Canetti, R., Dodis, Y., Pass, R., Walfish, S.: Universally composable security with global setup. In: Vadhan, S.P. (ed.) TCC 2007. LNCS, vol. 4392, pp. 61–85. Springer, Heidelberg (2007). https://doi.org/10.1007/978-3-540-70936-7_4
12. Canetti, R., Feige, U., Goldreich, O., Naor, M.: Adaptively secure multi-party computation. In: 28th ACM STOC, pp. 639–648. ACM Press, May 1996
13. Canetti, R., Fischlin, M.: Universally composable commitments. In: Kilian, J. (ed.) CRYPTO 2001. LNCS, vol. 2139, pp. 19–40. Springer, Heidelberg (2001). https://doi.org/10.1007/3-540-44647-8_2
14. Canetti, R., Goldwasser, S., Poburinnaya, O.: Adaptively secure two-party computation from indistinguishability obfuscation. In: Dodis, Y., Nielsen, J.B. (eds.) TCC 2015, Part II. LNCS, vol. 9015, pp. 557–585. Springer, Heidelberg (2015). https://doi.org/10.1007/978-3-662-46497-7_22
15. Canetti, R., Lindell, Y., Ostrovsky, R., Sahai, A.: Universally composable two-party and multi-party secure computation. In: 34th ACM STOC, pp. 494–503. ACM Press, May 2002
16. Canetti, R., Poburinnaya, O., Venkitasubramaniam, M.: Better two-round adaptive multi-party computation. In: Fehr, S. (ed.) PKC 2017, Part II. LNCS, vol. 10175, pp. 396–427. Springer, Heidelberg (2017). https://doi.org/10.1007/978-3-662-54388-7_14
17. Canetti, R., Poburinnaya, O., Venkitasubramaniam, M.: Equivocating yao: constant-round adaptively secure multiparty computation in the plain model. In: Hatami, H., McKenzie, P., King, V. (eds.) 49th ACM STOC, pp. 497–509. ACM Press, June 2017
18. Choi, S.G., Dachman-Soled, D., Malkin, T., Wee, H.: Improved non-committing encryption with applications to adaptively secure protocols. In: Matsui, M. (ed.) ASIACRYPT 2009. LNCS, vol. 5912, pp. 287–302. Springer, Heidelberg (2009). https://doi.org/10.1007/978-3-642-10366-7_17
19. Choi, S.G., Katz, J., Wee, H., Zhou, H.-S.: Efficient, adaptively secure, and composable oblivious transfer with a single, global CRS. In: Kurosawa, K., Hanaoka, G. (eds.) PKC 2013. LNCS, vol. 7778, pp. 73–88. Springer, Heidelberg (2013). https://doi.org/10.1007/978-3-642-36362-7_6
20. Clear, M., McGoldrick, C.: Multi-identity and multi-key leveled FHE from learning with errors. In: Gennaro, R., Robshaw, M. (eds.) CRYPTO 2015, Part II. LNCS, vol. 9216, pp. 630–656. Springer, Heidelberg (2015). https://doi.org/10.1007/978-3-662-48000-7_31

21. Cramer, R., Shoup, V.: Universal hash proofs and a paradigm for adaptive chosen ciphertext secure public-key encryption. In: Knudsen, L.R. (ed.) EUROCRYPT 2002. LNCS, vol. 2332, pp. 45–64. Springer, Heidelberg (2002). https://doi.org/10.1007/3-540-46035-7_4
22. Dachman-Soled, D., Katz, J., Rao, V.: Adaptively secure, universally composable, multiparty computation in constant rounds. In: Dodis, Y., Nielsen, J.B. (eds.) TCC 2015, Part II. LNCS, vol. 9015, pp. 586–613. Springer, Heidelberg (2015). https://doi.org/10.1007/978-3-662-46497-7_23
23. Damgård, I., Polychroniadou, A., Rao, V.: Adaptively secure multi-party computation from LWE (via equivocal FHE). In: Cheng, C.-M., Chung, K.-M., Persiano, G., Yang, B.-Y. (eds.) PKC 2016, Part II. LNCS, vol. 9615, pp. 208–233. Springer, Heidelberg (2016). https://doi.org/10.1007/978-3-662-49387-8_9
24. Garay, J.A., Wichs, D., Zhou, H.-S.: Somewhat non-committing encryption and efficient adaptively secure oblivious transfer. In: Halevi, S. (ed.) CRYPTO 2009. LNCS, vol. 5677, pp. 505–523. Springer, Heidelberg (2009). https://doi.org/10.1007/978-3-642-03356-8_30
25. Garg, S., Gentry, C., Halevi, S., Raykova, M.: Two-round secure MPC from indistinguishability obfuscation. In: Lindell, Y. (ed.) TCC 2014. LNCS, vol. 8349, pp. 74–94. Springer, Heidelberg (2014). https://doi.org/10.1007/978-3-642-54242-8_4
26. Garg, S., Polychroniadou, A.: Two-round adaptively secure MPC from indistinguishability obfuscation. In: Dodis, Y., Nielsen, J.B. (eds.) TCC 2015, Part II. LNCS, vol. 9015, pp. 614–637. Springer, Heidelberg (2015). https://doi.org/10.1007/978-3-662-46497-7_24
27. Garg, S., Srinivasan, A.: Garbled protocols and two-round MPC from bilinear maps. In: 58th FOCS, pp. 588–599. IEEE Computer Society Press (2017)
28. Garg, S., Srinivasan, A.: Two-round multiparty secure computation from minimal assumptions. In: Nielsen, J.B., Rijmen, V. (eds.) EUROCRYPT 2018, Part II. LNCS, vol. 10821, pp. 468–499. Springer, Cham (2018). https://doi.org/10.1007/978-3-319-78375-8_16
29. Goldreich, O., Micali, S., Wigderson, A.: How to play any mental game or a completeness theorem for protocols with honest majority. In: Aho, A. (ed.) 19th ACM STOC, pp. 218–229. ACM Press, May 1987
30. Goldwasser, S., Micali, S.: Probabilistic encryption. J. Comput. Syst. Sci. **28**(2), 270–299 (1984)
31. Dov Gordon, S., Liu, F.-H., Shi, E.: Constant-round MPC with fairness and guarantee of output delivery. In: Gennaro, R., Robshaw, M. (eds.) CRYPTO 2015, Part II. LNCS, vol. 9216, pp. 63–82. Springer, Heidelberg (2015). https://doi.org/10.1007/978-3-662-48000-7_4
32. Halevi, S., Kalai, Y.T.: Smooth projective hashing and two-message oblivious transfer. J. Cryptol. **25**(1), 158–193 (2012)
33. Hofheinz, D., Kiltz, E.: The group of signed quadratic residues and applications. In: Halevi, S. (ed.) CRYPTO 2009. LNCS, vol. 5677, pp. 637–653. Springer, Heidelberg (2009). https://doi.org/10.1007/978-3-642-03356-8_37
34. Mukherjee, P., Wichs, D.: Two round multiparty computation via multi-key FHE. In: Fischlin, M., Coron, J.-S. (eds.) EUROCRYPT 2016, Part II. LNCS, vol. 9666, pp. 735–763. Springer, Heidelberg (2016). https://doi.org/10.1007/978-3-662-49896-5_26
35. Naor, M., Pinkas, B.: Efficient oblivious transfer protocols. In: Kosaraju, S.R. (ed.) 12th SODA, pp. 448–457. ACM-SIAM, January 2001

36. Peikert, C., Shiehian, S.: Multi-key FHE from LWE, revisited. In: Hirt, M., Smith, A. (eds.) TCC 2016. LNCS, vol. 9986, pp. 217–238. Springer, Heidelberg (2016). https://doi.org/10.1007/978-3-662-53644-5_9
37. Peikert, C., Vaikuntanathan, V., Waters, B.: A framework for efficient and composable oblivious transfer. In: Wagner, D. (ed.) CRYPTO 2008. LNCS, vol. 5157, pp. 554–571. Springer, Heidelberg (2008). https://doi.org/10.1007/978-3-540-85174-5_31
38. Yao, A.C.C.: Theory and applications of trapdoor functions (extended abstract). In: 23rd FOCS, pp. 80–91. IEEE Computer Society Press, November 1982

Zero Knowledge

One-Message Zero Knowledge and Non-malleable Commitments

Nir Bitansky[1(✉)] and Huijia Lin[2(✉)]

[1] Tel Aviv University, Tel Aviv, Israel
nirbitan@tau.ac.il
[2] University of Santa Barbra, Santa Barbara, USA
rachel.lin@cs.ucsb.edu

Abstract. We introduce a new notion of *one-message zero-knowledge (1ZK) arguments* that satisfy a *weak soundness* guarantee—the number of false statements that a polynomial-time non-uniform adversary can convince the verifier to accept is not much larger than the size of its non-uniform advice. The zero-knowledge guarantee is given by a simulator that runs in (mildly) super-polynomial time. We construct such 1ZK arguments based on the notion of multi-collision-resistant *keyless* hash functions, recently introduced by Bitansky, Kalai, and Paneth (STOC 2018). Relying on the constructed 1ZK arguments, subexponentially-secure time-lock puzzles, and other standard assumptions, we construct *one-message fully-concurrent non-malleable commitments*. This is the first construction that is based on assumptions that do not already incorporate non-malleability, as well as the first based on (subexponentially) falsifiable assumptions.

1 Introduction

Zero-knowledge proofs [GMR89] are a cornerstone of modern cryptography. Their birth was enabled by introducing two new concepts to classical proofs—*interaction and randomness*. Indeed, both were shown [GO94] to be essential—for non-trivial languages, zero-knowledge proofs (or their computationally-sound counterparts known as *arguments*) require a randomized verifier that exchanges at least three messages with the prover. In particular, unlike classical proofs, zero-knowledge proofs cannot be transferred, published, nor stored.

The full version of this extended abstract can be found on Eprint [BL18].

N. Bitansky—Member of the Check Point Institute of Information Security. Supported by the Alon Young Faculty Fellowship and by Len Blavatnik and the Blavatnik Family foundation.

H. Lin—Supported by NSF grants CNS-1528178, CNS-1514526, CNS-1652849 (CAREER), a Hellman Fellowship, the Defense Advanced Research Projects Agency (DARPA) and Army Research Office (ARO) under Contract No. W911NF-15-C-0236, and a subcontract No. 2017-002 through Galois. The views expressed are those of the authors and do not reflect the official policy or position of the Department of Defense, the National Science Foundation, or the U.S. Government.

A. Beimel and S. Dziembowski (Eds.): TCC 2018, LNCS 11239, pp. 209–234, 2018.
https://doi.org/10.1007/978-3-030-03807-6_8

One setting in which this barrier can be circumvented is when a trusted setup (such as a *common random string*) is available [BFM88]. In the absence of a trusted setup, a natural approach to the problem is to relax the requirements of zero-knowledge protocols. Along this vein, Dwork and Naor [DN07] showed that for witness-indistinguishable (WI) proofs, two messages suffice, and by now, we know how to achieve them with no interaction at all [BOV07, GOS12]. Pass [Pas03] considered a stronger notion—zero-knowledge with a super-polynomial simulator (SPS). Indeed, WI proofs stand at the extreme of this notion, as they admit an exponential-time simulator (that can find a witness for the underlying statement by brute force). In contrast, based on subexponential hardness assumptions, Pass constructed two-message arguments where the zero-knowledge simulator runs in subexponential, or even quasi-polynomial time (without violating the hardness of the underlying language). Such SPS zero-knowledge has proven instrumental for central applications such as concurrent computation [Pas03, PS04, BS05, MMY06, CLP16, GGJS12, GKP17, BGI+17, BGJ+17] and non-malleable commitments [KS17].

While Pass' proofs break the three-message barrier, they still consist of two messages and do not enjoy the merits of completely non-interactive proofs. Following the introduction of non-interactive WI (NIWI) proofs, Barak and Pass [BP04] investigated the possibility that SPS zero-knowledge can also be made non-interactive (with no trusted setup). They observed that non-interactive proofs (or arguments) that satisfy the usual notion of soundness and have a T_{SPS}-time simulator are impossible to achieve against non-uniform adversaries, except for languages $\mathcal{L}$ decidable in time T_{SPS}. Indeed, if the simulator cannot decide $\mathcal{L}$, there must *exist* proofs π for false statements $x \notin \mathcal{L}$, and a non-uniform prover can have such proofs hardwired in its code. Accordingly, Barak and Pass define a notion of SPS zero-knowledge protocols satisfying a *weak* notion of soundness that only holds against efficient *uniform* provers. They show how to construct such protocols based on keyless hash functions that are collision-resistant against subexponential uniform adversaries (or more general uniform sampling problems).

This Work: Weak Soundness Against Non-uniform Provers. We introduce a new notion of weak soundness for one-message zero-knowledge (1ZK) *that also captures non-uniform adversaries.*

The notion is inspired by the notion of multi-collision resistance for keyless hash functions, introduced recently in [BKP18]. Roughly speaking, it requires that an efficient non-uniform adversary *cannot do more than hardwire false statements with their accepting proofs in its code.* That is, any non-uniform adversary, with description of polynomial size S and arbitrary polynomial running time $T \gg S$, should not be able to find (i.e., output in one shot) more than $K(S)$ false statements $x \notin \mathcal{L}$ together with an accepting proof π, where K is some blowup function (for concreteness, the reader may think of $K(S) = S^2$ throughout this introduction). In other words, *false statements with their accepting proofs cannot be significantly compressed.*

The zero-knowledge requirement is the same SPS requirement as before—the simulator is allowed to be mildly super-polynomial (and in particular, cannot decide the underlying language $\mathcal{L}$). We note that even with such weak soundness, the SPS relaxation is essential—languages $\mathcal{L}$ that are hard on average cannot have an efficient simulator.[1]

1.1 Results and Discussion

We construct 1ZK arguments satisfying the new notion of weak soundness based on the notion of multi-collision resistance and generalizations thereof. Then, relying on such arguments, we construct one-message (concurrently) non-malleable commitments, which has been a long standing problem. We now elaborate on each of these results.

Constructing 1ZK Arguments. We show how to construct 1ZK arguments from keyless hash functions that satisfy the notion of multi-collision resistance recently introduced in [BKP18]. Such a hash function $\mathsf{H} : \{0,1\}^\lambda \to \{0,1\}^{\lambda/2}$ guarantees that no relatively-efficient adversary with non-uniform description of polynomial size S can find more than $K(S)$ collisions in the underlying function.[2] Here, K is again a fixed polynomial (e.g., quadratic) and relatively-efficient means mildly superpolynomial-time (e.g. quasipolynomial or subexponential).

Theorem 1 (Informal). *Assuming multi-collision-resistant keyless hash functions, injective one-way functions, and non-interactive witness-indistinguishable proofs, all subexponentially-secure, there exist 1ZK arguments for NP with weak soundness and a subexponential-time simulator.*

As noted in [BKP18], while non-standard, multi-collision resistance is a falsifiable and relatively simple assumption. As candidates they suggest existing keyless hash functions such as SHA, or AES-based hashing, and point out directions for investigating additional candidates. We can, in fact, rely on a more general notion of *incompressible problems*, for which additional candidates may be found. At high-level, a (T, K, Δ)-incompressible problem is a collection $\mathcal{W} = \{\mathcal{W}_\lambda\}_\lambda$ of efficiently recognizable sets (one set for each security parameter λ) satisfying the following. On one hand, no T-time adversary with non-uniform description of polynomial size S can find more than $K(S)$ *solutions* $w \in \mathcal{W}_\lambda$. On the other hand, $\mathcal{W}_\lambda$ is relatively *dense* in $\{0,1\}^\lambda$, in the sense that a random $w \leftarrow \{0,1\}^\lambda$

[1] If there were such a simulator, then due to weak soundness, the simulator should fail to find accepting proofs for no-instances $\bar{x} \notin \mathcal{L}$ sampled from any efficiently samplable distribution. In contrast, for yes-instance $x \in \mathcal{L}$, it should succeed by the zero-knowledge guarantee. Thus, such a simulator would violate the average-case hardness of $\mathcal{L}$.

[2] To be exact, in [BKP18], they call this notion strong multi-collision resistance. They define (weak) multi-collision resistance as the problem of finding multiple inputs that all map to the same image. Throughout the introduction, we ignore this difference. In the body, we show that we can rely on either one, relying in addition on standard derandomization assumptions.

is in $\mathcal{W}_\lambda$ with relatively high probability $\Delta = 2^{-o(\lambda)}$.[3] For concreteness, the reader may think of $T = 2^{\lambda^{.01}} \ll 2^{\lambda^{.99}} = \Delta^{-1}$.

Theorem 2 (Informal). *Assuming (T, K, Δ)-incompressible problems, where $K \ll T \ll \Delta^{-1} \ll 2^{\lambda^{.99}}$, and subexponentially-secure injective one-way functions and non-interactive witness-indistinguishable proofs, there exist 1ZK arguments for NP with (T, K)-weak soundness and a* $\text{poly}(\Delta^{-1})$*-time simulator.*[4]

We also define and construct, under the same assumptions, a more general notion that we call *φ-tuned 1ZK* that admits a more flexible tradeoff between the level of soundness and simulation time, and will be useful when applying these arguments. We defer the details to the technical overview below.

One-Message Non-malleable Commitments. The question of the round complexity of non-malleable commitments [DDN03] has been long pursued. The past two decades have seen impressive progress [Bar02, PR05a, PR05b, LPV08a, LP09, PPV08, PW10, Wee10, Goy11, LP11, GLOV12, GRRV14, GPR16, COSV16, COSV17, Khu17], culminating in two recent constructions of *two-message* non-malleable commitments [KS17, LPS17] based on subexponential Decision-Diffie-Hellman or Quadratic Residuosity in the first, and subexponential *time-lock puzzles* [RSW00] in the second (which achieves also full concurrency).

Yet, one-message non-malleable commitments have remained somewhat elusive. So far, they have only been constructed starting from a non-falsifiable assumption that already incorporates non-malleability called *adaptive injective one-way functions*, against *uniform* adversaries [LPS17], or for a restricted class of algebraic mauling functions and entropic plaintexts [KY18]. Indeed, one-message non-malleable commitments would give rise to powerful features that cannot be achieved with interaction, such as the ability to publish them on public ledgers, transfer them from one hand to another, or store them for future use.

Relying on 1ZK arguments with weak soundness, we construct one-message fully-concurrent non-malleable commitments against *non-uniform* adversaries.

Theorem 3 (Informal). *Under the same assumptions as in Theorem 2 (or 1), as well as subexponential time-lock puzzles, there exist fully-concurrent one-message non-malleable commitments against all efficient non-uniform adversaries.*

We actually prove a more general theorem that transforms commitments satisfying a notion of *four-tag non-malleability* into full-fledge non-malleable commitments as stated in the above theorem. (More specifically, the former refers to

[3] To get subexponential density, we need to multi-collision-resistant hash functions with polynomial, rather than linear, shrinkage. In [BKP18], it is shown how polynomial compression can be achieved form linear compression.

[4] Here (T, K)-weak soundness refers to the expected generalization of the weak soundness notion discussed above where the prover may run in time at most $\text{poly}(T)$, and T may be superpolynomial and the blowup function is K.

non-malleability w.r.t. four tags, whereas full-fledged non-malleability can handle an exponential number of tags.) Such four-tag (or constant-tag) commitments are constructed in [LPS17] based on sub-exponentially secure time-lock puzzles and injective one-way functions. In addition, we present new candidate four-tag (or constant-tag) non-malleable commitments from a new assumption regarding *injective one-way functions that are amenable to hardness amplification*, which can replace time-lock puzzles in the above theorem. This yields new candidates from natural one-way functions such as discrete logarithms, RSA, or Rabin. See further details in the technical overview below.

On the Underlying Assumptions. The assumptions that we rely on, most notably incompressible problems, are not standard. Nevertheless, we do find them simple and plausible. Bitansky, Kalai, and Paneth give evidence that multi-collision resistance may hold for existing cryptographic hash functions and in particular does not require any special algebraic structure—they show that this property is satisfied by random oracles, even in the auxiliary-input model [Unr07] (where the adversary may first store arbitrary polynomial information about the oracle).

We also note that all of our assumptions are *subexponentially-falsifiable* (i.e., falsifiable w.r.t. sub-exponential time adversaries). Here we note that Pass [Pas13] showed that non-malleable commitments in less than three messages cannot be shown secure based on black-box reductions to polynomially-falsifiable assumptions.

A more conservative view of our results would be that to rule out the existence of one-message non-malleable commitments, one must show that incompressible problems do not exist. That is, any efficiently recognizable, somewhat dense, set must have a non-trivial sampler (where by non-trivial we mean that it can output more samples then its non-uniform size). In particular, one would have to show that for any keyless hash function, it is possible to compress collisions. This would also constitute a strong (and non-contrived) separation between random oracles and any keyless hash function.

Using Weak Soundness. Weak soundness is the best one could hope for when considering one-message zero-knowledge without trusted setup and non-uniform cheating provers, *but when is it useful?* Generally speaking, weak soundness could be leveraged in settings where a prover does not fully determine proven statements, namely, *statements have some non-trivial entropy.*

This gives some intuition on why weak soundness is useful in our application of non-malleable commitments. Roughly speaking, to maul a commitment c to a value v, the attacker is required to generate a new commitment c' to a related value v', and prove that the new commitment is well-formed. As long as the attacker does not always produce a fixed commitment c', or rather a commitment c' from some fixed polynomial-size set $\mathcal{Z}$, proven statements are sufficiently entropic and weak soundness kicks in. In contrast, mauling c into c' from such a set $\mathcal{Z}$ would not constitute a meaningful attack—the distribution of the value v' in the commitment c' cannot depend on the committed value v in c, or a reduction that has the set $\mathcal{Z}$ hardcoded could break the hiding of c. See more details in the technical overview below.

It is plausible that weak soundness will be found useful in other settings with entropic statements or in different man-in-the-middle attack models.

Robustness Beyond Human Ignorance. When considering the possibility of integrating non-interactive zero-knowledge in real-world systems, the need for a trusted common reference string may present a serious hurdle (certainly in decentralized applications whose essence is to avoid central trust). The system of Barak and Pass [BP04], when instantiated, say, with SHA256, already avoids the need for central trust and suggests a meaningful guarantee of *soundness in the face of human ignorance* (a term coined by Rogaway [Rog06]). Namely, as long as humanity fails to find collisions in SHA256, it will also fail to find accepting proofs for false statements. However, the moment even a single collision in SHA256 is found, the Barak and Pass system would completely lose soundness—it will be possible to easily prove *any false statement.*

Our system has a more robust guarantee—finding a few collisions only allows finding a few false statements with accepting proofs, and the mapping from collisions to false statements is deterministic and efficiently computable.

1.2 Technical Overview

We now give an overview of the main ideas and techniques behind our results.

Throughout this overview, it will be convenient to consider a slight variant of incompressible problems requiring that for any efficient adversary $\mathcal{A}$ with a non-uniform description of polynomial size S, there exists a set $\mathcal{Z}$ of size at most $K(S)$, such that $\mathcal{A}$ cannot find solutions $w \in \mathcal{W}\backslash\mathcal{Z}$. In the body, we show that this variant is indeed equivalent to requiring that the adversary fails to find more than K solutions w. We consider a similar variant for the definition of weak soundness, where the adversary cannot output a false statement and accepting proof (x, π), except for statements x from some size-K set.

One-Message Zero-Knowledge

The starting point for our construction is the Barak-Pass [BP04] construction against uniform provers. They follow the common [FLS99] paradigm in which the prover provides a WI proof that

"Either $x \in \mathcal{L}$ or the prover knows some trapdoor".

The trapdoor should be such that it is too hard for an efficient prover to compute, but only mildly hard, so that a super-polynomial simulator can obtain it relatively fast in time $T_{\text{td}} \ll 2^{o(|x|)}$. The hardness of obtaining the trapdoor, and the soundness of the proof, guarantee the soundness of the argument, whereas as the WI property, along with the simulator's ability to find the trapdoor, give rise to SPS simulation. To realize this idea, the prover sends a commitment c and proves that $x \in \mathcal{L}$ or c is a commitment to the trapdoor. The commitment is only mildly hard—the committed value could be extracted by brute force in time $T_{\text{com}} \ll T_{\text{td}}$, which does not suffice to find the trapdoor. Therefore, violating soundness requires violating the hardness of finding a trapdoor in T_{td}.

The question is *what could be the trapdoor.* Focusing on uniform provers, Barak and Pass rely on problems that are hard for uniform algorithms. For instance finding collisions of certain keyless hash functions is conjectured to be hard for uniform algorithms (or more generally, algorithms whose description is smaller than the function's input), even in time $\text{poly}(T_{\text{com}})$. This of course miserably fails against non-uniform provers who could simply have such a trapdoor (e.g., a collision) hardwired in their code and use it to cheat.

Leveraging Incompressible Problems. Recall that we are only interested in a weak notion of soundness—we wish to guarantee that there is only a small set of false statements for which the prover may give false proofs (where small is some polynomial $K(S)$ in the prover's non-uniform description size S). A first natural idea is to simply replace the trapdoor problem with an incompressible problem $\mathcal{W}$ (for instance, replace collision-resistance against uniform adversaries with multi-collision resistance against non-uniform ones).

This first attempt, however, fails. The problem is that any *single* solution in $\mathcal{W}$ allows to efficiently generate accepting proofs for *all* statements x. Thus, a non-uniform attacker with one such hardwired solution, can convince the verifier of accepting any number of false statement, thereby violating the weak soundness requirement. The problem stems from the fact that in such a protocol, the concept of a useful trapdoor is completely detached from the proven statement x. We solve this by binding trapdoors and statements, so that, finding accepting proofs for different false statements requires finding different solutions in $\mathcal{W}$. Thus, an attacker who can only find a small set of solutions, can only generate proofs for a small number of corresponding false statements.

More specifically, we aim to achieve two goals. First, every trapdoor $w \in \mathcal{W}$ is associated with a specific statement $x = f(w)$ determined by some efficiently computable function f—this would ensure that the prover could only provide accepting proofs for false statements from a small set $\mathcal{X} = f(\mathcal{Z})$ determined by the small set $\mathcal{Z}$ of trapdoors it may be able to find. Second, we would like to guarantee that for any $x \in \mathcal{L}$, the simulator would be able to reverse sample a trapdoor $w \in \mathcal{W}$ such that $x = f(w)$, and it should do so relatively fast.

We achieve the above combinatorial properties as follows. For instances x of size ℓ, we choose f to be a *two-source extractor* $\mathsf{2Ext} : \{0,1\}^n \times \{0,1\}^n \rightarrow \{0,1\}^\ell$, where n is a parameter dictated by the quality of the extractor (in our actual construction $n = 4\ell$). We then choose our incompressible problem to be pairs of solutions $\mathcal{W} \times \mathcal{W} \subseteq \{0,1\}^n \times \{0,1\}^n$ for some underlying incompressible problem $\mathcal{W}$. It is easy to see that the product of incompressible problems is itself an incompressible problem, and so weak soundness is obtained according to the above reasoning. Furthermore, by choosing an appropriate extractor, we can guarantee that as long as $\mathcal{W}$ has density $\Delta \geq 2^{-o(\ell)}$, for any $x \in \{0,1\}^\ell$, it is possible to sample $(w, w') \in \mathcal{W}$ such that $\mathsf{2Ext}(w, w') = x$ in time $O(\Delta^{-2})$, as required.

The above is satisfied by any extractor with the following two properties. First, it has an exponentially small error—for independent sources with min-entropy $n - o(\ell)$, the output is $2^{-\ell-\Omega(1)}$-close to uniform. Second, it admits efficient reverse sampling—for any x, it is possible to efficiently sample from the uniform distribution on $U_n \times U'_n$ conditioned on $2\mathsf{Ext}(U, U') = x$. These properties are both satisfied by the classical Hadamard extractor [CG88, Vaz85]. See further details in the full version of this paper.

To recap, the final proof (c, π) consists of a commitment c to a string of length $2n$, and a NIWI that

$$\text{“}\textit{Either}\, x \in \mathcal{L}\, \textit{or}\, c\, \textit{is a commitment to}\, (w, w') \in \mathcal{W} \times \mathcal{W}\, \textit{such that}\, 2\mathsf{Ext}(w, w') = x\text{”}.$$

Starting from a $(T_{\mathcal{W}}, K, \Delta)$-incompressible problem, we choose a mildly-hard commitment so that it is extractable in time $T_{\mathsf{com}} \ll T_{\mathcal{W}}$. The resulting system is then $(T_{\mathcal{W}}, K)$-weakly-sound and has a Δ^{-2}-time simulator. In particular, for the discussed setting of parameters $K \ll T \ll \Delta^{-1} \ll 2^{\ell^{.99}}$, we get a subexponential-time simulator.

φ-Tuned 1ZK. We also consider a generalization of the 1ZK definition that admits a more flexible soundness vs. simulation-time tradeoff. Specifically, we parameterize our system by a projection function $\varphi(x)$ and obtain the following augmented guarantees:

- *Weaker Soundness:* we are only guaranteed that the prover produces accepting proofs for false statements x whose projection $\varphi(x)$ is taken from a small set $\mathcal{Z}$ (but x itself is not restricted to any small set).
- *Faster Simulation:* simulation time is only subexponential in $|\varphi(x)|$ and not in $\ell = |x|$. Furthermore, fixing any projection y, there is a corresponding trapdoor state st_y that allows simulating any $x \in \varphi^{-1}(y)$ *in polynomial time.* A bit more formally, simulation for x can be split into a long preprocessing step $\mathsf{S}_{\mathsf{pre}}$, subexponential in $|\varphi(x)|$, that produces $\mathsf{st}_{\varphi(x)}$, and a short postprocessing step $\mathsf{S}_{\mathsf{pos}}$ that takes polynomial time given the trapdoor state $\mathsf{st}_{\varphi(x)}$.

Note that the above is indeed a generalization of the previous notion when considering the identity as the projection φ. As we shall see later on, the flexibility of choosing φ differently, with the above tradeoff, will be useful in our application to non-malleable commitments. The construction of such φ-tuned 1ZK is identical to the construction described above only that we require that the trapdoor (w, w') fixes $\varphi(x)$ rather than x. See further details in the full version.

One-Message Non-malleable Commitments

We now give an overview of how to use our 1ZK arguments to construct one-message non-malleable commitments. We adopt a standard formulation of non-malleable commitments where players have identities, and the commitment protocol depends on the identity of the committer, which is referred to as the *tag* of the interaction. Non-malleability [DDN03] ensures that no man-in-the-middle attacker can “maul” a commitment it receives *on the left* into a commitment of a related value it gives *on the right*, as long as the tags of the left and right commitments are different. More formally, for any two values u and w, the values the man-in-the-middle commits to after receiving left commitments to u or w, along with the commitments it sees on the left, are indistinguishable. The notion of *concurrent non-malleability* [DDN03, PR05a] further requires that no attacker can "maul" a set of left commitments into a set of right commitments so that the joint distribution of right committed values depends on the left committed values.

The number γ of tags a scheme supports can be viewed as a quantitative measure of how non-malleable it is: A γ-tag non-malleable commitment gives a family of γ commitment schemes—each with a hardwired tag—that are "mutually non-malleable" to each other. Therefore, the fewer tags, the easier it is to construct a corresponding non-malleable commitment. Indeed, as shown by [LPS17], non-interactive non-malleable commitments for a constant number of tags can be constructed from subexponentially-secure injective one-way functions and time-lock puzzles [RSW00]. Full-fledged non-malleable commitments, in contrast, have an exponential number of tags $\gamma = 2^{\lambda}$. Thus, the main challenge lies in increasing the number of tags from a constant to exponential.

Techniques for amplifying the number of tags have been explored in the literature [DDN03, LP11, KS17, LPS17]. They show that a non-malleable commitment scheme for γ tags can be transformed into one for $2^{\tilde{\Omega}(\gamma)}$ tags. Thus, starting from constant-tag non-malleable commitments, applying the transformation iteratively for $O(\log^* \lambda)$ times yields non-malleable commitments for exponentially many tags. However, all existing tag-amplification techniques crucially rely on interaction—even if the initial constant-tag non-malleable commitments are non-interactive, the transformation increases the message-complexity to at least two. For instance, the tag-amplification technique of Khurana and Sahai makes use of 2-message SPS zero-knowledge arguments. In this work, we show how to replace the 2-message SPS ZK arguments with our 1ZK arguments, which gives a non-interactive tag-amplification technique, and hence non-interactive non-malleable commitments.

Two-Message Tag-Amplification. We start with reviewing the Khurana and Sahai (KS) 2-message tag-amplification technique, which transforms a non-interactive input scheme iNM for γ tags into a 2-message output scheme oNM for $\binom{\gamma}{\gamma/2} = 2^{\Omega(\gamma)}$ tags. Each tg' of oNM consists of a subset of $\gamma/2$ tags $\mathsf{tg}' = (\mathsf{tg}_1, \cdots, \mathsf{tg}_{\gamma/2})$ of iNM. To commit to a value v, oNM computes $\gamma/2$ commitments to v using iNM with respect to tags $\mathsf{tg}_1, \cdots, \mathsf{tg}_{\gamma/2}$, followed by a 2-message SPS argument that all commitments are consistent. More precisely,

KS 2-message tag-amplification—oNM:

- The receiver R sends the first message π_1 of a 2-message SPS argument.
- To commit to v using $\mathsf{tg}' = (\mathsf{tg}_1, \cdots, \mathsf{tg}_{\gamma/2})$, the committer C generates $\{\mathrm{nm}_j \leftarrow \mathsf{iNM}(\mathsf{tg}_j, v)\}_{j\in[\gamma/2]}$ and the second message π_2 of a 2-message SPS argument that all iNM commitments commit to the same value.
  The committed value is defined to be the value committed in nm_1.

To see that oNM is non-malleable, consider a man-in-the-middle receiving a left commitment using $\mathsf{tg}' = (\mathsf{tg}_1, \cdots, \mathsf{tg}_{\gamma/2})$ and giving a right commitment using $\tilde{\mathsf{tg}}' = (\tilde{\mathsf{tg}}_1, \cdots, \tilde{\mathsf{tg}}_{\gamma/2})$. If $\mathsf{tg}' \neq \tilde{\mathsf{tg}}'$, there must exist $i^\star$, such that, $\tilde{\mathsf{tg}}_{i^\star} \neq \mathsf{tg}_i$ for all i—the $i^\star$'th right iNM commitment uses a tag different from all left tags.

Then, they reduce the non-malleability of oNM to the non-malleability of iNM. To do so, they rely on the soundness of the 2-message SPS argument to argue that in *left-honest* man-in-the-middle executions, the attacker must send consistent iNM commitments $\{\widetilde{\mathrm{nm}}_j\}$ on the right, or else it would fail in the SPS argument. (Here by *left-honest*, we mean the proofs on the left are honestly generated and not simulated.) Thus, to show that the right committed values do not change in two left-honest executions with different left committed values u or w, it suffices to show that the value committed in any right iNM commitment—in particular, the $i^\star$'th one $\widetilde{\mathrm{nm}}_{i^\star}$—does not change (in a distinguishable manner). To show this, they gradually simulate components in the left commitment in a sequence of hybrids, while maintaining that $\tilde{v}_{i^\star}$ committed in $\widetilde{\mathrm{nm}}_{i^\star}$ does not change throughout hybrids.

In the first hybrid, the left SPS argument (π_1, π_2) is simulated. To ensure that $\tilde{v}_{i^\star}$ does not change, they rely on *complexity leveraging* to make simulated proofs "harder to distinguish" than extracting from the commitment iNM; that is, the indistinguishability of SPS simulation holds even when $\tilde{v}_{i^\star}$ is extracted by brute force. Once the left SPS argument is simulated, the left iNM commitments are switched to committing to 0 in following hybrids. By the non-malleability of iNM and the fact that $\widetilde{\mathrm{nm}}_{i^\star}$ uses a tag $\tilde{\mathsf{tg}}_{i^\star}$ different from all left tags, its committed value $\tilde{v}_{i^\star}$ does not change through these hybrids. Note that this requires the non-malleability of iNM to hold against T_{iNM}-time attackers for $T_{\mathsf{iNM}} \gg T_{\mathsf{SPS}}$. Using SPS ZK where simulation-time only depends on the underlying security parameter (and not the size of the instance), the above can be satisfied by appropriately choosing the relation between the iNM security parameter n and the SPS security parameter $\bar{n}$.

Non-interactive Tag-Amplification. To obtain non-interactive tag-amplification, a natural idea is replacing the 2-message SPS in the KS transformation with our 1ZK argument. However, two challenges arise:

- Challenge 1: Our 1ZK is only weakly sound. Thus, the man-in-the-middle attacker is able to generate an accepting 1ZK argument $\tilde{\pi}$ even when the right iNM commitments $\{\widetilde{\mathrm{nm}}_j\}$ are inconsistent (i.e., committing to different values).
- Challenge 2: In our basic 1ZK, the simulation time is subexponential in the length of the statement $|x|$ (and the security parameter). This makes it difficult to guarantee that the simulator cannot break the underling non-malleable commitment, i.e. $T_{\mathsf{iNM}} \gg T_{\mathsf{SPS}}$.

  Specifically, the statement x concerns the consistency of $\gamma/2$ iNM commitments, and thus the simulation time is at least $T_{\mathsf{SPS}} = 2^{(\gamma \times \ell_{\mathrm{nm}}/2)^\varepsilon}$, where

$\ell_{\text{nm}} = \ell_{\text{nm}}(n)$ is the length of iNM commitments and could scale polynomially with the security parameter n of iNM. It could well be that $T_{\mathsf{iNM}} \ll T_{\text{SPS}}$.

In a nutshell, to solve the first problem, we rely on the weak soundness of 1ZK to argue that whenever the right iNM commitments are not consistent (that is, the statement is false), the right commitments are taken from a small "apriori known" set, and their underlying values can be non-uniformly hardcoded into the reduction. To solve the second problem, we make the security of iNM independent of the simulation time, by introducing an extra commitment under another scheme Com and using the φ-tuned version of 1ZK to reduce the simulation time to only depend on the length of commitments in Com, instead of commitments in iNM.

The Actual Tag-Amplification and Resulting Scheme oNM:
To commit to v using $\mathsf{tg}' = (\mathsf{tg}_1, \cdots, \mathsf{tg}_{\gamma/2})$, the committer C generates $c \leftarrow \mathsf{Com}(v)$, $\{\text{nm}_j \leftarrow \mathsf{iNM}(\mathsf{tg}_j, v)\}_{j\in[\gamma/2]}$, and a 1ZK argument π showing that c and all iNM commitments commit to the same value. The 1ZK statement is given by $x = (c, \text{nm}_1, \cdots, \text{nm}_{\gamma/2})$ and we consider its projection $\varphi(x) = c$ that only fixes the Com commitment c.
The committed value is defined to be the value committed in c.

Let us see how the above two problems are resolved.

Resolving Challenge 1: The weak soundness of φ-tuned 1ZK guarantees that for any attacker $\mathcal{A}$ of polynomial size S, there is a set $\mathcal{Z}$ consisting of a polynomial number $K(S)$ of Com commitments c (the so called projections) such that $\mathcal{A}$ cannot prove a false statement x where the corresponding commitment c is not in $\mathcal{Z}$. This means that in left-honest man-in-the-middle executions, one of the following two cases occurs: Either the right Com commitment $\tilde{c}$ and the iNM commitments are all consistent, or the commitment $\tilde{c}$ belongs to $\mathcal{Z}$. In the latter case, the right committed value must belong to the polynomial-sized set $\{\tilde{v} : \tilde{v} \text{ is the value in } \tilde{c} \in \mathcal{Z}\}$, which can be hardwired non-uniformly into the reduction. In the first case, showing the indistinguishability of the right committed values again reduces to showing that of $\tilde{v}_{i^\star}$ committed in $\widetilde{\text{nm}}_{i^\star}$.

Resolving Challenge 2: Recall that φ-tuned 1ZK enjoys a simulation speedup. Specifically, simulation consists of (i) a $2^{|c|^\delta}$-time preprocessing phase that depends only on the projection c and computes a trapdoor state $\mathsf{st} \leftarrow \mathsf{S}_{\mathsf{pre}}(c)$, and (ii) a polynomial $\text{poly}(|x|, \bar{n})$-time postprocessing phase that generates the simulated proof $\widehat{\pi} \leftarrow \mathsf{S}_{\mathsf{pos}}(x, \mathsf{st})$. With this speed-up, let us examine again the sequence of hybrids where the left Com and iNM commitments are gradually switched to committing to 0, while the 1ZK argument on the left is simulated. We need to ensure that $\tilde{v}_{i^\star}$ does not change.

To change the Com commitment, we require that its hiding holds even in the presence of 1ZK simulation and (brute-force) extraction from $\tilde{v}_{i^\star}$:

$$T_{\mathsf{Com}} \gg T_{\text{SPS}} = 2^{|c|^\delta} + \text{poly}(|x|, \bar{n}) \quad \text{and} \quad T_{\mathsf{Com}} \gg T_{\mathsf{iNM.E}}$$

The latter can be satisfied by setting the security parameter $\bar{n}$ of Com to be sufficiently larger than the security parameter n of iNM. The former is more subtle as it requires Com to be at least $2^{|c|^\delta}$-secure, where $|c|$ is the length of Com commitments. Such a commitment scheme for strings of length ℓ, can be instantiated by the classical Blum-Micali bit commitment scheme [BM84] (recall that a commitment to b is $f(r), \mathrm{hc}(r) \oplus b$, where hc is a hardcore bit of an injective one-way function f), instantiated with any 2^{k^ρ}-hard injective one-way function, and sufficiently large security parameter $k > \Omega(\ell^{\delta/\rho-\delta})$.

Next, when changing the left iNM commitments, we can circumvent the requirement that $T_{\mathsf{iNM}} \gg T_{\mathsf{SPS}}$ by leveraging the efficient postprocessing of 1ZK simulation. Recall that given a trapdoor state $\mathsf{st} \leftarrow \mathsf{S}_{\mathsf{pre}}(c)$ that depends only on the projection c, simulating the proof $\widehat{\pi} \leftarrow \mathsf{S}_{\mathsf{pos}}(x, \mathsf{st})$ takes only polynomial time. When changing the values committed in left iNM commitments, the left Com commitment c is independent—it is by now a commitment to 0. If in two neighboring hybrids, the value $\tilde{v}_{i^\star}$ on the right changes, there must exist a commitment c (committing to 0) such that conditioned on c occurring in the hybrids the value $\tilde{v}_{i^\star}$ still changes. With respect to this specific c, 1ZK simulation can now be done in polynomial time, given as non-uniform advice the preprocessed state $\mathsf{st} \leftarrow \mathsf{S}_{\mathsf{pre}}(c)$ depending on c. This suffices for the security reduction, as now, the non-malleability of iNM is detached from the 1ZK simulation time.

A Subtle Issue. The above description captures the main idea, but misses a subtle issue. Roughly speaking, in order to apply our tag-amplification iteratively, across different iterations, we need to increase the level of security of the Com schemes used in each iteration. In particular, the security parameter k for the one-way functions underlying Com needs to grow polynomially in each iteration. If we start with $k > \ell^{\delta/(\rho-\delta)} = \ell^{\Omega(1)}$, after a super-constant number of iterations (out of the $\log^* n$ iterations needed), k would grow to be super-polynomial in ℓ.

To avoid this, we modify the scheme oNM to have a separate 1ZK argument for each bit commitment c_j (committing to a bit v_j of the committed value), proving that all iNM commitments are consistent with it, in the sense that, the j'th bit of their committed strings equals to the bit committed in c_j. By doing so, c_j only needs to be $2^{|c_j|^\delta}$-secure, independent of the length ℓ of committed values. Thus, we no longer need to set k to be $k = \ell^{\Omega(1)}$, but instead to $k = \ell^{o(1)}$. Though k still increases through $O(\log^* n)$ iterations, it is always kept polynomial in ℓ. See section for a formal description of the final transformation.

Achieving Concurrency. Applying our non-interactive tag amplification to the 4-tag non-malleable commitments of [LPS17] gives a full-fledged non-interactive non-malleable commitment, which however, is only stand-alone (i.e., one-one) but not concurrently non-malleable. This is because the basic commitments of [LPS17] are not concurrently non-malleable.

To obtain concurrent non-malleability, we give another transformation from non-malleable commitments in a restricted concurrent setting, called *same-tag concurrency* into *fully concurrent* ones. Roughly speaking, in the same-tag concurrent setting, we require non-malleability to hold with respect to attackers who always use the *same tag* in all commitments on the right. We observe that the 4-tag commitments of [LPS17] actually are same-tag non-malleable, and our tag amplification preserves this property. Therefore, by applying the same-tag to full-concurrency transformation after tag amplification, we obtain concurrent non-malleability.

Our transformation is inspired by the *2-round* non-malleability strengthening transformation in [LPS17], but works in one message and is simpler and more modular; in particular, the transformation of [LPS17] relies directly on time-lock puzzles, whereas we work with any non-malleable commitment satisfying the intermediate notion of same-tag non-malleability.

At a high level, starting from a same-tag non-malleable input scheme iNM, our transformation follows the Naor-Yung paradigm for constructing CCA encryption, producing an output scheme oNM as follows. oNM fixes two arbitrary tags $\mathsf{tg}_0^\star, \mathsf{tg}_1^\star$ of iNM for special use, and commitments are computed using to other tags $\mathsf{tg} \neq \mathsf{tg}_0^\star, \mathsf{tg}_1^\star$.

The Same-Tag to Fully-Concurrent Transformation and Resulting Scheme oNM (Simplified):

- On input v and tag tg, the committer C commits to v using iNM with the two special tags:

$$\mathrm{nm}_0 \leftarrow \mathsf{iNM}(\mathsf{tg}_0^\star, v) \qquad \mathrm{nm}_1 \leftarrow \mathsf{iNM}(\mathsf{tg}_1^\star, v),$$

  and proves that both iNM commitments commit to the same value v. The proof is computed using a *simulation-sound* variant of our 1ZK argument relative to the tag tg.

To argue the concurrent non-malleability of oNM, it suffices to argue one-many non-malleability [LPV08a] (that is, the man-in-the-middle receives a single commitment on the left and gives many commitments on the right.)

The two commitments of iNM using special tags $\mathsf{tg}_0^\star$ and $\mathsf{tg}_1^\star$ are the counterparts of the as two public-key encryptions in the Naor-Yung paradigm, and the proof of non-malleability follows similarly to the proof of CCA security. The simulation soundness of 1ZK ensures that the man-in-the-middle attacker can only send consistent $\widetilde{\mathrm{nm}}_{0,j}$ and $\widetilde{\mathrm{nm}}_{1,j}$ in every right commitment j, *even when the left 1ZK argument is simulated.* Therefore, as the left commitment nm_0 is simulated (by committing to 0), one can argue that the right committed values do not change by showing that values in $\{\widetilde{\mathrm{nm}}_{1,j}\}$ do not change. Similarly, as the left commitment nm_1 is simulated, one can switch to showing that values in $\{\widetilde{\mathrm{nm}}_{0,j}\}$ do not change. Here same-tag non-malleability is essential for arguing that the joint distribution of all right committed values does not change (in a distinguishable manner).

To achieve simulation-soundness, we open the construction of our 1ZK arguments. Recall that these arguments rely on a basic commitment scheme, a NIWI, and an incompressible language. We show that by replacing the basic commitment scheme with a non-malleable one (such as the input scheme iNM), our 1ZK arguments become simulation-sound. For this approach to work, we additionally need "mutual non-malleability" between the commitment in our simulation-sound 1ZK arguments and the iNM commitments using $\mathsf{tg}_0^\star, \mathsf{tg}_1^\star$. That is, (i) simulating the 1ZK argument on the left does not change the values that the attacker commits to in iNM commitments $\{\widetilde{\mathsf{nm}}_{0,j}, \widetilde{\mathsf{nm}}_{1,j}\}$ on the right, and (ii) changing the values committed in the iNM commitments on the left does not allow the attacker to break (weak) soundness on the right. Such "mutual non-malleability" is achieved again relying on the same-tag non-malleability of iNM and the fact that the iNM commitments use two special tags $\mathsf{tg}_0^\star, \mathsf{tg}_1^\star$ different from the tags we use for iNM commitments in 1ZK arguments.

The above discussion is overly-simplified. Indeed, this transformation also has to deal with the challenges presented before in the tag-amplification transformation. They are dealt with using similar techniques. See Sect. ?? for details.

New Candidate Constant-Tag Non-malleable Commitments. As explained above, our transformations start from non-malleable commitments for a constant number of tags, which were previously known based on time-lock puzzles [LPS17]. We also provide new candidate constant-tag non-malleable commitments, based on a new assumption on hardness amplification of (injective) one-way functions.

Known results on hardness amplification have shown ways of strengthening weak one-way functions to strong ones, via direct product lemmas or XOR lemmas. However, these results have a common weakness—hardness does not amplify beyond negligible. Concretely, starting from a function f that is δ-hard against T-time attackers, the k-fold combined function f' is $(\mathrm{poly}(\frac{T'}{T})+(1-\delta)^k))$-hard for $(T' \ll T)$-time attackers. As the number k of copies increases, the hardness approaches the limit of $\mathrm{poly}(\frac{T'}{T})$.

The work of [DJMW12] showed that this limit is inherent for certain contrived one-way functions, but there is no evidence that this limit should bound natural one-way functions, such as, discrete logarithm, RSA, or Rabin. We put forward the notion of *amplifiable one-way functions and hardcore bits*: Roughly speaking, we say that a one-way function f is amplifiable, if there is a way to combine (e.g. XOR), say ℓ, hardcore bits, corresponding to ℓ independent images $f(x_1), \ldots, f(x_\ell)$, so that the combined bit is 2^{ℓ^ε}-unpredictable; that is, the level of unpredictability increases at least subexponentially as more hardcore bits are combined and beyond the limit $\mathrm{poly}(\frac{T'}{T})$.

We show that amplifiable one-way functions are useful for constructing non-malleable commitments. They essentially allow us to construct commitment schemes $(\mathsf{Com}, \mathsf{Com}')$, such that, Com is "harder" than Com' *in the time axis*—Com remains hiding in time needed for extracting from Com', whereas Com' is "harder" than Com *in the distinguishing axis*—the maximum distinguishing advantage of Com' is smaller than the probability that one can guess a decommitment of Com. As shown in [LPS17], commitments that are harder than each other under different measures are essentially non-malleable. This yields new candidate constant-tag non-malleable commitments with one-way functions that are believed to have amenable hardness amplification behavior, such as, discrete logarithm, RSA, or Rabin.

1.3 Concurrent Work

In concurrent and independent work, Holmgren and Lombardi [HL18] study *one-way product functions*, which are related to our notion of amplifiable one-way functions. Their notion requires that ℓ independent images $f(x_1), \ldots, f(x_\ell)$ cannot be inverted simultaneously by efficient algorithms, except with exponentially small probability in the input size. They show how to use such functions in different parameter regimes to obtain several applications ranging form collision-resistant hashing to correlation intractability (when combined with indistinguishability obfuscation). (The exact inversion probability and choice of ℓ depends on the specific application. Most of their applications are in the regime where ℓ is small, e.g. constant, and the inversion probability is at most $2^{-n-\omega(\log n)}$.)

While their one-way product functions and our amplifiable one-way functions are very related, there are some notable differences. For once, we make a stronger requirement than the hardness of inversion, namely, the hardness of predicting a combined hardcore bit. (Note that this gap cannot be bridged by the classic Goldreich-Levin theorem, where the adversary's distinguishing advantage ε translates to a reduction running in time at least $\mathrm{poly}(\varepsilon^{-1})$ to invert the underlying function.) On the other hand, since we allow ℓ to grow polynomially, our notion could potentially hold for one-way functions where a single copy is only mildly hard to invert, whereas for many of their applications (like collision-resistant hashing), ℓ is required to be small, and accordingly the one-way function has to be hard to invert except with exponentially small probability.

Organization. The rest of this extended abstract is organized as follows. In Sect. 2, we give some of the basic definitions used in the paper, including the definition of non-malleable commitments that we achieve. In Sect. 3, we define the notion of incompressible problems. In Sect. 4, we define and construct our new notion of one-message zero knowledge. Our constructions of non-malleable commitments, as well as all proofs, can be found in the full version of the paper.

2 Preliminaries

We rely on the following standard computational concepts:

- We model algorithms as (possibly probabilistic and possibly interactive) Turing machines. A *non-uniform* algorithm M is given by a family of algorithms $\mathsf{M} = \{\mathsf{M}_\lambda\}_{\lambda \in \mathbb{N}}$, where λ is a security parameter, and each M_λ corresponds to an input size $n(\lambda)$ and has description-size related to λ.
  - M is T-time, if for every $\lambda \in \mathbb{N}$, M_λ performs at most $T(\lambda)$ steps.
  - M is S-size if for every $\lambda \in \mathbb{N}$, M_λ has description size at most $S(\lambda)$.

  Throughout, we assume w.l.o.g. that the description-size of a non-uniform algorithm is bounded by its running time $S(\lambda) \leq T(\lambda)$ for all λ.

  A *uniform* algorithm M is a special-case of a non-uniform algorithm where for all $\lambda \in \mathbb{N}$, $\mathsf{M}_\lambda = \mathsf{M}$ is a single, constant-size, algorithm. A PPT is a probabilistic polynomial-time uniform algorithm. By default, algorithms in cryptographic schemes are PPTs.

- We model T-time adversaries as arbitrary non-uniform T-time algorithms $\mathcal{A} = \{\mathcal{A}_\lambda\}_{\lambda\in\mathbb{N}}$. Efficient adversaries have polynomial time. Throughout this work, we consider polynomial-size adversaries, and assume w.l.o.g. that their sizes are at least λ, i.e., $|A_\lambda| \geq \lambda$ (via padding).
- We say that a function $f : \mathbb{N} \to \mathbb{R}$ is negligible if for all constants $c > 0$, there exists $N \in \mathbb{N}$ such that for all $n > N$, $f(n) < n^{-c}$. We sometimes denote negligible functions by negl.
- We say that a function $f : \mathbb{N} \to \mathbb{R}$ is noticeable if there exists a constant $c > 0$ and $N \in \mathbb{N}$ such that for all $n > N$, $f(n) \geq n^{-c}$.
- For two functions $T(\lambda), T'(\lambda)$, we write that $T' \ll T$ if $T' = T^{o(1)}$, when $\lambda \to \infty$.

In this paper, we will sometimes consider security of primitives against general poly(T)-time adversaries, as illustrated in the definition of T-indistinguishability below.

Definition 1 ((T,μ)-Indistinguishability). *Let $\mathcal{X}^{(b)} = \{X_\lambda^{(b)}\}_{\lambda\in\mathbb{N}}$ for $b \in \{0,1\}$ be two ensembles of random variables indexed by $\lambda \in \mathbb{N}$. We say that $\mathcal{X}^{(0)}$ and $\mathcal{X}^{(1)}$ are (T,μ)-indistinguishable for functions T, μ, if for all* poly(T)*-time distinguishers $\mathcal{D}$, and all large enough λ,*

$$\left|\Pr[\mathcal{D}(X_\lambda^{(0)}) = 1] - \Pr[\mathcal{D}(X_\lambda^{(1)}) = 1]\right| \leq \mu(\lambda)^{\Omega(1)}.$$

We say that $\mathcal{X}^{(0)}$ and $\mathcal{X}^{(1)}$ are T-indistinguishable if it is (T,μ)-indistinguishable for some negligible function μ. We say that they are computational indistinguishable if they are T-indistinguishable for every polynomial T.

We denote the above notions of indistinguishability by $\mathcal{X}^{(0)} \approx_{T,\mu} \mathcal{X}^{(1)}$, $\mathcal{X}^{(0)} \approx_T \mathcal{X}^{(1)}$, and $\mathcal{X}^{(0)} \approx \mathcal{X}^{(1)}$, respectively.

2.1 Commitments

We define non-interactive commitments.

Definition 2 (Commitment Scheme). *A non-interactive commitment scheme consists of two polynomial-time algorithms* (Com, Open)*, with the following syntax:*

- $(c, d) \leftarrow \mathsf{Com}(v, 1^\lambda)$*: Given 1^λ and $v \in \{0,1\}^*$,* Com *samples a commitment c and a decommitment string d.*
- $b = \mathsf{Open}(c, v, d)$*: Given a commitment c, value v, and decommitment string d,* Open *outputs a bit b, where $b = 1$ indicates acceptance. We say that a commitment c is valid, if there exists a decommitment (v, d), such that* $\mathsf{Open}(c, v, d) = 1$.

We make the following requirements:

Correctness: *For any $\lambda \in \mathbb{N}$, $v \in \{0,1\}^*$,*

$$\Pr[\mathsf{Open}(c, v, d) \; : \; (c, d) \leftarrow \mathsf{Com}(v, 1^\lambda)] = 1.$$

Binding: *For any string c, values v, v', and decommitment strings d, d',*

$$\text{if } \mathsf{Open}(c, v, d) = \mathsf{Open}(c, v', d') = 1 \text{ then } v = v'.$$

T-hiding: *For any polynomial $n = n(\lambda)$,*

$$\left\{\mathsf{Com}(v, 1^\lambda)\right\}_{\lambda \in \mathbb{N}, v, v' \in \{0,1\}^{n \times 2}} \approx_T \left\{\mathsf{Com}(v', 1^\lambda)\right\}_{\lambda \in \mathbb{N}, v, v' \in \{0,1\}^{n \times 2}}.$$

Tag-Based Commitments. We consider "tag-based" commitment schemes.

Definition 3 (Tag-based commitment scheme). *A commitment scheme $(\mathsf{Com}, \mathsf{Open})$ is a tag-based scheme with t-bit tags if, in addition to 1^λ, Com also receive a "tag" (a.k.a. identity) $\mathsf{tg} \in \{0,1\}^{t(\lambda)}$ as input, $c \leftarrow \mathsf{Com}(\mathsf{tg}, v, 1^\lambda)$. We assume w.l.o.g that commitments generated by Com contains the tag used for generating them. For any sequence of fixed tags $\mathsf{tg} = \{\mathsf{tg}_\lambda\}_\lambda$, the corresponding $(\mathsf{Com}_{\mathsf{tg}}, \mathsf{Open}_{\mathsf{tg}}) = \left\{(\mathsf{Com}_{\mathsf{tg}_\lambda}, \mathsf{Open}_{\mathsf{tg}_\lambda})\right\}_\lambda$ satisfy correctness, binding, and hiding as defined for plain commitment schemes. By default, a tag-based commitment scheme has t-bit tags for some polynomial t.*

2.2 Non-malleable Commitments

The Man-in-the-Middle (MIM) Execution: Let $\mathsf{NM} = (\mathsf{Com}, \mathsf{Open})$ be a commitment scheme for t-bit tags, and $\mathcal{A} = \{\mathcal{A}_\lambda\}_{\lambda \in \mathbb{N}}$ an arbitrary non-uniform adversary. For a security parameter λ, and $m = m(\lambda)$, $\mathcal{A}_\lambda$ on input 1^λ, receives m commitments from an honest committer C to values $v_1, \ldots, v_m \in \{0,1\}^\lambda$, and sends m commitments to R to values $\tilde{v}_1, \ldots, \tilde{v}_m \in \{0,1\}^\lambda$. The commitments received by the adversary are called *the left commitments* and those sent are called *the right commitments.* The left and right commitments use $t = t(\lambda)$-bit tags $\mathsf{tg}_1, \mathsf{tg}_2, \ldots, \mathsf{tg}_m$ and $\tilde{\mathsf{tg}}_1, \tilde{\mathsf{tg}}_2, \ldots, \tilde{\mathsf{tg}}_m$ chosen adaptively by $\mathcal{A}_\lambda$ for each commitment. The values $\tilde{v}_j$ in the j'th right commitment $\tilde{c}_j$ is defined as

$$\tilde{v}_j = \begin{cases} \perp & \text{if } \exists i, \; \mathsf{tg}_i = \tilde{\mathsf{tg}}_j \\ \mathsf{val}(\tilde{c}_j) & \text{otherwise} \end{cases}.$$

That is, $\tilde{v}_j$ is either the unique committed value if the commitment $\tilde{c}_j$ is valid and uses a tag different from all left tags, or $\perp$ otherwise. (Recall that by binding, $\tilde{v}_j$ is uniquely defined whenever $\tilde{c}_j$ is valid.)

We denote by $\mathsf{MIM}^{\mathcal{A}}_{\mathsf{NM}}(v_1, \ldots, v_m, 1^\lambda)$ the above described man-in-the-middle experiment.

Non-malleability with Respect to Commitment. Let $\mathsf{mim}^{\mathcal{A}}_{\mathsf{NM}}(v_1, \ldots, v_m, 1^\lambda)$ denote the random variable that describes the view of $\mathcal{A}_\lambda$ (consisting of all left commitments) and the values $\tilde{v}_1, \ldots, \tilde{v}_m$ it commits to on the right in the above man-in-the-middle experiment.

Definition 4 (Non-Malleability). *A commitment scheme* NM *for* t*-bit tags is concurrent* T*-non-malleable if for any non-uniform* $\text{poly}(T)$*-time adversary* $\mathcal{A} = \{\mathcal{A}_\lambda\}_{\lambda \in \mathbb{N}}$ *and for every polynomial* $m = m(\lambda)$*, it holds that:*

$$\left\{\mathsf{mim}^{\mathcal{A}}_{\mathsf{NM}}(v_1, \dots, v_m, 1^\lambda)\right\}_{\lambda \in \mathbb{N}, v_1, \dots, v_m, v'_1, \dots, v'_m \in \{0,1\}^\lambda}$$
$$\approx_c \left\{\mathsf{mim}^{\mathcal{A}}_{\mathsf{NM}}(v'_1, \dots, v'_m, 1^\lambda)\right\}_{\lambda \in \mathbb{N}, v_1, \dots, v_m, v'_1, \dots, v'_m \in \{0,1\}^\lambda} .$$

2.3 Non-interactive Witness-Indistinguishable Proofs

We define non-interactive witness-indistinguishable proofs (NIWIs).

Definition 5 (NIWI). *A non-interactive witness-indistinguishable proof system* (P, V) *for an* ***NP*** *relation* $\mathcal{R}(x, w)$ *consists of two polynomial-time algorithms:*

- $\pi \leftarrow \mathsf{P}(x, w, 1^\lambda)$*: Given an instance* x*, witness* w*, and security parameter* 1^λ*,* P *produces a proof* π*.*
- $b = \mathsf{V}(x, \pi)$*: Given a proof* π *for instance* x*,* V *outputs a bit* b*, where* $b = 1$ *indicates acceptance.*

We make the following requirements:

Completeness: For every $\lambda \in \mathbb{N}, (x, w) \in \mathcal{R}$*,*

$$\Pr_{\mathsf{P}}[\mathsf{V}(x, \pi) = 1 : \pi \leftarrow \mathsf{P}(x, w, 1^\lambda)] = 1.$$

Soundness: For every $x \notin \mathcal{L}(\mathcal{R})$ *and* $\pi \in \{0,1\}^*$*:*

$$\mathsf{V}(x, \pi) \neq 1.$$

T-Witness-Indistinguishability: For any sequence

$$\mathcal{I} = \left\{(\lambda, x, w_0, w_1) : \begin{array}{c} \lambda \in \mathbb{N}, x, w_0, w_1 \in \{0,1\}^{\text{poly}(\lambda)}, \\ (x, w_0), (x, w_1) \in \mathcal{R} \end{array}\right\}$$

It holds that

$$\left\{\pi_0 \leftarrow \mathsf{P}(x, w_0, 1^\lambda)\right\}_{(\lambda, x, w_0, w_1) \in \mathcal{I}} \approx_T \left\{\pi_1 \leftarrow \mathsf{P}(x, w_1, 1^\lambda)\right\}_{(\lambda, x, w_0, w_1) \in \mathcal{I}} .$$

Barak, Ong, and Vadhan [BOV07] constructed NIWIs based on NIZK and the worst-case assumption that there exists a problem solvable in deterministic time $2^{O(n)}$ with non-deterministic circuit complexity $2^{\Omega(n)}$ (or more generally the existence of hitting set generators that fool non-deterministic distinguishers). Groth, Ostrovsky, and Sahai [GOS12] then constructed NIWIs based on standard assumptions on bilinear maps such as the Decision Linear Assumption, the Symmetric External Diffie Hellman assumption, or the Subgroup Decision Assumption. Bitansky and Paneth [BP15] constructed NIWIs from indistinguishability obfuscation and one-way permutations.

2.4 Two-Source Extractors

We rely on the standard notion of two-source extractors.

Definition 6 (Two-Source Extractor). *A polynomial-time computable function* $\mathsf{2Ext} : \{0,1\}^n \times \{0,1\}^n \to \{0,1\}^m$ *is a* (k_1, k_2, ε)*-two-source extractor, if for any two independent sources* X_1, X_2 *with min-entropies at least* k_1 *and* k_2*, respectively, it holds that*

$$\|\mathsf{2Ext}(X_1, X_2) - U_m\|_1 \le \varepsilon,$$

where U_m *is the uniform distribution over* $\{0,1\}^m$.

We also require *efficient reverse sampling*, which says that given any y in the image of the extractor $\mathsf{2Ext}$ we can efficiently sample uniformly random and independent sources X_1 and X_2 conditioned on $\mathsf{2Ext}(X_1, X_2) = y$.

Definition 7 (Efficient Reverse Sampling). *A function* $\mathsf{2Ext} : \{0,1\}^n \times \{0,1\}^n \to \{0,1\}^m$ *is efficiently reverse-samplable if there exists a PPT that given* $y \in \mathsf{Image}(\mathsf{2Ext})$ *outputs a uniformly random pair* x_1, x_2 *such that* $\mathsf{2Ext}(x_1, x_2) = y$.

Two source extractors with efficient reverse sampling and an exponentially small error are known based on the Hadamard code over an appropriate field.

3 Incompressible Problems

Following [BKP18], we consider a notion of incompressible problems. Here every security parameter λ, defines a search problem $\mathcal{W}_\lambda$ with superpolynomially many solutions $w \in \mathcal{W}_\lambda$. Since the problem is fixed, a non-uniform adversary $\mathcal{A} = \{\mathcal{A}_\lambda\}$ may always have hardwired solutions $w \in \mathcal{W}_\lambda$ in its code. We require, however, that it is *impossible to significantly compress solutions*—an adversary with description size at most S and bounded running time T, larger than S, should fail to produce more than S solutions (or $K(S)$ solutions for some polynomial blowup function $K(\cdot)$).

Definition 8 (Incompressible Problem). *An incompressible problem* $\mathcal{W}$ *is associated with a polynomial-time verifier algorithm* $\mathcal{V}$ *and a collection of sets* $\{\mathcal{W}_\lambda\}_\lambda$*, such that* $\mathcal{W}_\lambda \subseteq \{0,1\}^\ell$ *for some polynomial* $\ell = \ell(\lambda)$*, and for any* $w \in \{0,1\}^\ell$*,* $\mathcal{V}(w) = 1$ *if and only if* $w \in \mathcal{W}_\lambda$*. For any function* $T = T(\lambda) \ge \lambda$ *and polynomial* K*, we make the following incompressibility requirement.*
(T, K)-Incompressibility: for any non-uniform $\mathrm{poly}(T)$*-time, polynomial-size, probabilistic adversary* $\mathcal{A} = \{\mathcal{A}_\lambda\}$*, there is a negligible function* μ*, such that for any* $\lambda \in \mathbb{N}$*, letting* $K = K(|\mathcal{A}_\lambda|)$*,*

$$\Pr_{\mathcal{A}_\lambda}\left[\begin{matrix} W \subseteq \mathcal{W}_\lambda \\ |W| \ge K \end{matrix} \;\middle|\; W \leftarrow \mathcal{A}_\lambda\right] \le \mu(\lambda).$$

We say that $\mathcal{W}$ *has density* $\Delta = \Delta(\lambda)$*, if for every sufficiently large* $\lambda \in \mathbb{N}$*, letting* $\ell = \ell(\lambda)$*, it holds that* $|\mathcal{W}_\lambda| \ge \Delta 2^\ell$*. We say that* $\mathcal{W}$ *has subexponential density if it has density* $\Delta = 2^{-\ell^\varepsilon}$ *for some constant* ε.

Remark 1 (Parameters). The parameters T, K, Δ that we consider will always be such that

$$K \leq T \ll K\Delta^{-1}.$$

Indeed, when $T < K$ the requirement trivializes and when $T \geq \text{poly}(K\Delta^{-1})$ the requirement becomes impossible.

Candidates. Candidates for incompressible problems were introduced in [BKP18]. The problems addressed there come from *keyless* (shrinking) hash functions where collisions are incompressible in some sense. We can rely on more general incompressible problems, which may give rise to additional candidates. The problems considered in [BKP18] and a discussion of additional possible candidates can be found in the full version of the paper.

4 One-Message Zero Knowledge

In this section, we give a new definition of a one-message zero-knowledge (1ZK) system, and construct such a system based on incompressible problems. The definition relaxes both the zero knowledge requirement and soundness. Here the zero knowledge definition is the standard super-polynomial simulation (SPS) definition [Pas03]. The soundness definition is new and roughly says that a (relatively) efficient adversary of description size S shouldn't be able to sample more than S (or $K(S)$ for some polynomial blowup K) false statements x together with an accepting proof π. As discussed in the introduction, both of these relaxations are necessary.

We proceed to the formal definition.

Definition 9 (1ZK). *A one-message zero-knowledge argument system* (P, V) *for an* ***NP*** *relation* $\mathcal{R}(x, w)$ *consists of two polynomial-time algorithms:*

- $\pi \leftarrow \mathsf{P}(x, w, 1^\lambda)$*: Given an instance* x*, witness* w*, and security parameter* 1^λ*,* P *produces a proof* π*.*
- $b = \mathsf{V}(x, \pi, 1^\lambda)$*: Given a proof* π *for instance* x*,* V *outputs a bit* b*, where* $b = 1$ *indicates acceptance.*

The system is parameterized by functions $T_{\mathsf{D}}(\cdot), T_{\mathsf{S}}(\cdot), T_{\mathsf{P}}(\cdot), K(\cdot)$*.*

We make the following requirements:

Completeness: For every $\lambda \in \mathbb{N}, (x, w) \in \mathcal{R}$*,*

$$\Pr_{\mathsf{P}}[\mathsf{V}(x, \pi, 1^\lambda) = 1 : \pi \leftarrow \mathsf{P}(x, w, 1^\lambda)] = 1.$$

$(T_{\mathsf{D}}, T_{\mathsf{S}})$-Zero-Knowledge: There exists a uniform $\text{poly}(T_{\mathsf{S}})$*-time simulator* S*, such that,*

$$\left\{\pi \leftarrow \mathsf{P}(x, w, 1^\lambda)\right\}_{\substack{(x,w)\in\mathcal{R}\\ \lambda\in\mathbb{N}}} \approx_{T_{\mathsf{D}}} \left\{\widehat{\pi} \leftarrow \mathsf{S}(x, 1^\lambda)\right\}_{\substack{(x,w)\in\mathcal{R}\\ \lambda\in\mathbb{N}}}.$$

<u>(T_{P}, K)-*Weak-Soundness:*</u> *For any non-uniform* $\mathrm{poly}(T_{\mathsf{P}})$*-time, polynomial-size, probabilistic adversary* $\mathcal{A} = \{\mathcal{A}_\lambda\}_\lambda$ *there exists a negligible* μ *and a collection of sets* $\mathcal{Z} = \{\mathcal{Z}_\lambda\}_\lambda$*, where* $|\mathcal{Z}_\lambda| \leq K(|\mathcal{A}_\lambda|)$*, such that for any* $\lambda \in \mathbb{N}$*,*

$$\Pr_{\mathcal{A}_\lambda}\left[\begin{array}{l} x \notin \mathcal{L}(\mathcal{R}) \cup \mathcal{Z}_\lambda \\ \mathsf{V}(x, \pi, 1^\lambda) = 1 \end{array} \middle| \, (x, \pi) \leftarrow \mathcal{A}_\lambda \right] \leq \mu(\lambda).$$

φ-Tuning: Relaxed Soundness and Speeding-up Simulation. We in fact consider a more general definition that allows to get faster simulators on the account of relaxing soundness. Here the argument system is associated with a non-expanding (typically, shrinking) projection function $\varphi(\cdot)$ defined over instances x. Soundness is relaxed and guarantees that the adversary could only output accepting pairs (x, π) for false statements *whose projection* $\varphi(x)$ falls in a set of size at most $K(S)$. Simulation is performed in two steps—a first preprocessing step that depends only on $\varphi(x)$, and a postprocessing step that depends on the instance x itself and the state produced in the preprocessing phase. The preprocessing phase takes superpolynomial time, but only depends on $\ell := |\varphi(x)|$ and not on $|x|$; the postprocessing phase takes polynomial time.

Note that the previous basic definition is indeed a special case of this definition by considering the identity projection (in this case the entire simulation is done in the preprocessing phase, and takes superpolynomial time in $|x|$). We gain from this definitions in scenarios where $\varphi : \{0,1\}^{>\ell} \to \{0,1\}^\ell$ is a shrinking projection—here when $\ell \ll |x|$, simulation can become significantly faster; furthermore, in settings where $\varphi(x)$, and its preprocessing are known ahead of time (but x isn't), we can get efficient simulation. On the other hand, we will only get the above relaxed soundness guarantee. In our application to non-malleable commitments, relaxed soundness will be enough, and we'll indeed benefit from the above simulation speedup.

We proceed with the definition.

Definition 10 (φ-tuned 1ZK). *A one-message zero-knowledge argument system* (P, V) *for an* ***NP*** *relation* $\mathcal{R}(x, w)$ *is* φ*-tuned for a polynomial-time projection function* $\varphi = \{\varphi_\lambda : \{0,1\}^{\geq \ell(\lambda)} \to \{0,1\}^{\ell(\lambda)}\}_\lambda$ *if it satisfies:*

<u>*Simulation Speedup:*</u> *The system is* $(T_{\mathsf{D}}, T_{\mathsf{S}})$*-zero-knowledge with a uniform simulator* $\mathsf{S} = (\mathsf{S}_{\mathsf{pre}}, \mathsf{S}_{\mathsf{pos}})$ *such that* $\mathsf{S}(x, 1^\lambda)$ *consists of two phases:*

- $\mathsf{st} \leftarrow \mathsf{S}_{\mathsf{pre}}(\varphi_\lambda(x), 1^\lambda)$ *is a preprocessing phase whose running time* $T_{\mathsf{S}_{\mathsf{pre}}}(\ell(\lambda))$ *depends on* $\ell(\lambda) = |\varphi_\lambda(x)|$*, but not on* $|x|$*.*
- $\widehat{\pi} \leftarrow \mathsf{S}_{\mathsf{pos}}(x, \mathsf{st})$ *is a postprocessing phase that takes time* $\mathrm{poly}(|x| + \lambda)$*.*

Overall, $T_{\mathsf{S}}(|x|, \lambda) = \mathrm{poly}(T_{\mathsf{S}_{\mathsf{pre}}}(\ell(\lambda)), |x|)$ *depends only polynomially on* $|x|$ *(and superpolynomially on* $|\varphi_\lambda(x)|$*).*

<u>$(T_{\mathsf{P}}, K, \varphi, t)$-*Weak-Soundness:*</u> *For any non-uniform* $\mathrm{poly}(T_{\mathsf{P}})$*-time, polynomial-size, probabilistic adversary* $\mathcal{A} = \{\mathcal{A}_\lambda\}_\lambda$ *there exists a negligible* μ *and a collection of sets* $\mathcal{Z} = \{\mathcal{Z}_\lambda\}_\lambda$*, where* $|\mathcal{Z}_\lambda| \leq K(|\mathcal{A}_\lambda|)$*, such that for any* $\lambda \in \mathbb{N}$*,*

$$\Pr_{\mathcal{A}_\lambda}\left[\begin{array}{l} x \notin \mathcal{L}(\mathcal{R}), \varphi_\lambda(x) \notin \mathcal{Z}_\lambda \\ \mathsf{V}(x, \pi, 1^\lambda) = 1 \end{array} \middle| \, (x, \pi) \leftarrow \mathcal{A}_\lambda \right] \leq \mu(\lambda).$$

4.1 Construction

We now construct a φ-tuned 1ZK based on incompressible problems and other standard primitives. The parameters of the construction are derived from those of the underlying building blocks, and in particular on the density and incompressability of the incompressible problem.

Building Blocks. In what follows, let $\varphi = \{\varphi_\lambda : \{0,1\}^{\geq \ell(\lambda)} \to \{0,1\}^{\ell(\lambda)}\}_\lambda$ be a polynomial-time projection. Our transformation will make use the following building blocks:

- An incompressible problem $\mathcal{W} = \{\mathcal{W}_\lambda \subseteq \{0,1\}^{4\ell(\lambda)}\}_\lambda$ with associated verifier $\mathcal{V}$, density Δ, and $(T_\mathcal{W}, K_\mathcal{W})$ incompressability, where $K_\mathcal{W} \ll T_\mathcal{W} \ll \Delta^{-1}$.
- A commitment scheme (Com, Open) that is T_R-hiding and $T_{\mathsf{Com.E}}$-extractable where $T_\mathsf{R} \ll T_{\mathsf{Com.E}} \ll T_\mathcal{W}$.
- A $T_\mathsf{D}^{\mathsf{niwi}}$-indistinguishable NIWI system for an **NP** language, specified in the construction below.
- A two-source extractor $\mathsf{2Ext} = \{\mathsf{2Ext} : \{0,1\}^{4\ell(\lambda)} \times \{0,1\}^{4\ell(\lambda)} \to \{0,1\}^{\ell(\lambda)}\}_\lambda$ with error $\varepsilon(\lambda) = 2^{-\ell(\lambda)-2}$ for sources of min-entropies $k_1 = k_2 > 4\ell(\lambda) - \log \Delta^{-1}$, and efficient reverse sampling.

The Proof System. We now describe the system (P, V) for an **NP** relation $\mathcal{R}$.

- **The prover** $\mathsf{P}(x, w, 1^\lambda)$:
  - Computes a commitment $c \leftarrow \mathsf{Com}(0^{8\ell})$.
  - Computes a NIWI proof π for the statement

    $\psi_{x,c} :=$

    "*Either* $x \in \mathcal{L}(\mathcal{R})$ *or*

    c is a commitment to $(\mathrm{td}_1, \mathrm{td}_2) \in \mathcal{W}_\lambda \times \mathcal{W}_\lambda$ *such that* $\mathsf{2Ext}(\mathrm{td}_1, \mathrm{td}_2) = \varphi_\lambda(x)$."

    The prover uses the witness w to compute π.
  - Overall the proof consists of (c, π).
- **The verifier** $\mathsf{V}(x, (c, \pi), 1^\lambda)$:
  - Applies the NIWI verifier to verify the statement $\psi_{x,c}$.

Theorem 4. *The above is a* φ*-tuned 1ZK for* $\mathcal{R}$ *that is* $(T_\mathsf{S}, T_\mathsf{D})$*-zero-knowledge and* $(T_\mathsf{P}, K, \varphi)$*-weakly sound for*

$$T_\mathsf{S} = \Delta^{-1}, T_\mathsf{D} = \min\{T_\mathsf{R}, T_\mathsf{D}^{\mathsf{niwi}}\}, \qquad T_\mathsf{P} = T_\mathcal{W}, K = O(K_\mathcal{W}).$$

A Concrete Setting of Parameters. A natural setting of parameters that will be considered throughout this paper is subexponential $\Delta(\ell) = 2^{-\ell^\delta}$. We can accordingly set $T_\mathsf{R}, T_{\mathsf{Com.E}}, T_\mathcal{W}, T_\mathsf{D}^{\mathsf{niwi}}$ to be super-polynomial functions satisfying:

$$T_\mathsf{R} \ll T_{\mathsf{Com.E}} \ll T_\mathcal{W} \ll \Delta^{-1} = 2^{\ell(\lambda)^\delta}.$$

Indeed, the main tradeoff is between the simulation time T_S and the density Δ of the incompressible problem $\mathcal{W}$. On one hand, we aim for a short as possible simulation time $T_S \ll 2^{\ell(\lambda)}$.[5] On the other hand, shorter simulation time requires higher density, which strengthens the corresponding incompressibility assumption. (In terms of existing candidates for incompressible problems based on fixed hash functions, subexponential density corresponds to polynomially-compressing hash functions.)

Acknowledgments. We thank Ilan Komargodski for pointing out [KY18].

References

Bar02. Barak, B.: Constant-round coin-tossing with a man in the middle or realizing the shared random string model. In: Proceedings of the 43rd Symposium on Foundations of Computer Science (FOCS 2002), Vancouver, BC, Canada, 16–19 November 2002, pp. 345–355 (2002)

BFM88. Blum, M., Feldman, P., Micali, S.: Non-interactive zero-knowledge and its applications (extended abstract). In: Proceedings of the 20th Annual ACM Symposium on Theory of Computing, Chicago, Illinois, USA, 2–4 May 1988, pp. 103–112 (1988)

BGI+17. Badrinarayanan, S., Garg, S., Ishai, Y., Sahai, A., Wadia, A.: Two-message witness indistinguishability and secure computation in the plain model from new assumptions. In: Takagi, T., Peyrin, T. (eds.) ASIACRYPT 2017. LNCS, vol. 10626, pp. 275–303. Springer, Cham (2017). https://doi.org/10.1007/978-3-319-70700-6_10

BGJ+17. Badrinarayanan, S., Goyal, V., Jain, A., Khurana, D., Sahai, A.: Round optimal concurrent MPC via strong simulation. In: Kalai, Y., Reyzin, L. (eds.) TCC 2017. LNCS, vol. 10677, pp. 743–775. Springer, Cham (2017). https://doi.org/10.1007/978-3-319-70500-2_25

BKP18. Bitansky, N., Kalai, Y.T., Paneth, O.: Proceedings of the 50th Annual ACM Symposium on Theory of Computing, STOC 2018, Los-Angeles, CA, USA, 25–29 June 2018 (2018)

BL18. Bitansky, N., Lin, H.: One-message zero knowledge and non-malleable commitments. IACR Cryptology ePrint Archive, vol. 2018, p. 613 (2018)

BM84. Blum, M., Micali, S.: How to generate cryptographically strong sequences of pseudo-random bits. SIAM J. Comput. **13**(4), 850–864 (1984)

BOV07. Barak, B., Ong, S.J., Vadhan, S.P.L.: Derandomization in cryptography. SIAM J. Comput. **37**(2), 380–400 (2007)

BP04. Barak, B., Pass, R.: On the possibility of one-message weak zero-knowledge. In: Naor, M. (ed.) TCC 2004. LNCS, vol. 2951, pp. 121–132. Springer, Heidelberg (2004). https://doi.org/10.1007/978-3-540-24638-1_7

BP15. Bitansky, N., Paneth, O.: ZAPs and non-interactive witness indistinguishability from indistinguishability obfuscation. In: Dodis, Y., Nielsen, J.B. (eds.) TCC 2015. LNCS, vol. 9015, pp. 401–427. Springer, Heidelberg (2015). https://doi.org/10.1007/978-3-662-46497-7_16

[5] Note that when φ is the identity, a witness for $x \in \{0,1\}^{\ell(\lambda)}$ can already be found by brute force in time $2^{O(\ell(\lambda))}$, in which case the zero-knowledge requirement collapses to witness indistinguishability.

BS05. Barak, B., Sahai, A.: How to play almost any mental game over the net - concurrent composition via super-polynomial simulation. In: Proceedings of the 46th Annual IEEE Symposium on Foundations of Computer Science (FOCS 2005), Pittsburgh, PA, USA, 23–25 October 2005, pp. 543–552 (2005)

CG88. Chor, B., Goldreich, O.: Unbiased bits from sources of weak randomness and probabilistic communication complexity. SIAM J. Comput. **17**(2), 230–261 (1988)

CLP16. Canetti, R., Lin, H., Pass, R.: Adaptive hardness and composable security in the plain model from standard assumptions. SIAM J. Comput. **45**(5), 1793–1834 (2016)

COSV16. Ciampi, M., Ostrovsky, R., Siniscalchi, L., Visconti, I.: Concurrent non-malleable commitments (and more) in 3 rounds. In: Robshaw, M., Katz, J. (eds.) CRYPTO 2016. LNCS, vol. 9816, pp. 270–299. Springer, Heidelberg (2016). https://doi.org/10.1007/978-3-662-53015-3_10

COSV17. Ciampi, M., Ostrovsky, R., Siniscalchi, L., Visconti, I.: Four-round concurrent non-malleable commitments from one-way functions. In: Katz, J., Shacham, H. (eds.) CRYPTO 2017. LNCS, vol. 10402, pp. 127–157. Springer, Cham (2017). https://doi.org/10.1007/978-3-319-63715-0_5

DDN03. Dolev, D., Dwork, C., Naor, M.: Nonmalleable cryptography. SIAM Rev. **45**(4), 727–784 (2003)

DJMW12. Dodis, Y., Jain, A., Moran, T., Wichs, D.: Counterexamples to hardness amplification beyond negligible. In: Cramer, R. (ed.) TCC 2012. LNCS, vol. 7194, pp. 476–493. Springer, Heidelberg (2012). https://doi.org/10.1007/978-3-642-28914-9_27

DN07. Dwork, C., Naor, M.: Zaps and their applications. SIAM J. Comput. **36**(6), 1513–1543 (2007)

FLS99. Feige, U., Lapidot, D., Shamir, A.: Multiple noninteractive zero knowledge proofs under general assumptions. SIAM J. Comput. **29**(1), 1–28 (1999)

GGJS12. Garg, S., Goyal, V., Jain, A., Sahai, A.: Concurrently secure computation in constant rounds. In: Pointcheval, D., Johansson, T. (eds.) EUROCRYPT 2012. LNCS, vol. 7237, pp. 99–116. Springer, Heidelberg (2012). https://doi.org/10.1007/978-3-642-29011-4_8

GKP17. Garg, S., Kiyoshima, S., Pandey, O.: On the exact round complexity of self-composable two-party computation. In: Coron, J.-S., Nielsen, J.B. (eds.) EUROCRYPT 2017. LNCS, vol. 10211, pp. 194–224. Springer, Cham (2017). https://doi.org/10.1007/978-3-319-56614-6_7

GLOV12. Goyal, V., Lee, C.-K., Ostrovsky, R., Visconti, I.: Constructing non-malleable commitments: a black-box approach. In: 53rd Annual IEEE Symposium on Foundations of Computer Science, FOCS 2012, New Brunswick, NJ, USA, 20–23 October 2012, pp. 51–60 (2012)

GMR89. Goldwasser, S., Micali, S., Rackoff, C.: The knowledge complexity of interactive proof systems. SIAM J. Comput. **18**(1), 186–208 (1989)

GO94. Goldreich, O., Oren, Y.: Definitions and properties of zero-knowledge proof systems. J. Cryptol. **7**(1), 1–32 (1994)

GOS12. Groth, J., Ostrovsky, R., Sahai, A.: New techniques for noninteractive zero-knowledge. J. ACM **59**(3), 11 (2012)

Goy11. Goyal, V.: Constant round non-malleable protocols using one way functions. In: Proceedings of the 43rd ACM Symposium on Theory of Computing, STOC 2011, San Jose, CA, USA, 6–8 June 2011, pp. 695–704 (2011)

GPR16. Goyal, V., Pandey, O., Richelson, S.: Textbook non-malleable commitments. In: Proceedings of the 48th Annual ACM SIGACT Symposium on Theory of Computing, STOC 2016, Cambridge, MA, USA, 18–21 June 2016, pp. 1128–1141 (2016)

GRRV14. Goyal, V., Richelson, S., Rosen, A., Vald, M.: An algebraic approach to non-malleability. In: 55th IEEE Annual Symposium on Foundations of Computer Science, FOCS 2014, Philadelphia, PA, USA, 18–21 October 2014, pp. 41–50 (2014)

HL18. Holmgren, J., Lombardi, A.: Cryptographic hashing from strong one-way functions. IACR Cryptology ePrint Archive, vol. 2018, p. 385 (2018)

Khu17. Khurana, D.: Round optimal concurrent non-malleability from polynomial hardness. In: Kalai, Y., Reyzin, L. (eds.) TCC 2017. LNCS, vol. 10678, pp. 139–171. Springer, Cham (2017). https://doi.org/10.1007/978-3-319-70503-3_5

KS17. Khurana, D., Sahai, A.: How to achieve non-malleability in one or two rounds. In: 58th IEEE Annual Symposium on Foundations of Computer Science, FOCS 2017, Berkeley, CA, USA, 15–17 October 2017, pp. 564–575 (2017)

KY18. Komargodski, I., Yogev, E.: Another step towards realizing random oracles: non-malleable point obfuscation. In: Nielsen, J.B., Rijmen, V. (eds.) EUROCRYPT 2018. LNCS, vol. 10820, pp. 259–279. Springer, Cham (2018). https://doi.org/10.1007/978-3-319-78381-9_10

LP09. Lin, H., Pass, R.: Non-malleability amplification. In: Proceedings of the 41st Annual ACM Symposium on Theory of Computing, STOC 2009, Bethesda, MD, USA, 31 May–2 June 2009, pp. 189–198 (2009)

LP11. Lin, H., Pass, R.: Constant-round non-malleable commitments from any one-way function. In: Proceedings of the 43rd ACM Symposium on Theory of Computing, STOC 2011, San Jose, CA, USA, 6–8 June 2011, pp. 705–714 (2011)

LPS17. Lin, H., Pass, R., Soni, P.: Two-round and non-interactive concurrent non-malleable commitments from time-lock puzzles. In: 58th IEEE Annual Symposium on Foundations of Computer Science, FOCS 2017, Berkeley, CA, USA, 15–17 October 2017, pp. 576–587 (2017)

LPV08a. Lin, H., Pass, R., Venkitasubramaniam, M.: Concurrent non-malleable commitments from any one-way function. In: Canetti, R. (ed.) TCC 20086. LNCS, vol. 4948, pp. 571–588. Springer, Heidelberg (2008). https://doi.org/10.1007/978-3-540-78524-8_31

MMY06. Malkin, T., Moriarty, R., Yakovenko, N.: Generalized environmental security from number theoretic assumptions. In: Halevi, S., Rabin, T. (eds.) TCC 2006. LNCS, vol. 3876, pp. 343–359. Springer, Heidelberg (2006). https://doi.org/10.1007/11681878_18

Pas03. Pass, R.: Simulation in quasi-polynomial time, and its application to protocol composition. In: Biham, E. (ed.) EUROCRYPT 2003. LNCS, vol. 2656, pp. 160–176. Springer, Heidelberg (2003). https://doi.org/10.1007/3-540-39200-9_10

Pas13. Pass, R.: Unprovable security of perfect NIZK and non-interactive non-malleable commitments. In: Sahai, A. (ed.) TCC 2013. LNCS, vol. 7785, pp. 334–354. Springer, Heidelberg (2013). https://doi.org/10.1007/978-3-642-36594-2_19

PPV08. Pandey, O., Pass, R., Vaikuntanathan, V.: Adaptive one-way functions and applications. In: Wagner, D. (ed.) CRYPTO 2008. LNCS, vol. 5157, pp. 57–74. Springer, Heidelberg (2008). https://doi.org/10.1007/978-3-540-85174-5_4

PR05a. Pass, R., Rosen, A.: Concurrent non-malleable commitments. In: Proceedings of the 46th Annual IEEE Symposium on Foundations of Computer Science (FOCS 2005), Pittsburgh, PA, USA, 23–25 October 2005, pp. 563–572 (2005)

PR05b. Pass, R., Rosen, A.: New and improved constructions of non-malleable cryptographic protocols. In: Proceedings of the 37th Annual ACM Symposium on Theory of Computing, Baltimore, MD, USA, 22–24 May 2005, pp. 533–542 (2005)

PS04. Prabhakaran, M., Sahai, A.: New notions of security: achieving universal composability without trusted setup. In: Proceedings of the 36th Annual ACM Symposium on Theory of Computing, Chicago, IL, USA, 13–16 June 2004, pp. 242–251 (2004)

PW10. Pass, R., Wee, H.: Constant-round non-malleable commitments from subexponential one-way functions. In: Gilbert, H. (ed.) EUROCRYPT 2010. LNCS, vol. 6110, pp. 638–655. Springer, Heidelberg (2010). https://doi.org/10.1007/978-3-642-13190-5_32

Rog06. Rogaway, P.: Formalizing human ignorance. In: Nguyen, P.Q. (ed.) VIETCRYPT 2006. LNCS, vol. 4341, pp. 211–228. Springer, Heidelberg (2006). https://doi.org/10.1007/11958239_14

RSW00. Rivest, R.L., Shamir, A., Wagner, D.A.: Time-lock puzzles and timed-release crypto. Technical Report MIT/LCS/TR-684, MIT, February 2000

Unr07. Unruh, D.: Random oracles and auxiliary input. In: Menezes, A. (ed.) CRYPTO 2007. LNCS, vol. 4622, pp. 205–223. Springer, Heidelberg (2007). https://doi.org/10.1007/978-3-540-74143-5_12

Vaz85. Vazirani, U.V.: Towards a strong communication complexity theory or generating quasi-random sequences from two communicating slightly-random sources (extended abstract). In: Proceedings of the 17th Annual ACM Symposium on Theory of Computing, Providence, Rhode Island, USA, 6–8 May 1985, pp. 366–378 (1985)

Wee10. Wee, H.: Black-box, round-efficient secure computation via non-malleability amplification. In: 51th Annual IEEE Symposium on Foundations of Computer Science, FOCS 2010, Las Vegas, Nevada, USA, 23–26 October 2010, pp. 531–540 (2010)

Smooth NIZK Arguments

Charanjit S. Jutla[1(✉)] and Arnab Roy[2]

[1] IBM T. J. Watson Research Center, Yorktown Heights, NY, USA
csjutla@us.ibm.com

[2] Fujitsu Laboratories of America, Sunnyvale, CA, USA
aroy@us.fujitsu.com

Abstract. We introduce a novel notion of smooth (-verifier) non- interactive zero-knowledge proofs (NIZK) which parallels the familiar notion of smooth projective hash functions (SPHF). We also show that the single group element quasi-adaptive NIZK (QA-NIZK) of Jutla and Roy (CRYPTO 2014) and Kiltz and Wee (EuroCrypt 2015) for linear subspaces can be easily extended to be computationally smooth. One important distinction of the new notion from SPHFs is that in a smooth NIZK the public evaluation of the hash on a language member using the projection key does not require the witness of the language member, but instead just requires its NIZK proof.

This has the remarkable consequence that if one replaces the traditionally employed SPHFs with the novel smooth QA-NIZK in the Gennaro-Lindell paradigm of designing universally-composable password- authenticated key-exchange (UC-PAKE) protocols, one gets highly efficient UC-PAKE protocols that are secure even under adaptive corruption. This simpler and modular design methodology allows us to give the first single-round *asymmetric* UC-PAKE protocol, which is also secure under adaptive corruption in the erasure model. Previously, all asymmetric UC-PAKE protocols required at least two rounds. In fact, our protocol just requires each party to send a single message asynchronously. In addition, the protocol has short messages, with each party sending only four group elements. Moreover, the server password file needs to store only one group element per client. The protocol employs asymmetric bilinear pairing groups and is proven secure in the (limited programmability) random oracle model and under the standard bilinear pairing assumption SXDH.

Keywords: QA-NIZK · Bilinear pairings · SXDH · MDDH
UC-PAKE · Online attack · Server compromise · Dual-system

1 Introduction

Ever since the remarkably efficient non-interactive zero knowledge (NIZK) proofs [BFM88] for algebraic statements were developed by Groth and Sahai (GS-NIZK) [GS12], there have been significant efficiency improvements and innovations in the construction of cryptographic protocols. Jutla and Roy [JR13, JR14]

A. Beimel and S. Dziembowski (Eds.): TCC 2018, LNCS 11239, pp. 235–262, 2018.
https://doi.org/10.1007/978-3-030-03807-6_9

and Libert, Peters, Joye and Yung [LPJY14] further improved the efficiency of algebraic NIZK proofs, culminating in *constant* size NIZK proofs for linear subspaces, independent of the number of equations and witnesses. This efficiency improvement came in the weaker Quasi-Adaptive setting [JR13], which nevertheless proved sufficient for many applications.

Quasi-adaptive NIZK (QA-NIZK) proofs were further extended to provide simulation soundness [LPJY14,KW15] and dual-system simulation soundness [JR15], thus lending applicability to many more applications, such as structure preserving signatures, password authenticated key exchange in the UC model, and keyed homomorphic CCA-secure encryption.

In this paper, we further extend (QA-)NIZK proofs to provide an additional property called *smooth soundness*. The idea is to force the verification step to consist of computing hashes in two different ways and comparing the result. To this end, the verifier is split into three algorithms: a randomized hash-key generation algorithm, a public hashing algorithm and a private hashing algorithm. The verification step starts off by generating two hash-keys, the private key and the projection key. Next, the setting allows computation of a private hash given the private hash-key and the word, and computation of the public hash using the projection key and just a QA-NIZK proof for the word - the witness for the word is *not* required. Completeness states that the private hash is equal to the public hash for a language member and correct (QA-)NIZK proof. Computational soundness states that it is hard to come up with a proof such that a non-language word passes the same equality check. The new *smoothness* property states that for any non-language word, the private hash algorithm outputs a value (computationally) indistinguishable from uniformly random, even when the projection key is given to the adversary.

Comparison with SPHFs. The new primitive is modeled after smooth projective hash functions (SPHF [CS02]). An SPHF also generates private and projection hash-keys and defines a private hash and a public hash. Further, similar properties hold where (1) for a member word, private hash equals public hash, (2) for a non-member word, private hash is uniformly random (even given projection hash-key). The crucial difference is that[1], whereas the SPHF public hash computation requires a witness of the member word, the smooth (QA-)NIZK public hash requires only a NIZK proof of the word. This allows for hiding of the witness, even when computing using the projection hash-key. In contrast, trapdoor-SPHFs as introduced by [BBC+13] allow a simulation world to have a trapdoor to evaluate a hash over a word without a witness and using only projection hash-key. As shown in Fig. 1, where trapdoor-SPHFs are compared with smooth QA-NIZK, their notion does not allow "erasure" of the witness w in the real world (if only projection hash-key is available).

While Fig. 1 is self-explanatory, it brings up an interesting alternative interpretation of smooth (QA)-NIZK. In the common reference string (CRS) setting, one can have a *composite*-SPHF, which is composed of two SPHFs: the first

[1] On the other hand, our constructions only allow computational smooth-soundness, while for SPHFs these properties hold information-theoretically.

SPHF's projection hash-key is published in the CRS, that enables one to compute an intermediate-hash using the witness w of a language member x. At this point, the witness can be erased. Next, the real projection hash-key hp is revealed (possibly, generated by another party along with the private hash-key hk). Then, a final hash on input x can be computed using hp and the intermediate-hash. If x is a language member then the final hash is same as that computed from x using hk. The question then arises as to why the intermediate-hash is depicted as a (QA)-NIZK in Fig. 1. However, we note that this first SPHF is already publicly verifiable, as the private hash-key of the first SPHF is generated by the CRS generator, and if it has to be used in any form in a private hash evaluation (and in the real world) it must be publicly available in the CRS. Indeed, in our construction the private hash-key k is given in the CRS as a commitment to k (this interpretation of QA-NIZK as a publicly-verifiable SPHF was given in [KW15]).

We remark that this interpretation of smooth (QA)-NIZK is similar to constructions of structure-preserving SPHF in [BC16a]. In that work, the intermediate-hash is a GS-NIZK proof in the commit and prove framework [GS12], and hence the (second) private-hash takes the commitments also as input. Although the first hash is not a SPHF, their construction can still be viewed as a smooth NIZK (as per our definition[2]). Since their construction also works only for linear subspaces, our smooth QA-NIZK construction turns out to be more efficient, namely that no commitments need to be given for private hash computation.

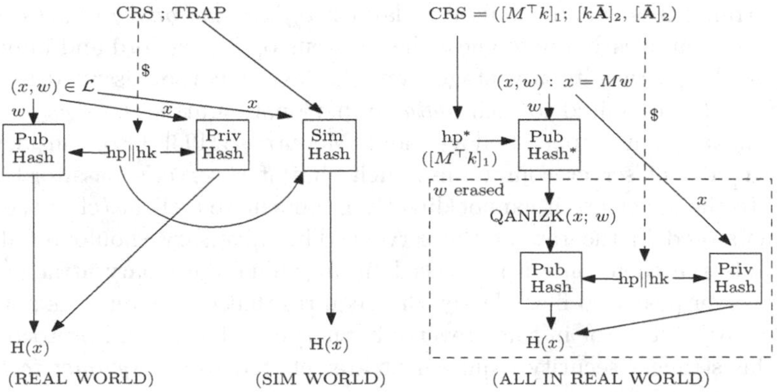

Fig. 1. Trapdoor-SPHF [BBC+13] vs Smooth QANIZK

Our Construction. In this work, we show that the single group element QA-NIZK arguments of [JR14, KW15] can be easily extended to be smooth. As a

[2] Since their construction uses the commit and prove paradigm of GS-NIZK proofs, their (composite-) construction is a smooth NIZK with a small tweak: they obtain information-theoretic smoothness, but computational zero-knowledge.

first application, we show that in the Gennaro-Lindell paradigm of designing universally-composable password-authenticated key exchange (UC-PAKE) protocols, if one replaces the traditional SPHFs with the novel smooth QA-NIZK, then one gets highly efficient single-round UC-PAKE protocols which are adaptively secure in the erasure model. At a high level, the UC simulator must emulate each party's outgoing commitment to the password, without knowing the password. This is not difficult, as one can use ElGamal encryption to achieve a hiding commitment. However, if the party is corrupted after its message has been sent, the simulator is at a loss to produce a witness which each party must retain to eventually compute the SPHF public hash. In our new protocol, the parties need only save the QA-NIZK and not the witness, as that suffices to compute the public hash. This nicely captures the main idea behind the single-round adaptively secure UC-PAKE of [JR15]. In this work, the novel abstraction further allows us to obtain a single-round adaptively secure *asymmetric* UC-PAKE, which is a much more difficult notion to understand even from a definitional perspective, let alone constructing one.

(Asymmetric) Password-Authenticated Key-Exchange. The problem of setting up a secure channel between two parties that only share a human-memorizable password (or a low-entropy secret) was first studied by Bellovin and Merritt [BM92], and later by Jiang and Gong [JG04]. Since then, this problem has been extensively studied and is called the *password-authenticated key-exchange* (PAKE) problem. One of the main challenges in designing such protocols is the intricacy in the natural security definition which requires that the protocol transcripts cannot be used to launch *offline dictionary attacks.* While an adversary can clearly try to guess the (low-entropy) password and impersonate one of the parties, its advantage from the fact that the password is of low entropy should be limited to such *online* impersonation attacks.

In a subsequent paper, Bellovin and Merritt [BM93] also considered a stronger model of server compromise such that if a server's password file is revealed to the adversary it cannot directly impersonate a client (cf. if the password was stored in the raw at the server). The adversary should be able to impersonate the client only if it succeeds in an offline dictionary attack on the revealed server password file. Clearly, this requires that the server does not store the password as it is (or in some reversibly-encrypted form), and protocols satisfying this stronger security requirement are referred to as *asymmetric PAKE* protocols.

Canetti et al. [CHK+05] also considered designing (symmetric) UC-PAKE protocols in the universally-composable (UC) framework [Can01]. One of their main contributions was the definition of a natural UC-PAKE ideal functionality ($\mathcal{F}_{\text{PAKE}}$). Gentry et al. [GMR06] extended the functionality of symmetric UC-PAKE [CHK+05] to the asymmetric setting ($\mathcal{F}_{\mathsf{apwKE}}$) and gave a general method of extending any symmetric UC-PAKE protocol to an asymmetric UC-PAKE protocol (from now on referred to as UC-APAKE). Their general method adds an additional round to the UC-PAKE protocol.

Our Contributions. In this paper, we give the first single-round UC-APAKE protocol (realizing $\mathcal{F}_{\mathsf{apwKE}}$). In fact, both parties just send a single message asynchronously. The protocol is realized in the (limited programmability[3]) random-oracle (RO) [BR93] hybrid-model under standard static assumptions for bilinear groups, namely SXDH [BBS04] and the general MDDH [EHK+13] assumption. Our protocol is also secure against adaptive corruption (in the erasure model) and is very succinct, with each message consisting of only four group elements. Moreover, for each client the server need store only *one* group elements as a "password hash". Many non-UC asymmetric PAKE protocols are at least two rounds [HK98, BPR00, BMP00, Mac01, Boy09]. Benhamouda and Pointcheval [BP13] proposed the first single round asymmetric PAKE protocol, but in a game-based model built on the BPR model [BPR00].

The first single-round UC-secure *symmetric* PAKE protocol was given in [KV11] (using bilinear pairings), which was then further improved (in the number of group elements) in subsequent papers [JR12, BBC+13]. Recently in [JR15], a single round UC-PAKE protocol (in the standard model and using bilinear pairings) was also proven secure against adaptive corruption using ideas from the dual-system IBE construction of Waters [Wat09]. However, the [JR15] construction did not employ their dual-system simulation-sound QA-NIZK proofs (DSS-QA-NIZK) in a black box manner. Instead, it used ideas from the DSS-QA-NIZK construction and properties as the underlying intuition for the proof.

In this paper, we show that the UC-PAKE of [JR15] can be built in a black-box manner using smooth QA-NIZK arguments. Next, we build on the verifier-based PAKE (VPAKE) construction of [BP13], to construct the first adaptively-secure UC-APAKE protocol, which in addition has a single (asynchronous) round. Since, in the UC framework, the simulator has to detect offline password guesses by an adversary that steals the server password file, for provable security this seems to inevitably require the RO model, and indeed our security proof is in the (limited programmability) RO model.

In our protocol, each party sends an ElGamal style encryption of the (hash of) the password *pw* to the other party, along with an SPHF of the underlying language and a projection verification hash-key of a smooth QA-NIZK of the underlying language (ElGamal augmented with the SPHF). If such a message is adversarially inserted, the simulator must have the capability to extract password *pw′* from it, so that it can feed the ideal functionality $\mathcal{F}_{\mathsf{apwKE}}$ to test this guess of the password. Thus, the NIZK proof must have simulation-sound extractability. It was shown in [JR15] that dual-system simulation soundness suffices for this purpose (and that makes the protocol very simple). When using smooth QA-NIZK, this dual-system simulation-soundness can be attained by simply sending an SPHF.

Detailed explanations can be found in Sect. 5 with proof details in the full version [JR16], where we also explain how the random oracle is used to extract the password efficiently from the exponent. This leads to a security reduction

[3] Basically, the output values of the random oracle are all randomly chosen, but different inputs can be assigned dynamically to these outputs [FLR+10].

which has an additive computational overhead of $n * m * \text{poly}(q)$, where n is the number of random oracle calls, m is the number of online attacks and q is the security parameter.

Recent Related Work. Recently, [JKX18] formulated a stronger UC-APAKE functionality that disallows use of pre-computation to attack a stolen password file. Using an ideal functionality for oblivious pseudo-random functions (OPRF), they give a compiler that converts any standard UC-APAKE realization (such as in this paper) into one that satisfies their stronger definition (in the OPRF-hybrid model). Thus, if the OPRF can be realized with adaptive corruption, then we obtain a adaptive corruption secure (strong) UC-APAKE realization. However, to the best of our knowledge, no adaptive corruption secure (UC-) OPRF realization is known, and hence the problem of realizing adaptive corruption secure strong UC-APAKE remains open.

Organization. The rest of the paper is organized as follows. In Sect. 2, we introduce the new notion of smooth QA-NIZK proofs. In Sect. 3, we recall the MDDH assumptions and establish a useful *boosting* theorem relating the assumptions. In Sect. 4, we give the single group element smooth QA-NIZK construction for linear subspaces. In Sect. 5, we describe the ideal functionality $\mathcal{F}_{\mathsf{apwKE}}$ for asymmetric password-authenticated key-exchange and construct the new single-round UC-APAKE protocol. Preliminaries and proofs of many of the theorems are relegated to the Appendix.

2 Smooth Quasi-Adaptive NIZK Proofs

We start by reviewing the definition of Quasi-Adaptive computationally-sound NIZK proofs (QA-NIZK) [JR13]. A witness relation is a binary relation on pairs of inputs, the first called a (potential) language member and the second called a witness. Note that each witness relation R defines a corresponding language L which is the set of all x for which there exists a witness w, such that $R(x, w)$ holds.

We will consider QA-NIZK proofs for a probability distribution $\mathcal{D}$ on a collection of (witness-) relations $\mathcal{R} = \{R_\rho\}$ (with corresponding languages L_ρ). Recall that in a QA-NIZK, the CRS can be set after the language parameter has been chosen according to $\mathcal{D}$. We recall the formal definition of Quasi-Adaptive NIZK below from [JR13].

Definition 1 (QA-NIZK [JR13]**).** *We call a tuple of efficient algorithms* (pargen, crsgen, prover, ver) *a* quasi-adaptive non-interactive zero-knowledge *(QA-NIZK) proof system for witness-relations $\mathcal{R}_\lambda = \{R_\rho\}$ with parameters sampled from a distribution $\mathcal{D}$ over associated parameter language* Lpar, *if there exist simulators* crssim *and* sim *such that for all non-uniform PPT adversaries $\mathcal{A}_1, \mathcal{A}_2, \mathcal{A}_3$, we have (in all of the following probabilistic experiments, the experiment starts by setting λ as $\lambda \leftarrow \mathsf{pargen}(1^m)$, and choosing ρ as $\rho \leftarrow \mathcal{D}_\lambda$):*

Quasi-Adaptive Completeness:

$$\Pr\left[\begin{array}{l}\textsc{crs} \leftarrow \mathsf{crsgen}(\lambda,\rho)\\ (x,w) \leftarrow \mathcal{A}_1(\textsc{crs},\rho)\\ \pi \leftarrow \mathsf{prover}(\textsc{crs},x,w)\end{array} : \begin{array}{c}\mathit{ver}(\textsc{crs},x,\pi)=1 \ \textit{if}\\ R_\rho(x,w)\end{array}\right] = 1$$

Quasi-Adaptive Soundness:

$$\Pr\left[\begin{array}{l}\textsc{crs} \leftarrow \mathsf{crsgen}(\lambda,\rho)\\ (x,\pi) \leftarrow \mathcal{A}_2(\textsc{crs},\rho)\end{array} : \begin{array}{c}x \notin L_\rho \ \textit{and}\\ \mathit{ver}(\textsc{crs},x,\pi)=1]\end{array}\right] \approx 0$$

Quasi-Adaptive Zero-Knowledge:

$$\Pr\left[\textsc{crs} \leftarrow \mathsf{crsgen}(\lambda,\rho) \ : \ \mathcal{A}_3^{\mathsf{prover}(\textsc{crs},\cdot,\cdot)}(\textsc{crs},\rho)=1\right]$$
$$\approx$$
$$\Pr\left[(\textsc{crs},\mathsf{trap}) \leftarrow \mathsf{crssim}(\lambda,\rho) \ : \ \mathcal{A}_3^{\mathit{sim}^*(\textsc{crs},\mathsf{trap},\cdot,\cdot)}(\textsc{crs},\rho)=1\right],$$

where $\mathit{sim}^*(\textsc{crs},\mathsf{trap},x,w) = \mathsf{sim}(\textsc{crs},\mathsf{trap},x)$ *for* $(x,w) \in R_\rho$ *and both oracles (i.e.* prover *and* sim^**) output failure if* $(x,w) \notin R_\rho$.

We call a QA-NIZK **smooth (-verifier)** if the verifier ver consists of three efficient algorithms ver = (hkgen, pubH, privH), and it satisfies the following modified completeness and soundness conditions. Here, hkgen is a probabilistic algorithm that takes a CRS as input and outputs two keys, hp, a projection hash key, and hk, a private hash key. The algorithm privH takes as input a word (e.g. a potential language member), and a (private hash) key, and outputs a string. Similarly, the algorithm pubH takes as input a word, a proof (for instance generated by prover), and a (projection hash) key hp, and outputs a string.

The **completeness** property is now defined as:

$$\Pr\left[\begin{array}{l}\textsc{crs} \leftarrow \mathsf{crsgen}(\lambda,\rho)\\ (x,w) \leftarrow \mathcal{A}_1(\textsc{crs},\rho)\\ \pi \leftarrow \mathsf{prover}(\textsc{crs},x,w)\\ (\mathsf{hp},\mathsf{hk}) \leftarrow \mathsf{hkgen}(\textsc{crs})\end{array} : \begin{array}{c}\mathsf{privH}(\mathsf{hk},x) = \mathsf{pubH}(\mathsf{hp},x,\pi)\\ \textbf{if } R_\rho(x,w)\end{array}\right] = 1$$

The QA-NIZK is said to satisfy **smooth-soundness** if for all words $x \notin L_\rho$, $\mathsf{privH}(\mathsf{hk},x)$ is computationally indistinguishable to the Adversary from uniformly random, even when the Adversary is given hp, and even if it produces x after receiving hp.

More precisely, **Quasi-Adaptive Smooth-Soundness** is the following property (let $\mathcal{U}$ be the uniform distribution on the range of privH, which is assumed to be of cardinality exponential in m): for every two-stage efficient oracle adversary $\mathcal{A}$

$$\Pr\left[\begin{array}{l}\textsc{crs} \leftarrow \mathsf{crsgen}(\lambda,\rho), \ (\mathsf{hp},\mathsf{hk}) \leftarrow \mathsf{hkgen}(\textsc{crs})\\ (x^*,\sigma) \leftarrow \mathcal{A}^{\mathcal{O}}(\textsc{crs},\rho,\mathsf{hp}), \ u \leftarrow \mathcal{U}\end{array} : \mathcal{A}^{\mathcal{O}}(\mathsf{privH}(\mathsf{hk},x^*),\sigma) = 1 \mid Q\right]$$
$$\approx$$
$$\Pr\left[\begin{array}{l}\textsc{crs} \leftarrow \mathsf{crsgen}(\lambda,\rho), \ (\mathsf{hp},\mathsf{hk}) \leftarrow \mathsf{hkgen}(\textsc{crs})\\ (x^*,\sigma) \leftarrow \mathcal{A}^{\mathcal{O}}(\textsc{crs},\rho,\mathsf{hp}), \ u \leftarrow \mathcal{U}\end{array} : \mathcal{A}^{\mathcal{O}}(u,\sigma) = 1 \mid Q\right]$$

where the oracle $\mathcal{O}$ is instantiated with $\mathsf{privH}(\mathsf{hk}, \cdot)$, and Q is the condition that x^* is not in the language L_ρ **and** all oracle calls by the adversary in both stages are with L_ρ-language members. Here, σ is a local state of $\mathcal{A}$.

Note that as opposed to the information-theoretic smoothness property of projective hash functions, one cannot argue here that $\mathsf{privH}(\mathsf{hk}, x)$ for $x \in L_\rho$ can instead just be computed using hp, as that would also require efficiently computing a witness for x. Hence, the need to provide oracle access to $\mathsf{privH}(\mathsf{hk}, \cdot)$ for language members.

Also, note that smooth-soundness implies the earlier definition of soundness [JR13] if verification of (x, π) is defined as $\mathsf{privH}(\mathsf{hk}, x) = \mathsf{pubH}(\mathsf{hp}, x, \pi)$.

To differentiate the functionalities of the verifier of a QA-NIZK from similar functionalities of an SPHF, we will prepend the SPHF functionalities with keyword sphf and the QA-NIZK verifier functionalities with the keyword ver.

3 Matrix Decisional Assumptions

We will consider bilinear groups that consist of three cyclic groups of prime order q, $\mathbb{G}_1, \mathbb{G}_2$ and $\mathbb{G}_T$ with an efficient bilinear map $\mathsf{e} : \mathbb{G}_1 \times \mathbb{G}_2 \to \mathbb{G}_T$. Group elements $\mathbf{g}_1$ and $\mathbf{g}_2$ will typically denote generators of the group $\mathbb{G}_1$ and $\mathbb{G}_2$ respectively. Following [EHK+13], in this section and the next we will use the notations $[a]_1, [a]_2$ and $[a]_T$ to denote $a\mathbf{g}_1, a\mathbf{g}_2$, and $a \cdot \mathsf{e}(\mathbf{g}_1, \mathbf{g}_2)$ respectively and use additive notations for group operations. When talking about a general group $\mathbb{G}$ with generator $\mathbf{g}$, we will just use the notation $[a]$ to denote $a\mathbf{g}$. However, in the UC-APAKE constructions, we will switch to multiplicative notation for easy readability.

For two vector or matrices A and B, we will denote the product $A^\top B$ as $A \cdot B$. The pairing product $\mathsf{e}([A]_1, [B]_2)$ evaluates to the matrix product $[AB]_T$ in the target group with pairing as multiplication and target group operation as addition.

We recall the *Matrix Decisional Diffie Hellman* or MDDH assumptions from [EHK+13]. A matrix distribution $\mathcal{D}_{l,k}$, where $l > k$, is defined to be an efficiently samplable distribution on $\mathbb{Z}_q^{l \times k}$ which is full-ranked with overwhelming probability. The $\mathcal{D}_{l,k}-$MDDH *assumption* in group $\mathbb{G}$ states that with samples $\mathbf{A} \leftarrow \mathcal{D}_{l,k}$ and $(\mathbf{s},\ \mathbf{s}') \leftarrow \mathbb{Z}_q^k \times \mathbb{Z}_q^l$, the tuple $([\mathbf{A}], [\mathbf{As}])$ is computationally indistinguishable from $([\mathbf{A}], [\mathbf{s}'])$. A matrix distribution $\mathcal{D}_{k+1,k}$ is simply denoted by $\mathcal{D}_k$.

Intuitively, a $\mathcal{D}_{l,k}-$MDDH assumption allows us to generate l (computationally) independently random group elements from an initial k independently random exponents. A $\mathcal{D}_k-$MDDH assumption allows us to generate one extra random group element. In this section, we will establish that, in fact, a $\mathcal{D}_k-$MDDH assumption can be *boosted* to generate additional (computationally) independently random elements. This will be useful to us in the next section to prove the smoothness property of our construction.

We remark that boosting is different from the random self-reducibility of $\mathcal{D}_{l,k}-$MDDH assumptions, as described by [EHK+13]. While the former aims to generate extra randomness from the same initial sample of vector of random exponents, the latter talks about results from several independent samples of vector of random exponents. Boosting can be seen as an abstraction of the *switching lemma* of [JR14] and follows the same blueprint for the proof.

For an $l \times k$ matrix $\mathbf{A}$, we denote $\bar{\mathbf{A}}$ to be the top $k \times k$ square sub-matrix of $\mathbf{A}$ and $\underline{\mathbf{A}}$ to be the bottom $(l-k) \times k$ sub-matrix of $\mathbf{A}$.

Theorem 1. *Let $\mathcal{D}_k$ be a matrix distribution on $\mathbb{Z}_q^{(k+1)\times k}$. Define another matrix distribution $\mathcal{D}_{l,k}$ on $\mathbb{Z}_q^{l\times k}$ as follows: First sample matrices $\mathbf{A} \leftarrow \mathcal{D}_k$ and $\mathbf{R} \leftarrow \mathbb{Z}_q^{(l-k)\times k}$ and then output $\begin{pmatrix} \bar{\mathbf{A}} \\ \mathbf{R} \end{pmatrix}$. Then the $\mathcal{D}_k$−MDDH assumption implies the $\mathcal{D}_{l,k}$−MDDH assumption.*

We will call *boosting* to be the process of stretching $\mathcal{D}_k$ to $\mathcal{D}_{l,k}$ as above. This theorem is proved as a corollary of an even more general theorem which we will describe after defining the notion of 'boostable'-ity as follows.

Definition 2. *We say that a matrix distribution $\mathcal{D}_k$ on $\mathbb{Z}_q^{(k+1)\times k}$ is* boostable *to a matrix distribution $\mathcal{D}_{l,k}$ on $\mathbb{Z}_q^{l\times k}$, where $l > k$, if there are efficiently samplable distributions $\mathcal{E}$ on $\mathbb{Z}_q^{(l-k)\times k}$ and $\mathcal{F}$ on $\mathbb{Z}_q^{(l-k)\times(k+1)}$, such that the following hold:*

- *For $\mathbf{A} \leftarrow \mathcal{D}_k, \mathbf{B} \leftarrow \mathcal{D}_{l,k}, \mathbf{E} \leftarrow \mathcal{E}, \mathbf{F} \leftarrow \mathcal{F}$, we have:*

$$\bar{\mathbf{B}} \approx \bar{\mathbf{A}}, \quad \underline{\mathbf{B}} \approx \mathbf{E}\bar{\mathbf{A}} \approx \mathbf{F}\mathbf{A}.$$

- *For $\mathbf{F} \leftarrow \mathcal{F}$, with overwhelming probability, all entries of the rightmost column $\mathbf{F}_r$ of $\mathbf{F}$ are non-zero.*

Theorem 2. *If a matrix distribution $\mathcal{D}_k$ on $\mathbb{Z}_q^{(k+1)\times k}$ is boostable to a matrix distribution $\mathcal{D}_{l,k}$ on $\mathbb{Z}_q^{l\times k}$ then the $\mathcal{D}_k$-MDDH assumption implies the $\mathcal{D}_{l,k}$-MDDH assumption.*

Proof. We prove this by a sequence of hybrids, where in the i-th hybrid we transform row $k+i$ from that of $[\mathbf{Bs}]$ to uniformly random. We start off with $i = 0$, where we have the real output $[\mathbf{Bs}]$ and end with $i = l-k$ where we have the fake output which is uniformly random in $\mathbb{Z}_q^l$.

The i-th hybrid $([\mathbf{B}], [\mathbf{b}])$ is computed as follows. We sample $[\mathbf{A}]$ from $\mathcal{D}_k$ and $\mathbf{s}$ from $\mathbb{Z}_q^k$. We set $[\bar{\mathbf{B}}]$ as $[\bar{\mathbf{A}}]$ and, if $i \neq 0$, the row i of $[\underline{\mathbf{B}}]$ as the row i of $\mathbf{F}[\mathbf{A}]$. All other rows $j \neq i$ of $[\underline{\mathbf{B}}]$ are set to the j-th row of $\mathbf{E}[\bar{\mathbf{A}}]$. We set the top k elements of $[\mathbf{b}]$ to be $[\bar{\mathbf{A}}\mathbf{s}]$ and choose all the $(k+j)$-th elements, where $j < i$, of $[\mathbf{b}]$ uniformly at random from $\mathbb{Z}_q$. If $i \neq 0$, we set the $(k+i)$-th element of $[\mathbf{b}]$ to be the i-th element of $\mathbf{F}[\mathbf{As}]$. For all $j > i$, we set the $(k+j)$-th element of $[\mathbf{b}]$ to be the j-th element of $\mathbf{E}[\bar{\mathbf{A}}\mathbf{s}]$. To summarize, $[\mathbf{b}]$ is computed as:

$$\begin{bmatrix} [\bar{\mathbf{A}}\mathbf{s}] \\ \$ \\ \vdots \\ \$ \\ (\mathbf{F}[\mathbf{As}])_i \\ (\mathbf{E}[\bar{\mathbf{A}}\mathbf{s}])_{j=(i+1) \text{ to } (l-k)} \end{bmatrix}$$

We observe that the 0-th hybrid has the distribution of $([\mathbf{B}], [\mathbf{Bs}])$ and the $(l-k)$-th hybrid has the distribution of $([\mathbf{B}], [\mathbf{s}'])$, with $\mathbf{s}'$ uniform in $\mathbb{Z}_q^l$.

Now, $(\mathbf{F}[\mathbf{As}])_i = (\mathbf{F}_l)_i[\bar{\mathbf{A}}\mathbf{s}] + (\mathbf{F}_r)_i[\underline{\mathbf{A}}\mathbf{s}]$, where $\mathbf{F}_l$ is the first k-column sub-matrix of $\mathbf{F}$ and $\mathbf{F}_r$ is the last column of $\mathbf{F}$. Suppose we are given a $\mathcal{D}_k$-MDDH challenge $([\mathbf{A}], \chi = [\mathbf{As}] \text{ or } [\mathbf{s}'])$. If $\chi = [\mathbf{As}]$, then $(\mathbf{F}\chi)_i$ is distributed as $(\mathbf{F}[\mathbf{As}])_i$. Else, if $\chi = [\mathbf{s}']$, then $(\mathbf{F}\chi)_i$ is distributed uniformly randomly in $\mathbb{Z}_q$, since $(\mathbf{F}_r)_i$ is overwhelmingly non-zero by design. Next we transition to an intermediate hybrid i' where $[\mathbf{b}]$ is computed as:

$$\begin{bmatrix} [\bar{\mathbf{A}}\mathbf{s}] \\ \$ \\ \vdots \\ \$ \\ \$ \\ (\mathbf{E}[\bar{\mathbf{A}}\mathbf{s}])_{j=(i+1) \text{ to } (l-k)} \end{bmatrix}$$

As shown above, the hybrid i' is indistinguishable from hybrid i by the $\mathcal{D}_k$-MDDH assumption. Next we transition to the hybrid $i+1$ where $[\mathbf{b}]$ is computed as:

$$\begin{bmatrix} [\bar{\mathbf{A}}\mathbf{s}] \\ \$ \\ \vdots \\ \$ \\ \$ \\ (\mathbf{F}[\mathbf{As}])_{(i+1)} \\ (\mathbf{E}[\bar{\mathbf{A}}\mathbf{s}])_{j=(i+2) \text{ to } (l-k)} \end{bmatrix}$$

The hybrid $i+1$ is indistinguishable from hybrid i', as $\mathbf{E}\bar{\mathbf{A}}$ is identically distributed as $\mathbf{FA}$. The theorem is thus established by chaining all the hybrids.

Corollary 1. *Any $\mathcal{D}_k$ distribution can be boosted to a $\mathcal{D}_{l,k}$ distribution which inherits the distribution of the top $k \times k$ matrix of the samples.*

This can be seen by setting the top $k \times k$ matrix of a $\mathcal{D}_{l,k}$ sample to be the top $k \times k$ matrix of a $\mathcal{D}_k$ sample and setting the bottom $(l-k) \times k$ sub-matrix of the $\mathcal{D}_{l,k}$ sample to be uniformly random in $\mathbb{Z}_q^{(l-k)\times k}$. The required distributions $\mathcal{E}$ and $\mathcal{F}$ are just the uniform distributions on their respective domains.

This corollary allows us to retain the *representation size* of the top square matrix of a $\mathcal{D}_k$ distribution sample, while boosting it to an assumption required for security proofs. In particular, in applications such as this paper, this can lead to shorter public keys.

Finally, observe that Theorem 2 and the justification of Corollary 1 establishes Theorem 1.

4 Smooth Quasi-Adaptive NIZK Constructions

In this section we show that the single element QA-NIZK [JR14, KW15] for witness-samplable linear subspaces can easily be extended to be smooth QA-NIZK. Particularly, under SXDH, the public hash key hp generated by $\mathsf{ver.hkgen}$ consists of a single group element. We follow the construction of Kiltz and Wee [KW15] and prove the result under the more general MDDH assumption in bilinear groups.

We follow additive notation for group operations in this section. In later sections we will use product notation.

Linear Subspace Languages. We first consider languages that are linear subspaces of vectors of $\mathbb{G}_1$ elements. In other words, the languages we are interested in can be characterized as languages parametrized by $[\mathbf{M}]_1$ as below:

$$L_{[\mathbf{M}]_1} = \{[\mathbf{M}]_1\mathbf{x} \in \mathbb{G}_1^n \mid \mathbf{x} \in \mathbb{Z}_q^t\}, \text{ where } [\mathbf{M}]_1 \text{ is an } n \times t \text{ matrix of } \mathbb{G}_1 \text{ elements.}$$

Here $[\mathbf{M}]_1$ is an element of the associated *parameter language* Lpar, which is all $n \times t$ matrices of $\mathbb{G}_1$ elements. The parameter language Lpar also has a corresponding witness relation $\mathcal{R}_{\text{par}}$, where the witness is a matrix of $\mathbb{Z}_q$ elements: $\mathcal{R}_{\text{par}}([\mathbf{M}]_\infty, \mathbf{M}')$ iff $\mathbf{M} = \mathbf{M}'$.

Robust and Efficiently Witness-Samplable Distributions. Let the $t \times n$ dimensional matrix $[\mathbf{M}]_1$ be chosen according to a distribution $\mathcal{D}$ on Lpar. The distribution $\mathcal{D}$ is called *robust* if with probability close to one the left-most t columns of $[\mathbf{M}]_1$ are full-ranked. A distribution $\mathcal{D}$ on Lpar is called *efficiently witness-samplable* if there is a probabilistic polynomial time algorithm such that it outputs a pair of matrices $([\mathbf{M}]_1, \mathbf{M}')$ that satisfy the relation $\mathcal{R}_{\text{par}}$ (i.e., $\mathcal{R}_{\text{par}}([\mathbf{M}]_1, \mathbf{M}')$ holds), and further the resulting distribution of the output $[\mathbf{M}]_1$ is same as $\mathcal{D}$. For example, the uniform distribution on Lpar is efficiently witness-samplable, by first picking $\mathbf{M}$ at random, and then computing $[\mathbf{M}]_1$.

Smooth QA-NIZK Construction. We now describe a smooth computationally-sound Quasi-Adaptive NIZK $(\mathsf{pargen}, \mathsf{crsgen}, \mathsf{prover}, \mathsf{ver})$ for linear subspace languages $\{L_{[\mathbf{M}]_1}\}$ with parameters sampled from a robust and efficiently witness-samplable distribution $\mathcal{D}$ over the associated parameter language Lpar and given a $\mathcal{D}_k$-MDDH assumption.

crsgen: The crsgen algorithm generates the CRS as follows. Let $[\mathbf{M}^{n\times t}]_1$ be the parameter supplied to crsgen. It generates an $n \times k$ matrix $\mathbf{K}$ with all elements chosen randomly from $\mathbb{Z}_q$ and a $(k+1) \times k$ matrix $\mathbf{A}$ from the MDDH distribution $\mathcal{D}_k$. Let $\bar{\mathbf{A}}$ be the top $k \times k$ square matrix of $\mathbf{A}$.

The common reference string (CRS) has two parts CRS_p and CRS_v which are to be used by the prover and the verifier respectively.

$$\mathsf{CRS}_p^{t\times k} := ([\mathbf{P}]_1 = [\mathbf{M}^\top \mathbf{K}]_1) \qquad \mathsf{CRS}_v := ([\mathbf{C}]_2^{n\times k} = [\mathbf{K}\bar{\mathbf{A}}]_2, \quad [\bar{\mathbf{A}}]_2^{k\times k})$$

prover: Given candidate $[\mathbf{y}]_1 = [\mathbf{M}]_1\mathbf{x}$ with witness vector $\mathbf{x}^{t\times 1}$, the prover generates the following proof consisting of k elements in $\mathbb{G}_1$:

$$\pi := \mathbf{x}^\top \mathsf{CRS}_p$$

ver: The algorithm hkgen is as follows: Sample $\mathbf{s} \leftarrow \mathbb{Z}_q^k$. Given CRS_v as above, compute hk and hp as follows:

$$\mathsf{hk} := [\mathbf{C}]_2\, \mathbf{s}, \qquad \mathsf{hp} := [\bar{\mathbf{A}}]_2\, \mathbf{s}$$

The algorithms pubH and privH are as follows: Given candidate $[\mathbf{y}]_1$, and proof π, compute:

$$\mathsf{privH}(\mathsf{hk}, [\mathbf{y}]_1) := \mathsf{e}([\mathbf{y}^\top]_1, \mathsf{hk}) \qquad \mathsf{pubH}(\mathsf{hp}, \pi) := \mathsf{e}(\pi, \mathsf{hp})$$

Theorem 3. *The above algorithms* (pargen, crsgen, prover, *ver*) *constitute a smooth computationally -sound Quasi-Adaptive NIZK proof system for linear subspace languages* $\{L_{[\mathbf{M}]_1}\}$ *with parameters* $[\mathbf{M}]_1$ *sampled from a robust and efficiently witness-samplable distribution* $\mathcal{D}$ *over the associated parameter language* Lpar, *given any group generation algorithm for which the* $\mathcal{D}_k$−MDDH *assumption holds for group* $\mathbb{G}_2$.

The proofs of completeness, zero knowledge and soundness are same as [KW15]. The proof of smooth soundness follows.

Proof (Smooth Soundness). First, note that the range of privH is exponential in the security parameter, for otherwise an adversarial circuit can compute discrete logarithms with non-negligible probability. We prove smoothness by transforming the system over a sequence of games. Game $\mathbf{G_0}$ just replicates the construction, but samples $\mathbf{A}$ from a distribution $\mathcal{D}_{k+n-t,k}$ obtained by boosting the given distribution $\mathcal{D}_k$ by Theorem 1. The construction only uses the top $k \times k$ sub-matrix $\bar{\mathbf{A}}$ of the sample which is distributed identically for both $\mathcal{D}_k$ and $\mathcal{D}_{k+n-t,k}$. Let $\underline{\mathbf{A}}$ be the bottom $(n-t) \times k$ sub-matrix of $\mathbf{A}$.

In Game $\mathbf{G_1}$, the challenger efficiently samples $[\mathbf{M}]_1$ according to distribution $\mathcal{D}$, along with witness $\mathbf{M}$ (since $\mathcal{D}$ is an efficiently witness samplable distribution). Since $\mathbf{M}$ is an $n \times t$ dimensional rank t matrix, there is a rank $n-t$ matrix $\mathbf{M}^\perp$ of dimension $n \times (n-t)$ whose columns form a complete basis for the kernel of $\mathbf{M}^\top$, which means $\mathbf{M}^\top \mathbf{M}^\perp = \mathbf{0}^{t\times(n-t)}$. In this game, the NIZK CRS is computed as follows: Generate matrix $\mathbf{K}'^{\,n\times k}$ and compute the matrix $\mathbf{T}^{(n-t)\times k}$, such that $\mathbf{T}\bar{\mathbf{A}} = \underline{\mathbf{A}}$. Implicitly set: $\mathbf{K} = \mathbf{K}' + \mathbf{M}^\perp \mathbf{T}$. Therefore we have,

$$\mathsf{CRS}_p^{t\times k} = [\mathbf{M}^\top \mathbf{K}]_1 = [\mathbf{M}^\top(\mathbf{K}' + \mathbf{M}^\perp \mathbf{T})]_1 = [\mathbf{M}^\top \mathbf{K}']_1$$
$$[\mathbf{C}]_2^{n\times k} = [(\mathbf{K}' + \mathbf{M}^\perp \mathbf{T})\bar{\mathbf{A}}]_2 = \mathbf{K}'[\bar{\mathbf{A}}]_2 + \mathbf{M}^\perp[\underline{\mathbf{A}}]_2,$$
$$\mathsf{hk} = [\mathbf{C}]_2\ \mathbf{s}, \quad \mathsf{hp} = [\bar{\mathbf{A}}]_2\ \mathbf{s}$$

In Game $\mathbf{G_2}$, we sample fresh random vectors $\mathbf{s}'$ in $\mathbb{Z}_q^k$ and $\mathbf{s}''$ in $\mathbb{Z}_q^{n-t}$ and modify the simulated computations as follows:

$$\mathsf{CRS}_p^{t\times k} = [\mathbf{M}^\top \mathbf{K}']_1, \qquad [\mathbf{C}]_2^{n\times k} = \mathbf{K}'[\bar{\mathbf{A}}]_2 + \mathbf{M}^\perp[\underline{\mathbf{A}}]_2,$$
$$\mathsf{hk} = \mathbf{K}'[\mathbf{s}']_2 + \mathbf{M}^\perp[\mathbf{s}'']_2, \quad \mathsf{hp} = [\mathbf{s}']_2$$

Given a $\mathcal{D}_{k+n-t,k}$ challenge which is either "real": $([\mathbf{A}]_2, [\bar{\mathbf{A}}\mathbf{s}]_2, [\underline{\mathbf{A}}\mathbf{s}]_2)$ or "fake": $([\mathbf{A}]_2, [\mathbf{s}']_2, [\mathbf{s}'']_2)$, we observe that the real tuple can be used to simulate Game $\mathbf{G_1}$, while the fake tuple can be used to simulate Game $\mathbf{G_2}$. Thus the games $\mathbf{G_1}$ and $\mathbf{G_2}$ are indistinguishable by the $\mathcal{D}_{k+n-t,k}$-MDDH assumption, which in turn is implied by the $\mathcal{D}_k$-MDDH assumption by Theorem 2.

Now in Game $\mathbf{G_2}$ we have,

$$\mathsf{privH}(\mathsf{hk}, [\mathbf{y}^*]_1) = \mathsf{e}\left([\mathbf{y}^{*\top}]_1, \mathbf{K}'[\mathbf{s}']_2 + \mathbf{M}^\perp[\mathbf{s}'']_2\right)$$

For the oracle queries where $[\mathbf{y}^*]_1 \in L_{[\mathbf{M}]_1}$, we have $\mathbf{y}^{*\top}\mathbf{M}^\perp = 0^{1\times(n-t)}$. Hence the simulator responds with $\mathsf{e}\left([\mathbf{y}^*]_1^\top, \mathbf{K}'[\mathbf{s}']_2\right)$. Note that $\mathbf{s}''$ does not appear in this response.

For the adversary supplied $[\mathbf{y}^*]_1 \notin L_{[\mathbf{M}]_1}$, we have $\mathbf{y}^{*\top}\mathbf{M}^\perp \neq 0^{1\times(n-t)}$. Therefore $\mathsf{privH}(\mathsf{hk}, \mathbf{y}^*)$ is uniformly random, as $\mathbf{s}''$ is independently random of everything else given to the adversary.

Smooth Split-CRS QA-NIZK for Tagged Affine Languages. QA-NIZKs for linear subspaces were also extended by [JR13] to integer tag-based languages as well as provided split-CRS[4] instantiation for affine languages. In [JR16], we combine all these extensions and describe a smooth computationally-sound Quasi-Adaptive NIZK ($\mathsf{pargen}, \mathsf{crsgen}, \mathsf{prover}, \mathsf{ver}$) for tagged affine linear subspace languages $\{L\}$, parametrized by $([\mathbf{M}_0]_1, [\mathbf{M}_1]_1, [\mathbf{M}_2]_1, [\mathbf{M}_3]_1, [\mathbf{a}]_1)$ and consisting of words of the form:

$$([\mathbf{M}_0\mathbf{x}]_1, [\mathbf{M}_1\mathbf{x} + \mathbf{a}]_1, [(\mathbf{M}_2 + \textsc{tag}.\mathbf{M}_3)\mathbf{x}]_1, \ \textsc{tag} \in \mathbb{Z}_q),$$

with parameters sampled from a robust and efficiently witness-samplable distribution $\mathcal{D}$ over $(\mathbf{M}_0, \mathbf{M}_1, \mathbf{M}_2, \mathbf{M}_3, \mathbf{a})$ and given a $\mathcal{D}_k$–MDDH assumption. We assume that $\mathbf{M}_0$ is a square matrix and the robustness of $\mathcal{D}$ is defined by $\mathbf{M}_0$ being non-singular. The smooth QA-NIZK will be split-CRS [JR13], so that CRS_v is independent of the language parameters.

5 Asymmetric UC-PAKE: UC-APAKE

Based on the UC-PAKE functionality of [CHK+05], Gentry et al. [GMR06] gave another UC functionality for asymmetric PAKE (UC-APAKE). A salient feature of the UC-PAKE functionality [CHK+05] is that it models the security requirement that an adversary cannot perform efficient off-line computations on protocol transcripts to verifiably guess the low-entropy password. An adversary can only benefit from the low-entropy of the password by actually conducting an on-line attack (i.e. by impersonating one of the parties with a guessed password). This is modeled in the ideal world with a $\mathsf{TestPwd}$ capability available to the ideal world adversary: if $\mathsf{TestPwd}$ is called with the correct password, the ideal world adversary is allowed to set the session key. Moreover, in this functionality if any of the parties is corrupted, then the ideal world adversary is given the registered password.

---

[4] A split-CRS QA-NIZK allows the verifier CRS to be generated independent of the language.

5.1 The UC Ideal Functionality for Asymmetric PAKE

In asymmetric PAKE [GMR06], the ideal functionality also allows an adversary to steal the password file stored at the server (while not necessarily corrupting the server). However, this by itself does not directly provide the actual password to the adversary. However, after this point the adversary is allowed to perform OfflineTestPwd tests to mimic a similar capability in the real world (in fact, the ideal world adversary is even allowed to perform OfflineTestPwd tests before it steals the password file, but it does not get a confirmation of the guess being correct until after it steals the password file).

Moreover, after the "steal password file" event the adversary is also allowed to impersonate the server to a *correctly guessed* client, even without providing the actual password (as it can clearly do so in the real world). However, compromising impersonation of the client still requires providing a correct password. This differentiation in capabilities also becomes important when characterizing the complexity of a simulator in terms of the real world adversary, as we will see later.

The $\mathcal{F}_{\text{PAKE}}$ functionality for UC-PAKE was a single-session functionality. However, asymmetric PAKE requires that a password file be used across multiple sessions, so the $\mathcal{F}_{\mathsf{apwKE}}$ functionality for UC-APAKE is defined as a multiple-session functionality. Note that this cannot be accomplished simply using composition with joint state [CR03] because the functionality itself requires shared state that needs to be maintained between sessions. The complete UC-APAKE functionality $\mathcal{F}_{\mathsf{apwKE}}$ is described in detail in Fig. 2.

5.2 UC-APAKE Based on VPAKE and Smooth-NIZK

We now design an asymmetric UC-PAKE based on Verifier-based PAKE or VPAKE of Benhamouda and Pointcheval [BP13] and the novel Smooth NIZK proofs. The essential idea of [BP13] is that while the Client holds the actual password, the Server does not hold password in the clear. Instead the Server stores a hard to invert function called PHash (password hash) evaluated over the password and a random "salt" (PSalt) published in the CRS. While executing a session, the client sends encryptions of the password or another function called PPreHash (password pre-hash) evaluated on the password. Correspondingly, the server sends encryptions of the stored PHash.

Of course, some kind of zero-knowledge proof must accompany these encryptions, and to that end [BP13] can utilize the new smooth projective hash functions (SPHF) for CCA2-encryption [BBC+13] such as Cramer-Shoup encryption [CS02]. In each session, both parties generate fresh SPHF private and projection keys (to be employed on incoming messages). The projection key is sent (piggybacked) along with the encrypted message. If the encrypted messages use the correct password (meaning both parties have the same password or its PHash), then SPHF computed on the message by the receiving party using the SPHF hash key it generated equals the SPHF computed on the message by the sending party using the SPHF projection key it received. Thus, these SPHF hashes can be

Functionality $\mathcal{F}_{\mathsf{apwKE}}$

The functionality $\mathcal{F}_{\mathsf{apwKE}}$ is parameterized by a security parameter k. It interacts with an adversary S and a set of parties via the following queries:

Password Storage and Authentication Sessions

Upon receiving a query (StorePwdFile, sid, P_i, pw) **from party** P_j**:**
If this is the first StorePwdFile query, store password data record (file, P_i, P_j, pw) and mark it uncompromised.

Upon receiving a query (CltSession, sid, ssid, P_i, P_j, pw) **from party** P_i**:**
Send (CltSession, sid, ssid, P_i, P_j) to S. In addition, if this is the first CltSession query for ssid, then store session record (Clt, ssid, P_i, P_j, pw) and mark this record fresh.

Upon receiving a query (SvrSession, sid, ssid, P_i) **from party** P_j**:**
If there is a password data record (file, P_i, P_j, pw), then send (SvrSession, sid, ssid, P_j, P_i) to S, and if this is the first SvrSession query for ssid, store session record (Svr, ssid, P_j, P_i, pw), and mark it fresh.

Stealing Password Data

Upon receiving a query (StealPwdFile, sid) **from adversary** S**:**
If there is no password data record reply to S with 'no password file'. Otherwise, do the following: If the password data record (file, P_i, P_j, pw) is marked uncompromised, mark it compromised. If there is a tuple (offline, pw') stored with $pw' = pw$ then send pw to S, otherwise reply to S with 'password file stolen'.

Upon receiving a query (OfflineTestPwd, sid, pw') **from Adversary** S**:**
If there is no password data record, or if there is a password data record (file, P_i, P_j, pw) that is marked uncompromised, then store (offline, pw'). Otherwise do: if $pw = pw'$, send pw back to S. If $pw \neq pw'$, reply with 'wrong guess'.

Active Session Attacks

Upon receiving a query (TestPwd, sid, ssid, P_i, pw') **from the adversary** S**:**
If there is a session record of the form (role, ssid, P_i, P_j, pw) which is fresh, then do: If $pw = pw'$, mark the record compromised and reply to S with "correct guess". If $pw \neq pw'$, mark the record interrupted and reply with "wrong guess".

Upon receiving a query (Impersonate, sid, ssid)
If there is a session record of the form (Clt, ssid, P_i, P_j, pw) which is fresh, then do: then if there is a password data record file (file, P_i, P_j, pw) that is marked compromised, mark the session record compromised and reply to S with 'correct guess', else mark the session record interrupted and reply with wrong guess.

Key Generation and Authentication

Upon receiving a query (NewKey, sid, ssid, P_i, sk) **from** S**, where** $|sk| = k$**:**
If there is a session record of the form (role, ssid, P_i, P_j, pw) that is not marked completed,

- If this record is compromised, or either P_i or P_j is corrupted, then output (sid, ssid, sk) to player P_i.
- If this record is fresh, and there is a session record (role, ssid, P_j, P_i, pw') with $pw' = pw$, and a key sk' was sent to P_j, and (role, ssid, P_j, P_i, pw) was fresh at the time, then output (sid, ssid, sk') to P_i.
- In any other case, pick a new random key sk' of length k and send (sid, ssid, sk') to P_i.

Either way, mark the record (P_i, P_j, pw) as completed.

Upon receiving (Corrupt, sid, P) **from** S**:** if there is a (Clt, sid, P, P', pw) recorded, return pw to S, and mark P_i corrupted. If there is a (Svr, sid, P, P', pw) recorded, then mark P corrupted and (internally) call (StealPwdFile, sid).

Fig. 2. The password-based key-exchange functionality $\mathcal{F}_{\mathsf{apwKE}}$

used to compute the session key. Smoothness property of the SPHF guarantees security of the VPAKE scheme.

Unfortunately, each party must retain the witness used in the CCA2 encryption, as computing the SPHF projection-hash of its outgoing encrypted message

Generate $\mathbf{g} \leftarrow \mathbb{G}_1$; $a_1, a_2, b_C, b_S \leftarrow \mathbb{Z}_q$ and let $\rho = \{\mathbf{a}_1 = \mathbf{g}^{a_1}, \mathbf{a}_2 = \mathbf{g}^{a_2}, \mathbf{b}_C = \mathbf{g}^{b_C}, \mathbf{b}_S = \mathbf{g}^{b_S}\}$.

Define languages $\begin{bmatrix} L_C = \{(R, S, H) \mid \exists r, p : R = \mathbf{g}^r, S = \mathbf{a}_1^r \mathbf{b}_C^p, H = \mathbf{b}_S^p\} \\ L_S = \{(R, S) \mid \exists r : R = \mathbf{g}^r, S = \mathbf{a}_2^r\} \end{bmatrix}$

Let $(\mathsf{hk_C}, \mathsf{hp_C}) \leftarrow \mathsf{sphf}(L_C).\mathsf{hkgen}$ and $(\mathsf{hp_S}, \mathsf{hk_S}) \leftarrow \mathsf{sphf}(L_S).\mathsf{hkgen}$.

Define languages:

$$\begin{bmatrix} L_C^+ = \{(R, S, H, T, l) \mid \exists r, p : R = \mathbf{g}^r, S = \mathbf{a}_1^r \mathbf{b}_C^p, H = \mathbf{b}_S^p, T = \mathsf{sphf.pubH}(\mathsf{hp_C}, \langle R, S, H \rangle, l; r, p)\} \\ L_S^+ = \{(R, S, T, l) \mid \exists r : R = \mathbf{g}^r, S = \mathbf{a}_2^r, T = \mathsf{sphf.pubH}(\mathsf{hp_S}, \langle R, S \rangle, l; r)\} \end{bmatrix}$$

Let $(\mathsf{pargen}_P, \mathsf{crsgen}_P, \mathsf{prover}_P, \mathsf{ver}_P)$ be Smooth QA-NIZKs for languages L_P^+, with $P \in \{C, S\}$.

Let $\mathrm{CRS}_P \leftarrow \mathsf{crsgen}_P(\rho)$ and $\mathcal{H}$ be a collision resistant hash function.

Let $\mathcal{RO}$ be a random oracle and let $\mathsf{phash} = \mathcal{RO}(sid, P_i, P_j, \mathsf{pwd})$.

Note that there are several sessions, designated by unique ssid-s, within the scope of a single *sid*. Thus, phash is the same across all these sessions.

$$\mathrm{CRS} := (\rho, \mathsf{hp_C}, \mathsf{hp_S}, \mathrm{CRS_C}, \mathrm{CRS_S}, \mathcal{H}).$$

$$\text{Server Persistent State} := \mathbf{b}_S^{\mathsf{phash}}.$$

Client P_i	Network
Input $(\mathsf{CltSession}, sid, \mathsf{ssid}, P_i, P_j, \mathsf{pwd})$. Choose $r_1 \leftarrow \mathbb{Z}_q$ and $(\mathrm{HK}_1, \mathrm{HP}_1) \leftarrow \mathsf{ver_S.hkgen}(\mathrm{CRS_S})$. Set $R_1 = \mathbf{g}^{r_1}$, $S_1 = \mathbf{a}_1^{r_1} \mathbf{b}_C^{\mathsf{phash}}$, $T_1 = \mathsf{sphf_C.pubH}(\mathsf{hp_C}, \langle R_1, S_1, \mathbf{b}_S^{\mathsf{phash}} \rangle, i_1; r_1, \mathsf{phash})$, $W_1 = \mathsf{prover_C}(\mathrm{CRS_C}, \langle R_1, S_1, \mathbf{b}_S^{\mathsf{phash}}, T_1, i_1 \rangle; r_1, \mathsf{phash})$, where $i_1 = \mathcal{H}(sid, \mathsf{ssid}, P_i, P_j, R_1, S_1, \mathrm{HP}_1)$. Erase r_1, send $(R_1, S_1, T_1, \mathrm{HP}_1)$ and retain (W_1, HK_1).	$\xrightarrow{R_1, S_1, T_1, \mathrm{HP}_1} P_j$
Receive $(R_2', S_2', T_2', \mathrm{HP}_2')$. If any of $R_2', S_2', T_2', \mathrm{HP}_2'$ is not in their respective group or is 1, set $\mathsf{sk}_1 \xleftarrow{\$} \mathbb{G}_T$, else compute $i_2' = \mathcal{H}(sid, \mathsf{ssid}, P_j, P_i, R_2', S_2', \mathrm{HP}_2')$, and $\mathsf{sk}_1 = \mathsf{ver_S.privH}(\mathrm{HK}_1, \langle R_2', S_2'/\mathbf{b}_S^{\mathsf{phash}}, T_2', i_2' \rangle) \cdot \mathsf{ver_C.pubH}(\mathrm{HP}_2', W_1)$. Output $(sid, \mathsf{ssid}, \mathsf{sk}_1)$.	$\xleftarrow{R_2', S_2', T_2', \mathrm{HP}_2'} P_j$
Server P_j	**Network**
Input $(\mathsf{SvrSession}, sid, \mathsf{ssid}, P_j, P_i, \text{Server Persistent State})$. Choose $r_2 \leftarrow \mathbb{Z}_q$ and $(\mathrm{HK}_2, \mathrm{HP}_2) \leftarrow \mathsf{ver_C.hkgen}(\mathrm{CRS_C})$. Set $R_2 = \mathbf{g}^{r_2}$, $S_2 = \mathbf{a}_2^{r_2} \mathbf{b}_S^{\mathsf{phash}}$, $T_2 = \mathsf{sphf_S.pubH}(\mathsf{hp_S}, \langle R_2, S_2/\mathbf{b}_S^{\mathsf{phash}} \rangle, i_2; r_2)$, $W_2 = \mathsf{prover_S}(\mathrm{CRS_S}, \langle R_2, S_2/\mathbf{b}_S^{\mathsf{phash}}, T_2, i_2 \rangle; r_2)$, where $i_2 = \mathcal{H}(sid, \mathsf{ssid}, P_j, P_i, R_2, S_2, \mathrm{HP}_2)$. Erase r_2, send $(R_2, S_2, T_2, \mathrm{HP}_2)$ and retain (W_2, HK_2).	$\xrightarrow{R_2, S_2, T_2, \mathrm{HP}_2} P_i$
Receive $(R_1', S_1', T_1', \mathrm{HP}_1')$. If any of $R_1', S_1', T_1', \mathrm{HP}_1'$ is not in their respective group or is 1, set $\mathsf{sk}_2 \xleftarrow{\$} \mathbb{G}_T$, else compute $i_1' = \mathcal{H}(sid, \mathsf{ssid}, P_i, P_j, R_1', S_1', \mathrm{HP}_1')$, and $\mathsf{sk}_2 = \mathsf{ver_C.privH}(\mathrm{HK}_2, \langle R_1', S_1', \mathbf{b}_S^{\mathsf{phash}}, T_1', i_1' \rangle) \cdot \mathsf{ver_S.pubH}(\mathrm{HP}_1', W_2)$. Output $(sid, \mathsf{ssid}, \mathsf{sk}_2)$.	$\xleftarrow{R_1', S_1', T_1', \mathrm{HP}_1'} P_i$

Fig. 3. Single round RO-hybrid UC-APAKE protocol under SXDH assumption.

using the received projection key requires this witness. In the strong simulation paradigm of universally composable security, this leads to a problem if an Adversary can corrupt a session dynamically after the outgoing message has been sent and the incoming message has not yet been received. Thus, this SPHF methodology can only handle static corruption. While Jutla and Roy [JR15] have recently given an efficient UC-PAKE protocol which can handle dynamic corruption, the construction uses ideas from dual-system simulation-sound QA-NIZK that they introduce there. These ideas are rather intricate and do not seem to allow a modular or generic design of such UC password-authenticated protocols.

In this paper, we show that the new notion of Smooth QA-NIZK allows easy to understand (and equally efficient) modular or generic design. Just as QA-NIZK proofs can be seen as generalization of projective hash proof systems to public verifiability (and also assuring zero-knowledge), the novel notion of Smooth QA-NIZK naturally generalizes the notion of smooth projective hash functions where instead of the witness, the publicly verifiable proof can be used to evaluate the projection-hash. The zero-knowledge property of this publicly verifiable proof assures that this proof and hence the projection-hash can be generated by a simulator with no access to the witness. In particular, each party in the UC-PAKE protocol can generate an encryption of the password and generate this publicly verifiable QA-NIZK proof, send the encryption to the other party, erase the witness and retain just the proof for later generation of session key.

The natural question that arises is whether one needs a notion of smooth-soundness under simulation. Indeed, one does need some form of unbounded simulation-soundness as the UC simulator generates QA-NIZK proofs on non-language members without access to the password. Unfortunately, the recent efficient unbounded simulation sound QA-NIZK construction of [KW15] does not extend to be smooth under unbounded simulation (or at least current techniques do not seem to allow one to prove so). The dual-system simulation sound QA-NIZK [JR15] does satisfy smoothness property, but it would need introduction of various new intricate definitions and complicated proofs. One may also ask whether CCA2 encryption by itself provides the required simulation soundness, but that is also not the case, as CCA2 encryption by itself does not give a privately-verifiable (say, via its underlying SPHF as in Cramer-Shoup encryption) proof that it is the password that is being encrypted.

In light of this, it turns out that the simplest way to design the UC-APAKE (or UC-PAKE) protocol is to use an ElGamal encryption of the password (or its PPreHash or PHash) and augment it with an SPHF proof of its consistency, and finally a Smooth QA-NIZK on this augmented ElGamal encryption. (If the reader is interested in the simpler UC-PAKE protocol secure under dynamic corruption in the new Smooth QA-NIZK framework, the UC-PAKE definition and protocol are provided in [JR16]).

We will also need the random oracle hybrid model to achieve the goal of a UC-APAKE protocol, as explained next. The focus of [BP13] was to design protocols which can be proven secure in the standard model. They formalized a security notion for APAKEs modifying the game-based BPR model [BPR00]. However, our focus is to construct an APAKE protocol in the UC model. In the UC model of [GMR06], the UC simulator must be able to detect offline password guess attempts of the adversary. This is not possible in the standard model as offline tests can be internally performed by the adversary. In order to intercept offline tests by the adversary, it thus becomes inevitable to use an idealized model, such as the random oracle model.

So in particular, we adapt the random oracle-based password hashing scheme of [BP13]. In the scheme, the public parameters are $param = \mathbf{b}_\mathsf{c}, \mathbf{b}_\mathsf{s}$ randomly sampled from $\mathbb{G}_1$ and a random oracle $\mathcal{RO}$. Define phash = $\mathcal{RO}$(*sid*, Client-id, Server-id, pwd), where Client-id, Server-id are the ids of the participating parties, *sid* is the common session-id for all sessions between these parties and pwd is the password of the client. Note that there are several sessions designated by unique ssid-s within the scope of a single *sid*. Thus phash is the same across all these sessions. We set:

$$\mathsf{PPreHash}(param, \mathsf{pwd}) = \mathbf{b}_{\mathsf{c}}^{\mathsf{phash}}$$
$$\mathsf{PSalt}(param) = \mathbf{b}_{\mathsf{s}}$$
$$\mathsf{PHash}(param, \mathsf{pwd}) = \mathbf{b}_{\mathsf{s}}^{\mathsf{phash}}$$

Corresponding to the asymmetric storages of the client and the server, we define the following languages, one for each party, which implicitly check the consistency of correct elements being used ($\mathbf{a}_1$ and $\mathbf{a}_2$ are essentially public keys for ElGamal encryption):

$$L_{\mathsf{c}} = \{(R, S, H) \mid \exists r, p : R = \mathbf{g}^r, S = \mathbf{a}_1^r \mathbf{b}_{\mathsf{c}}^p, H = \mathbf{b}_{\mathsf{s}}^p\}$$
$$L_{\mathsf{s}} = \{(R, S) \mid \exists r : R = \mathbf{g}^r, S = \mathbf{a}_2^r\}$$

We now plug these languages into UC-PAKE methodology described above. The client sends ElGamal encryption of $\mathbf{b}_{\mathsf{c}}^p$, as in (R, S) of L_{c}, while the server supplies the last element H for forming a word of L_{c}. The server sends ElGamal encryption of $\mathbf{b}_{\mathsf{s}}^p$, while the client divides out $\mathbf{b}_{\mathsf{s}}^p$ from the second component to form a word of L_{s}.

The CRS provides public smooth$_2$ SPHF keys for the languages L_{c} and L_{s}, which are used by the client and server respectively to compute T_1 and T_2 for their flows.

Lastly, we use Smooth QA-NIZK proofs for generating a public hash key and a private hash key over the above languages augmented with the SPHFs as below:

$$L_{\mathsf{c}}^{+} = \left\{ (R, S, H, T, l) \mid \exists r, p : \begin{array}{c} R = \mathbf{g}^r, S = \mathbf{a}_1^r \mathbf{b}_{\mathsf{c}}^p, H = \mathbf{b}_{\mathsf{s}}^p, \\ T = \mathsf{sphf.pubH}(\mathsf{hp}_{\mathsf{c}}, \langle R, S, H \rangle, l; r, p) \end{array} \right\}$$
$$L_{\mathsf{s}}^{+} = \{(R, S, T, l) \mid \exists r : R = \mathbf{g}^r, S = \mathbf{a}_2^r, T = \mathsf{sphf.pubH}(\mathsf{hp}_{\mathsf{s}}, \langle R, S \rangle, l; r)\}$$

The client generates a Smooth QA-NIZK verification key pair for the server language L_{s}^{+}, retains the private key HK_1 and sends the public key HP_1 along with the ElGamal encryption and the SPHF. The client computes a QA-NIZK proof W_1 of $(R_1, S_1, \mathbf{b}_{\mathsf{s}}^{\mathsf{phash}}, T_1) \in L_{\mathsf{c}}^{+}$ with label $i_1 = \mathcal{H}(sid, \mathsf{ssid}, P_i, P_j, R_1, S_1, T_1, \text{HP}_1)$ and retains that for later key computation.

Similarly, the server generates a Smooth QA-NIZK verification key pair for the client language L_{c}^{+}, retains the private key HK_2 and sends the public key HP_2 along with the ElGamal encryption and the SPHF. The server computes a QA-NIZK proof W_2 of $(R_2, S_2/\mathbf{b}_{\mathsf{s}}^{\mathsf{phash}}, T_2) \in L_{\mathsf{s}}^{+}$ with label $i_2 = \mathcal{H}(sid, \mathsf{ssid}, P_j, P_i, R_2, S_2, T_2, \text{HP}_2)$ and retains that for later key computation.

In the second part of the protocol, after receiving the peer flow, each party computes the final secret key as the product of the private Smooth QA-NIZK hash of the peer flow with own private Smooth QA-NIZK key and the public Smooth QA-NIZK hash of the (retained) QA-NIZK proof of own flow with the peer public Smooth QA-NIZK hash key. Formally the client computes:

$$\mathsf{ver_s.privH}(\mathrm{HK}_1, \langle R_2', S_2'/\mathbf{b}_\mathsf{s}^{\mathsf{phash}}, T_2', i_2' \rangle) \cdot \mathsf{ver_c.pubH}(\mathrm{HP}_2', W_1).$$

Similarly, the server computes:

$$\mathsf{ver_c.privH}(\mathrm{HK}_2, \langle R_1', S_1', \mathbf{b}_\mathsf{s}^{\mathsf{phash}}, T_1', i_1' \rangle) \cdot \mathsf{ver_s.pubH}(\mathrm{HP}_1', W_2).$$

Given the completeness property of the Smooth QA-NIZK, it is not difficult to see that legitimately completed peer sessions end up with equal keys. In the next section, we prove that this protocol securely realizes $\mathcal{F}_{\mathsf{apwKE}}$, as stated in the theorem below.

The complete protocol is described in detail in Fig. 3. The SPHF sphf is required to be a smooth$_2$ projective hash function (see [JR16] for definitions). For simplicity, in this paper we focus on constructions based on $\mathcal{D}_1$−MDDH assumptions, and in particular the SXDH assumption.

Theorem 4. *Under the $\mathcal{D}_1$−MDDH assumption SXDH, the protocol in Fig. 3 securely realizes the $\mathcal{F}_{\mathsf{apwKE}}$ functionality in the $(\mathcal{F}_{\mathrm{CRS}}, \mathcal{F}_{\mathrm{RO}})$-hybrid model, in the presence of adaptive corruption adversaries. The number of unique password arguments passed to* TestPwd *and* OfflineTestPwd *of $\mathcal{F}_{\mathsf{apwKE}}$ combined in the ideal world is at most the number of random oracle calls in the $(\mathcal{F}_{\mathrm{CRS}}, \mathcal{F}_{\mathrm{RO}})$-hybrid world.*

We describe the intuition of the proof below and describe the UC simulator, while detailed formal steps proving indistinguishability of the real and the ideal world are relegated to the full version [JR16].

5.3 Main Idea of the UC Simulator

The UC simulator $\mathcal{S}$works as follows: It simulates the random oracle calls and records all the query response pairs. It will generate the CRS for $\widehat{\mathcal{F}}_{\mathrm{PAKE}}$ using the real world algorithms, except for the Smooth QA-NIZK, for which it uses the simulated CRS generator. It also retains the private hash keys of the SPHF's. The next main difference is in the simulation of the outgoing message of the real world parties: $\mathcal{S}$ uses a dummy message μ instead of the real password which it does not have access to. Further, it postpones computation of W till the session-key generation time. Finally, another difference is in the processing of the incoming message, where $\mathcal{S}$ decrypts the incoming message R_2', S_2' and runs through the list of random oracle queries to search for a pwd', such that the decryption is $\mathbf{b}_\mathsf{s}^{\mathcal{RO}(sid, P_i, P_j, \mathsf{pwd}')}$, which it uses to call the ideal functionality's test function. It next generates an sk similar to how it is generated in the real-world. It sends sk to the ideal functionality to be output to the party concerned.

Since the (R_1, S_1) that it sends out is no longer such that $(R_1, S_1, \mathbf{b}_\mathsf{s}^{\mathsf{phash}})$ in the language L_c, it has to use the private key of the SPHF in order to compute T_1 on $(R_1, S_1, \mathbf{b}_\mathsf{s}^{\mathsf{phash}})$ and the QA-NIZK proof simulator to compute W_1.

There are other special steps designed to simulate stealing the password file and then impersonating the server to the client. Specifically, when the password file is stolen, the simulator still may not know pwd. It then preemptively sets phash to a random value and pretends that this is the random oracle response with the correct pwd query. Later on when there is a successful pwd query, which the simulator can find out by the online or offline testpwd ideal functionality calls, it sets the record accordingly.

In case of a stolen password file, the simulator includes a "Client Only Step" which lets it test (modified) server flows for consistency and call the Impersonate functionality if consistency checks out. The server simulation steps do not include such a step to model the security notion that even if the password file is stolen, the adversary should still not be able to impersonate the client.

5.4 Main Idea of the Proof of UC Realization

The proof that the simulator $\mathcal{S}$ described above simulates the Adversary in the real-world protocol, follows essentially from the properties of the Smooth QA-NIZK and smooth$_2$ SPHF, and we give a broad outline here. The proof will describe various experiments between a challenger $\mathcal{C}$ and the adversary, which we will just assume to be the environment $\mathcal{Z}$ (as the adversary $\mathcal{A}$ can be assumed to be just dummy and following $\mathcal{Z}$'s commands). In the first experiment the challenger $\mathcal{C}$ will just be the combination of the code of the simulator $\mathcal{S}$ above and $\widehat{\mathcal{F}}_{\text{PAKE}}$. In particular, after the environment issues a CltSession request with a password pwd, the challenger gets that password. So, while in the first experiment, the challenger (copying $\mathcal{S}$) does not use pwd directly, from the next experiment onwards, it can use pwd. Thus, the main goal of the ensuing experiments is to modify the fake tuples $\mathbf{g}^{r_1}, \mathbf{g}^{r'}$ by real tuples (as in real-world) $\mathbf{g}^{r_1}, \mathbf{a}_1^{r_1}\mathbf{b}_\mathsf{c}^{\mathsf{phash}}$, since the challenger has access to pwd, and hence phash. This is accomplished by a hybrid argument, modifying one instance at a time using DDH assumption in group $\mathbb{G}_1$.

The guarantee that the client cannot be impersonated by the adversary, even when the password file is stolen is established by noting that $\mathbf{b}_\mathsf{c}^{\mathsf{phash}}$, which is what the client encrypts in its flows, is hard to compute given the server persistent state $\mathbf{b}_\mathsf{s}^{\mathsf{phash}}$. This is formally captured in the proof by using a DDH transition from $(\mathbf{b}_\mathsf{s}, \mathbf{b}_\mathsf{c}, \mathbf{b}_\mathsf{s}^{\mathsf{phash}}, \mathbf{b}_\mathsf{c}^{\mathsf{phash}})$ to $(\mathbf{b}_\mathsf{s}, \mathbf{b}_\mathsf{c}, \mathbf{b}_\mathsf{s}^{\mathsf{phash}}, \mathbf{b}_\mathsf{c}^{z})$, where z is independently random from phash.

Once all the instances are corrected, i.e. R_1, S_1 are generated as $\mathbf{g}^{r_1}, \mathbf{a}_1^{r_1}\mathbf{b}_\mathsf{c}^{\mathsf{phash}}$, the challenger can switch to the real-world because the tuples $R_1, S_1, \mathbf{b}_\mathsf{s}^{\mathsf{phash}}$ are now in the language L_c. This implies that the session keys are generated exactly as in the real-world.

5.5 Adaptive Corruption

The UC protocol described above is also UC-secure against adaptive corruption of parties by the Adversary in the erasure model. In the real-world when the adversary corrupts a client (with a Corrupt command), it gets the internal state of the client. Clearly, if the party has already been invoked with a $\mathsf{CltSession}$ command then the password pwd is leaked at the minimum, and hence the ideal functionality $\mathcal{F}_{\text{PAKE}}$ leaks the password to the Adversary in the ideal world. In the protocol described above, the Adversary also gets W_1 and HK_1, as this is the only state maintained by each client between sending $R_1, S_1, T_1, \text{HP}_1$, and the final issuance of session-key. Simulation of HK_1 is easy for the simulator $\mathcal{S}$ since $\mathcal{S}$ generates HK_1 exactly as in the real world. For generating W_1, which $\mathcal{S}$ had postponed to computing till it received an incoming message from the adversary, it can now use the pwd which it gets from $\widehat{\mathcal{F}}_{\text{PAKE}}$ by issuing a $\mathsf{Corrupt}$ call to $\widehat{\mathcal{F}}_{\text{PAKE}}$. More precisely, it issues the $\mathsf{Corrupt}$ call, and gets pwd, and then calls the QA-NIZK simulator with the tuple $(R_1, S_1, \mathbf{b}_{\mathsf{s}}^{\mathsf{phash}}, T_1, i_1)$ to get W_1. Note that this computation of W_1 is identical to the postponed computation of W_1 in the computation of client factor of sk_1 (which is really used in the output to the environment when $\mathsf{pwd}' = \mathsf{pwd}$).

In case of server corruption, the simulator does not get pwd, but is able to set phash which also enables it to compute W_2 using the QA-NIZK simulator on $(R_2, S_2/\mathbf{b}_{\mathsf{s}}^{\mathsf{phash}}, T_2, i_2)$.

We first define a simulator which interfaces with the ideal functionality and the adversary and then through a series of experiments convert it to just the real world protocol interacting with the same adversary.

5.6 Simulator for the Protocol

We will assume that the adversary $\mathcal{A}$ in the UC protocol is dummy, and essentially passes back and forth commands and messages from the environment $\mathcal{Z}$. Thus, from now on we will use environment $\mathcal{Z}$ as the real adversary, which outputs a single bit. The simulator $\mathcal{S}$ will be the ideal world adversary for $\mathcal{F}_{\mathsf{apwKE}}$. It is a universal simulator that uses $\mathcal{A}$ as a black box. For each instance (session and a party), we will use a prime, to refer to variables received in the message from $\mathcal{Z}$ (i.e. $\mathcal{A}$). We will call a message *legitimate* if it was not altered by $\mathcal{Z}$, and delivered in the correct session and to the correct party.

Responding to Random Oracle Queries. Let the input be m. If there is a record of the form (m, r), that is, m was queried before and was responded with r, then just return r.

Otherwise, if m is of the form (sid, P_i, P_j, x), for some x and the password file has been stolen then call $\mathsf{OfflineTestPwd}$ with x. If the test succeeds then return phash, which must already have been set (see Stealing Password File below), and record (m, phash).

In all other cases, generate $r \leftarrow \mathbb{Z}_q$, record (m, r) and return r.

Setting the CRS. The simulator $\mathcal{S}$ picks the CRS just as in the real world, except the QA-NIZK CRS-es are generated using the crs-simulators, which also generate simulator trapdoors $\mathsf{trap}_{\mathsf{c}}, \mathsf{trap}_{\mathsf{s}}$. It retains $a_1, a_2, \mathsf{trap}_{\mathsf{c}}, \mathsf{trap}_{\mathsf{s}}, \mathsf{hk}_{\mathsf{c}}, \mathsf{hk}_{\mathsf{s}}$ as trapdoors.

New Client Session: Sending a Message to $\mathcal{Z}$. On message (CltSession, *sid*, ssid, P_i, P_j) from $\mathcal{F}_{\mathsf{apwKE}}$, $\mathcal{S}$ starts simulating a new instance of the protocol for client P_i, server P_j, session identifier ssid, and CRS set as above. We will denote this instance by (P_i, ssid) and call it a *client instance*.

To simulate this instance, $\mathcal{S}$ chooses r_1, r_1', r_1'' at random, and sets $R_1 = \mathbf{g}^{r_1}$, $S_1 = \mathbf{g}^{r_1'}$ and $T_1 = \mathbf{g}^{r_1''}$. Next, $\mathcal{S}$ generates $(\text{HK}_1, \text{HP}_1) \leftarrow \mathsf{ver_s.hkgen}(\text{CRS}_\mathsf{s})$ and sets $i_1 = \mathcal{H}(sid, \mathsf{ssid}, P_i, P_j, R_1, S_1, \text{HP}_1)$. It retains (i_1, HK_1). It then hands $(R_1, S_1, T_1, \text{HP}_1)$ to $\mathcal{Z}$ on behalf of this instance.

New Server Session: Sending a Message to $\mathcal{Z}$. On message (SvrSession, *sid*, ssid, P_j, P_i) from $\mathcal{F}_{\mathsf{apwKE}}$, $\mathcal{S}$ starts simulating a new instance of the protocol for client P_i, server P_j, session identifier ssid, and CRS set as above. We will denote this instance by (P_j, ssid) and call it a *server instance*.

To simulate this instance, $\mathcal{S}$ chooses r_2, r_2', r_2'' at random, and sets $R_2 = \mathbf{g}^{r_2}$, $S_2 = \mathbf{g}^{r_2'}$ and $T_2 = \mathbf{g}^{r_2''}$. Next, $\mathcal{S}$ generates $(\text{HK}_2, \text{HP}_2) \leftarrow \mathsf{ver_c.hkgen}(\text{CRS}_\mathsf{c})$ and sets $i_2 = \mathcal{H}(sid, \mathsf{ssid}, P_j, P_i, R_2, S_2, \text{HP}_2)$. It retains (i_2, HK_2). It then hands $(R_2, S_2, T_2, \text{HP}_2)$ to $\mathcal{Z}$ on behalf of this instance.

On Receiving a Message from $\mathcal{Z}$. On receiving a message $R_2', S_2', T_2', \text{HP}_2'$ from $\mathcal{Z}$ intended for a **client instance** (P, ssid), the simulator S does the following:

1. If any of the the real world protocol checks, namely group membership and non-triviality fail it goes to the step "Other Cases"below.
2. If the message received from $\mathcal{Z}$ is same as message sent by $\mathcal{S}$ on behalf of peer P' in session ssid, then $\mathcal{S}$ just issues a NewKey call for P.
3. ("Client Only Step"): If StealPwdFile has already taken place then do the following: If $S_2' = R_2'^{a_2} \mathbf{b}_\mathsf{s}^{\mathsf{phash}}$, then $\mathcal{S}$ calls $\mathcal{F}_{\mathsf{apwKE}}$ with (Impersonate, P, *sid*, ssid) and skips to the "Key Setting" step below, and otherwise go to the step "Other Cases".
4. It searches its random oracle query response pairs $\{(m_k, h_k)\}_k$ and checks whether for some $k = x$ we have $S_2' = R_2'^{a_2} \mathbf{b}_\mathsf{s}^{h_x}$ and m_x is of the form $(sid, P_i, P_j, \mathsf{pwd}')$. If so, then $\mathcal{S}$ calls $\mathcal{F}_{\mathsf{apwKE}}$ with (TestPwd, ssid, P, pwd$'$) else it goes to the step "Other Cases" below. If the test passes, it sets $\mathsf{phash} = h_x$ and goes to the "Key Setting" step below, else it goes to the step "Other Cases" below.
5. ("Key Setting Step"): Compute $i_2' = \mathcal{H}(sid, \mathsf{ssid}, P_j, P_i, R_2', S_2', \text{HP}_2')$.
If $T_2' \neq \mathsf{sphf_s.privH}(\mathsf{hk_s}, \langle R_2', S_2'/\mathbf{b}_\mathsf{s}^{\mathsf{phash}} \rangle, i_2')$ then goto the step "Other Cases". Else, compute $W_1 = \mathsf{sim}(\text{CRS}_\mathsf{c}, \mathsf{trap_c}, \langle R_1, S_1, \mathbf{b}_\mathsf{s}^{\mathsf{phash}}, T_1, i_1 \rangle)$. Issue a NewKey call to $\widehat{\mathcal{F}}_{\text{PAKE}}$ with key
$$\mathsf{ver_s.privH}(\text{HK}_1, \langle R_2', S_2'/\mathbf{b}_\mathsf{s}^{\mathsf{phash}}, T_2', i_2' \rangle) \cdot \mathsf{ver_c.pubH}(\text{HP}_2', W_1)$$
6. ("Other Cases"): $\mathcal{S}$ issues a TestPwd call to $\widehat{\mathcal{F}}_{\text{PAKE}}$ with the dummy password μ, followed by a NewKey call with a random session key, which leads to the functionality issuing a random and independent session key to the party P.

On receiving a message $R'_1, S'_1, T'_1, \text{HP}'_1$ from $\mathcal{Z}$ intended for a **server instance** (P, ssid), the response of the simulator $\mathcal{S}$ is symmetric to the response described above for client instances, except the above step "Client Only Step" is skipped.

Stealing Password File. If there was a successful online TestPwd call by the simulator, before this StealPwdFile call, the corresponding random oracle response h_k was already assigned to the variable phash. Otherwise, the simulator runs through the set of random oracle query response set of the adversary $\{(m_k, h_k)\}_k$, which were not used for an online TestPwd call. For all the m_k's of the form $(sid, P_i, P_j, \mathsf{pwd}')$, it calls $(\mathsf{OfflineTestPwd}, sid, \mathsf{pwd}')$. Next, $\mathcal{S}$ calls StealPwdFile. If StealPwdFile returns pwd then it must equal pwd$'$ in some m_k. Assign to the variable phash the value h_k from the earlier recorded random oracle response to m_k. Otherwise, phash is assigned a fresh random value. The Server Persistent State $\mathbf{b}_\mathsf{s}^{\mathsf{phash}}$ is computed accordingly and given to the adversary.

Client Corruption. On receiving a Corrupt call from $\mathcal{Z}$ for client instance P_i in session ssid, the simulator $\mathcal{S}$ calls the Corrupt routine of $\mathcal{F}_{\mathsf{apwKE}}$ to obtain pwd. If $\mathcal{S}$ had already output a message to $\mathcal{Z}$, and not output sk_1 it computes

$$W_1 = \mathsf{sim}_\mathsf{c}(\text{CRS}_\mathsf{c}, \mathsf{trap}_\mathsf{c}, \langle R_1, S_1, \mathbf{b}_\mathsf{s}^{\mathsf{phash}}, T_1, i_1\rangle).$$

and outputs this W_1 along with pwd, and HK_1 as internal state of P_i. Note that this computation of W_1 is identical to the computation of W_1 in the computation of sk_1 (which is really output to $\mathcal{Z}$ only when $\mathsf{pwd}' = \mathsf{pwd}$).

Without loss of generality, we can assume that in the real-world if the Adversary (or Environment $\mathcal{Z}$) corrupts an instance before the session key is output then the instance does not output any session key. This is so because the Adversary (or $\mathcal{Z}$) either sets the key for that session or can compute it from the internal state it broke into.

Server Corruption. On receiving a Corrupt call from $\mathcal{Z}$ for server instance P_j in session ssid, the simulator $\mathcal{S}$ first performs the steps in the section on Stealing Password File above. In particular this sets the value of phash. It then calls the Corrupt routine of $\mathcal{F}_{\mathsf{apwKE}}$. If $\mathcal{S}$ had already output a message to $\mathcal{Z}$, and not output sk_1 it computes

$$W_2 = \mathsf{sim}_\mathsf{s}(\text{CRS}_\mathsf{s}, \mathsf{trap}_\mathsf{s}, \langle R_2, S_2/\mathbf{b}_\mathsf{s}^{\mathsf{phash}}, T_2, i_2\rangle).$$

and outputs this W_2 along with HK_2 as internal state of P_j. Note that pwd is not given out.

Complexity of the Simulator. Observe that on stealing the password file, the function OfflineTestPwd is only called once for each random oracle input, which was not already tested by calling TestPwd. Hence the number of unique password arguments passed to TestPwd and OfflineTestPwd of $\mathcal{F}_{\mathsf{apwKE}}$ combined in the ideal world is at most the number of random oracle calls in the hybrid model.

Time complexity-wise, most of the simulator steps are $\log q$-time, where q is the security parameter. Due to Step 4 of the simulator code, where for each of the m sessions, in the worst case, it might go through all the n random oracle calls, there is an additive component of $m * n * \log q$ time. So the simulator runs in $O(mn \log q)$-time.

5.7 Proof of Indistinguishability

We now describe a series of experiments between a probabilistic polynomial time challenger $\mathcal{C}$ and the environment $\mathcal{Z}$, starting with Expt_0 which we describe next. We will show that the view of $\mathcal{Z}$ in Expt_0 is same as its view in UC-APAKE ideal-world setting with $\mathcal{Z}$ interacting with $\mathcal{F}_{\mathsf{apwKE}}$ and the UC-APAKE simulator $\mathcal{S}$ described above in Sect. 5.6. We end with an experiment which is identical to the real world execution of the protocol in Fig. 3. We prove that environment has negligible advantage in distinguishing between these series of experiments, leading to a proof of realization of $\mathcal{F}_{\mathsf{apwKE}}$ by the protocol Π. Due to space limitations, in this version we only describe Expt_0, and rest of the experiments and related proofs of indistinguishability can be found in the full version [JR16].

Here is the complete code in Expt_0 (stated as it's overall experiment with $\mathcal{Z}$):

1. Responding to a random oracle query on input m: If there is a record of the form (m, r), then just return r. Otherwise, generate $r \leftarrow \mathbb{Z}_q$, record (m, r) and return r.
2. The challenger $\mathcal{C}$ picks the CRS just as in the real world, except the QA-NIZK CRS-es are generated using the crs-simulators, which also generate simulator trapdoors $\mathsf{trap_c}, \mathsf{trap_s}$. It retains $a_1, a_2, \mathsf{trap_c}, \mathsf{trap_s}, \mathsf{hk_c}, \mathsf{hk_s}$ as trapdoors.
   Next, (on StorePwdFile) the challenger calls the random oracle with query $(sid, P_i, P_j, \mathsf{pwd})$. It sets phash equal to the random oracle response and sets the server persistent state as $\mathbf{b}_{\mathsf{s}}^{\mathsf{phash}}$.
   Define PHASHISSET to be true after either StealPwdFile has been called or the random oracle has been called with $(sid, P_i, P_j, \mathsf{pwd})$ by the adversary, and false before.
   Define PWDCALLED to be true after the random oracle has been called with $(sid, P_i, P_j, \mathsf{pwd})$ by the adversary, and false before.
3. On receiving (CltSession, sid, ssid, P_i, P_j) from $\mathcal{Z}$, $\mathcal{C}$ generates $(\mathrm{HK}_1, \mathrm{HP}_1) \leftarrow \mathsf{ver_s.hkgen}(\mathrm{CRS_s})$. Next, $\mathcal{C}$ chooses r_1, r_1', r_1'' at random, and sets $R_1 = \mathbf{g}^{r_1}$, $S_1 = \mathbf{g}^{r_1'}$ and $T_1 = \mathbf{g}^{r_1''}$. It then hands $(R_1, S_1, T_1, \mathrm{HP}_1)$ to $\mathcal{Z}$ on behalf of this instance.
4. On receiving $(R_2', S_2', T_2', \mathrm{HP}_2')$ from $\mathcal{Z}$, intended for client session (P_i, ssid) (and assuming no corruption of this instance):
   (a) If the received elements are either not in their respective groups, or are trivially 1, output $\mathrm{sk}_1 \leftarrow \mathbb{G}_T$.
   (b) If the message received is identical to message sent by $\mathcal{C}$ in the same session (i.e. same ssid) on behalf of the peer, then output $\mathrm{sk}_1 \leftarrow \mathbb{G}_T$

(unless the simulation of peer also received a legitimate message and its key has already been set, in which case the same key is used to output sk_1 here).

(c) If *PhashIsSet* is false, then output $\mathrm{sk}_1 \leftarrow \mathbb{G}_T$.

(d) Compute: $i'_2 = \mathcal{H}(sid, \mathsf{ssid}, P_j, P_i, R'_2, S'_2, \mathrm{HP}'_2)$. If $S'_2 = R'^{a_2}_2 \mathbf{b}^{\mathsf{phash}}_{\mathsf{s}}$ and $T'_2 = \mathsf{sphf_s.privH}(\mathsf{hk_s}, \langle R'_2, S'_2/\mathbf{b}^{\mathsf{phash}}_{\mathsf{s}} \rangle, i'_2)$, compute:

$$W_1 = \mathsf{sim_c}(\mathrm{CRS_c}, \mathsf{trap_c}, \langle R_1, S_1, \mathbf{b}^{\mathsf{phash}}_{\mathsf{s}}, T_1, i_1 \rangle).$$

Output:

$$\mathrm{sk}_1 = \mathsf{ver_s.privH}(\mathrm{HK}_1, \langle R'_2, S'_2/\mathbf{b}^{\mathsf{phash}}_{\mathsf{s}}, T'_2, i'_2 \rangle) \cdot \mathsf{ver_c.pubH}(\mathrm{HP}'_2, W_1)$$

(e) If the above check failed then output $\mathrm{sk}_1 \leftarrow \mathbb{G}_T$.

5. On a Corrupt call for client P_i, output pwd. If Step 3 has already happened then also output HK_1 and $W_1 = \mathsf{sim_c}(\mathrm{CRS_c}, \mathsf{trap_c}, \langle R_1, S_1, \mathbf{b}^{\mathsf{phash}}_{\mathsf{s}}, T_1, i_1 \rangle)$.
6. On receiving (SrvSession, *sid*, ssid, P_j, P_i) from $\mathcal{Z}$, follow steps symmetric to Step 4, swapping subscripts and languages accordingly and replacing the condition *PhashIsSet* by *PwdCalled* in Step 4c. Also, in step 4d, the condition becomes: if $S'_1 = R'^{a_1}_1 \mathbf{b}^{\mathsf{phash}}_{\mathsf{c}}$ and $T'_1 = \mathsf{sphf_c.privH}(\mathsf{hk_c}, \langle R'_1, S'_1, \mathbf{b}^{\mathsf{phash}}_{\mathsf{s}} \rangle, i'_1)$,
7. On a Corrupt call for server P_j, if Step 3 has already happened then output HK_2, and $W_2 = \mathsf{sim_s}(\mathrm{CRS_s}, \mathsf{trap_s}, \langle R_2, S_2/\mathbf{b}^{\mathsf{phash}}_{\mathsf{s}}, T_2, i_2 \rangle)$. Finally, execute a StealPwdFile call, as described below.
8. On a StealPwdFile call, return $\mathbf{b}^{\mathsf{phash}}_{\mathsf{s}}$ as the Server Persistent State to the adversary.

All outputs of sk_1 are also accompanied with *sid*, ssid (but are not mentioned above for ease of exposition).

Note that each instance has two asynchronous phases: a phase in which $\mathcal{C}$ outputs $R_1, S_1, ...$ to $\mathcal{Z}$, and a phase where it receives a message from $\mathcal{Z}$. However, $\mathcal{C}$ cannot output sk_1 until it has completed both phases. These orderings are dictated by $\mathcal{Z}$. We will consider two different kinds of temporal orderings. A temporal ordering of different instances based on the order in which $\mathcal{C}$ outputs sk_1 in an instance will be called **temporal ordering by key output**. A temporal ordering of different instances based on the order in which $\mathcal{C}$ outputs its first message (i.e. $R_1, S_1, ...$) will be called **temporal ordering by message output**. It is easy to see that $\mathcal{C}$ can dynamically compute both these orderings by maintaining a counter (for each ordering).

We now claim that the view of $\mathcal{Z}$ in Expt_0 is statistically indistinguishable from its view in its combined interaction with $\mathcal{F}_{\mathsf{apwKE}}$ and $\mathcal{S}$. The CRS is set identically by both $\mathcal{C}$ and $\mathcal{S}$. While $\mathcal{C}$ has access to pwd from the outset and sets up the random oracle output phash corresponding to $(sid, P_i, P_j, \mathsf{ssid})$ at the beginning, $\mathcal{S}$ doesn't have access to pwd at the beginning and hence defers this step till the point where either (1) a correct online guess has been made, (2) the password file was stolen and a correct offline guess was made, (3) the client was corrupted. In all these three cases the simulator gets to know pwd and has the chance to set phash. At the point when password file is stolen, the correct pwd may not have been guessed, but phash has to be set in order to output the server persistent state. In that case $\mathcal{S}$ generates a random phash, remembers it and assigns it to the correct input when the actual password is queried. At all points, although their algorithms differ, we can see that $\mathcal{C}$ and $\mathcal{S}$ respond to random oracle queries identically.

Both $\mathcal{C}$ and $\mathcal{S}$ generate the client and server flows identically. In particular, observe that the condition PHASHISSET exactly captures the state of $\mathcal{S}$ for a client session where it knows phash and can compute the relevant elements and keys. $\mathcal{C}$ uses the condition PHASHISSET to do the same computations. Similarly for the server sessions with the condition PWDCALLED. The stronger condition for the server reflects the absence of the "Client Only Step" in the server sessions simulation. In the steps where a party receives a message from the adversary, both $\mathcal{C}$ and $\mathcal{S}$ end up computing keys identically. While $\mathcal{C}$ directly checks by exponentiation with phash in the case that pwd was guessed correctly, $\mathcal{S}$ goes through the list of random oracle calls to see which response was used for exponentiation as it may not know pwd or phash at this point.

Due to space limitations, the rest of the experiments and related proofs of indistinguishability are relegated to the full version [JR16].

References

[BBC+13] Benhamouda, F., Blazy, O., Chevalier, C., Pointcheval, D., Vergnaud, D.: New techniques for SPHFs and efficient one-round PAKE protocols. In: Canetti, R., Garay, J.A. (eds.) CRYPTO 2013. LNCS, vol. 8042, pp. 449–475. Springer, Heidelberg (2013). https://doi.org/10.1007/978-3-642-40041-4_25

[BBS04] Boneh, D., Boyen, X., Shacham, H.: Short group signatures. In: Franklin, M. (ed.) CRYPTO 2004. LNCS, vol. 3152, pp. 41–55. Springer, Heidelberg (2004). https://doi.org/10.1007/978-3-540-28628-8_3

[BC16a] Blazy, O., Chevalier, C.: Structure-preserving smooth projective hashing. In: Cheon, J.H., Takagi, T. (eds.) ASIACRYPT 2016. LNCS, vol. 10032, pp. 339–369. Springer, Heidelberg (2016). https://doi.org/10.1007/978-3-662-53890-6_12

[BFM88] Blum, M., Feldman, P., Micali, S.: Non-interactive zero-knowledge and its applications (extended abstract). In: 20th ACM STOC, pp. 103–112. ACM Press, May 1988

[BM92] Bellovin, S.M., Merritt, M.: Encrypted key exchange: password-based protocols secure against dictionary attacks. In: 1992 IEEE Symposium on Security and Privacy, pp. 72–84. IEEE Computer Society Press, May 1992

[BM93] Bellovin, S.M., Merritt, M.: Augmented encrypted key exchange: a password-based protocol secure against dictionary attacks and password file compromise. In: Ashby, V. (ed.) ACM CCS 93, pp. 244–250. ACM Press, November 1993

[BMP00] Boyko, V., MacKenzie, P., Patel, S.: Provably secure password-authenticated key exchange using diffie-hellman. In: Preneel, B. (ed.) EUROCRYPT 2000. LNCS, vol. 1807, pp. 156–171. Springer, Heidelberg (2000). https://doi.org/10.1007/3-540-45539-6_12

[Boy09] Boyen, X.: HPAKE: password authentication secure against cross-site user impersonation. In: Garay, J.A., Miyaji, A., Otsuka, A. (eds.) CANS 09. LNCS, vol. 5888, pp. 279–298. Springer, Heidelberg (2009). https://doi.org/10.1007/978-3-642-10433-6_19

[BP13] Benhamouda, F., Pointcheval, D.: Verifier-based password-authenticated key exchange: new models and constructions. Cryptology ePrint Archive, Report 2013/833 (2013). http://eprint.iacr.org/2013/833

[BPR00] Bellare, M., Pointcheval, D., Rogaway, P.: Authenticated key exchange secure against dictionary attacks. In: Preneel, B. (ed.) EUROCRYPT 2000. LNCS, vol. 1807, pp. 139–155. Springer, Heidelberg (2000). https://doi.org/10.1007/3-540-45539-6_11

[BR93] Bellare, M., Rogaway, P.: Random oracles are practical: a paradigm for designing efficient protocols. In: Ashby, V. (ed.) ACM CCS 93, pp. 62–73. ACM Press, November 1993

[Can01] Canetti, R.: Universally composable security: a new paradigm for cryptographic protocols. In: 42nd FOCS, pp. 136–145. IEEE Computer Society Press, October 2001

[CHK+05] Canetti, R., Halevi, S., Katz, J., Lindell, Y., MacKenzie, P.: Universally composable password-based key exchange. In: Cramer, R. (ed.) EUROCRYPT 2005. LNCS, vol. 3494, pp. 404–421. Springer, Heidelberg (2005). https://doi.org/10.1007/11426639_24

[CR03] Canetti, R., Rabin, T.: Universal composition with joint state. In: Boneh, D. (ed.) CRYPTO 2003. LNCS, vol. 2729, pp. 265–281. Springer, Heidelberg (2003). https://doi.org/10.1007/978-3-540-45146-4_16

[CS02] Cramer, R., Shoup, V.: Universal hash proofs and a paradigm for adaptive chosen ciphertext secure public-key encryption. In: Knudsen, L.R. (ed.) EUROCRYPT 2002. LNCS, vol. 2332, pp. 45–64. Springer, Heidelberg (2002). https://doi.org/10.1007/3-540-46035-7_4

[EHK+13] Escala, A., Herold, G., Kiltz, E., Ràfols, C., Villar, J.: An algebraic framework for diffie-hellman assumptions. In: Canetti, R., Garay, J.A. (eds.) CRYPTO 2013. LNCS, vol. 8043, pp. 129–147. Springer, Heidelberg (2013). https://doi.org/10.1007/978-3-642-40084-1_8

[FLR+10] Fischlin, M., Lehmann, A., Ristenpart, T., Shrimpton, T., Stam, M., Tessaro, S.: Random oracles with(out) programmability. In: Abe, M. (ed.) ASIACRYPT 2010. LNCS, vol. 6477, pp. 303–320. Springer, Heidelberg (2010). https://doi.org/10.1007/978-3-642-17373-8_18

[GMR06] Gentry, C., MacKenzie, P., Ramzan, Z.: A method for making password-based key exchange resilient to server compromise. In: Dwork, C. (ed.) CRYPTO 2006. LNCS, vol. 4117, pp. 142–159. Springer, Heidelberg (2006). https://doi.org/10.1007/11818175_9

[GS12] Groth, J., Sahai, A.: Efficient non-interactive proof systems for bilinear groups. SIAM J. Comput. **41**(5), 1193–1232 (2012)

[HK98] Halevi, S., Krawczyk, H.: Public-key cryptography and password protocols. In: ACM CCS 98, pp. 122–131. ACM Press, November 1998

[JG04] Jiang, S., Gong, G.: Password Based key exchange with mutual authentication. In: Handschuh, H., Hasan, M.A. (eds.) SAC 2004. LNCS, vol. 3357, pp. 267–279. Springer, Heidelberg (2004). https://doi.org/10.1007/978-3-540-30564-4_19

[JKX18] Jarecki, S., Krawczyk, H., Xu, J.: OPAQUE: an asymmetric pake protocol secure against pre-computation attacks. In: Nielsen, J.B., Rijmen, V. (eds.) EUROCRYPT 2018. LNCS, vol. 10822, pp. 456–486. Springer, Cham (2018). https://doi.org/10.1007/978-3-319-78372-7_15

[JR12] Jutla, C., Roy, A.: Relatively-sound NIZKs and password-based key-exchange. In: Fischlin, M., Buchmann, J., Manulis, M. (eds.) PKC 2012. LNCS, vol. 7293, pp. 485–503. Springer, Heidelberg (2012). https://doi.org/10.1007/978-3-642-30057-8_29

[JR13] Jutla, C.S., Roy, A.: Shorter quasi-adaptive NIZK proofs for linear subspaces. In: Sako, K., Sarkar, P. (eds.) ASIACRYPT 2013. LNCS, vol. 8269, pp. 1–20. Springer, Heidelberg (2013). https://doi.org/10.1007/978-3-642-42033-7_1

[JR14] Jutla, C.S., Roy, A.: Switching lemma for bilinear tests and constant-size NIZK proofs for linear subspaces. In: Garay, J.A., Gennaro, R. (eds.) CRYPTO 2014. LNCS, vol. 8617, pp. 295–312. Springer, Heidelberg (2014). https://doi.org/10.1007/978-3-662-44381-1_17

[JR15] Jutla, C.S., Roy, A.: Dual-system simulation-soundness with applications to UC-PAKE and more. In: Iwata, T., Cheon, J.H. (eds.) ASIACRYPT 2015. LNCS, vol. 9452, pp. 630–655. Springer, Heidelberg (2015). https://doi.org/10.1007/978-3-662-48797-6_26

[JR16] Jutla, C., Roy, A.: Smooth NIZK arguments with applications to asymmetric UC-PAKE. Cryptology ePrint Archive, Report 2016/233 (2016). http://eprint.iacr.org/2016/233

[KV11] Katz, J., Vaikuntanathan, V.: Round-optimal password-based authenticated key exchange. In: Ishai, Y. (ed.) TCC 2011. LNCS, vol. 6597, pp. 293–310. Springer, Heidelberg (2011). https://doi.org/10.1007/978-3-642-19571-6_18

[KW15] Kiltz, E., Wee, H.: Quasi-adaptive NIZK for linear subspaces revisited. In: Oswald, E., Fischlin, M. (eds.) EUROCRYPT 2015. LNCS, vol. 9057, pp. 101–128. Springer, Heidelberg (2015). https://doi.org/10.1007/978-3-662-46803-6_4

[LPJY14] Libert, B., Peters, T., Joye, M., Yung, M.: Non-malleability from malleability: simulation-sound quasi-adaptive NIZK proofs and CCA2-secure encryption from homomorphic signatures. In: Nguyen, P.Q., Oswald, E. (eds.) EUROCRYPT 2014. LNCS, vol. 8441, pp. 514–532. Springer, Heidelberg (2014). https://doi.org/10.1007/978-3-642-55220-5_29

[Mac01] MacKenzie, P.: More efficient password-authenticated key exchange. In: Naccache, D. (ed.) CT-RSA 2001. LNCS, vol. 2020, pp. 361–377. Springer, Heidelberg (2001). https://doi.org/10.1007/3-540-45353-9_27

[Wat09] Waters, B.: Dual system encryption: realizing fully secure IBE and HIBE under simple assumptions. In: Halevi, S. (ed.) CRYPTO 2009. LNCS, vol. 5677, pp. 619–636. Springer, Heidelberg (2009). https://doi.org/10.1007/978-3-642-03356-8_36

Round-Optimal Fully Black-Box Zero-Knowledge Arguments from One-Way Permutations

Carmit Hazay[1] and Muthuramakrishnan Venkitasubramaniam[2(✉)]

[1] Bar-Ilan University, Ramat Gan, Israel
carmit.hazay@biu.ac.il

[2] University of Rochester, Rochester, USA
muthuv@cs.rochester.edu

Abstract. In this paper, we revisit the round complexity of designing zero-knowledge (ZK) arguments via a black-box construction from minimal assumptions. Our main result implements a 4-round ZK argument for any language in NP, based on injective one-way functions, that makes black-box use of the underlying function. As a corollary, we also obtain the first 4-round perfect zero-knowledge argument for NP based on claw-free permutations via a black-box construction and 4-round input-delayed commit-and-prove zero-knowledge argument based on injective one-way functions.

Keywords: One-way permutations · Zero-knowledge arguments
Black-box constructions

1 Introduction

Zero-knowledge (ZK) interactive proofs [GMR89] are paradoxical constructs that allow one player (called the prover) to convince another player (called the verifier) of the validity of a mathematical statement $x \in L$, while providing zero additional knowledge to the verifier. This is formalized by requiring that the view of every "efficient" adversary verifier $\mathcal{V}^*$ interacting with the honest prover $\mathcal{P}$ be simulated by an "efficient" machine $\mathcal{S}$ (a.k.a. the simulator). The idea behind this definition is that whatever $\mathcal{V}^*$ might have learned from interacting with $\mathcal{P}$, it could have actually learned by itself (by running the simulator $\mathcal{S}$). As "efficient" adversaries are typically modelled as probabilistic polynomial-time machines (PPT), the traditional definition of ZK models both the verifier and the simulator as PPT machines.

Several variants of ZK systems have been studied in literature. In this work, we are interested in computational ZK argument systems with black-box simulation, where the soundness is required to hold only against non-uniform PPT provers whereas the zero-knowledge property holds against PPT verifiers which get an auxiliary input. Such systems are referred to as computational zero-knowledge argument systems. We will further focus on the case of black-box

A. Beimel and S. Dziembowski (Eds.): TCC 2018, LNCS 11239, pp. 263–285, 2018.
https://doi.org/10.1007/978-3-030-03807-6_10

constructions[1] and black-box simulation.[2] The main question we address is the the round-complexity of computational zero-knowledge argument systems based on minimal assumptions via a fully black-box construction. First, we survey prior work in this area.

Goldreich et al. [GMW91] constructed the first zero-knowledge proof systems for all of NP based on the minimal assumption of one-way functions, where they required polynomially many rounds to achieve negligible soundness. For arguments, Feige and Shamir [FS89] provided a 4-round zero-knowledge system based on algebraic assumptions. In [BJY97], Bellare, Jackobson and Yung showed how to achieve the same assuming only one-way functions.

On the negative side, Goldreich and Oren [GO94] demonstrated that three rounds are necessary for designing zero-knowledge for any non-trivial language (i.e. outside BPP) against non-uniform verifiers. When further restricting to black-box simulation, Goldreich and Krawcyzk [GK96b] showed that four rounds are necessary for achieving zero-knowledge of non-trivial languages. For the specific case of proofs (i.e. unconditional soundness), Katz [Kat12] showed that only languages in MA can have 4-round zero-knowledge proof systems.

As such, the works of [BJY97] and [GK96b] identify the round-complexity of zero-knowledge arguments as four when restricting to black-box simulation. However, when considering constructions that are black-box in the underlying primitives, Pass and Wee [PW09] provided the first black-box construction of a 6-round zero-knowledge argument for NP based on one-way permutations[3] and seven rounds based on one-way functions. Ishai, Mahmoody and Sahai provided the first black-box sublinear zero-knowledge arguments based on collision-resistant hash-functions [IMS12]. Ostrovsky, Richelson and Scafuro [ORS15] showed how to construct black-box two-party secure computation protocols in four rounds where only one party receives the output from enhanced trapdoor permutations. As zero-knowledge can be seen as an instance of such a secure computation, their work provides a round-optimal black-box construction based on enhanced trapdoor permutations.

This sequence of prior works leaves the following fundamental question regarding black-box constructions of zero-knowledge arguments open:

What is the weakest hardness assumption for a black-box construction of a 4-round zero-knowledge argument system for all of NP?

We remark that when considering non-black-box simulation, a recent work due to Bitansky et al. [BKP18] demonstrates how to obtain 3-round zero-knowledge arguments for NP based on multi-collision resistance hash functions. On the negative side, Fleischhacker et al. [FGJ18] proved that 3-round private-coin ZK proofs for NP do not exist, even with respect to non-black-box simulation assuming the existence of certain program obfuscation primitives.

[1] Where the construction is agnostic of the specific implementation and relies only on its input/output behavior.

[2] Where the simulator is only allowed to make black-box use of the verifier's code.

[3] Where injective one-way functions are sufficient.

Our Results. In this work we present the first 4-round ZK argument of knowledge protocols based on one-way permutations (injective one-way functions) and claw-free permutations. Specifically,

Theorem 1.1 (Informal). *Assuming injective one-way functions, there exists a fully black-box 4-round black-box computational zero-knowledge argument for all of* NP.

As a corollary we obtain the following result regarding perfect zero-knowledge argument systems.

Corollary 1.2 (Informal). *Assuming claw-free permutations, there exists a fully black-box 4-round black-box perfect zero-knowledge argument for all of* NP.

Commit-and-Prove Input-Delayed ZK Proofs. In [LS90], Lapidot and Shamir provided a three-round witness-indistinguishable (WI) proof for Graph Hamiltonicity with a special "input-delayed" property: namely, the prover uses the statement to be proved only in the last round. Recently, in [CPS+15] it was shown how to obtain efficient input-delayed variants of the related "Sigma protocols" when used in a restricted setting of an OR-composition. In [HV16], starting from a randomized encoding scheme with an additional robustness property and security against adaptive inputs, it was shown how to obtain general constructions of input-delayed zero-knowledge proofs that yield an efficient version of the protocol of [LS90] for arbitrary NP-relations.

The "commit-and-prove" paradigm considers a prover that first commits to a witness w and then, in a second phase upon receiving a statement x asserts whether a particular relation $R(x, w) = 1$ without revealing the committed value. This paradigm, which is implicit in the work of [GMW87] and later formalized in [CLOS02], is a powerful mechanism to strengthen semi-honest secure protocols to maliciously secure ones. The MPC-in-the-head approach of [IKOS09] shows how to obtain a commit-and-prove protocol based on one-way functions that relies on the underlying primitives in a black-box way. In [HV16] it was further shown how to extend the above input-delayed ZK proof to further support the commit-and-prove paradigm which is additionally black-box in the underlying one-way functions or permutations.

Instantiating the 3-round honest verifier zero-knowledge proof required in Theorem 1.1 with the commit-and-proof and input-delayed protocol from [HV16] implies the following corollary.

Corollary 1.3 (Informal). *Assuming injective one-way functions, there exists a fully black-box 4-round black-box commit-and-prove input-delayed zero-knowledge argument for all of* NP.

We prove the main theorem in Sect. 3 and the corollaries in Sect. 4.

1.1 Our Techniques

We begin with an overview of our 4-round ZK argument that is obtained by compiling 3-round (i.e. sigma) protocols of some special form. Consider a sigma protocol where the prover simply relies on commitments to generate its first round message and decommits to some subset of the commitments depending on the challenge provided by the verifier. Following [PW09], we require a special soundness guarantee in the protocol, where there exists at most one "easy challenge" that allows the prover to cheat for false instances. Furthermore, this easy challenge can be efficiently reconstructed from the set of messages committed to by the prover. An example of a sigma protocol with these properties, is the Blum Hamiltonicity zero-knowledge protocol [Blu]. Here, the prover commits to the adjacency matrix of a permutation of the underlying graph in the first round, and either decommits all entries in the matrix along with the permutation or decommits just the entries that form a Hamiltonian cycle depending on the verifier's challenge. Given the prover's commitments, the easy challenge can be extracted by observing whether the prover commits to the adjacency matrix of the permutation of original graph or just the entries of a Hamiltonian cycle.

This 3-round protocol already yields a zero-knowledge argument system, but only with constant soundness. To amplify soundness, one can have the entire protocol repeated in parallel, and have the verifier commit to all the parallel challenges in a first round of the protocol while decommitting in the third round. This 4-round protocol will indeed be zero-knowledge. However, one cannot prove that it is negligibly sound. Specifically, there could be a malleability attack, where, the prover upon receiving the verifier's commitment in the first round, can maul it to another commitment that can be open to a valid accepting response depending on the decommitment provided by the verifier in the third round. Another way of looking at this is that, one cannot have a black-box reduction of a cheating prover to the hiding property of the commitment used by the verifier in the first round to commit to the challenge. A standard way to circumvent this issue would be to require the verifier to use a perfectly hiding commitment and the prover a statistically binding commitment. However, this will result in a 5-round protocol (as perfectly hiding commitments require two rounds), and stronger assumptions, such as collision resistant hash functions.

The approach taken by Pass and Wee is to have the prover and verifier commit using a computationally hiding commitment scheme (that can be based on injective one-way functions) but additionally require the prover to prove "knowledge" of the messages in its commitment before the verifier decommits its challenge. This can be done generically using an extractable commitment scheme (introduced in the same work) which is a commitment scheme that has a "proof-of-knowledge" property. Before we go into the details of this construction, we point out that an extractable commitment scheme can be constructed from injective one-way function in three rounds which results in an overall zero-knowledge argument system with six rounds.

To collapse this protocol into four rounds we follow a *cut-and-choose* paradigm. Namely, our protocol will comprise of n parallel instances of the basic

4-round protocol. In the third round, the verifier chooses a random $S \subseteq [n]$ of some size t and decommits to the challenges made in those indices while providing a challenge for the extractable commitment for repetitions outside S. Then in the fourth round, the prover will complete the zero-knowledge protocol for the parallel repetitions with indexes in S and respond to the proof-of-knowledge challenge for the extractable commitment for the remaining indexes. The high-level idea here is that this allows to regain soundness in a simple way. Since the prover does not know the subset S revealed by the verifier in the third round, the prover has to "cheat" in most of the parallel invocations. This means we can argue by a simple averaging argument that there is an index $i \in [n]$ such that the probability that the prover cheats in the ith repetition, i is not included in S and the prover convinces the verifier of a false statement is non-negligible. This means that we can now use the prover to violate the hiding of the commitment made by the verifier for the ith repetition by running the proof-of-knowledge extractor on the prover's commitment in the ith repetition and extracting the easy challenge.

However, proving zero-knowledge of this compilation is subtle and non-trivial. Recall that the verifier only reveals the challenges for a chosen subset S in the third round. A simple strategy for the simulator is to obtain the challenge, i.e. "trapdoor" for the indexes in S rewind and setup the prover messages in such a way that will allow for it to cheat in all repetitions in S. Now, the simulator can conclude with an accepting transcript if the verifier opens the same set S. However, the verifier can choose to reveal different subsets in different "rewindings". Nevertheless, in any rewinding, either the simulator has succeeded in cheating in all the indexes of the subset revealed by the verifier or has learned a new trapdoor. Now it suffices to show that the simulator will only require to perform a bounded number of rewindings before it has extracted most (if not all) trapdoors to complete the execution. A minor subtlety arises as a malicious verifier can abort before revealing the third message and this affects the number of rewindings that needs to be performed. However, this can be dealt with via a standard probability analysis. There is, however, a bigger issue in proving indistinguishability of this simulation. As described above, the simulator tries to extract trapdoors and outputs the "first" accepting transcript when it has managed to cheat in all indexes in the revealed subset. This simple idea however has a subtle flaw. The issue is that one can come up with a strategy for a malicious verifier where the distribution of the views output by the simulator is not indistinguishable from the real view. Roughly speaking, the distribution of the subset S in the transcript output by the simulator will be biased towards indexes revealed earlier in the rewindings. Our main technical contribution is to determine a "stopping" condition for the simulator that will result in the right distribution and we describe this below.

We abstract the simulation strategy to the following game. The game proceeds in iterations where in the ith iteration the adversary outputs a subset $S_i \subset [n]$ from some unknown but pre-determined distribution D. The goal is to determine the iteration j to stop the game and output S_j such that the following two conditions are met:

- First, $S_j \subseteq S_1 \cup \cdots \cup S_{j-1}$, and
- Second, if D' is the distribution of the subset S_j output, then $D' = D$. In other words, the distribution of the subset output when the game is stopped is identical to the original distribution D.

Our main technical contribution is to show that the following simple strategy achieves the required goal.

- In any iteration if $S_j \subseteq S_1 \cup \cdots \cup S_{j-1}$, then halt if $S_j \not\subseteq S_1 \cup \cdots \cup S_{j-2}$, and proceed to the next iteration otherwise.

We prove this formally in Sect. 3.

2 Preliminaries

Basic Notations. We denote the security parameter by n. We say that a function $\mu : \mathbb{N} \to \mathbb{N}$ is *negligible* if for every positive polynomial $p(\cdot)$ and all sufficiently large n it holds that $\mu(n) < \frac{1}{p(n)}$. We use the abbreviation PPT to denote probabilistic polynomial-time. We further denote by $a \leftarrow A$ the random sampling of a from a distribution A, and by $[n]$ the set of elements $\{1, \ldots, n\}$. For an NP relation $\mathcal{R}$, we denote by $\mathcal{R}_x$ the set of witnesses of x and by $\mathcal{L}_\mathcal{R}$ its associated language. That is, $\mathcal{R}_x = \{\omega \mid (x, \omega) \in \mathcal{R}\}$ and $\mathcal{L}_\mathcal{R} = \{x \mid \exists\, \omega \ s.t.\ (x, \omega) \in \mathcal{R}\}$. We specify next the definition of computationally indistinguishable.

Definition 2.1. *Let $X = \{X(a,n)\}_{a\in\{0,1\}^*, n\in\mathbb{N}}$ and $Y = \{Y(a,n)\}_{a\in\{0,1\}^*, n\in\mathbb{N}}$ be two distribution ensembles. We say that X and Y are* computationally indistinguishable, *denoted $X \stackrel{c}{\approx} Y$, if for every* PPT *machine $\mathcal{D}$, every $a \in \{0,1\}^*$, every positive polynomial $p(\cdot)$ and all sufficiently large n:*

$$\left|\Pr\left[\mathcal{D}(X(a,n), 1^n, a) = 1\right] - \Pr\left[\mathcal{D}(Y(a,n), 1^n, a) = 1\right]\right| < \frac{1}{p(n)}.$$

2.1 Commitment Schemes

Commitment schemes are used to enable a party, known as the *sender* Sen, to commit itself to a value while keeping it secret from the *receiver* Rec (this property is called *hiding*). Furthermore, in a later stage when the commitment is opened, it is guaranteed that the "opening" can yield only a single value determined in the committing phase (this property is called *binding*). In this work, we consider commitment schemes that are *statistically binding*, namely while the hiding property only holds against computationally bounded (non-uniform) adversaries, the binding property is required to hold against unbounded adversaries. Formally,

Definition 2.2 (Commitment schemes). *A* PPT *machine* $\mathsf{Com} = \langle S, R\rangle$ *is said to be a non-interactive commitment scheme if the following two properties hold.*

Computational hiding: *For every (expected)* PPT *machine* Rec^*, *it holds that the following ensembles are computationally indistinguishable.*
- $\{\mathbf{View}^{\text{Rec}^*}_{\mathsf{Com}}(m_1, z)\}_{\kappa\in N, m_1, m_2 \in \{0,1\}^\kappa, z\in\{0,1\}^*}$
- $\{\mathbf{View}^{\text{Rec}^*}_{\mathsf{Com}}(m_2, z)\}_{\kappa\in N, m_1, m_2 \in \{0,1\}^\kappa, z\in\{0,1\}^*}$

where $\mathbf{View}^{R^*}_{\mathsf{Com}}(m, z)$ *denotes the random variable describing the output of* Rec^* *after receiving a commitment to* m *using* Com.

Statistical binding: *For any (computationally unbounded) malicious sender* Sen^* *and auxiliary input* z, *it holds that the probability that there exist valid decommitments to two different values for a view* v, *generated with an honest receiver while interacting with* $\text{Sen}^*(z)$ *using* Com, *is negligible.*

We refer the reader to [Gol01] for more details. We recall that non-interactive perfectly binding commitment schemes can be constructed based on one-way permutation, whereas two-round statistically binding commitment schemes can be constructed based on one-way functions [Nao91]. To set up some notations, we let $\mathsf{com}_m \leftarrow \mathsf{Com}(m; r_m)$ denote a commitment to a message m, where the sender uses uniform random coins r_m. The decommitment phase consists of the sender sending the decommitment information $\mathsf{decom}_m = (m, r_m)$ which contains the message m together with the randomness r_m. This enables the receiver to verify whether decom_m is consistent with the transcript com_m. If so, it outputs m; otherwise it outputs $\perp$. For simplicity of exposition, in the sequel, we will assume that random coins are an implicit input to the commitment functions, unless specified explicitly.

2.2 Extractable Commitment Schemes

A core building block of our protocol is an extractable commitment scheme ExtCom introduced by Pass and Wee in [PW09].

Definition 2.3 (Extractable commitment schemes). *Let* $\mathsf{ExtCom} = (\text{Sen}, \text{Rec})$ *be a statistically binding commitment scheme. We say that* ExtCom *is an extractable commitment scheme if there exists an expected* PPT *oracle machine (the extractor)* E *that given oracle access to any* PPT *cheating sender* Sen^* *outputs a pair* (τ, m^*) *such that:*

Simulation: τ *is identically distributed to the view of* Sen^* *at the end of interacting with an honest receiver* Rec *in commit phase.*

Extraction: *The probability that* τ *is accepting and* $m^* = \perp$ *is negligible. We remark here that, we only need a weak extraction property where the extraction succeeds if the commitment is well formed. In other words, we allow for "over extraction" where the commitment could be invalid, yet, the extraction returns a value.*

Binding: *If $m^* \neq \perp$, then it is statistically impossible to open τ to any value other than m^*.*

In Fig. 1 we describe their 3-round extractable commitment scheme ExtCom that is based on one-way permutations. In order to commit to a bit m the sender splits m into two shares which are committed using a statistically binding commitment scheme Com. Next, the receiver sends a challenge bit e where the sender must open one of the two commitments that lie in the eth position. Later, in the decommit phase the sender opens the remaining commitments enabling the receiver to verify that all opening are valid and that all pairs correspond to the same bit m. Loosely speaking, hiding follows from hiding of the underlying commitment scheme Com. Whereas extractability follows from repetitively rewinding the sender obtaining two shares of a particular instance.

Extractable Commitment Scheme ExtCom **[PW09]**

The commitment scheme ExtCom uses a statistically binding commitment scheme Com and runs between sender Sen and receiver Rec.

Input: Sen holds a message $m \in \{0,1\}$.
Commit Phase:

Sen $\rightarrow$ Rec: Sen proceeds as follows:

1. Sen chooses $\eta_1, \ldots, \eta_\kappa \leftarrow \{0,1\}^\kappa$.
2. For all $i \in [\kappa]$, Sen commits to the following matrix:

$$\left(\mathsf{com}_{\eta_i}\ \mathsf{com}_{m\oplus\eta_i}\right) = \left(\mathsf{Com}(\eta_i)\ \mathsf{Com}(m\oplus\eta_i)\right).$$

Rec $\rightarrow$ Sen: Rec sends a challenge $e = e_1, \ldots, e_\kappa \leftarrow \{0,1\}^\kappa$ to Sen.

For all $i \in [\kappa]$, Sen sends the decommitment information $\mathsf{decom}_{(e_i\cdot m)\oplus\eta_i}$ for which the receiver checks the validity of openings.

Decommit Phase:

1. The sender sends m and opens the commitments to all κ pairs of strings.
2. The receiver checks that all the openings are valid, and also that all pairwise decommitments correspond to m.

Fig. 1. Extractable commitment scheme

2.3 Zero-Knowledge Arguments

We denote by $\langle A(\omega), B(z)\rangle(x)$ the random variable representing the (local) output of machine B when interacting with machine A on common input x, when the random-input to each machine is uniformly and independently chosen, and A (resp., B) has auxiliary input ω (resp., z).

Definition 2.4 (Interactive argument system). *A pair of* PPT *interactive machines* $(\mathcal{P}, \mathcal{V})$ *is called an* interactive proof system for a language $\mathcal{L}$ *if there exists a negligible function* negl *such that the following two conditions hold:*

1. COMPLETENESS: *For every* $x \in \mathcal{L}$ *there exists a string* ω *such that for every* $z \in \{0,1\}^*$,

$$\Pr[\langle \mathcal{P}(\omega), \mathcal{V}(z)\rangle(x) = 1] \geq 1 - \mathsf{negl}(|x|).$$

2. SOUNDNESS: *For every* $x \notin \mathcal{L}$, *every interactive* PPT *machine* $\mathcal{P}^*$, *and every* $\omega, z \in \{0,1\}^*$

$$\Pr[\langle \mathcal{P}^*(\omega), \mathcal{V}(z)\rangle(x) = 1] \leq \mathsf{negl}(|x|).$$

Definition 2.5 (Zero-knowledge). *Let* $(\mathcal{P}, \mathcal{V})$ *be an interactive proof system for some language* $\mathcal{L}$. *We say that* $(\mathcal{P}, \mathcal{V})$ *is* computational zero-knowledge with respect to an auxiliary input *if for every* PPT *interactive machine* $\mathcal{V}^*$ *there exists a* PPT *algorithm* $\mathcal{S}$, *running in time polynomial in the length of its first input, such that*

$$\{\langle \mathcal{P}(\omega), \mathcal{V}^*(z)\rangle(x)\}_{x\in\mathcal{L},\omega\in\mathcal{R}_x,z\in\{0,1\}^*} \stackrel{c}{\approx} \{\langle \mathcal{S}\rangle(x,z)\}_{x\in\mathcal{L},z\in\{0,1\}^*}$$

(when the distinguishing gap is considered as a function of $|x|$*). Specifically, the left term denote the output of* $\mathcal{V}^*$ *after it interacts with* $\mathcal{P}$ *on common input* x *whereas, the right term denote the output of* $\mathcal{S}$ *on* x.

If further the distributions are identically distributed, we refer to the proof system as perfect zero-knowledge.

Definition 2.6 (Σ-protocol). *A protocol* π *is a* Σ-protocol *for relation* $\mathcal{R}$ *if it is a 3-round public-coin protocol and the following requirements hold:*

- COMPLETENESS: *If* $\mathcal{P}$ *and* $\mathcal{V}$ *follow the protocol on input* x *and private input* ω *to* $\mathcal{P}$ *where* $\omega \in \mathcal{R}_x$, *then* $\mathcal{V}$ *always accepts.*
- SPECIAL SOUNDNESS: *There exists a polynomial-time algorithm* A *that given any* x *and any pair of accepting transcripts* $(a, e, t), (a, e', t')$ *on input* x, *where* $e \neq e'$, *outputs* ω *such that* $\omega \in \mathcal{R}_x$.
- SPECIAL HONEST-VERIFIER ZERO KNOWLEDGE: *There exists a* PPT *algorithm* $\mathcal{S}$ *such that*

$$\{\langle \mathcal{P}(\omega), \mathcal{V}(e)\rangle(x)\}_{x\in\mathcal{L}} \stackrel{c}{\approx} \{\mathcal{S}(x,e)\}_{x\in\mathcal{L}}$$

where $\mathcal{S}(x,e)$ *denotes the output of* $\mathcal{S}$ *upon input* x *and* e, *and* $\langle \mathcal{P}(\omega), \mathcal{V}(e)(x)\rangle$ *denotes the output transcript of an execution between* $\mathcal{P}$ *and* $\mathcal{V}$, *where* $\mathcal{P}$ *has input* (x, ω), $\mathcal{V}$ *has input* x, *and* $\mathcal{V}$*'s random tape (determining its query) equals* e.

2.4 Claw-Free Permutations

Definition 2.7 (Claw-free permutations). *A triple of algorithms, (I, D, F), is called a claw-free collection if the following conditions hold.*

- *Both I and D are probabilistic polynomial-time, whereas F is deterministic polynomial-time. We denote by $f_i^\sigma(x)$ the output of F on input (σ, i, x), and by D_i^σ the support of the random variable $D(\sigma, i)$.*
- *For every i in the range of algorithm I, the random variables $f_i^0(D(0,i))$ and $f_i^1(D(1,i))$ are identically distributed.*
- *For every probabilistic polynomial-time algorithm, A', every polynomial $p(\cdot)$, and all sufficiently large n's*

$$\Pr[f_{I_n}^0(X_n) = f_{I_n}^1(Y_n)] \leq 1/p(n)$$

where I_n is a random variable describing the output distribution of algorithm I on input 1^n, and (X_n, Y_n) is a random variable describing the output of algorithm A' on input (random variable) I_n.

A construction for perfectly hiding commitment scheme based on claw-free permutations can be found in [GK96a].

3 The Feasibility of 4-Round BB ZK Arguments from OWPs

In this section we will prove our main theorem, demonstrating the feasibility of black-box 4-round zero-knowledge argument of knowledge. More formally, we prove the following theorem.

Theorem 3.1. *Assuming one-way permutations, Protocol 1 is a 4-round fully black-box zero-knowledge argument for any* NP *language.*

Building Blocks. Our protocol will employ the following cryptographic primitives.

Non-interactive perfectly binding commitment scheme: Such commitment schemes can be based on one-way permutations. We denote this scheme by Com and employ it for the verifier in the first message of our protocol.

Extractable commitment scheme: We recall that an extractable commitment scheme is a commitment scheme that has in addition an extraction algorithm, such that given an adversarial sender Sen*, can extract the committed message or output $\perp$ if the commitment is invalid. A 3-round extractable commitment scheme can be constructed based on any non-interactive commitment scheme [PW09]. We denote this scheme by ExtCom; see Sect. 2.2 for more details. We employ that commitment scheme for the prover.

3-round public-coin honest-verifier zero-knowledge proof: A 3-round zero-knowledge proof with constant soundness for any language in NP, denoted by $\pi_{\text{ZK}} = (a, e, t)$, that can be constructed starting from a non-interactive commitment scheme Com and where the witness is only used to in computing the third message t. For instance, the Blum's Hamiltonicity protocol [Blu] or [IKOS07,HV16]. For concreteness, let us consider the former protocol, where given a public input graph G, proceeds as follows. In the first message, the prover commits to the elements of the adjacency matrix $\{\mathsf{com}_{a_{ij}}\}_{i,j\in[m]}$ of a random permutation of the input graph G. The verifier responds with a challenge bit e. If $e = 0$, then the prover decommits all entries of the matrix and gives the permutation, and the verifier accepts if the permutation maps the input graph to the revealed graph. If $e = 1$, then the prover only decommits to elements in the adjacency matrix that form a Hamiltonian cycle. The verifier accepts if the revealed entries form an Hamiltonian cycle.

Protocol's Description: Our protocol executes the honest verifier zero-knowledge proof π_{ZK} in parallel n times, where a t subset of these executions (that is picked by the verifier) are completed till end while the rest are used for completing the extractable commitment algorithm.

Protocol 1 (Black-box 4-round zero-knowledge argument)

- **Inputs:** *A public statement* $x \in \mathcal{L}$ *for both and a witness* $\omega \in \mathcal{R}_x$ *for the prover* $\mathcal{P}$.
- **The protocol:**
  1. $\mathcal{V} \to \mathcal{P}$: *The verifier picks* n *challenges for the parallel invocations of protocol* π_{ZK}*, say* $e_1, \ldots, e_n$*, and commits to them using algorithm* Com*. Denote this set of commitments by* $(\mathsf{com}_{e_1}, \ldots, \mathsf{com}_{e_n})$.
  2. $\mathcal{P} \to \mathcal{V}$: *The prover generates* n *first-messages* $(a_1, \ldots, a_n)$ *according to* π_{ZK}*. Here each* a_i *contains commitments to entries of an adjacency matrix* $\{\mathsf{extcom}_{a_i[r,c]}\}_{r,c\in[m]}$ *of an independently and randomly chosen permutation of the input graph G where the commitment is computed using* ExtCom *where* m *is the number of nodes in the graph.*
  3. $\mathcal{V} \to \mathcal{P}$: *The verifier chooses a random* t *subset* $T \subset \{1, \ldots, n\}$ *and sends* $\{\mathsf{decom}_{e_i}\}_{i\in T}$ *where* decom_{e_i} *is the decommitment of* com_{e_i}*. It also sends a challenge* $\mathsf{ch} \in ([n] - T)$ *for all the extractable commitments.*
  4. $\mathcal{P} \to \mathcal{V}$: *Condition on valid decommitments sent by the verifier, for every ZK iteration* $i \in T$*, the prover completes protocol* π_{ZK}*, answering challenge* e_i *with the message* t_i *and sends* $\{t_i, \mathsf{decom}_{a_i}\}_{i\in T}$*. For the remaining ZK iterations, the prover simply responds to the challenge* ch *according to the extractable commitment protocol* ExtCom*.*

     The verifier accepts if all decommitments are valid, if (a_i, e_i, t_i) *is a valid transcript for* π_{ZK} *for all* $i \in T$ *and if the extractbale commitments protocol has been concluded correctly for all remaining iterations* $i \notin T$.

Proof (**Theorem** 3.1). Completeness follows directly from the completeness of the underlying honest verifier zero knowledge protocol π_{ZK}. Below we prove soundness and zero-knowledge of our protocol.

Soundness. On a high-level, the special soundness of the underlying zero-knowledge protocol implies that, on a false statement, and a set of commitments provided by the prover in its first message, there is only one "easy challenge" for which the prover can complete the protocol and convince the verifier. Pass and Wee in [PW09] formalized the notion of "easy challenge" by requiring that the zero-knowledge protocol satisfies the property that there is an efficient procedure that given the input statement x and values in the commitments made by the prover in the second message $v_1, \ldots, v_k$, outputs a string e such that if an easy challenge exists then it must equal e, and if this challenge is revealed by the verifier the (malicious) prover can convince the verifier even on a false statement. For example, the Blum Hamiltonicity zero-knowledge protocol satisfies this requirement and the easy challenge can be extracted as follows. If the value committed to by the prover is a permutation π and the adjacency matrix A such that A represents the graph $\pi(G)$, then set the easy challenge to be 0 and otherwise 1. We argue soundness based on the following two steps.

1. We show that for a false statement an adversarial prover has to guess the challenge from the commitments made by the verifier before it is revealed in the third message for most of the n parallel instances. More precisely, the "easy challenge" extracted from the messages committed by the prover in most of the n iterations must match exactly the challenge committed to by the verifier.
2. There is an extraction procedure to extract the messages committed by the prover in one of these iterations without having to reveal the challenge committed to in the first message.

Combining these two ideas, we can reduce the soundness of the zero-knowledge to the hiding property of the commitments made by the verifier. We remark that our protocol and proof are different from those presented in [PW09] in that the verifier only reveals a subset of the challenges, where essentially the prover is only required to convince the verifier in the executions corresponding to this subset. In contrast, in the protocol presented in [PW09] the verifier opens all challenges. Specifically, as their protocol includes additional rounds between the prover's second message and when the verifier reveals the challenge in order to extract the prover's committed message, their analysis becomes easier. In our protocol, on the other hand, we will be able to extract the values in the commitments made by the prover only in the repetitions for which the challenge was not revealed by the verifier. We now proceed to the formal proof.

Assume for contradiction that there exists a PPT prover $\mathcal{P}^*$ and polynomial $p(\cdot)$ such that for infinitely many n's, there exists $x_n \notin \mathcal{L} \cap \{0,1\}^n$ such that the prover successfully convinces the verifier on the statement x_n with probability $\frac{1}{p(n)}$. Fix an arbitrary n for which this happens. We will construct an adversary $\mathcal{B}$ that uses $\mathcal{P}^*$ to break the hiding property of the non-interactive commitment scheme Com. More formally, $\mathcal{B}$ will internally incorporate the code of the prover $\mathcal{P}^*$ on input $(1^n, x_n)$ and feed it with messages according to the honest verifier. That is, on input $(1^n, x_n)$ and a commitment c from the external challenger, $\mathcal{B}$ proceeds as follows.

1. It will begin an internal emulation with $\mathcal{P}^*$. To simulate the first message from the verifier, it will choose a random index i to feed the challenge commitment c and the rest of them it will generate honestly internally.
2. Next, it will continue the execution to completion where it picks a random subset $S_1 \subseteq [n]$ conditioned on $i \notin S_1$. Let ch_1 be the challenge it feeds for the extractable commitment. If the prover aborts in the internal emulation then $\mathcal{B}$ aborts.
3. Otherwise, it will record the response to challenge e_i for the extractable commitment in repetition i. Next, it will rewind the prover to the third message, giving another set $S_2 \subseteq [n]$ subject to $i \notin S_2$ and an independent challenge ch_2 for the extractable commitment. If the prover aborts, $\mathcal{B}$ aborts as well. Otherwise, it will use the extractor for the underlying extractable commitment scheme on the commitment made for iteration i and the responses given for two challenges. We remark here that our extractor could "over extract". Namely, extract in case of an invalid commitment. To deal with this, we stipulate that if the extractor extracts a valid graph, the bit b is set to 1 and otherwise 0. If the extractor successfully extracts the committed messages, then $\mathcal{B}$ extracts the easy challenge b, outputs b and halts.

We next prove in the claim that $\mathcal{B}$ breaks the hiding property of the challenge commitment c with non-negligible probability.

Claim 3.1. *There exists polynomial $q(\cdot)$ such that,*

$$\Pr[b \leftarrow \{0,1\}^n : c \leftarrow \mathsf{Com}(1^n, b) : \mathcal{B}(1^n, x, c) = b] \geq \frac{1}{q(n)}.$$

Proof: Define the random variable Γ to be the set that contains the indexes where the prover commits to the adjacency matrix according to the easy challenge. We will further restrict Γ to be those indices where if $b = 1$ (meaning the prover commits to the graph), the index will be included only if the commitment is valid. This means that the prover can successfully convince the verifier only if $T \subseteq \Gamma$. Note that this set (even if not efficiently computable) is well-defined as we rely on statistically binding commitments. Our analysis relies on the following two cases:

Case $|\Gamma| \leq \frac{3n}{4}$: Here the probability that $T \subseteq \Gamma$ can be bounded by $\frac{\binom{3n/4}{t}}{\binom{n}{t}}$ which is negligible. We remark here that if $b = 1$ and the commitment is invalid, then the Prover can not convince the verifier in that index because all the commitments are decommitted in the fourth message. Based on the observation that T must be contained in γ, the prover successfully completes the protocol only with negligible probability.

Case $|\Gamma| > \frac{3n}{4}$: We begin by showing that there exists an index $i \in \Gamma$ such that $\mathcal{P}^*$ convinces $\mathcal{V}$ with non-negligible probability conditioned on $i \notin T$. Define p_i to be the probability that $\mathcal{P}^*$ successfully convinces the verifier conditioned on $i \notin T$ where recall that T is the set of challenges revealed by the verifier. By a union bound, we have that $\sum_{i \in \Gamma} p_i \geq \frac{1}{p(n)}$. Therefore, there exists i

such that $p_i \geq \frac{1}{|\Gamma|p(n)} \geq \frac{4}{3np(n)}$.
Now, we have that if $\mathcal{B}$ picks this index i and the prover completes the proof in both the executions performed by $\mathcal{B}$, then with overwhelming probability the extractor reveals the messages committed to by the prover. This in turn reveals the easy challenge for all indexes outside $S_1 \cup S_2$. In particular, it will obtain the easy challenge b_i which $\mathcal{B}$ outputs as its guess for the challenge commitment c. By definition of Γ we have that b_i is correct.
$\mathcal{B}$ succeeds if it picks this index i to feed the external challenge, convinces $\mathcal{V}^*$ in the two executions, the extractor succeeds. The right index is chosen with probability $\frac{1}{2^n}$. for the specific extractable commitment used in the construction (namely, the construction from [PW09]), the extractor succeeds except with negligible probability if the $\mathsf{ch}_1 \neq \mathsf{ch}_2$ which happens with probability at most $1 - 2^{-n}$. Furthermore, even if the extractor "over-extracts", if the extracted value is the valid graph, it cannot be the case that the prover can convince with $b = 0$ and we know that if $i \in \Gamma$ and $b = 1$ then the commitment is valid. Therefore the probability that $\mathcal{B}$ succeeds is at least $\frac{1}{n}p_i^2 - \frac{1}{2^n} - \nu(n) \geq \frac{1}{2n^3(p(n))^2}$. □

This concludes the proof of soundness.

Zero-Knowledge. We describe our black-box simulator and prove correctness of simulation.

Description of Simulator $\mathcal{S}$: More formally, let $\mathcal{V}^*$ be a malicious verifier. We define simulator $\mathcal{S}$ as follows:

1. $\mathcal{S}$ receives the first message $\mathcal{V}^*(x, z)$ from the malicious verifier.
2. $\mathcal{S}$ continues the execution by generating the second message according to the honest prover's algorithm. If the verifier aborts, the simulator outputs the transcript and halts.
3. Otherwise, $\mathcal{S}$ records the challenges that the verifier reveals; denote this t subset by T_1. Set $T_0 = \emptyset$.
4. Next, $\mathcal{S}$ repeatedly rewinds the verifier to the second message to extract some trapdoor information, namely, decommitments of the challenges committed by the verifier. It proceeds in iterations. In iteration ℓ, we assume that the $\mathcal{S}$ holds the sets $T_1, \ldots, T_\ell$ and at the end of the iteration either the simulator learns a new trapdoor (and adds a new set $T_{\ell+1}$) or halts outputting a transcript. More precisely, for $\ell = 1$ through $n - t + 1$,[4] the simulator proceeds as follows:
   (a) It generates the second prover's message $(a_1, \ldots, a_n)$ as follows:
      - For $i \notin T_1 \cup \cdots \cup T_\ell$, run the honest prover strategy to generate the second message a_i. In the particular Blum's Hamiltonian proof that we use, this amounts to simply generating commitments to the adjacency matrix of a random permutation of the original graph G.

[4] Note that this is the maximum number of iterations as at least one new element is added in each iteration and $|T_1| = t$.

- For $i \in T_1 \cup \cdots \cup T_\ell$, let e_i be the challenge revealed for index i. The simulator runs $\mathcal{S}_{\text{ZK}}(x, e_i)$ of the underlying honest-verifier zero-knowledge proof in order to generate the second and fourth messages (p_2^i, p_4^i) using the knowledge of the challenge e_i. It then sets $a_i = p_2^i$.

Let T' be the challenge set revealed by the verifier. The simulator repeats until one of the following cases occur:

Case 1. $T' \not\subseteq T_1 \cup \cdots \cup T_\ell$: This case implies that the verifier reveals a challenge of a new ZK repetition that the simulator did not record before. In this case, the simulator sets $T_{\ell+1} = T'$ and proceeds to the next iteration under ℓ (i.e. go to Step 4).

Case 2. $T' \subseteq T_1 \cup \cdots \cup T_\ell$: This case implies two subcases.

Case 2.1. $T' \subseteq T_1 \cup \cdots \cup T_{\ell-1}$: The simulator ignores this case and continues to rewind, i.e. go to step 4(a). We remark here that in this case, the simulator could complete the execution as it has simulated all the second messages according to the challenges corresponding to the set T'. Nevertheless, we deliberately make the simulator ignore this case so as to not skew the probability distributions of the simulator's output.

Case 2.2. $T' \not\subseteq T_1 \cup \cdots \cup T_{\ell-1}$**and** $T' \subseteq T_1 \cup \cdots \cup T_\ell$: This case considers the event where the revealed subset T' is not contained in the first $\ell - 1$ collected sets, but is contained in first ℓ sets. In this case, the simulator continues the simulation and generates the fourth message $(r_1, \ldots, r_n)$ for every $i \in [n]$ as follows:

- If $i \notin T'$, the simulator needs to respond to the challenge given for the extractable commitment scheme. In this case, the simulator simply responds to the challenge honestly.
- If $i \in T'$, then recall that the second message a_i was set to p_2^i, where (p_2^i, p_4^i) were generated using the honest verifier zero-knowledge simulator based on the challenge e_i (which is implied by the fact that $T' \subseteq T_1 \cup \cdots \cup T_\ell$). Therefore, if the revealed challenge for this repetition i is e_i, then the simulator sets the fourth message $r_i = p_4^i$. On the other hand, if the verifier reveals a different challenge for repetition i, then the simulator aborts. Note that the simulator will never abort because the challenges are committed using a perfectly binding commitment scheme Com.

The simulator then feeds this last message and outputs the view of the verifier.

Proof of Indistinguishability. Denote by $\mathbf{View}_{\mathcal{V}^*}(\mathcal{P}(x, \omega), \mathcal{V}^*(x, z))$ the view of the verifier $\mathcal{V}^*(z)$ when interacting with the honest prover on input ω and common input x. We prove the indistinguishability of real and simulated proofs by defining the following intermediate hybrid experiments.

Hybrid Hyb_0: In this experiment, we consider the view of the verifier when it interacts with the honest prover with witness ω.

Hybrid Hyb_1: In this experiment, we define a simulator $\mathcal{S}_1$ that proceeds with the rewinding strategy as simulator $\mathcal{S}$ does, with the exception that the prover's messages are generated according to the honest prover's strategy. Define $\mathcal{S}_1(x, \omega, z)$ to be the output of the simulator $\mathcal{S}_1$ in this hybrid. We next prove indistinguishability and analyze the running time of $\mathcal{S}_1$ in the following claims.

Claim 3.2. *The following distributions are identical.*

- $\mathcal{D}_0 = \{\mathbf{View}_{\mathcal{V}^*}(\mathcal{P}(x, \omega), \mathcal{V}^*(x, z))\}_{x \in \mathcal{L}, \omega \in \mathcal{R}_x, z \in \{0,1\}^*}$
- $\mathcal{D}_1 = \{\mathcal{S}_1(x, \omega, z)\}_{x \in \mathcal{L}, \omega \in \mathcal{R}_x, z \in \{0,1\}^*}$

Proof: Fix a random tape r for $\mathcal{V}^*$. Let $\psi = (V_1, P_1^\psi, V_2, P_2^\psi)$ be the transcript of a random execution between $\mathcal{V}^*(x, z; r)$ and an honest prover $\mathcal{P}(x, \omega)$. We will show that the probability with which this transcript is returned is identical in both distributions. Let p_ψ be the probability with which this transcript appears in $\mathcal{D}_0$ conditioned on $\mathcal{V}^*$'s random tape being fixed to r. Clearly, the resulting first message will always be V_1, if $\mathcal{S}_1$ emulates the interaction with $\mathcal{V}^*$ on a random tape r. Then we prove that transcript $(V_1, P_1^\psi, V_2, P_2^\psi)$ is generated by $\mathcal{S}_1(x, \omega, z)$ with the same probability p_ψ conditioned on the random tape of $\mathcal{V}^*$ being r.

Note first, that by the definition of $\mathcal{S}_1$, the probability with which an aborting transcript appears in both distributions is identical. We therefore focus on non-aborting transcripts. Therefore, it suffices to compute the probability that $\mathcal{S}_1(x, \omega, z)$ outputs the (non-aborting) transcript of messages $(V_1, P_1^\psi, V_2, P_2^\psi)$ conditioned on $\mathcal{V}^*$'s random tape being fixed as r. We continue with some more conventions and notations:

- We denote by S the set that occurs in the target transcript ψ, namely, the set contained in message V_2.
- We denote by p_T the probability the subset T occurs in the real execution. We let $p_\perp$ denote the probability that the verifer aborts before sending its second message in the real execution. In this notation $p_T = \sum p_\psi$ where the summation is over all transcripts ψ that contains the subset T.
- We denote a tuple of sets by $\mathbf{T} = (T_1, \ldots, T_\ell)$ to denote the sets collected by the simulator before it enters the ℓth iteration. Typically, given a tuple $\mathbf{T}$, we use $\widetilde{\mathbf{T}}$ to denote the tuple $(T_1, \ldots, T_{\ell-1})$ and use :: for appending a set. In this notation, $\mathbf{T} = \widetilde{\mathbf{T}} :: T_\ell$.
- For $1 \leq \ell \leq n - t + 1$, let Valid_ℓ denote the set of all ℓ-tuples $(T_1, \ldots, T_\ell)$ that satisfy the following two conditions.
  1. All sets T_i are of size t.
  2. For every $1 \leq i \leq \ell$, it holds that $T_i \not\subseteq T_1, \ldots, T_{i-1}$. (Recall that the simulator moves to the next iteration only if it finds a new trapdoor).

  Intuitively, valid sequences captures all sequences that can be obtained by the simulator when entering the ℓth iteration.[5]

[5] By possibly we mean that it might be the case that the verifier never opens some particular t subset T in any execution, in which case any tuple that involves T will never occur in a simulation.

- For any ℓ-tuple $\mathbf{T} = (T_1, \ldots, T_\ell)$, we define $q_{\mathbf{T}}$ the probability *conditioned on not aborting* that in a random execution between $\mathcal{V}^*(x, z; r)$ and the honest prover, the set opened by the verifier is covered by the elements $T_1, \ldots, T_\ell$, i.e. $T \subseteq \cup_{i=1}^{\ell} T_i$. We set $q_{\{\emptyset\}} = 0$. We next observe that, for any tuple $\mathbf{T} = (T_1, \ldots, T_\ell)$, it holds that $q_{\mathbf{T}} = (\sum p_T)/(1 - p_\perp)$ where the summation is over all T such that $|T| = t$ and $T \subseteq \cup_{i=1}^{\ell} T_i$.
- For a tuple $\mathbf{T} = (T_1, \ldots, T_\ell)$, let $P_{\mathbf{T}}^{\psi}(\ell)$ denote the probability that, starting with sets $\mathbf{T}$ and iteration ℓ, the simulator $\mathcal{S}_1$ outputs the transcript ψ.

Without loss of generality we assume $p_\perp < 1$, since, if the verifier aborts w.p. 1, the simulator outputs the transcript from the first execution and will be distributed identically to the real execution. We begin with the following claim which will be sufficient to prove Claim 3.2.

Subclaim 3.3. *For* $1 \leq \ell \leq n - t + 1$ *and every tuple* $\mathbf{T} = (T_1, \ldots, T_\ell) \in \mathsf{Valid}_\ell$,

$$P_{\mathbf{T}}^{\psi}(\ell) = \begin{cases} \frac{p_\psi}{(1-p_\perp)(1-q_{\widetilde{\mathbf{T}}})} & \text{if } \widetilde{\mathbf{T}} \text{ does not cover } S, \text{ and} \\ 0 & \text{otherwise.} \end{cases}$$

where $\widetilde{\mathbf{T}} = (T_1, \ldots, T_{\ell-1})$.

Before we prove this claim, we conclude Claim 3.2 using the preceding subclaim. As argued above, the probability that the simulator outputs aborting transcripts is identical to the real execution. Observing that $q_\emptyset = 0$, conditioned on not aborting, the probability that the simulator outputs non-aborting ψ is given by $P_{\mathbf{T}}^{\psi}(0)$ which from the preceeding claim is $p_\psi/(1 - p_\perp)$. Since the probability that the simulator continues after the first execution is $(1 - p_\perp)$, Claim 3.2 follows.

Now we proceed to prove Subclaim 3.3.

Proof: Given $\mathbf{T} = (T_1, \ldots, T_\ell)$, suppose $\widetilde{\mathbf{T}} = (T_1, \ldots, T_{\ell-1})$ covers S, then from the description of our simulation it follows that it is not allowed to output ψ in iterations ℓ or higher. In other words, when $\widetilde{\mathbf{T}}$ covers S, $P_{\mathbf{T}}^{\psi}(\ell) = 0$ as in the claim.

Therefore, it suffices to prove the subclaim when $\widetilde{\mathbf{T}}$ does not cover S. We prove this case using a reverse induction on ℓ from $n - t + 1$ to 1.

Base Case: $\ell = n - t + 1$. Let $\mathbf{T} = (T_1, \ldots, T_{n-t+1})$ be an arbitrary valid tuple and let $\widetilde{\mathbf{T}} = (T_1, \ldots, T_{n-t})$. Recall that, for a general iteration ℓ, the simulator rewinds until it obtains $T \not\subseteq \cup_{i=1}^{\ell-1} T_i$. Then, if $T \subseteq \cup_{i=1}^{\ell} T_i$ it outputs the transcript. Otherwise, it has obtained a new trapdoor, sets T to be the new set T_{i+1} and proceeds to the next iteration. However, if $\ell = n - t + 1$, we have that $\cup_{i=1}^{n-t+1} T_i$ must be $[n]$ as at least one new element is added in each iteration and $|T_1| = t$. Therefore, in this base case, we have that $S \not\subseteq \cup_{i=1}^{n-t} T_i$ and $S \subseteq \cup_{i=1}^{n-t+1} T_i$. This means that if the simulator encounters the transcript

ψ in iteration $n-t+1$, it will output it. The probability can be computed as follows:

$$\begin{aligned}
&\Pr[\psi \text{ occurs in the iteration} \mid \text{no } t\text{ -subset of } \cup_{i=1}^{\ell-1} T_i \text{ occurs}] \\
&= \frac{\Pr[\psi \text{ occurs in the iteration }]}{\Pr[\text{ no } t\text{-subset of } \cup_{i=1}^{\ell-1} T_i \text{ occurs}]} \\
&= \frac{p_\psi}{(1-p_\perp)} \times \frac{1}{(1-q_{\widetilde{\mathbf{T}}})}
\end{aligned}$$

This completes our base case.

Induction Step: $1 \leq \ell \leq n-t$. Let $\mathbf{T} = (T_1, \ldots, T_\ell)$ be an arbitrary tuple in Valid_i. Set $\widetilde{\mathbf{T}} = (T_1, \ldots, T_{\ell-1})$. Recall that we only need to show the subclaim when $\widetilde{\mathbf{T}}$ does not cover S. There are two cases w.r.t $\mathbf{T}$:

Case 1: T covers S: In this case, the simulator can output ψ only in this iteration and not higher. Recall that the simulator in this iteration will rewind until it obtains a set $T \not\subseteq \widetilde{\mathbf{T}}$. Therefore, the probability that the simulator outputs ψ is same as in the base case and given by $p_\psi/((1-p_\perp)(1-q_{\widetilde{\mathbf{T}}}))$.
Case 2: T does not cover S: This means that the simulator can output ψ only in iterations $\ell+1$ or higher. Then for any subset T not covered by $\mathbf{T}$ the probability that the simulator outputs ψ in iteration $\ell+1$ or higher is given by

$$\begin{aligned}
&\Pr[T \text{ occurs in the current iteration} \mid \text{no } t\text{-subset of } \cup_{i=1}^{\ell-1} T_i \text{ occurs}] \\
&\times \Pr[\psi \text{ occurs in iteration } \geq \ell+1 \text{ with } \mathbf{T} :: T \text{ occuring in the first } \ell \text{ iterations}] \\
&= \Pr[T \text{ occurs in the current iteration} \mid \text{no } t\text{-subset of } \cup_{i=1}^{\ell-1} T_i \text{ occurs}] \\
&\times P^{\psi}_{\mathbf{T}::T}(\ell+1) \\
&= \frac{p_\psi}{(1-p_\perp)(1-q_{\widetilde{\mathbf{T}}})} \times P^{\psi}_{\mathbf{T}::T}(\ell+1)
\end{aligned}$$

This means that the overall probability can be obtained by summing the proceeding expression over all sets T not covered by $\mathbf{T}$, namely, $T \not\subseteq T_1, \ldots, T_\ell$.

$$\begin{aligned}
P^{\psi}_{\mathbf{T}}(\ell) &= \sum_{T \not\subseteq T_1 \cup \cdots \cup T_{\ell-1}} \frac{p_T}{(1-p_\perp)(1-q_{\widetilde{\mathbf{T}}})} \times P^{\psi}_{\mathbf{T}::T}(\ell+1) \\
&= \sum_{T \not\subseteq T_1 \cup \cdots \cup T_{\ell-1}} \frac{p_T}{(1-p_\perp)(1-q_{\widetilde{\mathbf{T}}})} \times \frac{p_\psi}{(1-p_\perp)(1-q_{\mathbf{T}})} \\
&= \frac{p_\psi}{(1-p_\perp)(1-q_{\mathbf{T}})} \times \frac{1-q_{\mathbf{T}}}{1-q_{\widetilde{\mathbf{T}}}} \\
&= \frac{p_\psi}{(1-p_\perp)(1-q_{\widetilde{\mathbf{T}}})}.
\end{aligned}$$

where in the second step we invoke our induction hypothesis that $P^{\psi}_{\mathbf{T}::T}(\ell+1) = p_\psi/((1-p_\perp)(1-q_{\mathbf{T}}))$.

This completes our inductive step and concludes the proof of our subclaim. □

Claim 3.4. *The expected running time of $\mathcal{S}_1$ is polynomial.*

Proof: We argue by induction on the iterations that the expected running time of the simulator $\mathcal{S}_1$ defined in this hybrid is polynomial. Define $\mathsf{RunTime}_{\mathbf{T}}(\ell)$ to be the expected total running time of the simulator in iterations ℓ and above conditioned on $\mathbf{T} = (T_1, \ldots, T_\ell)$ being the sets obtained by the simulator in the first $\ell - 1$ iterations.

Subclaim 3.5. *There exists a constant c such that, for any valid tuple $(T_1, \ldots, T_\ell)$, $\mathsf{RunTime}_{\mathbf{T}}(\ell) \leq \frac{n^c(n-\ell)}{(1-p_\perp)(1-q_{\widetilde{\mathbf{T}}})}$ where $1 \leq \ell \leq n - t + 1$ and $\widetilde{\mathbf{T}} = (T_1, \ldots, T_{\ell-1})$.*

Proof: As in the previous proof we do reverse induction on iteration ℓ.

Base Case $\ell = n - t + 1$**.** Let $\mathbf{T} = (T_1, \ldots, T_{n-t+1})$. Recall that in iteration $\ell = n - t + 1$ we have $\cup_{i=1}^{n-t+1} T_i = [n]$. Therefore, there are no more iterations and the simulator stops whenever it finds any T such that $T \not\subseteq \cup_{i=1}^{n-t} T_i$. The probability of observing such an execution using our notation defined above is given by $(1-p_\perp)(1-q_{\widetilde{\mathbf{T}}})$. Therefore, the expected number of rewindings that the simulator needs to perform in the $(n-t+1)^{st}$ iteration is $1/((1-p_\perp)(1-q_{\widetilde{\mathbf{T}}}))$. This in turn means the expected time spent by the simulator conditioned on entering iteration $n - t + 1$ with sets $(T_1, \ldots, T_{n-t+1})$, i.e.

$$\mathsf{RunTime}_{\mathbf{T}}(n-t+1) = \frac{n^c}{(1-p_\perp)(1-q_{\widetilde{\mathbf{T}}})}$$

where n^c is an upper bound on the time spent by the simulator in a single rewinding with the verifier.

Induction Step: $1 \leq \ell \leq n-t$. We will compute the expected time spent in this iteration. Suppose that the simulator collected the sets $(T_1, \ldots, T_\ell)$ in the first $\ell - 1$ iterations. Recall that the simulator rewinds until it obtains $T \not\subseteq \cup_{i=1}^{\ell-1} T_i$ and either outputs the transcript (if $T \subseteq \cup_{i=1}^{\ell} T_i$) or moves on to the next iteration otherwise. The number of rewindings in this iteration is therefore $\frac{1}{1-q_{\widetilde{\mathbf{T}}}}$ in expectation. Now, the total expected running time in iterations ℓ and above can be computed as

$$\begin{aligned}
&E[\#\text{rewindings in iteration } \ell \text{ until it obtains } T \not\subseteq \cup_{i=1}^{\ell-1} T_i] \times n^c \\
&\quad + E[\text{time spent in iterations } > \ell \text{ with } T] \\
&\quad = \frac{n^c}{(1-p_\perp)(1-q_{\widetilde{\mathbf{T}}})} + \sum_{T' \not\subseteq \cup_{i=1}^{\ell} T_i} \Pr[T = T' | T \not\subseteq \cup_{i=1}^{\ell-1} T_i] \times \mathsf{RunTime}_{\mathbf{T}::T}(\ell+1) \\
&\quad \leq \frac{n^c}{(1-p_\perp)(1-q_{\widetilde{\mathbf{T}}})} + \frac{n^c(n-\ell-1)}{(1-p_\perp)(1-q_{\mathbf{T}})} \times \sum_{T' \not\subseteq \cup_{i=1}^{\ell} T_i} \Pr[T = T' | T \not\subseteq \cup_{i=1}^{\ell-1} T_i]
\end{aligned}$$

$$= \frac{n^c}{(1-p_\perp)(1-q_{\tilde{\mathbf{T}}})} + \frac{n^c(n-\ell-1)}{(1-p_\perp)(1-q_{\mathbf{T}})} \times \frac{\sum_{T' \not\subseteq \cup_{i=1}^{\ell} T_i} \Pr[T=T']}{1-q_{\tilde{\mathbf{T}}}}$$

$$= \frac{n^c}{(1-p_\perp)(1-q_{\tilde{\mathbf{T}}})} + \frac{n^c(n-\ell-1)}{(1-p_\perp)(1-q_{\mathbf{T}})} \times \frac{1-q_{\mathbf{T}}}{1-q_{\tilde{\mathbf{T}}}}$$

$$= \frac{n^c(n-\ell)}{(1-p_\perp)(1-q_{\tilde{\mathbf{T}}})}$$

where the third step follows from the induction hypothesis. □

The expected total running time of the simulation is given by

$$p_\perp \times n^c + (1-p_\perp) \times \mathsf{RunTime}_\emptyset(1) = n^c + n^c(n-1)$$

and this concludes the proof of the claim. □

Hybrid Hyb_2: In this experiment we consider the actual simulation as defined by $\mathcal{S}(x,z)$. The output of the experiment will then be $\mathcal{S}(x,z)$.

Claim 3.6. *The following distributions are identical.*

- $\{\mathcal{S}_1(x,\omega,z)\}_{x\in\mathcal{L},\omega\in\mathcal{R}_x,z\in\{0,1\}^*}$
- $\{\mathcal{S}(x,z)\}_{x\in\mathcal{L},\omega\in\mathcal{R}_x,z\in\{0,1\}^*}$

Proof. Assume for contradiction that there exists a malicious verifier $\mathcal{V}^*$, a distinguisher $\mathcal{D}$ and a polynomial $p(n)$ such that for infinitely many n's, $\mathcal{D}$ distinguishes $\mathcal{S}_1(x,\omega,z) = \langle \mathcal{S}_1(\omega), \mathcal{V}^*(z)\rangle(x)$ and $\mathcal{S}(x,z) = \mathcal{S}^{\mathcal{V}^*}(x,z)$ with probability $\frac{1}{p(n)}$. Fix any n for which this event occurs.

First, we consider truncated experiments $\overline{\mathsf{Hyb}}_1(n,x,z)$ (resp. $\overline{\mathsf{Hyb}}_2(n,x,z)$) which proceeds exactly as $\mathsf{Hyb}_1(n,x,z)$ (resp. $\mathsf{Hyb}_2(n,x,z)$) with the exception that the simulation is aborted if it runs more than $np(n)t(n)$ steps where $t(n)$ is the polynomial bounding the expected running time of $\mathcal{S}_1$. If the experiment is aborted then $\overline{\mathsf{Hyb}}_1$ (resp. $\overline{\mathsf{Hyb}}_2$) is set to a special symbol $\perp$. By an averaging argument we can conclude that the truncated experiments $\overline{\mathsf{Hyb}}_1(n,x,z)$ and $\overline{\mathsf{Hyb}}_2(n,x,z)$ can be distinguished with probability at least $\frac{1}{2p(n)}$ by the distinguisher $\mathcal{D}$.

Next, we consider a sequence of intermediate hybrids $\mathsf{Hyb}_1^0, \ldots, \mathsf{Hyb}_1^{n-t+1}$, where in Hybrid Hyb_1^ℓ, we define a simulator $\mathcal{S}_1^\ell$ that will follow the real simulator's strategy $\mathcal{S}$ in the first ℓ iterations of the for loop and the remaining according to the honest prover using the real witness. If $\mathcal{S}_1^\ell$ runs over $np(n)t(n)$ steps then we stop the simulation and output $\perp$. Let $\overline{\mathsf{Hyb}}_1^\ell(n,x,z)$ be the output of the $\mathcal{S}_1^\ell$ in Hyb_1^ℓ. It follows from definition that $\overline{\mathsf{Hyb}}_1^0 = \overline{\mathsf{Hyb}}_1$ and $\overline{\mathsf{Hyb}}_1^{n-t+1} = \overline{\mathsf{Hyb}}_2$. Therefore, if $\mathcal{D}$ distinguishes $\overline{\mathsf{Hyb}}_1^0$ from $\overline{\mathsf{Hyb}}_1^{n-t+1}$ then there exists an index i such that $\mathcal{D}$ distinguishes $\overline{\mathsf{Hyb}}_1^i$ from $\overline{\mathsf{Hyb}}_1^{i+1}$ with probability $\frac{1}{2np(n)}$. Since the experiments are truncated after $np(n)t(n)$ steps the maximum number of rewindings that can occur in iteration i where the two experiments differ is

$np(n)t(n)$. We show that using $\mathcal{V}^*$ and $\mathcal{D}$ we can contradict the honest verifier zero-knowledge property (for many parallel repetitions).

Consider an adversary $\mathcal{A}$ that begins an emulation of $\overline{\mathsf{Hyb}}_1^i(n,x,z)$ until it reaches iteration i. If it halts before, $\mathcal{A}$ simply outputs the output of the experiment. Otherwise, let $T_1,\ldots,T_i$ be the set of indexes that were obtained by the simulator in the internal emulation. Let $T = T_1 \cup \cdots \cup T_i$ and let $\{e_t\}_{t\in T}$ be the challenges in the indexes in T. $\mathcal{A}$ forwards these challenges to an external challenger $\mathcal{C}$. The challenger then produces $np(n)t(n)$ transcripts of the honest-verifier zero-knowledge protocol for each challenge e_t for $t \in T$. $\mathcal{A}$ uses the prover's messages in these transcripts to generate the prover messages in the internal emulation in iteration i. Then it completes the experiment, where from iteration $i+1$ the adversary plays the honest prover strategy and uses the real witness, and outputs the output of the experiment. By our construction, if the external challenger $\mathcal{C}$ produces transcripts according to the honest prover, then the internal emulation by $\mathcal{A}$ is identical to $\overline{\mathsf{Hyb}}_1^i$. On the other hand if the transcripts received from $\mathcal{C}$ is according to the honest verifier simulator, then the internal emulation is identical to $\overline{\mathsf{Hyb}}_1^{i+1}$. Therefore, $\mathcal{D}$ and $\mathcal{A}$ violates the honest verifier zero-knowledge property of π_{ZK}.

Claim 3.7. *The expected running time of $\mathcal{S}$ is polynomial.*

Proof: Assume for contradiction, the expected running time of $\mathcal{S}$ is not polynomial. Recall that the expected running time of $\mathcal{S}_1$ is some polynomial $t(n)$. Then we can construct a distinguisher that distinguishes the truncated experiments $\overline{\mathsf{Hyb}}_1(n,x,z)$ and $\overline{\mathsf{Hyb}}_2(n,x,z)$ defined above and this is a contradiction to the previous claim. We consider truncated experiments $\overline{\mathsf{Hyb}}_1(n,x,z)$ and $\overline{\mathsf{Hyb}}_2(n,x,z)$ where the experiments are truncated after $2t(n)$ steps. Next, consider a distinguisher $\mathcal{D}$ that outputs 1 if the experiment's output is $\perp$ and 0 otherwise. $\mathcal{D}$ on input view from $\overline{\mathsf{Hyb}}_1(n,x,z)$ outputs 1 with probability at least $\frac{1}{2}$. However, $\mathcal{D}$ on input a view from $\overline{\mathsf{Hyb}}_2(n,x,z)$ outputs 1 is negligible. Therefore, $\mathcal{D}$ distinguishes $\overline{\mathsf{Hyb}}_1(n,x,z)$ and $\overline{\mathsf{Hyb}}_2(n,x,z)$ with non-negligible probability and this is a contradiction. □

4 Corollaries

In this section, we provide corollaries to our main techniques. We obtain the first round optimal fully black-box constructions of perfect zero-knowledge arguments and input-delayed commit-and-prove zero-knowledge argument.

4-round Perfect Zero-Knowledge Argument from Claw-free Permutations. As a corollary of Theorem 3.1, we prove that there exists a 4-round perfect zero-knowledge argument based on claw-free permutations. This is achieved by replacing the prover's commitments in Protocol 1 with perfectly hiding commitments which can be based on claw-free permutations. More formally,

Corollary 4.1. *Assuming claw-free permutations, there exists a 4-round fully black-box perfect zero-knowledge argument for any NP language.*

The protocol for the perfect zero-knowledge case is identical to the protocol described in Sect. 3 with the only exception that the commitments made by the prover is replaced with perfectly hiding commitments that can be based on claw-free permutations [GK96a]. The proof follows is analogous to the proof of Theorem 3.1. The soundness argument essentially remains unchanged; we only need to handle the case when the prover violates the binding property of the underlying commitment scheme. The zero-knowledge property follows essentially as before. We observe that the distributions in Hyb_0 and Hyb_1 are already proved to be identical. To conclude we observe that the distributions in Hyb_1 and Hyb_2 are also identical because the underlying commitment scheme is perfectly hiding.

4-round Input-Delayed Commit-and-Prove ZK Argument. As a second corollary, we prove that there exists a 4-round input delayed commit-and-prove zero-knowledge argument. This is achieved by replacing the three-round honest-verifier zero-knowledge argument based on Blum-Hamiltonicity with the three-round commit-and-prove input-delayed protocol of Hazay and Venkitasubramaniam [HV16] in Sect. 6.2. More formally,

Corollary 4.2. *Assuming injective one-way functions, there exists a fully black-box 4-round input-delayed commit-and-prove zero-knowledge argument for any* NP *language.*

Acknowledgments. We thank the anonymous TCC reviewers for their detailed comments and Rafael Pass for helpful suggestions. The first author was supported by the BIU Center for Research in Applied Cryptography and Cyber Security in conjunction with the Israel National Cyber Bureau in the Prime Minister's Office. The second author was supported by Google Faculty Research Grant and NSF Award CNS-1526377. This work was partly carried out by the second author during a visit to DIMACS supported by the National Science Foundation under grant number CNS-1523467.

References

[BJY97] Bellare, M., Jakobsson, M., Yung, M.: Round-optimal zero-knowledge arguments based on any one-way function. In: Fumy, W. (ed.) EUROCRYPT 1997. LNCS, vol. 1233, pp. 280–305. Springer, Heidelberg (1997). https://doi.org/10.1007/3-540-69053-0_20

[BKP18] Bitansky, N., Kalai, Y.T., Paneth, O.: Multi-collision resistance: a paradigm for keyless hash functions. In: STOC (2018)

[Blu] Blum, M.: How to prove a theorem so no one else can claim it. In: Proceedings of the International Congress of Mathematicians, USA, pp. 1444–1451 (1986). http://citeseerx.ist.psu.edu/viewdoc/download?doi=10.1.1.469.9048&rep=rep1&type=pdf

[CLOS02] Canetti, R., Lindell, Y., Ostrovsky, R., Sahai, A.: Universally composable two-party and multi-party secure computation. In: STOC, pp. 494–503 (2002)

[CPS+15] Ciampi, M., Persiano, G., Scafuro, A., Siniscalchi, L., Visconti, I.: Improved OR composition of sigma-protocols. IACR Cryptol. ePrint Arch. **2015**, 810 (2015)

[FGJ18] Fleischhacker, N., Goyal, V., Jain, A.: On the existence of three round zero-knowledge proofs. In: Nielsen, J.B., Rijmen, V. (eds.) EUROCRYPT 2018. LNCS, vol. 10822, pp. 3–33. Springer, Cham (2018). https://doi.org/10.1007/978-3-319-78372-7_1

[FS89] Feige, U., Shamir, A.: Zero knowledge proofs of knowledge in two rounds. In: Brassard, G. (ed.) CRYPTO 1989. LNCS, vol. 435, pp. 526–544. Springer, New York (1990). https://doi.org/10.1007/0-387-34805-0_46

[GK96a] Goldreich, O., Kahan, A.: How to construct constant-round zero-knowledge proof systems for NP. J. Cryptol. **9**(3), 167–190 (1996)

[GK96b] Goldreich, O., Krawczyk, H.: On the composition of zero-knowledge proof systems. SIAM J. Comput. **25**(1), 169–192 (1996)

[GMR89] Goldwasser, S., Micali, S., Rackoff, C.: The knowledge complexity of interactive proof systems. SIAM J. Comput. **18**(1), 186–208 (1989)

[GMW87] Goldreich, O., Micali, S., Wigderson, A.: How to play any mental game or A completeness theorem for protocols with honest majority. In: STOC, pp. 218–229, (1987)

[GMW91] Goldreich, O., Micali, S., Wigderson, A.: Proofs that yield nothing but their validity for all languages in NP have zero-knowledge proof systems. J. ACM **38**(3), 691–729 (1991)

[GO94] Goldreich, O., Oren, Y.: Definitions and properties of zero-knowledge proof systems. J. Cryptol. **7**(1), 1–32 (1994)

[Gol01] Goldreich, O.: Foundations of Cryptography: Basic Tools. Cambridge University Press, Cambridge (2001)

[HV16] Hazay, C., Venkitasubramaniam, M.: On the power of secure two-party computation. In: Robshaw, M., Katz, J. (eds.) CRYPTO 2016. LNCS, vol. 9815, pp. 397–429. Springer, Heidelberg (2016). https://doi.org/10.1007/978-3-662-53008-5_14

[IKOS07] Ishai, Y., Kushilevitz, E., Ostrovsky, R., Sahai, A.: Zero-knowledge from secure multiparty computation. In: STOC, pp. 21–30 (2007)

[IKOS09] Ishai, Y., Kushilevitz, E., Ostrovsky, R., Sahai, A.: Zero-knowledge proofs from secure multiparty computation. SIAM J. Comput. **39**(3), 1121–1152 (2009)

[IMS12] Ishai, Y., Mahmoody, M., Sahai, A.: On efficient zero-knowledge PCPs. In: Cramer, R. (ed.) TCC 2012. LNCS, vol. 7194, pp. 151–168. Springer, Heidelberg (2012). https://doi.org/10.1007/978-3-642-28914-9_9

[Kat12] Katz, J.: Which languages have 4-round zero-knowledge proofs? J. Cryptology **25**(1), 41–56 (2012)

[LS90] Lapidot, D., Shamir, A.: Publicly verifiable non-interactive zero-knowledge proofs. In: Menezes, A.J., Vanstone, S.A. (eds.) CRYPTO 1990. LNCS, vol. 537, pp. 353–365. Springer, Heidelberg (1991). https://doi.org/10.1007/3-540-38424-3_26

[Nao91] Naor, M.: Bit commitment using pseudorandomness. J. Cryptology **4**(2), 151–158 (1991)

[ORS15] Ostrovsky, R., Richelson, S., Scafuro, A.: Round-optimal black-box two-party computation. In: Gennaro, R., Robshaw, M. (eds.) CRYPTO 2015. LNCS, vol. 9216, pp. 339–358. Springer, Heidelberg (2015). https://doi.org/10.1007/978-3-662-48000-7_17

[PW09] Pass, R., Wee, H.: Black-Box constructions of two-party protocols from one-way functions. In: Reingold, O. (ed.) TCC 2009. LNCS, vol. 5444, pp. 403–418. Springer, Heidelberg (2009). https://doi.org/10.1007/978-3-642-00457-5_24

Round Optimal Black-Box "Commit-and-Prove"

Dakshita Khurana[1(✉)], Rafail Ostrovsky[2], and Akshayaram Srinivasan[3]

[1] Microsoft Research, New England, USA
dakshkhurana@gmail.com
[2] UCLA, Los Angeles, USA
[3] UC Berkeley, Berkeley, USA
akshayaram@berkeley.edu

Abstract. Motivated by theoretical and practical considerations, an important line of research is to design secure computation protocols that only make black-box use of cryptography. An important component in nearly all the black-box secure computation constructions is a *black-box commit-and-prove* protocol. A commit-and-prove protocol allows a prover to commit to a value and prove a statement about this value while guaranteeing that the committed value remains hidden. A black-box commit-and-prove protocol implements this functionality while only making black-box use of cryptography.

In this paper, we build several tools that enable constructions of *round-optimal*, black-box commit and prove protocols. In particular, assuming injective one-way functions, we design the first round-optimal, black-box commit-and-prove arguments of knowledge satisfying strong privacy against malicious verifiers, namely:

– Zero-knowledge in four rounds and,
– Witness indistinguishability in three rounds.

Prior to our work, the best known black-box protocols achieving commit-and-prove required more rounds.

We additionally ensure that our protocols can be used, if needed, in the *delayed-input* setting, where the statement to be proven is decided only towards the end of the interaction. We also observe simple applications

R. Ostrovsky—Research supported in part by NSF grant 1619348, DARPA SafeWare subcontract to Galois Inc., DARPA SPAWAR contract N66001-15-1C-4065, US-Israel BSF grant 2012366, OKAWA Foundation Research Award, IBM Faculty Research Award, Xerox Faculty Research Award, B. John Garrick Foundation Award, Teradata Research Award, and Lockheed-Martin Corporation Research Award. The views expressed are those of the authors and do not reflect position of the Department of Defense or the U.S. Government.

A. Srinivasan—Research supported in part from Sanjam Garg's 2017 AFOSR YIP Award, DARPA/ARL SAFEWARE Award W911NF15C0210, AFOSR Award FA9550-15-1-0274, and research grants by the Okawa Foundation, Visa Inc., and Center for Long-Term Cybersecurity (CLTC, UC Berkeley). The views expressed are those of the author and do not reflect the official policy or position of the funding agencies.

A. Beimel and S. Dziembowski (Eds.): TCC 2018, LNCS 11239, pp. 286–313, 2018.
https://doi.org/10.1007/978-3-030-03807-6_11

of our protocols towards achieving black-box four-round constructions of extractable and equivocal commitments.

We believe that our protocols will provide a useful tool enabling several new constructions and easy round-efficient conversions from non-black-box to black-box protocols in the future.

1 Introduction

Secure computation [13,42] allows a set of mutually distrusting parties to compute a joint function of their private inputs such that nothing else apart from the function's output is leaked. The constructions of secure computation protocols (where the majority of the parties can be corrupted) may make use of cryptographic primitives in one out of the following two ways. The construction can either make *black-box* use of the primitive by referring only to the input/output behavior of that primitive or it can make *non-black-box* use of the primitive by using the code computing this primitive.

Typically, non black-box use of a cryptographic primitive is made to protect against malicious adversaries who may deviate arbitrarily from the protocol specification. In such scenarios, a zero-knowledge proof [14] showing correct computation of this primitive (which in turn requires access to the code computing this primitive) is used. This part is computationally expensive and further, the complexity of this step depends on the actual implementation of this cryptographic functionality.

The advantage of black-box constructions is that their complexity is independent of the complexity of implementation of the underlying primitive. In fact, such protocols are sometimes considered as the first step towards practical implementations. There has been an impressive body of research [7,15,16,19,25–28,36] on constructing secure computation protocols that make black-box use of underlying primitives. However, most of these works incur several additional rounds of interaction when compared to non-black-box protocols.

A very natural question, which is still far from being resolved, is whether there exist *black-box* protocols that match the exact round complexity of their non-black-box counterparts.[1] In this paper, we ask this question for a key cryptographic functionality that lies at the center of nearly all black-box constructions: *the commit-and-prove functionality.*

1.1 Commit-and-Prove Functionalities

A "commit-and-prove" functionality [6,13] is generally used to prevent malicious behaviour by forcing participants to prove correctness of their protocol messages w.r.t. the committed inputs. Informally, a commit-and-prove functionality allows

[1] Two notable exceptions are the works of [34] and [18] who construct round-optimal secure computation, and non-malleable commitments respectively via black-box use of cryptography. However, these works developed techniques very specific to their respective settings.

a party to commit to some secret value x and prove that value satisfies some predicate P. In order to maintain secrecy, such a proof must additionally hide the secret input x, in other words it must be *zero-knowledge*.

Very roughly, any commit-and-prove protocol is said to be zero-knowledge if there exists an associated simulator that given the commitment externally, is able to generate a proof without access to the witness (or the value being committed via the commitment). We note that such protocols have been a core primitive in nearly all previous works on obtaining black-box constructions, including [16, 25,27,36]. In addition to zero-knowledge, we also consider the weaker privacy property of witness indistinguishability [9].[2]

Despite the above mentioned fascinating advances in constructing such protocols, we still do not know round-optimal black-box constructions of zero-knowledge commit-and-prove functionalities. Indeed, in the black-box regime, the best known result is due to Hazay and Venkitasubramaniam [21] which requires 6 rounds of interaction. In fact, when not restricted to black-box use of primitives, we have known for more than 25 years that four rounds are necessary [12][3] and sufficient [5,8] for constructing zero-knowledge commit-and-prove arguments.

However, so many years later, in the regime of *black-box commit-and-prove*, the following question is still open:

"Do there exist round-optimal, black-box commit-and-prove zero-knowledge protocols?"

1.2 Our Results

We provide a positive answer to this question. In particular, assuming injective one-way functions, we construct the first:

- Four round black-box commit-and-prove zero-knowledge arguments of knowledge against malicious verifiers, and
- Three round black-box commit-and-prove witness-indistinguishable arguments of knowledge against malicious verifiers. These commitments satisfy only a weaker notion of binding (that we call 1-of-2 binding), which nevertheless suffices for all our applications, and which we detail in Definition 4.

Our protocols satisfy correctness and soundness even in the *delayed-input* setting, where the predicate to be proved can be decided even in the last round of the protocol, however, the witness or message to be committed must be known before the prover sends his first message. Additionally, as simple applications of these protocols, we give the first constructions of four round extractable and equivocal commitments that only make black-box use of injective one-way functions.

[2] Please refer to Sect. 3 for a formal definition of witness indistinguishable commit-and-prove protocols.

[3] Due to limitations on the round-complexity required to implement existing non black-box techniques, we restrict ourselves to black-box reductions in this paper.

Discussion. Our construction makes non-black-box use of the predicate, similar to all previous constructions in this line of work. With respect to constructions making black-box use of the predicate, we would like to point to the negative result of Rosulek [39] which shows that any (honest-verifier) zero-knowledge argument for the NP language $L = \{x : \exists w s.t. f(w) = x\}$ and f is a one-way function must make use of the code of the function f.

We note that similar to previous work using MPC-in-the-head [IKOS07] and follow-ups, our techniques can be used directly to build black-box protocols in cases where the predicate is information theoretic. There are several settings in literature where the predicate is indeed information theoretic. A few simple examples include:

- A commit-and-prove protocol for checking equality of two committed values (This is in fact used in our construction of equivocal commitments).
- A commit-and-prove protocol for checking that one committed value corresponds to a fixed polynomial evaluated on a different committed value (Eg, in the ZK arguments that achieve four round non-malleable commitments in GRRV14.)
- Comparison queries or range proofs, showing that a committed value lies in a certain fixed range (Such proofs have become increasingly popular in recent years).
- These techniques may also be relevant to distributed secure protocols with information-theoretic guarantees.

Furthermore, as we note in the paper, in many other situations, where the predicate itself involves cryptography, cut-and-choose techniques have been extensively explored (Please see [1,22,23,30–33,40,41] and references therein). Specifically, the works of [16,17,35] used cut-and-choose to separate such predicates into cryptographic components, for which malicious security was obtained using cut-and-choose, and information-theoretic components, for which tailored commit-and-prove protocols were built. In this paper, we concentrate on the latter and build round-optimal, black-box commit-and-prove ZK protocols to generically solve the problem of commit-and-prove for information-theoretic predicates. As simple applications of these results, in the paper, we construct the first four round extractable and equivocal commitments from injective one-way functions.

1.3 Related Works

Goldreich and Krawcyzk [12] showed that four rounds are necessary to construct zero-knowledge argument system that make black-box use of a verifier for languages outside of BPP. Bellare et al. [5] and Feige et al. [8] gave protocols that matches this round complexity from the minimum assumption that one-way functions exist.

The commit and prove functionality was first used implicitly in [13] and was later formalized in [6]. The constructions given in these works made non-black-box use of one-way functions. A constant round black-box commit and prove zero-knowledge proof was implicit in the work of Ishai et al. [27] assuming collision resistant hash functions. Later works of [16,17,35] improved the concrete round complexity of this construction and also constructed zero-knowledge argument systems from one-way functions. More recently, Hazay and Venkitasubramaniam [21] constructed a six-round black-box commit and prove zero-knowledge argument from injective one-way functions. This work represents the state of the art in terms of round complexity of black-box commit and prove.

2 Our Techniques

Our starting point is the work of Hazay and Venkitasubramaniam [21], who constructed three-message black-box commit-and-prove ZK protocols with constant soundness, by making use of *robust offline/online randomized encodings.*

Starting Point: Robust Offline/Online Encoding. A randomized encoding [2–4,24,42] of a boolean circuit f is a function $\widehat{f}$ along with a decoding algorithm Dec such that for any input x in the domain of the function f, with overwhelming probability it holds that $\mathrm{Dec}(\widehat{f}(x; U_m)) = f(x)$, where U_m denotes the uniform distribution over m bits. Moreover, the encoding $\widehat{f}$ required to satisfy computational privacy, meaning that the encoding $\widehat{f}(x, U_m)$ reveals no information about x and f, except $f(x)$. A randomized encoding is called offline/online if it has two components: an offline component that does not depend on the input, and an online component which is a function of the input. We will denote these by two functions $\widehat{f}_{\mathrm{off}}$ and $\widehat{f}_{\mathrm{on}}$ such that $\widehat{f}(x;r) = (\widehat{f}_{\mathrm{off}}(r), \widehat{f}_{\mathrm{on}}(x,r))$. Such an encoding is called *robust*, if additionally the following is true: when there exists no x such that $f(x) = a$, then for any r, there does not exist any z such that $\mathrm{Dec}(\widehat{f}_{\mathrm{off}}(r), z) = a$. The work of [21] showed that robust randomized encodings can be instantiated in multiple ways, including the use of adaptive garbled circuits.

Black-Box Commit and Prove with Constant Soundness. Let us now explain how the work of [21] used offline/online randomized encodings to construct black-box commit and prove ZK proofs with constant soundness error. Additionally, if the encodings are robust then this zero-knowledge proof satisfies correctness and soundness in the *delayed-input* setting.

The prover $\mathcal{P}$ has a message m and wants to convince the verifier that $\phi(m) = 1$ where ϕ is some predicate. The protocol is as follows:

1. In the first round, $\mathcal{P}$ secret shares m into two shares m_0 and m_1. It then constructs a function f which has hardwired a secret share m_0 of m, and obtains as input the other share m_1 and the predicate ϕ. This function outputs $(1, \phi, m_1)$ if and only if $\phi(m_0 \oplus m_1) = 1$; otherwise it outputs $\perp$. It constructs an offline encoding of this function $\widehat{f}_{\mathrm{off}}(r)$ and sends $\widehat{f}_{\mathrm{off}}(r)$ and also sends a (standard) non-interactive commitment to m_1.
2. The verifer $\mathcal{V}$ sends a random single bit challenge b.

3. If $b := 0$ then the prover sends f, r and the verifier checks if $\widehat{f}_{\text{off}}(r)$ is computed correctly. Otherwise, $\mathcal{P}$ opens the commitment to m_1 and also sends $\widehat{f}_{\text{on}}((m_1, \phi), r)$. $\mathcal{V}$ checks if the opening is valid and also runs $\text{Dec}(\widehat{f}_{\text{off}}(r), \widehat{f}_{\text{on}}((m_1, \phi), r))$ and checks if this output is $(1, m_1, \phi)$.

In the case where $b = 0$, the commitment computationally hides m_1, whereas when $b = 1$, the privacy of the randomized encoding ensures that m_0 remains hidden. As shown in [21], this can indeed be formalized to prove that the protocol satisfies zero-knowledge. However, the protocol is only 1/2 sound: in particular, a cheating prover can guess the verifier's challenge in advance, and use this to generate an accepting proof of a false statement.

Boosting Soundness. In order to boost soundness to close to 1, a natural idea is to parallel repeat this basic protocol to achieve negligible soundness error. But this idea does not work because we want a commit-and-prove: meaning that a malicious prover should be forced to commit to a single value and prove that it satisfies the predicate. In a naïve parallel repetition, a cheating prover could use different m's to compute the first message in different parallel repetitions. Therefore, we must find a way to ensure consistency of messages used across different parallel executions.

To achieve this, we augment the constant soundness protocol in the following way:

1. Instead of secret sharing m, the prover now secret shares $w := (m\|r)$ where r is a random element from a finite field $\mathbb{F}$.[4] Let w_0 and w_1 be the secret shares. The prover constructs a function f that has w_0 hardwired in its description and takes as input the other share w_1 along with an augmented predicate ϕ' (which we will define later). f outputs $(1, w_1, \phi')$ if and only if $\phi'(w_0 \oplus w_1) = 1$. It constructs an offline encoding of this function $\widehat{f}_{\text{off}}(r)$ and sends $\widehat{f}_{\text{off}}(r)$ and also sends a (standard) non-interactive commitment to w_1.
2. The verifier chooses a random bit b as before and additionally chooses a random element $\alpha \leftarrow \mathbb{F} \setminus \{0\}$ and sends b, α to $\mathcal{P}$.
3. The prover computes $\gamma := r\alpha + m$ and sets the predicate $\phi'((m\|r))$ to check if $\phi(m) = 1$ and if γ is correctly computed. The prover sends γ and responds to the verifier's challenge bit as before.

In the parallel repetition of the above protocol, $\mathcal{P}$ chooses a "global" r that remains the same for each of the repetitions and also sends a single $\gamma := r\alpha + m$ in the third round; in each repetition, the predicate ϕ' shows that this "global" γ is consistent with the value w used in that repetition. We now show that the above augmented constant soundness protocol can force a prover to use consistent witness across multiple parallel executions. Say, the prover tries to use different witnesses $(r', m') \neq (r, m)$ across parallel repetitions. Then, with overwhelming probability $r\alpha + m \neq r'\alpha + m'$ by the Schwartz-Zippel lemma. Thus, the predicate that the prover is trying to prove in those repetitions is false and hence he will

[4] We assume that the message m also belongs to the same finite field.

be caught if he tries to use inconsistent witness in many repetitions. We show that this parallel repetition satisfies witness indistinguishability.

Achieving Zero-Knowledge. As mentioned earlier, our three round parallel repetition of the augmented constant soundness protocol satisfies witness indistinguishability. Indeed, in order for it to achieve zero-knowledge property, it is necessary to have an additional round of interaction [11].

Our four round commit and prove ZK protocol follows the FLS paradigm [8] i.e., we run two special purpose witness indistinguishable protocols in opposite directions between the prover $\mathcal{P}$ and the verifier $\mathcal{V}$. Recall that in the FLS paradigm the first protocol is a WI-PoK run by the verifier proving the knowledge of some trapdoor information. The second WI-PoK protocol run by the prover shows the knowledge of a witness for the statement x or the knowledge of verifier's trapdoor information. Intuitively, the soundness of the protocol follows from the security of the first WI-PoK and the zero-knowledgeness property follows from the observation that the simulator can rewind and extract the trapdoor information from the first WI-PoK and then use it in the second protocol.

In our construction, the first WI protocol run by $\mathcal{V}$ is a 3-round two-com protocol. Intuitively, the two-com protocol is a commitment to two random strings s_0 and s_1 such that commitment to s_b for a random $b \in \{0, 1\}$ is binding whereas the commitment to the other string s_{1-b} is equivocal. The trapdoor information is the string s_b. We demonstrate how to construct this primitive with black-box use of statistically binding commitment scheme using ideas from [34]. We additionally show that this trapdoor information can be extracted in expected polynomial time by rewinding the verifier. We wish to emphasize that the trapdoor that we use is in some sense "information theoretic" in nature and in contrast, the trapdoors usually used in the FLS paradigm are "crytographic" in nature such as the inverse of a given one-way function, or a signature under a public verification key, etc. Indeed, using such cryptographic trapdoors in the FLS paradigm leads to non-black-box use of one-way functions.

The second WI protocol run by $\mathcal{P}$ is essentially the 3-round WI protocol that we constructed earlier which proves that either the committed message m satisfies the predicate or m is the trapdoor. We show that a combination of these two special purpose WI protocols is a zero-knowledge commit and prove by carefully relying on the timing of the messages exchanged and the delayed input property of the second WI. We refer the reader to the main body for the details.

3 Preliminaries

In this section, we recall some preliminaries and tools that will be useful in our constructions. We will denote the security parameter by λ, and we will say that a function $f : \mathbb{N} \rightarrow \mathbb{N}$ is negligible if for every polynomial $p(\cdot)$ and all sufficiently large n it holds that $f(n) < \frac{1}{p(n)}$. We use the abbreviation PPT to denote probabilistic polynomial-time.

3.1 Commitment Schemes

A commitment scheme enables a party, known as the *sender* S, to commit to a value while keeping it secret from the *receiver* R – this property is called *hiding*. Furthermore, it is guaranteed that at a later stage, the opening of the commitment can only yield a single value – this property is called *binding*. We consider commitment schemes that are statistically binding and computationally hiding.

Definition 1 (Commitment schemes). *A commitment scheme* $\langle C(m), R\rangle$ *is a two-phase protocol between a committer* $\mathcal{C}$ *and receiver* $\mathcal{R}$. *At the beginning of the protocol,* $\mathcal{C}$ *obtains as input a message* $m \in \{0,1\}^p$. *Next,* $\mathcal{C}$ *and* $\mathcal{R}$ *execute the commit phase, and obtain commitment transcript* $\tau \leftarrow \mathsf{Commit}\langle\mathcal{C}(m), \mathcal{R}\rangle$. *They also store (private) randomness used respectively by* $\mathcal{C}$ *and* $\mathcal{R}$ *as* $\mathsf{state}_{\mathcal{C},\tau}$ *and* $\mathsf{state}_{\mathcal{R},\tau}$. *At the end of this phase,* $\mathcal{R}$ *outputs* 0 *or* 1, *where* 1 *denotes that* $\mathcal{R}$ *accepted the commitment phase. The view of the receiver (including its coins, any auxiliary information* z *and transcript) at the end of this phase is denoted by* $\mathsf{View}_{\mathcal{R}}\langle\mathcal{C}(M), \mathcal{R}(z)\rangle$.

Later, $\mathcal{C}$ *and* $\mathcal{R}$ *possibly engage in another (interactive) decommit phase, which we denote by* $\mathsf{Decommit}\langle\tau, \mathcal{C}(m, \mathsf{state}_{\mathcal{C},\tau}), \mathcal{R}(\mathsf{state}_{\mathcal{R},\tau})\rangle$ *at the end of which* $\mathcal{R}$ *outputs* $\perp$ *or a message* $\widetilde{m} \in \{0,1\}^p$.

We require these algorithms to satisfy the following properties:

- **Correctness.** *If* $\mathcal{C}, \mathcal{R}$ *honestly follow the protocol,* Pr[$\mathcal{R}$ *accepts the decommitment*] $= 1 - \mathsf{negl}(\lambda)$.
- **Computational hiding.** *For every PPT machine* R^* *with auxiliary information* z, *the distributions* $\{\mathsf{View}_{\mathcal{R}}\langle\mathcal{C}(m), \mathcal{R}(z)\rangle\}$ *and* $\{\mathsf{View}_{\mathcal{R}}\langle\mathcal{C}(0), \mathcal{R}(z)\rangle\}$ *are computationally indistinguishable.*
- **Statistical binding.** *For any (unbounded) malicious* $\mathcal{C}^*$,

$$\Pr\left[\mathcal{R} \textit{ accepts decommitment to } \widetilde{m}_1 \textit{ and } \widetilde{m}_2 \textit{ where } \widetilde{m}_1 \neq \widetilde{m}_2\right] \leq \mathsf{negl}(\lambda)$$

where the probability is over the randomness of sampling ($\tau \leftarrow \mathsf{Commit}\langle\mathcal{C}^*, \mathcal{R}\rangle$), ($\widetilde{m}_1 \leftarrow \mathsf{Decommit}\langle\tau, \mathcal{C}^*, \mathcal{R}(\mathsf{state}_{\mathcal{R},\tau})\rangle$) *and* ($\widetilde{m}_2 \leftarrow \mathsf{Decommit}\langle\tau, \mathcal{C}^*, \mathcal{R}(\mathsf{state}_{\mathcal{R},\tau})\rangle$). *We will say that the scheme satisfies computational binding if the above holds for any PPT committer* $\mathcal{C}^*$ *with auxiliary input* z.

We now define an extractable commitment scheme [37,38]. Intuitively, a commitment scheme is extractable if there exists an expected polynomial time machine that can extract the value committed by a cheating committer.

Definition 2 (Extractable Commitments). *A commitment scheme is said to be extractable, if there exists a PPT oracle algorithm* E *that given* $\tau \leftarrow \mathsf{Commit}\langle\mathcal{C}^*, \mathcal{R}\rangle$ *and oracle access to* $\mathcal{C}^*$, *outputs* $\widetilde{m}, r$ *such that* $\exists r$ *where* $\tau = \mathsf{Commit}\langle\mathcal{C}(\widetilde{m}), \mathcal{R}\rangle$ *using randomness* r *for* $\mathcal{C}$.

An equivocal commitment scheme allows an expected polynomial time machine called as the *equivocator* to equivocate a commitment transcript to any chosen committed value. Equivocal commitments have been extensively used to obtain round optimal constructions of secure two-party and multiparty computations [10,29].

Definition 3 (Equivocal Commitments). *A commit-and-prove scheme is equivocal if there exists a PPT oracle algorithm* Eq *that interacts with oracle access to any malicious receiver* $\mathcal{R}^*$ *to output a commitment transcript* $\widetilde{\tau}$*. Next, it obtains externally generated string* m'*, and then runs* $\mathsf{Decommit}\langle\widetilde{\tau}, \mathsf{Eq}^{\mathcal{R}^*}, \mathcal{R}^*\rangle$*. Then, we require that the distributions*

$$\mathsf{View}_{\mathcal{R}^*}(\tau \leftarrow \mathsf{Commit}\langle\mathcal{C}(M'), \mathcal{R}^*\rangle, \mathsf{Decommit}\langle\tau, \mathcal{C}, \mathcal{R}^*\rangle) \text{ and}$$
$$\mathsf{View}_{\mathcal{R}^*}(\widetilde{\tau} \leftarrow \mathsf{Commit}\langle\mathsf{Eq}^{\mathcal{R}^*}, \mathcal{R}^*\rangle, \mathsf{Decommit}\langle\widetilde{\tau}, \mathsf{Eq}^{\mathcal{R}^*}, \mathcal{R}^*\rangle)$$

are computationally indistinguishable.

3.2 Commit-and-Prove Protocols

We start with the definition of commit and prove witness indistinguishable proof of knowledge. Our construction of commit and prove witness indistinguishable proof of knowledge satisfies a weaker notion of 1-of-2 binding. Intuitively, 1-of-2 binding states that there exists at most two different messages that a committed transcript can be opened to.

Definition 4 (Commit-and-Prove Witness Indistinguishable Proof of Knowledge). *A commit-and-prove witness indistinguishable proof of knowledge is a protocol between a prover* $\mathcal{P}$ *and verifier* $\mathcal{V}$*. It consists of two phases, a commit phase and reveal phase.*

In the commit phase, $\mathcal{P}$ *interacts with* $\mathcal{V}$ *to commit to a message* m*. It also proves that the* m *satisfies some predicate* ϕ*, in other words it proves that* $\phi(m) = 1$*. Let* τ *denote the transcript* $\tau \leftarrow \mathsf{Commit\text{-}and\text{-}Prove}\langle\mathcal{P}(m, \phi), \mathcal{V}(\phi)\rangle$*. They also store (private) randomness used respectively by* $\mathcal{P}$ *and* $\mathcal{V}$ *as* $\mathsf{state}_{\mathcal{P},\tau}$ *and* $\mathsf{state}_{\mathcal{V},\tau}$*. At the end of this phase,* $\mathcal{V}$ *outputs* 0 *or* 1*, where* 1 *denotes that* $\mathcal{V}$ *accepted the commit-and-prove phase.*

Later, the parties $\mathcal{P}$ *and* $\mathcal{V}$ *possibly engage in another decommit phase, which we denote by* $\mathsf{Decommit}\langle\tau, \mathcal{P}(m, \mathsf{state}_{\mathcal{P},\tau}), \mathcal{V}(\mathsf{state}_{\mathcal{V},\tau})\rangle$*, at the end of which* $\mathcal{V}$ *outputs* $\perp$ *or* $\widetilde{m} \in \{0,1\}^p$*.*

We require the protocol to satisfy the following conditions:

- **Completeness.** *If* $\mathcal{P}, \mathcal{V}$ *honestly follow the protocol,* $\Pr[\mathcal{V}$ *accepts the proof*$] = 1 - \mathsf{negl}(\lambda)$.
- **Witness Indistinguishability.** *Let the view of a malicious verifier* $\mathcal{V}^*$ *at the end of the commit phase when the honest prover has input message* m *be denoted by* $\mathsf{View}_{\mathcal{V}^*}(\mathsf{Commit\text{-}and\text{-}Prove}\langle\mathcal{P}(m), \mathcal{V}^*(z)\rangle)$*. For any malicious*

verifier V^**, and any two messages* m_1, m_2 *such that* $\phi(m_1) = 1$ *and* $\phi(m_2) = 1$*, the distributions* $\{P(m_1), V^*(z)\}$ *and* $\{P(m_2), V^*(z)\}$ *are computationally indistinguishable.*

- **Proof of Knowledge.** *There exists a PPT oracle algorithm* E *that given oracle access to* $\mathcal{P}^*$ *and* $\tau \leftarrow \mathsf{Commit\text{-}and\text{-}Prove}\langle \mathcal{P}^*, \mathcal{R}(\phi)\rangle$ *outputs* $\widetilde{m}$ *such that the following properties are satisfied for every PPT* $\mathcal{P}^*$*:*
  - $\phi(\widetilde{m}) = 1$.
  - **1-of-2-Binding.** *This requires that the committer cannot decommit to two values* m_1, m_2*, both of which are different from* $\widetilde{m}$*. In other words, we require the commit-and-prove to bind any malicious committer to at least one out of two values. Formally,* $\Pr[\widetilde{m} \notin \{m_1, m_2\}] \leq \mathsf{negl}(\lambda)$*, whenever* $m_1 \leftarrow \mathsf{Decommit}\langle \tau, \mathcal{P}^*, \mathcal{V}(\mathsf{state}_{\mathcal{V},\tau})\rangle$*, and also when* $m_2 \leftarrow \mathsf{Decommit}\langle \tau, \mathcal{P}^*, \mathcal{V}(\mathsf{state}_{\mathcal{V},\tau})\rangle$.

We now give the definition of commit and prove zero-knowledge argument of knowledge. We include the equivocality property into our zero-knowledge condition. This will be helpful when proving the security of our construction of equivocal commitment scheme.

Definition 5 (Commit-and-Prove Zero-Knowledge Arguments of Knowledge). *A commit-and-prove zero-knowledge argument of knowledge is a protocol between a prover* $\mathcal{P}$ *and verifier* $\mathcal{V}$*. It consists of two phases, a commit phase and reveal phase.*

In the commit phase, $\mathcal{P}$ *interacts with* $\mathcal{V}$ *to commit to a message* m*. It also proves that the* m *satisfies some predicate* ϕ*, in other words it proves that* $\phi(m) = 1$*. Let* τ *denote the transcript* $\tau \leftarrow \mathsf{Commit\text{-}and\text{-}Prove}\langle \mathcal{P}(m,\phi), \mathcal{V}(\phi)\rangle$*. They also store (private) randomness used respectively by* $\mathcal{P}$ *and* $\mathcal{V}$ *as* $\mathsf{state}_{\mathcal{P},\tau}$ *and* $\mathsf{state}_{\mathcal{V},\tau}$*. At the end of this phase,* $\mathcal{V}$ *outputs* 0 *or* 1*, where* 1 *denotes that* $\mathcal{V}$ *accepted the commit-and-prove phase.*

Later, the parties $\mathcal{P}$ *and* $\mathcal{V}$ *possibly engage in another decommit phase, which we denote by* $\mathsf{Decommit}\langle \tau, \mathcal{P}(m, \mathsf{state}_{\mathcal{P},\tau}), \mathcal{V}(\mathsf{state}_{\mathcal{V},\tau})\rangle$*, at the end of which* $\mathcal{V}$ *outputs* $\perp$ *or* $\widetilde{m} \in \{0,1\}^p$*.*

We require the protocol to satisfy the following conditions:

- **Completeness.** *If* $\mathcal{P}, \mathcal{V}$ *honestly follow the protocol,* $\Pr[\mathcal{V}$ *accepts the proof*$] = 1 - \mathsf{negl}(\lambda)$.
- **Argument of Knowledge.** *There exists a PPT oracle algorithm* E *that given oracle access to* $\mathcal{P}^*$ *and* $\tau \leftarrow \mathsf{Commit\text{-}and\text{-}Prove}\langle \mathcal{P}^*, \mathcal{R}(\phi)\rangle$ *outputs* $\widetilde{m}$ *such that the following properties are satisfied for every PPT* $\mathcal{P}^*$*:*
  - $\phi(\widetilde{m}) = 1$.
  - **Computational Binding.** $\Pr\left[m \leftarrow \mathsf{Decommit}\langle \tau, \mathcal{P}^*, \mathcal{R}(\mathsf{state}_{\mathcal{R},\tau})\rangle \wedge m \neq \widetilde{m}\right] \leq \mathsf{negl}(\lambda)$.
- **Zero-Knowledge.** *Let* $\mathsf{View}_{\mathcal{V}^*}(\mathsf{Commit\text{-}and\text{-}Prove}\langle \mathcal{P}(m), \mathcal{V}^*(z)\rangle)$ *denote the view of a malicious verifier* $\mathcal{V}^*$ *at the end of the commit phase when the honest prover has input message* m *such that* $\phi(m) = 1$*. There exists a simulator*

Sim *that outputs* $\mathsf{View}_{\mathsf{Commit}}(\mathsf{Sim}^{\mathcal{V}^*})$. *Next, it obtains input* m *and outputs* $\mathsf{View}_{\mathsf{Decommit}}(\mathsf{Sim}^{\mathcal{V}^*}(m))$. *Then, we require that for all values* m,

$$\Big(\mathsf{View}_{\mathsf{Commit}}(\mathsf{Sim}^{\mathcal{V}^*}), \mathsf{View}_{\mathsf{Decommit}}(\mathsf{Sim}^{\mathcal{V}^*}(m))\Big) \overset{c}{\approx}$$
$$(\mathsf{View}_{\mathcal{V}^*}(\mathsf{Commit\text{-}and\text{-}Prove}\langle \mathcal{P}(m), \mathcal{V}^*(z)\rangle), \mathsf{Decommit}\langle \tau, \mathcal{P}(\mathsf{state}_{\mathcal{P},\tau}), \mathcal{V}^*)$$

In particular, this also implies that any malicious verifier V^*, *and any two messages* m_1, m_2 *such that* $R(\phi, m_1) = 1$ *and* $R(\phi, m_2) = 1$, *the distribution* $\mathsf{View}_{\mathcal{V}^*}(\mathsf{Commit\text{-}and\text{-}Prove}\langle \mathcal{P}(m_1), \mathcal{V}^*(z)\rangle)$ *and the distribution* $\mathsf{View}_{\mathcal{V}^*}(\mathsf{Commit\text{-}and\text{-}Prove}\langle \mathcal{P}(m_2), \mathcal{V}^*(z)\rangle)$ *are computationally indistinguishable.*

Remark 1. A commit-and-prove protocol is said to satisfy delayed-input completeness, if $\mathcal{P}, \mathcal{V}$ obtain the predicate ϕ in the last round of a protocol.

3.3 Robust Offline/Online Randomized Encoding

We start with the definition of a randomized encoding [2,3,24].

Definition 6 (Randomized Encoding). *Let* $f : \{0,1\}^n \to \{0,1\}^\ell$ *be a function. Then a function* $\hat{f} : \{0,1\}^n \times \{0,1\}^m \to \{0,1\}^s$ *is said to be a randomized encoding of* f, *if:*

- **Correctness:** *There exists a decoder algorithm* Dec *such that for any input* $x \in \{0,1\}^n$, *except with negligible probability over the randomness of the encoding and the random coins of* Dec, *it holds that* $\mathsf{Dec}(\hat{f}(x, U_m)) = f(x)$.
- **Computational (statistical) privacy:** *There exists a PPT simulator* $\mathcal{S}$, *such that for any input* $x \in \{0,1\}^n$ *the following distributions are computationally (statistically) indistinguishable:*
  - $\{\hat{f}(x, U_m)\}_{n\in\mathbb{N}, x\in\{0,1\}^n}$, *and,*
  - $\{\mathcal{S}(f(x))\}_{n\in\mathbb{N}, x\in\{0,1\}^n}$

We recall the definition of robust randomized encoding from [21].

Definition 7 (Robust Offline/Online Randomized Encoding). *[21] A randomized encoding is called an online/offline encoding, if there exists functions* $\widehat{f}_{\mathrm{off}}$ *and* $\widehat{f}_{\mathrm{on}}$ *such that* $\widehat{f}(x; r) = (\widehat{f}_{\mathrm{off}}(r), \widehat{f}_{\mathrm{on}}(x, r))$. *That is, there exists an offline component that does not depend on the input, and an online component which is a function of the input. It is called robust if additionally, it holds that: if there exists no* x *such that* $f(x) = a$, *then for any* r, *there does not exist any* z *such that* $\mathsf{Dec}(\widehat{f}_{\mathrm{off}}(r), z) = a$.

In Appendix A, we describe a simplified variant of the construction of robust offline/online randomized encodings from [21], that only assumes one-way functions.

4 Three-Round Black-Box Commit-and-Prove WIPoK

In this section, we describe a three-round black-box commit-and-prove witness indistinguishable proof of knowledge protocol.

4.1 Construction

The construction is described in Fig. 1, and uses a robust randomized encoding $(\widehat{f}^{\text{off}}, \widehat{f}^{\text{on}})$, secure in the presence of adaptive choice of inputs.

We have the following theorem.

Input: The prover $\mathcal{P}$ and verifier $\mathcal{V}$ have common input a predicate ϕ. $\mathcal{P}$ additionally obtains input $m \in \mathbb{F}$ (where $\mathbb{F}$ is a finite field) such that $\phi(m) = 1$.

Definition of f: The function f has $w_0 \in \mathbb{F}^3$ hardwired. It takes as input the predicate ϕ, two elements $\alpha, \beta \in \mathbb{F}$, an element $w_1 \in \mathbb{F}^3$, two values $(a, b) \in \mathbb{F}$, and does the following:

1. Set $(m\|r\|s) = w_0 + w_1$.
2. If $a \neq (r + \alpha m)$ and $b \neq (s + \beta m)$ output $\perp$.
   Else, output $(\phi(m), \phi, \alpha, \beta, w_1, (a, b))$.

Protocol:

1. $\mathcal{P}$ chooses $r \xleftarrow{\$} \mathbb{F}$. For $i \in [\lambda]$, $\mathcal{P}$ does the following:
   (a) Choose $w_0^i \xleftarrow{\$} \mathbb{F}^3$ and compute $w_1^i := w_0^i \oplus (m\|r\|\perp)$.
   (b) Choose $\omega_i \xleftarrow{\$} \{0,1\}^*$ and compute $\widehat{f}^{\text{off}}(\omega_i)$ and $\tau_i \leftarrow \mathsf{Com}(w_1^i)$.
   (c) Send $(\widehat{f}^{\text{off}}(\omega_i), \tau_i)$.
2. $\mathcal{V}$ sends $\mathsf{ch} \xleftarrow{\$} \{0,1\}^\lambda$, $\alpha \xleftarrow{\$} \mathbb{F}$ and $\beta \leftarrow \mathbb{F}$.
3. $\mathcal{P}$ chooses $b \xleftarrow{\$} \mathbb{F}$, and sets $a = (r + \alpha m)$. It sends a, b. Additionally, for every $i \in [\lambda]$, $\mathcal{P}$ does the following:
   (a) If $\mathsf{ch}_i = 0$, send w_0^i, ω_i.
   (b) If $\mathsf{ch}_i = 1$, send $\widehat{f}^{\text{on}}(\phi||\alpha||\beta||w_1^i||(a, b), \omega_i)$, and decommit to τ_i.

Verification Phase:

– Output 1 if the following checks pass for every $i \in [\lambda]$:
  1. If $\mathsf{ch}_i = 0$, check if the received w_0^i is embedded in the circuit $\widehat{f}^{\text{off}}$ computed using randomness r_i.
  2. If $\mathsf{ch}_i = 1$, run $\text{Dec}(\widehat{f}^{\text{off}}, \widehat{f}^{\text{on}})$ and accept if the evaluation outputs $(1, \phi, \alpha, \beta, w_1^i, (a, b))$ where w_1^i is obtained from the decommitment to τ_i.

Fig. 1. Black-box witness indistinguishable proof of knowledge

Theorem 1. *The protocol described in Fig. 1 is a black-box commit-and-prove witness indistinguishable argument of knowledge according to Definition 4.*

The completeness of the protocol can be easily verified from inspection. Furthermore, the protocol only makes black-box access to a non-interactive commitment scheme and a robust randomized encoding. Recall that a robust randomized encoding can be constructed from black-use of a one-way function. We now show witness indistinguishability.

Lemma 1. *The protocol described in Fig. 1 satisfies witness indistinguishability according to Definition 4.*

Proof. To prove witness indistinguishability of this protocol, we consider the following sequence of hybrid experiments.

The first hybrid Hyb_0 corresponds to the view of a (malicious) verifier interacting with an honest prover that follows the protocol in Fig. 1 using the message m_0 for the predicate ϕ.

We define a hybrid $\mathsf{Hyb}_{0,k}$ for each $k \in [0, \lambda]$ that corresponds to the view of a (malicious) verifier interacting with a prover that uses the message m_1 in the first k instances and the message m_0 in the remaining instances. To be more precise, the prover in $\mathsf{Hyb}_{0,k}$ does the following:

- In round-1,
  1. $\mathcal{P}$ chooses $r, s \xleftarrow{\$} \mathbb{F}$.
  2. For $i \in [k]$, $\mathcal{P}$ does the following:
     (a) Choose $w_0^i \xleftarrow{\$} \mathbb{F}^3$ and compute $w_1^i := w_0^i \oplus (m_1 \| \bot \| s)$.
     (b) Choose $\omega_i \xleftarrow{\$} \{0,1\}^*$ and compute $\widehat{f}^{\text{off}}(\omega_i)$ and $\tau_i \leftarrow \mathsf{Com}(w_1^i)$.
     (c) Send $(\widehat{f}^{\text{off}}(\omega_i), \tau_i)$.
  3. For $i \in [k+1, \lambda]$, $\mathcal{P}$ does the following:
     (a) Choose $w_0^i \xleftarrow{\$} \mathbb{F}^3$ and compute $w_1^i := w_0^i \oplus (m_0 \| r \| \bot)$.
     (b) Choose $\omega_i \xleftarrow{\$} \{0,1\}^*$ and compute $\widehat{f}^{\text{off}}(\omega_i)$ and $\tau_i \leftarrow \mathsf{Com}(w_1^i)$.
     (c) Send $(\widehat{f}^{\text{off}}(\omega_i), \tau_i)$.
- In round-3,
  1. $\mathcal{P}$ sends $b := s + \beta m_1$ and $a = r + \alpha m_0$. Additionally, for every $i \in [\lambda]$, $\mathcal{P}$ does the following:
     (a) If $\mathsf{ch}_i = 0$, send w_0^i, ω_i.
     (b) If $\mathsf{ch}_i = 1$, send $\widehat{f}^{\text{on}}(\phi \| \alpha \| \beta \| w_1^i \| (a, b), \omega_i)$, and decommit to τ_i.

Claim. Assuming the hiding property of Com and the adaptive security of robust randomized encoding, $\mathsf{Hyb}_{0,k-1} \stackrel{c}{\approx} \mathsf{Hyb}_{0,k}$ for each $k \in [\lambda]$.

Proof. Assume for the sake of contradiction that there exists a malicious verifier that can distinguish $\mathsf{Hyb}_{0,k-1}$ and $\mathsf{Hyb}_{0,k}$ with non-negligible probability. We will construct an adversary $\mathcal{B}$ that breaks the security of either the robust randomized encoding or the hiding property of Com with non-negligible probability. $\mathcal{B}$ chooses a bit $b_k \xleftarrow{\$} \{0,1\}$.

Case-1: $b_k = 0$. In this case, $\mathcal{B}$ does the following:

1. For all $i \neq k$, $\mathcal{B}$ generates the commitments and the randomized encoding as in $\mathsf{Hyb}_{0,k-1}$. For $i = k$, it does the following:
   (a) Choose $w_0^i \xleftarrow{\$} \mathbb{F}^3$ and compute $w_1^i := w_0^i \oplus (m_0\|r\|\bot)$ and $\widehat{w}_1^i := w_0^i \oplus (m_1\|\bot\|s)$. Give the two messages $w_0^i, \widehat{w}_1^i$ as the challenge messages to the hiding property of Com. Obtain the challenge commitment τ_i.
   (b) Choose $\omega_i \xleftarrow{\$} \{0,1\}^*$ and compute $\widehat{f}^{\text{off}}(\omega_i)$ and $\tau_i \leftarrow \mathsf{Com}(w_1^i)$.
   (c) Send $(\widehat{f}^{\text{off}}(\omega_i), \tau_i)$.
2. If ch_k obtained from the receiver is not equal to b_k, we abort and output a random bit. Else, continue the protocol as per the description of $\mathsf{Hyb}_{0,k-1}$. Output whatever the verifier outputs
3. Note that if τ_k is a commitment to w_1^i then the distribution is identical to $\mathsf{Hyb}_{0,k-1}$; else, it is identical to distribution $\mathsf{Hyb}_{0,k}$. Thus, if the malicious verifier can distinguish between $\mathsf{Hyb}_{0,k-1}$ and $\mathsf{Hyb}_{0,k}$ with probability p then $\mathcal{B}$ breaks the hiding of the commitment scheme with probability at least $p/2$.

Case-2: $b_k = 1$. In this case, $\mathcal{B}$ does the following:

1. For all $i \neq k$, $\mathcal{B}$ generates the commitments and the randomized encoding as in $\mathsf{Hyb}_{0,k-1}$. For $i = k$, it does the following:
   (a) Choose $w_1^i \xleftarrow{\$} \mathbb{F}^3$ and computes $w_0^i := w_1^i \oplus (m_0\|r\|s)$ and $\widehat{w}_0^i := w_1^i \oplus (m_1\|r\|s)$. Give to the randomized encoding challenger two circuits $f[w_0^i]$ and $f[\widehat{w}_0^i]$ as the challenge circuits. Obtain $\widehat{f}^{\text{off}}$ as the challenge circuit.
   (b) Send $\widehat{f}^{\text{off}}$ and $\tau_i \leftarrow \mathsf{Com}(w_1^i)$.
2. If ch_k obtained from the receiver is not equal to b_k, we abort and output a random bit. Else,
   (a) Obtain α from the verifier.
   (b) Send $\phi\|\alpha\|\beta\|w_1^i\|(a,b), \omega_i$ as the challenge input to the randomized encoding challenger and obtain $\widehat{f}^{\text{on}}$.
   (c) Send $\widehat{f}^{\text{on}}$ as response to ch_k and decommit to τ_k.
3. Finally, output whatever the verifier outputs.

Notice that the output of the two circuits $f[w_0^i]$ and $f[\widehat{w}_0^i]$ on the challenge input is exactly the same. Thus, $\mathcal{B}$ constitutes a valid challenger to the adaptive security of randomized encoding. Thus, if $\widehat{f}^{\text{off}}$ corresponds to a offline randomized encoding of $f_{w_0^i}$, the view of the malicious verifier is identical to $\mathsf{Hyb}_{0,k-1}$. Else, the view is identical to $\mathsf{Hyb}_{0,k}$. Thus, a malicious verifier distinguishing $\mathsf{Hyb}_{0,k-1}$ and $\mathsf{Hyb}_{0,k}$ can be used to break the security of robust randomized encodings.

We now prove that $\mathsf{Hyb}_{0,0}$ is identically distributed to Hyb_0. Notice that $\mathsf{Hyb}_{0,0}$ is the same as Hyb_0, except that the prover sends $b = s + \beta m_1$ instead of sampling b uniformly at random. Since s is information theoretically hidden in both $\mathsf{Hyb}_{0,0}$ and Hyb_0 it follows that both these distributions are identical. A similar argument shows that $\mathsf{Hyb}_{0,\lambda}$ is identical to Hyb_1. This completes the proof of the claim.

The proof of WI follows by noting that $\mathsf{Hyb}_{0,\lambda}$ is distributed identically to the case where the prover uses the witness W_1 to generate the proof.

We will now prove that it is an argument of knowledge:

Lemma 2. *The protocol in Fig. 1 is a proof of knowledge against PPT provers, even for statements chosen adaptively by such a prover in the last round, according to Definition 4.*

Proof. We begin by describing the extractor (having oracle access to a PPT prover $\mathcal{P}^*$) that takes as input an accepted transcript $\mathbb{T}$ and outputs a value $\widetilde{m}$ such that $\phi(\widetilde{m}) = 1$ and there exists at most two messages $\widetilde{m}_1, \widetilde{m}_2$ such that $\widetilde{m} \in \{\widetilde{m}_1, \widetilde{m}_2\}$ and either $\mathcal{P}^*$ will decommit to $\widetilde{m}_1$ or $\widetilde{m}_2$.

The extractor rewinds the cheating prover $\mathcal{P}^*$ to the beginning of the third round multiple times, and gives different uniformly chosen challenge messages $ch \xleftarrow{\$} \{0,1\}^\lambda$. It stops when it obtains for some $i \in [\lambda]$, two decommitments w_0^i, w_1^i such that $w_0^i \oplus w_1^i = (m\|r\|s)$, and outputs m if $\phi(m)$, and $r + \alpha m = a$ or $s + \beta m = b$ from the main thread.

Let $\mathbb{T}$ be the accepted protocol transcript. Because of robustness of the randomized encoding and a simple averaging argument, we note that with overwhelming probability over the choice of random challenge $ch \in \mathbb{T}$, at least $\lambda - O(\log^2 \lambda)$ indices i are such that $f_{w_0^i}(\phi, \alpha, \beta, w_1^i, a, b) \neq \bot$. Let S be the set of indices i such that the above is true. Then, we have for each $i \in S$, let $w_1^i \oplus w_0^i = (m_i\|r_i\|s_i)$ where $\phi(m_i) = 1$. Further, for every $i \in S$, we now have from the definition of f that, $r_i + \alpha m_i = a$ and $s_i + \beta m_i = b$. With overwhelming probability over α, β, this is possible only if there exists at most two values $\widetilde{m}_1, \widetilde{m}_2$ such that $m_i \in \{\widetilde{m}_1, \widetilde{m}_2\}$ for all $i \in S$ (by Schwartz-Zippel lemma).

We finally argue that the extractor runs in expected polynomial time. Let p be the probability that conditioned on the first two messages of the protocol, the prover $\mathcal{P}^*$ generates an accepting proof. Since the running time of the extractor in each rewind is bounded by some polynomial $\mathrm{poly}(\lambda)$, we have that the expected running time of the extractor is $p \cdot \frac{\mathrm{poly}(\lambda)}{p} = \mathrm{poly}(\lambda)$.

4.2 Black-Box One-Binding Commitment to Two Strings

In this section, we describe how to use the black-box commit-and-prove WIPoK to generate a commitment to two strings such that one of the two commitments is binding, and the other can be freely equivocated by a simulator. Such a protocol can also be built using ideas from [34], however, we give a direct instantiation via a slight modification of our black-box commit-and-prove WIAoK. This scheme is referred to as two-com, and is described in Fig. 2.

We also note that unlike [34], when we use scheme two-com, honest parties will never need to rely on equivocation, and equivocation will only be used in the proof of security.

Witness indistinguishability of the argument of binding of one of the two commitments follows directly via witness indistinguishability of the underlying protocol, using an identical proof to the one in Lemma 1.

Input: Committer $\mathcal{C}$ has input two messages m_0, m_1.

Definition of f**:** The function f has $w_0 \in \mathbb{F}^2$ hardwired. *The relation* $R(x, w) = 1$ *if and only if* $(x_1 = w$ *OR* $x_2 = w)$*, where* $x = x_1||x_2$.
The function f takes as input an instances $x \in \mathbb{F}^2$, an element $\alpha \in \mathbb{F}$, an element $w_1 \in \mathbb{F}^2$, two values $(a, \widetilde{a}) \in \mathbb{F}^2$, and does the following:

1. Compute $(w\|r\|\widetilde{r}) = w_0 + w_1$.
2. If $a \neq (r + \alpha w)$ and $\widetilde{a} \neq (\widetilde{r} + \alpha_1 w)$, output $\perp$. Else, output $(R(x, w), x, \alpha, w_1, (a, \widetilde{a}))$.

Protocol:

1. $\mathcal{C}$ chooses $r \xleftarrow{\$} \mathbb{F}$. For $i \in [\lambda]$, $\mathcal{P}$ does the following with $w = m_0$:
   (a) Chooses $w_0^i \xleftarrow{\$} \mathbb{F}$ and computes $w_1^i := w_0^i \oplus (w\|r)$.
   (b) Chooses $r_i \xleftarrow{\$} \{0,1\}^*$ and computes $\widehat{f}^{\text{off}}_{w_0^i}(r_i)$, $\sigma_i \leftarrow \mathsf{Com}(r_i)$ and $\tau_i \leftarrow \mathsf{Com}(w_1^i)$.
   (c) Sends $(\widehat{f}^{\text{off}}_{w_0^i}(r_i), \sigma_i, \tau_i)$.
2. $\mathcal{R}$ sends $\mathsf{ch} \xleftarrow{\$} \{0,1\}^\lambda$ and $\alpha \xleftarrow{\$} \mathbb{F}$.
3. $\mathcal{P}$ sends the opening $x = (m_0||m_1)$. Additionally, $\mathcal{P}$ chooses $\widetilde{a} \xleftarrow{\$} \mathbb{F}$ sends $\widetilde{a}$ and $a = r + \alpha w$. Additionally, for every $i \in [\lambda]$, $\mathcal{P}$ does the following:
   (a) If $\mathsf{ch}_i = 0$, sends w_0^i, s_0^i and decommits to σ_i.
   (b) If $\mathsf{ch}_i = 1$, sends $\widehat{f}^{\text{on}}_{w_0^i}(x||\alpha||w_1^i||(a, \widetilde{a}); r_i)$, and decommits to τ_i.

Verification Phase:

– Output 1 if the following checks pass for every $i \in [\lambda]$:
   1. If $\mathsf{ch}_i = 0$, check if the received w_0^i is embedded in the circuit $\widehat{f}^{\text{off}}_{w_0^i}$ computed using randomness r_i. Check that the decommitment information to σ_i is correct.
   2. If $\mathsf{ch}_i = 1$, run the evaluation algorithm for randomized encoding $\widehat{f}^{\text{off}}_{w_0^i}$ with $\widehat{f}^{\text{on}}_{w_0^i}$ as input and accept if the evaluation outputs $(1, x, \alpha, w_1^i, (a, \widetilde{a}))$ where w_1^i is obtained from the decommitment to τ_i.

Fig. 2. Commitment to two strings where one is binding

We will now argue why the protocol in Fig. 2 is such that any (malicious) committer is bound to one of the two openings $m \in \{m_0, m_1\}$, by the end of the first round. This relies on soundness of the witness indistinguishable argument. Specifically, by the Schwartz-Zippel lemma, there exist at most two witnesses W, W' such that at least $(\lambda - \log^2 n)$ parallel executions generated by a malicious committer, have a commitment to either W or W', or both. Now, because of the soundness of individual WI arguments, once the first message has been committed, in the third message, any (malicious) committer can only open to m_0, m_1 such that:

- If in the first message, all but $\log^2 n$ commitments were to the same witness W, then either $W = m_0$ or $W = m_1$.
- If in the first message, all but $\log^2 n$ commitments were to two witnesses W, W' then $W = m_0, W' = m_1$ or vice-versa.

5 Four-Round Black-Box Commit-and-Prove Zero-Knowledge

In this section, we describe a black-box commit-and-prove zero-knowledge argument in four rounds based on injective one-way functions. We start with a description of the main tools used in the construction.

5.1 Construction

Our construction is described formally in Fig. 3, and makes use of the following primitives:

- A non-interactive, statistically binding commitment Com.
- A three-round commitment to two strings, together with a black-box witness-indistinguishable proof that one of the two commitments is binding by the end of the first round. We also require the other commitment to be equivocal. Such a scheme is described in [34], Sect. 3. Let $\mathsf{two\text{-}com}(s_1, s_2)$ denote such a scheme for committing to strings s_1 and s_2.
- A robust randomized encoding $\widehat{f}^{\text{off}}, \widehat{f}^{\text{on}}$ according to Definition 6.

5.2 Proof of Security

We start with the lemma which shows that the protocol described in Fig. 1 is a commitment to the witness w.

Lemma 3. *The protocol described in Fig. 3 is a statistically binding commitment to the element $w \in \mathbb{F}$.*

Proof. We start with the description of the decommit phase and then argue statistical binding and computational hiding of the protocol.

The decommit phase involves opening the commitments σ_i, σ_i' and σ_i^* and sending w_0^i for every $i \in [\lambda]$. For each $i \in [\lambda]$, compute $w_i \| r_i := w_0^i + w_1^i$ (where a value is substituted with a default symbol if the decommitment information is not valid) and output the value w that occurs in more than $\lambda/2$ positions. If there is no w that occurs in more that $\lambda/2$ positions then we reject the decommitment information.

Since the commitment sent in the second round of the protocol is statistically binding and we have defined the decommitment phase to output the majority of the committed values, we note that there can exist at most one valid decommitment to a protocol transcript except with negligible probability. Thus, the protocol is statistically binding. We note that computational hiding property follows the zero-knowledge property we later show.

Input: The prover $\mathcal{P}$ and verifier $\mathcal{V}$ have common input x and relation R. $\mathcal{P}$ additionally obtains input w such that $R(x, w) = 1$. We assume that $w \in \mathbb{F}$ where $\mathbb{F}$ is a finite field.

Definition of f: The function f has hardwired a share of the witness w_0, and a share of trapdoor information s_0. It takes as input the instance x, a challenge α, a share of the witness w_1, a share of trapdoor information s_1, a value a, $\widehat{s}_0, \widehat{s}_1$ (recovered from the third message of the two-com) and does the following:

1. Compute $s = s_0 \oplus s_1$. If $\widehat{s}_0 = s$ or $\widehat{s}_1 = s$, output $(1, x, w_1, s_1, a)$. Else, continue.
2. Compute $w\|r = w_0 \oplus w_1$. If $a \neq (r\alpha + w)$, output $\bot$. Else, output $(R(x, w), x, w_1, s_1, a)$.

Protocol:

1. $\mathcal{V}$ picks strings $\widehat{s}_0, \widehat{s}_1 \xleftarrow{\$} \{0,1\}^{2\lambda}$ and sends the first message π_1 of $\mathsf{two\text{-}com}(\widehat{s}_0, \widehat{s}_1)$.
2. $\mathcal{P}$ chooses $r \xleftarrow{\$} \mathbb{F}$, and $s \leftarrow \{0,1\}^{\lambda}$. For $i \in [\lambda]$ it does the following:
   (a) Choose w_0^i uniformly at random and compute $w_1^i := w_0^i \oplus (w\|r)$.
   (b) Choose s_0^i uniformly at random and compute $s_1^i := s_0^i \oplus s$.
   (c) Choose $r_i \xleftarrow{\$} \{0,1\}^*$, compute $\widehat{f}^{\text{off}}_{w_0^i, s_0^i}(r_i)$, $\sigma_i := \mathsf{Com}(r_i)$, $\sigma_i' := \mathsf{Com}(w_1^i)$ and $\sigma_i^* := \mathsf{Com}(s_1^i)$.

   Send $(\widehat{f}^{\text{off}}_{w_0^i, s_0^i}(r_i), \sigma_i, \sigma_i', \sigma_i^*)$ for each $i \in [\lambda]$ along with the second message π_2 of two-com.
3. $\mathcal{V}$ sends the strings $\widehat{s}_0$ and $\widehat{s}_1$, the third message π_3 of two-com to $\mathcal{P}$, together with $\mathsf{ch} \xleftarrow{\$} \{0,1\}^{\lambda}$ and $\alpha \xleftarrow{\$} \mathbb{F} \setminus \{0\}$.
4. $\mathcal{P}$ sends $a = r + \alpha w$ (in the field $\mathbb{F}$), and does the following for every $i \in [\lambda]$:
   (a) If $\mathsf{ch}_i = 0$, send w_0^i, s_0^i and decommit σ_i.
   (b) If $\mathsf{ch}_i = 1$, send $\widehat{f}^{\text{on}}_{w_0^i, s_0^i}(x\|\alpha\|a\|\widehat{s}_0\|\widehat{s}_1, w_1^i, s_1^i; r_i)$ and the decommitment to σ_i' and σ_i^*.

Check Phase:

- For every $i \in [\lambda]$:
  1. If $\mathsf{ch}_i = 0$, check if the received w_0^i, s_0^i are embedded in the circuit $\widehat{f}^{\text{off}}_{w_0^i, s_0^i}$ computed using randomness r_i. Also check that the decommitment information to σ_i is correct.
  2. If $\mathsf{ch}_i = 1$, run the evaluator for the garbled circuit by providing with $\widehat{f}^{\text{on}}_{w_0^i, s_0^i}$ and $\widehat{f}^{\text{off}}_{w_0^i, s_0^i}$ as inputs and accept if the evaluation outputs $(1, x, w_1^i, s_1^i)$ where w_1^i and s_1^i are obtained from the decommitment to σ_i' and σ_i^*.

Fig. 3. Four round black-box commit-and-prove ZKAoK

Lemma 4. *The protocol in Fig. 3 is an argument of knowledge against PPT provers, even for statements chosen adaptively by such a prover in the last round, according to Definition 5.*

Proof. We begin by describing the extractor (having oracle access to a PPT prover $\mathcal{P}^*$) that takes as input an accepted transcript $\mathbb{T}$ and outputs a value $w \in \mathbb{F}$ that occurs in majority of the positions and is such that $R(x, w) = 1$.

The extractor rewinds the cheating prover $\mathcal{P}^*$ to the beginning of the third round and gives different uniformly chosen challenge messages $ch \xleftarrow{\$} \{0,1\}^\lambda$. The extractor stops when it obtains for some $i \in [\lambda]$, two decommitments w_0^i, w_i^1 such that $w_0^i \oplus w_1^i = (w \| r)$ and outputs w if $r + \alpha w = a$ from the main thread.

We will now prove that for any PPT prover, the extracted w is such that $R(x, w) = 1$ – in particular, we will show that for any PPT prover, $\Pr[s = \widehat{s}_0 \text{ or } s = \widehat{s}_1] \le \mathsf{negl}(\lambda)$. Suppose for contradiction there exists a polynomial poly$(\cdot)$ and $\beta \in \{0,1\}$ such that $\Pr[s = \widehat{s}_\beta] \ge \frac{1}{\text{poly}(\lambda)}$. We will use this to contradict witness indistinguishability of $\mathsf{two\text{-}com}$, or the hiding of the commitments in $\mathsf{two\text{-}com}$. We consider the following sequence of hybrid experiments.

Hyb_0 corresponds to the real experiment, where the challenger generates the verifier messages according to the honest verifier strategy, such that the commitment $\widehat{s}_0$ is equivocable and the commitment $\widehat{s}_1$ is binding for $\gamma \in \{0,1\}$. It then uses the extraction strategy described above to extract s such that $\Pr[s = \widehat{s}_\beta] \ge \frac{1}{\text{poly}(\lambda)}$ for some $\beta \in \{0,1\}$.

In Hyb_{1a}, the challenger sends messages exactly the same way as Hyb_0, except that it samples $\widehat{s} \xleftarrow{\$} \{0,1\}^\lambda$, and in the third message, equivocates $\widehat{s}_0$ to $\widehat{s}$. The value extracted by the challenger must remain indistinguishable between Hyb_0 and Hyb_1, because of the equivocation property of the commitment to $\widehat{s}_0$. However, since $\widehat{s}$ was chosen uniformly at random and independent of $\widehat{s}_0$, the probability that $\widehat{s}$ equals $s_1^i \oplus s_0^i$ (which are both fixed before $\widehat{s}$ is chosen), is at most $2^{-\lambda}$. Otherwise, $\beta = 1$ and we consider the following sequence of hybrids.

In Hyb_{1b}, the challenger sends messages the same way as Hyb_0, except that the commitment $\widehat{s}_0$ is binding and the commitment $\widehat{s}_1$ is equivocable for $\gamma \in \{0,1\}$. It then uses the extraction strategy described above to extract s. By witness indistinguishability of the argument, this is such that $\Pr[s = \widehat{s}_1] \ge \frac{1}{\text{poly}(\lambda)}$.

In Hyb_2, the challenger sends messages exactly the same way as Hyb_{1b}, except that it samples $\widehat{s} \xleftarrow{\$} \{0,1\}^\lambda$, and in the third message, equivocates $\widehat{s}_1$ to $\widehat{s}$. The value extracted by the challenger must remain indistinguishable between Hyb_{1b} and Hyb_2, because of the equivocation property of the commitment to $\widehat{s}_1$. However, since $\widehat{s}$ was chosen uniformly at random and independent of $\widehat{s}_0$, the probability that $\widehat{s}$ equals $s_1^i \oplus s_0^i$ (which are both committed by the prover even before $\widehat{s}$ is chosen), is at most $2^{-\lambda}$.

We now argue that the extracted w occurs in the majority of positions. Let $\mathbb{T}$ be the accepted protocol transcript. We note that with overwhelming probability over the choice of random challenge $ch \in \mathbb{T}$, at least $\lambda - O(\log^2 \lambda)$ positions are such that $f_{w_0^i, s_0^i}(x, \alpha, w_1^i, s_1^i, a, \widehat{s}_0, \widehat{s}_1) = (1, x, \alpha, w_1^i, s_1^i, (a, \widetilde{a}))$. This follows from the robustness property of the randomized encoding scheme. Let S be the set of positions such that the above is true. Additionally, we showed above that for any i (in particular, for any $i \in S$) $s_0^i \oplus s_1^i$ is not equal to $\widehat{s}_0$ or $\widehat{s}_1$ with overwhelming probability. Thus, we have for each $i \in S$, let $w_1^i \oplus w_0^i = (w_i \| r_i)$ where $R(x, w_i) = 1$. Since $f_{w_0^i, s_0^i}(x, \alpha, w_1^i, s_1^i, a, \widehat{s}_0, \widehat{s}_1) = (1, x, \alpha, w_1^i, s_1^i, (a, \widetilde{a}))$ for every $i \in S$, we now have from the definition of f that, $w_i\alpha + r_i = a$. With overwhelming probability over α, this is possible only if there exists $(w, r) \in \mathbb{F}$ such that $w_i = w$ and $r_i = r$ for all $i \in S$ (by Schwartz-Zippel lemma).

We finally argue that the extractor runs in expected polynomial time. Let p be the probability that conditioned on fixing the first two messages of the main thread the prover $\mathcal{P}^*$ gives an accepted proof. Since the running time of the extractor in each rewind is bounded by some polynomial poly(λ), we have that the expected running time of the extractor is $p \cdot \frac{\text{poly}(\lambda)}{p} = \text{poly}(\lambda)$.

This completes the proof of soundness, and of the argument of knowledge property.

Lemma 5. *The protocol in Fig. 3 is zero-knowledge against all PPT verifiers $\mathcal{V}$.*

Proof. We begin with a brief overview of the simulation strategy (for simplicity in this overview we only consider non-aborting verifiers). The simulator runs the verifier on randomly chosen prover message for the second round, and observes the openings $\widehat{s}_0^{(1)}$ and $\widehat{s}_1^{(1)}$. On learning $\widehat{s}_0^{(1)}, \widehat{s}_1^{(1)}$, the simulator rewinds and sends a prover message by setting $s = \widehat{s}_0^{(1)}$. If the verifier responds with $\widehat{s}_0^{(2)} \neq \widehat{s}_0^{(1)}$, the simulator rewinds again and sets $s = \widehat{s}_1^{(1)}$. Denote the response of the verifier in the second rewinding by $\widehat{s}_0^{(3)}, \widehat{s}_1^{(3)}$.

Since the first message of two-com is binding to at least one string, if $\widehat{s}_0^{(2)} \neq \widehat{s}_0^{(1)}$, then with overwhelming probability, it must be the case that the commitment to $\widehat{s}_1$ is binding. In other words, $s = \widehat{s}_1^{(1)} = \widehat{s}_1^{(3)}$ with overwhelming probability. In this case, the simulator uses s as witness to complete the proof. The general simulation strategy is detailed in Fig. 4.

Proof of Simulation Security. The proof that the simulated distribution is indistinguishable from the real distribution will rely on the witness indistinguishability of a three round sub-protocol that is being executed within the main protocol. Let us give the details.

It was shown in [21] that the single execution (i.e., for each $i \in [\lambda]$) of the sub-protocol is zero-knowledge with soundness error 1/2. Hence, this sub-protocol is also witness indistinguishable. The parallel repetition of any witness indistinguishable protocol preserves the WI property. This also directly proves that conditioned on not aborting, a real transcript is indistinguishable from an ideal transcript.

Next, we prove that the probability of abort is at most negl(λ)-far between the real and ideal worlds. Note that by binding property of two-com, the simulator obtains one opening out of $\widehat{s}_0$ and $\widehat{s}_1$ correctly. Therefore, the simulation proceeds to Step 4(b) after at most two non-aborting rewinds. Now, the simulator rewinds the verifier in Step 4(*b*): by computational hiding of the second message of the

Input: The simulator Simu and verifier $\mathcal{V}$ have common input x and relation R.

Definition of f: The function f has hardwired a share of the witness w_0, and a share of trapdoor information s_0. It takes as input the instance x, a challenge α, a share of the witness w_1, a share of trapdoor information s_1, a value a, $\widehat{s}_0, \widehat{s}_1$ (recovered from the third message of the two-com) and does the following:

1. Compute $s = s_0 \oplus s_1$. If $\widehat{s}_0 = s$ or $\widehat{s}_1 = s$, output $(1, x, w_1, s_1)$. Else, continue.
2. Compute $w \| r = w_0 \oplus w_1$. If $a \neq (r + \alpha w)$, output $\perp$. Else, output $(R(x, w), x, w_1, s_1)$.

Protocol:

1. Obtain the first message π_1 of two-com from $\mathcal{V}$.
2. Simu chooses $r \xleftarrow{\$} \mathbb{F}$, and $s \leftarrow \{0,1\}^\lambda$. For $i \in [\lambda]$ it does the following:
   (a) Choose w_0^i uniformly at random and compute $w_1^i := w_0^i \oplus 0^{|w|+|r|}$.
   (b) Choose s_0^i uniformly at random and compute $s_1^i := s_0^i \oplus s$.
   (c) Choose $r_i \xleftarrow{\$} \{0,1\}^*$, compute $\widehat{f}^{\text{off}}_{w_0^i, s_0^i}(r_i)$, $\sigma_i := \mathsf{Com}(r_i)$, $\sigma_i' := \mathsf{Com}(w_1^i)$ and $\sigma_i^* := \mathsf{Com}(s_1^i)$.
   Send $(\widehat{f}^{\text{off}}_{w_0^i, s_0^i}(r_i), \sigma_i, \sigma_i', \sigma_i^*)$ for each $i \in [\lambda]$ and the message π_2 of two-com.
3. If the verifier $\mathcal{V}$ aborts or does not send a valid message, then abort and end the simulation. Otherwise, obtain strings $\widehat{s}_0$ and $\widehat{s}_1$, the third message π_3 of two-com from $\mathcal{V}$, together with $\mathsf{ch} \xleftarrow{\$} \{0,1\}^\lambda$ and $\alpha \xleftarrow{\$} \mathbb{F}$. Set $s = \widehat{s}_0$, and rewind the verifier to the end of Step 1.
4. (a) Repeat the following until the verifier sends a valid message for Step 3.
   – With s set to $\widehat{s}_0$ as described above, compute and send $(\widehat{f}^{\text{off}}_{w_0^i, s_0^i}(r_i), \sigma_i, \sigma_i', \sigma_i^*)$ for each $i \in [\lambda]$ along with the second message π_2 of two-com.
   On obtaining a valid message from the verifier, parse it as $\widehat{s}_0^{(2)}, \widehat{s}_1^{(2)}$. If $s = \widehat{s}_0^{(2)}$, continue to Step 5, using s as witness. Else, if $\widehat{s}_1 \neq \widehat{s}_1^{(2)}$, abort and end the simulation. Else, set $s = \widehat{s}_1$ and go to Step 4b.
   (b) Repeat the following until the verifier sends a valid message for Step 3.
   – With s set to $\widehat{s}_1$ as described above, compute and send $(\widehat{f}^{\text{off}}_{w_0^i, s_0^i}(r_i), \sigma_i, \sigma_i', \sigma_i^*)$ for each $i \in [\lambda]$ along with the second message π_2 of two-com.
   On obtaining a valid message from the verifier, parse it as $\widehat{s}_0^{(3)}, \widehat{s}_1^{(3)}$. If $s = \widehat{s}_1^{(3)}$, continue to Step 5, using s as witness. Else, abort.
5. Simu sends $a = r + \alpha w$ (in the field $\mathbb{F}$), and for every $i \in [\lambda]$:
   (a) If $\mathsf{ch}_i = 0$, send w_0^i, s_0^i and decommit σ_i.
   (b) If $\mathsf{ch}_i = 1$, send $\widehat{f}^{\text{on}}_{w_0^i, s_0^i}(x \| \alpha \| a \| \widehat{s}_0 \| \widehat{s}_1, w_1^i, s_1^i; r_i)$ and the decommitment to σ_i' and σ_i^*.

Fig. 4. Simulation strategy for black-box commit-and-prove ZKAoK

protocol, the probability that the simulated view aborts in these rewindings at the end of Step 3 is at most $p \pm \mathsf{negl}(\lambda)$, where p is the probability that the verifier aborts after the second message, when interacting with an honest prover. Conditioned on the verifier not aborting in step 3, the simulator persists after rewinding until the verifier sends a non-aborting message. Thus, the probability of abort in the ideal world remains $p \pm \mathsf{negl}(\lambda)$.

However, this strategy still suffers from the problem that the simulator may not be expected polynomial time. This issue, akin to [11] is resolved by ensuring that the simulator does not run for too long. Specifically, if the adversary did not abort in Step 3, and the simulator proceeds to the rewinding phase, then it first estimates the value of p, which is the probability that the verifier V^* did not abort given commitments to 0 values. This is done by repeating Steps 2 and 3 of the simulation (with fresh random commitments to all zeroes) until $m = 12\lambda$ successful decommits occur (to the same string q that it decommitted to in the main thread). Then, an estimate $\widetilde{\epsilon}$ of p is taken to be m/T, where T is the overall number of attempts until m successful decommits occured. This suffices to ensure that the probability that $\widetilde{\epsilon}$ is not within a constant factor of p is at most $2^{-\lambda}$. An exact analyses of the probabilities can be found in Sect. 6.5.3 in [20].

Finally, we can switch the simulator to using the trapdoor witness in the three-round WI sub-protocol. More formally, we consider an intermediate hybrid Hyb_1, where the simulator follows the strategy above but continues to use the real witness in the WI argument.

Claim. Hyb_1 is computationally indistinguishable from the ideal world.

Proof. To prove that Hyb_1 and the ideal world are computationally indistinguishable, we build the following reduction R to the witness indistinguishability of the underlying protocol. The reduction R first completes the experiment by rewinding the adversary using the [11] strategy described above to extract the value $s = \widehat{s}_0$ or $\widehat{s}_1$. Next, the reduction rewinds back to the beginning of Step 2, and commits to s. It obtains the first message of the (delayed-input) WI argument externally, giving it both witnesses w, s. In the third round, it computes $a = r\alpha + w$ externally and obtains the WI argument externally proving at either $a = r\alpha + w$ or $s = \widehat{s}_0$ or $s = \widehat{s}_1$.

Note that if w is used as witness, this corresponds to Hyb_1. If s is used as witness, the only difference between this and the simulation strategy is that the simulator computes a completely at random, instead of computing it as $a = r\alpha + w$. These are perfectly indistinguishable because r completely hides w. Thus, any adversary that distinguishes Hyb_1 from the ideal world breaks the witness indistinguishability of $\mathsf{two\text{-}com}$.

6 Extractable and Equivocal Commitments

We describe direct applications of our black-box commit-and-prove protocols to four round black-box extractable and equivocal commitments.

Extractable Commitments. The construction of black-box commit-and-prove ZK, given in Fig. 3, is already an extractable commitment to the witness w (proved in Lemma 4). The hiding of the extractable commitment scheme follows from

Input: The committer $\mathcal{C}$ has an input $m \in \{0,1\}$.
Definition of f: The function f has hardwired a share of the witness w_0, and a share of trapdoor information s_0. It takes as input a challenge α, a share of the witness w_1, a share of trapdoor information s_1, a value a, $\widehat{s}_0, \widehat{s}_1$ (recovered from the third message of the two-com) and does the following:

1. Compute $s = s_0 \oplus s_1$. If $\widehat{s}_0 = s$ or $\widehat{s}_1 = s$, output $(1, w_1, s_1, a)$. Else, continue.
2. Compute $m_0 \| m_1 \| r = w_0 \oplus w_1$. If $a \neq (r + \alpha(m_0 \| m_1))$, output $\perp$. Else, output $((m_0 \stackrel{?}{=} m_1), w_1, s_1, a)$.

Commit Phase:

1. $\mathcal{R}$ picks strings $\widehat{s}_0, \widehat{s}_1 \stackrel{\$}{\leftarrow} \{0,1\}^{2\lambda}$ and sends the first message π_1 of $\mathsf{two\text{-}com}(\widehat{s}_0, \widehat{s}_1)$.
2. $\mathcal{C}$ chooses $r \stackrel{\$}{\leftarrow} \mathbb{F}$, and $s \leftarrow \{0,1\}^{\lambda}$. For $i \in [\lambda]$ it does the following:
   (a) Choose w_0^i uniformly at random and compute $w_1^i := w_0^i \oplus (m\|m\|r)$.
   (b) Choose s_0^i uniformly at random and compute $s_1^i := s_0^i \oplus s$.
   (c) Choose $r_i \stackrel{\$}{\leftarrow} \{0,1\}^*$, set $\widehat{f}^{\mathrm{off}}_{w_0^i, s_0^i}(r_i)$, $\sigma_i := \mathsf{Com}(r_i)$, $\sigma_i' := \mathsf{Com}(w_1^i)$, $\sigma_i^* := \mathsf{Com}(s_1^i)$.

   Send $(\widehat{f}^{\mathrm{off}}_{w_0^i, s_0^i}(r_i), \sigma_i, \sigma_i', \sigma_i^*)$ for each $i \in [\lambda]$ along with the second message π_2 of $\mathsf{two\text{-}com}$.

Decommit Phase:

1. $\mathcal{R}$ sends the strings $\widehat{s}_0$ and $\widehat{s}_1$, the third message π_3 of $\mathsf{two\text{-}com}$ to $\mathcal{P}$, together with $\mathsf{ch} \stackrel{\$}{\leftarrow} \{0,1\}^{\lambda}$ and $\alpha \stackrel{\$}{\leftarrow} \mathbb{F} \setminus \{0\}^8$.
2. $\mathcal{C}$ sends $a = r + \alpha(m\|m)$ (in the field $\mathbb{F}$), and does the following for every $i \in [\lambda]$:
   (a) If $\mathsf{ch}_i = 0$, send w_0^i, s_0^i and decommit σ_i.
   (b) If $\mathsf{ch}_i = 1$, send $\widehat{f}^{\mathrm{on}}_{w_0^i, s_0^i}(\alpha \| a \| \widehat{s}_0 \| \widehat{s}_1, w_1^i, s_1^i; r_i)$ and the decommitment to σ_i' and σ_i^*.

Check Phase: The receiver accepts the commitment if the following checks pass:

- For every $i \in [\lambda]$:
  1. If $\mathsf{ch}_i = 0$, check if the received w_0^i, s_0^i are embedded in the circuit $\widehat{f}^{\mathrm{off}}_{w_0^i, s_0^i}$ computed using randomness r_i. Also check that the decommitment information to σ_i is correct.
  2. If $\mathsf{ch}_i = 1$, run the evaluator for the garbled circuit by providing with $\widehat{f}^{\mathrm{on}}_{w_0^i, s_0^i}$ and $\widehat{f}^{\mathrm{off}}_{w_0^i, s_0^i}$ as inputs and accept if the evaluation outputs $(1, w_1^i, s_1^i, a)$ where w_1^i and s_1^i are obtained from the decommitment to σ_i' and σ_i^*.

Fig. 5. Black box equivocal commitment

the computational hiding of the commitment and the zero-knowledge property of the protocol proven in Lemma 5.

Equivocal Commitments. We give a construction of equivocal *bit* commitments in Fig. 5. This can be extended to an equivocal string commitments by committing to every bit using the protocol in Fig. 5. Our construction of equivocal bit commitment is standard: commit to two bits m_0 and m_1, and prove in zero-knowledge (via our round-optimal black-box commit-and-prove strategy) that $m_0 = m_1$.

Lemma 6. *The protocol in Fig. 5 is an equivocal commitment scheme.*

Proof. The (computational) binding property of the scheme follows by the binding property of commit-and-prove ZK. The hiding of the equivocal commitment scheme follows directly based on the computational hiding of Com (since the ZK proofs are not even completed in the commit phase).

The equivocal property is the most interesting, we now describe how this follows by simulating the zero-knowledge proof and generating a commitment to $m_0 \neq m_1$. That is, we consider an intermediate hybrid Hyb_1 where the challenger commits to $m_0 = m_1$ (just as in the real experiment), but starts simulating the underlying proof. This is indistinguishable from the real experiment by simulation security of the commit-and-prove protocol.

In the next hybrid, the challenger continues to simulate the ZK proof but sets $m_0 \neq m_1$. This remains indistinguishable by the computational hiding of com. Note that the challenger can freely equivocate in this experiment. This completes our proof of security.

A Robust Randomized Encodings

We reiterate (a simplified variant of) the construction of online-offline robust randomized encodings from [21]. While they describe a complex protocol that uses adaptive garbled circuits in order to provide improved efficiency, in this paper we present a simplication of the scheme that does not rely on adaptive garbling.

The randomized encoding of function f consists of two functions $\widehat{f}^{\mathrm{off}}, \widehat{f}^{\mathrm{on}}$ and makes use of two components.

- Let Eqcom denote a non-interactive equivocal commitment scheme for string commitments, for which a commitment transcript can be opened in two modes. In binding mode, the opening must remain statistically binding against any malicious committer. In equivocal mode, a commitment transcript can be equivocated freely by a simulator.
  Such a scheme can be constructed using any non-interactive statistically binding commitment scheme, where the (honest) commitment algorithm requires committing to each bit of the string twice. In an equivocal mode, the committer is only required to reveal, for every bit in the string, *one* randomly chosen

commitment to the bit. While generating an opening in the equivocal mode, a simulator can commit to two different values for every bit of the string and use these to freely equivocate.
- A garbling scheme for circuits, with its algorithms denoted by Yao.Garble and Yao.labels.

Using this scheme, the construction of online-offline randomized encodings (which follows the ideas in [21]) is as follows:

- $\widehat{f}^{\text{off}}(r)$ generates a commitment to a Yao's garbled circuit for the function f, using scheme Eqcom. The output of this phase is Eqcom.Commit (Yao.Garble($f; r$)).
- $\widehat{f}^{\text{on}}(r)$ consists of the decommitment information (in equivocal mode) for the garbled circuit, that is, this phase outputs $y = \mathsf{Eqcom.EquivOpen}(\widehat{f}^{\text{off}}(r))$ that was generated in the offline phase. Additionally, given an input x, $\widehat{f}^{\text{on}}(r)$ consists of the wire-labels for this input corresponding to Yao's garbled circuit, that is, it also outputs Yao.labels($x; r$).

Recall that robustness requires that, for a correctly computed $\widehat{f}^{\text{off}}(r)$ (that is, when the commitment to Yao's garbled circuit are generated honestly and the Eqcom.Commit value is correctly generated), there should not exist *any* (maliciously computed) string $\widehat{f}^{\text{on}}$ such that $(\widehat{f}^{\text{off}}, \widehat{f}^{\text{on}})$ generates an output outside the range of f. This is guaranteed by the perfect correctness of Yao's garbling scheme. We refer the reader to [21] for more details and for schemes with improved efficiency.

References

1. Afshar, A., Hu, Z., Mohassel, P., Rosulek, M.: How to efficiently evaluate RAM programs with malicious security. In: Oswald, E., Fischlin, M. (eds.) EUROCRYPT 2015. LNCS, vol. 9056, pp. 702–729. Springer, Heidelberg (2015). https://doi.org/10.1007/978-3-662-46800-5_27
2. Applebaum, B., Ishai, Y., Kushilevitz, E.: Cryptography in NC^0. In: 45th FOCS, pp. 166–175. IEEE Computer Society Press, Rome, Italy, 17–19 October 2004 (2004)
3. Applebaum, B., Ishai, Y., Kushilevitz, E.: Computationally private randomizing polynomials and their applications. In: 20th Annual IEEE Conference on Computational Complexity (CCC 2005), 11–15 June 2005, San Jose, CA, USA, pp. 260–274 (2005), https://doi.org/10.1109/CCC.2005.9
4. Bellare, M., Hoang, V.T., Rogaway, P.: Foundations of garbled circuits. In: Yu, T., Danezis, G., Gligor, V.D. (eds.) ACM CCS 2012, pp. 784–796. ACM Press, Raleigh, NC, USA, 16–18 October 2012 (2012)
5. Bellare, M., Jakobsson, M., Yung, M.: Round-optimal zero-knowledge arguments based on any one-way function. In: Fumy, W. (ed.) EUROCRYPT 1997. LNCS, vol. 1233, pp. 280–305. Springer, Heidelberg (1997). https://doi.org/10.1007/3-540-69053-0_20

6. Canetti, R., Lindell, Y., Ostrovsky, R., Sahai, A.: Universally composable two-party and multi-party secure computation. In: 34th ACM STOC, pp. 494–503. ACM Press, Montréal, Québec, Canada, 19–21 May 2002 (2002)
7. Choi, S.G., Dachman-Soled, D., Malkin, T., Wee, H.: Simple, black-box constructions of adaptively secure protocols. In: Reingold, O. (ed.) TCC 2009. LNCS, vol. 5444, pp. 387–402. Springer, Heidelberg (2009). https://doi.org/10.1007/978-3-642-00457-5_23
8. Feige, U., Lapidot, D., Shamir, A.: Multiple noninteractive zero knowledge proofs under general assumptions. SIAM J. Comput. **29**(1), 1–28 (1999). https://doi.org/10.1137/S0097539792230010
9. Feige, U., Shamir, A.: Witness indistinguishable and witness hiding protocols. In: 22nd ACM STOC, pp. 416–426. ACM Press, Baltimore, MD, USA, 14–16 May 1990 (1990)
10. Garg, S., Mukherjee, P., Pandey, O., Polychroniadou, A.: The exact round complexity of secure computation. In: Fischlin, M., Coron, J.-S. (eds.) EUROCRYPT 2016. LNCS, vol. 9666, pp. 448–476. Springer, Heidelberg (2016). https://doi.org/10.1007/978-3-662-49896-5_16
11. Goldreich, O., Kahan, A.: How to construct constant-round zero-knowledge proof systems for NP. J. Cryptol. **9**(3), 167–190 (1996)
12. Goldreich, O., Krawczyk, H.: On the composition of zero-knowledge proof systems. SIAM J. Comput. **25**, 169–192 (1990)
13. Goldreich, O., Micali, S., Wigderson, A.: How to play any mental game or a completeness theorem for protocols with honest majority. In: Aho, A. (ed.) 19th ACM STOC, pp. 218–229. ACM Press, New York City, 25–27 May 1987 (1987)
14. Goldwasser, S., Micali, S., Rackoff, C.: The knowledge complexity of interactive proof-systems (extended abstract). In: 17th ACM STOC, pp. 291–304. ACM Press, Providence, RI, USA, 6–8 May 1985 (1985)
15. Goyal, V.: Constant round non-malleable protocols using one way functions. In: Fortnow, L., Vadhan, S.P. (eds.) 43rd ACM STOC, pp. 695–704. ACM Press, San Jose, CA, USA, 6–8 June 2011 (2011)
16. Goyal, V., Lee, C., Ostrovsky, R., Visconti, I.: Constructing non-malleable commitments: a black-box approach. In: 53rd Annual IEEE Symposium on Foundations of Computer Science, FOCS 2012, New Brunswick, NJ, USA, 20–23 October 2012, pp. 51–60. IEEE Computer Society (2012). https://doi.org/10.1109/FOCS.2012.47
17. Goyal, V., Ostrovsky, R., Scafuro, A., Visconti, I.: Black-box non-black-box zero knowledge. In: Shmoys, D.B. (ed.) 46th ACM STOC, pp. 515–524. ACM Press, New York, 31 May–3 Jun 2014 (2014)
18. Goyal, V., Pandey, O., Richelson, S.: Textbook non-malleable commitments. In: Wichs, D., Mansour, Y. (eds.) Proceedings of the 48th Annual ACM SIGACT Symposium on Theory of Computing, STOC 2016, Cambridge, MA, USA, 18–21 June 2016, pp. 1128–1141. ACM (2016). https://doi.org/10.1145/2897518.2897657
19. Haitner, I.: Semi-honest to malicious oblivious transfer—the black-box way. In: Canetti, R. (ed.) TCC 2008. LNCS, vol. 4948, pp. 412–426. Springer, Heidelberg (2008). https://doi.org/10.1007/978-3-540-78524-8_23
20. Hazay, C., Lindell, Y.: Efficient Secure Two-Party Protocols - Techniques and Constructions. Information Security and Cryptography, Springer, Heidelberg (2010). https://doi.org/10.1007/978-3-642-14303-8

21. Hazay, C., Venkitasubramaniam, M.: On the power of secure two-party computation. In: Robshaw, M., Katz, J. (eds.) CRYPTO 2016. LNCS, vol. 9815, pp. 397–429. Springer, Heidelberg (2016). https://doi.org/10.1007/978-3-662-53008-5_14
22. Huang, Y., Katz, J., Evans, D.: Efficient secure two-party computation using symmetric cut-and-choose. In: Canetti, R., Garay, J.A. (eds.) CRYPTO 2013. LNCS, vol. 8043, pp. 18–35. Springer, Heidelberg (2013). https://doi.org/10.1007/978-3-642-40084-1_2
23. Huang, Y., Katz, J., Kolesnikov, V., Kumaresan, R., Malozemoff, A.J.: Amortizing garbled circuits. In: Garay, J.A., Gennaro, R. (eds.) CRYPTO 2014. LNCS, vol. 8617, pp. 458–475. Springer, Heidelberg (2014). https://doi.org/10.1007/978-3-662-44381-1_26
24. Ishai, Y., Kushilevitz, E.: Randomizing polynomials: a new representation with applications to round-efficient secure computation. In: 41st Annual Symposium on Foundations of Computer Science, FOCS 2000, 12–14 November 2000, Redondo Beach, California, USA, pp. 294–304. IEEE Computer Society (2000). https://doi.org/10.1109/SFCS.2000.892118
25. Ishai, Y., Kushilevitz, E., Lindell, Y., Petrank, E.: Black-box constructions for secure computation. In: Kleinberg, J.M. (ed.) Proceedings of the 38th Annual ACM Symposium on Theory of Computing, Seattle, WA, USA, 21–23 May 2006, pp. 99–108. ACM (2006). https://doi.org/10.1145/1132516.1132531
26. Ishai, Y., Kushilevitz, E., Ostrovsky, R., Prabhakaran, M., Sahai, A.: Efficient non-interactive secure computation. In: Paterson, K.G. (ed.) EUROCRYPT 2011. LNCS, vol. 6632, pp. 406–425. Springer, Heidelberg (2011). https://doi.org/10.1007/978-3-642-20465-4_23
27. Ishai, Y., Kushilevitz, E., Ostrovsky, R., Sahai, A.: Zero-knowledge from secure multiparty computation. In: Johnson, D.S., Feige, U. (eds.) Proceedings of the 39th Annual ACM Symposium on Theory of Computing, San Diego, California, USA, 11–13 June 2007, pp. 21–30. ACM (2007). https://doi.org/10.1145/1250790.1250794
28. Ishai, Y., Prabhakaran, M., Sahai, A.: Founding cryptography on oblivious transfer - efficiently. In: Wagner, D. (ed.) CRYPTO 2008. LNCS, vol. 5157, pp. 572–591. Springer, Heidelberg (2008). https://doi.org/10.1007/978-3-540-85174-5_32
29. Katz, J., Ostrovsky, R.: Round-optimal secure two-party computation. In: Franklin, M. (ed.) CRYPTO 2004. LNCS, vol. 3152, pp. 335–354. Springer, Heidelberg (2004). https://doi.org/10.1007/978-3-540-28628-8_21
30. Lindell, Y.: Fast cut-and-choose based protocols for malicious and covert adversaries. In: Canetti, R., Garay, J.A. (eds.) CRYPTO 2013. LNCS, vol. 8043, pp. 1–17. Springer, Heidelberg (2013). https://doi.org/10.1007/978-3-642-40084-1_1
31. Lindell, Y., Pinkas, B.: An efficient protocol for secure two-party computation in the presence of malicious adversaries. In: Naor, M. (ed.) EUROCRYPT 2007. LNCS, vol. 4515, pp. 52–78. Springer, Heidelberg (2007). https://doi.org/10.1007/978-3-540-72540-4_4
32. Lindell, Y., Pinkas, B.: Secure two-party computation via cut-and-choose oblivious transfer. J. Cryptol. **25**(4), 680–722 (2012)
33. Nielsen, J.B., Orlandi, C.: LEGO for two-party secure computation. In: Reingold, O. (ed.) TCC 2009. LNCS, vol. 5444, pp. 368–386. Springer, Heidelberg (2009). https://doi.org/10.1007/978-3-642-00457-5_22

34. Ostrovsky, R., Richelson, S., Scafuro, A.: Round-optimal black-box two-party computation. In: Gennaro, R., Robshaw, M. (eds.) CRYPTO 2015. LNCS, vol. 9216, pp. 339–358. Springer, Heidelberg (2015). https://doi.org/10.1007/978-3-662-48000-7_17
35. Ostrovsky, R., Scafuro, A., Venkitasubramanian, M.: Resettably sound zero-knowledge arguments from OWFs - the (semi) black-box way. In: Dodis, Y., Nielsen, J.B. (eds.) TCC 2015. LNCS, vol. 9014, pp. 345–374. Springer, Heidelberg (2015). https://doi.org/10.1007/978-3-662-46494-6_15
36. Pass, R., Wee, H.: Black-box constructions of two-party protocols from one-way functions. In: Reingold, O. (ed.) TCC 2009. LNCS, vol. 5444, pp. 403–418. Springer, Heidelberg (2009). https://doi.org/10.1007/978-3-642-00457-5_24
37. Prabhakaran, M., Rosen, A., Sahai, A.: Concurrent zero knowledge with logarithmic round-complexity. In: 43rd FOCS, pp. 366–375. IEEE Computer Society Press, Vancouver, British Columbia, Canada, 16–19 November 2002 (2002)
38. Rosen, A.: A note on constant-round zero-knowledge proofs for NP. In: Naor, M. (ed.) TCC 2004. LNCS, vol. 2951, pp. 191–202. Springer, Heidelberg (2004). https://doi.org/10.1007/978-3-540-24638-1_11
39. Rosulek, M.: Must you know the code of f to securely compute f? In: Safavi-Naini, R., Canetti, R. (eds.) CRYPTO 2012. LNCS, vol. 7417, pp. 87–104. Springer, Heidelberg (2012). https://doi.org/10.1007/978-3-642-32009-5_7
40. shelat, A., Shen, C.: Two-output secure computation with malicious adversaries. In: Paterson, K.G. (ed.) EUROCRYPT 2011. LNCS, vol. 6632, pp. 386–405. Springer, Heidelberg (2011). https://doi.org/10.1007/978-3-642-20465-4_22
41. Woodruff, D.P.: Revisiting the efficiency of malicious two-party computation. In: Naor, M. (ed.) EUROCRYPT 2007. LNCS, vol. 4515, pp. 79–96. Springer, Heidelberg (2007). https://doi.org/10.1007/978-3-540-72540-4_5
42. Yao, A.C.C.: How to generate and exchange secrets (extended abstract). In: 27th FOCS, pp. 162–167. IEEE Computer Society Press, Toronto, Ontario, Canada, 27–29 October 1986 (1986)

Information-Theoretic Cryptography

On the Power of Amortization in Secret Sharing: d-Uniform Secret Sharing and CDS with Constant Information Rate

Benny Applebaum(✉) and Barak Arkis

Tel-Aviv University, Tel Aviv, Israel
bennyap@post.tau.ac.il, barakark@mail.tau.ac.il

Abstract. Consider the following secret-sharing problem. Your goal is to distribute a long file s between n servers such that $(d-1)$-subsets cannot recover the file, $(d+1)$-subsets can recover the file, and d-subsets should be able to recover s if and only if they appear in some predefined list L. How small can the information ratio (i.e., the number of bits stored on a server per each bit of the secret) be?

We advocate the study of such d-uniform access structures as a useful scaled-down version of general access structures. Our main result shows that, for constant d, any d-uniform access structure admits a secret sharing scheme with a *constant* asymptotic information ratio of c_d that does not grow with the number of servers n. This result is based on a new construction of d-party Conditional Disclosure of Secrets (CDS) for arbitrary predicates over n-size domain in which each party communicates at most four bits per secret bit.

In both settings, previous results achieved a non-constant information ratio that grows asymptotically with n, even for the simpler (and widely studied) special case of $d = 2$. Moreover, our multiparty CDS construction yields the first example of an access structure whose amortized information ratio is constant, whereas its best-known non-amortized information ratio is sub-exponential, thus providing a unique evidence for the potential power of *amortization* in the context of secret sharing.

Our main result applies to exponentially long secrets, and so it should be mainly viewed as a barrier against amortizable lower-bound techniques. We also show that in some natural simple cases (e.g., low-degree predicates), amortization kicks in even for quasi-polynomially long secrets. Finally, we prove some limited lower-bounds, point out some limitations of existing lower-bound techniques, and describe some applications to the setting of private simultaneous messages.

1 Introduction

Secret sharing schemes (SS), introduced by [Sha79,Bla79], are a central cryptographic tool with a wide range of applications (see [Bei11] and references therein).

The full version of this paper appears in [AA18]. Research supported by the European Union's Horizon 2020 Programme (ERC-StG-2014-2020) under grant agreement no. 639813 ERC-CLC, and the Check Point Institute for Information Security.

A. Beimel and S. Dziembowski (Eds.): TCC 2018, LNCS 11239, pp. 317–344, 2018.
https://doi.org/10.1007/978-3-030-03807-6_12

In its general form, an n-party secret sharing scheme for a family of authorized sets $\mathcal{A} \subseteq 2^{[n]}$ (referred to as *access structure*) allows to distribute a secret $s \in \mathcal{S}$ into n shares, $s_1, \ldots, s_n$, one for each party, such that: (1) every authorized set of parties, $A \in \mathcal{A}$, can reconstruct s from its shares; and (2) every unauthorized set of parties A not in $\mathcal{A}$ cannot reveal any partial information on the secret even if the parties are computationally unbounded. A canonical example is the case of threshold secret-sharing in which $\mathcal{A}$ contains all the sets whose cardinality is at least a certain threshold. For this case, Shamir's scheme [Sha79] provides an optimal solution since each party gets a share whose length equals to the length of the secret s which is the best that one can hope for.

It is known that any monotone access structure $\mathcal{A}$ admits a secret sharing scheme [ISN87].[1] However, the communication complexity of general access structures has remained wide open. It is known that the *information ratio*, $\max_i |s_i|/|s|$, of an access structure is at most polynomial in the representation size of $\mathcal{A}$ as a monotone formula [BL88] or as a monotone span program [KW93]. This leads to an exponential upper-bound of $2^{n(1-o(1))}$ for any $\mathcal{A}$. This upper-bound was recently improved by [LV18] to $2^{(1-\alpha)n}$ for some small constant $\alpha > 0$. On the other hand, despite much efforts, the best known lower-bound on the information ratio of an n-party access structure is $\Omega(n/\log n)$ due to [Csi97]. Consequently, we do not know which of the following hypotheses holds:

Hypothesis 1 (SS is short). *Every access structure over n parties is realizable with small information ratio (say $2^{o(n)}$).*

Hypothesis 2 (SS is long). *Some access structures over n parties require large information ratio (e.g., $2^{\Omega(n)}$).*

It is widely believed that the second "SS is long" hypothesis holds [Bei11]. However, proving any super-linear lower-bound (even for a non-explicit access structure) has remained an intriguing open problem.

Does amortization help? We take a closer fine-grained look at the complexity of secret-sharing by taking into account the *length* of the secret. While Hypotheses 1 and 2 are typically understood as addressing the case of a single-bit secret, we consider the case of *long* secrets. Specifically, we explore the following new hypothesis:

Hypothesis 3 (SS is amortizable). *For every access structure over n parties, and every sufficiently long secret s, there exists a secret sharing scheme with small information ratio (e.g., sub-exponential in n).*

Hypothesis 3 can be viewed as a weak (yet bold) version of Hypothesis 1 that does not exclude Hypothesis 2. Indeed, it may be the case that both Hypothesis 3 and 2 hold. That is, sharing a single-bit requires (say exponentially) long shares,

[1] Monotonicity here means that for any $A \subset B$ it holds that $A \in \mathcal{A} \Rightarrow B \in \mathcal{A}$. It is not hard to see that a non-monotone access structure does not admit an SS, and therefore this requirement is necessary.

but once the secret is sufficiently long, the information ratio becomes much smaller. This may explain why proving lower-bounds is such a hard task: typical lower-bounds techniques "fail to distinguish" between short secrets and very long secrets, and thus, under Hypothesis 3, cannot yield strong lower-bounds. Moreover, since huge gaps between amortized communication and non-amortized communication are common in other related settings (e.g., coding theory), one may expect to see such gaps in the context of secret sharing as well.

Perhaps surprisingly, the rich literature of secret sharing hardly contains examples in which amortization significantly helps. In fact, to the best of our knowledge, it is unknown whether there is a super-logarithmic (let alone super-polynomial) gap between the amortized information ratio and the non-amortized information ratio, and this question is open even for restricted special cases of secret-sharing schemes.[2]

In this paper we study the power of amortization in secret sharing. Since the case of general access structures seems highly complicated, we focus on two concrete families of (related) access structures: the family of *d-uniform* access structures and access structures that correspond to *Conditional Disclosure of Secrets*.

1.1 Uniform Access Structures

A d-uniform access structure $\mathcal{A}$ is represented by a d-uniform hypergraph G over $[n]$ and has the following semantics:

- All sets of $d+1$ parties (or more) are authorized.
- All sets of $d-1$ parties (or less) are unauthorized.
- A set of size d is authorized if it appears as an hyperedge in G.

The family of *d-uniform* access structures is rich enough to capture an arbitrary relation on d-size sets. By focusing on a constant d (that does not grow with the number of parties n), we get a scaled-down "toy" version of the more general problem of arbitrary access structures.

Previous Works. The case of $d = 2$ was presented by Sun and Shieh [SS97] under the terminology of graph forbidden access structure and was further studied in several works. For single-bit secrets and linear schemes (in which the secret is viewed as a field element and each share can be written as a linear combination of the secret and several independent random field elements), we know that an information ratio of $\Theta(\sqrt{n})$ is both sufficient [BIKK14, GKW15] and necessary [BFMP17, Min12] for 2-uniform access structures. Recently, it was shown in [LVW17a] that a non-linear scheme can achieve a sub-polynomial information ratio of $2^{O(\sqrt{\log n \log\log n})}$. Based on extensions of this result [LVW17b], an

[2] A logarithmic gap appears, for example, for threshold access structures. Indeed, sharing a single bit requires a share-size of $\Omega(\log n)$ as shown by Kilian and Naor (in an unpublished work) whereas Shamir's scheme provides an information ratio of 1 in the amortized setting (whenever the secret length exceeds $\log n$).

information ratio of $2^{\tilde{O}(\sqrt{n})}$ for d-uniform access structures with arbitrary d was obtained in [BKN18].[3]

Most relevant to us is the work of [AARV17]. There it was shown that if the secret is sufficiently long (exponential in n), then any 2-uniform access structure can the realized with information ratio of $O(\log n)$. At the same paper, it was shown that some non-explicit 2-uniform access structures require an information ratio of $\Omega(\log n)$ for a single-bit secret. (An explicit version of this bound appears in [AHMS18].)

Our Contribution. We show that the asymptotic information ratio (for sufficiently long secrets) of any d-uniform access structure can be reduced to a *constant.*

Theorem 4. *Any n-party d-uniform access structure $\mathcal{A}$ can be realized by a secret sharing scheme that achieves a constant information ratio of $c_d \leq 6\frac{d^d+1}{d!} \leq O(e^d)$ for sufficiently long secrets of length exponential in n^d.*[4]

Theorem 4 (whose proof appears in Sect. 4) validates Hypothesis 3 for the special case of d-uniform access structures as long as d is not too large. Moreover, it provides a rare example for a natural class of access structures $\mathcal{F}$ that can be realized with information rate much smaller than its bit-representation length $\log|\mathcal{F}|$ (i.e., $\log(\binom{n}{d}) = \Omega(n^d)$ for d-uniform access structures). Another such example (in the non-amortized setting) was recently obtained in the concurrent work of [LVW17b].[5]

Interestingly, the scheme constructed in Theorem 4 is *multilinear*, namely, the secret is viewed as a vector of field elements and each share can be written as a linear combination of the secret and several independent random field elements.[6] By observing that the lower-bound of [BFMP17, Min12] for 2-uniform linear schemes extends to multilinear SS for d-uniform access structures, we prove:

Theorem 5. *For every $d \geq 2$, there exists a d-uniform access structure for which every multilinear secret sharing scheme has a share size of at least $\frac{n^{(d-1)/2}}{2d^{d+1/2}}$.*

Together with Theorem 4, this yields the first provable separation between the amortized complexity and the non-amortized complexity for the natural family of multilinear secret sharing schemes. Specifically, for constant d we get a polynomial gap, and for $d = \log n$, a super-polynomial gap! This result also implies that the amortization point of any multilinear scheme (like in Theorem 4) must be at least polynomial in n. (See Sect. 5 for details.)

---

[3] In [BKN18] such access structures are referred to as strongly d-homogenous.

[4] Although we did not try to optimize the constant c_d, we mention that, for the special case of $d = 2$, we get an information ratio c_d of at most 12.5.

[5] Both works were submitted to Eurocrypt 2018.

[6] While this notion of multilinearity is standard in the secret sharing literature (cf. [Bei11]), the reader should note that this is different from the common mathematical notion of multilinearity.

We believe that d-uniform access structures form a good candidate for general separation between amortized and non-amortized information ratio. Unfortunately, proving a general lower-bound against non-linear secret sharing seems quite hard. Indeed, the mere existence of good amortized upper-bounds (Theorem 4) forms a barrier against lower-bound techniques that apply to the amortized setting. This is the case, for example, with typical information theoretic based arguments. In Sect. 5, we further show that a standard information-theoretic method [CSGV93,KGH83] based on Shannon's information inequalities cannot prove a lower-bound better than d for d-uniform access structures.

1.2 Conditional Disclosure of Secrets

The proof of Theorem 4 is based on a new construction of Conditional Disclosure of Secrets (CDS) [GIKM00]. In this model, Alice and Bob hold a shared secret s and private inputs x and y, respectively, and they wish to let Carol learn the secret s if and only if the inputs (x, y) satisfy some predefined predicate $f : X \times Y \to \{0, 1\}$. The inputs x, y are known to Carol, and, in addition, she gets a single message, a, from Alice and a single message, b, from Bob. These messages depend on the party's input, on the secret s, and on a random string r that is shared between Alice and Bob but is hidden from Carol. Given (a, b, x, y), Carol should be able to recover s if $f(x, y) = 1$ but should learn nothing on the secret otherwise. The parties are assumed to be computationally unbounded, and the goal is to minimize the communication complexity of Alice and Bob. (See Sect. 2 for a formal definition.)

CDS schemes have found useful applications in various contexts such as information-theoretically private information retrieval [CKGS98], priced oblivious transfer [AIR01], and attribute based encryption [GPSW06,SW05]. Focusing on the last application, it turns out that the communication complexity of CDS for natural predicates is tightly connected to the parameters (private-key/ciphertext length) achievable by natural constructions of attribute based encryption. (See the discussion in [GKW15].) As a result, the communication complexity of CDS has recently attracted a noticeable amount of research.

CDS*as a Secret Sharing.* CDS can be viewed as a (simpler) variant of 2-uniform access structure. Specifically, consider an access structure over the set of players $X \times Y$ in which every pair of parties $(x, y) \in X \times Y$ should be able to recover the secret s if and only if $f(x, y) = 1$. We further assume that singletons are not authorized, but other than that we do not require any privacy/correctness condition for other subsets of parties. Then, we can represent the secret-sharing problem as the problem of realizing a CDS for the predicate f and vice-versa by setting the share of the x-th player (resp., y-th player) to be the message $a(x, s; r)$ (resp., $b(y, s; r)$). The communication complexity of the CDS protocol therefore corresponds to the maximal size of the shares.

The worst-case complexity of CDS (over all predicates $f : [n] \times [n] \to \{0, 1\}$) matches, up to a constant multiplicative factor, the complexity of the worst-case

2-uniform SS over $2n$ players (as shown implicitly in [BIKK14]).[7] In particular, for single bit secrets, the best known communication complexity is sub-polynomial in the domain size [LVW17a], and for exponentially long secrets the best upper-bound on the information ratio (i.e., communication divided by the length of the secret) is logarithmic in n [AARV17]. (In fact, these results were first established for the CDS setting and then were exported to the more general 2-uniform setting via [BIKK14].)

Our Contribution. We prove that any predicate admits a CDS with asymptotic information ratio of 4. Moreover, this result applies to multiparty CDS where Alice and Bob are replaced with k parties. (See Sect. 2 for formal definitions.)

Theorem 6. *Any k-party predicate $f : X_1 \times \ldots \times X_k \to \{0,1\}$ admits a k-party* CDS *in which, for sufficiently large secrets (whose length is exponential in the function's domain), each party communicates at most 4 bits per each bit of the secret. For the special case of $k = 2$, the information ratio can be improved to 3.*

The theorem is quite general: It achieves an information ratio of 4 for any function f, regardless of the number of parties or their domain. This validates Hypothesis 3 for the class of access structures induced by general CDS, including the special case of k-party CDS in which each party holds a single bit. For this setting (sometimes known as *non-monotone secret sharing* [BI01, VV15]) the best non-amortized communication complexity is $2^{\tilde{O}(\sqrt{k})}$ [LVW17b]. This leaves a huge (almost maximal) gap between the amortized communication and non-amortized communication.

From CDS *to Partial* PSM. Finally, we ask whether highly efficient CDS protocols can be used to improve the complexity of more challenging tasks such as *Private Simultaneous Message Protocols* [FKN94]. This setting is similar to the CDS setting except that here, the inputs x, y are treated as private data (not known to Carol), and the goal is to let Carol learn the function $f(x, y)$ without learning any additional information. (The communication pattern is one-way just as the case of CDS.) This setting is much more challenging (just like functional encryption is more challenging than attribute based encryption). For an arbitrary function $f : [n] \times [n] \to \{0,1\}$, the best upper-bound is $O(\sqrt{n})$ [BIKK14] and no amortization results are known.

Following [IW14], we consider a hybrid model (partial PSM) in which Alice's input x is partitioned into a public part x_1 that is known to Carol (but not to Bob) and to a private part x_2, and similarly Bob's input, y, is partitioned into a public part y_1 (known to Carol but not to Alice) and a private part y_2. Trivially, partial PSM complexity is upper bounded by PSM complexity in the sense that one can apply a PSM protocol to hide all of Alice's and Bob's input (both the private and public parts). Adapting known PSM protocols to the partial PSM model in a way that communication complexity is reduced, does

[7] The reader should note that CDS complexity is sometimes measured in terms of the bit-length of the x and y (i.e., $\log|X| + \log|Y|$). In our context it is more natural to use the cardinality of the alphabet as the main parameter.

not seem like an easy task. As explained in Sect. 6, CDS turns out to be a natural tool for accomplishing this task. In Sect. 6 we reduce partial PSM to CDS with an overhead that is roughly linear in the domain of the private input. (We obtain better results for families of predicates that can be computed by small/shallow Boolean circuits.) Our results improve upon the reduction of [AARV17] whose overhead is exponential in the domain of the private parts.

1.3 Overview of Our Constructions

We briefly sketch the outline of our main theorems starting with Theorem 6.

Amortized CDS. Theorem 6 is proved by strengthening the amortization techniques of [AARV17]. In particular, Applebaum et al. reduce the problem of amortizing the complexity of two-party CDS to the problem of constructing a two-party *batch*-CDS scheme. In the latter setting Alice holds a single input x, Bob holds a single input y, and both parties hold 2^{2n} secrets, one for each predicate in $\mathcal{F} = \{f : [n] \times [n] \rightarrow \{0,1\}\}$. The scheme releases the secret s_f if and only if f evaluates to 1 on (x, y). In [AARV17] such a scheme is realized by recursing over the inputs (x, y) in a bit-by-bit manner. Loosely speaking, once Alice knows that the last bit of x is, say, zero, she can complete the task by invoking a batch-CDS for the residual functions $\mathcal{G} = \{g : [n/2] \times [n] \rightarrow \{0,1\}\}$ with random secrets r_g and release $s_f \oplus r_g$. In fact, many functions f will be simplified to the same $g \in \mathcal{G}$, and therefore, in order to deliver the secret s_f for each such f, Alice will have to use many copies of g with a different secret $r_{g,i}$ for each copy. The crucial point is that each $g \in \mathcal{G}$ accounts for the same number $D = |\mathcal{F}|/|\mathcal{G}|$ of functions $f \in \mathcal{F}$, and so we can use D copies of batch-CDS over $\mathcal{G}$. This bit-by-bit recursion leads to a batch-CDS with communication complexity of $O(|\mathcal{F}| \log n)$, and the logarithmic overhead is carried over to the setting of amortized CDS for long secrets.

In order to get rid of this overhead, we modify the construction of batch-CDS, and instead of treating Alice's inputs in a bit-by-bit manner, we treat it as a single element from $[n]$. Abstracting the above argument, the transformation works as long as each residual function g over Bob's inputs accounts for the same number of original functions in $\mathcal{F}$. We further abstract this property of $\mathcal{F}$ and extend the argument to k parties (recursing over the parties instead of the bits of the inputs). This allows us to shave the logarithmic factor and to obtain a constant overhead for any function family $\mathcal{F}$ that satisfies some regularity and closure conditions. (See Sect. 3.1 for details.)

These results are used to obtain multilinear CDS for any predicate f in $\mathcal{F}$ with information ratio of at most 4 as long as the secret is larger than $|\mathcal{F}|$. Taking $\mathcal{F}$ to be the class of *all* predicates (a class that is shown to satisfy the required conditions) we derive Theorem 6. In this case, amortization kicks in only when the secret is exponential in the domain size of f. This can be significantly improved when f is taken from a small family $\mathcal{F}$ of predicates that satisfies our conditions. For example, we show that when f is a low-degree multivariate polynomial amortization kicks in even for secrets of length quasi-polynomial in the size of the domain. (See Sect. 3 for details.)

Amortized d-uniform SS. Amortized secret sharing schemes for d-uniform access structures (Theorem 4) are obtained via a reduction to d-party CDS. Recall that a d-uniform access structure corresponds to a d-uniform hypergraph (in which d-size authorized sets appear as hyperedges). Similarly, d-party CDS essentially corresponds to the special case of d-partite hypergraph, that is, hypergraphs whose vertices can be partitioned into d parts $V_1, \dots, V_d$ such that every hyperedge is an element of $V_1 \times \dots \times V_d$. Therefore, ignoring some technicalities, the reduction boils down to a graph covering problem. That is, it suffices to show that any d-uniform hypergraph G can be covered by a collection of d-partite hypergraphs $(G_1, \dots, G_t)$. If we can further show that each hyperedge of G is covered by a constant fraction of the graphs in the collection, then the communication blow-up of the reduction will be constant.

This approach was implemented by [BIKK14] in the case of $d = 2$. In this case, a good covering can be obtained via an error-correcting code. In the multiparty setting, standard codes do not solve the problem. Instead, we established the existence of a good covering via the probabilistic method. As a result, we get a general reduction from d-uniform access structure to d-party CDS with an overhead of $O(e^d)$. (See Sect. 4 for details.)

We mention that, concurrently to our work, [BKN18] describe an incomparable reduction from d-uniform access structures over n parties to n-party CDS (aka non-monotone secret sharing) with a non-constant multiplicative overhead of $\tilde{O}(n)$ which is independent of d.

2 Definitions

In this section we define *Secret-Sharing*, *multiparty* CDS, and *partial*-PSM. In all of our definitions, we consider only perfect correctness and perfect privacy. (Relaxations to the case of imperfect privacy and imperfect correctness can be obtained in a natural manner.)

2.1 Secret-Sharing

The following definitions are based on [Bei11].

Access Structures and Distribution Schemes. Let $p_1, \dots, p_n$ be a set of parties. A collection $\mathcal{A} \subset 2^{\{p_1,\dots,p_n\}}$ is monotone if $B \in A$ and $B \subset C$ imply that $C \in \mathcal{A}$. An access structure is a monotone collection $\mathcal{A} \subset 2^{\{p_1,\dots,p_n\}}$ of non-empty subsets of $\{p_1, \dots, p_n\}$. Sets in $\mathcal{A}$ are called authorized, and sets not in $\mathcal{A}$ are called unauthorized. A distribution scheme $\Sigma = (\Pi, \mu)$ with domain of secrets $\mathcal{S}$ is a pair, where μ is a probability distribution on some finite set $\mathcal{R}$ called the set of random strings and Π is a mapping from $\mathcal{S} \times \mathcal{R}$ to a set of n-tuples $\mathcal{Z}_1 \times \mathcal{Z}_2 \times \dots \times \mathcal{Z}_n$, where $\mathcal{Z}_j$ is called the domain of shares of p_j. A dealer distributes a secret $s \in S$ according to Σ by first sampling a random string $r \in \mathcal{R}$ according to μ, computing a vector of shares $\Pi(s,r) = (z_1, ..., z_n)$, and privately communicating each share z_j to party p_j. For a set $A \subset \{p_1, \dots, p_n\}$, we denote $\Pi(s,r)_A$ as the restriction of $\Pi(s,r)$ to its A-entries. The *information ratio* of a distribution scheme is $max_{1 \leq j \leq n} \frac{\log |\mathcal{Z}j|}{\log |\mathcal{S}|}$.

Definition 1 (Secret Sharing). *Let $\mathcal{S}$ be a finite set of secrets, where $|\mathcal{S}| \geq 2$. A distribution scheme (Π, μ) with domain of secrets $\mathcal{S}$ is a secret-sharing scheme realizing an access structure $\mathcal{A}$ if the following two requirements hold:*

- ***Correctness.*** *For every authorized set $B \in \mathcal{A}$ (where $B = \{p_{i_1}, \dots, p_{i_{|B|}}\}$), there exists a reconstruction function $\mathsf{Rec}_B : \mathcal{Z}_{i_1} \times \ldots \times \mathcal{Z}_{i_{|B|}} \to \mathcal{S}$ such that for every $s \in \mathcal{S}$,*

$$\Pr[Recon_B(\Pi(s,r)_B) = s] = 1.$$

- ***Privacy.*** *For any unauthorized set $T \notin \mathcal{A}$, every two secrets $a, b \in \mathcal{S}$, the random variables*

$$\Pi(a,r)_T \quad \text{and} \quad \Pi(b,r)_T,$$

induced by sampling r according to μ, are identically distributed.

A secret sharing scheme is *linear* (resp., *multilinear*) over a finite field $\mathbb{F}$, if the secret domain $\mathcal{S}$ is $\mathbb{F}$ (resp., $\mathbb{F}^i$ for some $i \geq 1$), the randomness domain $\mathcal{R}$ is $\mathbb{F}^j$ for some $j \geq 1$, and the mapping Π is linear over $\mathbb{F}$. By default, we always assume that the domain $\mathcal{S}$ can be associated with some finite field.

Uniform access structures. Our main focus will be on *Uniform Access Structures*. Formally, an access structure $\mathcal{A}$ is *d-uniform* if every authorized set of $\mathcal{A}$ is of size at least d, and every set of size at least $d+1$ is authorized. A secret-sharing scheme for a d-uniform access structure is referred to as a d-uniform secret sharing scheme.

2.2 Conditional Disclosure of Secrets

Definition 2 (multiparty CDS). *Let $f : \mathcal{X}_1 \times \ldots \times \mathcal{X}_k \to \{0,1\}$ be a predicate. For $1 \leq i \leq k$ let $F_i : \mathcal{X}_i \times \mathcal{S} \times \mathcal{R} \to \mathcal{Z}_i$ be deterministic encoding algorithms ($\mathcal{S}$ is the secret domain and $\mathcal{R}$ is the shared randomness domain). We say that the tuple $(F_1, \dots, F_k)$ is a k-party* CDS *for f, if the function $F(x_1, \dots, x_k, s, r) = (F_1(x_1, s, r), \dots, F_k(x_k, s, r))$ satisfies the following conditions:*

- ***Correctness.*** *There exists a deterministic algorithm* Dec, *called the decoder, such that for every input $(x_1, \dots, x_k)$ such that $f(x_1, \dots, x_k) = 1$, every secret $s \in \mathcal{S}$, and every random string $r \in \mathcal{R}$ we have that*

$$\mathsf{Dec}(x_1, \dots, x_k, F(x_1, \dots, x_k, s, r)) = s.$$

- ***Privacy.*** *There exists a randomized simulator* Sim *such that for every input* $(x_1, \ldots, x_k)$ *such that* $f(x_1, \ldots, x_k) = 0$ *and any secret* $s \in \mathcal{S}$ *the random variables*

$$F(x_1, \ldots, x_k, s, r) \quad \text{and} \quad \mathsf{Sim}(x_1, \ldots, x_k),$$

induced by a random choice of $r \in \mathcal{R}$ *and a uniform choice of the internal randomness of the simulator, are identically distributed.*

The communication complexity *of party* i *is* $\log(|\mathcal{Z}_i|)$ *and its* amortized communication *complexity (or* information ratio*) is* $\frac{\log(|\mathcal{Z}_i|)}{\log(|\mathcal{S}|)}$. *The information ratio of the protocol is the maximum information ratio of all parties.*

A important property of CDS is whether or not it is linear. We distinguish between linear CDS and multilinear CDS. A multiparty CDS is *multilinear* over a finite field $\mathbb{F}$ if:

1. The secret and the randomness domains are both vectors over $\mathbb{F}$.
2. The encoding functions F_i are linear in the secret and randomness. That is, fixing the input x_i, F_i's output is a vector over $\mathbb{F}$ in which every coordinate is a linear combination of the secret and the random field elements.

A multilinear CDS is *linear* if the secret is a *single* field element (i.e., $\mathcal{S} = \mathbb{F}$). By default, we always assume that the domain $\mathcal{S}$ can be associated with some finite field. To simplify notation, we will use the term CDS instead of multiparty CDS when the number of parties is clear from the context.

Remark 1. It is sometimes useful to consider a variant of CDS in which only a single party (say the last one) holds the secret. Formally, this means that F_k depends on the secret (and randomness) and $F_1, \ldots, F_{k-1}$ depend only in the randomness. Being a special case of the original definition, any construction of this variant of CDS, also satisfies the general notion of CDS. We mention that all the constructions in this paper natively admit a CDS in which only the last party holds the secret. More generally, it is not hard to turn any standard CDS into a single-party-holds-the-secret type with a minor loss of $|s|$ in the total communication complexity. Indeed, one can just run the standard CDS with a random secret s', and let the last party send, in addition, the value $s + s'$.

2.3 Partial Simultaneous Message Protocols

Lastly, we define a variant of PSM called *partial*-PSM that adopts the notion of partial garbling [IW14] to the three-party setting of [FKN94].

Definition 3 (partial-PSM). *Let* $f : (\mathcal{X} \times \mathcal{W}) \times (\mathcal{Y} \times \mathcal{T}) \to \{0, 1\}$ *be a function. We say that a pair of deterministic encoding algorithms* $F_1 : (\mathcal{X} \times \mathcal{W}) \times \mathcal{R} \to \mathcal{Z}_1$ *and* $F_2 : (\mathcal{Y} \times \mathcal{T}) \times \mathcal{R} \to \mathcal{Z}_2$ *are partial-*PSM *for* f *if the function* $F(x, w, y, t, r) = (F_1(x, w, r), F_2(y, t, r))$ *that corresponds to the joint computation of* F_1 *and* F_2 *on a common* r, *satisfies the following properties:*

– ***Correctness.*** *There exists a deterministic algorithm* Dec, *called the decoder, such that for every input* (x, w, y, t) *and every* $r \in \mathcal{R}$ *we have that*

$$\mathsf{Dec}(w, t, F(x, w, y, t, r)) = f(x, w, y, t).$$

– ***Privacy.*** *There exists a randomized algorithm (simulator)* Sim *such that for any input* (x, w, y, t) *the random variables*

$$F(x, w, y, t, r) \qquad \textit{and} \qquad \mathsf{Sim}(w, t, f(x, w, y, t)),$$

induced by a random choice of $r \in \mathcal{R}$ *and a uniform choice of the internal randomness of the simulator, are identically distributed.*

We refer to $\mathcal{X}$ *and* $\mathcal{Y}$ *as the* private domain *of* f*, and to* $\mathcal{W}$ *and* $\mathcal{T}$ *as the* public domain *of* f*. When the public domain is empty, we get the standard definition for* PSM *(as all input is required to be hidden). The* communication complexity *of the protocol is defined as the total encoding length* $(\log|\mathcal{Z}_1| + \log|\mathcal{Z}_2|)$*, and the* randomness complexity *is defined as the length* $\log|\mathcal{R}|$ *of the common randomness.*

*Remark 2 (*PSM *as randomized encoding of functions).* A PSM protocol for f can be alternatively viewed as a special type of *randomized encoding* [IK00, AIK06] of f, where the output of f is encoded by the output of a randomized function $F((x, y), r)$ such that F can be written as $F((x, y), r) = (F_1(x, r), F_2(y, r))$. This is referred to as a "2-decomposable" encoding in [Ish13]. Similarly, the notion of partial PSM can be derived by considering 2-decomposable *partial encoding* (or garbling).

3 Constant Information Ratio for CDS

In this section we show that, for sufficiently long secrets, any d-ary predicate f admits a d-party CDS with constant information ratio. Following [AARV17], we begin (in Sect. 3.1) by constructing a highly efficient *batch* version of CDS (that simultaneously handles a class of different predicates) and then show (in Sect. 3.2) how to transform it into a standard CDS with low amortized complexity.

3.1 Batch-CDS and Regular Function Families

A k-party *batch*-CDS for a class of predicates $\mathcal{F}$ takes as an input a vector of secrets $(s_f)_{f \in \mathcal{F}}$ and a single input tuple $x = (x_1, \ldots, x_k)$ where x_i belongs to the i-th party, and delivers to Carol all the secrets s_f for which $f(x) = 1$.

Definition 4 (batch-CDS [AARV17]). *Let* $\mathcal{F} = (f_1, \ldots, f_m)$ *be an* m*-tuple of predicates over the domain* $\mathcal{X}_1 \times \ldots \times \mathcal{X}_k$*. For* $i \in [k]$ *let* $F_i : \mathcal{X}_i \times \mathcal{S}^m \times \mathcal{R} \to \mathcal{Z}_i$ *be deterministic encoding algorithms, where* $\mathcal{S}$ *is the secret domain. Then,* $(F_1, \ldots, F_k)$ *is a* k*-party batch-*CDS *scheme for* $\mathcal{F}$ *if the function* $F(x, y, s, r) = (F_1(x_1, s, r), \ldots, F_k(x_k, s, r))$*, where* $s \in \mathcal{S}^m$ *, satisfies the following properties:*

1. ***Correctness.*** *There exists a deterministic algorithm* Dec*, called a decoder, such that for every $i \in [m]$, every input $x = (x_1, \ldots, x_k)$ that satisfies f_i and every vector of secrets $s \in \mathcal{S}^m$, we have that:*

$$\Pr_{r \xleftarrow{R} \mathcal{R}} [\mathsf{Dec}(i, x, y, F(x, y, s, r)) = s_i] = 1.$$

2. ***Privacy.*** *There exists a randomized simulator* Sim *such that for every input $x = (x_1, \ldots, x_k)$ and every vector of secrets $s \in \mathcal{S}^m$, the following distributions are identical*

$$\mathsf{Sim}(x, \hat{s}) \quad \text{and} \quad F(x, s, r),$$

where $r \xleftarrow{R} \mathcal{R}$ and $\hat{s}$ is an m-long vector whose i-th component equals to s_i if $f_i(x, y) = 1$, and $\perp$ otherwise.

The communication complexity *of the party i is* $\log |\mathcal{Z}_i|$.

We generalize the ideas of [AARV17] and show that every family of functions that satisfy some closure properties (detailed in Definition 5) admits a highly efficient batch-CDS.

Definition 5 (regular function family). *Let $\mathcal{X}_1, \ldots, \mathcal{X}_k$ be a tuple of input domains and let $\mathcal{F} = (\mathcal{F}_1, \ldots, \mathcal{F}_k)$ be a sequence of function families where, for every i, the family $\mathcal{F}_i$ contains functions of the form $f : \mathcal{X}_1 \times \ldots \times \mathcal{X}_i \to \{0, 1\}$. We say that $\mathcal{F}$ is* regular *if it satisfies the following conditions:*

1. *$\mathcal{F}$ is closed under addition. That is, for every $i \in [k]$ and $f_1, f_2 \in \mathcal{F}_i$, we have that $f_1 + f_2 \in \mathcal{F}_i$ (addition is over the binary field).*
2. *For every $i \in [k]$, $\mathcal{F}_i$ contains the constant function 1.*
3. *For every $i \in [k-1]$ and every function $g \in \mathcal{F}_i$ and $a \in \mathcal{X}_{i+1}$, let $R(g, a)$ be the set of functions $f \in \mathcal{F}_{i+1}$ that simplify to g when their last input is substituted by a. (That is, $f(x_1, \ldots, x_i, a) = g(x_1, \ldots, x_i)$ for every $(x_1, \ldots, x_i) \in \mathcal{X}_1 \times \ldots \times \mathcal{X}_i$). Then the size of $R(g, a)$ is independent of g and a, and depends only on the arity i. We let R_i denote this size.*

We refer to the first two properties as closure properties, *and to the third property as* downward regularity.

Remark 3. It is useful to think of the last property of Definition 5 in graph-theoretic terms. Consider a k-layered graph in which the i-th layer contains a node for every function $f \in \mathcal{F}_i$, and add an edge, labeled by $a \in \mathcal{X}_{i+1}$, from $f \in \mathcal{F}_{i+1}$ to $g \in \mathcal{F}_i$ if $f(\cdots, a)$ simplifies to g. Then, each layer i should be regular in the sense that, for every edge label $a \in \mathcal{X}_{i+1}$, every node $f \in \mathcal{F}_i$ has exactly R_i incoming edges that are labeled by a. (This, in particular, implies that $|\mathcal{F}_{i+1}| = R_i |\mathcal{F}_i|$.)

An important example of a regular function family is the family of all functions.

Proposition 1. *Let $\mathcal{X}_1, \ldots, \mathcal{X}_k$ be a sequence of finite sets, and let $\mathcal{F}_i$ denote the family of all predicates over $\mathcal{X}_1 \times \ldots \times \mathcal{X}_i$. Then the family $\mathcal{F} = (\mathcal{F}_i)_{i\in[k]}$ is regular.*

The proof is deferred to the full version [AA18].

Another regular function family is polynomials of degree at most D over the binary field.

Proposition 2. *Let $(\ell_1, \ldots, \ell_k)$ be a k-tuple of positive integers and let $\mathcal{X}_i = \{0,1\}^{\ell_i}$. For an integer D let $\mathcal{P}_i$ be the family of all functions over $\mathcal{X}_1 \times \ldots \times \mathcal{X}_i$ that can be expressed as multivariate polynomials over the binary field with $\sum_{j=1}^{i} \ell_j$ variables and total degree of at most D. Then the family $\mathcal{P}_{\ell,D} = (\mathcal{P}_i)_{i\in[k]}$ is regular.*

The proof is deferred to the full version [AA18].

We continue by showing that every regular function family has an efficient batch-CDS. From now on, we work with secrets (and randomness) that are taken from some arbitrary finite field $\mathbb{F}$ (e.g., the binary field).

Lemma 1. *Let $\mathcal{F} = \{\mathcal{F}_i\}_{i=1}^{k}$ be a regular function family over the input domains $\mathcal{X}_1, \ldots, \mathcal{X}_k$. There is a batch-CDS for $\mathcal{F}_k$ such that the communication of each party consists of at most $|\mathcal{F}_k|$ field elements. Moreover, one of the parties (e.g., the first) communicates only $|\mathcal{F}_k|/2$ field elements.*

Proof. Denote by s_f the secret field element associated with some function $f \in \mathcal{F}_k$. We show (inductively) how to construct a batch-CDS for $\mathcal{F}_k$. For $k = 1$ a single party holds the entire input and can send s_f for every f that satisfies $f(x_1) = 1$, using communication at most $|\mathcal{F}_1|$ field elements. In fact, the regularity conditions (1 and 2) guarantee that exactly half of the functions are satisfied by x_1, and therefore only $|\mathcal{F}_1|/2$ field elements will be sent by the first party.

Let us assume that the claim holds for $k - 1$. To extend the protocol to k parties we make use of the following family of mappings. For every $a \in \mathcal{X}_k$ let T_a be an injective mapping that maps a function $f \in \mathcal{F}_k$ to $(g, i) \in \mathcal{F}_{k-1} \times [R_{k-1}]$, such that f is the i-th function in $R(g, a)$ according to some fixed predefined order. (Recall that $f \in R(g, a)$ if $f(\cdot, a) = g(\cdot)$.) By the third regularity condition, $|R(g, a)| = R_{k-1}$ for every g, a, and therefore T_a is well defined. The existence of such mappings T_a gives us the ability to use the batch-CDS inductively:

1. Players $1, \ldots, k-1$ run the batch-CDS for $\mathcal{F}_{k-1}$, R_{k-1} times with random field elements $r_{g,i}$ for $(g, i) \in \mathcal{F}_{k-1} \times [R_{k-1}]$ to release $r_{g,i}$ if and only if $g(x_1, \ldots, x_{k-1}) = 1$.
2. For every function $f \in \mathcal{F}_k$ player k computes $(g, i) = T_{x_k}(f)$ and releases $s_f + r_{g,i}$.

The decoding procedure is simple. If the input $(x_1, \ldots, x_k)$ satisfies $f \in \mathcal{F}_k$, the decoder does the following: (1) Computes $(g, i) = T_{x_k}(f)$ and retrieves the value of $r_{g,i}$ that is released by the batch-CDS since $g(x_1, \ldots, x_{k-1}) =$

$f(x_1, \ldots, x_k) = 1$; (2) Collects the values $s_f + r_{g,i}$ sent during the second step, and recovers the value of s_f.

It is not hard to verify that perfect privacy holds. Indeed, suppose that $(x_1, \ldots, x_k)$ does not satisfy f. Then, the only s_f-dependent value that is released is $s_f + r_{g,i}$ where g is the restriction of f to x_k. However, since $(x_1, \ldots, x_k)$ fails to satisfy f, its prefix does not satisfy g and therefore $r_{g,i}$ remains hidden from the receiver.

We complete the proof by analyzing the communication complexity. The last party sends exactly $|\mathcal{F}_k|$ field elements. By the induction hypothesis, each of the other parties sends at most $R_{k-1} \cdot |\mathcal{F}_{k-1}| = |\mathcal{F}_k|$ field elements, and the first party sends $R_{k-1} \cdot |\mathcal{F}_{k-1}|/2 = |\mathcal{F}_k|/2$ field elements, as required. □

Remark 4 (On the use of regularity). We mention that (without the "Moreover" part) Lemma 1 holds even if $\mathcal{F}$ satisfies only the property of downward regularity.

3.2 Amortization for CDS

We use the above lemma to amortize the complexity of CDS over long secrets.

Theorem 7. *Let $\mathcal{F} = \{\mathcal{F}_i\}_{i=1}^k$ be a regular family of functions, and let $f \in \mathcal{F}_k$. Then for $m = |\mathcal{F}_k|/2$ there exists a multilinear (k-party) CDS that supports m field element secrets with information ratio of 4. Moreover, one of the parties has information ratio of 2.*

Proof. Given a secret vector $s \in \mathbb{F}^m$, we duplicate each secret twice and index the secrets by predicates $p \in \mathcal{F}_m$ such that $s_p = s_{\bar{p}}$ (i.e., a predicate and its complement index the same secret). Note that properties (1) and (2) guarantee that $\mathcal{F}_k$ is closed under complement. On inputs $x_1, \ldots, x_k$, the parties make two calls to $\mathcal{F}_k$-batch CDS. In the first call the secret associated with a predicate $p \in \mathcal{F}_k$ is a random value $r_p \in \mathbb{F}$. In the second call, for every predicate $f+p+1 \in \mathcal{F}_k$, we release $s_p + r_p$. Since the mapping $p \mapsto p + f + 1$ is a bijection, the second call associates exactly one secret to each function.

Correctness. Suppose that $f(x_1, \ldots, x_k) = 1$. Recall that each of the original secrets s_i appears in two copies $(s_p, s_{\bar{p}})$ for some predicate p. Since one of these copies is satisfied by $x = (x_1, \ldots, x_k)$, it suffices to show that, whenever $p(x) = 1$, the secret s_p can be recovered. Indeed, for such a predicate p, the value r_p is released by the first batch-CDS, and the value $s_p + r_p$ is released by the second batch-CDS. The latter follows by noting that x satisfies the predicate $p + f + 1$ (since it satisfies both f and p). It follows that s_p can be recovered for every p that is satisfied by x, as required.

Privacy. Suppose that $f(x) = 0$. We show that all the "virtual secrets" s_p remain perfectly hidden in this case. Indeed, for every $p \in \mathcal{F}_k$, it holds that whenever $f(x) = 0$, either $(f + p + 1)(x) = 0$ or $p(x) = 0$, and therefore, for any p, either r_p or $s_p + r_p$ are released, but never both.

Finally, using Lemma 1.5, the total communication complexity of each party is $2|\mathcal{F}_k| = 4m$ and the first party has communication complexity of

$2|\mathcal{F}_k|/2 = 2m$, as claimed. Also note that our protocol is multilinear. Indeed, our construction uses batch-CDS on "virtual" secrets that are linear in the original secrets and the randomness. In addition, batch-CDS itself is multilinear in the sense that the output of every player is a vector with coordinates of the form $s + r$ or r for some secret s and random element r. □

Remark 5 (On the use of regularity). We mention that Theorem 7 relies on the closure properties of $\mathcal{F}$. Indeed, the proof actually shows that these properties alone suffice for reducing the problem of amortizing CDS to the problem of batch-CDS.

Plugging in the regular family of all functions, we get the following corollary.

Corollary 1 (Theorem 6 restated). *Every function $f : [N]^k \to \{0,1\}$ has a multilinear k-party* CDS *protocol that supports secrets of length 2^{N^k-1} with information ratio of 4. Moreover, for secrets of length $k2^{N^k-1}$, one can get an information ratio of $4 - \frac{2}{k}$ (i.e., 3 for the case of $k = 2$).*

Proof. The first part follows directly from Theorem 7. To prove the "Moreover" part, we exploit the fact that in Theorem 7 one of the parties (say the first) has information ratio of 2. In particular, partition the $k2^{N^k-1}$-long secret to k blocks of length $B = 2^{N^k-1}$ and run the protocol k times (one for each block) where in each invocation a different party plays the role of the first party. This way each party communicates $4(k-1)B + 2B$ elements for a secret of length kB, and the information ratio is $4 - \frac{2}{k}$. □

Applying Theorem 7 to the class of all degree-D multivariate polynomials (that was shown to be regular in Proposition 2), we conclude:

Corollary 2. *Every multivariate polynomial $p : \{0,1\}^{\ell_1} \times \cdots \times \{0,1\}^{\ell_k} \to \{0,1\}$ over $\ell = \sum_i \ell_i$ variables with total degree of at most D admits a k-party* CDS *protocol with information ratio of 4 for secrets of length $P(\ell, D)/2$ where $P(\ell, D)$ denotes the number of multivariate polynomials with ℓ variables and total degree of at most D over the binary field.*

Note that $P(\ell, D) \leq 2^{D \cdot \ell^D}$ which, for constant D, is quasipolynomial in the size of the total domain $L = 2^\ell$ (as opposed to exponential in the size of the domain as in Corollary 1). Overall, in order to construct an amortized CDS for a target function f, it is beneficial to employ Theorem 7 with the smallest regular family of functions that constrains f. Smaller families can significantly improve the amortization starting point.

4 From Multiparty CDS to d-uniform Secret-Sharing

As shown by [BIKK14] CDS is closely related to secret-sharing. We further extend this relation by using our multiparty CDS to construct efficient secret-sharing for d-uniform access structures (here, efficiency is measured by the information ratio of the scheme).

Hypergraph Representation. Every access structure $\mathcal{A}$ can be represented as a hypergraph $\mathcal{H} = (V, E)$ whose vertices correspond to parties of $\mathcal{A}$ and hyperedges correspond to **minimal** authorized sets of $\mathcal{A}$ (a minimal authorized set is a set for which no subset is authorized). In the case of d-uniform access structure $\mathcal{A}$, it is convenient to restrict the attention to minimal authorized sets of size exactly d while keeping in mind that all larger sets are always authorized. Under this convention, we represent d-uniform access structures by d-uniform hypergraphs.

Hypergraph Decomposition. A sub-hypergraph $\mathcal{G} = (V', E')$ of a hypergraph $\mathcal{H} = (V, E)$ is a hypergraph such that $V' \subset V$ and $E' \subset E$. Decomposing a "complicated" hypergraph into a set of "simple" sub-hypergraphs is a common way to achieve secret-sharing schemes for the former. For that matter, Stinson's theorem [Sti94] is commonly used. In this paper, a "complicated" hypergraph is a d-uniform hypergraph, and a "simple" hypergraph is a *d-partite hypergraph* - a hypergraph whose vertices can be partitioned into d parts $V_1, \ldots, V_d$ such that every hyperedge is an element of $V_1 \times \ldots \times V_d$. The following fact follows from Stinson's theorem.

Fact 8. *Let $\mathcal{H}$ be a hypergraph, and let $\mathcal{H}_1, \ldots, \mathcal{H}_t$ be sub-hypergraphs of $\mathcal{H}$ such that for some $0 < c \leq 1$ every edge $e \in E$ appears in at least $c \cdot t$ different sub-hypergraphs. Assume in addition that every sub-hypergraph $\mathcal{H}_i$ has a secret-sharing scheme with information ratio of at most r for secrets whose domain $\mathcal{S}$ is of size at least t.*[8] *Then $\mathcal{H}$ has secret-sharing scheme with information ratio at most $\frac{r}{c}$ for secrets taken from $\mathcal{S}^{ct}$. In addition, if the schemes for $\mathcal{H}_i$ are multilinear, the new scheme is multilinear as well.*

The proof is deferred to the full version [AA18].

4.1 Secret-Sharing for d-partite Hypergraphs

For a d-partite hypergraph $\mathcal{H} = (V = (V_1, \ldots, V_d), E)$ we define $f_{\mathcal{H}} : V_1 \times \ldots \times V_d \to \{0, 1\}$ to be the function that outputs 1 on an input $e = (v_1, \ldots, v_d)$ if and only if $e \in E$.

Lemma 2. *Suppose that $f_{\mathcal{H}}$ has a d-party* CDS *scheme $(F_1, \ldots, F_d)$ with information ratio w for secrets whose domain $\mathcal{S}$ is of size at least n where n is the number of nodes in $\mathcal{H}$. Then, there is a secret sharing scheme for $\mathcal{H}$ with information ratio $w+2$ for secrets in $\mathcal{S}$. Moreover, if the* CDS *scheme is linear (resp., multilinear) then the secret sharing scheme is also linear (resp., multilinear).*

Proof. Let $\mathcal{S}$ be the secret domain of the CDS for $f_{\mathcal{H}}$ and let $|V| = n$. Given a secret $s \in \mathcal{S}$ we share it as follows. First, we use $(d+1)$-out-of-$(d+1)$ secret sharing to share s into $(s_0, \ldots, s_d)$. Next, we sample randomness r for the CDS and distribute the secret s_0; That is, for each vertex $v \in V_i$, we generate the

[8] This condition can be completely waived at the expense of losing a constant factor in the final rate.

share $a_v = F_i(v, s_0, r)$. Finally, we use $(d+1)$-out-of-n Shamir's secret sharing to share the secret s into n shares $(b_v)_{v \in V}$. (For this we view $\mathcal{S}$ as a field and use the fact that $|\mathcal{S}| \geq n$.) Overall, the share of the vertex $v \in V_i$ is the triplet (s_i, a_v, b_v). Observe that the information ratio is $w+2$ (since threshold access structures can be realized with information ratio of 1).

Correctness: Consider an authorized coalition parties $e \subset V$. If e contains more than d parties then the secret can be recovered based on the b parts. Otherwise, $e \in E$. In this case, the CDS allows the coalition to recover s_0. Moreover, since e must contain exactly one vertex from each part V_i of the graph the parties also have the shares $s_1, \ldots, s_d$ and they can recover s.

Privacy: Consider an unauthorized coalition of parties $e \subset V$. In any case e is smaller than $d+1$ and so the b parts reveal no information. If the size of e is smaller than d then e does not contain a vertex from V_i for some $i \in [d]$, and so s_i remains hidden and no information is revealed about s. If e is of size d then $e \notin E$ and so the CDS keeps s_0 hidden, and no information is revealed about s. □

Corollary 3. *Every d-partite hypergraph has a d-uniform, multilinear secret-sharing scheme with information ratio of 6 for secrets of domain size 2^{n^d-1}, where n is the number of nodes in $\mathcal{H}$.*

Proof. Let $\mathcal{H}$ be a d-partite hypergraph with n vertices $V = (V_1, \ldots, V_d)$. Since each V_i contains at most n vertices, the function $f_{\mathcal{H}}$ can be viewed as a binary function over $[n]^d$. We construct a d-party CDS for $f_{\mathcal{H}}$ using Corollary 1, and then use Lemma 2 to get the required secret-sharing scheme. □

4.2 Secret-Sharing for d-uniform Hypergraphs

Recall that Fact 8 shows that the case of general d-uniform hypergraphs reduces to the case of d-partite hypergraphs provided that we have a "good" covering of hypergraphs by d-partite hypergraphs. The following lemma uses a probabilistic argument to establish the existence of such a good covering.

Lemma 3. *Let $\mathcal{H} = (V, E)$ be a d-uniform hypergraph with n vertices. Let $t = 3\frac{d^d(d^d+1)^2}{d!} \cdot \ln(n^d)$. There exists a set of sub-hypergraphs of $\mathcal{H}$ denoted by $\{\mathcal{H}_1, \ldots, \mathcal{H}_t\}$ such that every $\mathcal{H}_i$ is d-partite and every edge of $\mathcal{H}$ appears in at least $\frac{d!}{d^d+1} \cdot t$ sub-hypergraphs.*

The constant $\frac{d!}{d^d+1}$ can be replaced with any constant strictly smaller than $\frac{d!}{d^d}$. The proof is deferred to the full version [AA18].

We can now prove Theorem 4 (restated here for convenience).

Theorem 9. *Every d-uniform hypergraph $\mathcal{H}$ has a multilinear d-uniform secret-sharing scheme with information ratio $6 \cdot \frac{d^d+1}{d!}$ for secrets of length $\exp(O(n^d \cdot \log n \cdot d^{2d+1}))$ where n is the number of nodes in $\mathcal{H}$.*

Proof. First, we use Lemma 3 to decompose $\mathcal{H}$ into $t = 3\frac{d^d(d^d+1)^2}{d!} \cdot \ln(n^d)$ sub-hypergraphs that are d-partite, such that every edge of $\mathcal{H}$ appears in at least $c \cdot t$ different sub-hypergraphs where $c = \frac{d!}{d^d+1}$. Following Corollary 3, every sub-hypergraph in the decomposition has a multilinear d-uniform secret-sharing scheme with information ratio of 6 for secrets of domain size 2^{n^d-1}. Finally, we use Fact 8 to establish a multilinear d-uniform secret-sharing scheme for $\mathcal{H}$ with information ratio $\frac{6}{c} = 6 \cdot \frac{d^d+1}{d!}$ for secrets domain of size $(2^{n^d}-1)^{ct} = 2^{(n^d-1)3d^d(d^d+1)\ln(n^d)} = \exp(O(n^d \cdot \log n \cdot d^{2d+1}))$. □

For the special case of $d = 2$ (i.e., forbidden graph access structure) we get the following corollary.

Corollary 4. *Every forbidden graph access structure has a multilinear secret-sharing scheme with information ratio of* 12.5.

Proof. As explained in Corollary 1 there exists a multilinear 2-party CDS with information ratio of 3. □

Remark 6. There are some tweaks that can be applied to our secret-sharing construction to get (minor) improvements in the information ratio. Since these modifications complicate the statements and their proofs, we briefly describe them here instead:

1. In our construction of secret-sharing for d-partite hypergraphs, as described in Lemma 2, each party is given a $(d+1)$-out-of-n share of Shamir's secret sharing. This is done to promise that any $d+1$ parties can reconstruct the secret. As we use the construction from Lemma 2 multiple times in our final construction for d-uniform hypergraphs, this creates a redundancy. Instead, we can drop this step at Lemma 2, apply Lemma 3, and add a Shamir secret sharing for $d+1$ sets at the end. This gives us an overall information ratio of $5 \cdot \frac{d^d+1}{d!} + 1$.
2. In Lemma 3 we used Chernoff bound to show the existence of our desired decomposition. We chose a value for δ that is $1 - \frac{d^d}{d^d+1}$. In general, every value of δ smaller than 1 would suffice. Hence, the information ratio can be arbitrarily close to $5 \cdot \frac{d^d}{d!} + 1$. (Naturally, when the information ratio gets closer to $5 \cdot \frac{d^d}{d!} + 1$, longer secrets are required in order to achieve amortization).
3. An additional improvement can be obtained by plugging-in the optimized $4 - \frac{2}{k}$ bound on the information ratio of k-party CDS (Corollary 1). This yields a secret-sharing scheme for d-uniform hypergraphs with an information ratio $(5 - \frac{2}{d}) \cdot \frac{d^d}{d!} + 1 + \epsilon$ for every $\epsilon > 0$.

5 Lower Bounds for *d*-uniform Secret Sharing

In this section we discuss the possibility of proving lower-bounds against d-uniform secret sharing.

5.1 Lower Bound for the Share Size of d-uniform Linear SS

We start by showing a lower bound on the *share size* (in bits) of linear d-uniform secret sharing. This immediately implies a similar lower-bound on the share size of multilinear schemes. (Since one can turn a multilinear scheme into a linear scheme by fixing all but a single secret). The following definitions are needed:

Definition 6. *Let $\mathcal{A}$ be an access structure and q be a prime power. Define $\rho_q(\mathcal{A})$ to be the minimal information ratio of all* **linear** *secret sharing schemes realizing $\mathcal{A}$ over the field $\mathbb{F}_q$ (the finite field over q elements).*

Definition 7. *For an access structure $\mathcal{A}$, we say that $\mathcal{A}$ has* rank r, *if every minimal authorized set of $\mathcal{A}$ is of size at most r.*

The following theorem is proved in [BFM16]:

Theorem 10. *Let q be a prime power, and s, r, n be integers such that $s > \log(n)$. Denote by $T(q, s, r, n)$ the number of access structures with n parties, rank r and $\rho_q(\mathcal{A}) \leq s$. Then $T(q, s, r, n) \leq 2^{2rns^2 \log(q)}$.*

From this theorem, it is easy to get a lower bound for the maximum share size of linear d-uniform secret sharing schemes. The following corollary is presented by [BFM16] for the case of forbidden graphs. We generalize this result to d-uniform access structures:

Corollary 5 (Theorem 5 restated). *For every n and $d \geq 2$, there exists a d-uniform access structure $\mathcal{A}$ such that the maximal share size of every linear secret sharing scheme realizing it (and therefore of every multilinear scheme as well), is at least*

$$\sqrt{\frac{n^{d-1}}{2d^d(d+1)}} \geq \frac{n^{(d-1)/2}}{2d^{(d+1)/2}}.$$

Proof. Fix some prime power q. Suppose that every d-uniform access structure admits a linear scheme over $\mathbb{F}_q$ with maximal share size of $z = s\log(q)$. Every d-uniform access structure, is a rank $d+1$ access structure. Therefore we get that on one hand the number of d uniform access structures such that $\rho_q(\mathcal{A}) < s$ is at most $T(q, s, d+1, n) \leq 2^{2(d+1)nz^2}$. On the other hand, the number of d-uniform access structures is $2^{\binom{n}{d}}$. Therefore, $2^{2(d+1)nz^2} \geq 2^{\binom{n}{d}}$ which in turn means that $z \geq \sqrt{\frac{n^{d-1}}{2d^d(d+1)}}$. For the case of multilinear schemes, observe that any such scheme simplifies to a linear scheme after we fix all but a single entry of the vector of secrets. □

For a constant d, we conclude that the share size of d-uniform linear (or multilinear) SS must be at least $\Omega_d(n^{\frac{d-1}{2}})$. We conclude that multilinear SS (like the one from Theorem 4) cannot achieve constant information rate for secrets shorter than $\Omega_d(n^{\frac{d-1}{2}})$. Note that in our scheme amortization begins only for exponentially long secrets. Narrowing this gap, even for multilinear schemes, remains an interesting open problem.

5.2 Limitations of Shannon's Inequalities Based Lower-Bounds

A commonly used technique for proving secret sharing lower bounds is by analyzing the entropy of the shares (induced by a uniform choice of the secret). In particular, one typically relies on the following claim. (Below H denotes Shannon's entropy).

Claim 11. *Let $\mathcal{A}$ be an access structure and let Σ be a (perfect) secret sharing scheme for $\mathcal{A}$ with secret domain of $\mathcal{S}$. For a set of parties A, denote by S_A the joint distribution of the shares of parties in A induced by a uniformly chosen secret $S \xleftarrow{R} \mathcal{S}$, and by the internal randomness of Σ. Define $f(A) = \frac{H(S_A)}{H(S)}$. Then the following holds:*

1. *Monotonicity. If $A \subset B$, then $f(B) \geq f(A) \geq f(\emptyset) = 0$.*
2. *Submodularity. $f(A) + f(B) \geq f(A \cup B) + f(A \cap B)$.*
3. *Strong Monotonicity. If $A \notin \mathcal{A}, B \in \mathcal{A}$, and $A \subset B$, then $f(B) \geq f(A) + 1$.*
4. *Strong Submodularity. If $A, B \in \mathcal{A}$ and $A \cap B \notin \mathcal{A}$, then $f(A) + f(B) \geq f(A \cup B) + f(A \cap B) + 1$.*

These inequalities are called Shannon inequalities, and a proof of the claim is given by Csirmaz [Csi97]. The claim is typically used to lower-bound, for some party a, the value of $f(a)$ and conclude a lower-bound on the (normalized) entropy value of a's share, which implies a lower-bound on the share size. Indeed, this technique was used by Csirmaz to prove the best known lower-bound ($\frac{n}{\log n}$) on the information ratio of some n-party access structure. Csirmaz also showed that this method cannot prove superlinear lower-bounds since there is a "semi-entropy" function g that satisfies the conditions of Claim 11 but assign to each singleton a value of $O(n)$. We use the same idea to show a barrier of d for the case of d-uniform access structures.

Theorem 12. *Let $d \geq 2$. Then Shannon inequalities cannot give a better lower bound than d for the information ratio of d-uniform secret sharing.*

Proof. Let $\mathcal{A}$ be a d-uniform access structure, and let A be a non-empty set of parties. For $t = min\{|A|, d+1\}$ we define

$$g(A) = \left(\sum_{i=0}^{t-1} (d+1-i) \right) - 1$$

For the empty set, we define $g(\emptyset) = 0$. Note that $g(\{p\}) = d$ for every party p. Thus, showing that g satisfies the Shannon inequalities will prove the theorem. Clearly g is monotone and non-negative, so (1) is satisfied. For (3), we assume $A \notin \mathcal{A}, B \in \mathcal{A}$, and $A \subset B$. The set A contains at most d parties (since it is unauthorized), and the set B contains more parties than A, therefore (3) follows.

For (2) and (4), we first ignore the -1 at the definition of g and consider the following cases:

1. $|A| \geq d+1$. In this case, $g(A) = g(A \cup B)$ and we reduce (2) and (4) to (1) and (3) respectively. The case where $|B| \geq d+1$ is symmetric.

2. $A \subset B$. In this case $A = A \cap B$ and $B = A \cup B$. (2) follows. In addition, if $A \in \mathcal{A}$ then $A \cap B \in \mathcal{A}$ and so (4) vacuously follows. The case where $B \subset A$ is symmetric.
3. Assume $|A|, |B| \leq d+1$ and that $A \cup B \neq A, B$. We show that $g(A) - g(A \cap B) \geq g(A \cup B) - g(B) + 1$, thus showing both (4) and (2). We denote $C = A - (A \cap B)$ and $D = (A \cup B) - B$. Note that $C = D$ and let $\ell := |C| = |D|$. This implies that $g(A) - g(A \cap B)$ is the sum of the last ℓ consecutive integers of $g(A)$, denote this sum by $x_1 + \cdots + x_\ell$. Also, $g(A \cup B) - g(B)$ is the sum of the last ℓ consecutive integers of $g(A \cup B)$, denote this sum by $y_1 +, \ldots, + y_\ell$. Since A is a strict subset of $A \cup B$, it holds that for every i, $x_i > y_i$, and so (2) and (4) follow.

Returning to the original definition of g (with the -1), we note that this substraction matters only if one of the sets is empty. The cases where $A = \emptyset$ or $B = \emptyset$ are easily validated. In case $A \cap B = \emptyset$ we argue that

$$g(A) + g(B) \geq g(A \cup B) + 1.$$

Denote $a = \min\{|A|, d+1\}$, $b = \min\{|B|, d+1\}$ and $c = \min\{a+b, d+1\}$. On the LHS we have $(\sum_{i=0}^{a-1}(d+1-i) + \sum_{i=0}^{b-1}(d+1-i)) - 2$, and on the RHS we have $(\sum_{i=0}^{c-1}(d+1-i)) - 1$. One can easily verify that the LHS is indeed at least as big as the RHS, with equality in case $a = b = 1, c = 2$. □

6 Reducing Partial-PSM to CDS

In this section we show how to reduce partial-PSM to CDS with better overhead than the one achieved in [AARV17]. Let $f : (\mathcal{X} \times \mathcal{W}) \times (\mathcal{Y} \times \mathcal{Z}) \to \{0,1\}$ be the target function where $\mathcal{X}$ and $\mathcal{Y}$ are the private domains and $\mathcal{W}$ and $\mathcal{Z}$ are the public domains. We associate with f the function family

$$\mathcal{F} = \{f(\cdot, w, \cdot, z) : w \in \mathcal{W}, z \in \mathcal{Z}\} \tag{1}$$

that consists of all two-party functions that can be derived from f after fixing some values for the public domains. For the sake of simplicity, we assume the private input domains $\mathcal{X}$ and $\mathcal{Y}$ are both $\{0,1\}^t$, and the public domains $\mathcal{W}$ and $\mathcal{Z}$ are both $\{0,1\}^{\ell-t}$. That is, Alice and Bob each hold ℓ bits, out of which t bits are considered private. By abuse of notation, we sometimes view the domain of f as $\{0,1\}^\ell \times \{0,1\}^\ell$. We will use the following notations:

- We denote by $\mathsf{CDS}(f, b)$ the minimal total communication complexity of a perfect CDS for f supporting b-bit secrets.
- We denote by $\mathsf{CDS}(\ell, b)$ the maximal value of $\mathsf{CDS}(f, b)$ over all functions $f : \{0,1\}^\ell \times \{0,1\}^\ell \to \{0,1\}$.

Overview. The general idea behind the reductions is as follows: Let (x, w_0) and (y, z_0) be the input for Alice and Bob respectively. Let f_{w_0,z_0} be the function f restricted to $w = w_0, z = z_0$. The function f_{w_0,z_0} is known to Carol, but not to Alice and Bob. Suppose that we have a family of PSM protocols $\{F_{(w,z)} = (F_{(w,z),1}, F_{(w,z),2})\}_{w,z}$ for all possible functions $f_{w,z}$. The idea is to release only the transcript of $F_{(w_0,z_0)}(x, y, r)$ via the aid of CDS. Naively, this can be done by letting Alice generate, for every (w, z), the PSM messages $F_{(w,z),1}$ and use the result as a secret for a CDS over the 2-party predicate "Is (w_0, z_0) equal to (w, z)?", and do the same with Bob's messages. Clearly, the overhead in this case is huge (exponential in the length of the public input (w, z)). To see how this overhead can be reduced, imagine that the underlying PSM has the property that Alice's (resp., Bob's) computation can be decomposed to blocks where in the i-th block we compute one of L functions $g_1(x, r), \ldots, g_L(x; r)$ depending on the value of (w, z). Then, we can release each block of $F_{(w,z),1}$ by making only L calls to a CDS. We start with a formalization of this idea with the notion of PSM *compilers*, and then give concrete examples of this approach.

6.1 PSM Compilers

Definition 8 (PSM Compiler). *Let $\mathcal{F}$ be a function family. We say that C is a* PSM *compiler for $\mathcal{F}$, if C maps every function $f \in \mathcal{F}$ to a (fully secure)* PSM *$F = (F_1, F_2)$. As usual, let x and y be Alice's and Bob's inputs respectively, and let r be the randomness of the* PSM. *We say that C is (c, v, b, L)-uniform if there exist v families of functions $\mathcal{G}_1, ..., \mathcal{G}_v$ and a pair of functions h_A, h_B with the following properties:*

1. *Every* PSM *$F = (F_1, F_2)$ in the image of C can be written as a concatenation of functions $(h_A, h_B, g_1, ..., g_v)$, where $g_i \in \mathcal{G}_i$ is chosen based on f (and h_A and h_B are identical for all $f \in \mathcal{F}$). Every function $g_i \in \mathcal{G}_i$ depends either on (x, r) or on (y, r), and the functions h_A and h_B depend on (x, r) and (y, r) respectively.*
2. *Every function family $\mathcal{G}_i$ contains at most L functions.*
3. *The output length of every function $g \in \cup\mathcal{G}_i$ is at most b bits, and the total output length of h_A and h_B is at most c bits.*

Lemma 4. *Let f be a two-party predicate whose private and public domains are $\{0,1\}^t$ and $\{0,1\}^{\ell-t}$, for each party. Let $\mathcal{F}$ be the function family associated with f as in Eq. (1). Then, a (c, v, b, L)-uniform* PSM *compiler for $\mathcal{F}$ implies a partial-*PSM *for f with communication complexity $O(c + L \cdot v \cdot \mathsf{CDS}(\ell - t, b))$.*

Proof. Let x and y be the private inputs of Alice and Bob, and let w and z denote their public inputs. Let $(h_A, h_B, g_1, ..., g_v)$ be the compiled representation of the PSM for $f_{w,z} = f(\cdot, w, \cdot, z)$ and let r be the randomness used by that PSM. Recall that for every i, g_i is chosen from $\mathcal{G}_i$ according to the public inputs w, z. Hence, for every g, i, we can define a predicate $P_{g,i}$ that given w, z as an input outputs 1 if $g_i = g$. To execute a partial PSM, Alice and Bob sample joint randomness r and send the following messages:

- Alice sends $h_A(x,r)$ and Bob sends $h_B(y,r)$.
- For every $i \in [v]$ and $g \in \mathcal{G}_i$ the parties invoke a CDS (with fresh randomness) on the public inputs w and z, predicate $P_{g,i}$ (i.e.,"Is g equal to g_i?"), and secret $g(x,r)$ (if g depends on Alice's input) or $g(y,r)$ (if g depends on Bob's input).

Note that the secret is known either to Alice or Bob, but not to both. Hence we should use a proper CDS that operates even if the secret is known only to one of the parties. Recall that this feature can be obtained from any (standard) CDS at the expense of increasing the total communication by $|s|$, the length of the secret (see Remark 1). It follows that the overall communication complexity is at most $c+L\cdot v\cdot(\mathsf{CDS}(\ell-t,b)+b) \leq c+2L\cdot v\cdot \mathsf{CDS}(\ell-t,b)$, as required. (The inequality follows by noting that $\mathsf{CDS}(\ell-t,b) \geq b$.).

The correctness of CDS guarantees that Carol, who knows w and z, can recover the value

$$\hat{f}_{w,z}(x,y;r) = (h_A(x,r), h_B(y,r), g_1(x,y,r), ..., g_v(x,y,r)),$$

which, by the correctness of the PSM for $f_{w,z}$, can decoded to $f(x,w,y,z)$.

On the other hand, we can perfectly simulate the view of Carol based on w, z and $f(x,w,y,z)$ as follows. First sample $\hat{f}_{w,z}(x,y;r)$ using the PSM simulator; Then, use the corresponding values to perfectly sample the transcript of the CDS calls in which the predicate was satisfied. Finally, use the CDS simulator to sample the transcripts for the CDS calls that did not satisfy the predicate. The lemma follows. □

6.2 Partial-PSM for General Functions

Our first reduction employs a simple PSM compiler that reduces the evaluation of an arbitrary function to the case of inner product. (This can be viewed as a special case of the multilinear PSM from [BIKK14].)

Theorem 13. *Every two-party functionality $f : \{0,1\}^\ell \times \{0,1\}^\ell \to \{0,1\}$ with private domain of $\{0,1\}^t$ admits a prefect partial-PSM with communication complexity $O(2^t + 2^{2t} \cdot \mathsf{CDS}(\ell-t,1))$.*

Proof. By Lemma 4 it suffices to show that the family $\mathcal{F}_t$ of all all two-party functionality over $\{0,1\}^t \times \{0,1\}^t$ admit a (c,v,b,L)-uniform PSM compiler PSM with $c = O(2^t), v = O(2^{2t})$ and $b = L = O(1)$.

We describe the compiler in two steps beginning with following PSM compiler (that does not achieve the required efficiency properties).

- **Public input:** A function $f : \{0,1\}^t \times \{0,1\}^t \to \{0,1\}$, represented as its truth table $P \in \{0,1\}^{2^{2t}}$.
- **Alice's inputs:** $x \in \{0,1\}^t$ represented as the indicator vector $e_x \in \{0,1\}^{2^t}$.
- **Bob's inputs:** $y \in \{0,1\}^t$ represented as the indicator vector $e_y \in \{0,1\}^{2^t}$.
- **Carol's output:** $f(x,y)$ represented by the inner product $\langle P, e_x \otimes e_y \rangle$, where $\otimes$ denotes tensor product.
- **Shared randomness:** random bit r and random strings $a', b' \in \{0,1\}^{2^t}$.

The Protocol:

– Alice and Bob send to Carol

$$\alpha = e_x + a' \quad \text{and} \quad \beta = e_y + b', \tag{2}$$

respectively. In addition, Alice sends

$$\gamma = -\langle P, (e_x + a') \otimes b' \rangle + r, \tag{3}$$

and Bob sends

$$\delta = -\langle P, a' \otimes e_y \rangle - r. \tag{4}$$

– Carol outputs the value $\alpha\beta + \gamma + \delta$.

Correctness follows directly from the construction, by noting that the product $\alpha\beta$ simplifies to

$$\langle P, (e_x + a') \otimes (e_y + b') \rangle = \langle P, e_x \otimes e_y \rangle + \langle P, (e_x + a') \otimes b' \rangle + \langle P, a' \otimes e_y \rangle.$$

Privacy is due to the fact that the messages α, β, γ are uniform, and the last message δ is uniquely determined by all other messages and $f(x, y)$. Hence, there exists a simulator S_f that, given $f(x, y)$ perfectly samples the transcript $(\alpha, \beta, \gamma, \delta)$.

The protocol above forms a $(2 \cdot 2^t, 2, 1, 2^{2^{2t}})$-uniform PSM compiler for $\mathcal{F}_t$. Indeed, $h_A = e_x + a'$, $h_B = e_y + b'$ and the function families $\mathcal{G}_1$ and $\mathcal{G}_2$ correspond to computations of $-\langle P, (e_x + a') \otimes b' \rangle + r$ and $-\langle P, e_y \otimes a' \rangle - r$ respectively, with all possible values for P. To avoid this double-exponential blow-up, we replace the inner-product computations in (3) and (4) by their randomized encoding. Concretely, letting $u = (e_x + a') \otimes b'$ we replace (3) by

$$\left(P_i \cdot u_i + s_i\right)_{i=1}^{2^{2t}}, \tag{5}$$

where $s = (s_1, \ldots, s_{2^{2t}-1})$ is a string of random bits (added to the shared randomness) and $s_{2^{2t}} = r - \sum_{i=1}^{2^{2t}-1} s_i$. Similarly, letting $u' = a' \otimes e_y$ we replace (4) by

$$\left(-P_i \cdot u'_i + s'_i\right)_{i=1}^{2^{2t}-1}, \tag{6}$$

where $s' \in \{0,1\}^{2^{2t}-1}$ is a string of random bits (added to the shared randomness) and $s'_{2^{2t}} = -r - \sum_{i=1}^{2^{2t}-1} s'_i$.

The resulting PSM protocol is still correct since Carol can recover the original messages of (3) and (4) by summing-up the entries in (5) and (6) sent by Alice and Bob in the modified protocol. To see that privacy is preserved, observe that, given $f(x, y)$, we can first sample a transcript $(\alpha, \beta, \gamma, \delta)$ for the original protocol, and then sample (5) and (6) by sampling 2^{2t} random bits that sum up to γ together with 2^{2t} random bits that sum up to δ. It is not hard to verify that this simulation is perfect. (Indeed, this is just a special case of the general composition property of randomized encoding, cf. [AIK06].)

The modified compiler now uses $2 \cdot 2^{2t}$ function families $\mathcal{G}_i$ where each family consists of exactly 2 functions (selected according to the i-th bit of P) whose output is a single bit. Hence, we get $(2 \cdot 2^t, 2 \cdot 2^{2t}, 1, 2)$-uniform PSM compiler for $\mathcal{F}_m$, as required. □

Plugging in the CDS construction of [LVW17a] to Theorem 13, we derive the following corollary.

Corollary 6. *For every two-party predicate f with input domains $\mathcal{X} = \mathcal{Y} = \{0,1\}^{2t}$ there exists a partial-PSM protocol with overall complexity of $(2^{2t})^{1+o(1)}$.*

The resulting partial-PSM is is quasilinear in the alphabet size, $|\mathcal{X} \times \mathcal{Y}|$, of the private inputs. Note that a direct application of the fully secure PSM of [BIKK14] yields a complexity of $O(2^{\ell/2})$, hence our construction becomes useful only when the length of the secret part t is smaller than $\ell/4$.

6.3 Partial-PSM for Formulas

Our second reduction is based on an information theoretic version of Yao's garbled circuit [IK02]. Recall that a *formula* is a Boolean circuit in which every non-input gate has a fan-out of 1. The *size* of a formula is the number of gates, and its *depth* is the length of longest path from a leaf to the root.

Theorem 14. *Let f be a two-party predicate whose private and public domains are $\{0,1\}^t$ and $\{0,1\}^{\ell-t}$, for each party. Let $\mathcal{F}$ be the function family associated with f as in Eq. (1), and assume that every function in $\mathcal{F}$ can be computed by a formula of size B and depth D. Then there is a partial-PSM for f with communication complexity of $O(B^3 \cdot \mathsf{CDS}(\ell - t, 2^D))$.*

Proof. By Lemma 4, the theorem follows from the existence of a PSM compiler for formulas of size B and depth D that achieves $(O(1), B, 2^D, O(B^2))$-uniformity. Such a compiler follows immediately from the information-theoretic variant of garbled circuits that is presented in [IK02]. See the full version for details. □

References

[AA18] Applebaum, B., Arkis, B.: Conditional disclosure of secrets and d-uniform secret sharing with constant information rate. IACR Cryptology ePrint Archive 2018/1 (2018)

[AARV17] Applebaum, B., Arkis, B., Raykov, P., Vasudevan, P.N.: Conditional disclosure of secrets: amplification, closure, amortization, lower-bounds, and separations. In: Katz, J., Shacham, H. (eds.) CRYPTO 2017. LNCS, vol. 10401, pp. 727–757. Springer, Cham (2017). https://doi.org/10.1007/978-3-319-63688-7_24

[AHMS18] Applebaum, B., Holenstein, T., Mishra, M., Shayevitz, O.: The communication complexity of private simultaneous messages, revisited. In: Nielsen, J.B., Rijmen, V. (eds.) EUROCRYPT 2018. LNCS, vol. 10821, pp. 261–286. Springer, Cham (2018). https://doi.org/10.1007/978-3-319-78375-8_9. https://eprint.iacr.org/2018/144

[AIK06] Applebaum, B., Ishai, Y., Kushilevitz, E.: Cryptography in NC^0. SIAM J. Comput. **36**(4), 845–888 (2006)

[AIR01] Aiello, B., Ishai, Y., Reingold, O.: Priced oblivious transfer: how to sell digital goods. In: Pfitzmann, B. (ed.) EUROCRYPT 2001. LNCS, vol. 2045, pp. 119–135. Springer, Heidelberg (2001). https://doi.org/10.1007/3-540-44987-6_8

[Bei11] Beimel, A.: Secret-sharing schemes: a survey. In: Chee, Y.M., Guo, Z., Ling, S., Shao, F., Tang, Y., Wang, H., Xing, C. (eds.) IWCC 2011. LNCS, vol. 6639, pp. 11–46. Springer, Heidelberg (2011). https://doi.org/10.1007/978-3-642-20901-7_2

[BFM16] Beimel, A., Farràs, O., Mintz, Y.: Secret-sharing schemes for very dense graphs. J. Cryptol. **29**(2), 336–362 (2016)

[BFMP17] Beimel, A., Farràs, O., Mintz, Y., Peter, N.: Linear secret-sharing schemes for forbidden graph access structures. In: Kalai, Y., Reyzin, L. (eds.) TCC 2017. LNCS, vol. 10678, pp. 394–423. Springer, Cham (2017). https://doi.org/10.1007/978-3-319-70503-3_13

[BI01] Beimel, A., Ishai, Y.: On the power of nonlinear secrect-sharing. In: Proceedings of the 16th Annual IEEE Conference on Computational Complexity, Chicago, Illinois, USA, 18–21 June 2001, pp. 188–202. IEEE Computer Society (2001)

[BIKK14] Beimel, A., Ishai, Y., Kumaresan, R., Kushilevitz, E.: On the cryptographic complexity of the worst functions. In: Lindell, Y. (ed.) TCC 2014. LNCS, vol. 8349, pp. 317–342. Springer, Heidelberg (2014). https://doi.org/10.1007/978-3-642-54242-8_14

[BKN18] Beimel, A., Kushilevitz, E., Nissim, P.: The Complexity of Multiparty PSM Protocols and Related Models. In: Nielsen, J.B., Rijmen, V. (eds.) EUROCRYPT 2018. LNCS, vol. 10821, pp. 287–318. Springer, Cham (2018). https://doi.org/10.1007/978-3-319-78375-8_10. https://eprint.iacr.org/2018/148

[BL88] Benaloh, J., Leichter, J.: Generalized secret sharing and monotone functions. In: Goldwasser, S. (ed.) CRYPTO 1988. LNCS, vol. 403, pp. 27–35. Springer, New York (1990). https://doi.org/10.1007/0-387-34799-2_3

[Bla79] Blakley, G.R.: Safeguarding cryptographic keys. In: Proceedings AFIPS 1979 National Computer Conference, pp. 313–317. AFIPS (1979)

[CKGS98] Chor, B., Kushilevitz, E., Goldreich, O., Sudan, M.: Private information retrieval. J. ACM **45**(6), 965–981 (1998)

[CSGV93] Capocelli, R.M., Santis, A.D., Gargano, L., Vaccaro, U.: On the size of shares for secret sharing schemes. J. Cryptol. **6**(3), 157–167 (1993)

[Csi97] Csirmaz, L.: The size of a share must be large. J. Cryptol. **10**(4), 223–231 (1997)

[FKN94] Feige, U., Kilian, J., Naor, M.: A minimal model for secure computation (extended abstract). In: Leighton, F.T., Goodrich, M.T. (eds.) Proceedings of the Twenty-Sixth Annual ACM Symposium on Theory of Computing, 23–25 May 1994, Montréal, Québec, Canada, pp. 554–563. ACM (1994)

[GIKM00] Gertner, Y., Ishai, Y., Kushilevitz, E., Malkin, T.: Protecting data privacy in private information retrieval schemes. J. Comput. Syst. Sci. **60**(3), 592–629 (2000)

[GKW15] Gay, R., Kerenidis, I., Wee, H.: Communication complexity of conditional disclosure of secrets and attribute-based encryption. In: Gennaro, R., Robshaw, M. (eds.) CRYPTO 2015. LNCS, vol. 9216, pp. 485–502. Springer, Heidelberg (2015). https://doi.org/10.1007/978-3-662-48000-7_24

[GPSW06] Goyal, V., Pandey, O., Sahai, A., Waters, B.: Attribute-based encryption for fine-grained access control of encrypted data. In Juels, A., Wright, R.N., di Vimercati, S.D.C. (eds.) Proceedings of the 13th ACM Conference on Computer and Communications Security, CCS 2006, Alexandria, VA, USA, 30 october–3 November 2006, pp. 89–98. ACM (2006)

[IK00] Ishai, Y., Kushilevitz, E.: Randomizing polynomials: A new representation with applications to round-efficient secure computation. In: 41st Annual Symposium on Foundations of Computer Science, FOCS 2000, 12–14 November 2000, Redondo Beach, California, USA, pp. 294–304. IEEE Computer Society (2000)

[IK02] Ishai, Y., Kushilevitz, E.: Perfect constant-round secure computation via perfect randomizing polynomials. In: Widmayer, P., Eidenbenz, S., Triguero, F., Morales, R., Conejo, R., Hennessy, M. (eds.) ICALP 2002. LNCS, vol. 2380, pp. 244–256. Springer, Heidelberg (2002). https://doi.org/10.1007/3-540-45465-9_22

[Ish13] Ishai, Y.: Randomization techniques for secure computation. In: Prabhakaran, M., Sahai, A. (eds.) Secure Multi-Party Computation, Volume 10 of Cryptology and Information Security Series, pp. 222–248. IOS Press (2013)

[ISN87] Ito, M., Saito, A., Nishizeki, T.: Secret sharing scheme realizing general access structure. In: Proceedings IEEE Globecom 1987, pp. 99–102. IEEE (1987)

[IW14] Ishai, Y., Wee, H.: Partial garbling schemes and their applications. In: Esparza, J., Fraigniaud, P., Husfeldt, T., Koutsoupias, E. (eds.) ICALP 2014. LNCS, vol. 8572, pp. 650–662. Springer, Heidelberg (2014). https://doi.org/10.1007/978-3-662-43948-7_54

[KGH83] Karnin, E.D., Greene, J.W., Hellman, M.E.: On secret sharing systems. IEEE Trans. Inf. Theor. **29**(1), 35–41 (1983)

[KS17] Katz, J., Shacham, H. (eds.): CRYPTO 2017. LNCS, vol. 10401. Springer, Cham (2017). https://doi.org/10.1007/978-3-319-63688-7

[KW93] Karchmer, M., Wigderson, A.: On span programs. In: Proceedings of the Eigth Annual Structure in Complexity Theory Conference, San Diego, CA, USA, 18–21 May 1993, pp. 102–111. IEEE Computer Society (1993)

[LV18] Liu, T., Vaikuntanathan, V.: Breaking the circuit-size barrier in secret sharing. In: To appear in STOC2018 (2018). https://eprint.iacr.org/2018/333

[LVW17a] Liu, T., Vaikuntanathan, V., Wee, H.: Conditional disclosure of secrets via non-linear reconstruction. In: Katz, J., Shacham, H. (eds.) CRYPTO 2017. Lecture Notes in Computer Science, vol. 10401, pp. 758–790. Springer, Cham (2017). https://doi.org/10.1007/978-3-319-63688-7_25

[LVW17b] Liu, T., Vaikuntanathan, V., Wee, H.: Towards breaking the exponential barrier for general secret sharing. In: Nielsen, J.B., Rijmen, V. (eds.) EUROCRYPT 2018. LNCS, vol. 10820, pp. 567–596. Springer, Cham (2018). https://doi.org/10.1007/978-3-319-78381-9_21

[Min12] Mintz, Y.: Information ratios of graph secret-sharing schemes. Master's thesis, Department of Computer Science, Ben Gurion University (2012)

[Sha79] Shamir, A.: How to share a secret. Commun. ACM **22**(11), 612–613 (1979)

[SS97] Sun, H., Shieh, S.: Secret sharing in graph-based prohibited structures. In: Proceedings IEEE INFOCOM 1997, The Conference on Computer Communications, Sixteenth Annual Joint Conference of the IEEE Computer and Communications Societies, Driving the Information Revolution, Kobe, Japan, 7–12 April 1997, pp. 718–724. IEEE (1997)

[Sti94] Stinson, D.R.: Decomposition constructions for secret-sharing schemes. IEEE Trans. Inf. Theor. **40**(1), 118–125 (1994)

[SW05] Sahai, A., Waters, B.: Fuzzy identity-based encryption. In: Cramer, R. (ed.) EUROCRYPT 2005. LNCS, vol. 3494, pp. 457–473. Springer, Heidelberg (2005). https://doi.org/10.1007/11426639_27

[VV15] Vaikuntanathan, V., Vasudevan, P.N.: Secret sharing and statistical zero knowledge. In: Iwata, T., Cheon, J.H. (eds.) ASIACRYPT 2015. LNCS, vol. 9452, pp. 656–680. Springer, Heidelberg (2015). https://doi.org/10.1007/978-3-662-48797-6_27

Information-Theoretic Secret-Key Agreement: The Asymptotically Tight Relation Between the Secret-Key Rate and the Channel Quality Ratio

Daniel Jost[1](✉), Ueli Maurer[1], and João L. Ribeiro[2]

[1] Department of Computer Science, ETH Zurich, 8092 Zurich, Switzerland
{dajost,maurer}@inf.ethz.ch

[2] Department of Computing, Imperial College London, London SW7 2AZ, UK
j.lourenco-ribeiro17@imperial.ac.uk

Abstract. Information-theoretic secret-key agreement between two parties Alice and Bob is a well-studied problem that is provably impossible in a plain model with public (authenticated) communication, but is known to be possible in a model where the parties also have access to some correlated randomness. One particular type of such correlated randomness is the so-called satellite setting, where uniform random bits (e.g., sent by a satellite) are received by the parties and the adversary Eve over inherently noisy channels. The antenna size determines the error probability, and the antenna is the adversary's limiting resource much as computing power is the limiting resource in traditional complexity-based security. The natural assumption about the adversary is that her antenna is at most Q times larger than both Alice's and Bob's antenna, where, to be realistic, Q can be very large.

The goal of this paper is to characterize the secret-key rate per transmitted bit in terms of Q. Traditional results in this so-called satellite setting are phrased in terms of the error probabilities ϵ_A, ϵ_B, and ϵ_E, of the binary symmetric channels through which the parties receive the bits and, quite surprisingly, the secret-key rate has been shown to be strictly positive unless Eve's channel is perfect ($\epsilon_E = 0$) or either Alice's or Bob's channel output is independent of the transmitted bit (i.e., $\epsilon_A = 0.5$ or $\epsilon_B = 0.5$). However, the best proven lower bound, if interpreted in terms of the channel quality ratio Q, is only exponentially small in Q. The main result of this paper is that the secret-key rate decreases asymptotically only like $1/Q^2$ if the per-bit signal energy, affecting the quality of all channels, is treated as a system parameter that can be optimized. Moreover, this bound is tight if Alice and Bob have the same antenna sizes.

Motivated by considering a fixed sending signal power, in which case the per-bit energy is inversely proportional to the bit-rate, we also propose a definition of the secret-key rate per second (rather than per transmitted bit) and prove that it decreases asymptotically only like $1/Q$.

J. L. Ribeiro—Part of the work was performed while at ETH Zurich.

A. Beimel and S. Dziembowski (Eds.): TCC 2018, LNCS 11239, pp. 345–369, 2018.
https://doi.org/10.1007/978-3-030-03807-6_13

1 Introduction

1.1 Motivation for Information-Theoretic Security

In cryptography, one generally considers two types of security of cryptographic schemes. *Unconditional* or *information-theoretic* security means that not even an adversary with unbounded computing power can cause a violation of the security property, whereas *computational* security means that the violation of the security property is impossible for an adversary with (suitably) bounded computing power, but is usually possible for a computationally unbounded adversary. Information-theoretic security was first defined and considered in Shannon's ground-breaking paper [22].

While for the most part cryptographic research is focused on computational security, actually the state of the art in complexity theory is that no cryptographic scheme has been proven to be computationally secure for a general and realistic model of computation. Instead, the term "provable security" is often used for schemes for which a reduction from a commonly agreed conjectured hard problem (such as factoring large integers) is known: Any adversary breaking the cryptographic scheme could be transformed (by the reduction), with reasonable efficiency loss, into an algorithm solving the hard problem with noticeable probability. Therefore, under the assumption that the problem is indeed hard, the scheme is secure.

In summary, there are two main advantages of information-theoretic security:

- Information-theoretic security is stronger because, compared to computational security, the security holds against a larger class of adversaries.
- The security proof does not require an unproven computational assumption.

1.2 Circumventing Impossibility Results

Unfortunately, information-theoretic security is in many settings unachievable, often provably so, at least for practical settings. For instance, Shannon's famous impossibility result [22] states that perfectly secure encryption is impossible unless the secret key has at least as much entropy as the message. This result is often quoted as showing that information-theoretic security is not practical since exchanging a fresh truly random key for every message is generally completely impractical.

The significance of such an impossibility result depends on the generality of the conditions underlying the impossibility proof. For example, Shannon's impossibility result was stated (and proven) only under the restriction that the communication between sender and receiver is one-way. That this result also holds in the more realistic setting with interactive communication between sender and receiver has been proven by Maurer only in 1993 [11]. It is therefore possible that a careful re-examination of impossibility results allows to circumvent them by a slight change of the model, where such a change should be as realistic as possible and should not destroy the practicality of schemes proven secure in the model.

A prominent such modification is quantum key distribution (QKD), where one assumes that the honest parties can exchange quantum information and thereby achieves perfect security. Given that being able to exchange quantum information is a very strong assumption for many practical scenarios, however, classical settings are still of great interest. One such model, proposed by Maurer [15] and investigated by many researchers in different contexts, is the so-called bounded-storage model. Here one assumes that the adversary's memory resources are bounded, but no assumption about the adversary's computing power is needed. Unfortunately, it seems very hard to argue that schemes proven secure in this model are practical for a reasonable bound on the adversary's memory capacity.

Other notable earlier attempts include the works of Wyner [25] and Csiszár and Körner [4], where all parties are connected by noisy channels (and only one-way communication between the two honest parties is allowed), and the work of Ozarow and Wyner [19], where the adversary is allowed to observe a bounded subset of the message's encoding. In these models, perfectly secure encryption is possible only when the adversary is at a disadvantage compared to the honest parties, which is rarely the case in practice.

A more promising approach in the context of secret-key agreement is the so-called *secret-key agreement by public discussion* model proposed by Maurer [11, 16]. In this model, two parties Alice and Bob wish to agree on a secret key by communicating over a public authenticated channel perfectly accessible to the adversary Eve. In this setting, without further assumptions, key agreement is provably impossible. However, by a slight modification of the model, namely by considering a setting where Alice, Bob, and Eve have access to correlated random variables X, Y, and Z, respectively, with joint probability distribution P_{XYZ}, secret-key agreement becomes possible, even if X and Y are almost not correlated and even if Z is strongly correlated with both X and Y.

Often one considers a setting where the experiment generating X, Y, and Z is repeated many times (independently), and one then considers the *secret-key rate*, the maximal rate (per realization of the random experiment) at which Alice and Bob can generate secret-key bits. Surprisingly, in this model, secret-key agreement (and thus perfectly secure encryption) is also possible in many cases where Eve starts with an advantage over Alice and Bob.

1.3 The Satellite Setting

A setting of particular interest is the so-called satellite setting: A satellite (or for instance a deep-space radio source) broadcasts a sequence of uniformly random bits that Alice, Bob, and Eve receive via antennas of different sizes.

In order to achieve a meaningfully large secret-key rate in this setting, one has to assume that the adversary's resources are bounded. While in computationally secure cryptography the bounded resource is the computing power, in the satellite model the natural bounded resource of the adversary is her antenna quality, that closely corresponds to the antenna size. Given that for most practical settings the honest parties' antenna sizes are more or less fixed, we specify in the following, for simplicity, this bound on Eve's antenna size as the maximal ratio Q between Eve's antenna size and the size of the smaller one of either Alice's or Bob's antennas. Analogously to the computational setting where the ratio between the adversary's and the honest parties' computing power must be assumed to be quite large, this antenna size ratio Q can be very large as well, in realistic settings. If the honest parties use for instance mobile phones, then it is very well imaginable that Q is in the order of magnitude of a million.

The satellite setting is modeled as a sequence of uniform random bits being generated and Alice, Bob, and Eve receiving them over independent binary symmetric channels with error probabilities ϵ_A, ϵ_B, and ϵ_E, respectively. Traditionally, the secret-key rate in the satellite model has then been specified in terms of the error probabilities ϵ_A, ϵ_B, and ϵ_E, respectively, capturing the fact that the antenna sizes clearly affect those error probabilities. However, it is natural to consider the signal strength of the satellite, i.e., the amount of energy it uses to broadcast each bit, as a design parameter we can control, implying that the error probabilities are no longer a priori fixed. Moreover, this highlights an interesting trade-off, as increasing the energy per bit means that the error probabilities of Alice, Bob, and Eve all decrease simultaneously, which is at the same time advantageous (Alice and Bob getting more information) and disadvantageous (Eve getting more information). As a consequence, the essential question in the satellite setting is: What is the best secret-key rate for given antenna sizes of the honest parties if we are willing to assume an upper bound on Eve's antenna size, but consider the signal strength as a design parameter to maximize over?

1.4 Contributions

Quite surprisingly, it has been shown by Maurer and Wolf [11,14] that in the satellite model secret-key agreement is possible even if Eve's channel is almost perfect, i.e., if ϵ_E is arbitrarily close to 0 but not exactly 0, and if Alice's and Bob's channels have arbitrarily high error probability but still some information (i.e., ϵ_A and ϵ_B are close to 0.5 but not exactly 0.5). However, the lower bound for the secret-key rate obtained via the original repeater-code protocol in [11], when interpreted in terms of the ratio Q, is only exponentially small in Q. In contrast, the secret-key ratio as a function of Q has already been briefly considered by Maurer and Gander [6], who conjectured based on numerical results that the rate of the parity-check protocol (introduced in [16]) asymptotically decreases like $1/Q^2$, for a setting where Alice's and Bob's antennas are assumed to be of equal size.

As our main technical contribution, we prove that both the rate of the parity-check protocol and the optimal secret-key rate are indeed inversely proportional to Q^2 in Sect. 4. This matches the numerical results and the conjecture by Gander and Maurer. We point out that the lower bound on the secret-key rate is proved by showing that the parity-check protocol, which is an explicit and simple protocol, achieves this rate in the given setting, rather than providing a pure existence proof of a protocol achieving this rate.

In the full version [9], we also generalize the secret-key rate as a function of the antenna ratio Q to the case where Alice and Bob can have antennas of different sizes, by specifying well motivated and relevant quantities for both lower and upper bounds.

In addition, we consider the setting where the power consumption of the satellite is bounded; for instance, by the size of its solar panels. Nevertheless, we can adjust the energy used to broadcast each bit by adjusting the bit-rate, i.e., the number of bits broadcast per second, while maintaining a fixed power consumption. Hence, the energy used to broadcast each bit is inversely proportional to the bit-rate. This motivates the study of the secret-key rate per second rather than the secret-key rate per bit. In order to investigate the secret-key rate per second, we introduce a novel quantity that approximates it in Sect. 5. We then show that this quantity decreases inversely proportional to Q, rather than Q^2, which makes a significant difference, since Q must be assumed to be very large.

1.5 A Note on the Practicality of the Satellite Setting

While the satellite setting attempts to mimic a real-world scenario, it also abstracts away many practical issues which affect its immediate applicability. For instance, the satellite setting encodes some basic assumptions on the adversary that might not necessarily hold in practice, such as the assumption that Eve will quantize the signal she receives. Moreover, the setting basically assumes a passive adversary, by assuming that the adversary can neither influence the bits the honest parties receive from the satellite, nor tamper with their communication. While the former restriction could be translated into some sort of physical assumption, the authenticated communication is something that can easily be obtained in a separate step. We can allow Alice and Bob to start with a small shared secret-key, which they can then use to authenticate the channel with information-theoretic security [23]. In this case, the goal of a protocol is to amplify a short initial secret-key into a very long secret-key, like in quantum key distribution.

As a consequence, even if one could imagine proving stronger results that hold if the channels can be to a certain degree dependent, or consider a setting where the adversary tries to get an advantage by considering the actual analog signal she receives, we nevertheless believe that proving theoretical results in our setting is meaningful. Showing that the secret-key rate under a channel quality constraint is reasonably large, and that the rate of a simple protocol asymptotically behaves like the secret-key rate in this setting can be seen as a step towards showing that the satellite setting is practical. In short, we feel that the problem studied in this paper is one of the most relevant and natural scientific problems extractable from the general setting.

1.6 Related Work

There have been considerable efforts to find good approximations for the secret-key rate, both in the satellite setting and for more general probability distributions, and also for settings with more than three parties.

The first bounds on the secret-key rate were proved by Maurer [11,13], and by Ahlswede and Csiszár [1], who studied the secret-key rate when only one-way communication from Alice to Bob is allowed. Later, Maurer and Wolf [12] and Renner, Skripsky, and Wolf [20] introduced improved upper bounds for general distributions, called the *intrinsic mutual information* and the *reduced intrinsic mutual information*, respectively. Csiszár and Narayan [5] extended the study of the secret-key rate to settings with more than three parties, and exhibited connections between information-theoretic secret-key agreement and the problem of *communication for omniscience*. Then, Gohari and Anantharam [7] showcased new lower and upper bounds on the secret-key rate for an arbitrary number of parties, which in particular are strict improvements over the previously known bounds for our setting.

There has been some recent interest in the secret-key rate in the finite blocklength setting, where the number of available realizations (X, Y, Z) is bounded. Tyagi and Watanabe [24] showcase a connection between the secret-key rate in this setting and binary hypothesis testing, and use it to obtain an upper bound on the secret-key rate for a bounded number of realizations. Later, Hayashi, Tyagi, and Watanabe [8] used this connection to better understand how the gap between the secret-key rate in the finite blocklength and asymptotic settings decreases as the number of available realizations increases, for certain probability distributions.

For the satellite setting, there exist better lower bounds on the secret-key rate due to the study of several *advantage distillation protocols*. The first such protocol, called the *repeater-code protocol*, was introduced and studied by Maurer [11,16]. An improved version of this protocol, called the *parity-check protocol*, was studied by Gander and Maurer [6,16]. Later, Liu, Van Tilborg, and Van Dijk [10] proposed another protocol that seems to outperform the parity-check protocol. However, the rate achieved by the proposed protocol was only numerically computed in a simulation where Eve follows a certain fixed strategy, which is not known to be optimal. Furthermore, finding a clean expression for the rate of this protocol that can be analyzed (as is done for the rate of the parity-check protocol) appears infeasible, and so it is very difficult to extract tangible rate lower bounds, even when assuming that the proposed strategy for Eve is optimal.

The scenario where Alice, Bob, and Eve receive the random bits in the satellite setting through Gaussian channels, instead of binary symmetric channels, was first considered by Maurer and Wolf [12]. Later, Naito et al. [18] showed that Alice and Bob can extract more secret-key rate in the Gaussian scenario than in the BSC scenario, as they are able to make use of soft-decoding.

2 Preliminaries

2.1 Notation

We denote random variables by uppercase letters such as X, Y, and Z. We may denote sequences of random variables $X_1, X_2, \ldots, X_N$ as X^N. We say that $X_1, X_2, \ldots, X_N$ are i.i.d. if all the X_i are independent random variables and they all have the same distribution. Most sets are denoted by uppercase calligraphic letters such as $\mathcal{S}$. The set of real numbers is denoted by $\mathbb{R}$ and for a natural number $n \in \mathbb{N}$, $[n]$ denotes the set $\{1, \ldots, n\}$. Given a set $\mathcal{S}$, the size of $\mathcal{S}$ is denoted by $|\mathcal{S}|$. For a string $x \in \{0,1\}^*$, $|x|$ denotes the length of x. The (Hamming) weight of a string $x \in \{0,1\}^*$ is defined as $w(x) := |\{i : x_i = 1\}|$, where x_i is the i-th entry of x. We denote the logarithm to the base 2 by log and the natural logarithm by ln. The closed interval in $\mathbb{R}$ between two real numbers a and b is denoted by $[a, b]$.

Given an event A, we denote the probability that A happens by $\Pr[A]$, which is the sum of the probabilities of all outcomes in event A. Given two events A and B, the probability that A and B happen simultaneously is denoted by $\Pr[A, B]$. The conditional probability of A given B, provided $\Pr[B] > 0$, is $\Pr[A|B] := \frac{\Pr[A, B]}{\Pr[B]}$.

The probability distribution of a finite random variable X is denoted by P_X, and so $P_X(x)$ denotes the probability that X takes the value x. Given an event A, $P_{X|A}$ denotes the conditional probability distribution of X conditioned on A. For two finite random variables X and Y, $P_{X|Y}(\cdot, y)$ denotes the probability distribution of X conditioned on the event $Y = y$.

2.2 Information Theory

Throughout this paper we will make use of some fundamental concepts from information theory. We briefly define the required notions in this section; a more detailed exposition of this field can be found in [3].

Fix a finite random variable X with range $\mathcal{X}$. The *entropy of* X, denoted by $H(X)$, is defined as

$$H(X) := -\sum_{x \in \mathcal{X}} P_X(x) \log P_X(x).$$

Intuitively, the entropy measures the uncertainty about a given random variable. In fact, a finite random variable X with range $\mathcal{X}$ satisfies $0 \leq H(X) \leq \log|\mathcal{X}|$ with equality in the lower bound if and only if $P_X(x) = 1$ for some $x \in \mathcal{X}$, and with equality in the upper bound if and only if X is uniform over $\mathcal{X}$. We call

$$h(p) := -p \log(p) - (1-p)\log(1-p)$$

the *binary entropy function* and note that for a binary random variable X with $P_X(1) = p$ we have that $H(X) = h(p)$.

Given two finite random variables X and Y with ranges $\mathcal{X}$ and $\mathcal{Y}$, respectively, we define the *conditional entropy of* X *given* Y, denoted by $H(X|Y)$, as

$$H(X|Y) := \sum_{y\in\mathcal{Y}} P_Y(y)H(X|Y=y).$$

Given an event A, $H(X|Y,A)$ is defined as

$$H(X|Y,A) := \sum_{y\in\mathcal{Y}} P_{Y|A}(y)H(X|Y=y,A).$$

We define the *mutual information between* X *and* Y, denoted by $I(X;Y)$, as

$$I(X;Y) := H(X) - H(X|Y).$$

Intuitively, the mutual information measures how independent two random variables are, and we have $I(X;Y) = 0$ if and only if X and Y are independent. Given an event A, $I(X;Y|A)$ is defined as

$$I(X;Y|A) := H(X|A) - H(X|Y,A).$$

Finally, if additionally Z is a finite random variable with range $\mathcal{Z}$, the *conditional mutual information between* X *and* Y *given* Z, denoted by $I(X;Y|Z)$, is defined as

$$I(X;Y|Z) := \sum_{z\in\mathcal{Z}} P_Z(z)I(X;Y|Z=z).$$

We will be dealing with a simple instance of a *discrete memoryless channel.* A discrete memoryless channel with input X and output W is characterized by a conditional probability distribution $P_{W|X}$. The term *memoryless* stems from the fact that the channel's output depends only on the current input, and so is independent of previous channel utilizations. The *binary symmetric channel with error probability* ϵ is the discrete memoryless channel with input $X \in \{0,1\}$ and conditional probability distribution such that $P_{W|X}(b,b) = 1-\epsilon$ and $P_{W|X}(1-b,b) = \epsilon$ for $b \in \{0,1\}$. Intuitively, the binary symmetric channel receives a bit as input and flips it with a certain error probability.

The *capacity* is a fundamental quantity associated to every channel. Informally, the capacity of a channel is the optimal rate at which one can communicate through the channel while ensuring that the decoding error probability goes to zero as the number of channel uses increases. Shannon [21] proved that the capacity of a channel $P_{W|X}$ is given by $\max_{P_X} I(X;W)$. In particular, it is easily shown that the capacity of the binary symmetric channel with error probability ϵ is $1-h(\epsilon)$, where h is the binary entropy function.

3 Secret-Key Agreement by Public Discussion

In the following section, we revisit the basic models of information-theoretically secure secret-key agreement on which we will build in Sects. 4 and 5.

3.1 The Source Model and the Secret-Key Rate

We study information-theoretic secret-key agreement, in which Alice and Bob want to agree on a shared secret-key, about which Eve has (almost) no information. To circumvent the trivial impossibility results, we consider the model introduced by Maurer [11,16], called *secret-key agreement by public discussion from common information.* In this model, we assume that in addition to a bidirectional authenticated noiseless channel, which Eve can listen in to but not tamper with, the parties also share some form of correlated randomness. More specifically, we will look at the setting where the correlated randomness of Alice, Bob, and Eve consists of several independent and identically distributed realizations of discrete random variables X, Y, and Z, respectively, distributed according to some joint probability distribution P_{XYZ}.

Remark 1. As already mentioned, the assumption that an authenticated channel exists between Alice and Bob is not a significant drawback in the model. We can allow Alice and Bob to start with a small shared secret-key, which they can then use to authenticate the channel with information-theoretic security [23]. In this case, the goal of a protocol is to amplify a short initial secret-key into a very long secret-key, analogous to quantum key distribution.

In this setting, the main quantity of interest is the maximal rate (per number of realizations of X, Y, and Z received) at which Alice and Bob can generate secret-key bits, about which Eve has almost no information, as a function of the probability distribution P_{XYZ}. We first define what we mean by a secret-key agreement protocol. The following definition is taken from [17], and we show in the full version [9] that it is actually a composable definition, and hence the obtained key can be securely used in any context.

Definition 1. *Given a finite probability distribution* P_{XYZ}*, an* (N, R, ϵ)-secret-key agreement protocol for P_{XYZ} *is an interactive protocol for Alice and Bob, who receive* $X^N = (X_1, \ldots, X_N)$ *and* $Y^N = (Y_1, \ldots, Y_N)$*, respectively, as input. Then they generate a communication transcript* $C^M = (C_1, \ldots, C_M)$ *(where* M *is also a random variable) by sending messages over authenticated channels in an alternating manner. After the interaction is finished, Alice and Bob produce outputs* S_A *and* S_B *over the finite range* $\mathcal{S}$*, respectively.*

We require that if for $i \in [N]$,[1] *the random variables* (X_i, Y_i, Z_i) *are i.i.d. according to* P_{XYZ}*, then the following properties must hold:*

1. $H(S_A) \geq N(R - \epsilon)$;
2. $H(S_A) \geq \log|\mathcal{S}| - \epsilon$;
3. $\Pr[S_A = S_B] \geq 1 - \epsilon$;
4. $I(S_A; Z^N C^M) \leq \epsilon$.

[1] We denote by $[n]$ the set $\{1, 2, \ldots, n\}$, see Sect. 2 for an exhaustive introduction on the notation we use.

Intuitively, property 1 in Definition 1 states that, on average, Alice and Bob extract at least $R - \epsilon$ secret bits per realization of (X, Y, Z), i.e., the rate is at least $R - \epsilon$. Property 2 enforces that S_A is almost uniform over $\mathcal{S}$, property 3 implies that S_A and S_B should coincide with high probability, and property 4 means that Eve's information, which consists of Z^N and the transcript C^M, gives almost no information about the secret keys S_A and S_B. We are now ready to define the secret-key rate.

Definition 2. *Given a finite probability distribution P_{XYZ}, the* secret-key rate *for P_{XYZ} (abbreviated as the* secret-key rate *when the context is clear), denoted by $S(X;Y\|Z)$, is the supremum of all real numbers R such that for all $\epsilon > 0$ and large enough N there exists an (N, R, ϵ)-secret-key agreement protocol for P_{XYZ}.*

The secret-key rate was first studied by Maurer [11,16], while Csiszár and Körner [1] studied the *one-way* secret-key rate, where only one-way communication from Alice to Bob is allowed.

The following theorem states basic bounds for the secret-key rate. The lower bound was proved by Maurer [11,13] and Csiszár and Körner [1], while the upper bound was proved by Maurer [11].

Lemma 1 **([11, Theorem 2] and [13, Theorem 4]).** *For all finite probability distributions P_{XYZ}, we have*

$$I(X;Y) - \min(I(X;Z), I(Y;Z)) \le S(X;Y\|Z) \le \min(I(X;Y), I(X;Y|Z)).$$

Note that our definition of the secret-key rate corresponds to the so-called strong secret-key rate, which Maurer and Wolf [17] have proven to be equivalent to the weak one initially considered in the lower bounds.

3.2 A Special Case: The Satellite Setting

Our focus will lie on the secret-key rate of a conceptually simple, but realistic and interesting, class of distributions P_{XYZ}, named the *satellite setting.*

Fix real numbers $\epsilon_A, \epsilon_B, \epsilon_E \in [0, 1/2]$ and consider the following experiment:

1. Sample a bit $R \in \{0, 1\}$ uniformly at random;
2. Send R to Alice, Bob, and Eve through independent binary symmetric channels with error probabilities ϵ_A, ϵ_B, and ϵ_E, respectively. The random variables X, Y, and Z are the output of these three channels.

This class of distributions was introduced by Maurer [11,16]. The satellite setting earned its name because a realistic implementation of such a scenario would consist of having a satellite orbiting the Earth which broadcasts random bits. On the ground, Alice, Bob, and Eve would be in possession of their own antennas, which they can use to listen to the satellite broadcasts. The quality of a party's antenna would then dictate how reliably they receive the random bits from the satellite. For instance, a better antenna leads to a smaller error probability.

An additional surprising benefit of this model is that secret-key agreement is possible whenever it is not trivially impossible, as stated in the following theorem of Maurer and Wolf [11,14].

Theorem 1 ([14, Theorem 2, adapted]). *We have* $S(X;Y\|Z) > 0$ *if and only if* $\epsilon_E > 0$ *and* $\epsilon_A, \epsilon_B < 1/2$.

This stands in stark contrast to the well-known fact that secret-key agreement with one-way communication from Alice to Bob (in the sense of [1]) is impossible whenever Eve's antenna is better than both Alice's and Bob's antennas, i.e., whenever $\epsilon_E < \epsilon_A$ and $\epsilon_E < \epsilon_B$.

While Theorem 1 assures that the secret-key rate is positive in all non-trivial settings, computing (or even approximating) it has proven to be a surprisingly difficult problem for most parameters ϵ_A, ϵ_B, and ϵ_E.

3.3 Advantage Distillation Protocols

In the following section, we present some required background to understand the proofs in Sects. 4 and 5, and in particular we introduce the parity-check protocol that we use to lower bound the secret-key rate.

The parity-check protocol is an example of a so-called *advantage-distillation protocol*, which is a type of protocol introduced in [11,14] to prove Theorem 1 in the satellite setting.

Definition 3. *Let* P_{XYZ} *denote a finite probability distribution. An* advantage-distillation protocol *for* P_{XYZ} *is then an interactive protocol for Alice and Bob, who receive* $X^N = (X_1, \ldots, X_N)$ *and* $Y^N = (Y_1, \ldots, Y_N)$*, respectively, as input for some* N*. Then they generate a communication transcript* $C^M = (C_1, \ldots, C_M)$ *by sending messages over authenticated channels in an alternating manner. Afterwards, Alice and Bob produce outputs* $\hat{X}$ *and* $\hat{Y}$*, respectively.*

For all large enough N*, if the random variables* (X_i, Y_i, Z_i) *are i.i.d. according to* P_{XYZ}*, we require that*

$$I(\hat{X}; \hat{Y}) - I(\hat{X}; \hat{Z}) > 0,$$

where $\hat{Z} = (Z^N, C^M)$ *denotes Eve's total information at the end of the protocol.*

Intuitively, Bob ends up with more information about Alice than Eve does, and so the protocol "distills" an advantage for Alice and Bob over Eve.

Note that such an advantage-distillation protocol itself is not a secret-key agreement protocol according to Definition 1, as it neither guarantees that Alice and Bob output the same key, nor guarantees that Eve has arbitrary small information about Alice's output. However, for any probability distribution P_{XYZ} and advantage-distillation protocol, we can consider the induced probability distribution $P_{\hat{X}\hat{Y}\hat{Z}}$ from running the protocol on N i.i.d. realizations of P_{XYZ}, and then simply apply a secret-key agreement protocol for this distribution. Along this line, we can then also introduce the secret-key rate of an advantage-distillation protocol.

Definition 4. *Given a finite probability distribution P_{XYZ} and an advantage-distillation protocol, the* secret-key rate of the advantage-distillation protocol for P_{XYZ} *is the supremum of all real numbers R such that for all $\epsilon > 0$ and large enough N there exists a secret-key agreement protocol for $P_{\hat{X}\hat{Y}\hat{Z}}$, such that the composed protocol is an (N, R, ϵ)-secret-key agreement protocol for P_{XYZ}.*

The existence of an advantage-distillation protocol implies $S(X;Y\|Z) > 0$, since we have

$$S(X;Y\|Z) \geq \frac{S(\hat{X};\hat{Y}\|\hat{Z})}{N} \geq \frac{I(\hat{X};\hat{Y}) - I(\hat{X};\hat{Z})}{N} > 0,$$

where the second inequality follows from Lemma 1.

The Repeater-Code Protocol. The first advantage distillation protocol was the *repeater-code protocol* [11,16]. It works as follows:

1. Alice samples $R \in \{0,1\}$ uniformly at random and sends $R \oplus X^N = (R \oplus X_1, \ldots, R \oplus X_N)$ to Bob over the authenticated channel;
2. Bob computes $R \oplus X^N \oplus Y^N = (R \oplus X_1 \oplus Y_1, \ldots, R \oplus X_N \oplus Y_N)$ and sets $A = 1$ if $R \oplus X^N \oplus Y^N = 0^N$ or $R \oplus X^N \oplus Y^N = 1^N$. Otherwise, Bob sets $A = 0$. Then, Bob sends A to Alice through the authenticated channel;
3. If $A = 1$, then Alice sets $\hat{X} = R$ and Bob sets $\hat{Y} = R \oplus X_1 \oplus Y_1$. Otherwise, if $A = 0$, then Alice and Bob set $\hat{X} = \hat{Y} = \perp$.

Maurer and Wolf [14] proved that, in the satellite setting, for all triples $(\epsilon_A, \epsilon_B, \epsilon_E)$ with $\epsilon_A < 1/2$, $\epsilon_B < 1/2$, and $\epsilon_E > 0$ and for N large enough we have

$$I(\hat{X};\hat{Y}) - I(\hat{X};\hat{Z}) > 0,$$

where $\hat{Z} := (Z^N, R \oplus X^N, A)$ denotes Eve's total information.

While the repeater-code protocol is good enough to prove that secret-key agreement is possible in the satellite setting, it guarantees only a very small lower bound on the secret-key rate, especially when ϵ_A and ϵ_B are much larger than ϵ_E. This issue motivated the search for better advantage distillation protocols in the satellite setting.

The Parity-Check Protocol. Gander and Maurer [6,16] studied an improved protocol, called the *parity-check protocol.* The parity-check protocol with ℓ rounds works as follows:

1. Alice and Bob start with initially empty strings U_A and U_B, respectively;
2. Alice and Bob divide X^N and Y^N into pairs (X_{2i-1}, X_{2i}) and (Y_{2i-1}, Y_{2i}), respectively, for $i = 1, \ldots, \lfloor N/2 \rfloor$;
3. For each i, Alice sends $X_{2i-1} \oplus X_{2i}$ to Bob via the authenticated channel;
4. Bob sets $A_i = 1$ if $X_{2i-1} \oplus X_{2i} = Y_{2i-1} \oplus Y_{2i}$. Otherwise, Bob sets $A_i = 0$. Then, he sends A_i to Alice;
5. If $A_i = 1$, Alice adds X_{2i-1} to her string U_A and Bob adds Y_{2i-1} to his string U_B, and they discard X_{2i} and Y_{2i}, respectively (i.e., these bits are not added to U_A and U_B, respectively). If $A_i = 0$, Alice and Bob discard the bits (X_{2i-1}, X_{2i}) and (Y_{2i-1}, Y_{2i}), respectively;

6. If $\ell = 1$, then Alice and Bob stop the protocol. Alice sets $\hat{X} = U_A$ and Bob sets $\hat{Y} = U_B$;
7. If $\ell > 1$ and $|U_A| \geq 2^{\ell-1}$, Alice and Bob run the parity-check protocol with $\ell - 1$ rounds on the strings U_A and U_B. Otherwise, if $|U_A| < 2^{\ell-1}$, then Alice and Bob set $\hat{X} = \perp$ and $\hat{Y} = \perp$, respectively.

If $\hat{X}$ and $\hat{Y}$ are the outputs of the parity-check protocol with ℓ rounds, then each pair of bits $(\hat{X}_i, \hat{Y}_i)$ behaves like the output of a successful run of the repeater-code protocol with $N := 2^\ell$. Furthermore, all pairs $(\hat{X}_i, \hat{Y}_i)$ are identically distributed and independent of each other.

Again, consider the satellite setting and assume, without loss of generality, that $\epsilon_A \geq \epsilon_B$. Analogous to [6], let us now introduce a couple of useful quantities in the setting of running the parity-check protocol.

Definition 5. *Consider the satellite setting with error probabilities ϵ_A, ϵ_B, and ϵ_E respectively. Let (X, Y, Z) be distributed according to the thereby induced distribution P_{XYZ}. Then we define*

$$\beta := \Pr[X \neq Y] = \epsilon_A(1 - \epsilon_B) + (1 - \epsilon_A)\epsilon_B$$

and for $r, s \in \{0, 1\}$

$$\alpha_{rs} := \Pr[X \oplus Y = r, X \oplus Z = s],$$

which satisfy

$$\begin{aligned}
\alpha_{00} &= \epsilon_A\epsilon_B\epsilon_E + (1 - \epsilon_A)(1 - \epsilon_B)(1 - \epsilon_E) \\
\alpha_{01} &= \epsilon_A\epsilon_B(1 - \epsilon_E) + (1 - \epsilon_A)(1 - \epsilon_B)\epsilon_E \\
\alpha_{10} &= \epsilon_A(1 - \epsilon_B)\epsilon_E + (1 - \epsilon_A)\epsilon_B(1 - \epsilon_E) \\
\alpha_{11} &= \epsilon_A(1 - \epsilon_B)(1 - \epsilon_E) + (1 - \epsilon_A)\epsilon_B\epsilon_E.
\end{aligned}$$

Moreover, considering L independent draws from P_{XYZ}, and let

$$\beta_L := \Pr[X^L \oplus Y^L = 1^L | X^L \oplus Y^L \in \{0^L, 1^L\}] = \frac{\beta^L}{\beta^L + (1 - \beta)^L},$$

and $p_{L,w}$ denote the probability that $X^L \oplus Y^L \in \{0^L, 1^L\}$ and $X^L \oplus Z^L$ is a specific codeword of Hamming weight w, i.e.,

$$p_{L,w} := \alpha_{00}^{L-w}\alpha_{01}^{w} + \alpha_{10}^{L-w}\alpha_{11}^{w}.$$

Using those quantities, we can now express the secret-key rate of the parity-check protocol.

Theorem 2 (rephrased form [6]). *Let $R(\ell, \epsilon_A, \epsilon_B, \epsilon_E)$ denote the secret-key rate of the parity-check protocol when using ℓ rounds, and Alice, Bob, and Eve having error probabilities ϵ_A, ϵ_B, and ϵ_E, respectively. We then have*

$$R(\ell, \epsilon_A, \epsilon_B, \epsilon_E) \geq 2^{-\ell}\,\Phi(2^\ell, \epsilon_A, \epsilon_B, \epsilon_E)\prod_{i=0}^{\ell-1}\left(\beta_{2^i}^2 + (1 - \beta_{2^i})^2\right),$$

where

$$\Phi(L, \epsilon_A, \epsilon_B, \epsilon_E) := \sum_{w=0}^{L} \binom{L}{w} \frac{p_{L,w}}{\beta^L + (1-\beta)^L} h\left(\frac{p_{L,w}}{p_{L,w} + p_{L,L-w}}\right) - h(\beta_L),$$

and β, β_L, *and* $p_{L,w}$ *are according to Definition 5.*

The intuition behind Theorem 2 is the following: Suppose there are N_i bits left after i rounds of the parity-check protocol. These N_i bits are partitioned into $\lfloor N_i/2 \rfloor$ pairs (if N_i is even, Alice and Bob discard a bit), and, in round $i+1$, Alice and Bob keep a bit from a given pair with probability $\beta_{2^i}^2 + (1-\beta_{2^i})^2$. Therefore, we have

$$\mathrm{E}[N_{i+1} \mid N_i \text{ bits after } i \text{ rounds}] \approx \frac{\beta_{2^i}^2 + (1-\beta_{2^i})^2}{2} \cdot N_i,$$

where N_{i+1} is the random variable denoting the number of bits after $i+1$ rounds of the parity-check protocol.

The lower bound on the secret-key rate obtained through the parity-check protocol is, for most choices of error probabilities in the satellite setting, much better than the lower bound given by the repeater-code protocol. Note that the parity-check protocol consists of the iterative application of the repeater-code protocol with length 2 to pairs of bits of X^N and Y^N. This protocol can be further improved in a natural way for some interesting choices of error probabilities in the satellite setting by modifying the length of the repeater-code protocol that is applied iteratively, and reutilizing discarded bits from failed runs of the repeater-code protocol which are "almost" successful. We do not expand on this, since the original parity-check protocol suffices for our needs.

4 The Secret-Key Rate Under a Fixed Channel Quality Ratio

4.1 Modeling a Fixed Channel Quality Ratio

In this section, we formally define the main quantity used in this work. Recall that we want to consider a setting where we assume that the antenna sizes of the honest parties are fixed, but where the energy the satellite uses to send a bit is a design parameter that we can adjust in order to achieve an optimal secret-key rate. To obtain a meaningful lower bound on the secret-key rate in this setup, however, we need to make an assumption about Eve's capabilities, which in the satellite setting correspond to her antenna size. In order to simplify the model, we moreover do not consider the actual antenna sizes, but the ratio between Eve's antenna size and Alice's and Bob's. Therefore, in the following we want to assume that Eve's antenna is exactly Q times larger than both Alice's and Bob's antennas. For ease of exposition, we will also assume that Alice and Bob have antennas of the same size. This was the setting considered by Gander and

Maurer [6]. In the full version [9], we analyze the general setting where Alice's and Bob's antennas may differ in size, and also where Eve's antenna is only known to be *at most*, or *at least*, Q times larger than Alice's and Bob's, instead of exactly Q times larger.

To model the antenna size ratio, we choose the ratio of the channel capacities, which reflect the qualities of the respective channels. Recall that the satellite model with BSC's is a simplification of the more realistic analog model with Additive White Gaussian Noise (AWGN) channels (if the channel input is X, then the output is $X + Z$, where Z is distributed according to a normal distribution with mean zero and variance N, where N is also called the noise power). It is well-known that the capacity (in bits per second) of an AWGN channel is given by $C_{\mathsf{AWGN}} = B \log(1 + S/N)$, where B is the bandwidth (in the spectrum), S is the signal power, and N is the noise power (see [3, Chap. 9]). The signal power is proportional to the total antenna surface, independently of whether the antenna consists of several independent small antennas or one large one. In the low-signal regime, i.e., if $S/N \ll 1$, we have that C is essentially proportional to S (for fixed noise power N), and hence to the antenna size too. In short, in such a regime the channel capacity is essentially proportional to the product of the surface of the receiver's antenna and the energy used to transmit the bits. Hence, when considering two of the antennas, the ratio of their capacity stays approximately constant when adjusting the energy that is used to transmit each bit and, therefore, this ratio is a good approximation of the ratio of the antenna sizes.

While this justification is based on the AWGN model, we assume that it essentially carries over to the BSC model of the satellite setting. Observe that the satellite setting using BSC's can be interpreted in a natural way as a version of the satellite setting with AWGN channels where Alice, Bob, and Eve quantize the signals they receive.

This leads us to the following definition of the channel quality ratio between two binary symmetric channels.

Definition 6. *The* channel quality ratio between the BSC with error probability α and the BSC with error probability γ, *denoted* $\rho(\alpha, \gamma)$, *is defined as*

$$\rho(\alpha, \gamma) := \frac{1 - h(\gamma)}{1 - h(\alpha)}.$$

Assume a fixed antenna size ratio Q between Eve's and Alice's antennas, and hence between Eve's and Bob's antennas, since Alice and Bob are assumed to have antennas of the same size. Considering the energy spent per bit as a design parameter then corresponds to freely choosing $\alpha = \epsilon_A = \epsilon_B$ and $\gamma = \epsilon_E$ under the constraint that $\rho(\alpha, \gamma) = Q$. This leads to the following definition, where the supremum corresponds to choosing the energy per bit in an optimal manner.

Definition 7. *The* secret-key rate for an adversary with an exactly Q times better channel, *denoted by* $S(Q)$, *is defined as*

$$S(Q) := \sup_{\substack{\alpha, \gamma \\ \rho(\alpha, \gamma) = Q}} S(\alpha, \alpha, \gamma).$$

In the following sections, we will give an exact characterization (up to a multiplicative constant) of the asymptotic behavior of $S(Q)$ when Q increases. In particular, we settle the conjecture of Gander and Maurer [6] in the affirmative.

4.2 A Lower Bound on $S(Q)$

Our first main result is that $S(Q)$ decreases at most inversely proportional to Q^2. We omit or shorten most proofs of intermediate results in this section. Detailed proofs can be found in the full version [9].

Theorem 3. *There exist a constant $c > 0$ such that*

$$\frac{c}{Q^2} \leq S(Q)$$

for all $Q \geq 1$.

To prove this result, we actually show that the parity-check protocol [16] (c.f. Sect. 3.3) achieves this rate, which was first conjectured to be true by Gander and Maurer [6], based on numerical evidence.

Definition 8. *The* secret-key rate of the parity-check protocol for an adversary with an exactly Q times better channel, *denoted by $R(Q)$, is defined as*

$$R(Q) := \sup_{\substack{\ell,\alpha,\gamma \\ \rho(\alpha,\gamma)=Q}} R(\ell,\alpha,\alpha,\gamma),$$

where $R(\ell, \epsilon_A, \epsilon_B, \epsilon_E)$ denotes the rate per random bit achieved by the parity-check protocol using ℓ rounds when Alice, Bob, and Eve have error probabilities ϵ_A, ϵ_B, and ϵ_E, respectively.

Since the secret-key rate $S(\epsilon_A, \epsilon_B, \epsilon_E)$ is defined as the secret-key rate of the best possible protocol, we trivially get the following lower bound.

Lemma 2. *Let $Q \geq 1$. Then, we have $R(Q) \leq S(Q)$.*

We now proceed by proving that there exists a constant $c > 0$ such that $\frac{c}{Q^2} \leq R(Q)$ for all $Q \geq 1$, which will eventually conclude the proof. In order to prove such a lower bound, we need to lower bound the supremum in the definition of $R(Q)$. We achieve this by carefully choosing a sequence of triples $(\ell_k, \alpha_k, \gamma_k)$ such that $R\left(\frac{1-h(\gamma_k)}{1-h(\alpha_k)}\right)$ does not decrease too quickly when compared to $\frac{1-h(\gamma_k)}{1-h(\alpha_k)}$. Namely, in the first step we will show that

$$R\left(\frac{1-h(\gamma_k)}{1-h(\alpha_k)}\right) \geq \frac{c_1}{k^4}$$

for some constant $c > 0$, and then in a second step use that $\frac{1-h(\gamma_k)}{1-h(\alpha_k)}$ increases like k^2, in order to derive the desired result.

Lower Bounding the Secret-Key Rate of the Parity-Check Protocol with Concrete Parameters. In this section we show that for $\ell_k = 2\log(k)$ rounds, in the satellite setting with $\epsilon_A = \epsilon_B = \alpha_k = 1/2 - 1/k$, and $\epsilon_E = \gamma_k = 2/5$, the secret-key rate of the parity-check protocol $R(\ell_k, \alpha_k, \alpha_k, \gamma_k)$ decreases inversely proportional to k^4. For simplicity, we drop the subscript k in most terms from now on.

Before deriving the actual lower bound on $R(\ell, \alpha, \alpha, \gamma)$, we introduce an auxiliary quantity and prove some properties about it. Recall the definition of α_{rs} for $r, s \in \{0,1\}$ and $p_{L,w}$ from Definition 5 in Sect. 3.3. In the following, let

$$p'_{L,w} := \alpha_{00}^{L-w}\alpha_{01}^{w}. \tag{1}$$

We now present a few lemmas about $p_{L,w}$, $p'_{L,w}$, and their relation.

Lemma 3. *Let $\alpha = \epsilon_A = \epsilon_B = 1/2 - 1/k$. Then we have*

$$p_{L,w} = \alpha_{00}^{L-w}\alpha_{01}^{w} + (\alpha(1-\alpha))^L = p'_{L,w} + (\alpha(1-\alpha))^L > p'_{L,w}.$$

Lemma 4. *Let $p'_{L,w}$ as defined in (1). Then $p'_{L,w}$ is equal to the probability that $X^L \oplus Z^L$ is a particular codeword of weight w and $X^L = Y^L$, i.e. for any $c \in \{0,1\}^L$ with $w(c) = w$, where $w(c)$ denotes the Hamming weight of c, we have*

$$\Pr[X^L \oplus Z^L = c, X^L = Y^L] = p'_{L,w}.$$

Lemma 5. *We have*

$$h\left(\frac{p_{L,w}}{p_{L,w} + p_{L,L-w}}\right) \geq h\left(\frac{p'_{L,w}}{p'_{L,w} + p'_{L,L-w}}\right)$$

for all L and w.

Lemma 6. *Let $0 \leq \delta \leq L/2$. Then*

$$\frac{p'_{L,L/2+\delta}}{p'_{L,L/2-\delta}} = \left(\frac{\alpha_{01}}{\alpha_{00}}\right)^{2\delta}.$$

Lemma 7. *For all $L/2 \geq x \geq y \geq 0$ the following two properties hold*

1. $h\left(\frac{p'_{L,L/2-x}}{p'_{L,L/2-x} + p'_{L,L/2+x}}\right) \leq h\left(\frac{p'_{L,L/2-y}}{p'_{L,L/2-y} + p'_{L,L/2+y}}\right)$
2. $h\left(\frac{p'_{L,L/2-x}}{p'_{L,L/2-x} + p'_{L,L/2+x}}\right) = h\left(\frac{p'_{L,L/2+x}}{p'_{L,L/2+x} + p'_{L,L/2-x}}\right).$

Next, we lower bound $R(\ell, \alpha, \alpha, \gamma)$, i.e., the rate of the parity-check protocol when using ℓ rounds, Alice and Bob have the same error probability α, and Eve has error probability γ, in a sequence of lemmas.

Lemma 8. *For all $k \in \{2^j : j \in \mathbb{N}\}$, let $\ell_k = 2\log(k)$, $\alpha_k = 1/2 - 1/k$, and $\gamma_k = 2/5$. We then have*

$$R(\ell_k, \alpha_k, \alpha_k, \gamma_k) \geq \frac{1}{k^4}\Phi(k^2, \alpha_k, \alpha_k, \gamma_k),$$

where Φ is defined as in Theorem 2.

Lemma 9. *For $k \in \{2^j : j \in \mathbb{N}\}$, let $\ell_k = 2\log(k)$, $\alpha_k = 1/2 - 1/k$, and $\gamma_k = 2/5$. Then there exists a positive constant $c > 0$ such that*

$$\Phi(k^2, \alpha_k, \alpha_k, \gamma_k) \geq c$$

for large enough $k \in \{2^j : j \in \mathbb{N}\}$, where Φ is defined as in Theorem 2.

Proof. We present a sketch of the proof. The complete proof can be found in the full version [9]. First, it holds that

$$\lim_{k\to\infty} h\left(\beta_{k^2}\right) = h\left(\lim_{k\to\infty} \frac{1}{1 + (1 + 8/k^2)^{k^2}}\right) = h\left(\frac{1}{1+e^8}\right) < 5 \cdot 10^{-3}. \quad (2)$$

Furthermore, using Lemmas 3 and 5 to 7 it can be seen that

$$\sum_{w=0}^{k^2} \binom{k^2}{w} \frac{p_{k^2,w}}{\beta^{k^2} + (1-\beta)^{k^2}} \cdot h\left(\frac{p_{k^2,w}}{p_{k^2,w} + p_{k^2,k^2-w}}\right)$$
$$\geq \frac{1}{2} \sum_{w=k^2(1/2-2/k)}^{k^2(1/2+2/k)} \binom{k^2}{w} \frac{p'_{k^2,w}}{(1-\beta)^{k^2}} \cdot h\left(\frac{1}{1 + \left(\frac{\alpha_{01}}{\alpha_{00}}\right)^{4k}}\right) \quad (3)$$

for large enough k.

In order to lower bound the binary entropy term in (3), we can use the definition of α_{rs} (recall Definition 5) to show that

$$\lim_{k\to\infty} h\left(\frac{1}{1 + \left(\frac{\alpha_{01}}{\alpha_{00}}\right)^{4k}}\right) = h\left(\frac{1}{1 + e^{-32/5}}\right) > 1.7 \cdot 10^{-2}. \quad (4)$$

We now define $W := (w(X^{k^2} \oplus Z^{k^2}) \mid X^{k^2} = Y^{k^2})$ as the random variable denoting the Hamming weight of $X^{k^2} \oplus Z^{k^2}$ conditioned on $X^{k^2} = Y^{k^2}$, i.e., W is defined in the modified random experiment obtained by conditioning on $X^{k^2} = Y^{k^2}$. Through Lemma 4, we have

$$\sum_{w=k^2(1/2-2/k)}^{k^2(1/2+2/k)} \binom{k^2}{w} \frac{p'_{k^2,w}}{(1-\beta)^{k^2}} = \Pr[|W - k^2/2| \leq 2k]. \quad (5)$$

It suffices now to find a suitable lower bound for $\Pr[|W - k^2/2| \leq 2k]$. In order to do that, we will apply Chebyshev's inequality. It can be shown that

$$\frac{k^2}{2} - 2k \leq \mathrm{E}[W] - k \leq \mathrm{E}[W] + k \leq \frac{k^2}{2} + 2k,$$

and hence

$$\Pr[|W - k^2/2| \leq 2k] \geq \Pr[|W - \mathrm{E}[W]| \leq k] \geq 1 - \frac{\mathrm{Var}[W]}{k^2} \geq \frac{3}{4}, \tag{6}$$

where the second inequality follows from Chebyshev's inequality, and the third inequality follows from the fact that $\mathrm{Var}[W] \leq k^2/4$.

Combining (3), (4), (5), and (6) yields

$$\sum_{w=0}^{k^2} \binom{k^2}{w} \frac{p_{k^2,w}}{\beta^{k^2} + (1-\beta)^{k^2}} \cdot h\left(\frac{p_{k^2,w}}{p_{k^2,w} + p_{k^2,k^2-w}}\right)$$
$$> \frac{1}{2} \cdot \frac{3}{4} \cdot 1.7 \cdot 10^{-2} > 5 \cdot 10^{-3} > h(\beta_{k^2})$$

for large enough $k \in \{2^j : j \in \mathbb{N}\}$, which concludes the proof. □

Combining Lemmas 8 and 9 yields the main result of this subsection.

Lemma 10. *For all $k \in \{2^j : j \in \mathbb{N}\}$, let $\ell_k = 2\log(k)$, $\alpha_k = 1/2 - 1/k$, and $\gamma_k = 2/5$. Then there exists a constant $c > 0$ such that we have*

$$R(\ell_k, \alpha_k, \alpha_k, \gamma_k) \geq \frac{c}{k^4}$$

for large enough $k \in \{2^j : j \in \mathbb{N}\}$.

Deriving a Lower Bound in Q. It now remains to show that Lemma 10 actually implies the desired lower bound in Q. We can prove this by using the fact that $\frac{1-h(\gamma_k)}{1-h(\alpha_k)}$ increases like k^2, and then substituting this term by Q.

Lemma 11. *For all $k \in \{2^j : j \in \mathbb{N}\}$, let $\ell_k = 2\log(k)$, $\alpha_k = 1/2 - 1/k$, and $\gamma_k = 2/5$. We then have*

$$R\left(\frac{k^2}{200}\right) \geq R(\ell_k, \alpha_k, \alpha_k, \gamma_k).$$

We are now ready to prove Theorem 3 by substituting $k^2/200$ in place of Q.

Proof (Theorem 3). Follows by combining Lemmas 10 and 11, and extending the result to all $Q \geq 1$. □

4.3 An Upper Bound on $S(Q)$

As a second main result, we show that $S(Q)$ decreases at least inversely proportional to Q^2.

Theorem 4. *We have*

$$S(Q) \leq \frac{4\ln(2)^2}{Q^2} < \frac{2}{Q^2}$$

for all $Q \geq 1$.

Before we can prove Theorem 4, we need the following auxiliary result.

Lemma 12. ([2, Theorem 2.2]). *If* $p = 1/2 - \epsilon$, *we have*

$$\frac{2\epsilon^2}{\ln(2)} \leq 1 - h(p) \leq 4\epsilon^2.$$

We now proceed by showing two lemmas that we will reuse later.

Lemma 13. *Let* $Q \geq 1$, $\alpha, \gamma \in [0, 1/2]$ *such that* $\frac{1-h(\gamma)}{1-h(\alpha)} = Q$, *and* $\delta := 1/2 - \alpha$. *We then have*

$$S(\alpha, \alpha, \gamma) \leq 16\delta^4.$$

Proof. Note that

$$S(\alpha, \alpha, \gamma) \leq I(X;Y) = 1 - h(\beta),$$

where X and Y are Alice's and Bob's random variables in the satellite setting with $\epsilon_A = \epsilon_B = \alpha$, and, as before, $\beta := \Pr[X \neq Y] = 2\alpha(1-\alpha)$. Since $\beta = 2\alpha(1-\alpha) = 1/2 - 2\delta^2$, using $\epsilon := 2\delta^2$, it follows by Lemma 12 that

$$1 - h(\beta) \leq 16\delta^4,$$

concluding the proof. □

It remains to bound δ^4 by a function of Q.

Lemma 14. *Let* $Q \geq 1$, $\alpha, \gamma \in [0, 1/2]$ *such that* $\frac{1-h(\gamma)}{1-h(\alpha)} = Q$, *and* $\delta := 1/2 - \alpha$. *We then have*

$$2\delta^2 \leq \frac{\ln(2)}{Q}.$$

Proof. Using Lemma 12 we obtain

$$\frac{2\delta^2}{\ln(2)} \leq 1 - h(\alpha) = \frac{1 - h(\gamma)}{Q} \leq \frac{1}{Q}.$$

□

We are now ready to conclude the overall proof of Theorem 4.

Proof (Theorem 4). Combining Lemmas 13 and 14 yields

$$S(Q) = \sup_{\substack{\alpha,\gamma \\ \rho(\alpha,\gamma)=Q}} S(\alpha, \alpha, \gamma) \leq 16\delta^4 \leq \frac{4\ln(2)^2}{Q^2} < \frac{2}{Q^2}$$

for all $Q \geq 1$. □

4.4 Combining All Bounds

Recall that, by Definition 7, $S(Q)$ denotes the secret-key rate in the setting where Alice's and Bob's channels are identical (i.e., $\epsilon_A = \epsilon_B$ always), and Eve's channel is exactly Q times better than both of Alice's and Bob's. Moreover, by Definition 8, $R(Q)$ denotes the secret-key rate of the parity-check protocol in the same setting. In Sects. 4.2 and 4.3, we have overall proven the following bounds on $S(Q)$ and $R(Q)$:

$$\frac{c}{Q^2} \leq R(Q) \leq S(Q) \leq \frac{2}{Q^2}$$

for some $c > 0$. Thus, in this setting we have determined the secret-key rate $S(Q)$ up to a multiplicative constant, and on the way proved the conjecture by Gander and Maurer.

Corollary 1. *We have* $S(Q) = \Theta(1/Q^2)$. *Moreover, the parity-check protocol from [6] achieves rate* $\Omega(1/Q^2)$ *in this setting.*

5 The Secret-Key Rate per Second Under a Fixed Channel Quality Ratio

In this section, we consider the scenario where the power consumption of the satellite is bounded; for instance, due to the size of its solar panels. Nevertheless, we can adjust the energy used to broadcast each bit by adjusting the bit-rate, i.e., the number of bits broadcast per second, while maintaining a fixed power consumption. In this setting, the natural quantity to optimize for is clearly the secret-key rate per second, rather than the secret-key rate per random bit.

5.1 Defining the Secret-Key Rate per Second

When defining the secret-key rate per second in the satellite model, there is one inherent issue: the abstraction using BSC's instead of AWGN channels actually abstracted away any notion of time. Hence, to nevertheless devise a quantity that can serve as a heuristic of the secret-key rate per second, expressed as a function of the error probabilities, we once again consider the AWGN setting. In contrast to the capacity of the BSC, which is measured as the number of bits that can be reliably transmitted per bit sent, the capacity of an AWGN channel is measured in bits that can be reliably transmitted per second.

As mentioned in Sect. 4.1, the capacity of an AWGN channel is $C_{\mathsf{AWGN}} = B \log(1 + S/N)$, where B is the bandwidth (in the spectrum), S is the signal power, and N is the noise power. Importantly, the capacity of the AWGN channel is a physical property of the channel that is not influenced by the way we encode and decode. A BSC can be seen as an AWGN channel where all parties perform hard decoding, i.e., measure the signal over a given interval in time and output a 1 if the average value in this time is above a certain threshold and 0 otherwise. Hence, we can also look at the capacity per bit in the AWGN model by normalizing by the "bit-rate", meaning the number of bits the parties output per second when applying their hard decoding. If we now double this bit-rate, the capacity per second has to remain constant, hence the capacity per bit must decrease by a factor of two. Therefore, the capacity per bit is inversely proportional to the bit-rate. Moreover, this capacity per bit of the AWGN channel roughly corresponds to the capacity of the BSC, as long as hard decoding is not too far from an optimal encoding scheme, which is the case in a regime with small signal to noise ratio. Thus, for a BSC with significant error probabilities, the capacity is inversely proportional to the bit-rate. This implies that, asymptotically, the secret-key rate per second, which is equal to the secret-key rate per bit times the bit-rate, behaves like the secret-key rate per bit divided by the capacity of the binary symmetric channel.

As a consequence, we can define the secret-key rate per second by dividing the secret-key rate per bit by the capacity of the honest parties' channel, which we assume to have larger error probabilities than Eve's channel, and hence deliver the better approximation.

Definition 9. *The* secret-key rate per second for an adversary with an exactly Q times better channel, *denoted by $S^*(Q)$, is defined as*

$$S^*(Q) := \sup_{\substack{\alpha,\gamma \\ \rho(\alpha,\gamma)=Q}} \frac{S(\alpha,\alpha,\gamma)}{1-h(\alpha)}.$$

where $S(\epsilon_A, \epsilon_B, \epsilon_E)$ is the secret-key rate of the satellite setting with error probabilities ϵ_A, ϵ_B, and ϵ_E for Alice, Bob, and Eve, respectively.

5.2 Bounds on the Secret-Key Rate per Second

In this section, we establish the exact asymptotic behavior of $S^*(Q)$ as a function of Q, up to a multiplicative constant. For the lower bound, we will, analogously to Sect. 4.2, make use of the fact that the secret-key rate achieved by the parity-check protocol is a lower bound of the secret-key rate. Therefore, we also introduce the secret-key rate per second of the parity-check protocol.

Definition 10. *The* secret-key rate per second of the parity-check protocol for an adversary with an exactly Q times better channel, *denoted by $R^*(Q)$, is defined as*

$$R^*(Q) := \sup_{\substack{\ell,\alpha,\gamma \\ \rho(\alpha,\gamma)=Q}} \frac{R(\ell,\alpha,\alpha,\gamma)}{1-h(\alpha)}.$$

where $R(\ell, \epsilon_A, \epsilon_B, \epsilon_E)$ denotes the rate per random bit achieved by the parity-check protocol using ℓ rounds.

We then obtain the following asymptotically exact characterization of the secret-key rate per second.

Theorem 5. *There exist constants* $c_1, c_2 > 0$ *such that*

$$\frac{c_1}{Q} \leq R^*(Q) \leq S^*(Q) \leq \frac{c_2}{Q}$$

for all $Q \geq 1$.

6 Conclusions and Open Problems

In this paper we investigated the secret-key rate in the satellite setting with the additional property that the satellite can freely choose the energy spent when transmitting a bit. In order to study this setting, we assumed there is a "quality ratio" Q between Eve's and the honest parties' antennas, which is an intrinsic property of the system that must stay fixed over all possible choices for the satellite. We model this quality ratio as the ratio of the capacities of the BSC's associated to Eve and the honest parties. Therefore, in our model, the extra degree of freedom for the satellite means that he can choose the error probabilities for Eve and the honest parties as long as the BSC's induced by them have capacity ratio Q. This setting was briefly considered for the first time by Gander and Maurer [6].

We motivated and introduced the quantity $S(Q)$ as a secret-key rate measure for the modified satellite setting just described. While even approximating the secret-key rate of the original satellite setting appears to be very complex, we are actually able to show that $S(Q) = \Theta(1/Q^2)$ when Q grows. This proves a conjecture of Gander and Maurer [6]. The mild decrease of the secret-key rate as a function of Q, coupled with the fact that our lower bound is obtained by considering a simple, explicit advantage distillation protocol, can be interpreted as a first step towards showing that information-theoretic secret-key agreement may be more practical than what is usually believed. We also propose a heuristic definition of the secret-key rate per second, instead of "per random bit", and show that this quantity behaves like $\Theta(1/Q)$. In the full version of this paper [9], we generalize our results to the more general setting where Alice's and Bob's antennas may have different sizes, and furthermore one does not know the exact ratio between Eve's and the honest parties' antennas – only whether it is at most, or at least, some value.

In terms of future work, we envision several main problems. First, one should extend our analysis to settings where Alice and Bob have antennas of vastly different sizes, addressing the typical client-server scenarios. Second, there is a need for a better model of the secret-key rate per second, which should be built on an abstraction level that does not abstract away time, thereby allowing one to verify our conjecture that the secret-key rate per second behaves like $1/Q$ in practice. Finally, and most importantly, one should address the issues that still prevent the satellite model from being used in practice, for instance by studying the secret-key rate in a similar setting to ours when the adversary does not quantize her analog signal, or by investigating the potential effect of an active adversary jamming the signal.

References

1. Ahlswede, R., Csiszár, I.: Common randomness in information theory and cryptography. I. Secret sharing. IEEE Trans. Inf. Theory **39**(4), 1121–1132 (1993)
2. Calabro, C.: The exponential complexity of satisfiability problems. Ph.D. thesis, University of California, San Diego (2009)
3. Cover, T., Thomas, J.: Elements of Information Theory (Wiley Series in Telecommunications and Signal Processing). Wiley, Hoboken (2006)
4. Csiszár, I., Körner, J.: Broadcast channels with confidential messages. IEEE Trans. Inf. Theory **24**(3), 339–348 (1978)
5. Csiszár, I., Narayan, P.: Secrecy capacities for multiple terminals. IEEE Trans. Inf. Theory **50**(12), 3047–3061 (2004)
6. Gander, M.J., Maurer, U.M.: On the secret-key rate of binary random variables. In: Proceedings of the 1994 IEEE International Symposium on Information Theory (ISIT 1994), p. 351. IEEE (1994)
7. Gohari, A.A., Anantharam, V.: Information-theoretic key agreement of multiple terminals: Part I. IEEE Trans. Inf. Theory **56**(8), 3973–3996 (2010)
8. Hayashi, M., Tyagi, H., Watanabe, S.: Secret key agreement: general capacity and second-order asymptotics. IEEE Trans. Inf. Theory **62**(7), 3796–3810 (2016)
9. Jost, D., Maurer, U., Ribeiro, J.L.: Information-theoretic secret-key agreement: the asymptotically tight relation between the secret-key rate and the channel quality ratio. Cryptology ePrint Archive, Report 2017/1130 (2017). https://eprint.iacr.org/2017/1130
10. Liu, S., Van Tilborg, H.C.A., Van Dijk, M.: A practical protocol for advantage distillation and information reconciliation. Des. Codes Cryptogr. **30**(1), 39–62 (2003). https://doi.org/10.1023/A:1024755209150
11. Maurer, U.M.: Secret key agreement by public discussion from common information. IEEE Trans. Inf. Theory **39**(3), 733–742 (1993)
12. Maurer, U.M., Wolf, S.: Unconditionally secure key agreement and the intrinsic conditional information. IEEE Trans. Inf. Theory **45**(2), 499–514 (1999)
13. Maurer, U.: The strong secret key rate of discrete random triples. In: Blahut, R.E., Costello, D.J., Maurer, U., Mittelholzer, T. (eds.) Communications and Cryptography. The Springer International Series in Engineering and Computer Science (Communications and Information Theory), vol. 276, pp. 271–285. Springer, Boston, MA (1994). https://doi.org/10.1007/978-1-4615-2694-0_27
14. Maurer, U., Wolf, S.: Towards characterizing when information-theoretic secret key agreement is possible. In: Kim, K., Matsumoto, T. (eds.) ASIACRYPT 1996. LNCS, vol. 1163, pp. 196–209. Springer, Heidelberg (1996). https://doi.org/10.1007/BFb0034847
15. Maurer, U.M.: Conditionally-perfect secrecy and a provably-secure randomized cipher. J. Cryptol. **5**(1), 53–66 (1992). https://doi.org/10.1007/BF00191321
16. Maurer, U.M.: Protocols for secret key agreement by public discussion based on common information. In: Brickell, E.F. (ed.) CRYPTO 1992. LNCS, vol. 740, pp. 461–470. Springer, Heidelberg (1993). https://doi.org/10.1007/3-540-48071-4_32
17. Maurer, U., Wolf, S.: Information-theoretic key agreement: from weak to strong secrecy for free. In: Preneel, B. (ed.) EUROCRYPT 2000. LNCS, vol. 1807, pp. 351–368. Springer, Heidelberg (2000). https://doi.org/10.1007/3-540-45539-6_24
18. Naito, M., Watanabe, S., Matsumoto, R., Uyematsu, T.: Secret key agreement by reliability information of signals in Gaussian Maurer's Model. In: Proceedings of the 2008 IEEE International Symposium on Information Theory (ISIT 2008), pp. 727–731. IEEE (2008)

19. Ozarow, L.H., Wyner, A.D.: Wire-tap channel II. In: Beth, T., Cot, N., Ingemarsson, I. (eds.) EUROCRYPT 1984. LNCS, vol. 209, pp. 33–50. Springer, Heidelberg (1985). https://doi.org/10.1007/3-540-39757-4_5
20. Renner, R., Skripsky, J., Wolf, S.: A new measure for conditional mutual information and its properties. In: Proceedings of the 2003 IEEE International Symposium on Information Theory (ISIT 2003), p. 259. IEEE (2003)
21. Shannon, C.: A mathematical theory of communication. Bell Syst. Tech. J. **27**(3), 379–423 (1948)
22. Shannon, C.: Communication theory of secrecy systems. Bell Syst. Tech. J. **28**(4), 656–715 (1949)
23. Stinson, D.: Universal hashing and authentication codes. Des. Codes Cryptogr. **4**(3), 369–380 (1994)
24. Tyagi, H., Watanabe, S.: A bound for multiparty secret key agreement and implications for a problem of secure computing. In: Nguyen, P.Q., Oswald, E. (eds.) EUROCRYPT 2014. LNCS, vol. 8441, pp. 369–386. Springer, Heidelberg (2014). https://doi.org/10.1007/978-3-642-55220-5_21
25. Wyner, A.D.: The wire-tap channel. Bell Syst. Tech. J. **54**(8), 1355–1387 (1975)

Information-Theoretic Broadcast with Dishonest Majority for Long Messages

Wutichai Chongchitmate[1(✉)] and Rafail Ostrovsky[2]

[1] Department of Mathematics and Computer Science, Faculty of Science, Chulalongkorn University, Bangkok, Thailand
wutichai.ch@chula.ac.th

[2] Department of Computer Science and Department of Mathematics, University of California, Los Angeles, Los Angeles, CA, USA
rafail@cs.ucla.edu

Abstract. Byzantine broadcast is a fundamental primitive for secure computation. In a setting with n parties in the presence of an adversary controlling at most t parties, while a lot of progress in optimizing communication complexity has been made for $t < n/2$, little progress has been made for the general case $t < n$, especially for information-theoretic security. In particular, all information-theoretic secure broadcast protocols for ℓ-bit messages and $t < n$ and optimal round complexity $\mathcal{O}(n)$ have, so far, required a communication complexity of $\mathcal{O}(\ell n^2)$. A *broadcast extension* protocol allows a long message to be broadcast more efficiently using a small number of single-bit broadcasts. Through broadcast extension, so far, the best achievable round complexity for $t < n$ setting with the optimal communication complexity of $\mathcal{O}(\ell n)$ is $\mathcal{O}(n^4)$ rounds.

In this work, we construct a new broadcast extension protocol for $t < n$ with information-theoretic security. Our protocol improves the round complexity to $\mathcal{O}(n^3)$ while maintaining the optimal communication complexity for long messages. Our result shortens the gap between the information-theoretic setting and the computational setting, and between the optimal communication protocol and the optimal round protocol in the information-theoretic setting for $t < n$.

W. Chongchitmate—Work done while the author was at Department of Computer Science, University of California, Los Angeles.

R. Ostrovsky—Research supported in part by NSF grant 1619348, DARPA SafeWare subcontract to Galois Inc., DARPA SPAWAR contract N66001-15-1C-4065, US-Israel BSF grant 2012366, OKAWA Foundation Research Award, IBM Faculty Research Award, Xerox Faculty Research Award, B. John Garrick Foundation Award, Teradata Research Award, and Lockheed-Martin Corporation Research Award. The views expressed are those of the authors and do not reflect position of the Department of Defense or the U.S. Government.

A. Beimel and S. Dziembowski (Eds.): TCC 2018, LNCS 11239, pp. 370–388, 2018.
https://doi.org/10.1007/978-3-030-03807-6_14

1 Introduction

A (Byzantine) broadcast protocol allows a party, called "sender," to distribute a message among n parties such that (1) all honest parties receive the same message, and (2) if the sender is honest, the received message is indeed sent from the sender. This guarantee holds even in the presence of a malicious adversary corrupting up to t parties, possibly including the sender. The adversary controls the behavior of the corrupted parties and may divert from the protocol.

Broadcast is one of the most fundamental primitives used in cryptographic protocols—especially secure multi-party computation (MPC). Most MPC protocols assume broadcast is given by default. However, without a specific hardware setup, broadcast must be built from point-to-point communications. While efficient broadcast can be done with an honest majority, the opposite case is much more common in applications.

Although a lot of progress has been made to improve broadcast protocol in the honest majority case, the best-known result for any number of corruptions has not seen any improvement since [4] for computational security and [15] for information-theoretic security.

Traditionally, broadcast protocols are designed for single bits [13]. However, most applications that use broadcast as a subprotocol often broadcast long messages. While any broadcast protocol can be used multiple times in parallel to broadcast messages of any length, it leads to inefficiency, especially in communication complexity.

Broadcast extension protocol, introduced in [16], uses bit broadcast (or broadcast for fixed-length messages) as a subprotocol, similar to oblivious transfer (OT) extension [1,8,10,11]. The goal is to reduce the communication complexity of broadcasting long messages, compared to trivially executing multiple broadcast protocols.

Broadcast with Dishonest Majority. Unlike when the number of corrupted parties $t < n/3$, it has been shown that broadcast for $t < n$ cannot be achieved in the plain model [13]. To circumvent the impossibility result, Dolev and Strong considered the broadcast protocol in the setup model [4]. They implemented broadcast from any public-key signature assuming public-key infrastructure (PKI) for distributing signing and verification keys for the signature scheme. Their protocol achieves the lower bound $\Omega(n)$ on the round complexity, and $\Omega(n^2)$ on the number of messages exchanged.

For the information-theoretic case, Pfitzmann and Waidner introduce the notion of pseudosignature [14], formalizing unconditionally secure signature in [2], to replace the public-key signature in [4]. The resulting protocol [14,15] is in the correlated randomness model where each party holds a random string generated from some joint distribution instead of PKI. Similar to the computational case, this protocol achieves the lower bound on the round complexity and the number of messages exchanged.

In terms of communication complexity, the broadcast protocol of [15] uses $\mathcal{O}(\ell n^2 + n^6\lambda)$ bits of communication, while that of [4] uses $\mathcal{O}(\ell n^2 + n^3\lambda)$ bits to broadcast a message of length ℓ. In both protocols, a sender sends a message and a corresponding signature to every party, who then sign and pass the message to all other parties in the first two rounds.

In fact, [3] shows that any broadcast protocol must communicate at least $\Omega(n^2)$ bits. Thus, to broadcast a message of length ℓ directly using such protocol requires at least $\Omega(\ell n^2)$ bits of communication. To circumvent this limitation, an extension protocol is designed to reduce the multiplicative factor to the length ℓ of the message to lower than n^2 while increasing the part that is independent of ℓ, thus reducing the overall communication complexity when $\ell \gg \lambda$. Since every party must receive the message, the lower bound on the communication complexity is $\Omega(\ell n)$.

Broadcast Extension. While Turpin and Coan [16] introduced the construction of a broadcast protocol for long messages from bit broadcast, their protocol tolerating $t < n/3$ has the communication complexity of $\mathcal{O}(\ell n^2 + n(B(1)))$, where $B(s)$ is the communication complexity of s-bit broadcast. Fitzi and Hirt [5] first showed how to achieve broadcast with communication complexity $\mathcal{O}(\ell n + poly(n, \lambda))$ in an information-theoretic setting tolerating $t < n/2$ with $poly(n, \lambda) = n^3\lambda + nB(n + \lambda)$. Liang and Vaidya [9] later constructed perfectly secure broadcast tolerating $t < n/3$ with communication complexity $\mathcal{O}(\ell n + \sqrt{\ell}n^2 B(1) + n^4 B(1))$, and Patra [12] improved it to $\mathcal{O}(\ell n + n^2 B(1))$. As mentioned earlier, the best result for communication complexity in an information-theoretic setting tolerating $t < n$ is by Hirt and Raykov [7] with communication complexity $\mathcal{O}(\ell n + (n^4 + n^3\lambda)B(1))$ and round complexity $\mathcal{O}(n^4)$. They also constructed another protocol based on collision-resistant hash functions (CRHF) in the same setting with communication complexity $\mathcal{O}(\ell n + (n^2 + n\lambda)B(1))$ and round complexity $\mathcal{O}(n^3)$. The CRHF-based construction is later improved in round complexity by Ganesh and Patra [6] to $\mathcal{O}(n^2)$, while communication complexity slightly increases to $\mathcal{O}(\ell n + (n\lambda + n^3 \log n)B(1))$.

Round Complexity of Broadcast Protocols. While broadcast can be accomplished in constant round with honest majority, [4] shows that a broadcast protocol secure against an adversary corrupting any number of parties requires at least $\mathcal{O}(n)$ rounds. In the $t < n/3$ and $t < n/2$ settings, the broadcast extension protocols achieve optimal constant round complexity similar to that of bit broadcast [6]. [7] first achieved broadcast protocols for ℓ-bit messages using $\mathcal{O}(\ell n)$ communication complexity for $t < n$ with round complexity $\mathcal{O}(n^3)$ for computational security and $\mathcal{O}(n^4)$ for information-theoretic security, respectively. They left an open question:

Are there broadcast protocols with $\mathcal{O}(\ell n)$ communication complexity for $t < n$ with round complexity lower than $\mathcal{O}(n^3)$ for computational security and lower than $\mathcal{O}(n^4)$ for information-theoretic security?

[6] answered the first part of the question: they constructed a computationally secure protocol with communication complexity of $\mathcal{O}(n^2)$. This result still leaves the second part of the open question unsolved.

1.1 Our Results

We construct a broadcast extension protocol in the information-theoretic setting against adversaries corrupting up to $t < n$ parties. Our result improves the current best-known result in the same setting of [7] in round complexity by a multiplicative factor of n while maintaining the same communication complexity. More formally, we obtain the following theorem.

Theorem 1. *Assuming an oracle for broadcasting short messages, there exists a broadcast protocol achieving information-theoretic security in $t < n$ setting for an ℓ-bit message in $\mathcal{O}(n^2)$ rounds by communicating $\mathcal{O}(\ell n + n^3(B(\lambda) + nB(\log n)))$ bits, where $B(l)$ is the communication complexity of broadcasting l bits.*

Thus, combining the above result with the broadcast protocol of [15] gives the following corollary.

Corollary 1. *There exists a broadcast protocol achieving information-theoretic security in $t < n$ setting for an ℓ-bit message in $\mathcal{O}(n^3)$ rounds by communicating $\mathcal{O}(\ell n + n^{10}\lambda)$ bits.*

This result shortens the gap in round complexity between the information-theoretic case and the computational case where $\mathcal{O}(n^2)$ rounds is achieved in [6]. Closing this gap entirely is left as an open question.

1.2 Our Techniques

Block Broadcast. The traditional broadcast protocol of [4] for $t < n$ prevents a corrupted sender from sending different values to different receivers using signature (or pseudosignature for information-theoretic security [14,15]). The receivers then send their signed values to each other. This means in order to broadcast a message m, both m and the corresponding signature need to be sent and received $\mathcal{O}(n^2)$ times. Thus, the communication complexity of broadcasting a message of length ℓ is at least $\mathcal{O}(\ell n^2)$. Similar to the existing broadcast extension protocols in literature [6,7], a sender in our broadcast protocol cuts a long message into multiple blocks. Each block is sent via point-to-point channels—first from the sender, and later from any parties publicly known to hold the block. Then a broadcast protocol for short messages (multiple times, but independent of ℓ) is used to verify the correctness of the blocks using a universal hash function as in [7]. This keeps the multiplicative factor in the communication complexity linear in n instead of n^2. Similar to [7], our protocol processes one block at a time sequentially.

Multi-party Block Sending. In [7], each block is sent between one pair of parties at a time. In order to improve the round complexity, we use the technique in [6] for the computational security setting where a block is sent between multiple pairs of parties at the same time. In each round, a block is sent to every party not holding the block and satisfying a certain condition from a designated party that holds the block and is still trusted by the receiving party. In particular, if all parties are honest, they will all receive a block in one round.

Checking Block Validity. In order to ensure that all honest parties receive each message block with the same value, we use a universal hash function similar to the protocol in [7]. Once a party receives a block from the designated party, it will randomly generate and broadcast a universal hash function key. The original sender P_s will respond by broadcasting the hash value of the block. All parties holding a block will also compute the hash values of their own blocks and compare to the value broadcast by P_s. They then broadcast whether or not the values are the same. Unlike in [7], multiple sessions of this correspondence can happen in parallel—one for each pair of parties transmitting a block. In order to guarantee that blocks received by multiple honest parties in the same round have the same value, we also require parties that just receive blocks to broadcast their hash checking result as well.

Trust Graph. We combine and expand the techniques for keeping track of a party's interactions in [7] and [6]. As in [7], each party collectively keeps track of conflict between each pair of parties. A conflict occurs between two parties P_a and P_b—both holding a block with P_b receiving a block from P_a earlier in the protocol—if one approves a hash value from P_s while another rejects it. In [6], each party instead keeps track of a set of corrupted parties from their own perspective. In both constructions, a party only tries to obtain a block from another party if it is not in conflict with that party or the party is not corrupted. We expand this idea to the concept of the public trust graph. A trust graph starts as a complete graph where vertices are all parties. When a pair of parties are in conflict in the same sense as in [7], an edge between them is removed. If a party publicly does not follow the protocol, it will be isolated in the trust graph. While the conflict set in [7] can be directly translated to our trust graph, we make additional use of the graph property to strengthen our protocol.

Condition to Forfeit a Block. Unlike the collision-resistant hash function used in [6], a universal hash function cannot be computed once and for all. If an adversary knows a hash key before it chooses whether to send a block, it can find a different block that hashes to the same value. In order to get around this limitation, the protocol in [7] lets the receiver choose a new hash key after it receives a block via point-to-point channel.

However, the verification in [7] is done separately for each receiver. In the situation where the sender P_s and block holders P_a and P_b collude, they can approve two different block values for honest P_i and P_j, who receive blocks from P_a and P_b, respectively. When P_j learns of the conflict between P_a and P_i, it cannot tell which of P_a and P_i is corrupted. In this case, P_j removes an edge $\{P_a, P_i\}$ from its trust graph. Since the conflict is known to every honest party via broadcast, the honest parties can maintain a consistent trust graph locally. In [7], whenever such conflict occurs, P_j must forfeit the block it has. Any pairs of parties in conflict do not send or receive a block from one another ever again across all message blocks. This guarantees that any two honest parties hold message blocks with the same value. As in [7], this means that each honest party may need to receive a block more than once. Since the trust graph has

$\mathcal{O}(n^2)$ edges, such a conflict can occur at most $\mathcal{O}(n^2)$ times. By dividing the message into blocks appropriately, [7] can keep the communication complexity to the optimal $\mathcal{O}(\ell n + poly(n, \lambda))$. However, our parallel block sending further increases the number of such forfeits as more than one party may try to get a block and fail at the same time. We solve this problem by implementing a stronger condition for a party to forfeit a block. Namely, P_j only forfeits a block when there is no trust path of block holders from P_j to P_s. Together with the next technique to increase the number of such paths, we can also keep the communication complexity the same as in [7].

Condition to Receive a Block. In order to reduce the number of forfeits which leads to an increase in communication complexity, we add additional conditions for when a party is to be sent a block. The idea is to make it harder for an adversary to force a party, who has already received a block, to forfeit it in a later round. The protocol in [7] uses a tree with P_s as a root to represent how a block is sent between parties. However, their protocol entirely resets this tree whenever a conflict occurs. Doing so, along with the parallel block sending technique, leads to an increase in both round complexity and communication complexity by a factor of n. Our first solution is, instead of resetting the tree, to disconnect the pair in conflict and remove those no longer connected to P_s. Unfortunately, this does not solve the problem. An adversary can still force a long path between P_s and honest parties, and repeatedly disconnect them from P_s. Instead, our protocol uses a graph H^j to represent the connection for jth block. H^j is an induced subgraph of the trust graph G on a subset of parties that have received a block. Due to the verification via universal hash function, all honest parties in H^j hold a block with the same value. When a party P_i is added to H^j, we add all edges between P_i and all parties in H^j that connect to P_i in G as well. Thus, in order for a party to be removed from H^j—which is equivalent to forfeiting a block—all of its neighbors in H^j need to be removed as well.

Varying Block Size. Our protocol takes $\mathcal{O}(d_j + \Delta_j)$ rounds to broadcast the jth block, where d_j is the maximum distance between the sender and receiving parties in the trusted graph and Δ_j is the number of edges removed from the graph while broadcasting the block. If the blocks are of the same size either ℓ/n^2, as in [7], or ℓ/n, as in [6], the resulting protocol will provide no improvement in round complexity. We solve this problem by using a non-constant block size of $\ell d_{j-1}/n^2$. Since $1 \leq d_{j-1} \leq n$, our block size is between that of [7] and [6]. In the case of an honest sender, $d_j = 1$ for all j, we get the same block size as in [7]. Intuitively, as the corrupted parties are known and the distance from receiving parties in G grows, we want to send a larger block because the number of edges that can be disconnected is smaller. It is more difficult for the corrupted parties to make the honest parties resend a block.

2 Definitions

Let λ denote the security parameter. A *negligible* function $\nu(\lambda)$ is a non-negative function such that for any constant $c < 0$ and for all sufficiently large λ, $\nu(\lambda) < \lambda^c$. We will denote by $\Pr_r[X]$ the probability of an event X over coins r, and $\Pr[X]$ when r is not specified. For a randomized algorithm A, let $A(x; r)$ denote running A on an input x with random coins r. If r is chosen uniformly at random with an output y, we denote $y \leftarrow A(x)$. Let $\mathcal{P}$ be a set of n parties $\{P_1, \ldots, P_n\}$. For a finite subset $A \subset U$, let $\overline{A}$ denote $U \setminus A$ when U is clear from context. For a vertex v of a graph G, we may use $v \in G$ to denote $v \in V(G)$.

Definition 1 (Byzantine Broadcast). *A protocol Π for a set of n parties $\mathcal{P}$, with secure private channel between every pair of parties, and a distinguished party P_s for some $s \in [n]$, called a sender, who holds an input $m \in \mathcal{M}$, is a* secure (Byzantine) broadcast *protocol if, at the end of the protocol, the following holds except with negligible probability:*

- *All honest parties output the same value $m' \in \mathcal{M} \cup \{\perp\}$; and*
- *If the sender P_s is honest, $m' = m$.*

Definition 2 (Universal Hash Function). *A family of functions $\{H_k\}_{k \in S_H}$ where $H_k : \mathcal{M} \to Y$ is* ϵ-universal *if for any two distinct $m, m' \in \mathcal{M}$,*

$$\Pr[k \leftarrow S_H : H_k(m) = H_k(m')] \leq \epsilon.$$

A universal hash function can be constructed as follows. Let $S_H = Y = \mathbb{F} = \mathbb{F}_{2^\lambda}$. Let $m \in \mathcal{M} = \{0,1\}^\ell$ be represented by a polynomial $m(x)$ over $\mathbb{F}$ by cutting m in blocks of size λ. We compute $H_k(m) = m(k) \in Y$.

3 Broadcast Extension

In this section we give an overview of the broadcast constructions of [7] and [6].

3.1 Information-Theoretic Secure Broadcast in $\mathcal{O}(n^4)$ Rounds

We first describe the broadcast extension protocol of [7]. Informally, the sender P_s cuts a long message into blocks. The protocol broadcasts each block sequentially using ITBlockBC. The subprotocol ITBlockBC works as follows. In each loop, a party P_a who has the block sends it to another party P_b that has not received it. P_b then generates and broadcasts a key k for information-theoretically secure universal hash function. Next, P_s computes and broadcasts the hash value of the block using the received key. Every party that has the block responds as to whether the block they have gives the same hash value. If there is a pair of parties P_c and P_d where P_d has received a block from P_c and the two disagree on the hash value, the subprotocol is restarted and $\{P_c, P_d\}$ is added to a "dispute set" where they will not interact again. This set is kept across multiple executions of ITBlockBC—one for each block. Thus, the conflict can only occur at most $\mathcal{O}(n^2)$ times across the executions. When no such conflict occurs, each execution of ITBlockBC takes $\mathcal{O}(n)$ rounds with oracle access to (short) broadcast. By cutting the message into n^2 blocks, the protocol gives $\mathcal{O}(n^3)$ rounds with the oracle access, and $\mathcal{O}(n^4)$ rounds when the oracle is substituted by an $\mathcal{O}(n)$-round broadcast protocol of [15].

Let $\{H_k\}_{k \in S_H}$ be a family of universal hash functions with seeds in S_H. Let $\mathcal{P} = \{P_1, \ldots, P_n\}$ be a set of all parties. We describe the protocol ITBlockBC in Fig. 1.

ITBlockBC(P_s, m)

For each party P_i on input dispute set Δ.

1. Initialize a set $H = \{P_s\}$ and $T = \emptyset$.
2. While $\exists P_x, P_y \in \mathcal{P}$ such that $P_x \in H$, $P_y \in \overline{H}$ and $\{P_x, P_y\} \notin \Delta$ do the following:

Round 1: P_x sends m_x to P_y via point-to-point channel. P_y sets $m_y := m_x$. Add (P_x, P_y) to T.

Round 2: P_y generates and broadcasts $k \leftarrow S_H$.

Round 3: P_s broadcasts $h := H_k(m)$.

Round 4: $\forall P_i \in H \cup \{P_y\} \setminus \{P_s\}$ if $h = H_k(m_i)$ broadcasts 1; otherwise, 0.

Round 5: If all parties broadcast 1, add P_y to H. Else,
- for all $(P_i, P_j) \in T$ such that P_i broadcast 1 or $P_i = P_s$ and P_j broadcast 0, add $\{P_i, P_j\}$ to Δ; and
- set $H = \{P_s\}$ and $T = \emptyset$.

3. $\forall P_i \in \mathcal{P}$, if $P_i \in H$, output m_i; otherwise, output $\perp$.

Fig. 1. Information-theoretic block broadcast of [7]

The broadcast protocol can be obtained by running ITBlockBC n^2 times as shown in Fig. 2.

LongBC(P_s, m)

1. Parties initialize dispute set $\Delta = \emptyset$.
2. Sender P_s cuts m into n^2 equal pieces $m^1, \ldots, m^{n^2}$ (padding if required).
3. For $c = 1, \ldots, n^2$, invoke ITBlockBC(P_s, m^c) and let m_i^c be the output of P_i.
4. For each $P_i \in \mathcal{P}$, if $m_i^j = \perp$ for some j, output $\perp$. Otherwise, output $m_i^1 || \ldots || m_i^{n^2}$.

Fig. 2. Broadcast extension using ITBlockBC

Theorem 2 ([7]). *Assuming an oracle for broadcasting short messages, there exists a broadcast protocol* LongBC *achieving information-theoretic security in* $t < n$ *setting for an* ℓ*-bit message in* $\mathcal{O}(n^3)$ *rounds by communicating* $\mathcal{O}(\ell n + n^3(B(\lambda) + nB(1)))$ *bits.*

Corollary 2 ([7]). *There exists a broadcast protocol achieving information-theoretic security in* $t < n$ *setting for an* ℓ*-bit message in* $\mathcal{O}(n^4)$ *rounds by communicating* $\mathcal{O}(\ell n + n^{10}\lambda)$ *bits.*

3.2 Computationally Secure Broadcast in $\mathcal{O}(n^2)$ Rounds

The construction of [6] improves on the computational case of [7]. In [7] a long message is broadcast in blocks similar to the information-theoretic case above. Instead of generating a new key for universal hash function every time a party receives a block, the sender P_s broadcasts a hash value of the block using collision-resistant hash function (CRHF) at the beginning of the subprotocol. When a party P_b receives a block from P_a, he can verify it locally with no additional interaction. If the verification fails, P_b knows that P_a is corrupted. Thus, the failure can occur at most $\mathcal{O}(n)$ times. By cutting the message into n blocks, the protocol gives $\mathcal{O}(n^2)$ rounds with the oracle access, and $\mathcal{O}(n^3)$ rounds when the oracle is substituted by $\mathcal{O}(n)$-round broadcast protocol of [15].

In [6] this protocol is improved by allowing multiple parties to send and receive a block in the same round. Several checks are added to ensure that this parallel process does not break the correctness and security. This technique speeds up the protocol by a factor of n.

Let Hash be a collision-resistant hash function. We describe the protocol CryptoBC in Fig. 3.

Theorem 3 ([6]). *Assuming an oracle for broadcasting short messages and CRHFs, there exists a broadcast protocol* CryptoBC *against a PPT adversary corrupting* $t < n$ *parties for an* ℓ*-bit message in* $\mathcal{O}(n)$ *rounds by communicating* $\mathcal{O}(\ell n + (n\lambda + n^3 \log n)B(1))$ *bits.*

Corollary 3 ([6]). *Assuming CRHFs, there exists a broadcast protocol against a PPT adversary corrupting* $t < n$ *parties for an* ℓ*-bit message in* $\mathcal{O}(n^2)$ *rounds by communicating* $\mathcal{O}(\ell n + n^6\lambda \log n)$ *bits.*

4 Our Construction

In this section we show how to improve information-theoretic secure broadcast for long messages in [7]. In [6], Ganesh et al. show that it is possible to broadcast a message of arbitrary length ℓ using $\mathcal{O}(n)$ rounds having $\mathcal{O}(n)$ black-box access to a broadcast protocol for single bit, assuming CRHF. Thus, combining the result with [4] gives a broadcast protocol for a message of arbitrary length in $\mathcal{O}(n^2)$ rounds under the same assumption. On the other hand, the best result for information-theoretic broadcast for arbitrary long messages by [7] uses $\mathcal{O}(n^3)$

CryptoBC(P_s, m)

Hash Agreement phase:

1. P_s cuts m into n equal pieces $m^1, \ldots, m^n$ (padding if required).
2. For $c = 1, \ldots, n$, P_s computes and broadcasts $h^c = \mathsf{Hash}(m^c)$ to all parties.

Block Agreement phase: For each party P_i

1. Initialize
   - $C_i = \emptyset$, $c_i = 1$, $r = 1$;
   - $T_i^k[j, l] = 1$ for $j, l, k \in [n]$;
   - $H_i^k = \{P_s\}$ for $k \in [n]$;
2. While $r \leq n + t$ do
   (a) If $P_i \in \overline{H}_i^{c_i}$, $\exists P_j \in H_i^{c_i} \setminus C_i$ and $|H_i^{c_i} \cup C_i| \geq r - c_i + 1$, broadcast (send, j, c_i).
   (b) Let (send, x, y) be the output of the broadcast from $P_j \notin C_i$.
      i. if $T_i^y[x, j] = 1$ and there is only one broadcast from P_j, then set $T_i^y[x, j] = 0$, and if $x = i$ and $P_i \in H_i^y$, send m_i^y to P_j via point-to-point channel;
      ii. else, add P_j to C_i.
   (c) If P_i broadcast (send, j, c_i) in Step 2(a), let $\overline{m}_j^{c_i}$ be the message block received from P_j
      i. if $h^{c_i} = \mathsf{Hash}(\overline{m}_j^{c_i})$, then increment c_i by 1, set $m_i^{c_i} = \overline{m}_j^{c_i}$ and broadcast $(\mathsf{happy}, H_i^{c_i}, C_i, c_i)$;
      ii. else, broadcast $(\mathsf{unhappy}, c_i)$ and add P_j to C_i.
   (d) Let v be the output of the broadcast from $P_j \notin C_i$ in Step 2(c) who broadcast $(\mathsf{send}, \star, \star)$ in Step 2(a) this round
      i. if $v = (\mathsf{happy}, H_j^x, C_j, x)$, $H_j^x \cup C_j \subseteq H_i^x \cup C_i$ and $|H_j^x \cup C_j| \geq r - x + 1$, then add $H_j^x \cup \{P_j\}$ to H_i^x;
      ii. if $v = (\mathsf{unhappy}, x)$ do nothing;
      iii. else, add P_j to C_i.
   (e) If $r = c_i + t$ and $P_i \in \overline{H}_i^{c_i}$, then exit while loop.
3. If $m_i^k = \bot$ for some $k \in [n]$, output $\bot$. Otherwise, output $m_i^1 || \ldots || m_i^n$.

Fig. 3. Computationally secure broadcast of [6] against $t < n$ corruption

rounds having $\mathcal{O}(n^3)$ black-box access to a broadcast protocol for single bit. Thus, combining the result with [14,15] gives a broadcast protocol in $\mathcal{O}(n^4)$ rounds. We show that several techniques, including parallel block broadcast in [6], can be used to improve this result to $\mathcal{O}(n^3)$ rounds.

We first describe a protocol ImprovedBlockBC that broadcasts a block of a long message using an oracle broadcasting short messages. Besides the message block as an input of the sender, each party P_i maintains a trust graph G_i across executions of ImprovedBlockBC for all message blocks. While our trust graph and the dispute set in [7] provide similar information, our protocol takes into account some properties of graph such as the length of a shortest path between a pair of nodes. Finally, we describe our broadcast protocol ImprovedLongBC running ImprovedBlockBC as a subprotocol. This protocol is similar to LongBC (in Sect. 3) but with a varying number of blocks depending on the state of the trust graph at the end of each execution of ImprovedBlockBC.

4.1 Improved Block Broadcast

The protocol ImprovedBlockBC modifies ITBlockBC (in Sect. 3) using several techniques. Similar to ITBlockBC, each party uses a universal hash function to verify whether a block it receives is "correct"—meaning that all honest parties agree on the value of the message block. To speed up the protocol, it also employs some of the parallel processing technique in [6]. Similar to CryptoBC of [6], ImprovedBlockBC allows multiple pair of parties to send and receive blocks at the same time. Additional conditions are checked to ensure that all honest parties agree on which parties sending and receiving blocks at all time. When all parties follow the protocol honestly, every party receives the block concurrently and ImprovedBlockBC terminates in $\mathcal{O}(1)$ round (with oracle access to short broadcast). On the other hand, ImprovedBlockBC operates on one block at time, unlike CryptoBC where different pairs of parties may send and receive different blocks at the same time. This is unavoidable due to the weaker guarantee of universal hash functions compared to that of collision-resistant hash functions.

We replace the dispute set Δ, the set H of parties that have already received a block, and the history set T with a trust graph G_i and a graph H_i. While they contain the same information, we utilize the graph properties including connectivity and path length in our protocol. Similar to ITBlockBC, a party may forfeit a block due to conflict in universal hash value. Instead of resetting the block broadcast entirely as in ITBlockBC—which can lead to larger round complexity—we minimize the number of such forfeits using two techniques. First, a party P_j is only sent a block when all of its neighbors in the trust graph that are closer to the sender already have the block. (In that case, we say P_j is "ready to receive a block.") Second, P_j only forfeits a block if it is disconnected to P_s in H_i, which only occurs when all of the neighbors above are also disconnected.

Let $\{H_k\}_{k \in S_H}$ be a family of universal hash functions with seeds in S_H. Let $\mathcal{P} = \{P_1, \ldots, P_n\}$ be a set of all parties with fixed ordering, e.g., $P_1 > P_2 > \ldots > P_n$. Each party P_i keeps its trusted graph G_i, where each node represents a party in $\mathcal{P}$, throughout ImprovedBlockBC for all message blocks. In the beginning of the first block, G_i is initialized to a complete graph C_n. If a broadcast protocol from P_a fails, P_i isolates P_a in G_i by removing all edges connecting to P_a. Let $G(P_s)$ denote the connected component of G containing P_s. We describe the protocol ImprovedBlockBC in Fig. 4. Note that all broadcasts in the same step can be done in parallel. P_i ignores all messages it does not expect as specified by the protocol.

Definition 3. *Let G be a graph on $\mathcal{P}$ and $H \subseteq G(P_s)$. We say P_j is* ready to receive a block from P_i *with respect to (H, G, P_s) if all of the following holds:*

- *P_j is a neighbor of P_i in G_i;*

- *$P_j \notin H$;*
- *For every shortest path from P_j to P_s, $(P_j, P_{j_k}, \ldots, P_s)$, $P_{j_k} \in H$;*
- *P_i is the maximal such P_{j_k} (with respect to the ordering given above).*

Now we prove the following properties of ImprovedBlockBC. The following lemma shows that G_i and H_i of honest parties are the same as they are only updated using information that is broadcast.

Lemma 1. *Suppose all honest parties hold the same G_i at the beginning of* ImprovedBlockBC*. Then, at the end of each while loop, all honest parties hold the same G_i and H_i.*

Proof. Assuming all honest parties hold the same G_i and H_i at the beginning of a while loop. Then in Round 1, 2 and 3, all honest parties agree whether P_y is ready to receive a block from P_x. Then, by the agreement property of broadcast, all honest parties agree on edge removal of G_i in Round 3 and hold the same recording (k_y, P_x, P_y)'s. Also by the agreement property, all honest parties agree on edge removal of G_i in Round 4 and 5. Finally, by the agreement property and the consistency of G_I, they also agree on modification of H_i in Round 5. Since the honest parties hold the same G_i and initialize the same H_i at the beginning of the protocol, the consistency of G_i and H_i holds at the end of each while loop. □

From this point onward, we assume all honest parties hold the same G_i at the beginning of ImprovedBlockBC, and denote the same G_i and H_i for all honest P_i by G and H, respectively. The following lemma shows the consistency of the values hold by honest parties. We use the property of universal hash functions when the keys are chosen uniformly at random by honest parties.

Lemma 2. *Except with negligible probability, at the end of each while loop, all honest parties in H hold the same value m.*

Proof. Assume that at the beginning of a loop, all honest parties in H hold the same value m. Suppose P_i is an honest party added to H in this loop. The statement holds trivially if there is no other honest party in H at the end of the loop. Suppose there is another honest party P_j in H at the end of the loop. Then P_i broadcasts (k_j, P_a) for some $P_a \in H$ in Round 2 and P_s broadcasts (h_i, P_i) in Round 3. Also, P_j broadcasts (true, P_i) in Round 4; otherwise, P_j would be removed from or not added to H_i. Since P_i and P_j are honest $H_{k_i}(m_a) = H_{k_i}(m_j) = h_i$. By the property of universal hash function, since k_i is chosen honestly independent of the messages, except with negligible probability, $m_a = m_j = m$. The result follows as the first loop has $V(H) = \{P_s\}$. □

Let Good be the event that, at the end of each while loop, all honest parties in H hold the same value m.

ImprovedBlockBC(P_s, m)

For each party P_i on input a trust graph G_i.

1. Initialize a graph $H_i \subseteq G_i(P_s)$ with only one vertex P_s and no edge.
2. While $P_i \in G_i(P_s)$ and $|V(H_i)| < |V(G_i(P_s))|$, clear all records and do

Round 1: If $P_i \in H_i$, for each P_j ready to receive a block from P_i with respect to (H_i, G_i, P_s) P_i sends m_i to P_j via point-to-point channel.

Round 2: If $P_i \notin H_i$ and is ready to receive a block from P_j with respect to (H_i, G_i, P_s),
   (a) if P_i does not receive m_j or receive more than one block from P_j in Round 1, broadcast (fail, P_j) and remove $\{P_i, P_j\}$ from $E(G_i)$;
   (b) else, sample $k \leftarrow S_H$ and broadcast (k, P_j) and record (k, P_j, P_i).

Round 3: When P_i outputs (A_y, P_x) broadcast by P_y, if $\{P_x, P_y\} \notin E(G_i)$ or P_y is not ready to receive a block from P_x with respect to (H_i, G_i, P_s), isolate P_y in G_i. Else
   (a) if $A_y =$ fail, remove $\{P_x, P_y\}$ from $E(G_i)$;
   (b) if $A_y = k_y$, record (k_y, P_x, P_y);
   (c) if $P_i = P_s$, broadcast $(H_{k_y}(m), P_y)$;
   (d) if P_i receives multiple broadcast messages from P_y this round or A_y is not one of the above, isolate P_y in G_i.

Round 4: When P_i outputs (h_y, P_y) broadcast by P_s, if (k_y, P_x, P_y) is not recorded, output $\perp$ and abort; else if $P_i \in H_i$ or received m_j in Round 1, check if $H_{k_y}(m_i) = h_y$ or $H_{k_y}(m_j) = h_y$, respectively. Broadcast (true, P_y) or (false, P_y) accordingly. If there exists a record (k_y, P_x, P_y) without (h_y, P_y) broadcast, output $\perp$ and abort.

Round 5: When P_i outputs (true, P_y) or (false, P_y) with (k_y, P_x, P_y) recorded broadcast by P_b either in H_i or with (k_b, P_a, P_b) recorded, P_i appends (P_b, true/false) to the recording (k_y, P_x, P_y). Isolate any P_b broadcasting both (true, P_y) and (false, P_y), or P_b either in H_i or with (k_b, P_a, P_b) recorded broadcasting neither. At the end of this round, P_i processes each recorded $(k_y, P_x, P_y, \ldots)$ one by one in the order of P_y as follows.
   (a) For each $P_b \in H_i$ whose (P_b, false) is appended,
      i. for each P_a, P_b's neighbor in G_i, if (P_a, true) is appended (or $P_a = P_s$), remove $\{P_a, P_b\}$ from $E(G_i)$ and $E(H_i)$;
      ii. remove P_b from H_i.
   (b) For each P_b with $(k_b, P_a, P_b, \ldots)$ recorded, if (P_a, true) is appended (or $P_a = P_s$), remove $\{P_a, P_b\}$ from $E(G_i)$ and append fail to $(k_b, P_a, P_b, \ldots)$.
   (c) Ignore P_b that is removed from H_i earlier this round.

   After processing all records, remove any P_a no longer connected to P_s in H_i from H_i. For each recorded $(k_y, P_x, P_y, \ldots)$, if P_x is still in H_i, $\{P_x, P_y\}$ is still in $E(G_i)$ and no fail appended, add P_y to $V(H_i)$ and $\{P_x, P_y\}$ to $E(H_i)$ and if $P_i = P_y$, set $m_i = m_y$.

3. If $P_i \in H_i$, output m_i. Otherwise, output $\perp$.

Fig. 4. Improved block broadcast

Lemma 3. *Assuming the event* Good *occurs, for any two different honest parties* P_i *and* P_j, $\{P_i, P_j\} \in E(G)$ *at any point in the protocol. Furthermore, at the end of the protocol, either all honest parties are in* H *and output the same* m*, or output* $\perp$.

Proof. An honest P_a removes $\{P_i, P_j\}$ from $E(G)$ when one of the following holds:

1. P_j is ready to receive a block from P_i but does not get one or get more than one in Round 1 and broadcasts (fail, P_i) in Round 2;
2. P_j broadcasts malformed or multiple messages in Round 2;
3. P_i and P_j broadcast different $(\mathsf{true}/\mathsf{false}, P_y)$ with (k_y, P_x, P_y) recorded in Round 4.

By Lemma 1, the first two conditions do not occur for honest P_i and P_j. By Lemma 2, the last condition does not occur for honest P_i and P_j. Thus, $\{P_i, P_j\}$ is never removed from $E(G)$.

By the agreement property of broadcast, honest parties agree on the abort condition in Round 4. If the abort condition does not occur, the protocol ends when $P_i \notin G(P_s)$ or $|V(H)| = |V(G(P_s))|$. Since honest parties are connected in G, they agree on the first condition. The honest parties also agree on the second condition by Lemma 1, and if the first condition does not hold, it implies $P_i \in H = G(P_s)$ for all honest P_i. By Lemma 2, they all output m. □

Let G^* be the trust graph G at the end of the protocol. Let $H^* = G^*(P_s)$. We let $d(P_i)$ denote the length of the shortest path from P_i to P_s in H^* and $d = \max_i d(P_i)$. For $j = 1, \ldots, d$, let Δ_j be the number of edges removed from G when all parties P_i with $d(P_i) \leq j$ are last added to H (i.e., not removed later in the protocol). We have $0 \leq \Delta_1 \leq \Delta_2 \leq \ldots \leq \Delta_d \leq \Delta$.

Lemma 4. *Suppose a party* P_i *is in* H *at the end of the protocol, then* P_i *is last added to* H *in* $t_i = t(P_i) \leq d(P_i) + \Delta_{d(P_i)}$ *loops. In particular, assuming the event* Good *occurs, the protocol ends in* $5(d + \Delta)$ *rounds.*

Proof. We prove the statement by induction on $d(P_i)$. Clearly, when $d(P_i) = 1$, $(P_i, P_s) \in E(G^*)$ and P_s sends a block to P_i every loop until P_i is added to H. If P_i fails to be added, a neighbor of P_i broadcasts (false, P_i), and thus there must be an edge (P_a, P_b) that gets removed from $E(G)$. Thus, $t_i = t(P_i) \leq d(P_i) + \Delta_1$. Suppose any P_j with $d(P_j) = d(P_i) - 1$ is last added to H in $t_j \leq d(P_j) + \Delta_{d(P_j)} = d(P_i) + \Delta_{d(P_j)} - 1$ loops. In the $(t_j + 1)$th loop, either $P_i \in H$ or $P_i \notin H$. Suppose $P_i \in H$. Then P_i is not removed in or after this loop as P_j is not. Otherwise, a neighbor P_j of P_i on the shortest path will have to be added after t_jth loop, which is a contradiction. Thus, $t_i \leq t_j \leq d(P_i) + \Delta_{d(P_i)}$. Now suppose $P_i \notin H$. Then P_i is ready to receive a block from one of its neighbors every loop after t_j as all of its neighbors on the shortest path are in H and have never been removed. Thus, in every loop after t_j, either P_i gets a block or an edge gets removed from $E(G)$. Therefore, $t_i = t_j + 1 + (\Delta_{d(P_i)} - \Delta_{d(P_i)-1}) \leq d(P_i) + \Delta_{d(P_i)}$.

Now assume that the event Good occurs. If an honest party is in H at the end of the protocol, then by Lemma 3, all honest parties are in H at the end of the protocol. The last honest party is last added to H in $d + \Delta$ loops, i.e., $5(d + \Delta)$ rounds. Otherwise, suppose all honest parties are not in H at the end of the protocol. By Lemma 3 and the agreement property of broadcast, honest parties terminate at the same time. Let t^* be the last loop before the termination. Suppose that every party follows the protocol correctly from the next loop onward. Then an honest party P_i will stay in $G_i(P_s)$ and be added to H within $t' \leq d + \Delta$ loops. We have $t^* \leq t' \leq d + \Delta$ as well. □

Lemma 5. *Let d_0 be the maximum length of the shortest path from any honest party to P_s at the beginning of the protocol. Let d_1 be the maximum length of the shortest path from any honest party to P_s at the end of the protocol. The number of times a block is sent to and from honest parties is at most $\mathcal{O}(n+\Delta+n(d_1-d_0))$.*

Proof. Every party in $G^*(P_s)$ must receive a block at least once. Thus, we need n times. A party receives a block more than once under two conditions:

1. $P_j \notin H$ is ready to receive a block from P_i but fails due to
   (a) P_i does not send a block; or
   (b) (P_i, P_j) is removed from $E(G)$; or
   (c) P_i is removed from H.
2. $P_j \in H$ is removed from H.

For 1(a) and 1(b), $|E(G)|$ decreases by 1. For 1(c) and 2, the shortest path of some party increases by at least 1. Thus, the number of additional times a party needs to get a block is bounded by $\Delta + n(d_1 - d_0)$. □

4.2 Improved Broadcast Extension

Now we are ready to describe our main construction of broadcast extension using block broadcast ImprovedBlockBC as a subprotocol. As in [7], in order to broadcast a message m of arbitrary length ℓ, we cut m into q blocks. Unlike in [7], the block size will vary depending on the trust graph G at the end of the previous block. In particular, each block m_j has length $\ell_j = \ell d_{j-1}/n^2$ where d_j is the maximum length of the shortest path from P_s to any P_i connected to P_s at the end of jth execution of ImprovedBlockBC. We let $d_0 = 1$ and allow the last block to be shorter so that the length of all q blocks add up to ℓ. We then run ImprovedBlockBC in Fig. 4 q times sequentially as shown in Fig. 5.

Now we prove the round complexity and communication complexity of ImprovedLongBC. Let d_j be the maximum length of the shortest path from P_s to any P_i connected to P_s at the end of jth execution of ImprovedBlockBC, and Δ_i be the decrease in number of edges of G.

Lemma 6. *Assuming an oracle for broadcasting short messages,* ImprovedLongBC *takes at most $\mathcal{O}(n^2)$ rounds.*

ImprovedLongBC(P_s, m)

1. Each party P_i initializes a trust graph $G_i = C_n$, a complete graph on $V = \mathcal{P}$.
2. Sender P_s initializes m_1, the first ℓ_1 bits of m where $\ell_1 = \ell/n^2$ (padding if ℓ is not divisible by n^2), and sets $c = 1$.
3. While $\sum_{j=1}^{c} \ell_j < \ell$, do the following:
   (a) Invoke ImprovedBlockBC(P_s, m_c) and let m_c^i be the output of P_i.
   (b) If $|m_c^i| \neq \ell_c$, P_i aborts.
   (c) Compute d_c the maximum length of the shortest path from P_s to any P_i connected to P_s.
   (d) Let $\ell_{c+1} = \ell d_c/n^2$ and m_{c+1} be the next ℓ_{c+1} bits of m.
   (e) increase c by 1.
4. For each P_i, if $m_j^i = \perp$ for some j, output $\perp$. Otherwise, output $m_1^i||\ldots||m_q^i$ where q is the number of ImprovedBlockBC invoked.

Fig. 5. Broadcast extension using ImprovedBlockBC

Proof. The round complexity of LongBC is the sum of the round complexity of ImprovedBlockBC. By Lemma 4, the round complexity is

$$\sum_{j=1}^{q} 5(d_j + \Delta_j) = 5\left(\sum_{j=1}^{q} d_j + \sum_{j=1}^{q} \Delta_j\right)$$

Since $\ell = \sum_{j=1}^{q} \ell_j = \ell(1 + \sum_{j=1}^{q-1} d_j)/n^2$,

$$\sum_{j=1}^{q} d_j = n^2 - 1 + d_q \leq n^2 + n - 1$$

and $\sum_{j=1}^{q} \Delta_j \leq |E(C_n)| \leq n^2/2$. We have the round complexity $\mathcal{O}(n^2)$. □

Let d'_j be the maximum length of the shortest path from P_s to any *honest* P_i connected to P_s at the end of jth execution of ImprovedBlockBC. Let $B(l)$ be the communication complexity of broadcasting l bits.

Lemma 7. *The number of bits sent and received by honest parties in* Improved LongBC *is at most* $\mathcal{O}(\ell n + n^3(B(\lambda) + nB(\log n)))$.

Proof. The communication complexity of ImprovedLongBC is the sum of the communication complexity of ImprovedBlockBC.

By Lemma 5, the number of blocks communicated is $b_j \leq n + \Delta_j + n(d_j - d_{j-1})$ where each block incurs the communication of $\ell_j + B(|k| + \log n) + B(|h| + \log n) + nB(1 + \log n)$. Thus, the communication complexity is

$$\sum_{j=1}^{q} b_j \ell_j + \sum_{j=1}^{q} b_j \left(B(|k| + \log n) + B(|h| + \log n) + nB(1 + \log n)\right)$$

The first sum is

$$\begin{aligned}\sum_{j=1}^{q} d_j \ell_j &\leq \sum_{j=1}^{q} (n + \Delta_j + n(d_j - d_{j-1})) \frac{\ell d_{j-1}}{n^2} \\ &= \ell \left(\frac{\sum_{j=1}^{q} d_{j-1}}{n} + \frac{\sum_{j=1}^{q} \Delta_j d_{j-1}}{n^2} + \frac{\sum_{j=1}^{q} d_{j-1}(d'_j - d'_{j-1})}{n} \right) \\ &\leq \ell \left(\frac{n^2}{n} + \frac{n \sum_{j=1}^{q} \Delta_j}{n^2} + \frac{\left(\sum_{j=1}^{q} d_{j-1}\right)\left(\sum_{j=1}^{q} (d'_j - d'_{j-1})\right)}{nq} \right) \\ &\leq \ell \left(n + n + \frac{n^3}{nq} \right) \leq 3\ell n.\end{aligned}$$

as $d'_j \leq d_j \leq n$ and $q \geq n$. Since $\sum_{j=1}^{q} b_j \leq nq + \sum_{j=1}^{q} \Delta_j + nd'_q \leq n^3 + 2n^2$, the communication complexity is

$$\begin{aligned}&3\ell n + (n^3 + 2n^2)\left(B(|k| + \log n) + B(|h| + \log n) + nB(1 + \log n)\right) \\ &= \mathcal{O}(\ell n + n^3(B(\lambda) + nB(\log n))).\end{aligned}$$

□

Since the correctness of ImprovedLongBC follows directly from the correctness of ImprovedBlockBC from Lemma 2 and 3, we get the following theorem.

Theorem 4. *Assuming an oracle for broadcasting short messages, there exists a broadcast protocol achieving information-theoretic security in $t < n$ setting for an ℓ-bit message in $\mathcal{O}(n^2)$ rounds by communicating $\mathcal{O}(\ell n + n^3(B(\lambda) + nB(\log n)))$ bits.*

Combining the above result with the broadcast protocol of [15] gives the following corollary.

Corollary 4. *There exists a broadcast protocol achieving information-theoretic security in $t < n$ setting for an ℓ-bit message in $\mathcal{O}(n^3)$ rounds by communicating $\mathcal{O}(\ell n + n^{10}\lambda)$ bits.*

This result improves round complexity from instantiating the broadcast extension protocol in [7] with the broadcast protocol in [15] while maintaining the communication complexity.

5 Conclusion

We studied the broadcast protocols for long messages in the $t < n$ setting with the information-theoretic security. We modify and improve the broadcast extension protocol in [7], with the previously best-known round complexity of $\mathcal{O}(n^3)$ assuming an oracle for short messages. Our broadcast extension protocol has round complexity of $\mathcal{O}(n^2)$ while maintaining the same communication complexity. Combining our result with the broadcast protocol of [15] gives a broadcast extension protocol in the $t < n$ setting that achieves the communication complexity $\mathcal{O}(\ell n + n^{10}\lambda)$ and the round complexity of $\mathcal{O}(n^3)$. We leave an open question on how to further improve the round complexity to $\mathcal{O}(n^2)$ matching the computational case in [6] or to the optimal round complexity of $\mathcal{O}(n)$.

References

1. Beaver, D.: Correlated pseudorandomness and the complexity of private computations. In: Proceedings of the Twenty-Eighth Annual ACM Symposium on Theory of Computing, pp. 479–488. ACM (1996)
2. Chaum, D., Roijakkers, S.: Unconditionally-secure digital signatures. In: Menezes, A.J., Vanstone, S.A. (eds.) CRYPTO 1990. LNCS, vol. 537, pp. 206–214. Springer, Heidelberg (1991). https://doi.org/10.1007/3-540-38424-3_15
3. Dolev, D., Reischuk, R.: Bounds on information exchange for byzantine agreement. J. ACM (JACM) **32**(1), 191–204 (1985)
4. Dolev, D., Strong, H.R.: Authenticated algorithms for byzantine agreement. SIAM J. Comput. **12**(4), 656–666 (1983)
5. Fitzi, M., Hirt, M.: Optimally efficient multi-valued byzantine agreement. In: Proceedings of the Twenty-Fifth Annual ACM Symposium on Principles of Distributed Computing, pp. 163–168. ACM (2006)
6. Ganesh, C., Patra, A.: Optimal extension protocols for byzantine broadcast and agreement. IACR Cryptol. ePrint Arch. **2017**, 63 (2017)
7. Hirt, M., Raykov, P.: Multi-valued byzantine broadcast: The $t<n$ case. In: Sarkar, P., Iwata, T. (eds.) ASIACRYPT 2014. LNCS, vol. 8874, pp. 448–465. Springer, Berlin (2014). https://doi.org/10.1007/978-3-662-45608-8_24
8. Ishai, Y., Kilian, J., Nissim, K., Petrank, E.: Extending oblivious transfers efficiently. In: Boneh, D. (ed.) CRYPTO 2003. LNCS, vol. 2729, pp. 145–161. Springer, Heidelberg (2003). https://doi.org/10.1007/978-3-540-45146-4_9
9. Liang, G., Vaidya, N.: Error-free multi-valued consensus with byzantine failures. In: Proceedings of the 30th Annual ACM SIGACT-SIGOPS Symposium on Principles of Distributed Computing, pp. 11–20. ACM (2011)
10. Lindell, Y., Zarosim, H.: On the feasibility of extending oblivious transfer. In: Sahai, A. (ed.) TCC 2013. LNCS, vol. 7785, pp. 519–538. Springer, Heidelberg (2013). https://doi.org/10.1007/978-3-642-36594-2_29
11. Nielsen, J.B., Nordholt, P.S., Orlandi, C., Burra, S.S.: A new approach to practical active-secure two-party computation. In: Safavi-Naini, R., Canetti, R. (eds.) CRYPTO 2012. LNCS, vol. 7417, pp. 681–700. Springer, Heidelberg (2012). https://doi.org/10.1007/978-3-642-32009-5_40
12. Patra, A.: Error-free multi-valued broadcast and byzantine agreement with optimal communication complexity. In: Fernàndez Anta, A., Lipari, G., Roy, M. (eds.) OPODIS 2011. LNCS, vol. 7109, pp. 34–49. Springer, Heidelberg (2011). https://doi.org/10.1007/978-3-642-25873-2_4
13. Pease, M., Shostak, R., Lamport, L.: Reaching agreement in the presence of faults. J. ACM (JACM) **27**(2), 228–234 (1980)

14. Pfitzmann, B., Waidner, M.: Unconditional byzantine agreement for any number of faulty processors. In: Finkel, A., Jantzen, M. (eds.) STACS 1992. LNCS, vol. 577, pp. 337–350. Springer, Heidelberg (1992). https://doi.org/10.1007/3-540-55210-3_195
15. Pfitzmann, B., Waidner, M.: Information-Theoretic Pseudosignatures and Byzantine Agreement for $t>n/3$. IBM, Armonk (1996)
16. Turpin, R., Coan, B.A.: Extending binary byzantine agreement to multivalued byzantine agreement. Inf. Process. Lett. **18**(2), 73–76 (1984)

Oblivious Transfer in Incomplete Networks

Varun Narayanan(✉) and Vinod M. Prabahakaran

Tata Institute of Fundamental Research, Mumbai, India
{varun.narayanan,vinodmp}@tifr.res.in

Abstract. Secure message transmission and Byzantine agreement have been studied extensively in incomplete networks. However, information theoretically secure multiparty computation (MPC) in *incomplete* networks is less well understood. In this paper, we characterize the conditions under which a pair of parties can compute *oblivious transfer (OT)* information theoretically securely against a general adversary structure in an incomplete network of reliable, private channels. We provide characterizations for both semi-honest and malicious models. A consequence of our results is a complete characterization of networks in which a given subset of parties can compute any functionality securely with respect to an adversary structure in the semi-honest case and a partial characterization in the malicious case.

1 Introduction

Secure message transmission (SMT) [12,13,28,34–37] and Byzantine agreement [12,14,15,31,38] in incomplete networks have been studied extensively. However, information theoretically secure multiparty computation (MPC) in *incomplete* networks is less well studied with a few notable exceptions [3,6,17,26]. In this paper we consider the problem of realizing *oblivious transfer (OT)* between a given pair of parties in an incomplete network of reliable, private links with unconditional security with respect to a general adversary structure. We characterize networks in which a given pair of parties may securely compute OT in both the semi-honest and malicious models. For the malicious case, our characterization is limited to statistical security.

For a pair of parties A and B to compute OT securely in an incomplete network, an approach which might suggest itself is the following. Try to complete the network (or a part of the network which includes A and B) by using SMT to realize the missing private links. Then, use a protocol for complete networks [4,9,24] on the 'completed' (part of the) network to realize OT between A and B. It turns out that such a direct approach is, in general, not adequate. In particular, Fig. 1 shows a network where this approach fails, but it is still possible to realize OT securely.

In the graph G (Fig. 1), vertices represent parties and edges represent private authenticated communication links. Our characterization (Theorem 1) shows

A. Beimel and S. Dziembowski (Eds.): TCC 2018, LNCS 11239, pp. 389–418, 2018.
https://doi.org/10.1007/978-3-030-03807-6_15

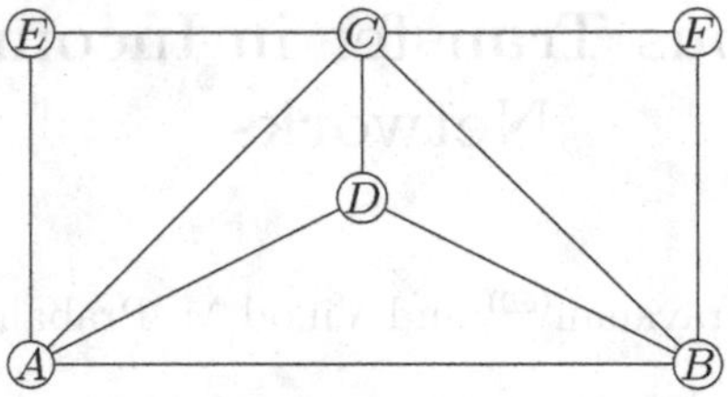

Fig. 1. Semi-honest 2-secure OT between A and B is possible in G by Theorem 1. However, a 'direct' approach of completing (a part of) the network using semi-honest SMT with 2-security and applying a standard MPC protocol for complete networks does not work.

that A and B can realize 2-secure OT in G in the semi-honest case. However, we cannot achieve this using the aforementioned direct approach. Observe that the pairs of vertices that are not already connected by an edge are only 2-connected, hence no new semi-honest 2-secure links can be established in this network using SMT. Thus, the biggest complete network containing A and B that can be obtained by such a 'completion' is the subgraph induced by vertices A, B, C, D. Theorem 1 also shows that 2-secure OT between A and B is impossible in this induced subgraph. Alternatively, this impossibility can be seen as follows. If 2-secure OT can be realized between a pair of parties in a complete network with 4 parties, then, by symmetry, it is possible to set up 2-secure OT between every pair of parties in the network. This would imply semi-honest 2-secure MPC in a network with 4 parties [18,19], which is impossible [4,9].

Standard results [11,18–20,25] allow reduction of MPC to establishing pairwise OT between the parties wishing to compute securely. In the semi-honest case, a consequence of our result is a complete characterization of networks in which a given subset of parties can compute any functionality with perfect privacy with respect to a given adversary structure. When the adversary is malicious, our results imply a condition that is necessary for statistically secure computation of any functionality among a given subset of parties in an incomplete network. This condition is also sufficient for statistically secure computation of any functionality, but *with abort and no fairness*.

1.1 Our Model and Results

Consider a simple graph $G(\mathcal{V}, \mathcal{E})$ on a set $\mathcal{V}$ of n parties (or vertices), where each undirected edge $\{u, v\} \in \mathcal{E}$ represents a private, authenticated, synchronous, bidirectional communication link between the distinct parties u and v. Let $A, B \in \mathcal{V}$ be two distinct parties. Given an adversary structure $\mathbb{Z} \subseteq 2^{\mathcal{V}}$, we seek necessary and sufficient conditions on G so that A and B may compute OT with unconditional security with respect to (w.r.t.) the adversary structure $\mathbb{Z}$. By security w.r.t. $\mathbb{Z}$, we mean security against the corruption of every set of parties in $\mathbb{Z}$. We restrict our attention to static adversaries, but consider both the semi-honest and malicious cases.

Given a vertex $u \in \mathcal{V}$ and a subset of vertices $\mathcal{Z} \subseteq \mathcal{V}$, we define *u-blocked vertices of* $\mathcal{Z}$, denoted by $\Gamma_u(\mathcal{Z})$, as the set of vertices whose every path to u contains some vertex in $\mathcal{Z}$. Our main result for the semi-honest case is the following:

Theorem 1. *Given a graph $G(\mathcal{V}, \mathcal{E})$ and an adversary structure $\mathbb{Z}$, two distinct parties $A, B \in \mathcal{V}$ can compute OT with perfect unconditional security in the semi-honest, static adversary setting if and only if the following conditions are satisfied:*

1. *For every $\mathcal{Z} \in \mathbb{Z}$ such that $A, B \notin \mathcal{Z}$, there exists a path from A to B that does not have any vertex from $\mathcal{Z}$.*
2. *There do not exist sets of parties $\mathcal{Z}_A, \mathcal{Z}_B \in \mathbb{Z}$ such that $A \in \mathcal{Z}_A$, $B \notin \mathcal{Z}_A$, $B \in \mathcal{Z}_B$, $A \notin \mathcal{Z}_B$, and*

$$\Gamma_B(\mathcal{Z}_A) \cup \Gamma_A(\mathcal{Z}_B) = \mathcal{V}.$$

Moreover, when these conditions are satisfied and $|\mathbb{Z}| = \mathsf{poly}(n)$, there is an efficient ($\mathsf{poly}(n)$ complexity) protocol to compute OT securely.

Standard results [18,19] imply that if every pair in a set of vertices can realize oblivious transfer with security w.r.t. $\mathbb{Z}$, then these vertices can compute any functionality with security w.r.t. $\mathbb{Z}$.

Corollary 1. *Given a graph $G(\mathcal{V}, \mathcal{E})$ and a subset of vertices $\mathcal{K} \subseteq \mathcal{V}$, any functionality can be computed among the vertices in $\mathcal{K}$ with perfect security with respect to a semi-honest adversary structure $\mathbb{Z}$ if and only if the conditions in Theorem 1 are satisfied by every pair of vertices in $\mathcal{K}$.*

Please refer to the full version [33] for a proof. When G is complete, $\Gamma_u(\mathcal{Z}) = \mathcal{Z}$ whenever $u \notin Z \subset \mathcal{V}$. Hence, when $\mathcal{K} = \mathcal{V}$, the condition in Corollary 1 is equivalent to non-existence of sets $\mathcal{Z}_1, \mathcal{Z}_2 \in \mathbb{Z}$ such that $\mathcal{Z}_1 \cup \mathcal{Z}_2 = \mathcal{V}$. Thus, for this case, we retrieve the $\mathcal{Q}^2$ condition of Hirt and Maurer [24].

While the focus of this paper is on deriving tight necessary and sufficient conditions on the network which permit information theoretically secure computation, we consider efficiency in two regimes for t-privacy (i.e., semi-honest adversary structures of the form $\mathbb{Z}^t := \{\mathcal{Z} \subset \mathcal{V} : |\mathcal{Z}| \leq t\}$). Theorem 1 already gives an efficient protocol for $t = O(1)$. We separately consider the case of $n = 2t + O(1)$ and give an efficient protocol in this setting as well (when the conditions of Theorem 1 are satisfied). The case of other regimes of t remains open.

The following is our result for the malicious case:

Theorem 2. *Two vertices A, B in $G(\mathcal{V}, \mathcal{E})$ can realize OT with statistical security (with guaranteed output delivery) against an adversary structure $\mathbb{Z}$ in the malicious static adversary setting if and only if the following conditions are satisfied:*

1. *For every $\mathcal{Z}_1, \mathcal{Z}_2 \in \mathbb{Z}$ such that $A, B \notin \mathcal{Z}_1 \cup \mathcal{Z}_2$, there exists a path from A to B that does not have any vertex from $\mathcal{Z}_1 \cup \mathcal{Z}_2$.*

2. *There do not exist* $\mathcal{Z}_A, \mathcal{Z}_B, \mathcal{Z} \in \mathbb{Z}$ *such that* $A \in \mathcal{Z}_A$, $B \notin \mathcal{Z}_A$, $B \in \mathcal{Z}_B$, $A \notin \mathcal{Z}_B$, $A, B \notin \mathcal{Z}$, *and*

$$\Gamma_B(\mathcal{Z}_A \cup \mathcal{Z}) \cup \Gamma_A(\mathcal{Z}_B \cup \mathcal{Z}) = \mathcal{V}.$$

Moreover, when these conditions are satisfied and $|\mathbb{Z}| = \mathsf{poly}(n)$, *there is an efficient* ($\mathsf{poly}(n)$ *complexity) protocol to compute OT securely.*

This characterization can be easily extended to 2-party functionalities with output only at one party since standard results [27] allow reduction of such functionalities to establishing OT between the parties. Unlike in the semi-honest case, the availability of secure OT between every pair of parties does not directly imply that any functionality may be computed securely in the malicious case. Hence, we have a more modest implication in this case using standard results in [11,20] and [25].

Corollary 2. *Consider a graph* $G(\mathcal{V}, \mathcal{E})$, *a subset of vertices* $\mathcal{K} \subseteq \mathcal{V}$ *and a malicious adversary structure* $\mathbb{Z}$.

1. *The vertices in* $\mathcal{K}$ *can statistically securely compute any functionality w.r.t.* $\mathbb{Z}$ *only if every pair of vertices in* $\mathcal{K}$ *satisfies the conditions in Theorem 2.*
2. *The vertices in* $\mathcal{K}$ *can statistically securely compute any functionality* with abort and no fairness *w.r.t.* $\mathbb{Z}$ *if every pair of vertices in* $\mathcal{K}$ *satisfies the conditions in Theorem 2.*

Please refer to the full version [33] for a proof. When G is complete and $\mathcal{K} = \mathcal{V}$, we indeed recover the $\mathcal{Q}^3$ condition of Hirt and Maurer [24]. Note that, for this case, [24] shows that $\mathcal{Q}^3$ condition is sufficient to achieve perfect security.

1.2 Technical Overview

We now give a quick overview of the technical details of our results.

Necessity of Conditions: Semi-honest Case. The first condition in Theorem 1 is simply the necessary (and sufficient) condition for SMT between A and B in the semi-honest setting. To show the necessity of the second condition, we observe that security w.r.t. the adversary structure $\{\mathcal{Z}_A, \mathcal{Z}_B\}$ implies security w.r.t. $\{\Gamma_B(\mathcal{Z}_A), \Gamma_A(\mathcal{Z}_B)\}$, i.e., we may throw into $\mathcal{Z}_A$ those vertices which it blocks from reaching B, and, similarly, for $\mathcal{Z}_B$ and A. Our condition simply says that this should not be a $\mathcal{Q}^2$ adversary structure [24].

Sufficiency of Conditions: Semi-honest Case. To show the sufficiency of these conditions, we first observe (Lemma 1) that if one could find a vertex C which cannot be blocked from an honest A or B, then C can provide A and B with precomputed OT through SMT channels. But, in general, the conditions in Theorem 1 do not guarantee that such a C exists. Our approach is to find a set of such C's such that a majority of them will work against each member of the adversary structure. This will allow us to employ the idea of *OT combiner* [22, 23, 32, 39] to obtain one protocol which is secure w.r.t. the adversary structure. The bulk of our proof is in showing that there is a set of such C's. In fact, we do this for a special class of adversary structures (Lemma 3) – those with only one member which contains A (B, respectively). We show that, in this case, the vertices C of interest are precisely those that are not blocked from B (A, respectively) the unique member of the adversary structure which contains A (B, respectively). We then obtain a protocol for OT in the general case by employing the idea of OT combiner again, this time on the protocols constructed for the special class of adversary structures above.

Efficiency of t-privacy. Our protocol has complexity which is polynomial in the size of the graph and the size of the adversary structure. So, it is efficient for t-privacy when $t = O(1)$. We also give a t-private protocol which is efficient when $n = 2t+O(1)$. For this, we first consider adversary structures where all the members which contain A (B, respectively) block the same set of vertices. We show that for such an adversary structure, using OT combiner, we may construct an efficient protocol for OT. We show that, similar to the construction in the general case, we may combine these protocols to get a t-private OT protocol. If $n = 2t + O(1)$, the number of such adversary structures is polynomial in n, thereby making the combiner efficient.

Necessity of Conditions: Malicious Case. The first condition of Theorem 2 is just the necessary (and sufficient) condition for SMT between A and B in the malicious setting. We show the necessity of the second condition by reducing the problem to the case of an OT in a specific graph and showing that such an OT cannot be computed securely in that graph using arguments similar to the proof of impossibility of Byzantine agreement by Fischer *et al.* in [15]. For ease of exposition, in Sect. 3, we consider a special case (the general case is proved in the full version [33] along similar lines), which we reduce to the case of the graph H_{OT} in Fig. 2 (Lemma 6). To show that A and B cannot compute OT in H_{OT} securely w.r.t. the malicious adversary structure $\{\{C\}, \{A, D\}, \{B, D\}\}$, we

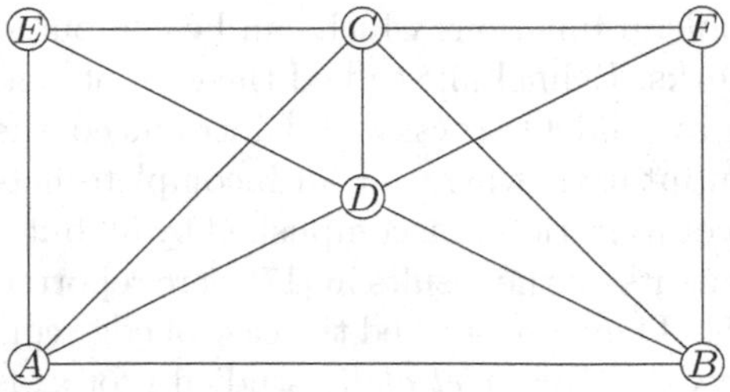

Fig. 2. H_{OT}: OT between A and B is not possible with security against the malicious adversary structure $\{\{C\}, \{A, D\}$ and $\{B, D\}\}$.

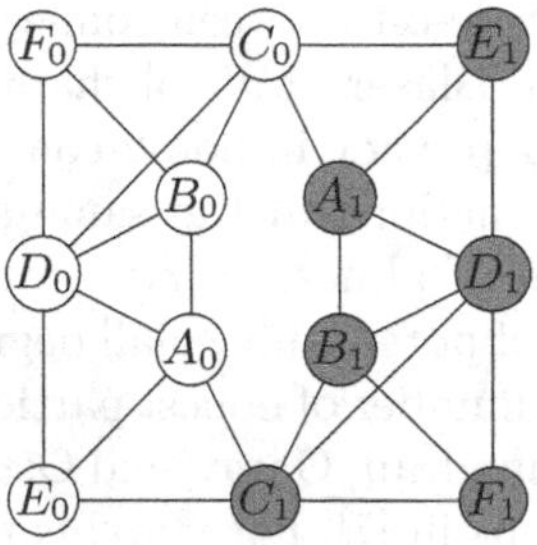

Fig. 3. S_{OT}: constructed by interconnecting two copies of H_{OT}.

interconnect two copies of H_{OT} (see Fig. 3) and consider (a pair of) executions of a purported OT protocol to argue that this would give a secure two-party OT protocol in the semi-honest setting (Lemma 5).

Sufficiency of Conditions: Malicious Case. To show the sufficiency of these conditions, we proceed along the lines of the semi-honest case. But here, we construct a separate OT protocol corresponding to each set in the adversary structure which does not contain either A or B. The parties in this set do not participate in the protocol thereby ensuring that it is perfectly secure against their corruption. However, the corruption of any other set in the adversary structure may force this protocol to abort. But, if the protocol does not abort, it is guaranteed to compute OT with statistical security w.r.t $\mathbb{Z}$. Our final protocol iterates over every protocol of this kind. If the OT is computed in any iteration, it is guaranteed to be statistically secure. If every iteration is aborted, either A or B is corrupt, in which case, a honest B may output a random bit.

1.3 Related Work

Secure multiparty computation in complete networks is addressed in a large body of literature. Ben-Or, Goldwasser, and Wigderson [4] and Chaum, Crépeau, and Damgård [9] showed that every function can be computed with perfect information theoretic security against a semi-honest adversary whenever there is an honest majority; and against a malicious adversary if more than two-third of the parties are honest. Hirt and Maurer [24] extended these results and characterized adversary structures, in both semi-honest and malicious settings, that allow perfectly secure computation. Keeping these results in view, our problem formulation is a natural one. However, to the best of our knowledge, there is no prior work on the characterization problem we address even in restricted settings of graph topologies other than the complete graph. We list below the works in the literature that come closest to our problem.

Franklin and Yung [16] studied private message exchange in incomplete networks of hypergraph communication channels with the goal of performing secure computation over such networks. Jakoby, Liśkiewicz, and Reischuk [26] studied the trade-off between connectivity and randomness required for private computation. Bläser *et al.* [6] characterized Boolean functions which can be computed with 1-privacy in non-2-connected networks. Beimel [3] studied the case of general functions in the same setting. Garay and Ostrovsky [17] introduced the notion of almost-everywhere secure computation where, in an incomplete network of potentially small degree, secure computation is accomplished by all but a small number of honest parties. Improvements on the results in [17] were reported by Chandran, Garay, and Ostrovsky in [8]. They also studied the case of edge corruptions in [7]. For non-2-connected networks, Bläser *et al.* [5] studied protocols that provide a relaxed notion of privacy for functions that cannot be privately computed in an incomplete network. Harnik, Ishai, and Kushilevitz [22] and Kumaresan, Raghuraman, and Sealfon [29] characterized incomplete networks of OT channels which, when used along with a *complete* pairwise communication network, allow t-secure computation. Halevi *et al.* [21] studied notions of security in multiparty computation with restricted interaction patterns.

Privacy and reliability of communication over incomplete networks has been extensively studied. The problems of reliable and private message transmission have been studied for threshold adversary structures [1,12,13,30,34–37] and for arbitrary adversary structures [28]. The problem of Byzantine agreement was studied in [12,14,15,31,38].

2 Semi-honest Case

In this section we prove Theorem 1. We start with some notation and definitions which will be used throughout the sequel. We define the following subclasses of an adversary structure $\mathbb{Z}$.

$$\begin{aligned} \mathbb{Z}_A &:= \{\mathcal{Z} \in \mathbb{Z} \mid A \in \mathcal{Z}\}, \\ \mathbb{Z}_B &:= \{\mathcal{Z} \in \mathbb{Z} \mid B \in \mathcal{Z}\}, \\ \mathbb{Z}_{\neg A \neg B} &:= \{\mathcal{Z} \in \mathbb{Z} \mid A, B \notin \mathcal{Z}\}. \end{aligned}$$

Clearly if $\mathcal{Z} \in \mathbb{Z}_A \cup \mathbb{Z}_B$, then it cannot be in $\mathbb{Z}_{\neg A \neg B}$ by definition. If $\mathcal{Z} \in \mathbb{Z}_A \cap \mathbb{Z}_B$, then $A, B \in \mathcal{Z}$, but any protocol is trivially secure against the corruption of such a set since only A and B have inputs and outputs. Hence, without loss of generality, we consider only adversary structures $\mathbb{Z}$ that do not contain such sets. Thus, $\mathbb{Z}_A, \mathbb{Z}_B$, and $\mathbb{Z}_{\neg A \neg B}$ form a partition of $\mathbb{Z}$.

Definition 1. *Given a pair of vertices $u, v \in \mathcal{V}$ in an undirected graph $G(\mathcal{V}, \mathcal{E})$, a* ***path*** *from u to v is a sequence of distinct vertices such that u is the first vertex and v is the last vertex and there is an edge between every pair of consecutive vertices. The length-one sequence u is a path from u to u.*

Definition 2. *Given a vertex $u \in \mathcal{V}$ and a subset of vertices $\mathcal{Z} \subseteq \mathcal{V}$, we define* ***$u$-blocked vertices of $\mathcal{Z}$*** *as the set of vertices whose every path to u includes some vertex in $\mathcal{Z}$. We denote this set by $\Gamma_u(\mathcal{Z})$.*

$$\Gamma_u(\mathcal{Z}) := \{v \in \mathcal{V} \mid \textit{every path from } v \textit{ to } u \textit{ has a vertex from } \mathcal{Z}\}.$$

2.1 Necessity of Conditions

Necessity of the First Condition. Secure OT can be used for secure communication, i.e., secure message transmission (SMT). So a necessary condition for SMT is also a necessary condition for OT. SMT between A and B is possible (if and) only if for every $\mathcal{Z} \in \mathbb{Z}_{\neg A \neg B}$ there is a path from A to B that has no vertex from $\mathcal{Z}$ [13]. Hence, OT between A and B with security w.r.t. $\mathbb{Z}$ is possible only if the first condition in Theorem 1 is satisfied.

Necessity of the Second Condition. We show that if the second condition in Theorem 1 is not satisfied, a protocol that can realize OT between A and B would imply a 2-party OT protocol. The necessity then follows from the impossibility of 2-party OT. Suppose the second condition is not satisfied, then there are $\mathcal{Z}_A \in \mathbb{Z}_A$ and $\mathcal{Z}_B \in \mathbb{Z}_B$ such that $\Gamma_B(\mathcal{Z}_A) \cup \Gamma_A(\mathcal{Z}_B) = \mathcal{V}$. Let Π be an OT protocol that is secure against the corruption of $\mathcal{Z}_A$ and $\mathcal{Z}_B$.

Claim 1. Π is secure against the corruption of $\Gamma_B(\mathcal{Z}_A)$ and of $\Gamma_A(\mathcal{Z}_B)$.

Proof. We prove that Π is secure against the corruption of $\Gamma_B(\mathcal{Z}_A)$, the other case can be proved in a similar manner. Let u be a vertex in $\Gamma_B(\mathcal{Z}_A) \setminus \mathcal{Z}_A$ and v be any vertex outside $\Gamma_B(\mathcal{Z}_A)$. By the definition of B-blocked vertices of $\mathcal{Z}_A$ (*i.e.*, $\Gamma_B(\mathcal{Z}_A)$), every path from u to B has a vertex from $\mathcal{Z}_A$ and v has a path to B that has no vertex from $\mathcal{Z}_A$. Hence, every path from u to v must have a vertex from $\mathcal{Z}_A$. Also, no vertex in $\Gamma_B(\mathcal{Z}_A) \setminus \mathcal{Z}_A$ has inputs since $A \in \mathcal{Z}_A$ and $B \notin \Gamma_B(\mathcal{Z}_A)$. Hence we may conclude that the vertices in $\Gamma_B(\mathcal{Z}_A) \setminus \mathcal{Z}_A$ do not have inputs or outputs and are separated from $\mathcal{V} \setminus \Gamma_B(\mathcal{Z}_A)$ by $\mathcal{Z}_A$. Consequently, the *view* of $\Gamma_B(\mathcal{Z}_A) \setminus \mathcal{Z}_A$ may be simulated by $\mathcal{Z}_A$. Since Π is secure against the corruption of $\mathcal{Z}_A$, it must also be secure against the corruption of $\Gamma_B(\mathcal{Z}_A)$. □

Now consider three parties $\mathcal{P}_1, \mathcal{P}_2$, and $\mathcal{P}_3$. Let $\mathcal{P}_3$ simulate vertices in the set $\mathcal{Z} := \Gamma_B(\mathcal{Z}_A) \cap \Gamma_A(\mathcal{Z}_B)$ and $\mathcal{P}_1$ and $\mathcal{P}_2$ simulate $\Gamma_B(\mathcal{Z}_A) \setminus \mathcal{Z}$ and $\Gamma_A(\mathcal{Z}_B) \setminus \mathcal{Z}$ respectively. By Claim 1, there is a 3-party protocol Π_3 that computes OT between $\mathcal{P}_1$ and $\mathcal{P}_2$ that is secure against the corruption of $\{\mathcal{P}_1, \mathcal{P}_3\}$ and that of $\{\mathcal{P}_2, \mathcal{P}_3\}$. Since $\mathcal{P}_3$ does not have any input, Π_3 is also secure against the corruption of $\{\mathcal{P}_1\}$ (and $\{\mathcal{P}_2\}$); see [22, Lemma 2]. From Π_3 we can get a 2-party OT protocol Π_2 by letting one party simulate $\mathcal{P}_1$ and the other party simulate $\{\mathcal{P}_2, \mathcal{P}_3\}$ (see [22, Sect. 3.2]), yielding a contradiction.

2.2 Sufficiency of Conditions

Next, we construct a protocol Π_{sh} for OT between A and B that is secure w.r.t. an adversary structure $\mathbb{Z}$ if the conditions in Theorem 1 are met. If the size of $\mathbb{Z}$ is polynomial in n, the Π_{sh} constructed is efficient. We first consider a few special cases that will lead us up to the general case.

For the complete graph on 3 vertices A, B, C, 1-secure OT between A and B can be realized as follows: Vertex C samples a *precomputed OT* uniformly at random and sends it privately to A and B, who use this to securely realize OT [2]. i.e., C samples independent, uniform bits r_0, r_1, c and then sends (r_0, r_1) to A and (c, r_c) to B privately. B sends to A the sum $u := b \oplus c$ of its input b with c, where $\oplus$ denotes addition in the binary field. Let (x_0, x_1) be the input to A, then A replies with $(y_0, y_1) := (x_0 \oplus r_u, x_1 \oplus r_{1 \oplus u})$. B reconstructs x_b as $y_b \oplus r_c$.

We first generalize the above protocol to networks and adversary structures where we can find a node C which can not be corrupted together with A or B, and such that it can communicate to A with privacy against $\mathbb{Z}_B$ and to B with privacy against $\mathbb{Z}_A$.

Lemma 1. *Consider $G(\mathcal{V}, \mathcal{E})$ with vertices $A, B \in \mathcal{V}$ and a semi-honest adversary structure $\mathbb{Z}$ that satisfy the conditions in Theorem 1. Suppose there exists a vertex C such that*

(i) $\forall \mathcal{Z}_A \in \mathbb{Z}_A, C \notin \Gamma_B(\mathcal{Z}_A)$, and
(ii) $\forall \mathcal{Z}_B \in \mathbb{Z}_B, C \notin \Gamma_A(\mathcal{Z}_B)$.

Then, there is an efficient protocol Π^C for securely computing OT between A and B.

The protocol Π^C involves C sending precomputed OT to A and B using SMT. A and B use it to carry out OT by using the standard protocol from [2] mentioned above. In carrying out the OT, A and B communicate with each other using SMT; something which the first condition of Theorem 1 guarantees is possible. The conditions in the lemma ensure that if C is corrupt, A and B must be honest and, since they carry out OT over SMT, they have privacy. If A is corrupt, the conditions in the lemma guarantee that both C and B are honest, and have a path of honest vertices between them ensuring the privacy of SMT from C to B used to deliver the precomputed OT. The privacy of B's input then follows. A similar argument can be made for the case when B is corrupt. The full proof, which includes a formal description of Π^C, is deferred to the full version [33]. Note that A is a valid candidate for the choice of C in Lemma 1 if (and only if) $\mathbb{Z}_A$ is empty, i.e., A is honest. Similarly, B is a valid choice if and only if $\mathbb{Z}_B$ is empty, i.e., B is honest. The protocols, Π^A and Π^B, for these cases will play a role in the sequel.

In general, the conditions in Theorem 1 do not imply the existence of a vertex C that satisfies the conditions in Lemma 1. Our approach is to next consider several protocols of the kind used in the proof of this lemma, each corresponding to a potentially different choice of C. In general, no such protocol on its own may be secure against the corruption of each set in $\mathbb{Z}$. We invoke the idea of *OT combiner* [22,23,32,39] to obtain one protocol which is secure w.r.t. $\mathbb{Z}$. An OT combiner is a compiler of OT protocols which produces one OT protocol which is secure w.r.t. $\mathbb{Z}$ by 'combining' many OT protocols, none of which is secure against the corruption of every set in $\mathbb{Z}$.

Lemma 2 [22,23,32,39]
Let $\Pi_1, \ldots, \Pi_m$ be m protocols for OT between A and B, such that against the passive corruption of every $\mathcal{Z} \in \mathbb{Z}$, a majority of $\Pi_1, \ldots, \Pi_m$ is secure. Then, there exists a protocol Combiner$(\Pi_1, \ldots, \Pi_m)$ *for OT between A and B which is secure w.r.t. the semi-honest adversary structure $\mathbb{Z}$. Moreover, this protocol is efficient if m is polynomial in n, and Π_i is efficient for each $i \in [m]$.*

We proceed in two steps. We first consider adversary structures $\mathbb{Z}$ such that $\mathbb{Z}_A$ (or $\mathbb{Z}_B$) is a singleton set. Specifically, we first prove our result for adversary structure $\mathbb{Z} = \{\mathcal{Z}_A\} \cup \mathbb{Z}_B \cup \mathbb{Z}_{\neg A \neg B}$ where $\mathcal{Z}_A$ is such that $A \in \mathcal{Z}_A$; similarly, we consider $\mathbb{Z} = \{\mathcal{Z}_B\} \cup \mathbb{Z}_A \cup \mathbb{Z}_{\neg A \neg B}$, where $\mathcal{Z}_B$ is such that $B \in \mathcal{Z}_B$. We will later use this to prove our general result.

Lemma 3. *Consider $G(\mathcal{V}, \mathcal{E})$ with vertices $A, B \in \mathcal{V}$ and a semi-honest adversary structure $\mathbb{Z} = \{\mathcal{Z}_A\} \cup \mathbb{Z}_B \cup \mathbb{Z}_{\neg A \neg B}$, where $A \in \mathcal{Z}_A$, ($\mathbb{Z} = \{\mathcal{Z}_B\} \cup \mathbb{Z}_A \cup \mathbb{Z}_{\neg A \neg B}$, $B \in \mathcal{Z}_B$, respectively) that satisfy the conditions in Theorem 1. There is an efficient protocol $\Pi^{\mathcal{Z}_A}$ ($\Pi^{\mathcal{Z}_B}$, respectively) that securely realizes OT between A and B.*

Before we present the construction of the protocols, we make the following claims.

Claim 2. For every $C \notin \Gamma_B(\mathcal{Z}_A)$, the protocol Π^C is secure w.r.t. $\{\mathcal{Z}_A\} \cup \mathbb{Z}_{\neg A \neg B}$.

Proof. If $C \notin \Gamma_B(\mathcal{Z}_A)$, then C satisfies both the conditions in Lemma 1 for the adversary structure $\{\mathcal{Z}_A\} \cup \mathbb{Z}_{\neg A \neg B}$. This proves the claim. □

Claim 3. Let $\mathcal{Z}'_B \in \mathbb{Z}_B$, then there exists $C \notin \Gamma_B(\mathcal{Z}_A) \cup \Gamma_A(\mathcal{Z}'_B)$. The protocol Π^C is secure w.r.t. $\{\mathcal{Z}_A\} \cup \mathbb{Z}_{\neg A \neg B} \cup \{\mathcal{Z}'_B\}$.

Proof. If there exists a $C \notin \Gamma_B(\mathcal{Z}_A) \cup \Gamma_A(\mathcal{Z}'_B)$, then C satisfies both the conditions in Lemma 1 for the adversary structure $\{\mathcal{Z}_A\} \cup \mathbb{Z}_{\neg A \neg B} \cup \{\mathcal{Z}'_B\}$ and second part of the claim follows. Such a C must exist, since $\Gamma_B(\mathcal{Z}_A) \cup \Gamma_A(\mathcal{Z}'_B) \neq \mathcal{V}$ by the second condition in Theorem 1. □

Similar claims can be made regarding the adversary structure $\{\mathcal{Z}_B\} \cup \mathbb{Z}_A \cup \mathbb{Z}_{\neg A \neg B}$, and the proof for these claims are similar.

Claims 2 and 3 directly imply the following observations. For $\mathcal{Z}_A \in \mathbb{Z}_A$, let $\mathcal{V} \setminus \Gamma_B(\mathcal{Z}_A) = \{C^1, \ldots, C^{k_A}\}$. Note that $\mathcal{V} \setminus \Gamma_B(\mathcal{Z}_A)$ is non-empty since $B \notin \Gamma_B(\mathcal{Z}_A)$. Then, by Claim 2, Π^{C^i} is secure w.r.t. $\{\mathcal{Z}_A\} \cup \mathbb{Z}_{\neg A \neg B}$ for all $i \in [k_A]$. By Claim 3, for each $\mathcal{Z}'_B \in \mathbb{Z}_B$, there exists $i \in [k_A]$ such that Π^{C^i} is secure w.r.t. $\{\mathcal{Z}_A\} \cup \mathbb{Z}_{\neg A \neg B} \cup \{\mathcal{Z}'_B\}$. Similarly, for $\mathcal{Z}_B \in \mathbb{Z}_B$, let $\mathcal{V} \setminus \Gamma_A(\mathcal{Z}_B) = \{C^1, \ldots, C^{k_B}\}$. Then Π^{C^i} is secure w.r.t. $\{\mathcal{Z}_B\} \cup \mathbb{Z}_{\neg A \neg B}$ for all $i \in [k_B]$. For each, $\mathcal{Z}'_A \in \mathbb{Z}_A$ there exists $i \in [k_B]$ such that Π^{C^i} is secure w.r.t. $\{\mathcal{Z}'_A\} \cup \mathbb{Z}_{\neg A \neg B} \cup \{\mathcal{Z}_B\}$.

Proof (Proof of Lemma 3)

Consider a collection of protocols $\Pi_1, \ldots \Pi_{2k_A-1}$, where $\Pi_i := \Pi^{C^i}$ for $i \in [k_A]$ and $\Pi_i := \Pi^A$ for $i = k_A + 1, \ldots, 2k_A - 1$. We construct the protocol $\Pi^{\mathcal{Z}_A}$ as $\mathsf{Combiner}(\Pi_1, \ldots, \Pi_{2k_A-1})$. Since $\Pi_1, \ldots \Pi_{2k_A-1}$ are protocols for OT between A and B, this is a valid combiner. As we argued above, $\Pi_1, \ldots, \Pi_{k_A}$ $(= \Pi^{C^1}, \ldots, \Pi^{C^{k_A}})$ are secure w.r.t. $\{\mathcal{Z}_A\} \cup \mathbb{Z}_{\neg A \neg B}$. Hence a majority of the protocols (k_A out of $2k_A - 1$ protocols) used in the combiner is secure w.r.t. $\{\mathcal{Z}_A\} \cup \mathbb{Z}_{\neg A \neg B}$. The security of $\Pi^{\mathcal{Z}_A}$ w.r.t. $\{\mathcal{Z}_A\} \cup \mathbb{Z}_{\neg A \neg B}$ now follows from Lemma 2. Consider the corruption of any $\mathcal{Z}'_B \in \mathbb{Z}_B$. Since A is honest (i.e., $A \notin \mathcal{Z}'_B$), the $k_A - 1$ copies of Π^A used in the combiner are secure against the corruption of $\mathcal{Z}'_B$. As we previously observed, for each $\mathcal{Z}'_B \in \mathbb{Z}_B$, at least one of the protocols $\Pi_1, \ldots, \Pi_{k_A}$ is secure against the corruption of $\mathcal{Z}'_B$. Hence, at least k_A protocols used in the combiner are secure against the corruption of each $\mathcal{Z}'_B \in \mathbb{Z}_B$. From Lemma 2, it follows that $\Pi^{\mathcal{Z}_A}$ is secure w.r.t. $\mathbb{Z}_B$ and hence against $\{\mathcal{Z}_A\} \cup \mathbb{Z}_{\neg A \neg B} \cup \mathbb{Z}_B$. Observe that $\Pi^{\mathcal{Z}_A}$ is a combiner of $2k_A - 1 < 2n$

protocols of the kind Π^C. Since, by Lemma 1, each of these protocols is efficient, $\Pi^{\mathcal{Z}_A}$ is efficient according to Lemma 2.

Similarly, the protocol $\Pi^{\mathcal{Z}_B} := \mathsf{Combiner}(\Pi_1, \ldots \Pi_{2k_B-1})$, where $\Pi_i := \Pi^{C^i}$ for $i \in [k_B]$ and $\Pi_i := \Pi^B$ for $i = k_B + 1, \ldots, 2k_B - 1$ will efficiently realize OT between A and B with security w.r.t. $\{\mathcal{Z}_B\} \cup \mathbb{Z}_{\neg A \neg B} \cup \mathbb{Z}_A$. □

We are finally ready to prove Theorem 1. The idea is to combine protocols of the kind $\Pi^{\mathcal{Z}_A}, \mathcal{Z}_A \in \mathbb{Z}_A$ and $\Pi^{\mathcal{Z}_B}, \mathcal{Z}_B \in \mathbb{Z}_B$ in a way such that a majority of these protocols is secure against the corruption of every set of vertices in $\mathbb{Z}$.

Proof (Proof of Theorem 1). If the adversary structure $\mathbb{Z}$ is such that $\mathbb{Z}_A$ ($\mathbb{Z}_B$), respectively) is empty then, we have already seen that Π^A (Π^B, respectively) is secure w.r.t. $\mathbb{Z}$. So, let $\mathbb{Z}_A = \{\mathcal{Z}_A^1, \ldots, \mathcal{Z}_A^{\ell_A}\}$ and $\mathbb{Z}_B = \{\mathcal{Z}_B^1, \ldots, \mathcal{Z}_B^{\ell_B}\}$. We consider the following pairs of protocols.

$$(\Pi_{1,1}, \Pi_{1,2}), \ldots, (\Pi_{\ell_A,1}, \Pi_{\ell_A,2}), (\Pi_{\ell_A+1,1}, \Pi_{\ell_A+1,2}), \ldots, (\Pi_{\ell_A+\ell_B,1}, \Pi_{\ell_A+\ell_B,2}),$$

where

$$(\Pi_{i,1}, \Pi_{i,2}) := (\Pi^{\mathcal{Z}_A^i}, \Pi^B), \text{ for } 1 \leq i \leq \ell_A, \tag{1}$$

$$(\Pi_{\ell_A+i,1}, \Pi_{\ell_A+i,2}) := (\Pi^{\mathcal{Z}_B^i}, \Pi^A), \text{ for } 1 \leq i \leq \ell_B. \tag{2}$$

Let $\Pi_{\mathsf{sh}} := \mathsf{Combiner}((\Pi_{1,1}, \Pi_{1,2}) \ldots, (\Pi_{\ell_A+\ell_B,1}, \Pi_{\ell_A+\ell_B,2}))$. All the protocols used in the combiner realize OT between A and B, hence the combiner is valid. For all $\mathcal{Z}_A \in \mathbb{Z}_A$ and $\mathcal{Z}_B \in \mathbb{Z}_B$, $\Pi^{\mathcal{Z}_A}$ and $\Pi^{\mathcal{Z}_B}$ are secure w.r.t. $\mathbb{Z}_{\neg A \neg B}$ by Lemma 3. Π^A and Π^B are also secure w.r.t. $\mathbb{Z}_{\neg A \neg B}$. Therefore, by Lemma 2, Π_{sh} is secure w.r.t. $\mathbb{Z}_{\neg A \neg B}$. The essential idea for the proof of security of Π_{sh} w.r.t. $\mathbb{Z}_A \cup \mathbb{Z}_B$ is the fact that for each $\mathcal{Z} \in \mathbb{Z}_A \cup \mathbb{Z}_B$, both protocols in the pair corresponding to $\mathcal{Z}$ are secure against the corruption of $\mathcal{Z}$ and at least one protocol from every other pair is also secure against the corruption of $\mathcal{Z}$. Hence, a majority of protocols used in the combiner is secure against the corruption of $\mathcal{Z}$.

Formally, let $\mathcal{Z}_A^j$ be any set in $\mathbb{Z}_A$. Note that $(\Pi_{j,1}, \Pi_{j,2}) = (\Pi^{\mathcal{Z}_A^j}, \Pi^B)$. By Lemma 3, $\Pi^{\mathcal{Z}_A^j}$ is secure against the corruption of $\mathcal{Z}_A^j$. Also, Π^B is secure against the corruption of $\mathcal{Z}_A^j$ since $B \notin \mathcal{Z}_A^j$. Hence, the pair of protocols $(\Pi_{j,1}, \Pi_{j,2})$ is secure against the corruption of $\mathcal{Z}_A^j$. Among the other pairs, for $1 \leq i \leq \ell_A$, the protocols $\Pi_{i,2}$ are copies of Π^B and hence, secure against the corruption of $\mathcal{Z}_A^j$. For the remaining pairs, note that $\Pi_{\ell_A+i,1} = \Pi^{\mathcal{Z}_B^i}, 1 \leq i \leq \ell_B$ are also secure against the corruption of $\mathcal{Z}_A^j$ by Lemma 3. Thus, at least $\ell_A + \ell_B + 1$ protocols (among $2(\ell_A + \ell_B)$) protocols used in the combiner are secure against the corruption of $\mathcal{Z}_A^j$. Hence, by Lemma 2, Π_{sh} is secure against the corruption of this set. This proves that the protocol Π_{sh} is secure w.r.t. $\mathbb{Z}_A$. The proof of security against $\mathbb{Z}_B$ is similar.

If the size of $\mathbb{Z}_A \cup \mathbb{Z}_B$ is polynomial in n, Π_{sh} is a combiner of $\mathsf{poly}(n)$ protocols, each of which is efficient by Lemma 3. Hence, in this case Π_{sh} is efficient by Lemma 2. □

2.3 Efficiency of t-privacy

A protocol is said to be *t-private* if it is secure w.r.t. the semi-honest adversary structure $\mathbb{Z}^t := \{\mathcal{Z} \subseteq \mathcal{V} : |\mathcal{Z}| \leq t\}$. Without loss of generality, we restrict our attention to $t < n/2$ since OT cannot be computed with $\lceil n/2 \rceil$-privacy even in a complete graph [4,9]. We have the following result:

Theorem 3. *Given a communication graph $G(\mathcal{V}, \mathcal{E})$, vertices $A, B \in \mathcal{V}$ can compute OT with perfect t-privacy if and only if the following conditions are satisfied:*

1. *There exists an edge or at least $t+1$ vertex disjoint paths between A and B.*
2. *There do not exist $\mathcal{Z}_A, \mathcal{Z}_B \subset \mathcal{V}$ of size at most t such that $A \in \mathcal{Z}_A, B \notin \mathcal{Z}_A, A \notin \mathcal{Z}_B, B \in \mathcal{Z}_B$, and $\Gamma_B(\mathcal{Z}_A) \cup \Gamma_A(\mathcal{Z}_B) = \mathcal{V}$.*

Moreover, this can be performed using an efficient protocol if $t = O(1)$ or $n = 2t + O(1)$.

The conditions 1 and 2 above are just restatements of the conditions in Theorem 1 for $\mathbb{Z}^t$. The efficiency when $t = O(1)$ follows from Theorem 1 as the size of the adversary structure in this case is $\mathsf{poly}(n)$. It only remains to construct an efficient t-private OT protocol for the case of $n = 2t + O(1)$. As in Sect. 2.2, we first consider certain specific adversary structures and construct efficient protocols for these. We will then use these protocols to construct protocols for the general case. For a set $\mathcal{S} \subseteq \mathcal{V}$, let

$$\mathbb{Z}^t_A(\mathcal{S}) := \{\mathcal{Z}_A \in \mathbb{Z}^t_A \mid \Gamma_B(\mathcal{Z}_A) \setminus \mathcal{Z}_A = \mathcal{S}\}, \text{ where } \mathbb{Z}^t_A := \{\mathcal{Z}_A \in \mathbb{Z}^t \mid A \in \mathcal{Z}_A\},$$
$$\mathbb{Z}^t_B(\mathcal{S}) := \{\mathcal{Z}_B \in \mathbb{Z}^t_B \mid \Gamma_A(\mathcal{Z}_B) \setminus \mathcal{Z}_B = \mathcal{S}\}, \text{ where } \mathbb{Z}^t_B := \{\mathcal{Z}_B \in \mathbb{Z}^t \mid B \in \mathcal{Z}_B\}.$$

To interpret this, $\mathbb{Z}^t_A(\mathcal{S})$ are sets containing A and of size at most t (i.e., they can be corrupted) such that the set of additional vertices they block off from reaching B is precisely $\mathcal{S}$. Loosely, $\mathcal{S}$ is the "shadow" of sets in $\mathbb{Z}^t_A(\mathcal{S})$. Now we define the collections of such "shadow" sets.

$$\mathbb{S}^t_A := \{\mathcal{S} \subseteq \mathcal{V} \mid \mathbb{Z}^t_A(\mathcal{S}) \neq \emptyset\}, \qquad \text{and} \qquad \mathbb{S}^t_B := \{\mathcal{S} \subseteq \mathcal{V} \mid \mathbb{Z}^t_B(\mathcal{S}) \neq \emptyset\}.$$

It is clear that $\mathbb{Z}^t_A = \cup_{\mathcal{S}_A \in \mathbb{S}^t_A} \mathbb{Z}^t_A(\mathcal{S}_A)$ and $\mathbb{Z}^t_B = \cup_{\mathcal{S}_B \in \mathbb{S}^t_B} \mathbb{Z}^t_B(\mathcal{S}_B)$.

Claim 4. Let $k = n - 2t$. $|\mathcal{S}_A| < k$ for all $\mathcal{S}_A \in \mathbb{S}^t_A$, and $|\mathcal{S}_B| < k$ for all $\mathcal{S}_B \in \mathbb{S}^t_B$. Sizes of $\mathbb{S}^t_A$ and $\mathbb{S}^t_B$ are $O(n^k)$.

Proof. Let $\mathcal{S}_A \in \mathbb{S}^t_A$. Then, there exists $\mathcal{Z}_A \in \mathbb{Z}^t_A$ such that $\Gamma_B(\mathcal{Z}_A) \setminus \mathcal{Z}_A = \mathcal{S}_A$, so clearly $B \notin \mathcal{S}_A$. Suppose $|\mathcal{S}_A| \geq k$.

If $|\mathcal{V} \setminus (\mathcal{S}_A \cup \{B\})| < t$, the size of $\mathcal{V} \setminus \mathcal{S}_A$ is at most t. Since $\mathcal{S}_A \subseteq \Gamma_B(\mathcal{Z}_A)$, $\mathcal{V} \setminus \Gamma_B(\mathcal{Z}_A)$ is of size at most t with B as an element. Hence, $\mathcal{V} \setminus \Gamma_B(\mathcal{Z}_A) \in \mathbb{Z}^t_B$; call this set $\mathcal{Z}_B$. Then $\Gamma_B(\mathcal{Z}_A) \cup \Gamma_A(\mathcal{Z}_B) = \mathcal{V}$ which violates the second condition in Theorem 1.

Therefore, $|\mathcal{V} \setminus (\mathcal{S}_A \cup \{B\})| \geq t$. This implies that there is $\mathcal{Z}'_A \subseteq \mathcal{V} \setminus \mathcal{S}_A \cup \{B\}$ of size t such that $\mathcal{Z}_A \subseteq \mathcal{Z}'_A$. Since, $\Gamma_B(\mathcal{Z}'_A) \supseteq \mathcal{S}_A \cup \mathcal{Z}'_A$, size of $\Gamma_B(\mathcal{Z}'_A)$ is at least $t+k$. But then, $|\mathcal{V} \setminus \Gamma_B(\mathcal{Z}'_A)| \le n-(t+k) = t$ and B is a member of this set. Hence $\mathcal{V} \setminus \Gamma_B(\mathcal{Z}'_A) \in \mathbb{Z}^t_B$; call this set $\mathcal{Z}_B$. Then $\Gamma_A(\mathcal{Z}_B) \cup \Gamma_B(\mathcal{Z}'_A) = \mathcal{V}$, a contradiction. Thus, $|\mathcal{S}_A| < k$ for all $\mathcal{S}_A \in \mathbb{S}^t_A$. Further, this implies that $|\mathbb{S}^t_A|$ is $O(n^k)$. The proof for sizes of $\mathcal{S}_B \in \mathbb{S}^t_B$ and $\mathbb{S}^t_B$ is similar. □

We next construct efficient protocols for OT between A and B that are secure w.r.t. adversary structures of the kind $\mathbb{Z}^t_A(\mathcal{S}_A) \cup \mathbb{Z}^t_B \cup \mathbb{Z}^t_{\neg A \neg B}$, where $\mathcal{S}_A \in \mathbb{S}^t_A$, and adversary structures of the kind $\mathbb{Z}^t_A \cup \mathbb{Z}^t_B(\mathcal{S}_B) \cup \mathbb{Z}^t_{\neg A \neg B}$, where $\mathcal{S}_B \in \mathbb{S}^t_B$. Then, we use a combiner of these protocols to construct an efficient protocol Π'_{sh} that is secure w.r.t. $\mathbb{Z}^t$. The efficiency of Π'_{sh} will follow from Claim 4 which shows that the sizes of the adversary structures $\mathbb{S}_A$ and $\mathbb{S}_B$ are of the order n^k.

Lemma 4. *For every $\mathcal{S}_A \in \mathbb{S}^t_A$ ($\mathcal{S}_B \in \mathbb{S}^t_B$, respectively) there is an efficient protocol $\Pi^{\mathcal{S}_A}$ ($\Pi^{\mathcal{S}_B}$, respectively) that realizes OT between A and B with security w.r.t. a semi-honest adversary structure $\mathbb{Z} = \mathbb{Z}^t_A(\mathcal{S}_A) \cup \mathbb{Z}_B \cup \mathbb{Z}_{\neg A \neg B}$, ($\mathbb{Z} = \mathbb{Z}^t_B(\mathcal{S}_B) \cup \mathbb{Z}_A \cup \mathbb{Z}_{\neg A \neg B}$, respectively) if the conditions in Theorem 3 are satisfied.*

Proof. Refer to the full version [33] for the proof. □

Proof. (Proof of Theorem 3). The construction of Π'_{sh} is similar to that of Π_{sh} in the proof of Theorem 1. Let $\mathbb{S}^t_A = \{\mathcal{S}^1_A, \ldots, \mathcal{S}^{\ell_A}_A\}$ and $\mathbb{S}^t_B = \{\mathcal{S}^1_B, \ldots, \mathcal{S}^{\ell_B}_B\}$. We construct Π'_{sh} as

$$\Pi'_{\mathsf{sh}} := \mathsf{Combiner}((\Pi_{1,1}, \Pi_{1,2}), \ldots, (\Pi_{\ell_A+\ell_B,1}, \Pi_{\ell_A+\ell_B,2})),$$
$$\text{where } (\Pi_{i,1}, \Pi_{i,2}) := (\Pi^{\mathcal{S}^i_A}, \Pi^B), \text{ for } 1 \le i \le \ell_A, \text{ and}$$
$$(\Pi_{i,1}, \Pi_{i,2}) := (\Pi^{\mathcal{S}^i_B}, \Pi^B), \text{ for } \ell_A + 1 \le i \le \ell_A + \ell_B.$$

From Lemma 4 and the properties of Π^A, Π^B, it is easy to see that against the corruption of every $\mathcal{Z} \in \mathbb{Z}^t$, a majority of the protocols in the combiner are secure. A pair of efficient protocols are contributed by every $\mathcal{S} \in \mathbb{S}^t_A \cup \mathbb{S}^t_B$ to the combiner, but as we previously observed, the size of $\mathbb{S}^t_A \cup \mathbb{S}^t_B$ is of the order n^k. Hence the combiner is efficient, this proves that Π'_{sh} is efficient. □

3 Malicious Case

In this section, we characterize graphs in which a given pair of vertices may realize OT with statistical security w.r.t. an adversary structure $\mathbb{Z}$ in the static malicious setting.

3.1 Necessity of Conditions

Necessity of the First Condition. If A and B can compute OT with statistical security, then they can communicate with non-trivial (greater than 1/2) probability of success. Necessity of the condition follows from the fact that in a graph, if A and B are disconnected by removing two vertices C and D from the graph, then A and B cannot communicate with non-trivial probability of success w.r.t the adversary structure $\{\{C\}, \{D\}\}$ in the malicious setting [15]. Note that although the proof in [15] is for communication with zero-error, it also works for communication with non-trivial probability of success. A proof of the necessity of this condition is included in the full version [33].

Necessity of the Second Condition. We show that in a graph G, it is impossible to realize OT between two of its vertices A and B with statistical security w.r.t. the adversary structure $\mathbb{Z}$ if the second condition is not satisfied, *i.e.*, there exists $\mathcal{Z}_A \in \mathbb{Z}_A, \mathcal{Z}_B \in \mathbb{Z}_B$, and $\mathcal{Z} \in \mathbb{Z}_{\neg A \neg B}$ such that

$$\Gamma_B(\mathcal{Z}_A \cup \mathcal{Z}) \cup \Gamma_A(\mathcal{Z}_B \cup \mathcal{Z}) = \mathcal{V}. \tag{3}$$

For the ease of exposition, we provide a proof for a special case where the following additional conditions hold for the sets $\mathcal{Z}_A, \mathcal{Z}_B$ and $\mathcal{Z}$ satisfying (3).[1]

$$(\Gamma_B(\mathcal{Z}_A \cup \mathcal{Z}) \setminus (\mathcal{Z}_A \cup \mathcal{Z})) \cap \Gamma_A(\mathcal{Z}_B \cup \mathcal{Z}) = \emptyset, \tag{4}$$

$$(\Gamma_A(\mathcal{Z}_B \cup \mathcal{Z}) \setminus (\mathcal{Z}_B \cup \mathcal{Z})) \cap \Gamma_B(\mathcal{Z}_A \cup \mathcal{Z}) = \emptyset. \tag{5}$$

Please refer to the full version [33] for a proof of the general case. The proof technique is identical, but uses a more elaborate construction (Fig. 10).

The proof proceeds in two steps: First we show the impossibility of OT between A and B in the graph H_{OT} of Fig. 4 with security w.r.t. a certain adversary structure (Lemma 5), then we use this observation to prove the necessity of the second condition in Theorem 2 for the special case through a reduction argument (Lemma 6).

Lemma 5. *In $H_{\text{OT}}(\mathcal{V}_{H_{\text{OT}}}, \mathcal{E}_{H_{\text{OT}}})$ (Fig. 4), it is impossible to realize OT between A and B with statistical security w.r.t. the malicious adversary structure $\{\{C\}, \{A, D\}, \{B, D\}\}$.*

Proof. The proof uses ideas from the proof for impossibility of Byzantine agreement by Fischer *et al.* in [15]. We first consider the case of perfect security for clarity and later argue the case of statistical security. We will show that a protocol for OT between A and B with perfect security w.r.t. the malicious adversary structure $\{\{C\}, \{A, D\}, \{B, D\}\}$ would imply a secure 2-party OT protocol for the semi-honest case. The impossibility will then follow from the impossibility of secure 2-party semi-honest OT. To prove a contradiction, let Π be a protocol that realizes OT between A and B with *perfect* security w.r.t. $\{\{C\}, \{A, D\}, \{B, D\}\}$. Similar to the construction used in [15], we construct a graph $S_{\text{OT}}(\mathcal{V}_{S_{\text{OT}}}, \mathcal{E}_{S_{\text{OT}}})$ by interconnecting two copies of H_{OT} as shown in Fig. 5. Consider the map $\phi : \mathcal{V}_{S_{\text{OT}}} \to \mathcal{V}_{H_{\text{OT}}}$ such that $\phi(v_i) = v, i = 0, 1$, *i.e.*, $\phi(A_0) = \phi(A_1) = A$, $\phi(B_0) = \phi(B_1) = B$ and so on. Then S_{OT} looks locally like H_{OT}. For example, A_0 has edges to B_0, D_0, E_0 and C_1 in S_{OT}, whereas in H_{OT}, $\phi(A_0)$ has edges to $\phi(B_0), \phi(D_0), \phi(E_0)$, and $\phi(C_1)$. Let each vertex v in S_{OT} run the instruction

[1] $\Gamma_B(\mathcal{Z}_A \cup \mathcal{Z}) \setminus (\mathcal{Z}_A \cup \mathcal{Z})$ is the set of vertices outside $\mathcal{Z}_A \cup \mathcal{Z}$ that have no paths to B except through vertices in $\mathcal{Z}_A \cup \mathcal{Z}$, similarly for $\Gamma_B(\mathcal{Z}_A \cup \mathcal{Z}) \setminus (\mathcal{Z}_A \cup \mathcal{Z})$.

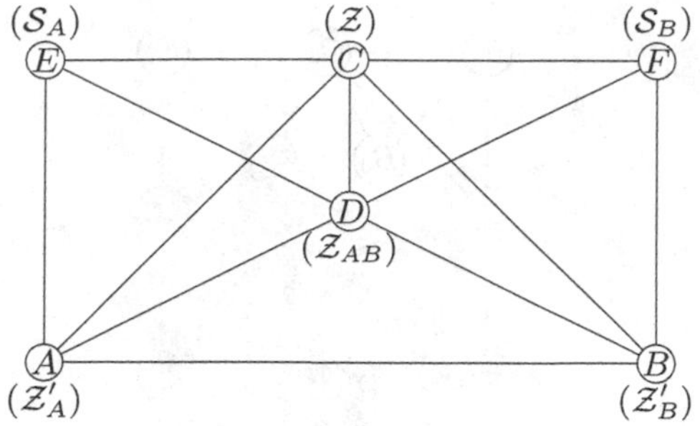

Fig. 4. $H_{\mathrm{OT}}(\mathcal{V}_{H_{\mathrm{OT}}}, \mathcal{E}_{H_{\mathrm{OT}}})$: OT between A and B with security w.r.t. malicious adversary structure $\{\{C\}, \{A, D\}, \{B, D\}\}$ is impossible (Lemma 5). The sets shown inside brackets correspond to the vertex identification used in the proof of Lemma 6.

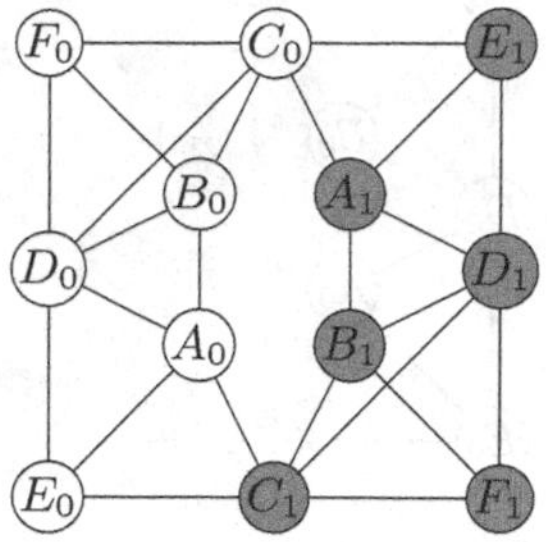

Fig. 5. $S_{\mathrm{OT}(\mathcal{V}_{S_{\mathrm{OT}}}, \mathcal{E}_{S_{\mathrm{OT}}})}$: Constructed by interconnecting two copies of H_{OT}. We analyze the scenario where $v_i, i = 0, 1$ in S_{OT} execute the instructions for v in H_{OT} for protocol Π faithfully.

for $\phi(v)$ in the protocol Π. We *fix* the input to A_1 as $(0, 0)$ and input to B_1 as 0 and let the input to A_0 be (X_0, X_1) and that to B_0 be Q, where X_0, X_1, Q are independent uniformly random bits. We call this the execution of a protocol Π' in S_{OT}. Clearly Π' is not the same as Π (Π is defined for 6 parties), but it is easy to see that this execution is well-defined.

Claim 5. The output at B_0 is X_Q.

Proof. In Fig. 6, it can be verified none of the vertices in the yellow region has any inputs or outputs in the protocol (inputs of A_1, B_1 have been fixed) and that all the edges that enter the yellow region (edges in red) are incident on either C_0 or C_1. Hence, all the vertices in the yellow region may be thought of as being simulated by a malicious C. The execution of Π' in S_{OT} can be interpreted as an execution of Π among honest vertices A_0, B_0, D_0, E_0, F_0, and a corrupted set $\{C\}$ as shown in Fig. 6. Π is assumed to be secure against the corruption of C, therefore A_0, B_0, D_0, E_0, F_0 halt and realize OT between A_0 and B_0; hence B_0 outputs X_Q. This proves the claim. □

Claim 6. Let $\mathcal{A}_{\{A,D\}} := \{A_0, A_1, D_0, D_1, B_1, C_1, F_1, E_0\}$, the vertices in the blue region of Fig. 7. Then Q is independent of the view of $\mathcal{A}_{\{A,D\}}$.

Proof. In Fig. 7, the only vertex in the blue region with input or output to the protocol Π' is A_0. Also, A_0, D_0, A_1, D_1 are the only vertices to which there are edges (red edges in the figure) from the vertices outside the blue region. Hence, the execution of Π' in S_{OT} can also be interpreted as an execution of Π by honest B_0, C_0, E_1, F_0, and a corrupted set $\{A, D\}$ that simulates $\mathcal{A}_{\{A,D\}}$ (the vertices in the blue region) and communicates with the honest vertices accordingly. Since Π is secure against the corruption of $\{A, D\}$, the input Q of B_0 is independent of the view of $\{A, D\}$. Hence Q is independent of the view of $\mathcal{A}_{\{A,D\}}$. □

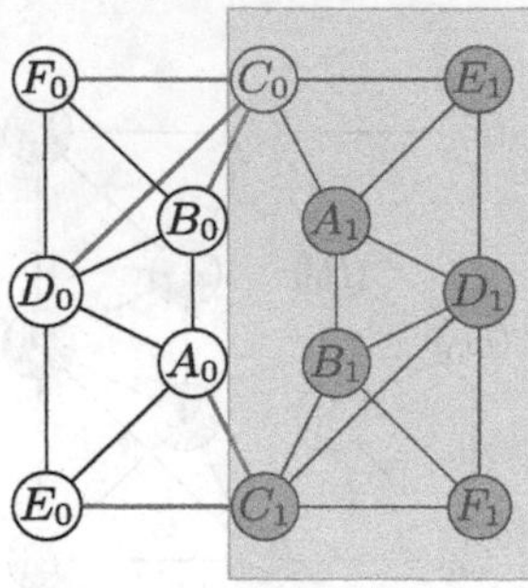

Fig. 6. We may visualize the execution of Π' as vertices A_0, B_0, D_0, E_0, F_0 following Π honestly and the corrupted set $\{C\}$ simulating all the vertices in the yellow region. Since Π is secure against the corruption of $\{C\}$, A_0 and B_0 must have computed OT correctly.

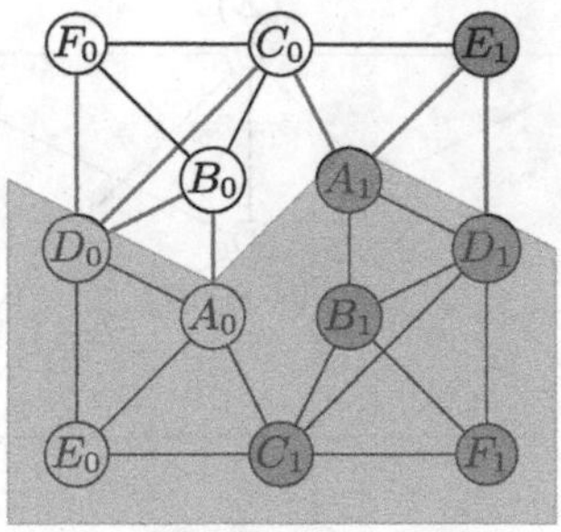

Fig. 7. We may also visualize the execution of Π' as vertices B_0, C_0, F_0, E_1 following Π honestly and the corrupted set $\{A, D\}$ simulating all the vertices in the blue region. Since Π is secure against the corruption of $\{A, D\}$, view of all vertices in the blue region is independent of B_0's input. (Color figure online)

Claim 7. Let $\mathcal{A}_{\{B,D\}} := \{B_0, B_1, D_0, D_1, A_1, C_0, E_1, F_0\}$, the vertices in the yellow region of Fig. 8. X_0, X_1 is independent of the view of $\mathcal{A}_{\{B,D\}}$ conditioned on Q, X_Q.

Proof. Similar to the previous claims, as shown in Fig. 8, the execution of Π' in S_{OT} can also be interpreted as an execution of Π by honest parties A_0, E_0, C_1, F_1 and a corrupted set $\{B, D\}$ simulates the vertices in the yellow region ($\mathcal{A}_{\{B,D\}}$) and communicates with the honest vertices accordingly. Notice that the view of this set contains the input Q and output X_Q of B_0. Since Π is secure against the corruption of $\{B, D\}$, the input (X_0, X_1) of A_0 is independent of the view of $\{B, D\}$ conditioned on its input and output. Hence (X_0, X_1) is independent of the view of $\mathcal{A}_{\{B,D\}}$ conditioned on Q, X_Q. □

We show that Claims 5, 6, and 7 lead to a contradiction. To see this, let parties $\mathcal{P}_1$ and $\mathcal{P}_2$ simulate the vertices in the blue region ($\mathcal{A}_{\mathcal{P}_1}$) and yellow region ($\mathcal{A}_{\mathcal{P}_2}$) respectively in Fig. 9. Let them execute Π' faithfully with $\mathcal{P}_1$ setting the input to the simulated A_0 as X_0, X_1 and that to the simulated B_1 as 0, and $\mathcal{P}_2$ setting the input to the simulated B_0 as Q and that to the simulated A_1 as $(0, 0)$. Then,

(i) The output at B_0 is X_Q.
(ii) Q is independent of the view of $\mathcal{A}_{\mathcal{P}_1}$.
(iii) X_0, X_1 is independent of the view of $\mathcal{A}_{\mathcal{P}_2}$ conditioned on Q, X_Q.

Here (i) follows from Claim 5. Claim 6 implies (ii) since the vertices $\mathcal{A}_{\mathcal{P}_1}$ (the blue region in Fig. 9) is contained in $\mathcal{A}_{\{A,D\}}$ (the blue region in Fig. 7) and the only vertex in $\mathcal{A}_{\{A,D\}}$ with input or output is A_0. Similarly, Claim 7 implies (iii) because $\mathcal{A}_{\mathcal{P}_2}$ (the blue region in Fig. 9) is contained in $\mathcal{A}_{\{B,D\}}$ (the blue region in Fig. 8) and the only vertex in $\mathcal{A}_{\{B,D\}}$ with input or output in $\mathcal{A}_{\{B,D\}}$ is B_0. But,

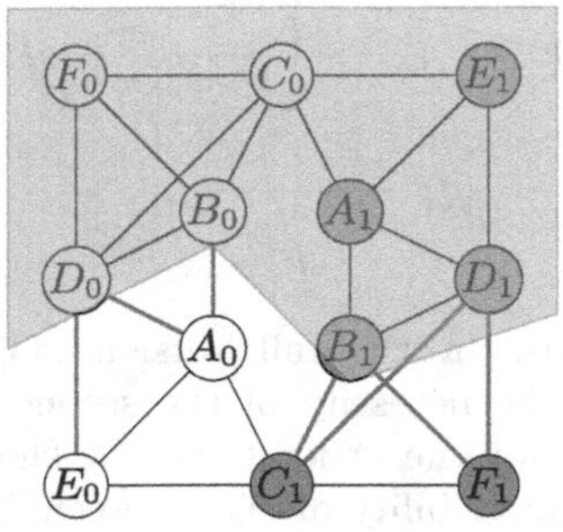

Fig. 8. We may visualize the execution of Π' as vertices A_0, C_1, E_0, F_1 following Π honestly and the corrupted set $\{B, D\}$ simulating all the vertices in the yellow region. Since Π is secure against the corruption of $\{B, D\}$, the view of vertices in the yellow region must be conditionally independent of A_0's input conditioned on B_0's input and output. (Color figure online)

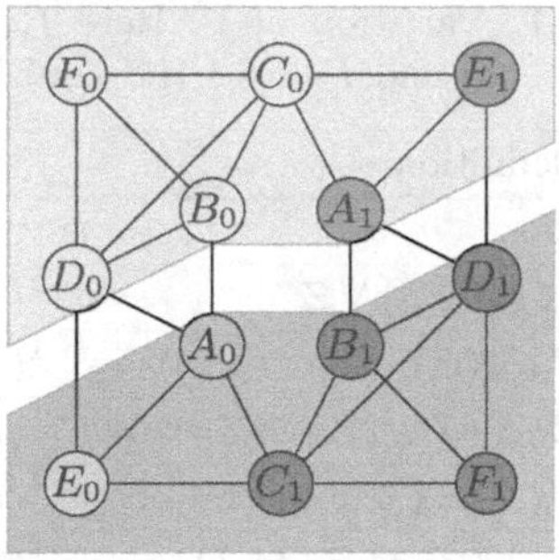

Fig. 9. $\mathcal{P}_1$ and $\mathcal{P}_2$ simulate the vertices in the blue and yellow regions respectively and run Π' faithfully by setting their inputs as inputs to A_0 and B_0 respectively to securely realize a 2-party OT, a contradiction. (Color figure online)

(i), (ii), and (iii) together imply that parties $\mathcal{P}_1$ and $\mathcal{P}_2$ can securely realize a 2-party OT in the semi-honest setting. Hence a protocol for OT between A and B with perfect security w.r.t. the adversary structure $\{\{C\}, \{A, D\}, \{B, D\}\}$ in the graph H_{OT} in the malicious setting implies a perfectly secure 2-party OT protocol in the semi-honest setting. By the same line of reasoning, a protocol for statistically secure OT between A and B in the same setting would imply a statistically secure 2-party OT protocol in the semi-honest setting. The lemma now follows from the impossibility of statistically secure semi-honest 2-party OT. □

Lemma 6 below shows that if $\mathcal{Z}_A \in \mathbb{Z}_A, \mathcal{Z}_B \in \mathbb{Z}_B$, and $\mathcal{Z} \in \mathbb{Z}_{\neg A \neg B}$ satisfy conditions (3), (4), and (5), then any protocol for OT between A and B in G with security w.r.t. $\mathbb{Z}$ may be simulated in H_{OT} to realize OT between A and B with security w.r.t. $\{\{C\}, \{A, D\}, \{B, D\}\}$. The necessity of the second condition in Theorem 2 for the special case when (4) and (5) is satisfied will then follow from Lemma 6.

Lemma 6. *Let $\mathcal{Z}_A \in \mathbb{Z}_A, \mathcal{Z}_B \in \mathbb{Z}_B$, and $\mathcal{Z} \in \mathbb{Z}_{\neg A \neg B}$ be such that conditions (3), (4), and (5) are satisfied. If OT between A and B in $G(\mathcal{V}, \mathcal{E})$ can be computed with statistical security w.r.t. the malicious adversary structure $\{\mathcal{Z}_A, \mathcal{Z}_B, \mathcal{Z}\}$ then A and B in $H_{\mathsf{OT}}(\mathcal{V}_{H_{\mathsf{OT}}}, \mathcal{E}_{H_{\mathsf{OT}}})$ (Fig. 4) can realize OT with statistical security w.r.t. the malicious adversary structure $\{\{C\}, \{A, D\}, \{B, D\}\}$.*

Table 1. Partition of $\mathcal{V}$. Here $\Gamma_A := \Gamma_B(\mathcal{Z}_A \cup \mathcal{Z})$ and $\Gamma_B := \Gamma_A(\mathcal{Z}_B \cup \mathcal{Z})$.

Set	Definition	
$\mathcal{Z}$	$\mathcal{Z}$	$= \psi^{-1}(C)$
$\mathcal{Z}_{AB}$	$(\mathcal{Z}_A \cap \mathcal{Z}_B) \setminus \mathcal{Z}$	$=\psi^{-1}(D)$
$\mathcal{Z}'_A$	$\mathcal{Z}_A \setminus (\mathcal{Z} \cup (\mathcal{Z}_A \cap \mathcal{Z}_B))$	$=\psi^{-1}(A)$
$\mathcal{Z}'_B$	$\mathcal{Z}_B \setminus (\mathcal{Z} \cup (\mathcal{Z}_A \cap \mathcal{Z}_B))$	$=\psi^{-1}(B)$
$\mathcal{S}_A$	$\Gamma_A \setminus (\mathcal{Z}_A \cup \mathcal{Z}_B \cup \mathcal{Z})$	$=\psi^{-1}(E)$
$\mathcal{S}_B$	$\Gamma_B \setminus (\mathcal{Z}_A \cup \mathcal{Z}_B \cup \mathcal{Z})$	$=\psi^{-1}(F)$

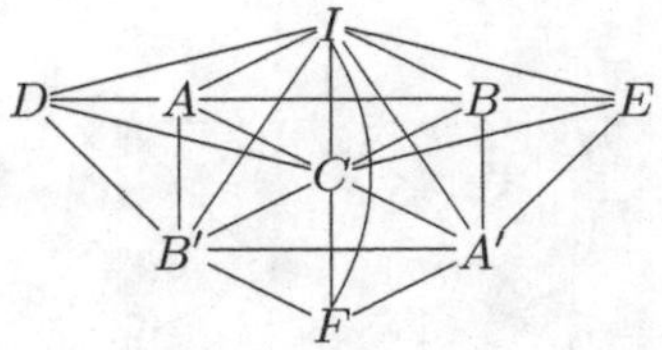

Fig. 10. In the full version [33], we show the necessity of the second condition for the general case by showing the impossibility of OT between A and B in this graph with statistical security w.r.t. the malicious adversary structure $\{\{C\}, \{A, A', I\}, \{B, B', I\}\}$.

Proof. Consider the subsets of $\mathcal{V}$ defined in Table 1. We show the following:

(i) $\mathcal{Z}'_A, \mathcal{Z}'_B, \mathcal{Z}, \mathcal{Z}_{AB}, \mathcal{S}_A$, and $\mathcal{S}_B$ form a partition of $\mathcal{V}$ and $A \in \mathcal{Z}'_A, B \in \mathcal{Z}'_B$.

(ii) Let the map $\psi : \mathcal{V} \to \mathcal{V}_{H_{\mathsf{OT}}}$ be as given in Fig. 4, *i.e.*, for $v \in \mathcal{Z}'_A, \psi(v) = A$ and so on. (i) implies that ψ is well-defined. For $u, v \in \mathcal{V}$, edge $\{u, v\}$ is in G only if $\psi(u) = \psi(v)$ or edge $\{\psi(u), \psi(v)\}$ is present in H_{OT}. In short, H_{OT} (or a subgraph of H_{OT}) is obtained from G on applying *vertex contraction* to every subset of $\mathcal{V}$ given in Table 1.

(iii) If Π realizes OT between A and B in G securely w.r.t. malicious adversary structure $\{\mathcal{Z}, \mathcal{Z}_A, \mathcal{Z}_B\}$, then it is also secure w.r.t. malicious adversary structure $\{\mathcal{Z}, \mathcal{Z}'_A \cup \mathcal{Z}_{AB}, \mathcal{Z}'_B \cup \mathcal{Z}_{AB}\} = \{\psi^{-1}(\{C\}), \psi^{-1}(\{A, D\}), \psi^{-1}(\{B, D\})\}$.

Assuming (i), (ii), and (iii), it is easy to see that the vertices in H_{OT} can simulate Π and realize OT between A and B with statistical security w.r.t. the malicious adversary $\{\{C\}, \{A, D\}, \{B, D\}\}$. It remains to show (i), (ii), and (iii).

Proof of (i) – From their definitions, it can be easily verified that $\mathcal{Z}, \mathcal{Z}_{AB}, \mathcal{Z}'_A, \mathcal{Z}'_B$ are disjoint and that their union is $\mathcal{Z} \cup \mathcal{Z}_A \cup \mathcal{Z}_B$. By definition of $\mathcal{S}_A, \mathcal{S}_B$, their union is $\Gamma_B(\mathcal{Z}_A \cup \mathcal{Z}) \cup \Gamma_A(\mathcal{Z}_B \cup \mathcal{Z}) \setminus (\mathcal{Z}_A \cup \mathcal{Z}_B \cup \mathcal{Z})$. By condition (3), this union is equal to $\mathcal{V} \setminus (\mathcal{Z} \cup \mathcal{Z}_A \cup \mathcal{Z}_B)$. Finally, the fact that $\mathcal{S}_A$ and $\mathcal{S}_B$ are disjoint follows from (4) since $\mathcal{S}_A \subseteq \Gamma_B(\mathcal{Z}_A \cup \mathcal{Z}) \setminus (\mathcal{Z}_A \cup \mathcal{Z})$ and $\mathcal{S}_B \subseteq \Gamma_A(\mathcal{Z}_B \cup \mathcal{Z})$.

Proof of (ii) – Note that the only edges missing in H_{OT} are $\{F, A\}, \{F, E\}$ and $\{E, B\}$. We will now show that there is no edge between any vertex in $\psi^{-1}(F) = \mathcal{S}_B$ and any vertex in $\psi^{-1}(A) = \mathcal{Z}'_A$ or $\psi^{-1}(E) = \mathcal{S}_A$. The fact that there is no edge between any vertex in $\psi^{-1}(E) = \mathcal{S}_A$ and any vertex in $\psi^{-1}(B) = \mathcal{Z}'_B$ follows similarly. Suppose there exists $u \in \mathcal{S}_B$ and $v \in \mathcal{Z}'_A \cup \mathcal{S}_A$ such that $\{u, v\}$ is an edge in G. Since $\mathcal{Z}_B \cup \mathcal{Z} \subseteq \Gamma_A(\mathcal{Z}_B \cup \mathcal{Z})$, we have

$$\begin{aligned}
\mathcal{Z}_A \cap \Gamma_A(\mathcal{Z}_B \cup \mathcal{Z}) &= (\mathcal{Z}_A \cap (\mathcal{Z}_B \cup \mathcal{Z})) \cup (\mathcal{Z}_A \cap (\Gamma_A(\mathcal{Z}_B \cup \mathcal{Z}) \setminus (\mathcal{Z}_B \cup \mathcal{Z}))) \\
&= (\mathcal{Z}_A \cap (\mathcal{Z}_B \cup \mathcal{Z})) \cup \emptyset \text{ (by (5) since } \mathcal{Z}_A \subset \Gamma_B(\mathcal{Z}_A \cup \mathcal{Z})) \\
&\subseteq \mathcal{Z} \cup (\mathcal{Z}_A \cap \mathcal{Z}_B) \\
\implies \mathcal{Z}'_A &= \mathcal{Z}_A \setminus (\mathcal{Z} \cup (\mathcal{Z}_A \cap \mathcal{Z}_B)) \subseteq \mathcal{V} \setminus \Gamma_A(\mathcal{Z}_B \cup \mathcal{Z}). \\
\mathcal{S}_A &= \Gamma_B(\mathcal{Z}_A \cup \mathcal{Z}) \setminus (\mathcal{Z} \cup \mathcal{Z}_A \cup \mathcal{Z}_B) \subseteq \Gamma_B(\mathcal{Z}_A \cup \mathcal{Z}) \setminus (\mathcal{Z}_A \cup \mathcal{Z}) \\
\implies \mathcal{S}_A &\subseteq \mathcal{V} \setminus \Gamma_A(\mathcal{Z}_B \cup \mathcal{Z}), \text{ by (4).}
\end{aligned}$$

Hence we have $v \in \mathcal{Z}'_A \cup \mathcal{S}_A \subseteq \mathcal{V} \setminus \Gamma_A(\mathcal{Z}_B \cup \mathcal{Z})$ and $u \in \mathcal{S}_B \subseteq \Gamma_A(\mathcal{Z}_B \cup \mathcal{Z}) \setminus (\mathcal{Z}_B \cup \mathcal{Z})$. Since $v \in \mathcal{V} \setminus \Gamma_A(\mathcal{Z}_B \cup \mathcal{Z})$, there is a path from v to A that does not have any vertex from $\mathcal{Z}_B \cup \mathcal{Z}$. Since edge $\{u, v\}$ is present in G, u has a path via v to A that does not contain any vertex from $\mathcal{Z}_B \cup \mathcal{Z}$ (note that $u \notin \mathcal{Z}_B \cup \mathcal{Z}$). But $u \in \mathcal{S}_B$ and hence $u \in \Gamma_A(\mathcal{Z}_B \cup \mathcal{Z})$, a contradiction.

Proof of (iii) – $A \in \mathcal{Z}'_A$ and $B \in \mathcal{Z}'_B$ are the only vertices with input or output in Π. Also, $\mathcal{Z}'_A \cup \mathcal{Z}_{AB} \subseteq \mathcal{Z}_A$ and $\mathcal{Z}'_B \cup \mathcal{Z}_{AB} \subseteq \mathcal{Z}_B$. Hence, if Π is secure w.r.t. $\{\mathcal{Z}, \mathcal{Z}_A, \mathcal{Z}_B\}$, then it is also secure w.r.t. $\{\mathcal{Z}, \mathcal{Z}'_A \cup \mathcal{Z}_{AB}, \mathcal{Z}'_B \cup \mathcal{Z}_{AB}\}$. □

General Case: The necessity of the second condition for the general case is proved in a similar manner. We first show that it is impossible to realize OT between A and B in the graph shown in Fig. 10 with statistical security w.r.t. the malicious adversary structure $\{\{C\}, \{A, A', I\}, \{B, B', I\}\}$. This is shown using an argument similar to the one used in Lemma 5 on a graph constructed by interconnecting *three copies* of this graph. Then we use this observation to prove the necessity of the second condition in Theorem 2 for the general case through a reduction argument. This proof is included in the full version [33].

3.2 Sufficiency of Conditions

In this section, we consider a graph $G(\mathcal{V}, \mathcal{E})$ with $A, B \in \mathcal{V}$ and a malicious adversary structure $\mathbb{Z}$ that satisfies the conditions in Theorem 2 and construct a protocol Π_{mal} that realizes OT between A and B with statistical security w.r.t. $\mathbb{Z}$. First we comment on two protocols we use extensively in this section: for realizing secure communication and for computing OT from sampled OT.

Realizing Perfectly Secure Communication: In the previous section, we saw that the first condition in Theorem 2 is necessary for statistically correct communication. In [28], Kumar *et al.* showed that this condition is sufficient for perfectly secure communication. We will use their protocol for realizing secure communication between A and B in all the protocols that follow. This protocol is guaranteed to be efficient if the size of $\mathbb{Z}$ is polynomial in n. We note here that their protocol can be shown to be composable.

OT Computation Using Sampled OT: A *sampled OT* or a precomputed OT between A and B is a functionality that generates r_0, r_1, c independently and uniformly at random and sends the ordered pair (r_0, r_1) to A and the ordered pair

(c, r_c) to B. The following protocol describes a well known technique for realizing OT between A with input (x_0, x_1) and B with input b using this sampled OT. The OT computed by this protocol is statistically secure as long as the sampled OT was computed with statistical security [2].

Protocol 4 $(\mathsf{SampledOT} \rightarrow \mathsf{OT}\,(A : (x_0, x_1; r_0, r_1), B : (b; c, r_c)))$.[2]

1. B: Sends $p := b \oplus c$ to A securely.
2. A: Sends $(y_0, y_1) := (x_0 \oplus r_p, x_1 \oplus r_{1 \oplus p})$ securely.
3. B: Stores the messages it received as (y_0, y_1) and outputs $y_b \oplus r_c$.

Overview of the Section: The protocol Π_{mal} constructed in this section executes many sub-protocols which in turn execute other sub-protocols. Figure 11 shows the sub-protocols that are used in the construction of each of the protocols described in the section. All the protocols that follow, except Π, Π^A, and Π^B have the property that they either compute OT with statistical security or *abort* depending on the malicious behavior of the adversary. A protocol is said to have aborted if both A and B output $\perp$ while guaranteeing *perfect privacy* of the inputs of A and B.

Π^A, Π^B		Π^A, Π^B				
$\Pi^{\mathsf{path}(C,A),\mathsf{path}(C,B)}$	Combiner $\longrightarrow$	$\Pi^{\mathcal{Z}_A,\mathcal{Z}}, \Pi^{\mathcal{Z}_B,\mathcal{Z}}$	Combiner $\longrightarrow$	$\Pi^{\mathcal{Z}}$	Iteration $\longrightarrow$	Π_{mal}

Fig. 11. Protocols in each column (except the ones in blue) make calls to the protocols in the previous column.

First we demonstrate the construction Π_{mal} assuming the following lemma which claims the existence of protocols $\Pi^{\mathcal{Z}}, \mathcal{Z} \in \mathbb{Z}_{\neg A \neg B}$ with certain properties. We prove this lemma later in the section by giving an explicit construction for $\Pi^{\mathcal{Z}}, \mathcal{Z} \in \mathbb{Z}_{\neg A \neg B}$. The construction and analysis of $\Pi^{\mathcal{Z}}, \mathcal{Z} \in \mathbb{Z}_{\neg A \neg B}$ is very similar to that of protocol Π_{sh} described in the semi-honest section.

Lemma 7. *Consider a pair of vertices A, B in $G(\mathcal{V}, \mathcal{E})$, and a malicious adversary structure $\mathbb{Z}$ such that the conditions in Theorem 2 hold. For each $\mathcal{Z} \in \mathbb{Z}_{\neg A \neg B}$, there is a protocol $\Pi^{\mathcal{Z}}$ such that*

(i) $\Pi^{\mathcal{Z}}$ computes OT between A and B with perfect security against the corruption of $\mathcal{Z}$.
(ii) $\Pi^{\mathcal{Z}}$ is either aborted or it computes OT between A and B with statistical security w.r.t. $\mathbb{Z} \setminus \{\mathcal{Z}\}$.

This protocol is efficient if the size of $\mathbb{Z}$ is polynomial in n.

---

[2] A and B treat missing and incorrect messages as 0.

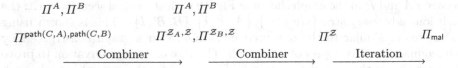

Protocol Π_{mal}. This protocol computes OT between A and B with statistical security with guaranteed output delivery. For each $\mathcal{Z} \in \mathbb{Z}_{\neg A \neg B}$, A and B attempts to compute a sampled OT by executing $\Pi^{\mathcal{Z}}$ with independent uniform bits as input. If, for some $\mathcal{Z} \in \mathbb{Z}_{\neg A \neg B}, \Pi^{\mathcal{Z}}$ succeeds in computing a sampled OT, A and B use this sampled OT to realize the OT. Since the sampled OT is statistically secure by Lemma 7 (ii), the OT computed using it is also statistically secure. By Lemma 7 (i), $\Pi^{\mathcal{Z}}$ aborts for all $\mathcal{Z} \in \mathbb{Z}_{\neg A \neg B}$ only if the corrupted set is not in $\mathbb{Z}_{\neg A \neg B}$, *i.e.*, either A or B is corrupt. In that case, B (if honest) may output a random bit and the computation is still secure. Let $\mathbb{Z}_{\neg A \neg B} = \{\mathcal{Z}_1, \ldots, \mathcal{Z}_\ell\}$, we formally describe Π_{mal} as follows:

Protocol 5 $(\Pi_{\mathsf{mal}}(A : (x_0, x_1), B : (b)))$

1. For $i = 1, \ldots, \ell$:
   (a) A generates bits r_0^i, r_1^i uniformly and independently and B generates a bit c^i uniformly and executes $\Pi^{\mathcal{Z}^i}(A : (r_0^i, r_1^i), B : c^i)$.
   (b) If for some $i \le \ell, B$ receives $\bar{r}_c^i$ as output (*i.e.*, $\Pi^{\mathcal{Z}^i}$ does not abort) then A and B execute $\mathsf{SampledOT} \to \mathsf{OT}\left(A : (x_0, x_1; r_0^i, r_1^i), B : (b; c^i, \bar{r}_c^i)\right)$, output whatever the protocol outputs and terminate.
2. If for all $i \le \ell$, $\Pi^{\mathcal{Z}^i}$ aborts, then B outputs a bit uniformly at random.

Proof (Proof of the sufficiency part of Theorem 2). We show that Π_{mal} computes OT between A and B with statistical security w.r.t. $\mathbb{Z}$. For every $i = 1, \ldots \ell$, the inputs of A and B to $\Pi^{\mathcal{Z}^i}$ are random bits independent of their real inputs. Hence their input remains perfectly private after the execution of $\Pi^{\mathcal{Z}^i}$ irrespective of whether it is aborted or not. We consider two cases.

Case 1 – For some iteration $i \in \{1, \ldots, \ell\}$, $\Pi^{\mathcal{Z}^i}$ does not abort: By Lemma 7 (ii), the sampled OT computed by $\Pi^{\mathcal{Z}^i}$ is statistically secure, hence the OT computed using this sampled OT is also statistically secure.

Case 2 – For $i = 1, \ldots \ell$, $\Pi^{\mathcal{Z}^i}$ aborts: By Lemma 7 (i), for any $\mathcal{Z} \in \mathbb{Z}_{\neg A \neg B}$, $\Pi^{\mathcal{Z}}$ realizes OT with perfect security against the corruption of $\mathcal{Z}$. Hence, $\Pi^{\mathcal{Z}^i}$ aborts for all i only if the corrupted set is in $\mathbb{Z} \setminus \mathbb{Z}_{\neg A \neg B}$ *i.e.*, either A or B is corrupted. In this case, an honest B may output a random bit and the protocol remains perfectly secure.

Hence Π_{mal} computes OT between A and B with statistical security w.r.t. $\mathbb{Z}$. The efficiency claim follows from the fact that Π_{mal} runs at most $|\mathbb{Z}_{\neg A \neg B}|$ protocols of the kind $\Pi^{\mathcal{Z}}$, each of which is efficient when $\mathbb{Z}$ is of size $\mathsf{poly}(n)$ according to Lemma 7. □

In the rest of this section, we prove Lemma 7 by explicitly constructing $\Pi^{\mathcal{Z}}, \mathcal{Z} \in \mathbb{Z}_{\neg A \neg B}$. As a first step, we construct a protocol $\Pi^{\mathsf{path}(C,A),\mathsf{path}(C,B)}$ that is defined for $C \in \mathcal{V} \setminus \{A, B\}$, and paths $\mathsf{path}(C, A)$ and $\mathsf{path}(C, B)$ from C to A and B, respectively.

Protocol $\Pi^{\mathsf{path}(C,A),\mathsf{path}(C,B)}$ (*analogous to* Π^C *in Lemma* 1). In this protocol vertex C facilitates an OT computation between A and B by providing them with a sampled OT similar to protocol Π^C described in the semi-honest case. The protocol either computes OT with statistical security or aborts in a precomputation phase unless A and a vertex in $\mathsf{path}(C, B)$ are corrupted simultaneously or B and a vertex in $\mathsf{path}(C,A)$ are corrupted simultaneously.

The protocol has two phases; a precomputation phase and an OT computation phase. In the precomputation phase, vertex C generates a sampled OT and distributes it to A and B by communicating with A and B along $\mathsf{path}(C, A)$ and $\mathsf{path}(C, B)$ respectively. Unlike in the semi-honest case, the correctness of the sampled OT has to be verified, lest A and B compute OT using an incorrect sampled OT. If the verification succeeds, A and B enter the OT computation phase in which they use the sampled OT to compute OT with their real inputs, else the protocol aborts. The verification step accepts an incorrect sampled OT with positive probability, but this probability can be made as small as needed.

Protocol 6 ($\Pi^{\mathsf{path}(C,A),\mathsf{path}(C,B)}(A : (x_0, x_1), B : b)$)

- **Precomputation Phase**[3]
  1. C: Generates uniformly random bits r_0, r_1, c, and chooses a_0, a_1 independently and uniformly at random from $\mathbb{F}$ of size at least 3. Define $p_0(x) := a_0x + r_0$, and $p_1(x) := a_1x + r_1$. C sends (p_0, p_1) to A along $\mathsf{path}(C, A)$ and (c, p_c) to B along $\mathsf{path}(C, B)$.
  2. A: Stores the received polynomials as $\bar{p}_0^A, \bar{p}_1^A$. B: Stores the received bit as $\bar{c}$ and polynomial as $\bar{p}_{\bar{c}}^B$.
  3. B: Generates α uniformly at random from $\mathbb{F} \setminus \{0\}$. B sends α to C along $\mathsf{path}(C, B)$ and sends α to A securely.
  4. C: Sends α received from B to A along $\mathsf{path}(C, A)$. If α is non-zero, it sends $(p_0(\alpha), p_1(\alpha))$ to B along $\mathsf{path}(C, B)$ else it sends $\perp$ to B.
  5. A: If α received from B and C are identical and non-zero, A sends $(p_0^A(\alpha), p_1^A(\alpha))$ to B securely, otherwise it sends $\perp$ to B securely and aborts by outputting $\perp$.
  6. B: Stores evaluations received from A as y_0^A, y_1^A and evaluations from C as y_0^C, y_1^C. If $y_i^A = y_i^C, i = 0, 1$ and $y_{\bar{c}}^A = \bar{p}_{\bar{c}}^B(\alpha)$:
     - Then: Sends ACCEPT to A securely and stores the sampled OT $(\bar{c}, \bar{p}_{\bar{c}}^B(0))$.
     - Else: Sends REJECT to A securely and aborts by outputting $\perp$.
  7. A: If REJECT is received from B, then it aborts by outputting $\perp$ else it stores the sampled OT $(\bar{p}_0^A(0), \bar{p}_1^A(0))$.
- **OT computation Phase**:
  Execute $\mathsf{SampledOT} \to \mathsf{OT}\big(A : (x_0, x_1; \bar{p}_0^A(0), \bar{p}_1^A(0), B : (b; \bar{c}, \bar{p}_{\bar{c}}^B(0))\big)$ and return the output.

Lemma 8. *Consider a network $G(\mathcal{V}, \mathcal{E})$, vertices $A, B \in \mathcal{V}$ and a malicious adversary structure $\mathbb{Z}$ such that the conditions in Theorem 2 hold. Suppose there exists a vertex $C \in \mathcal{V} \setminus \{A, B\}$, and paths $\mathsf{path}(C, A)$ and $\mathsf{path}(C, B)$ from C to A and B respectively such that, for every set $\mathcal{Z} \in \mathbb{Z}$, at least one of the following conditions is satisfied.*

[3] If A or B receives an invalid message at any stage, it sends an abort message to the other party and aborts by outputting $\perp$.

(i) $A, B \notin \mathcal{Z}$,
(ii) $A \in \mathcal{Z}$ *but* $\mathsf{path}(C, B) \cap \mathcal{Z} = \emptyset$,
(iii) $B \in \mathcal{Z}$ *but* $\mathsf{path}(C, A) \cap \mathcal{Z} = \emptyset$.

Then, the protocol $\Pi^{\mathsf{path}(C,A),\mathsf{path}(C,B)}$ *is either aborted in the precomputation phase while guaranteeing perfect privacy of inputs or computes OT between A and B with statistical security w.r.t.* $\mathbb{Z}$ *with error probability* $\frac{1}{|\mathbb{F}|-1}$. *Moreover, this protocol is efficient as long as the size of* $\mathbb{Z}$ *is polynomial in n.*

Proof. Refer to the full version [33] for the proof. □

The probability of error in this protocol can be brought down to $\left(\frac{1}{|\mathbb{F}|-1}\right)^k$ if C distributes k pairs of independent and uniformly random polynomials with r_0, r_1 as constant terms and the verification steps are carried out independently for each pair of polynomials with a fresh sample of α.

We define OT protocols Π^A, Π^B as follows. In both these protocols, A and B interpret missing or invalid messages as 0.

Protocol 7 $(\Pi^A(A : (x_0, x_1), B : b))$

1. B: Sends b to A securely.
2. A: Sends x_b to B securely.
3. B: Outputs x_b.

Protocol 8 $(\Pi^B(A : (x_0, x_1), B : b))$

1. A: Sends (x_0, x_1) to B securely.
2. B: Outputs x_b.

It is easy to see that Π^A is perfectly secure as long as A is honest and communication between A and B is secure, similarly Π^B is perfectly secure as long as B is honest and communication between A and B is secure. Specifically, if A, B satisfy the conditions in Theorem 2 for an adversary structure $\mathbb{Z}$, then Π^A is secure w.r.t. $\mathbb{Z}_B \cup \mathbb{Z}_{\neg A \neg B}$ and Π^B is secure w.r.t. $\mathbb{Z}_A \cup \mathbb{Z}_{\neg A \neg B}$. These protocols are also efficient as long as $|\ \mathbb{Z}\ | = \mathsf{poly}(n)$ since the secure communication between A and B can be carried out efficiently.

We construct the protocol $\Pi^{\mathcal{Z}}$ corresponding to each $\mathcal{Z} \in \mathbb{Z}_{\neg A \neg B}$ in two steps along the lines of the construction of OT protocol Π_{sh} in the semi-honest case. In the first step, the protocol will be secure w.r.t. some specific adversary structures. Then we use these protocols to construct a protocol for the general case. In both these protocols, similar to the semi-honest case, we invoke the idea of compiling many protocols that are not individually secure w.r.t. the adversary structure to create a protocol that is secure. For this, we use an OT combiner for malicious setting as described in [23].

Lemma 9 [23, Corollary 7]
Given a malicious adversary structure $\mathbb{Z}$ *and protocols* $\Pi_1, \ldots, \Pi_m$ *realizing OT between A and B such that against the corruption of every set* $\mathcal{Z} \in \mathbb{Z}$, *a*

majority of protocols $\Pi_1, \ldots, \Pi_m$ are statistically secure, there is a hybrid protocol $\mathsf{Combiner}_{\mathsf{mal}}(\Pi_1, \ldots, \Pi_m)$ *that makes calls to $\Pi_1, \ldots, \Pi_m$ and computes OT between A and B with statistical security w.r.t. $\mathbb{Z}$. Moreover, if m is polynomial in n and each Π_i is efficient for $i \in [m]$, then the combiner is efficient.*

In the first step, for $\mathcal{Z} \in \mathbb{Z}_{\neg A \neg B}$ and $\mathcal{Z}_A \in \mathbb{Z}_A$ ($\mathcal{Z}_B \in \mathbb{Z}_B$, respectively), we construct a protocol $\Pi^{\mathcal{Z},\mathcal{Z}_A}$ ($\Pi^{\mathcal{Z},\mathcal{Z}_B}$, respectively) that runs in two stages. It is either aborted in the first stage or computes OT between A and B with security w.r.t. the adversary structure $\{\mathcal{Z}_A\} \cup \mathbb{Z}_{\neg A \neg B} \cup \mathbb{Z}_B$ ($\{\mathcal{Z}_B\} \cup \mathbb{Z}_{\neg A \neg B} \cup \mathbb{Z}_A$, respectively). The protocol has the additional property that it computes OT with *perfect security* against the corruption of $\mathcal{Z}$.

Protocol $\Pi^{\mathcal{Z},\mathcal{Z}_A}$ (analogous to $\Pi^{\mathcal{Z}_A}$ in Lemma 3). The protocol involves only the vertices in $\mathcal{V} \setminus \mathcal{Z}$, hence it is perfectly secure against the corruption of $\mathcal{Z}$. It is a combiner of a set of protocols of the kind defined in Protocol 6 and copies of Π^A. It runs in two phases. In the first phase, A and B compute and store sufficient number of sampled OTs for each protocol of the kind $\Pi^{\mathsf{path}(C,A),\mathsf{path}(C,B)}$ used in the combiner by running their precomputation phases. $\Pi^{\mathcal{Z},\mathcal{Z}_B}$ is aborted if any of the precomputation phases abort. Otherwise, A and B proceed to compute the combiner with each call to $\Pi^{\mathsf{path}(C,A),\mathsf{path}(C,B)}$ being realized by executing the OT computation phase of Protocol 6. Analysis of this protocol is very similar to $\Pi^{\mathcal{Z}_A}$ described in Lemma 3. Since the protocol $\Pi^{\mathcal{Z},\mathcal{Z}_B}$ is similar, with the roles of A and B reversed, we omit its description.

Consider the adversary structure $\{\mathcal{Z}_A\} \cup \mathbb{Z}_{\neg A \neg B} \cup \mathbb{Z}_B$, such that $A \in \mathcal{Z}_A$ and a set $\mathcal{Z} \in \mathbb{Z}_{\neg A \neg B}$. For every $\mathcal{Z}_B \in \mathbb{Z}_B$, there exists a vertex $C_{\mathcal{Z}_B}$ and paths $\mathsf{path}_{\mathcal{Z}_B}(C_{\mathcal{Z}_B}, B)$ and $\mathsf{path}_{\mathcal{Z}_B}(C_{\mathcal{Z}_B}, A)$ such that $\mathsf{path}_{\mathcal{Z}_B}(C_{\mathcal{Z}_B}, A)$ does not have any vertex from set $\mathcal{Z}_B \cup \mathcal{Z}$ and $\mathsf{path}_{\mathcal{Z}_B}(C_{\mathcal{Z}_B}, B)$ does not have any vertex from set $\mathcal{Z}_A \cup \mathcal{Z}$. Otherwise, for each vertex $v \in \mathcal{V}$, we have $v \in \Gamma_A(\mathcal{Z}_B \cup \mathcal{Z})$ or $v \in \Gamma_B(\mathcal{Z}_A \cup \mathcal{Z})$. This would lead to the contradiction that $\Gamma_A(\mathcal{Z}_B \cup \mathcal{Z}) \cup \Gamma_B(\mathcal{Z}_A \cup \mathcal{Z}) = \mathcal{V}$. Note that, since $C_{\mathcal{Z}_B} \notin \Gamma_A(\mathcal{Z}_B \cup \mathcal{Z}) \cup \Gamma_B(\mathcal{Z}_A \cup \mathcal{Z})$, it can not be A or B, hence $\Pi^{\mathsf{path}_{\mathcal{Z}_B^i}(C_{\mathcal{Z}_B^i},A),\mathsf{path}_{\mathcal{Z}_B^i}(C_{\mathcal{Z}_B^i},B)}$ are well-defined.

Let $\mathbb{Z}_B = \{\mathcal{Z}_B^1, \ldots, \mathcal{Z}_B^{\ell_B}\}$. Consider the protocols $\Pi_1, \ldots, \Pi_{2\ell_B-1}$, where

$$\Pi_i := \Pi^{\mathsf{path}_{\mathcal{Z}_B^i}(C_{\mathcal{Z}_B^i},A),\mathsf{path}_{\mathcal{Z}_B^i}(C_{\mathcal{Z}_B^i},B)}, \text{ for } 1 \le i \le \ell_B,$$
$$\Pi_i := \Pi^A, \text{ for } \ell_B + 1 \le j \le 2\ell_B - 1.$$

Consider the combiner of these $2\ell_B - 1$ protocols for OT between A and B. Let $\mathsf{Calls}(\Pi_i)$ represent the number of calls made to the protocol Π_i during an execution of the combiner. Then we construct the protocol $\Pi^{\mathcal{Z},\mathcal{Z}_A}$ as follows.

Protocol 9 ($\Pi^{\mathcal{Z},\mathcal{Z}_A}(A : (x_0, x_1), B : b)$)

1. For $1 \le i \le \ell_B$, perform $\mathsf{Calls}(\Pi_i)$ number of independent executions of the precomputation phase of $\Pi^{\mathsf{path}_{\mathcal{Z}_B^i}(C_{\mathcal{Z}_B^i},A),\mathsf{path}_{\mathcal{Z}_B^i}(C_{\mathcal{Z}_B^i},B)}$.
2. If any of the executions is aborted: abort the protocol otherwise execute the protocol $\mathsf{Combiner}_{\mathsf{mal}}(\Pi_1, \ldots, \Pi_{2\ell_B-1})$ with (x_0, x_1) and b as input from A

and B respectively and output what the combiner outputs.
Note: Every call to $\Pi_i, 1 \leq i \leq \ell_B$ is realized by executing the OT computation phase of $\Pi^{\mathsf{path}_{\mathcal{Z}_B^i}(C_{\mathcal{Z}_B^i},A),\mathsf{path}_{\mathcal{Z}_B^i}(C_{\mathcal{Z}_B^i},B)}$ with the sampled OT from step 1. All other protocols in the combiner are copies of Π^A, which are executed online.

Lemma 10. *Consider a pair of vertices A, B in a graph $G(\mathcal{V}, \mathcal{E})$, and a malicious adversary structure $\mathbb{Z} = \{\mathcal{Z}_A\} \cup \mathbb{Z}_{\neg A \neg B} \cup \mathbb{Z}_B$ where $A \in \mathcal{Z}_A$ ($\mathbb{Z} = \mathbb{Z}_A \cup \mathbb{Z}_{\neg A \neg B} \cup \{\mathcal{Z}_B\}$ where $B \in \mathcal{Z}_B$, respectively) such that the conditions in Theorem 2 hold. Let $\mathcal{Z} \in \mathbb{Z}_{\neg A \neg B}$, then the following hold:*

(i) $\Pi^{\mathcal{Z},\mathcal{Z}_A}$ ($\Pi^{\mathcal{Z},\mathcal{Z}_B}$, respectively) computes OT between A and B with perfect security against the corruption of $\mathcal{Z}$.
(ii) $\Pi^{\mathcal{Z},\mathcal{Z}_A}$ ($\Pi^{\mathcal{Z},\mathcal{Z}_B}$, respectively) is either aborted in step 1 or computes OT between A and B with statistical security w.r.t. $\mathbb{Z} \setminus \{\mathcal{Z}\}$.

The protocol $\Pi^{\mathcal{Z},\mathcal{Z}_A}$ ($\Pi^{\mathcal{Z},\mathcal{Z}_B}$, respectively) is efficient if the size of $\mathbb{Z}$ is polynomial in n.

Proof. Refer to the full version [33] for the proof. □

Protocol $\Pi^{\mathcal{Z}}$ (analogous to Π_{sh} in the proof of Theorem 1). Now we are ready to prove Lemma 7 which will complete the proof of the sufficiency of Theorem 2. We do this by constructing $\Pi^{\mathcal{Z}}$ for each $\mathcal{Z} \in \mathbb{Z}_{\neg A \neg B}$ using protocols $\Pi^{\mathcal{Z},\mathcal{Z}_A}, \mathcal{Z}_A \in \mathbb{Z}_A$, $\Pi^{\mathcal{Z},\mathcal{Z}_B}, \mathcal{Z}_B \in \mathbb{Z}_B$ and copies of Π^A and Π^B. This protocol realizes OT between A and B with perfect security against corruption of $\mathcal{Z}$ and guarantees statistical security w.r.t. $\mathbb{Z} \setminus \{\mathcal{Z}\}$ whenever it is not aborted. The construction of this protocol and its analysis is similar to the construction of Π_{sh} from $\Pi^{\mathcal{Z}_A}, \mathcal{Z}_A \in \mathbb{Z}_A, \Pi^{\mathcal{Z}_B}, \mathcal{Z}_A \in \mathbb{Z}_B$ and copies of Π^A, Π^B in the semi-honest case (Proof of Theorem 1). Let $\mathbb{Z}_A = \{\mathcal{Z}_A^1, \ldots, \mathcal{Z}_A^{\ell_A}\}$ and $\mathbb{Z}_B = \{\mathcal{Z}_B^1, \ldots, \mathcal{Z}_B^{\ell_B}\}$. Consider the following set of protocols

$$(\Pi_{1,1}, \Pi_{1,2}), \ldots, (\Pi_{\ell_A,1}, \Pi_{\ell_A,2}), (\Pi_{\ell_A+1,1}, \Pi_{\ell_A+1,2}), \ldots, (\Pi_{\ell_A+\ell_B,1}, \Pi_{\ell_A+\ell_B,2}),$$
$$\text{where } (\Pi_{i,1}, \Pi_{i,2}) := (\Pi^{\mathcal{Z},\mathcal{Z}_A}, \Pi^B), \text{ for } 1 \leq i \leq \ell_A,$$
$$(\Pi_{\ell_A+i,1}, \Pi_{\ell_A+i,2}) := (\Pi^{\mathcal{Z},\mathcal{Z}_B}, \Pi^A), \text{ for } 1 \leq i \leq \ell_B.$$

Let $\mathsf{Calls}(\Pi_{i,j})$ represent the maximum number of calls made to the protocol $\Pi_{i,j}$ during any execution of $\mathsf{Combiner}_{\mathsf{mal}}(\Pi_{1,1}, \Pi_{1,2}, \ldots, \Pi_{\ell_A+\ell_B,1}, \Pi_{\ell_A+\ell_B,2})$.

Protocol 10 ($\Pi^{\mathcal{Z}}(A : (x_0, x_1), B : b)$)

- **Precomputation Phase**
  1. For $1 \leq i \leq \ell_A$: Execute $\mathsf{Calls}(\Pi_{i,1})$ instances of $\Pi^{\mathcal{Z},\mathcal{Z}_A}$ with uniformly random independent bits as inputs by A and B.
     (a) If any of the executions abort: abort the protocol.
     (b) Else: Store the sampled OT from each execution.

2. For $1 \leq i \leq \ell_B$: Execute $\mathsf{Calls}(\Pi_{\ell_A+i,1})$ instances of $\Pi^{\mathcal{Z},\mathcal{Z}_B}$ with uniformly random independent bits as inputs by A and B.
   (a) If any of the executions abort: abort the protocol.
   (b) Else: Store the sampled OT from each execution.

– **OT Computation Phase**
  1. Run $\mathsf{Combiner_{mal}}(\Pi_{1,1}, \Pi_{1,2}, \ldots, \Pi_{\ell_A+\ell_B,1}, \Pi_{\ell_A+\ell_B,2})$ and output what the combiner outputs. Calls to $\Pi_{i,1}, 1 \leq i \leq \ell_A + \ell_B$ are realized by computing OT using the sampled OT from the corresponding protocol.

Proof (Proof of Lemma 7). The protocol involves only vertices in $\mathcal{V} \backslash \mathcal{Z}$, hence it is perfectly secure against the corruption of $\mathcal{Z}$. Consider any set $\mathcal{Z}' \in \mathbb{Z} \backslash \{\mathcal{Z}\}$. If the protocol aborts during the precomputation phase, the inputs of honest vertices are private since the real inputs are not used in this phase. Suppose the protocol is not aborted in the precomputation phase. Using the same argument we used in the proof of security of Π_{sh} in the semi-honest case, one could verify that against the corruption of any $\mathcal{Z}' \in \mathbb{Z} \setminus \{\mathcal{Z}\}$, a majority of the protocols used in the combiner is secure. Hence, the combiner computes OT with statistical security by Lemma 9. Moreover, if the size of $\mathbb{Z}$ is polynomial in n, then the protocols that are combined are all efficient by Lemma 10 and properties of Π^A, Π^B. Since, $\Pi^{\mathcal{Z}}$ is a combiner of $2(|\mathbb{Z}_A| + |\mathbb{Z}_B|)$ protocols, Lemma 9 implies that it is efficient in this case. This proves the lemma. □

4 Discussion

In this section we address some of the limitations of our results and scope for further improvements.

- In the semi-honest case, Theorem 1 provides a complete characterization of incomplete networks that allow a given pair of parties to compute OT. Furthermore, this result implies the more general result (Corollary 1) regarding the characterization of networks in which a given subset may realize MPC. As we previously observed, this generalizes the result by Hirt and Maurer [24] on feasibility of MPC with respect to a general adversary structure in complete networks.
  However, in the malicious case, our characterization is limited to the notion of statistical security. Our results leave open the possibility that the necessary and sufficient condition for OT with perfect security between a given pair of parties in an incomplete network might be different from the one in Theorem 2. As previously observed, our characterization directly extends to statistically secure computation of 2-party functionalities with output only at one party. However, the problem of 2-party secure computation with output at both parties remains open. Although our current technique using OT combiners is unable to realize secure computation (with fairness), we conjecture that the conditions in Theorem 2 might be sufficient for statistically secure MPC of such functionalities too.

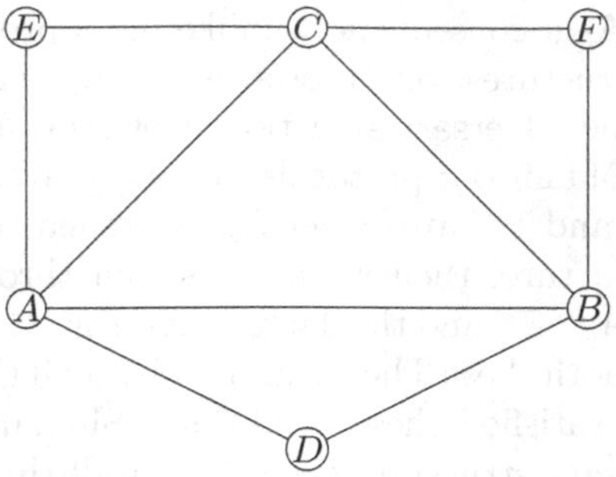

Fig. 12. Consider the problem of MPC among the parties $\{A, B, C\}$ with statistical security w.r.t. the malicious adversary structure $\mathbb{Z} = \{\{A\}, \{B\}, \{C\}\}$. Every pair of parties in $\{A, B, C\}$ satisfies the conditions in Theorem 2, hence the condition given in Corollary 2 is satisfied. However, an argument almost identical to the one presented by Fischer *et al.* in [15] can be used to show the impossibility of Byzantine agreement among $\{A, B, C\}$ in this network. This shows that the conditions given in Corollary 2 are not sufficient for a given subset of parties in an incomplete network to do MPC with statistical security w.r.t. a given adversary structure, with guaranteed output delivery.

Corollary 2 only partially solves the problem of the characterization of networks in which a given subset of parties may realize statistically secure MPC. The characterization of networks in which a given subset of parties may realize statistically secure MPC *without abort and with fairness* (guaranteed output delivery) still remains open. The example given in Fig. 12 shows that the necessary and sufficient condition for this must be strictly stronger than the condition given in Corollary 2. We also leave open the problem of whether the conditions in Corollary 2 are sufficient for a given subset of parties to realize statistically secure MPC with fairness, but with abort.

- Section 2.3 addresses efficiency for threshold adversarial structures when the threshold is a constant or when $n = 2t+O(1)$. Except for these cases, the communication complexity of our protocols are polynomial in the size of adversary structure. Efficiency of the protocol in the case of large adversary structures is an important aspect which needs further study. Being the first work on this problem, our focus has been mostly on the characterization. We hope that future work will address the efficiency question more thoroughly; we believe this might require a different set of tools.
- Protocols for general adversary structures often have the following property: if they are secure against the corruption of a set of parties, then they would be secure against the corruption of a subset of these parties. This is not true, in general, for the protocols we construct, neither in the semi-honest nor in the malicious setting. Consider a graph $G(\mathcal{V}, \mathcal{E})$, where $\mathcal{V} = \{A, B, 1\}$ and $\mathcal{E} = \{\{A, 1\}, \{1, B\}\}$. It can be verified that semi-honest OT is feasible between A and B with security against corruption of vertices $\{A, 1\}$. However, OT between A and B is impossible with security against the corruption of vertex 1, as SMT between A and B with security against such a corruption

itself is impossible. As a consequence, unlike most protocols constructed for general adversary structures, our protocols are not efficient in the number of maximal sets in the adversary structure. However, a more limited form of monotonicity does hold for our protocols. It is easy to see from the conditions in both Theorems 2 and 1 that if a set $\mathcal{Z}_A \subset \mathcal{V}$ such that $A \in \mathcal{Z}_A$ is present in the adversary structure, then we may as well throw in sets of the kind $\mathcal{Z}'_A \subset \mathcal{Z}_A$ such that $A \in \mathcal{Z}'_A$ and this larger adversary structure will satisfy the conditions stated in both these Theorems if and only if the adversary structure we started out with satisfied these conditions. Similarly, if $B \in C_B \subset \mathcal{V}$ is present in the adversary structure, we may as well throw in sets of the kind $\mathcal{Z}'_B \subset C_B$ such that $B \in \mathcal{Z}'_B$. Also, if $\mathcal{Z}$ such that $A, B \notin \mathcal{Z}$ is present in the adversary structure, then throwing in every subset of $\mathcal{Z}$ will not make any difference. Indeed, with some modifications, our protocols can be made efficient w.r.t. the size of 'maximal' adversary structure in the above sense. Another consequence of this lack of monotonicity is that our protocols do not, in general, continue to be secure when the adversary is adaptive rather than static (see [10, Chap. 4.5]). To see this, we again consider the graph $G(\mathcal{V}, \mathcal{E})$, where $\mathcal{V} = \{A, B, 1\}$ and $\mathcal{E} = \{\{A, 1\}, \{1, B\}\}$ along with the adversary structure $\{\{A, 1\}\}$. Semi-honest OT between A and B is feasible w.r.t this adversary structure when the adversary is static. However, there exists no protocol that is secure against an adaptive adversary who corrupts 1 at the beginning of the protocol and waits for B to output before corrupting A.

Acknowledgments. We acknowledge useful discussions with Manoj Prabhakaran, IIT Bombay.

References

1. Agarwal, S., Cramer, R., de Haan, R.: Asymptotically optimal two-round perfectly secure message transmission. In: Dwork, C. (ed.) CRYPTO 2006. LNCS, vol. 4117, pp. 394–408. Springer, Heidelberg (2006). https://doi.org/10.1007/11818175_24
2. Beaver, D.: Precomputing oblivious transfer. In: Coppersmith, D. (ed.) CRYPTO 1995. LNCS, vol. 963, pp. 97–109. Springer, Heidelberg (1995). https://doi.org/10.1007/3-540-44750-4_8
3. Beimel, A.: On private computation in incomplete networks. J. Distrib. Comput. **19**(3), 237–252 (2007)
4. Ben-Or, M., Goldwasser, S., Wigderson, A.: Completeness theorems for non-cryptographic fault-tolerant distributed computation. In: STOC, pp. 1–10 (1988)
5. Bläser, M., et al.: Privacy in non-private environments. J. Theory Comput. Syst. **48**(1), 211–245 (2011)
6. Bläser, M., et al.: Private computation: k-connected versus 1-connected networks. J. Cryptol. **19**(3), 341–357 (2006)
7. Chandran, N., Garay, J., Ostrovsky, R.: Edge fault tolerance on sparse networks. In: Czumaj, A., Mehlhorn, K., Pitts, A., Wattenhofer, R. (eds.) ICALP 2012. LNCS, vol. 7392, pp. 452–463. Springer, Heidelberg (2012). https://doi.org/10.1007/978-3-642-31585-5_41

8. Chandran, N., Garay, J., Ostrovsky, R.: Improved fault tolerance and secure computation on sparse networks. In: Abramsky, S., Gavoille, C., Kirchner, C., Meyer auf der Heide, F., Spirakis, P.G. (eds.) ICALP 2010. LNCS, vol. 6199, pp. 249–260. Springer, Heidelberg (2010). https://doi.org/10.1007/978-3-642-14162-1_21
9. Chaum, D., Crépeau, C., Damgård, I.: Multiparty unconditionally secure protocols. In: STOC, pp. 11–19 (1988)
10. Cramer, R., Damgård, I., Nielsen, J.: Secure Multiparty Computation and Secret Sharing. Cambridge University Press, Cambridge (2015)
11. Crépeau, C., van de Graaf, J., Tapp, A.: Committed oblivious transfer and private multi-party computation. In: Coppersmith, D. (ed.) CRYPTO 1995. LNCS, vol. 963, pp. 110–123. Springer, Heidelberg (1995). https://doi.org/10.1007/3-540-44750-4_9
12. Dolev, D.: The Byzantine generals strike again. J. Algorithms **3**(1), 14–30 (1982)
13. Dolev, D., et al.: Perfectly secure message transmission. J. ACM **40**(1), 17–47 (1993)
14. Dwork, C., et al.: Fault tolerance in networks of bounded degree. SIAM J. Comput. **17**(5), 975–988 (1988)
15. Fischer, M.J., Lynch, N.A., Merritt, M.: Easy impossibility proofs for distributed consensus problems. J. Distrib. Comput. **1**(1), 26–39 (1986)
16. Franklin, M.K., Yung, M.: Secure hypergraphs: privacy from partial broadcast. SIAM J. Discret. Math. **18**(3), 437–450 (2004)
17. Garay, J.A., Ostrovsky, R.: Almost-everywhere secure computation. In: Smart, N. (ed.) EUROCRYPT 2008. LNCS, vol. 4965, pp. 307–323. Springer, Heidelberg (2008). https://doi.org/10.1007/978-3-540-78967-3_18
18. Goldreich, O., Micali, S., Wigderson, A.: How to play any mental game or a completeness theorem for protocols with honest majority. In: STOC, pp. 218–229 (1987)
19. Goldrcich, O., Vainish, R.: How to solve any protocol problem - an efficiency improvement (extended abstract). In: Pomerance, C. (ed.) CRYPTO 1987. LNCS, vol. 293, pp. 73–86. Springer, Heidelberg (1988). https://doi.org/10.1007/3-540-48184-2_6
20. Goldwasser, S., Lindell, Y.: Secure computation without agreement. In: Malkhi, D. (ed.) DISC 2002. LNCS, vol. 2508, pp. 17–32. Springer, Heidelberg (2002). https://doi.org/10.1007/3-540-36108-1_2
21. Halevi, S., et al.: Secure multiparty computation with general interaction patterns. In: ITCS, pp. 157–168 (2016)
22. Harnik, D., Ishai, Y., Kushilevitz, E.: How many oblivious transfers are needed for secure multiparty computation? In: Menezes, A. (ed.) CRYPTO 2007. LNCS, vol. 4622, pp. 284–302. Springer, Heidelberg (2007). https://doi.org/10.1007/978-3-540-74143-5_16
23. Harnik, D., Ishai, Y., Kushilevitz, E., Nielsen, J.B.: OT-combiners via secure computation. In: Canetti, R. (ed.) TCC 2008. LNCS, vol. 4948, pp. 393–411. Springer, Heidelberg (2008). https://doi.org/10.1007/978-3-540-78524-8_22
24. Hirt, M., Maurer, U.M.: Complete characterization of adversaries tolerable in secure multi-party computation (extended abstract). In: PODC, pp. 25–34 (1997)
25. Ishai, Y., Prabhakaran, M., Sahai, A.: Founding cryptography on oblivious transfer – efficiently. In: Wagner, D. (ed.) CRYPTO 2008. LNCS, vol. 5157, pp. 572–591. Springer, Heidelberg (2008). https://doi.org/10.1007/978-3-540-85174-5_32

26. Jakoby, A., Liśkiewicz, M., Reischuk, R.: Private computations in networks: topology versus randomness. In: Alt, H., Habib, M. (eds.) STACS 2003. LNCS, vol. 2607, pp. 121–132. Springer, Heidelberg (2003). https://doi.org/10.1007/3-540-36494-3_12
27. Kilian, J.: Founding cryptography on oblivious transfer. In: STOC, pp. 20–31 (1988)
28. Kumar, M.V.N.A., et al.: On perfectly secure communication over arbitrary networks. In: PODC, pp. 193–202 (2002)
29. Kumaresan, R., Raghuraman, S., Sealfon, A.: Network oblivious transfer. In: Robshaw, M., Katz, J. (eds.) CRYPTO 2016. LNCS, vol. 9815, pp. 366–396. Springer, Heidelberg (2016). https://doi.org/10.1007/978-3-662-53008-5_13
30. Kurosawa, K., Suzuki, K.: Truly efficient 2-round perfectly secure message transmission scheme. IEEE Trans. Inf. Theor. **55**(11), 5223–5232 (2009)
31. Lamport, L., Shostak, R., Pease, M.: The Byzantine generals problem. ACM Trans. Program. Lang. Syst. **4**, 382–401 (1982)
32. Meier, R., Przydatek, B., Wullschleger, J.: Robuster combiners for oblivious transfer. In: Vadhan, S.P. (ed.) TCC 2007. LNCS, vol. 4392, pp. 404–418. Springer, Heidelberg (2007). https://doi.org/10.1007/978-3-540-70936-7_22
33. Narayanan, V., Prabhakaran, V.M.: Oblivious Transfer in Incomplete Networks. Cryptology ePrint Archive, Report 2018/875. https://eprint.iacr.org/2018/875 (2018)
34. Rabin, T., Ben-Or, M.: Verifiable secret sharing and multiparty protocols with honest majority. In: STOC, pp. 73–85 (1989)
35. Sayeed, M.H., Abu-Amara, H.: Efficient perfectly secure message transmission in synchronous networks. J. Inf. Comput. **126**(1), 53–61 (1996)
36. Spini, G., Zémor, G.: Perfectly secure message transmission in two rounds. In: Hirt, M., Smith, A. (eds.) TCC 2016. LNCS, vol. 9985, pp. 286–304. Springer, Heidelberg (2016). https://doi.org/10.1007/978-3-662-53641-4_12
37. Srinathan, K., Narayanan, A., Rangan, C.P.: Optimal perfectly secure message transmission. In: Franklin, M. (ed.) CRYPTO 2004. LNCS, vol. 3152, pp. 545–561. Springer, Heidelberg (2004). https://doi.org/10.1007/978-3-540-28628-8_33
38. Upfal, E.: Tolerating linear number of faults in networks of bounded degree. In: PODC, pp. 83–89 (1992)
39. Wullschleger, J.: Oblivious-transfer amplification. In: Naor, M. (ed.) EUROCRYPT 2007. LNCS, vol. 4515, pp. 555–572. Springer, Heidelberg (2007). https://doi.org/10.1007/978-3-540-72540-4_32

Trapdoor Permutations and Signatures

Injective Trapdoor Functions via Derandomization: How Strong is Rudich's Black-Box Barrier?

Lior Rotem(✉) and Gil Segev

School of Computer Science and Engineering, Hebrew University of Jerusalem, 91904 Jerusalem, Israel
{lior.rotem,segev}@cs.huji.ac.il

Abstract. We present a cryptographic primitive $\mathcal{P}$ satisfying the following properties:

- Rudich's seminal impossibility result (PhD thesis '88) shows that $\mathcal{P}$ cannot be used in a black-box manner to construct an injective one-way function.
- $\mathcal{P}$ can be used in a *non-black-box* manner to construct an injective one-way function assuming the existence of a hitting-set generator that fools deterministic circuits (such a generator is known to exist based on the *worst-case* assumption that $\mathrm{E} = \mathrm{DTIME}(2^{O(n)})$ has a function of deterministic circuit complexity $2^{\Omega(n)}$).
- Augmenting $\mathcal{P}$ with a trapdoor algorithm enables a non-black-box construction of an injective *trapdoor* function (once again, assuming the existence of a hitting-set generator that fools deterministic circuits), while Rudich's impossibility result still holds.

The primitive $\mathcal{P}$ and its augmented variant can be constructed based on any injective one-way function and on any injective trapdoor function, respectively, and they are thus unconditionally essential for the existence of such functions. Moreover, $\mathcal{P}$ can also be constructed based on various known primitives that are secure against related-key attacks, thus enabling to base the strong structural guarantees of injective one-way functions on the strong security guarantees of such primitives.

Our application of derandomization techniques is inspired mainly by the work of Barak, Ong and Vadhan (CRYPTO '03), which on one hand relies on any one-way function, but on the other hand only results in a non-interactive perfectly-binding commitment scheme (offering significantly weaker structural guarantees compared to injective one-way functions), and does not seem to enable an extension to public-key primitives.

L. Rotem and G. Segev—Supported by the European Union's 7th Framework Program (FP7) via a Marie Curie Career Integration Grant (Grant No. 618094), by the European Union's Horizon 2020 Framework Program (H2020) via an ERC Grant (Grant No. 714253), by the Israel Science Foundation (Grant No. 483/13), by the Israeli Centers of Research Excellence (I-CORE) Program (Center No. 4/11), by the US-Israel Binational Science Foundation (Grant No. 2014632), and by a Google Faculty Research Award.

A. Beimel and S. Dziembowski (Eds.): TCC 2018, LNCS 11239, pp. 421–447, 2018.
https://doi.org/10.1007/978-3-030-03807-6_16

The key observation underlying our approach is that Rudich's impossibility result applies not only to one-way functions as the underlying primitive, but in fact to a variety of "unstructured" primitives. We put forward a condition for identifying such primitives, and then subtly tailor the properties of our primitives such that they are both sufficiently unstructured in order to satisfy this condition, and sufficiently structured in order to yield injective one-way and trapdoor functions. This circumvents the basic approach underlying Rudich's long-standing evidence for the difficulty of constructing injective one-way functions (and, in particular, injective trapdoor functions) based on seemingly weaker or unstructured assumptions.

1 Introduction

Over the last few decades the cryptography community has been successful in constructing a wide variety of cryptographic primitives based on the minimal assumption that one-way functions exist. For example, the existence of one-way functions has been shown equivalent to the existence of private-key encryption schemes [GGM84], pseudorandom functions and permutations [GGM86,LR88,NR99], message authentication codes [GGM86], pseudorandom generators [BM84,HIL+99], universal one-way hash functions and signature schemes [NY89,Rom90], commitment schemes [Nao91,HIL+99,HNO+09], and many other symmetric primitives (also known as "MiniCrypt" primitives [Imp95]).

Despite the great progress in basing symmetric cryptography on one-way functions, the existence of one-way functions is still not known to imply the existence of all symmetric cryptographic primitives. A prime example is that of injective one-way functions (and, in particular, one-way permutations), whose existence seems to require somewhat more structured assumptions (e.g., specific number-theoretic assumptions [GLN11]).[1] Moreover, the seminal work by Rudich [Rud88], within the framework of Impagliazzo and Rudich modeling black-box constructions [IR89,RTV04], provided substantial evidence that the existence of injective one-way functions may not be "naturally implied" by the existence of arbitrary one-way functions. Specifically, Rudich proved that one-way functions cannot be used in a black-box manner to construct injective one-way functions.[2]

Black-box impossibility results are clearly inherently limited, and do not capture non-black-box techniques (e.g., [GMW86,Yao86,NY90,Bar01,AIK06,BP12,CPS16]). Thus, it may still be the case that one-way functions can be used in a non-black-box manner to construct injective one-way functions (and even one-way permutations). Given that Rudich's black-box barrier is currently

[1] An additional example is that of collision-resistant hash functions, whose existence also seems to require somewhat stronger assumptions [Sim98].

[2] Although Rudich formalized his statements for one-way permutations, his proof relies only on the injectivity of the resulting functions, and thus applies to injective one-way functions.

the main evidence for explaining our lack of success in constructing injective one-way functions based on seemingly weaker assumptions, this naturally raises the fundamental question of whether or not Rudich's black-box barrier can be circumvented using non-black-box techniques.

Significant progress towards obtaining a better understanding of the above question was made in the work of Barak, Ong and Vadhan [BOV07]. Their work demonstrated that derandomization techniques can be fundamentally useful in cryptographic constructions by enabling to eliminate interaction from certain two-message cryptographic protocols. Relying on the existence of a hitting-set generator that fools co-non-deterministic algorithms,[3] they derandomized Naor's statistically-binding commitment scheme [Nao91] for obtaining a non-interactive perfectly-binding commitment scheme (in addition, relying on the existence of a hitting-set generator that fools co-non-deterministic circuits, they derandomized Dwork and Naor's ZAPs [DN07] for obtaining a non-interactive witness-indistinguishable proof system for NP).

In particular, as observed by Barak, Ong and Vadhan, a non-interactive perfectly-binding commitment scheme naturally implies a somewhat weak form of an injective one-way function, to which they refer to as a "partially-injective" one-way function. Such a function f is a two-input function $f(x, y)$, which is injective with respect to its first input x but not necessarily with respect to its second input y (thus offers significantly weaker structural guarantees compared to an injective one-way function), and for which it is hard to recover x given $f(x, y)$ where both x and y are distributed uniformly. This shows that non-black-box techniques are useful for constructing a somewhat weak form of injective one-way functions, but the problem of whether or not such techniques can be useful for constructing (fully) injective one-way functions (and even trapdoor functions) based on seemingly weaker assumptions has been left completely open.

1.1 Our Contributions

We show that non-black-box techniques can be used to circumvent the basic approach underlying Rudich's long-standing evidence for the difficulty of constructing injective one-way functions (and, in particular, injective trapdoor functions) based on seemingly weaker or unstructured assumptions. In addition, whereas separations between the black-box and non-black-box power of cryptographic constructions were known to exist for private-key primitives [MP12], our work provides in particular such a separation for public-key primitives.

Specifically, we present a cryptographic primitive $\mathcal{P}$ and prove that it satisfies the following properties:

[3] Such a generator is known to exist based on the worst-case assumption that $\mathrm{E} = \mathrm{DTIME}(2^{O(n)})$ has a function that is not computable for infinitely many input lengths by a probabilistic non-deterministic algorithm that runs in sub-exponential time [NW94, IW97, MV99, GSTS03].

- Rudich's seminal impossibility result shows that $\mathcal{P}$ cannot be used in a black-box manner to construct an injective one-way function.
- $\mathcal{P}$ can be used in a non-black-box manner to construct an injective one-way function assuming the existence of a hitting-set generator that fools deterministic circuits. The non-black-box aspect of our construction is quite modest, asking for an upper bound on the size of $\mathcal{P}$'s implementation.
- Augmenting $\mathcal{P}$ with a trapdoor algorithm enables a non-black-box construction of an injective trapdoor function (once again, assuming the existence of a hitting-set generator that fools deterministic circuits), while Rudich's impossibility result still holds.

Generally speaking, a hitting-set generator that fools deterministic circuits is known to exist based on the worst-case assumption that $\mathrm{E} = \mathrm{DTIME}(2^{O(n)})$ has a function of deterministic circuit complexity $2^{\Omega(n)}$ (see Sect. 2.1 for more details). For our construction, however, it suffices to assume the existence of a hitting-set generator that fools a rather simple computation involving the primitive $\mathcal{P}$ (two parallel invocations of $\mathcal{P}$ followed by a comparison of their outputs). Thus, if a hitting-set generator that fools this specific computation is known to exist *unconditionally* then we do not need to rely on the above worst-case assumption.

Our application of derandomization techniques is inspired mainly by the work of Barak, Ong and Vadhan [BOV07], which on one hand relies on any one-way function, but on the other hand only results in a non-interactive perfectly-binding commitment scheme (offering a significantly weaker structural guarantee when compared to injective one-way functions), and does not seem to enable an extension to public-key primitives (see Sect. 1.3 for an in-depth discussion and comparison to previous applications of derandomization techniques in cryptography).

The Primitive $\mathcal{P}$. Our primitive $\mathcal{P}$ is a predicate $\mathcal{P} : \{0,1\}^* \rightarrow \{0,1\}$ that satisfies two rather natural properties, and we refer to this primitive as a *correlated-input balanced one-way predicate*. We show that such a predicate $\mathcal{P}$ can be constructed based on any injective one-way function without relying on any additional assumptions, and thus the existence of such a predicate is unconditionally essential for the existence of an injective one-way function. Therefore, under a standard worst-case hardness assumption, the existence of our primitive is equivalent to that of an injective one-way function, although it is strictly weaker when restricted to black-box constructions.

Moreover, we also show that $\mathcal{P}$ can be constructed in a black-box manner from various known primitives that are secure against related-secret attacks (e.g., related-key pseudorandom functions and related-seed pseudorandom generators). Although these primitives seem rather unstructured, it turns out that we can rely on their strong *security guarantees* to achieve the relatively modest *structural guarantee* of $\mathcal{P}$, and then apply derandomization techniques to obtain the more robust structure of injective one-way functions.

In addition to the primitive $\mathcal{P}$, we also introduce a natural "public-key" variant of $\mathcal{P}$ which is obtained by augmenting $\mathcal{P}$ with a trapdoor algorithm. We show that this augmented primitive can be constructed based on any injective trapdoor function without relying on any additional assumptions, and thus the existence of this primitive is unconditionally essential for the existence of an injective trapdoor one-way function. Therefore, similarly to the above, under a standard worst-case hardness assumption, the existence of our augmented primitive is equivalent to that of an injective trapdoor function, although it is strictly weaker when restricted to black-box constructions.

Our Approach. The key observation underlying our approach is that Rudich's black-box impossibility result applies not only to rule out black-box constructions of injective one-way functions from general one-way functions as the underlying primitive class, but in fact from a wide variety of "unstructured" primitive classes. As basic examples, these include one-way functions and "almost-injective" one-way functions,[4] and obviously do not include injective one-way functions. At a very high level, as we discuss in Sect. 1.2 in more detail, Rudich's impossibility applies to any primitive class $\mathfrak{S}$ satisfying the following condition: For any $\mathcal{O}, \mathcal{O}' \in \mathfrak{S}$ and for any two *disjoint* sets of inputs X and X' *of polynomial size*, there exists an $\mathcal{O}'' \in \mathfrak{S}$ that agrees with $\mathcal{O}$ on the set X and agrees with $\mathcal{O}'$ on the set X'.

Equipped with this observation, a significant part of our effort in this work focuses on carefully identifying a primitive $\mathcal{P}$ that on one hand is sufficiently unstructured in order to satisfy the above condition, whereas on the other hand it is sufficiently structured in order to yield an injective one-way function (via a non-black-box construction). As we pointed out, one-way functions and almost-injective one-way functions are examples for primitive classes that satisfy the above condition, but it is still a long-standing open problem to use them in order to construct an injective one-way function. Instead, we specifically tailor the properties of our primitive $\mathcal{P}$ in order to simultaneously satisfy the above condition and yield an injective one-way function via derandomization techniques.

1.2 Overview of Our Approach

In this section we provide an overview of our main contributions. First, we describe our new notion of a correlated-input balanced one-way predicate, as well as our non-black-box construction of an injective one-way function. We emphasize that we view the introduction and the specific formalization of our new primitive as a central contribution given that: (1) it is sufficiently unstructured in order to satisfy the above-mentioned condition for Rudich's impossibility result, (2) it is sufficiently structured in order to yield an injective one-way function, and (3) its existence is essential for the existence of an injective one-way function.

Then, we describe the application of Rudich's impossibility proof to correlated-input balanced one-way predicates, and discuss the observation that Rudich's impossibility result applies to a wide variety of primitives. In fact,

[4] We denote by an "almost-injective" function a function that is injective for each input length on all but a negligible fraction of its domain.

we prove a stronger result, showing that there is no black-box construction of a *partially-injective* one-way function (as defined by Barak, Ong and Vadhan [BOV07]) from these primitives.

Correlated-Input Balanced One-Way Predicates. The new primitive at the heart of our approach is an efficiently-computable predicate $\mathcal{P} : \{0,1\}^* \rightarrow \{0,1\}$ that can be viewed as a two-input predicate $\mathcal{P}(x, r)$, where $r \in \{0,1\}^{\ell(|x|)}$, which satisfies the following two natural requirements with respect to correlated inputs:

- The first requirement is that the predicate $\mathcal{P}$ has to be rather balanced in the sense that $|\Pr[\mathcal{P}(x, r) = \mathcal{P}(x', r)] - 1/2|$ is bounded for every distinct $x, x' \in \{0,1\}^n$, where the probability is taken over the choice of a uniform $r \in \{0,1\}^{\ell(n)}$.
  This requirement (on its own) is easy to satisfy by making sure that $\mathcal{P}$ is pair-wise independent over the choice of $r \in \{0,1\}^{\ell(n)}$. For example, this requirement can be satisfied by defining $\mathcal{P}(x, r) = \langle f(x), r \rangle$, where f may be any *injective* function mapping n-bit inputs to $\ell(n)$-bit outputs.
- The second requirement is that for adversarially-chosen values $r_1, \ldots, r_T \in \{0,1\}^{\ell(n)}$, the function mapping x to the sequence of values $\mathcal{P}(x, r_1), \ldots, \mathcal{P}(x, r_T)$ is a one-way function of x.
  This requirement (on its own) is easy to satisfy by making sure that $\mathcal{P}$ first applies any given one-way function to its first input x, and only then involves its second input r in the computation. For example, this requirement can be satisfied by defining $\mathcal{P}(x, r) = \langle f(x), r \rangle$, where f may be any *one-way* function mapping n-bit inputs to $\ell(n)$-bit outputs (note that this predicate fails to satisfy the first requirement whenever f is not an injective function).

The following definition formalizes these two requirements:

Definition 1.1. *Let $\mathcal{P} : \{0,1\}^* \rightarrow \{0,1\}$ be an efficiently-computable predicate, and let $\ell = \ell(n)$ and $\delta = \delta(n)$ be functions of the security parameter $n \in \mathbb{N}$. Then, $\mathcal{P}$ is a* correlated-input (ℓ, δ)-balanced one-way predicate *if it satisfies the following two requirements:*

- *For any $n \in \mathbb{N}$ and for any $x, x' \in \{0,1\}^n$ such that $x \neq x'$ it holds that*
$$\left| \Pr_{r \leftarrow \{0,1\}^{\ell(n)}} [\mathcal{P}(x, r) = \mathcal{P}(x', r)] - \frac{1}{2} \right| \leq \delta(n).$$
- *For any probabilistic polynomial-time algorithm A there exists a negligible function $\nu(\cdot)$ such that*
$$\Pr\left[\mathsf{Invert}_{\mathcal{P},A}(n) = 1\right] \leq \nu(n)$$
for all sufficiently large $n \in \mathbb{N}$, where the experiment $\mathsf{Invert}_{\mathcal{P},A}(n)$ is defined as follows:
  1. $(\mathsf{state}, r_1, \ldots, r_T) \leftarrow A(1^n)$ *for $r_1, \ldots, r_T \in \{0,1\}^{\ell(n)}$, where $T = T(n)$ may be any polynomial determined by A.*

2. $x' \leftarrow A(\mathsf{state}, \mathcal{P}(x, r_1), \ldots, \mathcal{P}(x, r_T))$ *where* $x \leftarrow \{0,1\}^n$.
3. *If* $x' = x$ *then output* 1, *and otherwise output* 0.

As demonstrated above, each of the two requirements on its own can be easily satisfied, but it seems significantly more difficult to simultaneously satisfy both requirements. However, putting together our examples for predicates that satisfy each requirement on its own, we observe that for any injective one-way function f mapping n-bit inputs to $\ell(n)$-bit outputs, it holds that $\mathcal{P}(x,r) = \langle f(x), r\rangle$ is a correlated-input $(\ell(n), \delta(n))$-balanced one-way predicate, where $\delta(n) = 0$.[5] This shows that the existence of such a predicate is unconditionally essential for the existence of an injective one-way function.

In addition, in the full version of the paper [RS18] we show that the existence of a correlated-input balanced one-way predicate is also implied by that of various primitives that are secure against related-key attacks. These include, for example, related-key pseudorandom functions (e.g., [BK03, Luc04, BC10, LMR14, AW14]) and related-seed pseudorandom generators (e.g., [GL10]). Unlike injective one-way functions, these primitives seem rather unstructured, yet still suffice for constructing correlated-input balanced one-way predicates.

Our Injective One-Way Function. Given any correlated-input $(\ell, 1/4)$-balanced one-way predicate $\mathcal{P}$, we present a construction of an injective one-way function by relying on a hitting-set generator H that fools deterministic circuits whose size is roughly that of $\mathcal{P}$'s given implementation. Our construction applies to any function $\ell = \ell(n)$ of the security parameter $n \in \mathbb{N}$ (recall that $\ell(n)$ denotes the length of $\mathcal{P}$'s second input r), as long as it is upper bounded by some polynomial (e.g., $\ell(n) = \log^2(n)$, $\ell(n) = n^2$). In what follows we first describe the construction assuming that $\ell(n) = O(\log n)$, as this case already sheds initial light on some of the main ideas underlying the construction. In fact, assuming that $\ell(n) = O(\log n)$ the construction is fully black box, and the hitting-set generator is not needed. Then, we show that the construction extends to any polynomial $\ell(n)$ by relying on a hitting-set generator.

Let $\mathcal{P}$ be a correlated-input $(\ell, 1/4)$-balanced one-way predicate where $\ell(n) = O(\log n)$, and denote by $r_{n,1}, \ldots, r_{n,L(n)}$ all $L(n) = 2^{\ell(n)}$ possible $\ell(n)$-bit strings for any $n \in \mathbb{N}$ (note that $L = L(n)$ is polynomial given that $\ell(n) = O(\log n)$). Then, we claim that the function

$$g(x) = \left(\mathcal{P}(x, r_{|x|,1}), \ldots, \mathcal{P}(x, r_{|x|,L(|x|)})\right)$$

is both injective and one way:

- The injectivity of g follows from the fact that $\mathcal{P}$ is balanced: For any distinct $x, x' \in \{0,1\}^n$, as long as $\Pr[\mathcal{P}(x,r) = \mathcal{P}(x',r)] < 1$, where the probability is taken over the choice of a uniform $r \in \{0,1\}^{\ell(n)}$, this means that there exists at least one value $r \in \{0,1\}^{\ell(n)}$ for which $\mathcal{P}(x,r) \neq \mathcal{P}(x',r)$, and therefore $g(x) \neq g(x')$.

[5] This follows from our above observation that $\mathcal{P}(x,r) = \langle f(x), r\rangle$ satisfies the first requirement for any injective f, and satisfies the second requirement for any one-way f.

- The one-wayness of g follows from the fact that $\mathcal{P}$ is one-way for correlated inputs: For any sequence of values $r_1, \ldots, r_T$ the function mapping x to the sequence of values $\mathcal{P}(x, r_1), \ldots, \mathcal{P}(x, r_T)$ is a one-way function of x. This holds, in particular, for the sequence of values $r_{n,1}, \ldots, r_{n,L(n)}$, and thus g is a one-way function.

Now suppose that $\mathcal{P}$ is a correlated-input $(\ell, 1/4)$-balanced one-way predicate where $\ell(n)$ may be any polynomial. Here, we can no longer define g as above by enumerating over all possible $\ell(n)$-bit strings to be used as $\mathcal{P}$'s second input r. All we need, however, is to enumerate over a carefully-chosen set $r_1, \ldots, r_T$ such that for any distinct $x, x' \in \{0,1\}^n$ there exists a value $r \in \{r_1, \ldots r_T\}$ such that $\mathcal{P}(x, r) \neq \mathcal{P}(x', r)$. This is exactly the type of guarantee that is provided by a hitting-set generator, and enables us to argue that the following function g is both injective and one way: On input $x \in \{0,1\}^n$ our function $g : \{0,1\}^* \to \{0,1\}^*$ first uses a hitting-set generator H that fools circuits whose size is roughly the size of $\mathcal{P}$'s implementation for obtaining a sequence of values $r_1, \ldots, r_{T(n)} \in \{0,1\}^{\ell(n)}$, and then outputs the value

$$g(x) = \left(\mathcal{P}(x, r_1), \ldots, \mathcal{P}(x, r_{T(n)})\right).$$

In Sect. 3 we prove that the injectivity of g follows from the fact that $\mathcal{P}$ is balanced and H is a hitting-set generator, whereas the one-wayness of g follows from the fact that $\mathcal{P}$ is one way for correlated inputs as above. Moreover, we show that by augmenting $\mathcal{P}$ with a trapdoor argument, our construction generalizes to an injective trapdoor function. We refer the reader to Sect. 3 for the formal details.

Applying Rudich's Impossibility to Correlated-Input Predicates. We now briefly overview Rudich's approach while pointing out the adjustments required in order to apply it to correlated-input balanced one-way predicates. Let $\mathcal{O} = \{\mathcal{O}_n\}_{n \in \mathbb{N}}$ be an oracle, where each $\mathcal{O}_n$ is uniformly chosen from some function family $\mathfrak{S}_n$, and let C be an oracle-aided circuit guaranteeing that $C^{\mathcal{O}}$ implements an injective function for any $\mathcal{O} \in \{\mathfrak{S}_n\}_{n \in \mathbb{N}}$. In the case of Rudich's proof, $\mathfrak{S}_n$ is the family of all functions mapping n bits to n bits, and hence $\mathcal{O}$ is simply a random length-preserving function. In our case, $\mathfrak{S}_n$ is the set of all $(\ell(n) = n, \delta(n) = 2^{-n/3})$-balanced predicates; i.e., predicates taking inputs in $\{0,1\}^n \times \{0,1\}^n$, such that for every distinct $x, x' \in \{0,1\}^n$ it holds that $\left|\Pr_{r \leftarrow \{0,1\}^n}\left[\mathcal{O}_n(x, r) = \mathcal{O}_n(x', r)\right] - 1/2\right| \leq 2^{-n/3}$. We set $\ell(n) = n$ for the sake of simplicity, but the proof holds for any super-logarithmic ℓ with minor adjustments.

Rudich's proof then considers an adversary that makes a polynomial number of queries to $\mathcal{O}$ and always succeeds in inverting $C^{\mathcal{O}}(x^*)$ for any input x^*. On input $y^* = C^{\mathcal{O}}(x^*)$, the adversary A proceeds in iterations, where in each iteration it arbitrarily picks a value x and a possible oracle $\mathcal{O}'$ that is consistent with what it has learned so far on $\mathcal{O}$, such that $y^* = C^{\mathcal{O}'}(x)$. A then checks if $C^{\mathcal{O}}(x) = y^*$ (if so $x = x^*$), and if not, queries $\mathcal{O}$ with all queries in the execution of $C^{\mathcal{O}'}(x)$ that were not already known. The main observation is that in each iteration, the adversary either learns a new query made in the evaluation of $C^{\mathcal{O}}(x^*)$, or finds the correct pre-image $x = x^*$ of y^*. Hence, if C makes at most q oracle queries, then A is guaranteed to find x^* within $q + 1$ iterations.

In order to prove this main observation, suppose that in some iteration A does not learn a new query made in the evaluation of $C^{\mathcal{O}}(x^*)$ nor does it hold that $x = x^*$. This means that from A's point of view, the oracles have so far been defined on disjoint sets of inputs. Now, the idea is that $\mathcal{O}$ and $\mathcal{O}'$ can be "glued" together to form a third oracle $\mathcal{O}'' \in \mathfrak{S}$ such that $C^{\mathcal{O}''}(x) = C^{\mathcal{O}''}(x^*) = y^*$, contradicting the injectivity guarantee of C. In the case of Rudich's proof, this is straightforward: since $\mathfrak{S}$ is the family of *all* length-preserving functions, $\mathcal{O}''$ can simply be any oracle that is consistent with the answers of $\mathcal{O}$ and $\mathcal{O}'$ to the queries made during the evaluations of $C^{\mathcal{O}}(x^*)$ and $C^{\mathcal{O}'}(x)$, respectively, and can be arbitrarily defined everywhere else. In our case, we need to show that we can complete $\mathcal{O}''$ to be balanced for every input length.

More generally, this shows that Rudich's proof does not only apply to length-preserving functions or to correlated-input balanced predicates, but in fact to any function family $\mathfrak{S}$ that is "sufficiently unstructured" in order to guarantee the following property: For any two functions $\mathcal{O}, \mathcal{O}' \in \mathfrak{S}$ and for any two *disjoint* sets of "not too short" inputs X and X' *of polynomial size*, there exists a function $\mathcal{O}'' \in \mathfrak{S}$ that agrees with $\mathcal{O}$ on the set X and agrees with $\mathcal{O}'$ on the set X'. We have provided two examples for such families: All length-preserving functions (i.e., where $\mathcal{O}$ a random oracle) and all balanced predicates. Of course, not all families exhibit this property as some primitives—and in particular injective one-way functions—do imply injective one-way functions in a black-box manner. For example, if we consider $\mathfrak{S} = \{\mathfrak{S}_n\}_{n \in \mathbb{N}}$ where $\mathfrak{S}_n$ is the set of all permutations on n-bit strings, then this is obviously not the case even for X and X' of size one. For any $n \in \mathbb{N}$ and any distinct $x, x' \in \{0,1\}^n$, if $\mathcal{O}(x) = \mathcal{O}'(x')$, then no function $\mathcal{O}'' \in \mathfrak{S}$ can agree both with $\mathcal{O}$ on input x and with $\mathcal{O}'$ on input x', as this will contradict the injectivity of $\mathcal{O}''$.

Two final remarks are in order. First, one still needs to show that our balanced predicate oracle is hard to invert for correlated inputs. Roughly speaking, this follows from the fact that a truly uniform predicate is correlated-input one way, and is also balanced with an overwhelming probability. Second, our proof readily extends to rule out black-box constructions of the seemingly weaker *partially-injective one-way functions* from our strengthened variant of $\mathcal{P}$ that is augmented with a trapdoor algorithm. We refer the reader to Sect. 4 for the formal details.

1.3 Related Work

The Power of Black-Box vs. Non-black-Box Constructions. Our work shows a gap between the power of black-box constructions and the power of non-black-box constructions both in the private-key setting and in the public-key setting.

Such a gap in the private-key setting was previously identified by Mahmoody and Pass [MP12] who proved that one-way functions cannot be used in a black-box manner for constructing a non-interactive commitment scheme. Combining their negative result with the above-mentioned positive result of Barak et al. implies that, under a standard worst-case hardness assumption, the existence of a one-way function is equivalent to that of a non-interactive commitment scheme, although it is strictly weaker when restricted to black-box constructions.[6]

Our work identifies such a gap in the public-key setting as well, by showing that augmenting our primitive $\mathcal{P}$ with a trapdoor algorithm enables a non-black-box construction of a trapdoor function (while Rudich's impossibility result still holds), whereas the construction of Barak et al. does not seem to enable an extension to the public-key setting. An additional such gap in the public-key setting was identified by Döttling and Garg [DG17] who presented a breakthrough construction of an identity-based encryption scheme based on the computational Diffie-Hellman assumption, circumventing the impossibility result of Papakonstantinou et al. [PRV12] in the generic-group model.

Derandomization in Cryptography. When compared to the work of Barak, Ong and Vadhan [BOV07] and other applications of derandomization in similar scenarios (e.g., [Lau83, Nao91, DN07, DNR04, BV17]), our work exhibits the following main differences.

- The underlying cryptographic building block and the resulting primitive in our work are incomparable to those in their work: We rely on a seemingly stronger cryptographic building block (specifically, a correlated-input balanced one-way predicate in our work vs. a one-way function in their work), and obtain a seemingly stronger primitive (an injective one-way function in our work vs. a partially-injective one-way function in their work). A natural question that arises in this context is whether or not our two approaches can be combined and yield a non-black-box construction of an injective one-way function based on any one-way function.
- We rely on the existence of a hitting-set generator that fools *deterministic circuits*, whereas Barak et al. rely on the seemingly incomparable assumption that there exists a hitting-set generator that fools *co-non-deterministic algorithms.* In turn, our transformation relies on the assumption that $\mathrm{E} = \mathrm{DTIME}(2^{O(n)})$ has a function of deterministic circuit complexity $2^{\Omega(n)}$, whereas Barak et al. rely on the assumption that $\mathrm{E} = \mathrm{DTIME}(2^{O(n)})$ has a function that is not computable for infinitely many input lengths by a probabilistic non-deterministic algorithm that runs in sub-exponential time.
- Following the work of Barak et al. derandomization using pseudorandom generators was also applied in the recent work of Bitansky and Vaikuntanathan [BV17] (both motivated by the classic applications of derandomization techniques in similar settings [Lau83, Nao91, DN07, DNR04]). The common theme underlying these applications is to derandomize an "almost perfectly correct" primitive into a "perfectly correct" one. This seems somewhat incomparable to our work, where our starting point is not an "almost perfectly correct"

[6] As pointed out by Mahmoody and Pass [MP12], this is different from the results of Barak [Bar01] and Goldreich and Krawczyk [GK96] which provide separations between the power of black-box and non-black-box *proofs of security.*

injective one-way function, but rather our new notion of a correlated-input balanced one-way predicate.
Indeed, it would seem that using an "almost perfectly correct" injective one-way function as our starting point is not enough. Consider for example a collection of functions, where all of them are one way, and most of them are injective. A standard attempt to apply derandomization techniques to construct an injective one-way function from such a collection may naturally rely on the following idea: Given an input x, use a hitting-set generator to choose a small subset of the functions in the collection, evaluate all of these functions on the same input x, and concatenate their outputs. The properties of the hitting-set generator indeed guarantee that the resulting function is injective (since at least one of the functions chosen by the generator is injective), but unfortunately there is no guarantee that this function is actually one way. A similar problem will arise when trying to start with a single function that is almost injective in the sense that it has only a few collisions. Our new primitive $\mathcal{P}$ is just strong enough to enable the construction of an injective one-way function by applying such techniques, yet still weak enough so that Rudich's black-box separation directly applies to it.

Strengthening the Framework of Black-Box Constructions. In recent years there have been several approaches for extending the framework of black-box impossibility results to capture various non-black-box techniques. For example, Brakerski et al. [BKS+11] and Asharov and Segev [AS15] showed that various non-black-box constructions that are based on non-interactive zero-knowledge proofs and indistinguishability obfuscation [BGI+12, GGH+13], respectively, can in fact be modeled in a black-box manner. This enabled them to prove various limitations on the power of these two primitives even when used in a particular non-black-box manner. Subsequently, Garg et al. [GMM17] refined the framework of Asharov and Segev to also account for "self-calls" of some primitives that might receive circuits as input (e.g., indistinguishability obfuscation).

Baecher, Brzuska and Fischlin [BBF13] considered more fine-grained variants of black-box constructions. Among their definitions, they considered constructions where the correctness or security guarantees need hold only for the case when the underlying primitive or the adversary in the security reduction are assumed to be efficient. They also went a step further, to consider a more subtle definition in which the security reduction may depend on some parameters of the assumed adversary (such as running time, success probability, etc.), even though its *access* to the adversary may still be black box. These notions seem related to, but do not precisely capture our non-black-box construction of an injective one-way function, which makes use of knowledge of the implementation size *of the underlying primitive* (with a security proof that makes black-box use of the adversary).

Most relevant to our work is the work of Pass, Tseng and Venkitasubramaniam [PTV11] that rules out constructions of various cryptographic primitives (e.g., one-way permutations, collision-resistant hash functions, constant-round statistically-hiding commitments, and constant-round black-box zero-knowledge proofs for NP) based on one-way functions, where the implementation of the underlying one-way function can be used in an arbitrary manner both within the construction and within the security proof, but the adversary may only be used in a black-box manner within the proof of security.[7] Their results are based on average-case strengthenings of the traditional assumption that coNP is not contained in AM. As Pass et al. pointed out, their approach does not seem to extend to ruling out constructions of injective one-way functions (as such functions may not be size-verifiable in general).

More recently, the work of Dachman-Soled [Dac16] strengthened the black-box barrier of constructing a public-key encryption scheme based on one-way functions [IR89] by relying on somewhat similar assumptions. Roughly speaking, her work considers non-adaptive constructions, where both the underlying one-way function and the adversary are used in a black-box manner by the construction and the security proof, respectively, but the security proof is allowed to rely on the implementation of the underlying one-way function in an arbitrary manner (this class of constructions seems orthogonal to our construction).

1.4 Open Problems

Circumventing Other Black-Box Barriers. A natural question that arises is whether we can rely on worst-case assumptions and similar techniques to those we use in order to circumvent other known and long-standing black-box impossibility results. In particular, can such techniques be useful in obtaining a key-agreement protocol from any one-way function or from slightly stronger yet symmetric-key primitives, or in constructing collision-resistant hash functions from any one-way function; circumventing the black-box separation results of Impagliazzo and Rudich [IR89] and of Simon [Sim98], respectively? Conversely, can one enhance the aforementioned impossibility results in a way that will provide evidence that such constructions are unlikely to exist? We refer the reader to Sect. 1.3 for a discussion on recent approaches to broaden the black-box separations framework.

Correlated-Input Balanced One-Way Predicates vs. One-Way Functions. Our new primitive $\mathcal{P}$ seems to be somewhat stronger than "plain" one-way functions, yet at least from a structural point of view, the added requirement is fairly modest and it seems much weaker than the injectivity requirement of injective one-way functions. A central open question is then the following: Can one construct a correlated-input balanced one-way predicate from any one-way function, resulting – when combined with our result (and a worst-case complexity assumption) – in a construction of an injective one-way function from any one-way function? Alternatively, can it be shown that such a construction

7 This is exactly our case: We need a bound on the size of the underlying primitive's implementation both for the construction and for security proof, but the adversary is used in a black-box manner.

is impossible in a black-box manner, thus establishing that a black-box barrier between general one-way functions and their injective counterparts still exists?

Per the latter possibility, it seems that the structural properties of $\mathcal{P}$ are weak enough, so that at least the techniques underlying Rudich's approach cannot be applied to ruling out black-box constructions of $\mathcal{P}$ from one-way functions. More broadly, any separation that aims to derive a contradiction to $\mathcal{P}$'s balance requirement (the first property in Definition 1.1) will have to fundamentally deviate from Rudich's technique due to the following observation. Suppose C is a candidate implementation of an (ℓ, δ)-balanced predicate with respect to some oracle $\mathcal{O}$, and say we partially fix $\mathcal{O}$ so that the output of $C^{\mathcal{O}}$ is determined for a subset X of its possible inputs of length $n + \ell(n)$. Even if X is of exponential size (in n), then $C^{\mathcal{O}}$ might still be (ℓ, δ)-balanced for a non-negligible δ, which is enough for our needs of constructing an injective one-way function.

Constructing Correlated-Input Balanced Trapdoor Predicates. In the current state of affairs, candidates for injective trapdoor functions are scarce. Most candidates rely on specific number-theoretic or lattice based assumptions, and general constructions from other cryptographic primitives either rely on very strong assumptions such as sub-exponential indistinguishability obfuscation [BPW16] or are proven in the random oracle model [BHS+98]. We thus view the construction of our trapdoor version of $\mathcal{P}$ from new assumptions as a very interesting open problem, as this will imply new constructions for injective trapdoor functions. More specifically, can the trapdoor version of $\mathcal{P}$ be obtained from public-key encryption (perhaps with additional symmetric primitives)? Can enhancing the latter's security properties help in such a transformation (similarly to the symmetric case, in which we were able to trade strong security guarantees of related-key secure pseudorandom functions for the structural ones of $\mathcal{P}$)?

Weakening the Derandomization-Related Assumption. Our construction of an injective one-way function is based on the existence of a hitting-set generator, which in turn is known to exist under the assumption of a non-uniform circuit lower bound (namely, that $\mathsf{E} = \mathrm{DTIME}(2^{O(n)})$ has a function of deterministic circuit complexity $2^{\Omega(n)}$). Can this assumption be weakened? More specifically, can similar results be obtained using weaker types of hitting-set generators or pseudorandom generators, known to exist under seemingly weaker complexity assumptions? For example, can results of similar nature be based on the seemingly weaker assumption that $\mathsf{P} = \mathsf{BPP}$, which Goldreich [Gol11] showed to yield certain uniform versions of pseudorandom generators?

Implications to Extensions of Rudich's Work. A variety of extensions have been developed to Rudich's impossibility result, including for example [BKS+11, MM11, AS15, AS16, BDV17, RSS17]. Our result does not directly imply that all of these extensions may be circumvented as well, since they deal with primitives that seem either significantly stronger than injective one-way functions (e.g., public-key primitives [BKS+11, AS15] and specific forms of injective one-way functions [MM11, AS16]), or incomparable to injective one-way functions (e.g., bounded-TFNP instances [RSS17]), and are currently not known to be implied by our notion of a correlated-input balanced one-way predicate. An interesting problem that arises given these extensions is to extend our approach to such stronger or incomparable primitives.

1.5 Paper Organization

The remainder of this paper is organized as follows. In Sect. 2 we introduce our notation as well as the basic cryptographic primitives that we consider in this paper. In Sect. 3 we present our constructions of an injective one-way function and of an injective trapdoor function. Finally, in Sect. 4 we show that Rudich's impossibility result applies not only to constructions based on one-way functions, but also to constructions based on correlated-input balanced one-way predicates (and even when augmented with a trapdoor algorithm).

2 Preliminaries

In this section we present the notation and basic definitions that are used in this work. For a distribution X we denote by $x \leftarrow X$ the process of sampling a value x from the distribution X. Similarly, for a set $\mathcal{X}$ we denote by $x \leftarrow \mathcal{X}$ the process of sampling a value x from the uniform distribution over $\mathcal{X}$. The *statistical distance* between two distributions X and Y over a finite domain Ω is $\mathsf{SD}(X,Y) = \frac{1}{2}\sum_{\omega \in \Omega} |X(\omega) - Y(\omega)|$. For an integer $n \in \mathbb{N}$ we denote by $[n]$ the set $\{1, \ldots, n\}$. A function $\nu : \mathbb{N} \rightarrow \mathbb{R}^+$ is *negligible* if for any polynomial $p(\cdot)$ there exists an integer N such that for all $n > N$ it holds that $\nu(n) \leq 1/p(n)$.

2.1 Hitting-Set Generators

We rely on the following standard notion of a hitting-set generator, as formalized by Goldreich et al. [GVW11], for the class of deterministic circuits (see also [Sip88, CG89, And94, ACR+97, LLS+97, ACR98, GVW11] and the references therein).

Definition 2.1. *A deterministic polynomial-time algorithm H is a* hitting-set generator that fools deterministic circuits *if for every $n, t \in \mathbb{N}$ the generator H on input $(1^n, 1^t)$ outputs a set $\mathcal{S}$ such that the following hold:*

- *$\mathcal{S} \subseteq \{0,1\}^n$.*
- *For every circuit $C : \{0,1\}^n \rightarrow \{0,1\}$ of size at most t for which*

$$\Pr_{x \leftarrow \{0,1\}^n} [C(x) = 1] \geq 1/4,$$

there exists some $x^* \in \mathcal{S}$ such that $C(x^*) = 1$.

Any *pseudorandom* generator [NW94] that fools deterministic circuits and has a logarithmic seed length immediately gives rise to such a hitting-set generator (by having H enumerate over all possible seeds). This implies the following corollary on which we rely for our constructions in Sect. 3:

Corollary 2.2 ([NW94,IW97]). *If there exists a function* $f \in DTIME(2^{O(n)})$ *with deterministic circuit complexity* $2^{\Omega(n)}$, *then there exists a hitting-set generator that fools deterministic circuits.*

2.2 Injective and Partially-Injective One-Way Functions

In this paper we rely on the following standard notions of one-way functions and injective one-way functions (see, for example, [Gol01]), as well as on the notion of partially-injective one-way functions due to Barak, Ong and Vadhan [BOV07].

Definition 2.3. *An efficiently-computable function* $f : \{0,1\}^* \to \{0,1\}^*$ *is* one way *if for every probabilistic polynomial-time algorithm A there exists a negligible function* $\nu(\cdot)$ *such that*

$$\Pr_{x \leftarrow \{0,1\}^n} \left[A(1^n, f(x)) \in f^{-1}(f(x))\right] \leq \nu(n)$$

for all sufficiently large $n \in \mathbb{N}$.

An injective one-way function is a function that is both injective and one way. Barak, Ong, and Vadhan [BOV07] introduced the following notion of a partially-injective one-way function.

Definition 2.4 ([BOV07]). *Let* $m = m(n)$ *be a function of the security parameter* $n \in \mathbb{N}$. *An efficiently-computable function* $f : \{0,1\}^* \times \{0,1\}^* \to \{0,1\}^*$ *is a* partially-injective one-way function *if it satisfies the following two requiremets:*

1. *For every* $n \in \mathbb{N}$, *every* $x, x' \in \{0,1\}^n$ *such that* $x \neq x'$, *and every* $y, y' \in \{0,1\}^{m(n)}$, *it holds that* $f(x, y) \neq f(x', y')$ *(i.e., f is injective with respect to its first input).*
2. *For every probabilistic polynomial-time algorithm A there exits a negligible function* $\nu(\cdot)$ *such that*

$$\Pr_{(x,y) \leftarrow \{0,1\}^{n+m(n)}} \left[A\left(f(x, y)\right) = x\right] \leq \nu(n)$$

for all sufficiently large $n \in \mathbb{N}$.

Note that a partially-injective one-way function with $m(n) = 0$ is in fact an injective one-way function, but for general $m(n)$ this notion seems potentially weaker than that of an injective one-way function. Barak et al. observed that any perfectly-binding non-interactive commitment scheme yields a partially-injective one-way function. Since Barak et al. derandomized Naor's commitment scheme [Nao91] into a perfectly-binding non-interactive one assuming the existence of a hitting-set generator that fools co-non-deterministic algorithms (recall Sect. 2.1), the following corollary follows.

Corollary 2.5 ([BOV07]). *Assuming the existence of a hitting-set generator that fools co-non-deterministic algorithms, then one-way functions imply partially-injective one-way functions.*

2.3 Injective Trapdoor Functions

We also rely in this paper on the following standard notion of a collection of trapdoor functions (see, for example, [Gol01]).

Definition 2.6. *Let $m = m(n)$ be a function of the security parameter $n \in \mathbb{N}$. A* collection of trapdoor functions *is a triplet of efficient algorithms $\mathcal{F} = (G, F, F^{-1})$ satisfying the following requirements:*

1. *G is a probabilistic algorithm that on input 1^n, samples and outputs a public key $pk \in \{0,1\}^n$ and a corresponding trapdoor $td \in \{0,1\}^n$.*[8]
2. *F is a deterministic algorithm that receives as input a public key $pk \in \{0,1\}^n$ and an additional input value $x \in \{0,1\}^n$ and outputs a value $y \in \{0,1\}^{m(n)}$. We require that for every probabilistic polynomial-time algorithm A there exists a negligible function ν such that*
$$\Pr_{\substack{(td,pk)\leftarrow G(1^n)\\ x\leftarrow\{0,1\}^n}}\left[F(pk, A(1^n, pk, F(pk, x))) = F(pk, x)\right] \leq \nu(n)$$
for all sufficiently large $n \in \mathbb{N}$.
3. *F^{-1} is a deterministic algorithm that on input $(td, F(pk, x))$ has the following guarantee: For any $n \in \mathbb{N}$, (td, pk) in the range of $G(1^n)$ and $x \in \{0,1\}^n$, it holds that $F^{-1}(td, F(pk, x))$ outputs $x' \in \{0,1\}^n$ such that $F(pk, x') = F(pk, x)$.*

We say that $\mathcal{F}$ is a collection of injective trapdoor functions if for every $n \in \mathbb{N}$ and any (td, pk) in the range of $G(1^n)$ the function $F(pk, \cdot)$ is injective.

3 Our Constructions

In this section we present our non-black-box constructions of an injective one-way function (see Sect. 3.1) and an injective trapdoor function (see Sect. 3.2).

3.1 An Injective One-Way Function

In this section we present our non-black-box construction of an injective one-way function from any correlated-input balanced one-way predicate and any hitting-set generator that fools deterministic circuits. More formally, our construction relies on the following two building blocks:

- A correlated-input $(\ell, 1/4)$-balanced one-way predicate $\mathcal{P}$ (recall Definition 1.1), where $\ell(n)$ may be upper bounded by any fixed polynomial (e.g., $\ell(n) = \log^2(n)$, $\ell(n) = n^2$). Let $t = t(n)$ be an upper bound on the size of the circuit computing $\mathcal{P}(x, r)$ for inputs $x \in \{0,1\}^n$ (recall that $r \in \{0,1\}^{\ell(n)}$).

[8] Definition 2.6 assumes that the lengths of the public key and of the trapdoor are equal to the security parameter n. This is for simplicity only, and in both cases one may replace n with any length that is polynomial in n.

- A hitting-set generator H that fools deterministic circuits. Denote by $T = T(n)$ the size of the set $\mathcal{S}$ that is produced by the generator H on input $(1^{\ell(n)}, 1^{2t(n)+c})$ for a constant c to be determined later. As discussed in Sect. 2.1, such a generator exists based on the worst-case assumption that $\mathrm{E} = \mathrm{DTIME}(2^{O(n)})$ has a function with deterministic circuit complexity $2^{\Omega(n)}$.

We note that the choice of the constant 1/4 that parameterizes both of our building blocks is rather arbitrary. More generally, the construction may rely on any (ℓ, δ)-balanced predicate and on any ϵ-hitting-set generator as long as $\delta + \epsilon \geq 1/2$ (in Definition 2.1 we fixed ϵ to be 1/4, but the definition readily extends to any $\epsilon \in [0, 1]$).

The Construction. On input $x \in \{0,1\}^n$ our function $g : \{0,1\}^* \to \{0,1\}^*$ first computes

$$H\left(1^{\ell(n)}, 1^{2t(n)+c}\right) = \left(r_1, \ldots, r_{T(n)}\right) \in \{0,1\}^{\ell(n) \times T(n)},$$

where $c > 0$ is a fixed constant that we determine later on, and then outputs the value

$$g(x) = \left(\mathcal{P}(x, r_1), \ldots, \mathcal{P}(x, r_{T(n)})\right) \in \{0,1\}^{T(n)}.$$

The following theorem, which is proved in the full version of this work [RS18], states that g is an injective one-way function based on our assumptions on the underlying building blocks $\mathcal{P}$ and H:

Theorem 3.1. *Assuming that $\mathcal{P}$ is a correlated-input $(\ell, 1/4)$-balanced one-way predicate and that H is a hitting-set generator that fools deterministic circuits, the function g is an injective one-way function.*

3.2 An Injective Trapdoor Function

We now turn to extend our approach to injective *trapdoor* functions. Loosely speaking, we augment our primitive $\mathcal{P}$ with a trapdoor algorithm $\mathcal{P}^{-1}$, and show that an extension of the construction presented in Sect. 3.1 yields an injective trapdoor function. Informally, knowledge of a trapdoor enables $\mathcal{P}^{-1}$ to find an $x \in \{0,1\}^n$ such that $\mathcal{P}(x, r) = b$ for each pair $(r, b) \in \{0,1\}^{\ell(n)} \times \{0,1\}$ in a set S of such pairs that is given as input to the algorithm, with the proviso that S provides "sufficient information" about x. This last condition may be formalized as a boolean set function $\phi : \left(\{0,1\}^{\ell}\right)^* \to \{0,1\}$ with the interpretation that a set is mapped to 1 if and only if it is "sufficiently rich". Informally, a reasonable choice of a function ϕ should meet two criteria:

1. For every $n \in \mathbb{N}$, it should be possible to efficiently come up with a set that satisfy ϕ. Otherwise, $\mathcal{P}^{-1}$ seems of little use.
2. ϕ should be monotone; i.e., if $S \subseteq T$ and $\phi(S) = 1$, then $\phi(T) = 1$. Intuitively, if $\phi(S) = 1$ has the interpretation that S generates "enough information" on x, then surely this is also the case for T.

A natural choice for ϕ, which we will adopt in our definition below, is a function that checks whether or not the input set contains a basis for $\mathbb{F}_2^{\ell(n)}$ (when each element $r \in \{0,1\}^{\ell(n)}$ is viewed a vector in $\mathbb{F}_2^{\ell(n)}$); that is, $\phi(S) = 1$ if and only if S contains a subset of $\ell(n)$ linearly independent r's. This choice, other than satisfying the aforementioned criteria, enables us to construct a correlated-input balanced *trapdoor* predicate (as will be defined shortly in Definition 3.2) from any injective trapdoor function, making our trapdoor predicate with respect to that choice of ϕ essential for the existence of injective trapdoor functions.

It should be noted, however, that any choice of ϕ that satisfies the above two criteria yields a predicate that can be used in a non-black-box manner to construct an injective trapdoor function via our transformation, yet (a strengthened version of) Rudich's proof shows that this is not the case when restricting ourselves to black-box constructions. Indeed, in Sect. 4 we show that this augmented variant of $\mathcal{P}$ cannot be used in a black-box manner to construct even a partially-injective one-way function.

The following definition naturally extends Definition 1.1 by considering a family of predicates equipped with a trapdoor algorithm, as discussed above:

Definition 3.2. *Let $\ell = \ell(n)$ and let $\delta = \delta(n)$ be functions of the security parameter. A* correlated-input (ℓ, δ)-balanced trapdoor predicate *is a triplet $\mathcal{T} = (G, P, P^{-1})$ of efficiently-computable algorithms such that:*

- *The algorithm G on input 1^n outputs a pair $(pk, td) \in \{0,1\}^*$.*
- *For every $n \in \mathbb{N}$ and for every $pk \in \{0,1\}^*$ produced by $G(1^n)$, the function $P(pk,\cdot,\cdot) : \{0,1\}^n \times \{0,1\}^{\ell(n)} \to \{0,1\}$ is an (ℓ, δ)-balanced predicate. That is, for any $x, x' \in \{0,1\}^n$ such that $x \neq x'$ it holds that*

$$\left| \Pr_{r \leftarrow \{0,1\}^{\ell(n)}} \left[\mathcal{P}(pk, x, r) = \mathcal{P}(pk, x', r) \right] - \frac{1}{2} \right| \leq \delta(n).$$

- *For every $n, T \in \mathbb{N}$, and for every (pk, td) that is produced by $G(1^n)$, the algorithm P^{-1} satisfies the following guarantee:*
  On input td and $\{(r_i, b_i)\}_{i=1}^T \in \left(\{0,1\}^{\ell(n)} \times \{0,1\}\right)^T$, if the set $\{r_i\}_{i=1}^T$ contains a subset of $\ell(n)$ linearly independent elements and there exists an $x \in \{0,1\}^n$ such that $P(pk, r_i) = b_i$ for every $i \in [T]$, then P^{-1} outputs such an x. Otherwise, P^{-1} outputs $\perp$.
- *For any probabilistic polynomial-time algorithm A there exists a negligible function $\nu(\cdot)$ such that*

$$\Pr\left[\mathsf{Invert}_{\mathcal{T},A}(n) = 1\right] \leq \nu(n)$$

  for all sufficiently large $n \in \mathbb{N}$, where the experiment $\mathsf{Invert}_{\mathcal{T},A}(n)$ is defined as follows:
  1. *$(\mathsf{state}, r_1, \ldots, r_T) \leftarrow A(1^n, pk)$ for $r_1, \ldots, r_T \in \{0,1\}^{\ell(n)}$, where $T = T(n)$ may be any polynomial determined by A and $(pk, td) \leftarrow G(1^n)$.*
  2. *$x' \leftarrow A\left(\mathsf{state}, P_{pk}(x, r_1), \ldots, P_{pk}(x, r_T)\right)$ where $x \leftarrow \{0,1\}^n$.*
  3. *If $x' = x$ then output 1, and otherwise output 0.*

Observe that the existence of $\mathcal{T}$ is indeed essential for the existence of an injective trapdoor function. Let $\mathcal{F} = (G_F, F, F^{-1})$ be any collection of injective trapdoor functions, and consider the construction $P_{pk}(x, r) = \langle F_{pk}(x), r\rangle$. This is essentially (a keyed version of) the same construction that we had in the symmetric case, and P is thus both balanced for every pk and correlated-input one way for the same reasons as before. As for the inversion algorithm P^{-1}, note that given the construction P, every pair (r, b) in the input to P^{-1} may be interpreted as a linear equation with $\ell(n)$ variables over $\mathbb{F}_2$: $\langle F_{pk}(x), r\rangle = b$. Hence, when the input to P^{-1} contains $\ell(n)$ linearly independent r's (which is only then that it is required to return a pre-image x), it can uniquely recover $z = F_{pk}(x)$ and invoke $F_{td}^{-1}(z)$ to find x.

Similarly to Sect. 3.1, our construction of an injective trapdoor function is based a hitting-set-generator against deterministic circuits H, but we replace the correlated-product $(\ell, 1/4)$-balanced *one-way* predicate $\mathcal{P}$, with a correlated-product $(\ell, 1/4)$-balanced *trapdoor* predicate $\mathcal{T} = (G, P, P^{-1})$. As before, we let $t = t(n)$ be an upper bound on the size of the circuit computing $P_{pk}(x, r)$ for $x \in \{0,1\}^n$ and let $T = T(n)$ denote the size of $\mathcal{S} = \{r_1, \ldots, r_T\}$ - the output set of H on input $(1^{\ell(n)}, 1^{2t(n)+c})$.

The Construction. The construction extends that of an injective one-way function presented in Sect. 3.1. The main difference is that we need to make sure that the output of $F_{pk}(x)$ encodes "enough information" on x so that we may use P_{td}^{-1} to implement the inversion algorithm F_{td}^{-1}. To ensure that, when computing $F_{pk}(x)$, we will also invoke P_{pk} on $(x, e_1), \ldots, (x, e_{\ell(n)})$, where $e_1, \ldots, e_{\ell(n)}$ are the standard basis vectors, interpreted as binary strings of length $\ell(n)$. The output of $F_{pk}(x)$ will then consist of two parts: The first part $P_{pk}(x, r_1), \ldots, P_{pk}(x, r_T)$ ensures injectivity (as in Sect. 3.1), while the second part $P_{pk}(x, e_1), \ldots, P_{pk}(x, e_{\ell(n)})$ ensures efficient invertibility.

Concretely, given the aforementioned ingredients, we construct an injective trapdoor function $\mathcal{F} = (G_F, F, F^{-1})$ as follows:

- The algorithm G_F on input 1^n invokes $G(1^n)$, and outputs its output (pk, td).
- The algorithm F on input $(pk, x) \in \{0,1\}^n \times \{0,1\}^n$ computes $H(1^{\ell(n)}, 1^{2t(n)+c}) = (r_1, \ldots, r_T)$, and outputs

$$F_{pk}(x) = \left(P_{pk}(x, r_1), \ldots P_{pk}(x, r_T), P_{pk}(x, e_1), \ldots, P_{pk}(x, e_{\ell(n)})\right).$$

- The algorithm F^{-1} on input $(td, y) \in \{0,1\}^n \times \{0,1\}^{T+\ell(n)}$ computes $H(1^{\ell(n)}, 1^{2t(n)+c}) = (r_1, \ldots, r_T)$, and outputs

$$F_{td}^{-1}(y) = P_{td}^{-1}\left((r_1, y_1), \ldots, (r_T, y_T), (e_1, y_{T+1}), \ldots, (e_{\ell(n)}, y_{T+\ell(n)})\right)$$

where y_i denotes the ith bit of y for every $i \in \{1, \ldots, T + \ell(n)\}$.

Theorem 3.3. *Assuming that $\mathcal{T} = (G, P, P^{-1})$ is a correlated-input $(\ell, 1/4)$-balanced trapdoor predicate and that H is a hitting-set generator that fools deterministic circuits, the triplet $\mathcal{F} = (G_F, F, F^{-1})$ is an injective trapdoor function.*

The proof of Theorem 3.3 can be found in the full version [RS18].

4 Applying Rudich's Impossibility to Correlated-Input Predicates

In this section we show that Rudich's impossibility result [Rud88] can be applied to correlated-input balanced trapdoor predicates. That is, we show that there is no black-box construction of an injective one-way function from such a predicate. In fact, we prove a stronger result, showing that there is no black-box construction of a *partially-injective* one-way function (as defined by Barak, Ong and Vadhan [BOV07]) from such a predicate (recall Definition 2.4). Since any injective trapdoor function is also an injective (and a partially-injective) one-way function, it trivially follows that the former also cannot be constructed in a black-box manner from our predicate. We prove the following theorem:

Theorem 4.1. *There is no black-box construction of a partially-injective one-way function based on a correlated-input* $(\ell(n), \delta(n))$*-balanced trapdoor predicate, where* $\ell(n) = n$ *and* $\delta(n) = 2^{-n/3}$.

We note that, as with Rudich's original statement, the above theorem applies even to *semi*-black-box constructions (i.e., cases where the construction itself is black box, but adversaries may be used in a non-black-box manner within the proof of security – see [RTV04] for more details). In addition, we note that our choice of $\ell(n) = n$ is done purely for simplicity, and our proof applies to any super-logarithmic $\ell(n)$ (recall that a logarithmic $\ell(n)$ does imply an injective one-way function in a black-box manner – see Sect. 1.2).

In what follows we first describe the oracle that enables us to prove our result (essentially replacing Rudich's random function with a random predicate and complementing it with a trapdoor oracle). We describe and analyze (a slightly modified version of) Rudich's attacker with respect to this oracle, showing that it can invert any partially-injective one-way function. Then, we show that this oracle is an exponentially-secure correlated-input balanced trapdoor predicate for poly-query adversaries. Theorem 4.1 then immediately follows (see, for example, [Rud88, IR89, RTV04]). Throughout our proof we rely on the following standard notion of a q-query algorithm:

Definition 4.2. *Let A be an oracle-aided algorithm and let $q = q(n)$ be a function of the security parameter $n \in \mathbb{N}$. Then, A is a q-*query algorithm *if for any $n \in \mathbb{N}$ it holds that A issues at most $q(n)$ oracle queries when invoked on inputs of length n.*

The Oracle. Our oracle is a triplet $\mathcal{T} = (\mathcal{G}, \mathcal{P}, \mathcal{P}^{-1}) = \{(\mathcal{G}_n, \mathcal{P}_n, \mathcal{P}_n^{-1})\}_{n \in \mathbb{N}}$ of three sub-routines. For every $n \in \mathbb{N}$, the functions $\mathcal{G}_n, \mathcal{P}_n$ and $\mathcal{P}_n^{-1}$ are defined as follows:

- The function $\mathcal{G}_n : \{0,1\}^n \to \{0,1\}^n$ is a uniformly chosen function from $\{0,1\}^n$ to $\{0,1\}^n$. Looking ahead, $\mathcal{G}_n$ will be used for mapping trapdoors to corresponding public keys.

– For any $pk \in \{0,1\}^n$ the function $\mathcal{P}_n(pk,\cdot,\cdot) : \{0,1\}^n \times \{0,1\}^n \to \{0,1\}$ is a predicate sampled uniformly at random from all predicates of suitable input-length that are correlated-input $\delta(n)$-balanced, independently of $\mathcal{P}_n(pk',\cdot,\cdot)$ for any $pk' \neq pk$. That is, for any $pk \in \{0,1\}^n$, the predicate $\mathcal{P}_n(pk,\cdot,\cdot)$ is sampled uniformly subject to the condition that for any distinct $x, x' \in \{0,1\}^n$ it holds that

$$\left| \Pr_{r \leftarrow \{0,1\}^n} [\mathcal{P}_n(pk,x,r) = \mathcal{P}_n(pk,x',r)] - \frac{1}{2} \right| \leq 2^{-n/3}.$$

– For any $td \in \{0,1\}^n$, the function $\mathcal{P}^{-1}(td,\cdot) : (\{0,1\}^n \times \{0,1\})^* \to \{0,1\}^n \cup \{\perp\}$ is defined as follows. For $R = \{(r_i,b_i)\}_i \in (\{0,1\}^n \times \{0,1\})^*$ define the set:

$$X_{td,R} = \{\ x \in \{0,1\}^n : \exists pk \in \{0,1\}^n \text{ s.t. } \mathcal{G}(td) = pk \wedge \forall i, \mathcal{P}(pk,x,r_i) = b_i\}.$$

Then, for every $R \in (\{0,1\}^n \times \{0,1\})^*$, if $X_{td,R} \neq \emptyset$, $\mathcal{P}_n^{-1}(td,R)$ returns a uniformly chosen element in the set. Otherwise, it returns $\perp$.

We denote the set of all such oracles by $\mathfrak{S}$.

4.1 Inverting Partially-Injective One-Way Functions

Suppose F is an s-size, q-query black-box implementation of a partially-injective one-way function from the oracle $\mathcal{T}$ for some polynomially bounded $s = s(n)$ and $q = q(n)$. We assume without loss of generality that before each query of the form $(td, \{(r_i,b_i)\}_i)$ that F makes to $\mathcal{P}^{-1}$, it also obtains $pk = \mathcal{G}(td)$ via a single query to $\mathcal{G}$, and after learning $x = \mathcal{P}^{-1}(td,\{(r_i,b_i)\}_i)$ it also queries $\mathcal{P}$ with (pk,x,r_i) for each r_i (if $x = \perp$, we forgo these queries to $\mathcal{P}$). Note that as F makes at most $q(n)$ queries to $\mathcal{P}^{-1}$ and each of which involves at most $s(n)$ values of r, this adds at most $q(n) \cdot (s(n)+1)$ queries to the computation. For ease of notation we simply assume F makes the afore-described queries and continue to bound on the total number of queries made by F by $q(n)$.

The following lemma shows that for every black-box implementation F of a partially-injective one-way function from the oracle $\mathcal{T}$, there exists a poly-query adversary that on input $F^{\mathcal{T}}(x,y)$ always finds x.

Lemma 4.3. *Let $q = q(n), s = s(n)$ and let F be an s-size, q-query algorithm such that for every $\mathcal{T} \in \mathfrak{S}$ it holds that $F^{\mathcal{T}} : \{0,1\}^* \to \{0,1\}^*$ is partially injective. Then, there exists an $O(q^6 \cdot s^6)$-query algorithm A such that*

$$\Pr_{(x,y) \leftarrow \{0,1\}^{n+m(n)}} \left[A^{\mathcal{T}}\left(F^{\mathcal{T}}(x,y)\right) = x\right] = 1$$

for all sufficiently large $n \in \mathbb{N}$.

Consider the following attacker A, that on input v^* finds x^* such that there exists some y^* for which $F^{\mathcal{T}}(x^*,y^*) = v^*$:

- **Input:** A string $v^* \in \{0,1\}^*$, which is the output of $F^{\mathcal{T}}$ on input $(x^*, y^*) \in \{0,1\}^{n+m(n)}$.
- **Initialize:** A initializes a set $Q(A) = \emptyset$, to hold all query/answer pairs to $\mathcal{T}$ that A learns throughout the attack.
- **Learning:** Let $n' = 2\log(2q(n) \cdot s(n))$. A queries $\mathcal{P}$ with all queries of length at most $3n' = n' + n' + \ell(n')$, and updates $Q(A)$ accordingly.
- **Iteration:** A runs $q(n) + 1$ iterations of the following three steps:
  1. Simulation: A finds a possible execution of F that is consistent with $Q(A)$ and v^*. That is, A finds inputs x, y, and an oracle $\widehat{\mathcal{T}} = (\widehat{\mathcal{G}}, \widehat{\mathcal{P}}, \widehat{\mathcal{P}}^{-1}) \in \mathfrak{S}$ that is consistent with $Q(A)$, such that $F^{\widehat{\mathcal{T}}}(x, y) = v^*$.
  2. Evaluation: A evaluates $F^{\mathcal{T}}(x, y)$ (note that the evaluation is done with the true oracle $\mathcal{T}$). In case $F^{\mathcal{T}}(x, y) = v^*$, A terminates and outputs x.
  3. Update: A queries the true oracle $\mathcal{T}$ with all queries made in the execution of $F^{\widehat{\mathcal{T}}}(x, y)$ and are not in $Q(A)$, and updates $Q(A)$ accordingly. Additionally, for any query of the form $u = (td, \{(r_i, b_i)\}_i)$ that A makes to (the true oracle) $\mathcal{P}^{-1}$ in the update phase, it also queries $\mathcal{P}$ with (pk, x, r_i) for each r_i, where x is the answer to u according to $\widehat{\mathcal{P}}^{-1}$ (if $x = \perp$, A forgoes these queries to $\mathcal{P}$), and pk is the public-key associated with td according to $\widehat{\mathcal{G}}$; i.e., $pk = \widehat{\mathcal{G}}(td)$.[9]

The success and query efficiency of A follow immediately by the following claim, a proof for which is given in the full version [RS18].

Claim 4.4. *In each iteration, at least one of the following events occur:*

1. A queries $\mathcal{T}$ with a query that is made by the execution of $F^{\mathcal{T}}(x^*, y^*)$, but was not in $Q(A)$ at the beginning of the iteration.
2. A finds x^* and some y for which $F^{\mathcal{T}}(x^*, y) = v^*$, and terminates.

Proof of Lemma 4.3 from Claim 4.4. Since $F^{\mathcal{T}}(x^*, y^*)$ makes at most $q(n)$ queries to $\mathcal{T}$, by Claim 4.4 and the pigeon-hole principle, there exists an iteration in which A finds x^* and terminates. Moreover, during the learning phase, A queries the oracle with $O\left(q(n)^6 \cdot s(n)^6\right)$ queries, and in each iteration it queries the oracle with at most $q(n) \cdot (s(n) + 2)$ new queries. Since there are at most $q(n) + 1$ iterations, A is an $O(q^6 \cdot s^6)$-query algorithm. □

4.2 $\mathcal{T}$ is One Way for Correlated Inputs

The proof that the oracle $\mathcal{T}$ is one way for correlated inputs (according to Definition 3.2) consists of the following two steps. First, we show that a uniformly-chosen predicate (not necessarily balanced) is one way with an extremely high probability. Then, we show that the uniform distribution over predicates is statistically close to the uniform distribution over balanced predicates (for our choice of $\ell(n) = n$ and $\delta(n) = 2^{-n/3}$).

---

[9] Recall that we assumed that before each query to $\mathcal{P}^{-1}$ that contains some trapdoor td, F queries $\mathcal{G}$ with td. Hence, this is also the case in the execution chosen by A in the simulation step.

In more detail, recall that the trapdoor and public key in the experiment $\mathsf{Invert}_{\mathcal{T},A^{\mathcal{T}}}(n)$ are chosen as follows: First, the trapdoor td is chosen uniformly at random from the set $\{0,1\}^n$ and then the public key is set to be $pk = \mathcal{G}(td)$. Now, let R_n denote the uniform distribution over predicates mapping a triplet of strings of length n each, to an output bit (i.e., if $\mathcal{P}_n$ is a predicate drawn from R_n, then for every $pk \in \{0,1\}^n$ and $x, r \in \{0,1\}^n$ it holds that $\mathcal{P}(pk, x, r)$ is a uniformly-chosen bit which is independent of the value of $\mathcal{P}_n$ on all other inputs). The following lemma shows that when $\mathcal{P}_n$ is sampled from R_n, then any poly-query adversary inverts $\mathcal{P} = \{\mathcal{P}_{n'}\}_{n' \in \mathbb{N}}$ on inputs of length n (vis-à-vis Definition 3.2) with probability that is negligible in n, regardless of how $\mathcal{P}_{-n}$ is chosen (where we use $\mathcal{P}_{-n}$ to denote $\mathcal{P} \setminus \{\mathcal{P}_n\}$).

Lemma 4.5. *Let $q = q(n)$ be a function of the security parameter $n \in \mathbb{N}$. For any q-query algorithm A, any $n \in \mathbb{N}$ and any fixing of $\mathcal{P}_{-n}$, it holds that*

$$\Pr\left[\mathsf{Invert}_{\mathcal{T},A^{\mathcal{T}}}(n) = 1\right] \leq \frac{2q(n)}{2^n - q(n)}$$

where $\mathcal{P}_n \leftarrow R_n$.

The proof of Lemma 4.5 is provided in the full version [RS18].

Acknowledgments. We thank Iftach Haitner and Moni Naor for useful discussions in various stages of this work.

References

[ACR+97] Andreev, A., Clementi, A., Rolim, J., Trevisan, L.: Weak random sources, hitting sets, and BPP simulations. In: Proceedings of the 38th Annual IEEE Symposium on Foundations of Computer Science, pp. 264–272 (1997)

[ACR98] Andreev, A., Clementi, A., Rolim, J.: A new general derandomization method. J. ACM **45**(1), 179–213 (1998)

[AIK06] Applebaum, B., Ishai, Y., Kushilevitz, E.: Cryptography in NC^0. SIAM J. Comput. **36**(4), 845–888 (2006)

[And94] Andreev, A.: Complexity of nondeterministic functions. BRICS Report Series, 1(2) (1994)

[AS15] Asharov, G., Segev, G.: Limits on the power of indistinguishability obfuscation and functional encryption. In: Proceedings of the 56th Annual IEEE Symposium on Foundations of Computer Science, pp. 191–209 (2015)

[AS16] Asharov, G., Segev, G.: On constructing one-way permutations from indistinguishability obfuscation. In: Proceedings of the 13th Theory of Cryptography Conference, pp. 512–541 (2016)

[AW14] Applebaum, B., Widder, E.: Related-key secure pseudorandom functions: the case of additive attacks. Cryptology ePrint Archive, Report 2014/478 (2014)

[Bar01] Barak, B.: How to go beyond the black-box simulation barrier. In: Proceedings of the 42nd Annual IEEE Symposium on Foundations of Computer Science, pp. 106–115 (2001)

[BBF13] Baecher, P., Brzuska, C., Fischlin, M.: Notions of black-box reductions, revisited. In: Advances in Cryptology - ASIACRYPT 2013, pp. 296–315 (2013)

[BC10] Bellare, M., Cash, D.: Pseudorandom functions and permutations provably secure against related-key attacks. In: Rabin, T. (ed.) CRYPTO 2010. LNCS, vol. 6223, pp. 666–684. Springer, Heidelberg (2010). https://doi.org/10.1007/978-3-642-14623-7_36

[BDV17] Bitansky, N., Degwekar, A., Vaikuntanathan, V.: Structure vs. hardness through the obfuscation lens. In: Katz, J., Shacham, H. (eds.) CRYPTO 2017. LNCS, vol. 10401, pp. 696–723. Springer, Cham (2017). https://doi.org/10.1007/978-3-319-63688-7_23

[BGI+12] Barak, B., et al.: On the (im)possibility of obfuscating programs. J. ACM **59**(2), 6 (2012)

[BHS+98] Bellare, M., Halevi, S., Sahai, A., Vadhan, S.: Many-to-one trapdoor functions and their relation to public-key cryptosystems. In: Krawczyk, H. (ed.) CRYPTO 1998. LNCS, vol. 1462, pp. 283–298. Springer, Heidelberg (1998). https://doi.org/10.1007/BFb0055735

[BK03] Bellare, M., Kohno, T.: A theoretical treatment of related-key attacks: RKA-PRPs, RKA-PRFs, and applications. In: Biham, E. (ed.) EUROCRYPT 2003. LNCS, vol. 2656, pp. 491–506. Springer, Heidelberg (2003). https://doi.org/10.1007/3-540-39200-9_31

[BKS+11] Brakerski, Z., Katz, J., Segev, G., Yerukhimovich, A.: Limits on the power of zero-knowledge proofs in cryptographic constructions. In: Ishai, Y. (ed.) TCC 2011. LNCS, vol. 6597, pp. 559–578. Springer, Heidelberg (2011). https://doi.org/10.1007/978-3-642-19571-6_34

[BM84] Blum, M., Micali, S.: How to generate cryptographically strong sequences of pseudo-random bits. SIAM J. Comput. **13**(4), 850–864 (1984)

[BOV07] Barak, B., Ong, S.J., Vadhan, S.P.: Derandomization in cryptography. SIAM J. Comput. **37**(2), 380–400 (2007)

[BP12] Bitansky, N., Paneth, O.: From the impossibility of obfuscation to a new non-black-box simulation technique. In: Proceedings of the 53rd Annual IEEE Symposium on Foundations of Computer Science, pp. 223–232 (2012)

[BPW16] Bitansky, N., Paneth, O., Wichs, D.: Perfect structure on the edge of chaos - trapdoor permutations from indistinguishability obfuscation. In: Proceedings of the 13th Theory of Cryptography Conference, pp. 474–502 (2016)

[BV17] Bitansky, N., Vaikuntanathan, V.: A note on perfect correctness by derandomization. In: Coron, J.-S., Nielsen, J.B. (eds.) EUROCRYPT 2017. LNCS, vol. 10211, pp. 592–606. Springer, Cham (2017). https://doi.org/10.1007/978-3-319-56614-6_20

[CG89] Chor, B., Goldreich, O.: On the power of two-point based sampling. J. Complex. **5**(1), 96–106 (1989)

[CPS16] Chung, K., Pass, R., Seth, K.: Non-black-box simulation from one-way functions and applications to resettable security. SIAM J. Comput. **45**(2), 415–458 (2016)

[Dac16] Dachman-Soled, D.: Towards non-black-box separations of public key encryption and one way function. In: Hirt, M., Smith, A. (eds.) TCC 2016. LNCS, vol. 9986, pp. 169–191. Springer, Heidelberg (2016). https://doi.org/10.1007/978-3-662-53644-5_7

[DG17] Döttling, N., Garg, S.: Identity-based encryption from the Diffie-Hellman assumption. In: Katz, J., Shacham, H. (eds.) CRYPTO 2017. LNCS, vol. 10401, pp. 537–569. Springer, Cham (2017). https://doi.org/10.1007/978-3-319-63688-7_18

[DN07] Dwork, C., Naor, M.: Zaps and their applications. SIAM J. Comput. **36**(6), 1513–1543 (2007)

[DNR04] Dwork, C., Naor, M., Reingold, O.: Immunizing encryption schemes from decryption errors. In: Cachin, C., Camenisch, J.L. (eds.) EUROCRYPT 2004. LNCS, vol. 3027, pp. 342–360. Springer, Heidelberg (2004). https://doi.org/10.1007/978-3-540-24676-3_21

[GGH+13] Garg, S., Gentry, C., Halevi, S., Raykova, M., Sahai, A., Waters, B.: Candidate indistinguishability obfuscation and functional encryption for all circuits. In: Proceedings of the 54th Annual IEEE Symposium on Foundations of Computer Science, pp. 40–49 (2013)

[GGM84] Goldreich, O., Goldwasser, S., Micali, S.: On the cryptographic applications of random functions (extended abstract). In: Blakley, G.R., Chaum, D. (eds.) CRYPTO 1984. LNCS, vol. 196, pp. 276–288. Springer, Heidelberg (1985). https://doi.org/10.1007/3-540-39568-7_22

[GGM86] Goldreich, O., Goldwasser, S., Micali, S.: How to construct random functions. J. ACM **33**(4), 792–807 (1986)

[GK96] Goldreich, O., Krawczyk, H.: On the composition of zero-knowledge proof systems. SIAM J. Comput. **25**(1), 169–192 (1996)

[GL10] Goldenberg, D., Liskov, M.: On related-secret pseudorandomness. In: Micciancio, D. (ed.) TCC 2010. LNCS, vol. 5978, pp. 255–272. Springer, Heidelberg (2010). https://doi.org/10.1007/978-3-642-11799-2_16

[GLN11] Goldreich, O., Levin, L.A., Nisan, N.: On constructing 1-1 one-way functions. In: Goldreich, O. (ed.) Studies in Complexity and Cryptography. Miscellanea on the Interplay between Randomness and Computation. LNCS, vol. 6650, pp. 13–25. Springer, Heidelberg (2011). https://doi.org/10.1007/978-3-642-22670-0_3

[GMM17] Garg, S., Mahmoody, M., Mohammed, A.: Lower bounds on obfuscation from all-or-nothing encryption primitives. In: Katz, J., Shacham, H. (eds.) CRYPTO 2017. LNCS, vol. 10401, pp. 661–695. Springer, Cham (2017). https://doi.org/10.1007/978-3-319-63688-7_22

[GMW86] Goldreich, O., Micali, S., Wigderson, A.: How to prove all NP statements in zero-knowledge and a methodology of cryptographic protocol design (extended abstract). In: Odlyzko, A.M. (ed.) CRYPTO 1986. LNCS, vol. 263, pp. 171–185. Springer, Heidelberg (1987). https://doi.org/10.1007/3-540-47721-7_11

[Gol01] Goldreich, O.: Foundations of Cryptography - Volume 1: Basic Techniques. Cambridge University Press, Cambridge (2001)

[Gol11] Goldreich, O.: In a world of P=BPP. In: Goldreich, O. (ed.) Studies in Complexity and Cryptography. Miscellanea on the Interplay between Randomness and Computation. LNCS, vol. 6650, pp. 191–232. Springer, Heidelberg (2011). https://doi.org/10.1007/978-3-642-22670-0_20

[GSTS03] Gutfreund, D., Shaltiel, R., Ta-Shma, A.: Uniform hardness versus randomness tradeoffs for Arthur-Merlin games. Comput. Complex. **12**(3), 85–130 (2003)

[GVW11] Goldreich, O., Vadhan, S., Wigderson, A.: Simplified derandomization of BPP using a hitting set generator. In: Goldreich, O. (ed.) Studies in Complexity and Cryptography. Miscellanea on the Interplay between Randomness and Computation. LNCS, vol. 6650, pp. 59–67. Springer, Heidelberg (2011). https://doi.org/10.1007/978-3-642-22670-0_8

[HIL+99] Håstad, J., Impagliazzo, R., Levin, L.A., Luby, M.: A pseudorandom generator from any one-way function. SIAM J. Comput. **28**(4), 1364–1396 (1999)

[HNO+09] Haitner, I., Nguyen, M., Ong, S.J., Reingold, O., Vadhan, S.P.: Statistically hiding commitments and statistical zero-knowledge arguments from any one-way function. SIAM J. Comput. **39**(3), 1153–1218 (2009)

[Imp95] Impagliazzo, R.: A personal view of average-case complexity. In: Proceedings of the 10th Annual Structure in Complexity Theory Conference, pp. 134–147 (1995)

[IR89] Impagliazzo, R., Rudich, S.: Limits on the provable consequences of one-way permutations. In: Proceedings of the 21st Annual ACM Symposium on Theory of Computing, pp. 44–61 (1989)

[IW97] Impagliazzo, R., Wigderson, A.: P = BPP if E requires exponential circuits: Derandomizing the XOR lemma. In: Proceedings of the 29th Annual ACM Symposium on Theory of Computing, pp. 220–229 (1997)

[Lau83] Lautemann, C.: BPP and the polynomial hierarchy. Inf. Process. Lett. **17**(4), 215–217 (1983)

[LLS+97] Linial, N., Luby, M., Saks, M., Zuckerman, D.: Efficient construction of a small hitting set for combinatorial rectangles in high dimension. Combinatorica **17**(2), 215–234 (1997)

[LMR14] Lewi, K., Montgomery, H., Raghunathan, A.: Improved constructions of PRFs secure against related-key attacks. In: Boureanu, I., Owesarski, P., Vaudenay, S. (eds.) ACNS 2014. LNCS, vol. 8479, pp. 44–61. Springer, Cham (2014). https://doi.org/10.1007/978-3-319-07536-5_4

[LR88] Luby, M., Rackoff, C.: How to construct pseudorandom permutations from pseudorandom functions. SIAM J. Comput. **17**(2), 373–386 (1988)

[Luc04] Lucks, S.: Ciphers secure against related-key attacks. In: Roy, B., Meier, W. (eds.) FSE 2004. LNCS, vol. 3017, pp. 359–370. Springer, Heidelberg (2004). https://doi.org/10.1007/978-3-540-25937-4_23

[MM11] Matsuda, T., Matsuura, K.: On black-box separations among injective one-way functions. In: Ishai, Y. (ed.) TCC 2011. LNCS, vol. 6597, pp. 597–614. Springer, Heidelberg (2011). https://doi.org/10.1007/978-3-642-19571-6_36

[MP12] Mahmoody, M., Pass, R.: The curious case of non-interactive commitments – on the power of black-box vs. non-black-box use of primitives. In: Safavi-Naini, R., Canetti, R. (eds.) CRYPTO 2012. LNCS, vol. 7417, pp. 701–718. Springer, Heidelberg (2012). https://doi.org/10.1007/978-3-642-32009-5_41

[MV99] Miltersen, P.B., Vinodchandran, N.V.: Derandomizing Arthur-Merlin games using hitting sets. In: Proceedings of the 40th Annual IEEE Symposium on Foundations of Computer Science, pp. 71–80 (1999)

[Nao91] Naor, M.: Bit commitment using pseudorandomness. J. Cryptol. **4**(2), 151–158 (1991)

[NR99] Naor, M., Reingold, O.: On the construction of pseudorandom permutations: Luby-Rackoff revisited. J. Cryptol. **12**(1), 29–66 (1999)

[NW94] Nisan, N., Wigderson, A.: Hardness vs randomness. J. Comput. Syst. Sci. **49**(2), 149–167 (1994)

[NY89] Naor, M., Yung, M.: Universal one-way hash functions and their cryptographic applications. In: Proceedings of the 21st Annual ACM Symposium on Theory of Computing, pp. 33–43 (1989)

[NY90] Naor, M., Yung, M.: Public-key cryptosystems provably secure against chosen ciphertext attacks. In: Proceedings of the 22nd Annual ACM Symposium on Theory of Computing, pp. 427–437 (1990)

[PRV12] Papakonstantinou, P.A., Rackoff, C.A., Vahlis, Y.: How powerful are the DDH hard groups? Cryptology ePrint Archive, Report 2012/653 (2012)

[PTV11] Pass, R., Tseng, W.-L.D., Venkitasubramaniam, M.: Towards non-black-box lower bounds in cryptography. In: Ishai, Y. (ed.) TCC 2011. LNCS, vol. 6597, pp. 579–596. Springer, Heidelberg (2011). https://doi.org/10.1007/978-3-642-19571-6_35

[Rom90] Rompel, J.: One-way functions are necessary and sufficient for secure signatures. In: Proceedings of the 22nd Annual ACM Symposium on Theory of Computing, pp. 387–394 (1990)

[RS18] Rotem, L., Segev, G.: Injective trapdoor functions via derandomization: how strong is Rudich's black-box barrier? Cryptology ePrint Archive, Report 2018/812 (2018)

[RSS17] Rosen, A., Segev, G., Shahaf, I.: Can PPAD hardness be based on standard cryptographic assumptions? In: Kalai, Y., Reyzin, L. (eds.) TCC 2017. LNCS, vol. 10678, pp. 747–776. Springer, Cham (2017). https://doi.org/10.1007/978-3-319-70503-3_25

[RTV04] Reingold, O., Trevisan, L., Vadhan, S.: Notions of reducibility between cryptographic primitives. In: Naor, M. (ed.) TCC 2004. LNCS, vol. 2951, pp. 1–20. Springer, Heidelberg (2004). https://doi.org/10.1007/978-3-540-24638-1_1

[Rud88] Rudich, S.: Limits on the provable consequences of one-way functions. Ph.D. thesis, EECS Department, University of California, Berkeley (1988)

[Sim98] Simon, D.R.: Finding collisions on a one-way street: can secure hash functions be based on general assumptions? In: Nyberg, K. (ed.) EUROCRYPT 1998. LNCS, vol. 1403, pp. 334–345. Springer, Heidelberg (1998). https://doi.org/10.1007/BFb0054137

[Sip88] Sipser, M.: Expanders, randomness, or time versus space. J. Comput. Syst. Sci. **36**(3), 379–383 (1988)

[Yao86] Yao, A.C.: How to generate and exchange secrets. In: Proceedings of the 27th Annual IEEE Symposium on Foundations of Computer Science, pp. 162–167 (1986)

Enhancements are Blackbox Non-trivial: Impossibility of Enhanced Trapdoor Permutations from Standard Trapdoor Permutations

Mohammad Hajiabadi[1,2](✉)

[1] University of California Berkeley, Berkeley, USA
mdhajiabadi@berkeley.edu

[2] University of Virginia, Charlottesville, USA

Abstract. Trapdoor permutations (TDP) are a fundamental primitive in cryptography. Several variants of this notion have emerged as a result of different applications. However, it is not clear whether these variants can be based on the standard notion of TDPs.

We study the question of whether enhanced trapdoor permutations can be based on classical trapdoor permutations. The main motivation of our work is in the context of existing TDP-based constructions of oblivious transfer and non-interactive zero knowledge protocols, which require enhancements to the classical TDP notion. We prove that these enhancements are non-trivial, in the sense that there does not exist fully blackbox constructions of enhanced TDPs from classical TDPs.

On the technical side, we show that the enhanced TDP security of any construction in the random TDP oracle world can be broken via a polynomial number of queries to the TDP oracle as well as a weakening oracle, which provides inversion with respect to randomness. We also show that the standard one-wayness of the random TDP oracle stays intact in the presence of this weakening oracle.

1 Introduction

Trapdoor permutations (TDPs) [RSA78,Rab79] are a family of permutations, where each permutation in the family is easy to compute given the underlying index key, and also easy to invert given a corresponding trapdoor key. The classical notion of one-wayness for TDPs states that it is hard to invert a randomly chosen permutation from the family on a random image. While classical TDPs suffice for many applications, such as public-key encryption (PKE) [Yao82], parallel constructions of pseudorandom synthesizers [NR99], etc., for certain applications we need to strengthen this basic one-wayness notion. The main reason is that in protocols in which TDPs are used, the adversary may sometimes have some side information about the underlying image element, which may give her some advantage.

A. Beimel and S. Dziembowski (Eds.): TCC 2018, LNCS 11239, pp. 448–475, 2018.
https://doi.org/10.1007/978-3-030-03807-6_17

Technically, TDPs come with a sampling algorithm S, which, on input an index key IK and random coins R, outputs an element from the domain Dom_{ik} of the permutation $\mathsf{E}(\mathrm{IK}, \cdot)$. We call a TDP *enhanced* if it is hard to find the pre-image of a random image element $\mathrm{Y} := \mathsf{S}(\mathrm{IK}; \mathrm{R})$ even if the inverter is given the randomness R (along with IK). Intuitively, enhanced TDPs allow a sampler, given only the underlying index key, to sample an image point obliviously to its pre-image: if we sample $\mathrm{Y} = \mathsf{S}(\mathrm{IK}; \mathrm{R})$ for a random R, then even given R, we are still oblivious to the corresponding pre-image of Y.

To see when this need of enhancement arises, consider the classical construction of hones-but-curious oblivious transfer (OT) protocols [EGL82, GMW87]. In this setting, a receiver $\mathsf{Alice}(\mathrm{b}, \cdot)$ with input bit b wishes to secretly learn the message $\mathrm{m_b}$ of Bob's two messages $(\mathrm{m_0}, \mathrm{m_1})$. She does so by sending two image elements $\mathrm{Y_1}$ and $\mathrm{Y_2}$ of a TDP $\mathsf{E}(\mathrm{IK}, \cdot)$, where IK's trapdoor key is only known to Bob, in such a way that Alice knows the pre-image of $\mathrm{Y_b}$ but not of $\mathrm{Y_{1-b}}$. She does so by sampling $\mathrm{Y_{1-b}}$ *obliviously* and by sampling $\mathrm{Y_b}$ by applying $\mathsf{E}(\mathrm{IK}, \cdot)$ on a random domain element X. Bob sends to Alice encryptions $\mathrm{c_1}$ and $\mathrm{c_2}$ of the two bits $\mathrm{m_0}$ and $\mathrm{m_1}$ under the standard TDP-based PKE construction, using $\mathrm{Y_0}$ and $\mathrm{Y_1}$ as the 'encoded randomness.' Alice can open $\mathrm{c_b}$ to recover $\mathrm{Y_b}$. In order to ensure privacy for Bob, we need to assume that the underlying TDP is enhanced one-way.

The need for strengthening the notion of TDPs was first discovered by Bellare and Yung [BY93], noting that the previous TDP-based non-interactive zero knowledge (NIZK) construction in [FLS90] requires the set of valid permutations to be *certifiable.* Goldreich [Gol04] was the first to realize the need for enhanced TDPs in the context of OT constructions. It was also later discovered that for the TDP-based non-interactive zero knowledge (NIZK) protocol [FLS90] the zero-knowledge property relies on the TDP being *doubly enhanced* [Gol11], in addition to the certifiability property. Informally, doubly-enhanced TDPs are enhanced TDPs that provide the feature that given an index key IK it is possible to sample random coins R_y together with the pre-image of $\mathsf{S}(\mathrm{IK}, \mathrm{R}_y)$. As noted in [Gol11, GR13] the main reason these requirements were not noticed earlier is because TDPs had implicitly been assumed to be permutations over $\{0,1\}^\kappa$ (or over domains which enable trivial sampling algorithms). While these idealized TDPs are doubly enhanced, we do not have any candidate constructions for them.

Faced with this difficulty, Haitner [Hai04] gives a more complicated OT protocol which works with respect to any classical TDP with *dense domains.* It is not however clear whether such TDPs can be built from classical one-way TDPs.

In summary, the possibility of basing OT or NIZK on classical TDPs remains unknown. One way to address these is to investigate whether enhanced TDPs can be constructed from standard TDPs.

1.1 Our Result and Discussion

We take a first step toward understanding the relationships between various notions of TDPs. Our main result shows that enhanced TDPs cannot be constructed from classical TDPs in a fully blackbox way (in the taxonomy of [RTV04]). We give an overview of our result and techniques in Sect. 1.2. In what follows, we discuss the significance of our work.

TDPs are rather coarse as a primitive, since the set of assumptions from which TDPs can be built is relatively small, being limited to factoring-related assumptions [RSA78, Rab79] and obfuscation-based assumptions [BPW16]. Also, variants of the popular RSA and Rabin TDPs (see e.g., [KKM12]) as well as variants of iO-based TDPs are already doubly enhanced [GR13, BPW16].[1] Given this state of affairs, one may ask about the motivations of this work. We provide the following motivations.

- In a similar vein, Hsiao and Reyzin [HR04] draw attention to the distinction between secret-coin collision resistant hash functions (CRHF) and public-coin CRHF by showing that the latter cannot be constructed from the former in a blackbox way. Prior to their work, these two notions had been deemed to be equivalent. In some sense, our result shows that a similar situation relating to public-versus-secret coins holds in the TDP setting as well, emphasizing the need of rigorously showing which version is required in each application and achieved by a future construction.
- Goldreich and Rothblum [Gol11] show that the TDP-based PKE construction, when instantiated with enhanced TDPs, offer properties, such as *oblivious ciphertext samplability*, that have useful applications. This gives applications beyond the OT and NIZK settings, and serves as another motivation for studying the possibility of basing enhanced TDPs on standard TDPs.
- TDPs turn out to be tricky objects to define, because after several decades of research, still new aspects of this primitive are revealed, which turn out to be required by some applications, but which were overlooked before. (See for example the recent work of [CL17]). Faced with this landscape of TDP with various properties, from a theoretical point of view, one would like to understand to what extent these notions relate to each other, elucidating and simplifying the landscape.

Open Problems. Our work leads to the following open problem: is it possible to prove that OT cannot be based on standard TDPs in a blackbox way? Since our work removes one path toward this goal, our techniques may be useful in an eventual separation (if at all possible).

Other Related Work. There is a rich body of research on understanding the limitations of TDPs. In particular, we know that TDPs cannot be used in a blackbox way to construct two-message statistically-hiding commitments [Fis02], identity-based encryption [BPR+08], correlated-secure trapdoor functions [Vah10] and verifiable random functions [FS12]. To the best of our knowledge, all these separations still hold even if the base TDP is doubly enhanced. Haitner et al. [HHRS07] give lower-bounds on the round complexity of statistically-hiding

[1] The TDP construction in [BPW16] does not satisfy doubly-enhanced one-wayness, but a relaxed version of it, which nevertheless suffices for their respective application.

commitments making blackbox use of TDPs. There is a positive construction of TDPs from indistinguishability obfuscations (IO) and one-way functions [BPW16], which is not so-called *domain invariant.* The result of Asharov and Segev [AS16] justifies this, showing that current non-blackbox iO-based techniques are not sufficient to give us domain-invariant TDPs.

Gertner et al. [GKM+00] show that TDPs cannot be built from trapdoor functions (TDFs) in a blackbox way. Their result is incomparable to ours (and their techniques are also different), because their base primitive is TDFs, and in their proof they make essential of the fact that the domain of a TDF can be different from the range. Our result in contrast is about a separation between two notions of TDPs.

1.2 Technical Overview

As common in blackbox impossibility results, we will prove our impossibility by giving an oracle relative to which the base primitive exists, but not the target primitive. Consider a random TDP oracle $\mathbf{O} = (\mathbf{g}, \mathbf{s}, \mathbf{e}, \mathbf{d})$ with the following sub-oracles. The key-generation oracle $\mathbf{g} : \{0,1\}^{\kappa} \mapsto \{0,1\}^{\kappa}$ is a random injective function mapping a trapdoor key tk to an index key ik. The evaluation oracle $\mathbf{e}(\mathrm{ik}, \cdot) : \{0,1\}^{5\kappa} \mapsto \{0,1\}^{5\kappa}$ on an index key ik is defined over all elements in $\{0,1\}^{5\kappa}$; however, $\mathbf{e}(\mathrm{ik}, \cdot)$ is a permutation only over a *sparse* subset $\mathsf{Dom}_{\mathrm{ik}}$ of $\{0,1\}^{5\kappa}$, where $|\mathsf{Dom}_{\mathrm{ik}}| = 2^{\kappa}$ (hence the name sparseness). That is, we have $\mathbf{e}(\mathrm{ik}, \mathsf{Dom}_{\mathrm{ik}}) = \mathsf{Dom}_{\mathrm{ik}}$.

The sampling oracle $\mathbf{s}(\mathrm{ik}, \cdot)$ is a random injective function which allows us to sample from $\mathsf{Dom}_{\mathrm{ik}}$: given a string $\mathrm{r} \in \{0,1\}^{\kappa}$, $\mathbf{s}(\mathrm{ik}, \mathrm{r})$ returns an element in $\mathsf{Dom}_{\mathrm{ik}}$. Finally, the inversion oracle $\mathbf{d}$ is defined in a manner consistent with the other oracles.

The Oracle $\mathbf{O}$ *by Itself is Too Strong.* Such a randomly chosen oracle $\mathbf{O}$ is overly strong, satisfying already all enhanced forms of one-wayness. Thus, it cannot be taken as is for deriving an impossibility. To address this problem, we will add a weakening oracle $\mathbf{u}$, which does not harm the standard one-wayness of $\mathbf{O}$, but which helps us break the enhanced one-wayness of any blackbox construction $(\mathsf{G}^{\mathbf{O}}, \mathsf{S}^{\mathbf{O}}, \mathsf{E}^{\mathbf{O}}, \mathsf{D}^{\mathbf{O}})$. Our blackbox separation will then follow from this.

Intuition Behind the Weakening Oracle $\mathbf{u}$. As a starter, suppose we are content with $\mathbf{u}$ only breaking the enhanced one-wayness of $\mathbf{O}$ (as opposed to any TDP construction from $\mathbf{O}$). Thus, $\mathbf{u}$ should provide help for an inverter who has the randomness of the challenge image. A natural choice for $\mathbf{u}$ would be the following: on input $\mathbf{u}(\mathrm{ik}, \mathrm{r})$, let $\mathrm{y} := \mathbf{s}(\mathrm{ik}, \mathrm{r})$ and return $\mathrm{x} \in \mathsf{Dom}_{\mathrm{ik}}$ for which we have $\mathbf{e}(\mathrm{ik}, \mathrm{x}) = \mathrm{y}$.

Indeed, the above oracle $\mathbf{u}$ breaks the enhanced one-wayness of $\mathbf{O}$. We can also see that the oracle $\mathbf{u}$ does not harm the standard one-wayness of $\mathbf{O}$. This is because of the sparse and random nature of the outputs of the oracles, making the oracle $\mathbf{u}$ effectively useless for standard one-wayness. However, this oracle $\mathbf{u}$ is not much useful beyond this simple scenario. In particular, imaging a self-composing

TDP construction, whose evaluation algorithm $\mathsf{E}^{\mathbf{e}}$ is the self-composition of $\mathbf{e}(\mathrm{ik}, \cdot)$; i.e., $\mathsf{E}^{\mathbf{e}}(\mathrm{ik}, \mathrm{x}) = \mathbf{e}(\mathrm{ik}, \mathbf{e}(\mathrm{ik}, \mathrm{x}))$. An adversary $\mathcal{A}$ against enhanced one-wayness is given $(\mathrm{ik}, \mathrm{r}, \mathrm{y})$, and should find x such that $\mathrm{y} = \mathbf{e}(\mathrm{ik}, \mathbf{e}(\mathrm{ik}, \mathrm{x}))$. Given the randomness r, the adversary $\mathcal{A}$ can find x_0 such that $\mathbf{e}(\mathrm{ik}, \mathrm{x}_0) = \mathrm{y}$ by calling $\mathbf{u}(\mathrm{ik}, \mathrm{r})$, but $\mathcal{A}$ cannot continue to get to x, because $\mathcal{A}$ does not have the randomness of x_0.

Description of the Oracle **u**. The above discussion directs us toward a natural choice of **u**: on input $(\mathrm{ik}, \mathrm{r})$, letting $\mathrm{y} := \mathbf{s}(\mathrm{ik}, \mathrm{r})$, the oracle $\mathbf{u}(\mathrm{ik}, \mathrm{r})$ returns the randomness of the pre-image of y, not the pre-image itself. That is, letting $\mathrm{x} \in \mathsf{Dom}_{\mathrm{ik}}$ be such that $\mathbf{e}(\mathrm{ik}, \mathrm{x}) = \mathrm{y}$, the oracle $\mathbf{u}(\mathrm{ik}, \mathrm{r})$ returns r_0, where $\mathbf{s}(\mathrm{ik}, \mathrm{r}_0) = \mathrm{x}$.

Returning to the construction example above, it is not hard to see that this new oracle **u** not only breaks the enhanced one-wayness of the self-composition construction, but that of more general k-composition constructions, in which we compose $\mathbf{e}(\mathrm{ik}, \cdot)$ k times. One would just need to sequentially call **u** k times to get down to the base pre-image.

The Construction does not Call **u** *Itself.* We will assume that the construction $(\mathsf{G}^{\mathbf{O}}, \mathsf{S}^{\mathbf{O}}, \mathsf{E}^{\mathbf{O}}, \mathsf{D}^{\mathbf{O}})$, which we want to show that can be broken by a polynomial number of queries to $(\mathbf{O}, \mathbf{u})$, does not call **u** itself. This is sufficient for deriving a fully blackbox separation because the base oracle **O** *by itself* is a one-way TDP against all poly-query adversaries with access to $(\mathbf{O}, \mathbf{u})$. Our separation model is close to those of [GMR01,HR04], which only rule out fully-blackbox constructions, as opposed to the earlier models of [IR89,Sim98,GKM+00], which also rule out relativizing reductions.

Main Techniques. We now give a high-level sketch of how to attack a general construction $(\mathsf{G}^{\mathbf{O}}, \mathsf{S}^{\mathbf{O}}, \mathsf{E}^{\mathbf{O}}, \mathsf{D}^{\mathbf{O}})$. Let $(\mathrm{IK}, \mathrm{R})$ be the challenge input to the adversary: if $\mathrm{Y} := \mathsf{S}^{\mathbf{O}}(\mathrm{IK}; \mathrm{R})$, the adversary should invert Y w.r.t. IK. The main difficult part in inverting Y is to reply to queries for which we need to invert some image y w.r.t. the oracle $\mathbf{e}(\mathrm{ik}, \cdot)$. We denote such queries as $\mathbf{e}^{-1}(\mathrm{ik}, \mathrm{y})$: namely, if $\mathbf{e}(\mathrm{ik}, \mathrm{x}) = \mathrm{y}$, then $\mathbf{e}^{-1}(\mathrm{ik}, \mathrm{y}) = \mathrm{x}$.

As in the above k-composition construction example, suppose (informally) one can start the decryption execution of Y without having the underlying inversion key; namely, it is just a matter of answering a few oracle queries of the form $\mathbf{e}^{-1}(\mathrm{ik}, \mathrm{y})$ for various $(\mathrm{ik}, \mathrm{y})$. Roughly, for any meaningful query $\mathrm{qu} := \mathbf{e}^{-1}(\mathrm{ik}, \mathrm{y})$ during this execution we will have two cases: (I) y was generated during the process which produced $(\mathrm{IK}, *) \xleftarrow{\$} \mathsf{G}^{\mathbf{O}}(1^{\kappa})$: namely, during this process there was a query/response $((\mathrm{ik}, \mathrm{x}) \xrightarrow[\mathbf{e}]{} \mathrm{y})$ or $((\mathrm{ik}, \mathrm{r}) \xrightarrow[\mathbf{s}]{} \mathrm{y})$ for some x and r, and (II) y was generated during the execution of $\mathrm{Y} := \mathsf{S}^{\mathbf{O}}(\mathrm{IK}; \mathrm{R})$.

We will show that cases (I) and (II) are the only likely cases; this is roughly because otherwise one can forge such a valid $(\mathrm{ik}, \mathrm{y})$ without making a corresponding query: This is very unlikely because of the sparseness of the oracle outputs.

Let Q_s be the set of all queries/responses during $\mathsf{S}^{\mathbf{O}}(\mathrm{IK}; \mathrm{R})$. If during the inversion of Y Case (II) holds, then either $((\mathrm{ik}, \mathrm{x}) \xrightarrow[\mathbf{e}]{} \mathrm{y})$ in Q_s, in which case the answer to the query qu is clear, or $((\mathrm{ik}, \mathrm{r}) \underset{\mathbf{s}}{\rightarrow} \mathrm{y})$ is in Q_s, which can be used along with the oracle $\mathbf{u}$ to reply to the query qu.

The main difficult part of our analysis involves handling Case (I): in this case the adversary does not have enough information to reply to qu correctly. At a high-level, our solution is as follows. We will distinguish between two types of such qu queries: *important* and *immaterial*. We say qu is important if a query/response $((\mathrm{ik}, *) \underset{\mathbf{s}}{\rightarrow} \mathrm{y})$ or $((\mathrm{ik}, *) \underset{\mathbf{e}}{\rightarrow} \mathrm{y})$ happens with 'good' probability during a random execution of $\mathrm{X}' \xleftarrow{\$} \mathsf{S}^{\mathbf{O}}(\mathrm{IK})$ followed by $\mathsf{E}^{\mathbf{O}}(\mathrm{IK}, \mathrm{X}')$. If qu is important, then $\mathbf{e}^{-1}(\mathrm{ik}, \mathrm{y})$ is likely to be determined by performing these two preceding executions many times. If qu is immaterial (namely, it will not be picked up during these many sample executions), then we will show that during the inversion of Y one may reply to qu with a random answer without making the result of the overall inversion of Y significantly skewed. The intuition is: in this case neither of $((\mathrm{ik}, *) \underset{\mathbf{s}}{\rightarrow} \mathrm{y})$ and $((\mathrm{ik}, *) \underset{\mathbf{e}}{\rightarrow} \mathrm{y})$ are likely to happen during the sampling algorithm that produced the challenge pre-image X and during $\mathsf{E}^{\mathbf{O}}(\mathrm{IK}, \mathrm{X})$ which results in Y. We will use this intuition to build hybrid oracles, denoted $\mathbf{O}\Diamond\widetilde{\mathbf{O}}$, which provide random answers to such immaterial queries but relative to which all of IK, X and Y are valid.

In Sect. 4 we will give a more concrete overview of our techniques and approach by showing how to break the enhanced one-wayness of any construction whose oracle access is of the form $(\mathsf{G}^{\mathbf{g}}, \mathsf{S}^{\mathbf{s}}, \mathsf{E}^{\mathbf{e}}, \mathsf{D}^{\mathbf{d}})$. We will then give the general attack against all constructions in Sect. 5.

2 Preliminaries

If $\mathcal{D}$ is a distribution, we use $\mathrm{x} \xleftarrow{\$} \mathcal{D}$ to indicate x is sampled according to $\mathcal{D}$ and we use $\mathrm{x}' \in \mathcal{D}$ to indicate $\mathrm{x}' \in \mathsf{support}(\mathcal{D})$. If $\mathsf{R}(\mathrm{x}_1, \ldots, \mathrm{x}_n)$ is a randomized algorithm, then $\mathsf{R}(\mathrm{a}_1, \ldots, \mathrm{a}_n)$ denotes the random variable $\mathsf{R}(\mathrm{a}_1, \ldots, \mathrm{a}_n; \mathrm{r})$, where $\mathrm{r} \xleftarrow{\$} \{0,1\}^*$.

If f is a function and Dom is a set, then $f(\mathsf{Dom}) \triangleq \{f(x) \mid x \in \mathsf{Dom}\}$.

We start with the definition of a family of trapdoor permutations. Each function $\mathsf{E}(\mathrm{IK}, \cdot)$ in the family acts as a permutation over a domain $\mathsf{Dom}_{\mathrm{IK}} \subseteq \{0,1\}^w$ (for some fixed polynomial w specified by the permutation family), where the domain $\mathsf{Dom}_{\mathrm{IK}}$ may possibly depend on IK. Moreover, this induced permutation can be inverted using any matching trapdoor key for IK. Finally, there is a sampling algorithm S, where $\mathsf{S}(\mathrm{IK})$ allows one to sample from $\mathsf{Dom}_{\mathrm{IK}}$.

Definition 1 (Trapdoor Permutations). *Let $w = w(\kappa)$ be an arbitrary polynomial. A family of trapdoor permutations* TDP *consists of four PPT algorithms* G, S, E *and* D *defined as follows.*

- $\mathsf{G}(1^\kappa)$*: The key generation algorithm* G *takes as input a security parameter* 1^κ *and outputs a pair* (IK, TK) *of index/trapdoor keys.*

- $\mathsf{S}(\mathrm{IK};\mathrm{R})$: *The sampling algorithm* S *takes as input an index key* IK *and randomness* $\mathrm{R} \in \{0,1\}^\kappa$ *and outputs an element* $\mathrm{X} \in \{0,1\}^w$. *We use* $\mathsf{Dom}_{\mathrm{IK}}$ *to denote the set of values* X *which are outputted by* $\mathsf{S}(\mathrm{IK};\cdot)$.
- $\mathsf{E}(\mathrm{IK},\mathrm{X})$: *The evaluation algorithm* E *takes as input an index key* IK *and an element* $\mathrm{X} \in \{0,1\}^w$ *and outputs* $\mathrm{Y} \in \{0,1\}^w \cup \{\bot\}$.
- $\mathsf{D}(\mathrm{TK},\mathrm{Y})$: *The inversion algorithm* D *takes as input a trapdoor key* TK, *and an element* $\mathrm{Y} \in \{0,1\}^w$ *and outputs* $\mathrm{X} \in \{0,1\}^w \cup \{\bot\}$.

We will now define the notion of correctness, as well as two one-wayness notions. As terminology, we say that an index key IK *is valid if* $(\mathrm{IK}, *) = \mathsf{G}(1^\kappa;\mathrm{R})$ *for some randomness* R.

- ***Correctness.*** *For any valid index key* IK, *the function* $\mathsf{E}(\mathrm{IK},\cdot)$ *induces a permutation over* $\mathsf{Dom}_{\mathrm{IK}}$. *Moreover, for any security parameter* κ *we have* $\Pr[\mathsf{D}(\mathrm{TK},\mathsf{E}(\mathrm{IK},\mathrm{X})) = \mathrm{X}] = 1$, *where* $(\mathrm{IK},\mathrm{TK}) \xleftarrow{\$} \mathsf{G}(1^\kappa)$, $\mathrm{R} \xleftarrow{\$} \{0,1\}^\kappa$ *and* $\mathrm{X} := \mathsf{S}(\mathrm{IK};\mathrm{R})$.
- ***Standard one-wayness.*** *For any PPT adversary we have* $\mathcal{A}$ $\Pr[\mathcal{A}(\mathrm{IK},\mathrm{Y}) = \mathsf{D}(\mathrm{TK},\mathrm{Y})] = \mathrm{negl}(\kappa)$, *where* $(\mathrm{IK},\mathrm{TK}) \xleftarrow{\$} \mathsf{G}(1^\kappa)$, $\mathrm{R} \xleftarrow{\$} \{0,1\}^\kappa$ *and* $\mathrm{Y} := \mathsf{S}(\mathrm{IK};\mathrm{R})$.
- ***Enhanced one-wayness.*** *For any PPT adversary* $\mathcal{A}$.

$$\Pr[\mathcal{A}(\mathrm{IK},\mathrm{Y},\mathrm{R}) = \mathsf{D}(\mathrm{TK},\mathrm{Y})] = \mathrm{negl}(\kappa),$$

  where $(\mathrm{IK},\mathrm{TK}) \xleftarrow{\$} \mathsf{G}(1^\kappa)$, $\mathrm{R} \xleftarrow{\$} \{0,1\}^\kappa$, $\mathrm{Y} := \mathsf{S}(\mathrm{IK};\mathrm{R})$. *Note that* Y *can be computed from* IK *and* R, *but we include it separately just for notational convenience.*

We now define the notion of fully-blackbox constructions, tailored to our setting. See [RTV04,BBF13] for more general notions.

Definition 2 (Fully blackbox constructions). *A fully-blackbox (shortly, a blackbox) construction of an enhanced TDP from a standard TDP consists of a PPT oracle-aided construction* $(\mathsf{G},\mathsf{S},\mathsf{E},\mathsf{D})$ *and a PPT oracle-aided reduction algorithm* Red *satisfying the following. For any correct TDP oracle* $\mathbf{O} = (\mathbf{g},\mathbf{s},\mathbf{e},\mathbf{d})$ *(where correctness is defined in Definition 1) we have*

1. ***Correctness:*** $(\mathsf{G}^{\mathbf{O}},\mathsf{S}^{\mathbf{O}},\mathsf{E}^{\mathbf{O}},\mathsf{D}^{\mathbf{O}})$ *is a correct TDP;*
2. ***Security:*** *for any adversary* $\mathcal{A}$ *breaking the enhanced one-wayness of the oracle-aided scheme* $(\mathsf{G}^{\mathbf{O}},\mathsf{S}^{\mathbf{O}},\mathsf{E}^{\mathbf{O}},\mathsf{D}^{\mathbf{O}})$, *the oracle algorithm* $\mathsf{Red}^{\mathbf{O},\mathcal{A}}$ *breaks the standard one-wayness of* $\mathbf{O}$.

3 Main Theorem and Proofs Roadmap

In this section we describe our main theorem and the roadmap of the proofs.

As common in impossibility results, we prove our main theorem by showing the existence of an oracle relative to which the base primitive exists (namely, standard TDPs), but not the target primitive (namely, enhanced TDPs). Technically, our separation model is closest to that of [HR04], which only results in fully-blackbox separations, as opposed to the more general *relativizing* separations, considered in most previous work, e.g., [IR89, Sim98, GKM+00].

Theorem 1 (Impossibility of Enhanced TDPs from Standard TDPs). *There exists oracles* $(\mathbf{O}, \mathbf{u}, \mathbf{v})$, *where* $\mathbf{O} := (\mathbf{g}, \mathbf{s}, \mathbf{e}, \mathbf{d})$, *such that both the following conditions hold.*

1. $\mathbf{O}$ *is a standard TDP against every polynomial-query adversary* $\mathcal{A}^{\mathbf{O},\mathbf{u},\mathbf{v}}$*: That is, the probability that* $\mathcal{A}^{\mathbf{O},\mathbf{u},\mathbf{v}}(\mathrm{ik}, \mathrm{y}) = \mathrm{x}$ *is at most negligible, where* $(\mathrm{ik}, \mathrm{tk}) \xleftarrow{\$} \mathbf{g}(1^\kappa)$, $\mathrm{x} \xleftarrow{\$} \mathbf{s}(\mathrm{ik})$ *and* $\mathrm{y} := \mathbf{e}(\mathrm{ik}, \mathrm{x})$.
2. *The enhanced one-wayness of any construction* $(\mathsf{G}^{\mathbf{O}}, \mathsf{S}^{\mathbf{O}}, \mathsf{E}^{\mathbf{O}}, \mathsf{D}^{\mathbf{O}})$ *can be broken by a poly-query adversary* $\mathsf{Break}^{\mathbf{O},\mathbf{u},\mathbf{v}}$. *That is, the probability that* $\mathsf{Break}^{\mathbf{O},\mathbf{u},\mathbf{v}}(\mathrm{IK}, \mathrm{R}, \mathrm{Y}) = \mathsf{D}^{\mathbf{O}}(\mathrm{TK}, \mathrm{Y})$ *is non-negligible, where* $(\mathrm{IK}, \mathrm{TK}) \xleftarrow{\$} \mathsf{G}^{\mathbf{O}}(1^\kappa)$, $\mathrm{R} \xleftarrow{\$} \{0,1\}^*$ *and* $\mathrm{Y} := \mathsf{S}^{\mathbf{O}}(\mathrm{IK}; \mathrm{R})$.

As a result, there exists no fully-blackbox construction of enhanced TDPs from standard TDPs.

Roadmap: Proof of Theorem 1. The "as a result" part follows immediately from Parts 1 and 2 of the theorem, and thus we focus on proving these two parts. (For completeness, we show how to derive the "as a result" part below.) As common in impossibility results, we show the existence of the oracles $(\mathbf{O}, \mathbf{u}, \mathbf{v})$, required by Theorem 1, by first describing a distribution of oracles, and then proving results for oracles randomly chosen from this distribution. We will first start by describing a distribution Ψ of oracles $(\mathbf{g}, \mathbf{s}, \mathbf{e}, \mathbf{d}, \mathbf{u}, \mathbf{v})$. A randomly chosen $\mathbf{O} = (\mathbf{g}, \mathbf{s}, \mathbf{e}, \mathbf{d})$ from this distribution will allow one to implement an ideal version of a TDP, which not only satisfies standard one-wayness, but also enhanced-one-wayness. We then introduce two weakening oracles $\mathbf{u}$ and $\mathbf{v}$, so that the oracle $\mathbf{O}$ still provides standard one-wayness in the presence of $\mathbf{u}$ and $\mathbf{v}$, but the enhanced one-wayness of any TDP construction instantiated with $\mathbf{O}$ can be broken by making a polynomial number of queries to $(\mathbf{O}, \mathbf{u}, \mathbf{v})$.

In the following definition, whenever we say a function $f\colon \mathsf{Dom} \to \mathsf{Ran}$ with property P (e.g., injectivity) is a randomly chosen function we mean f is chosen uniformly at random from the space of all functions from Dom to Ran having property P.

Definition 3. *We define an oracle distribution* Ψ *that produces an ensemble of oracles* $(\mathbf{O}_\kappa, \mathbf{u}_\kappa, \mathbf{v}_\kappa)_\kappa$. *For all* κ *and all* $\mathrm{ik} \in \{0,1\}^\kappa$, *choose a set* D_{ik} *uniformly at random under the conditions that* $\mathsf{D}_{\mathrm{ik}} \subseteq \{0,1\}^{5\kappa}$ *and that* $|\mathsf{D}_{\mathrm{ik}}| = 2^\kappa$.

- $\mathbf{g}_\kappa\colon \{0,1\}^\kappa \to \{0,1\}^\kappa$ *is a random injective function, mapping a trapdoor key to an index key.*
- $\mathbf{s}_\kappa\colon \{0,1\}^\kappa \times \{0,1\}^\kappa \to \{0,1\}^{5\kappa}$ *is a random function, where for all* $\mathrm{ik} \in \{0,1\}^\kappa$*:* $\mathbf{s}_\kappa(\mathrm{ik}, \cdot)$ *is 1-1 and for all* $\mathrm{r} \in \{0,1\}^\kappa$*:* $\mathbf{s}_\kappa(\mathrm{ik}, r) \in \mathsf{D}_{\mathrm{ik}}$.

- $\mathbf{e}_\kappa \colon \{0,1\}^\kappa \times \{0,1\}^{5\kappa} \to \{0,1\}^{5\kappa} \cup \{\perp\}$ *is a random function, satisfying the following two conditions: for all* $\mathrm{ik} \in \{0,1\}^\kappa$*:* $\mathbf{e}_\kappa(\mathrm{ik}, \mathsf{D}_{\mathrm{ik}}) = \mathsf{D}_{\mathrm{ik}}$ *and for all* $\mathrm{x} \notin \mathsf{D}_{\mathrm{ik}}$*:* $\mathbf{e}_\kappa(\mathrm{ik}, \mathrm{x}) = \perp$.
- $\mathbf{d}_\kappa \colon \{0,1\}^\kappa \times \{0,1\}^{5\kappa} \to \{0,1\}^{5\kappa} \cup \{\perp\}$ *is a function, where* $\mathbf{d}_\kappa(\mathrm{tk}, \mathrm{y})$ *is defined as follows. Letting* $\mathrm{ik} := \mathbf{g}_\kappa(\mathrm{tk})$, *if* $\mathrm{y} \in \mathsf{D}_{\mathrm{ik}}$, *then letting* x *be the unique string satisfying* $\mathbf{e}_\kappa(\mathrm{ik}, \mathrm{x}) = \mathrm{y}$, *set* $\mathbf{d}_\kappa(\mathrm{tk}, \mathrm{y}) := \mathrm{x}$. *Otherwise (i.e., if* $\mathrm{y} \notin \mathsf{D}_{\mathrm{ik}}$*), set* $\mathbf{d}_\kappa(\mathrm{tk}, \mathrm{y}) := \perp$.
- $\mathbf{u}_\kappa \colon \{0,1\}^\kappa \times \{0,1\}^\kappa \to \{0,1\}^\kappa$ *is defined as follows. For* $\mathrm{ik} \in \{0,1\}^\kappa$ *and* $\mathrm{r} \in \{0,1\}^\kappa$, *letting* $\mathrm{y} := \mathbf{s}_\kappa(\mathrm{ik}, \mathrm{r})$ *and* r_0 *be such that* $\mathrm{y} = \mathbf{e}_\kappa(\mathrm{ik}, \mathbf{s}_\kappa(\mathrm{ik}, \mathrm{r}_0))$, *set* $\mathbf{u}_\kappa(\mathrm{ik}, \mathrm{r}) := \mathrm{r}_0$.
- $\mathbf{v}_\kappa \colon \{0,1\}^\kappa \times \{0,1\}^{5\kappa} \to \{\perp, \top\}$ *is defined as follows:* $\mathbf{v}_\kappa(\mathrm{ik}, \mathrm{x})$ *checks whether the given input* x *is in* D_{ik} *or not: set* $\mathbf{v}_\kappa(\mathrm{ik}, \mathrm{x}) := \top$ *if* $\mathrm{x} \in \mathsf{D}_{\mathrm{ik}}$, *and* $\mathbf{v}_\kappa(\mathrm{ik}, \mathrm{x}) := \perp$, *otherwise.*

Redundancy of the Oracle $\mathbf{v}_\kappa$. Note that the oracle $\mathbf{v}_\kappa$ can be simulated by $\mathbf{e}_\kappa$. We only include this oracle as it will simplicity notation.

Convention and Notation. We will often drop the security parameter κ as a sub-index to the oracles whenever the underlying security parameter is clear from the context. For an oracle algorithm $A^{\mathbf{g},\mathbf{s},\mathbf{e},\mathbf{d}}$ we use notation such as $(\mathrm{qu} \underset{\mathbf{g}}{\longrightarrow} \mathrm{an})$ to indicate that $\mathcal{A}$ queries $\mathbf{g}$ on qu and receives an as the answer. We also use $(\mathrm{qu} \underset{\mathbf{g}}{\longrightarrow} ?)$ to indicate that the query qu is asked.

We will now give a simple-information theoretic lemma showing that a randomly chosen TDP $\mathbf{O}$ is standard one-way even in the presence of the oracle $\mathbf{u}$. The proof of the following theorem is based on simple information theoretic arguments and so is omitted.

Lemma 1 (O is one-way relative to $(\mathbf{O}, \mathbf{u}, \mathbf{v})$). *For any polynomial query adversary* $\mathcal{A}$ *we have*

$$\Pr[\mathcal{A}^{\mathbf{O},\mathbf{u},\mathbf{v}}(\mathrm{ik}, \mathrm{y}) = \mathrm{x} \text{ and } \mathbf{e}(\mathrm{ik}, \mathrm{x}) = \mathrm{y}] \leq \tfrac{1}{2^{\kappa/3}},$$

where $(\mathbf{g}, \mathbf{s}, \mathbf{e}, \mathbf{d}, \mathbf{u}, \mathbf{v}) \leftarrow \Psi$, $\mathbf{O} := (\mathbf{g}, \mathbf{s}, \mathbf{e}, \mathbf{d})$, $\mathrm{tk} \xleftarrow{\$} \{0,1\}^\kappa$ *and* $\mathrm{ik} = \mathbf{g}(\mathrm{tk})$. *This bound holds so long as* $\mathcal{A}$ *is poly-query bounded (and unbounded otherwise).*

The following lemma shows how to break the enhanced one-wayness of any candidate construction.

Lemma 2 (Breaking enhanced one-wayness of any construction). *Let* $(\mathsf{G}, \mathsf{S}, \mathsf{E}, \mathsf{D})$ *be a candidate blackbox construction of a TDP. There exists a polynomial query adversary* Break *such that*

$$\Pr[\mathsf{Break}^{\mathbf{O},\mathbf{u},\mathbf{v}}(1^\kappa, \mathrm{IK}, \mathrm{R}, \mathrm{Y}) = \mathrm{X}] \geq 1 - \frac{1}{\kappa^2},$$

where $(\mathbf{g}, \mathbf{s}, \mathbf{e}, \mathbf{d}, \mathbf{u}, \mathbf{v}) \xleftarrow{\$} \Psi$, $\mathbf{O} := (\mathbf{g}, \mathbf{s}, \mathbf{e}, \mathbf{d})$, $(\mathrm{IK}, \mathrm{TK}) \xleftarrow{\$} \mathsf{G}^{\mathbf{O}}(1^\kappa)$, $\mathrm{R} \xleftarrow{\$} \{0,1\}^*$, $\mathrm{Y} := \mathsf{S}^{\mathbf{O}}(\mathrm{IK}; \mathrm{R})$ *and* $\mathrm{X} := \mathsf{D}^{\mathbf{O}}(\mathrm{TK}, \mathrm{Y})$.

Completing the Proof of Theorem 1. The proof of Theorem 1 follows easily by combining Lemmas 1 and 2, as given below.

Proof (of Theorem 1). We will first prove the "as a result" part of the theorem. Suppose to the contrary that there exists an enhanced TDP construction $(\mathsf{G}, \mathsf{S}, \mathsf{E}, \mathsf{D})$, and let Red be the PPT security reduction algorithm guaranteed to exist by Definition 2. Let $(\mathbf{O}, \mathbf{u}, \mathbf{v})$ be the oracle shown to exist by Parts 1 and 2 of the theorem. By Part 2 of the theorem we know that there exists a polynomial query adversary $\mathsf{Break}^{\mathbf{O},\mathbf{u},\mathbf{v}}$ which breaks the enhanced one-wayness of $(\mathsf{G}^{\mathbf{O}}, \mathsf{S}^{\mathbf{O}}, \mathsf{E}^{\mathbf{O}}, \mathsf{D}^{\mathbf{O}})$. Thus, by definition of blackbox constructions, $\mathsf{Red}^{\mathsf{Break},\mathbf{O}}$ should break the standard one-wayness of $\mathbf{O}$. This however is a contradiction to Part 1, because $\mathsf{Red}^{\mathsf{Break},\mathbf{O}}$ can be simulated by a polynomial query adversary $\mathcal{A}^{\mathbf{O},\mathbf{u},\mathbf{v}}$.

We now prove Parts 1 and 2. To show the existence of the oracles $(\mathbf{g}, \mathbf{s}, \mathbf{e}, \mathbf{d}, \mathbf{u}, \mathbf{v})$ required by the theorem, we show

1. For a measure-one of oracles $(\mathbf{g}, \mathbf{s}, \mathbf{e}, \mathbf{d}, \mathbf{u}, \mathbf{v})$, the oracle $(\mathbf{g}, \mathbf{s}, \mathbf{e}, \mathbf{d})$ is standard oneway against all polynomial-query adversaries with oracle access to $(\mathbf{g}, \mathbf{s}, \mathbf{e}, \mathbf{d}, \mathbf{u}, \mathbf{v})$.
2. For a measure-one of oracles $(\mathbf{g}, \mathbf{s}, \mathbf{e}, \mathbf{d}, \mathbf{u}, \mathbf{v})$, the adversary $\mathsf{Break}^{\mathbf{O},\mathbf{u},\mathbf{v}}$ breaks the enhanced one-wayness of $(\mathsf{G}^{\mathbf{O}}, \mathsf{S}^{\mathbf{O}}, \mathsf{E}^{\mathbf{O}}, \mathsf{D}^{\mathbf{O}})$.

The above two statements implies the existence of a specific oracle $(\mathbf{g}, \mathbf{s}, \mathbf{e}, \mathbf{d}, \mathbf{u}, \mathbf{v})$, meeting the requirement of the theorem.

We show how to derive Condition 2 from Lemma 2. The proof of Condition 1 follows similarly from Lemma 1.

By Lemma 2 we have

$$\Pr_{(\mathbf{O},\mathbf{u},\mathbf{v}),\mathrm{IK},\mathrm{R}}[\mathsf{Break}^{\mathbf{O},\mathbf{u},\mathbf{v}}(1^\kappa, \mathrm{IK}, \mathrm{R}) = \mathrm{X}] \geq 1 - \frac{1}{\kappa^2}. \tag{1}$$

Using a simple averaging argument we may obtain

$$\Pr_{(\mathbf{O},\mathbf{u},\mathbf{v})}\left[\Pr_{\mathrm{IK},\mathrm{R}}[\mathsf{Break}^{\mathbf{O},\mathbf{u},\mathbf{v}}(1^\kappa, \mathrm{IK}, \mathrm{R}) = \mathrm{X}] \geq \frac{1}{\kappa^3}\right] \geq 1 - \frac{1}{\kappa^{1.5}}. \tag{2}$$

Thus, for at most a $\frac{1}{\kappa^{1.5}}$ fraction of all oracles $(\mathbf{O}, \mathbf{u}, \mathbf{v})$, the adversary $\mathsf{Break}^{\mathbf{O},\mathbf{u},\mathbf{v}}$, on security parameter 1^κ, recovers the pre-image correctly with probability less than $\frac{1}{\kappa^3}$. Since $\sum \frac{1}{\kappa^{1.5}}$ converges, by the Borel-Cantelli Lemma we have that for a measure-one of oracles $(\mathbf{O}, \mathbf{u}, \mathbf{v})$, the adversary $\mathsf{Break}^{\mathbf{O},\mathbf{u},\mathbf{v}}$ breaks the enhanced-onewayness of $(\mathsf{G}^{\mathbf{O}}, \mathsf{S}^{\mathbf{O}}, \mathsf{E}^{\mathbf{O}}, \mathsf{D}^{\mathbf{O}})$: for all sufficiently large κ, the adversary recovers X from $\mathsf{Break}^{\mathbf{O},\mathbf{u},\mathbf{v}}(1^\kappa, \mathrm{IK}, \mathrm{R}, \mathrm{Y})$ with probability at least $\frac{1}{\kappa^3}$. □

Roadmap for the Proof of Lemma 2. We are left with proving Lemma 2, which constitutes the main technical bulk of our work. As a warp up, first in Sect. 4 we will prove and give an overview of our techniques for a special case of Lemma 2: that in which the oracle access of the construction is of the form $(\mathsf{G}^{\mathbf{g}}, \mathsf{S}^{\mathbf{s}}, \mathsf{E}^{\mathbf{e}}, \mathsf{D}^{\mathbf{d}})$. Then, we will give the proof for the general case in Sect. 5.

4 Proof of Lemma 2: Special Case $(\mathsf{G}^{\mathbf{g}}, \mathsf{S}^{\mathbf{s}}, \mathsf{E}^{\mathbf{e}}, \mathsf{D}^{\mathbf{d}})$

In this section we show how to break the enhanced one-wayness of a simple class of TDP constructions, those in which the oracle access is of the form $(\mathsf{G}^{\mathbf{g}}, \mathsf{S}^{\mathbf{s}}, \mathsf{E}^{\mathbf{e}}, \mathsf{D}^{\mathbf{d}})$. We call such constructions *type-1*. We first start with a general overview.

Setup. The input to the adversary $\mathsf{Break}^{\mathbf{O},\mathbf{u},\mathbf{v}}$ is (IK, R, Y), where $(\mathrm{IK}, \mathrm{TK}) \xleftarrow{\$} \mathsf{G}^{\mathbf{g}}(1^{\kappa})$, $\mathrm{R} \xleftarrow{\$} \{0,1\}^*$ and $\mathrm{Y} := \mathsf{S}^{\mathbf{s}}(\mathrm{IK}; \mathrm{R})$. The goal of Break is to find X such that $\mathrm{X} := \mathsf{D}^{\mathbf{d}}(\mathrm{TK}, \mathrm{Y})$.

High-Level Idea of Break's ***Strategy***. Consider a partial fake oracle $\mathbf{g}'$ and randomness R′ under which we have $\mathsf{G}^{\mathbf{g}'}(\mathrm{R}') = (\mathrm{IK}, \widetilde{\mathrm{TK}})$ for some $\widetilde{\mathrm{TK}}$. By a partial oracle we mean an oracle that is defined only on a small set of all queries, those that occur exactly during the execution of $\mathsf{G}^{\mathbf{g}'}(\mathrm{R}')$. Such a fake oracle $\mathbf{g}'$ and corresponding matching randomness R′ can be found by doing expensive offline computation and without interacting at all with the real oracles $(\mathbf{O}, \mathbf{u}, \mathbf{v})$.

Now consider the effect of super-imposing $\mathbf{g}'$ on the real oracle $\mathbf{g}$ to get an oracle $\widetilde{\mathbf{g}}$. This oracle $\widetilde{\mathbf{g}}$ is defined according to $\mathbf{g}'$ on all queries defined in $\mathbf{g}'$, and otherwise is defined as in $\mathbf{g}$.

For this perturbed oracle $\widetilde{\mathbf{g}}$, we will define a correspondingly perturbed oracle $\widetilde{\mathbf{d}}$ so that $(\widetilde{\mathbf{g}}, \mathbf{s}, \mathbf{e}, \widetilde{\mathbf{d}})$ is a valid TDP. Now since we know $\mathsf{G}^{\widetilde{\mathbf{g}}}(\mathrm{R}') = (\mathrm{IK}, \widetilde{\mathrm{TK}})$, we must have $\mathrm{X} = \mathsf{D}^{\widetilde{\mathbf{d}}}(\widetilde{\mathrm{TK}}, \mathrm{Y})$, and thus recovering the challenge pre-image X amounts to one's ability to perform the execution of $\mathsf{D}^{\widetilde{\mathbf{d}}}(\widetilde{\mathrm{TK}}, \mathrm{Y})$ by only making a polynomial number queries to $(\mathbf{O}, \mathbf{u}, \mathbf{v})$. As we will see, the naive way of performing this execution will result in an exponential number of queries to $(\mathbf{O}, \mathbf{u}, \mathbf{v})$. Our main technique will allow us to get around this problem by making use of the oracle $\mathbf{u}$ and knowledge of R (which is the randomness underlying the image point Y).

Organization of Section 4. In Sect. 4.1 we will give a more detailed (but still informal) overview of the above approach for the case in which each of the algorithms (G, S, E, D) makes only one query. We will then formally describe an attack against any candidate many-query construction $(\mathsf{G}^{\mathbf{g}}, \mathsf{S}^{\mathbf{s}}, \mathsf{E}^{\mathbf{e}}, \mathsf{D}^{\mathbf{d}})$ in the next two subsections.

4.1 General Overview: One Query Case

We will now give a concrete overview of the above abstract approach for the following type of construction: We assume each of the algorithms $(\mathsf{G}^{\mathbf{g}}, \mathsf{S}^{\mathbf{s}}, \mathsf{E}^{\mathbf{e}}, \mathsf{D}^{\mathbf{d}})$ makes only one query. The input to the adversary $\mathsf{Break}^{\mathbf{O},\mathbf{u},\mathbf{v}}$ is (IK, R, Y), where $(\mathrm{IK}, \mathrm{TK}) \xleftarrow{\$} \mathsf{G}^{\mathbf{g}}(1^{\kappa})$, $\mathrm{R} \xleftarrow{\$} \{0,1\}^*$ and $\mathrm{Y} := \mathsf{S}^{\mathbf{s}}(\mathrm{IK}; \mathrm{R})$. Let X denote Break's challenge image point; namely, we have $\mathsf{E}^{\mathbf{e}}(\mathrm{IK}, \mathrm{X}) = \mathrm{Y}$.

We sketch the main steps taken by Break, and will explain about each of them.

Sampling a Fake Oracle and a Trapdoor Key. Sample an oracle $\mathbf{g}'$ and a randomness value R' uniformly at random in such a way that

$$\mathsf{G}^{\mathbf{g}'}(1^\kappa; \mathrm{R}') = (\mathrm{IK}, \widetilde{\mathrm{TK}}), \tag{3}$$

for some $\widetilde{\mathrm{TK}}$. Since G makes only one query, we may think of $\mathbf{g}'$ as only one query/response pair $\mathsf{qa} := (\mathrm{tk} \xrightarrow[\mathbf{g}]{} \mathrm{ik})$. Thus, we may write Eq. 3 as $\mathsf{G}^{\mathsf{qa}}(1^\kappa; \mathrm{R}') = (\mathrm{IK}, \widetilde{\mathrm{TK}})$.

Defining the Oracle $\widetilde{\mathbf{g}}$. Consider an oracle $\widetilde{\mathbf{g}} := \mathsf{qa}\Diamond^*\mathbf{g}$, where the *composed* oracle $\mathsf{qa}\Diamond^*\mathbf{g}$ is defined as follows: $(\mathsf{qa}\Diamond^*\mathbf{g})(\mathrm{tk}') = \mathrm{ik}$ if $\mathrm{tk}' = \mathrm{tk}$; otherwise, $(\mathsf{qa}\Diamond^*\mathbf{g})(\mathrm{tk}') = \mathbf{g}(\mathrm{tk}')$. Briefly, the oracle $\mathsf{qa}\Diamond^*\mathbf{g}$ first forwards a given query to qa, and if the query is not defined there, the query will be forwarded to $\mathbf{g}$.

Defining the Oracle $\widetilde{\mathbf{d}}$. We now define $\widetilde{\mathbf{d}}$ in such a way that $(\widetilde{\mathbf{g}}, \mathbf{s}, \mathbf{e}, \widetilde{\mathbf{d}})$ forms a valid TDP oracle. For any tk' and y', the value of $\widetilde{\mathbf{d}}(\mathrm{tk}', \mathrm{y}')$ is formed as follows. Letting $\mathrm{ik}' = \widetilde{\mathbf{g}}(\mathrm{tk}')$:

- If $\mathbf{v}(\mathrm{ik}', \mathrm{y}') = \bot$, then set $\widetilde{\mathbf{d}}(\mathrm{tk}', \mathrm{y}') = \bot$;
- Otherwise, letting x' be the unique string for which we have $\mathbf{e}(\mathrm{ik}', \mathrm{x}') = \mathrm{y}'$, set $\widetilde{\mathbf{d}}(\mathrm{tk}', \mathrm{y}') = \mathrm{x}'$. Note that since we know $\mathbf{v}(\mathrm{ik}', \mathrm{y}') = \top$ (because otherwise the previous check would hold), by definition of $\mathbf{e}$ (Definition 3) such x' does exist and it is unique.

Performing the Execution $\mathsf{D}^{\widetilde{\mathbf{d}}}(\widetilde{\mathrm{TK}}, \mathrm{Y})$ is Enough. It is straightforward to verify that $(\widetilde{\mathbf{g}}, \mathbf{s}, \mathbf{e}, \widetilde{\mathbf{d}})$ forms a valid TDP oracle. Moreover, by definition of $\widetilde{\mathbf{g}}$ and R', we have $\mathsf{G}^{\widetilde{\mathbf{g}}}(\mathrm{R}') = (\mathrm{IK}, \widetilde{\mathrm{TK}})$. Now since $\mathsf{E}^{\mathbf{e}}(\mathrm{IK}, \mathrm{X}) = \mathrm{Y}$, by completeness of the construction, we will have $\mathsf{D}^{\widetilde{\mathbf{d}}}(\widetilde{\mathrm{TK}}, \mathrm{Y}) = \mathrm{X}$, where X is Break's challenge image point.

Executing $\mathsf{D}^{\widetilde{\mathbf{d}}}(\widetilde{\mathrm{TK}}, \mathrm{Y})$ *efficiently?* Can we execute $\mathsf{D}^{\widetilde{\mathbf{d}}}(\widetilde{\mathrm{TK}}, \mathrm{Y})$ by making only a polynomial number of queries to $(\mathbf{g}, \mathbf{s}, \mathbf{e}, \mathbf{d}, \mathbf{u})$? Let us look at all the possibilities for a possible encountered query $((\mathrm{tk}', \mathrm{y}') \xrightarrow[\widetilde{\mathbf{d}}]{} ?)$ below. Let $\mathrm{ik}' := \widetilde{\mathbf{g}}(\mathrm{tk}')$, which can be computed by making at most one query to $\mathbf{g}$.

1. **Simple case**: $\mathrm{ik}' \neq \mathrm{ik}$ (recall that ik is defined in the query/response set qa, which in turn forms $\widetilde{\mathbf{g}}$): in this case by inspection we can see that we indeed have $\mathbf{d}(\mathrm{tk}', \mathrm{y}') = \widetilde{\mathbf{d}}(\mathrm{tk}', \mathrm{y}')$, and so the answer can be determined by calling $\mathbf{d}$ directly.
2. **Simple case**: $\mathrm{ik}' = \mathrm{ik}$ and $\mathbf{v}(\mathrm{ik}, \mathrm{y}') = \bot$: in this case we can again easily see that $\mathbf{d}(\mathrm{tk}', \mathrm{y}') = \bot$.
3. **Problematic case**: $\mathrm{ik}' = \mathrm{ik}$ and $\mathbf{v}(\mathrm{ik}, \mathrm{y}') \neq \bot$: in this case Break cannot right away compute the value of $\widetilde{\mathbf{d}}(\mathrm{tk}', \mathrm{y}')$ because in order to do so, Break must find an x' such that $\mathbf{e}(\mathrm{ik}, \mathrm{x}') = \mathrm{y}'$.

The Oracle* u *and Randomness* R *to the Rescue. From the above discussion, the attacker Break only needs to handle Case 3. That is, from the pair $(\mathrm{ik}, \mathrm{y}')$, upon which Line 3 is hit, and without knowledge of ik's trapdoor key $\mathbf{g}^{-1}(\mathrm{ik})$, the attacker Break should find an x' such that $\mathbf{e}(\mathrm{ik}, \mathrm{x}') = \mathrm{y}'$. Recall that D makes only one query, and so if Break gets past this "one-time" problematic case, it will be done.

Recall that the input to Break is (IK, R, Y), where R is the randomness underlying the image point Y. We claim that with all but negligible probability the following must hold: letting $(\mathrm{ik}, \mathrm{y}')$ be the pair upon which Line 3 was hit, during the execution of $\mathsf{S}^{\mathbf{s}}(\mathrm{IK}; \mathrm{R})$ we must have a query/response pair $((\mathrm{ik}, \mathrm{r}) \underset{\mathbf{s}}{\rightarrow} \mathrm{y}')$ for some r. Assuming that this claim holds, Break may then simply call $((\mathrm{ik}, \mathrm{r}) \underset{\mathbf{u}}{\rightarrow} ?)$ to get r', and then call $((\mathrm{ik}, \mathrm{r}') \underset{\mathbf{s}}{\rightarrow} ?)$ to get x', completing its attack.

It remains to prove the above claim. We show that if the claim does not hold, then one may efficiently produce a pair $(\mathrm{ik}', \mathrm{y}')$, where y' is a valid image of $\mathbf{s}(\mathrm{ik}', *)$, *without* ever calling $\mathbf{s}(\mathrm{ik}', \cdot)$ on the corresponding pre-image of y', and without ever calling $\mathbf{e}$ and $\mathbf{d}$ at all. Due to the sparse and random nature of the oracle $\mathbf{s}$, the probability of this event is at most negligible. To produce $(\mathrm{ik}', \mathrm{y}')$, do the following.

- Sample $(\mathrm{IK}, \mathrm{TK}) \xleftarrow{\$} \mathsf{G}^{\mathbf{g}}(1^\kappa)$, $\mathrm{R} \xleftarrow{\$} \{0,1\}^*$ and set $\mathrm{Y} := \mathsf{S}^{\mathbf{s}}(\mathrm{IK}; \mathrm{R})$.
- Form $\widetilde{\mathrm{TK}}$ and $\widetilde{\mathbf{d}}$ as above. (This step is done offline, without interacting with the real oracles).
- Run $\mathsf{D}^{\widetilde{\mathbf{d}}}(\widetilde{\mathrm{TK}}, \mathrm{Y})$ and as soon as as query $((\mathrm{tk}', \mathrm{y}') \underset{\widetilde{\mathbf{d}}}{\longrightarrow} ?)$ is made, return $(\mathrm{ik}', \mathrm{y}')$, where $\mathrm{ik}' := \mathbf{g}(\mathrm{tk}')$.

Our claim about the pair $(\mathrm{ik}', \mathrm{y})$ now follows.

4.2 Definitions and Simple Lemmas

In this section we will give some definitions and simple lemmas, which will then be used in Sect. 4.3. Some of these were informally reviewed in Sect. 4.1.

TDP-Valid and Ψ-Valid Oracles. Recall the distribution Ψ on oracles $(\mathbf{O}, \mathbf{u}, \mathbf{v})$ given in Definition 3. We say that an oracle $\mathbf{O}_1 := (\mathbf{g}_1, \mathbf{s}_1, \mathbf{e}_1, \mathbf{d}_1)$ is *Ψ-valid* if $\mathbf{O}_1$ is a possible output of Ψ. This means in particular that the input and output sizes of the sub-routines of $\mathbf{O}_1$ match those specified in Definition 3. We say that an oracle $\mathbf{O}_2 := (\mathbf{g}_2, \mathbf{s}_2, \mathbf{e}_2, \mathbf{d}_2)$ is *TDP valid* if $\mathbf{O}_2$ satisfies the completeness condition of Definition 1. Note that if an oracle is Ψ-valid then it is also TDP-valid, but the converse is not true.

Similarly, we say that a partial oracle $\mathbf{O}'$ (which is not defined on all points) is Ψ-valid (resp., TDP-valid) if there exists a full Ψ-valid (resp., a full TDP-valid) oracle $\mathbf{O}$ such that $\mathbf{O}' \subseteq \mathbf{O}$. Here, $\mathbf{O}' \subseteq \mathbf{O}$ means that $\mathbf{O}$ agree with $\mathbf{O}'$.

Definition 4 (Composed Oracles $\lozenge^*$). *Let* $\mathbf{O} := (\mathbf{g}, \mathbf{s}, \mathbf{e}, \mathbf{d})$ *be a* Ψ*-valid oracle and let*

$$\mathbf{g}' := \{(\mathrm{tk}_1 \underset{\mathbf{g}}{\rightarrow} \mathrm{ik}_1), \dots, (\mathrm{tk}_w \underset{\mathbf{g}}{\rightarrow} \mathrm{ik}_w)\}$$

be a partial Ψ*-valid oracle consisting of only* $\mathbf{g}$*-type queries. We define the composed oracle* $\mathbf{g}'\lozenge^*\mathbf{O} := (\widetilde{\mathbf{g}}, \mathbf{s}, \mathbf{e}, \widetilde{\mathbf{d}})$*, which has perturbed key-generation and inversion oracles, as follows.*

- $\widetilde{\mathbf{g}}(\cdot)$*: for a given* tk*, let* $\widetilde{\mathbf{g}}(\mathrm{tk}) \triangleq \mathrm{ik}_i$ *if* $\mathrm{tk} = \mathrm{tk}_i$ *for* $i \in [w]$*; otherwise,* $\widetilde{\mathbf{g}}(\mathrm{tk}) \triangleq \mathbf{g}(\mathrm{tk})$.
- $\widetilde{\mathbf{d}}(\cdot,\cdot)$*: for a given pair* $(\mathrm{tk}, \mathrm{y})$*, define* $\widetilde{\mathbf{d}}(\mathrm{tk}, \mathrm{y})$ *as follows. Assuming* $\mathrm{ik} = \widetilde{\mathbf{g}}(\mathrm{tk})$*, let* $\widetilde{\mathbf{d}}(\mathrm{tk}, \mathrm{y}) \triangleq \mathbf{e}^{-1}(\mathrm{ik}, \mathrm{y})$*. Here,* $\mathbf{e}^{-1}(\mathrm{ik}, \cdot)$ *is the inverse function of* $\mathbf{e}(\mathrm{ik}, \cdot)$*— i.e.,* $\mathbf{e}^{-1}(\mathrm{ik}, \mathrm{y}) = \mathrm{x}$ *if for some* x*,* $\mathbf{e}(\mathrm{ik}, \mathrm{x}) = \mathrm{y}$*; otherwise,* $\mathbf{e}^{-1}(\mathrm{ik}, \mathrm{y}) = \bot$*. Note that by definition of* Ψ*, the function* $\mathbf{e}^{-1}(\mathrm{ik}, \cdot)$ *is indeed well-defined.*

It is straightforward to verify that the operation $\lozenge^*$ preserves completeness.

Lemma 3. *Let* $\mathbf{O}$ *and* $\mathbf{g}'$ *be as in Definition 4. Then, the composed oracle* $\mathbf{g}'\lozenge^*\mathbf{O}$ *is TDP-valid.*

Proof. The proof is straightforward and so is omitted. □

Consider a random Ψ-valid oracle $(\mathbf{g}, \mathbf{s}, \mathbf{e}, \mathbf{d}, \mathbf{u}, \mathbf{v})$. Imagine an adversary that wants to come up with a pair $(\mathrm{ik}, \mathrm{y}) \in \{0,1\}^\kappa \times \{0,1\}^{5\kappa}$ of an index-key/image such that y lies in the support of $\mathbf{s}(\mathrm{ik})$. The following lemma shows that the probability that an adversary can do this in non-trivial way is exponentially small.

Lemma 4. *For any polynomial query oracle adversary* $\mathcal{B}$ *with access only to the oracles* $(\mathbf{g}, \mathbf{s}, \mathbf{u}, \mathbf{v})$ *we have*

$$\Pr\left[(\mathrm{ik}, \mathrm{y}) \xleftarrow{\$} \mathcal{B}^{\mathbf{g},\mathbf{s},\mathbf{u},\mathbf{v}}(1^\kappa) \text{ s.t. } \left(((\mathrm{ik}, *) \underset{\mathbf{s}}{\rightarrow} \mathrm{y}) \notin \mathsf{Que}\right) \wedge (\mathbf{v}(\mathrm{ik}, \mathrm{y}) = \top) \wedge (|\mathrm{ik}| = \kappa))\right] \le \frac{1}{2^{3\kappa}}, \tag{4}$$

where $(\mathbf{g}, \mathbf{s}, \mathbf{e}, \mathbf{d}, \mathbf{u}, \mathbf{v}) \xleftarrow{\$} \Psi$ *and* Que *is the set of all query/response pairs that* $\mathcal{B}^{\mathbf{g},\mathbf{s},\mathbf{u},\mathbf{v}}$ *makes. We stress that* $\mathcal{B}$ *is not allowed to make* $\mathbf{e}$ *or* $\mathbf{d}$ *queries.*[2]

Proof. The proof is based on a simple information-theoretic argument and so we sketch the main idea. Assume w.l.o.g. that $\mathcal{B}$ before returning its guess $(\mathrm{ik}, \mathrm{y})$, it calls the oracle $\mathbf{v}$ on $(\mathrm{ik}, \mathrm{y})$. This only increases the number of queries by one.

At any point of execution, say the next query of $\mathcal{B}$ is a *hit* if the next query is a $\mathbf{v}$ query, say $((\mathrm{ik}', \mathrm{y}') \underset{\mathbf{v}}{\rightarrow} ?)$, which is a valid forgery; namely, (a) $((\mathrm{ik}', *) \underset{\mathbf{s}}{\rightarrow} \mathrm{y}') \notin \mathsf{Que}$, (b) $|\mathrm{ik}'| = \kappa$ and (c) $\mathbf{v}(\mathrm{ik}', \mathrm{y}') = \top$.

At any point, the probability that the next query is a hit given we had no hits before is at most $\frac{2^\kappa}{2^{5\kappa} - 2^\kappa}$. The proof now follows by a union bound. □

[2] We may define and prove a version of this lemma which allows the adversary $\mathcal{B}$ to also make $\mathbf{e}$ and $\mathbf{d}$ queries. This current version however suffices for what we need for the simple separation we show in this section.

4.3 Many-Query Case

Fix the candidate type-1 construction $(\mathsf{G}^{\mathbf{g}}, \mathsf{S}^{\mathbf{s}}, \mathsf{E}^{\mathbf{e}}, \mathsf{D}^{\mathbf{d}})$. We will build an adversary $\mathsf{Break}^{\mathbf{g},\mathbf{s},\mathbf{u},\mathbf{v}}$ which breaks the enhanced one-wayness of $(\mathsf{G}^{\mathbf{g}}, \mathsf{S}^{\mathbf{s}}, \mathsf{E}^{\mathbf{e}}, \mathsf{D}^{\mathbf{d}})$ by making a polynomial number of queries to its oracles. The attacker Break does not need to call the oracles $\mathbf{e}$ and $\mathbf{d}$ during its attack, so we did not put them as superscripts to Break.

For simplicity we assume the following for all constructions $(\mathsf{G}, \mathsf{S}, \mathsf{E}, \mathsf{D})$ discussed in this paper. This assumption is made only for simplicity and all our results can be proved without it.

Assumption 2. Each of the algorithms $\mathsf{G}^{\mathbf{O}}$, $\mathsf{S}^{\mathbf{O}}$, $\mathsf{E}^{\mathbf{O}}$ and $\mathsf{D}^{\mathbf{O}}$ on a security parameter 1^{κ} call their oracle $\mathbf{O}$ always on the same security parameter 1^{κ}.

We will now describe the attacker Break. We will use notation and concepts from Definition 4.

Attacker $\mathsf{Break}^{\mathbf{g},\mathbf{s},\mathbf{u},\mathbf{v}}(\mathrm{IK}, \mathrm{R}, \mathrm{Y})$:

Oracles: $(\mathbf{g}, \mathbf{s}, \mathbf{u}, \mathbf{v})$, **where** $(\mathbf{g}, \mathbf{s}, \mathbf{e}, \mathbf{d}, \mathbf{u}, \mathbf{v}) \xleftarrow{\$} \Psi$. **Set** $\mathbf{O} := (\mathbf{g}, \mathbf{s}, \mathbf{e}, \mathbf{d})$.

Input: $(\mathrm{IK}, \mathrm{R}, \mathrm{Y})$, where $(\mathrm{IK}, *) \xleftarrow{\$} \mathsf{G}^{\mathbf{g}}(1^{\kappa})$, $\mathrm{R} \xleftarrow{\$} \{0,1\}^{\kappa}$ and $\mathrm{Y} := \mathsf{S}^{\mathbf{s}}(\mathrm{IK}; \mathrm{R})$.

Operations:

1. Sample (in an offline manner) a pair $(\mathbf{g}', \mathrm{R}')$ uniformly at random, where $\mathbf{g}'$ is a partial Ψ-valid oracle and $\mathrm{R}' \in \{0,1\}^{\kappa}$, under the condition that $(\mathrm{IK}, \widetilde{\mathrm{TK}}) = \mathsf{G}^{\mathbf{g}'}(1^{\kappa}; \mathrm{R}')$, for some $\widetilde{\mathrm{TK}}$. Let $\mathbf{g}' \Diamond^* \mathbf{O} := (\widetilde{\mathbf{g}}, \mathbf{s}, \mathbf{e}, \widetilde{\mathbf{d}})$ be formed as in Definition 4.
2. Let $\mathsf{L} := \emptyset$. Run $\mathsf{S}^{\mathbf{s}}(\mathrm{IK}; \mathrm{R})$ and for any query/response pair $((\mathrm{ik}, \mathrm{r}) \xrightarrow[\mathbf{s}]{} \mathrm{y})$ made, add $((\mathrm{ik}, \mathrm{r}) \xrightarrow[\mathbf{s}]{} \mathrm{y})$ to L.
3. Simulate the execution of $\mathsf{D}^{\widetilde{\mathbf{d}}}(\widetilde{\mathrm{TK}}, \mathrm{Y})$ using the oracles $\mathbf{g}, \mathbf{s}, \mathbf{u}, \mathbf{v}$ as follows. For any encountered query $\mathsf{qu} := ((\mathrm{tk}, \mathrm{y}) \xrightarrow[\widetilde{\mathbf{d}}]{} ?)$, first compute $\widetilde{\mathbf{g}}(\mathrm{tk})$ to get ik; this can be done by making at most one query to $\mathbf{g}$. Then,
   (a) if $\mathbf{v}(\mathrm{ik}, \mathrm{y}) = \bot$, then reply to qu with $\bot$ and continue the execution;
   (b) else if $((\mathrm{ik}, \mathrm{r}) \xrightarrow[\mathbf{s}]{} \mathrm{y}) \in \mathsf{L}$ for some r, then call $((\mathrm{ik}, \mathrm{r}) \xrightarrow[\mathbf{u}]{} ?)$ to receive r_0 and call $((\mathrm{ik}, \mathrm{r}_0) \xrightarrow[\mathbf{s}]{} ?)$ to get x. Return x as the response to the query qu, add $((\mathrm{ik}, \mathrm{r}_0) \xrightarrow[\mathbf{s}]{} \mathrm{x})$ to L and continue the execution.
   (c) else (i.e., if $\mathbf{v}(\mathrm{ik}, \mathrm{y}) = \top$ and $((\mathrm{ik}, *) \xrightarrow[\mathbf{s}]{} \mathrm{y}) \notin \mathsf{L}$), then halt the execution and return Fail.
4. If the simulation has not halted yet, return $\widetilde{\mathrm{X}}$, the output of $\mathsf{D}^{\widetilde{\mathbf{d}}}(\widetilde{\mathrm{TK}}, \mathrm{Y})$.

Theorem 3. *The attacker* Break *is successful with probability at least* $1 - \frac{1}{2^{3\kappa}}$. *Namely,*

$$\Pr[\mathsf{Break}^{\mathbf{g},\mathbf{s},\mathbf{u},\mathbf{v}}(\mathrm{IK}, \mathrm{R}, \mathrm{Y}) = \mathrm{X}] \geq 1 - \frac{1}{2^{3\kappa}},$$

where the probability is taken over $(\mathbf{g}, \mathbf{s}, \mathbf{e}, \mathbf{d}, \mathbf{u}, \mathbf{v}) \leftarrow \Psi$, $(\mathrm{IK}, \mathrm{TK}) \leftarrow \mathsf{G}^{\mathbf{g}}(1^{\kappa})$, $\mathrm{R} \leftarrow \{0,1\}^{\kappa}$, $\mathrm{Y} := \mathsf{S}^{\mathbf{s}}(\mathrm{IK}, \mathrm{R})$ *and* $\mathrm{X} := \mathsf{D}^{\mathbf{d}}(\mathrm{TK}, \mathrm{Y})$.

Proof Roadmap. We show that if the execution of Break never halts due to Line 3c, then the retrieved string $\widetilde{X}$ is indeed the correct pre-image of Y. We will then show that the probability that Line 3c is ever hit (which we call the event Bad) is at most $\frac{1}{2^{3\kappa}}$, by "reducing" it to Lemma 4. These two will complete the proof.

Lemma 5. *Let* Bad *be the event that line (3c) is hit during the execution of* $\mathsf{Break}^{\mathbf{g},\mathbf{s},\mathbf{u},\mathbf{v}}(\mathrm{IK},\mathrm{R},\mathrm{Y})$. *Then*

$$\Pr[\mathrm{Bad}] \leq \frac{1}{2^{3\kappa}},$$

where the probability is taken over $(\mathbf{g},\mathbf{s},\mathbf{e},\mathbf{d},\mathbf{u},\mathbf{v}) \leftarrow \Psi$, $(\mathrm{IK},*) \leftarrow \mathsf{G}^{\mathbf{g}}(1^\kappa)$, $\mathrm{R} \leftarrow \{0,1\}^\kappa$, $\mathrm{Y} := \mathsf{S}^{\mathbf{s}}(\mathrm{IK},R)$ *and over* Break*'s random coins.*

We first show how to derive Theorem 3 from Lemma 5 and we will then prove Lemma 5.

Proof of Theorem 3. All probabilities that appear below are taken over the variables sampled in the theorem. We claim

$$\alpha \triangleq \Pr[\mathsf{Break}^{\mathbf{g},\mathbf{s},\mathbf{u},\mathbf{v}}(\mathrm{IK},\mathrm{R},\mathrm{Y}) = X \mid \overline{\mathrm{Bad}}] = 1.$$

Assuming the claim is true, we may combine it with Lemma 5 to get

$$\Pr[\mathsf{Break}^{\mathbf{g},\mathbf{s},\mathbf{u},\mathbf{v}}(\mathrm{IK},\mathrm{R},\mathrm{Y}) = X] \geq (1 - \frac{1}{2^{3\kappa}})\alpha = 1 - \frac{1}{2^{3\kappa}},$$

as desired. To prove the above claim first note that by Lemma 3 we have $\mathbf{g}'\Diamond^*\mathbf{O} := (\widetilde{\mathbf{g}},\mathbf{s},\mathbf{e},\widetilde{\mathbf{d}})$ is a valid TDP-oracle, where $\mathbf{g}'$ is formed in Step 1 of Break's execution. Moreover, recall that $\mathrm{Y} = \mathsf{E}^{\mathbf{e}}(\mathrm{IK},X)$ and that $(\mathrm{IK},\widetilde{\mathrm{TK}}) \in \mathsf{G}^{\widetilde{\mathbf{g}}}(1^\kappa)$. Thus, by the correctness condition of the blackbox construction (G, S, E, D) (Definition 2) we have $X = \mathsf{D}^{\widetilde{\mathbf{d}}}(\widetilde{\mathrm{TK}},\mathrm{Y})$. The claim now follows by noting that if the event Bad does not hold, then the simulated execution of $\mathsf{D}^{\widetilde{\mathbf{d}}}(\widetilde{\mathrm{TK}},\mathrm{Y})$ performed by Break proceeds identically to the real decryption. The proof is now complete. □

Proof of Lemma 5. Let $\beta := \Pr[\mathrm{Bad}]$. We show how to construct an adversary $\mathcal{B}^{\mathbf{g},\mathbf{s},\mathbf{u},\mathbf{v}}$ with oracle access to $(\mathbf{g},\mathbf{s},\mathbf{u},\mathbf{v})$ which makes a poly number of queries and with probability at least β forges some $(\mathrm{ik},\mathrm{y}) \in \{0,1\}^\kappa \times \{0,1\}^{5\kappa}$ in the sense of Lemma 4. Applying the lemma we will then obtain $\beta \leq \frac{1}{2^{3\kappa}}$, as desired.

The adversary $\mathcal{B}^{\mathbf{g},\mathbf{s},\mathbf{u},\mathbf{v}}(1^\kappa)$ first samples a random input (IK, R, Y) for Break: namely, $(\mathrm{IK},\mathrm{TK}) \xleftarrow{\$} \mathsf{G}^{\mathbf{g}}(1^\kappa)$, $\mathrm{R} \xleftarrow{\$} \{0,1\}^*$ and $\mathrm{Y} := \mathsf{S}^{\mathbf{s}}(\mathrm{IK};\mathrm{R})$. Then, $\mathcal{B}^{\mathbf{g},\mathbf{s},\mathbf{u},\mathbf{v}}$ simulates the execution of $\mathsf{Break}^{\mathbf{g},\mathbf{s},\mathbf{u},\mathbf{v}}(\mathrm{IK},\mathrm{R},\mathrm{Y})$ with the only deviation that whenever Break's execution hits Line (3c) with the underlying strings ik and y, then $\mathcal{B}$ halts and returns (ik, y). If Break's execution is successfully completed without ever hitting Line (3c), then $\mathcal{B}^{\mathbf{g},\mathbf{s},\mathbf{u},\mathbf{v}}$ gives up and returns $\perp$. Let Que be the set of all query/response pairs that $\mathsf{Break}^{\mathbf{g},\mathbf{s},\mathbf{u},\mathbf{v}}$ makes to its oracles, and note |Que| is polynomial.

Validity of $\mathcal{B}$'s Forgery Output. As per Lemma 4, we need to show three things: that, (a) $((\mathrm{ik}, *) \underset{\mathbf{s}}{\rightarrow} \mathrm{y}) \notin \mathsf{Que}$, (b) $\mathbf{v}(\mathrm{ik}, \mathrm{y}) = \top$ and (c) $|\mathrm{ik}| = \kappa$.

Condition (a) holds because for any $\mathbf{s}$ query $((\mathrm{ik}', \mathrm{r}') \underset{\mathbf{s}}{\rightarrow} \mathrm{y}')$ ever made by $\mathcal{B}$, this query/response is added to the set L. By the underlying if-condition of Line (3c), we have $((\mathrm{ik}, *) \underset{\mathbf{s}}{\rightarrow} \mathrm{y}) \notin \mathsf{L}$ and hence $((\mathrm{ik}, *) \underset{\mathbf{s}}{\rightarrow} \mathrm{y}) \notin \mathsf{Que}$. Condition (b) also holds immediately by the underlying if-condition of Line (3c). Finally, by Assumption 2 $|\mathrm{ik}| = \kappa$. To see this, recall from the description of Break that $\mathrm{ik} = \widetilde{\mathbf{g}}(\mathrm{tk})$ and that $|\mathrm{tk}| = \kappa$. Thus, by definition of $\widetilde{\mathbf{g}}$ we have $|\mathrm{ik}| = \kappa$, as desired. The proof is now complete. □

5 Proof of Lemma 2: General Case

Sketch of the Attack. Let $(\mathrm{IK}, \mathrm{R}, \mathrm{Y})$ be the inputs to $\mathsf{Break}^{\mathbf{O},\mathbf{u},\mathbf{v}}$, where $(\mathrm{IK}, \mathrm{TK}) \xleftarrow{\$} \mathsf{G}^{\mathbf{O}}(1^\kappa)$ and $\mathrm{Y} := \mathsf{S}^{\mathbf{O}}(\mathrm{IK}; \mathrm{R})$. Let Q be the set of all query/response pairs during $\mathsf{S}^{\mathbf{O}}(\mathrm{IK}; \mathrm{R}) = \mathrm{Y}$. Let $\mathrm{X} := \mathsf{D}^{\mathbf{O}}(\mathrm{TK}, \mathrm{Y})$. Let us first try to proceed as before: sample $(\mathbf{O}', \widetilde{\mathrm{TK}})$ such that $(\mathrm{IK}, \widetilde{\mathrm{TK}}) \xleftarrow{\$} \mathsf{G}^{\mathbf{O}'}(1^\kappa)$ and attempt to perform $\mathsf{D}^{\mathbf{O}' \diamond^* \mathbf{O}}$. However, things are not as simple as before. Previously, we were able to show that for any meaningful query which asks for the value of $\mathbf{e}^{-1}(\mathrm{ik}, \mathrm{y})$, we must have $((\mathrm{ik}, *) \underset{\mathbf{s}}{\rightarrow} \mathrm{y})$, and so Break can simulate the answer using $\mathbf{u}$. However, this does not hold here, because y may be coming from the queries made by $\mathsf{G}^{\mathbf{O}}$, to which Break does not have access.

Our solution at a high level is as follows. We work with a partial oracle $\widetilde{\mathbf{O}}$ for which initially we have $(\mathrm{IK}, \widetilde{\mathrm{TK}}) \xleftarrow{\$} \mathsf{G}^{\widetilde{\mathbf{O}}}(1^\kappa)$. This oracle will then be used to invert Y (using $\widetilde{\mathrm{TK}}$) as the secret key, but since $\widetilde{\mathbf{O}}$ is not necessarily defined on all encountered queries (since it is a partial oracle) we need to "make up" answers as we go on in a *consistent* manner. Ideally, we would like to produce answers by directly resorting to $\mathbf{O}$, so to make the whole execution as close to the real execution as possible. However, this is not always possible, and so at times we need to fake some answers. Whenever, a new answer is generated (either by directly calling $\mathbf{O}$ or by faking it) we add the new query/answer pair to $\widetilde{\mathbf{O}}$ and will continue. Let us elaborate more.

Consider the execution of $\mathsf{D}^{\widetilde{\mathbf{O}}}(\widetilde{\mathrm{TK}}, \mathrm{Y})$: Suppose we encounter a query qu that is not defined in $\widetilde{\mathbf{O}}$ yet. We have two cases. If qu is of type $\mathbf{g}$, $\mathbf{s}$ or $\mathbf{e}$—namely, a query which does not require any "trapdoor" information to reply to—we will use the oracle $\mathbf{O}$ directly to answer to this query but with some case to make sure we do not introduce inconsistencies. (Remember that $\widetilde{\mathbf{O}}$ fakes some answers, so "blind" use of $\mathbf{O}$ may potentially creat inconsistencies.) If, however, qu is of $\mathbf{d}$-type, we will make use of our trapdoor-based accumulated knowledge of the oracle $\mathbf{O}$ along with the oracle $\mathbf{u}$ if we happened to have the required information. Let us give a more detailed explanation.

1. Suppose $\mathrm{qu} := ((\mathrm{ik}', \mathrm{r}') \underset{\mathbf{s}}{\rightarrow} ?)$, but $\widetilde{\mathbf{O}}(\mathrm{qu})$ is not defined yet. Suppose $\mathrm{x}' = \mathbf{s}(\mathrm{ik}', \mathrm{r}')$. We may think we can simply reply to qu with x' and add

the query/response pair qua $:= ((\mathrm{ik}', \mathrm{r}') \underset{\mathbf{s}}{\rightarrow} \mathrm{x}')$ to $\widetilde{\mathbf{O}}$. However, we may get the following problem: There may already be a (fake) query/response $\mathrm{qua}_1 := ((\mathrm{ik}', \mathrm{x}') \underset{\mathbf{e}}{\rightarrow} \perp) \in \widetilde{\mathbf{O}}$, which would be inconsistent with qua. Thus, $\widetilde{\mathbf{O}} \cup \{\mathrm{qua}\}$ will not be TDP-consistent, and so we cannot guarantee correct inversion w.r.t. this oracle. We handle this as follows: In case of such inconsistencies, we will reply to qu with a random answer (which is unlikely to create inconsistencies) and will add the result to $\widetilde{\mathbf{O}}$.

A same situation may hold for an **e** query and we will handle such inconsistencies in a similar manner. For **g** queries, however, we will preempt the possibility of inconsistencies by putting Break in "normal form"; see Assumption 5.

2. Suppose qu $:= ((\mathrm{tk}', \mathrm{y}') \underset{\mathbf{d}}{\rightarrow} ?)$, and qua $:= (\mathrm{tk}' \underset{\mathbf{g}}{\rightarrow} \mathrm{ik}) \in \widetilde{\mathbf{O}}$. (We will force qua to already be in $\widetilde{\mathbf{O}}$ by putting Break in normal form.) We have two cases: (a) trapdoor-available: $\mathbf{g}(\mathrm{tk}') = \mathrm{ik}$ (i.e., tk' is the real trapdoor key); or (b) trapdoor-absent: $\mathbf{g}(\mathrm{tk}') \neq \mathrm{ik}$: That is, the trapdoor key tk' has been "faked" before.

   If case (a) holds, we call the real oracle **O** on qu and will use the result as is if it leads to no inconsistencies—we, however, now have many more cases of inconsistencies, as compared to Part 1; if an inconsistency occurs, we will fake the answer.

   For case (b) we need to resort to our side trapdoor-information about **O** (e.g., set Q above: the set of all query/response pairs during $\mathsf{S}^{\mathbf{O}}(\mathrm{IK}; \mathrm{R}) = \mathrm{Y}$). Also, to handle case (b), we will also need to collect all frequent trapdoor information that happen during random executions of $\mathsf{S}^{\mathbf{O}}$ and $\mathsf{E}^{\mathbf{O}}$. This collection of information is done in Step 1 of the algorithm Break.

For our analysis, we will show w.h.p. the union of $\widetilde{\mathbf{O}}_{\mathrm{uni}} \triangleq \widetilde{\mathbf{O}} \cup \mathsf{W}_1 \cup \mathsf{W}_2$ is TDP-valid, where W_1 is the (hidden) set of all queries/responses made to sample the challenge pre-image X and W_2 is the (hidden) set of all query/response pairs in $\mathsf{E}^{\mathbf{O}}(\mathrm{IK}, \mathrm{X})$. Note that W_1 and W_2 are not available to Break (which is the reason we called them hidden). Proving this will show that w.h.p. the decrypted result, $\widetilde{\mathrm{X}}$, by Break will be equal to X. This is because relative to $\widetilde{\mathbf{O}}_{\mathrm{uni}}$, $(\mathrm{IK}, \widetilde{\mathrm{TK}})$ is valid, X is valid (i.e., outputted by $\mathsf{S}^{\widetilde{\mathbf{O}}_{\mathrm{uni}}}(\mathrm{IK})$), $\mathrm{Y} = \mathsf{E}^{\mathbf{O}}(\mathrm{IK}, \mathrm{X})$ and $\widetilde{\mathrm{X}} = \mathsf{D}^{\mathbf{O}}(\widetilde{\mathrm{TK}}, \mathrm{Y})$.

We now proceed to describe the attack formally. We start with the following assumption.

Assumption 4. We assume that $\mathsf{G}^{\mathbf{g},\mathbf{s},\mathbf{e},\mathbf{d}}$ never calls the oracle **d**. (It can predict the answer with high probability.) For notational convenience we keep **d** as a superscript to G.

We first start by describing two procedures that will be used by Break. The first procedure samples many executions of S and E in order to collect frequent trapdoors. The second procedure allows one to sample a fake secret key w.r.t. a priori information about the real oracle **O**.

Definition 5 (Sampling frequent queries). *We define a probabilistic oracle procedure* $\mathsf{SFreq}^{\mathbf{O}}$*:*

- ***Input:*** $(1^\kappa, p, \mathrm{IK})$, *where* p *is an integer.*
- ***Output:*** *A set of query/response pairs* $\mathsf{Freq} \leftarrow \mathsf{SFreq}^{\mathbf{O}}(1^\kappa, p, \mathrm{IK})$ *sampled as follows. Let* $\mathsf{Freq} = \emptyset$*. Do the following* p *times:*
  - *Sample* $\mathrm{X} \leftarrow \mathsf{S}^{\mathbf{O}}(\mathrm{IK})$ *and execute* $\mathsf{E}^{\mathbf{O}}(\mathrm{IK}, \mathrm{X})$ *and record all query/response pairs to* Freq.

Definition 6. *We define the procedure* SOrc.

- ***Input:*** $(\mathsf{Freq}, \mathrm{IK})$*: A set of query/answer pairs* Freq *and an index key* IK.
- ***Output:*** $(\mathrm{TK}', \mathsf{Q}_g, \mathsf{Q}_s, \mathsf{Q}_e)$, *produced as follows.* Q_e *sampled as follows. Sample a* Ψ*-generated* $\mathbf{O}' = (\mathbf{g}', \mathbf{s}', \mathbf{e}', \mathbf{d}')$ *and* TK' *uniformly at random subject to the conditions that (a)* $\mathbf{O}'$ *is consistent with* Freq *(i.e.,* $\mathbf{O}' \cup \mathsf{Freq}$ *is a valid TDP) and (b)* $\mathsf{G}^{\mathbf{O}'} = (\mathrm{IK}, \mathrm{TK}')$*. Let* Q_g*,* Q_s *and* Q_e *contain, respectively, the* $\mathbf{g}$*,* $\mathbf{s}$ *and* $\mathbf{e}$ *query/response pairs made during the execution of* $\mathsf{G}^{\mathbf{O}'}$*. (Recall that by Assumption 4 no* $\mathbf{d}$ *queries are made).*

We need the following normal-form condition for our attack algorithm.

Assumption 5. We assume the following for any oracle algorithm A with oracle access to $(\mathbf{g}, \mathbf{s}, \mathbf{e}, \mathbf{d})$: Any query $((\mathrm{tk}, \mathrm{y}) \underset{\mathbf{d}}{\rightarrow} ?)$ is preceded by a query $(\mathrm{tk} \underset{\mathbf{g}}{\rightarrow} ?)$. Moreover, if $\mathbf{d}(\mathrm{tk}, \mathrm{y}) = \mathrm{x} \neq \perp$, then A will make the query $((\mathrm{ik}, \mathrm{x}) \underset{\mathbf{e}}{\rightarrow} ?)$ after making the query $((\mathrm{tk}, \mathrm{y}) \underset{\mathbf{d}}{\rightarrow} ?)$.

Partial Oracles. In the algorithm Break below we will work with partial oracles, defined only on a subset of their input queries. Specifically, for a partial oracle $\widetilde{\mathbf{O}}$ we define the following notation: We write $\widetilde{\mathbf{O}}(\mathrm{qu}) = \mathrm{null}$ to indicate $\widetilde{\mathbf{O}}$ is not defined on the query qu. This should not be confused with $\widetilde{\mathbf{O}}(\mathrm{qu}) = \perp$ as we use $\widetilde{\mathbf{O}}(\mathrm{qu}) = \perp$ to indicate that the output of $\widetilde{\mathbf{O}}(\mathrm{qu})$ is a fixed invalid symbol. We say $\widetilde{\mathbf{O}}$ is TDP consistent, if there exists a full TDP oracle $\widetilde{\mathbf{O}}_{\mathrm{full}}$ such that $\widetilde{\mathbf{O}} \subseteq \widetilde{\mathbf{O}}_{\mathrm{full}}$.

Parameter γ. For any Ψ-valid oracle $\mathbf{O}$ we assume that each of the algorithms $\mathsf{G}^{\mathbf{O}}$, $\mathsf{S}^{\mathbf{O}}$, $\mathsf{E}^{\mathbf{O}}$ and $\mathsf{D}^{\mathbf{O}}$ on inputs corresponding to the security parameter 1^κ make exactly κ^γ oracle queries.

The Attack Algorithm $\mathsf{Break}^{\mathbf{g},\mathbf{s},\mathbf{e},\mathbf{d},\mathbf{u},\mathbf{v}}$: We describe all components of the attack algorithm.
Oracles. $(\mathbf{O}, \mathbf{u}, \mathbf{v})$. Parse $\mathbf{O} := (\mathbf{g}, \mathbf{s}, \mathbf{e}, \mathbf{d})$.
Input. $(1^\kappa, \mathrm{IK}, \mathrm{R})$
Output. $(\widetilde{\mathrm{X}}, \mathsf{Freq}, \widetilde{\mathbf{O}})$.[3]

[3] $\widetilde{\mathrm{X}}$ is the final result of inversion. The other two outputs, namely $\mathsf{Freq}, \widetilde{\mathbf{O}}$, are partial oracles, which are included in the output so to help us later state our security statements easier.

1. Sample $\mathsf{Freq} \leftarrow \mathsf{SFreq}^{\mathbf{O}}(1^{\kappa}, \kappa^{2\gamma+8}, \mathrm{IK})$. Let $\widetilde{\mathbf{O}}$ and Real be two partial oracles, both initially empty.
2. Sample $(\widetilde{\mathrm{TK}}, \mathsf{Q_g}, \mathsf{Q_s}, \mathsf{Q_e}) \leftarrow \mathsf{SOrc}(\mathsf{Freq}, \mathrm{IK})$. Add $\mathsf{Q_g} \cup \mathsf{Q_s} \cup \mathsf{Q_e} \cup \mathsf{Freq}$ to $\widetilde{\mathbf{O}}$.
3. Run $\mathsf{S}^{\mathbf{O}}(\mathrm{R})$—which gives us the challenge image Y—and add all the underlying query/response pairs to Real. Also, add all elements of Freq to Real. From this point on, all the queries made to the real oracles $(\mathbf{g}, \mathbf{s}, \mathbf{e}, \mathbf{d}, \mathbf{u}, \mathbf{v})$ will be recorded in Real.
4. Simulate the execution of $\mathsf{D}^{\cdot}(\widetilde{\mathrm{TK}}, \mathrm{Y})$ and answer an encountered query qu as follows:
   4.1 **Already answered in $\widetilde{\mathbf{O}}$**: if for some ans, $(\mathrm{qu}, \mathrm{ans}) \in \widetilde{\mathbf{O}}$, then reply to qu with ans;
   4.2 **g-type query**: if qu is of **g**-type, then reply to qu by calling the real oracle **g** and add the query/response pair to $\widetilde{\mathbf{O}}$;
   4.3 **s-type query**: if $\mathrm{qu} := ((\mathrm{ik}, \mathrm{r}) \underset{\mathbf{s}}{\rightarrow} ?)$, then call $((\mathrm{ik}, \mathrm{r}) \underset{\mathbf{s}}{\rightarrow} \mathrm{x})$. If $((\mathrm{ik}, \mathrm{x}) \underset{\mathbf{e}}{\rightarrow} \perp) \notin \widetilde{\mathbf{O}}$, then reply to qu with x and add $((\mathrm{ik}, \mathrm{r}) \underset{\mathbf{s}}{\rightarrow} \mathrm{x})$ to $\widetilde{\mathbf{O}}$. Otherwise, reply to qu with $\mathrm{x}' \leftarrow \{0,1\}^{5\kappa}$ and add $((\mathrm{ik}, \mathrm{r}) \underset{\mathbf{s}}{\rightarrow} \mathrm{x}')$ to $\widetilde{\mathbf{O}}$.
   4.4 **e-type query**: if $\mathrm{qu} := ((\mathrm{ik}, \mathrm{x}) \underset{\mathbf{e}}{\rightarrow} ?)$ for some ik and x: Call the real oracle $((\mathrm{ik}, \mathrm{x}) \underset{\mathbf{e}}{\rightarrow} ?)$ to get y;
      4.4.1 if $\mathrm{y} = \perp$ or $((*, *) \underset{\mathbf{e}}{\rightarrow} \mathrm{y}) \notin \widetilde{\mathbf{O}}$, then reply to qu with y add $((\mathrm{ik}, \mathrm{x}) \underset{\mathbf{e}}{\rightarrow} \mathrm{y})$ to $\widetilde{\mathbf{O}}$;
      4.4.2 Otherwise, reply to qu with a random $\mathrm{y}' \leftarrow \{0,1\}^{5\kappa}$ and add $((\mathrm{ik}, \mathrm{x}) \underset{\mathbf{e}}{\rightarrow} \mathrm{y}')$ to $\widetilde{\mathbf{O}}$.
   4.5 **d-type query**: if $\mathrm{qu} := ((\mathrm{tk}, \mathrm{y}) \underset{\mathbf{d}}{\rightarrow} ?)$ for some tk and y: letting ik be such that $(\mathrm{tk} \underset{\mathbf{g}}{\rightarrow} \mathrm{ik}) \in \widetilde{\mathbf{O}}$.
      4.5.1 if $((\mathrm{ik}, \mathrm{x}) \underset{\mathbf{e}}{\rightarrow} \mathrm{y}) \in \widetilde{\mathbf{O}}$, then reply to qu with x and add $((\mathrm{tk}, \mathrm{y}) \underset{\mathbf{d}}{\rightarrow} \mathrm{x})$ to $\widetilde{\mathbf{O}}$.
      4.5.2 else if $((\mathrm{ik}, \mathrm{y}) \underset{\mathbf{e}}{\rightarrow} \perp) \in \widetilde{\mathbf{O}}$ then reply to qu with $\perp$ and add $((\mathrm{tk}, \mathrm{y}) \underset{\mathbf{d}}{\rightarrow} \perp)$ to $\widetilde{\mathbf{O}}$.
      4.5.3 otherwise,
         4.5.3.1 if for some tk′: $(\mathrm{tk}' \underset{\mathbf{g}}{\rightarrow} \mathrm{ik}) \in \mathsf{Real}$ then call $((\mathrm{tk}', \mathrm{y}) \underset{\mathbf{d}}{\rightarrow} ?)$ to get x:
            (A) if $((\mathrm{ik}, \mathrm{x}) \underset{\mathbf{e}}{\rightarrow} *) \notin \widetilde{\mathbf{O}}$, then reply to qu with x and add $((\mathrm{ik}, \mathrm{x}) \underset{\mathbf{e}}{\rightarrow} \mathrm{y})$ to $\widetilde{\mathbf{O}}$.
            (B) if $((\mathrm{ik}, \mathrm{x}) \underset{\mathbf{e}}{\rightarrow} *) \in \widetilde{\mathbf{O}}$ then reply to qu with a random $\mathrm{x}' \leftarrow \{0,1\}^{5\kappa}$ and add $((\mathrm{ik}, \mathrm{x}') \underset{\mathbf{e}}{\rightarrow} \mathrm{y})$ to $\widetilde{\mathbf{O}}$.
         4.5.3.2 else if $((\mathrm{ik}, \mathrm{x}) \underset{\mathbf{e}}{\rightarrow} \mathrm{y}) \in \mathsf{Real}$, then
            (A) if $((\mathrm{ik}, \mathrm{x}) \underset{\mathbf{e}}{\rightarrow} *) \notin \widetilde{\mathbf{O}}$ then reply to qu with x and add $((\mathrm{ik}, \mathrm{x}) \underset{\mathbf{e}}{\rightarrow} \mathrm{y})$ to $\widetilde{\mathbf{O}}$.

(B) if $((\text{ik}, \text{x}) \underset{\mathbf{e}}{\to} *) \in \widetilde{\mathbf{O}}$ then reply to qu with a random $\text{x}' \leftarrow \{0,1\}^{5\kappa}$ and add $((\text{ik}, \text{x}') \underset{\mathbf{e}}{\to} \text{y})$ to $\widetilde{\mathbf{O}}$.

4.5.3.3 else if for some r: $((\text{ik}, \text{r}) \underset{\mathbf{s}}{\to} \text{y}) \in \mathsf{Real}$, then call $((\text{ik}, \text{r}) \underset{\mathbf{u}}{\to} ?)$ to get r_0 and call $((\text{ik}, \text{r}_0) \underset{\mathbf{s}}{\to} ?)$ to get x_0:

(A) if $((\text{ik}, \text{x}_0) \underset{\mathbf{e}}{\to} *) \notin \widetilde{\mathbf{O}}$, then reply to qu with x_0 and add $((\text{ik}, \text{x}_0) \underset{\mathbf{e}}{\to} \text{y})$ to $\widetilde{\mathbf{O}}$.

(B) if $((\text{ik}, \text{x}_0) \underset{\mathbf{e}}{\to} *) \in \widetilde{\mathbf{O}}$, then reply to qu with a random $\text{x}' \leftarrow \{0,1\}^{5\kappa}$ and add $((\text{ik}, \text{x}') \underset{\mathbf{e}}{\to} \text{y})$ to $\widetilde{\mathbf{O}}$.

4.5.3.4 else if $\mathbf{v}(\text{ik}, \text{y}) = \perp$ then reply to qu with $\perp$;

4.5.3.5 otherwise, reply to qu with a random $\text{x}' \leftarrow \{0,1\}^{5\kappa}$ and add both of $((\text{tk}, \text{y}) \underset{\mathbf{d}}{\to} \text{x}')$ and $((\text{ik}, \text{x}') \underset{\mathbf{e}}{\to} \text{y})$ to $\widetilde{\mathbf{O}}$.

5. Letting $\widetilde{\text{X}}$ be the result of the simulated execution of $\mathsf{D}^{\cdot}(\widetilde{\text{TK}, Y})$, return $(\widetilde{\text{X}}, \mathsf{Freq}, \widetilde{\mathbf{O}})$.

5.1 Proof of Attack Effectiveness

We now focus on proving Lemma 2. We first start with a simple information theoretic lemma, which generalizes Lemma 4 to the case in which the "forger" may call all the underlying oracles. For that lemma, we need the following definition.

Definition 7. *Let* Q *be a set of query/response pairs obtained from oracles* $(\mathbf{g}, \mathbf{s}, \mathbf{e}, \mathbf{d}, \mathbf{u}, \mathbf{v})$. *We say that* (ik, x) *is embedded in* Q *if*

- $((\text{ik}, *) \underset{\mathbf{s}}{\to} \text{x}) \in \text{Q}$, *or*
- $((\text{ik}, *) \underset{\mathbf{e}}{\to} \text{x}) \in \text{Q}$ *or*
- *for some* tk: $(\text{tk} \underset{\mathbf{g}}{\to} \text{ik}) \in \text{Q}$ *and* $((\text{tk}, *) \underset{\mathbf{d}}{\to} \text{x}) \in \text{Q}$.

The following lemma generalizes Lemma 4. The proof again follows using standard information-theoretic arguments and so is omitted.

Lemma 6. *Let* $\mathcal{B}$ *be a a polynomial-query oracle adversary. We have*

$$\Pr_{(\mathbf{O},\mathbf{u},\mathbf{v})\leftarrow\Psi}[(\text{ik}, \text{y}) \xleftarrow{\$} \mathcal{B}^{\mathbf{g},\mathbf{s},\mathbf{e},\mathbf{d},\mathbf{u},\mathbf{v}}(1^\kappa) \ \textit{s.t.}\ |\text{ik}| = \kappa$$

$$\textit{and}\ \ \mathbf{v}(\text{ik}, \text{y}) = \top \ \textit{and}\ \ (\text{ik}, \text{y}) \ \textit{is not embedded in}\ \ \mathsf{Que}] \leq \frac{1}{2^{3\kappa}}, \quad (5)$$

where Que *is the set of all query/answer pairs of* $\mathcal{B}$.

We define the following environment that specifies a random choice of the oracles $(\mathbf{g}, \mathbf{s}, \mathbf{e}, \mathbf{d}, \mathbf{u}, \mathbf{v})$ as well as random variables used to form a random input to an adversary against enhanced one-wayness of the construction.

Environment. The environment $\mathsf{Env}(\kappa)$ specifies the following random variables: $(\text{IK}, \mathsf{Query}, \text{R}_y, \text{Y}, \text{R}_x, \text{X}, \mathbf{O})$:

- $(\mathbf{g}, \mathbf{s}, \mathbf{e}, \mathbf{d}, \mathbf{u}, \mathbf{v}) \leftarrow \Psi$. Let $\mathbf{O} := (\mathbf{g}, \mathbf{s}, \mathbf{e}, \mathbf{d})$;
- $(\mathrm{IK}, \mathrm{TK}) \leftarrow \mathsf{G}^{\mathbf{O}}(1^\kappa)$ and let Query be the set of all query/response pairs asked during the execution;
- $\mathrm{R}_y \leftarrow \{0,1\}^*$;
- $\mathrm{Y} := \mathsf{S}^{\mathbf{O}}(\mathrm{IK}, \mathrm{R}_y)$;
- $\mathrm{X} := \mathsf{D}^{\mathbf{O}}(\mathrm{TK}, \mathrm{Y})$
- $\mathrm{R}_x \leftarrow \mathsf{S}$, where

$$\mathsf{S} := \{\mathrm{R} \mid \mathsf{S}^{\mathbf{O}}(\mathrm{IK}, \mathrm{R}) = \mathrm{X}\}.$$

Notation HitQ. For an oracle algorithm $\mathsf{A}^{\mathbf{O}}$ we let $\mathsf{HitQ}(\mathsf{A}^{\mathbf{O}}(\mathrm{X}))$ denote the set of all query response pairs made during the execution of $\mathsf{A}^{\mathbf{O}}(\mathrm{X})$. If A is a randomized algorithm, then $\mathsf{HitQ}(\mathsf{A}^{\mathbf{O}}(\mathrm{X}))$ will be a random variable.

Notation $\Diamond$. For a partial oracle $\widetilde{\mathbf{O}}$ and full oracle $\mathbf{O}$ we let $\widetilde{\mathbf{O}}\Diamond\mathbf{O}$ denote the oracle that responds to a query qu as follows: if $\widetilde{\mathbf{O}}(\mathrm{qu}) \neq \mathrm{null}$ then $\widetilde{\mathbf{O}}\Diamond\mathbf{O}(\mathrm{qu}) = \widetilde{\mathbf{O}}(\mathrm{qu})$; otherwise, $\widetilde{\mathbf{O}}\Diamond\mathbf{O}(\mathrm{qu}) = \mathbf{O}(\mathrm{qu})$. Note that even if both $\widetilde{\mathbf{O}}$ and $\mathbf{O}$ are TDP consistent, $\widetilde{\mathbf{O}}\Diamond\mathbf{O}$ is not necessarily so.

Lemma 7. *Let* $(\mathrm{IK}, \mathsf{Query}, \mathrm{R}_y, \mathrm{Y}, \mathrm{R}_x, \mathrm{X}, \mathbf{O}, \mathbf{u}, \mathbf{v}) \leftarrow \mathsf{Env}(\kappa)$ *and* $(\widetilde{\mathrm{X}}, \mathsf{Freq}, \widetilde{\mathbf{O}}) \leftarrow \mathsf{Break}^{\mathbf{O},\mathbf{u},\mathbf{v}}(1^\kappa, \mathrm{IK}, \mathrm{R})$.

1.

$$\Pr[\mathrm{X} = \mathsf{S}^{\widetilde{\mathbf{O}}\Diamond\mathbf{O}}(\mathrm{IK}, \mathrm{R}_\mathrm{x}) \textit{ and } \mathsf{E}^{\widetilde{\mathbf{O}}\Diamond\mathbf{O}}(\mathrm{IK}, \mathrm{X}) = \mathrm{Y}] \geq 1 - \frac{1}{4\kappa^2} \tag{6}$$

2. Letting

$$\mathsf{ALLQ} := \widetilde{\mathbf{O}} \cup \mathsf{HitQ}(\mathsf{S}^{\widetilde{\mathbf{O}}\Diamond\mathbf{O}}(\mathrm{IK}, \mathrm{R}_\mathrm{x})) \cup \mathsf{HitQ}(\mathsf{E}^{\widetilde{\mathbf{O}}\Diamond\mathbf{O}}(\mathrm{IK}, \mathrm{X}))$$

we have $\Pr[\mathsf{ALLQ}$ *is TDP consistent* $] \geq 1 - \frac{1}{2\kappa^2}$.

Let us first show how to use Lemma 7 to prove Lemma 2. We will then prove Lemma 7.

Proof ***(Proof of Lemma** 2**).*** Let all the variables be sampled as in Lemma 2. Let $\mathrm{R}_x \leftarrow \mathsf{S}$, where

$$\mathsf{S} := \{\mathrm{R} \mid \mathsf{S}^{\mathbf{O}}(\mathrm{IK}, \mathrm{R}) = \mathrm{X}\}.$$

Let Evnt_1 and Evnt_2 denote the events of Parts 1 and 2 of Lemma 7. That is,

- $\mathrm{Evnt}_1 : \mathrm{X} = \mathsf{S}^{\widetilde{\mathbf{O}}\Diamond\mathbf{O}}(\mathrm{IK}, \mathrm{R}_\mathrm{x})$ and $\mathsf{E}^{\widetilde{\mathbf{O}}\Diamond\mathbf{O}}(\mathrm{IK}, \mathrm{X}) = \mathrm{Y}$
- $\mathrm{Evnt}_2 : \mathsf{ALLQ}$ is TDP consistent .

We claim if $\mathrm{Evnt}_1 \wedge \mathrm{Evnt}_2$ holds, then $\widetilde{\mathrm{X}} = \mathrm{X}$. This implies our result since

$$\Pr[\widetilde{\mathrm{X}} = \mathrm{X}] \geq \Pr[\mathrm{Evnt}_1 \wedge \mathrm{Evnt}_2] \geq 1 - \Pr[\overline{\mathrm{Evnt}_1}] - \Pr[\overline{\mathrm{Evnt}_2}] \geq 1 - \frac{1}{\kappa^2}.$$

It remains to prove the above claim. We show if $\mathrm{Evnt}_1 \wedge \mathrm{Evnt}_2$ then (I) ALLQ is TDP consistent, (II) $(\mathrm{IK}, \widetilde{\mathrm{TK}}) \in \mathsf{G}^{\mathsf{ALLQ}}(1^\kappa)$, (III) $\widetilde{\mathrm{X}} = \mathsf{D}^{\mathsf{ALLQ}}(\widetilde{\mathrm{TK}}, Y)$, (IV) $\mathrm{X} = \mathsf{S}^{\mathsf{ALLQ}}(\mathrm{IK}, \mathrm{R_x})$, (V) $\mathsf{E}^{\mathsf{ALLQ}}(\mathrm{IK}, \mathrm{X}) = \mathrm{Y}$. Then, by the correctness of the construction $(\mathsf{G}, \mathsf{S}, \mathsf{E}, \mathsf{D})$ we obtain $\widetilde{\mathrm{X}} = \mathrm{X}$, and the proof will be complete.

First, note that (I) follows by definition of Evnt_2.

To prove (II) and (III), first note that we have $(\mathrm{IK}, \widetilde{\mathrm{TK}}) \in \mathsf{G}^{\widetilde{\mathbf{O}}}(1^\kappa)$ and $\widetilde{\mathrm{X}} = \mathsf{D}^{\widetilde{\mathbf{O}}}(\widetilde{\mathrm{TK}}, \mathrm{Y})$. Now since $\widetilde{\mathbf{O}} \subseteq \mathsf{AllQ}$ and since ALLQ is TDP consistent, we have $(\mathrm{IK}, \widetilde{\mathrm{TK}}) \in \mathsf{G}^{\mathsf{ALLQ}}$ and $\widetilde{\mathrm{X}} = \mathsf{D}^{\mathsf{ALLQ}}(\widetilde{\mathrm{TK}}, \mathrm{Y})$. Note that the mere fact that $\widetilde{\mathbf{O}} \subseteq \mathsf{ALLQ}$ will not be sufficient to conclude these two last statements (II) and (III); the reason is that there may be collisions between $\widetilde{\mathbf{O}}$ and $\mathsf{ALLQ} \setminus \widetilde{\mathbf{O}}$ (e.g., a query qu may receive different responses from the two oracles), rendering the corresponding executions ambiguous.

Similarly, from the facts that ALLQ is TDP consistent and that Evnt_1 holds, we conclude (IV) and (V). □

We now show how to prove Lemma 7, starting with Part 1. We give the proof of Part 2 of the lemma in the full version. To this end, we define some variables and events to help us describe things more concisely.

Sub-oracles $\widetilde{\mathbf{O}_1}$, $\widetilde{\mathbf{O}_2}$, $\widetilde{\mathbf{O}_3}$, $\widetilde{\mathbf{O}_4}$ and set Rand. We define four sub-oracles of $\widetilde{\mathbf{O}}$, which capture some of the query/response pairs that were added to $\widetilde{\mathbf{O}}$ as a result of faking answers for those queries that created conflict with the real oracle $\mathbf{O}$. Recall that for removing such conflicts, we sampled elements uniformly at random from $\{0,1\}^{5\kappa}$ and used those for faking answers. Informally, the set Rand contain those points sampled for these purposes. We now formally define these pieces of notation.

- $\widetilde{\mathbf{O}_1}$: We let $\widetilde{\mathbf{O}_1}$ contain any query/response pair $((\mathrm{ik}, \mathrm{x}) \underset{\mathsf{e}}{\to} \mathrm{y}')$ added to $\widetilde{\mathbf{O}}$ as a result of Line 4.4.2..
- $\widetilde{\mathbf{O}_2}$: We let $\widetilde{\mathbf{O}_2}$ contain any query/response pair added to $\widetilde{\mathbf{O}}$ as a result of Condition (B) of Line 4.5.3.1..
- $\widetilde{\mathbf{O}_3}$: We let $\widetilde{\mathbf{O}_3}$ contain any query/response pair added to $\widetilde{\mathbf{O}}$ as a result of Condition (B) of Line 4.5.3.3..
- $\widetilde{\mathbf{O}_4}$: We let $\widetilde{\mathbf{O}_4}$ contain any query/response pair $((\mathrm{ik}, \mathrm{x}) \underset{\mathsf{e}}{\to} \mathrm{y})$ added to $\widetilde{\mathbf{O}}$ as a result of Line 4.5.3.5..
- Rand: We let Rand contain all x such that $((*, \mathrm{x}) \underset{\mathsf{e}}{\to} *) \in \widetilde{\mathbf{O}_2} \cup \widetilde{\mathbf{O}_3}$ or $((*, *) \underset{\mathsf{e}}{\to} \mathrm{x}) \in \widetilde{\mathbf{O}_1}$. Intuitively, the set Rand contains all points that were sampled uniformly at random for making up fake answers.

Events Surp_1, Surp_2, Surp_3, Surp_4. We define some events which we will prove can only happen with negligible probability.

- Surp_1: the event that for some $((\mathrm{ik}, *) \underset{\mathsf{e}}{\to} \mathrm{y}') \in \widetilde{\mathbf{O}_1}$ we have $\mathbf{v}(\mathrm{ik}, \mathrm{y}') = \top$ or for some $((\mathrm{ik}, \mathrm{x}') \underset{\mathsf{e}}{\to} *) \in \widetilde{\mathbf{O}_2} \cup \widetilde{\mathbf{O}_3} \cup \widetilde{\mathbf{O}_4}$ we have $\mathbf{v}(\mathrm{ik}, \mathrm{x}') = \top$.

- Surp_2: the event that during the execution $\mathsf{S}^{\mathbf{O}}(\mathrm{IK};\mathrm{R}_{\mathrm{x}})$ a query $qu = ((\mathrm{ik},\mathrm{x}) \underset{\mathbf{e}}{\rightarrow} ?)$ or a query $((*,\mathrm{x}) \underset{\mathbf{d}}{\rightarrow} ?)$ is made where $\mathrm{x} \in \mathsf{Rand}$;
- Surp_3: the event that there exists $((\mathrm{ik},\mathrm{x}) \underset{\mathbf{e}}{\rightarrow} \mathrm{y}) \in \widetilde{\mathbf{O}_4}$ such that (ik,y) is not embedded in Query.
- Surp_4: For $\mathrm{x} \neq \mathrm{x}'$ and $\mathrm{y} \neq \perp$: $((\mathrm{ik},\mathrm{x}) \underset{\mathbf{e}}{\rightarrow} \mathrm{y}) \in \widetilde{\mathbf{O}}$ and $((\mathrm{ik},\mathrm{x}') \underset{\mathbf{e}}{\rightarrow} \mathrm{y}) \in \widetilde{\mathbf{O}}$.

Let $\mathrm{Surp} = \mathrm{Surp}_1 \vee \mathrm{Surp}_2 \vee \mathrm{Surp}_3 \vee \mathrm{Surp}_4$.

Set Dif. Let $\mathsf{Q} := \mathsf{Q}_{\mathsf{g}} \cup \mathsf{Q}_{\mathsf{s}} \cup \mathsf{Q}_{\mathsf{e}}$, where recall that the sets Q_{g}, Q_{s} and Q_{e} are formed during Line 2 of the algorithm Break. Let Dif be the set of queries formed as follows: For any query/response pair $(qu \underset{*}{\rightarrow} *) \in \mathsf{Q}$, add the query qu to Dif. Moreover, for any (ik,x) that occurs in $\mathsf{Query} \cup \mathsf{Q}$:

(A) if for some r: $\mathbf{s}(\mathrm{ik},\mathrm{r}) = \mathrm{x}$ add $((\mathrm{ik},\mathrm{r}) \underset{\mathbf{s}}{\rightarrow} ?)$ to Dif;
(B) add $((\mathrm{ik},\mathrm{x}) \underset{\mathbf{e}}{\rightarrow} ?)$ to Dif;
(C) add $((\mathrm{tk},\mathrm{x}) \underset{\mathbf{d}}{\rightarrow} ?)$ to Dif, where $\mathrm{tk} = \mathbf{g}^{-1}(\mathrm{ik})$;
(D) if for some x': $\mathbf{e}(\mathrm{ik},\mathrm{x}') = \mathrm{x}$, add $((\mathrm{ik},\mathrm{x}') \underset{\mathbf{e}}{\rightarrow} ?)$ to Dif.[4]

Events Match and MissQ. Equipped with the set Dif we now define the following two events.

- Match: $\widetilde{\mathbf{O}} \Diamond \mathbf{O}$ agrees with $\mathsf{HitQ}(\mathsf{S}^{\mathbf{O}}(\mathrm{IK};\mathrm{R}_{\mathrm{x}})) \cup \mathsf{HitQ}(\mathsf{E}^{\mathbf{O}}(\mathrm{IK},\mathrm{X}))$.
- MissQ:

$$\exists \langle qu \rangle \in \mathsf{Dif} \text{ s.t. } \langle qu \rangle \notin \mathsf{Freq} \text{ and } \langle qu \rangle \in \mathsf{HitQ}(\mathsf{S}^{\mathbf{O}}(\mathrm{IK};\mathrm{R}_{\mathrm{x}})) \cup \mathsf{HitQ}(\mathsf{E}^{\mathbf{O}}(\mathrm{IK},\mathrm{X})).$$

Lemma 8. *If* $\overline{\mathrm{Match}}$ *holds, then* $\mathrm{MissQ} \vee \mathrm{Surp}$ *holds.*

Lemma 9. *We have* $\Pr[\mathrm{MissQ}] \leq \frac{1}{8\kappa^2}$.

Lemma 10. *We have* $\Pr[\mathrm{Surp}] \leq \frac{1}{2^\kappa}$.

Proof (of Part 1 of Lemma 7). Let $\alpha(n)$ denote the probability of this part of the lemma. We have $\alpha(n) \geq \Pr[\mathrm{Match}]$. From Lemmas 8, 9 and 10 $\Pr[\overline{\mathrm{Match}}] \leq \frac{1}{4\kappa^2}$. The proof is complete. □

We give the proof of Lemma 8 in the full version. We now prove Lemma 9, for which we will use the following standard lemma.

Lemma 11. *Let* $x_1, \ldots, x_{t+1}$ *be independent, Bernoulli random variables, where* $\Pr[x_i = 1] = p$, *for all* $i \leq t+1$. *Then*

$$\Pr[x_1 = 0 \wedge \cdots \wedge x_t = 0 \wedge x_{t+1} = 1] \leq \frac{1}{t}.$$

[4] Note that we do not claim that Dif can be built efficiently. We merely introduce Dif to define a related event.

Proof (of Lemma 9). Let $\mathsf{Exec}^{\mathbf{O}}(\mathrm{IK})$ be the following random execution: Sample $\mathrm{X}' \leftarrow \mathsf{S}^{\mathbf{O}}(\mathrm{IK})$ and run $\mathsf{E}^{\mathbf{O}}(\mathrm{IK}, \mathrm{X}')$. Recall that Freq is formed by running $\mathsf{Exec}^{\mathbf{O}}(\mathrm{IK})$ independently $t := \kappa^{2\gamma+8}$ times. Also, note that R_x is a uniformly random string, and thus $(\mathsf{S}^{\mathbf{O}}(\mathrm{IK}; \mathrm{R}_{\mathrm{x}}); \mathsf{E}^{\mathbf{O}}(\mathrm{IK}, X))$ corresponds to a random execution of $\mathsf{Exec}^{\mathbf{O}}(\mathrm{IK})$.

Using simple inspection, we may verify $|\mathsf{Dif}| \leq 6\kappa^{\gamma}$. Now applying Lemma 11 for each element of Dif and taking a union bound, we will have $\Pr[\mathrm{MissQ}] \leq 6\kappa^{\gamma}\frac{1}{\kappa^{2\gamma+8}} \leq \frac{1}{8\kappa^2}$, as desired. □

Proof (of Lemma 10). We can easily show that each of the events Surp_1, Surp_2 and Surp_4 happens with probability at most $\frac{1}{2^{3n}}$: Arguing about the probability of each of these events amounts to arguing that a randomly chosen element in $\{0,1\}^{5\kappa}$ happens to lie in a sparse subset of $\{0,1\}^{5\kappa}$. Thus, we omit the details for these parts.

We focus on bounding the probability of Surp_3. Recall that

- Surp_3: a query $((\mathrm{tk}, \mathrm{y}) \underset{\mathbf{d}}{\rightarrow} ?)$ is made for which Line 4.5.3.5. is hit and for which $(\mathrm{ik}, \mathrm{y})$ is not embedded in Query, where $(\mathrm{ik}, \mathrm{y})$ is defined as in Line 4.5.3.5.. Also, recall that the notion of embeddedness from Definition 7.

We will show that whenever the event Surp_3 holds, we can forge a pair $(\mathrm{ik}, \mathrm{y})$ in the sense of Lemma 4, obtaining $\Pr[\mathrm{Surp}_3] \leq \frac{1}{2^{3n}}$.

In order for Line 4.5.3.5.—during the simulated execution of $\mathsf{D}^{\cdot}(\widetilde{\mathrm{TK}}, \mathrm{Y})$—to be hit with the underlying values $(\mathrm{ik}, \mathrm{y})$, all of the following must hold at that point:

(I) $((\mathrm{ik}, *) \underset{\mathbf{e}}{\rightarrow} \mathrm{y}) \notin \mathsf{Real}$—this is because otherwise Line 4.5.3.2. would have been hit.
(II) $((\mathrm{ik}, *) \underset{\mathbf{s}}{\rightarrow} \mathrm{y}) \notin \mathsf{Real}$—this is because otherwise Line 4.5.3.3. would have been hit.
(III) $((\mathrm{tk}_{\mathrm{real}}, *) \underset{\mathbf{d}}{\rightarrow} *) \notin \mathsf{Real}$, where $\mathrm{tk}_{\mathrm{real}} = \mathbf{g}^{-1}(\mathrm{ik})$—this is because otherwise Line 4.5.3.1. would have been hit (by Assumption 5).
(IV) $\mathbf{v}(\mathrm{ik}, \mathrm{y}) = \top$—this is because otherwise Line 4.5.3.4. would have been hit.

We now show show how the above conditions enable us to forge in the sense of Lemma 4. In particular, the above conditions immediately imply that $(\mathrm{ik}, \mathrm{y})$ is not embedded in Real. Also, notice that the set Real contains all those query/response pairs made by $\mathsf{Break}^{\mathbf{O},\mathbf{u},\mathbf{v}}(1^{\kappa}, \mathrm{IK}, \mathrm{R})$ (to its real oracles) up to the point the event Surp_3 holds. Moreover, since Surp_3 holds, then, by definition, the pair $(\mathrm{ik}, \mathrm{y})$ is not embedded in Query either, which contains all the query/response pairs used to produce IK. We may now design a forgery attack as follows. The forger $\mathcal{B}^{\mathbf{O},\mathbf{u},\mathbf{v}}(1^{\kappa})$ first samples $(\mathrm{IK}, *) \leftarrow \mathsf{G}^{\mathbf{O}}(1^{\kappa})$ and then simulates $\mathsf{Break}^{\mathbf{O},\mathbf{u},\mathbf{v}}(1^{\kappa}, \mathrm{IK}, \mathrm{R})$ for $\mathrm{R} \leftarrow \{0,1\}^*$. Whenever the event Surp_3 holds with the underlying pair $(\mathrm{ik}, \mathrm{y})$, then $\mathcal{B}$ will halt and return $(\mathrm{ik}, \mathrm{y})$. Note that $\mathsf{Break}^{\mathbf{O},\mathbf{u},\mathbf{v}}(1^{\kappa}, \mathrm{IK}, \mathrm{R})$ can efficiently recognize the occurrence of the event Surp_3. The success probability of $\mathcal{B}^{\mathbf{O},\mathbf{u},\mathbf{v}}(1^{\kappa})$ is the probability that Bad holds. □

Acknowledgements. I am grateful to the anonymous reviewers for their useful comments, and especially to one reviewer for their very elaborate comments. I would also like to thank Bruce Kapron for commenting on an earlier draft of the paper.

References

[AS16] Asharov, G., Segev, G.: On constructing one-way permutations from indistinguishability obfuscation. In: Kushilevitz, E., Malkin, T. (eds.) TCC 2016. LNCS, vol. 9563, pp. 512–541. Springer, Heidelberg (2016). https://doi.org/10.1007/978-3-662-49099-0_19

[BBF13] Baecher, P., Brzuska, C., Fischlin, M.: Notions of black-box reductions, revisited. In: Sako, K., Sarkar, P. (eds.) ASIACRYPT 2013. LNCS, vol. 8269, pp. 296–315. Springer, Heidelberg (2013). https://doi.org/10.1007/978-3-642-42033-7_16

[BPR+08] Boneh, D., Papakonstantinou, P.A., Rackoff, C., Vahlis, Y., Waters, B.: On the impossibility of basing identity based encryption on trapdoor permutations. In: 49th FOCS, 25–28 October 2008, Philadelphia, PA, USA, pp. 283–292. IEEE Computer Society Press (2008)

[BPW16] Bitansky, N., Paneth, O., Wichs, D.: Perfect structure on the edge of chaos. In: Kushilevitz, E., Malkin, T. (eds.) TCC 2016. LNCS, vol. 9562, pp. 474–502. Springer, Heidelberg (2016). https://doi.org/10.1007/978-3-662-49096-9_20

[BY93] Bellare, M., Yung, M.: Certifying cryptographic tools: the case of trapdoor permutations. In: Brickell, E.F. (ed.) CRYPTO 1992. LNCS, vol. 740, pp. 442–460. Springer, Heidelberg (1993). https://doi.org/10.1007/3-540-48071-4_31

[CL17] Canetti, R., Lichtenberg, A.: Certifying trapdoor permutations, revisited. Cryptology ePrint Archive, Report 2017/631 (2017). http://eprint.iacr.org/2017/631

[EGL82] Even, S., Goldreich, O., Lempel, A.: A randomized protocol for signing contracts. In: Chaum, D., Rivest, R.L., Sherman, A.T. (eds.) CRYPTO 1982, Santa Barbara, CA, USA, pp. 205–210. Plenum Press, New York (1982)

[Fis02] Fischlin, M.: On the impossibility of constructing non-interactive statistically-secret protocols from any trapdoor one-way function. In: Preneel, B. (ed.) CT-RSA 2002. LNCS, vol. 2271, pp. 79–95. Springer, Heidelberg (2002). https://doi.org/10.1007/3-540-45760-7_7

[FLS90] Feige, U., Lapidot, D., Shamir, A.: Multiple non-interactive zero knowledge proofs based on a single random string (extended abstract). In: 31st FOCS, 22–24 October 1990, St. Louis, Missouri, pp. 308–317. IEEE Computer Society Press (1990)

[FS12] Fiore, D., Schröder, D.: Uniqueness is a different story: impossibility of verifiable random functions from trapdoor permutations. In: Cramer, R. (ed.) TCC 2012. LNCS, vol. 7194, pp. 636–653. Springer, Heidelberg (2012). https://doi.org/10.1007/978-3-642-28914-9_36

[GKM+00] Gertner, Y., Kannan, S., Malkin, T., Reingold, O., Viswanathan, M.: The relationship between public key encryption and oblivious transfer. In: 41st FOCS, 12–14 November 2000, Redondo Beach, CA, USA, pp. 325–335. IEEE Computer Society Press (2000)

[GMR01] Gertner, Y., Malkin, T., Reingold, O.: On the impossibility of basing trapdoor functions on trapdoor predicates. In: 42nd FOCS, 14–17 October 2001, pp. 126–135, Las Vegas, NV, USA. IEEE Computer Society Press (2001)

[GMW87] Goldreich, O., Micali, S., Wigderson, A.: How to play any mental game or a completeness theorem for protocols with honest majority. In: Aho, A. (ed.) 19th ACM STOC, pp. 218–229, 25–27 May 1987, New York City, NY, USA. ACM Press, New York (1987)

[Gol04] Goldreich, O.: Foundations of Cryptography: Basic Applications, vol. 2. Cambridge University Press, Cambridge (2004)

[Gol11] Goldreich, O.: Basing non-interactive zero-knowledge on (enhanced) trapdoor permutations: the state of the art. In: Goldreich, O. (ed.) Studies in Complexity and Cryptography. Miscellanea on the Interplay between Randomness and Computation. LNCS, vol. 6650, pp. 406–421. Springer, Heidelberg (2011). https://doi.org/10.1007/978-3-642-22670-0_28

[GR13] Goldreich, O., Rothblum, R.D.: Enhancements of trapdoor permutations. J. Cryptol. **26**(3), 484–512 (2013)

[Hai04] Haitner, I.: Implementing oblivious transfer using collection of dense trapdoor permutations. In: Naor, M. (ed.) TCC 2004. LNCS, vol. 2951, pp. 394–409. Springer, Heidelberg (2004). https://doi.org/10.1007/978-3-540-24638-1_22

[HHRS07] Haitner, I., Hoch, J.J., Reingold, O., Segev, G.: Finding collisions in interactive protocols - a tight lower bound on the round complexity of statistically-hiding commitments. In: 48th FOCS, pp. 669–679, 20–23 October 2007, Providence, RI, USA. IEEE Computer Society Press (2007)

[HR04] Hsiao, C.-Y., Reyzin, L.: Finding collisions on a public road, or do secure hash functions need secret coins? In: Franklin, M. (ed.) CRYPTO 2004. LNCS, vol. 3152, pp. 92–105. Springer, Heidelberg (2004). https://doi.org/10.1007/978-3-540-28628-8_6

[IR89] Impagliazzo, R., Rudich, S.: Limits on the provable consequences of one-way permutations. In: 21st ACM STOC, 15–17 May, Seattle, WA, USA, pp. 44–61. ACM Press (1989)

[KKM12] Kakvi, S.A., Kiltz, E., May, A.: Certifying RSA. In: Wang, X., Sako, K. (eds.) ASIACRYPT 2012. LNCS, vol. 7658, pp. 404–414. Springer, Heidelberg (2012). https://doi.org/10.1007/978-3-642-34961-4_25

[NR99] Naor, M., Reingold, O.: Synthesizers and their application to the parallel construction of pseudo-random functions. J. Comput. Syst. Sci. **58**(2), 336–375 (1999)

[Rab79] Rabin, M.O.: Digital signatures and public key functions as intractable as factorization. Technical report MIT/LCS/TR-212, Massachusetts Institute of Technology, January 1979

[RSA78] Rivest, R.L., Shamir, A., Adleman, L.M.: A method for obtaining digital signature and public-key cryptosystems. Commun. Assoc. Comput. Mach. **21**(2), 120–126 (1978)

[RTV04] Reingold, O., Trevisan, L., Vadhan, S.: Notions of reducibility between cryptographic primitives. In: Naor, M. (ed.) TCC 2004. LNCS, vol. 2951, pp. 1–20. Springer, Heidelberg (2004). https://doi.org/10.1007/978-3-540-24638-1_1

[Sim98] Simon, D.R.: Finding collisions on a one-way street: can secure hash functions be based on general assumptions? In: Nyberg, K. (ed.) EUROCRYPT 1998. LNCS, vol. 1403, pp. 334–345. Springer, Heidelberg (1998). https://doi.org/10.1007/BFb0054137

[Vah10] Vahlis, Y.: Two Is a crowd? a black-box separation of one-wayness and security under correlated inputs. In: Micciancio, D. (ed.) TCC 2010. LNCS, vol. 5978, pp. 165–182. Springer, Heidelberg (2010). https://doi.org/10.1007/978-3-642-11799-2_11

[Yao82] Yao, A.C.-C.: Theory and applications of trapdoor functions (extended abstract). In: 23rd FOCS, pp. 80–91, 3–5 November, Chicago, Illinois. IEEE Computer Society Press (1982)

Certifying Trapdoor Permutations, Revisited

Ran Canetti[1,2](✉) and Amit Lichtenberg[2](✉)

[1] Boston University, Boston, USA
canetti@bu.edu
[2] Tel Aviv University, Tel Aviv, Israel
amitlich@post.tau.ac.il

Abstract. The modeling of trapdoor permutations has evolved over the years. Indeed, finding an appropriate abstraction that bridges between the existing candidate constructions and the needs of applications has proved to be challenging. In particular, the notions of certifying permutations (Bellare and Yung, 96), enhanced and doubly enhanced trapdoor permutations (Goldreich, 04, 08, 11, Goldreich and Rothblum, 13) were added to bridge the gap between the modeling of trapdoor permutations and needs of applications. We identify an additional gap in the current abstraction of trapdoor permutations: Previous works implicitly assumed that it is easy to recognize elements in the domain, as well as uniformly sample from it, even for illegitimate function indices. We demonstrate this gap by using the (Bitansky-Paneth-Wichs, 16) doubly-enhanced trapdoor permutation family to instantiate the Feige-Lapidot-Shamir (FLS) paradigm for constructing non-interactive zero-knowledge (NIZK) protocols, and show that the resulting proof system is unsound. To close the gap, we propose a general notion of *certifiably injective* doubly enhanced trapdoor functions (DECITDFs), which provides a way of certifying that a given key defines an injective function over the domain defined by it, even when that domain is not efficiently recognizable and sampleable. We show that DECITDFs suffice for instantiating the FLS paradigm; more generally, we argue that certifiable injectivity is needed whenever the generation process of the function is not trusted. We then show two very different ways to construct DECITDFs: One is via the traditional method of RSA/Rabin with the Bellare-Yung certification mechanism, and the other using indistinguishability obfuscation and injective pseudorandom generators. In particular the latter is the first candidate injective trapdoor function, from assumptions other than factoring, that suffices for the FLS paradigm. Finally we observe that a similar gap appears also in other paths proposed in the literature for instantiating the FLS paradigm, specifically via verifiable pseudorandom generators and verifiable pseudorandom functions. Closing the gap there can be done in similar ways to the ones proposed here.

Research supported by the Check Point Institute for Information Security and ISF grant 1523/14.

R. Canetti—Supported by the NSF MACS project. Member of CPIIS.

A. Beimel and S. Dziembowski (Eds.): TCC 2018, LNCS 11239, pp. 476–506, 2018.
https://doi.org/10.1007/978-3-030-03807-6_18

Keywords: Non-interactive zero-knowledge · Trapdoor permutations
Indistinguishability obfuscation

1 Introduction

In the late-1970s, Rivest, Shamir and Adelman [RSA78] and Rabin [Rab79] suggested functions which are easy to evaluate, easy to invert when given a suitable secret trapdoor key, but are presumably hard to invert when only given the function description without the trapdoor. Both of these constructions use the same source of computational hardness: the hardness of factoring. These constructions were later abstracted to a formal notion of trapdoor functions [Yao82], which became one of the pillars of modern cryptography. In particular, trapdoor permutations (TDPs) were used as building blocks for public key encryption [Yao82, GM84, BG84], oblivious transfer [EGL85] and zero-knowledge protocols [FLS90].

One of the quintesential uses of the TDP astraction is in constructing Non-interactive zero knowledge (NIZK) protocols, introduced by Blum Feldman and Micali [BFM88, BSMP91]: While the first constructions were based on the hardness of factoring, Feige et al. [FLS90] demonstrated a more general construction based on any trapdoor permutation. Specifically, this proof system (henceforth the FLS protocol) treats the common reference string as a sequence of blocks, where each block represents an image of a trapdoor permutation selected by the prover. The prover then inverts a subset of these using the secret trapdoor. The verifier can validate that the pre-images it was given are correct by forward-evaluating the trapdoor function, but is unable to invert any other image due to the hardness of inverting the function without the secret trapdoor. By treating the common string as a series of sealed off boxes (aka the *hidden-bit-model*), the prover is able to provide a NIZK proof for an NP-Hard language. Soundness is based on the fact that, for any given permutation, each block in the reference string defines a unique pre-image. This construction assumes that the trapdoor permutation in use is *ideal*, namely its domain is $\{0,1\}^n$ for some n, hardness holds with respect to uniformly chosen n-bit strings, and any key (index) in an efficiently recognizable set describes a permutation.

Bellare and Yung [BY96] consider the case where it is not known how to recognize whether a given index defines a permutation, but the domain is still $\{0,1\}^n$. This relaxation is indeed essential, as even the first TDP candidates suggested by [RSA78, Rab79] do not have efficiently recognizable keys. They observe that in this case a malicious prover may be able to choose a key which evaluates to a many-to-one function, breaking the soundness of the protocol, and suggest a mechanism for certifying that a given index describes a permutation. Their mechanism, which is specific to the case of NIZK, is based on the prover providing the verifier with pre-images of a set of random images, which are taken from the common reference string. We refer to this mechanism as the Bellare-Yung protocol. We note however that this mechanism crucially needs the verifier to be able to detect whether an element is in the domain of the permutation (which is not an issue in their case of full domain).

Goldreich and Rothblum [Gol04, Gol08, Gol11, GR13] point out that when the domain of the permutation is not just $\{0,1\}^n$, additional mechanisms are required in order to base the Zero-Knowledge property of the FLS protocol on the one-wayness of the underlying TDP. Specifically, they define the notions of enhanced and doubly-enhanced trapdoor permutations, which require the existence of a domain sampling algorithm such that finding the pre-image of a sampled element is hard, even given the random coins used by the sampler. Furthermore, it should be possible to sample pairs of pre-image and random coins for the domain sampler, which both map to the same image (one under the forward evaluation and one via the domain sampler). They then show that the FLS protocol is zero-knowledge when using doubly-enhanced trapdoor permutations. For soundness, they rely on the Bellare-Yung protocol, and thus inherit the limitation that the domain of the permutation must be publicly recognizable; yet, they do not explicitly require that the domain be efficiently recognizable.

A number of other methods for implementing the hidden-bit model by way of cryptographic primitives have been proposed over the years, e.g. *invariant signatures* [BG90], *verifiable random generators* [DN00], *(weak) verifiable random functions* [BGRV09], or *publicly-verifiable trapdoor predicates* [CHK03]. However, in all of these methods (with the exception of invariant signatures, discussed below), soundness of the NIZK protocol crucially relies on the verifier's ability to recognize when an element is in the domain of a function chosen by the prover.

A natural question is then whether this gap in modeling TDPs is significant, and furthermore whether public verifiability is an essential property for realizing the hidden bit model. In particular, do doubly-enhanced TDPs where the domain is not publicly recognizable suffice for the FLS protocol?

This question is underlined by the recent doubly enhanced TDP of Bitansky et. al. [BPW16], where the domain is not efficiently recognizable given the public index. Interestingly, this is also the first TDP based on general assumptions which are not known to imply the hardness of factoring (specifically, subexponentially secure indistinguishability obfuscation and one-way functions).

1.1 Our Contributions

We start by demonstrating that the above gap is significant: We show that, when instantiated with the [BPW16] doubly enhanced trapdoor permutation family, the FLS protocol is unsound, even when combined with the [BY96] certification protocol. Indeed, this loss of soundness stems from the fact that the existing notion of doubly enhanced trapdoor permutations does not make sufficient requirements on indices that were not legitimately generated.

We then formulate a general property for trapdoor permutations, called *certifiable injectivity*. We show that this requirement suffices for the FLS paradigm even when the TDF is not necessarily a permutation, and does not have publicly recognizable domain. We then construct a doubly enhanced certifiably injective trapdoor function assuming indistinguishability obfuscation (iO) and injective pseudorandom generators. Interestingly, this is the first candidate trapdoor function that suffices for the FLS paradigm, and is based on assumptions other than factoring. Also, crucially, the co-domain of the function is not publicly recognizable.

In the rest of this subsection we present our contributions in more detail.

Unsoundness of FLS+BY with the [BPW16] *Trapdoor Permutations:* We instantiate the FLS+BY protocols using the [BPW16] iO-based doubly enhanced trapdoor function family, whose domain is not efficiently recognizable. We demonstrate how a malicious prover could choose an index α which describes a many-to-one function, wrongly certify it as a permutation by having the sampler sample elements only out of a restricted domain D_α which is completely invertible, but then invert any image in D_α into two pre-images - one in D_α and another outside of it. The verifier cannot detect the lie since D_α is not efficiently recognizable.

Certifiable Injective Trapdoor Functions: We formulate a new notion of *Certifiable Injectivity*, which captures a general abstraction of certifiability for doubly-enhanced injective trapdoor functions. This notion requires the function family to be accompanied by algorithms for generation and verification of certificates for indices, along with an algorithm for certification of individual points from the domain. It is guaranteed that if the index certificate is verified then, except for negligible probability, randomly sampled range points have only a single pre-image that passes the pointwise certification. We show that certifiable injectivity suffices for the FLS paradigm.

We show that the FLS+BY combination regains its soundness when instantiated with a specific class of trapdoor permutations, whose domain is recognizable using a poly-time algorithm, and is additionally almost-uniformly sampleable using a poly-time algorithm. We call such TDPs *public-domain*. We show that any public-domain TDP is certifiably injective. We note that the RSA and Rabin candidates are indeed public-domain, while the [BPW16] permutation is not.

We additionally suggest a strengthened notion of *Perfectly Certifiable Injectivity*, which guarantees that no point generated by the range sampler has two pre-images that pass the pointwise certification. We show that by implementing FLS using this notion, the resulting error in soundness is optimal, in that it is equal to the error incurred by implementing the FLS protocol with ideal trapdoor permutations.

Doubly Enhanced Perfectly Certifiable Trapdoor Functions from iO+: We construct a doubly-enhanced family of trapdoor functions which is perfectly certifiable injective. Our construction, inspired by the work of [SW14], is based on indistinguishability obfuscation and pseudorandom generators, and is perfectly certifiable injective under the additional assumption that the underlying pseudorandom generator is (a) injective and (b) its domain is either full, or efficiently sampleable and recognizable.

To provide an enhanced range sampler and a correlated pre-image sampler, we use a re-randomization technique by having the range-sampler be given as an obfuscated circle, which applies a length-preserving pseudorandom function on the random coins given to it, before inputting it to the forward evaluator. Using another round of re-randomization we augment our construction into a doubly-enhanced TDF. Our re-randomization technique can be applied to any trapdoor function with an efficiently sampleable domain to obtain a doubly-enhanced domain sampler, at the cost of using iO.

Finally, we show how using the assumption that the pseudorandom generator g is injective and that its domain is efficiently recognizable, we are able to provide a perfect pointwise certification algorithm for our trapdoor functions, proving it is perfectly certifiable injective. We then show how to construct such generators from standard assumptions (such as, e.g., hardness of discrete log). This makes our construction sufficient for NIZK.

1.2 On Alternative Methods for NIZK

We briefly present a number of alternative avenues proposed in the literature for obtaining NIZK, and specifically for instantiation the FLS protocol. We observe that the need for functions whose domain is publicly recognizable, even for maliciously generated indices, is common to all with the exception of one recent construction.

[DN00] suggest a different path for realizing the hidden-bit model, by using the notion of *verifiable random generators*. This notion provide the guarantee that every pre-image has only one (verified) image, in the sense that one cannot invert two different images into the same pre-image. They then suggest a construction of verifiable random generators from a particular type of trapdoor permutations, specifically from families of *certified* trapdoor permutations where all the functions in a given family share a common, efficiently recognizable and efficiently (publicly) sampleable domain. The latter assumption is crucial for this construction to work, or else the same attack we describe in our work would work in that case too. As we show in our work, assuming an efficiently recognizable and sampleable domain is indeed sufficient to soundly certify the permutation, however this assumption adds some limitation to the generalized abstraction of trapdoor permutations.

[BGRV09] use the notion of *(weak) verifiable random functions* to obtain NIZK using a very similar technique to that of [DN00]. Here too, they construct verifiable random functions from trapdoor permutations, but in this case the only assumption is that the trapdoor permutations are doubly enhanced.[1] Their construction assumes that the trapdoor permutation is efficiently certifiable, and that this construction can be made to work with any (doubly enhanced) trapdoor permutation, using the certification procedure of Bellare and Yung. However, as we show in out current work, the latter is not true, in that certifying

[1] In their original work, [BGRV09] only required that the trapdoor permutations be *enhanced*. Regardless of the findings in our work, in light of [GR13], this requirement should have been strengthened into *doubly-enhanced* to support the Bellare-Yung certification.

that an enhanced trapdoor permutation is indeed injective requires additional assumptions.

[CHK03] provides yet another alternative path for realizing the hidden-bit model. They suggest the notion of publicly-verifiable trapdoor predicates, which they construct based on the decisional bilinear Diffie-Hellman assumption. Not to confuse with our notion of certifiability, here the "verifiability" concerns the ability to check, given a pair (x, y), that x is indeed a pre-image of y (not necessarily the *sole* pre-image). This notion is suggested as a relaxation of the notion of trapdoor permutations, which suffices for NIZK. Still, it has the same weakness as the one pointed out here re DETDPs, namely it implicitly assumes that the trapdoor index is generated honestly (or that the domain of the predicate is efficiently recognizable and sampleable), thus it does not suffice in of itself for realizing the hidden-bit model.

Recently, [BP15] showed how to construct invariant signatures [BG90] from indistinguishability obfuscation and one-way functions. This, together with the technique of [GO92], gives yet another path for realizing the hidden-bit model from assumptions other than factoring. (Previously, the only known construction of invariant signatures was from NIZK.) Their construction not only gives an arguably more natural realization of the hidden-bit model then that obtained by trapdoor permutation, but also avoids the certification problems altogether (as invariant signatures handle the certification problem by definition). Still, the trapdoor-permutations-based paradigm of [FLS90] remains the textbook method for realizing non-interactive zero-knowledge proofs.

Over the years, additional approaches were suggested to obtaining non-interactive zero-knowledge proofs which are not based on the hidden-bit model. [GOS06] constructed non-interactive zero-knowledge proofs for circuit satisfiability with a short reference string, and non-interactive zero-knowledge arguments for any NP language. [GS08] constructed non-interactive zero-knowledge proofs from assumptions on bilinear groups. [GOS12] and [SW14] constructed non-interactive zero-knowledge arguments with a short reference string for any NP language. All of these protocols either use a structured CRS whose generation requires additional randomness that's trusted to never be revealed, or achieve zero-knowledge *arguments*, where the soundness holds only with respect to computationally bounded adversaries. This leaves the hidden-bit paradigm (along with the original protocols of [BFM88, BSMP91]) as the only known general way to achieve zero-knowledge proofs for NP in the uniform reference string model.

1.3 Alternative Notions of Certifiability for TDPs

[Abu13] define and discuss two notions of verifiability for doubly-enhanced trapdoor permutations, which indeed allow verifying, or certifying, that a given trapdoor index indeed describes an injective function: a strong (errorless) one, in which the verification is not allowed to accept any function which is not injective, and a weaker variant, with negligible error. The strong notion indeed suffices for realizing the hidden-bit model, but is overly strong - in particular the existing constructions from RSA and BY do not satisfy it. On the other hand, the weak notion suffers from the same weakness as the prior notions, in that it implicitly assumes that the range of the function is efficiently recognizable. In contrast, we provide a single notion that suffices for realizing the HBM model and is realizable by the factoring-based constructions, by the IO-based construction, and by the gap-DH based construction.

1.4 Other Applications of Trapdoor Permutations

The gap between ideal and general trapdoor permutations imposes a problem in other applications as well. [Rot10, GR13] discuss the security of the [EGL85] trapdoor-permutations-based 1-out-of-k oblivious transfer protocol, which breaks in the presence of partial-domain trapdoor functions when $k \geq 3$, and show how doubly enhanced trapdoor functions can be used to overcome this. The concern of certifying keys is irrelevant in the oblivious transfer applications, as the parties are assumed to be trusted. Still, certifiability concerns apply whenever dishonesty of one or more of the parties is considered an issue, such as the case of interactive proofs and multi-party computation. We note however that requiring that the trapdoor be certifiable does not suffice for making the [EGL85] protocol secure against Byzantine attacks.

1.5 Paper Organization

In Sect. 2 we review the basic notations used in our work, as well as previous results related to this work. In Sect. 3 we demonstrate how the soundness of the FLS protocol may be compromised when using general TDPs, and discuss the additional assumptions required to avoid this problem. In Sect. 4 we suggest the alternative notion of *certifiably injective* trapdoor functions, and use it to overcome the limitations of the FLS+BY combination and regain the soundness of the FLS protocol. In Sect. 5 we construct a doubly-enhanced, certifiable injective trapdoor function family based on indistinguishability obfuscation and injective pseudorandom generators.

2 Review of Basic Definitions and Constructs

The cryptographic definitions in this paper follow the convention of modeling security against non-uniform adversaries. A protocol P is said to be secure against (non-uniformly) polynomial-time adversaries, if it is secure against any adversary $A = \{A_\lambda\}_{\lambda \in \mathbb{N}}$, such that each circuit A_λ is of size polynomial in λ.

2.1 Notations

For a probabilistic polynomial time (PPT) algorithm A which operates on input x, we sometimes denote $A(x; r)$ as the (deterministic) evaluation A using random coins r.

We use the notation $\Pr[E_1; E_2; ...; E_n; R]$ to denote the probability of the resulting boolean event R, following a sequence of probabilistic actions $E_1, ..., E_n$. In other words, we describe a probability experiment as a sequence of actions from left to right, with a final boolean success predicate. We sometime combine this notion with the stacked version $\Pr_S[E_1; E_2; ...; E_n; R]$ in which case the sampling steps taken in S precede $E_1, ..., E_n$, and the random coins used for S are explicitly specified. (The choice of which actions are described in a subscript and which are described within the brackets is arbitrary and is done only for visual clarity).

2.2 Puncturable Pseudorandom Functions

We consider a simple case of puncturable pseudorandom functions (PPRFs) where any PRF may be punctured at a single point. The definition is formulated as in [SW14], and is satisfied by the GGM PRF [GGM86, BW13, KPTZ13, BGI14].

Definition 1 *(Puncturable PRFs). Let n, k be polynomially bounded length functions. An efficiently computable family of functions:*

$$PRF = \{PRF_S : \{0,1\}^{n(\lambda)} \to \{0,1\}^{\lambda} : S \in \{0,1\}^{k(\lambda)}, \lambda \in \mathbb{N}\}$$

associated with a PPT key sampler K_{PRF}, is a puncturable PRF if there exists a poly-time puncturing algorithm Punc that takes as input a key S and a point x^* and outputs a punctured key $S^* = S\{x^*\}$, so that the following conditions are satisfied:

1. ***Functionality is preserved under puncturing:*** *For every $x^* \in \{0,1\}^{n(\lambda)}$,*

   $$\Pr[S \leftarrow K_{PRF}(1^\lambda); S^* = Punc(S, x^*); \forall x \neq x^* : PRF_S(x) = PRF_{S^*}(x)] = 1$$

2. ***Indistinguishability at punctured points:*** *for any PPT distinguisher D there exists a negligible function μ such that for all $\lambda \in \mathbb{N}$, and any $x^* \in \{0,1\}^{n(\lambda)}$,*

   $$\Pr[D(x^*, S^*, PRF_S(x^*)) = 1] - \Pr[D(x^*, S^*, u) = 1] \leq \mu(\lambda)$$

   where the probability is taken over the choice of $S \leftarrow K_{PRF}(1^\lambda), S^* = Punc(S, x^*)$, $u \leftarrow \{0,1\}^\lambda$, and the random coins of D.

2.3 Indistinguishability Obfuscation

We define indistinguishability obfuscation (iO) with respect to a given class of circuits. The definition is formulated as in [BGI+01].

Definition 2 *(Indistinguishability Obfuscation [BGI+01]). A PPT algorithms iO is said to be an indistinguishability obfuscator for a class of circuits $\mathcal{C}$, if it satisfies:*

1. ***Functionality:*** *for any* $C \in \mathcal{C}$,

$$\Pr_{iO}[\forall x : iO(C)(x) = C(x)] = 1$$

2. ***Indistinguishability:*** *for any PPT distinguisher D there exists a negligible function* μ, *such that for any two circuits* $C_0, C_1 \in \mathcal{C}$ *that compute the same function and are of the same size* λ:

$$\Pr[D(iO(C_0)) = 1] - \Pr[D(iO(C_1)) = 1] \leq \mu(\lambda)$$

where the probability is taken over the coins of D and iO.

2.4 Injective TDFs and TDPs

Definition 3 *(Trapdoor Functions). A family of one-way trapdoor functions, or TDFs, is a collection of finite functions, denoted* $f_\alpha : \{D_\alpha \to R_\alpha\}$, *accompanied by PPT algorithm I (index),* S_D *(domain sampler),* S_R *(range sampler) and two (deterministic) polynomial-time algorithms F (forward evaluator) and B (backward evaluator or inverter) such that the following condition holds:*

1. *On input* 1^n, *algorithm* $I(1^n)$ *selects at random an index* α *of a function* f_α, *along with a corresponding trapdoor* τ. *Denote* $\alpha = I_0(1^n)$ *and* $\tau = I_1(1^n)$.
2. *On input* $\alpha = I_0(1^n)$, *algorithm* $S_D(\alpha)$ *samples an element from domain* D_α.
3. *On input* $\alpha = I_0(1^n)$, *algorithm* $S_R(\alpha)$ *samples an image from the range* R_α.
4. *On input* $\alpha = I_0(1^n)$ *and any* $x \in D_\alpha$, $F(\alpha, x) = f_\alpha(x)$.
5. *On input* $\tau = I_1(1^n)$ *and any* $y \in R_\alpha$, $B(\tau, y)$ *outputs x such that* $F(\alpha, x) = y$.

The standard hardness condition refers to the difficulty of inverting f_α on a random image, sampled by S_R or by evaluating $F(\alpha)$ on a random pre-image sampled by S_D, when given only the image and the index α but not the trapdoor τ. That is, it is required that, for every polynomial-time algorithm A, it holds that:

$$\Pr[\alpha \leftarrow I_0(1^n); x \leftarrow S_D(\alpha); y = F(\alpha, x); A(\alpha, y) = x' \text{ s.t. } F(\alpha, x') = y] \leq \mu(n) \quad (1)$$

Or, when sampling an image directly using the range sampler:

$$\Pr[\alpha \leftarrow I_0(1^n); y \leftarrow S_R(\alpha); A(\alpha, y) = x' \text{ s.t. } F(\alpha, x') = y] \leq \mu(n) \quad (2)$$

for some negligible function μ.

Additionally, it is required that, for any $\alpha \leftarrow I_0(1^n)$, the distribution sampled by $S_R(\alpha)$ should be *close* to from that sampled by $F(S_D(\alpha))$. In this context we require that the two distributions be computationally indistinguishable. We note that this requirement implies that the two hardness requirements given in Eqs. 1 and 2 are equivalent. The issue of closeness of the sampling distributions is discussed further at the end of this section.

If f_α is injective for all $\alpha \leftarrow I_0(1^n)$, we say that our collection describes an injective trapdoor function family, or iTDFs (in which case $B(\tau, \cdot)$ inverts any image to its sole pre-image). If additionally D_α and R_α coincide for any $\alpha \leftarrow I_0(1^n)$, the resulting primitive is a trapdoor permutation.

If for any $\alpha \leftarrow I_0(1^n)$, $D_\alpha = \{0,1\}^{p(n)}$ for some polynomial $p(n)$, that is, every $p(n)$-bit string describes a valid domain element, we say the function is full domain. Otherwise we say the domain is partial. Full and partial range and keyset are defined similarly. We say that a TDF (or TDP) is ideal if it has a full range and a full keyset.

Definition 4 *(Hard-Core Predicate). p is a hard-core predicate for f_α if its value is hard to predict for a random domain element x, given only α and $f_\alpha(x)$. That is, if for any PPT adversary A there exists a negligible function μ such that:*

$$\Pr[\alpha \leftarrow I_0(1^n); x \leftarrow S_D(\alpha); y = F(\alpha, x); A(\alpha, y) = p(x)] \leq 1/2 + \mu(n).$$

Enhancements. A trivial range-sampler implementation may just sample a domain element x by applying $S_D(\alpha)$, and then evaluate the TDF on it by applying $F(\alpha, x)$. This sampler, while fulfilling the standard one-way hardness condition, is not good enough for some applications. Specifically, for the case of NIZK, we require the ability to obliviously sample a range element in a way that does not expose its pre-image (without using the trapdoor). This trivial range sampler obviously does not qualify for this case.

Goldreich [Gol04] suggested the notion of enhanced TDPs, which can be used for cases where sampling is required to be available in a way that does not expose the pre-image. They then demonstrate how enhanced trapdoor permutations can be used to obtain NIZK proofs (as we describe later in Sect. 2.5). We revisit this notion, while extending it to the case of injective TDF (where the domain and range are not necessarily equal).

Definition 5 *(Enhanced injective TDF, [Gol04]). Let $\{f_\alpha : D_\alpha \to R_\alpha\}$ be a collection of injective TDFs, and let S_D be the domain sampler associated with it. We say that the collection is enhanced if there exists a range sampler S_R that returns random samples out of R_α, and such that, for every polynomial-time algorithm A, it holds that:*

$$\Pr[\alpha \leftarrow I_0(1^n); r \leftarrow \{0,1\}^n; y = S_R(\alpha; r); A(\alpha, r) = x' \ s.t. \ F(\alpha, x') = y] \leq \mu(n) \tag{3}$$

where μ is some negligible function.

The range sampler of an enhanced injective TDF has the property that its random coins do not reveal a corresponding pre-image, i.e. an adversary which is given an image along with the random coins which created it, still cannot inverse it with all but negligible probability.

[Gol11] additionally suggested enhancing the notion of hard-core predicates in order to adapt the FLS proof (that uses traditional hard-core predicates) to the case of enhanced trapdoor functions. Loosely speaking, such a predicate p is easy to compute, but given $\alpha \leftarrow I_0(1^n)$ and $r \leftarrow \{0,1\}^n$, it is hard to guess the value of the predicate on the pre-image of the image sampled by the range sampler using the coins r:

Definition 6 *(Enhanced Hard-Core Predicate, [Gol11]). Let $\{f_\alpha : D_\alpha \to R_\alpha\}$ be an enhanced collection of injective TDFs, with domain sampler S_D and range sampler S_R. We say that the predicate p is an enhanced hard-core predicate of f_α if it is efficiently computable and for any PPT adversary A there exists a negligible function μ such that*

$$\Pr[(\alpha,\tau) \leftarrow I(1^n); r \leftarrow \{0,1\}^n; y = S_R(\alpha; r); x = B(\tau, y); A(\alpha, r) = p(\alpha, x)] \leq 1/2 + \mu(n)$$

Or, equivalently, if the following two distribution ensembles are computationally indistinguishable:

1. $\{(\alpha, r, p(\alpha, B(\tau, S_R(\alpha; r)))) : (\alpha,\tau) \leftarrow I(1^n), r \leftarrow \{0,1\}^n\}_{n\in\mathbb{N}}$
2. $\{(\alpha, r, u) : \alpha \leftarrow I_0(1^n), r \leftarrow \{0,1\}^n, u \leftarrow \{0,1\}\}_{n\in\mathbb{N}}$

The hard-core predicates presented in [GL89] satisfy this definition without changes (as they do not use the trapdoor index).

Definition 7 *(Doubly Enhanced injective TDF, [Gol08]). Let $\{f_\alpha : D_\alpha \to R_\alpha\}$ be an enhanced collection of injective TDFs, with domain sampler S_D and range sampler S_R. We say that this collection is doubly-enhanced if it provides another polynomial-time algorithm S_{DR} with the following properties:*

- **Correlated pre-image sampling:** *for any $(\alpha,\tau) \leftarrow I(1^n)$, $S_{DR}(\alpha; 1^n)$ outputs pairs of (x, r) such that $F(\alpha, x) = S_R(\alpha; r)$*
- **Pseudorandomness:** *for any PPT distinguisher D there exists a negligible μ such that:*

$$\Pr[(\alpha,\tau) \leftarrow I(1^n); (x, r) \leftarrow S_{DR}(\alpha); D(x, r, \alpha) = 1] -$$
$$\Pr[(\alpha,\tau) \leftarrow I(1^n); r \leftarrow \{0,1\}^*; y = S_R(\alpha; r); x = B(\tau, y); D(x, r, \alpha) = 1] \leq \mu(n)$$

S_{DR} provides a way to sample pairs of an element x in the function's domain, along with random coins r which explain the sampling of the image $y = f_\alpha(x)$ in the function's range. Note that since the collection is enhanced, r must not reveal any information of x.

[GR13] review these enhanced notions of trapdoor permutations in light of applications for which they are useful, specifically oblivious transfer and NIZK, providing a comprehensive picture of trapdoor permutations and the requirements they should satisfy for each application. They additionally suggested a number of intermediate notions between idealized TDPs, enhanced TDPs and doubly-enhanced TDPs, and discussed notions of enhancements for general trapdoor and one-way functions.

On the Uniformity of Distributions Sampled by the Domain, Range and Correlated Pre-image Samplers: In Definitions 3 and 7 we required that the distribution sampled by (a) running the domain sampler S_D, (b) inverting images sampled by the range sampler S_R, and (c) taking pre-images sampled by the correlated pre-image sampler S_{DR}, are all *computationally indistinguishable.* This is a relaxation of the definition given in [Gol11,GR13], which require that all three of these distributions be *statistically close.* The relaxed notion is adapted from [BPW16], which indeed define and implement the computational-indistinguishable variant. While samplers that are statistically close to uniform are often needed in situations where the permutation is applied repeatedly, computational closeness suffices in our setting.

2.5 Non-interactive Zero-Knowledge

Definition

Definition 8 *(Non-Interactive Zero Knowledge, Blum-Feldman-Micali [BFM88]). A pair of PPT algorithms (P, V) provides an (efficient-prover) Non-Interactive Zero Knowledge (NIZK) proof system for language $L \in NP$ with relation R_L in the* Common Reference String *(CRS) Model if it provides:*

- ***Completeness:*** *for every $(x, w) \in R_L$ we have that:*

$$\Pr_{P,crs}\left[\pi \leftarrow P(x, w, crs); V(x, crs, \pi) = 0\right] \leq \mu(|x|)$$

where the probability is taken over the coins of P and the choice of the CRS as a uniformly random string, and $\mu(n)$ is some negligible function.
- ***Soundness:*** *for every $x \notin L$:*

$$\Pr_{crs}\left[\exists \pi : V(x, crs, \pi) = 1\right] \leq \mu(|x|)$$

where the probability is taken over the choice of the CRS as a uniformly random string, and $\mu(n)$ is some negligible function.
- ***Zero-Knowledge:*** *there exists a PPT algorithm S (simulator) such that the following two distribution ensembles are computationally indistinguishable:*
  - $\{(x, crs, \pi) : crs \leftarrow U, \pi \leftarrow P(x, w, crs)\}_{(x,w)\in R_L}$
  - $\{S(x)\}_{(x,w)\in R_L}$.

  Here U denotes the set of uniformly random strings of length polynomial in $|x|$.

While it sometimes makes sense to have a computationally unbounded prover, it should be stressed that the verifier and simulator should both be polynomial-time.

The common reference string is considered the practical one for NIZK proof systems, and is the one widely accepted as the appropriate abstraction. When discussing NIZK proof systems, we sometime omit the specific model being assumed, in which case we mean the CRS model.

NIZK in the Hidden-Bit Model. A fictitious abstraction, which is nevertheless very helpful for the design of NIZK proof systems, is the hidden-bits model. In this model the common reference-string is uniformly selected as before, but only the prover can see all of it. The prover generates, along with a proof π, a subset I of indices in the CRS, and passes them both to the verifier. The verifier may only inspect the bits of the CRS that reside in the locations that have been specified by the prover in I, while all other bits of the CRS are hidden to the verifier.

Definition 9 *(NIZK in the Hidden-Bit Model [FLS90, Gol98]). For a bit-string s and an index set I denote by s_I the set of values of s in the indexes given by I: $s_I := \{(i, s[i]) : i \in I\}$. A pair of PPT algorithms (P, V) constitute an (efficient-prover) NIZK proof system for language $L \in NP$ with relation R_L in the* Hidden-Bit *(HB) Model if it provides:*

- ***Completeness:*** *for every $(x, w) \in R_L$ we have that:*

$$\Pr_{P,crs}[(\pi, I) \leftarrow P(x, w, crs); V(x, I, crs_I, \pi) = 0] \leq \mu(|x|)$$

where the probability is taken over the coins of P and the choice of the CRS as a uniformly random string, and $\mu(n)$ is some negligible function.
- ***Soundness:*** *for every $x \notin L$:*

$$\Pr_{crs}[\exists \pi, I : V(x, I, crs_I, \pi) = 1] \leq \mu(|x|)$$

where the probability is taken over the choice of the CRS as a uniformly random string, and $\mu(n)$ is some negligible function.
- ***Zero-Knowledge:*** *there exists a PPT algorithm S (simulator) such that the following two distribution ensembles are computationally indistinguishable:*
  - $\{(x, crs_I, \pi) : crs \leftarrow U, (\pi, I) \leftarrow P(x, w, crs)\}_{(x,w) \in R_L}$
  - $\{S(x)\}_{(x,w) \in R_L}$.

  Here U denotes the set of uniformly random strings of length polynomial in $|x|$.

While the hidden-bit model is an unrealistic one, its importance lies in two facts. Firstly, it provides a clean abstraction for NIZK systems, which facilities the design of "clean" proof systems. Efficient-prover NIZK proof systems for NP-hard languages exist unconditionally in the hidden-bit model [FLS90, Gol98]:

Theorem 1 *([FLS90]). There exists a NIZK proof system in the hidden-bit model for any NP language (unconditionally). Furthermore, the protocol is statistical zero-knowledge and statistically sound.*

Secondly, proof systems in the hidden-bit model can be easily transformed into proof systems in the more realistic CRS model, using general hardness assumptions. Feige, Lapidot and Shamir [FLS90] suggests such a transformation. In the rest of this section, we describe their construction and the details of the underlying hardness assumptions. We remark that in the hidden-bit model, we can obtain both perfect soundness (with a negligible completeness error) and perfect completeness (with a negligible soundness error).

From Hidden-Bit to CRS. The following is a review of the full details of the FLS protocol and the enhancement that followed to adapt it to general trapdoor permutations. This follows the historic line of research by [FLS90, BY96, Gol98, Gol11, GR13]. We refer the reader to [CL17] for a more comprehensive overview.

The FLS Protocol: Assuming the existence of one-way permutations, Feige, Lapidot and Shamir [FLS90] constructed a NIZK proof-system in the CRS model for any NP language. The key to this protocol is having the prover provide the verifier with pre-images of random images taken from the one-way permutation's range. They also offer an efficient implementation of the prescribed prover, using trapdoor permutations, which allow the prover to efficiently invert random images using the secret trapdoor key. We refer to this construction as the FLS protocol. The full details of this protocol are given in [FLS90].

Theorem 2 *([FLS90]). Assuming the existence of* ***one-way permutations****, there exists a NIZK proof system in the CRS model with an* ***inefficient prover*** *for any NP language.*

Theorem 3 *([FLS90]). Assuming the existence of an* ***ideal trapdoor permutation*** *family, there exists a NIZK proof system in the CRS model (with an efficient prover) for any NP language.*

As shown by [FLS90], the FLS protocol provides a NIZK proof system assuming that the underlying TDP is ideal. However, existing instantiations of TDPs are *not* ideal, and in fact are far from it. Most reasonable constructions of TDPs have both partial keysets and partial domains. This leads to two gaps which arise when using general TDPs, in place of ideal ones.

Ideal Domains + General Keys: The Bellare-Yung Protocol: The first hurdle, discovered by Bellare and Yung [BY96], involves the use of general trapdoor keys (rather than ideal ones). The problem is that the soundness of the FLS protocol relies on the feasibility of recognizing permutations in the collection. If the permutation is ideal then every key describes a permutation, and therefore detecting a permutation is trivial. However, existing instantiations of TDPs require sampling keys of a certain form using a specific protocol. This brings us to the problem of *certifying permutations*, which aims to answer the question of how to certify that a given key indeed describes a valid permutation. Bellare and Yung [BY96] suggested a certification procedure for permutations, assuming nothing of the keyset, but requiring that the range remains full. We refer to this procedure as the Bellare-Yung protocol. In a nutshell, the prover in the Bellare-Yung protocol simply inverts random images taken from the CRS into their pre-images and presents the verifier with those pre-images. The verifier validates the pre-images. By having the prover inverts enough random pre-images, the verifier is convinced that only a negligible part of the range is non-invertitable, meaning the function is "almost" injective. [BY96] show that this property of almost-injectivity is strong enough for FLS.

Theorem 4 *([BY96]). Assuming the existence of a* ***full-domain trapdoor permutation*** *family (whose keys may be hard to recognize), there exists a NIZK proof system in the CRS model for any NP language (with an efficient prover).*

General Domains: Doubly Enhanced TDPs: The second gap concerns the case of partial domains, where the function's domain is comprised of elements of specific structure (and not just $\{0,1\}^n$). The FLS protocol treats the CRS as a sequence of range elements. In the case of the general abstraction of trapdoor permutations, an additional domain sampling algorithm is required. This problem is solved by requiring the use of doubly enhanced trapdoor permutations. Given the permutation index α, both the prover and the verifier use the enhanced sampling algorithm $S_R(\alpha)$ to sample elements from the permutation's range. They treat the CRS as a sequence $r_1, ..., r_l$, where each $r_l \in \{0,1\}^n$ is handled as random coins for the range sampler. They create a list of range items $y_i = S_R(\alpha; r_i)$ and use them for the rest of the FLS protocol. Using the range sampler solves the completeness issue of NIZK in the CRS model for permutations with general domains. However, the resulting protocol may no longer be zero-knowledge, as the verifier now obtains a list of random pairs (x_i, r_i) such that $f_\alpha(x_i) = S_\alpha(r_i)$, but it is not clear that it could have generated such pairs itself. The two enhancements solve just that, and allow the verifier to obtain such pairs on its own.

Theorem 5 *([GR13]). Assuming the existence of a general* ***doubly-enhanced trapdoor permutation*** *family with* ***efficiently recognizable keys****, there exists a NIZK proof system in the CRS model for any NP language (with an efficient prover).*

Moreover, in order to certify general keys, [Gol11, GR13] suggested combining between doubly enhanced permutations and the Bellare-Yung protocol, by using the doubly-enhanced domain sampler to sample images by the Bellare-Yung prover and verifier. We reexamine this suggestion in Sect. 3.

Basing FLS on Injective Trapdoor Functions: Before moving on, we mention that while the FLS protocol is originally described using (trapdoor) permutations, it may just as well be described and implemented using general injective trapdoor functions. In this case, since the CRS is used to generate range elements, there is no useful notion of "ideal" injective trapdoor functions; if f maps n-bit strings into m-bit strings, where $m > n$, then there must exists some m-bit strings which do not have a pre-image under f. However, using a doubly-enhanced general injective trapdoor function, the FLS protocol and the generalization into general TDPs will work without any changes, under assuming the keys are efficiently recognizable. In Sect. 5 we show an example for such a injective TDF and it's application to NIZK proof systems.

3 FLS with General Doubly Enhanced TDPs Is Unsound

We begin with a careful reexamination of the FLS protocol, in light of the work of [Gol11, GR13]. We discuss a crucial problem yet to be detected when applying the

Bellare-Yung protocol on general TDPs, which have both partial domains and partial keysets. Specifically, we identify that the soundness of the FLS protocol may be compromised when using such trapdoor functions.

3.1 The Counter Example

In preparation to describing the counter example, we first sketch the full details of the Bellare-Yung protocol, while allowing both partial range and partial keyset for the TDPs, as suggested by [GR13]. Recall that we are provided with a doubly-enhanced TDP family, described using the algorithms $I(1^n) \rightarrow (\alpha, \tau), F(\alpha, x) \rightarrow y, B(\tau, y) \rightarrow x, S(\alpha; r) \rightarrow y$. We treat the CRS as a sequence of random coins for the sampler S, and apply S both on the prover and on the verifier side to obtain range elements.

- Input: $(\alpha, \tau) \leftarrow I(1^n)$
- CRS: a sequence of l random strings $r_1, ..., r_l$, each acts as random coins for S.
- Prover: is given (α, τ) and does the following:
  1. Calculate $y_i := S(\alpha; r_i)$ for each $1 \leq i \leq l$.
  2. Calculate $x_i := B(\tau, y_i)$ for each $1 \leq i \leq l$.
  3. Output $\{(i, x_i) : 1 \leq i \leq l\}$
- Verifier: is given α and $\{(i, x_i) : 1 \leq i \leq l\}$, and does the following
  1. Calculate $y_i := S(\alpha; r_i)$ for each $1 \leq i \leq l$.
  2. Validate that $y_i = F(\alpha, x_i)$ for each $1 \leq i \leq l$. If any of the validations fail, reject the proof. Otherwise, accept it.

Looking into the details of the protocol, we detect a potential problem. We demonstrate it by instantiating the FLS+BY protocols using a specific family of doubly-enhanced trapdoor permutations, which was proposed by [BPW16]:

Let PRF_k be a pseudorandom function family, and iO an indistinguishability obfuscator. Let C_k be the circuit that, on input (i, t), if $t = PRF_k(i)$ outputs $(i+1, PRF_k(i+1))$ (where $i+1$ is computed modulo some T) and otherwise outputs $\perp$. Denote by $\tilde{C} := iO(C_k)$ the obfuscation of C_k. The BPW construction gives a DETDP F where $\tilde{C}$ is the public permutation index, and k is the trapdoor. To evaluate the permutation on a domain element $(i, PRF_k(i))$, just apply $\tilde{C}$. To invert $(i+1, PRF_k(i+1))$ given k, return $(i, PRF_k(i))$. The range sampler is given as an obfuscation of a circuit which samples out of a (sparse) subset of the function's range. One-wayness holds due to a hybrid puncturing argument: the obfuscation of the cycle $(i, PRF_k(i)) \rightarrow (i+1, PRF_k(i+1))$ (where $i+1$ is computed module T) is indistinguishable from that of the same cycle when punctured on a single spot i^*, by replacing the edge $(i^*, PRF_k(i^*)) \rightarrow (i^* + 1, PRF_k(i^*+1))$ with a self loop from $(i^*, PRF_k(i^*))$ to itself. By repeating the self-loops technique we obtain a punctured obfuscated cycle where arriving from

$(i, PRF_k(i))$ to its predecessor $(i-1, PRF_k(i-1))$ cannot be done efficiently without knowing k itself.[2]

Suppose that the [BPW16] construction is used to instantiate the FLS+BY protocols, and consider the following malicious prover: Let C'_k be a circuit which, given input (i,t), does the following: if $t = PRF_k(i)$ or $t = PRF_k(i-1)$, output $(i+1, PRF_k(i+1))$. Otherwise, output $\perp$. Denote $\tilde{C}' := iO(C'_k)$. We give out $\tilde{C}'$ as the public key and keep k as the trapdoor. We keep the domain sampler as it is, that is, it returns only items of the form $(i, PRF_k(i))$.

Denote $D_k = \{(i, PRF_k(i) : i \in [1...T])\}$ and $\tilde{D}_k = \{(i, PRF_k(i)) : i \in [1...T]\} \cup (i, PRF_k(i-1)) : i \in [1...T]\}$. It is easy to see that C'_k is a permutation when restricted to the domain D_k, but it is many-to-one when evaluated on the domain $\tilde{D}_k$: each item $(i+1, PRF_k(i+1)) \in D_k$ has 2 pre-images: $(i, PRF_k(i))$ and $(i, PRF_k(i-1))$. Note that the one-wayness of the trapdoor function is maintained even when extended to the domain $\tilde{D}_k$: For each image $(i+1, PRF_k(i+1))$ we now have two pre-images, one is $(i, PRF_k(i))$ which is hard to invert to due to the same puncturing argument as in the original BPW paper, and the second is $(i, PRF_k(i-1))$ which has no pre-image of its own, and therefore no path on the cycle can lead to it (keeping the same one-wayness argument intact).

Finally, our cheating prover can wrongly "certify" the function as a permutation. The domain sampler will always give an image in D_k as it was not altered. During the Bellare-Yung certification protocol, the prover can invert $y = (i+1, PRF_k(i+1)) \in D_k$ to, say, $(i, PRF_k(i))$, which will pass the validation. However, during the FLS protocol, the prover can choose to invert any $y \in D_k$ to one of its two distinct pre-images, one from D_k and another from $\tilde{D}_k \setminus D_k$, which breaks the soundness of the protocol. (Indeed, for natural hard-core predicates of F the predicate values for the two preimages associated with a random i are close to being statistically independent).

3.2 Discussion

We attribute the loss in soundness when applying the FLS+BY combination on the [BPW16] construction to a few major issues.

First, we observe that both the sampling and forward evaluation algorithms are required to operate even on illegitimate keys. However, the basic definition of trapdoor permutations (c.f. [Gol98]) does not address this case at all. Ignoring this case may make sense in settings where the party generating the index is trusted, but this is not so in the case of NIZK proof systems. We therefore generalize the basic definition of trapdoor permutations so that the forward

[2] In order to add an enhanced domain sampler, the BPW construction returns elements of the form $(PRG(r), PRF_k(PRG(r)))$, where PRG is a pseudorandom generator which lengthens the input by a significant factor. The domain sampler is just an obfuscation of a circuit which outputs the above pair on some random r. By augmenting the sampler even more, they were able to doubly-enhance their TDP, at the cost of creating a very sparse part of the domain which is sampleable. We leave the rest of the details to the reader.

evaluation and domain sampling definitions generalize to any α, rather than just those which were generated by running the index-generation algorithm. That is, for every α, D_α is some domain over which $F(\alpha, \cdot)$ is well defined, and $S(\alpha; r)$ returns elements from that domain.

We next claim that in order for the soundness of the complete FLS+BY protocol to be preserved, two additional requirements are needed: First, membership in D_α should be efficiently recognizable given α. That is, there should exist a polynomial-time algorithm which, given α and some string x, decides if x represents an element in D_α or not. Second, the domain sampler S should be guaranteed to sample (almost) uniformly out of D_α. We stress that both these requirements should hold with respect to *any* index α, in particular indices that were not generated truthfully. Furthermore, they are made *on top of* the existing requirements from doubly-enhanced trapdoor permutations.

We call doubly enhanced trapdoor permutations that have these properties *public domain*. We formalize this notion in Definition 13 and prove that it indeed suffices for regaining the soundness of the FLS+BY combination in Theorem 7 (see Sect. 4.3).

In the rest of this section, we show that these two requirements are indeed necessary, by demonstrating that if either of the two do not hold then the resulting proof system is not sound.

First, consider the case where S's sampling distribution is non-negligibly far from uniform over D_α. The soundness of Bellare-Yung depends on the observation that if the function is not an almost-permutation, then by sampling enough random images from the function's domain, there must be a sample with cannot be inverted (with all but negligible probability). However, if the sampler does not guarantee uniformity this claim no longer holds, as the prover may give out a sampler which samples only out of that portion of the range which is invertible.

Secondly, assume S indeed samples uniformly from the domain, and consider the case where D_α is not efficiently recognizable. As it turns out, both the Bellare-Yung protocol and the original FLS protocol require the verifier to determine whether pre-images provided by the prover are indeed in D_α. Otherwise, a malicious prover could certify the permutation under a specific domain, but later provide pre-images taken out of an entirely different domain, thus enabling it to invert some images to two or more pre-images of its choice.

Indeed, the attack described in Sect. 3.1 takes advantage of the loophole resulting from the fact that the domain of the [BPW16] is neither efficiently recognizable nor efficiently sampleable. The exact reason for the failure depends on how the domain of [BPW16] is defined with respect to illegitimate indices. Say for $\alpha = \tilde{C}$, we give out D_α which includes only pairs (i, x) such that $x = PRF_k(i)$ (for the specific k used to construct $\tilde{C}$). In that case, S indeed samples uniformly from D_α. However since D_α is not efficiently recognizable, the prover cannot check that the pre-image it was given is from D_α. In particular it cannot tell if it is from $D_k = D_\alpha$ or from $\tilde{D}_k$. On the other hand, if $D_\alpha = \{0,1\}^*$, then D_α may be trivially recognizable for any index, but S does not guarantee a uniform sample from D_α. Indeed, S may sample only from that subset of D_α which is invertible, thus breaking the soundness.

4 Certifying Injectivity of Trapdoor Functions

We go back to the original problem of certifying permutations in a way that is sufficient for the FLS protocol, while addressing the more general problem of certifying injectivity of trapdoor functions (which may or may not be permutations). We note that although this problem is motivated by the need to fill in the gaps in the FLS protocol, a solution for it might be interesting on its own.

In Sect. 4.1 we define the notion of *Certifiable Injectivity* as a general abstraction of certifiability for doubly-enhanced injective trapdoor functions. In Sect. 4.2 we prove that this notion indeed suffices for regaining the soundness of the FLS protocol. In Sect. 4.3 we show how certifiable injectivity can be realized by any trapdoor permutations whose domain provides certain additional properties, by using the Bellare-Yung certification protocol. In Sect. 4.4 we suggest the notion of *Perfectly Certifiable Injectivity* as a specific variant of certifiable injectivity, where there is no longer need for a certification protocol and the resulting soundness is optimal.

4.1 Certifiable Injectivity - Definition

We define a general notion of certifiability for injective trapdoor functions, which requires the existence of a general prover and verifier protocol for the function family. The verifier in our notion provides two levels of verification: a general verification procedure V for an index α, and then a pointwise certification procedure $ICert$ which, on index α and an image y, "certifies" that with all but negligible probability y has only one pre-image under α. The purpose of this protocol is to guarantee that if the verifier accepts the proof given by the prover on a certain index α, then with all but negligible probability (over the coins of the range sampler), the range sampler cannot sample images which are certified by $ICert$ and can be inverted to any two pre-images. We note that this certification must not assume recognizability of the domain.

Definition 10 *(Certifiable Injective Trapdoor Functions (CITDFs)). Let $\mathcal{F} = \{f_\alpha : D_\alpha \to R_\alpha\}$ be a collection of doubly enhanced injective trapdoor functions, given by way of algorithms I, F, B, S_D, S_R. We say that F is certifiably injective (in the common reference string model) if there exists a polynomial-time algorithm $ICert$ and a pair of PPT algorithms (P, V), which provides the following properties:*

- ***Completeness:*** *for any $(\alpha, \tau) \leftarrow I(1^n)$ we have:*
  1. $\Pr_{P,V,crs}[\pi \leftarrow P(\alpha, \tau, crs); V(\alpha, crs, \pi) = 1] = 1$, *where the probability is taken over the coins of P and V and the choice of the CRS, and*
  2. *For any $x \in D_\alpha$, $ICert(\alpha, x) = 1$.*

- ***Soundness:*** *there exists a negligible function* μ *such that the following holds for any* $\alpha \in \{0,1\}^*$:

$$\Pr_{crs,V,r}[\exists \pi, x_1 \neq x_2 \in \{0,1\}^* : V(\alpha, crs, \pi) = 1, F(\alpha, x_1) = F(\alpha, x_2) = S_R(\alpha; r), ICert(\alpha, x_1) = ICert(\alpha, x_2) = 1] \leq \mu(n)$$

where the probability is taken over the coins of V *the choice of the CRS, and the random coins given to the range sampler. Note that this must hold for any* α*, including those that* I *cannot output, and that* π *can be chosen adaptively given the common reference string.*
- ***Enhanced Hardness (even) given the Proof:*** *for any polynomial-time algorithm* A *there exists a negligible function* μ*, such that the following holds*

$$\Pr_{P,crs,r}[(\alpha, \tau) \leftarrow I(1^n); \pi \leftarrow P(\alpha, \tau, crs); x \leftarrow A(\alpha, r, crs, \pi); F(\alpha, x) = S_R(\alpha; r)] \leq \mu(n)$$

where the probability is taken over the coins of P*, the choice of the CRS and the randomness* r *for the range sampler.*

Certifiable injectivity gives a general way to certify that a given key describes an injective function, even when using general, partial-domain/range functions. The proof generated by P and verified by F is used to certify that the given key α is indeed injective, in the sense that if V accepts it then no two acceptable pre-images can map to the same image (with all but negligible probability). Note that our hardness condition only requires that inversion remains hard. Partial information on the preimage x can be leaked, and there is no "zero-knowledge-like" property.

4.2 Certifiable Injectivity Suffices for the Soundness of FLS

Our key theorem, stated next, shows how combining certifiable injectivity with the FLS protocol and doubly-enhanced permutations, we overcome the existing problems and obtain NIZK for NP from general permutations.

Theorem 6 *(DECITDFs → NIZK). Assuming the existence of doubly-enhanced, certifiably injective trapdoor functions, there exists a NIZK proof system in the CRS model for any NP language.*

Proof Sketch: We adapt the FLS protocol in an intuitive way: given a DECITDF, we treat the CRS as two separate strings. The first string is used to certify the injectivity of the trapdoor function, using the CI-prover and verifier, while the second is used for the FLS protocol. Moreover, we adapt the verifier part of the FLS protocol to pointwise-certify any pre-image presented to it by running $ICert$ on it. The soundness guarantee of CI notion ensures that a malicious prover must choose a trapdoor index which describes an injective (or at least an almost-injective) function over the domain of elements accepted by $ICert$, or otherwise the CI verifier would reject the first part of the proof. The hardness guarantee ensures that the FLS proof remains zero-knowledge, even in the presence of the CI proof.

Proof Let $\mathcal{F} = \{f_\alpha : D_\alpha \to R_\alpha\}$ be a collection of doubly-enhanced, certifiably injective trapdoor functions, and let L be an NP language.

We extend the definition of enhanced hard-core predicates to hold with respect to the CI proof (as well as the index):

Definition 11 *(CI-Enhanced Hard-Core Predicate). Let $\mathcal{F} = \{f_\alpha\}$ be a collection of doubly-enhanced certifiably injective trapdoor functions, with P being a CI-prover for it and S_R the enhanced range sampler. We say that the predicate p is a CI-enhanced hard-core predicate of f_α if it is efficiently computable, and for any PPT adversary A there exists a negligible function μ such that*

$$\Pr_{crs}[(\alpha,\tau) \leftarrow I(1^n); \pi \leftarrow P(\alpha,\tau,crs); r \leftarrow \{0,1\}^n; \\ A(\alpha,crs,\pi,r) = p(\alpha, f_\alpha^{-1}(S_R(\alpha;r)))] \leq 1/2 + \mu(n)$$

Similarly to (plain) enhanced hard-core predicates, this definition is unconditionally realizable for any doubly-enhanced certifiably injective TDF (e.g. using the [GL89] hard-core predicate, which does not use the function index).

Recall that by Theorem 1, there exists a hidden-bit-model proof system for L, denote it (P_{HB}, V_{HB}). Let p be a CI-enhanced hard-core predicate for f_α.

We treat the common reference string as two separate substrings c_{CI}, c_{FLS}. c_{CI} will be used by the CI-prover and CI-verifier (P_{CI}, V_{CI}) for F. c_{FLS} will be used by the prover-verifier pair from the FLS protocol, which is adapted to the use of doubly-enhanced trapdoor functions (based on the adaptation suggested by [Gol11]).

Let (P, V) be the following protocol:

- The prover P: given an instance-witness pair $(x, w) \in R_L$:
  1. Selects $(\alpha,\tau) \leftarrow I(1^n)$.
  2. Invoke $P_{CI}(\alpha,\tau,c_{CI})$ to obtain a proof π_{CI} for the injectivity of f_α.
  3. Treat c_{FLS} as a sequence of random strings $r_1, ..., r_l$, where each r_i is of length needed for the random coins for S_R (which is polynomial in n). For $i = 1, ..., l$, let $y_i = S_R(\alpha; r_i)$, $x_i = B(\tau, y_i)$, and $\sigma_i = p(x_i)$.
  4. Invoke P_{HB} on $\sigma = (\sigma_1, ..., \sigma_l)$, to obtain (I, π_{HB}) - I is a list of indices to reveal, and π_{HB} is the hidden-bit-model proof. Let π_{FLS} be the pair $(\pi_{HB}, \{(i, x_i) : i \in I\})$.
  5. Output $(\alpha, \pi_{CI}, \pi_{FLS})$.
- The verifier V: given an instance x and a proof $(\alpha, \pi_{CI}, \pi_{FLS})$:
  1. Invoke $V_{CI}(\alpha, c_{CI}, \pi_{CI})$ to check the proof π_{CI} for the injectivity of f_α. If the validation failed, reject the proof.
  2. $\pi_{FLS} := (\pi_{HB}, \{(i, x_i) : i \in I\})$. Treat c_{FLS} as a sequence of random strings $r_1, ..., r_m$.

3. Check that, for every $i \in I$, $y_i := S_R(\alpha; r_i) = F(\alpha, x_i)$ *and* $ICert(\alpha, x_i)$ accepts. If any of the validations failed, reject the proof.
4. Let $\sigma_i = p(x_i)$ for all $i \in I$. Let $\sigma_I = (i, \sigma_i)_{i \in I}$. Invoke V_{HB} on x, σ_I, π_{HB}, and accepts if and only if it accepts.

We next prove that (P, V) provide a NIZK proof system for L in the CRS model.

Completeness follows immediately from the completeness of the CI notion and of the FLS protocol.

For **Soundness**, we follow the line of [BY96], of bounding the extra error in soundness induced when the trapdoor function is not a permutation, adapting it to the notion of DECITDFs:

Definition 12. *Let* $\mathcal{F} = \{f_\alpha : \{0,1\}^m \to \{0,1\}^n\}$ *be a DECITDF family. The* Certified Collision Set *of an index* α *is the set of all* n*-bit strings which have more than one* certified *pre-image under* f_α*:*

$$CIC(\alpha) := \{y \in \{0,1\}^n : \exists x_1 \neq x_2 \in \{0,1\}^m \ s.t. \ f_\alpha(x_1) = f_\alpha(x_2) = y \\ and ICert(\alpha, x_1) = ICert(\alpha, x_2) = 1\} \tag{4}$$

We say that f_α *is (certified) almost-injective if* $|CIC(\alpha)|$ *is negligible.*

Lemma 1. *Let* F *be a DECITDF family with a CI verifier* V_{CI}*, and let* α *be some index such that* f_α *is not (certified) almost-injective. Then* $\Pr_{crs,V}[\exists \pi : V_{CI}(\alpha, crs, \pi) = 1] \leq \mu(n)$ *for some negligible function* μ*, where the probability is taken over the choice of the crs and the random coins of* V*.*

Proof. Follows directly from the soundness condition of Definition 10.

Next, suppose $x \notin L$, and let $(\alpha, \pi_{CI}, \pi_{FLS})$ be some proof given to V. We split our proof to cases:

- f_α is not (certified) almost-injective: then by Lemma 1, $V_{CI}(\alpha, crs, \pi)$ rejects with all but negligible probability.
- f_α is (certified) almost-injective. As shown by [FLS90], if $y_i \notin CIC(\alpha)$ for all $i = 1, ..., l$, then V_{HB} rejects the proof on x with all but negligible probability. This is so because on every presumed pre-image x_i presented to it by the prover, the verifier checks that $f_\alpha(x_i) = y_i$ and $ICert(\alpha, x_i) = 1$. As $y_i \notin CIC(\alpha)$, there can only exists one pre-image x_i that passes both certifications, thus each hidden-bit can be opened into only one certified pre-image, preserving the soundness of the underlying hidden-bit proof. Finally, we bound the additional error induced by the case where $y_i \in CIC(\alpha)$ for some i, by $\Pr[\exists 1 \leq i \leq l : y_i \in CIC(\alpha)]$. By our assumption, $|CIC(\alpha)|$ is negligible in n, thus the additional error is negligible as well.

This completes the proof of the soundness condition.

For **Zero Knowledge**, we follow the zero-knowledge proof given in [Gol11]. The proof is given using a hybrid argument, based on the security of the doubly-enhanced injective trapdoor function, and while handling the issue of additionally simulating the certifiable injectivity proof. We refer the reader to [CL17] for the full details of the zero-knowledge condition.

This completes the proof of Theorem 6.

4.3 Certifiable Injectivity for Public-Domain TDPs Using Bellare-Yung

Building on the discussion in Sect. 3.2, we formalize the notion of *public-domain* trapdoor permutations. We then show that, when applied to public-domain permutation, the BY certification mechanism suffices for guaranteeing Certifiably Injectivity (and, thus, also soundness of the FLS paradigm).

Definition 13 *(Public-Domain Trapdoor Permutations). Let $f_\alpha : \{D_\alpha \to D_\alpha\}$ be a trapdoor permutation family, given by (I, S, F, B). We say that it is public-domain if the following two additional properties hold:*

- **The domain is efficiently recognizable:** *that is, there exists an polynomial-time algorithm Rec which, for any index α and any string $x \in \{0,1\}^*$, accepts on (α, x) if and only if $x \in D_\alpha$. In other words, D_α is defined as the set of all strings x such that $Rec(\alpha, x)$ accepts.*
- **The domain is efficiently sampleable:** *that is, for any index α, $S(\alpha)$ samples almost uniformly from D_α.*

We stress that both properties should hold with respect to any α, including ones that were not generated by running I.

We show that indeed, for the case of public-domain doubly-enhanced trapdoor permutations, Bellare-Yung can be used to obtain certifiable injectiveness.

Theorem 7. *Any doubly-enhanced public-domain trapdoor permutation family is certifiably injective.*

Proof. Let F be a doubly enhanced public-domain trapdoor permutation. Let (P, V) the prover and verifier from the enhanced Bellare-Yung protocol for F, that is, the version of Bellare-Yung that uses the enhanced range sampler to generate images from the random coins given in the common reference string, as described in Sect. 3.1. Let *Rec* be a polynomial-time domain recognizer for D_α, for any index α (which exists since the permutation family is public-domain). We claim that F is certifiably injective, with $ICert(\alpha, x) = Rec(\alpha, x)$ and (P, V) giving the CI prover and verifier.

Completeness follows immediately from that of Bellare-Yung. The hardness-given-the-proof requirement follows from the Bellare-Yung protocol providing zero-knowledge secrecy, which implies an even stronger guarantee. For soundness, we note that if $\Pr_r[\exists x_1 \neq x_2 \in \{0,1\}^* : F(\alpha, x_1) = F(\alpha, x_2) = S_R(\alpha; r), ICert(\alpha, x_1) = ICert(\alpha, x_2) = 1]$ is non-negligible, then by definition

$F(\alpha, \cdot)$ is not almost-injective over D_α. As shown by [BY96], this implies that the verifier will reject any proof with all but negligible probability, which implies our soundness requirement.

We note that some existing candidate constructions, such as ones on the line of [BPW16], are not public-domain, as they inherently need the sampling algorithm to hold secrets. Indeed, as demonstrated in Sect. 3, Bellare-Yung does not suffice to guarantee soundness when instantiating FLS with such a candidate. On the other hand, the RSA TDPs are public-domain: the domain Z_N^* is indeed efficiently recognizable for any public index N, and a PPT certifiably uniform domain sampler can be described for any public key N of RSA, by mapping strings in $\{0,1\}^n$ to Z_N^* in a way that obtains (almost) uniform samples in Z_N^*.[3] For those constructions the FLS+BY combination is indeed sound.

4.4 Perfectly Certifiable Injectivity

While certifiable injectivity seems to capture the minimal requirement for a trapdoor permutation that suffices for FLS, the requirement of a prover and verifier algorithms are somewhat cumbersome when viewed purely in the context of trapdoor permutations. We thus suggest a strengthened notion of Perfectly Certifiable Injectivity, which is a variant of certifiable injectivity in which the pointwise certification algorithm $ICert$ provides a stronger guarantee, eliminating the need for an additional prover-verifier protocol.

Definition 14 *(Perfectly Certifiable Injective TDFs). A doubly-enhanced injective TDF family is perfectly certifiable injective if, in addition to the standard set of algorithms I, S_D, S_R, F, B, it defines a certification algorithm $ICert$.*

$ICert$ is given a permutation index α and a pre-image x, and accepts or rejects, providing the following two guarantees:

- ***Completeness:** If $\alpha \leftarrow I_0(1^n)$ and $x \leftarrow S_D(\alpha)$ then $ICert(\alpha, x) = 1$.*
- **Perfect Soundness:** *For any index α, there do not exist any $x_1 \neq x_2 \in \{0,1\}^*$ such that $F(\alpha, x_1) = F(\alpha, x_2)$ and $ICert(\alpha, x_1) = ICert(\alpha, x_2) = 1$. Note that α needs not be generated honestly by I.*

The standard hardness condition is required as usual (and must apply even in the presence of $ICert$).

Perfect CI is a special case of general CI, where the soundness of $ICert$ is absolute; for any α, x_1, if $ICert(\alpha, x_1) = 1$ then it is guaranteed that there exists no second pre-image x_2 which maps to $F(\alpha, x_1)$ and accepted by $ICert(\alpha, \cdot)$. It turns out that in the specific case where the trapdoor function family in use is perfectly certifiable injective with, the index certification protocol can

[3] Full details can be found in [BY96] and [GR13], appendix B.

be completely avoided. Indeed, the soundness requirement of Definition 10 is trivially fulfilled, as:

$$\Pr_r[\exists x_1, x_2 : F(\alpha, x_1) = F(\alpha, x_2) = S_R(\alpha; r), ICert(\alpha, x_1) = ICert(\alpha, x_2) = 1] = 0$$

An important property of this technique is that the soundness it provides is perfect, in that it is identical to the soundness obtained by using ideal trapdoor permutations. No additional error is incurred, since for every image there exists a single acceptable pre-image (unconditionally).

5 Doubly Enhanced Perfectly Certifiable Injective Trapdoor Functions from iO+

We construct doubly-enhanced injective trapdoor functions using iO + pseudorandom generators (which can be constructed from one way functions). Additionally, assuming the pseudorandom generator is injective, we show that the injectivity of our construction is perfectly certifiable. Using the additional certification procedure, our construction suffices for general NIZK proofs for NP-languages. This construction is motivated by the [SW14] CPA-secure public key encryption system.

For simplicity, in Sects. 5.1, 5.2 and 5.3, we assume that the PRGs and PPRFs being used by our construction are *full domain*; that is, every string in $\{0,1\}^{p(n)}$ (for some $p(n)$ polynomial in the security parameter n), can be mapped to a pre-image of the function. This assumption makes sense in the context of general pseudorandom generators and puncturable pseudorandom functions, where natural full-domain candidates exist (c.f. [GGM86]). However this is not the case for *injective* PRGs, which are required for our certifiable injectivity proof. In Sect. 5.4 we show how this assumption can be relaxed, by allowing injective PRGs with a domain which is efficiently sampleable and recognizable. We additionally demonstrate how these requirements can be realized by existing candidates.

5.1 Construction

Let g be an n-to-$2n$ bits PRG, d be a $n/2$-to-n PRG, $\{f_k : \{0,1\}^{2n} \rightarrow \{0,1\}^n\}_{k\in K}$ and $\{h_w : \{0,1\}^n \rightarrow \{0,1\}^n\}_{w\in W}$ puncturable PRF families, and iO an indistinguishability obfuscation scheme.

Let $T_k, S_{k,w}$ and Q_w be the following circuits:

$T_k(x)$: (Forward evaluator)
constants:
  puncturable PRF key k
$t = g(x)$
$s = f_k(t)$
return $(x \oplus s,\ t)$

$S_{k,w}(r)$: (Range Sampler)
constants:
  puncturable PRF key k for f
  puncturable PRF key w for h
$x = h_w(r)$
return $T_k(x)$

```
Q_w(ρ): (Correlated Pre-Image Sampler)
    constants:
        puncturable PRF keys w for h
    r  =  d(ρ)
    x  =  h_w(r)
    return (x, r)
```

We define our injective TDF in the following way:

- $I(1^n)$: Choose $k \leftarrow K$ as a PRF key for f, and $w \leftarrow W$ as a PRF key for h. Denote $\tilde{T} := iO(T_k)$, $\tilde{S} := iO(S_{k,w})$, $\tilde{Q} := iO(Q_w)$. Output $\alpha := (\tilde{T}, \tilde{S}, \tilde{Q})$ as the public TDP index, and $\tau := k$ as the trapdoor.
- $F(\alpha = (\tilde{T}, \tilde{S}, \tilde{Q}), x \in \{0,1\}^n)$: output $\tilde{T}(x)$.
- $B(\tau = k, y = (c \in \{0,1\}^n, t \in \{0,1\}^{2n}))$: output $c \oplus f_k(t)$.
- $S_D(\alpha = (\tilde{T}, \tilde{S}, \tilde{Q}), r \in \{0,1\}^n)$: output r.
- $S_R(\alpha = (\tilde{T}, \tilde{S}, \tilde{Q}), r \in \{0,1\}^n)$: output $\tilde{S}(r)$.

Motivation: $\tilde{T} = iO(T_k)$ is used as the forward evaluation algorithm, with the secret key k used to invert it. $\tilde{S} = iO(S_{k,w})$ is used as a range sampler providing the first enhancement, with h_w being used to re-randomize the random coins provided to in to create a secret pre-image. $\tilde{Q} = iO(Q_w)$ will be used to provide the second enhancement, using yet another round of re-randomization on the coins provided to it.

An interesting point about our construction is that both enhancements do not depend at all on the structure of the TDF itself. In fact, all the enhancements need in order to work is any full-domain, or even efficiently sampleable domain, TDF, and the proof remains the same. Hence, our technique of re-randomizing the input via a length-preserving PRF can be considered as a generic method for doubly-enhancing any efficiently-sampleable-domain TDF, using iO and one-way functions.

5.2 Completeness, Hardness and Enhancements

Theorem 8. *The function family described using (I, F, B, S_D, S_R) gives a doubly-enhanced injective trapdoor function family.*

Proof Sketch: using a hybrid argument, we reduce the hardness of inverting F to the (1) security of the iO scheme, (2) the selective security of a punctured PRF key at the punctured point, and (3) the pseudorandomness of the PRG g. The enhancements are shown using a similar argument. We refer the reader to [CL17] for the full details of this proof.

5.3 Certifiable Injectivity

We show that our construction is perfectly certifiable injective, under the assumption that the PRG g is injective. Moreover, the soundness of the certification protocol is perfect. This shows that our construction is sufficient for realizing the FLS paradigm.

Recall that, on input x, our TDF evaluation returns $(x \oplus s, t)$, where $t = g(x)$ (and s is determined by the secret trapdoor). The certifier $ICert$ is given x, obtains $y = F(\alpha, x)$, and compares the last $2n$ bits of y to $g(x)$. If they are equal, $ICert$ accepts. Otherwise it rejects.

Theorem 9. *Assuming g is a full-domain injective PRG, our TDF family, along with $ICert$, is perfectly certifiable injective.*

Proof. For $y \in \{0,1\}^{3n}$, denote by $y[n+1:3n]$ the last $2n$ bits of y.

1. Completeness: if $y = F(\alpha, x)$ for an honestly created α, then by the definition of our TDF we have $y = (c, t)$ for $t = g(x)$ and $c = x \oplus f_k(t)$. So $y[n+1: 3n] = t = g(x)$ and $ICert$ accepts.
2. Soundness: Suppose x_1, x_2, y such that $F(\alpha, x_1) = F(\alpha, x_2) = y$ and $ICert(\alpha, x_1) = ICert(\alpha, x_2) = 1$. By definition, since $ICert(\alpha, x_i) = 1$ for both x_1 and x_2, we have that $g(x_1) = y[n+1 : 3n] = g(x_2)$. Since g is injective, this means $x_1 = x_2$.

The soundness, hardness and enhancements proofs for the TDF are not harmed, as $ICert$ does not depend on the private key k.

5.4 On the Assumption of Full-Domain iPRGs

As mentioned in the opening of Sect. 5, our construction and security proof rely on the assumption that the underlying PRGs and PPRFs are full-domain; That is, every string in $\{0,1\}^{p(n)}$ (for some $p(n)$ polynomial in the security parameter n) can be mapped to a pre-image of the function. This assumption makes sense in the case of general PRGs and PPRFs, where natural full-domain candidates exists. However this is not the case for injective PRGs, which are required for our certifiable injectivity proof.

We first note that for the completeness, security and enhancements, the full-domain assumption can be relaxed by allowing functions with an efficiently sampleable domain. The domain sampler is then used to map random coins, as well as the output of some of the primitives we use, into domain items.

Secondly, we show that the certifiable injectivity of our construction is maintained under the relaxed assumption of an injective PRG with a domain which is *efficiently recognizable* (as well as sampleable). That is, we require that there exists a polynomial-time global domain recognizer algorithm *Rec* which, given some string $x \in \{0,1\}^n$, decides if that string is in the domain or not, and g is injective over the set of all strings which *Rec* accepts. Assuming the existence of such a recognizer algorithm *Rec*, we modify $ICert$ such that given a supposed pre-image x, $ICert$ first runs $Rec(x)$. Only after, $ICert$ continues to compare the last $2n$ bits of $y = F(\alpha, x)$ to $g(x)$. It accepts only if both conditions passed. The CI soundness requirement follows directly.

We point out that the recognizable domain requirement is indeed necessary for certifiable injectivity. Without it, a malicious prover might be able to cheat using a similar attack to the one described in Sect. 3: the prover can give pre-images taken outside of the PRG's supposed domain, on which $ICert$ might arbitrarily accept, and the verifier won't be able to tell the difference.

Finally, we demonstrate how injective pseudorandom generators with efficiently recognizable and sampleable domains can be constructed based on standard assumptions. We suggest two alternatives; one using a black-box construction from another primitive (one-way permutations), and another based on specific algebraic structure (the DDH assumption).

iPRGs from OWPs: Assuming one-way permutations with an efficiently sampleable domain, an injective length-doubling pseudorandom generator can be obtained using the textbook construction (c.f. [Gol98]). That is, let owp be a one-way permutation over domain $D_n \subseteq \{0,1\}^n$, and let p be a hard-core predicate for it. Then $prg_1(x) = (owp(x), p(x))$ is a pseudorandom generator which is single-bit expending. For $i > 1$, let $prg_i(x) := prg_{i-1}(owp(x)), p(x)$ be the result of recursively applying prg_q on the first n bits of the output. Using a hybrid argument, $prg_n(x)$ is a injective length-doubling PRG. Constructing an injective pseudorandom generator from primitives weaker then one-way permutations remains an open question.[4]

For the certifiable injectivity of our TDP construction, we require that the PRG's domain, D_n, be efficiently recognizable. However when this is the case additional attention is required, since the first n bits of $prg_n(x)$ describe an element in that domain, and hence they are clearly distinguishable from just any n-bit string. We circumvent this issue by defining our PRG as pseudorandom with respect to $D_n \circ U_n := \{(x, s) : x \leftarrow D_n, s \leftarrow \{0,1\}^n\}$. That is, we adapt the security requirement of the PRG to the following: for any PPT adversary A, $\Pr[x \leftarrow D_n : A(prg_n(x)) = 1] - \Pr[x \leftarrow D_n, s \leftarrow \{0,1\}^n : A((x, s)) = 1] \leq \mu(n)$, where $\mu(n)$ is negligible. Under the revised definition, our security proof remains sound, with the change that when replacing $t^* = prg_n(x^*)$ with a random t^*, the replaced value is taken out of $D_n \circ U_n$ (instead of a random $2n$-bit string).

A one-way permutation with an efficiently recognizable domain can be obtained, e.g., based on the discrete log assumption.

iPRGs from DDH: Based on the DDH assumption [DH76], [Bon98] suggested the the following candidate for injective PRGs. Let $G_p = \{x^2 : x \in Z_p\}$, where p is a safe prime (that is $p = 2q + 1$ for some prime q). We define the following

---

[4] [Rud84, KSS00, MM11] give a black-box separation between one-way permutations and weaker primitives, such as one-way functions.

enumeration from G_q to Z_q (see e.g. [CS03,CFGP05]):

$$i(x) = \begin{cases} x & \text{if } 1 \leq x \leq q \\ p - x & \text{if } q + 2 \leq x \leq p \\ 0 & \text{otherwise} \end{cases}$$

Let g be a generator for G_p. For $a, b \in Z_q$, let:

$$prg(a, b) = i(g^a), i(g^b), i(g^{ab})$$

Then by the DDH assumption, prg is an injective pseudorandom generator from $Z_q^2 \to Z_q^3$. Using the same technique, an injective length-doubling PRG from $Z_q^3 \to Z_q^6$ can be constructed by using

$$prg(a, b, c) = i(g^a), i(g^b), i(g^c), i(g^{ab}), i(g^{ac}), i(g^{bc})$$

Acknowledgments. We thank Oded Goldreich and Ron Rothblum for their very useful comments.

References

[Abu13] Abusalah, H.: Generic instantiations of the hidden bits model for non-interactive zero-knowledge proofs for np. Master's thesis, RWTH-Aachen (2013)

[BFM88] Blum, M., Feldman, P., Micali, S.: Non-interactive zero-knowledge and its applications. In: Proceedings of the Twentieth Annual ACM Symposium on Theory of Computing, pp. 103–112. ACM (1988)

[BG84] Blum, M., Goldwasser, S.: An *Efficient* probabilistic public-key encryption scheme which hides all partial information. In: Blakley, G.R., Chaum, D. (eds.) CRYPTO 1984. LNCS, vol. 196, pp. 289–299. Springer, Heidelberg (1985). https://doi.org/10.1007/3-540-39568-7_23

[BG90] Bellare, M., Goldwasser, S.: New paradigms for digital signatures and message authentication based on non-interactive zero knowledge proofs. In: Brassard, G. (ed.) CRYPTO 1989. LNCS, vol. 435, pp. 194–211. Springer, New York (1990). https://doi.org/10.1007/0-387-34805-0_19

[BGI+01] Barak, B., Goldreich, O., Impagliazzo, R., Rudich, S., Sahai, A., Vadhan, S., Yang, K.: On the (im)possibility of obfuscating programs. In: Kilian, J. (ed.) CRYPTO 2001. LNCS, vol. 2139, pp. 1–18. Springer, Heidelberg (2001). https://doi.org/10.1007/3-540-44647-8_1

[BGI14] Boyle, E., Goldwasser, S., Ivan, I.: Functional signatures and pseudorandom functions. In: Krawczyk, H. (ed.) PKC 2014. LNCS, vol. 8383, pp. 501–519. Springer, Heidelberg (2014). https://doi.org/10.1007/978-3-642-54631-0_29

[BGRV09] Brakerski, Z., Goldwasser, S., Rothblum, G.N., Vaikuntanathan, V.: Weak verifiable random functions. In: Reingold, O. (ed.) TCC 2009. LNCS, vol. 5444, pp. 558–576. Springer, Heidelberg (2009). https://doi.org/10.1007/978-3-642-00457-5_33

[Bon98] Boneh, D.: The decision Diffie-Hellman problem. In: Buhler, J.P. (ed.) ANTS 1998. LNCS, vol. 1423, pp. 48–63. Springer, Heidelberg (1998). https://doi.org/10.1007/BFb0054851

[BP15] Bitansky, N., Paneth, O.: ZAPs and non-interactive witness indistinguishability from indistinguishability obfuscation. In: Dodis, Y., Nielsen, J.B. (eds.) TCC 2015. LNCS, vol. 9015, pp. 401–427. Springer, Heidelberg (2015). https://doi.org/10.1007/978-3-662-46497-7_16

[BPW16] Bitansky, N., Paneth, O., Wichs, D.: Perfect structure on the edge of chaos. In: Kushilevitz, E., Malkin, T. (eds.) TCC 2016. LNCS, vol. 9562, pp. 474–502. Springer, Heidelberg (2016). https://doi.org/10.1007/978-3-662-49096-9_20

[BSMP91] Blum, M., De Santis, A., Micali, S., Persiano, G.: Noninteractive zero-knowledge. SIAM J. Comput. **20**(6), 1084–1118 (1991)

[BW13] Boneh, D., Waters, B.: Constrained pseudorandom functions and their applications. In: Sako, K., Sarkar, P. (eds.) ASIACRYPT 2013. LNCS, vol. 8270, pp. 280–300. Springer, Heidelberg (2013). https://doi.org/10.1007/978-3-642-42045-0_15

[BY96] Bellare, M., Yung, M.: Certifying permutations: noninteractive zero-knowledge based on any trapdoor permutation. J. Cryptol. **9**(3), 149–166 (1996)

[CFGP05] Chevassut, O., Fouque, P.-A., Gaudry, P., Pointcheval, D.: Key derivation and randomness extraction. IACR Cryptology ePrint Archive 2005:61 (2005)

[CHK03] Canetti, R., Halevi, S., Katz, J.: A forward-secure public-key encryption scheme. In: Biham, E. (ed.) EUROCRYPT 2003. LNCS, vol. 2656, pp. 255–271. Springer, Heidelberg (2003). https://doi.org/10.1007/3-540-39200-9_16

[CL17] Canetti, R., Lichtenberg, A.: Certifying trapdoor permutations, revisited. Cryptology ePrint Archive, Report 2017/631 (2017). https://eprint.iacr.org/2017/631

[CS03] Cramer, R., Shoup, V.: Design and analysis of practical public-key encryption schemes secure against adaptive chosen ciphertext attack. SIAM J. Comput. **33**(1), 167–226 (2003)

[DH76] Diffie, W., Hellman, M.: New directions in cryptography. IEEE Trans. Inf. Theory **22**(6), 644–654 (1976)

[DN00] Dwork, C., Naor, M.: Zaps and their applications. In: Proceedings of 41st Annual Symposium on Foundations of Computer Science, pp. 283–293. IEEE (2000)

[EGL85] Even, S., Goldreich, O., Lempel, A.: A randomized protocol for signing contracts. Commun. ACM **28**(6), 637–647 (1985)

[FLS90] Feige, U., Lapidot, D., Shamir, A.: Multiple non-interactive zero knowledge proofs based on a single random string. In: Proceedings of 31st Annual Symposium on Foundations of Computer Science, pp. 308–317. IEEE (1990)

[GGM86] Goldreich, O., Goldwasser, S., Micali, S.: How to construct random functions. J. ACM (JACM) **33**(4), 792–807 (1986)

[GL89] Goldreich, O., Levin, L.A.: A hard-core predicate for all one-way functions. In: Proceedings of the Twenty-First Annual ACM Symposium on Theory of Computing, pp. 25–32. ACM (1989)

[GM84] Goldwasser, S., Micali, S.: Probabilistic encryption. J. Comput. Syst. Sci. **28**(2), 270–299 (1984)

[GO92] Goldwasser, S., Ostrovsky, R.: *Invariant* signatures and non-interactive zero-knowledge proofs are equivalent. In: Brickell, E.F. (ed.) CRYPTO 1992. LNCS, vol. 740, pp. 228–245. Springer, Heidelberg (1993). https://doi.org/10.1007/3-540-48071-4_16

[Gol98] Goldreich, O.: Foundation of cryptography, February 1995

[Gol04] Goldreich, O.: Foundations of Cryptography. Basic Applications, vol. 2 (2004)

[Gol08] Goldreich, O.: Computational complexity: a conceptual perspective. ACM SIGACT News **39**(3), 35–39 (2008)

[Gol11] Goldreich, O.: Basing non-interactive zero-knowledge on (enhanced) trapdoor permutations: the state of the art. In: Goldreich, O. (ed.) Studies in Complexity and Cryptography. Miscellanea on the Interplay between Randomness and Computation. LNCS, vol. 6650, pp. 406–421. Springer, Heidelberg (2011). https://doi.org/10.1007/978-3-642-22670-0_28

[GOS06] Groth, J., Ostrovsky, R., Sahai, A.: Perfect non-interactive zero knowledge for NP. In: Vaudenay, S. (ed.) EUROCRYPT 2006. LNCS, vol. 4004, pp. 339–358. Springer, Heidelberg (2006). https://doi.org/10.1007/11761679_21

[GOS12] Groth, J., Ostrovsky, R., Sahai, A.: New techniques for noninteractive zero-knowledge. J. ACM (JACM) **59**(3), 11 (2012)

[GR13] Goldreich, O., Rothblum, R.D.: Enhancements of trapdoor permutations. J. Cryptol. **26**(3), 484–512 (2013)

[GS08] Groth, J., Sahai, A.: Efficient non-interactive proof systems for bilinear groups. In: Smart, N. (ed.) EUROCRYPT 2008. LNCS, vol. 4965, pp. 415–432. Springer, Heidelberg (2008). https://doi.org/10.1007/978-3-540-78967-3_24

[KPTZ13] Kiayias, A., Papadopoulos, S., Triandopoulos, N., Zacharias, T.: Delegatable pseudorandom functions and applications. In: Proceedings of the 2013 ACM SIGSAC Conference on Computer & Communications Security, pp. 669–684. ACM (2013)

[KSS00] Kahn, J., Saks, M., Smyth, C.: A dual version of Reimer's inequality and a proof of Rudich's conjecture. In: Proceedings of 15th Annual IEEE Conference on Computational Complexity, pp. 98–103. IEEE (2000)

[MM11] Matsuda, T., Matsuura, K.: On black-box separations among injective one-way functions. In: Ishai, Y. (ed.) TCC 2011. LNCS, vol. 6597, pp. 597–614. Springer, Heidelberg (2011). https://doi.org/10.1007/978-3-642-19571-6_36

[Rab79] Rabin, M.O.: Digitalized signatures and public-key functions as intractable as factorization. Technical report, DTIC Document (1979)

[Rot10] Rothblum, R.: A taxonomy of enhanced trapdoor permutations. In: Electronic Colloquium on Computational Complexity (ECCC), vol. 17, p. 145 (2010)

[RSA78] Rivest, R.L., Shamir, A., Adleman, L.: A method for obtaining digital signatures and public-key cryptosystems. Commun. ACM **21**(2), 120–126 (1978)

[Rud84] Rudich, S.: Limits on the provable consequences of one-way functions. Ph.D. thesis, Wesleyan University (1984)

[SW14] Sahai, A., Waters, B.: How to use indistinguishability obfuscation: deniable encryption, and more. In: Proceedings of the Forty-Sixth Annual ACM Symposium on Theory of Computing, pp. 475–484. ACM (2014)

[Yao82] Yao, A.C.: Theory and application of trapdoor functions. In: 23rd Annual Symposium on Foundations of Computer Science, SFCS 2008, pp. 80–91. IEEE (1982)

On the Security Loss of Unique Signatures

Andrew Morgan[1(✉)] and Rafael Pass[2]

[1] Cornell University, Ithaca, USA
asmorgan@cs.cornell.edu
[2] Cornell Tech, New York City, USA
rafael@cornell.edu

Abstract. We consider the question of whether the security of unique digital signature schemes can be based on game-based cryptographic assumptions using *linear-preserving* black-box security reductions—that is, black-box reductions for which the security loss (i.e., the ratio between "work" of the adversary and the "work" of the reduction) is some *a priori* bounded polynomial. A seminal result by Coron (Eurocrypt'02) shows limitations of such reductions; however, his impossibility result and its subsequent extensions all suffer from two notable restrictions: (1) they only rule out so-called "simple" reductions, where the reduction is restricted to only *sequentially* invoke "straight-line" instances of the adversary; and (2) they only rule out reductions to non-interactive (two-round) assumptions. In this work, we present the first full impossibility result: our main result shows that the existence of *any* linear-preserving black-box reduction for basing the security of unique signatures on some *bounded-round* assumption implies that the assumption can be broken in polynomial time.

1 Introduction

Digital signature schemes, whereby a party can "sign" a message in a publicly verifiable yet still adversarially unforgeable way, are one of the most basic and important classes of cryptographic primitives; their security has been studied since the 1970s. While the earliest constructions of digital signatures [16,38,40, 41] were heuristic in nature, modern constructions have tight proofs of security against all computationally bounded adversaries based on certain underlying assumptions.

Specifically, in a provably secure construction, we have a reduction $\mathcal{R}$, which, given any adversary $\mathcal{A}$ which breaks the security of a digital signature scheme Π, can break a certain underlying assumption $\mathcal{C}$; hence, if the assumption holds,

Supported in part by NSF Award CNS-1561209, NSF Award CNS-1217821, NSF Award CNS-1704788, AFOSR Award FA9550-18-1-0267, a Microsoft Faculty Fellowship, and a Google Faculty Research Award.

A. Beimel and S. Dziembowski (Eds.): TCC 2018, LNCS 11239, pp. 507–536, 2018.
https://doi.org/10.1007/978-3-030-03807-6_19

then the scheme must be secure. In this paper, we restrict our attention to *black-box* security reductions, where $\mathcal{R}$ only interacts with $\mathcal{A}$ as a "black box".[1] As far as we know, all security proofs for digital signatures rely on black-box security reductions.

We are interested in the *security loss* of such a reduction (a concept originally proposed as "security preservation" in [29]), or intuitively how "inefficient" it is in terms of running time and success probability compared to the adversary it runs. Informally, if, given a security parameter n, $\mathcal{R}$ (including the instances of $\mathcal{A}$ it runs) and $\mathcal{A}$ run in time $\mathsf{Time}_{\mathcal{R}^{\mathcal{A}}}(n)$ and $\mathsf{Time}_{\mathcal{A}}(n)$ respectively, and have success probabilities of $\mathsf{Success}_{\mathcal{R}^{\mathcal{A}}}(n)$ and $\mathsf{Success}_{\mathcal{A}}(n)$, then the security loss is given by the maximum over all adversaries $\mathcal{A}$ of:

$$\lambda_{\mathcal{R}}(n) = \frac{\mathsf{Success}_{\mathcal{A}}(n)}{\mathsf{Success}_{\mathcal{R}^{\mathcal{A}}}(n)} \frac{\mathsf{Time}_{\mathcal{R}^{\mathcal{A}}}(n)}{\mathsf{Time}_{\mathcal{A}}(n)}$$

Intuitively, if we define the "work factor" of the adversary $\mathcal{A}$ to be the ratio of its running time to its success probability, or $\mathsf{Work}_{\mathcal{A}}(n) = \frac{\mathsf{Time}_{\mathcal{A}}(n)}{\mathsf{Success}_{\mathcal{A}}(n)}$ (and respectively for $\mathcal{R}^{\mathcal{A}}$), then we can think of the security loss as

$$\lambda_{\mathcal{R}} = \frac{\mathsf{Work}_{\mathcal{R}^{\mathcal{A}}}(n)}{\mathsf{Work}_{\mathcal{A}}(n)}$$

or how much "work" the reduction $\mathcal{R}$ needs to do to break the underlying assumption compared to the amount of work that its adversary $\mathcal{A}$ does to break the primitive Π. So the higher the security loss, the easier the primitive is to break compared to the underlying assumption. As such, having security reductions with low security loss is essential for proving practical security of cryptographic primitives, since the security loss has a significant effect on the security parameter (i.e., the bit length of a key, size of a large prime for RSA, etc.) which must be used for the underlying assumption to achieve a particular level of security for the primitive.

The most efficient possible reductions are those which have *constant* security loss $\lambda_{\mathcal{R}}(n) \leq c$; these are commonly called *tight* reductions [5]. These reductions prove that $\mathsf{Work}_{\mathcal{A}}(n)$ is always directly proportional to $\mathsf{Work}_{\mathcal{R}^{\mathcal{A}}}(n)$, and so increasing the security parameter will always have the same effect on the security of the primitive as on the security of the underlying assumption.

A weaker notion of efficiency—introduced by Luby [29]—is that of a *linear-preserving* reduction, where the security loss is required to be bounded by some *a priori* fixed polynomial $p(\cdot)$ in just the security parameter; that is, $\lambda_{\mathcal{R}}(n) \leq p(n)$.

For instance, a security reduction that only runs the adversary $\mathcal{A}$ a fixed polynomial number of times (independent of A's running time and success probability) may not be tight, but is still linear-preserving.[2] While, with a linear-

[1] We note that Π need not be black-box itself in some underlying primitive; we only require the *reduction* $\mathcal{R}$ to be black-box.

[2] The name "linear-preserving" comes from the fact that $\mathsf{Work}_{\mathcal{R}^{\mathcal{A}}}$ is still linear in the quantity $\mathsf{Work}_{\mathcal{A}}(n)$, although it may depend polynomially on the security parameter n.

preserving reduction, the concrete security of the primitive Π is only comparable to that of the assumption if we use an increased security parameter for Π, Π still retains the same "asymptotic" security as the underlying assumption: for instance, if Π can be broken in time $poly(n) \cdot (2^{n/3})$, then so can the underlying assumption.

Unique Signatures. While the original provably secure construction of digital signatures in [21] was neither tight nor linear-preserving, more recent constructions [1,5,7,12,13,23] with tight reductions have been exhibited. However, while these modern constructions are quite efficient, they sacrifice some arguably important features of the original constructions in achieving this. Most notably, the earliest construction in [40] had the property that signatures were *unique*—that is, for every public key and every message, there exists at most one valid signature for that message. Whereas provably secure constructions of unique signatures exist [30,31], as well as constructions of verifiable random functions [9,26,31] (which [31] shows imply unique signatures), none of these have linear-preserving, let alone tight, security reductions. And unfortunately, for many recent applications of digital signatures (e.g., the recent applications to blockchains [19,34]), this uniqueness property is in fact necessary.

Can Unique Signatures Have Linear-Preserving Reductions? A natural question, given the fact that no linear-preserving reductions have been discovered, is whether a certain degree of security loss is *required* when proving the security of unique signatures. This question was first addressed in 2002 by Jean-Sébastien Coron in his seminal paper [14]. At a high level, Coron's goal was to demonstrate that any unique signature scheme with a black-box security reduction must have a security loss of $O(\ell(n))$, where $\ell(n)$ is the number of signing queries made by the adversary. This, in particular, would rule out all linear-preserving reductions for unique signature schemes because $\ell(n)$ depends on the specific adversary $\mathcal{A}$ and can be an arbitrarily large polynomial.

However, while Coron's proof rules out many "natural" reductions, it does not fully answer the question. In particular, it applies only to a quite restricted class of "simple" reductions which run the adversary in a "sequential straight-line" fashion—that is, they can run many instances of the adversary, but must run them sequentially (such that each must finish before the next starts) and cannot rewind the adversary. Furthermore, Coron's result applies only to reductions to the class of *non-interactive* (i.e., two-round) security assumptions (e.g., inverting a one-way function or breaking RSA). This latter restriction is necessary to some extent; if the security assumption may have arbitrarily many rounds, then it becomes trivial to base security on such an assumption (e.g., reducing the security of digital signatures to itself). However, there is still a large gap between non-interactive and "unbounded-round" security assumptions, leaving open the question of whether *bounded-round* assumptions [33] (that is, security assumptions modeled as security games with an *a priori* bounded number of communication rounds) can be used to prove the security of unique signatures.

Since Coron's seminal work, his result has been generalized to a number of related primitives [3,24], improved and simplified [3,27], and extended to rule out other notions of security tightness [42]. However, despite these extensions, improvements, and generalizations, the above restrictions—to simple reductions, and to non-interactive assumptions—have not yet been surmounted, leaving open the question:

Does there exist a linear-preserving security reduction for basing the security of unique digital signatures on some natural hardness assumption?

Main Theorem. In this work, we settle this question, ruling out *all* linear-preserving reductions from unique signatures to *any* bounded-round assumption.

Theorem 1 (Informal). *There does not exist a linear-preserving black-box reduction from the security of some unique signature scheme Π to a bounded-round intractability assumption $\mathcal{C}$, unless $\mathcal{C}$ can be broken in polynomial time.*

More precisely, we show that, unless $\mathcal{C}$ can be broken in polynomial time, the security loss of any black-box reduction from the security of some unique signature scheme Π to any bounded-round intractability assumption $\mathcal{C}$ must be at least $O(\sqrt{\ell(n)})$, where $\ell(n)$ is the number of signature queries the adversary uses (and thus not a fixed polynomial independent of the adversary). Moreover, we observe (deferred to the full version) that our main theorem, with minor alterations, can also be applied to the related notion of *rerandomizable* signatures, or non-unique signatures with the property that signatures can be efficiently "rerandomized".

1.1 Proof Outline

In proving our main theorem, we follow the "meta-reduction" paradigm, originally pioneered in [8] (see also [2,4,6,10,18,22] for related work concerning meta-reductions), though we note that work on black-box separations using other frameworks dates back much farther, to [25]. The core idea behind this approach is, given an arbitrary black-box reduction $\mathcal{R}$ that breaks the assumption $\mathcal{C}$ by using black-box access to some "ideal adversary" $\mathcal{A}$ (which itself breaks the security of the primitive Π), to create an efficient adversary $\mathcal{B}$ which breaks $\mathcal{C}$ *without using* $\mathcal{A}$: $\mathcal{B}$ will internally run $\mathcal{R}$ and, roughly speaking, internally (and efficiently) "emulate" $\mathcal{A}$ for $\mathcal{R}$. The implication then is that if such a reduction $\mathcal{R}$ exists and breaks $\mathcal{C}$ using the inefficient adversary $\mathcal{A}$, then $\mathcal{B}$ would likewise break $\mathcal{C}$, but in polynomial time, proving that $\mathcal{C}$ is not a secure assumption. See Fig. 1 for an illustration of the mechanics of this paradigm.

Of course, we cannot prove complete non-existence (since, indeed, provably secure unique signature schemes exist); instead, we show that, unless $\mathcal{R}$ makes many queries to $\mathcal{A}$—which already implies that the security loss is high—then we can efficiently emulate $\mathcal{A}$'s responses with "high" (but not overwhelming) probability, which in turn will imply that $\mathcal{B}$ breaks $\mathcal{C}$ unless $\mathcal{R}$'s success probability is relatively small (again implying that its security loss is high).

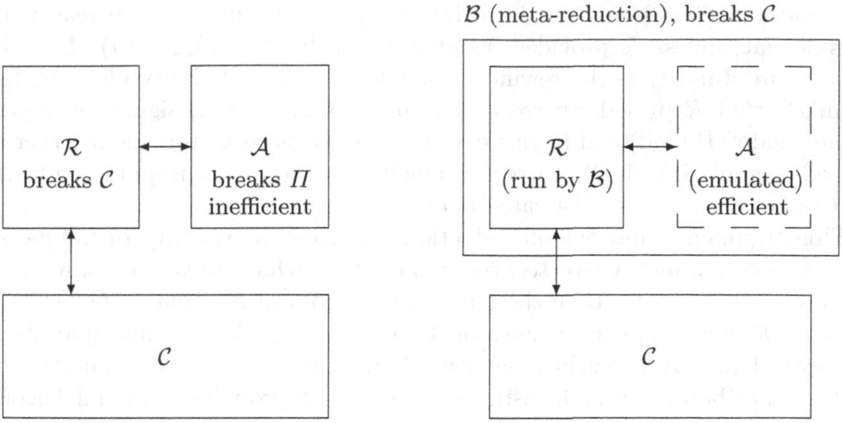

Fig. 1. The meta-reduction paradigm. *Left:* $\mathcal{R}$ breaks the assumption $\mathcal{C}$ by using the "ideal" but inefficient adversary $\mathcal{A}$ (against the signature scheme Π) as an oracle. *Right:* the meta-reduction $\mathcal{B}$ runs $\mathcal{R}$ (forwarding its communication with $\mathcal{C}$) and efficiently emulates $\mathcal{A}$ to break $\mathcal{C}$ with slightly less probability than in the left experiment.

Coron's Meta-reduction. As already mentioned, Coron, in [14], demonstrates how to employ this technique for a *restricted* class of reductions from the security of unique signatures. In particular, imagine an "ideal" inefficient adversary $\mathcal{A}$ which requests signatures for $\ell(n)$ randomly chosen messages, next uses a *brute-force search* to find a signature (i.e., a forgery) on a new random message, and finally returns the forgery. (Note that this adversary $\mathcal{A}$ is inefficient as it requires a brute-force search to recover the forgery.) In order to simulate $\mathcal{R}$'s interaction with $\mathcal{A}$ while running in polynomial time, $\mathcal{B}$ will run $\mathcal{R}$ normally and simulate $\mathcal{A}$ by first requesting signatures for $\ell(n)$ random messages. However, in order to extract a forgery without using brute force, $\mathcal{B}$ will pick a random message m^*, rewind the execution of $\mathcal{R}$ to before a randomly selected query, and try querying $\mathcal{R}$ for m^* instead of what it sent to $\mathcal{R}$ during the "main" (i.e., non-rewound) thread. If $\mathcal{R}$ returns a correct signature for m^* during this "rewinding", then $\mathcal{B}$ has succeeded in efficiently extracting a forgery and can return it to $\mathcal{R}$. In this case, $\mathcal{B}$ has succeeded in *perfectly* emulating $\mathcal{A}$; note that this relies on the fact that the signature scheme is unique and thus there exists at most one valid signature on m^*.

Of course, $\mathcal{R}$ may not always return a correct response to $\mathcal{A}$'s (or $\mathcal{B}$'s) queries; however, if $\mathcal{A}$ receives any incorrect responses in the "main" thread, it may simply return $\perp$ to $\mathcal{R}$ (as the security game for unique signatures only dictates that $\mathcal{A}$ must return a valid forgery when its queries are correctly answered), and so, in that case, $\mathcal{B}$ may also do so when emulating $\mathcal{A}$. The only time that $\mathcal{B}$ will fail to emulate $\mathcal{A}$ is, in fact, when $\mathcal{R}$ responds correctly to the original $\ell(n)$ queries by $\mathcal{B}$ during the "main" execution, but fails to respond to the rewound query of m^* in *any* rewinding (and so $\mathcal{B}$ can neither return $\perp$ or a forgery). Coron, through an elegant (yet complex) probabilistic argument, shows that the probability of this "bad event" is bounded above by $O(1)/\ell(n)$. Intuitively, the reason this holds is that, unless $\mathcal{R}$ provides signatures to a fraction $O(1)/\ell(n)$ of random messages m^* (and thus the rewinding succeeds with probability $O(1)/\ell(n)$), it is unlikely that $\mathcal{R}$ provides correct signatures to all the $\ell(n)$ signature requests on the "main" thread, and in this case $\mathcal{B}$ does not need to provide a forgery to succeed in emulating $\mathcal{A}$. Of course, formalizing this argument is quite non-trivial, and Coron presents a sophisticated analysis which does so.

This argument rules out all reductions $\mathcal{R}$ from the security of unique signatures to a non-interactive security assumption which break the assumption with probability greater than the failure probability of $\mathcal{B}$—that is, $O(1)/\ell(n)$—assuming $\mathcal{R}$ runs a single instance of its adversary. If $\mathcal{R}$ runs multiple, $M(n)$, instances of its adversary in a sequential (i.e., non-interleaved) manner, then by the union bound over all instances, the failure probability bound becomes $O(M(n))/\ell(n)$. Furthermore, in this case $\mathsf{Time}_{\mathcal{R}^{\mathcal{A}}}(n) \geq M(n)\mathsf{Time}_{\mathcal{A}}(n)$, and so (given $\mathsf{Success}_{\mathcal{A}}(n) = 1$) Coron's argument achieves a bound of

$$\lambda_{\mathcal{R}}(n) \geq O(\ell(n))$$

which thus rules out all linear-preserving reductions as there is no *a priori* polynomial bound on $\ell(n)$.

We note that while Coron's proof relies on a subtle and non-trivial analysis, a very recent and elegant work by Bader et al. [3] presents a much simpler proof of Coron's theorem. In their approach, however, they consider a quite different ideal adversary $\mathcal{A}'$, which is even more tailored to simple reductions and non-interactive assumptions.[3] Consequently, we focus on Coron's original approach, which we shall see can be generalized to deal with all reductions and all bounded-round assumptions.

The Problem with Interactive Assumptions and "Nesting". Note that, in the above argument, it is crucial that the security assumption is non-interactive. Otherwise, when we rewind $\mathcal{R}$, $\mathcal{R}$ may send a new message to $\mathcal{C}$ and may require a response before proceeding; if this happens, we can no longer perform the emulation (as we cannot rewind the communication with $\mathcal{C}$).

Additionally, the argument crucially relies on the fact that $\mathcal{R}$ talks to $\mathcal{A}$ in a "straight-line" fashion, and only considers sequential interactions with (multiple instances) of $\mathcal{A}$. If we did not have that restriction, $\mathcal{R}$ might simultaneously run multiple instances of $\mathcal{A}$ and "nest" these different executions. For instance, it might be the case that $\mathcal{R}$ receives a query from a particular instance of $\mathcal{A}$, begins an entirely different instance of $\mathcal{A}$ (or perhaps even multiple instances), makes queries, and potentially requests a forgery, all before returning a response to the first query. Rewinding this will be troublesome because, depending on the query, $\mathcal{R}$ could respond differently to the nested queries or even follow an entirely different execution pattern. Even more worrying is the fact that, if there

3 In fact, whereas it is not clear whether Coron's meta-reduction $\mathcal{B}$ fails under these more general conditions, the meta-reduction from [3] trivially breaks down under them.

are enough levels of nesting, rewinding every query for every instance may take super-polynomial time, which would invalidate the construction of $\mathcal{B}$ (since an inefficient adversary would not contradict the assumption $\mathcal{C}$). See Fig. 2 for an example illustrating this.

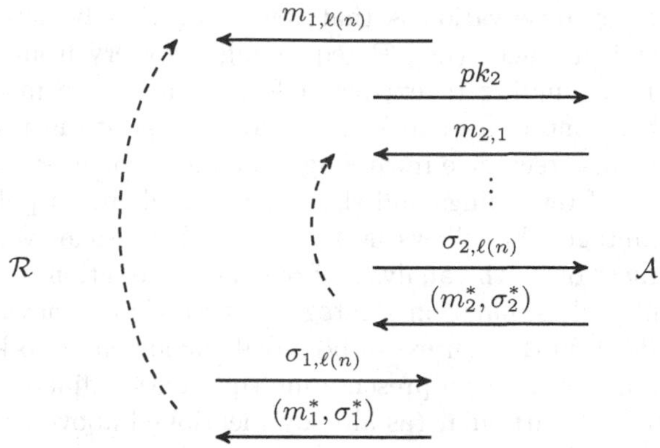

Fig. 2. A simple example of nested rewinding by $\mathcal{B}$ that might occur during interaction between $\mathcal{R}$ and two concurrent simulated instances of $\mathcal{A}$. Note that the inner rewinding must occur twice, once before the outer rewinding and once after, as the public key pk_2 might change based on the message $m_{1,\ell(n)}$. In fact, with m concurrent instances, up to 2^m rewindings may occur in this fashion.

Interestingly, this problem is also prevalent in research concerning concurrent zero-knowledge [17]. This connection was already noted in the earlier impossibility result for black-box reductions of [33], where a "recursive rewinding strategy" (similar to [11, 15, 36, 39]) is used to overcome this problem. The core idea behind this technique is to rewind *every* relevant query, but to "abort" the rewinding when "too many" nested queries take place during the rewinding. The limit on nested queries furthermore decreases by a factor of n with each recursive level of nesting, so, since the total number of messages is polynomial, the number of levels will always be bounded by a constant, providing the polynomial bound on running time.

One might be tempted to simply apply this technique directly to the problem at hand; unfortunately, due to a fundamental difference between the two results, this is not possible. Specifically, in [33], the result proven is a complete impossibility (and not just a bound on the security loss): more precisely, emulation of $\mathcal{A}$ can be shown to succeed with overwhelming probability. In our context, however, the probability that the emulation succeeds is some inverse polynomial (and inherently must be so, or else we would have shown a complete impossibility of black-box security reductions). The problem then with a recursive rewinding strategy is that the failure probabilities may "cascade". Additionally, we cannot rely on the technique from [33] of repeatedly rewinding until we obtain a correct response, since that would bias the distribution of the message m^* on which we output a forgery!

A Simple Rewinding Technique. We deal with the problem by using a different (and actually much simpler) rewinding strategy, inspired by a technique for "bounded-concurrent" zero-knowledge arguments originally introduced by Lindell [28]. The key observation is that rewinding is only necessary when $\mathcal{B}$ encounters an "end message" (i.e., $\mathcal{R}$ requesting a forgery from an instance of $\mathcal{A}$). If, during the rewinding to extract a forgery for some instance of $\mathcal{A}$, $\mathcal{B}$ avoids queries that contain an end message for a separate instance of $\mathcal{A}$ (i.e., those that would cause recursive rewinding), then it becomes straightforward to bound the number of rewindings and show that $\mathcal{B}$ will run in polynomial time; as an added advantage, this allows us to treat end messages very similarly to external communication in the analysis of our meta-reduction.

However, while this simulation strategy at first glance may seem straightforward (and, indeed, in the context of bounded-concurrent zero-knowledge, the analysis is simple), our scenario presents multiple major differences that make it quite non-trivial. In particular (as already mentioned above), unlike for zero-knowledge, we can no longer rewind queries with arbitrary messages; instead, in order to generate a forgery of a uniformly random message, we must choose a single forgery target m^* and rewind every query *only once* using this *same* message m^* (otherwise, as mentioned above, we would bias the distribution of the message m^* on which we output a forgery). Thus, to not bias the distribution of m^*, we must rewind each query with the same message m^* and consequently, we no longer have any independence between the rewindings, which severely complicates the analysis. (Indeed, recall that even in the simplified setting of Coron, his argument is already quite non-trivial).

Towards dealing with this, we present a new way of analyzing an ideal adversary which is quite similar to Coron's ideal adversary. Our analysis relies on a "randomness-switching" argument similar in spirit to that of [35,37], where we demonstrate that any "bad" sequence of randomness which causes the meta-reduction to fail can be permuted into many "good" sequences for which the meta-reduction succeeds. In particular, recall from our above discussion of Coron's meta-reduction that, if a sequence of messages is such that $\mathcal{B}$ fails to emulate $\mathcal{A}$, then *all* of its rewindings with the forgery target m^* must fail to extract a signature for the query to m^*. Hence, every rewound sequence beginning with a prefix $(m_1, \ldots, m_{i-1}, m^*)$ will either contain nesting or external communication during the query for m^*, or is such that $\mathcal{R}$ provides an incorrect signature for m^*. In the latter case, we can conclude as above that $\mathcal{A}$ and $\mathcal{B}$, having received an invalid signature, will both accordingly return $\perp$ (meaning that in fact $\mathcal{B}$ will succeed) if any sequence with that prefix is given in the (non-rewound) execution; thus, any such sequence cannot itself be a "bad" sequence. This, combined with the fact that the amount of nesting and external communication (and hence the possible number of rewound sequences which do *not* fall into the latter category) is bounded, will allow us to derive an upper bound for the possible number of "bad" sequences of randomness and hence for the probability of one of these sequences occurring (and causing the meta-reduction $\mathcal{B}$ to fail). This failure probability bound for $\mathcal{B}$ will ultimately allow us to upper-bound the success probability, and hence lower-bound the security loss, of the reduction $\mathcal{R}$. (In the full version, as an independent contribution and a warm-up, we sketch how an even simpler randomness-switching approach can be used to provide a simplified proof of a generalization of Coron's theorem to arbitrary reductions with *static* scheduling—where the order in which the reductions sends its sends messages is a-priori fixed).

Overview. In Sect. 2 we present key notation and definitions to be employed in our proof. We present and discuss our main result in Sect. 3, construct our "ideal" adversary $\mathcal{A}$ in Sect. 3.1, construct the meta-reduction $\mathcal{B}$ in Sect. 3.2, and complete our analysis and proof of the main theorem in Sect. 3.3. Lastly, we defer a synopsis of related work, as well as the details of an extension of our theorem to rerandomizable signatures, to the full version of this paper.

2 Preliminaries and Definitions

2.1 Notation

Let $\mathbb{N}$ denote the set of natural numbers (positive integers), and let $[n]$ denote the set of natural numbers at most n, or $\{1, 2, \ldots, n\}$. For $n \in \mathbb{N}$, we denote by 1^n the string of n ones, which will be used to provide a security parameter as input to an algorithm (this is by convention, so that the input length is bounded below by the security parameter). Given a set $S = \{s_1, \ldots, s_n\}$ of distinct elements, we shall let $|S|$ denote the number of elements n in S, and we refer to the set $\Pi_n(S)$ as the set of *permutations* of S, which contains any sequence which itself contains, in any order, each element of S exactly once.

When we say that a statement holds "for all sufficiently large $n \in \mathbb{N}$", by this we indicate that there exists an $N \in \mathbb{N}$ such that, for any integer $n \geq N$, the statement holds for n.

We recall that a function $\epsilon(\cdot)$ is *negligible* if, for any polynomial $p(\cdot)$, $\epsilon(n) < 1/p(n)$ for all sufficiently large $n \in \mathbb{N}$—that is, if $\epsilon(\cdot)$ is asymptotically smaller than any inverse polynomial. (For instance, an inverse exponential such as e^{-cn} is negligible in n for any constant $c > 0$).

Lastly, we assume a basic level of familiarity with the concepts of probabilistic algorithms and interactive Turing machines [20]. We will let $\mathcal{R}^{\mathcal{A}}(x)$ denote the probability distribution over the output of an oracle algorithm $\mathcal{R}$ given oracle access to a probabilistic $\mathcal{A}$. If $\mathcal{A}$ is a (deterministic) interactive algorithm, we instead assume $\mathcal{R}$ has oracle access to the function that, given the current partial transcript of (i.e., all messages sent up to a certain point in) interaction between $\mathcal{R}$ and $\mathcal{A}$, returns $\mathcal{A}$'s next message to $\mathcal{R}$.

Furthermore, we shall refer by $\langle \mathcal{A}, \mathcal{C} \rangle(x)$ to the probability distribution over the output of $\mathcal{C}$ after interaction between probabilistic interactive Turing machines $\mathcal{A}$ and $\mathcal{C}$, both given common input x (where the common input is also provided to any oracles, e.g., to $\mathcal{O}$ if $\mathcal{A}$ is an oracle machine given by $\mathcal{A}^{\mathcal{O}}$); the view of the respective experiment, or the transcript of all messages sent and all randomness consumed, shall be denoted as $[\mathcal{A} \leftrightarrow \mathcal{C}](x)$.

2.2 Unique Signatures

First, we define unique signature schemes. Recall that a signature scheme is a means by which a message can be signed with the signer's secret key and the signature can be verified using a public key. A unique signature scheme, then, is simply a signature scheme for which each message can only have one possible signature:

Definition 1. *A* ***unique signature scheme*** *is a triple* (Gen, Sign, Ver) *of probabilistic polynomial-time algorithms such that, for every $n \in \mathbb{N}$:*

- Gen, *on input 1^n, produces a pair (pk, sk).*
- Sign, *on input (sk, m) for any $m \in \{0,1\}^n$, produces a signature σ. (We write $\sigma \leftarrow \mathsf{Sign}_{sk}(m)$).*
- Ver, *on input (pk, m, σ), produces either* Accept *or* Reject. *(We write out $\leftarrow \mathsf{Ver}_{pk}(m, \sigma)$).*

and, in addition, the following properties hold:

- *Correctness: For every $n \in \mathbb{N}$ and $m \in \{0,1\}^n$:*

$$Pr[(pk, sk) \leftarrow \mathsf{Gen}(1^n) : \mathsf{Ver}_{pk}(m, \mathsf{Sign}_{sk}(m)) = \mathsf{Accept}] = 1$$

- *Uniqueness: For every $m \in \{0,1\}^*$, and $pk \in \{0,1\}^*$, there exists at most one $\sigma \in \{0,1\}^*$ for which $\mathsf{Ver}_{pk}(m, \sigma) = \mathsf{Accept}$.*

We next turn to discussing what it means for such a scheme to be secure. A natural definition of security is the notion of *existential unforgeability against adaptive chosen-message attacks* [21], which requires that an adversary knowing the public key, even if allowed to adaptively choose a bounded number of messages and observe their signatures, is unable to forge any signature for a message they have not yet queried. We formalize this by allowing the adversary access to an oracle for Sign, as follows:

Definition 2. *We say that a signature scheme is* ***unforgeable*** *if, for every non-uniform probabilistic polynomial-time oracle-aided algorithm $\mathcal{A}$, there is some negligible function $\epsilon(\cdot)$ such that for all $n \in \mathbb{N}$:*

$$Pr\left[(pk, sk) \leftarrow \mathsf{Gen}(1^n); (m, \sigma) \leftarrow \mathcal{A}^{\mathsf{Sign}_{sk}(\cdot)}(1^n, pk) : \mathsf{Ver}_{pk}(m, \sigma) = \mathsf{Accept} \wedge \mathsf{Valid}\right] \leq \epsilon(n)$$

where Valid *is the event that none of $\mathcal{A}$'s queries were for the signature of the output message m.*

*We will define a weaker notion of a signature scheme being $\ell(\cdot)$-**unforgeable** identically to the above, with the exception that* Valid *is the event that the following* two *conditions on $\mathcal{A}$ are true:*

- *$\mathcal{A}$ has queried its oracle at most $\ell(n)$ times.*
- *None of $\mathcal{A}$'s queries were for the signature of the output message m.*

The bounded notion of $\ell(\cdot)$-unforgeability is primarily useful to prove our concrete security loss bound, whereas our main result applies to the general notion of unforgeability. Furthermore, for the purposes of the impossibility result, we weaken the definition of unforgeability to a worst-case definition, as this will strengthen our main theorem (by showing that basing even this weak notion of security on standard assumptions will incur a security loss):

Definition 3. *We say that a signature scheme is* ***weakly unforgeable*** *(respectively, weakly $\ell(\cdot)$-unforgeable) if, for every non-uniform probabilistic polynomial-time oracle-aided algorithm $\mathcal{A}$ and every $n \in \mathbb{N}$:*

$$Pr\left[(pk, sk) \leftarrow \mathsf{Gen}(1^n); (m, \sigma) \leftarrow \mathcal{A}^{\mathsf{Sign}_{sk}(\cdot)}(1^n, pk) : \mathsf{Ver}_{pk}(m, \sigma) = \mathsf{Accept} \wedge \mathsf{Valid}\right] < 1$$

where Valid *is defined as above (and respectively for $\ell(\cdot)$-unforgeability). In particular, we say that a non-uniform probabilistic polynomial-time algorithm $\mathcal{A}$* breaks weak unforgeability *of a signature scheme* (Gen, Sign, Ver) *if the probability above is equal to 1.*

2.3 Intractability Assumptions

Next, we define intractability assumptions in a manner originally proposed in [32]. Formally, we can model an assumption as a "security game" involving an interaction between a probabilistic *challenger* $\mathcal{C}$ and *adversary* $\mathcal{A}$, after which $\mathcal{C}$ will output either Accept or Reject. We say that an adversary $\mathcal{A}$ breaks the assumption if $\mathcal{C}$ accepts with probability non-negligibly greater than a certain threshold.

For instance, an assumption that a function f is one-way could be modeled by a two-round interaction where $\mathcal{C}$ sends $\mathcal{A}$ the image $y = f(x)$ on a uniformly random input x, $\mathcal{A}$ sends a message x' to $\mathcal{C}$, and $\mathcal{C}$ accepts if and only if $f(x') = y$. In this case, $\mathcal{A}$ breaks the assumption if it inverts f (i.e., $\mathcal{C}$ accepts) with probability non-negligibly greater than zero.

As an example of an assumption that would have a non-zero threshold, an assumption that two distributions $\mathcal{D}_0$ and $\mathcal{D}_1$ are indistinguishable could be modeled by the two-round interaction where $\mathcal{C}$ picks a random $b \in \{0, 1\}$, sends $\mathcal{A}$ a sample from $\mathcal{D}_b$, receives b' from $\mathcal{A}$, and accepts if $b = b'$. Then $\mathcal{A}$ would only break the assumption if $\mathcal{C}$ accepts with probability non-negligibly greater than a threshold of $1/2$. Formally, we model these assumptions following [33]:

Definition 4. *For polynomial $r(\cdot)$, we denote an $r(\cdot)$-**round intractability assumption** by a pair $(\mathcal{C}, t(\cdot))$, where $t(\cdot)$ is a function and $\mathcal{C}$ is a probabilistic interactive algorithm with input 1^n and an* a priori *bound of $r(n)$ rounds of communication. We say that $(\mathcal{C}, t(\cdot))$ is* **secure** *if the following is true:*

For any non-uniform probabilistic polynomial-time interactive algorithm $\mathcal{A}$, there exists a negligible function $\epsilon(\cdot)$ such that, for all $n \in \mathbb{N}$:

$$Pr[\langle \mathcal{A}, \mathcal{C} \rangle (1^n) = \mathsf{Accept}] \leq t(n) + \epsilon(n)$$

Furthermore, we say that a specific $\mathcal{A}$ breaks *the assumption if the above inequality is not true with respect to that $\mathcal{A}$; in particular, for some polynomial $p(\cdot)$, we say that $\mathcal{A}$ breaks $(\mathcal{C}, t(\cdot))$ with probability $1/p(\cdot)$ if, for infinitely many $n \in \mathbb{N}$,*

$$Pr[\langle \mathcal{A}, \mathcal{C} \rangle (1^n) = \mathsf{Accept}] \geq t(n) + \frac{1}{p(n)}$$

We also call a pair $(\mathcal{C}, t(\cdot))$ a ***bounded-round intractability assumption*** *if there exists some polynomial $r(\cdot)$ such that $(\mathcal{C}, t(\cdot))$ is an $r(\cdot)$-round intractability assumption.*

We note that any standard cryptographic security assumption can be modeled as a pair $(\mathcal{C}, t(\cdot))$ of this form, including our definitions above of the security of signature schemes. (In this case, the threshold $t(n)$ would be zero, and $\mathcal{C}$ would have $r(n) = 2\ell(n) + 2$ rounds of communication, first generating (pk, sk) and sending pk to $\mathcal{A}$, then signing $\ell(n)$ messages for $\mathcal{A}$, and finally receiving (m, σ) and outputting the result of Ver, or Reject if it had already signed m.) In particular, this is why we require an *a priori* bound on the number of rounds $r(\cdot)$ of the assumption; it will allow us to avoid such trivial reductions as reducing unforgeability to itself (for which we could obviously not prove the impossibility result).

2.4 Black-Box Reductions

Finally, we briefly discuss what it means for one assumption to be based on another assumption. In particular, given two assumptions $(\mathcal{C}_1, t_1(\cdot))$ and $(\mathcal{C}_2, t_2(\cdot))$, basing the hardness of $\mathcal{C}_1$ on that of $\mathcal{C}_2$ in a black-box way would classically entail, given an arbitrary adversary $\mathcal{A}_2$ which can break $(\mathcal{C}_2, t_2(\cdot))$ constructing a polynomial-time procedure $\mathcal{A}_1$ that breaks $(\mathcal{C}_1, t_1(\cdot))$ through standard interactions with $\mathcal{A}_2$ (i.e., using $\mathcal{A}_2$ in a *black-box* manner).

Notably, there is no guarantee that $\mathcal{A}_1$ invoke $\mathcal{A}_2$ only once; it could be the case that there are polynomially many invocations, or even "nested" invocations (e.g., multiple concurrent invocations such that the rounds of communication may be interleaved or dependent on one another), of $\mathcal{A}_2$ during the execution of $\mathcal{A}_1$. We can formalize this by imagining $\mathcal{A}_1$ as a polynomial-time *reduction* $\mathcal{R}$ that has oracle access to the interactive algorithm $\mathcal{A}$ (formerly $\mathcal{A}_2$):

Definition 5. *We refer to a probabilistic polynomial-time oracle-aided algorithm $\mathcal{R}$ as a* ***black-box reduction for basing the hardness of assumption*** $(\mathcal{C}_1, t_1(\cdot))$ ***on that of*** $(\mathcal{C}_2, t_2(\cdot))$ *if, given any deterministic $\mathcal{A}$ that breaks $(\mathcal{C}_1, t_1(\cdot))$, $\mathcal{R}^{\mathcal{A}}$ breaks $(\mathcal{C}_2, t_2(\cdot))$. We refer to such a black-box reduction as* ***fixed-parameter*** *if, given common input 1^n, $\mathcal{R}^{\mathcal{A}}$ queries $\mathcal{A}$ only on input 1^n.*

We notably restrict our attention to oracles that are deterministic (or have some fixed randomness), as this allows us to consider cases where the reduction $\mathcal{R}$ can rewind or restart its oracle. We shall also restrict our attention, similarly to [33], to the case of *fixed-parameter* reductions where $\mathcal{R}$ invokes its adversary $\mathcal{A}$ only using a single security parameter (i.e., $\mathcal{A}$ must be the same algorithm in each instance); in particular, for security parameter n, we allow $\mathcal{R}$ to run up to $M(n)$ instances of some parameterized adversary $\mathcal{A}(1^n)$. Lastly, we can also apply the above concept to our definition of weak $\ell(\cdot)$-unforgeability (and define a fixed-parameter reduction identically for this case):

Definition 6. *We say that a probabilistic polynomial-time oracle-aided algorithm $\mathcal{R}$ is a* black-box reduction for basing weak unforgeability of a signature scheme $(\mathsf{Gen}, \mathsf{Sign}, \mathsf{Ver})$ on the hardness of an assumption $(\mathcal{C}, t(\cdot))$ *(resp. for weak $\ell(\cdot)$-unforgeability) if, for every deterministic algorithm $\mathcal{A}$ that breaks weak unforgeability of* $(\mathsf{Gen}, \mathsf{Sign}, \mathsf{Ver})$ *(i.e., forges a signature with probability 1), there is a polynomial $p(\cdot)$ such that, for infinitely many $n \in \mathbb{N}$, $\mathcal{R}^{\mathcal{A}}$ breaks $(\mathcal{C}, t(\cdot))$ with probability $1/p(n)$.*

Finally, we wish to formalize the *security loss* of such a reduction $\mathcal{R}$, or the loss in the reduction's success probability proportionate to its time efficiency. We state this as follows:

Definition 7. *Let $\mathcal{R}$ be a black-box reduction for basing the hardness of assumption $(\mathcal{C}_1, t_1(\cdot))$ on that of $(\mathcal{C}_2, t_2(\cdot))$. Given any deterministic $\mathcal{A}$ and for each $n \in \mathbb{N}$:*

- *Let* $\mathsf{Success}_{\mathcal{A}}(n) = \Pr[\langle \mathcal{A}, \mathcal{C}_1 \rangle (1^n) = \mathsf{Accept}] - t_1(n)$ *(that is, the probability with which $\mathcal{A}$ breaks $(\mathcal{C}_1, t_1(\cdot))$, taken over all randomness of $\mathcal{A}$ and $\mathcal{C}_1$).*
- *Let* $\mathsf{Query}_{\mathcal{A}}(n)$ *denote the maximum, over all randomness of $\mathcal{A}$ and $\mathcal{C}_1$, of the possible number of messages sent from $\mathcal{C}_1$ to $\mathcal{A}$ during the experiment $[\mathcal{A} \leftrightarrow \mathcal{C}_1](1^n)$.*
- *Let* $\mathsf{Success}_{\mathcal{R}^{\mathcal{A}}}(n) = \Pr[\langle \mathcal{R}^{\mathcal{A}}, \mathcal{C}_2 \rangle (1^n) = \mathsf{Accept}] - t_2(n)$ *(that is, the probability with which $\mathcal{R}^{\mathcal{A}}$ breaks $(\mathcal{C}_2, t_2(\cdot))$ taken over all randomness of $\mathcal{A}$, $\mathcal{C}_2$, and $\mathcal{R}$).*
- *Let* $\mathsf{Query}_{\mathcal{R}^{\mathcal{A}}}(n)$ *denote the maximum, over all randomness of $\mathcal{A}$, $\mathcal{C}_2$, and $\mathcal{R}$, of the possible number of messages sent from $\mathcal{R}$ to $\mathcal{A}$ during the experiment $[\mathcal{R}^{\mathcal{A}} \leftrightarrow \mathcal{C}_2](1^n)$.*

Then we say that the **security loss** *of $\mathcal{R}$ is given by:*

$$\lambda_{\mathcal{R}}(n) = max_{\mathcal{A}} \left(\frac{\mathsf{Success}_{\mathcal{A}}(n)}{\mathsf{Success}_{\mathcal{R}^{\mathcal{A}}}(n)} \frac{\mathsf{Query}_{\mathcal{R}^{\mathcal{A}}}(n)}{\mathsf{Query}_{\mathcal{A}}(n)} \right)$$

Furthermore, we say that $\mathcal{R}$ is **linear-preserving** *if its security loss is bounded above by a fixed polynomial independent of $\mathcal{A}$—that is, there is a polynomial $p(\cdot)$ for which, for all sufficiently large $n \in \mathbb{N}$ and every $\mathcal{A}$, $\lambda_{\mathcal{R}}(n) \leq p(n)$.*

We note that, as we consider black-box reductions, we consider the ratio between the communication complexities of $\mathcal{R}$ and $\mathcal{A}$ as opposed to the running times when determining the security loss. While many other recent works (e.g., [3,24]) use a definition which, though similar to the above, measures actual running time rather than rounds of communication, we note that our definition is at least as strong as time-based alternatives, and formally prove this fact in the full version.

3 Main Theorem

As our main theorem, we prove the following result:

Theorem 2. *Let $\Pi = (\mathsf{Gen}, \mathsf{Sign}, \mathsf{Ver})$ be a unique signature scheme, and let $(\mathcal{C}, t(\cdot))$ be some $r(\cdot)$-round intractability assumption for polynomial $r(\cdot)$. If there exists some fixed-parameter black-box reduction $\mathcal{R}$ for basing weak unforgeability of Π on the hardness of $(\mathcal{C}, t(\cdot))$, then either:*

(1) $\mathcal{R}$ is not a linear-preserving reduction, or
(2) there exists a polynomial-time adversary $\mathcal{B}$ that breaks $(\mathcal{C}, t(\cdot))$.

We note that this result also applies to the slightly more general notion of *rerandomizable* signatures through an almost identical argument; we discuss this in more detail in the full version. Theorem 2 follows in a straightforward manner from the following lemma, which is a concrete security loss bound analogous to Coron's in [14], but generalized so that it handles arbitrary (i.e., not just simple) reductions:

Lemma 1. *Let $\Pi = (\mathsf{Gen}, \mathsf{Sign}, \mathsf{Ver})$ be a unique signature scheme, and let $(\mathcal{C}, t(\cdot))$ be some $r(\cdot)$-round intractability assumption for polynomial $r(\cdot)$. If for some polynomial $\ell(\cdot)$ there exists some fixed-parameter black-box reduction $\mathcal{R}$ for basing weak $\ell(\cdot)$-unforgeability of Π on the hardness of $(\mathcal{C}, t(\cdot))$, then either $\mathcal{R}$'s security loss is at least*

$$\lambda_{\mathcal{R}}(n) \geq \sqrt{\ell(n)} - (r(n) + 1)$$

for all sufficiently large $n \in \mathbb{N}$, or there exists a polynomial-time adversary $\mathcal{B}$ that breaks the assumption $(\mathcal{C}, t(\cdot))$.

Lemma 1 implies Theorem 2 by the definition of a linear-preserving reduction (we defer the formal proof to the full version, however). Hence, the remainder of the section is dedicated to proving Lemma 1. Our proof of Lemma 1 follows four major steps, which we shall describe here at a high level before beginning the full argument.

Constructing an Ideal Adversary. First, we describe an "ideal" adversary $\mathcal{A}$ which is *guaranteed* to break the security of Π while sending $\ell(n)$ queries, but does so by brute force and hence does not run in polynomial time. Our objective then is to create a meta-reduction $\mathcal{B}$ that *almost* always emulates the interaction $\mathcal{R}^{\mathcal{A}}$ between $\mathcal{R}$ and $\mathcal{A}$. If it does so with, say, probability $1 - 1/p(n)$, then

$\mathcal{B}$ will break the assumption $(\mathcal{C}, t(\cdot))$ with probability at least $\mathsf{Success}_{\mathcal{R}^{\mathcal{A}}}(n) - 1/p(n)$. However, this means that $\mathcal{R}^{\mathcal{A}}$ itself cannot have success probability non-negligibly greater than $1/p(n)$; otherwise, $\mathcal{C}$ would be broken with non-negligible probability by $\mathcal{B}$.

The "ideal" $\mathcal{A}$ will pick $\ell(n)$ messages $(\vec{m})$ at random and query $\mathcal{R}$ for the signatures of each of these messages in turn, and will finally brute-force a secret key from the results and use that key to forge a signature for another random message m^*, which it will return. Crucially, $\mathcal{A}$ will also verify $\mathcal{R}$'s responses to its queries and return $\perp$ instead if not all are correct signatures. By construction $\mathcal{A}$ breaks $\ell(\cdot)$-weak unforgeability; however, due to the brute-force step, it (and consequently $\mathcal{R}^{\mathcal{A}}$) will not run in polynomial time.

Constructing a Meta-reduction. Hence, to *efficiently* emulate $\mathcal{R}^{\mathcal{A}}$, we create the meta-reduction $\mathcal{B}$. $\mathcal{B}$ will run $\mathcal{R}$ and forward communicate with $\mathcal{C}$ as normal; when $\mathcal{R}$ would start a new instance of its adversary $\mathcal{A}$, $\mathcal{B}$ will generate messages $\vec{m}$ and m^* randomly (i.e., identically to $\mathcal{A}$) and forward queries to $\mathcal{R}$ in the same manner as $\mathcal{A}$. However, when $\mathcal{R}$ requires an instance to provide a forged signature, $\mathcal{B}$ will also "rewind" the simulated execution to the start of each query for that instance and try to query $\mathcal{R}$ with m^* instead of the message it would normally query. If $\mathcal{R}$ gives a response to the rewound query, then $\mathcal{B}$ has (efficiently) found a forgery for m^*, which it can return to $\mathcal{R}$ when it requests a forgery from the corresponding instance of $\mathcal{A}$.

$\mathcal{B}$, while rewinding, will abort (and try rewinding the next slot instead) if either $\mathcal{R}$ would communicate externally with $\mathcal{C}$ (which $\mathcal{B}$ of course cannot rewind) or $\mathcal{R}$ would request a forgery for some other simulated instance of $\mathcal{A}$ during the simulated execution of $\mathcal{R}^{\mathcal{A}}$ (i.e., before responding to the rewound query). In particular, this strategy ensures that recursive rewinding as in [33] will not be required, since $\mathcal{B}$ will never attempt to start rewinding some instance while rewinding a different one.

Furthermore, $\mathcal{B}$ will "verify" all of $\mathcal{R}$'s responses to its signature queries (in the non-rewound part of the execution) in the same manner as $\mathcal{A}$, likewise returning $\perp$ from the simulated instance of $\mathcal{A}$ if not all responses are valid. So, whenever either $\mathcal{R}$ gives a simulated instance one or more incorrect responses or $\mathcal{B}$ successfully extracts a forgery (noting that, by the uniqueness property, the forgeries they return must be identical, which is crucial), $\mathcal{A}$ and $\mathcal{B}$'s simulations of $\mathcal{A}$ will be identically distributed to one another.

Bounding the Failure Probability. So, to bound the probability with which $\mathcal{B}$ does *not* successfully emulate some instance of $\mathcal{A}$, we must bound the probability that all of $\mathcal{B}$'s queries to $\mathcal{R}$ $(\vec{m})$ are correctly answered, yet the rewinding of *every one* of the queries fails due to either $\mathcal{R}$ responding badly to m^*, $\mathcal{R}$ communicating externally with $\mathcal{C}$, or a forgery request for another simulated instance of $\mathcal{A}$ occurring before $\mathcal{R}$ responds.

We bound this probability by using a counting argument similar to that exhibited in the introduction. In particular, we consider the messages $\vec{m}$ and m^*

for a particular instance, fixing the randomness outside of that instance arbitrarily. Then we show that, for any "bad" sequencing of these messages such that the non-rewound execution succeeds but every rewinding fails, many (though not all, because of the possibility for rewindings to fail due to an end message or external communication) of the rewindings of this sequence will correspond to "good" sequences where $\mathcal{B}$ returns $\perp$ due to receiving an incorrect response from $\mathcal{R}$.

What we intuitively show is that, in every set of $\ell(n)+1$ sequences corresponding to a sequence and its various rewindings, at most $M(n)+r(n)+1$ can be bad (since, informally, given a bad sequence, in expectation only $M(n)+r(n)$ of its rewindings can fail for reasons besides $\mathcal{R}$ responding incorrectly, i.e., due to nested end messages or external communication), where $M(n)$ is the maximum number of instances of $\mathcal{A}$ which $\mathcal{R}$ executes (which we show by our construction of $\mathcal{A}$ must be no less than the number of successful end messages). Hence we obtain a bound of $\frac{M(n)+r(n)+1}{\ell(n)+1}$ on the failure probability for each instance, which by the union bound over all $M(n)$ instances sums to an overall failure probability of less than $M(n)\left(\frac{M(n)+r(n)+1}{\ell(n)}\right)$.

Bounding the Security Loss. This does not immediately imply a bound on the security loss $\lambda_{\mathcal{R}}(n)$, since $M(n)$ can be arbitrarily large. However, as in the technical overview, we bound the security loss by showing that, if $M(n)$ is large, this requires a large enough running time of $\mathcal{R}$ that we still obtain a non-trivial lower bound on the security loss. Specifically, recalling that

$$\lambda_{\mathcal{R}}(n) \geq \frac{\mathsf{Success}_{\mathcal{A}}(n)}{\mathsf{Success}_{\mathcal{R}^{\mathcal{A}}}(n)} \frac{\mathsf{Query}_{\mathcal{R}^{\mathcal{A}}}(n)}{\mathsf{Query}_{\mathcal{A}}(n)}$$

we notice first that $\mathsf{Query}_{\mathcal{R}^{\mathcal{A}}}(n)/\mathsf{Query}_{\mathcal{A}}(n) \geq M(n)$, which follows (with some subtleties which we defer to the main proof) from the fact that $\mathcal{R}$ will in the worst case run $M(n)$ instances of $\mathcal{A}$. So, since $\mathsf{Success}_{\mathcal{A}}(n) = 1$ by construction, and since, as we discussed previously, $\mathsf{Success}_{\mathcal{R}^{\mathcal{A}}}(n)$ cannot be non-negligibly larger than the failure probability of $\mathcal{B}$, we have

$$\lambda_{\mathcal{R}}(n) \geq \frac{\ell(n)}{M(n)+r(n)+1}$$

which immediately implies the bound when $M(n) < \sqrt{\ell(n)} - (r(n)+1)$ (and so $\lambda_{\mathcal{R}}(n) > \sqrt{\ell(n)}$). On the other hand, we also know that $\mathsf{Success}_{\mathcal{R}^{\mathcal{A}}}(n) \leq 1$ trivially, and so it is also the case that $\lambda_{\mathcal{R}}(n) \geq M(n)$, which implies the bound when $M(n) \geq \sqrt{\ell(n)} - (r(n)+1)$, completing the proof of Lemma 1 and hence Theorem 2.

3.1 The "Ideal" Adversary

We now proceed to the formal proof of Lemma 1. First, we exhibit an inefficient adversary $\mathcal{A}$ that will break weak $\ell(\cdot)$-unforgeability, so that we can later construct an efficient $\mathcal{B}$ to simulate it while running $\mathcal{R}$ in order to break the assumption $(\mathcal{C}, t(\cdot))$.

Let $\Pi = (\mathsf{Gen}, \mathsf{Sign}, \mathsf{Ver})$ be a unique signature scheme, and let $(\mathcal{C}, t(\cdot))$ be some $r(\cdot)$-round intractability assumption for polynomial $r(\cdot)$. Assume that there exists some black-box reduction $\mathcal{R}$ for basing weak $\ell(\cdot)$-unforgeability of Π on the hardness of $(\mathcal{C}, t(\cdot))$ which, given an oracle breaking weak unforgeability, will break $(\mathcal{C}, t(\cdot))$ with probability $1/p(\cdot)$ for some polynomial $p(\cdot)$.

First, for any polynomial $\ell(n)$, we construct an inefficient but easily emulatable adversary $\mathcal{A}$ which sends at most $\ell(n)$ queries and is guaranteed to break weak unforgeability of Π. Since we will require $\mathcal{A}$ to be deterministic during execution yet generate random messages, we will assume that $\mathcal{A}$ is formally given by a deterministic interactive $\mathcal{A}^{\mathcal{O}}$ which has access to a random oracle $\mathcal{O}$ (of course, $\mathcal{O}$ is not needed for our actual constructions, as we shall emulate $\mathcal{A}$), which, as in [33], is given by a random variable which is uniformly distributed over functions $\{0,1\}^* \to \{0,1\}^\infty$. In particular, this ensures that the queries output by $\mathcal{A}^{\mathcal{O}}$ are uniformly distributed (i.e., over the randomness of $\mathcal{O}$), but are still preserved under rewinding.

We shall henceforth denote by $\mathcal{A}$ the specific adversary $\mathcal{A}^{\mathcal{O}}$ which, on input 1^n, behaves as described in Fig. 3. Informally, $\mathcal{A}$ makes $\ell(n)$ signature queries, generating the message for each query by applying $\mathcal{O}$ to the current partial transcript. Finally, after receiving responses for each query, $\mathcal{A}$ returns a brute-forced forgery, but only if it successfully "verifies" the transcript by ensuring that each query's response is valid and that each query in the transcript was generated in the correct manner (i.e., by $\mathcal{O}$ applied to the prior partial transcript).

It is straightforward to see that $\mathcal{A}$, given any fixed oracle $\mathcal{O}$, will break weak $\ell(\cdot)$-unforgeability; given an honest signing oracle (which will always send the correct partial transcript), it will always return some (m, σ) such that $\mathsf{Ver}_{pk}(m, \sigma) = \mathsf{Accept}$, m was not queried (as m^* is not equal to any of the queries m_i), and only $\ell(n)$ queries were made.

However, when interacting with $\mathcal{R}$, which is not bound by the rules of an honest oracle, the transcript verification is necessary to prevent $\mathcal{R}$ from "cheating" in certain ways during its interaction. First, we wish to ensure that $\mathcal{R}$ will return valid signatures to queries as often as possible. Also, we wish to ensure that $\mathcal{R}$ is actually required to answer $\ell(n)$ signature queries generated randomly by $\mathcal{A}$ and cannot, for instance, immediately send $\mathcal{A}$ an end message with an artificially generated transcript; this is done by using the oracle $\mathcal{O}$ to generate $\mathcal{A}$'s messages and ensuring that the transcript is consistent with the oracle. Formally, we make the following claim, which will be useful later:

Claim 1. *There exists a negligible function $\nu(\cdot)$ such that, for all $n \in \mathbb{N}$, the probability, over all randomness in the experiment $[\mathcal{R}^{\mathcal{A}^{\mathcal{O}}} \leftrightarrow \mathcal{C}](1^n)$, that some instance of $\mathcal{A}$ returns a forgery (i.e., something besides $\bot$) to $\mathcal{R}$ without having received $\ell(n)$ different responses to its signature queries from $\mathcal{R}$, is less than $\nu(n)$.*

The proof, which is straightforward, is deferred to the full version.

- Initially, receive a message pk, the public key; respond (i.e., generate m_1) according to the next step for $i = 1$.
- On receiving a message consisting of a partial transcript $\tau = (pk, m_1, \sigma_1, \cdots, m_{i-1}, \sigma_{i-1})$ for some $i \in [\ell(n)]$, do the following:
  - Generate m_i by taking the first n bits resulting from applying the oracle $\mathcal{O}$ to τ.
  - Return the new partial transcript $\tau || m_i$.
- On receiving a message consisting of a complete transcript $\tau = (pk, m_1, \sigma_1, \cdots, m_{\ell(n)}, \sigma_{\ell(n)})$ (we shall refer to such a message as a "forgery request" or "end message"), do the following:
  - Verify that, for each signature σ_i, $\mathsf{Ver}_{pk}(m_i, \sigma_i) = \mathsf{Accept}$. If not true for all i, return $\perp$.
  - Verify that, for each message m_i, m_i is equal to the first n bits resulting from applying the oracle $\mathcal{O}$ to the prefix transcript $\tau_{<i} = (pk, m_1, \sigma_1, \cdots, m_{i-1}, \sigma_{i-1})$. If not true for all i, then return $\perp$.
  - Finally, generate a random message m^* (distinct from each m_i in τ) by applying $\mathcal{O}$ to the transcript τ, use brute force to find a signature σ^* for which $\mathsf{Ver}_{pk}(m^*, \sigma^*) = \mathsf{Accept}$, and return the forgery (m^*, σ^*).

Fig. 3. Formal description of the "ideal" adversary $\mathcal{A}^{\mathcal{O}}$.

Furthermore, this construction of $\mathcal{A}$ (using the oracle $\mathcal{O}$) allows us to assume, without loss of generality, that the reduction $\mathcal{R}$ will never rewind an instance of $\mathcal{A}$—this is without loss of generality because there is a single accepting transcript for each choice of the oracle $\mathcal{O}$. Namely, given an oracle $\mathcal{O}$, if $\mathcal{R}$ always provides correct signatures, then $\mathcal{A}$'s messages (including the forgery it returns) and $\mathcal{R}$'s responses are fully determined by $\mathcal{O}$ and the uniqueness property of Π. Meanwhile, if $\mathcal{R}$ does not provide correct signatures, $\mathcal{A}$ will not return a forgery.

Because $\mathcal{A}$ breaks unforgeability, and by the assumed properties of $\mathcal{R}$ and the determinism of $\mathcal{A}^{\mathcal{O}}$ for any fixed oracle $\mathcal{O}$, it must be true that there exists polynomial $p(\cdot)$ such that

$$\Pr\left[\langle \mathcal{R}^{\mathcal{A}^{\mathcal{O}}}, \mathcal{C}\rangle(1^n) = \mathsf{Accept}\right] \geq t(n) + \frac{1}{p(n)}$$

for any oracle $\mathcal{O}$. As such, by the fact that $\mathcal{R}$ is fixed-parameter, we can observe that, for any n, averaging this probability over all possible oracles $\mathcal{O}$, we likewise have

$$\Pr\left[\langle \mathcal{R}^{\mathcal{A}}, \mathcal{C}\rangle(1^n) = \mathsf{Accept}\right] \geq t(n) + \frac{1}{p(n)}$$

even though $\mathcal{A}$ over a randomly-chosen $\mathcal{O}$ is not deterministic.

Of course, $\mathcal{A}$ is inefficient, so, in order to break the assumption $(\mathcal{C}, t(\cdot))$, we must construct an efficient $\mathcal{B}$ that is able to run $\mathcal{R}$ while emulating its interactions with $\mathcal{A}$ most of the time. Hence, the remainder of the proof will be dedicated to constructing this meta-reduction and analyzing the probability with which it succeeds in emulating the "ideal" $\mathcal{A}$. Intuitively, if $\mathcal{B}$ successfully emulates $\mathcal{A}$ at least $1 - 1/p'(n)$ of the time for some function $p'(\cdot)$, then:

$$\left|\Pr\left[\langle \mathcal{R}^{\mathcal{A}}, \mathcal{C}\rangle(1^n) = \mathsf{Accept}\right] - \Pr\left[\langle \mathcal{B}, \mathcal{C}\rangle(1^n) = \mathsf{Accept}\right]\right| \leq \frac{1}{p'(n)}$$

$$\Pr\left[\langle \mathcal{B}, \mathcal{C}\rangle(1^n) = \mathsf{Accept}\right] \geq t(n) + \frac{1}{p(n)} - \frac{1}{p'(n)}$$

meaning that $\mathcal{B}$ must break $\mathcal{C}$ with probability at least $1/p(n) - 1/p'(n)$, as desired. Hence, what we shall effectively show in the subsequent steps is that, unless the security loss of $\mathcal{R}$ is large, $1/p'(n)$ will be non-negligibly smaller than $1/p(n)$, and thus $\mathcal{B}$ will break the security of $(\mathcal{C}, t(\cdot))$.

Slots. As a notational aside, we shall for simplicity henceforth refer to the pair of a query made by $\mathcal{A}$ (or something, such as $\mathcal{B}$, which emulates $\mathcal{A}$) and its corresponding response by $\mathcal{R}$ as a *slot* (v_{open}, v_{close}). Such a slot is determined by two views: the "opening" of the slot, or the view v_{open} of the execution of $\mathcal{R}$ immediately before $\mathcal{A}$'s query to $\mathcal{R}$, and the "closing" of the slot, or the view v_{close} of the execution immediately after $\mathcal{R}$ responds to the respective query. (We will also often refer to the view of $\mathcal{R}$ immediately *after* the opening query of a message m, which we shall denote by the concatenation $v_{open}||m$).

3.2 The Meta-reduction

We next construct the meta-reduction $\mathcal{B}$ which will efficiently emulate $\mathcal{A}$. Let $\mathcal{B}$ be as described formally in Fig. 4; informally, $\mathcal{B}$ will run $\mathcal{R}$ internally, forwarding communication to $\mathcal{C}$ as $\mathcal{R}$ would while also internally simulating instances of $\mathcal{A}$ interacting with $\mathcal{R}$. The primary difference between $\mathcal{B}$ and the "ideal" execution of $\mathcal{A}$ interacting with $\mathcal{R}$ is that $\mathcal{B}$, being restricted to polynomial time, cannot brute-force forgeries as $\mathcal{A}$ does; instead, while simulating each instance of $\mathcal{A}$, $\mathcal{B}$ will select at random a message m^* for which to forge a signature and attempt to rewind each slot for that instance, substituting m^* for the original message.[4]

If $\mathcal{R}$ ever returns a valid signature σ^* for m^*, then $\mathcal{B}$ may store that signature and finally return (m^*, σ^*) when $\mathcal{R}$ requests a forgery for that instance. However, if one of the following "bad events" occurs:

- $\mathcal{R}$ fails to return a valid signature of m^*.
- $\mathcal{R}$ asks for a forgery for another instance before returning a signature.
- $\mathcal{R}$ requires external communication with $\mathcal{C}$ (which cannot be rewound) before returning a signature.

then $\mathcal{B}$ will abort and try the next slot. In this way we circumvent the issue of having to recursively rewind nested end messages as in [33].

First, we can show that $\mathcal{B}$, unlike $\mathcal{A}$, is efficient:

[4] That is, when "rewinding" a slot (v_{open}, v_{close}), $\mathcal{B}$ will simulate interaction with $\mathcal{R}$ starting from the view $v_{open}||m^*$.

- Set initial view $v \leftarrow \bot$ and set $k \leftarrow 1$. Execute $\mathcal{R}$, updating the current view v according to the following rules.
- When $\mathcal{R}$ begins a new instance of $\mathcal{A}$ and sends a public key pk, label this instance as instance k. Generate and store $\ell(n)$ random queries $\vec{m}_k = (m_{k,1}, \ldots, m_{k,\ell(n)})$ and a target forgery m_k^*. (Abort and return Fail if m_k^* is equal to a message in $\vec{m}_k$.) Also let $pk_k \leftarrow pk$ and initialize the forgery $f_k \leftarrow \{\}$. Lastly, respond with $\tau_k^* = pk_k || m_{k,1}$ and increment k.
- When $\mathcal{R}$ attempts to communicate externally with $\mathcal{C}$, forward the message, return $\mathcal{C}$'s response to $\mathcal{R}$, and update v accordingly.
- When $\mathcal{R}$ sends a transcript $\tau = (pk, m_{I,1}, \sigma_{I,1}, \cdots, m_{I,j}, \sigma_{I,j})$ to some simulated instance I of $\mathcal{A}$, store the signature $\sigma_{I,j}$ and do the following:
  - If $j = \ell(n)$ (i.e., this is an end message), then do the following:
    - If τ is an inconsistent transcript (i.e., $m_{I,i}$ or $\sigma_{I,i}$ in τ is different from the stored $m_{I,i}$ or $\sigma_{I,i}$ (respectively) for some $i \in [\ell(n)]$, or not all $\sigma_{I,i}$ have been stored) or $\mathcal{R}$'s response to some signature query j was invalid (i.e., $\mathsf{Ver}_{pk_I}(m_{I,i}, \sigma_{I,i}) = \mathsf{Reject}$ for some $i \in [\ell(n)]$), then return $\bot$.
    - Otherwise, if f_I is still empty (i.e., not $\bot$), run the procedure Rewind detailed below for the instance I.
    - If, at this point, there is a stored forgery $f_I = (m_I^*, \sigma_I^*)$, then return it and continue executing $\mathcal{R}$ as above. Otherwise, abort the entire execution of $\mathcal{B}$ and return Fail.
  - If $\mathsf{Ver}_{pk_I}(m_{I,j}, \sigma_{I,j}) = \mathsf{Reject}$, then store $f_I \leftarrow \bot$.
  - Lastly, respond with $\tau || m_{I,j+1}$ and continue the execution of $\mathcal{R}$.

Rewind procedure:

- Given instance I, for $j \in [\ell(n)]$ let $(v_{open}^j, v_{close}^j)$ denote the slot corresponding to the jth signature query for instance I.
- For each $j \in [\ell(n)]$, "rewind" the slot $(v_{open}^j, v_{close}^j)$ as follows: Let $k' \leftarrow k$, and begin executing $\mathcal{R}$ from the view $v' = v_{open}^j || m_I^*$ as in the main routine, with the following exceptions:
  - When $\mathcal{R}$ begins a new instance of $\mathcal{A}$, label this instance as instance k' and increment k'. (That is, continue creating new instances, but preserve the counter k in the outer execution for after the rewinding.)
  - When $\mathcal{R}$ attempts to communicate externally with $\mathcal{C}$, abort the rewinding and continue to the next j.
  - When $\mathcal{R}$ sends an end message for an instance $I' \neq I$ of $\mathcal{A}$, abort the rewinding and continue to the next j, *unless* $\mathcal{R}$ has not sent responses to $\ell(n)$ signature queries for I' (in which case reply with $\bot$).
  - If v' ever contains a message whose transcript contains a response σ_I^* to the query for m_I^*, then, if it is the case that $\mathsf{Ver}_{pk_I}(m_I^*, \sigma_I^*) = \mathsf{Accept}$, store $f_i \leftarrow (m_I^*, \sigma_I^*)$ and end the Rewind procedure (i.e., return to the outer execution); otherwise, if $\mathsf{Ver}_{pk_I}(m_I^*, \sigma_I^*) = \mathsf{Reject}$, store nothing to f_I and continue to the next j.

Fig. 4. Formal description of the meta-reduction $\mathcal{B}$.

Claim 2. *There exists a polynomial $t(n)$ such that, for all $n \in \mathbb{N}$, $\mathsf{Real}(1^n)$ is guaranteed to run in time at most $t(n)$.*

The proof, which is straightforward, is deferred to the full version.

Next, to reason about the failure probability of $\mathcal{B}$ (and through it the success probability of $\mathcal{R}^{\mathcal{A}}$), let us define the following experiments:

- Let $\mathsf{Ideal}(1^n)$ denote $[\mathcal{R}^{\mathcal{A}} \leftrightarrow \mathcal{C}](1^n)$—that is, the experiment where $\mathcal{R}(1^n)$, using the "ideal" adversary $\mathcal{A}(1^n)$ as a black box, communicates with $\mathcal{C}(1^n)$.
  - When we refer to probabilities in the context of this experiment, they are taken over a uniform distribution over random oracles $\mathcal{O}$ (which results in uniformly distributed messages $\vec{m}_I$ and m_I^*) for each instance I of $\mathcal{A}$ started by $\mathcal{R}$.
  - When we wish to fix the randomness of a particular execution of Ideal, we will denote this with the notation $\mathsf{Ideal}_{\{\mathcal{O}_I\}_{I \in [M(n)]}, \mathcal{O}_{ext}}(1^n)$, or, for more clarity, $\mathsf{Ideal}_{\{\vec{m}_I, m_I^*\}_{I \in [M(n)]}, \mathcal{O}_{ext}}(1^n)$. $\vec{m}_I$ and m_I^* are the messages and forgery generated for instance I by each oracle $\mathcal{O}_I$ given the (deterministic) prefix; $\mathcal{O}_{ext}$ is a random variable representing the random coins used by $\mathcal{R}$ and $\mathcal{C}$, containing a number of bits equal to the maximum number of coins needed (which must be polynomially many since $\mathcal{R}$ and $\mathcal{C}$ are polynomial-time). When all $\vec{m}_I$ and m_I^* are fixed, and $\mathcal{O}_{ext}$ is fixed, note that the execution of Ideal is deterministic for each instance.
- Let $\mathsf{Real}(1^n)$ denote $[\mathcal{B} \leftrightarrow \mathcal{C}](1^n)$—that is, the "real" experiment where $\mathcal{B}(1^n)$ communicates directly with $\mathcal{C}(1^n)$ by attempting to simulate the interaction between $\mathcal{A}(1^n)$ and $\mathcal{R}(1^n)$ while forwarding any external communications.
  - When we refer to probabilities in the context of this experiment, they are taken over uniformly distributed messages $\vec{m}_I$ and m_I^* for each simulated instance I of $\mathcal{A}$ started by $\mathcal{R}$ in the context of $\mathcal{B}$.
  - When we wish to fix the randomness of a particular execution of Real, we will again denote this with the notation $\mathsf{Real}_{\{\vec{m}_I, m_I^*\}_{I \in [M(n)]}, \mathcal{O}_{ext}}(1^n)$, where $\vec{m}_I$ and m_I^* are the messages and forgery for each simulated instance I of $\mathcal{A}$ and $\mathcal{O}_{ext}$ is again a random variable representing the random coins used by $\mathcal{R}$ and $\mathcal{C}$. When all $\vec{m}_I$ and m_I^* are fixed, and $\mathcal{O}_{ext}$ is fixed, note that the execution of Real is deterministic for each instance, just as with Ideal.
  - Furthermore, we may opt to isolate a particular simulated instance k by fixing all randomness *except for* that instance's; we denote this by $\mathsf{Real}^*_{\{\vec{m}_I, m_I^*\}_{-k}, \mathcal{O}_{ext}}(1^n)$ and note that the probability space in this altered experiment is over uniformly distributed $\vec{m}_k$ and m_k^*. Further note that in experiment Real^* the execution up to the start of the isolated instance k is deterministic, as is the execution for any choice of $\vec{m}_k$ and m_k^*.
- In all experiments, we will denote the *view*, or *execution*, as the transcript of all messages sent between, and all randomness consumed by, real or simulated machines (i.e., between $\mathcal{R}$, $\mathcal{A}$ or $\mathcal{B}$'s simulation of $\mathcal{A}$, and $\mathcal{C}$). We will notate this using just the notation for the experiment, e.g., $\mathsf{Real}(1^n)$.

– In all experiments, we will denote the *result*, or *output*, as either the final output of $\mathcal{C}$ (either Accept or Reject) if $\mathcal{C}$ finishes, or as Fail if $\mathcal{C}$ does not finish (i.e., when $\mathcal{B}$ aborts returning Fail). This will be notated by Output, e.g., $\mathsf{Output}[\mathsf{Real}(1^n)] = \mathsf{Accept}$.

3.3 Analyzing the Meta-reduction

Using this terminology, we wish to show that $\mathsf{Real}(1^n)$ is identically distributed to $\mathsf{Ideal}(1^n)$ with high probability. To that end, we make the following claim:

Claim 3. *For all* $n \in \mathbb{N}$*:*

$$|\Pr[\mathsf{Output}[\mathsf{Real}(1^n)] = \mathsf{Accept}] - \Pr[\mathsf{Output}[\mathsf{Ideal}(1^n)] = \mathsf{Accept}]| \leq \Pr[\mathsf{Output}[\mathsf{Real}(1^n)] = \mathsf{Fail}]$$

Proof Sketch. Intuitively, this follows from the uniqueness property of Π; for any message m^*, there is only a single possible signature σ^*. Thus, given some setting of the randomness in the experiments, Real must proceed identically to Ideal (that is, each instance of $\mathcal{A}$ in Real will have an identical view to the corresponding simulated instance in Ideal) *unless* $\mathcal{B}$'s attempt to extract a forgery fails for some m^*, in which case by construction Real must return Fail. The complete proof is deferred to the full version.

We can use this claim to bound $\mathcal{R}^{\mathcal{A}}$'s success probability by bounding the probability that $\mathcal{B}$ will return Fail for some simulated instance I of $\mathcal{A}$. Let $M(n)$ be the maximum, over all randomness of $\mathcal{A}$, $\mathcal{C}$, and $\mathcal{R}$, of the number of instances of $\mathcal{A}$ that $\mathcal{R}$ runs to completion (i.e., for which it responds to all $\ell(n)$ queries) during the experiment $\mathsf{Real}(1^n)$. Then we show the following:

Proposition 1. *There exists a negligible function* $\epsilon(\cdot)$ *such that, for all* $n \in \mathbb{N}$*:*

$$\Pr[\mathsf{Output}[\mathsf{Real}(1^n)] = \mathsf{Fail}] \leq M(n)\left(\frac{M(n) + r(n) + 1}{\ell(n) + 1}\right) + \epsilon(n)$$

Proof. We first prove the following claim for any $\mathsf{Real}^*_{\{\vec{m}_I, m^*_I\}_{-k}, \mathcal{O}_{ext}}(1^n)$ (i.e., for any fixed setting of all randomness aside from $\vec{m}_k$ and m^*_k), and notice that, since it applies to arbitrarily fixed randomness, it must thus apply over all possible randomness of the experiment $\mathsf{Real}(1^n)$:

Claim 4. *There exists a negligible* $\nu(\cdot)$ *such that, given any setting of the randomness in the experiment* $\mathsf{Real}^*_{\{\vec{m}_I, m^*_I\}_{-k}, \mathcal{O}_{ext}}(1^n)$*, the probability, over the uniformly chosen messages* $m_{k,1}, \ldots, m_{k,\ell(n)}, m^*_k$*, that the simulated instance* k *will return* Fail *is, for all* $n \in \mathbb{N}$*, at most*

$$\frac{M(n) + r(n) + 1}{\ell(n) + 1} + \nu(n)$$

Proof. Let us begin by assuming that other simulated instances (besides k) of $\mathcal{A}$ in the experiment $\mathsf{Real}^*_{\{\vec{m}_I, m_I^*\}_{-k}, \mathcal{O}_{ext}}(1^n)$ will never return Fail (i.e., that they will "magically" produce a correct forgery in the case where they otherwise would return Fail). Clearly, this can only increase the probability that instance k will return Fail by ensuring that the experiment never aborts early.

Now let us consider the messages $\vec{m^*}_k \triangleq (m_{k,1}, \ldots, m_{k,\ell(n)}, m_k^*)$ in instance k; note that by the definition of $\mathsf{Real}^*_{\{\vec{m}_I, m_I^*\}_{-k}, \mathcal{O}_{ext}}(1^n)$ the execution is fully determined by $\vec{m^*}_k$. Let us also define for $i \in [\ell(n) - 1]$ the "rewound" sequence

$$\rho(\vec{m^*}_k, i) \triangleq (m_{k,1}, \ldots, m_{k,i-1}, m_k^*)$$

that is, the rewinding of $\vec{m}_k$ where the message in slot i is replaced by m_k^* to attempt to extract a forgery.

In order for $\mathcal{B}$ to return Fail, one of the following "bad events" must occur for each $i \in [\ell(n)]$:

- $E_1(\rho(\vec{m^*}_k, i))$: $\mathcal{R}$ fails to return a valid signature of m_I^* in the rewinding of the last slot in the sequence (slot i).
- $E_2(\rho(\vec{m^*}_k, i))$: During the rewinding of the last slot in the sequence (slot i), $\mathcal{R}$ asks for a forgery for another instance $k' \neq k$ before returning a signature for m_I^*, *or* $\mathcal{R}$ requires external communication with $\mathcal{C}$ (which cannot be rewound) before returning a signature for m_I^*.

In addition, for k to fail, the non-rewound execution of the instance must succeed, in that the event $E_1(\vec{m}_{k,\leq i})$ (where $\mathcal{R}$ fails to return a valid signature) *cannot* occur for any prefix $\vec{m}_{k,\leq i} = (m_{k,1}, \ldots, m_{k,i})$, where $i \in [\ell(n)]$.

Since, as we have noted, the behavior of k in $\mathsf{Real}^*_{\{\vec{m}_I, m_I^*\}_{-k}, \mathcal{O}_{ext}}(1^n)$ is fully determined by $\vec{m^*}_k$, every sequence $\vec{m^*}_k$ will deterministically either result in instance k returning something (either a forgery or $\perp$) or aborting and returning Fail; we shall refer to the former type of sequence (where k succeeds) as a "good" sequence, and the latter type as a "bad" sequence. To describe the relationship between these "good" and "bad" sequences, we first introduce the following terminology:

For any $k > 0$ and any arbitrary set $\vec{m}$ of k distinct messages in $[2^n]$, let $\Pi_k(\vec{m})$ denote the set of ordered permutations of the elements of $\vec{m}$. Given a sequence $\pi = (m_1, \ldots, m_{k-1}, m^*) \in \Pi_k(\vec{m})$, we let the "rewinding" operator ρ for $i \in [k-1]$ be defined as before—that is:

$$\rho(\pi, i) \triangleq (m_1, \ldots, m_{i-1}, m^*)$$

(Note that this is a sequence of length i.) We shall say that a sequence $a = (a_1, \ldots, a_{k-1}, a^*) \in \Pi_k(\vec{m})$ *blocks* a sequence $b = (b_1, \ldots, b_{k-1}, b^*) \in \Pi_k(\vec{m})$ with respect to some $i \in [k-1]$ if

$$\rho(a, i) = (b_1, \ldots, b_i)$$

that is, if a has a rewinding equivalent to a prefix of b. If we wish to denote that a blocks b with respect to a particular i, we shall say that a blocks b *in slot* i. Furthermore, we will say that sequences $a^1, a^2, \ldots a^c \in \Pi_k(\vec{m})$ *c-block* a sequence $b \in \Pi_k(\vec{m})$ if there exist *distinct* $i_1, \ldots, i_c \in [k-1]$ such that, for any $j \in [c]$, a^j blocks b in slot i_j.

We next formalize the relationship between the "blocking" property and good/bad sequences that will allow us to use this property to bound the number of bad sequences that may occur. Specifically, we prove the following lemma:

Lemma 2. *Any sequence that is* $(M(n)+r(n)+1)$*-blocked by bad sequences must be a good sequence.*

Proof. Consider a sequence $\vec{m'}_k$ which is $(M(n)+r(n)+1)$-blocked by bad sequences. This means that $\vec{m'}_k$ must have $M(n)+r(n)+1$ distinct slots i_j for which E_1 or E_2 occurs in its (non-rewound) execution, as the execution is at each of those points identical to a rewinding of one of the bad sequences by the fact that the sequence blocks $\vec{m'}_k$ in slot i_j. However, because at most $M(n)$ end messages (to completed instances of $\mathcal{A}$, note that others are answered with $\perp$) and at most $r(n)$ rounds of external communication can occur in any given execution, we observe that E_2 can happen for at most $M(n)+r(n)$ of these slots, and thus that E_1 must happen for at least one slot. In this case, we can deduce that $\vec{m'}_k$ must be a *good* sequence, because it must contain some slot for which $\mathcal{R}$ fails to return a correct response (meaning that $\mathcal{B}$ can successfully emulate $\mathcal{A}$ by returning $\perp$)—that is, the event $E_1(\vec{m}_{k,\leq i})$ must occur for that slot, which we have previously stated cannot be the case for bad $\vec{m^*}_k$. □

Consider, then, a set S of "bad" sequences $\vec{m^*}_k$ which are permutations of any set of $\ell(n)+1$ distinct messages (i.e., an unordered set containing $\vec{m}_{k,i}$ and m^*_k). The following lemma, combined with Lemma 2, allows us to bound the size of such a set S:

Lemma 3. *Let* $\vec{m}$ *be an arbitrary set of* $\ell+1$ *distinct messages in* $[2^n]$*, and let* $S \subset \Pi_{\ell+1}(\vec{m})$ *be a set of permutations of* $\vec{m}$*. If it is the case that, for some* $B \in \mathbb{N}$*, any member of* $\Pi_{\ell+1}(\vec{m})$ *which is* $(B+1)$*-blocked by a subset of* S *cannot itself lie in* S*, then* $|S| \leq (B+1)\ell!$

Proof. We begin with the following crucial claim: □

Subclaim 1. *No member of* $\Pi_{\ell+1}(\vec{m})$ *is* $(B+2)$*-blocked by a subset of* S*.*

Proof. Assume for the sake of contradiction that there exists some $\pi \in \Pi_{\ell+1}(\vec{m})$, $B+2$ sequences $\pi^1, \ldots, \pi^{B+2} \in S$, and $B+2$ distinct integers $i_1, \ldots, i_{B+2} \in [\ell]$ such that each partial sequence $\rho(\pi^j, i_j)$ is equivalent to the first i_j elements of π.

Assume without loss of generality that the integers i_j are in strictly ascending order. Consider the last sequence $\pi^{B+2} = (\pi_1^{B+2}, \ldots, \pi_*^{B+2})$; we shall show that π^{B+2} is $(M+1)$-blocked by sequences in S, leading to a contradiction because by definition no element of S can be $(M+1)$-blocked by other members of S.

We know that, since by assumption the first i_{B+2} elements of π are equivalent to $\rho(\pi^{B+2}, i_{B+2}) = (\pi_1^{B+2}, \ldots, \pi_{i_{B+2}-1}^{B+2}, \pi_*^{B+2})$, then the first $i_{B+2}-1$ elements of π^{B+2} and π must be identical. However, notice that, for any $j < B+2$, we have that $\rho(\pi^j, i_j)$ is identical to π in the first i_j elements, which, since by assumption $i_j \leq i_{B+2} - 1$, also indicates that $\rho(\pi^j, i_j)$ is identical to π^{B+2} in the first i_j elements.

This in turn implies that π^{B+2} is $(B+1)$-blocked by $\pi^1, \ldots, \pi^{B+1} \in S$, contradicting that $\pi^{B+2} \in S$ by the requisite property of S. □

So, we know that any member of S can be at most B-blocked by a subset of S, while any non-member can be at most $(B+1)$-blocked by a subset of S. We will combine this fact (an effective upper bound on the number of blocked sequences) with the subsequent claim (a respective lower bound) to derive our final bound on $|S|$.

Subclaim 2. *For each $i \in [\ell]$, there exist $|S|$ distinct sequences blocked in slot i by sequences in S.*

Proof. Beginning with $i = 1$, we observe that sequences with at least $|S|/\ell!$ different last elements m^* must occur in S (as there are only $\ell!$ sequences with any given last element). Furthermore, any sequence in S with a certain last element m^* must block in slot 1 a total of $\ell!$ different sequences (i.e., anything beginning with m^*), and different m^* will produce disjoint sets of sequences blocked. Thus, we conclude that the sequences in S will block in slot 1 at least $(|S|/\ell!)\ell! = |S|$ distinct sequences.

For the remaining slots $i > 1$, we can apply the same logic to the distinct arrangements of the elements $(m_1, \ldots, m_{i-1})$ and m^*. Among the sequences in S there must be a minimum of $|S|/(\ell+1-i)!$ such arrangements (since, given a fixed $(m_1, \ldots, m_{i-1}, m^*)$, there are $(\ell+1-i)!$ sequences possible), and sequences with each arrangement will block in slot i a total of $(\ell+1-i)!$ distinct sequences (i.e., any sequence beginning with $(m_1, \ldots, m_{i-1}, m^*)$). Hence, the sequences in S will block in slot i at least $(|S|/(\ell+1-i)!)(\ell+1-i)! = |S|$ distinct sequences. □

In total, we notice that at least $|S|$ distinct sequences are blocked in slot i for any $i \in [\ell]$, and so there are at least $|S|\ell$ distinct pairs (π, i) such that the sequence π is blocked in slot i by sequences in S. Furthermore, we recall that the sequences in S are each blocked in slot i by sequences in S for at most B different i, while the remaining $(\ell+1)! - |S|$ elements are each blocked in slot i by sequences in S for at most $B+1$ different i. This provides an upper bound of $B|S| + ((\ell+1)! - |S|)(B+1)$ on the number of "blocking" pairs (π, i). We lastly combine these lower and upper bounds (noting that, if the lower bound exceeded the upper bound, there would be a contradiction) to bound $|S|$:

$$|S|\ell \leq B|S| + ((\ell+1)! - |S|)(B+1) = B(\ell+1)! + (\ell+1)! - |S|$$
$$|S|(\ell+1) \leq (B+1)(\ell+1)!$$
$$|S| \leq (B+1)\ell!$$

□

Recall that, if S is the set of all bad sequences which are permutations of some set $\vec{m^*}$ of $\ell(n)+1$ distinct messages, we have by Lemma 2 that any sequence which is $(M(n)+r(n)+1)$-blocked by bad sequences in S must be good and thus lie outside of S. Hence, by Lemma 3, S has size at most $(M(n)+r(n)+1)\,(\ell(n))!$. Given any set of $\ell(n)+1$ distinct messages, then, the above applies to show that at most an

$$\frac{(M(n)+r(n)+1)\,(\ell(n))!}{(\ell(n)+1)!} = \frac{M(n)+r(n)+1}{\ell(n)+1}$$

fraction of the sequences defined by the permutations of this set can be bad, and the remainder must be good. Applying this to every possible set of $\ell(n)+1$ distinct messages, we get that at most the same fraction of *all* sequences of distinct messages can be bad. While the property that messages are distinct is not necessarily guaranteed, we note that the probability that they are not over uniformly randomly chosen messages is negligible—specifically, we notice that the probability of any pair of elements colliding is 2^{-n}, and so, by the union bound, the probability that any of the $\frac{\ell(n)(\ell(n)+1)}{2}$ pairs of elements can collide is smaller than $\nu(n) \triangleq \ell(n)^2 2^{-n}$ (which is negligible in n because $\ell(\cdot)$ is polynomial).

Hence, the chance that a sequence chosen at random is bad, which by definition is equal to the probability that a randomly chosen sequence of messages $\vec{m^*}_k = (m_{k,1}, \ldots, m_{k,\ell(n)}, m_k^*)$ will result in instance k returning Fail, can be at most the fraction of sequences without repeated elements which are bad plus the fraction of sequences with repeated elements, or $\frac{M(n)+r(n)+1}{\ell(n)+1} + \nu(n)$, as desired. □

Recall that, because this result holds for any execution of the experiment $\mathsf{Real}^*_{\{\vec{m}_I, m_I^*\}_{-k}, \mathcal{O}_{ext}}(1^n)$, it must also hold over a *random* such execution—i.e., the actual execution $\mathsf{Real}(1^n)$ of $\mathcal{B}$, where the messages for all instances are chosen uniformly at random. Furthermore, it holds for any instance k of $\mathcal{A}$.

To conclude the proof of the proposition, by Claim 1 we know that $\mathcal{R}$ must send a total of at least $\ell(n)$ messages to each instance of $\mathcal{A}$ in order for the failure probability of $\mathcal{B}$ to emulate that instance to be more than negligible; if not, then $\mathcal{B}$ will always respond with $\bot$ (having not received $\ell(n)$ signature query responses), while $\mathcal{A}$ will return $\bot$ with all but negligible probability. Recall that $M(n)$ is an upper bound to the number of instances of $\mathcal{A}$ to which $\mathcal{R}$ sends $\ell(n)$ messages. By Claim 4 and a union bound over all $M(n)$ completed instances of $\mathcal{A}$, the failure probability of $\mathcal{B}$ for those instances is at most

$$M(n)\left(\frac{M(n)+r(n)+1}{\ell(n)+1} + \nu(n)\right)$$

for negligible $\nu(\cdot)$, and the failure probability for all other instances (of which there can only be a polynomial number by the time constraint on $\mathcal{R}$) is negligible by the union bound applied to Claim 1. Hence the overall failure probability of Real (i.e., the execution of $\mathcal{B}$) must be bounded above by

$$\Pr[\mathsf{Output}[\mathsf{Real}(1^n)] = \mathsf{Fail}] \leq M(n)\left(\frac{M(n)+r(n)+1}{\ell(n)+1} + \nu(n)\right) + \nu'(n)$$
$$< M(n)\left(\frac{M(n)+r(n)+1}{\ell(n)+1}\right) + \epsilon(n)$$

for some negligible functions $\nu'(\cdot)$ and $\epsilon(\cdot)$. □

Completing the Proof of Lemma 1. Finally, in order to bound the security loss, we note that, if the probability $\mathsf{Success}_{\mathcal{R}^{\mathcal{A}}}(n)$ (which specifically is by definition a lower bound to the probability $\Pr[\mathsf{Output}[\mathsf{Ideal}(1^n)] = \mathsf{Accept}] - t(n)$; recall that $t(\cdot)$ is the threshold for the underlying assumption $\mathcal{C}$) is non-negligibly greater than the failure probability of Real, there exists a polynomial $p(\cdot)$ such that:

$$\Pr[\mathsf{Output}[\mathsf{Ideal}(1^n)] = \mathsf{Accept}] - t(n) \geq \Pr[\mathsf{Output}[\mathsf{Real}(1^n)] = \mathsf{Fail}] + \frac{1}{p(n)}$$

But, by Claim 3, this would imply that

$$\Pr[\mathsf{Output}[\mathsf{Real}(1^n)] = \mathsf{Accept}] - t(n) \geq \frac{1}{p(n)}$$

that is, that $\mathcal{B}$ breaks the security of $(\mathcal{C}, t(\cdot))$. So, by Proposition 1, unless $\mathcal{B}$ breaks the security of $(\mathcal{C}, t(\cdot))$, the above cannot be the case—that is, there must exist negligible $\epsilon(\cdot), \epsilon'(\cdot)$ such that, for sufficiently large n:

$$\mathsf{Success}_{\mathcal{R}^{\mathcal{A}}}(n) \leq \Pr[\mathsf{Output}[\mathsf{Real}(1^n)] = \mathsf{Fail}] + \epsilon'(n)$$
$$< M(n)\left(\frac{M(n)+r(n)+1}{\ell(n)+1}\right) + (\epsilon(n)+\epsilon'(n)) < M(n)\left(\frac{M(n)+r(n)+1}{\ell(n)}\right)$$

Of course, $\mathsf{Success}_{\mathcal{R}^{\mathcal{A}}}(n)$, being a probability, is also trivially bounded above by 1. Furthermore, by the definition of $M(n)$, we know that $\mathsf{Query}_{\mathcal{R}^{\mathcal{A}}}(n) \geq M(n)\ell(n)$. Lastly, we consider two cases to derive our bound on the security loss.

Case 1. If $M(n) \geq \sqrt{\ell(n)} - (r(n)+1)$, then:

$$\lambda_{\mathcal{R}}(n) \geq \frac{\mathsf{Success}_{\mathcal{A}}(n)}{\mathsf{Success}_{\mathcal{R}^{\mathcal{A}}}(n)} \frac{\mathsf{Query}_{\mathcal{R}^{\mathcal{A}}}(n)}{\mathsf{Query}_{\mathcal{A}}(n)} \geq \frac{1}{1} \frac{M(n)\ell(n)}{\ell(n)}$$
$$= M(n) \geq \sqrt{\ell(n)} - (r(n)+1)$$

Case 2. Otherwise, if $M(n) < \sqrt{\ell(n)} - (r(n)+1)$ we have $M(n) + r(n) + 1 < \sqrt{\ell(n)}$, and so:

$$\lambda_{\mathcal{R}}(n) \geq \frac{\mathsf{Success}_{\mathcal{A}}(n)}{\mathsf{Success}_{\mathcal{R}^{\mathcal{A}}}(n)} \frac{\mathsf{Query}_{\mathcal{R}^{\mathcal{A}}}(n)}{\mathsf{Query}_{\mathcal{A}}(n)} \geq \frac{1}{M(n)\left(\frac{M(n)+r(n)+1}{\ell(n)}\right)} \frac{M(n)\ell(n)}{\ell(n)}$$
$$= \frac{\ell(n)}{M(n)+r(n)+1} > \frac{\ell(n)}{\sqrt{\ell(n)}} = \sqrt{\ell(n)}$$

Either way, we observe that $\lambda_{\mathcal{R}}(n) \geq \sqrt{\ell(n)} - (r(n)+1)$, thus completing the proof of both Lemma 1 and Theorem 2.

References

1. Abdalla, M., Fouque, P.-A., Lyubashevsky, V., Tibouchi, M.: Tightly-secure signatures from lossy identification schemes. In: Pointcheval, D., Johansson, T. (eds.) EUROCRYPT 2012. LNCS, vol. 7237, pp. 572–590. Springer, Heidelberg (2012). https://doi.org/10.1007/978-3-642-29011-4_34
2. Abe, M., Groth, J., Ohkubo, M.: Separating short structure-preserving signatures from non-interactive assumptions. In: Lee, D.H., Wang, X. (eds.) ASIACRYPT 2011. LNCS, vol. 7073, pp. 628–646. Springer, Heidelberg (2011). https://doi.org/10.1007/978-3-642-25385-0_34
3. Bader, C., Jager, T., Li, Y., Schäge, S.: On the impossibility of tight cryptographic reductions. In: Fischlin, M., Coron, J.-S. (eds.) EUROCRYPT 2016, Part II. LNCS, vol. 9666, pp. 273–304. Springer, Heidelberg (2016). https://doi.org/10.1007/978-3-662-49896-5_10
4. Baecher, P., Brzuska, C., Fischlin, M.: Notions of black-box reductions, revisited. In: Sako, K., Sarkar, P. (eds.) ASIACRYPT 2013, Part I. LNCS, vol. 8269, pp. 296–315. Springer, Heidelberg (2013). https://doi.org/10.1007/978-3-642-42033-7_16
5. Bellare, M., Rogaway, P.: The exact security of digital signatures-how to sign with RSA and Rabin. In: Maurer, U. (ed.) EUROCRYPT 1996. LNCS, vol. 1070, pp. 399–416. Springer, Heidelberg (1996). https://doi.org/10.1007/3-540-68339-9_34
6. Bernhard, D., Fischlin, M., Warinschi, B.: On the hardness of proving CCA-security of signed ElGamal. In: Cheng, C.-M., Chung, K.-M., Persiano, G., Yang, B.-Y. (eds.) PKC 2016, Part I. LNCS, vol. 9614, pp. 47–69. Springer, Heidelberg (2016). https://doi.org/10.1007/978-3-662-49384-7_3
7. Bernstein, D.J.: Proving tight security for Rabin-Williams signatures. In: Smart, N. (ed.) EUROCRYPT 2008. LNCS, vol. 4965, pp. 70–87. Springer, Heidelberg (2008). https://doi.org/10.1007/978-3-540-78967-3_5
8. Boneh, D., Venkatesan, R.: Breaking RSA may not be equivalent to factoring. In: Nyberg, K. (ed.) EUROCRYPT 1998. LNCS, vol. 1403, pp. 59–71. Springer, Heidelberg (1998). https://doi.org/10.1007/BFb0054117
9. Brakerski, Z., Goldwasser, S., Rothblum, G.N., Vaikuntanathan, V.: Weak verifiable random functions. In: Reingold, O. (ed.) TCC 2009. LNCS, vol. 5444, pp. 558–576. Springer, Heidelberg (2009). https://doi.org/10.1007/978-3-642-00457-5_33
10. Bresson, E., Monnerat, J., Vergnaud, D.: Separation results on the "one-more" computational problems. In: Malkin, T. (ed.) CT-RSA 2008. LNCS, vol. 4964, pp. 71–87. Springer, Heidelberg (2008). https://doi.org/10.1007/978-3-540-79263-5_5
11. Canetti, R., Lin, H., Pass, R.: Adaptive hardness and composable security in the plain model from standard assumptions. In: 2010 IEEE 51st Annual Symposium on Foundations of Computer Science, pp. 541–550, October 2010
12. Chen, J., Gong, J., Weng, J.: Tightly secure IBE under constant-size master public key. In: Fehr, S. (ed.) PKC 2017. LNCS, vol. 10174, pp. 207–231. Springer, Heidelberg (2017). https://doi.org/10.1007/978-3-662-54365-8_9
13. Chen, J., Wee, H.: Fully, (almost) tightly secure IBE and dual system groups. In: Canetti, R., Garay, J.A. (eds.) CRYPTO 2013. LNCS, vol. 8043, pp. 435–460. Springer, Heidelberg (2013). https://doi.org/10.1007/978-3-642-40084-1_25
14. Coron, J.-S.: Optimal security proofs for PSS and other signature schemes. In: Knudsen, L.R. (ed.) EUROCRYPT 2002. LNCS, vol. 2332, pp. 272–287. Springer, Heidelberg (2002). https://doi.org/10.1007/3-540-46035-7_18

15. Deng, Y., Goyal, V., Sahai, A.: Resolving the simultaneous resettability conjecture and a new non-black-box simulation strategy. In: Proceedings of the 2009 50th Annual IEEE Symposium on Foundations of Computer Science, FOCS 2009, pp. 251–260. IEEE Computer Society, Washington, DC (2009)
16. Diffie, W., Hellman, M.: New directions in cryptography. IEEE Trans. Inf. Theor. **22**(6), 644–654 (2006)
17. Dwork, C., Naor, M., Sahai, A.: Concurrent zero-knowledge. In: Proceedings of the Thirtieth Annual ACM Symposium on Theory of Computing, STOC 1998, pp. 409–418. ACM, New York (1998)
18. Fischlin, M., Schröder, D.: On the impossibility of three-move blind signature schemes. In: Gilbert, H. (ed.) EUROCRYPT 2010. LNCS, vol. 6110, pp. 197–215. Springer, Heidelberg (2010). https://doi.org/10.1007/978-3-642-13190-5_10
19. Gilad, Y., Hemo, R., Micali, S., Vlachos, G., Zeldovich, N.: Algorand: scaling byzantine agreements for cryptocurrencies. In: Proceedings of the 26th Symposium on Operating Systems Principles, SOSP 2017, pp. 51–68. ACM, New York (2017)
20. Goldwasser, S., Micali, S., Rackoff, C.: The knowledge complexity of interactive proof-systems. In: Proceedings of the Seventeenth Annual ACM Symposium on Theory of Computing, STOC 1985, pp. 291–304. ACM, New York (1985)
21. Goldwasser, S., Micali, S., Rivest, R.L.: A digital signature scheme secure against adaptive chosen-message attacks. SIAM J. Comput. **17**(2), 281–308 (1988)
22. Haitner, I., Rosen, A., Shaltiel, R.: On the (im)possibility of Arthur-Merlin witness hiding protocols. In: Reingold, O. (ed.) TCC 2009. LNCS, vol. 5444, pp. 220–237. Springer, Heidelberg (2009). https://doi.org/10.1007/978-3-642-00457-5_14
23. Hofheinz, D., Jager, T.: Tightly secure signatures and public-key encryption. In: Safavi-Naini, R., Canetti, R. (eds.) CRYPTO 2012. LNCS, vol. 7417, pp. 590–607. Springer, Heidelberg (2012). https://doi.org/10.1007/978-3-642-32009-5_35
24. Hofheinz, D., Jager, T., Knapp, E.: Waters signatures with optimal security reduction. In: Fischlin, M., Buchmann, J., Manulis, M. (eds.) PKC 2012. LNCS, vol. 7293, pp. 66–83. Springer, Heidelberg (2012). https://doi.org/10.1007/978-3-642-30057-8_5
25. Impagliazzo, R., Rudich, S.: Limits on the provable consequences of one-way permutations. In: Proceedings of the Twenty-First Annual ACM Symposium on Theory of Computing, STOC 1989, pp. 44–61. ACM, New York (1989)
26. Jager, T.: Verifiable random functions from weaker assumptions. In: Dodis, Y., Nielsen, J.B. (eds.) TCC 2015, Part II. LNCS, vol. 9015, pp. 121–143. Springer, Heidelberg (2015). https://doi.org/10.1007/978-3-662-46497-7_5
27. Kakvi, S.A., Kiltz, E.: Optimal security proofs for full domain hash, revisited. In: Pointcheval, D., Johansson, T. (eds.) EUROCRYPT 2012. LNCS, vol. 7237, pp. 537–553. Springer, Heidelberg (2012). https://doi.org/10.1007/978-3-642-29011-4_32
28. Lindell, Y.: Bounded-concurrent secure two-party computation without setup assumptions. In: Proceedings of the Thirty-Fifth Annual ACM Symposium on Theory of Computing, STOC 2003, pp. 683–692. ACM, New York (2003)
29. Luby, M.: Pseudorandomness and Cryptographic Applications. Princeton University Press, Princeton (1996)
30. Lysyanskaya, A.: Unique signatures and verifiable random functions from the DH-DDH separation. In: Yung, M. (ed.) CRYPTO 2002. LNCS, vol. 2442, pp. 597–612. Springer, Heidelberg (2002). https://doi.org/10.1007/3-540-45708-9_38
31. Micali, S., Vadhan, S., Rabin, M.: Verifiable random functions. In: Proceedings of the 40th Annual Symposium on Foundations of Computer Science, FOCS 1999, p. 120–130. IEEE Computer Society, Washington, DC (1999)

32. Naor, M.: On cryptographic assumptions and challenges. In: Boneh, D. (ed.) CRYPTO 2003. LNCS, vol. 2729, pp. 96–109. Springer, Heidelberg (2003). https://doi.org/10.1007/978-3-540-45146-4_6
33. Pass, R.: Limits of provable security from standard assumptions. In: Proceedings of the Forty-Third Annual ACM Symposium on Theory of Computing, STOC 2011, pp. 109–118. ACM, New York (2011)
34. Pass, R., Shi, E.: The sleepy model of consensus. In: Takagi, T., Peyrin, T. (eds.) ASIACRYPT 2017. LNCS, vol. 10625, pp. 380–409. Springer, Cham (2017). https://doi.org/10.1007/978-3-319-70697-9_14
35. Pass, R., Tseng, W.-L., Venkitasubramaniam, M.: Concurrent zero knowledge, revisited. J. Cryptol. **27**(1), 45–66 (2014)
36. Pass, R., Venkitasubramaniam, M.: On constant-round concurrent zero-knowledge. In: Canetti, R. (ed.) TCC 2008. LNCS, vol. 4948, pp. 553–570. Springer, Heidelberg (2008). https://doi.org/10.1007/978-3-540-78524-8_30
37. Prabhakaran, M., Rosen, A., Sahai, A.: Concurrent zero knowledge with logarithmic round-complexity. In: Proceedings of the 43rd Symposium on Foundations of Computer Science, FOCS 2002, pp. 366–375. IEEE Computer Society, Washington, DC (2002)
38. Rabin, M.: Digitalized signatures and public-key functions as intractable as factorization. Technical report, Cambridge, MA, USA (1979)
39. Richardson, R., Kilian, J.: On the concurrent composition of zero-knowledge proofs. In: Stern, J. (ed.) EUROCRYPT 1999. LNCS, vol. 1592, pp. 415–431. Springer, Heidelberg (1999). https://doi.org/10.1007/3-540-48910-X_29
40. Rivest, R., Shamir, A., Adleman, L.: A method for obtaining digital signatures and public-key cryptosystems. Commun. ACM **21**(2), 120–126 (1978)
41. Shamir, A.: A fast signature scheme. Technical report, Cambridge, MA, USA (1978)
42. Wang, Y., Matsuda, T., Hanaoka, G., Tanaka, K.: Memory lower bounds of reductions revisited. In: Nielsen, J.B., Rijmen, V. (eds.) EUROCRYPT 2018, Part I. LNCS, vol. 10820, pp. 61–90. Springer, Cham (2018). https://doi.org/10.1007/978-3-319-78381-9_3

Coin-Tossing and Fairness

On the Complexity of Fair Coin Flipping

Iftach Haitner[1(✉)], Nikolaos Makriyannis[1], and Eran Omri[2]

[1] School of Computer Science, Tel Aviv University, Tel Aviv, Israel
iftachh@cs.tau.ac.il, n.makriyannis@gmail.com
[2] Department of Computer Science, Ariel University, Ariel, Israel
omrier@ariel.ac.il

Abstract. A two-party coin-flipping protocol is ε-fair if no efficient adversary can bias the output of the honest party (who always outputs a bit, even if the other party aborts) by more than ε. Cleve [STOC '86] showed that r-round $o(1/r)$-fair coin-flipping protocols do not exist. Awerbuch et al. [Manuscript '85] constructed a $\Theta(1/\sqrt{r})$-fair coin-flipping protocol, assuming the existence of one-way functions. Moran et al. [Journal of Cryptology '16] constructed an r-round coin-flipping protocol that is $\Theta(1/r)$-fair (thus matching the aforementioned lower bound of Cleve [STOC '86]), assuming the existence of oblivious transfer.

The above gives rise to the intriguing question of whether oblivious transfer, or more generally "public-key primitives", is required for an $o(1/\sqrt{r})$-fair coin flipping. This question was partially answered by Dachman-Soled et al. [TCC '11] and Dachman-Soled et al. [TCC '14], who showed that *restricted* types of fully black-box reductions cannot establish $o(1/\sqrt{r})$-fair coin-flipping protocols from one-way functions. In particular, for constant-round coin-flipping protocols, [10] yields that black-box techniques from one-way functions can only guarantee fairness of order $1/\sqrt{r}$.

We make progress towards answering the above question by showing that, for any constant $r \in \mathbb{N}$, the existence of an $1/(c \cdot \sqrt{r})$-fair, r-round coin-flipping protocol implies the existence of an infinitely-often key-agreement protocol, where c denotes some universal constant (independent of r). Our reduction is non black-box and makes a novel use of the recent dichotomy for two-party protocols of Haitner et al. [FOCS '18] to facilitate a two-party variant of the attack of Beimel et al. [FOCS '18] on multi-party coin-flipping protocols.

Keywords: Coin-flipping · Fairness · Key-agreement

1 Introduction

In a two-party coin flipping protocol, introduced by Blum [6], the parties wish to output a common (close to) uniform bit, even though one of the parties

I. Haitner and N. Makriyannis—Research supported by ERC starting grant 638121.
I. Haitner and N. Makriyannis—Research supported by the Check Point Institute for Information Security.
E. Omri—Research supported by ISF grant 152/17.

A. Beimel and S. Dziembowski (Eds.): TCC 2018, LNCS 11239, pp. 539–562, 2018.
https://doi.org/10.1007/978-3-030-03807-6_20

may be corrupted and try to bias the output. Slightly more formally, an ε-fair coin flipping protocol should satisfy the following two properties: first, when both parties behave honestly (i.e., follow the prescribed protocol), they both output the *same* uniform bit. Second, in the presence of a corrupted party that may deviate from the protocol arbitrarily, the distribution of the honest party's output may deviate from the uniform distribution (unbiased bit) by at most ε. We emphasize that the above notion requires an honest party to *always* output a bit, regardless of what the corrupted party does, and, in particular, it is not allowed to abort if a cheat is detected.[1] Coin flipping is a fundamental primitive with numerous applications, and thus lower bounds on coin flipping protocols yield analogous bounds for many basic cryptographic primitives, including other inputless primitives and secure computation of functions that take input (e.g., XOR).

In his seminal work, Cleve [8] showed that, for *any* efficient two-party r-round coin flipping protocol, there exists an efficient adversarial strategy that biases the output of the honest party by $\Theta(1/r)$. The above lower bound on coin flipping protocols was met for the two-party case by Moran, Naor, and Segev [20] improving over the $\Theta(n/\sqrt{r})$-fairness achieved by the majority protocol of Awerbuch, Blum, Chor, Goldwasser, and Micali [2]. The protocol of [20], however, uses oblivious transfer; to be compared with the protocol of [2] that can be based on any one-way function. An intriguing open question is whether oblivious transfer, or more generally "public-key primitives", is required for an $o(1/\sqrt{r})$-fair coin flip. The question was partially answered in the black-box setting by Dachman-Soled, Lindell, Mahmoody, and Malkin [10] and Dachman-Soled, Mahmoody, and Malkin [11], who showed that *restricted* types of fully black-box reductions cannot establish $o(1/\sqrt{r})$-bias coin flipping protocols from one-way functions. In particular, for constant-round coin flipping protocols, [10] yields that black-box techniques from one-way functions can only guarantee fairness of order $1/\sqrt{r}$.

1.1 Our Results

Our main result is that constant-round coin flipping protocols with better bias compared to the majority protocol of [2] imply the existence of infinitely-often key-agreement. We recall that infinitely-often key-agreement protocols satisfy correctness (parties agree on a common bit with overwhelming probability), and, for an infinite number of security parameters, no efficient eavesdropper can deduce the output with probability noticeably far from a random guess.[2]

Theorem 1.1 (Main result, informal). *For any (constant)* $r \in \mathbb{N}$, *the existence of an* $1/(c \cdot \sqrt{r})$*-fair,* r*-round coin flipping protocol implies the existence*

[1] Such protocols are typically addressed as having *guaranteed output delivery*, or, abusing terminology, as *fair*.

[2] While infinitely-often key-agreement protocols are useless from a cryptographic point of view, constructing such protocols appears to be as hard as obtaining full-blown key agreement.

an infinitely-often key-agreement protocol, for $c > 0$ being a universal constant (independent of r).

As in [8,10,11], our result extends via a simple reduction to general multi-party coin flipping protocols (with more than two-parties) without an honest majority. Our non black-box reduction makes a novel use of the recent dichotomy for two-party protocols of Haitner et al. [12]. Specifically, assuming that io-key-agreement does not exist and applying Haitner et al.'s dichotomy, we show that a two-party variant of the recent multi-party attack of Beimel et al. [3] yields a $1/(c \cdot \sqrt{r})$-bias attack.

1.2 Our Technique

Let $\Pi = (\mathsf{A}, \mathsf{B})$ be a r-round two-party coin flipping protocol. We show that the nonexistence of key-agreement protocols yields an efficient $\Theta(1/\sqrt{r})$-bias attack on Π. We start by describing the $1/\sqrt{r}$-bias *inefficient* attack of Cleve and Impagliazzo [9], and the approach of Beimel et al. [3] towards making this attack efficient. We then explain how to use the recent results by Haitner et al. [12] to obtain an efficient attack (assuming the nonexistence of io-key-agreement protocols).

Cleve and Impagliazzo's Inefficient Attack. We describe the inefficient $1/\sqrt{r}$-bias attack due to Cleve and Impagliazzo [9]. Let $M_1, \ldots, M_r$ denote the messages in a random execution of Π, and let C denote the (without loss of generality) always common output of the parties in a random honest execution of Π. Let $X_i = \mathbf{E}[C \mid M_{\leq i}]$. Namely, $M_{\leq i} = M_1, \ldots, M_i$ denotes the partial transcript of Π up to and including round i, and X_i is the expected outcome of the parties in Π given $M_{\leq i}$. It is easy to see that $X_0, \ldots, X_r$ is a martingale sequence: $\mathbf{E}[X_i \mid X_0, \ldots, X_{i-1}] = X_{i-1}$ for every i. Since the parties in an honest execution of Π output a uniform bit, it holds that $X_0 = \Pr[C = 1] = 1/2$ and $X_r \in \{0, 1\}$. Cleve and Impagliazzo [9] (see Beimel et al. [3] for an alternative simpler proof) prove that, for such a sequence (omitting absolute values and constant factors),

$$\text{Gap:} \qquad \Pr\left[\exists i \in [r] \colon X_i - X_{i-1} \geq 1/\sqrt{r}\right] \geq 1/2. \tag{1}$$

Let the ith *backup value* of party P, denoted Z_i^{P}, be the output of party P if the other party aborts prematurely *after* the ith message was sent (recall that the honest party must always output a bit, by definition). In particular, Z_r^{P} denotes the final output of P (if no abort occurred). We claim that without loss of generality for both $\mathsf{P} \in \{\mathsf{A}, \mathsf{B}\}$ it holds that

Backup values approximate outcome:

$$\Pr\left[\exists i \in [r] \colon \left|X_i - \mathbf{E}\left[Z_i^{\mathsf{P}} \mid M_{\leq i}\right]\right| \geq 1/2\sqrt{r}\right] \leq 1/4. \tag{2}$$

To see why, assume Eq. (2) does not hold. Then, the (possibly inefficient) adversary controlling $\overline{\mathsf{P}} \in \{\mathsf{A}, \mathsf{B}\} \setminus \mathsf{P}$ that aborts at the end of round i if

$(-1)^{1-z} \cdot (X_i - \mathbf{E}[Z_i^{\mathsf{P}} \mid M_{\leq i}]) \geq 1/\sqrt{r}$, for suitable $z \in \{0,1\}$, biases the output of P towards $1 - z$ by $\Theta(1/\sqrt{r})$.

Finally, since the coins of the parties are *independent* conditioned on the transcript (a fundamental fact about protocols), if party A sends the $(i+1)$ message then

$$\text{Independence:} \qquad \mathbf{E}\left[Z_i^{\mathsf{B}} \mid M_{\leq i}\right] = \mathbf{E}\left[Z_i^{\mathsf{B}} \mid M_{\leq i+1}\right]. \tag{3}$$

Combining the above observations yields that without loss of generality:

$$\Pr\left[\exists i \in [r] \colon \mathsf{A} \text{ sends the } i^{\text{th}} \text{ message} \wedge X_i - \mathbf{E}\left[Z_{i-1}^{\mathsf{B}} \mid M_{\leq i}\right] \geq 1/2\sqrt{r}\right] \geq 1/8. \tag{4}$$

Equation (4) yields the following (possibly inefficient) attack for a corrupted party A biasing B's output towards zero: before sending the ith message M_i, party A aborts if $X_i - \mathbf{E}\left[Z_{i-1}^{\mathsf{B}} \mid M_{\leq i}\right] \geq 1/2\sqrt{r}$. By Eq. (4), this attack biases B's output towards zero by $\Omega(1/2\sqrt{r})$.

The clear limitation of the above attack is that, assuming one-way functions exist, the value of $X_i = \mathbf{E}\left[C \mid M_{\leq i} = (m_1, \ldots, m_i)\right]$ and the value of $\mathbf{E}\left[Z_i^{\mathsf{P}} \mid M_{\leq i} = (m_1, \ldots, m_i)\right]$ might *not* be efficiently computable as a function of t.[3] Facing this difficulty, Beimel et al. [3] considered the martingale sequence $X_i = \mathbf{E}\left[C \mid Z_{\leq i}^{\mathsf{P}}\right]$ (recall that Z_i^{P} is the ith backup value of P). It follows that, for constant-round protocols, the value of X_i is only a function of a constant size string, and thus it is efficiently computable ([3] have facilitated this approach for protocols of super-constant round complexity, see Footnote 4). The price of using the alternative sequence $X_1, \ldots, X_r$ is that the independence property (Eq. (3)) might no longer hold. Yet, [3] manage to facilitate the above approach into an efficient $\widetilde{\Omega}(1/\sqrt{r})$-attack on *multi-party* protocols. In the following, we show how to use the dichotomy of Haitner et al. [12] to facilitate a two-party variant of the attack from [3].

Nonexistence of Key-Agreement Implies an Efficient Attack. Let U_p denote the Bernoulli random variable taking the value 1 with probability p, and let $P \stackrel{\mathrm{c}}{\approx}_\rho Q$ stand for Q and P are ρ-computationally indistinguishability (i.e., an efficient distinguisher cannot tell P from Q with advantage better than ρ). We are using two results by Haitner et al. [12]. The first one given below holds for any two-party protocol.

Theorem 1.2 (Haitner et al. [12]'s forecaster, informal). *Let $\Delta = (\mathsf{A}, \mathsf{B})$ be a single-bit output (each party outputs a bit) two-party protocol. Then, for any constant $\rho > 0$, there exists a constant output-length poly-time algorithm (forecaster) F mapping transcripts of Δ into (the binary description of) pairs in $[0,1] \times [0,1]$ such that the following holds: let (X, Y, T) be the parties outputs and transcript in a random execution of Δ, then*

[3] For instance, the first two messages might contain commitments to the parties' randomness.

– $(X,T) \stackrel{c}{\approx}_\rho (U_{p^{\mathsf{A}}},T)_{(p^{\mathsf{A}},\cdot)\leftarrow \mathsf{F}(T)}$, *and*
– $(Y,T) \stackrel{c}{\approx}_\rho (U_{p^{\mathsf{B}}},T)_{(\cdot,p^{\mathsf{B}})\leftarrow \mathsf{F}(T)}$.

Namely, given the transcript, F forecasts the output-distribution for each party in a way that is computationally indistinguishable from (the distribution of) the real output.

Consider the $(r+1)$-round protocol $\widetilde{\Pi} = (\widetilde{\mathsf{A}},\widetilde{\mathsf{B}})$, defined by $\widetilde{\mathsf{A}}$ sending a random $i \in [r]$ to $\widetilde{\mathsf{B}}$ as the first message and then the parties interact in a random execution of Π for the first i rounds. At the end of the execution, the parties output their i^{th} backup values z_i^{A} and z_i^{B} and halt. Let F be the forecaster for $\widetilde{\Pi}$ guaranteed by Theorem 1.2 for $\rho = 1/r^2$ (note that ρ is indeed constant). A simple averaging argument yields that

$$(Z_i^{\mathsf{P}}, M_{\leq i}) \stackrel{c}{\approx}_{1/r} (U_{p^{\mathsf{P}}}, M_{\leq i})_{(p^{\mathsf{A}},p^{\mathsf{B}})\leftarrow \mathsf{F}(M_{\leq i})} \tag{5}$$

for both $\mathsf{P} \in \{\mathsf{A},\mathsf{B}\}$ and every $i \in [r]$, letting $\mathsf{F}(m_{\leq i}) = \mathsf{F}(i, m_{\leq i})$. Namely, F is a good forecaster for the partial transcripts of Π.

Let $M_1,\ldots,M_r$ denote the messages in a random execution of Π and let C denote the output of the parties in Π. Let $F_i = \left(F_i^{\mathsf{A}}, F_i^{\mathsf{B}}\right) = \mathsf{F}(M_{\leq i})$ and let $X_i = \mathbf{E}\left[C \mid F_{\leq i}\right]$. It is easy to see that $X_1,\ldots,X_r$ is a martingale sequence and that $X_0 = 1/2$. We assume without loss of generality that the last message of Π contains the common output. Thus, it follows from Eq. (5) that $F_r \approx (C,C) \in \{(0,0),(1,1)\}$ (otherwise, it will be very easy to distinguish the forecasted outputs from the real ones, given M_r). Hence, similarly to Sect. 1.2, it holds that

$$\text{Gap:} \qquad \Pr\left[\exists i \in [r]\colon X_i - X_{i-1} \geq 1/\sqrt{r}\right] \geq 1/2. \tag{6}$$

Since F_i has constant-size support and since Π is constant round, it follows that X_i is efficiently computable from $M_{\leq i}$.[4]

Let Z_i^{P} denote the backup value computed by party P in round i of a random execution of Π. The indistinguishability of F yields that $\mathbf{E}\left[Z_i^{\mathsf{P}} \mid F_{\leq i}\right] \approx F_i^{\mathsf{P}}$. Similarly to Sect. 1.2, unless there is a simple $1/\sqrt{r}$-attack, it holds that

Backup values approximate outcome:

$$\Pr\left[\exists i \in [r]\colon \left|X_i - \mathbf{E}\left[Z_i^{\mathsf{P}} \mid F_{\leq i}\right]\right| \geq 1/2\sqrt{r}\right] \leq 1/4. \tag{7}$$

Thus, for an efficient variant of [9]'s attack, it suffices to show that

$$\text{Independence:} \qquad \mathbf{E}\left[Z_i^{\mathsf{P}} \mid F_{\leq i}\right] \approx \mathbf{E}\left[Z_i^{\mathsf{P}} \mid F_{\leq i+1}\right]. \tag{8}$$

[4] In the spirit of Beimel et al. [3], we could have modified the definition of the X_i's to make them efficiently computable even for non constant-round protocols. The idea is to define $X_i = \mathbf{E}\left[C \mid F_i, X_{i-1}\right]$. While the resulting sequence might not be a martingale, [3] proves that a $1/\sqrt{r}$-gap also occurs with constant probability for such a sequence. Unfortunately, we cannot benefit from this improvement, since the results of Haitner et al. [12] only guarantees indistinguishability for constant ρ, which makes it useful only for attacking constant-round protocols.

for every $\mathsf{P} \in \{\mathsf{A}, \mathsf{B}\}$ and round i in which party $\overline{\mathsf{P}} \in \{\mathsf{A}, \mathsf{B}\} \setminus \{\mathsf{P}\}$ sends the $(i+1)$ message. However, unlike Eq. (3) in Sect. 1.2, Eq. (8) does not hold unconditionally (in fact, assuming oblivious transfer exists, the implied attack must fail for some protocols, yielding that Eq. (8) is false for these protocols). Rather, we relate Eq. (8) to the existence of a key-agreement protocol. Specifically, we show that if Eq. (8) is not true, then there exists a key-agreement protocol.

Proving that F_{i+1} and Z_i^{P} are Approximately Independent Given $F_{\leq i}$. The next (and last) argument is the most technically challenging part of our proof. At this time, we provide a brief yet meaningful overview of the technique. The full details are provided in the main body (Claim 3.8 in Sect. 3).

We show that assuming nonexistence of io-key-agreement, F_{i+1} and Z_i^{P} are approximately independent given $F_{\leq i}$. In more detail, the triple $(Z_i^{\mathsf{P}}, F_{i+1}, F_{\leq i})$ is ρ-indistinguishable from $(Y_1, Y_2, F_{\leq i})$ where (Y_1, Y_2) is a pair of random variables that are mutually independent given $F_{\leq i}$. It would then follow that $\mathbf{E}\left[Z_i^{\mathsf{P}} \mid F_{i+1}, F_{\leq i}\right] \approx \mathbf{E}\left[Y_1 \mid Y_2, F_{\leq i}\right] = \mathbf{E}\left[Y_1 \mid F_{\leq i}\right] \approx \mathbf{E}\left[Z_i^{\mathsf{P}} \mid F_{\leq i}\right]$ as required. To this end, we use a second result by Haitner et al. [12].[5]

Theorem 1.3 (Haitner et al. [12]'s dichotomy, informal). Let $\Delta = (\mathsf{A}, \mathsf{B})$ be an efficient single-bit output two-party protocol and assume infinitely-often key-agreement protocol does not exist. Then, for any constant $\rho > 0$, there exists a poly-time algorithm (*decorrelator*) Dcr mapping transcripts of Δ into $[0,1] \times [0,1]$ such that the following holds: let (X, Y, T) be the parties' outputs and transcript in a random execution of Δ, then

$$(X, Y, T) \overset{\mathsf{C}}{\approx}_{\rho} (U_{p^{\mathsf{A}}}, U_{p^{\mathsf{B}}}, T)_{(p^{\mathsf{A}}, p^{\mathsf{B}}) \leftarrow \mathsf{Dcr}(T)}.$$

Namely, assuming io-key-agreement does not exist, the distribution of the parties' output given the transcript is ρ-close to the product distribution given by Dcr. We assume for simplicity that the theorem holds for *many-bit* output protocols and not merely single bit (we get rid of this assumption in the actual proof).

We define another variant $\widehat{\Pi}$ of Π that internally uses the forecaster F, and show that the existence of a decorrelator for $\widehat{\Pi}$ implies that F_{i+1} and Z_i^{P} are approximately independent given $F_{\leq i}$, and Eq. (8) follows. For concreteness, we focus on party $\mathsf{P} = \mathsf{B}$.

Fix i such that A sends the $(i+1)$ message in Π and define protocol $\widehat{\Pi} = (\widehat{\mathsf{A}}, \widehat{\mathsf{B}})$ according to the following specifications: the parties interact just as in Π for the first i rounds; then $\widehat{\mathsf{B}}$ outputs the ith backup value of B and $\widehat{\mathsf{A}}$ internally computes m_{i+1} and outputs $f_{i+1} = \mathsf{F}(m_{\leq i+1})$. By Theorem 1.3 there exists an efficient decorrelator Dcr for $\widehat{\Pi}$ with respect to $\rho = 1/r$. That is:

$$(F_{i+1}, Z_i^{\mathsf{B}}, M_{\leq i}) \overset{\mathsf{C}}{\approx}_{1/r} (U_{p^{\widehat{\mathsf{A}}}}, U_{p^{\widehat{\mathsf{B}}}}, M_{\leq i})_{(p^{\widehat{\mathsf{A}}}, p^{\widehat{\mathsf{B}}}) \leftarrow \mathsf{Dcr}(M_{\leq i})}, \tag{9}$$

[5] Assuming the nonexistence of key-agreement protocols, Theorem 1.3 implies Theorem 1.2. Yet, we chose to use both results to make the text more modular.

where now $p^{\widehat{\mathsf{A}}}$ describes a non-Boolean distribution, and $U_{p^{\widehat{\mathsf{A}}}}$ denotes an independent sample from this distribution.

Since F and Dcr both output an estimate of (the expectation of) $Z_i^{\mathsf{B}}|M_{\leq i}$ in a way that is indistinguishable from the real distribution of Z_i^{B} (given $M_{\leq i}$), both algorithms output essentially the same value. Otherwise, the "accurate" algorithm can be used to distinguish the output of the "inaccurate" algorithm from the real output. It follows that

$$(U_{p^{\widehat{\mathsf{A}}}}, U_{p^{\widehat{\mathsf{B}}}}, M_{\leq i})_{(p^{\widehat{\mathsf{A}}}, p^{\widehat{\mathsf{B}}}) \leftarrow \mathsf{Dcr}(M_{\leq i})} \overset{\mathrm{C}}{\approx}_{1/r} (U_{p^{\widehat{\mathsf{A}}}}, U_{F_i^{\mathsf{B}}}, M_{\leq i})_{(p^{\widehat{\mathsf{A}}}, \cdot) \leftarrow \mathsf{Dcr}(M_{\leq i})} \tag{10}$$

Using a data-processing argument in combination with Eqs. (9) and (10), we deduce that

$$(F_{i+1}, Z_i^{\mathsf{B}}, F_{\leq i}) \overset{\mathrm{C}}{\approx}_{1/r} \left(U_{p^{\widehat{\mathsf{A}}}}, U_{p^{\widehat{\mathsf{B}}}}, F_{\leq i}\right)_{(p^{\widehat{\mathsf{A}}}, p^{\widehat{\mathsf{B}}}) \leftarrow \mathsf{Dcr}(M_{\leq i})} \tag{11}$$

$$\overset{\mathrm{C}}{\approx}_{1/r} \left(U_{p^{\widehat{\mathsf{A}}}}, U_{F_i^{\mathsf{B}}}, F_{\leq i}\right)_{(p^{\widehat{\mathsf{A}}}, \cdot) \leftarrow \mathsf{Dcr}(M_{\leq i})}. \tag{12}$$

Finally, conditioned on $F_{\leq i}$, we observe that the pair of random variables $(U_{p^{\widehat{\mathsf{A}}}}, U_{F_i^{\mathsf{B}}})_{(p^{\widehat{\mathsf{A}}}, \cdot) \leftarrow \mathsf{Dcr}(M_{\leq i})}$ are mutually independent since $U_{F_i^{\mathsf{B}}}$ is sampled independently according to F_i^{B}, and F_i^{B} is fully determined by $F_{\leq i}$.

1.3 Related Work

We review some of the relevant work on fair coin flipping protocols.

Necessary Hardness Assumptions. This line of work examines the minimal assumptions required to achieve an $o(1/\sqrt{r})$-bias two-party coin flipping protocols, as done in this paper. The necessity of one-way functions for weaker variants of coin flipping protocol where the honest party is allowed to abort if the other party aborts or deviates from the prescribed protocol, were considered in [5,13,17,18]. More related to our bound is the work of Dachman-Soled et al. [10] who showed that any fully black-box construction of $O(1/r)$-bias two-party protocols based on one-way functions (with r-bit input and output) needs $\Omega(r/\log r)$ rounds, and the work of Dachman-Soled et al. [11] showed that there is no fully black-box and function *oblivious* construction of $O(1/r)$-bias two-party protocols from one-way functions (a protocol is function oblivious if the outcome of protocol is independent of the choice of the one-way function used in the protocol). For the case we are interested in, i.e. constant-round coin flipping protocols, [10] yields that black-box techniques from one-way functions can only guarantee fairness of order $1/\sqrt{r}$.

Lower Bounds. Cleve [8] proved that, for every r-round two-party coin flipping protocol, there exists an efficient adversary that can bias the output by $\Omega(1/r)$. Cleve and Impagliazzo [9] proved that, for every r-round two-party coin flipping protocol, there exists an inefficient fail-stop adversary that biases the output by $\Omega(1/\sqrt{r})$. They also showed that a similar attack exists if the parties have access to an ideal commitment scheme. All above bounds extend to the multi-party case (with no honest majority) via a simple reduction. Very recently, Beimel et al. [3] showed that *any* r-round n-parties coin flipping with $n^k > r$, for some $k \in \mathbb{N}$, can be biased by $1/(\sqrt{r} \cdot (\log r)^k)$. Ignoring logarithmic factors, this means that if the number of parties is $r^{\Omega(1)}$, the majority protocol of [2] is optimal.

Upper Bounds. Blum [6] presented a two-party two-round coin flipping protocol with bias 1/4. Awerbuch et al. [2] presented an n-party r-round protocol with bias $O(n/\sqrt{r})$ (the two-party case appears also in Cleve [8]). Moran et al. [19] solved the two-party case by giving a two-party r-round coin flipping protocol with bias $O(1/r)$. Haitner and Tsfadia [14] solved the three-party case up to poly-logarithmic factor by giving a three-party coin flipping protocol with bias $O(\text{polylog}(r)/r)$. Buchbinder et al. [7] showed an n-party r-round coin flipping protocol with bias $\widetilde{O}(n^3 2^n / r^{\frac{1}{2}+\frac{1}{2^{n-1}-2}})$. In particular, their protocol for four parties has bias $\widetilde{O}(1/r^{2/3})$, and for $n = \log\log r$ their protocol has bias smaller than Awerbuch et al. [2].

For the case where less than 2/3 of the parties are corrupt, Beimel et al. [4] showed an n-party r-round coin flipping protocol with bias $2^{2^k}/r$, tolerating up to $t = (n+k)/2$ corrupt parties. Alon and Omri [1] showed an n-party r-round coin flipping protocol with bias $\widetilde{O}(2^{2^n}/r)$, tolerating up to t corrupted parties, for constant n and $t < 3n/4$.

1.4 Open Questions

We show that constant-round coin flipping protocol with "small" bias (i.e., $o(1/\sqrt{r})$-fair, for r round protocol) implies io-key-agreement. Whether such a reduction can be extended to protocols with super-constant round complexity remains open. The barrier to extending our results is that the dichotomy result of Haitner et al. [12] only guarantees indistinguishablility with constant advantage (as opposed to vanishing or negligible advantage). It is worth mentioning that for protocols of super-constant round complexity, even a black-box separation between optimal (and thus between small bias) coin flipping protocol and one-way functions is not known.

The question of reducing oblivious transfer to optimally-fair coin flip is also open. We recall that all known small bias coin flipping protocols rely on it [7,15,20]. It is open whether the techniques of Haitner et al. [12] can provide a similar dichotomy with respect to (io-) oblivious transfer (as opposed to io-key-agreement) allowing for the realization of oblivious transfer from $o(1/\sqrt{r})$-fair (constant round) coin flip via the techniques of the present paper.

Paper Organization

Basic definitions and notation used through the paper are given in Sect. 2. The formal statement and proof of the main theorem are given in Sect. 3.

2 Preliminaries

2.1 Notation

We use calligraphic letters to denote sets, uppercase for random variables and functions, lowercase for values. For $a, b \in \mathbb{R}$, let $a \pm b$ stand for the interval $[a - b, a + b]$. For $n \in \mathbb{N}$, let $[n] = \{1, \ldots, n\}$ and $(n) = \{0, \ldots, n\}$. Let poly denote the set of all polynomials, let PPT stand for probabilistic polynomial time and PPTM denote a PPT algorithm (Turing machine). A function $\nu\colon \mathbb{N} \to [0, 1]$ is *negligible*, denoted $\nu(n) = \text{neg}(n)$, if $\nu(n) < 1/p(n)$ for every $p \in \text{poly}$ and large enough n. For a sequence $x_1, \ldots, x_r$ and $i \in [r]$, let $x_{\leq i} = x_1, \ldots, x_i$ and $x_{<i} = x_1, \ldots, x_{i-1}$.

Given a distribution, or random variable, D, we write $x \leftarrow D$ to indicate that x is selected according to D. Given a finite set $\mathcal{S}$, let $s \leftarrow \mathcal{S}$ denote that s is selected according to the uniform distribution over $\mathcal{S}$. The support of D, denoted $\text{Supp}(D)$, be defined as $\{u \in \mathcal{U} : D(u) > 0\}$. The *statistical distance* between two distributions P and Q over a finite set $\mathcal{U}$, denoted as $\text{SD}(P, Q)$, is defined as $\max_{\mathcal{S} \subseteq \mathcal{U}} |P(\mathcal{S}) - Q(\mathcal{S})| = \frac{1}{2} \sum_{u \in \mathcal{U}} |P(u) - Q(u)|$. Distribution ensembles $X = \{X_\kappa\}_{\kappa \in \mathbb{N}}$ and $Y = \{Y_\kappa\}_{\kappa \in \mathbb{N}}$ are *δ-computationally indistinguishable in the set* $\mathcal{K}$, denoted by $X \overset{\text{C}}{\approx}_{\mathcal{K},\delta} Y$, if for every PPTM D and sufficiently large $\kappa \in \mathcal{K}$: $|\Pr[\mathsf{D}(1^\kappa, X_\kappa) = 1] - \Pr[\mathsf{D}(1^\kappa, Y_\kappa) = 1]| \leq \delta$.

2.2 Protocols

Let $\Pi = (\mathsf{A}, \mathsf{B})$ be a two-party protocol. The protocol Π is PPT if the running time of both A and B is polynomial in their input length (regardless of the party they interact with). We denote by $(\mathsf{A}(x), \mathsf{B}(y))(z)$ a random execution of Π with private inputs x and y, and common input z, and sometimes abuse notation and write $(\mathsf{A}(x), \mathsf{B}(y))(z)$ for the parties' output in this execution.

We will focus on no-input two-party single-bit output PPT protocol: the only input of the two PPT parties is the common security parameter given in unary representation. At the end of the execution, each party outputs a single bit. Throughout, we assume without loss of generality that the transcript contains 1^κ as the first message. Let $\Pi = (\mathsf{A}, \mathsf{B})$ be such a two-party single-bit output protocol. For $\kappa \in \mathbb{N}$, let $C_\Pi^{\mathsf{A},\kappa}$, $C_\Pi^{\mathsf{B},\kappa}$ and T_Π^κ denote the outputs of A, B and the transcript of Π, respectively, in a random execution of $\Pi(1^\kappa)$.

Fair Coin Flipping Protocols. Since we are concerned with a lower bound, we only give the game-based definition of coin flipping protocols (see [15] for the stronger simulation-based definition).

Definition 2.1 (Fair coin flipping protocols). A PPT single-bit output two-party protocol $\Pi = (\mathsf{A}, \mathsf{B})$ is an ε-fair coin flipping protocol if the following holds.

Output delivery: The honest party always outputs a bit (even if the other party acts dishonestly, or aborts).

Agreement: The parties always output the same bit in an honest execution.
Uniformity: $\Pr\left[C_\Pi^{\mathsf{A},\kappa} = b\right] = 1/2$ (and thus $\Pr\left[C_\Pi^{\mathsf{B},\kappa} = b\right] = 1/2$), for both $b \in \{0,1\}$ and all $\kappa \in \mathbb{N}$.
Fairness: For any PPT A^* and $b \in \{0,1\}$, for sufficiently large $\kappa \in \mathbb{N}$ it holds that $\Pr\left[C_\Pi^{\mathsf{B},\kappa} = b\right] \leq 1/2 + \varepsilon$, and the same holds for the output bit of A.

Key-Agreement. We focus on single-bit output key-agreement protocols.

Definition 2.2 (Key-agreement protocols). A PPT single-bit output two-party protocol $\Pi = (\mathsf{A}, \mathsf{B})$ is io-key-agreement, if there exist an infinite $\mathcal{K} \subseteq \mathbb{N}$ such that the following hold for κ's in $\mathcal{K}$:

Agreement. $\Pr\left[C_\Pi^{\mathsf{A},\kappa} = C_\Pi^{\mathsf{B},\kappa}\right] \geq 1 - \operatorname{neg}(\kappa)$.
Secrecy. $\Pr\left[\mathsf{Eve}(T_\Pi^\kappa) = C_\Pi^{\mathsf{A},\kappa}\right] \leq 1/2 + \operatorname{neg}(\kappa)$, for every PPT Eve.

2.3 Martingales

Definition 2.3 (Martingales). Let $X_0, \ldots, X_r$ be a sequence of random variables. We say that $X_0, \ldots, X_r$ is a martingale sequence if $\mathbf{E}\left[X_{i+1} \mid X_{\leq i} = x_{\leq i}\right] = x_i$ for every $i \in [r-1]$.

In plain terms, a sequence is a martingale if the expectation of the next point conditioned on the entire history is exactly the last observed point. One way to obtain a martingale sequence is by constructing a *Doob martingale*. Such a sequence is defined by $X_i = \mathbf{E}\left[f(Z) \mid Z_{\leq i}\right]$, for arbitrary random variables $Z = (Z_1, \ldots, Z_r)$ and a function f of interest. We will use the following fact proven by [9] (we use the variant as proven in [3]).

Theorem 2.1. *Let $X_0, \ldots, X_r$ be a martingale sequence such that $X_i \in [0,1]$, for every $i \in [r]$. If $X_0 = 1/2$ and $\Pr[X_r \in \{0,1\}] = 1$, then*

$$\Pr\left[\exists i \in [r] \ s.t. \ |X_i - X_{i-1}| \geq \frac{1}{4\sqrt{r}}\right] \geq \frac{1}{20}.$$

3 Fair Coin Flipping to Key-Agreement

In this section, we prove our main result: if there exist constant-round coin flipping protocols which improve over the $1/\sqrt{r}$-bias majority protocol of [2], then infinitely-often key-agreement exists as well. Formally, we prove the following theorem.

Theorem 3.1. *The following holds for any (constant) $r \in \mathbb{N}$: if there exists an r-round, $\frac{1}{25600\sqrt{r}}$-fair two-party coin flipping protocol, see Definition 2.1, then there exists an infinitely-often key-agreement protocol.*[6,7]

[6] Definition 2.1 requires perfect uniformity: the common output in an honest execution is an unbiased bit. The proof given below, however, easily extends to any non-trivial uniformity condition, e.g., the common output equals 1 with probability 3/4.

[7] We remark that we did not optimize the value of the constant.

Before formally proving Theorem 3.1, we briefly recall the outline of the proof as presented in the introduction (we ignore certain constants in this outline). We begin with a good forecaster for the coin flipping protocol Π (which must exist, according to [12]), and we define an efficiently computable conditional expected outcome sequence $X = (X_0, \ldots, X_r)$ for Π, conditioned on the forecaster's outputs. Then, we show that (1) the ith backup value (default output in case the opponent aborts) should be close to X_i; otherwise, an efficient attacker can use the forecaster to bias the output of the other party (this attack is applicable regardless of the existence of infinitely-often key-agreement). And (2), since X is a martingale sequence, "large" $1/\sqrt{r}$-gaps are bound to occur in some round, with constant probability. Hence, combining (1) and (2), with constant probability, for some i, there is a $1/\sqrt{r}$-gap between X_i and the forecasters' prediction for one party *at the preceding round* $i-1$. Therefore, unless protocol Π implies io-key-agreement, the aforementioned gap can be exploited to bias that party's output by $1/\sqrt{r}$, by instructing the opponent to abort as soon as the gap is detected. In more detail, the success of the attack requires that (3) the event that a gap occurs is (almost) *independent* of the backup value of the honest party. It turns out that if Π does not imply io-key-agreement, this third property is guaranteed by the dichotomy theorem of [12]. In summary, if io-key-agreement does not exist, then protocol Π is at best $1/\sqrt{r}$-fair.

Moving to the formal proof, fix an r-round, two-party coin flipping protocol $\Pi = (\mathsf{A}, \mathsf{B})$ (we assume nothing about its fairness parameter for now). We associate the following random variables with a random honest execution of $\Pi(1^\kappa)$. Let $M^\kappa = (M_1^\kappa, \ldots, M_r^\kappa)$ denote the messages of the protocol and let C^κ denote the (always) common output of the parties. For $i \in \{0, \ldots, r\}$ and $\mathsf{P} \in \{\mathsf{A}, \mathsf{B}\}$, let $Z_i^{\mathsf{P},\kappa}$ be the "backup" value party P outputs, if the other party aborts after the ith message was sent. In particular, $Z_r^{\mathsf{A},\kappa} = Z_r^{\mathsf{B},\kappa} = C^\kappa$ and $\Pr[C^\kappa = 1] = 1/2$.

Forecaster for Π. We are using a *forecaster* for Π, guaranteed by the following theorem (proof readily follows from Haitner et al. [12, Theorem 3.8]).

Theorem 3.2 (Haitner et al. [12], existence of forecasters). *Let Δ be a no-input, single-bit output two-party protocol. Then for any constant $\rho > 0$, there exists a* PPT *constant output-length algorithm* F *(forecaster) mapping transcripts of Δ into (the binary description of) pairs in $[0,1] \times [0,1]$ and an infinite set $\mathcal{K} \in \mathbb{N}$ such that the following holds: let $C^{\mathsf{A},\kappa}$, $C^{\mathsf{B},\kappa}$ and T^κ denote the parties' outputs and protocol transcript, respectively, in a random execution of $\Delta(1^\kappa)$. Let $m(\kappa) \in$* poly *be a bound on the number of coins used by* F *on transcripts in* $\operatorname{supp}(T^\kappa)$*, and let S^κ be a uniform string of length $m(\kappa)$. Then,*

- $(C^{\mathsf{A},\kappa}, T^\kappa, S^\kappa) \overset{\mathsf{c}}{\approx}_{\rho,\mathcal{K}} (U_{p^{\mathsf{A}}}, T^\kappa, S^\kappa)_{(p^{\mathsf{A}},\cdot)=\mathsf{F}(T^\kappa;S^\kappa)}$, *and*
- $(C^{\mathsf{B},\kappa}, T^\kappa, S^\kappa) \overset{\mathsf{c}}{\approx}_{\rho,\mathcal{K}} (U_{p^{\mathsf{B}}}, T^\kappa, S^\kappa)_{(\cdot,p^{\mathsf{B}})=\mathsf{F}(T^\kappa;S^\kappa)}$.

letting U_p be a Boolean random variable taking the value 1 *with probability* p.[8]

Since we require a forecaster for all (intermediate) backup values of Π, we apply Theorem 3.2 with respect to the following variant of protocol Π, which simply stops the execution at a random round.

Protocol 3.3 $(\widetilde{\Pi} = (\widetilde{\mathsf{A}}, \widetilde{\mathsf{B}}))$
Common input: security parameter 1^κ.
Description:

1. $\widetilde{\mathsf{A}}$ samples $i \leftarrow [r]$ and sends it to $\widetilde{\mathsf{B}}$.
2. The parties interact in the first i rounds of a random execution of $\Pi(1^\kappa)$, with $\widetilde{\mathsf{A}}$ and $\widetilde{\mathsf{B}}$ taking the role of A and B receptively.
   Let z_i^{A} and z_i^{B} be the ith backup values of A and B as computed by the parties in the above execution.
3. $\widetilde{\mathsf{A}}$ outputs z_i^{A}, and $\widetilde{\mathsf{B}}$ outputs z_i^{B}.

Let $\rho = 10^{-6} \cdot r^{-5/2}$. Let $\mathcal{K} \subseteq \mathbb{N}$ and a PPT F be the infinite set and PPT forecaster resulting by applying Theorem 3.2 with respect to protocol $\widetilde{\Pi}$ and ρ, and let S^κ denote a long enough uniform string to be used by F on transcripts of $\widetilde{\Pi}(1^\kappa)$. The following holds with respect to Π.

Claim 3.4. For $I \leftarrow [r]$, it holds that

- $(Z_I^{\mathsf{A},\kappa}, M_{\leq I}^\kappa, S^\kappa) \overset{\mathrm{C}}{\approx}_{\rho,\mathcal{K}} (U_{p^{\mathsf{A}}}, M_{\leq I}^\kappa, S^\kappa)_{(p^{\mathsf{A}},\cdot)=\mathsf{F}(M_{\leq I};S^\kappa)}$, and
- $(Z_I^{\mathsf{B},\kappa}, M_{\leq I}^\kappa, S^\kappa) \overset{\mathrm{C}}{\approx}_{\rho,\mathcal{K}} (U_{p^{\mathsf{B}}}, M_{\leq I}^\kappa, S^\kappa)_{(\cdot,p^{\mathsf{B}})=\mathsf{F}(M_{\leq I};S^\kappa)}$,

letting $\mathsf{F}(m_{\leq i}; r) = \mathsf{F}(i, m_{\leq i}; r)$.

Proof. Immediate, by Theorem 3.2 and the definition of $\widetilde{\Pi}$. □

We assume without loss of generality that the common output appears on the last message of Π (otherwise, we can add a final message that contains this value, which does not hurt the security of Π). Hence, without loss of generality it holds that $\mathsf{F}(m_{\leq r}; \cdot) = (b, b)$, where b is the output bit as implied by $m_{\leq r}$ (otherwise, we can change F to do so without hurting its forecasting quality).

For $\kappa \in \mathbb{N}$, we define the random variables $F_0^\kappa, \ldots, F_r^\kappa$, by

$$F_i^\kappa = (F_i^{\mathsf{A},\kappa}, F_i^{\mathsf{B},\kappa}) = \mathsf{F}(M_{\leq i}; S^\kappa) \tag{13}$$

[8] Haitner et al. [12] do not limit the output-length of F. Nevertheless, by applying [12] with parameter $\rho/2$ and chopping each of the forecaster's outputs to the first $\lceil \log 1/\rho \rceil + 1$ (most significant) bits, yields the desired constant output-length forecaster.

The Expected Outcome Sequence. To attack the protocol, it is useful to evaluate at each round the expected outcome of the protocol conditioned on the forecasters' outputs so far. To alleviate notation, we assume that the value of κ is determined by $|S^\kappa|$.

Definition 3.1 (Expected outcome function). For $\kappa \in \mathbb{N}$, $i \in [r]$, $f_{\leq i} \in \operatorname{supp}(F^\kappa_{\leq i})$ and $s \in \operatorname{Supp}(S^\kappa)$, let

$$g(f_{\leq i}, s) = \mathbf{E}\left[C^\kappa \mid F^\kappa_{\leq i} = f_{\leq i}, S^\kappa = s\right].$$

Namely, $g(f_{\leq i}, s)$ is the probability that the output of the protocol in a random execution is 1, given that $\mathsf{F}(M_{\leq j}; s) = f_j$ for every $j \in (i)$ and $M_1, \ldots, M_r$ being the transcript of this execution.

Expected Outcome Sequence is Approximable. The following claim, proven in Sect. 3.1, yields that the expected outcome sequence can be approximated efficiently.

Claim 3.5. There exists PPTM G such that

$$\Pr\left[\mathsf{G}(F^\kappa_{\leq i}, S^\kappa) \notin g(F^\kappa_{\leq i}, S^\kappa) \pm \rho\right] \leq \rho,$$

for every $\kappa \in \mathbb{N}$ and $i \in [r]$.

Algorithm G approximates the value of g on input $(f_{\leq i}, s) \in \operatorname{supp}(F^\kappa_{\leq i}, S^\kappa)$ by running multiple independent instances of protocol $\Pi(1^\kappa)$ and keeping track of the number of times it encounters $f_{\leq i}$ and the protocol outputs one. Standard approximation techniques yield that, unless $f_{\leq i}$ is very unlikely, the output of G is close to $g(f_{\leq i}, s)$. Claim 3.5 follows by carefully choosing the number of iterations for G and bounding the probability of encountering an unlikely $f_{\leq i}$.

Forecasted Backup Values are Close to Expected Outcome Sequence. The following claim bounds the probability that the expected outcome sequence and the forecaster's outputs deviate by more than $1/8\sqrt{r}$. The proof is given in Sect. 3.2.

Claim 3.6. Assuming Π is $\frac{1}{6400\sqrt{r}}$-fair, then

$$\Pr\left[\exists i \in [r] \text{ s.t. } \left|g(F^\kappa_{\leq i}, S^\kappa) - F^{\mathsf{P},\kappa}_i\right| \geq 1/8\sqrt{r}\right] < 1/100$$

for both $\mathsf{P} \in \{\mathsf{A}, \mathsf{B}\}$ and large enough $\kappa \in \mathcal{K}$.

Loosely speaking, Claim 3.6 states that the expected output sequence and the forecaster's outputs are close for a fair protocol. If not, then either of the following attackers P^*_0, P^*_1 can bias the output of party P: for fixed randomness $s \in \operatorname{supp}(S^\kappa)$, attacker P^*_z computes $f_i = \mathsf{F}(m_{\leq i}, s)$ for partial transcript $m_{\leq i}$ at round $i \in [r]$, and aborts as soon as $(-1)^{1-z}(\mathsf{G}(f^\kappa_{\leq i}, s) - f_i) \geq 1/8\sqrt{r} - \rho$. The desired bias is guaranteed by the accuracy of the forecaster (Claim 3.4), the accuracy of algorithm G (Claim 3.5) and the presumed frequency of occurrence of a suitable gap. The details of the proof are given in Sect. 3.2.

Expected Outcome Sequence has Large Gap. Similarly to [9], the success of our attack depends on the occurrence of large gaps in the expected outcome sequence. The latter is guaranteed by [9] and [3], since the expected outcome sequence is a suitable martingale.

Claim 3.7. For every $\kappa \in \mathbb{N}$, it holds that

$$\Pr\left[\exists i \in [r]\colon \left|g(F^{\kappa}_{\leq i}, S^{\kappa}) - g(F^{\kappa}_{\leq i-1}, S^{\kappa})\right| \geq 1/4\sqrt{r}\right] > 1/20.$$

Proof. Consider the sequence of random variables $G^{\kappa}_0, \ldots, G^{\kappa}_r$ defined by $G^{\kappa}_i = g(F^{\kappa}_{\leq i}, S^{\kappa})$. Observe that this is a Doob (and hence, strong) martingale sequence, with respect to the random variables $Z_0 = S^{\kappa}$ and $Z_i = F^{\kappa}_i$ for $i \in [r]$, and the function $f(S^{\kappa}, F^{\kappa}_{\leq r}) = g(F^{\kappa}_{\leq r}, S^{\kappa}) = F^{\kappa}_r[0]$ (i.e., the function that outputs the actual output of the protocol, as implied by F^{κ}_r). Clearly, $G^{\kappa}_0 = 1/2$ and $G^{\kappa}_r \in \{0,1\}$ (recall that we assume that $\mathsf{F}(M_{\leq r}; \cdot) = (b, b)$, where b is the output bit as implied by $M_{\leq r}$). Thus, the proof follows by Theorem 2.1. □

Independence of Attack Decision. Claim 3.4 immediately yields that the expected values of F_i and Z^{P}_i are close, for both $\mathsf{P} \in \{\mathsf{A}, \mathsf{B}\}$ and every $i \in [r]$. Assuming io-key-agreement does not exist, the following claim essentially states that F_i and Z^{P}_i remain close in expectation, even if we condition on some event that depends on the other party's next message. This observation will allow us to show that, when a large gap in the expected outcome is observed by one of the parties, the (expected value of the) backup value of the other party still lags behind. The following claim captures the core of the novel idea in our attack, and its proof is the most technical aspect towards proving our main result.

Claim 3.8 (Independence of attack decision). Let D be a single-bit output PPTM. For $\kappa \in \mathbb{N}$ and $\mathsf{P} \in \{\mathsf{A}, \mathsf{B}\}$, let $E^{\mathsf{P},\kappa}_1, \ldots, E^{\mathsf{P},\kappa}_r$ be the sequence of random variables defined by $E^{\mathsf{P},\kappa}_i = \mathsf{D}(F^{\kappa}_{\leq i}, S^{\kappa})$ if P sends the ith message in $\Pi(1^{\kappa})$, and $E^{\mathsf{P},\kappa}_i = 0$ otherwise.

Assume io-key-agreement protocols do not exist. Then, for any $\mathsf{P} \in \{\mathsf{A}, \mathsf{B}\}$ and infinite subset $\mathcal{K}' \subseteq \mathcal{K}$, there exists an infinite set $\mathcal{K}'' \subseteq \mathcal{K}'$ such that

$$\mathbf{E}\left[E^{\mathsf{P},\kappa}_{i+1} \cdot (Z^{\overline{\mathsf{P}},\kappa}_i - F^{\overline{\mathsf{P}},\kappa}_i)\right] \in \pm 4r\rho$$

for every $\kappa \in \mathcal{K}''$ and $i \in (r-1)$, where $\overline{\mathsf{P}} \in \{\mathsf{A}, \mathsf{B}\} \setminus \{\mathsf{P}\}$.

Since $\mathbf{E}\left[E^{\mathsf{P},\kappa}_{i+1} \cdot (Z^{\overline{\mathsf{P}},\kappa}_i - F^{\overline{\mathsf{P}},\kappa}_i)\right] = \mathbf{E}\left[E^{\mathsf{P},\kappa}_{i+1} \cdot \mathbf{E}\left[Z^{\overline{\mathsf{P}},\kappa}_i - F^{\mathsf{P},\kappa}_i \mid E^{\mathsf{P},\kappa}_{i+1} = 1\right]\right]$, Claim 3.8 yields that the expected values of F_i and Z^{P}_i remain close, even when conditioning on a likely-enough-event over the next message of P.

The proof of Claim 3.8 is given in Sect. 3.3. In essence, we use the recent dichotomy of Haitner et al. [12] to show that if io-key-agreement does not exist, then the values of $E^{\mathsf{P},\kappa}_{i+1}$ and $Z^{\overline{\mathsf{P}},\kappa}_i$ conditioned on $M_{\leq i}$ (which determines the value of $F^{\overline{\mathsf{P}},\kappa}_i$), are (computationally) close to be in a product distribution.

Putting Everything Together. Equipped with the above observations, we prove Theorem 3.1.

Proof of Theorem 3.1. Let Π be an $\varepsilon = \frac{1}{25600\sqrt{r}}$-fair coin flipping protocol. By Claims 3.6 and 3.7, we can assume without loss of generality that there exists an infinite subset $\mathcal{K}' \subseteq \mathcal{K}$ such that

$$\Pr\left[\exists i \in [r] \colon \mathsf{A} \text{ sends } i^{\text{th}} \text{ message in } \Pi(1^\kappa) \wedge g(F^\kappa_{\leq i}, S^\kappa) - F^{\mathsf{B},\kappa}_{i-1} \geq \frac{1}{8\sqrt{r}}\right]$$

$$\geq \frac{1}{80} - \frac{1}{100} = \frac{1}{400} \tag{14}$$

We define the following PPT fail-stop attacker A^* taking the role of A in Π. We will show below that assuming io-key-agreement do not exist, algorithm A^* succeeds in biasing the output of B towards zero by ε for all $\kappa \in \mathcal{K}''$, contradicting the presumed fairness of Π. In the following, let G be the PPTM guaranteed to exist by Claim 3.5.

Algorithm 3.9 (A^*)

Input: security parameter 1^κ.
Description:

1. *Sample* $s \leftarrow S^\kappa$ *and start a random execution of* $\mathsf{A}(1^\kappa)$.
2. *Upon receiving the* $(i-1)$ *message* m_{i-1}, *do*
   (a) *Forward* m_{i-1} *to* A, *and let* m_i *be the next message sent by* A.
   (b) *Compute* $f_i = (f_i^{\mathsf{A}}, f_i^{\mathsf{B}}) = \mathsf{F}(m_{\leq i}, s)$.
   (c) *Compute* $\widetilde{g}_i = \mathsf{G}(f_{\leq i}, s)$.
   (d) *If* $\widetilde{g}_i \geq f^{\mathsf{B}}_{i-1} + 1/16\sqrt{r}$, *abort (without sending further messages). Otherwise, send* m_i *to* B *and proceed to the next round.*

It is clear that A^* is a PPTM. We conclude the proof showing that assuming io-key-agreement do not exist, B's output when interacting with A^* is biased towards zero by at least ε.

The following random variables are defined with respect to a a random execution of $(\mathsf{A}^*, \mathsf{B})(1^\kappa)$. Let S^κ and $F^\kappa = (F^\kappa_1, \ldots, F^\kappa_r)$ denote the values of s and $f_1, \ldots, f_r$ sampled by A^*. Let $Z^{\mathsf{B},\kappa} = (Z^{\mathsf{B},\kappa}_1, \ldots, Z^{\mathsf{B},\kappa}_r)$ denote the backup values computed by B. For $i \in [r]$, let E^κ_i be the event that A^* decides to abort in round i. Finally, let J^κ be the index i with $E^\kappa_i = 1$, setting it to $r+1$ if no such index exist. Below, if we do not quantify over κ, it means that the statement holds for any $\kappa \in \mathbb{N}$.

By Claim 3.5 and Eq. (14),

$$\Pr\left[J^\kappa \neq r+1\right] > \frac{1}{400} - \rho \geq \frac{1}{800} \tag{15}$$

for every $\kappa \in \mathcal{K}'$. Where since the events E_i^κ and E_j^κ for $i \neq j$ are disjoint,

$$\begin{aligned}
\mathbf{E}\left[Z_{J^\kappa-1}^{\mathsf{B},\kappa} - F_{J^\kappa-1}^{\mathsf{B},\kappa}\right] &= \mathbf{E}\left[\sum_{i=1}^{r+1} E_i^\kappa \cdot (Z_{i-1}^{\mathsf{B},\kappa} - F_{i-1}^{\mathsf{B},\kappa})\right] \\
&= \sum_{i=1}^{r+1} \mathbf{E}\left[E_i^\kappa \cdot (Z_{i-1}^{\mathsf{B},\kappa} - F_{i-1}^{\mathsf{B},\kappa})\right] \\
&= \sum_{i=1}^{r} \mathbf{E}\left[E_i^\kappa \cdot (Z_{i-1}^{\mathsf{B},\kappa} - F_{i-1}^{\mathsf{B},\kappa})\right]. \qquad (16)
\end{aligned}$$

The last inequality holds since the protocol's output appears in the last message, by assumption, and thus without loss of generality $Z_r^{\mathsf{B},\kappa} = F_r^{\mathsf{B},\kappa}$. Consider the single-bit output PPTM D defined as follows: on input $(f_{\leq i}, s)$ where $f_{\leq i}$ is a sequence of pairs of values, i.e., $f_{\leq i} = (f_1^{\mathsf{A}}, f_1^{\mathsf{B}}), \ldots, (f_i^{\mathsf{A}}, f_i^{\mathsf{B}})$), it outputs 1 if $\mathsf{G}(f_{\leq i}, s) - f_{i-1}^{\mathsf{B}} \geq 1/16\sqrt{r}$, and $\mathsf{G}(f_{\leq j}, s) - f_{j-1}^{\mathsf{B}} < 1/16\sqrt{r}$ for all $j < i$. Otherwise, it outputs zero. Observe that E_i^κ is the indicator of the event A sends the ith message in $\Pi(1^\kappa)$ and $\mathsf{D}(F_{\leq i}^\kappa, S^\kappa) = 1$, for any fixing of $(F^\kappa, S^\kappa, Z^{\mathsf{B},\kappa})$. Thus, assuming io-key-agreement protocols do not exist, Claim 3.8 yields that that there exists an infinite set $\mathcal{K}'' \subset \mathcal{K}'$ such that

$$\mathbf{E}\left[E_{i+1}^\kappa \cdot (Z_i^{\mathsf{B},\kappa} - F_i^{\mathsf{B},\kappa})\right] \in \pm 4r\rho \qquad (17)$$

for every $\kappa \in \mathcal{K}''$ and $i \in [r-1]$. Putting together Eqs. (16) and (17), we conclude that, for every $\kappa \in \mathcal{K}''$,

$$\mathbf{E}\left[Z_{J^\kappa-1}^{\mathsf{B},\kappa} - F_{J^\kappa-1}^{\mathsf{B},\kappa}\right] \in \pm 4r^2\rho. \qquad (18)$$

Recall that our goal is to show that $\mathbf{E}\left[Z_{J^\kappa-1}^{\mathsf{B},\kappa}\right]$ is significantly smaller than 1/2. We do so by showing that it is significantly smaller than $\mathbf{E}\left[g(F_{\leq J^\kappa}^\kappa, S^\kappa)\right]$ which equals 1/2, since, by tower law (total expectation),

$$\mathbf{E}\left[g(F_{\leq J^\kappa}^\kappa, S^\kappa)\right] = \mathbf{E}\left[C^\kappa\right] = 1/2. \qquad (19)$$

Finally, let G_i be the value of $\mathsf{G}(F_{\leq i}, S^\kappa)$ computed by A^* in the execution of $(\mathsf{A}^*, \mathsf{B})(1^\kappa)$ considered above, letting $G_{r+1} = g(F_{\leq r+1}^\kappa, S^\kappa)$. Claim 3.5 yields that

$$\mathbf{E}\left[g(F_{\leq J^\kappa}^\kappa, S^\kappa) - G_{J^\kappa}\right] \leq 2r\rho. \qquad (20)$$

Putting all the above observations together, we conclude that, for every $\kappa \in \mathcal{K}''$,

$$\begin{aligned}
&\mathbf{E}\left[Z^{\mathsf{B},\kappa}_{J^\kappa-1}\right]\\
&= \mathbf{E}\left[g(F^\kappa_{\leq J^\kappa}, S^\kappa)\right] - \mathbf{E}\left[G_{J^\kappa} - F^{\mathsf{B},\kappa}_{J^\kappa-1}\right]\\
&\qquad + \mathbf{E}\left[Z^{\mathsf{B},\kappa}_{J^\kappa-1} - F^{\mathsf{B},\kappa}_{J^\kappa-1}\right] - \mathbf{E}\left[g(F^\kappa_{\leq J^\kappa}, S^\kappa) - G_{J^\kappa}\right]\\
&\leq \frac{1}{2} - \mathbf{E}\left[G_{J^\kappa} - F^{\mathsf{B},\kappa}_{J^\kappa-1} \mid J^\kappa \neq r+1\right] \cdot \Pr\left[J^\kappa \neq r+1\right] + 4r^2\rho + 2r\rho\\
&\leq \frac{1}{2} - (1/16\sqrt{r}) \cdot (1/800) + 4r^2\rho + 2r\rho\\
&< \frac{1}{2} - \frac{1}{25600\sqrt{r}}.
\end{aligned}$$

The first inequality holds by Eqs. (18) to (20). The second inequality holds by the definition of J^κ and Eq. (15). The last inequality holds by our choice of ρ.□

3.1 Approximating the Expected Outcome Sequence

In this section we prove Claim 3.5, restated below.

Claim 3.10 (Claim 3.5, restated). There exists PPTM G such that

$$\Pr\left[\mathsf{G}(F^\kappa_{\leq i}, S^\kappa) \notin g(F^\kappa_{\leq i}, S^\kappa) \pm \rho\right] \leq \rho,$$

for every $\kappa \in \mathbb{N}$ and $i \in [r]$.

The proof of Claim 3.10 is straightforward. Since there are only constant number of rounds and F has constant output-length, when fixing the randomness of F, the domain of G has constant size. Hence, the value of of g can be approximated well via sampling. Details below.

Let c be a bound on the number of possible outputs of F (recall that F has constant output-length). We are using the following implementation for G. In the following, let $\overline{\mathsf{F}}((m_1, \ldots, m_i); s) = (\mathsf{F}(m_1; s), \ldots, (\mathsf{F}(m_i; s))$ (i.e., $\overline{\mathsf{F}}(M_{\leq i}; S^\kappa) = F_{\leq i}$).

Algorithm 3.11 (G)

Parameters: $v = \left\lceil \frac{1}{2} \cdot \left(\frac{2c^r}{\rho}\right)^4 \cdot \ln\left(\frac{8}{\rho}\right)\right\rceil$.
Input: $f_{\leq i} \in \operatorname{supp}(F^\kappa_{\leq i})$ *and* $s \in \operatorname{Supp}(S^\kappa)$.
Description:

1. *Sample* v *transcripts* $\left\{m^j, c^j\right\}_{j\in[v]}$ *by taking the (full) transcripts and outputs of* v *independent executions of* $\Pi(1^\kappa)$.
2. *For every* $j \in [v]$ *let* $f^j_i = \overline{\mathsf{F}}(m^j_{\leq i}; s)$.
3. *Let* $q = \left|\left\{j \in [v] \colon f^j_{\leq i} = f_{\leq i}\right\}\right|$ *and* $p = \left|\left\{j \in [v] \colon f^j_{\leq i} = f_{\leq i} \wedge c^j = 1\right\}\right|$.
4. *Set* $\widetilde{g} = p/q$. *(Set* $\widetilde{g} = 0$ *if* $q = p = 0$.*)*
5. *Output* $\widetilde{g}$.

Remark 3.1 (A more efficient approximator.). The running time of algorithm G above is exponential in r. While this does not pose a problem for our purposes here, since r is constant, it might leave the impression that out approach cannot be extended to protocols with super-constant round complexity. So it is worth mentioning that the running time of G can be reduced to be polynomial in r, by using the augmented weak martingale paradigm of Beimel et al. [3]. Unfortunately, we currently cannot benefit from this improvement, since the result of [12] only guarantees indistinguishability for constant ρ, which makes it useful only for attacking constant-round protocols.

We prove Claim 3.10 by showing that the above algorithm approximates g well.

Proof of Claim 3.10. To prove the quality of G in approximating g, it suffices to prove the claim for every every $\kappa \in \mathbb{N}$, $i \in [r]$ and fixed $s \in \operatorname{supp}(S^\kappa)$. That is

$$\Pr\left[\left|g(\overline{\mathsf{F}}(M_{\leq i}, s), s) - \mathsf{G}(\overline{\mathsf{F}}(M_{\leq i}, s), s)\right| \geq \rho\right] \leq \rho, \tag{21}$$

where the probability is also taken over the random coins of G.

Fix $\kappa \in \mathbb{N}$ and omit it from the notation, and fix $i \in [r]$ and $s \in S^\kappa$. Let $\mathcal{D}_i = \left\{f_{\leq i} \colon \Pr\left[\overline{\mathsf{F}}(M_{\leq i}, s) = f_{\leq i}\right] \geq \rho/2c^r\right\}$. By Hoeffding's inequality [16], for every $f_{\leq i} \in \mathcal{D}$, it holds that

$$\begin{aligned}\Pr\left[|g(f_{\leq i}, s) - \mathsf{G}(f_{\leq i}, s)| \geq \rho\right] &\leq 4 \cdot \exp\left(-2 \cdot v \cdot (\rho/2c^r)^4\right)\\ &\leq 4 \cdot \exp\left(-\frac{v\rho^4}{8c^{4r}}\right)\\ &\leq \rho/2. \end{aligned} \tag{22}$$

It follows that

$$\begin{aligned}&\Pr\left[\left|g(\overline{\mathsf{F}}(M_{\leq i}, s), s) - \mathsf{G}(\overline{\mathsf{F}}(M_{\leq i}, s), s)\right| \geq \rho\right]\\ &\leq \Pr\left[(\overline{\mathsf{F}}(M_{\leq j}, s) \notin \mathcal{D}\right] + \rho/2\\ &\leq \left|\operatorname{Supp}(\overline{\mathsf{F}}(M_{\leq j}, s))\right| \cdot \rho/2c^r + \rho/2\\ &\leq c^r \cdot \rho/2c^r + \rho/2 = \rho.\end{aligned}$$

□

3.2 Forecasted Backup Values Are Close to Expected Outcome Sequence

In this section, we prove Claim 3.6 (restated below).

Claim 3.12 (Claim 3.6, restated). Assuming Π is $\frac{1}{6400\sqrt{r}}$-fair, then

$$\Pr\left[\exists i \in [r] \text{ s.t. } \left|g(F^\kappa_{\leq i}, S^\kappa) - F_i^{\mathsf{P},\kappa}\right| \geq 1/8\sqrt{r}\right] < 1/100$$

for both $\mathsf{P} \in \{\mathsf{A}, \mathsf{B}\}$ and large enough $\kappa \in \mathcal{K}$.

Proof. Assume the claim does not holds for $\mathsf{P} = \mathsf{B}$ and infinitely many security parameters $\mathcal{K}$ (the case $\mathsf{P} = \mathsf{A}$ is proven analogously). That is, for all $\kappa \in \mathcal{K}$ and without loss of generality, it holds that

$$\Pr\left[\exists i \in [r] \text{ s.t. } g(F^{\kappa}_{\leq i}, S^{\kappa}) - F^{\mathsf{B},\kappa}_i \geq \frac{1}{8\sqrt{r}}\right] \geq \frac{1}{200}. \tag{23}$$

Consider the following PPT fail-stop attacker A^* taking the role of A in Π to bias the output of B towards zeros.

Algorithm 3.13 (A^*)

Input: security parameter 1^κ.
Description:

1. *Samples* $s \leftarrow S^\kappa$ *and start a random execution of* $\mathsf{A}(1^\kappa)$.
2. *For* $i = 1 \ldots r$:
   After sending (or receiving) the prescribed message m_i:
   (a) *Let* $f_i = \mathsf{F}(m_{\leq i}; s)$ *and* $\mu_i = \mathsf{G}(f_{\leq i}, s) - f_i$.
   (b) *Abort if* $\mu_i \geq \frac{1}{8\sqrt{r}} - \rho$ *(without sending further messages).*
   Otherwise, proceed to the next round.

In the following, we fix a large enough $\kappa \in \mathcal{K}$ such that Eq. (23) holds, and we omit it from the notation when the context is clear. We show that algorithm A^* biases the output of B towards zero by at least $1/(6400\sqrt{r})$.

We associate the following random variables with a random execution of $(\mathsf{A}^*, \mathsf{B})$. Let J denote the index where the adversary aborted, i.e., the smallest j such that $\mathsf{G}(F_{\leq j}, S) - F^{\mathsf{B}}_j \geq \frac{1}{8\sqrt{r}} - \rho$, or $J = r$ if no abort occurred. The following expectations are taken over $(F_{\leq i}, S)$ and the random coins of G. We bound $\mathbf{E}\left[Z^{\mathsf{B}}_J\right]$, i.e. the expected output of the honest party.

$$\begin{aligned}
&\mathbf{E}\left[Z^{\mathsf{B}}_J\right] \\
&= \mathbf{E}\left[Z^{\mathsf{B}}_J\right] + \mathbf{E}\left[g(F_{\leq J}, S)\right] - \mathbf{E}\left[g(F_{\leq J}, S)\right] + \mathbf{E}\left[\mathsf{G}(F_{\leq J}, S) - F^{\mathsf{B}}_J\right] - \mathbf{E}\left[\mathsf{G}(F_{\leq J}, S) - F^{\mathsf{B}}_J\right] \\
&= \mathbf{E}\left[g(F_{\leq J}, S)\right] - \mathbf{E}\left[\mathsf{G}(F_{\leq J}, S) - F^{\mathsf{B}}_J\right] + \mathbf{E}\left[\mathsf{G}(F_{\leq J}, S) - g(F_{\leq J}, S)\right] + \mathbf{E}\left[Z^{\mathsf{B}}_J - F^{\mathsf{B}}_J\right] \\
&= \frac{1}{2} - \mathbf{E}\left[\mathsf{G}(F_{\leq J}, S) - F^{\mathsf{B}}_J\right] + \mathbf{E}\left[\mathsf{G}(F_{\leq J}, S) - g(F_{\leq J}, S)\right] + \mathbf{E}\left[Z^{\mathsf{B}}_J - F^{\mathsf{B}}_J\right].
\end{aligned} \tag{24}$$

The last equation follows from $\mathbf{E}\left[g(F_{\leq J}, S)\right] = \mathbf{E}\left[C\right]$ and thus $\mathbf{E}\left[g(F_{\leq J}, S)\right] = \frac{1}{2}$ (for a more detailed argument see Eq. (19) and preceding text). We bound each of the terms above separately. First, observe that

$$\begin{aligned}
&\Pr[J \neq r] \\
&\geq \Pr\left[(\forall i \in [r] : |\mathsf{G}(F_{\leq i}, S) - g(F_{\leq i}, S)| \leq \rho) \right. \\
&\qquad \left. \wedge \left(\exists j \in [r] : g(F_{\leq j}, S) - F_j^{\mathsf{B}} \geq \frac{1}{8\sqrt{r}}\right)\right] \\
&\geq \Pr\left[\exists j \in [r] : g(F_{\leq j}, S) - F_j \geq \frac{1}{8\sqrt{r}}\right] \\
&\qquad - \Pr[\exists i \in [r] : |\mathsf{G}(F_{\leq i}, S) - g(F_{\leq i}, S)| > \rho] \\
&\geq \frac{1}{200} - \rho \\
&\geq \frac{1}{400}. \qquad (25)
\end{aligned}$$

The penultimate inequality is by Eq. (24) and Claim 3.5. It follows that

$$\begin{aligned}
\mathbf{E}\left[g(F_{\leq J}, S) - F_J^{\mathsf{B}}\right] &= \Pr[J \neq r] \cdot \mathbf{E}\left[g(F_{\leq J}, S) - F_J^{\mathsf{B}} \mid J \neq r\right] \\
&\geq \frac{1}{400} \cdot \left(\frac{1}{8\sqrt{r}} - \rho\right) - \mathbf{E}\left[\mathsf{G}(F_{\leq J}, S) - g(F_{\leq J}, S)\right] \\
&\geq \frac{1}{400} \cdot \frac{1}{8\sqrt{r}} - 3\rho. \qquad (26)
\end{aligned}$$

The penultimate inequality is by Claim 3.5. Finally, since we were taking κ large enough, Claim 3.4 and a data-processing argument yields that

$$\mathbf{E}\left[Z_J^{\mathsf{B}} - F_J^{\mathsf{B}}\right] \leq r\rho \qquad (27)$$

We conclude that $\mathbf{E}\left[g(F_{\leq J}, S) - F_J^{\mathsf{B}}\right] \geq \frac{1}{400} \cdot \frac{1}{8\sqrt{r}} - (r+3)\rho > 1/(6400\sqrt{r})$, in contradiction to the assumed fairness of Π. □

3.3 Independence of Attack Decision

In this section, we prove Claim 3.8 (restated below).

Claim 3.14 (Claim 3.8, restated). Let D be a single-bit output PPTM. For $\kappa \in \mathbb{N}$ and $\mathsf{P} \in \{\mathsf{A}, \mathsf{B}\}$, let $E_1^{\mathsf{P},\kappa}, \ldots, E_r^{\mathsf{P},\kappa}$ be the sequence of random variables defined by $E_i^{\mathsf{P},\kappa} = \mathsf{D}(F_{\leq i}^{\kappa}, S^{\kappa})$ if P sends the ith message in $\Pi(1^{\kappa})$, and $E_i^{\mathsf{P},\kappa} = 0$ otherwise.

Assume io-key-agreement protocols do not exist. Then, for any $\mathsf{P} \in \{\mathsf{A}, \mathsf{B}\}$ and infinite subset $\mathcal{K}' \subseteq \mathcal{K}$, there exists an infinite set $\mathcal{K}'' \subseteq \mathcal{K}'$ such that

$$\mathbf{E}\left[E_{i+1}^{\mathsf{P},\kappa} \cdot (Z_i^{\overline{\mathsf{P}},\kappa} - F_i^{\overline{\mathsf{P}},\kappa})\right] \in \pm 4r\rho$$

for every $\kappa \in \mathcal{K}''$ and $i \in (r-1)$, where $\overline{\mathsf{P}} \in \{\mathsf{A}, \mathsf{B}\} \setminus \{\mathsf{P}\}$.

We prove for $\mathsf{P} = \mathsf{A}$. Consider the following variant of Π in which the party playing A is outputting E_i^{A} and the party playing B is outputting its backup value.

Protocol 3.15 ($\widehat{\Pi} = \left(\widehat{\mathsf{A}}, \widehat{\mathsf{B}}\right)$)

Common input: security parameter 1^κ.
Description:

1. Party $\widehat{\mathsf{A}}$ samples $i \leftarrow [r]$ and $s \leftarrow S^\kappa$, and sends them to $\widehat{\mathsf{B}}$.
2. The parties interact in the first $i-1$ rounds of a random execution of $\Pi(1^\kappa)$, with $\widehat{\mathsf{A}}$ and $\widehat{\mathsf{B}}$ taking the role of A and B respectively.
   Let $m_1, \ldots, m_{i-1}$ be the messages, and let z_{i-1}^{B} be the $(i-1)$ backup output of B in the above execution.
3. $\widehat{\mathsf{A}}$ sets the value of e_i^{A} as follows:
   If A sends the $i-1$ message above, then it sets $e_i^{\mathsf{A}} = 0$.
   Otherwise, it
   (a) Continues the above execution of Π to compute its next message m_i.
   (b) Computes $f_i = \mathsf{F}(m_{\leq i}, s)$.
   (c) Let $e_i^{\mathsf{A}} = \mathsf{D}(f_{\leq i}, s)$.

(4) $\widehat{\mathsf{A}}$ outputs e_i^{A} and B outputs z_{i-1}^{B}.

We apply the the following dichotomy result of Haitner et al. [12] on the above protocol.

Theorem 3.16 (Haitner et al.[12], Theorem 3.18, dichotomy of two-party protocols). *Let Δ be an efficient single-bit output two-party protocol. Assume io-key-agreement protocol do not exist, then for any constant $\rho > 0$ and infinite subset $\mathcal{K} \subseteq \mathbb{N}$, there exists a* PPT *algorithm* Dcr *(decorelator) mapping transcripts of Δ into (the binary description of) pairs in $[0,1] \times [0,1]$ and an infinite set $\mathcal{K}' \in \mathbb{N}$, such that the following holds: let $C^{\mathsf{A},\kappa}$, $C^{\mathsf{B},\kappa}$ and T^κ denote the parties' output and protocol transcript in a random execution of $\Delta(1^\kappa)$. Let $m(\kappa) \in \mathrm{poly}$ be a bound on the number of coins used by* Dcr *on transcripts in $\mathrm{supp}(T^\kappa)$, and let S^κ be a uniform string of length $m(\kappa)$. Then*

$$(C^{\mathsf{A},\kappa}, C^{\mathsf{B},\kappa}, T^\kappa, S^\kappa) \overset{\mathsf{C}}{\approx}_{\rho,\mathcal{K}'} (U_{p^{\mathsf{A}}}, U_{p^{\mathsf{A}}}, T^\kappa, S^\kappa)_{(p^{\mathsf{A}},p^{\mathsf{B}})=\mathsf{Dcr}(T^\kappa;S^\kappa)}$$

letting U_p be a Boolean random variable taking the value 1 with probability p.

Proof of Claim 3.14. Assume io-key-agreement does not exits, and let $\mathcal{K}'' \subseteq \mathcal{K}'$ and a PPT Dcr be the infinite set and PPT decorrelator resulting by applying Theorem 3.16 with respect to protocol $\widehat{\Pi}$ and ρ. Let $\widehat{S}^\kappa$ denote a long enough uniform string to be used by Dcr on transcripts of $\widehat{\Pi}(1^\kappa)$. Then for $I \leftarrow (r-1)$, letting $\mathsf{Dcr}(m_{\leq i}, s; \widehat{s}) = \mathsf{Dcr}(i, s, m_{\leq i}; \widehat{s})$, it holds that

$$(E_{I+1}^{\mathsf{A},\kappa}, Z_I^{\mathsf{B},\kappa}, M_{\leq i}^\kappa, S^\kappa, \widehat{S}^\kappa) \overset{\mathsf{C}}{\approx}_{\rho,\mathcal{K}''} (U_{p^{\mathsf{A}}}, U_{p^{\mathsf{B}}}, M_{\leq I}^\kappa, S^\kappa, \widehat{S}^\kappa)_{(p^{\mathsf{A}},p^{\mathsf{B}})=\mathsf{Dcr}(M_{\leq I},S^\kappa;\widehat{S}^\kappa)}. \tag{28}$$

For $i \in [r]$, let $W_i^\kappa = (W_i^{\mathsf{A},\kappa}, W_i^{\mathsf{B},\kappa}) = \mathsf{Dcr}(M_{\leq i}, S^\kappa; \widehat{S}^\kappa)$. The proof of Claim 3.17 follows by the following three observations, proven below, that hold for large enough $\kappa \in \mathcal{K}''$.

Claim 3.17. $\mathbf{E}\left[E_{I+1}^{\mathsf{A},\kappa} \cdot Z_I^{\mathsf{B},\kappa} - W_I^{\mathsf{A},\kappa} \cdot W_I^{\mathsf{B},\kappa}\right] \in \pm\rho$.

Claim 3.18. $\mathbf{E}\left[W_I^{\mathsf{A},\kappa} \cdot F_I^{\mathsf{B},\kappa} - E_{I+1}^{\mathsf{A},\kappa} \cdot F_I^{\mathsf{B},\kappa}\right] \in \pm\rho$.

Claim 3.19. $\mathbf{E}\left[W_I^{\mathsf{A},\kappa} \cdot W_I^{\mathsf{B},\kappa} - W_I^{\mathsf{A},\kappa} \cdot F_I^{\mathsf{B},\kappa}\right] \in \pm 2\rho$.

We conclude that $\mathbf{E}\left[E_{I+1}^{\mathsf{P},\kappa} \cdot Z_I^{\overline{\mathsf{P}},\kappa} - E_{I+1}^{\mathsf{P},\kappa} \cdot F_I^{\overline{\mathsf{P}},\kappa}\right] \in \pm 4\rho$, and thus $\mathbf{E}\left[E_{i+1}^{\mathsf{P},\kappa} \cdot Z_i^{\overline{\mathsf{P}},\kappa} - E_{i+1}^{\mathsf{P},\kappa} \cdot F_i^{\overline{\mathsf{P}},\kappa}\right] \in \pm 4r\rho$ for every $i \in (r-1)$. □

Proving Claim 3.17.

Proof of Claim 3.17. Consider algorithm D that on input $(z^{\mathsf{A}}, z^{\mathsf{B}}, \cdot)$, outputs (the product) $z^{\mathsf{A}} z^{\mathsf{B}}$. By definition,

1. $\Pr\left[\mathsf{D}(U_{W_I^{\mathsf{A},\kappa}}, U_{W_I^{\mathsf{B},\kappa}}, M_{\leq I}^{\kappa}, S^{\kappa}) = 1\right] = \mathbf{E}\left[U_{W_I^{\mathsf{A},\kappa}} \cdot U_{W_I^{\mathsf{B},\kappa}}\right] = \mathbf{E}\left[W_I^{\mathsf{A},\kappa} \cdot W_I^{\mathsf{B},\kappa}\right]$,
2. $\Pr\left[\mathsf{D}(E_{I+1}^{\mathsf{A},\kappa}, Z_I^{\mathsf{B},\kappa}, M_{\leq I}^{\kappa}, S^{\kappa}) = 1\right] = \mathbf{E}\left[E_{I+1}^{\mathsf{A},\kappa} \cdot Z_I^{\mathsf{B},\kappa}\right]$.

Hence, the proof follows by Eq. (28). □

Proving Claim 3.18.

Proof of Claim 3.18. Consider the algorithm D that on input $(z^{\mathsf{A}}, z^{\mathsf{B}}, (m_{\leq I}, s))$: (1) computes $(\cdot, f^{\mathsf{B}}) = \mathsf{F}(m_{\leq I}; s)$, (2) samples $u \leftarrow U_{f^{\mathsf{B}}}$, and (3) outputs $z^{\mathsf{A}} \cdot u$. By definition,

1. $\Pr\left[\mathsf{D}(U_{W_I^{\mathsf{A},\kappa}}, U_{W_I^{\mathsf{B},\kappa}}, M_{\leq I}^{\kappa}, S^{\kappa}) = 1\right] = \mathbf{E}\left[U_{W_I^{\mathsf{A},\kappa}} \cdot U_{F_I^{\mathsf{B},\kappa}}\right] = \mathbf{E}\left[W_I^{\mathsf{A},\kappa} \cdot F_I^{\mathsf{B},\kappa}\right]$,
2. $\Pr\left[\mathsf{D}(E_{I+1}^{\mathsf{A},\kappa}, Z_I^{\mathsf{B},\kappa}, M_{\leq I}^{\kappa}, S^{\kappa}) = 1\right] = \mathbf{E}\left[E_{I+1}^{\mathsf{A},\kappa} \cdot U_{F_I^{\mathsf{B},\kappa}}\right] = \mathbf{E}\left[E_{I+1}^{\mathsf{A},\kappa} \cdot F_I^{\mathsf{B},\kappa}\right]$.

Hence, also in this case the proof follows by Eq. (28). □

Proving Claim 3.19.

Proof of Claim 3.19. Since $\left|W_I^{\mathsf{A},\kappa}\right| \leq 1$, it suffices to prove $\mathbf{E}\left[\left|W_I^{\mathsf{B},\kappa} - F_I^{\mathsf{B},\kappa}\right|\right] \leq 2\rho$. We show that if $\mathbf{E}\left[\left|W_I^{\mathsf{B},\kappa} - F_I^{\mathsf{B},\kappa}\right|\right] > 2\rho$, then there exists a distinguisher with advantage greater than ρ for either the real outputs of $\widehat{\Pi}$ and the emulated outputs of Dcr, or, the real outputs of $\widetilde{\Pi}$ and the emulated outputs of F, in contradiction with the assumed properties of Dcr and F.

Consider algorithm D that on input $(z^{\mathsf{A}}, z^{\mathsf{B}}, m_{\leq i}, s)$ acts as follows: (1) samples $\widehat{s} \leftarrow \widehat{S}^{\kappa}$, (2) computes $(\cdot, f^{\mathsf{B}}) = \mathsf{F}(m_{\leq i}; s)$ and $(\cdot, w^{\mathsf{B}}) = \mathsf{Dcr}(m_{\leq i}, s; \widehat{s})$, (3) outputs z^{B} if $w^{\mathsf{B}} \geq f^{\mathsf{B}}$, and $1 - z^{\mathsf{B}}$ otherwise. We compute the difference in probability that D outputs 1 given a sample from $\mathsf{Dcr}(M^{\kappa}_{\leq I})$ or a sample from $\mathsf{F}(M^{\kappa}_{\leq I})$ (we omit the superscript κ and subscript I below to reduce clutter)

$$
\begin{aligned}
&\Pr\left[\mathsf{D}(U_{W_I^{\mathsf{A},\kappa}}, U_{W_I^{\mathsf{B},\kappa}}, M^{\kappa}_{\leq I}, S^{\kappa}) = 1\right] - \Pr\left[\mathsf{D}(U_{F_I^{\mathsf{A},\kappa}}, U_{F_I^{\mathsf{B},\kappa}}, M^{\kappa}_{\leq I}, S^{\kappa}) = 1\right] \\
&= \mathbf{E}\left[U_{W^{\mathsf{B}}} \mid W^{\mathsf{B}} \geq F^{\mathsf{B}}\right] \cdot \Pr\left[W^{\mathsf{B}} \geq F^{\mathsf{B}}\right] \\
&\quad + \mathbf{E}\left[1 - U_{W^{\mathsf{B}}} \mid W^{\mathsf{B}} < F^{\mathsf{B}}\right] \cdot \Pr\left[W^{\mathsf{B}} < F^{\mathsf{B}}\right] \\
&\quad - \mathbf{E}\left[U_{F^{\mathsf{B}}} \mid W^{\mathsf{B}} \geq F^{\mathsf{B}}\right] \cdot \Pr\left[W^{\mathsf{B}} \geq F^{\mathsf{B}}\right] \\
&\quad - \mathbf{E}\left[1 - U_{F^{\mathsf{B}}} \mid W^{\mathsf{B}} < F^{\mathsf{B}}\right] \cdot \Pr\left[W^{\mathsf{B}} < F^{\mathsf{B}}\right] \\
&= \mathbf{E}\left[W^{\mathsf{B}} \mid W^{\mathsf{B}} \geq F^{\mathsf{B}}\right] \cdot \Pr\left[W^{\mathsf{B}} \geq F^{\mathsf{B}}\right] \\
&\quad - \mathbf{E}\left[W^{\mathsf{B}} \mid W^{\mathsf{B}} < F^{\mathsf{B}}\right] \Pr\left[W^{\mathsf{B}} < F^{\mathsf{B}}\right] \\
&\quad - \mathbf{E}\left[F^{\mathsf{B}} \mid W^{\mathsf{B}} \geq F^{\mathsf{B}}\right] \cdot \Pr\left[W^{\mathsf{B}} \geq F^{\mathsf{B}}\right] \\
&\quad + \mathbf{E}\left[F^{\mathsf{B}} \mid W^{\mathsf{B}} < F^{\mathsf{B}}\right] \cdot \Pr\left[W^{\mathsf{B}} < F^{\mathsf{B}}\right] \\
&= \mathbf{E}\left[W^{\mathsf{B}} - F^{\mathsf{B}} \mid W^{\mathsf{B}} \geq F^{\mathsf{B}}\right] \cdot \Pr\left[W^{\mathsf{B}} \geq F^{\mathsf{B}}\right] \\
&\quad + \mathbf{E}\left[-W^{\mathsf{B}} + F^{\mathsf{B}} \mid W^{\mathsf{B}} < F^{\mathsf{B}}\right] \Pr\left[W^{\mathsf{B}} < F^{\mathsf{B}}\right] \\
&= \mathbf{E}\left[\left|W^{\mathsf{B}} - F^{\mathsf{B}}\right|\right] \\
&> 2\rho.
\end{aligned}
$$

An averaging argument yields that either D is a distinguisher for the tuples $(U_{F_I^{\mathsf{A},\kappa}}, U_{F_I^{\mathsf{B},\kappa}}, M^{\kappa}_{\leq I}, S^{\kappa})$ and $(Z_I^{\mathsf{A},\kappa}, Z_I^{\mathsf{B},\kappa}, M^{\kappa}_{\leq I}, S^{\kappa})$ with advantage greater than ρ, in contradiction with Claim 3.4, or, algorithm D is a distinguisher for the tuples $(U_{W_I^{\mathsf{A},\kappa}}, U_{W_I^{\mathsf{B},\kappa}}, M^{\kappa}_{\leq I}, S^{\kappa})$ and $(E_I^{\mathsf{A},\kappa}, Z_I^{\mathsf{B},\kappa}, M^{\kappa}_{\leq I}, S^{\kappa})$ with advantage greater than ρ, in contradiction with Eq. (28). □

References

1. Alon, B., Omri, E.: Almost-optimally fair multiparty coin-tossing with nearly three-quarters malicious. In: Hirt, M., Smith, A. (eds.) TCC 2016. LNCS, vol. 9985, pp. 307–335. Springer, Heidelberg (2016). https://doi.org/10.1007/978-3-662-53641-4_13
2. Awerbuch, B., Blum, M., Chor, B., Goldwasser, S., Micali, S.: How to implement Bracha's $O(\log n)$ byzantine agreement algorithm (1985). Unpublished manuscript
3. Beimel, A., Haitner, I., Makriyannis, N., Omri, E.: Tighter bounds on multi-party coin flipping via augmented weak martingales and differentially private sampling. In: Proceedings of the 59th Annual Symposium on Foundations of Computer Science (FOCS) (2018)
4. Beimel, A., Omri, E., Orlov, I.: Protocols for multiparty coin toss with a dishonest majority. J. Cryptol. **28**(3), 551–600 (2015)
5. Berman, I., Haitner, I., Tentes, A.: Coin flipping of any constant bias implies one-way functions. J. ACM **65**(3), 14 (2018)
6. Blum, M.: How to exchange (secret) keys. ACM Trans. Comput. Syst. **1**, 175–193 (1983)

7. Buchbinder, N., Haitner, I., Levi, N., Tsfadia, E.: Fair coin flipping: tighter analysis and the many-party case. In: Proceedings of the 28th Annual ACM-SIAM Symposium on Discrete Algorithms (SODA), pp. 2580–2600 (2017)
8. Cleve, R.: Limits on the security of coin flips when half the processors are faulty. In: Proceedings of the 18th Annual ACM Symposium on Theory of Computing (STOC), pp. 364–369 (1986)
9. Cleve, R., Impagliazzo, R.: Martingales, collective coin flipping and discrete control processes (extended abstract) (1993). http://citeseerx.ist.psu.edu/viewdoc/summary?doi=10.1.1.51.1797
10. Dachman-Soled, D., Lindell, Y., Mahmoody, M., Malkin, T.: On the black-box complexity of optimally-fair coin tossing. In: Ishai, Y. (ed.) TCC 2011. LNCS, vol. 6597, pp. 450–467. Springer, Heidelberg (2011). https://doi.org/10.1007/978-3-642-19571-6_27
11. Dachman-Soled, D., Mahmoody, M., Malkin, T.: Can optimally-fair coin tossing be based on one-way functions? In: Lindell, Y. (ed.) TCC 2014. LNCS, vol. 8349, pp. 217–239. Springer, Heidelberg (2014). https://doi.org/10.1007/978-3-642-54242-8_10
12. Haitner, I., Nissim, K., Omri, E., Shaltiel, R., Silbak, J.: Computational two-party correlation. In: Proceedings of the 59th Annual Symposium on Foundations of Computer Science (FOCS) (2018)
13. Haitner, I., Omri, E.: Coin flipping with constant bias implies one-way functions. SIAM J. Comput. **43**(2), 389–409 (2014)
14. Haitner, I., Tsfadia, E.: An almost-optimally fair three-party coin-flipping protocol. In: Proceedings of the 46th Annual ACM Symposium on Theory of Computing (STOC), pp. 817–836 (2014)
15. Haitner, I., Tsfadia, E.: An almost-optimally fair three-party coin-flipping protocol. SIAM J. Comput. **46**(2), 479–542 (2017)
16. Hoeffding, W.: Probability inequalities for sums of bounded random variables. J. Am. Stat. Assoc. **58**, 13–30 (1963)
17. Impagliazzo, R., Luby, M.: One-way functions are essential for complexity based cryptography. In: Proceedings of the 30th Annual Symposium on Foundations of Computer Science (FOCS), pp. 230–235 (1989)
18. Maji, H.K., Prabhakaran, M., Sahai, A.: On the computational complexity of coin flipping. In: Proceedings of the 51st Annual Symposium on Foundations of Computer Science (FOCS), pp. 613–622 (2010)
19. Moran, T., Naor, M., Segev, G.: An optimally fair coin toss. In: Reingold, O. (ed.) TCC 2009. LNCS, vol. 5444, pp. 1–18. Springer, Heidelberg (2009). https://doi.org/10.1007/978-3-642-00457-5_1
20. Moran, T., Naor, M., Segev, G.: An optimally fair coin toss. J. Cryptol. **29**(3), 491–513 (2016)

Game Theoretic Notions of Fairness in Multi-party Coin Toss

Kai-Min Chung[2(✉)], Yue Guo[1], Wei-Kai Lin[1], Rafael Pass[1,3], and Elaine Shi[1]

[1] Cornell University, Ithaca, NY, USA
{yueguo,wklin,rafael,elaine}@cs.cornell.edu
[2] Institute of Information Science, Academia Sinica, Taipei, Taiwan
kmchung@iis.sinica.edu.tw
[3] CornellTech, New York, NY, USA

Abstract. Coin toss has been extensively studied in the cryptography literature, and the well-accepted notion of fairness (henceforth called *strong fairness*) requires that a corrupt coalition cannot cause non-negligible bias. It is well-understood that two-party coin toss is impossible if one of the parties can prematurely abort; further, this impossibility generalizes to multiple parties with a corrupt majority (even if the adversary is computationally bounded and fail-stop only).

Interestingly, the original proposal of (two-party) coin toss protocols by Blum in fact considered a weaker notion of fairness: imagine that the (randomized) transcript of the coin toss protocol defines a winner among the two parties. Now Blum's notion requires that a corrupt party cannot bias the outcome in its favor (but self-sacrificing bias is allowed). Blum showed that this weak notion is indeed attainable for two parties assuming the existence of one-way functions.

In this paper, we ask a very natural question which, surprisingly, has been overlooked by the cryptography literature: can we achieve Blum's weak fairness notion in *multi-party* coin toss? What is particularly interesting is whether this relaxation allows us to circumvent the corrupt majority impossibility that pertains to strong fairness. Even more surprisingly, in answering this question, we realize that it is not even understood how to define weak fairness for multi-party coin toss. We propose several natural notions drawing inspirations from game theory, all of which equate to Blum's notion for the special case of two parties. We show, however, that for multiple parties, these notions vary in strength and lead to different feasibility and infeasibility results.

 This work is supported in part by NSF grants CNS-1514261 and CNS-1561209. This is the conference version. The full version of this paper is available online.

A. Beimel and S. Dziembowski (Eds.): TCC 2018, LNCS 11239, pp. 563–596, 2018.
https://doi.org/10.1007/978-3-030-03807-6_21

1 Introduction

The study of coin toss protocols was initiated in Blum's ground-breaking work [16]. Consider the following scenario: Alice and Bob had concurrent and independent results that solved a difficult open question in cryptography. Both submitted their papers to the prestigious Theory of Cryptography Conference (TCC) 2018 conference with the most amazing program committee (PC). The wise PC urged Alice and Bob to merge their results into one paper and provided them with a single presentation slot at the conference. Now Alice and Bob would like to toss a random coin to decide who goes to the most fabulous conference venue ever, Goa, and present the paper. Since Alice and Bob are not in the same room, they would like to complete the coin toss by sending messages to each other (slowly) over the Ethereum blockchain, such that anyone who observes the transcript can determine the outcome of the coin flip. Now either party would like to make sure that he/she has a fair chance of winning even when the other cheats and deviates from the protocol. The academic literature has since referred to Blum's notion of fairness as *weak fairness*; and Blum showed that assuming the existence of one-way functions a weakly-fair, 2-party coin toss protocol can be constructed [16]. Interestingly, however, the vast majority of subsequent cryptography literature has focused on a stronger notion of fairness than Blum's, that is, a corrupt party cannot bias the outcome of the coin toss—henceforth we refer to this notion as *strong fairness* [19]. It is not difficult to see that a strongly fair coin toss protocol must also be weakly fair; but not the other way round. In particular, a weakly fair protocol allows a corrupt party to bias the outcome of the remaining honest party—but the bias must not be in the corrupt party's favor. Unfortunately for the strongly fair notion, Cleve's celebrated result [19] proved its impossibility in a 2-party setting even for computationally bounded, fail-stop adversaries.

In this paper, we consider multi-party extensions of Blum's notion of weak fairness. We ask a very natural question that seems to have been overlooked by the literature so far:

> *Can we achieve Blum's weak fairness notion in multi-party coin toss protocols?*

By contrast, the strong fairness notion has been extensively studied in the multi-party context [12,27]. Well-known results tell us that the strong notion is attainable assuming honest majority and existence of one-way functions. On the other hand, Cleve's 2-party impossibility extends to multiple parties with a corrupt majority [19]. Therefore, a more refined question is

> *Can we overcome Cleve's impossibility for corrupt majority multi-party coin toss with weak fairness?*

Of course, to answer the above questions, we must first answer

> *How do we even define weak fairness in multi-party coin toss protocols?*

Intriguingly, even the definition itself is non-trivial! In this paper, we propose several natural notions of fairness that are inspired by the line of work on game theory [15,35,36,48]. Interestingly, all of these notions equate to Blum's notion for the special case of 2 parties; however, in general, they differ in strengths for multiple parties and thus lead to differing feasibility and infeasibility results.

1.1 Our Results and Contributions

Consider the following scenario: n parties would like to play a 1-bit roulette game over the Internet: First, each party puts down 1 Ether as stake and places a *publicly visible*[1] bet (also referred to as the party's *preference*) on one of the bits $b \in \{0, 1\}$. Without loss of generality *we assume that not everyone bets on the same bit.* Next, they run an n-party coin toss protocol by exchanging messages over the Ethereum blockchain, and transcript of the protocol determines an outcome bit. Now, those who betted correctly are called winners; and those who betted wrongly are called losers. Finally, every loser loses its stake to the house (e.g., owner of the smart contract); and each winner gets paid 1 Ether by the house. We require that *in an honest execution, each bit is chosen with probability* 1/2. Henceforth in the paper for simplicity we shall think of the Ethereum blockchain as a broadcast medium with identifiable abort, i.e., a public bulletin board that allows parties to post messages.

How should we define fairness for this 1-bit roulette game? Cryptography and game theory provide different answers. The standard notion from cryptography is again strong fairness [19], that is, any corrupt coalition should not be able to bias the outcome by more than a negligible amount. As mentioned strong fairness is unattainable under a corrupt majority even for fail-stop adversaries [19]. Most of game theory, on the other hand, considers (computational) Nash Equilibrium [48], that is, no corrupt *individual* can noticeably improve its expected reward by deviating, assuming that everyone else is playing honestly. Although Nash Equilibrium is indeed attainable by adopting a standard, strongly fair multi-party coin toss protocol that tolerates deviation by any single party [27], such a notion might be too weak. In particular, no guarantee is provided when two or more parties collude (e.g., in cryptocurrency applications, an individual user can always make up any number of pseudonyms and control the majority in a game). Therefore we would like to explore notions in between that allow us to resist majority coalitions and provide meaningful fairness guarantees in practical applications. In this paper, we define several notions of fairness—all of them equate to Blum's notion [16] for the special case of 2 parties. Thus for all of our notions, in the 2-party case Blum's result applies: assuming one-way functions, all notions are attainable against malicious, computationally bounded adversaries that control one of the two parties; moreover, for fail-stop adversaries, all our notions are attainable against even unbounded adversaries that control one of the two parties.

[1] Unless otherwise noted, we consider public preference profiles. For completeness, however, we present results for private preference profiles in the appendices, Sect. 7.

Henceforth for our fairness notions, we are concerned about feasibility and infeasibility results for 3 or more parties, and particularly for the case of *corrupt majority* (since for honest majority, feasibility is known even for strong fairness, against malicious, computationally bounded adversaries, due to the celebrated result by Goldreich et al. [27]). As a final remark before we introduce our notions, all our notions (as well as Blum's notion) can be easily ruled out for computationally unbounded, malicious adversaries [33,44].

1.2 Maximin Fairness

Definition. A natural notion, which seems to be a good fit for cryptocurrency applications, is to require the following: an honest Alice should not be harmed even when everyone else is colluding against her. In other words, any individual's expected reward should not noticeably decrease (relative to an all-honest execution) even when all others are colluding against her. This notion has a game theoretic interpretation: the honest strategy maximizes a player's worst-case expected payoff (even when everyone else is colluding against her); and moreover, by playing honest, the player's worst-case expected payoff is not noticeably worse than an all-honest execution. For maximin fairness, we present a complete characterization of feasibilities/infeasibilties.

Feasibility and Infeasibility for Almost Unanimous Preference Profiles. For 3 or more parties, if everyone agrees in preference except one party, we say that the preference profile is *almost unanimous.* When the preference profile is almost unanimous, maximin fairness is possible for fail-stop adversaries and without relying on cryptographic assumptions. Recall that a fail-stop adversary may prematurely abort from the protocol but would otherwise follow the honest protocol [19]. The corresponding protocol is very simple: without loss of generality assume that one party prefers 0 (called the 0-supporter) and all others prefer 1 (called the 1-supporters). Now, the 0-supporter chooses a random bit and broadcasts it. If the broadcast indeed happens, the bit broadcast is declared as the outcome. Otherwise, the outcome is defined to be 1.

We then prove that for an almost unanimous preference profile, maximin fairness is impossible for malicious adversaries even when allowing cryptographic assumptions. This result is somewhat counter-intuitive in light of the earlier feasibility for fail-stop (and the proof rather non-trivial too). In particular, in most of the cryptography literature, we are familiar with techniques that compile fail-stop (or semi-honest) protocols to attain full, malicious security [12,27]—but these compilation techniques *do not preserve maximin fairness* and thus are inapplicable here.

Note that for the special case of 3 parties, unless everyone has the same preference any preference profile is almost unanimous—thus for the case of 3 parties we already have a complete characterization. For 4 or more parties, we need to consider the case when the preference profile is more mixed.

Infeasibility for Amply Divided Preference Profiles. If there are at least two 0-supporters and at least two 1-supporters, we say that the parties have an *amply divided* preference profile. Note that for 3 or more parties, unless everyone has the same preference, then every preference profile is either almost unanimous or amply divided. For an amply divided preference profile, we show infeasibility even against computationally bounded, fail-stop adversaries by reduction to Cleve's impossibility result for strong fairness [19].

We summarize our results for maximin fairness in the following theorems—although not explicitly noted, all theorems are concerned about an adversary that may control up to $n-1$ players.

Theorem 1 (Maximin fairness: upper bound (informal)). *For any $n \geq 3$ and any almost unanimous preference profile, there is an n-party coin toss protocol that achieves maximin fairness against fail-stop and computationally unbounded adversaries.*

Theorem 2 (Maximin fairness: lower bound (informal)). *For any $n \geq 3$ and any almost unanimous preference profile, no n-party coin toss protocol can achieve maximin fairness against malicious and even polynomially bounded adversaries. Further, for any $n \geq 4$ and any amply divided preference profile, no n-party coin toss protocol can achieve maximin fairness against fail-stop and even polynomially bounded adversaries.*

Summary. While maximin fairness appears to provide strong guarantees in cryptocurrency and smart contract applications, we showed rather broad infeasibility results. Nonetheless it gives us a glimpse of hope: for the case of almost unanimous preference profiles and fail-stop adversaries, we are able to achieve positive results for corrupt majority while strong fairness cannot! We thus continue to explore alternative notions in hope of finding one that leads to broader feasibility results. Our high-level idea is the following: earlier, maximin fairness aims to rule out coalitions that *harm honest parties*; instead we now consider notions that rule out coalitions capable of *improving its own wealth*—this gives rise to two new notions, cooperative-strategy-proof fairness and Strong Nash Equilibrium, as we discuss subsequently in Sects. 1.3 and 1.4.

1.3 Cooperative-Strategy-Proof Fairness

Definition. Cooperative-strategy-proof (CSP) fairness requires that no deviation by a corrupt coalition of size up to $n-1$ can noticeably improve the coalition's total expected reward relative to an honest execution. It is not difficult to see that CSP fairness is equivalent to maximin fairness for zero-sum cases: when exactly half prefer 0 and half prefer 1. However, the two notions are incomparable in general.

Feasibility for Almost Unanimous Preference Profiles. When almost everyone prefers the same bit except for one party, we show that the following simple protocol achieves CSP fairness against malicious adversaries. For simplicity, our description below assumes an ideal commitment functionality $\mathcal{F}_{\text{idealcomm}}$—but this idealized oracle can be replaced with suitable non-malleable concurrent commitment schemes [42,43] with some additional work. Without loss of generality we assume that a single party prefers 0 and everyone else prefers 1: First, everyone picks a random bit upfront and commits the bit to $\mathcal{F}_{\text{idealcomm}}$. In round 0, the single 0-supporter opens its committed bit and broadcasts it. In round 1, everyone else opens its committed bit and broadcasts the opening. The outcome is defined to be 0 if one or more 1-supporter(s) aborted; else it is defined to be the XOR of all bits that have been correctly opened.

Finally, for fail-stop adversaries, a variant of the above protocol without commitment can achieve CSP fairness against even unbounded adversaries.

Infeasibility for Amply Divided Preference Profiles. For any amply divided preference profile, we prove that it is impossible to achieve CSP fairness against even fail-stop, polynomially bounded adversaries.

We summarize results for CSP fairness in the following theorem.

Theorem 3 (CSP fairness (informal)). *For any almost unanimous preference profile, it is possible to attain CSP fairness against fail-stop, unbounded adversaries, and against malicious, polynomially bounded adversaries assuming one-way permutations. By contrast, for any amply divided preference profile, it is impossible to attain CSP fairness against even fail-stop, polynomially bounded adversaries.*

1.4 Strong Nash Equilibrium

Due to earlier impossibility results for maximin fairness and CSP fairness, we ask if there is a notion for which we can enjoy broad feasibility. To this end we consider a fairness notion inspired by Strong Nash Equilibrium (SNE) [35], henceforth referred to as SNE fairness. SNE fairness requires that no deviation by a coalition can improve every coalition member's expected reward. It is not difficult to see that for SNE fairness, we only need to resist *unanimous* coalitions, i.e., coalitions in which every member prefers the same bit. Further, SNE fairness is also strictly weaker than CSP fairness in general.

We show that a simple dueling protocol achieves SNE fairness against malicious (but polynomially bounded) adversaries: pick two parties with opposing preferences (i.e., pick the two with smallest possible party identifiers), and then have the two run Blum's weak coin toss protocol. Further, the computational assumptions can be removed for fail-stop adversaries and thus SNE fairness can be guaranteed unconditionally for the fail-stop case. We summarize our results on SNE fairness in the following theorem.

Theorem 4 (SNE fairness (informal)). *For any $n \geq 3$ and any preference profile: (1) there is an n-party coin toss protocol that achieves SNE fairness against malicious, polynomially-bounded adversaries assuming the existence of one-way permutations; and (2) there is an n-party coin toss protocol that achieves SNE fairness against fail-stop, unbounded adversaries.*

Alternative Formulation: Cooperative-Coalition-Proof Fairness. While SNE fairness aims to rule out coalitions that improve every coalition member's wealth, an alternative notion would be to resist *self-enforcing* coalitions that aim to improve the coalition's overall wealth. In particular, a coalition is said to be self-enforcing iff no *self-enforcing* sub-coalition can gain by deviating from the coalition's original strategy. Such coalitions are stable and will not implode due to internally misaligned incentives. We formalize this notion in our online full version [18] which we call *cooperative-coalition-proof fairness* (CCP fairness). Since CCP fairness considers complex coalition and sub-coalition behavior, we can no longer use the familiar protocol execution model used in the standard cryptography literature—we instead propose a new, suitable protocol execution model that allows us to characterize complex coalition structures. Our CCP fairness notion is inspired by the notion of coalition-proof Nash equilibrium (CPNE) [15] in game theory—but unlike CPNE which considers self-enforcing coalitions that seek to improve every member's gain, our CCP notion considers self-enforcing coalitions that seek to improve its overall gain, and thus our notion is stronger (i.e., demands stronger solution concepts).

Although for general games, SNE fairness and CCP fairness are incomparable, we prove that for the special case of multi-party coin toss, the two notions are in fact equivalent! In this context both notions effectively rule out *unanimous* coalitions where everyone prefers the same outcome.

1.5 Technical Highlight

Conceptual, Definitional Contributions. First, we make a conceptual contribution by introducing several natural, game-theoretical notions of fairness for multi-party coin toss—our work thus opens a new avenue for connecting game theory and cryptography. Earlier efforts at connecting game theory and multi-party computation typically model the correctness and/or confidentiality of multi-party protocols as a game (see Sect. 8 for more discussions), whereas we consider a model in which each party independently declares the utility for various outcomes.

A New Framework for Proving Lower Bounds. Our upper bounds are simple and intuitive in hindsight (but note that several upper bounds were not immediately obvious to us in the beginning). Our main lower bound results, however, are rather non-trivial to prove. The most non-trivial proofs are (1) the impossibility of maximin fairness for almost unanimous preference profiles, against malicious, computationally bounded adversaries; and (2) the impossibility of CSP fairness for amply divided preference profiles, this time against fail-stop and computationally bounded adversaries.

We develop a new proof framework and apply this framework to rule out both maximin fairness (for almost unanimous, malicious) and CSP fairness (for amply divided, fail-stop)[2]. In this proof framework, we would carefully group nodes into three partitions such that we can view the execution as a 3-party protocol (between the partitions). In both impossibility proofs, we show that

[2] Interestingly, later in our online full version [18] we again reuse the same proof framework to prove lower bounds for private-preference protocols too.

the requirements of maximin or CSP fairness imposes a set of conditions that are by nature self-contradictory and thus cannot co-exist.

Since the lower bound proofs are highly non-trivial, to help the reader we give an informal narrative of the maximin proof in Sect. 4.4. Then, in Sect. 5.3, we intuitively explain the additional challenges that arise for ruling out CSP fairness (for amply divided, fail-stop)—this proof is even more challenging than maximin fairness (for almost unanimous, malicious) partly because we need to rule out even fail-stop adversaries in this case. The full formal proofs are deferred to the appendices due to lack of space.

2 Preliminaries

2.1 Protocol Execution Model

A protocol is a system of Interactive Turing Machines (ITMs) where each ITM is also referred to as a *party* or a *player*. Each party is either *honest* or *corrupt*. Honest parties correctly follow the protocol to the end without aborting. Corrupt parties, on the other hand, are controlled by an adversary $\mathcal{A}$. Corrupt parties forward all received messages to $\mathcal{A}$ and send messages or abort based on $\mathcal{A}$'s instructions. In this way, we can view the set of all corrupt parties as a single coalition that collude with one another.

A protocol's execution is parametrized by a security parameter $\kappa \in N$ that is public known to all parties including the adversary $\mathcal{A}$. A protocol's execution may be randomized where all parties and the adversary $\mathcal{A}$ receive and consume a string of random bits.

We assume a *round-based* execution model. In each round, every honest party can perform any polynomial in κ amount of computation. At the end of the round, every party may broadcast a message whose length must be polynomial in κ as well. We assume a *synchronous broadcast* medium (with identifiable abort) for parties to communicate with each other. Messages sent by honest parties in round r will be delivered to all honest parties at the beginning of round $r + 1$. If a party i aborts the protocol in round r without sending any message, then all honest parties can detect such abort by detecting the absence of i's message at the beginning of round $r + 1$. As an example, one can imagine that parties communicate by posting messages to a public blockchain such as Bitcoin [26,47,50,51][3].

2.2 Corruption Models

The adversary can corrupt any number of parties. Without loss of generality, we assume that for any fixed adversary algorithm $\mathcal{A}$, the set of parties it wants to corrupt is deterministically encoded in the description of $\mathcal{A}$ (i.e., for any fixed adversary $\mathcal{A}$, there is no randomness in the choice of the corrupt coalition). We

[3] Although a blockchain typically requires honest majority assumptions to retain security, the parties involved in the coin-toss protocol can be majority corrupt.

assume that the adversary is capable of a *rushing* attack[4], i.e., in any round r, the adversary is allowed to view messages sent by honest parties in round r, before deciding what messages corrupt parties will send in round r.

Depending on the adversary's capability, we say that the adversary is failstop or malicious. More formally, let Π denote the honest protocol under consideration. An adversarial algorithm $\mathcal{A}$ is said to be *fail-stop* or *malicious* w.r.t. Π iff the following holds:

- *Fail-stop:* Corrupt nodes always follow the honest protocol but may abort in the middle of the protocol. The decision to abort (or not) can depend on the corrupt parties' view in the protocol so far.
- *Malicious:* The adversary can make corrupt parties deviate arbitrarily from the prescribed protocol, including sending arbitrary messages, choosing randomness arbitrarily, and aborting prematurely.

2.3 Additional Notations and Assumptions

Throughout the paper, we assume that the number of parties is polynomially bounded, i.e., $n = \mathsf{poly}(\kappa)$ for some polynomial function $\mathsf{poly}(\cdot)$. We consider protocols that terminate in polynomially many rounds. Specifically, there exists some polynomial $R(\cdot)$ that denotes the round complexity of the protocol, such that with probability 1, honest parties complete execution in $R(\kappa)$ even in the presence of any (possibly computationally unbounded) adversary controlling any corrupt coalition.

We say that a function $\nu(\cdot)$ is a *negligible* function iff for every polynomial function $p(\cdot)$, there exists some $\kappa_0 \in \mathbb{N}$ such that $\nu(\kappa) \leq 1/p(\kappa_0)$ for all $\kappa \geq \kappa_0$.

3 Definitions: Multi-party Coin Toss

As in the standard cryptography literature, we model protocol execution as a system of Interactive Turing Machines. We consider a synchronous model with a broadcast medium. Messages broadcast by honest parties in the current round are guaranteed to be delivered at the beginning of the next round. We assume *identifiable abort*, that is, failure to send a message is publicly detectable.

We assume that the adversary, denoted $\mathcal{A}$, can control any number of parties. Without loss of generality, we assume that the set of parties $\mathcal{A}$ wants to corrupt is hard-wired in the description of $\mathcal{A}$. We assume a simultaneous messaging model with the possibility of *rushing attacks*, that is, the adversary can observe honest nodes' messages before deciding corrupt nodes' actions (including what messages to send and whether to abort) in any round.

Recall that a *fail-stop* party is one that could abort prematurely but would otherwise follow the honest protocol. By contrast, a *malicious* party is one that can deviate arbitrarily from the honest protocol.

[4] We note that in a simultaneous message model where the adversary is not capable of rushing attacks, even the standard notion of (strong) fairness [19] (which is stronger than all notions considered in this paper) is trivial to achieve for 2-party or multi-party coin toss, even against any majority corrupt coalition.

3.1 Multi-party Coin Toss

Preference Profile. Suppose that each party starts with a *preference* among the two outcomes 0 and 1. The vector of all parties' preferences, denoted $\mathcal{P} := \{0,1\}^n$, is referred to as a preference profile. We sometimes refer to a party that prefers 1 as a *1-supporter* and we refer to one that prefers 0 as a *0-supporter*. In a preference profile $\mathcal{P} := \{0,1\}^n$, if the number of 0-supporters and the number of 1-supporters are the same, we say that $\mathcal{P}$ is *balanced*; else we say that it is *unbalanced*.

Unless otherwise noted, we assume that all parties' preferences are predetermined and *public*. We discuss the private-preference case in the appendices, Sect. 7.

Coin-Toss Protocol. Consider a protocol Π where n parties jointly decide an outcome between 0 and 1. Such a protocol Π is said to be a coin toss protocol, there is a polynomial-time computable deterministic function, which, given the transcript of the protocol execution, outputs a bit $b \in \{0,1\}$, often said to be the *outcome* of the protocol. For correctness, we require that an honest execution outputs each bit with probability exactly $\frac{1}{2}$ unless all parties have the same preference. More formally, correctness requires that

1. If some parties have differing preferences, in an all-honest execution (when all parties are honest), the probability that the outcome is 0 (or 1) is exactly[5] 1/2.
2. If all parties happen to prefer the same bit $b \in \{0,1\}$, the honest execution should output the preferred bit b with probability 1.

Payoff Function. If the protocol's outcome is b, a party who prefers b receive a reward (or payoff) of 1; else it receives a reward (or payoff) of 0. Note that earlier in Sect. 1, our 1-bit roulette example had a -1 utility (rather than 0) for losing, but the two definitions are in fact equivalent; and for simplicity the remainder of the paper will assume 0 utility for losing.

3.2 Discussions

Trivial Case: Unanimous Preference Profile. When everyone has the same preference, we say that the preference profile is *unanimous*; otherwise we say that it is *mixed*. In this case, we do not require that an honest execution produce an unbiased coin, since it makes sense for the outcome to be the bit that is globally preferred. In the remainder of the paper, for the case of public preference: if everyone prefers the same bit $b \in \{0,1\}$, we assume that *the protocol simply fixes the outcome to be the universally preferred bit b* regardless of how parties act. In this way, everyone obtains a payoff of 1, and no deviation from the protocol can influence the outcome—therefore all game-theoretic fairness notions we consider are trivially satisfied when the preference profile is unanimous.

[5] Our upper bounds achieve perfect correctness, but our lower bounds in fact extend easily even when allowing negligible correctness failure.

On Public Verifiability. Our definition implies public verifiability of the coin toss's outcome. Anyone who can observe messages sent over the broadcast medium (e.g., a public blockchain) can independently compute the outcome of the protocol. Note that under this definition, the outcome of the protocol is well-defined even when all parties are corrupt. Alternatively, we can define a weaker notion where we do not require such public verifiability—instead we require that honest parties output a bit at the end of the execution, and that they output the same bit (said to be the *outcome* of the execution) with probability 1 even in the presence of an arbitrary (possibly unbounded) adversary that corrupts up to $n-1$ parties. Under this weaker notion, the outcome of an execution is not well-defined when all parties are corrupt. We note that all lower bounds in this paper in fact apply to this weaker notion too (which makes the lower bounds stronger).

3.3 Strong Fairness

We quickly review the classical notion of strong fairness [19]. Roughly speaking, strong fairness requires that the outcome of the coin toss protocol be unbiased even in the presence of an adversary (assuming that parties have mixed preferences). In the definition of strong fairness, we consider a single adversarial coalition that corrupts up to $n-1$ parties.

Definition 1 (Strong fairness [19]). *Let* $\mathfrak{A}$ *a family of adversaries that corrupt at most* $n-1$ *parties. An* n*-party coin toss protocol is said to be strongly fair against the family* $\mathfrak{A}$*, iff for every adversary* $\mathcal{A} \in \mathfrak{A}$*, there exists a negligible function* $\mathsf{negl}(\cdot)$ *such that (as long as not all parties have the same preference) the probability that the outcome is* 1 *is within* $[\frac{1}{2} - \mathsf{negl}(\kappa), \frac{1}{2} + \mathsf{negl}(\kappa)]$ *when playing with* $\mathcal{A}$.

4 Maximin Fairness: Feasibilities and Infeasibilities

4.1 Definition of Maximin Fairness

Maximin fairness requires that no honest party should be harmed by any corrupt coalition. In other words, a corrupt coalition should not be able to (non-negligibly) decrease the expected payoff for any honest party relative to an all-honest execution. In maximin fairness, we consider a single adversarial coalition that controls up to $n-1$ parties.

Definition 2 (Maximin fairness). *Let* $\mathfrak{A}$ *be a family of adversaries that corrupt up to* $n-1$ *parties; and let* $\mathcal{P} \in \{0,1\}^n$ *denote any mixed preference profile. We say that an* n*-party coin toss protocol is maximin fair for* $\mathcal{P}$ *against the family* $\mathfrak{A}$*, iff for every adversary* $\mathcal{A} \in \mathfrak{A}$*, there exists some negligible function* $\mathsf{negl}(\cdot)$ *such that in an execution with the preference profile* $\mathcal{P}$ *and the adversary* $\mathcal{A}$*, the expected reward for any honest party is at least* $\frac{1}{2} - \mathsf{negl}(\kappa)$*. More specifically, we have the following special cases:*

- *Computational maximin fairness. If $\mathfrak{A}$ is the family of all non-uniform, probabilistic polynomial-time (henceforth denoted p.p.t.) fail-stop (or malicious resp.) adversaries that can corrupt as many as $n-1$ parties, we say that the protocol is computationally maximin fair for $\mathcal{P}$ against any fail-stop (or malicious resp.) adversaries.*
- *Statistical maximin fairness. If $\mathfrak{A}$ is the family of all fail-stop (or malicious resp.) adversaries (including even computationally unbounded ones) that can corrupt as many as $n-1$ parties, we say that the protocol is statistically maximin fair for $\mathcal{P}$ against any fail-stop (or malicious resp.) adversaries.*
- *Perfect maximin fairness. If a protocol is statistically maximin fair against fail-stop (or malicious resp.) adversaries, and moreover the above definition is satisfied with a choice of 0 for the negligible function, we say that the protocol is perfectly maximin fair for $\mathcal{P}$ against fail-stop (or malicious resp.) adversaries. A perfectly maximin fair protocol does not allow any single honest party to have even negligibly small loss in its expected payoff in comparison with an all-honest execution.*

A straightforward observation is that classical strong fairness (Definition 1) implies maximin fairness:

Fact 1. *If an n-party coin toss protocol Π is strongly fair against a family of adversaries $\mathcal{F}$, then Π is maximin fair against $\mathcal{F}$ for any mixed preference profile $\mathcal{P} \in \{0,1\}^n$.*

Sometimes we also say that a protocol is computationally (or statistically, perfectly resp.) maximin fair for $\mathcal{P}$ against any fail-stop (or malicious resp.) coalition of size K—and this means the most obvious where in the above definitions, the family of adversaries $\mathfrak{A}$ we consider is additionally restricted to corrupting exactly K parties.

Claim. Let $\mathcal{P} \in \{0,1\}^n$ be any mixed preference profile. An n-party coin toss protocol Π satisfies computational (or statistical, perfect resp.) maximin fairness for $\mathcal{P}$ against any fail-stop (or malicious resp.) coalition, iff Π satisfies computational (or statistical, perfect resp.) maximin fairness for $\mathcal{P}$ against any fail-stop (or malicious resp.) coalition of size exactly $n-1$.

Game Theoretic Interpretation. If a coin-toss protocol is maximin fair, then the following hold:

1. First, the honest strategy maximizes a player's worst-case expected payoff (even when everyone else is colluding against the player); this explains the name "maximin fairness".
2. Moreover, when playing the honest strategy, a player's worst-case payoff is what it would have gained in an all-honest execution—note that a player's worst-case (expected) payoff obviously cannot be more than its payoff in an all-honest execution.

Equivalence to Group Maximin Fairness. An alternative way to define "no-harm to honest parties" is to require that any corrupt coalition cannot decrease (by more than a negligible amount) the expected overall wealth (i.e., total payoff) of the honest parties. We prove that this notion, called group maximin fairness, is in fact equivalent to maximin fairness in the context of coin toss. We defer the formal definition and proofs to our online full version [18].

4.2 The Case of Amply Divided Preference Profiles

As mentioned, feasibility for 2 parties or multiple parties but honest majority are already implied by existing literature [16,27]. Henceforth we focus on the case of three or more parties and corrupt majority.

First, we consider amply divided preference profiles, where at least two people prefer 0 and at least two prefer 1 respectively (and hence there must be at least 4 people). It is not too difficult to rule out maximin fairness for amply divided preference profiles, even against fail-stop, computationally bounded adversaries, leading to the following theorem.

Theorem 5 (Maximin fairness: amply divided preference profiles). *For any $n \geq 4$ and for any amply divided preference profile $\mathcal{P} \in \{0,1\}^n$, no n-party coin toss protocol can achieve even computational maximin fairness for $\mathcal{P}$ against even fail-stop adversaries.*

Proof (sketch). We show that if there is a maximin fair protocol for any amply mixed preference profile, we can construct a 2-party strongly fair coin toss protocol (and thus violating Cleve's lower bound [19]). The proof follows from a standard partitioning argument: consider two partitions, each containing at least one 0-supporter and at least one 1-supporter. Now, we can view the protocol as a two-party protocol between the two partitions, and by maximin fairness, if either partition aborts, it must not create any non-negligible bias towards either direction. We defer the full proof to our online full version [18].

4.3 The Case for Almost Unanimous Preference Profiles

Possibility of Perfect Maximin Fairness for Fail-Stop Adversaries. First, we show that for fail-stop adversaries, we can achieve perfect maximin-fairness for almost unanimous preference profiles. Without loss of generality, assume that a single party prefers 0 and everyone else prefers 1. The following simple protocol can guarantee perfect maximin fairness:

1. In the first round, the single 0-supporter flips a random coin b and broadcasts b;
2. If the single 0-supporter successfully broadcast a message b, then the outcome is b; else the outcome is 1.

It is not difficult to see that this simple protocol satisfies perfect maximin fairness against fail-stop adversaries: all the 1-supporters do not take any actions and they do not influence the outcome of the protocol. For the single 0-supporter, if it deviates (by aborting), then the outcome will be 1 with probability 1, and all honest parties utility are guaranteed to be 1. Thus we derive the following theorem:

Theorem 6 (Possibility of perfect maximin fairness for almost unanimous preferences and fail-stop adversaries). *For any $n \geq 3$, any almost unanimous preference profile $\mathcal{P} \in \{0,1\}^n$, there exists an n-party coin toss protocol that achieves perfect maxmin fairness for $\mathcal{P}$ against fail-stop adversaries.*

Impossibility of Computational Maximin Fairness for Malicious Adversaries. Next, we show that maximin fairness is impossible to achieve for almost unanimous preference profiles against malicious adversaries, even when allowing computational assumptions.

Theorem 7 (Impossibility of maximin fairness for almost unanimous preferences and malicious adversaries). *For $n \geq 3$ and any almost unanimous preference profile $\mathcal{P} \in \{0,1\}^n$, no n-party coin-toss protocol Π can ensure computational maximin fairness for $\mathcal{P}$ against malicious adversaries.*

4.4 Informal Proof Roadmap for Theorem 7

We in fact prove a stronger lower bound than stated in Theorem 7: we show that maximin fairness is impossible for any almost unanimous preference profile (for 3 or more parties), even against *semi-malicious*, polynomially bounded adversaries. In particular, a semi-malicious adversary can (1) choose corrupt parties' random coins arbitrarily upfront, and (2) prematurely abort; but otherwise it follows the honest protocol.

For simplicity, we focus on the case of 3 parties but the proof generalizes directly to more parties. Suppose that the 3 parties are called P_1, P_2 and P_3, and they come with the preferences $1, 0$, and 1 respectively.

We now present an informal proof roadmap, deferring the formal proof to our online full version [18]. We begin by assuming that a maximin fair protocol exists for 3 parties, resisting semi-malicious, computationally bounded adversaries. Our proof will seek to reach a contradiction, effectively showing that the various conditions imposed by maximin fairness cannot co-exist.

Almost All Random Coins of a Lone Semi-malicious 0-Supporter are Created Equal. By a direct application of maximin fairness, if the single 0-supporter is semi-malicious and allowed to program his random coins, then he should not bias the remaining two parties towards 0. However, perhaps somewhat surprisingly at first sight, we can prove a result that is much stronger, that the single 0-supporter in fact (almost) cannot cause bias towards *either* direction by programming its random coins!

Henceforth, we shall use the notations T_1, T_2, T_3 to denote the three parties' random coins, where T_2 belongs to the single 0-supporter P_2. Consider an honest execution of the protocol conditioned on the fact that the single 0-supporter has its randomness fixed to T_2, and let $f(T_2)$ denote the expected outcome (where the probability is taken over P_1 and P_3's randomness). We prove the following lemma stating that (except for a negligible fraction of choices), all choices of T_2 are equal if P_2 is the lone semi-malicious party.

Lemma 1 (Almost all random coins of a lone semi-malicious P_2 are created equal). *Suppose that the protocol under consideration satisfies computational maximin fairness against semi-malicious adversaries. Then, there exists a negligible function* $\mathsf{negl}(\cdot)$ *such that except for* $\mathsf{negl}(\kappa)$ *fraction of* T_2*'s, it must be that* $|f(T_2) - 0.5|$ *is a negligible function in* κ.

Proof (sketch). We present a proof sketch: by maximin fairness, we know that for all T_2's, $f(T_2) \geq 0.5 - \mathsf{negl}(\kappa)$. Now, notice that $\mathbf{E}_{T_2} f(T_2) = \frac{1}{2}$ by honest execution, i.e., the expected value of $f(T_2)$ is $\frac{1}{2}$ when averaging over T_2. This means that if there is a non-negligible fraction of T_2's that cause non-negligible bias towards 1, then there must be a non-negligible fraction of T_2's that cause non-negligible bias towards 0 and the latter violates maximin fairness for a semi-malicious P_2.

The Lone-Wolf Condition and Wolf-Minion Conditions. Henceforth, our general plan is to show that if the above T_2-equality lemma holds, then the following two conditions, implied by the definition of maximin fairness, cannot co-exist.

- *Lone-wolf condition.* When P_1 (or P_3) is the only fail-stop party, it cannot cause non-negligible bias towards either direction. Such an attack is also called a lone-wolf attack.
- *Wolf-minion condition.* When P_1 and P_2 (or P_2 and P_3) form a fail-stop coalition, they cannot cause non-negligible bias towards 0. In fact we only care about attacks where P_2 is a silent accomplice (called a *minion* [25]) that never aborts but shares information with P_1 (or P_3); and P_1 (or P_3) may abort depending on its view in the execution (called a *wolf* [25]). Such attacks are called wolf-minion attacks.

Note that both conditions above consider only fail-stop adversaries, and in fact in the entire proof the only place we rely on a semi-malicious adversary is in the proof of the aforementioned T_2-equality lemma.

Non-blackbox Application of Cleve's Lower Bound Conditioned on T_2. Recall that we assume that a maximin fair, 3-party protocol Π exists for the sake of reaching a contradiction. Now consider an execution of this protocol when P_2's randomness is fixed to T_2, and further, assume that P_2 never aborts and always follows the honest protocol to completion. We now view this 3-party protocol as a 2-party protocol between P_1 and P_3, where P_2's randomness T_2 is public and hard-wired in P_1 and P_3's program—more specifically both P_1 and P_3 would run the 3-party protocol Π, and they each independently simulate the actions of P_2 and compute all messages that P_2 wants to send.

Due to the T_2-equality lemma, if P_1 and P_3 are honest, we know that the expected outcome would be $\frac{1}{2}$ for almost all T_2's. Now, in this 2-party protocol defined by a fixed T_2 (that does not belong to the negligible fraction of bad T_2's), Cleve [19] showed that there must exist a polynomial-time attack by one of the parties, that causes non-negligible bias—but the bias can be either towards 0 or 1. Unfortunately, the direct implication of Cleve's lower bound is not quite so useful for us: it shows that a semi-malicious P_2 can collude with a fail-stop P_1 (or P_3) and cause bias for the remaining honest party, that is P_3 (or P_1)—but unless this bias is towards 0, it does not lend to a contradiction.

Our plan is the following: we will nonetheless apply Cleve's impossibility, but in a non-blackbox manner. First, we will show that for any fixed T_2 (except for a negligible fraction of bad ones), either P_1 or P_3 can bias towards 1 with an aborting attack. Specifically, we define a sequence of adversaries like in Cleve's proof, denoted $\{\mathcal{A}_i^b(1^\kappa, T_2), \mathcal{B}_i^b(1^\kappa, T_2)\}_{i\in[R]}, \cup\{\mathcal{A}_0(1^\kappa, T_2)\}$ where R is the protocol's round complexity. Adversaries $\mathcal{A}_i^b(1^\kappa, T_2)$, $\mathcal{B}_i^b(1^\kappa, T_2)$, and $\mathcal{A}_0(1^\kappa, T_2)$ are defined when P_2's randomness is fixed to T_2:

- Adversary $\mathcal{A}_i^b(1^\kappa, T_2)$:
  - $\mathcal{A}_i^b$ executes the honest protocol on behalf of P_1 and P_2 (whose randomness is fixed to T_2) until the moment right before P_1 is going to broadcast its i-th message.
  - At this moment, $\mathcal{A}_i^b$ computes α_i, that is, imagine that P_3 aborted right after sending its $(i-1)$-th message, what would be the outcome of parties P_1 and P_2.
  - If $\alpha_i = b$, then P_1 aborts after sending the i-th message; else P_1 aborts right now without sending the i-th message.
- Adversary $\mathcal{B}_i^b(1^\kappa, T_2)$: The definition is symmetric to that of $\mathcal{A}_i^b(1^\kappa, T_2)$ but now P_3 is the fail-stop party.
- Adversary $\mathcal{A}_0(1^\kappa, T_2)$: P_1 aborts upfront prior to speaking at all.

Cleve [19] showed that one of these above adversaries must be able to cause non-negligible bias towards either 0 or 1. However, due to the requirement of maximin fairness, we may conclude that the bias must be towards 1 except for a negligible fraction of the T_2's. Suppose this is not the case, i.e., the bias is towards 0 for a non-negligible fraction of the T_2's—then we could easily construct an attack (for the 3-party protocol) where a semi-malicious P_2 colluding with a fail-stop P_1 (or P_3) can bias the remaining party towards 0—in fact, in our formal proof later, we show that such an attack is even possible with a fail-stop P_1 and a silent accomplice P_2 who just shares information with P_1 but would otherwise follow the protocol honestly (i.e., a wolf-minion attack). Proving this stronger statement would require a little more effort—but looking forward, later we would like to rule out CSP fairness for even fail-stop adversaries. There we have a similar agenda: (1) reprove the T_2-equality lemma but for fail-stop adversaries and CSP fairness, and (2) show that under the T_2-equality lemma, the lone-wolf condition and the wolf-minion condition cannot co-exist. Thus in our formal proof later we will actually rely on a wolf-minion (fail-stop) attack to rule out the 0-bias attack.

Averaging over T_2: A Wolf-Minion Attack with Benign Bias. Next, we consider the above adversaries but now averaging over T_2. In other words, let $\overline{\mathcal{A}}_i^b(1^\kappa)$ be the following attacker: choose a random T_2; now consider the protocol execution with P_2's randomness fixed to T_2 and with the adversary $\mathcal{A}_i^b(1^\kappa, T_2)$. $\overline{\mathcal{B}}_i^b(1^\kappa)$ and $\overline{\mathcal{A}}_0(1^\kappa)$ are similarly defined by averaging over T_2.

Now, we prove that among these adversaries $\{\overline{\mathcal{A}}_i^b(1^\kappa), \overline{\mathcal{B}}_i^b(1^\kappa)\}_{i\in[R]}$ and $\overline{\mathcal{A}}_0(1^\kappa)$, one of them must be able to bias the remaining party, either P_1 or P_3, towards 1. This proof follows in a somewhat standard manner from an averaging argument and we defer the details to the appendices. Note that reflecting in the 3-party protocol, this corresponds to a wolf-minion attack that creates benign bias: P_1 (or P_3) acts as a fail-stop wolf, and P_2 acts as a silent accomplice (i.e., the minion) that follows the honest protocol to completion but shares information with P_1 (or P_3). Although this wolf-minion is able to create bias, the bias is benign and does not violate the definition of maximin fairness. Thus to reach a contradiction, it still remains to show an attack that creates harmful bias.

Applying the Lone-Wolf Condition: A Wolf-Minion Attack with Harmful Bias. We now argue that if there is a wolf-minion attack that creates benign bias, there must be one that creates harmful bias, assuming that the lone-wolf condition holds. To show this, we consider the adversary that flips the decisions (to abort in the present or next round) of the benign wolf-minion attack. Without loss of generality, assume that $\overline{\mathcal{A}}_i^1$ is the successful wolf-minion attack that creates non-negligible bias towards 1. We now consider $\overline{\mathcal{A}}_i^0$ which flips $\overline{\mathcal{A}}_i^1$'s decision whether to abort in round i or $i+1$, and we argue that $\overline{\mathcal{A}}_i^0$ must create non-negligible bias towards 0. At a very high level, the proof will show that the lone-wolf condition acts like a balancing condition.

Let Q be the set of sample paths (defined by choices of T_1, T_2, and T_3) over which $\overline{\mathcal{A}}_i^1$ decides to abort in round i, and let $\overline{Q}$ be the remaining sample paths. Now, consider a hybrid adversary that takes $\overline{\mathcal{A}}_i^1$'s decisions on Q and takes $\overline{\mathcal{A}}_i^0$'s decisions on $\overline{Q}$: in other words, P_1 basically always aborts in round i! Due to the lone-wolf condition, whatever average bias towards 1 $\overline{\mathcal{A}}_i^1$ has on Q, $\overline{\mathcal{A}}_i^0$ must create almost the same bias towards 0 on $\overline{Q}$. By a symmetric argument and considering a lone wolf P_1 that always aborts in round $i+1$, whatever average bias towards 1 $\overline{\mathcal{A}}_i^1$ has on $\overline{Q}$, $\overline{\mathcal{A}}_i^0$ must create almost the same bias towards 0 on Q. With this, it is not difficult to see that $\overline{\mathcal{A}}_i^0$ can bias towards 0 (almost) as well as $\overline{\mathcal{A}}_i^1$ can bias towards 1.

5 Cooperative-Strategy-Proof Fairness

5.1 Definition of Cooperative-Strategy-Proof Fairness

In a cooperative strategy, a corrupt coalition deviates from the honest protocol in an attempt to improve the coalition's overall wealth (i.e., the total reward). Cooperative strategies naturally arise in contexts where a corrupt coalition is allowed to have binding side contracts that allow the coalition to redistribute (e.g., equally) the overall wealth among its members. If a protocol is cooperative-strategy-proof fair (or CSP-fair), it intuitively means that any corrupt coalition should not be able to improve its overall wealth by more than negligible amounts (if the remaining parties are faithfully following the honest protocol).

Definition 3 (Cooperative-strategy-proof fairness or CSP-fairness). *Let $\mathfrak{A}$ be a family of adversaries that corrupt up to $n-1$ parties and let $\mathcal{P} \in \{0,1\}^n$ denote any mixed preference profile. We say that an n-party coin toss protocol is cooperative-strategy-proof fair (or CSP-fair) for $\mathcal{P}$ and against the family $\mathfrak{A}$, iff for any adversary $\mathcal{A} \in \mathfrak{A}$, there exists some negligible function* $\mathsf{negl}(\cdot)$, *such that in an execution with the preference profile $\mathcal{P}$ and the adversary $\mathcal{A}$, the expected total reward for the set of corrupt parties (denoted C) is at most $\sigma(C) + \mathsf{negl}(\kappa)$ where $\sigma(C)$ denotes the expected total reward for all nodes in C in an all-honest execution.*

Similar as before, now depending on the family $\mathfrak{A}$ of adversaries that we are concerned about, we can define computational, statistical, or perfect notions for cooperative-strategy-proof fairness, and for fail-stop, semi-malicious, or malicious adversaries respectively. We omit the detailed definitions for conciseness.

Remark 1 (The case of a global coalition for CSP-fairness). Unless otherwise noted, the definition of CSP-fairness considers coalitions of size up to $n-1$. One could alternatively define a variant of CSP-fairness where the corrupt coalition can contain up to n parties, i.e., CSP-fairness is desired even against a global coalition where everyone is corrupt. For any *balanced* preference profile, this variant is equivalent to the definition where not all can be corrupt since the global coalition is indifferent to either outcome. For any *unbalanced* preference profile, this variant where all can be corrupt is a stronger notion—in fact, one could easily rule out feasibility against (even computationally bounded) semi-malicious adversaries due to the following argument. By correctness, there must exist some joint randomness $\boldsymbol{\rho}$ of all parties, such that an honest execution fixing the randomness to $\boldsymbol{\rho}$ would lead to the outcome that is preferred by the global coalition. Now a semi-malicious adversary can receive this $\boldsymbol{\rho}$ as advice and program the parties' joint randomness to $\boldsymbol{\rho}$. Interestingly, however, for fail-stop adversaries, we will show the feasibility of perfect CSP-fairness even when all parties can be corrupt (see Corollary 1).

For any *balanced* preference profile, if the corrupt coalition gains in terms of overall wealth (i.e., total payoff) then honest overall wealth must be harmed (relative to an honest execution in both cases). Therefore, CSP-fairness is equivalent to maximin fairness for balanced preference profiles. The following fact is therefore straightforward:

Fact 2 (Equivalence of maximin fairness and CSP fairness for balanced preference profiles). *Let $\mathfrak{A}$ denote a family of adversaries that corrupt up to $n-1$ parties and let $\mathcal{P} \in \{0,1\}^n$ denote any balanced profile. Then, an n-party coin toss protocol Π is maximin fair for $\mathcal{P}$ against the family $\mathfrak{A}$ iff Π is CSP-fair for $\mathcal{P}$ against the family $\mathfrak{A}$.*

For *unbalanced* preference profiles, however, the two notions are not equivalent (and this will become obvious later in the paper).

As mentioned, for two parties, all our fairness notions equate to Blum's weak fairness notion [16], and therefore the results stated in our online full version [18] directly apply to CSP fairness too. In the remainder of this section, we focus on three or more parties.

5.2 Almost Unanimous Preference Profile

Recall that we consider 3 or more parties, i.e., $n \geq 3$.

Possibility of Perfect CSP-Fairness Against Semi-malicious Adversaries. First, we show that for almost unanimous preference profiles and any $n \geq 3$, perfect CSP-fairness is possible against any coalition of size up to $n-1$.

Let $P_0, \ldots, P_{n-1}$ denote the $n \geq 3$ players. Without loss of generality, suppose that P_0 is the single 0-supporter (i.e., prefers 0), and everyone else prefers 1 (all other cases are equivalent by flipping the bit and renumbering players). Consider the following simple protocol denoted Π_{csp}.

1. In the first round, every party i where $i \in [0, 1, \ldots, n-1]$ locally tosses a random coin b_i. Further, the single 0-supporter P_0 reveals its coin b_0.
2. In the second round, every 1-supporter (i.e., P_i where $i \neq 0$) reveals coin b_i.
3. The outcome of the protocol is defined as follows: if any 1-supporter aborted without revealing its bit, output 0. Else, output the XOR of all bits that have been revealed by the parties — note that if P_0 aborted without revealing its bit b_0, then we simply do not include b_0 in the XOR.

It is straightforward that under an honest execution, the expected outcome is $\frac{1}{2}$.

Theorem 8 (Possibility of perfect CSP-fairness against semi-malicious corruptions for almost unanimous preference profiles). *For any $n \geq 3$, there is an n-party coin toss protocol that achieves perfect CSP-fairness for any almost unanimous preference profile $\mathcal{P} \in \{0,1\}^n$ against the family of all semi-malicious adversaries that control at most $n-1$ parties.*

Proof. We analyze the aforementioned protocol Π_{csp} by considering the following cases:

1. **P_0 is the lone corrupt party.** In this case, all parties who prefer 1 are honest, and since P_0 makes its decision to abort prior to seeing the remaining parties' random bits, equivalently, we can think of the remaining parties flip their random coins after P_0 makes its decision whether to abort. Thus, regardless of P_0's strategy, the expected outcome must be $\frac{1}{2}$.
2. **P_0 and a single 1-supporter are corrupt.** In this case, the definition of CSP-fairness is trivially satisfied since the corrupt coalition would obtain a payoff of exactly 1 no matter what the outcome of the protocol is.
3. **P_0 is honest and one or more 1-supporters are corrupt.** Let $\mathbf{b} := (b_0, \ldots, b_{n-1})$ denote the random coin tosses of all the parties. For semi-malicious corruption, we can imagine that each party P_i chooses b_i and other randomness related to aborting decisions upfront prior to protocol start—honest parties sample them at random and corrupt parties choose the random strings arbitrarily. Let C denote the corrupt coalition and let $-C$ denote its complement. We consider an alternative adversary $\mathcal{B}$ that just receives $\mathbf{b}^C := \{b_i\}_{i \in C}$ as advice but all corrupt parties follow the protocol to the end—note that such a $\mathcal{B}$ needs to consume only $\mathbf{b}^C$ and no additional randomness. For any fixed $\mathbf{b}^C$, and for any fixed $\mathbf{b}^{-C}$, if playing with the adversary $\mathcal{B}$ who never aborts, the outcome is 0, then playing with any adversary $\mathcal{A}$ (who might abort), the outcome cannot be 1. Thus for every $(\mathbf{b}^C, \mathbf{b}^{-C})$, no adversary $\mathcal{A}$ can obtain a higher outcome than $\mathcal{B}$. The proof follows by seeing that for $\mathcal{B}$ and for any fixed $\mathbf{b}^C$, the expected outcome (averaging over honest parties' random coin flips) is $\frac{1}{2}$.
4. **P_0 and at least two 1-supporters are corrupt.** In this case it must be that $n \geq 4$ since if $n = 3$ all parties would be corrupt. Similar to the above case, here we can argue that for every fixed $(\mathbf{b}^C, \mathbf{b}^{-C})$ and P_0's decision whether to abort, the adversary $\mathcal{B}$ such that all other corrupt (besides P_0) execute to the end makes the outcome at least as high as any other adversary $\mathcal{A}$. Additionally, for $\mathcal{B}$ and for any fixed $\mathbf{b}^C$ and P_0's decision whether to abort, the expected outcome (averaging over honest parties' random coin flips) is $\frac{1}{2}$.

Corollary 1. *There is an 3-party coin toss protocol that achieves perfect CSP-fairness for any mixed preference profile against the family of all semi-malicious adversaries that control at most $n - 1$ parties.*

Proof. Note that for 3 parties, any mixed preference profile must be almost unanimous. The corollary now follows from Theorem 8.

We observe that for fail-stop adversaries, a variant of the aforementioned protocol Π_{csp} actually achieves perfect CSP-fairness even when all parties can be corrupt: Suppose that only parties in $\{P_1, \ldots, P_{n-1}\}$ flip a random coin and publish the coin; and P_0 does nothing. If any of these parties abort, the outcome is defined to be 0; else the outcome is defined to be the XOR of all published coins. We thus have the following corollary:

Corollary 2. *For any $n \geq 3$, there is an n-party coin toss protocol that achieves perfect CSP-fairness for any almost unanimous preference profile $\mathcal{P} \in \{0,1\}^n$ against the family of all fail-stop adversaries that control up to n parties.*

Proof. If no 1-supporter is corrupt, then obviously the expected outcome is $\frac{1}{2}$. If at least one 1-supporter is corrupt, then for every choice of the joint randomness of all 1-supporters, having any 1-supporter abort does no better for the adversary than having no 1-supporter abort.

Possibility of Computational CSP-Fairness Against Malicious Adversaries. It is also easy to see that for three or more parties, *statistical* CSP fairness is impossible against malicious adversaries much as the 2-party case [33,44]. Therefore for malicious adversaries we have to make computational assumptions.

For conceptual simplicity, we first describe our protocol assuming an idealized commitment scheme—in our online full version [18], we describe how to dispense with this idealized primitive and realize it from concurrent non-malleable commitments that can be constructed one-way permutations. For the time being, imagine that there is a special trusted party called $\mathcal{F}_{\text{idealcomm}}$ that has the following interface:

- In the first round (i.e., the commitment round), if $\mathcal{F}_{\text{idealcomm}}$ receives $(\texttt{commit}\ b)$ from some party i, it tells everyone $(\texttt{committed}, i)$.
- In any of the subsequent rounds (i.e., the opening rounds), if $\mathcal{F}_{\text{idealcomm}}$ receives $\texttt{open}$ from any party i who has committed b_i in the first round, it tells everyone $(\texttt{open}, i, b_i)$.

We can now upgrade our semi-malicious protocol earlier to resist even malicious adversaries (w.l.o.g. assume that there is a single 0-supporter and everyone else is a 1-supporter):

1. In round 0, everyone commits a bit to $\mathcal{F}_{\text{idealcomm}}$;
2. In round 1, the single 0-supporter opens its commitment;
3. In round 2, everyone else opens;
4. If any 1-supporter aborted, the outcome is 0; else the outcome is the XOR of all bits that have been opened.

Since the commitment round basically forces corrupt parties to commit to their randomness upfront; it is easy to see that this new protocol is CSP-fair against malicious adversaries (for the same reason why the earlier protocol is CSP-fair against semi-honest adversaries). Note that CSP fairness holds even for unbounded adversaries assuming the $\mathcal{F}_{\text{idealcomm}}$ ideal functionality; but in our online full version [18], we show how to remove the $\mathcal{F}_{\text{idealcomm}}$ and replace it with concurrent non-malleable commitments [42], the resulting protocol would secure only against computationally bounded adversaries as stated in the following theorem.

Theorem 9 (Computational CSP fairness against malicious adversaries). *Assume that one-way permutations exist, then for any $n \geq 3$, there exists an n-party protocol that achieves computational CSP fairness for any almost unanimous preference profile $\mathcal{P} \in \{0,1\}^n$ against malicious coalitions of size up to $n-1$.*

The proof is deferred to our online full version [18].

5.3 Amply Divided Preference Profile

For $n = 3$, any mixed preference profile must be almost unanimous. For $n \geq 4$, we need to consider amply divided preference profiles: i.e., at least two parties prefer 0 and at least two parties prefer 1. We now show a strong impossibility for mixed preference profiles, that is, for any mixed preference profile $\mathcal{P}$, no n-party coin toss can achieve even computational CSP-fairness for $\mathcal{P}$ against even fail-stop adversaries.

We note that for the special case of amply divided and *balanced* preference profiles, the impossibility for CSP fairness is already implied by the impossibility of maximin fairness for the same preference profiles (Theorem 5)—recall that the two notions are equivalent for balanced preference profiles. However, this observation does not rule out the feasibility of CSP fairness for *unbalanced* and amply divided preference profiles. Thus the following theorem is non-trivial even in light of Theorem 5.

Theorem 10 (Impossibility of CSP-fairness for $n \geq 4$). *Let $n \geq 4$, and let $\mathcal{P} \in \{0,1\}^n$ be any amply divided preference profile. Then, no n-party coin-toss protocol can achieve even computational CSP-fairness for $\mathcal{P}$, against even fail-stop adversaries.*

Proof Roadmap. Although for *balanced* and amply mixed preference profiles, the infeasibility of CSP fairness is already implied by the infeasibility of maximin fairness for the same profiles (since the two notions are equivalent for balanced preference profiles), here we would like to prove impossibility for *any* amply mixed preference profile, even *unbalanced* ones. At a very high level, our approach is to group the parties into three partitions called P_1, P_2, and P_3, such that we can view the execution as a 3-party protocol. This partitioning is carefully crafted such that the definition of CSP fairness would imply the T_2-equality lemma, the lone-wolf condition, and the wolf-minion conditions like in the impossibility proof for maximin fairness—and if this is the case, the same proof would apply and rule out CSP fairness.

Among these conditions, the T_2-equality lemma is the most challenging to prove. Specifically, earlier we relied on maximin fairness against a *semi-malicious* P_2 to prove the T_2-equality lemma; and here would like to prove the same lemma for CSP fairness but now against a *fail-stop* adversary[6]. This seems almost counter-intuitive at first sight since at the surface, the T_2-equality lemma is stating that *if a semi-malicious adversary were to program T_2 to specific strings, almost for all such strings it would not help.* But now how can we prove it by relying on CSP fairness against only *fail-stop* adversaries? In our formal proof later, we will show that for any two neighboring T_2 and T_2' (except for a negligibly small bad fraction), it must be that $|f(T_2) - f(T_2')| \leq \mathsf{negl}(\kappa)$, where T_2 and T_2' are said to be neighboring iff they differ only in one party's contribution

6 Note that the T_2-equality lemma does not even hold for maximin fairness against *fail-stop* adversaries since we have an explicit construction for almost pure preference profiles and fail-stop.

of random coins, and $f(T_2)$ is defined similarly as before, i.e., the expected outcome of an honest execution conditioned on P_2's randomness being fixed to T_2. Now if we can show this, we can then show, through a hybrid argument, that $|f(T_2) - f(T_2')| \leq \mathsf{negl}(\kappa)$ for any T_2 and T_2' (except for a negligibly small bad fraction), and this would complete the proof.

Thus the challenge is to show $|f(T_2) - f(T_2')| \leq \mathsf{negl}(\kappa)$ for almost all *neighboring* T_2 and T_2' pairs. To do this, suppose that T_2 and T_2' differ in the i-th player's contribution where $i \in P_2$—our intuition is to compare an honest execution involving T_2 with the execution where the i-th player aborts upfront (and P_2's randomness still fixed to T_2). Let $g^i(T_2)$ denote the expected outcome in the latter execution. Through a somewhat non-trivial argument, we will prove that for almost all T_2s, it must be that $|f(T_2) - g^i(T_2)| \leq \mathsf{negl}(\kappa)$—otherwise we can construct a *fail-stop* adversary in control of P_2, and this adversary, upon generating an honest random T_2, emulates polynomially many honest executions conditioned on T_2 to estimate $f(T_2)$ and $g^i(T_2)$ respectively, and informed by the estimates, decide to either have i abort upfront or not. We prove that such an adversary can cause non-negligible bias that improves P_2's overall wealth.

Similarly, for T_2' that is almost identical as T_2 but differing in the i-th coordinate, we also have that $|f(T_2') - g^i(T_2')| \leq \mathsf{negl}(\kappa)$. Finally, the proof follows by observing that, if the i-th party aborts upfront, then its random coins do not affect the expected outcome of the execution, i.e., $g^i(T_2) = g^i(T_2')$.

We defer the full proof of this theorem to our online full version.

6 Fairness by Strong Nash Equilibrium

6.1 Definition of Strong Nash Equilibrium (SNE)

Strong Nash Equilibrium (SNE) requires that no coalition, corrupting up to n parties, can noticeably (i.e., non-negligibly) increase the payoff of all members of the coalition. SNE is weaker than the earlier CSP notion since the former only needs to resist a subset of the coalition strategies that latter must resist—CSP must not only defend against coalition strategies that benefit all of its members, but also defend against strategies that benefit coalition members on average[7]. More formally, we define SNE-fairness below.

Definition 4 (Strong Nash Equilibrium or SNE-fairness). *Let $\mathfrak{A}$ be a family of adversaries that corrupt up to n parties and let $\mathcal{P} \in \{0,1\}^n$ be any mixed preference profile. We say that an n-party coin toss protocol is SNE-fair for $\mathcal{P}$ and against the family of adversaries $\mathfrak{A}$ iff for any $\mathcal{A} \in \mathfrak{A}$, there exists a negligible function $\mathsf{negl}(\cdot)$, such that in an execution with the preference profile $\mathcal{P}$ and the adversary $\mathcal{A}$, there is at least one corrupt party whose expected payoff is less than $\frac{1}{2} + \mathsf{negl}(\kappa)$.*

[7] Since SNE only needs to defend against unanimous coalitions by Fact 3, for any mixed preference profile we in fact only need to consider coalitions of size $n-1$ rather than n.

Note that the definition of SNE-fairness requires that the notion be satisfied *even when all parties are corrupt*. Similar as before, depending on the family $\mathfrak{A}$ of adversaries that we are concerned about, we can define computational, statistical, or perfect notions for SNE-fairness, and for fail-stop, semi-malicious, or malicious adversaries respectively. We omit the detailed definitions for conciseness.

A coalition of parties is said to be *unanimous* iff every party in the coalition prefers the same bit.

Fact 3. *Let $\mathfrak{A}$ be a family of adversaries corrupting up to n parties and let $\mathfrak{A}' \subset \mathfrak{A}$ be the (maximal) subset of $\mathfrak{A}$ that corrupts only unanimous coalitions*[8]. *Let $\mathcal{P} \in \{0,1\}^n$ be any mixed preference profile. Then, an n-party coin toss protocol Π is CSP-fair for $\mathcal{P}$ against the family $\mathfrak{A}'$ iff Π is SNE-fair for $\mathcal{P}$ against the family $\mathfrak{A}$.*

Proof. For any adversary $\mathcal{A} \in \mathfrak{A}$ that corrupts a coalition that has mixed preferences, if the coalition members that prefer 0 have expected payoff more than $\frac{1}{2}$, then those who prefer 1 must have payoff at most $\frac{1}{2}$—thus SNE-fairness is trivially satisfied for mixed coalitions. We therefore conclude that a protocol Π to be SNE-fair for $\mathcal{P}$ against $\mathfrak{A}$, if and only if Π is SNE-fair for $\mathcal{P}$ against those adversaries in $\mathfrak{A}$ that control unanimous coalitions—and this latter notion is equivalent to CSP-fair for unanimous coalitions, by observing the following: since $\mathcal{P}$ is mixed, any adversary in $\mathfrak{A}$ that controls unanimous coalitions corrupts only up to $n-1$ parties (recall that the definition of CSP-fair considers adversaries that corrupts upto $n-1$ parties).

6.2 Feasibility Results for SNE Fairness

We show that for any $n \geq 2$, there is an n-party coin toss protocol that is computationally SNE-fair for any mixed preference profile $\mathcal{P} \in \{0,1\}^n$ against even malicious adversaries; further, there is an n-party coin toss protocol that is perfectly SNE-fair for any mixed preference profile $\mathcal{P} \in \{0,1\}^n$ against semi-malicious adversaries. On the other hand, the impossibility of statistical SNE fairness against malicious adversaries is implied in a straightforward fashion by known lower bounds [33,44].

Achieving Perfect SNE-Fairness Against Semi-malicious Adversaries. Let $n \geq 3$ and let $\mathcal{P} \in \{0,1\}^n$ be a mixed preference profile. We can consider a simple dueling protocol: pick two people with opposing preferences (i.e., the ones with the smallest party identifiers) and have them play the simple 2-party protocol: each party picks a random bit upfront and both broadcast their bit in the first round. Normally the outcome is the XOR of the two bits but if one party aborts, the outcome is the other party's preference.

[8] Recall that we assume that the choice of corrupt parties is hard-wired in an adversary's algorithm.

Theorem 11 (Perfect SNE-fairness against semi-malicious adversaries). *For any $n \geq 2$, there is an n-party coin toss protocol that is perfectly SNE-fair for any mixed preference profile $\mathcal{P} \in \{0,1\}^n$ against semi-malicious adversaries.*

Proof. By Fact 3, we only need to resist unanimous coalitions. Thus for the two parties selected to duel with opposing preferences, one of them must be honest. Further, recall that a semi-malicious adversary must select its random coins upfront without seeing any protocol message, and henceforth the only attack it can perform is aborting. Now in the 2-party protocol, for any choice of randomness of the 2 dueling parties, if the corrupt party aborts, it does no better than playing honestly till completion.

Achieving Computational SNE-Fairness Against Malicious Adversaries. The above protocol can be made secure against malicious adversaries using a cryptographic commitment scheme. The only change needed is that when the selected two parties duel, one of them (denoted P) commits to a bit in Phase 0, then the other party (denoted P') sends its bit in Phase 1, and finally P opens its commitment.

Theorem 12 (Computational SNE-fairness against malicious adversaries). *For any $n \geq 2$, there is an n-party coin toss protocol that achieves computational SNE-fairness for any mixed preference profile $\mathcal{P} \in \{0,1\}^n$ against malicious adversaries.*

Proof. Consider the dueling protocol Π_{duel}. By Fact 3, it suffices to prove that any unanimous coalition cannot non-negligibly improve the coalition's total reward. Notice that any unanimous coalition controls at most one party in the two parties selected to duel. By maximin fairness of the 2-party protocol (which we argue in our online full version [18]), if one of the dueling parties deviates, the deviating party cannot improve its expected payoff by more than a negligible amount.

7 The Case of Private Preference Profiles

Here we consider the case of private preference profiles, where each party's preference is private information only known to the party. In other words, we consider *private preference* coin toss protocols, where each party's preference is a private input, instead of public information. Clearly, this is a more challenging setting for achieving fairness. For example, a malicious party may lie about his preference or abort without revealing his preference. Indeed, as we shall see, we lose some feasibility results in the private preference setting.

Recall that in the public preference setting, coin toss protocols and fairness can be naturally defined with respect to a preference profile $\mathcal{P}$. However, this is not the case for private preference. Thus, we only consider (universal) n-party private preference coin toss protocols that are defined for every preference profiles $\mathcal{P} \in \{0,1\}^n$. All three fairness notions can be naturally defined for such protocols. Below we only state the definition of maximin fairness in the private preference setting formally for succinctness. The other two notions can be defined analogously.

Definition 5 (Maximin fairness). *Let $\mathfrak{A}$ be a family of adversaries that corrupt up to $n-1$ parties. We say that an n-party private preference coin toss protocol is private maximin fair against the family $\mathfrak{A}$, iff for every adversary $\mathcal{A} \in \mathfrak{A}$, there exists some negligible function $\mathsf{negl}(\cdot)$ such that for every mixed preference profile $\mathcal{P} \in \{0,1\}^n$, in an execution with the preference profile $\mathcal{P}$ and the adversary $\mathcal{A}$, the expected reward for any honest party is at least $\frac{1}{2} - \mathsf{negl}(\kappa)$. For unanimous preference profiles, the execution should output the common preference with probability* 1.

We proceed to discuss the feasibility and impossibility of fair coin toss for private preference protocols. As this is harder to achieve, all impossibility results in the public preference setting trivially hold here, and it suffices to investigate cases that are feasible in the public preference setting.

SNE-Fairness. Recall that even in the public preference setting, we can only achieve general feasibility result for the notion of SNE-fairness, where computational SNE-fairness against malicious adversary and statistical SNE-fairness against semi-malicious adversary are feasible for any $n \geq 2$ parties (whereas maximum and CSP-fairness are impossible for $n \geq 4$ even against fail stop adversary). In the private preference setting, we show that SNE-fairness against malicious adversary becomes impossible for $n \geq 3$ parties, whereas SNE-fairness against semi-malicious adversary remain feasible. Intuitively, the reason for the impossibility is that a malicious adversary may lie about his preference.

Theorem 13 (Impossibility of SNE-fairness against malicious adversary). *For any $n \geq 3$, no n-party private preference coin-toss protocol can achieve even computational SNE-fairness against malicious adversaries.*

Proof (sketch). We focus on the three-party case and discuss how to handle general $n \geq 4$ parties at the end of the proof. At a high level, the proof for the three-party case relies on the same argument as that of Theorem 7 for maximin-fairness. Recall that in the proof of Theorem 7, we consider preference profile $\mathcal{P} = (1,0,1)$. We show that maximin-fairness implies T_2-equality lemma (Lemma 1) and the lone-wolf and wolf-minion conditions. Then we use these properties to derive a contradiction by constructing an adversary that breaks the wolf-minion condition. Here, we follow the same strategy to consider preference profile $\mathcal{P} = (1,0,1)$. It suffices to show that private SNE-fairness implies the same set of properties, and a contradiction can be derived in the same way.

Let Π be a three-party private preference coin toss protocol. Recall that we use the notation $T_1, T_2, T_3 \in \{0,1\}^{\ell(\kappa)}$ to denote the randomness of P_1, P_2 and P_3, respectively, and $f(T_2)$ to denote the expected outcome when P_2 uses the randomness T_2 whereas P_1 and P_3 executed the protocol honestly (when the preference profile is $\mathcal{P} = (1,0,1)$).

It is not hard to see that Lemma 1 follows. Please see our online full version [18]. Thus, T_2-equality lemma is implied by private SNE-fairness as well. It remains to check the lone-wolf and wolf-minion conditions.

For the lone-wolf conditions, it may seem that SNE-fairness only implies that P_1 (or P_3) cannot cause non-negligible (in κ) bias towards 1 by a fail-stop attack. This is the place that an adversary can take the advantage of private preference. Suppose there P_1 can cause non-negligible bias towards 0 by a fail-stop attack when the preference profile is $(1, 0, 1)$. Consider the case that the preference profile is $(0, 0, 1)$. An malicious P_1 (with preference 0) can participate the protocol with a pretended preference 1 and perform the fail-stop attack to cause bias toward 0 to violate fairness. Thus, a fail stop P_1 (or P_3) cannot cause non-negligible bias towards either direction.

Recall that the wolf-minion condition says that when P_1 and P_2 (or P_2 and P_3) form a fail-stop coalition, they cannot cause a non-negligible (in κ) bias towards 0. Suppose this is not the case, e.g., a fail-stop coalition P_1 and P_2 can cause a non-negligible bias towards 0. We show that SNE-fairness can be violated when the preference profile is $(0, 0, 1)$. Indeed, in this case, an malicious adversary corrupting P_1 and P_2 can pretend the preference of P_1 is 1 and use the assumed fail-stop attack to cause a non-negligible bias towards 0, which violates SNE-fairness.

The above shows that for three-party protocols, the properties needed in the proof of Theorem 7 are implied by private SNE-fairness. A contradiction can then be derived by the same arguments as in Theorem 7, which proves the impossibility.

Finally, for general $n \geq 4$ parties, we can use the standard trick to group $P_4, \ldots, P_n$ together with P_2 to form a supernode of 0-supporters. This effectively reduce the number of parties to 3 and the same argument can be applied to show impossibility.

Theorem 14 (Perfect private SNE-fairness against semi-malicious adversaries). *For any $n \geq 2$, there is an n-party private preference coin toss protocol that is perfectly private SNE-fair against semi-malicious adversaries.*

Proof. We simply modify the public preference duelling protocol by first asking all parties to reveal their private preference. If any parties abort, we ignore them. For the remaining non-aborting parties, we proceed with the dueling protocol as in the public preference setting. Note that since we only consider semi-malicious adversaries, the revealed preferences must be the true preferences.

By Fact 3 (which can be verified to hold in the private preference setting with the same argument), we only need to resist unanimous coalitions. Hence, all aborting parties must share the same preference as their non-aborting coalition (if any), who do not gain any advantage by the fairness of the public preference protocol. If all non-aborting parties are honest, then correctness of the honest execution also implies that the aborting parties do not gain any advantage.

Note that Theorem 14 is proved by a protocol that first asks all parties to reveal their private preference and then executes a public preference protocol among the non-aborting parties, and intuitively, this works since the semi-malicious can only reveal their true preferences. However, while this intuition turns out to be true for SNE-fairness and maximin fairness (which we discuss later), it can be subtle for CSP-fairness since the adversary still has the advantage of aborting before revealing his preference. We discuss this next.

CSP-Fairness. Recall that in the public preference setting, Corollary 2 says that for $n \geq 3$, there exists an n-party coin toss protocol that achieves perfect CSP-fairness for any almost unanimous preference profile against all fail-stop adversaries that can control up to n parties. In particular, there exists a three-party perfect CSP-fair protocol against fail-stop adversaries who may corrupt all three parties[9]. Interesting, this becomes impossible in the private preference setting.

Theorem 15 (Impossibility of CSP-fairness against fail-stop all-corruption adversary). *No three-party private preference coin-toss protocol can achieve computational CSP-fairness against fail-stop adversaries that can corrupt up to three parties.*

Proof (sketch). For the sake of contradiction, suppose Π is a three-party private preference coin-toss protocol that achieve the claimed fairness. Let us consider a scenario where P_3 always abort at the beginning, and P_1 and P_2 has preference 0 and 1, respectively. Note that suppose P_1 and P_2 execute the protocol honestly, the outcome need to be unbiased: Suppose the outcome is biased towards b and the private preference of P_3 is also b, then the CSP-fairness is violated.

Thus, in this scenario where P_3 is aborting, honest P_1 and P_2 execute a two-party protocol and produce an unbiased outcome. We can apply Cleve's lower bound argument to show the existence of a fail-stop adversary P_a that can bias the outcome non-negligibly towards b, for some $a \in \{1, 2\}$ and $b \in \{0, 1\}$. Now, suppose the private preference of P_3 is b, and consider an adversary $\mathcal{A}$ that corrupts all three parties and does the following: (i) $\mathcal{A}$ lets P_3 aborts at the beginning, and (ii) $\mathcal{A}$ let P_a to perform the fail-stop attack to cause non-negligible bias of the outcome towards b. This violates CSP-fairness since the total utility of the corrupted parties is increased by a non-negligible amount.

On the positive side, we observe that Corollary 1 extends to the private preference setting.

Theorem 16. *There is an 3-party private preference coin toss protocol that achieves perfect CSP-fairness against the family of all semi-malicious adversaries that control at most 2 parties.*

Proof (sketch). We follow the same strategy to first ask each party reveal his preference, and then let the non-aborting parties to execute a fair public preference protocol. Specifically, if no party aborts, then we run the three-party CSP-fair

[9] We focus on the three-party case here since the case of four or more parties are impossible in the private preference setting due to the existence of amply divided preference profiles for four or more parties.

protocol in Corollary 1. If one party aborts and the remaining two parties have the same preference, then they output their preference. If one party aborts and the remaining two parties have different preferences, then they execute the dueling protocol. If two parties abort, then the remaining party simply output his preference. It is not hard to see by inspection that private CSP-fairness holds in all cases.

Maximin Fairness. We end this section with a brief discussion on the maximin fairness for the private preference protocols. Note that the only interesting question is whether Theorem 6, which states the existence of perfect maximin fair coin toss protocol against fail-stop adversaries, extends to the private preference setting. Now, observe that the definition of maximin fairness only concerns the honest party's utility, so an adversary who aborts without revealing his preference cannot hurt maximin fairness. Therefore, the strategy of first asking each party to reveal his preference, and then letting the non-aborting parties to execute a fair public preference protocol works directly for maximin fairness.

Theorem 17 (Possibility of perfect maximin fairness for 3 parties and fail-stop adversaries). *There exists a 3-party private preference coin toss protocol that achieves perfect maximin fairness against any fail-stop adversaries.*

8 Related Work

Related works on strongly fair coin toss [19,27] as well as Blum's notion of weak fair coin toss [16] have been discussed earlier in Sect. 1. In this section, we discuss additional related work.

Game Theory and Cryptography. Historically, game theory [36,48] and multi-party computation [27,52,53] were investigated by separate communities. Some recent efforts have investigated the marriage of game theory and cryptography (see the excellent surveys by Katz [37] and by Dodis and Rabin [24]). This line of work has focused on two broad types of questions:

- First, a line of works [1,4–6,32,38,49] investigated how to define game-theoretic notions of security (as opposed to cryptography-style security notions) for multi-party computation tasks such as secret sharing and secure function evaluation. Existing works consider a different notion of utility than us: specifically, these works make (a subset to all of) the following assumptions about players' utility: players prefer to compute the function correctly; further, they prefer to learn secrets, and prefer that other players do not learn secrets. These works then investigate how to design protocols such that rational players will be incentivized to follow the honest protocol.
- Second, a line of work has asked how cryptography can help traditional game theory. Particularly, many classical works in game theory [36,48] assumes the existence of a trusted mediator—and recent works have shown that under certain conditions, this trusted mediator can be implemented using cryptography [9,23,29,34].

In this paper, we investigate game-theoretic notions of fairness for coin toss protocols. Our notions are novel in comparison with the aforementioned related work. First, to the best of our knowledge, we are the first to apply game theory to coin toss protocols, and asking whether we can circumvent known impossibilities [19] by considering rational players. Second, the fairness notions proposed in this paper are novel and to the best of our knowledge have not been investigated before for multiple parties. Specifically, we consider a natural notion of utility for coin toss protocols, where players have a preference over the outcome of the coin toss. We require that an honest execution produces an unbiased coin (unless all parties prefer the same bit); however if one or more coalition(s) deviate from the honest protocol, the coin toss outcome need not be unbiased (but we want that certain fairness properties must be preserved). All notions of fairness defined in the paper consider *corrupt majority*—since in the case of honest majority, strongly fair coin toss is known to be possible assuming standard cryptography assumptions [27], and the standard strong fairness notion implies all game-theoretic notions considered in this paper. In comparison, most earlier works [1,4–6,9,23,29,32,34,38,49] at the intersection of cryptography and game theory consider only the popular Nash equilibrium notion that is concerned about coalitions of size 1. Our fairness definitions are inspired by equilibrium notions in game theory that resist coalitions in various capacities [15,35].

Other Notions of Fairness. Our work is inspired by the study of new, financially motivated fairness notions in blockchains and cryptocurrency applications [3,8,13,22,39–41,45]. Several recent works [13,22,39,40] show that to achieve a suitable notion of financial fairness, the protocol may require that parties place collateral on the blockchain to participate, and misbehaving parties can be penalized by taking away their collateral. Among these works, the most closely related to ours are those that investigate lottery-style protocols [8,13,22,39,45]. While earlier works [3,13] require quadratic amount of collateral, more recent works [8,45] showed that it is possible to realize fair lottery in the presence of a blockchain (i.e., a broadcast medium with identifiable abort) requiring no collateral at all, by relying on a folklore tournament-tree approach. Interestingly, although not explicitly noted, all these works on fair lottery over a blockchain [8,13,22,39,45] adopt a game theoretic notion of fairness, that is, although a deviating coalition can bias the outcome of toss of the n-sided dice, such bias must be towards a direction that harms the perpetrators. In fact, the implicit fairness notion in these papers is equivalent to our notion of maximin fairness and cooperative-strategy-proof (CSP) fairness—for 0-sum games like a lottery, these two notions are equivalent.

Other relaxations of strong fairness have also been considered for coin toss and multi-party computation. For example, several works [2,7,10,11,14,17,19–21,28,30,31,46] consider a notion of ϵ-fairness, i.e., the adversary can bias the coin by at most a non-negligible ϵ amount. Moran et al. [46] showed that for general R, there is an R-round, 2-party coin toss protocol that satisfies $O(1/R)$-fairness—and this is optimal since Cleve [19] showed that for every R-round

2-party coin toss protocol, there exists an efficient adversary that can bias the honest party's outcome by at least $\Omega(1/R)$.

9 Conclusion

In this paper we proposed several natural, game theoretic notions of fairness for multi-party coin toss protocols. In the case of two parties, all of these notions equate to Blum's notion of weakly fair coin toss [16]; however, for more than 2 parties, these notions differ in strength and lead to different feasibility and infeasibility results. We summarize the strengths of various notions from strongest to weakest (for general n and mixed preference profiles).

Maximin $\neq$ Cooperative-Strategy-Proof (CSP) $>$ Cooperative-Coalition-Proof (CCP) $=$ Strong Nash Equilibrium (SNE) $>$ Coalition-Proof $>$ Nash

Among the above notions, we show broad feasibility results for SNE-fairness (which directly implies feasibility for coalition-proof equilibrium and Nash Equilibrium too). For other notions, we give a complete characterization of their feasibilities and infeasibilities—and for all of them we prove infeasibilities for amply divided preference profiles.

Note that among these notions, cooperative-strategy-proof and cooperative-coalition-proof are new notions first proposed in this paper—although we study them in the context of coin toss protocols, they would make sense for general games with transferrable utilities too. Finally, although maximin fairness is incomparable to CSP-fairness in general, the two are equivalent for balanced preference profiles (analogous to zero-sum games).

References

1. Abraham, I., Dolev, D., Gonen, R., Halpern, J.: Distributed computing meets game theory: robust mechanisms for rational secret sharing and multiparty computation. In: PODC (2006)
2. Alon, B., Omri, E.: Almost-optimally fair multiparty coin-tossing with nearly three-quarters malicious. In: Hirt, M., Smith, A. (eds.) TCC 2016. LNCS, vol. 9985, pp. 307–335. Springer, Heidelberg (2016). https://doi.org/10.1007/978-3-662-53641-4_13
3. Andrychowicz, M., Dziembowski, S., Malinowski, D., Mazurek, L.: Secure multiparty computations on bitcoin. In: S&P (2013)
4. Asharov, G., Canetti, R., Hazay, C.: Towards a game theoretic view of secure computation. In: Paterson, K.G. (ed.) EUROCRYPT 2011. LNCS, vol. 6632, pp. 426–445. Springer, Heidelberg (2011). https://doi.org/10.1007/978-3-642-20465-4_24
5. Asharov, G., Lindell, Y.: Utility dependence in correct and fair rational secret sharing. In: Halevi, S. (ed.) CRYPTO 2009. LNCS, vol. 5677, pp. 559–576. Springer, Heidelberg (2009). https://doi.org/10.1007/978-3-642-03356-8_33

6. Asharov, G., Lindell, Y.: Utility dependence in correct and fair rational secret sharing. J. Cryptol. **24**(1), 157–202 (2011)
7. Awerbuch, B., Blum, M., Chor, B., Goldwasser, S., Micali, S.: How to implement brachas o (log n) byzantine agreement algorithm (1985, unpublished manuscript)
8. Bartoletti, M., Zunino, R.: Constant-deposit multiparty lotteries on bitcoin. In: Brenner, M., et al. (eds.) FC 2017. LNCS, vol. 10323, pp. 231–247. Springer, Cham (2017). https://doi.org/10.1007/978-3-319-70278-0_15
9. Beimel, A., Groce, A., Katz, J., Orlov, I.: Fair computation with rational players. https://eprint.iacr.org/2011/396.pdf. Full version of Eurocrypt 2012 proceeding version by Groce and Katz (2011)
10. Beimel, A., Haitner, I., Makriyannis, N., Omri, E.: Tighter bounds on multi-party coin flipping via augmented weak martingales and differentially private sampling. Technical report TR17-168, Electronic Colloquium on Computational Complexity (2017)
11. Beimel, A., Omri, E., Orlov, I.: Protocols for multiparty coin toss with a dishonest majority. J. Cryptol. **28**(3), 551–600 (2015)
12. Ben-or, M., Goldwasser, S., Wigderson, A.: Completeness theorems for non-cryptographic fault-tolerant distributed computation. In: STOC (1988)
13. Bentov, I., Kumaresan, R.: How to use bitcoin to design fair protocols. In: Garay, J.A., Gennaro, R. (eds.) CRYPTO 2014. LNCS, vol. 8617, pp. 421–439. Springer, Heidelberg (2014). https://doi.org/10.1007/978-3-662-44381-1_24
14. Berman, I., Haitner, I., Tentes, A.: Coin flipping of any constant bias implies one-way functions. JACM **65**(3), 14 (2018)
15. Bernheim, B., Peleg, B., Whinston, M.D.: Coalition-proof nash equilibria i. concepts. J. Econ. Theory **42**(1), 1–12 (1987)
16. Blum, M.: Coin flipping by telephone. In: CRYPTO (1981)
17. Buchbinder, N., Haitner, I., Levi, N., Tsfadia, E.: Fair coin flipping: tighter analysis and the many-party case. In: SODA (2017)
18. Chung, K.-M., Guo, Y., Lin, W.-K., Pass, R., Shi, E.: Game theoretic notions of fairness in multi-party coin toss. Cryptology ePrint Archive (2018)
19. Cleve, R.: Limits on the security of coin flips when half the processors are faulty. In: STOC (1986)
20. Dachman-Soled, D., Lindell, Y., Mahmoody, M., Malkin, T.: On the black-box complexity of optimally-fair coin tossing. In: Ishai, Y. (ed.) TCC 2011. LNCS, vol. 6597, pp. 450–467. Springer, Heidelberg (2011). https://doi.org/10.1007/978-3-642-19571-6_27
21. Dachman-Soled, D., Mahmoody, M., Malkin, T.: Can optimally-fair coin tossing be based on one-way functions? In: Lindell, Y. (ed.) TCC 2014. LNCS, vol. 8349, pp. 217–239. Springer, Heidelberg (2014). https://doi.org/10.1007/978-3-642-54242-8_10
22. Delmolino, K., Arnett, M., Kosba, A., Miller, A., Shi, E.: Step by step towards creating a safe smart contract: lessons and insights from a cryptocurrency lab. In: Clark, J., Meiklejohn, S., Ryan, P.Y.A., Wallach, D., Brenner, M., Rohloff, K. (eds.) FC 2016. LNCS, vol. 9604, pp. 79–94. Springer, Heidelberg (2016). https://doi.org/10.1007/978-3-662-53357-4_6
23. Dodis, Y., Halevi, S., Rabin, T.: A cryptographic solution to a game theoretic problem. In: Bellare, M. (ed.) CRYPTO 2000. LNCS, vol. 1880, pp. 112–130. Springer, Heidelberg (2000). https://doi.org/10.1007/3-540-44598-6_7
24. Dodis, Y., Rabin, T.: Cryptography and game theory. In: Algorithmic Game Theory (2007)

25. Games, B.: One-night werewolf. https://beziergames.com. Accessed 21 Oct 2018
26. Garay, J., Kiayias, A., Leonardos, N.: The bitcoin backbone protocol: analysis and applications. In: Oswald, E., Fischlin, M. (eds.) EUROCRYPT 2015. LNCS, vol. 9057, pp. 281–310. Springer, Heidelberg (2015). https://doi.org/10.1007/978-3-662-46803-6_10
27. Goldreich, O., Micali, S., Wigderson, A.: How to play any mental game. In: STOC (1987)
28. Gordon, S.D., Katz, J.: Partial fairness in secure two-party computation. J. Cryptol. **25**(1), 14–40 (2012)
29. Groce, A., Katz, J.: Fair computation with rational players. In: Pointcheval, D., Johansson, T. (eds.) EUROCRYPT 2012. LNCS, vol. 7237, pp. 81–98. Springer, Heidelberg (2012). https://doi.org/10.1007/978-3-642-29011-4_7
30. Haitner, I., Omri, E.: Coin flipping with constant bias implies one-way functions. SIAM J. Comput. **43**(2), 389–409 (2014)
31. Haitner, I., Tsfadia, E.: An almost-optimally fair three-party coin-flipping protocol. SIAM J. Comput. **46**(2), 479–542 (2017)
32. Halpern, J., Teague, V.: Rational secret sharing and multiparty computation. In: STOC (2004)
33. Impagliazzo, R., Luby, M.: One-way functions are essential for complexity based cryptography. In: FOCS (1989)
34. Izmalkov, S., Micali, S., Lepinski, M.: Rational secure computation and ideal mechanism design. In: FOCS (2005)
35. Aumann, R.J.: Acceptable points in general cooperative n-person games. In: Contributions to the Theory of Games IV. Princeton University Press, Princeton (1959)
36. Aumann, R.J.: Subjectivity and correlation in randomized strategies. J. Math. Econ. **1**(1), 67–96 (1974)
37. Katz, J.: Bridging game theory and cryptography: recent results and future directions. In: Canetti, R. (ed.) TCC 2008. LNCS, vol. 4948, pp. 251–272. Springer, Heidelberg (2008). https://doi.org/10.1007/978-3-540-78524-8_15
38. Kol, G., Naor, M.: Cryptography and game theory: designing protocols for exchanging information. In: Canetti, R. (ed.) TCC 2008. LNCS, vol. 4948, pp. 320–339. Springer, Heidelberg (2008). https://doi.org/10.1007/978-3-540-78524-8_18
39. Kosba, A.E., Miller, A., Shi, E., Wen, Z., Papamanthou, C.: Hawk: the blockchain model of cryptography and privacy-preserving smart contracts. In: S&P (2016)
40. Kumaresan, R., Bentov, I.: How to use bitcoin to incentivize correct computations. In: CCS (2014)
41. Kumaresan, R., Bentov, I.: Amortizing secure computation with penalties. In: CCS (2016)
42. Lin, H., Pass, R.: Constant-round nonmalleable commitments from any one-way function. J. ACM **62**(1), 5:1–5:30 (2015)
43. Lin, H., Pass, R., Venkitasubramaniam, M.: Concurrent non-malleable commitments from any one-way function. In: Canetti, R. (ed.) TCC 2008. LNCS, vol. 4948, pp. 571–588. Springer, Heidelberg (2008). https://doi.org/10.1007/978-3-540-78524-8_31
44. Maji, H.K., Prabhakaran, M., Sahai, A.: On the computational complexity of coin flipping. In: FOCS (2010)
45. Miller, A., Bentov, I.: Zero-collateral lotteries in bitcoin and ethereum. In: EuroS&P Workshops (2017)
46. Moran, T., Naor, M., Segev, G.: An optimally fair coin toss. J. Cryptol. **29**(3), 491–513 (2016)

47. Nakamoto, S.: Bitcoin: a peer-to-peer electronic cash system (2008)
48. Nash, J.: Non-cooperative games. Ann. Math. **54**(2), 286–295 (1951)
49. Ong, S.J., Parkes, D.C., Rosen, A., Vadhan, S.: Fairness with an honest minority and a rational majority. In: Reingold, O. (ed.) TCC 2009. LNCS, vol. 5444, pp. 36–53. Springer, Heidelberg (2009). https://doi.org/10.1007/978-3-642-00457-5_3
50. Pass, R., Seeman, L., Shelat, A.: Analysis of the blockchain protocol in asynchronous networks. In: Coron, J.-S., Nielsen, J.B. (eds.) EUROCRYPT 2017. LNCS, vol. 10211, pp. 643–673. Springer, Cham (2017). https://doi.org/10.1007/978-3-319-56614-6_22
51. Pass, R., Shi, E.: Rethinking large-scale consensus. In: CSF (2017)
52. Yao, A.C.-C.: Protocols for secure computations. In: FOCS (1982)
53. Yao, A.C.-C.: How to generate and exchange secrets. In: FOCS (1986)

Achieving Fair Treatment in Algorithmic Classification

Andrew Morgan[1(✉)] and Rafael Pass[2]

[1] Cornell University, Ithaca, USA
asmorgan@cs.cornell.edu
[2] Cornell Tech, New York City, USA
rafael@cornell.edu

Abstract. Fairness in classification has become an increasingly relevant and controversial issue as computers replace humans in many of today's classification tasks. In particular, a subject of much recent debate is that of finding, and subsequently achieving, suitable definitions of fairness in an algorithmic context. In this work, following the work of Hardt et al. (NIPS'16), we consider and formalize the task of *sanitizing* an unfair classifier $\mathcal{C}$ into a classifier $\mathcal{C}'$ satisfying an approximate notion of "equalized odds" or *fair treatment*. Our main result shows how to take any (possibly unfair) classifier $\mathcal{C}$ over a *finite outcome space*, and transform it—by just *perturbing* the output of $\mathcal{C}$—according to some distribution learned by just having black-box access to samples of labeled, and previously classified, data, to produce a classifier $\mathcal{C}'$ that satisfies fair treatment; we additionally show that our derived classifier is near-optimal in terms of accuracy. We also experimentally evaluate the performance of our method.

1 Introduction

As algorithmic decision-making becomes ever more popular and widely-used in today's society, concerns are being raised about whether, and to what extent, algorithms have the potential to discriminate, either as a result of malicious designers or perhaps from learning biases inherent in previous decisions on which an algorithm could be trained. In a well-known recent example, the COMPAS recidivism analysis tool, one of an increasingly popular set of algorithmic criminal "risk assessments" which are being used nationwide in sentencing and other decisions pertaining to defendants in the criminal justice system, was shown to exhibit highly disparate treatment between different races; a study by ProPublica [1,2] showed that African-American defendants who ultimately did not recidivate were almost twice as likely as white defendants to receive a high risk score from the algorithm.

R. Pass—Supported in part by NSF Award CNS-1561209, NSF Award CNS-1217821, NSF Award CNS-1704788, AFOSR Award FA9550-18-1-0267, a Microsoft Faculty Fellowship, and a Google Faculty Research Award.

A. Beimel and S. Dziembowski (Eds.): TCC 2018, LNCS 11239, pp. 597–625, 2018.
https://doi.org/10.1007/978-3-030-03807-6_22

As a result of these concerns, there has been extensive research in computer science and other fields pertaining to how *fairness*, or *non-discrimination*, should be defined in the context of a classification scenario. In this work, we will formalize and study one such definition, *fair treatment*, which is an approximate and distribution-based version of the notion of *equalized odds* [6] or *balance* [7].

Fair Treatment (a.k.a. approximate equalized odds). The originally proposed notion of fairness in classification is that of *statistical parity* [5] (which is essentially identical to the notion of causal effect [8]), which captures non-discrimination between groups. Given a classifier $\mathcal{C}$ which assigns to *individuals* σ from some distribution $\mathcal{D}$—each of which has some subset of *observable features* $O(\sigma)$—an *outcome* $\mathcal{C}(O(\sigma))$ (e.g., a risk score), and given a function $f(\sigma)$ representing an individual's *actual class* (e.g., whether they will recidivate), statistical parity simply requires that the output of the classifier be independent (or almost independent) of the group of the individual; that is, for any two groups X and Y, the distributions $\{\mathcal{C}(O(\boldsymbol{\sigma}_X))\}$ and $\{\mathcal{C}(O(\boldsymbol{\sigma}_Y))\}$ are ϵ-close in statistical distance. This is a very strong notion of fairness, and in many contexts it may not make sense. In particular, if the *base rates* (e.g., the base percentages of people from each race who actually recidivate) are different, we should perhaps not expect the output distribution of the classifier to be the same across groups. Indeed, as the ProPublica article points out, in the COMPAS example, the overall recidivism probability among African-American defendants was 56%, whereas it was 42% among white defendants. Thus, in such situations, one would reasonably expect a classifier to *on average* output a higher risk score for African-American defendants, which would violate statistical parity. Indeed, the issue raised by ProPublica authors was that, even after taking this base difference into account (more precisely, even after conditioning on individuals that did not recidivate), there was a significant difference in how the classifier treated the two races.

The notion of *equalized odds* due to Hardt et al. [6] formalizes the desiderata articulated by the authors of the ProPublica study (for the case of recidivism) in a general setting by requiring the output of the classifier to be independent of the group of the individuals, *after conditioning on the class of the individuals.* Very similar notions of fairness appear also in works such as [3,7] using different names; for instance, Kleinberg et al. [7] consider a notion of "balance" which is an approximate version of equalized odds, albeit one which is tailored to scoring-based classifiers over a binary class space and only requires the conditioned expectation of the outcome (i.e., the score) to be close between groups. We here consider a more general approximate version of this notion which applies to all classifiers with a finite outcome space, which we refer to as ϵ-*fair treatment.* This requires that, for any two groups X and Y and any class c, the distributions

- $\{\mathcal{C}(O(\boldsymbol{\sigma}_X)) \mid f(\boldsymbol{\sigma}_X) = c\}$
- $\{\mathcal{C}(O(\boldsymbol{\sigma}_Y)) \mid f(\boldsymbol{\sigma}_Y) = c\}$

are ϵ-close with respect to some appropriate distance metric to be defined shortly. That is, in the COMPAS example, if we restrict to individuals that actually do not recidivate (respectively, those that do), the output of the classifier ought to be essentially independent of the group of the individual (just as intuitively desired by the authors of the ProPublica study, and as explictly put forward in [6]).

We will effectively use the notion of *max-divergence* to determine the "distance" between distributions; this notion, often found in areas such as differential privacy (see [4]), represents this distance as (the logarithm of) the *maximum multiplicative gap* between the probabilities of some element in the respective distributions. We argue that using such a multiplicative distance is important to ensure fairness between groups that may be under-represented in the data (see Sect. 3.1). Furthermore, as we note in the same appendix, such a notion is closed under "post-processing": if a classifier $\mathcal{C}$ satisfies ϵ-fair treatment with respect to a context $\mathcal{P} = (\mathcal{D}, f, g, O)$, then for any (possibly probabilistic) function $\mathcal{M}$, $\mathcal{C}'(\cdot) = \mathcal{M}(\mathcal{C}(\cdot))$ will also satisfy ϵ-fair treatment with respect to $\mathcal{P}$. Closure under post-processing is important as we ultimately want the output of any subsequent classifier that uses only the output of a prior fair classifier to be fair as well[1].

Can we Sanitize an "unfair" Classifier? As shown in the ProPublica study, the COMPAS classifier has a considerably large error in balance between races and hence also has a large error in the stronger notion of fair treatment. A natural question, then, would be whether we can "post-process" the output of this unfair classifier (or others) to satisfy some notion of balance or fair treatment. Indeed, there is a considerable amount of research devoted to *achieving* various definitions of fairness in practice. This is a highly non-trivial problem, in fact; early naïve approaches, such as just removing protected attributes from the feature set, fail due to redundant encodings for such features in the data (as discussed in [5]).

This question was more recently addressed in the work of Hardt et al. [6], who examine various methods by which a potentially unfair classifier can be post-processed into a fair *binary* classifier. They formalized the notion of a $\mathcal{C}$-*derived classifier*: namely a classifier $\mathcal{C}'$ obtained from $\mathcal{C}$ by first running $\mathcal{C}$, and then "perturbing" the output of $\mathcal{C}$. More precisely, such a $\mathcal{C}$ derived classifier may be specified by a "perturbation matrix" P where entry $P_{i,j}$ indicates with what probability output i gets perturbed into output j. Hardt et al. showed that for classifiers $\mathcal{C}$ over a binary outcome spaces, we can construct non-trivial $\mathcal{C}$-derived classifiers that satisfy their notion of equalized odds (in our terminology "perfect" fair treatment). Subsequent work [9] using this method showed that, for a binary version of the COMPAS classifier (which only attempts to predict recidivism and not output a risk score), it can produce a perfectly fair classifier with only an overall loss in accuracy of roughly 1.5%. Their method, however, requires "perfect" knowledge of the distribution $\mathcal{D}$ as well as of the classifier $\mathcal{C}$

[1] Remarking once again on the earlier definition of Kleinberg et al., we note that while it is equivalent to our definition for the case of binary outcomes, it is weaker for non-binary outcomes (as in the case of the COMPAS classifier). Furthermore, as with most expectation-based definitions, it is not closed under post-processing.

in order to demonstrate optimality; additionally, as mentioned, it only applies to binary outcomes (and as such, does not directly apply to a risk assessment setting such as COMPAS)[2].

Thus, the literature leaves open the questions of (1) whether we can *efficiently* find a $\mathcal{C}$-derived classifier (without having perfect knowledge of $\mathcal{D}$ and $\mathcal{C}$), and (2) whether sanitization can be done for non-binary outputs.

Towards addressing this problem, we first formalize the notion of *black-box sanitization*: how to efficiently find a $\mathcal{C}$-derived classifier given just black-box access to a "sampling oracle" which samples random individuals $\sigma \leftarrow \mathcal{D}$ and outputs $(O(\sigma), f(\sigma), \mathcal{C}(O(\sigma)), g(\sigma))$ (that is, the individual's observable features, prior classification $\mathcal{C}$, actual class, and group, which is essentially the data used by the ProPublica authors to investigate the fairness of COMPAS).

Definition 1 (Informally stated). *We call an algorithm $\mathcal{B}$ a* ***black-box sanitizer*** *if, given a distribution $\mathcal{D}$ and a sequence of prior classifiers $\{\mathcal{C}_n\}$ such that $\mathcal{C}_n$ takes as input n-bit descriptions $O_n(\sigma)$ of individuals' features*[3]*, then, for each n, it:*

- *runs in time polynomial in n, and*
- *outputs some $\mathcal{C}_n$-derived classifier $\mathcal{C}'_n$ which, with overwhelming probability $1 - \nu(n)$ for some $\nu(\cdot)$ negligible*[4] *in n, satisfies approximate fair treatment (with some small error $\epsilon(n)$) for individuals $\sigma \leftarrow \mathcal{D}$,*

while only making "black-box" queries to the prior classifier. (That is, $\mathcal{B}$ cannot use any information about $\mathcal{D}$ or $\mathcal{C}_n$ aside from querying random samples $(O_n(\sigma'), f(\sigma'), \mathcal{C}_n(O_n(\sigma')), g(\sigma'))$ for $\sigma' \leftarrow \mathcal{D}$.)

Our key result is the construction of an efficient (i.e., polynomial-time in n) black-box sanitizer $\mathcal{B}$ that works for any distribution $\mathcal{D}$ and prior classifier sequence $\{\mathcal{C}_n\}$ *over a fixed outcome space*, and produces a classifier which not only satisfies approximate fair treatment but also can be shown to be near-optimal in terms of prediction accuracy (though the same also holds for a more general class of linear loss functions, which are formalized in the main statement of the result):

Theorem 1 (Informally stated). *For any fixed outcome space Ω, group space $\mathbb{G}$, and inverse polynomial $\epsilon(n)$, there exists a black-box sanitizer $\mathcal{B}$ with fair treatment error $\epsilon(n)$ such that, with probability at least $1 - \nu(n)$ over $\mathcal{B}$'s queries for some inverse-exponential $\nu(\cdot)$, the accuracy loss of the classifier $\mathcal{C}'$ output by $\mathcal{B}$ (compared to the optimal $\mathcal{C}$-derived classifier over the same $\mathcal{D}$, f, and $\mathcal{C}$) is bounded by $|\Omega|(\epsilon(n) + \epsilon(n)^4|\mathbb{G}|/32)$.*

[2] Hardt et al. [6] also presented a method for sanitizing a classifier outputting a risk-score (just as COMPAS), but the final, derived, classifier again would only output a single bit.

[3] Here we consider a sequence of classifiers for the sake of defining "computational efficiency" of a sanitizer; in particular, we would like the running time of our sanitizer to be polynomial in the feature length n.

[4] That is, asymptotically smaller than any inverse polynomial $1/p(n)$.

We note that while Hardt et al. demonstrate a classifier satisfying *errorless* fair treatment, our derived classifier only satisfies ϵ-approximate fair treatment for some small ϵ, but this is unavoidable as we do not assume knowledge of the distribution $\mathcal{D}$. In contrast, we show how this classifier can be *efficiently* found without this knowledge of $\mathcal{D}$; additionally, our method applies to classifiers over any finite outcome space, as opposed to just binary outcomes.

In the full version of this paper, we also experimentally evaluate the accuracy of our post-processing technique using a data set from the COMPAS recidivism analysis tool [1]. We investigate the fair treatment rates of the original data set and subsequently use the above technique to create classifiers satisfying fair treatment with varying errors while optimizing three different loss functions, amounting to overall accuracy (when considering a binary version of the classifier where scores 0–5 get mapped to a 0, and 6–10 get mapped to 1) and two notions of the similarity of the derived classification to the original classification. We find that our method is able to produce derived classifiers satisfying fair treatment with a relatively small amount of loss (with respect to this experimental data).

1.1 Proof Outline for Theorem 1

We show our sanitization theorem in three steps. First, we consider an arbitrary $\mathcal{C}$-derived classifier, and we demonstrate constraints for a linear program that can be used to efficiently find the optimal such classifier $\mathcal{C}'$ satisfying fair treatment. We note that these constraints are precisely a generalized version of those which Hardt et al. [6] demonstrate for *binary* classifiers $\mathcal{C}$ (though they also consider $\mathcal{C}$ with larger outcome spaces); we, however, also leverage our approximate definition to create constraints for *approximate* fair treatment. We further note that solving this linear program will require time polynomial in the number of possible outcomes $|\mathcal{O}|$.

Of course, our linear constraints, as well as the loss function we wish to optimize, may in general depend on features of $\mathcal{D}$ and $\mathcal{C}$ that we may in this model only approximate with black-box queries. So, towards approximating this optimal classifier in a black-box setting, we show that it suffices to use experimental probabilities derived from these queries rather than actual probabilities to build the linear program, since over sufficiently many queries, and as long as real probabilities are sufficiently large, it is overwhelmingly likely by a simple Chernoff bound that the experimental probabilities will be very close to accurate. To deal with the case when real probabilities may be quite small (and prone to large multiplicative error in estimation due to variance in samples), we additionally add a very small amount of random noise to the classifier in order to smooth out the multiplicative distance between real and experimental probabilities, effectively by increasing the minimum possible probability of events (noting that the noise is optional when the probabilities we wish to calculate experimentally are reasonably large). By solving this approximate version of the linear program, we may obtain a near-optimal derived classifier satisfying approximate fair treatment with respect to a given loss function.

However, the loss function we wish to minimize in the linear program is also potentially dependent on certain probabilities of events over $\mathcal{C}$ and $\mathcal{D}$ which require non-black-box knowledge to derive exactly; to overcome this, we show that the constructed sanitizer can in fact estimate these accurately using black-box queries by the same argument as that for the linear program's coefficients, and so, given enough samples, an approximate loss function derived from experimental probabilities is overwhelmingly likely to be close to the real loss function. Of course, while the approximation of the loss function is close, it is unclear as to whether the optimum of the approximate loss function is necessarily close to optimal over the real loss function; we show, through leveraging properties of the loss function and the space over which it is defined, that in fact this is the case for accuracy (and other loss functions, including natural classes of loss functions that are linear in the probabilities $\Pr[\sigma \leftarrow \mathcal{D} : f(\sigma) = i \wedge \mathcal{C}(O(\sigma)) = j]$), which completes our argument of near-optimality.

2 Preliminaries and Definitions

2.1 Notation

Conditional Probabilities. Given some random variable X and some event E, we let $\Pr[p(X) \mid E]$ denote the probability of a predicate $p(X)$ holding when conditioning the probability space on the event E. If the probability of E is 0, we slightly abuse notation and simply define $\Pr[p(X) \mid E] = 0$.

Multiplicative Distance. The following definition of multiplicative distance will be useful to us. We let the **multiplicative distance** $\mu(x, y)$ between two real numbers $x, y \geq 0$ be defined as

$$\mu(x,y) = \begin{cases} \ln\left(\max\left(\frac{x}{y}, \frac{y}{x}\right)\right) & \text{if } x > 0, y > 0 \\ 0 & \text{if } x = y = 0 \\ \infty & \text{otherwise} \end{cases}$$

2.2 Classification Contexts

We start by defining classification contexts and classifiers.

Definition 2. *A* ***classification context*** *$\mathcal{P}$ is denoted by a tuple $(\mathcal{D}, f, g, O)$ such that:*

- *$\mathcal{D}$ is a probability distribution with some finite support $\Sigma_{\mathcal{P}}$ (the set of all possible* ***individuals*** *to classify).*
- *$f : \Sigma_{\mathcal{P}} \to \Psi_{\mathcal{P}}$ is a surjective function that maps each individual to their* ***class*** *in a set $\Psi_{\mathcal{P}}$.*
- *$g : \Sigma_{\mathcal{P}} \to \mathbb{G}_{\mathcal{P}}$ is a surjective function that maps each individual to their* ***group*** *in a set $\mathbb{G}_{\mathcal{P}}$.*

– $O : \Sigma_{\mathcal{P}} \to \{0,1\}^* \times \mathbb{G}_{\mathcal{P}}$ *is a function that maps each individual* σ *to their* ***observable features*** $(O'(\sigma), g(\sigma))$; *note that we by default assume that an individual's group can be observed.*

We note that f and g are deterministic; this is without loss of generality as we can encode any probabilistic features that f and g may depend on into σ as "unobservable features" of the individual.

Given such a classification context $\mathcal{P}$, we let $\Psi_{\mathcal{P}}$ denote the range of f, and $\mathbb{G}_{\mathcal{P}}$ denote the range of g. Whenever the classification context $\mathcal{P}$ is clear from context, we drop the subscript; additionally, whenever the distribution $\mathcal{D}$ and group function g are clear from context, we use $\boldsymbol{\sigma}$ to denote a random variable that is distributed according to $\mathcal{D}$, and $\boldsymbol{\sigma}_X$ to denote the random variable distributed according to $\mathcal{D}$ conditioned on $g(\sigma) = X$.

2.3 Classifiers

A **classifier** $\mathcal{C}$ for a classification context $\mathcal{P} = (\mathcal{D}, f, g, O)$ is simply a (possibly randomized) algorithm that acts on the support of O (the observable description of an individual). We let $\Omega_{\mathcal{P}}^{\mathcal{C}}$ denote the support of the distribution $\{\mathcal{C}(O(\boldsymbol{\sigma}))\}$.

We also must formalize what it means for a classifier to be "derived" from another classifier; hence, we define the following notion of a classifier $\mathcal{C}'$ that "perturbs" the output of some original classifier $\mathcal{C}$. Given an individual σ, $\mathcal{C}'$ will run $\mathcal{C}$ and then "post-process" the output according only to the output $\mathcal{C}(O(\sigma))$ and σ's group.

Definition 3. *[6] Given a classifier $\mathcal{C}$, we say that a classifier $\mathcal{C}'$ is a $\mathcal{C}$-**derived** classifier if, in any context $\mathcal{P} = (\mathcal{D}, f, g, O)$, the outcome $\mathcal{C}'$ is only dependent on $\mathcal{C}(O(\sigma))$ and σ's group $g(\sigma)$. (Equivalently, $\mathcal{C}'$ is a classifier over the context $\mathcal{P}' = (\mathcal{D}, f, g, (\mathcal{C}(O(\cdot)), g(\cdot)))$.)*

Formally, we can represent this as a $|\Omega_{\mathcal{P}}^{\mathcal{C}}| \times |\Omega_{\mathcal{P}}^{\mathcal{C}}| \times |\mathbb{G}_{\mathcal{P}}|$ vector $\vec{P}_{\mathcal{C}'}$ of the probabilities

$$P_{i,j}^g = Pr[\mathcal{C}'(\mathcal{C}(O(\boldsymbol{\sigma}_g)), g) = j | \mathcal{C}(O(\boldsymbol{\sigma}_g)) = i]$$

and let $\mathcal{C}'$ be a classifier that, given an individual σ, runs $\mathcal{C}$ on that individual, observes its outcome $i = \mathcal{C}(O(\sigma))$ and group $g(\sigma)$, and assigns that individual the distribution of outcomes $\{j$ with pr. $P_{i,j}^g\}$.

3 Defining Fair Treatment

Next, we define the notion of *fair treatment* for a classifier $\mathcal{C}$, which is an approximate version of the notion of "equalized odds" from Hardt et al. [6] (which in turn was derived from notions implicit in the ProPublica study [2]).

Definition 4. *(Fair treatment, a.k.a. approximate equalized odds [6].) We say that a classifier $\mathcal{C}$ satisfies ϵ-**fair treatment** with respect to a context $\mathcal{P}$ =*

$(\mathcal{D}, f, g, O)$ *if, for any groups* $X, Y \in \mathbb{G}_\mathcal{P}$*, any class* $c \in \Psi_\mathcal{P}$*, and any outcome* $o \in \Omega^\mathcal{C}_\mathcal{P}$*, we have that*

$$\mu(Pr[\mathcal{C}(O(\boldsymbol{\sigma}_X)) = o \mid f(\boldsymbol{\sigma}_X) = c], Pr[\mathcal{C}(O(\boldsymbol{\sigma}_Y)) = o \mid f(\boldsymbol{\sigma}_Y) = c]) \leq \epsilon$$

For the case of binary classification tasks and binary classifiers (i.e., when $\Psi_\mathcal{P} = \Omega^\mathcal{C}_\mathcal{P} = \{0, 1\}$), fair treatment is equivalent to requiring "similar" false positive and false negative rates [7].

3.1 On the Use of Multiplicative Distance

As defined here, fair treatment essentially requires that the *max-divergence* between the conditional distributions of outcomes is small between groups. Max-divergence is a distance measure often found in areas such as differential privacy (see [4]); we stress here, through two arguments following very similar logic to differential privacy, that using such a multiplicative distance is important to ensure fairness between groups that may be under-represented in the data, and also that fair treatment defined using multiplicative distance exhibits desirable properties that other distance metrics may not.

First, to motivate our statement that multiplicative distances are important for parity between under-represented groups, consider as an example a classifier used to determine whether to search people for weapons. Assume such a classifier determined to search 1% of minorities at random, but *only* the minorities (and no others). Such a classifier would still have a fair treatment error of 0.01 if we used standard statistical distance, while the max-divergence would in fact be infinite (and indeed, such a classification would be blatantly discriminatory).

Our use of max-divergence between distributions for our definitions is reflective of the fact that, in cases where we have such small probabilities, discrimination should be measured multiplicatively, rather than additively. In addition, when we may have a large number of possible classes, the use of max-divergence (in particular, the *maximum* of the log-probability ratios) means that we always look at the class with the *most* disparity to determine how discriminatory a classification is, rather than potentially amortizing this disparity over a large number of classes.

3.2 Closure Under Post-processing

We also remark that our definition of fair treatment is closed under "post-processing". If a classifier $\mathcal{C}$ satisfies ϵ-fair treatment with respect to a context $\mathcal{P} = (\mathcal{D}, f, g, O)$, then any $\mathcal{C}$-derived classifier *which acts independently of an individual's group* (i.e., whose decision is based only on the outcome of $\mathcal{C}$) will also satisfy ϵ-fair treatment with respect to $\mathcal{P}$.

Theorem 2. *Let* $\mathcal{C}_1$ *be a classifier satisfying* ϵ*-fair treatment with respect to context* $\mathcal{P} = (\mathcal{D}, f, g, O)$*. Let* $\mathcal{C}_2$ *be any classifier whose output for an individual* σ *is strictly a (possibly probabilistic) function of* $\mathcal{C}_1(O(\sigma))$*. Then* $\mathcal{C}_2$ *satisfies* ϵ*-fair treatment with respect to* $\mathcal{P}$*.*

Proof. Let $\mathcal{C}_1$ be a classifier satisfying ϵ-fair treatment w.r.t. some context $\mathcal{P}$. Consider some groups $X, Y \in \mathbb{G}_{\mathcal{P}}$, some class $c \in \Psi_{\mathcal{P}}$, and some outcome $o \in \Omega_{\mathcal{P}}^{\mathcal{C}'}$; we need to show that

$$\mu(\Pr[\mathcal{C}_2(\mathcal{C}_1(O(\boldsymbol{\sigma}_X))) = o \mid f(\boldsymbol{\sigma}_X) = c], \Pr[\mathcal{C}_2(\mathcal{C}_1(O(\boldsymbol{\sigma}_Y))) = o \mid f(\boldsymbol{\sigma}_Y) = c]) \leq \epsilon$$

Towards doing this, note that

$$\begin{aligned}
&\Pr[\mathcal{C}_2(\mathcal{C}_1(O(\boldsymbol{\sigma}_X))) = o | f(\boldsymbol{\sigma}_X) = c] \\
&= \sum_{o_1 \in \Omega_{\mathcal{P}}^{\mathcal{C}_1}} \Pr[\mathcal{C}_2(o_1) = o | f(\boldsymbol{\sigma}_X) = c, \mathcal{C}_1(O(\boldsymbol{\sigma}_X)) = o_1] \Pr[\mathcal{C}_1(O(\boldsymbol{\sigma}_X)) = o_1 | f(\boldsymbol{\sigma}_X) = c] \\
&= \sum_{o_1 \in \Omega_{\mathcal{P}}^{\mathcal{C}_1}} \Pr[\mathcal{C}_2(o_1) = o] \Pr[\mathcal{C}_1(O(\boldsymbol{\sigma}_X)) = o_1 | f(\boldsymbol{\sigma}_X) = c]
\end{aligned}$$

where the last step follows from the fact that $\mathcal{C}_2$ depends only on $\mathcal{C}_1$. By the same argument applied to Y, we also have that:

$$\begin{aligned}
&\Pr[\mathcal{C}_2(\mathcal{C}_1(O(\boldsymbol{\sigma}_Y))) = o \mid f(\boldsymbol{\sigma}_Y) = c] \\
&= \sum_{o_1 \in \Omega_{\mathcal{P}}^{\mathcal{C}_1}} \Pr[\mathcal{C}_2(o_1) = o] \Pr[\mathcal{C}_1(O(\boldsymbol{\sigma}_Y)) = o_1 \mid f(\boldsymbol{\sigma}_Y) = c]
\end{aligned}$$

These two probabilities are ϵ-close since, by fair treatment, $\Pr[\mathcal{C}_1(O(\boldsymbol{\sigma}_X)) = o_1 \mid f(\boldsymbol{\sigma}_X) = c]$ and $\Pr[\mathcal{C}_1(O(\boldsymbol{\sigma}_Y)) = o_1 \mid f(\boldsymbol{\sigma}_Y) = c]$ are ϵ-close, and furthermore multiplicative distance is preserved under linear operations[5]. This proves the theorem. □

We also remark that, in general, earlier "expectation-based" definitions of fair treatment are not preserved under post-processing.

4 Black-Box Sanitization

Next, we provide a novel definition of the type of sanitizer we shall construct in our main theorem.

For the purposes of defining a "computationally efficient" sanitizer, let us define a notion of an "ensemble" of classification contexts, wherein we assume a parameter n (similar to the idea of a security parameter in cryptography) so that each individual's observable features can be represented in n bits. In particular, this means that, for some setting of n there may be up to 2^n distinct descriptions of individuals in a distribution $\mathcal{D}$, and so a *computationally efficient* black-box classifier which runs in polynomial time with respect to n could not, for instance, query every possible feature description.

Definition 5. *Let a **classification context ensemble** Π be given by a sequence of classification contexts $\{\mathcal{P}_n\}_{n \in \mathbb{N}} = \{(\mathcal{D}, f, g, O_n)\}_{n \in \mathbb{N}}$ (note that $\mathcal{D}, f, g$ remain the same as n varies), such that, whenever $2^n \geq |\mathbb{G}_{\mathcal{P}_n}|$ (i.e., n is sufficiently large to describe $g(\sigma)$), O_n maps the space $\Sigma_{\mathcal{P}_n}$ of individuals to $\{0,1\}^n$, the space of n-bit descriptions.*

[5] That is, if $\mu(a, b) \leq \epsilon$ and $\mu(a', b') \leq \epsilon$ then $\mu(\alpha a + \beta a', \alpha b + \beta b') \leq \epsilon$.

Notably, the contexts are effectively describing the same distribution of individuals, but using different feature lengths for each context in the ensemble. Also, because $\mathcal{D}$, f, and g are the same throughout, this implies that the space of individuals $\Sigma_{\mathcal{P}_n}$ and the class and group spaces $\Psi_{\mathcal{P}_n}$ and $\mathbb{G}_{\mathcal{P}_n}$ are likewise the same for every n.

In our proofs, we will also consider deriving our classifier from a *sequence* of prior classifiers $\chi = \{\mathcal{C}_n\}_{n\in\mathbb{N}}$, where the classifier $\mathcal{C}_i$ is used to classify individuals in the context $\mathcal{P}_i$ (that is, individuals having feature length i).

Lastly, we wish to represent the fact that a sanitizer may, given a prior classifier sequence χ over a distribution ensemble Π, wish to make black-box queries to a distribution of labeled "training data" representing individuals' observable features, classes, groups, and prior classifications. We shall denote this distribution for a specific parameter n by

$$\tau_{\chi,\Pi}(1^n) \triangleq \{\sigma \leftarrow \mathcal{D} : (O_n(\sigma), f(\sigma), \mathcal{C}_n(O_n(\sigma)), g(\sigma))\}$$

Notationally, let $\mathcal{B}^{\tau_{\chi,\Pi}}(1^n)$[6] denote that a sanitizer $\mathcal{B}$ may make black-box queries to the distribution $\tau_{\chi,\Pi}(1^n)$ for some parameter n. Finally, we are able to formalize the notion of a "black-box sanitizer" given the above:

Definition 6. *We say that an algorithm $\mathcal{B}^{(\cdot)}$ is an $\epsilon(\cdot)$-**black-box sanitizer** if it is:*

- Efficient: *there exists a polynomial $p(\cdot,\cdot)$ such that, for any $m \in \mathbb{N}$, and for any context ensemble $\Pi = \{\mathcal{P}_n\}_{n\in\mathbb{N}}$ and sequence $\chi = \{\mathcal{C}_n\}_{n\in\mathbb{N}}$ of classifiers for which $|\Psi_{\mathcal{P}_n}| \leq m$, $|\mathbb{G}_{\mathcal{P}_n}| \leq m$, and $|\Omega^{\mathcal{C}_n}_{\mathcal{P}_n}| \leq m$ (i.e., the class, group, and output spaces have size bounded by m), $\mathcal{B}^{\tau_{\chi,\Pi}}(1^n)$ runs in time at most $p(m,n)$ for all $n \in \mathbb{N}$.*
- Fair: *for any context ensemble $\Pi = \{\mathcal{P}_n\}_{n\in\mathbb{N}}$ and any sequence $\chi = \{\mathcal{C}_n\}_{n\in\mathbb{N}}$ of classifiers, there exists negligible $\nu(\cdot)$[7] such that, for all $n \in \mathbb{N}$, with probability at least $(1-\nu(n))$ over the samples it queries from $\tau_{\chi,\Pi}(1^n)$, $\mathcal{B}^{\tau_{\chi,\Pi}}(1^n)$ outputs a $\mathcal{C}_n$-derived classifier $\mathcal{C}'$[8] which satisfies $\epsilon(n)$-fair treatment with respect to $\mathcal{P}_n$.*

4.1 Loss Functions

Lastly, we need to define "optimality" for derived classifiers in this context. In particular, we assume some loss function $\ell(\cdot)$ bounded in $[0,1]$ which may either be fixed or based on $\mathcal{D}$, f, and $\mathcal{C}$ (in which case we write $\ell_{\mathcal{D},f,\mathcal{C}}(\cdot)$ for clarity). Intuitively, $\ell(\mathcal{C}')$ represents the "loss" in utility incurred by classifying an individual σ with outcome $\mathcal{C}'(O(\sigma))$ when their actual class is $f(\sigma)$. As a

[6] The input of 1^n, or a string of n ones, is provided simply as a cryptographic convention, so that we can assert that the running time of $\mathcal{B}$ is polynomial in its input length. When implicit or clear from context, we shall for notational simplicity omit this input.

[7] That is, $\nu(n) < 1/p(n)$ for every polynomial $p(\cdot)$ and sufficiently large n.

[8] That is, $\mathcal{B}$ outputs the probabilities $\vec{P}_{\mathcal{C}'}$ corresponding to the derived classifier $\mathcal{C}'$.

concrete example, if we consider classifiers which attempt to classify each individual according to their correct class $f(\sigma) \in \Psi$, one might consider the *overall inaccuracy* as a loss function, which is given by:

$$\ell_{\mathcal{D},f,\mathcal{C}}(\mathcal{C}') = 1 - \Pr\left[\mathcal{C}'(O(\boldsymbol{\sigma})) = f(\boldsymbol{\sigma})\right]$$

We can define the *error* of a derived classifier to be its loss compared to the optimal *perfectly fair* derived classifier, as follows:

Definition 7. *For some context $\mathcal{P} = (\mathcal{D}, f, g, O)$ and prior classifier $\mathcal{C}$, given some loss function $\ell_{\mathcal{D},f,\mathcal{C}}$ that maps any classifier to its loss in $[0, 1]$, letting $\mathcal{S}$ be the set of all $\mathcal{C}$-derived classifiers satisfying (errorless) 0-fair treatment, then we define the **error** of some $\mathcal{C}$-derived classifier $\mathcal{C}'$ with respect to $\ell_{\mathcal{D},f,\mathcal{C}}$ to be*

$$\Delta_{\ell,\mathcal{D},f,\mathcal{C}}(\mathcal{C}') = \ max_{\mathcal{C}^* \in \mathcal{S}}(\ell_{\mathcal{D},f,\mathcal{C}}(\mathcal{C}') - \ell_{\mathcal{D},f,\mathcal{C}}(\mathcal{C}^*))$$

We note that, because we compare a classifier (which may be only approximately fair) to the optimal *perfectly* fair classifier, certain particularly good classifiers may in fact have a negative loss. We could, when considering ϵ-approximately fair classifiers, generalize this notion to consider the loss over all $f(\epsilon)$-fair classifiers for some $f(\epsilon) < \epsilon$ and derive a similar optimality result to what we prove here, but for simplicity and consistency over different parameters ϵ we consider the case when $f(\epsilon) = 0$.

Linear Loss Functions. Furthermore, with respect to derived classifiers, we consider the class of loss functions $\ell_{\mathcal{D},f,\mathcal{C}}$ which are *linear* in the probabilities $P^g_{i,j}$ constituting the derived classifier—that is:

Definition 8. *We say that a loss function $\ell_{\mathcal{D},f,\mathcal{C}}(\cdot)$ is a **linear** loss function for a context $\mathcal{P} = (\mathcal{D}, f, g, O)$ and prior classifier $\mathcal{C}$ if it can be represented as some $|\Omega^{\mathcal{C}}_{\mathcal{P}}| \times |\Omega^{\mathcal{C}}_{\mathcal{P}}| \times |\mathbb{G}_{\mathcal{P}}|$ vector $\vec{\ell}_{\mathcal{D},f,\mathcal{C}}$ so that the loss of a derived classifier $\mathcal{C}'$ is given as the inner product*

$$\langle \vec{\ell}_{\mathcal{D},f,\mathcal{C}}, \vec{P}_{\mathcal{C}'} \rangle = \sum_{i,j \in \Omega^{\mathcal{C}}_{\mathcal{P}}, g \in \mathbb{G}_{\mathcal{P}}} (\vec{\ell}_{\mathcal{D},f,\mathcal{C}})^g_{i,j} P^g_{i,j}$$

of this vector with the probabilities constituting the derived classifier $\mathcal{C}'$.

We can define error slightly more specifically for linear loss functions using the vector form:

$$\Delta_{\vec{\ell},\mathcal{D},f,\mathcal{C}}(\mathcal{C}') = \ \max_{\mathcal{C}^* \in \mathcal{S}}(\langle \vec{\ell}_{\mathcal{D},f,\mathcal{C}}, \vec{P}_{\mathcal{C}'} \rangle - \langle \vec{\ell}_{\mathcal{D},f,\mathcal{C}}, \vec{P}_{\mathcal{C}^*} \rangle)$$

We will focus on the specific subclass of linear loss functions whose coefficients (the coefficients of $P^g_{i,j}$) can either be constant or up to d^{th}-degree polynomials in probabilities $\Pr[g(\boldsymbol{\sigma}) = \gamma]$ and $\Pr[f(\boldsymbol{\sigma}_g) = i \wedge \mathcal{C}(O(\boldsymbol{\sigma}_g)) = j]$, which can be formalized as follows:

Definition 9. *We shall define a* **linear loss function with** ***t*****-term coefficients of degree** d *as one that can be represented as*

$$\ell_{\mathcal{D},f,\mathcal{C}}(\mathcal{C}') = \sum_{i,j,g} q^g_{i,j}(\rho) P^g_{i,j}$$

or equivalently

$$(\vec{\ell}_{\mathcal{D},f,\mathcal{C}})^g_{i,j} = q^g_{i,j}(\rho)$$

where ρ *denotes the set of all variables given by the probabilities* $Pr[g(\boldsymbol{\sigma}) = \gamma]$ *and* $Pr[f(\boldsymbol{\sigma}_g) = x \wedge \mathcal{C}(O(\boldsymbol{\sigma}_g)) = y]$ *(for any* γ, x, y*),* $P^g_{i,j}$ *is the vector representation of* $\mathcal{C}'$*, and each* $q^g_{i,j}(\cdot)$ *is a* d^{th}*-degree polynomial in the variables of* ρ *which contains at most* t *monomials which themselves are bounded in* $[0, 1]$ *whenever the variables in* ρ *are likewise bounded.*

We note that overall inaccuracy as described above is in fact a linear loss function with $(|\Omega^{\mathcal{C}}_{\mathcal{P}}|-1)$-term coefficients of degree 2, as we shall shortly demonstrate; furthermore, a wide variety of other useful loss functions are also linear with degree-2 coefficients. Returning to the example of COMPAS from the introduction, for instance, we see that the space of outcomes is a "risk score" from 1 to 10, while the space of classes is binary (either recidivating or not), so rather than overall accuracy (which as noted above requires the spaces to be identical) we will need another notion of loss. We exhibit three useful loss functions for this scenario in the experimental evaluation section in the full version, all of which will have degree-2 coefficients, which we will use to evaluate the quality of the fair classifiers we derive from COMPAS. Returning to investigating the notion of overall inaccuracy:

Claim 1. *For a context* $\mathcal{P}$ *and for any classifier with* $\Omega^{\mathcal{C}}_{\mathcal{P}} = \Psi_{\mathcal{P}} = \mathcal{O}$*, the overall inaccuracy loss function*

$$\ell_{\mathcal{D},f,\mathcal{C}}(\mathcal{C}') = 1 - Pr[\mathcal{C}'(O(\boldsymbol{\sigma})) = f(\boldsymbol{\sigma})]$$

is a linear loss function with $(|\Omega^{\mathcal{C}}_{\mathcal{P}}| - 1)$*-term coefficients of degree 2.*

Proof. The inaccuracy of a classifier, conditioning on a group g, can be expressed as a linear function in $P^g_{i,j}$ if $\mathcal{D}, f, \mathcal{C}$ are fixed:

$$\begin{aligned}
\Pr[f(\boldsymbol{\sigma}_g) \neq \mathcal{C}'(O(\boldsymbol{\sigma}_g))] &= 1 - \Pr[f(\boldsymbol{\sigma}_g) = \mathcal{C}'(O(\boldsymbol{\sigma}_g))] \\
&= 1 - \sum_{j \in \mathcal{O}} \Pr[f(\boldsymbol{\sigma}_g) = j \wedge \mathcal{C}'(O(\boldsymbol{\sigma}_g)) = j] \\
&= 1 - \sum_{i,j \in \mathcal{O}} \Pr[f(\boldsymbol{\sigma}_g) = j \wedge \mathcal{C}(O(\boldsymbol{\sigma}_g)) = i \wedge \mathcal{C}'(O(\boldsymbol{\sigma}_g)) = j] \\
&= 1 - \sum_{i,j \in \mathcal{O}} \Pr[f(\boldsymbol{\sigma}_g) = j \wedge \mathcal{C}(O(\boldsymbol{\sigma}_g)) = i] \Pr[\mathcal{C}'(O(\boldsymbol{\sigma}_g)) \\
&= j | f(\boldsymbol{\sigma}_g) = j \wedge \mathcal{C}(O(\boldsymbol{\sigma}_g)) = i]
\end{aligned}$$

Recalling that the output of $\mathcal{C}'$ is based only on an individual's group and the output of $\mathcal{C}$:

$$= 1 - \sum_{i,j \in \mathcal{O}} \Pr\left[f(\boldsymbol{\sigma}_g) = j \wedge \mathcal{C}(O(\boldsymbol{\sigma}_g)) = i\right] \Pr\left[\mathcal{C}'(O(\boldsymbol{\sigma}_g)) = j | \mathcal{C}(O(\boldsymbol{\sigma}_g)) = i\right]$$

$$= 1 - \sum_{i,j \in \mathcal{O}} \Pr\left[f(\boldsymbol{\sigma}_g) = j \wedge \mathcal{C}(O(\boldsymbol{\sigma}_g)) = i\right] P^g_{i,j}$$

This can be expanded into the overall inaccuracy of $\mathcal{C}'$ if we sum over groups, i.e.,

$$1 - \sum_{i,j \in \mathcal{O}; \gamma \in \mathbb{G}_{\mathcal{P}}} \Pr\left[g(\boldsymbol{\sigma}) = \gamma\right] \Pr\left[f(\boldsymbol{\sigma}_\gamma) = j \wedge \mathcal{C}(O(\boldsymbol{\sigma}_\gamma)) = i\right] P^\gamma_{i,j}$$

or, equivalently,

$$\sum_{i,j \in \mathcal{O}; \gamma \in \mathbb{G}_{\mathcal{P}}} \Pr\left[g(\boldsymbol{\sigma}) = \gamma\right] \sum_{k \neq j} \Pr\left[f(\boldsymbol{\sigma}_\gamma) = k \wedge \mathcal{C}(O(\boldsymbol{\sigma}_\gamma)) = i\right] P^\gamma_{i,j}$$

This suggests that we can, as previously described, write this loss function as a vector $\vec{\ell}_{\mathcal{D},f,\mathcal{C}}$ over the space of probabilities $P^\gamma_{i,j}$, in particular such that

$$(\vec{\ell}_{\mathcal{D},f,\mathcal{C}})^\gamma_{i,j} = \Pr\left[g(\boldsymbol{\sigma}) = \gamma\right] \sum_{k \neq j} \Pr\left[f(\boldsymbol{\sigma}_\gamma) = k \wedge \mathcal{C}(O(\boldsymbol{\sigma}_\gamma)) = i\right]$$

Notably, each of these coefficients has $\mathcal{O} - 1 = |\Omega^{\mathcal{C}}_{\mathcal{P}}| - 1$ monomials bounded in $[0, 1]$ which are degree 2 in the probabilities of the form $\Pr\left[g(\boldsymbol{\sigma}) = \gamma\right]$ and $\Pr\left[f(\boldsymbol{\sigma}_g) = x \wedge \mathcal{C}(O(\boldsymbol{\sigma}_g)) = y\right]$, as desired. □

5 Theorem: Achieving Fair Treatment by Post-processing

We now show that it is possible to achieve fair treatment, even in non-binary classification scenarios, by post-processing starting from a prior classification that may be unfair. We note that, though our theorems only state existence, we provide our concrete construction of the black-box sanitizer in the body of the proof. Focusing first on the specific example above where we use inaccuracy as a loss function, we show the following positive result:

Theorem 3. *For any fixed outcome space Ω, any polynomial $q(n)$, and any $\epsilon(n) \in [\frac{1}{q(n)}, 1)$, there exists an $\epsilon(\cdot)$-black-box sanitizer $\mathcal{B}$ which, given any context ensemble $\Pi = \{\mathcal{P}_n\}_{n \in \mathbb{N}}$ (such that $|\mathbb{G}_{\mathcal{P}_n}| = m$) and any classifier sequence χ such that $\Psi_{\mathcal{P}_n} = \Omega^{\mathcal{C}_n}_{\mathcal{P}_n} = \Omega$, there exists negligible $\nu(\cdot)$ such that, with probability $1 - \nu(n)$ over the samples it queries from $\tau_{\chi,\Pi}(1^n)$, $\mathcal{B}$ outputs a classifier $\mathcal{C}''$ which both satisfies $\epsilon(n)$-fair treatment and has error*

$$\Delta_{\ell,\mathcal{D},f,\mathcal{C}}(\mathcal{C}'') \leq |\Omega|(\epsilon(n) + m(|\Omega| - 1)\epsilon(n)^4/32)$$

with respect to the overall inaccuracy loss function

$$\ell_{\mathcal{D},f,\mathcal{C}}(\mathcal{C}'') = 1 - Pr[\mathcal{C}''(O(\boldsymbol{\sigma})) = f(\boldsymbol{\sigma})]$$

This is in fact implied directly by the following more general result, which we shall prove in its stead:

Theorem 4. *For any fixed outcome space Ω, any polynomial $q(n)$, and any $\epsilon(n) \in [\frac{1}{q(n)}, 1)$, there exists an $\epsilon(\cdot)$-black-box sanitizer $\mathcal{B}$ which, given any context ensemble $\Pi = \{\mathcal{P}_n\}_{n\in\mathbb{N}}$ and any classifier sequence χ, there exists negligible $\nu(\cdot)$ such that, with probability $1 - \nu(n)$ over the samples it queries from $\tau_{\chi,\Pi}(1^n)$, $\mathcal{B}$ outputs a classifier $\mathcal{C}''$ which both satisfies $\epsilon(n)$-fair treatment and has error*

$$\Delta_{\ell,\mathcal{D},f,\mathcal{C}}(\mathcal{C}'') \leq |\Omega_{\mathcal{P}_n}^{\mathcal{C}_n}|(\epsilon(n) + |\mathbb{G}_{\mathcal{P}_n}|\epsilon(n)^4 dt/64)$$

with respect to any linear loss function with t-term coefficients of degree d.

In the example above where we consider overall inaccuracy, we have (by Claim 1) $d = 2$ and $t = |\Omega| - 1$, directly implying Theorem 3. Next, we outline the proof of Theorem 4:

Achieving Fair Treatment with Distributional Knowledge. We begin with the simplifying assumption that the sanitizer we construct does have perfect knowledge of the context Π and classifier $\chi = \{\mathcal{C}_n\}_{n\in\mathbb{N}}$, and we show (Claim 2) that for each n we can use the probabilities of events in those distributions to construct a set of linear constraints for fair treatment over the probabilities $P_{i,j}^g = \Pr[\mathcal{C}'(O(\boldsymbol{\sigma}_g)) = j | \mathcal{C}_n(O(\boldsymbol{\sigma}_g)) = i]$. Then, given a loss function which is also linear in $P_{i,j}^g$, we can construct a linear program (Corollary 1) to efficiently minimize loss subject to the constraints for fair treatment. Since, by construction, any $\mathcal{C}_n$-derived $\mathcal{C}'(\sigma)$ which satisfies fair treatment will lie within the region determined by our constraints, we have shown that it is possible to efficiently determine the optimal fair $\mathcal{C}_n$-derived classifier (with respect to any linear loss function) in a non-black-box setting.

Black-Box Approximation. Next, we work towards discarding the assumption of non-black-box knowledge of Π and χ. In particular, we use a Chernoff-type bound to show (Lemma 3) that, given a sufficiently large (yet still polynomial in n) number of labeled and classified samples from $\tau_{\chi,\Pi}(1^n)$, with very high probability (i.e., probability $1 - \nu(n)$) all of the experimental probabilities relevant to our linear program will be close enough to their actual counterparts so that any solution to the linear program formulated from the experimental probabilities will also satisfy approximate fair treatment with respect to the actual probabilities. However, we note that the Chernoff bound will only apply when the real probabilities of the events in question are sufficiently large; if we are not guaranteed that this is the case, we additionally add a very small amount of noise to the classifier $\mathcal{C}'$ to deal with the possibility that events with very small real probability are measured to have a wildly different experimental probability due to sampling variance. This random noise will ensure that these events are accounted for when approximating the linear program while adding only a minimal error to the approximation. So, combined with the previous step, this suggests the approach that we will use to construct the final sanitizer $\mathcal{B}$; specifically, we can do as follows:

- Use a sufficiently large (yet polynomial in n) number of samples from the training distribution $\tau_{\mathcal{X},\Pi}(1^n)$ to estimate the parameters of the linear constraints from the previous step, in particular using a fairness error significantly smaller than $\epsilon(n)$ in order to account for variance in samples and random noise that will be added, yet one large enough to not rule out optimal classifiers that may not be perfectly fair. Also use the samples to estimate any distributionally dependent parameters of the loss function.
- Use standard linear programming techniques to optimize the derived loss function over the derived constraint region in polynomial time, and take the optimal solution as the "transformation parameters" of a derived classifier $\mathcal{C}'$ (i.e., the probabilities $P_{i,j}^g$).
- Output the (slightly noisy) classifier $\mathcal{C}''$ which, except with a small probability, applies the transformation given by the above solution to the output of the prior classifier; the rest of the time, it returns a random outcome.

If parameterized correctly, this classifier will still satisfy ϵ-approximate fairness whenever all of the above Chernoff bounds hold; furthermore, as we subsequently show, the output will also not incur much loss due to estimating parameters and adding noise when these bounds hold.

Showing Near-Optimality. In particular, we must account both for the noise added to the solution $\mathcal{C}'$ to the linear program and for the fact that the loss function over which $\mathcal{B}$ optimizes may be imprecise, as we have remarked that loss functions such as accuracy are in general dependent on features of the context or the classifier (which our sanitizer must estimate using samples). However, once again, we show (Claim 5) that this can be overcome by using another Chernoff-type bound (Lemma 4) to show that, with high probability, the experimentally derived coefficients of the loss function are very close to the corresponding coefficients of the actual loss function. Then we demonstrate that a slightly noisy variant of the optimal $\mathcal{C}_n$-derived classifier is always derivable by $\mathcal{B}$ when the bounds hold, and furthermore use linearity to show that, in that case, the actual loss of the output $\mathcal{C}''$ must not differ by much from that of the optimal $\mathcal{C}_n$-derived classifier (in particular, the possible degree of difference depends on the degree and number of terms of the loss function's coefficients and the number of variables, i.e., the number of groups and outcomes possible), even when the intermediate classifier $\mathcal{C}'$ itself might differ from this classifier due to the optimum over the approximate loss function being different from the optimum over the actual loss function.

Notation. For brevity and notational simplicity, in the body of the proof we will abbreviate the probability $\Pr[E(\sigma_g)]$ (i.e., the probability of some event E holding for σ drawn from group g) as $\Pr_g[E(\sigma)]$, and the probability $\Pr[g(\sigma) = \gamma]$ as $\Pr[\gamma]$.

Furthermore, we abbreviate the event $f(\sigma) = i$ as f_i, and similarly for any classifier $\mathcal{C}$ abbreviate $\mathcal{C}(O(\sigma)) = i$ as $\mathcal{C}_i$.

5.1 Step 1: Achieving Fair Treatment

For our first step, we prove the following result, showing that an optimal derived classifier can always be found efficiently given "perfect" knowledge of a context and a prior classifier:

Claim 2. *Let $\mathcal{C}$ be an arbitrary classifier over context $\mathcal{P} = (\mathcal{D}, f, g, O)$. Then there exists a set of polynomially many (in $|\Psi_\mathcal{P}|$, $|\mathbb{G}_\mathcal{P}|$, and $|\Omega^\mathcal{C}_\mathcal{P}|$) satisfiable linear constraints in the variables $P^g_{i,j} = Pr_g[\mathcal{C}'(\sigma) = j | \mathcal{C}(\sigma) = i]$ that define the set of $\mathcal{C}$-derived classifiers $\mathcal{C}'$ which satisfy ϵ-fair treatment with respect to $\mathcal{P}$.*

Corollary 1. *Let $\mathcal{C}$ be an arbitrary classifier over context $\mathcal{P} = (\mathcal{D}, f, g, O)$, and let $\ell_{\mathcal{D},f,\mathcal{C}}$ be a loss function which is linear over the probabilities $P^g_{i,j}$ as defined above. Then the $\mathcal{C}$-derived $\mathcal{C}'$ which minimizes $\ell_{\mathcal{D},f,\mathcal{C}}(\cdot)$ while satisfying ϵ-fair treatment with respect to $\mathcal{P}$ can be found efficiently (i.e., in time polynomial in $|\Psi_\mathcal{P}|$, $|\mathbb{G}_\mathcal{P}|$, and $|\Omega^\mathcal{C}_\mathcal{P}|$)*[9].

The corollary will follow immediately from Claim 2 by the efficiency of solving linear programs (that is, the well-known fact that a linear program with a polynomial number of variables and constraints may be solved in polynomial time). We now prove Claim 2:

Proof. Assume we have a discrete classifier $\mathcal{C}$ that classifies individuals from a context $\mathcal{P} = (\mathcal{D}, f, g, O)$, and we wish to produce $\mathcal{C}'$ that satisfies ϵ-fair treatment with respect to $\mathcal{P}$. Consider the $\mathcal{C}$-derived classifier defined by the set of $|\mathbb{G}_\mathcal{P}||\Omega^\mathcal{C}_\mathcal{P}|^2$ variables

$$P^g_{i,j} = \Pr_g[\mathcal{C}'_j | \mathcal{C}_i]$$

for $i, j \in \Omega^\mathcal{C}_\mathcal{P}$ and $g \in \mathbb{G}_\mathcal{P}$.

Next, we directly translate the definition of fair treatment into a set of constraints, which represents the space of all possible derived classifiers satisfying ϵ-fair treatment:

$$\forall i, j \in \Omega^\mathcal{C}_\mathcal{P}, \forall g \in \mathbb{G}_\mathcal{P} : P^g_{i,j} \in [0, 1]$$

$$\forall i \in \Omega^\mathcal{C}_\mathcal{P}, \forall g \in \mathbb{G}_\mathcal{P} : \sum_{j \in \Omega^\mathcal{C}_\mathcal{P}} P^g_{i,j} = 1$$

$$\forall j \in \Omega^\mathcal{C}_\mathcal{P}, \forall k \in \Psi_\mathcal{P}, \forall X, Y \in \mathbb{G}_\mathcal{P} : \Pr_X[\mathcal{C}'_j | f_k] \leq e^\epsilon \Pr_Y[\mathcal{C}'_j | f_k]$$

[9] If $\ell_{\mathcal{D},f,\mathcal{C}}(\cdot)$ is not linear, it is of course findable, but not necessarily efficiently, as we no longer have a linear program.

Notice, however, that:

$$\Pr_g\left[\mathcal{C}'_j|f_k\right] = \frac{1}{\Pr_g\left[f_k\right]}\left(\Pr_g\left[f_k \wedge \mathcal{C}'_j\right]\right) = \frac{1}{\Pr_g\left[f_k\right]}\left(\sum_{i\in\Omega^{\mathcal{C}}_{\mathcal{P}}} \Pr_g\left[f_k \wedge \mathcal{C}'_j \wedge \mathcal{C}_i\right]\right)$$

As observed earlier (see the proof of Claim 1), because we assign outcomes in $\mathcal{C}'$ based only on $\mathcal{C}$ and $g(\sigma)$, it must be the case that $\Pr_g\left[\mathcal{C}'_j|\mathcal{C}_i\right] = \Pr_g\left[\mathcal{C}'_j|\mathcal{C}_i \wedge f_k\right]$, or, expanding using conditional probability,

$$\frac{\Pr_g\left[\mathcal{C}'_j \wedge \mathcal{C}_i\right]}{\Pr_g\left[\mathcal{C}_i\right]} = \frac{\Pr_g\left[f_k \wedge \mathcal{C}'_j \wedge \mathcal{C}_i\right]}{\Pr_g\left[f_k \wedge \mathcal{C}_i\right]}$$

which implies

$$\begin{aligned}\Pr_g\left[f_k \wedge \mathcal{C}'_j \wedge \mathcal{C}_i\right] &= \frac{\Pr_g\left[f_k \wedge \mathcal{C}_i\right]\Pr_g\left[\mathcal{C}'_j \wedge \mathcal{C}_i\right]}{\Pr_g\left[\mathcal{C}_i\right]}\\ &= \Pr_g\left[f_k \wedge \mathcal{C}_i\right]\Pr_g\left[\mathcal{C}'_j|\mathcal{C}_i\right] = \Pr_g\left[f_k \wedge \mathcal{C}_i\right]P^g_{i,j}\end{aligned}$$

So our conditions of the form $\Pr_X\left[\mathcal{C}'_j|f_k\right] \le e^{\epsilon}\Pr_Y\left[\mathcal{C}'_j|f_k\right]$ can be rewritten (after substituting and multiplying through) as

$$\Pr_Y\left[f_k\right]\left(\sum_{i\in\Omega^{\mathcal{C}}_{\mathcal{P}}} \Pr_X\left[f_k \wedge \mathcal{C}_i\right]P^X_{i,j}\right) \le e^{\epsilon}\Pr_X\left[f_k\right]\left(\sum_{i\in\Omega^{\mathcal{C}}_{\mathcal{P}}} \Pr_Y\left[f_k \wedge \mathcal{C}_i\right]P^Y_{i,j}\right)$$

We can also reformat the second set of conditions into inequality constraints by selecting $j^* \in \Omega^{\mathcal{C}}_{\mathcal{P}}$, replacing each P^g_{i,j^*} with $1 - \sum_{j\in\Omega^{\mathcal{C}}_{\mathcal{P}}\setminus j^*} P^g_{i,j}$, and requiring $\sum_{j\in\Omega^{\mathcal{C}}_{\mathcal{P}}\setminus j^*} P^g_{i,j} \le 1$. Then our final set of constraints becomes:

$$\forall i \in \Omega^{\mathcal{C}}_{\mathcal{P}}, \forall j \in \Omega^{\mathcal{C}}_{\mathcal{P}} \setminus j^*, \forall g \in \mathbb{G}_{\mathcal{P}} : P^g_{i,j} \ge 0, P^g_{i,j} \le 1$$

$$\forall i \in \Omega^{\mathcal{C}}_{\mathcal{P}}, \forall g \in \mathbb{G}_{\mathcal{P}} : \sum_{j\in\Omega^{\mathcal{C}}_{\mathcal{P}}\setminus j^*} P^g_{i,j} \le 1$$

$$\forall j \in \Omega^{\mathcal{C}}_{\mathcal{P}} \setminus j^*, \forall k \in \Psi_{\mathcal{P}}, \forall X, Y \in \mathbb{G}_{\mathcal{P}} :$$

$$\Pr_Y\left[f_k\right]\left(\sum_{i\in\Omega^{\mathcal{C}}_{\mathcal{P}}} \Pr_X\left[f_k \wedge \mathcal{C}_i\right]P^X_{i,j}\right) \le e^{\epsilon}\Pr_X\left[f_k\right]\left(\sum_{i\in\Omega^{\mathcal{C}}_{\mathcal{P}}} \Pr_Y\left[f_k \wedge \mathcal{C}_i\right]P^Y_{i,j}\right)$$

$$\forall k \in \Psi_{\mathcal{P}}, \forall X, Y \in \mathbb{G}_{\mathcal{P}} :$$

$$\begin{aligned}&\Pr_Y\left[f_k\right]\left(\sum_{i\in\Omega^{\mathcal{C}}_{\mathcal{P}}} \Pr_X\left[f_k \wedge \mathcal{C}_i\right]\left(1 - \sum_{j\in\Omega^{\mathcal{C}}_{\mathcal{P}}\setminus j^*} P^X_{i,j}\right)\right)\\ &\le e^{\epsilon}\Pr_X\left[f_k\right]\left(\sum_{i\in\Omega^{\mathcal{C}}_{\mathcal{P}}} \Pr_Y\left[f_k \wedge \mathcal{C}_i\right]\left(1 - \sum_{j\in\Omega^{\mathcal{C}}_{\mathcal{P}}\setminus j^*} P^Y_{i,j}\right)\right)\end{aligned}$$

which is a system of $2|\mathbb{G}_{\mathcal{P}}||\Omega^{\mathcal{C}}_{\mathcal{P}}|^2 + |\mathbb{G}_{\mathcal{P}}|^2|\Omega^{\mathcal{C}}_{\mathcal{P}}||\Psi_{\mathcal{P}}|$ equations in $|\mathbb{G}_{\mathcal{P}}||\Omega^{\mathcal{C}}_{\mathcal{P}}|(|\Omega^{\mathcal{C}}_{\mathcal{P}}|-1)$ variables.

Furthermore, we know that this system necessarily has a solution on its domain, since taking $P^g_{i,j} = 1/|\Omega^{\mathcal{C}}_{\mathcal{P}}|$ for each i, j, and g corresponds to a classifier $\mathcal{C}'$ where all individuals are offered a uniform distribution over outcomes; this classifier trivially satisfies fair treatment (and indeed, one can easily verify that it satisfies the above conditions for any $\mathcal{C}$ and $\mathcal{P}$). □

Thus, finding assignments for $P_{i,j}$ in order to construct a classifier $\mathcal{C}'$ satisfying fair treatment with respect to $\mathcal{C}$ becomes a linear optimization problem—that is, to find an assignment that satisfies the sets of conditions above while minimizing some linear loss function.

5.2 Step 2: Approximate Fairness from Experimental Probabilities

Of course, we have only established so far that $\mathcal{C}'$ constructed in such a manner satisfies fair treatment if we already know the exact probabilities $\Pr_g[f_k]$ and $\Pr_g[f_k \wedge \mathcal{C}_i]$ for each group g. This of course requires non-black-box knowledge of $\mathcal{P}$ and $\mathcal{C}$; however, we will now show by a Chernoff bound that, assuming $\mathcal{B}$ is given *experimental* probabilities $\Pr_g[f_k]$ and $\Pr_g[f_k \wedge \mathcal{C}_i]$ from a sufficiently large "training set" of individuals randomly drawn from the distribution $\tau_{\mathcal{X},\Pi}(1^n)$, $\mathcal{C}'$ constructed according to the above linear program, and with a small amount of random noise added to prevent interference due to experimental variance in observing extremely rare events, will still satisfy ϵ-*approximate* fair treatment with overwhelming probability. Specifically, it can be proven that the probability of $\mathcal{C}'$ *not* satisfying approximate fair treatment is extremely small given a sufficiently large number of random samples (i.e., a number inversely polynomial in the desired fair treatment error ϵ).

To formalize what we mean by adding "a small amount of random noise", given some derived classifier $\mathcal{C}'$ (which we recall can be expressed as an $|\Omega^{\mathcal{C}}_{\mathcal{P}}| \times |\Omega^{\mathcal{C}}_{\mathcal{P}}|$ perturbation matrix), and letting $(\mathbf{1})_{m\times n}$ be an $m \times n$ matrix of all ones, we shall let

$$Q_r(\mathcal{C}') \triangleq \frac{r}{|\Omega^{\mathcal{C}}_{\mathcal{P}}|}(\mathbf{1})_{|\Omega^{\mathcal{C}}_{\mathcal{P}}|\times|\Omega^{\mathcal{C}}_{\mathcal{P}}|} + (1-r)\mathcal{C}'$$

be the derived classifier that with probability r outputs a random outcome and otherwise outputs an outcome according to the classifier $\mathcal{C}'$. (Hence, $Q_r(\mathcal{C}')(\sigma)$ is identical to $\mathcal{C}'(\sigma)$ with probability $1-r$.)

We will herein make use of the following well-known bound (for ease of notation, we denote $\exp(x) = e^x$):

Lemma 1. *(Hoeffding Bound.) Let $X_1, \ldots, X_N$ be independent binary random variables (i.e., $X_i \in \{0,1\}$). Let m be the expected value of their average and X^* their actual average. Then, for any $\delta \in (0,1)$:*

$$Pr[|X^* - m| \geq \delta] \leq 2\ exp\left(-2\delta^2 N\right)$$

In particular, when δ and m are fixed, this probability is inversely exponential (i.e., *negligible*) in the number of random variables N. To take advantage of this, consider our scenario where we have some classifier $\mathcal{C}$ trained using some number of individuals drawn (independently) from the distribution from the distribution $\tau_{\mathcal{X},\Pi}(1^n)$, and we wish to measure the probability of some event E_1 occurring conditioned on a subgroup g. Notationally, we will henceforth denote by $\mathsf{Ex}[E]$ the experimental probability of an event E over a set of random samples—i.e., letting $\mathcal{S}$ be the set of samples and $\mathbf{1}_{E(s)}$ the indicator variable which is 1 if E is true for a sample s and 0 if not:

$$\frac{1}{|\mathcal{S}|}\sum_{s\in\mathcal{S}}\mathbf{1}_{E(s)}$$

We will denote by $\mathsf{Ex}_g[E]$ the experimental probability of E conditioned on a group g, or $\mathsf{Ex}[E \wedge g]/\mathsf{Ex}[g]$. Then we prove the following lemma:

Lemma 2. *Given a distribution $\mathcal{D}$, event E, and group g, then, letting* Ex *denote the experimental probability as derived from N independent samples from the distribution $\tau_{\mathcal{X},\Pi}(1^n)$, for any $\delta \in (0,1)$, with probability at least*

$$1 - 4\ exp\left(-2\left(\frac{\delta Pr[g]}{3}\right)^2 N\right)$$

over the samples, the following two conditions hold:

1. $|\mathsf{Ex}_g[E] - Pr_g[E]\,| < \delta$
2. $|\mathsf{Ex}[g] - Pr[g]\,| < \delta$.

Specifically, this states that the probability of the experimental and real probabilities diverging for some fixed event E is inverse-exponential in the size of $\mathcal{C}$'s training set.

Proof. First we prove the following claim:

Claim 3. *Given positive real numbers a, b, c, d, ϵ such that $|a-b| < \epsilon$ and $|c-d| < \epsilon$, then*

$$\left|\frac{a}{c} - \frac{b}{d}\right| < \frac{(a+c)\epsilon}{c(c-\epsilon)}$$

Proof. The following three facts suffice:

$$\left|\frac{a}{c} - \frac{b}{d}\right| = \frac{1}{cd}|ad - bc|$$
$$\frac{1}{cd} < \frac{1}{c(c-\epsilon)}$$
$$|ad - bc| < |a(c+\epsilon) - (a-\epsilon)c| = \epsilon(a+c)$$

□

So, as long as $|\mathsf{Ex}[g] - \Pr[g]| < \delta$ and $|\mathsf{Ex}[E \wedge g] - \Pr[E \wedge g]| < \delta$, then

$$|\mathsf{Ex}_g[E] - \Pr_g[E]| = \left|\frac{\Pr[E \wedge g]}{\Pr[g]} - \frac{\mathsf{Ex}[E \wedge g]}{\mathsf{Ex}[g]}\right| < \frac{(\Pr[E \wedge g] + \Pr[g])\delta}{\Pr[g](\Pr[g] - \delta)}$$

which means that, by Lemma 1,

$$\begin{aligned}
&\Pr\left[|\mathsf{Ex}_g[E] - \Pr_g[E]| \geq \frac{(\Pr[E \wedge g] + \Pr[g])\delta}{\Pr[g](\Pr[g] - \delta)}\right] \\
&\leq \Pr[|\mathsf{Ex}[g] - \Pr[g]| \geq \delta] + \Pr[|\mathsf{Ex}[E \wedge g] - \Pr[E \wedge g]| \geq \delta] \\
&\leq 4\exp\left(-2\delta^2 N\right)
\end{aligned}$$

This follows because, for each of the (unconditioned) probabilities in question, we can use a Chernoff bound with N variables $X_1, \ldots, X_n$ equal to 1 if the respective event occurs for a sampled individual and 0 otherwise; then X^* is equal to the experimental probability of the event and m (its expectation) is by definition equal to the actual probability.

Finally, let

$$\delta' = \frac{(\Pr[E \wedge g] + \Pr[g])\delta}{\Pr[g](\Pr[g] - \delta)} = \frac{(\Pr_g[E] + 1)\delta}{\Pr[g] - \delta}$$

Then

$$\begin{aligned}
\delta'(\Pr[g] - \delta) &= (\Pr_g[E] + 1)\delta \\
\delta'\Pr[g] &= (\Pr_g[E] + 1 + \delta')\delta \\
\frac{\delta'\Pr[g]}{\Pr_g[E] + 1 + \delta'} &= \delta
\end{aligned}$$

And so

$$\begin{aligned}
&\Pr[|\mathsf{Ex}_g[E] - \Pr_g[E]| \geq \delta'] \leq 4\exp\left(-2\delta^2 N\right) \\
&= 4\exp\left(-2\left(\frac{\delta'\Pr[g]}{\Pr_g[E] + 1 + \delta'}\right)^2 N\right) \leq 4\exp\left(-2\left(\frac{\delta'\Pr[g]}{3}\right)^2 N\right)
\end{aligned}$$

since $\delta' < 1$ by assumption and $\Pr_g[E] \leq 1$ trivially. Furthermore, when we show that $|\mathsf{Ex}_g[E] - \Pr_g[E]| < \delta'$, we do so by showing that

$$|\Pr[g] - \mathsf{Ex}[g]| \leq [\delta =] \frac{\delta'\Pr[g]}{\Pr_g[E] + 1 + \delta'} \leq \delta'$$

which completes the other part of the argument. □

Now we can prove our key lemmas using this consequence.

Lemma 3. *Given context $\mathcal{P} = (\mathcal{D}, f, g, O)$ and $\epsilon \in (0, 1)$, let $\mathcal{C}'$ be a $\mathcal{C}$-derived classifier satisfying a modification of the linear constraints in Corollary 1 for $(\epsilon^2/4)$-fair treatment where the coefficients are determined by the* experimental *(rather than actual) probabilities of the respective events given N random* *samples $(O(\sigma), f(\sigma), \mathcal{C}(\sigma), g(\sigma))$ from the distribution $\tau_{\mathcal{X},\Pi}(1^n)$. Then the classifier $Q_{2\epsilon|\Omega^{\mathcal{C}}_{\mathcal{P}}|/3}(\mathcal{C}')$ satisfies ϵ-approximate fair treatment with respect to $\mathcal{P}$ except with probability negligible in N over the selection of samples—in particular, with probability $1 - O(e^{(-c\epsilon^4 N)})$ for some constant c dependent only on $\mathcal{D}$.*

Proof. Let $c = \frac{2}{144^2}\min_g \Pr[g]^2$. Notice that c is not dependent on n or, for that matter, on anything besides the (fixed) distribution $\mathcal{D}$.

First let us consider the classifier $\mathcal{C}'$ before noise is added. Because $\mathcal{C}'$ is derived from $\mathcal{C}$ according to Corollary 1, we have, by the respective constraints for fair treatment for each $j \in \Omega^{\mathcal{C}}_{\mathcal{P}}$, $X, Y \in \mathbb{G}_{\mathcal{P}}$, and $k \in \Psi_{\mathcal{P}}$:

$$\mu\left(\mathsf{Ex}_Y[f_k]\left(\sum_{i\in\Omega^{\mathcal{C}}_{\mathcal{P}}} \mathsf{Ex}_X[f_k \wedge \mathcal{C}_i]P^X_{i,j}\right), \mathsf{Ex}_X[f_k]\left(\sum_{i\in\Omega^{\mathcal{C}}_{\mathcal{P}}} \mathsf{Ex}_Y[f_k \wedge \mathcal{C}_i]P^Y_{i,j}\right)\right) \le \frac{\epsilon^2}{4}$$

which, since both sides are at most 1 and thus can differ additively by at most $1 - e^{-\epsilon^2/4} \le \epsilon^2/4$, implies:

$$\left|\mathsf{Ex}_Y[f_k]\left(\sum_{i\in\Omega^{\mathcal{C}}_{\mathcal{P}}} \mathsf{Ex}_X[f_k \wedge \mathcal{C}_i]P^X_{i,j}\right) - \mathsf{Ex}_X[f_k]\left(\sum_{i\in\Omega^{\mathcal{C}}_{\mathcal{P}}} \mathsf{Ex}_Y[f_k \wedge \mathcal{C}_i]P^Y_{i,j}\right)\right| \le \frac{\epsilon^2}{4}$$

where $P^X_{i,j}$ and $P^Y_{i,j}$ are derived from solving the constraints. Applying Lemma 2 (1) once for each $k \in \Psi_{\mathcal{P}}$ to the event f_k and group Y (with $\delta = \epsilon^2/48$) then gives us that

$$\left|\Pr_Y[f_k]\left(\sum_{i\in\Omega^{\mathcal{C}}_{\mathcal{P}}} \mathsf{Ex}_X[f_k \wedge \mathcal{C}_i]P^X_{i,j}\right) - \mathsf{Ex}_X[f_k]\left(\sum_{i\in\Omega^{\mathcal{C}}_{\mathcal{P}}} \mathsf{Ex}_Y[f_k \wedge \mathcal{C}_i]P^Y_{i,j}\right)\right| \le \frac{\epsilon^2}{4} + \frac{\epsilon^2}{48}$$

except with probability no greater than

$$4\exp\left(-2\left(\frac{(\epsilon^2/48)\Pr[Y]}{3}\right)^2 N\right) \le 4\exp\left(-2\left(\frac{\epsilon^2(\min_g \Pr[g])}{144}\right)^2 N\right)$$
$$= 4\exp\left(-\left(\frac{2\epsilon^4(\min_g \Pr[g])^2}{144^2}\right) N\right) = 4(\exp(-c\epsilon^4 N))$$

for each choice of k, or, over all of the $|\Psi_{\mathcal{P}}|$ choices of k, no greater than $4|\Psi_{\mathcal{P}}|(\exp(-c\epsilon^4 N))$ by the union bound. Symmetrically for each event f_k and group X:

$$\left|\Pr_Y[f_k]\left(\sum_{i\in\Omega^{\mathcal{C}}_{\mathcal{P}}} \mathsf{Ex}_X[f_k \wedge \mathcal{C}_i]P^X_{i,j}\right) - \Pr_X[f_k]\left(\sum_{i\in\Omega^{\mathcal{C}}_{\mathcal{P}}} \mathsf{Ex}_Y[f_k \wedge \mathcal{C}_i]P^Y_{i,j}\right)\right| \le \frac{\epsilon^2}{4} + \frac{\epsilon^2}{24}$$

except with the same failure probability. We then do the same for the events $f_k \wedge \mathcal{C}_i$ (for each of the $|\Psi_{\mathcal{P}}|$ choices of k) conditioned on X and Y to obtain that

$$\left|\Pr_Y[f_k]\left(\sum_{i\in\Omega^{\mathcal{C}}_{\mathcal{P}}} \Pr_X[f_k \wedge \mathcal{C}_i]\,P^X_{i,j}\right) - \Pr_X[f_k]\left(\sum_{i\in\Omega^{\mathcal{C}}_{\mathcal{P}}} \Pr_Y[f_k \wedge \mathcal{C}_i]\,P^Y_{i,j}\right)\right|$$
$$\le \frac{\epsilon^2}{4} + \frac{\epsilon^2}{12} = \frac{\epsilon^2}{3}$$

except with probability $16(\exp(-c\epsilon^4 N))$ for each choice of k (or, over all choices, $16|\Psi_{\mathcal{P}}|(\exp(-c\epsilon^4 N)))$. By the union bound over all classes $k \in \Psi_{\mathcal{P}}$ and over all (fewer than $|\mathbb{G}_{\mathcal{P}}|^2$) pairs of groups X and Y, the total failure probability from applying these bounds to all constraints is at most $16|\mathbb{G}_{\mathcal{P}}|^2|\Psi_{\mathcal{P}}|(\exp(-c\epsilon^4 N)) = O(\exp(-c\epsilon^4 N))$, which is of course negligible in the number of samples N. So, with probability at least $1 - O(\exp(-c\epsilon^4 N))$ over the drawn samples, all of the above constraints will hold.

This is not quite identical to the statement

$$\mu\left(\Pr_X\left[\mathcal{C}'_j|f_k\right], \Pr_Y\left[\mathcal{C}'_j|f_k\right]\right) \leq \epsilon$$

(i.e., fair treatment for $\mathcal{C}'$); particularly, if the probability of some outcome is very small, then a bound on the *additive* distance between real and experimental probabilities has no impact on whether the *multiplicative* distance is bounded. To overcome this issue, we will consider the classifier $Q_{2|\Omega^{\mathcal{C}}_{\mathcal{P}}|\epsilon/3}(\mathcal{C}')$ that, as defined above, runs $\mathcal{C}'$ and outputs the result *except* with probability $2|\Omega^{\mathcal{C}}_{\mathcal{P}}|\epsilon/3$, in which case it will pick an output uniformly at random. This guarantees that the probability of any outcome occurring (even conditioned on any group) must be at least $2\epsilon/3$; hence, except with the aforementioned failure probability, the multiplicative distance between the real and experimental probabilities for any such conditional outcome can be at most either

$$\ln\left(\frac{2\epsilon/3 + \epsilon^2/3}{2\epsilon/3}\right) = \ln(1 + \epsilon/2) \leq \epsilon$$

or

$$\ln\left(\frac{2\epsilon/3}{2\epsilon/3 - \epsilon^2/3}\right) = \ln\left(\frac{1}{1 - \epsilon/2}\right) \leq \epsilon$$

for all $\epsilon < 1$. □

Remark. While it may seem counterintuitive for the classifier output by our sanitizer to output a uniformly random class with small probability, in fact this "random noise" is only necessary due to the possibility of arbitrarily small probabilities $\Pr_g[f_k \wedge \mathcal{C}_i]$ occurring in the distribution $\mathcal{D}$; specifically, if some such event occurs with small enough probability, it would likely be measured to have probability 0, potentially causing an unbounded multiplicative fairness error in the derived classifier. If there instead exists a constant lower bound for these probabilities (or even, once parameterized, an asymptotic lower bound of $\epsilon(n)$), then we can directly obtain the result above without having to add noise to the outcome of the derived classifier.

Importantly, we can also apply Lemma 3 in reverse, transforming from the exact conditions to the modified conditions with experimental probabilities, under precisely the same conditions. This will be useful to demonstrate optimality (i.e., that the optimal fair classifier is derivable by $\mathcal{B}$ as it is overwhelmingly likely to satisfy approximate versions of the constraints) in the following section.

Lemma 4. *Given context $\mathcal{P} = (\mathcal{D}, f, g, O)$, let $\mathcal{C}'$ be a $\mathcal{C}$-derived classifier satisfying the conditions in Corollary 1 for 0-fair treatment with respect to $\mathcal{P}$. Then, for any $\epsilon \in (0,1)$, the classifier $Q_{\epsilon^2|\Omega_{\mathcal{P}}^{\mathcal{C}}|/4}(\mathcal{C}')$, with at least probability $1-O(e^{(-c\epsilon^8 N)})$ (for some constant c dependent only on $\mathcal{D}$) over N random samples $(O(\sigma), f(\sigma), \mathcal{C}(\sigma), g(\sigma))$ from the distribution $\tau_{\chi,\Pi}(1^n)$, satisfies the modification of the linear constraints in Corollary 1 for $(\epsilon^2/4)$-fair treatment where the coefficients are determined by the* experimental *(rather than actual) probabilities of the respective events given the random samples.*

Proof. We proceed very similarly to Lemma 3, except changing the error parameter ϵ and reversing $\mathsf{Ex}[\ldots]$ with $\Pr[\ldots]$. Since we know that $\mathcal{C}'$ satisfies perfect fair treatment, we have, this time with respect to the real probabilities:

$$\left| \Pr_Y[f_k] \left(\sum_{i \in \Omega_{\mathcal{P}}^{\mathcal{C}}} \Pr_X[f_k \wedge C_i] P_{i,j}^X \right) - \Pr_X[f_k] \left(\sum_{i \in \Omega_{\mathcal{P}}^{\mathcal{C}}} \Pr_Y[f_k \wedge C_i] P_{i,j}^Y \right) \right| = 0$$

Next we apply Lemma 2 (1) with $\delta = \epsilon^4/128$ to all events f_k and $f_k \wedge C_i$ for groups X and Y just as in Lemma 3, obtaining that

$$\left| \mathsf{Ex}_Y[f_k] \left(\sum_{i \in \Omega_{\mathcal{P}}^{\mathcal{C}}} \mathsf{Ex}_X[f_k \wedge C_i] P_{i,j}^X \right) - \mathsf{Ex}_X[f_k] \left(\sum_{i \in \Omega_{\mathcal{P}}^{\mathcal{C}}} \mathsf{Ex}_Y[f_k \wedge C_i] P_{i,j}^Y \right) \right|$$
$$\leq 4\left(\frac{\epsilon^4}{128}\right) = \frac{\epsilon^4}{32}$$

except with probability $O(e^{(-c\epsilon^8 N)})$ over the N samples taken (for some small constant $\mathcal{C}$ dependent only on $\mathcal{D}$). To convert this into multiplicative distance, we use the classifier $Q_{\epsilon^2|\Omega_{\mathcal{P}}^{\mathcal{C}}|/4}(\mathcal{C}')$ so that the probability of any outcome is at least $\epsilon^2/4$. Then, as long as the conditions of Lemma 2 are true, the multiplicative distance between the real and experimental probabilities for any such conditional outcome can be at most either

$$\ln\left(\frac{\epsilon^2/4 + \epsilon^4/32}{\epsilon^2/4}\right) = \ln\left(1 + \epsilon^2/8\right) \leq \epsilon^2/4$$

or

$$\ln\left(\frac{\epsilon^2/4}{\epsilon^2/4 - \epsilon^4/32}\right) = \ln\left(\frac{1}{1-\epsilon^2/8}\right) \leq \epsilon^2/4$$

for all $\epsilon < 1$. □

5.3 Step 3: Optimality over Derived Classifiers

Now we can construct an $\epsilon(\cdot)$-black box sanitizer for any inverse polynomial $\epsilon(n)$ using Corollary 1 and Lemma 3. In particular, given some context ensemble $\Pi = \{(\mathcal{D}, f, g, O_n)\}_{n \in \mathbb{N}}$ and a sequence of classifiers $\chi = \{\mathcal{C}_n\}_{n \in \mathbb{N}}$, if, for any n, we use Corollary 1 on experimental probabilities (given enough samples from $\tau_{\mathcal{X},\Pi}(1^n)$) to produce a $\mathcal{C}_n$-derived classifier which is fair with respect to those probabilities, Lemma 3 allows us to assert that a slightly noisy version of the resulting classifier is still approximately fair, even though we only have black-box access to the training data set $\tau_{\mathcal{X},\Pi}(1^n)$ (whereas notably our original formulation in Corollary 1 requires non-black-box access to determine the exact probabilities $\Pr_g[f_k]$ and $\Pr_g[f_k \wedge \mathcal{C}_i]$ for the optimization constraints). We propose the following construction and subsequently prove its correctness as a black-box sanitizer, amounting to the first part (existence) of the proof of Theorem 4:

Constructing the Black-Box Sanitizer. Consider the following algorithm for $\mathcal{B}_{\tau_{\mathcal{X},\Pi}}$ on input 1^n, where we assume some fairness parameter $\epsilon(n) \geq \frac{1}{q(n)}$ for polynomial $q(\cdot)$ and some loss function $\ell_{\mathcal{D},f,\mathcal{C}}(\cdot)$ which is linear in the probabilities $P^g_{i,j}$ but may depend on probabilities observed in $\mathcal{D}$, f, and $\mathcal{C}$:

- *(Estimating constraints by sampling.)* Use queries to $\tau_{\mathcal{X},\Pi}(1^n)$ to produce (for some $\epsilon' > 0$ and polynomial $p(n) = \Omega(q(n)^{8+\epsilon'})$) $N = p(n)$ samples $(O_n(\sigma'), f(\sigma'), \mathcal{C}_n(O_n(\sigma')), g(\sigma'))$ for $\sigma' \leftarrow \mathcal{D}$, so that the failure probabilities described in both Lemmas 3 and 4 are negligible in n. (In particular, this failure probability will be at most $O(e^{-cp(n)/q(n)^8}) = O(e^{-cn^{\epsilon'}})$, which is negligible since c depends only on the fixed distribution $\mathcal{D}$)[10].
- *(Estimating the loss function.)* Furthermore, use the experimental probabilities of the samples to estimate any distributionally-dependent parameters of the loss function ℓ. Call the approximate loss function $\ell'(\cdot)$.
- *(Solving the derived constraints.)* Use Corollary 1 to produce probabilities $P^g_{i,j}$ for a $\mathcal{C}_n$-derived classifier which minimizes $\ell'(\cdot)$ with respect to the constraints for $(\epsilon(n)^2/4)$-fair treatment generated from the experimental probabilities $\mathsf{Ex}_g[f_k]$ and $\mathsf{Ex}_g[f_k \wedge \mathcal{C}_i]$ over the N samples.
- *(Adding noise and producing the derived classifier.)* Output the $\mathcal{C}_n$-derived classifier $\mathcal{C}'' = Q_{2\epsilon(n)|\Omega^{\mathcal{C}_n}_{\mathcal{P}_n}|/3}(\mathcal{C}')$ (which with probability $2\epsilon(n)|\Omega^{\mathcal{C}_n}_{\mathcal{P}_n}|/3$ outputs a uniformly random element of $\Omega^{\mathcal{C}_n}_{\mathcal{P}_n}$, and which otherwise uses the probabilities $P^g_{i,j}$ found from the optimization to classify σ according to $\mathcal{C}_n(O_n(\sigma))$ and σ's group $g(\sigma)$—i.e., draws from the distribution $\{j \text{ with pr. } P^g_{\mathcal{C}_n(\sigma),j}\}$).

Claim 4. *For any $\epsilon(n) \geq \frac{1}{q(n)}$ for polynomial $q(\cdot)$, the above construction of $\mathcal{B}_{(\cdot)}$ is an $\epsilon(\cdot)$-black-box sanitizer.*

Proof. By Lemma 3, the classifier $\mathcal{C}'' = Q_{2\epsilon(n)|\Omega^{\mathcal{C}_n}_{\mathcal{P}_n}|/3}(\mathcal{C}')$ output by $\mathcal{B}$ satisfies $\epsilon(n)$-fair treatment with probability at least $1 - \nu(n)$ (where $\nu(\cdot)$ is negligible) for any given n.

[10] We use $\omega(q(n)^8)$ samples so that we can later assert that Lemma 4 holds with all-but-negligible probability in the optimality step. For the current step, only $\omega(q(n)^4)$ samples are necessary.

Furthermore, we note that the algorithm for $\mathcal{B}$ is efficient; for any context ensemble Π and classifier sequence χ such that $|\mathbb{G}_{\mathcal{P}_n}| \leq m$, $|\Psi_{\mathcal{P}_n}| \leq m$, and $|\Omega_{\mathcal{P}_n}^{\mathcal{C}_n}| \leq m$, it runs in time polynomial in m and polynomial in n. The former bound comes from the running time of the linear program in Corollary 1, and the latter bound comes from Lemma 3 and the fact that we make $N = p(n)$ oracle queries to gather "training data". Hence $\mathcal{B}_{(\cdot)}$ must be an $\epsilon(\cdot)$-black-box sanitizer. □

Notably, the running time of this algorithm is proportional to $\frac{1}{\epsilon(n)^8}$, which is natural in that, to derive a more accurate approximation of the real probabilities with training data, more samples are required. (In fact, as we shall show, decreasing ϵ and/or respectively increasing the number of samples will reduce both the fairness and optimality errors.)

Finally, we remark on the loss function $\ell_{\mathcal{D},f,\mathcal{C}}(\cdot)$ and the optimality of our construction. Of course, the entries of $\vec{\ell}_{\mathcal{D},f,\mathcal{C}}$—that is, the probabilities $\Pr[g]$ and $\Pr_g[f(\sigma) = k \wedge \mathcal{C}(\sigma) = i]$—are in general unknown to the black-box sanitizer $\mathcal{B}$, and this is why our construction uses its training samples to also calculate the experimental probabilities needed to approximate the loss function. Now we will show that using the experimentally derived loss function (naturally) increases the error bound of $\mathcal{C}''$, but only slightly (albeit dependent on the degree and number of terms of the coefficients of $P_{i,j}^g$ in ℓ). The following claim essentially states that, as the optimum of a linear loss function changes at most minimally if the coefficients change minimally, the loss of the classifier output by $\mathcal{B}$ over the predicted loss function will not be much worse than the loss over the correct loss function. This fact, combined with the fact that (a slightly noisy version of) the optimal perfectly fair classifier can always be derived by $\mathcal{B}$ if it knows the correct loss function, suffices to show that the classifier actually derived by $\mathcal{B}$ will not be much worse than the optimal fair classifier, hence proving the final part of Theorem 4.

Claim 5. *With probability at least $1-\nu(n)$ (for negligible $\nu(\cdot)$) over $\mathcal{B}$'s queries, the $\mathcal{C}''$ output by $\mathcal{B}_{\tau_{\chi,\Pi}}(1^n)$ constructed above has error*

$$\Delta_{\ell,\mathcal{D},f,\mathcal{C}}(\mathcal{C}'') \leq |\Omega_{\mathcal{P}_n}^{\mathcal{C}_n}|(\epsilon(n) + |\mathbb{G}_{\mathcal{P}_n}|\epsilon(n)^4 dt/64)$$

with respect to any linear loss function with t-term coefficients of degree d given by $\ell_{\mathcal{D},f,\mathcal{C}}(\mathcal{C}'')$.

Proof. Herein we shall for consistency refer to the loss function optimized by $\mathcal{B}$ by deriving from the experimental probabilities as $\ell'(\cdot)$, and the "true" loss function as $\ell(\cdot)$.

Let $\mathcal{C}^*$ be the optimal $\mathcal{C}_n$-derived classifier satisfying perfect fair treatment, let $\mathcal{C}^{**} \triangleq Q_{\epsilon(n)^2|\Omega_{\mathcal{P}_n}^{\mathcal{C}_n}|/4}(\mathcal{C}^*)$ be a noisy version of $\mathcal{C}^*$, and, as in the construction of $\mathcal{B}$, let $\mathcal{C}'$ be the classifier that optimizes ℓ' over the experimentally derived constraints and $\mathcal{C}'' = Q_{2\epsilon(n)|\Omega_{\mathcal{P}_n}^{\mathcal{C}_n}|/3}(\mathcal{C}')$ the noisy version of $\mathcal{C}'$. Towards bounding the quantity $\ell(\mathcal{C}'') - \ell(\mathcal{C}^*)$ and thus the error, we bound the difference in loss between successive pairs of classifiers:

- Beginning with $\mathcal{C}''$, the actual output, we notice that the difference in loss between $\mathcal{C}'$ and $\mathcal{C}''$ must be small because $\mathcal{C}''$ is by definition identical to $\mathcal{C}'$ except with small probability.
- Next, we can bound the difference in loss between $\mathcal{C}^{**}$ and $\mathcal{C}'$ by noticing that Lemma 4 provides that $\mathcal{C}^{**}$ with high probability satisfies $(\epsilon^2/4)$-fair treatment with respect to the experimentally derived constraints and can thus be derived by $\mathcal{B}$. So this means that $\mathcal{B}$ must find a classifier which is as good as $\mathcal{C}^{**}$ or better with respect to ℓ'; by analyzing the similarity between ℓ and ℓ' we can also conclude that $\mathcal{C}^{**}$ is not much better than $\mathcal{C}'$ in terms of the true loss function ℓ.
- Finally, the difference in loss between $\mathcal{C}^*$ and $\mathcal{C}^{**}$ is once again bounded by the fact that $\mathcal{C}^{**}$ is nearly identical to $\mathcal{C}^*$.

Formally, we present the following subclaims:

Subclaim 1. *$\ell(\mathcal{C}'') - \ell(\mathcal{C}') \leq 2\epsilon(n)|\Omega_{\mathcal{P}_n}^{\mathcal{C}_n}|/3$ with probability 1.*

Proof. $\mathcal{C}''$ is identical to $\mathcal{C}'$ except with probability $2\epsilon(n)|\Omega_{\mathcal{P}_n}^{\mathcal{C}_n}|/3$ (i.e., no probability $P_{i,j}$ can differ between the two by more than that amount). As such, since the loss function ℓ is bounded in $[0, 1]$ by assumption and linear in the probabilities $P_{i,j}^g$, the subclaim follows by linearity. Formally:

$$\ell(Q_r(\mathcal{C}')) = \ell\left(\frac{r}{|\Omega_{\mathcal{P}}^{\mathcal{C}}|}(\mathbf{1})_{|\Omega_{\mathcal{P}}^{\mathcal{C}}|\times|\Omega_{\mathcal{P}}^{\mathcal{C}}|} + (1-r)\mathcal{C}'\right)$$
$$= r\ell\left(\frac{1}{|\Omega_{\mathcal{P}}^{\mathcal{C}}|}(\mathbf{1})_{|\Omega_{\mathcal{P}}^{\mathcal{C}}|\times|\Omega_{\mathcal{P}}^{\mathcal{C}}|}\right) + (1-r)\ell(\mathcal{C}')$$

and so:

$$\ell(Q_r(\mathcal{C}')) - \ell(\mathcal{C}') = r\ell\left(\frac{1}{|\Omega_{\mathcal{P}}^{\mathcal{C}}|}(\mathbf{1})_{|\Omega_{\mathcal{P}}^{\mathcal{C}}|\times|\Omega_{\mathcal{P}}^{\mathcal{C}}|}\right) - r\ell(\mathcal{C}') \leq r(1-0) = r$$

□

Subclaim 2. *$\ell(\mathcal{C}') - \ell(\mathcal{C}^{**}) \leq |\Omega_{\mathcal{P}_n}^{\mathcal{C}_n}||\mathbb{G}_{\mathcal{P}_n}|dt\epsilon(n)^4/64$ with probability at least $1 - \nu(n)$ (for negligible $\nu(\cdot)$) over $\mathcal{B}$'s queries.*

Proof. We show this through three lemmas.

First, it is important to observe how far the experimental loss function ℓ' might be from the real function ℓ. Denote by $\ell_{i,j}^g$ the entry of $\vec{\ell}$ corresponding to the coefficient of $P_{i,j}^g$ (resp. for $\vec{\ell'}$). Then:

Lemma 5. *With probability $1 - \nu'(n)$ (for negligible $\nu'(\cdot)$), if ℓ is a linear loss function with t-term coefficients of degree d, then for any i, j, g it is true that $|\ell'^g_{i,j} - \ell^g_{i,j}| \leq dt\epsilon(n)^4/128$.*

Proof. By Lemma 2 for each event $f_k \wedge C_i$ and each group g with $\delta = \epsilon(n)^4/128$, we have $|\mathsf{Ex}_g[f_k \wedge C_i] - \Pr_g[f_k \wedge C_i]| < \epsilon(n)^4/128$ and $|\Pr[g] - \mathsf{Ex}[g]| < \epsilon(n)^4/128$ for any i, k, g except with probability $\nu'(n) = O(e^{(-c\epsilon(n)^8 p(n))})$ (which is negligible in n as $\mathcal{B}$ takes $p(n) = \Omega(\epsilon(n)^{-(8+\epsilon')})$ samples for $\epsilon' > 0$).

As we consider loss functions whose coefficients are polynomial in the above probabilities, we can note the following identity to bound the error between the coefficients in ℓ and ℓ': if we have $x_1, \ldots, x_n, x'_1, \ldots, x'_n \in [0,1]$ and $|x_i - x'_i| \leq \epsilon_i$ for each i, then[11]:

$$\left|\prod_i x_i - \prod_i x'_i\right| \leq \sum_i \epsilon_i$$

So, given some coefficient $\ell^g_{i,j}$ in the loss function which is a polynomial in the respective probabilities, the respective additive error between the real and experimental value of any degree-d monomial in that coefficient (which is bounded in $[0,1]$, i.e., does not contain a constant term greater than 1) will be at most $d\epsilon(n)^4/128$; this can be seen by taking $n = d$ in the above identity, letting x_i represent a real probability, x'_i the corresponding experimental probability, and noting that as shown above $\epsilon_i \leq \epsilon(n)^4/128$ for each i. In turn, the coefficient itself, or the sum of t of these monomials, cannot have error greater than $dt\epsilon(n)^4/128$ (adding the error bounds from each individual monomial). So, for any variable $P^g_{i,j}$, except with the aforementioned negligible probability:

$$|\ell'^g_{i,j} - \ell^g_{i,j}| \leq dt\epsilon(n)^4/128$$

as desired. □

Next, we compare the value of the experimental loss function ℓ' between $\mathcal{C}^{**}$ and $\mathcal{C}'$, which is easily done since $\mathcal{B}$ optimizes $\mathcal{C}'$ with respect to ℓ' over a region that we can show includes $\mathcal{C}^{**}$:

Lemma 6. *$\ell'(\mathcal{C}') \leq \ell'(\mathcal{C}^{**})$ with probability at least $1 - \nu''(n)$ (for negligible $\nu''(\cdot)$) over $\mathcal{B}$'s queries.*

Proof. By Lemma 4, except with some negligible probability $\nu''(n)$ (again negligible since $\mathcal{B}$ takes $p(n) = \omega(\epsilon(n)^{-8})$ samples), $\mathcal{C}^{**} = Q_{\epsilon(n)^2|\Omega^{\mathcal{C}_n}_{\mathcal{P}_n}|/4}(\mathcal{C}^*)$ satisfies $\epsilon(n)^2/4$-fair treatment with respect to the *experimental* probabilities derived by

---

[11] *Proof:* If $x_1x_2 > x'_1x'_2$, then:

$$|x_1x_2 - x'_1x'_2| = x_1x_2 - x'_1x'_2 < x_1(x'_2 + \epsilon_2) - (x_1 - \epsilon_1)x'_2 = \epsilon_2 x_1 + \epsilon_1 x'_2 \leq \epsilon_1 + \epsilon_2$$

and otherwise:

$$|x_1x_2 - x'_1x'_2| = x'_1x'_2 - x_1x_2 < (x_1 + \epsilon_1)x'_2 - x_1(x'_2 - \epsilon_2) = \epsilon_1 x'_2 + \epsilon_2 x_1 \leq \epsilon_1 + \epsilon_2$$

Applying the same to x_1x_2 and x_3 gives $|(x_1x_2)x_3 - (x'_1x'_2)x'_3| \leq (\epsilon_1 + \epsilon_2) + \epsilon_3$, and iteratively repeating to include all i ultimately gives the conclusion.

$\mathcal{B}$, since $\mathcal{C}^*$ satisfies perfect (errorless) fair treatment with respect to the actual probabilities. However, recall that the $\mathcal{C}'$ recovered by $\mathcal{B}$ can by construction (Corollary 1) lie anywhere within the set of derived classifiers satisfying $\epsilon(n)^2/4$-fair treatment with respect to the same derived experimental probabilities. Since $\mathcal{B}$ optimizes ℓ' over that region, we know that, with all but the above negligible probability:

$$\ell'(\mathcal{C}') \leq \ell'(\mathcal{C}^{**})$$

as desired, because, since $\mathcal{C}^{**}$ is always findable by $\mathcal{B}$, $\mathcal{B}$ can always find either $\mathcal{C}^{**}$ itself or something with a smaller value of ℓ'. □

Finally, let $k \triangleq |\Omega_{\mathcal{P}_n}^{\mathcal{C}_n}|$ and recall the L_1-norm $||\vec{a} - \vec{b}||_1 = \sum_i (a_i - b_i)$ between two vectors. Henceforth let $(P_{\mathcal{C}'})_{i,j}^g$ denote the entry of the vector form $\vec{P}_{\mathcal{C}'}$ corresponding to $P_{i,j}^g$ for $\mathcal{C}'$, and respectively for $\mathcal{C}^{**}$. Towards relating $\ell'(\mathcal{C}') - \ell'(\mathcal{C}^{**})$ to $\ell(\mathcal{C}') - \ell(\mathcal{C}^{**})$ (the quantity we wish to bound), we show the following:

Lemma 7. $||\mathcal{C}' - \mathcal{C}^{**}||_1 \leq 2k|\mathbb{G}_{\mathcal{P}_n}|$.

Proof. Consider the $|\mathbb{G}_{\mathcal{P}_n}|k(k-1)$-dimensional space defined by the variables $P_{i,j}^g$, in which we have assumed the loss functions ℓ and ℓ' to be linear.[12] Consider moving between the points in this space which represent $\mathcal{C}^{**}$ and $\mathcal{C}'$. Each of the k sets of coordinates $(P_{i,1}^g, \ldots, P_{i,k-1}^g)$ must sum to at most 1, because each set represents a probability distribution; hence, considering that moving from $\mathcal{C}^{**}$ and $\mathcal{C}'$ may decrease some number of coordinates in each such set by up to a total of 1 and correspondingly add up to a total of 1, the L_1-norm between these two points is bounded by:

$$||\mathcal{C}' - \mathcal{C}^{**}||_1 = \sum_{i,j,g} |(P_{\mathcal{C}'})_{i,j}^g - (P_{\mathcal{C}^{**}})_{i,j}^g| \leq \sum_{i,g} |1 + 1| = 2k|\mathbb{G}_{\mathcal{P}_n}|$$

This completes the argument. □

Since ℓ and ℓ' are linear, we know that

$$\begin{aligned}\ell'(\mathcal{C}') - \ell'(\mathcal{C}^{**}) &= \langle \vec{\ell'}, \vec{P}_{\mathcal{C}'} \rangle - \langle \vec{\ell'}, \vec{P}_{\mathcal{C}^{**}} \rangle = \langle \vec{\ell'}, \vec{P}_{\mathcal{C}'} - \vec{P}_{\mathcal{C}^{**}} \rangle \\ &= \sum_{i,j,g} \ell'^g_{i,j}((P_{\mathcal{C}'})_{i,j}^g - (P_{\mathcal{C}^{**}})_{i,j}^g)\end{aligned}$$

Also, using Lemma 5's bound on the difference between entries of ℓ and ℓ':

$$\begin{aligned}&\ell(\mathcal{C}') - \ell(\mathcal{C}^{**}) = \sum_{i,j,g} \ell_{i,j}^g((P_{\mathcal{C}'})_{i,j}^g - (P_{\mathcal{C}^{**}})_{i,j}^g) \\ &\leq \sum_{i,j,g} \left(\ell'^g_{i,j} + \frac{dt\epsilon(n)^4}{128}\right)((P_{\mathcal{C}'})_{i,j}^g - (P_{\mathcal{C}^{**}})_{i,j}^g) \\ &= \ell'(\mathcal{C}') - \ell'(\mathcal{C}^{**}) + \frac{dt\epsilon(n)^4}{128} \sum_{i,j,g}((P_{\mathcal{C}'})_{i,j}^g - (P_{\mathcal{C}^{**}})_{i,j}^g) \leq 0 + \frac{dt\epsilon(n)^4}{128}||\mathcal{C}' - \mathcal{C}^{**}||_1\end{aligned}$$

---

[12] While there are $2k^2$ variables in total, notice that $P_{i,k}^g$ is fully determined by $P_{i,1}^g$ through $P_{i,k-1}^g$.

where the final step follows because, by Lemma 6, (except with negligible probability) $\ell'(\mathcal{C}') \leq \ell'(\mathcal{C}^{**})$, or $\ell'(\mathcal{C}') - \ell'(\mathcal{C}^{**}) \leq 0$. So, using Lemma 7's bound of $2k|\mathbb{G}_{\mathcal{P}_n}|$ on the L_1-norm, we obtain that

$$\begin{aligned}\ell(\mathcal{C}') - \ell(\mathcal{C}^{**}) &\leq 2k|\mathbb{G}_{\mathcal{P}_n}|(dt\epsilon(n)^4/128) \\ &= k|\mathbb{G}_{\mathcal{P}_n}|dt\epsilon(n)^4/64 = |\Omega_{\mathcal{P}_n}^{\mathcal{C}_n}||\mathbb{G}_{\mathcal{P}_n}|dt\epsilon(n)^4/64\end{aligned}$$

as desired, with all but negligible probability $\nu(n) \triangleq \nu'(n) + \nu''(n)$. □

Subclaim 3. *$\ell(\mathcal{C}^{**}) - \ell(\mathcal{C}^*) \leq \epsilon(n)^2|\Omega_{\mathcal{P}_n}^{\mathcal{C}_n}|/4$ with probability 1.*

Proof. $\mathcal{C}^{**} = Q_{\epsilon(n)^2|\Omega_{\mathcal{P}_n}^{\mathcal{C}_n}|/4}(\mathcal{C}^*)$, so this follows by linearity, similarly to Subclaim 1. □

So, adding the differences from the above subclaims (and recalling $\epsilon(n) \leq 1$), the error of $\mathcal{C}''$ is at most:

$$\begin{aligned}\ell(\mathcal{C}'') - \ell(\mathcal{C}^*) &= (\ell(\mathcal{C}'') - \ell(\mathcal{C}')) + (\ell(\mathcal{C}') - \ell(\mathcal{C}^{**})) + (\ell(\mathcal{C}^{**}) - \ell(\mathcal{C}^*)) \\ &\leq 2\epsilon(n)|\Omega_{\mathcal{P}_n}^{\mathcal{C}_n}|/3 + |\Omega_{\mathcal{P}_n}^{\mathcal{C}_n}||\mathbb{G}_{\mathcal{P}_n}|dt\epsilon(n)^4/64 + \epsilon(n)^2|\Omega_{\mathcal{P}_n}^{\mathcal{C}_n}|/4 \\ &\leq |\Omega_{\mathcal{P}_n}^{\mathcal{C}_n}|(\epsilon(n) + |\mathbb{G}_{\mathcal{P}_n}|\epsilon(n)^4 dt/64)\end{aligned}$$

with probability at least $1 - \nu(n)$ (as given in Subclaim 2) over $\mathcal{B}$'s queries, as desired. □

Claims 4 and 5 taken together suffice to prove Theorem 4.

References

1. Angwin, J., Larson, J., Mattu, S., Kirchner, L.: How we analyzed the COMPAS recidivism algorithm. ProPublica (2016). https://www.propublica.org/article/how-we-analyzed-the-compas-recidivism-algorithm
2. Angwin, J., Larson, J., Mattu, S., Kirchner, L.: Machine bias: risk assessments in criminal sentencing. ProPublica (2016). https://www.propublica.org/article/machine-bias-risk-assessments-in-criminal-sentencing
3. Chouldechova, A.: Fair prediction with disparate impact: a study of bias in recidivism prediction instruments. In: FATML (2016)
4. Dwork, C.: Differential privacy. In: Bugliesi, M., Preneel, B., Sassone, V., Wegener, I. (eds.) ICALP 2006. LNCS, vol. 4052, pp. 1–12. Springer, Heidelberg (2006). https://doi.org/10.1007/11787006_1
5. Dwork, C., Hardt, M., Pitassi, T., Reingold, O., Zemel, R.: Fairness through awareness. In: Proceedings of the 3rd Innovations in Theoretical Computer Science Conference, ITCS 2012, pp. 214–226. ACM, New York (2012)
6. Hardt, M., Price, E., Srebro, N.: Equality of opportunity in supervised learning. In: NIPS (2016)
7. Kleinberg, J., Mullainathan, S., Raghavan, M.: Inherent trade-offs in the fair determination of risk scores. In: ITCS (2017)
8. Pearl, J.: Direct and indirect effects. In: Proceedings of the Seventeenth Conference on Uncertainty in Artificial Intelligence, UAI 2001, pp. 411–420. Morgan Kaufmann Publishers Inc., San Francisco (2001)
9. Zafar, M.B., Valera, I., Gomez Rodriguez, M., Gummadi, K.P.: Fairness beyond disparate treatment and disparate impact: learning classification without disparate mistreatment (2016). https://arxiv.org/abs/1610.08452

Functional and Identity-Based Encryption

Upgrading to Functional Encryption

Saikrishna Badrinarayanan[1(✉)], Dakshita Khurana[2], Amit Sahai[1], and Brent Waters[3]

[1] UCLA, Los Angeles, USA
{saikrishna,sahai}@cs.ucla.edu
[2] MSR New England, Cambridge, USA
dakshkhurana@gmail.com
[3] UT Austin, Austin, USA
bwaters@cs.utexas.edu

Abstract. The notion of Functional Encryption (FE) has recently emerged as a strong primitive with several exciting applications. In this work, we initiate the study of the following question: Can existing public key encryption schemes be "upgraded" to Functional Encryption schemes without changing their public keys or the encryption algorithm? We call a public-key encryption scheme with this property to be *FE-compatible*. Indeed, assuming ideal obfuscation, it is easy to see that every CCA-secure public-key encryption scheme is FE-compatible. Despite the recent success in using indistinguishability obfuscation to replace ideal obfuscation for many applications, we show that this phenomenon most likely will not apply here. We show that assuming fully homomorphic encryption and the learning with errors (LWE) assumption, there exists a CCA-secure encryption scheme that is provably *not FE-compatible*. We also show that a large class of natural CCA-secure encryption schemes proven secure in the random oracle model are not FE-compatible in the random oracle model.

S. Badrinarayanan—Research supported in part by the IBM PhD Fellowship.
D. Khurana—Research done while at UCLA, supported in part by the UCLA Dissertation Year Fellowship.
A. Sahai—Research of first, second and third author supported in part from a DARPA/ARL SAFEWARE award, NSF Frontier Award 1413955, NSF grants 1619348, 1228984, 1136174, and 1065276, BSF grant 2012378, a Xerox Faculty Research Award, a Google Faculty Research Award, an equipment grant from Intel, and an Okawa Foundation Research Grant. This material is based upon work supported by the Defense Advanced Research Projects Agency through the ARL under Contract W911NF-15-C-0205. The views expressed are those of the authors and do not reflect the official policy or position of the Department of Defense, the National Science Foundation, or the U.S. Government.
B. Waters—Research supported by NSF CNS-1228599 and CNS-1414082, DARPA SafeWare, Microsoft Faculty Fellowship, and Packard Foundation Fellowship. Any opinions, findings, and conclusions or recommendations expressed in this material are those of the author(s) and do not necessarily reflect the views of the Department of Defense or the U.S. Government.

A. Beimel and S. Dziembowski (Eds.): TCC 2018, LNCS 11239, pp. 629–658, 2018.
https://doi.org/10.1007/978-3-030-03807-6_23

Nevertheless, we identify a key structure that, if present, is sufficient to provide FE-compatibility. Specifically, we show that assuming sub-exponentially secure iO and sub-exponentially secure one way functions, there exists a class of public key encryption schemes which we call *Special-CCA* secure encryption schemes that are in fact, FE-compatible. In particular, each of the following popular CCA secure encryption schemes (some of which existed even before the notion of FE was introduced) fall into the class of *Special-CCA* secure encryption schemes and are thus FE-compatible:

1. [CHK04] when instantiated with the IBE scheme of [BB04].
2. [CHK04] when instantiated with any Hierarchical IBE scheme.
3. [PW08] when instantiated with any Lossy Trapdoor Function.

1 Introduction

Functional Encryption (FE) [SW05,SW08] is a powerful framework that significantly expands the scope of public-key encryption. In an ordinary public-key encryption scheme, a user Alice first chooses a public key PK and a corresponding secret key SK using a (master) setup algorithm Setup. Then, any other user Bob can use Alice's public key to encrypt a message m to obtain a ciphertext $c = \mathsf{Enc}(\mathsf{PK}, m)$. Alice can decrypt this ciphertext using her secret key, yielding $m = \mathsf{Dec}(\mathsf{SK}, c)$.

In a functional encryption scheme, we give Alice key delegation capabilities: Alice can use a new key generation algorithm KeyGen to generate a *functional key* $\mathsf{SK}_f = \mathsf{FE.KeyGen}(\mathsf{SK}, f)$ for a function f that is, say, described by a circuit. Then Alice can hand this functional key SK_f to an associate Charlie, and Charlie can use this functional key together with a new decryption algorithm to only learn $f(m) = \mathsf{FE.Dec}(\mathsf{SK}_f, c)$ when given the ciphertext c. Intuitively speaking, nothing[1] beyond $f(m)$ should be learned by Charlie when given SK_f and c. This notion was fully formalized by [BSW11] in the setting where many functional keys and ciphertexts may be given to an adversary. The first work achieving functional encryption for general functions was [GGH+13], using the power of indistinguishability obfuscation.

The work of [BSW11] gave several compelling applications of functional encryption. For instance, Alice may want to store her e-mail in encrypted form, but she wants her cloud provider to be able to execute a phishing-detection circuit C on her email prior to sending it to her for decryption. She could accomplish this goal by providing her cloud provider with a functional key for SK_C, and the only thing the cloud provider would learn is whether any email received by Alice satisfies the phishing-detection circuit.

Applications of functional encryption become even more compelling when we think of Alice as representing a large organization or company. In such a

[1] Slightly more formally, functional encryption requires that encryptions of two messages m_0 and m_1 should be indistinguishable when given functional keys corresponding to any functions f that satisfy $f(m_0) = f(m_1)$. See Sect. 3 for more details.

scenario, the threat that functional encryption helps to address cryptographically is the insider threat. For example, consider an organization like a government tax authority, that regularly handles extremely sensitive information, but where individuals within the organization should only have access to limited digests or snippets of this sensitive information. For example, an analyst Dave at the tax authority may need only to compute statistical summaries of tax returns filed by a large set of people. Functional encryption would allow Dave to obtain a functional key SK_T, where T is the description of a function that produces statistical summaries of tax returns. The security of functional encryption would guarantee that even if Dave goes rogue, Dave's functional key would only allow him to learn and exfiltrate statistical summaries, and not any more personal information about individual tax returns beyond what could be deduced from the statistical summary.

Contrast this to the case where only ordinary public-key encryption is used to encrypt tax information. In this case, Dave would need the (master) secret key SK in order to decrypt tax information before processing it to obtain statistical summaries. And therefore a rogue Dave could exfiltrate the personal details of any person's tax return that was an input to the statistical summary he was supposed to compute. This is just one example, illustrative of many such scenarios where functional encryption could be beneficial for security.

Upgrading to Functional Encryption. Suppose that some time in the future, an organization, upon hearing about the advantages of functional encryption, wishes to "upgrade" to use functional encryption. Such an organization may face many challenges. First, the organization may already have infrastructure in place where partners and clients use an existing public-key encryption scheme to communicate with the organization. As such, the organization may have already amassed large amounts of encrypted data using a legacy public-key encryption system. Second, the organization may face regulatory burdens like HIPAA or other future regulations, that require the organization to use a particular encryption algorithm. Third, it could be that, even in this future time, existing key generation algorithms for general-purpose functional encryption (which typically currently use indistinguishability obfuscation) are too slow, but the organization wants to be ready for the day when such algorithms become practical.

In light of these concerns, what public-key encryption algorithm should the organization use now? While these are mostly societal challenges, security must exist in the context of human societies with traditions, rules, and regulations. And in this case, these concerns give rise to an intriguing theoretical question:

What (existing) public-key encryption algorithms can be "upgraded" to become functional encryption schemes, without changing the encryption algorithm or the public keys?

Our paper initiates the systematic study of this question. To formalize this, we say that a public-key encryption scheme E is *FE-compatible* if there exist new key generation and decryption algorithms that, when combined with the original setup and encryption algorithms of E, yield a (selectively) secure functional encryption scheme. (See Sect. 3 for details.)

Necessary Conditions. The technical starting point for our work is the folklore observation that any functional encryption scheme must satisfy a certain level of non-malleability. To see why, consider a functional encryption scheme for encrypting $(n+1)$-bit messages m, and consider the function f_1 that on input m simply outputs the first n bits of m. Suppose that we obtain a functional key SK_{f_1} for this function. Then functional encryption guarantees that encryptions of any two messages with identical n-bit prefixes should still be indistinguishable from each other.

But suppose there was a way for an adversary to modify any encryption $\mathsf{FE.Enc}(m)$ to obtain $\mathsf{FE.Enc}(m')$ where m' swapped the first and last bits of m. This would, for example, easily be possible if one tried to encrypt the message bit-by-bit. Then, by applying the functional key SK_{f_1} to $\mathsf{FE.Enc}(m')$, the adversary would learn the last bit of m, and break the security that is supposed to be guaranteed by functional encryption.

Indeed, it is not hard to see that the above argument generalizes to guarantee a type of security against chosen-ciphertext attacks. Thus, (a form of) CCA-security is a necessary requirement for an encryption scheme to be FE-compatible.

Universal Functional Encryption? At this point, it might be tempting to consider the possibility that CCA-security is also a *sufficient* condition for being FE-compatible. Indeed, this would be true if we had ideal obfuscation[2] [Had00] – that is, obfuscation that creates the equivalent of a virtual black box. It is not difficult to see why: To create a functional key SK_f, simply obfuscate the function that uses SK as a hardwired constant to decrypt the input ciphertext c to obtain the message m, and then simply output $f(m)$. If the obfuscation is ideal, then this functional key can easily be simulated as a black box just by using the CCA-decryption oracle for decryption. Thus, given ideal obfuscation, every CCA-secure public-key encryption scheme is FE-compatible. In this sense, we could hope to have a kind of universal functional encryption (in the sense of universal deniable encryption [SW14] or universal signature aggregators [HKW15]), where the key generation construction above could be applied to any CCA-secure encryption scheme.

Recently our field has had remarkable success in achieving results using indistinguishability obfuscation that were previously known to be possible only using ideal obfuscation, especially using the punctured programming paradigm of [SW14]. Is this just a matter of applying enough "$i\mathcal{O}$ gymnastics" to make this work?

Our Results. In our first result, somewhat surprisingly, we show that in this case, the intuition based on ideal obfuscation is wrong. Specifically, we show the following:

[2] Note that ideal obfuscation is impossible to build.

Informal Theorem 1. *Assuming CCA-secure public-key encryption, fully homomorphic encryption (FHE) and LWE, there exists a CCA-secure public-key encryption scheme that is provably not FE-compatible.*

The construction we give in the impossibility result above is quite contrived, like most impossibility results of this type. Could it be that all "natural" CCA-secure public-key encryption schemes are FE-compatible? Sadly, we do not know how to answer, or even formally define, this question. Nevertheless, one natural setting in which to consider this question is the well-studied random oracle model; this model allows for very simple and intuitive proofs of CCA-security, via the popular Fujisaki-Okamoto [FO99] transformation. In the random oracle model, however, we show an even stronger negative result: Every public-key encryption scheme, when converted into a CCA-secure encryption scheme in the random oracle model via the Fujisaki-Okamoto transformation, is provably not FE-compatible in the random oracle model. Thus, in the random oracle model, we obtain a large family of natural CCA-secure schemes[3] that are not FE-compatible.[4]

In light of the impossibility results above, we believe that a systematic study of FE-compatibility will need to proceed in a "bottom-up" manner, by looking at existing classes of CCA-secure encryption schemes and seeing if they can indeed be FE-compatible. We initiate this line of study by identifying a key structure that, if present, is sufficient to provide FE-compatibility. Specifically, we show the following:

Informal Theorem 2. *Assuming sub-exponentially secure one way functions and sub-exponentially secure iO, there exists a class of public key encryption schemes which we call* Special-CCA *secure encryption schemes that are FE-compatible.*

We then note that several existing CCA-secure encryption schemes fall into the class of *Special-CCA* secure encryption schemes. As a result, we get the following theorem:

Informal Theorem 3. *Assuming sub-exponentially secure indistinguishability obfuscation and sub-exponentially secure one way functions, each of the following existing CCA-secure encryption schemes are FE-compatible:*

- *[CHK04] when instantiated with the IBE scheme of [BB04].*
- *[CHK04] when instantiated with any Hierarchical IBE scheme.*
- *[PW08] when instantiated with any Lossy Trapdoor Function.*

[3] We believe similarly structured transformation such as RSA-OAEP [BR94] will have the same issues.

[4] Interestingly, if the scheme is instantiated with a particular hash function family it might actually be FE-compatible. This is somewhat the opposite of a typical RO infeasibility results where one usually finds a scheme is provably secure in the RO model, but is insecure under any concrete instantiation. Unfortunately, it is unclear how to argue positive security of any such concrete FO instantiations as the usual RO heuristic is now off limits.

It is interesting to note that the above CCA-secure encryption schemes are each at least 9 years old, and yet they can be used to build functional encryption schemes without changing the encryption mechanism. Contrast this to existing functional encryption schemes before our work, most of which have specifically designed encryption methods using "$i\mathcal{O}$-friendly" tools.

Finally, we also consider a weaker notion called *key-only FE-compatibility* where we retain only the public key and secret key of the public key encryption scheme and design new encryption, function secret key generation and decryption algorithms to "upgrade" it to a FE scheme. In the common random string model, we show that assuming polynomially hard iO, every public key encryption scheme is key-only FE compatible - that is, it can be upgraded to a selectively secure FE scheme for any function family. We refer the reader to the full version for details regarding this notion and the corresponding results we achieve.

Open Problems and Future Work. It would be interesting to understand if there exists other classes of encryption schemes that are FE-compatible. More generally, an interesting open problem would be to study what is the exact type of CCA-security needed for an encryption scheme to be FE-compatible.

While it is known that general purpose functional encryption implies indistinguishability obfuscation, another interesting direction would be to weaken the security requirement of functional encryption (for example, bounded-key secure FE) and understand what class of encryption schemes can be upgraded without the use of indistinguishability obfuscation. A solution in this setting might also be practical in today's world. Going in the other direction, an interesting feasibility question is whether we can upgrade existing encryption schemes to achieve general purpose multi-input functional encryption [GGG+14,BGJS15].

Finally, we observe that in our positive result, on upgrading the CCA secure encryption schemes into an FE scheme, it may potentially lose the CCA property. It is an interesting open problem to define and achieve FE-CCA compatibility[5].

2 Technical Overview

The question at the core of this paper is: what kinds of public-key encryption schemes can be "upgraded" to yield functional encryption schemes? Informally speaking, we say that a public-key encryption scheme PKE is *FE-compatible* if a functional encryption scheme can be generated where the setup and encryption algorithms of the functional encryption scheme are the same as the public-key encryption scheme. Namely, we have $\mathsf{FE.Setup} = \mathsf{PKE.Setup}$ and $\mathsf{FE.Enc} = \mathsf{PKE.Enc}$. Thus, only the functional encryption key generation and decryption algorithms are allowed to be newly specified.

As already noted, the technical starting point for our work is the folklore observation that any functional encryption scheme must satisfy a certain level

[5] Note that our negative result would still hold in this stronger model of FE-CCA compatibility.

of non-malleability. To remind ourselves why, consider a functional encryption scheme for encrypting $(n+1)$-bit messages m, and consider the function f_1 that on input m simply outputs the first n bits of m. Suppose that we obtain a functional key SK_{f_1} for this function. Then functional encryption guarantees that encryptions of any two messages with identical n-bit prefixes should still be indistinguishable from each other.

But suppose there was a way for an adversary to modify any encryption $\mathsf{FE.Enc}(m)$ to obtain $\mathsf{FE.Enc}(m')$ where m' swapped the first and last bits of m. This would, for example, easily be possible if one tried to encrypt the message bit-by-bit. Then, by applying the functional key SK_{f_1} to $\mathsf{FE.Enc}(m')$, the adversary would learn the last bit of m, and break the security that is supposed to be guaranteed by functional encryption.

An Impossibility Result. The most natural question to ask, then, is whether CCA-security is also a sufficient condition for FE-compatibility. In our first result, we prove that this is indeed not the case: we construct a counterexample public-key encryption scheme that satisfies CCA-security, but provably is not FE-compatible.

Let us build some intuition for how our impossibility result will proceed. The main difference between the CCA security game and the FE security game is that in the CCA security game, there is a decryption *oracle*, whereas in the FE security game, the adversary can actually obtain a circuit that will (at least partially) decrypt ciphertexts. This is reminiscent of the situation underlying the impossibility result of Barak et al. [BGI+01] for virtual black-box obfuscation: There, the ideal model gave oracle access to the function to be obfuscated, whereas the real model gave the adversary an actual circuit implementing that function. Indeed, we draw inspiration from [BGI+01] in devising our negative result, although we differ from it in almost every technical respect.

The idea behind our negative result will be to take an arbitrary CCA-secure encryption scheme $(\mathsf{Setup}_{\mathsf{CCA}}, \mathsf{Enc}_{\mathsf{CCA}}, \mathsf{Dec}_{\mathsf{CCA}})$ and somehow "damage" it to make it FE-incompatible, without disturbing its CCA security. This "damaged scheme" must somehow make use of the fact that an FE-adversary will be able to ask for and obtain a functional key SK_{f_1}, let us say for the same prefix-revealing function f_1 that we defined above. This functional key SK_{f_1} enables the FE-adversary to compute a prefix-decryption circuit D that outputs the first n bits of the message corresponding to any ciphertext.

Our first idea (which conceptually dates back to [BGI+01]) is to use fully homomorphic encryption (FHE) to help us take advantage of this situation. We first choose a random n-bit string α, and encrypt it $c = \mathsf{Enc}_{\mathsf{CCA}}(\alpha||0)$ using the CCA-secure encryption scheme. But then we re-encrypt this $c' = \mathsf{FHE}(c)$ using the fully homomorphic encryption scheme. We reveal c' as part of the public key of the "damaged scheme," but crucially both α and c are kept hidden.

Why does this help? Because now an FE-adversary that obtains the prefix-decryption circuit D can compute $\mathsf{FHE.Eval}(D, c') = \mathsf{FHE}(\alpha)$. While it is not yet clear that this is useful for any attack, we observe that, at least intuitively, a CCA-attacker has no obvious way to obtaining $\mathsf{FHE}(\alpha)$ from the public key and the decryption oracle (though formally proving this will be the main technical challenge of our impossibility result, as we will discuss shortly). This is because the only information that the CCA-attacker has about α is contained in c', but c' is an encryption under FHE and the decryption oracle only decrypts ciphertexts validly encrypted using $\mathsf{Enc}_{\mathsf{CCA}}$.

To enable a real attack, then, we also add to the public key an obfuscation of a program P that takes as input an FHE ciphertext e, decrypts it, and checks whether this decryption is equal to α. If so, it outputs the secret key needed for executing $\mathsf{Dec}_{\mathsf{CCA}}$, otherwise it outputs $\perp$. Because the FE-attacker can obtain $\mathsf{FHE}(\alpha)$ as noted above, it can then use the obfuscated program to obtain the full secret key for executing $\mathsf{Dec}_{\mathsf{CCA}}$, breaking the security of the FE scheme.

Why These Changes Preserve CCA Security. The changes above – adding the FHE ciphertext c' and the obfuscated program P to the public key – only provide an impossibility result if CCA security is preserved even after these two objects are added to the public key. While it is not obvious how a CCA-attacker could use these objects to break security, in order to prove CCA security, intuitively we will need to remove the dependence of c' on α. But $c' = \mathsf{FHE}(\mathsf{Enc}_{\mathsf{CCA}}(\alpha||0))$, and the obfuscated program P contains the secret key for FHE. But in order to remove these secret keys from P, intuitively we need to remove the "trigger" point $\mathsf{FHE}(\alpha)$ from the code of P, for which we first need to remove the dependence of c' on α. This chicken-and-egg situation is the primary technical obstacle that we need to overcome to finish the proof.

To deal with this problem, we draw inspiration from the work of Myers and Shelat [MS09] and Hohenberger, Lewko and Waters [HLW12] that considered the seemingly very different problem of converting any CCA-secure encryption scheme for single-bit messages into a CCA-secure encryption scheme for multi-bit messages. However, to implement our inspiration, we will need to make a technical change to the encryption system. Instead of using $\mathsf{Enc}_{\mathsf{CCA}}$ to encrypt the entire $n+1$-bit message, we will use the CCA-secure encryption schemes to encrypt the first n bits of the message, and use a separate encryption scheme $\mathsf{Enc}_{\mathsf{CPA}}$ to encrypt the last bit of the message. (In fact, we will use $\mathsf{Enc}_{\mathsf{CCA}}$ to jointly encrypt the first n bits of the message and the ciphertext produced by $\mathsf{Enc}_{\mathsf{CPA}}$. But we will ignore this detail for the purpose of this overview.) Finally, we will change our obfuscated program P to output just the secret key for executing $\mathsf{Dec}_{\mathsf{CPA}}$ to decrypt the last bit. This way, the secret key for executing $\mathsf{Dec}_{\mathsf{CCA}}$ is independent of the program P. Now, we will define a Bad Event to be when a CCA-attacker queries its decryption oracle on the ciphertext $c = \mathsf{Enc}_{\mathsf{CCA}}(\alpha)$. Looking ahead, we will first consider the situation when this Bad Event does not happen. Then, we will show that indeed the Bad Event can only occur with negligible probability.

Suppose that we know that the Bad Event cannot happen. Then, the decryption oracle given to the CCA-attacker is equivalent to a decryption oracle that would be given to a CCA-attacker if $c = \mathsf{Enc}_{\mathsf{CCA}}(\alpha)$ was the "challenge" ciphertext on which the attacker is not allowed to query. Note that in this case, the CCA security of $\mathsf{Enc}_{\mathsf{CCA}}$ already guarantees that $c = \mathsf{Enc}_{\mathsf{CCA}}(\alpha)$ is indistinguishable from $c = \mathsf{Enc}_{\mathsf{CCA}}(0^n)$, even to an adversary that is given the obfuscated program P as auxiliary information about α. Thus, we can already remove the dependence of c' on α.

Now, the only part of the public key that depends on α is the obfuscated program P, and we just need to get rid of it. This could be accomplished via $i\mathcal{O}$ using the fact that α is a uniformly random string, but in fact our job is made even easier due to the recent works on "lockable obfuscation" of Goyal et al. [GKW17] and Wichs and Zirdelis [WZ17]. These works consider obfuscating programs $C(x)$ whose structure is exactly such that, for some circuit Test if $\mathsf{Test}(x) = \alpha$, then some secret β is revealed, and otherwise the output is $\perp$. Lockable obfuscation states that if α is chosen uniformly (and, for our setting, no auxiliary information about α is revealed), then such obfuscated programs are indistinguishable from obfuscated programs that always output $\perp$ and have no secrets within them whatsoever. Furthermore, such lockable obfuscation is possible to construct just assuming LWE for suitable parameters. Thus, applying the security of lockable obfuscation, we are able to replace the obfuscated program P with a program that always outputs $\perp$, thereby completely removing any information about the secret keys of any encryption scheme and about α. This shows that the new scheme is CCA-secure, under the assumption that the Bad Event does not occur.

All that remains to be done is to prove that the Bad Event does not occur. Counterintuitively, we first observe that the lockable obfuscation argument above already shows that the Bad Event cannot occur if the ciphertext c had been $c = \mathsf{Enc}_{\mathsf{CCA}}(0^n)$ instead of $c = \mathsf{Enc}_{\mathsf{CCA}}(\alpha)$. In other words, if $c = \mathsf{Enc}_{\mathsf{CCA}}(0^n)$, then the adversary never queries the decryption oracle with c. Now, suppose for sake of contradiction, that the adversary does query c with noticeable probability if $c = \mathsf{Enc}_{\mathsf{CCA}}(\alpha)$. Then, we can use this to break CCA-security of $\mathsf{Enc}_{\mathsf{CCA}}$; take as a challenge ciphertext c that is either $c = \mathsf{Enc}_{\mathsf{CCA}}(\alpha)$ or $c = \mathsf{Enc}_{\mathsf{CCA}}(0^n)$. Then run the adversary until it attempts to query the oracle on c. If it ever does this, we can conclude that $c = \mathsf{Enc}_{\mathsf{CCA}}(\alpha)$. If it doesn't, then we can output a random guess. This will give us an nontrivial advantage in determining whether $c = \mathsf{Enc}_{\mathsf{CCA}}(\alpha)$ or $c = \mathsf{Enc}_{\mathsf{CCA}}(0^n)$.

This completes the impossibility proof. Full details can be found in Sect. 4.

For the impossibility result that applies to CCA secure encryption schemes built using the Fujisaki-Okamoto transformation in the random oracle model, we refer the reader to the full version of the paper.

Positive Results for FE-Compatibility. Our impossibility result shows that CCA security is not a sufficient condition for an encryption scheme to be FE-compatible. On the other hand, unfortunately positive results on FE in the literature (e.g. [GGH+13, Wat14]) typically construct special-purpose encryption methods that are atypical for achieving CCA security. For instance, even though the original general-purpose FE scheme of [GGH+13] follows the Naor-Yung paradigm [NY90, Sah99], instead of using a simulation-sound NIZK in the encryption, it uses a special object introduced in [GGH+13] called a statistically simulation-sound NIZK. Recall that our goal is to find existing CCA-secure encryption schemes that are already FE-compatible, rather than design special-purpose (sometimes called "$i\mathcal{O}$ friendly") primitives that would enable FE.

How can we go about this? Let us try to see if there are encryption mechanisms that were useful in achieving CCA-security that can also be sufficient for achieving FE.

Our key observation is that the notion of a *punctured* decryption key, which has implicitly been used for building CCA-security for over a decade, since (at least) the work of [CHK04], can also be useful for building FE functional keys. Roughly speaking, we consider the notion of a tag-based encryption, where every ciphertext is associated with a tag. Then, a punctured decryption key $\mathsf{SK}_{\mathsf{tag}^*}$ should allow a user to decrypt every ciphertext with $\mathsf{tag} \neq \mathsf{tag}^*$, but messages encrypted under tag tag^* should still be semantically secure. Intuitively, such punctured keys have been useful for building CCA-secure encryption because a punctured decryption key would allow the implementation of a decryption oracle that would still not be able to decrypt a challenge message that was encrypted under tag tag^*. In the literature, such schemes are combined with one-time signature schemes, where the tag is set to be the verification key of such a one-time signature scheme, and then the ciphertext is signed in a way that verifies with this key.

How can we use this idea for building FE functional keys? At a high level, we start with the most basic idea for building a functional key for a function f. We can simply obfuscate a program that has the decryption key built in, uses this decryption key to decrypt the message m, and then outputs $f(m)$. Now, we need to argue that the encryption of m_0 and the encryption of m_1 should be indistinguishable as long as $f(m_0) = f(m_1) = y$. The first idea is to fix the verification key VK^* in advance that will be used as the tag for the challenge ciphertext c^*. Now, we can reformulate the obfuscated program to first check whether the input ciphertext is equal to c^*, in which case the program should output y, but otherwise it should just use the decryption key to decrypt the message m, and then output $f(m)$ as before. This program is functionally equivalent to the previous one, and therefore indistinguishability of obfuscated programs follows from $i\mathcal{O}$.

Now, our goal will be to replace the decryption key within the program with the punctured decryption key $\mathsf{SK}_{\mathsf{VK}^*}$. However, note that we cannot do that immediately, because there are many valid ciphertexts for various messages m that could be signed under verification key VK^*, on which the program is supposed to output $f(m)$. However, we know that it should be hard for the adversary to actually find such valid ciphertexts, because of the security of the one-time signature scheme. Here, we can use sub-exponentially secure $i\mathcal{O}$ to complete the argument: Roughly speaking, the work of [BCP14] shows that if an $i\mathcal{O}$ scheme is secure against time $T \cdot \mathsf{poly}(\mathsf{n})$ adversaries, then $i\mathcal{O}(P_1)$ and $i\mathcal{O}(P_2)$ are indistinguishable as long as: (1) they only differ on at most T inputs, and (2) these inputs are hard to find even if given the code of both P_1 and P_2, even for machines whose running time far exceed T. By using this, assuming also sub-exponentially secure one-time signatures (which follow from sub-exponentially strong one-way functions), we can replace the program with one that first checks whether the input ciphertext is equal to c^*, in which case the program outputs y, but otherwise it uses the *punctured* decryption key $\mathsf{SK}_{\mathsf{VK}^*}$ to decrypt the message m, and then output $f(m)$ as before.

Now, since only this punctured decryption key $\mathsf{SK}_{\mathsf{VK}^*}$ is used, we can argue that an encryption of m_0 under tag VK^* is indistinguishable from an encryption of m_1 under tag VK^*. Thus, we show how to bootstrap punctured decryption keys as an existing method for building CCA-secure encryption, into a method for constructing functional keys without needing to change the underlying encryption scheme. Interestingly, the security of the encryption given a punctured decryption key needs to hold only against polynomial-time adversaries, as in standard proofs of CCA-security.

We observe that at least three different existing CCA-secure schemes from the literature, some dating back over a decade, already follow the punctured key approach to building CCA-secure encryption, and therefore are FE-compatible. Full details can be found in Sect. 5.

2.1 Preliminaries and Organization

We refer the reader to the full version for definitions of the following primitives: public key encryption, indistinguishability obfuscation, differing inputs obfuscation, lockable obfuscation and fully homomorphic encryption.

In Sect. 3, we define the notion of FE-compatibility. In Sect. 4 we show the impossibility result. Finally, in Sect. 5, we show the constructions of FE-compatible CCA secure encryption schemes.

3 Defining Functional Encryption Compatibility

Throughout, let the security parameter be denoted by n. Let $\mathcal{X} = \{\mathcal{X}_n\}_{n\in\mathbf{N}}$ and $\mathcal{Y} = \{\mathcal{Y}_n\}_{n\in\mathbf{N}}$ denote ensembles where each $\mathcal{X}_n$ and $\mathcal{Y}_n$ is a finite set. Let $\mathcal{F} = \{\mathcal{F}_n\}_{n\in\mathbf{N}}$ denote an ensemble where each $\mathcal{F}_n$ is a finite collection of functions, and each function $f \in \mathcal{F}_n$ takes as input a string $x \in \mathcal{X}_n$ and outputs $f(x) \in \mathcal{Y}_n$.

We first define the notion of functional encryption (FE) in the next subsection and then, we define what it means for a public key encryption scheme to be FE-Compatible.

3.1 Functional Encryption

A functional encryption scheme $\mathsf{FE} = (\mathsf{FE.Setup}, \mathsf{FE.Enc}, \mathsf{FE.Keygen}, \mathsf{FE.Dec})$ for a family of message spaces $\{\mathcal{X}_n\}$, a family of output spaces $\{\mathcal{Y}_n\}$ and a family of functions $\mathcal{F}$ consists of the following polynomial time algorithms:

- $\mathsf{FE.Setup}(1^n)$. The setup algorithm takes as input the security parameter n and outputs a master public key-secret key pair $(\mathsf{MPK}, \mathsf{MSK})$.
- $\mathsf{FE.Enc}(\mathsf{MPK}, x) \to \mathsf{CT}$. The encryption algorithm takes as input a message $x \in \mathcal{X}_n$ and the master public key MPK. It outputs a ciphertext CT.
- $\mathsf{FE.Keygen}(\mathsf{MSK}, f) \to \mathsf{SK}_f$. The key generation algorithm takes as input a function $f \in \mathcal{F}_n$ and the master secret key MSK. It outputs a function secret key SK_f.
- $\mathsf{FE.Dec}(\mathsf{SK}_f, \mathsf{CT}) \to y$. The decryption algorithm takes as input a secret key SK_f and a ciphertext CT. It outputs a string $y \in \mathcal{Y}_n$ or $\perp$.

Definition 1. *(Correctness) A functional encryption scheme* FE *for* $\mathcal{F}$ *is correct if for all* $f \in \mathcal{F}_n$ *and all* $x \in \mathcal{X}_n$

$$\Pr\left[\begin{array}{c} (\mathsf{MPK},\mathsf{MSK}) \leftarrow \mathsf{FE.Setup}(1^n) \\ \mathsf{SK}_f \leftarrow \mathsf{FE.Keygen}(\mathsf{MSK}, f) \\ \mathsf{FE.Dec}(\mathsf{SK}_f, \mathsf{FE.Enc}(\mathsf{MPK}, x)) = f(x) \end{array}\right] = 1$$

where the probability is over the random coins of $\mathsf{FE.Setup}, \mathsf{FE.Enc}, \mathsf{FE.Keygen}$ *and* $\mathsf{FE.Dec}$.

Security. We define the security notion for a functional encryption scheme using the following game $(\mathsf{Adaptive} - \mathsf{IND})$ between a challenger and an adversary.

Setup Phase: The challenger generates $(\mathsf{MPK}, \mathsf{MSK}) \leftarrow \mathsf{FE.Setup}(1^n)$ and then hands over the master public key MPK to the adversary.

Key Query Phase 1: The adversary makes function secret key queries by submitting functions $\mathsf{f} \in \mathcal{F}_n$. The challenger responds by giving the adversary the corresponding function secret key $\mathsf{SK_f} \leftarrow \mathsf{FE.KeyGen}(\mathsf{MSK}, \mathsf{f})$.

Challenge Phase: The adversary chooses two messages $(\mathsf{m}_0, \mathsf{m}_1)$ of the same size (each in $\mathcal{X}_n$) such that for all queried functions f in the key query phase, it holds that $\mathsf{f}(\mathsf{m}_0) = \mathsf{f}(\mathsf{m}_1)$. The challenger selects a random bit $\mathsf{b} \in \{0, 1\}$ and sends a ciphertext $\mathsf{CT} \leftarrow \mathsf{FE.Enc}(\mathsf{MPK}, \mathsf{m_b})$ to the adversary.

Key Query Phase 2: The adversary may submit additional key queries $\mathsf{f} \in \mathcal{F}_n$ as long as they do not violate the constraint described above. That is, for all queries f, it must hold that $\mathsf{f}(\mathsf{m}_0) = \mathsf{f}(\mathsf{m}_1)$.

Guess: The adversary submits a guess b' and wins if $b' = b$. The adversary's advantage in this game is defined to be $2 * |\Pr[\mathsf{b} = \mathsf{b}'] - 1/2|$.

We also define the *selective* security game, which we call $(\mathsf{Selective} - \mathsf{IND})$ where the adversary outputs the challenge message pair even before seeing the master public key.

Definition 2. *A functional encryption scheme* FE *is selective/adaptive secure if all PPT adversaries have at most a negligible advantage in the* $\mathsf{Selective} - \mathsf{IND}/\mathsf{Adaptive} - \mathsf{IND}$ *security game.*

We can also parameterize by the number of function secret key queries the adversary can make in the security game.

Compactness [AJ15]: A functional encryption scheme is said to be compact if the size of the ciphertext does not depend on the size of the functions that the scheme can handle. That is, let $p(\cdot)$ be a polynomial. Now, any functional encryption scheme FE for a class of functions $\mathcal{F}$ is said to be compact if $|\mathsf{FE.Enc}(\mathsf{MPK}, x)| = p(n, |x|)$ where n is the security parameter.

3.2 FE-Compatibility

In this section, we define a property called FE-Compatibility for any public key encryption scheme.

Definition 3. *A public key encryption scheme* $\mathsf{PKE} = (\mathsf{PKE.Setup}, \mathsf{PKE.Enc}, \mathsf{PKE.Dec})$ *is said to be selective/adaptive FE-Compatible relative to a family of functions* $\mathcal{F}$ *if there exists two algorithms* $(\mathsf{FE.Keygen}, \mathsf{FE.Dec})$ *such that* $(\mathsf{FE.Setup}, \mathsf{FE.Enc}, \mathsf{FE.Keygen}, \mathsf{FE.Dec})$ *is a selectively/adaptively secure functional encryption scheme for the family* $\mathcal{F}$ *where:*

- $\mathsf{FE.Setup}(n) = \mathsf{PKE.Setup}(n)$. *In particular, if* $\mathsf{PKE.Setup}(n)$ *outputs* $(\mathsf{PK}, \mathsf{SK})$, *the output of* $\mathsf{FE.Setup}(n)$ *is* $(\mathsf{MPK} = \mathsf{PK}, \mathsf{MSK} = \mathsf{SK})$.
- $\mathsf{FE.Enc}(\mathsf{MPK}, \mathsf{m}) = \mathsf{PKE.Enc}(\mathsf{PK}, \mathsf{m})$.

Remark: Moreover, any such FE scheme is also compact because the size of the ciphertext is determined by the scheme PKE and doesn't depend on the size of the functions being queried.

4 An Impossibility Result

In this section, we will construct an IND-CCA secure encryption scheme that is not FE-Compatible according to Definition 3. Consider a function f_1 that on any input x of length $(n+1)$ bits, outputs the first n bits of x. Formally, we prove the following theorem:

Theorem 1. *Assuming the existence of lockable obfuscation, fully homomorphic encryption and IND-CCA secure public key encryption, the scheme* $\mathsf{PKE} = (\mathsf{PKE.Setup}, \mathsf{PKE.Enc}, \mathsf{PKE.Dec})$ *described below is an IND-CCA secure public key encryption scheme that is not selective FE-Compatible even for a single function secret key query for any function family* $\mathcal{F}$ *such that* $f_1 \in \mathcal{F}$.

We know how to construct lockable obfuscation with perfect correctness from the learning with errors (LWE) assumption [GKW17, WZ17]. As a result, we get the following corollary:

Corollary 2. *Assuming LWE, fully homomorphic encryption and the existence of IND-CCA secure public key encryption, the scheme* $\mathsf{PKE} = (\mathsf{PKE.Setup}, \mathsf{PKE.Enc}, \mathsf{PKE.Dec})$ *described below is an IND-CCA secure public key encryption scheme that is not selective FE-Compatible even for a single function secret key query for any function family* $\mathcal{F}$ *such that* $f_1 \in \mathcal{F}$.

Notation: Let the security parameter be n. Let $(\mathsf{Setup_{CPA}}, \mathsf{Enc_{CPA}}, \mathsf{Dec_{CPA}})$ be an IND-CPA secure encryption scheme that encrypts 1 bit messages and produces ciphertexts of length $l_1(n)$, $(\mathsf{Setup_{CCA}}, \mathsf{Enc_{CCA}}, \mathsf{Dec_{CCA}})$ be a CCA secure encryption scheme that encrypts messages of length $(n+1+l_1(n))$ and produces ciphertexts of size $l_2(n)$. Let $\mathsf{FHE} = (\mathsf{FHE.Setup}, \mathsf{FHE.Enc}, \mathsf{FHE.Dec}\mathsf{FHE.Eval})$ be a fully homomorphic encryption scheme that encrypts messages of length $(l_1(n)+l_2(n))$ and can evaluate any $\mathsf{Poly}(n)$-sized circuit. Let $(\mathcal{O}, \mathsf{Eval})$ be a secure lockable obfuscator for all $\mathsf{Poly}(n)$-sized circuits that take inputs of size $l_2(n)$ and produce outputs of size n. Our scheme $\mathsf{PKE} = (\mathsf{PKE.Setup}, \mathsf{PKE.Enc}, \mathsf{PKE.Dec})$ that encrypts messages of length $(n+1)$ is as follows:

- $\mathsf{PKE.Setup}(1^n)$:
  1. Compute $(\mathsf{PK_{CPA}}, \mathsf{SK_{CPA}}) \leftarrow \mathsf{Setup_{CPA}}(1^n)$, $(\mathsf{PK_{CCA}}, \mathsf{SK_{CCA}}) \leftarrow \mathsf{Setup_{CCA}}(1^n)$ and $(\mathsf{PK_{FHE}}, \mathsf{SK_{FHE}}) \leftarrow \mathsf{FHE.Setup}(1^n)$.
  2. Choose a random string $\alpha \in \{0,1\}^n$.
  3. Compute $\mathsf{CT}'_{\mathsf{CPA}} = \mathsf{Enc_{CPA}}(\mathsf{PK_{CPA}}, 0)$ and $\mathsf{CT}'_{\mathsf{CCA}} = \mathsf{Enc_{CCA}}(\mathsf{PK_{CCA}}, \alpha||0||\mathsf{CT}'_{\mathsf{CPA}})$. Let $\mathsf{CT}' = (\mathsf{CT}'_{\mathsf{CCA}}, \mathsf{CT}'_{\mathsf{CPA}})$. (In fact, CT' is an encryption of $(\alpha||0)$ using the encryption algorithm $\mathsf{PKE.Enc}$ described next).
  4. Compute $\mathsf{CT}'_{\mathsf{FHE}} = \mathsf{FHE.Enc}(\mathsf{PK_{FHE}}, \mathsf{CT}')$.
  5. Generate $\tilde{P} = \mathcal{O}(n, P, \mathsf{SK_{CPA}}, \alpha)$ using the tester program P described in Fig. 1 where n is the security parameter, P is the program, $\mathsf{SK_{CPA}}$ is the message and α is the lock value. In particular, the functionality of the obfuscated program $\tilde{P}$ is described in Fig. 2. Note that Fig. 2 is just for intuition and does not correspond to a formal specification.
  6. Output the public key as $\mathsf{PK} = (\mathsf{PK_{CPA}}, \mathsf{PK_{CCA}}, \mathsf{PK_{FHE}}, \mathsf{CT}'_{\mathsf{FHE}}, \tilde{P})$. The secret key of the scheme is $\mathsf{SK} = \mathsf{SK_{CCA}}$.
- $\mathsf{PKE.Enc}(\mathsf{PK}, \mathsf{m})$:
  1. Given an $(n+1)$ bit message m, let p be the last bit of m.
  2. Compute $\mathsf{CT_{CPA}} = \mathsf{Enc_{CPA}}(\mathsf{PK_{CPA}}, p)$.
  3. Compute $\mathsf{CT_{CCA}} = \mathsf{Enc_{CCA}}(\mathsf{PK_{CCA}}, \mathsf{m}||\mathsf{CT_{CPA}})$.
  4. Output the ciphertext $\mathsf{CT} = (\mathsf{CT_{CCA}}, \mathsf{CT_{CPA}})$.
- $\mathsf{PKE.Dec}(\mathsf{SK}, \mathsf{CT})$:
  1. Parse $\mathsf{CT} = (\mathsf{CT_{CCA}}, \mathsf{CT_{CPA}})$. Recall that $\mathsf{SK} = \mathsf{SK_{CCA}}$.
  2. Let $(\mathsf{m}||\mathsf{y}) = \mathsf{Dec_{CCA}}(\mathsf{SK_{CCA}}, \mathsf{CT_{CCA}})$.
  3. If the above decryption outputs $\perp$ or if $y \neq \mathsf{CT_{CPA}}$, output $\perp$.
  4. Else, output the message m.

We now prove Theorem 1.

Correctness: It can be observed that if the schemes $(\mathsf{Setup_{CPA}}, \mathsf{Enc_{CPA}}, \mathsf{Dec_{CPA}})$ and $(\mathsf{Setup_{CCA}}, \mathsf{Enc_{CCA}}, \mathsf{Dec_{CCA}})$ are correct except with negligible probability, then PKE is correct except with negligible probability. That is, $\mathsf{PKE.Dec}(\mathsf{PKE.Enc}(\mathsf{PK}, \mathsf{m}), \mathsf{SK}) = \mathsf{m}$ for any message $\mathsf{m} \in \{0,1\}^{(n+1)}$.

To prove our theorem we need to show two things. First, we will show that any candidate functional encryption scheme that includes a "all but last bit reveal" functionality which shares the setup and encrypt algorithms with the above public key encryption scheme must be insecure. Second, we show that the scheme PKE actually does have IND-CCA security under certain assumptions. Putting these together will yield our theorem.

Program P

Input : FHE ciphertext $\mathsf{CT}_{\mathsf{FHE}}$
Constants : $\mathsf{SK}_{\mathsf{FHE}}$

1. Output $\mathsf{FHE.Dec}(\mathsf{SK}_{\mathsf{FHE}}, \mathsf{CT}_{\mathsf{FHE}})$.

Fig. 1. Tester program (as in lockable obfuscation notation)

Program $\tilde{P}$

Input : FHE ciphertext $\mathsf{CT}_{\mathsf{FHE}}$
Constants : $\mathsf{SK}_{\mathsf{FHE}}, \alpha, \mathsf{SK}_{\mathsf{CPA}}$

1. Compute $\mathsf{y} \leftarrow \mathsf{FHE.Dec}(\mathsf{SK}_{\mathsf{FHE}}, \mathsf{CT}_{\mathsf{FHE}})$.
2. If $\mathsf{y} = \alpha$, output $\mathsf{SK}_{\mathsf{CPA}}$. Else, output $\perp$.

Fig. 2. Functionality of lockable obfuscated tester program

4.1 An Attack

In this section, assuming the correctness of the encryption schemes used and correctness of the obfuscator, we show that the above scheme PKE is not FE-Compatible. Suppose it is indeed FE-Compatible. We will arrive at a contradiction. Formally, we prove the following lemma.

Lemma 1. *Any scheme* $\mathsf{FE} = (\mathsf{FE.Setup}, \mathsf{FE.Enc}, \mathsf{FE.Keygen}, \mathsf{FE.Dec})$ *where* $\mathsf{FE.Setup}(.) = \mathsf{PKE.Setup}(.)$ *and* $\mathsf{FE.Enc}(.) = \mathsf{PKE.Enc}(.)$ *is not selectively secure even for just 1 function secret key query for any function family* $\mathcal{F}$ *such that* $f_1 \in \mathcal{F}$.

Proof. Consider a FE adversary $\mathcal{A}$ who interacts with a FE challenger in the selective IND-security game as follows:

1. In the first round, $\mathcal{A}$ submits two messages $\mathsf{m}_0 = (0^n||0)$ and $\mathsf{m}_1 = (0^n||1)$.
2. $\mathcal{A}$ asks for a function secret key corresponding to the following function f_1: on input x of length $(n+1)$ bits, $f_1(x)$ outputs the first n bits of x. Note that since the first n bits of m_0 and m_1 are equal, this is a valid function secret key query.
3. The challenger runs the setup algorithm and generates PK, SK. He gives PK to the adversary along with the function secret key SK_{f_1}. Also, the challenger picks a bit b at random and sends $\mathsf{CT}^* = \mathsf{PKE.Enc}(\mathsf{PK}, \mathsf{m}_b)$.
4. Let the challenge ciphertext be $\mathsf{CT}^* = (\mathsf{CT}^*_{\mathsf{CCA}}, \mathsf{CT}^*_{\mathsf{CPA}})$. The adversary computes a FHE ciphertext $\mathsf{CT}_{\mathsf{FHE}} = \mathsf{FHE.Eval}(\mathsf{FE.Dec}(\mathsf{SK}_f, \cdot), \mathsf{CT}'_{\mathsf{FHE}})$ using the

ciphertext $\mathsf{CT}'_{\mathsf{FHE}}$ in the public key and the function secret key SK_f. $\mathcal{A}$ then runs the obfuscated program $\tilde{P}$ on input $\mathsf{CT}_{\mathsf{FHE}}$. That is, run $\mathsf{Eval}(\tilde{P}, \mathsf{CT}_{\mathsf{FHE}})$ to receive output $\mathsf{SK}'_{\mathsf{CPA}}$. It then computes $b' = \mathsf{Dec}_{\mathsf{CPA}}(\mathsf{SK}'_{\mathsf{CPA}}, \mathsf{CT}^*_{\mathsf{CPA}})$ and outputs b' to the challenger.

Analysis: We now show why the adversary's guess b' is equal to the challenger's random bit b except with negligible probability. From the correctness of the FE scheme, SK_{f_1} must be a correct function secret key for the function f_1. First, from the correctness of the FHE scheme, observe that $\mathsf{CT}_{\mathsf{FHE}} = \mathsf{FHE.Eval}(\mathsf{SK}_f, \mathsf{CT}'_{\mathsf{FHE}})$ is an encryption of the random string α using the algorithm FHE.Enc. Now, notice that when this ciphertext $\mathsf{CT}_{\mathsf{FHE}}$ is a correct encryption of α. So, when it is fed as input to the program $\tilde{P}$, from the correctness of lockable obfuscation, the program outputs the secret key of the IND-CPA secure encryption scheme - $\mathsf{SK}_{\mathsf{CPA}}$ (which we denoted as $\mathsf{SK}'_{\mathsf{CPA}}$). Therefore, now the adversary's strategy easily follows. $\mathcal{A}$ uses $\mathsf{SK}_{\mathsf{CPA}}$ to decrypt $\mathsf{CT}^*_{\mathsf{CPA}}$ and from the correctness of the IND-CPA secure encryption scheme, this decrypts to give the value b correctly, which is the adversary's output.

Hence, the adversary can break the selective IND-security of the FE scheme which is a contradiction. Note that the negligible error comes from the fact that the IND-CPA secure encryption scheme, the FE scheme, the lockable obfuscation scheme and the FHE scheme are all correct except with negligible probability. □

4.2 IND-CCA Security

We now prove that the scheme is IND-CCA secure. Our proof strategy is organized along the lines around detecting a bad query event which follows the work of Myers and Shelat [MS09] and Hohenberger, Lewko and Waters [HLW12] who proved multibit CCA security from the existence of 1-bit CCA security. Formally, we prove the following lemma:

Lemma 2. *Assuming the hardness of learning with errors (LWE),* $(\mathsf{Setup}_{\mathsf{CPA}}, \mathsf{Enc}_{\mathsf{CPA}}, \mathsf{Dec}_{\mathsf{CPA}})$ *is an IND-CPA secure public key encryption scheme and* $(\mathsf{Setup}_{\mathsf{CCA}}, \mathsf{Enc}_{\mathsf{CCA}}, \mathsf{Dec}_{\mathsf{CCA}})$ *is an IND-CCA secure public key encryption scheme,* $\mathsf{PKE} = (\mathsf{PKE.Setup}, \mathsf{PKE.Enc}, \mathsf{PKE.Dec})$ *is an IND-CCA secure public key encryption scheme.*

Proof. We begin our proof by defining a "Bad-Query" event that is defined within the context of the attacker playing the IND-CCA security game on the encryption scheme PKE. □

Definition 4. ***(Bad Query Event):*** *Let* PK *be the public key of the scheme* PKE *that is given to the adversary. We say that a bad query event has occurred during an execution of the IND-CCA security game between the adversary* $\mathcal{A}$ *and the challenger if* $\mathcal{A}$ *makes a decryption query of the form* $\mathsf{CT} = (\mathsf{CT}_1, \mathsf{CT}_2)$ *such that* $\mathsf{CT}_1 = \mathsf{CT}'_{\mathsf{CCA}}$, *where* $\mathsf{CT}'_{\mathsf{CCA}}$ *was created by the setup algorithm* PKE.Setup.

In order to prove IND-CCA security of our scheme, we will rely on the following claim:

Claim. A Bad Query Event does not take place except with negligible probability in n, where the probability is taken over the coins of the adversary and the challenger playing the IND-CCA security game.

We defer the proof of this claim to the next section. Here, we show that our scheme is IND-CCA secure assuming the claim holds true. We will prove this via a series of hybrid experiments where we show that every successive pair of hybrids is computationally indistinguishable and the final hybrid is independent of the challenge bit b and hence the attacker's advantage will be 0 in the final hybrid.

- Hyb_1: This is the real world experiment with challenge bit b chosen randomly. The challenge ciphertext is $\mathsf{CT}^* = (\mathsf{CT}^*_{\mathsf{CCA}}, \mathsf{CT}^*_{\mathsf{CPA}})$.
- Hyb_2: This hybrid is identical to the previous hybrid except that now, the decryption oracle rejects[6] for any ciphertext query $\mathsf{CT} = (\mathsf{CT}_1, \mathsf{CT}_2)$ if $\mathsf{CT}_1 = \mathsf{CT}'_{\mathsf{CCA}}$. Note that the oracle also continues to reject the challenge ciphertext as before.
- Hyb_3: This hybrid is identical to the previous hybrid except that during setup, $\mathsf{CT}'_{\mathsf{CCA}}$ is now computed as $\mathsf{CT}'_{\mathsf{CCA}} = \mathsf{Enc}_{\mathsf{CCA}}(\mathsf{PK}_{\mathsf{CCA}}, 0^{n+1} || \mathsf{CT}'_{\mathsf{CPA}})$.
- Hyb_4: This hybrid is identical to the previous hybrid except that in the public key, $\tilde{P}$ is replaced with the simulated obfuscated program - i.e. $\mathsf{Sim}(n, 1^{|P|}, 1^{|\mathsf{SK}_{\mathsf{CPA}}|})$ where Sim is the simulator of the lockable obfuscation scheme.
- Hyb_5: This hybrid is identical to the previous hybrid except that in the challenge ciphertext $\mathsf{CT}^* = (\mathsf{CT}^*_{\mathsf{CCA}}, \mathsf{CT}^*_{\mathsf{CPA}})$, $\mathsf{CT}^*_{\mathsf{CPA}}$ is now computed independent of the bit b as follows: $\mathsf{CT}^*_{\mathsf{CPA}} = \mathsf{Enc}_{\mathsf{CPA}}(\mathsf{PK}_{\mathsf{CPA}}, 0)$.
- Hyb_6: This hybrid is identical to the previous hybrid except that now, the decryption oracle also rejects any ciphertext query $\mathsf{CT} = (\mathsf{CT}_1, \mathsf{CT}_2)$ if $\mathsf{CT}_1 = \mathsf{CT}^*_{\mathsf{CCA}}$.
- Hyb_7: This hybrid is identical to the previous hybrid except that in the challenge ciphertext, $\mathsf{CT}^*_{\mathsf{CCA}}$ is now computed independent of the bit b as follows: $\mathsf{CT}^*_{\mathsf{CCA}} = \mathsf{Enc}_{\mathsf{CPA}}(\mathsf{PK}_{\mathsf{CCA}}, 0^{n+1} || \mathsf{CT}^*_{\mathsf{CPA}})$.

Observe that in this last hybrid, the challenge ciphertext is created independent of the bit b. Hence, the attacker's advantage in this hybrid is negligible.

We will now show the indistinguishability of every successive pair of hybrids.

Claim. Assuming Claim 4.2 holds, Hyb_1 is computationally indistinguishable from Hyb_2.

Proof. The only difference between the two hybrids is that in Hyb_2, the decryption oracle rejects queries of the form $\mathsf{CT} = (\mathsf{CT}_1, \mathsf{CT}_2)$ where $\mathsf{CT}_1 = \mathsf{CT}'_{\mathsf{CCA}}$ while such queries are not rejected by the oracle in Hyb_1. However, Claim 4.2 essentially proves that such queries (which we have defined as the occurrence of a bad query event) are never made by the adversary except with negligible probability. Therefore, if Claim 4.2 holds, Hyb_1 is computationally indistinguishable from Hyb_2. □

[6] Throughout the paper, we use rejecting an input and producing output $\perp$ for the input interchangeably.

Claim. Assuming that $(\mathsf{Setup}_{\mathsf{CCA}}, \mathsf{Enc}_{\mathsf{CCA}}, \mathsf{Dec}_{\mathsf{CCA}})$ is an IND-CCA secure encryption scheme, Hyb_2 is computationally indistinguishable from Hyb_3.

Proof. The only difference is that in Hyb_2, $\mathsf{CT}'_{\mathsf{CCA}} = \mathsf{Enc}_{\mathsf{CCA}}(\mathsf{PK}_{\mathsf{CCA}}, \alpha||0||\mathsf{CT}'_{\mathsf{CPA}})$ while in Hyb_3, $\mathsf{CT}'_{\mathsf{CCA}} = \mathsf{Enc}_{\mathsf{CCA}}(\mathsf{PK}_{\mathsf{CCA}}, 0^{n+1}||\mathsf{CT}'_{\mathsf{CPA}})$. We can show that if there exists an adversary $\mathcal{A}$ that can distinguish between these two hybrids, there exists an adversary $\mathcal{B}$ that can break the CCA security of the encryption scheme $(\mathsf{Setup}_{\mathsf{CCA}}, \mathsf{Enc}_{\mathsf{CCA}}, \mathsf{Dec}_{\mathsf{CCA}})$. We defer the details of the proof to the full version. □

Claim. Assuming that $(\mathcal{O}, \mathsf{Eval})$ is a secure lockable obfuscator, Hyb_3 is computationally indistinguishable from Hyb_4.

Proof. The only difference between the two hybrids is that in Hyb_3, the public key contains $\mathcal{O}(n, P, \mathsf{SK}_{\mathsf{CPA}}, \alpha)$ while in Hyb_4, it contains the simulated program - $\mathsf{Sim}(n, 1^{|P|}, 1^{|\mathsf{SK}_{\mathsf{CPA}}|})$. Since α is picked uniformly at random and is used only as the lock value in the obfuscated program and nowhere else, from the security of lockable obfuscation, the two hybrids will be computationally indistinguishable. We now describe the reduction.

Consider an adversary $\mathcal{A}$ that can distinguish between these two hybrids. We will now design a reduction $\mathcal{A}_{\mathsf{lock}}$ that uses $\mathcal{A}$ to break the security of the lockable obfuscation scheme. $\mathcal{A}_{\mathsf{lock}}$ interacts with $\mathcal{A}$ and runs the experiment exactly as in Hyb_3 except generating the obfuscated program. $\mathcal{A}_{\mathsf{lock}}$ interacts with a challenger $\mathcal{C}$ for the lockable obfuscation scheme. $\mathcal{A}_{\mathsf{lock}}$ sends the program P and the message $\mathsf{SK}_{\mathsf{CPA}}$ to the challenger $\mathcal{C}$. $\mathcal{C}$ sends back either $\mathcal{O}(n, P, \mathsf{SK}_{\mathsf{CPA}}, \alpha)$ where α is picked uniformly at random or a simulated obfuscated circuit $\mathsf{Sim}(n, 1^{|P|}, 1^{|\mathsf{SK}_{\mathsf{CPA}}|})$. $\mathcal{A}_{\mathsf{lock}}$ sets this as the obfuscated circuit $\tilde{P}$ and continues with the experiment as in Hyb_3. Now, it easily follows that if $\mathcal{A}$ can distinguish between the two hybrids, $\mathcal{A}_{\mathsf{lock}}$ can use the same distinguishing guess to break the security of the lockable obfuscation scheme which is a contradiction. □

Claim. Assuming that $(\mathsf{Setup}_{\mathsf{CPA}}, \mathsf{Enc}_{\mathsf{CPA}}, \mathsf{Dec}_{\mathsf{CPA}})$ is an IND-CPA secure encryption scheme, Hyb_4 is computationally indistinguishable from Hyb_5.

Proof. The only difference between the two hybrids is in the challenge ciphertexts. In Hyb_4, $\mathsf{CT}^*_{\mathsf{CPA}} = \mathsf{Enc}_{\mathsf{CPA}}(\mathsf{PK}_{\mathsf{CPA}}, p_b)$ while in Hyb_5, $\mathsf{CT}^*_{\mathsf{CPA}} = \mathsf{Enc}_{\mathsf{CCA}}(\mathsf{PK}_{\mathsf{CPA}}, 0)$. Here, p is the last bit of the message m_b. We can show that if there exists an adversary $\mathcal{A}$ that can distinguish between these two hybrids, there exists an adversary $\mathcal{B}$ that can break the CPA security of the encryption scheme $(\mathsf{Setup}_{\mathsf{CPA}}, \mathsf{Enc}_{\mathsf{CPA}}, \mathsf{Dec}_{\mathsf{CPA}})$. We defer the details of the proof to the full version. □

Claim. Hyb_5 is identical to Hyb_6.

Proof. The only difference between the two hybrids is that in Hyb_6, the decryption oracle rejects any ciphertext query $\mathsf{CT} = (\mathsf{CT}_1, \mathsf{CT}_2)$ if $\mathsf{CT}_1 = \mathsf{CT}^*_{\mathsf{CCA}}$. First, observe that if $\mathsf{CT}_2 = \mathsf{CT}^*_{\mathsf{CPA}}$, then CT is in fact the challenge ciphertext CT^* itself and hence even Hyb_6 would reject the query. On the other hand, if

$\mathsf{CT}_2 \neq \mathsf{CT}^*_{\mathsf{CPA}}$ but $\mathsf{CT}_1 = \mathsf{CT}^*_{\mathsf{CCA}}$, then, $\mathsf{Dec}_{\mathsf{CCA}}(\mathsf{SK}_{\mathsf{CCA}}, \mathsf{CT}_1)$ produces (m^*, y^*) such that $y^* \neq \mathsf{CT}_2$. This is because y^* would in fact be equal to $\mathsf{CT}^*_{\mathsf{CPA}}$. Hence, even Hyb_5 would reject these queries and so the two hybrids are identical. □

Claim. Assuming that $(\mathsf{Setup}_{\mathsf{CCA}}, \mathsf{Enc}_{\mathsf{CCA}}, \mathsf{Dec}_{\mathsf{CCA}})$ is an IND-CCA secure encryption scheme, Hyb_6 is computationally indistinguishable from Hyb_7.

Proof. The only difference between the two hybrids is in the challenge ciphertext $\mathsf{CT}^* = (\mathsf{CT}^*_{\mathsf{CCA}}, \mathsf{CT}^*_{\mathsf{CPA}})$. In Hyb_6, $\mathsf{CT}^*_{\mathsf{CCA}} = \mathsf{Enc}_{\mathsf{CCA}}(\mathsf{PK}_{\mathsf{CCA}}, \mathsf{m}_b || \mathsf{CT}^*_{\mathsf{CPA}})$ while in Hyb_7, $\mathsf{CT}^*_{\mathsf{CCA}} = \mathsf{Enc}_{\mathsf{CCA}}(\mathsf{PK}_{\mathsf{CCA}}, 0^{n+1} || \mathsf{CT}^*_{\mathsf{CPA}})$. We can show that if there exists an adversary $\mathcal{A}$ that can distinguish between these two hybrids, there exists an adversary $\mathcal{B}$ that can break the CCA security of the encryption scheme $(\mathsf{Setup}_{\mathsf{CCA}}, \mathsf{Enc}_{\mathsf{CCA}}, \mathsf{Dec}_{\mathsf{CCA}})$. We defer the details of the proof to the full version. □

4.3 Proof of Claim 4.2

Instead of proving the claim directly, we first prove it for an alternate IND-CCA security game and then show how it holds even in the actual IND-CCA security game.

Alternate IND-CCA Game. This is same as the original game except that the Challenger now computes $\mathsf{CT}'_{\mathsf{CCA}}$ during setup as follows: $\mathsf{CT}'_{\mathsf{CCA}} = \mathsf{Enc}_{\mathsf{CCA}}(\mathsf{PK}_{\mathsf{CCA}}, 0^{n+1} || \mathsf{CT}'_{\mathsf{CPA}})$. That is, α is no longer part of the message being encrypted. For this alternate IND-CCA game, the Bad Query Event remains the same: i.e., the event occurs if the adversary makes a query $\mathsf{CT} = (\mathsf{CT}_1, \mathsf{CT}_2)$ to the decryption oracle where $\mathsf{CT}_1 = \mathsf{CT}'_{\mathsf{CCA}}$. Now, via a sequence of hybrids, we show that Claim 4.2 holds for this alternate IND-CCA game. That is, we show that the Bad Query Event happens with negligible probability.

- Hyb_1: This hybrid corresponds to the alternate IND-CCA game as described above.
- Hyb_2: This hybrid is identical to the previous hybrid except that in the public key, $\tilde{P}$ is replaced with the simulated obfuscated program - i.e. $\mathsf{Sim}(n, 1^{|P|}, 1^{|\mathsf{SK}_{\mathsf{CPA}}|})$ where Sim is the simulator of the lockable obfuscation scheme.
- Hyb_3: This hybrid is identical to the previous hybrid except that the ciphertext $\mathsf{CT}'_{\mathsf{FHE}}$ is now computed as $\mathsf{CT}'_{\mathsf{FHE}} = \mathsf{FHE.Enc}(\mathsf{PK}_{\mathsf{FHE}}, 0^{l_1(n)+l_2(n)})$.

We now show that every successive pair of hybrids is computationally indistinguishable. This proves that the probability that the Bad Query Event occurs is the same for every pair of successive hybrids. Finally, we show that in the last hybrid Hyb_4, the probability that the Bad Query Event occurs is negligible.

Claim. Assuming that $(\mathcal{O}, \mathsf{Eval})$ is a secure lockable obfuscator, Hyb_1 is computationally indistinguishable from Hyb_2.

Proof. The proof is same as the proof of Claim 4.2. □

Claim. Assuming that ($\mathsf{FHE}.\mathit{setup}, \mathsf{FHE}.\mathit{enc}, \mathsf{FHE}.\mathit{dec}$) is an IND-CPA secure fully homomorphic encryption scheme, Hyb_2 is computationally indistinguishable from Hyb_3.

Proof. The proof is same as the proof of Claim 4.2. □

Claim. $\Pr[\text{Bad Query Event occurs in } \mathsf{Hyb}_3] = \text{negligible}(n)$.

Proof. This is because the ciphertext $\mathsf{CT}'_{\mathsf{CCA}}$ does not appear at all in the public key anymore! Even if the adversary knew the value of $(\mathsf{CT}'_{\mathsf{CPA}})$, the only information that the adversary has about $\mathsf{CT}'_{\mathsf{CCA}}$ is that it is an encryption of $(0^{n+1}||\mathsf{CT}'_{\mathsf{CPA}})$ using public key $\mathsf{PK}_{\mathsf{CCA}}$.

First, observe that the number of possible ciphertexts for the message $(0^{n+1}|| \mathsf{CT}'_{\mathsf{CPA}})$ must be at least super-polynomial in n. This follows from the CPA security of the encryption scheme ($\mathsf{Setup}_{\mathsf{CCA}}, \mathsf{Enc}_{\mathsf{CCA}}, \mathsf{Dec}_{\mathsf{CCA}}$) because if this wasn't true, a polynomial time adversary can break the CPA security by generating all possible ciphertexts for $(0^{n+1}||\mathsf{CT}'_{\mathsf{CPA}})$ and testing it with the challenge ciphertext.

Now, notice that to make the Bad Query Event occur, the adversary will just have to guess the value of $\mathsf{CT}'_{\mathsf{CCA}}$ (or the randomness that was used in the encryption to generate $\mathsf{CT}'_{\mathsf{CCA}}$) and this can be done only with negligible probability. □

Original IND-CCA Game. We show that the Bad Query Event happens only with negligible probability even in the original IND-CCA game. Formally, we prove the following lemma:

Lemma 3. *Assuming* ($\mathsf{Setup}_{\mathsf{CCA}}, \mathsf{Enc}_{\mathsf{CCA}}, \mathsf{Dec}_{\mathsf{CCA}}$) *is a CCA secure encryption scheme and that the Bad Query Event does not occur in the Alternate CCA game described above except with negligible probability, the Bad Query Event does not occur in the original CCA security game for the encryption scheme* PKE *except with negligible probability.*

Proof. Suppose there exists an adversary $\mathcal{A}$ that makes the Bad Query Event occur with non-negligible probability. We now construct an algorithm $\mathcal{B}$ that breaks the IND-CCA security of ($\mathsf{Setup}_{\mathsf{CCA}}, \mathsf{Enc}_{\mathsf{CCA}}, \mathsf{Dec}_{\mathsf{CCA}}$). $\mathcal{B}$ acts as the challenger of the IND-CCA security game for the scheme PKE in its interaction with $\mathcal{A}$. First, $\mathcal{B}$ interacts with its challenger and receives the public key $\mathsf{PK}_{\mathsf{CCA}}$. $\mathcal{B}$ then runs the setup algorithm $\mathsf{PKE.Setup}$,(except the $\mathsf{Setup}_{\mathsf{CCA}}$ part) to compute the public keys $\mathsf{PK}_{\mathsf{CPA}}, \mathsf{PK}_{\mathsf{FHE}}$. It computes $\mathsf{CT}'_{\mathsf{CPA}}$ as done by the setup algorithm. $\mathcal{B}$ then sends the pair $(\alpha||0||\mathsf{CT}'_{\mathsf{CPA}}, 0^{n+1}||\mathsf{CT}'_{\mathsf{CPA}})$ as the two challenge messages to the challenger and sets the response as $\mathsf{CT}'_{\mathsf{CCA}}$. $\mathcal{B}$ continues with the rest of the game acting as the challenger to $\mathcal{A}$. Whenever $\mathcal{A}$ makes a decryption query $(\mathsf{CT}_1, \mathsf{CT}_2)$, if $\mathsf{CT}_1 \neq \mathsf{CT}'_{\mathsf{CCA}}$, it queries the decryption oracle of its challenger with CT_1 and uses this to respond to $\mathcal{A}$ as done in the original game. Similarly, $\mathcal{B}$ also creates the challenge ciphertext. If $\mathcal{B}$ ever receives a query $(\mathsf{CT}_1, \mathsf{CT}_2)$ from $\mathcal{A}$ to the decryption oracle such that $\mathsf{CT}_1 = \mathsf{CT}'_{\mathsf{CCA}}$, it immediately halts the game with $\mathcal{A}$ and outputs the guess 0 to its challenger. If such a query never happens, it outputs 1 to the challenger after completing the game with $\mathcal{A}$.

We now analyze why this works. The algorithm $\mathcal{B}$ knows that if its challenger gave an encryption of 0^{n+1}, then its interaction with $\mathcal{A}$ corresponds to the alternate IND-CCA game described earlier. Here, we know that the adversary $\mathcal{A}$ can not make the Bad Query Event occur. Therefore, if the adversary $\mathcal{A}$ makes the Bad Query Event occur, then it must occur in the case that $\mathsf{CT}'_{\mathsf{CCA}}$ is an encryption of $(\alpha||0||\mathsf{CT}'_{\mathsf{CPA}})$. Hence, $\mathcal{B}$ guesses 0 in that case. On the other hand, if the adversary $\mathcal{A}$ does not make the Bad Query Event occur, then it must be the case that 0^{n+1} was encrypted. This is because we assumed that $\mathcal{A}$ can make the Bad Query Event occur with non-negligible probability in the original IND-CCA security game. This completes the proof.

Note that the reduction is actually not interested in completing the game with $\mathcal{A}$ in the event that $\mathcal{B}$ halts. That is, $\mathcal{B}$ does not care whether $\mathcal{A}$ wins the IND-CCA game but is rather more interested in whether $\mathcal{A}$ makes a Bad Query Event occur. □

Remark: At first glance, there seems to be a circularity issue in trying to prove IND-CCA security of our scheme. That is, in order to prove indistinguishability of the main hybrids, we require to first erase α which depends on no queries being made to the decryption oracle that contain $\mathsf{CT}'_{\mathsf{CCA}}$. On the other hand, it seems difficult to directly argue that no such queries are made because of the presence of α in $\mathsf{CT}'_{\mathsf{CCA}}$. This causes a circularity. We get around this issue using the alternate IND-CCA game where α is erased. In this game, we show that the bad query event can't occur and then using a reduction to the underlying encryption scheme's security, we can eventually show that the bad query event does not occur even in the original CCA security game.

This technique is very similar to [MS09,HLW12]. In these works, they construct CCA secure encryption and in the process, they run into a similar circularity issue. The analog of α was the randomness used for encryption and this randomness is in fact encrypted by an inner encryption scheme.

This completes the proof of Theorem 1. □

5 Building FE-Compatible Encryption Schemes

We first define a new notion called puncturable tag based encryption[7]. In the next subsection, we show how to construct a selective IND-CCA secure public key encryption scheme from any puncturable tag based encryption scheme. We call such a selective IND-CCA secure public key encryption scheme as "Special-CCA". In the following subsection, we show how to instantiate a "Special-CCA" secure encryption scheme with several existing popular encryption schemes in literature. Finally, we show that this "Special-CCA" secure public key encryption scheme is FE-Compatible.

[7] Previously, [MH14] also introduced a primitive called puncturable tag based encryption which is completely different from the one we define here.

5.1 Puncturable Tag Based Encryption

In this section, we define a new primitive called puncturable tag based encryption (PTBE) that is a modification of tag based encryption schemes [Kil06] but with two more algorithms. We then show how several well known encryption schemes in literature (based on various assumptions) do in fact fit into the framework of puncturable tag based encryption.

Let n denote the security parameter and $\mathcal{X} = \{\mathcal{X}_n\}_{n\in\mathbf{N}}$, $\mathcal{T} = \{\mathcal{T}_n\}_{n\in\mathbf{N}}$ denote ensembles where each $\mathcal{X}_n$ and $\mathcal{T}_n$ is a finite set. Formally, a puncturable tag based encryption scheme $\mathsf{PTBE} = (\mathsf{PTBE.Setup}, \mathsf{PTBE.Enc}, \mathsf{PTBE.Dec}, \mathsf{PTBE.Setup\text{-}Alt}, \mathsf{PTBE.Setup\text{-}Alt\text{-}1}, \mathsf{PTBE.Dec\text{-}Alt})$ consists of the following algorithms:

- $\mathsf{PTBE.Setup}(1^n)$:
  Given the security parameter n, it generates a public key PK and a secret key SK.
- $\mathsf{PTBE.Enc}(\mathsf{PK}, \mathsf{t}, \mathsf{m})$:
  Given a message $\mathsf{m} \in \mathcal{X}_n$, a tag $\mathsf{t} \in \mathcal{T}_n$ and the public key PK as input, the encryption algorithm outputs a ciphertext CT.
- $\mathsf{PTBE.Dec}(\mathsf{SK}, \mathsf{t}, \mathsf{CT})$:
  Given a ciphertext CT, a tag $\mathsf{t} \in \mathcal{T}_n$ and the secret key SK as input, the decryption algorithm outputs a string $y \in \mathcal{X}_n$ or $\perp$.
- $\mathsf{PTBE.Setup\text{-}Alt}(1^n, \mathsf{t}^*, \mathsf{m}^*)$:
  Given the security parameter n, a tag $\mathsf{t}^* \in \mathcal{T}_n$ and a message $\mathsf{m}^* \in \mathcal{X}_n$, it generates a public key PK, a secret key SK, an alternate secret key $\mathsf{SK\text{-}Alt}$ and a ciphertext CT^*.
- $\mathsf{PTBE.Setup\text{-}Alt\text{-}1}(1^n, \mathsf{t}^*, \mathsf{m}^*)$:
  Given the security parameter n, a tag $\mathsf{t}^* \in \mathcal{T}_n$ and a message $\mathsf{m}^* \in \mathcal{X}_n$, it generates a public key PK, a secret key SK, an alternate secret key $\mathsf{SK\text{-}Alt}$ and a ciphertext CT^*.
- $\mathsf{PTBE.Dec\text{-}Alt}(\mathsf{SK\text{-}Alt}, \mathsf{t}, \mathsf{CT})$:
  Given a ciphertext CT, a tag $\mathsf{t} \in \mathcal{T}_n$ and an alternate secret key $\mathsf{SK\text{-}Alt}$ as input, the alternate decryption algorithm outputs a string $y \in \mathcal{X}_n$ or $\perp$.

Remark: For technical reasons, to make our proofs simpler while instantiating our "Special-CCA" secure encryption schemes, we use two setup-alt algorithms (that albeit perform a very similar role). We provide more details about this in a remark at the end of Section ??. Alternatively, we could just use one setup-alt algorithm in the abstraction and make the proof a bit more complicated. We choose the former option in this writeup.

Correctness: A puncturable tag based encryption scheme PTBE is correct if for all messages $\mathsf{m} \in \mathcal{X}_n$ and all tags $\mathsf{t} \in \mathcal{T}_n$

$$\Pr\left[\begin{array}{c}(\mathsf{PK},\mathsf{SK}) \leftarrow \mathsf{PTBE.Setup}(1^n) \\ \mathsf{PTBE.Dec}(\mathsf{SK}, \mathsf{t}, \mathsf{PTBE.Enc}(\mathsf{PK}, \mathsf{t}, \mathsf{m})) = \mathsf{m}\end{array}\right] = 1$$

The probability is over the randomness used in the setup, encryption and decryption algorithms.

For security, we require the following four properties:

1. **Equivalent on all but challenge tag:** For any message $\mathsf{m}^* \in \mathcal{X}_n$, any tag $\mathsf{t}^* \in \mathcal{T}_n$, for all ciphertexts CT and all tags $\mathsf{t} \in \mathcal{T}_n$ such that $\mathsf{t} \neq \mathsf{t}^*$, we require that:
$$\Pr\left[\begin{array}{c}(\mathsf{PK}, \mathsf{SK}, \mathsf{SK\text{-}Alt}, \mathsf{CT}^*) \leftarrow \mathsf{PTBE.Setup\text{-}Alt}(1^n, \mathsf{t}^*, \mathsf{m}^*)\\ \mathsf{PTBE.Dec}(\mathsf{SK}, \mathsf{t}, \mathsf{CT}) = \mathsf{PTBE.Dec\text{-}Alt}(\mathsf{SK\text{-}Alt}, \mathsf{t}, \mathsf{CT})\end{array}\right] = 1$$
The probability is over the randomness used in all the above algorithms.
2. **Indistinguishability of parameters:** The output of the following two experiments must be computationally indistinguishable for all messages m^* and tags t^*:
   (a) **Experiment 1:**
   Run $\mathsf{PTBE.Setup}(1^n)$ to generate $(\mathsf{PK}, \mathsf{SK})$. Compute $\mathsf{CT}^* = \mathsf{PTBE.Enc}(\mathsf{PK}, \mathsf{t}^*, \mathsf{m}^*)$ and output $(\mathsf{PK}, \mathsf{SK}, \mathsf{CT}^*)$.
   (b) **Experiment 2:**
   Run $\mathsf{PTBE.Setup\text{-}Alt}(1^n, \mathsf{t}^*, \mathsf{m}^*)$ to generate $(\mathsf{PK}, \mathsf{SK}, \mathsf{SK\text{-}Alt}, \mathsf{CT}^*)$ and output $(\mathsf{PK}, \mathsf{SK}, \mathsf{CT}^*)$.
3. **Indistinguishability of alternate setups:** The output of the following two experiments must be indistinguishable for all messages m^* and tags t^*:
   (a) **Experiment 1:**
   Run $\mathsf{PTBE.Setup\text{-}Alt}(1^n, \mathsf{t}^*, \mathsf{m}^*)$ to generate $(\mathsf{PK}, \mathsf{SK}, \mathsf{SK\text{-}Alt}, \mathsf{CT}^*)$ and output $(\mathsf{PK}, \mathsf{SK\text{-}Alt}, \mathsf{CT}^*)$.
   (b) **Experiment 2:**
   Run $\mathsf{PTBE.Setup\text{-}Alt\text{-}1}(1^n, \mathsf{t}^*, \mathsf{m}^*)$ to generate $(\mathsf{PK}, \mathsf{SK}, \mathsf{SK\text{-}Alt}, \mathsf{CT}^*)$ and output $(\mathsf{PK}, \mathsf{SK\text{-}Alt}, \mathsf{CT}^*)$.
4. **Indistinguishability of messages:** For this property to hold, we require the adversary's advantage to be negligible in the following game between an adversary $\mathcal{A}$ and a challenger Ch:
   (a) $\mathcal{A}$ sends $(\mathsf{t}^*, \mathsf{m}_0^*, \mathsf{m}_1^*)$ to the challenger.
   (b) Ch chooses a random bit b and runs $\mathsf{PTBE.Setup\text{-}Alt\text{-}1}(1^n, \mathsf{t}^*, \mathsf{m}_b^*)$ to generate $(\mathsf{PK}, \mathsf{SK\text{-}Alt}, \mathsf{CT}^*)$ and gives the adversary $(\mathsf{PK}, \mathsf{SK\text{-}Alt}, \mathsf{CT}^*)$.
   (c) $\mathcal{A}$ submits a guess b' and wins if $b' = b$. The adversary's advantage in this game is defined to be $2 * |\Pr[\mathsf{b} = \mathsf{b}'] - 1/2|$.

5.2 Special-CCA Secure Encryption Scheme

In this section, we show how to build a selective CCA secure encryption scheme from any PTBE with the addition of one time signatures. Recall that we define selective CCA secure encryption schemes in the full version. We call such a CCA secure encryption scheme as "Special-CCA". Formally, we prove the following theorem:

Theorem 3. *Given a puncturable tag based encryption scheme* $\mathsf{PTBE} = (\mathsf{PTBE.Setup}, \mathsf{PTBE.Enc}, \mathsf{PTBE.Dec}, \mathsf{PTBE.Setup\text{-}Alt}, \mathsf{PTBE.Setup\text{-}Alt\text{-}1}, \mathsf{PTBE.Dec\text{-}Alt})$ *and a strongly secure one time signature scheme* $\mathsf{OTS} = (\mathsf{OTS.Setup}, \mathsf{OTS.Sign}, \mathsf{OTS.Verify})$, *the scheme* $\mathsf{PKE} = (\mathsf{PKE.Setup}, \mathsf{PKE.Enc}, \mathsf{PKE.Dec})$ *described below is a selective CCA secure encryption scheme.*

According to our notation, scheme PKE is a Special-CCA secure encryption scheme.

Notation: Let $\mathsf{PTBE} = (\mathsf{PTBE.Setup}, \mathsf{PTBE.Enc}, \mathsf{PTBE.Dec}, \mathsf{PTBE.Setup\text{-}Alt}, \mathsf{PTBE.Setup\text{-}Alt\text{-}1}, \mathsf{PTBE.Dec\text{-}Alt})$ be a puncturable tag based encryption scheme with message space $\mathcal{X}_n$, tag space $\mathcal{T}_n$ that outputs ciphertexts of size $l(n)$. Let $\mathsf{OTS} = (\mathsf{OTS.Setup}, \mathsf{OTS.Sign}, \mathsf{OTS.Verify})$ be a one time signature scheme that signs messages of length $l(n)$ and the space of verification keys is $\mathcal{T}_n$. Our new scheme PKE has message space $\mathcal{X}_n$.

We now describe the template for building Special-CCA secure encryption schemes from any puncturable tag based encryption. This template can be instantiated by several existing CCA secure encryption schemes in the literature [CHK04,Kil06,PW08].

Construction:

- $\mathsf{PKE.Setup}(1^n)$:
  1. Generate the public key and secret key as $(\mathsf{PK}, \mathsf{SK}) \leftarrow \mathsf{PTBE.Setup}(1^n)$.
- $\mathsf{PKE.Enc}(\mathsf{PK}, \mathsf{m})$:
  1. Generate $(\mathsf{VK}, \mathsf{SigK}) \leftarrow \mathsf{OTS.Setup}(1^n)$.
  2. Compute $\mathsf{CT}_1 = \mathsf{PTBE.Enc}(\mathsf{PK}, \mathsf{VK}, \mathsf{m})$ and $\sigma = \mathsf{OTS.Sign}(\mathsf{CT}_1, \mathsf{SigK})$.
  3. Output $\mathsf{CT} = (\mathsf{VK}, \mathsf{CT}_1, \sigma)$ as the ciphertext.
- $\mathsf{PKE.Dec}(\mathsf{SK}, \mathsf{CT})$:
  1. Parse $\mathsf{CT} = (\mathsf{VK}, \mathsf{CT}_1, \sigma)$.
  2. Output $\perp$ if $\mathsf{OTS.Verify}(\mathsf{VK}, \mathsf{CT}_1, \sigma) = 0$.
  3. Output $\mathsf{m} = \mathsf{PTBE.Dec}(\mathsf{SK}, \mathsf{VK}, \mathsf{CT}_1)$.

We prove that the above scheme is CCA-secure in the full version of the paper.

5.3 Instantiating Special-CCA Encryption

We show that several popular and well-studied CCA-secure encryption schemes are in fact Special-CCA. That is, they satisfy this property that they can be constructed using PTBE and one-time signatures as shown in the above construction. We now list the encryption schemes below and prove in the full version of the paper that they satisfy the necessary conditions. Formally,

Theorem 4. *The selective CCA-secure encryption schemes in the following popular works are in fact Special-CCA secure encryption schemes:*

- *[CHK04] when instantiated with the IBE scheme of [BB04].*
- *[CHK04] when instantiated with any Hierarchical IBE scheme.*
- *[PW08] when instantiated with any Lossy Trapdoor Function.*

5.4 Building Selectively Secure FE

In this section, we show that the "Special-CCA" secure encryption scheme $\mathsf{PKE} = (\mathsf{PKE.Setup}, \mathsf{PKE.Enc}, \mathsf{PKE.Dec})$ from the previous section is FE-Compatible. We prove the security of our construction in two different ways - the first is based on the assumption of sub-exponentially secure indistinguishability obfuscation. Additionally, it requires the one time signature scheme used in the construction of PKE to be a sub-exponentially secure unique signature scheme. On the other hand, the second proof is based on the existence of polynomially secure differing inputs obfuscation and just polynomially secure one time signatures.

Formally, we prove the following two theorems:

Theorem 5. *Any "Special-CCA" secure encryption scheme is selective FE-Compatible for any function family $\mathcal{F}_n$ and poly(n) function key queries assuming:*

- *Sub-exponentially secure indistinguishability obfuscation. (AND)*
- *Sub-exponentially secure unique one time signatures.*

Moreover, the resulting FE scheme is also compact.

Theorem 6. *Any "Special-CCA" secure encryption scheme is selective FE-Compatible for any function family $\mathcal{F}_n$ and poly(n) function key queries assuming:*

- *Polynomially secure differing inputs obfuscation. (AND)*
- *Polynomially secure strong one time signatures.*

Moreover, the resulting FE scheme is also compact.

One example of a one time signature scheme is the Lamport signature scheme [Lam79]. Observe that it is in fact a unique one time signature scheme if we rely on injective one way functions. Instantiating the Special-CCA scheme with the various schemes in Sect. 5.3, we get the following two corollaries:

Corollary 7. *Let X denote the CCA secure encryption scheme in any of the following popular works:*

- *[CHK04] when instantiated with the IBE scheme of [BB04].*
- *[CHK04] when instantiated with any Hierarchical IBE scheme.*
- *[PW08] when instantiated with any Lossy Trapdoor Function.*

Assuming the existence of sub-exponentially secure indistinguishability obfuscation and sub-exponentially secure injective one way functions, scheme X is selective FE-Compatible for any function family $\mathcal{F}_n$ and poly(n) function key queries. Moreover, the resulting FE scheme is also compact.

Corollary 8. *Let X denote the CCA secure encryption scheme in any of the following popular works:*

- *[CHK04] when instantiated with the IBE scheme of [BB04].*
- *[CHK04] when instantiated with any Hierarchical IBE scheme.*
- *[PW08] when instantiated with any Lossy Trapdoor Function.*

Assuming polynomially secure differing inputs obfuscation and polynomially secure one way functions, scheme X *is selective FE-Compatible for any function family* $\mathcal{F}_n$ *and poly(n) function key queries. Moreover, the resulting FE scheme is also compact.*

Construction: Let $(\mathcal{O}, \mathsf{Eval})$ be a secure obfuscator (note that we will use indistinguishability obfuscation in one proof and differing inputs obfuscation in the other). The functional encryption $\mathsf{FE} = (\mathsf{FE.Setup}, \mathsf{FE.Enc}, \mathsf{FE.Keygen}, \mathsf{FE.Dec})$ built from the Special-CCA scheme PKE is as follows. Recall that from the definition of FE-Compatibility, $\mathsf{FE.Setup}(\cdot) = \mathsf{PKE.Setup}(\cdot)$ and $\mathsf{FE.Enc}(\cdot) = \mathsf{PKE.Enc}(\cdot)$.

- $\mathsf{FE.Setup}(1^n)$: Run $\mathsf{PKE.Setup}(1^n)$ to generate $(\mathsf{PK}, \mathsf{SK})$.
- $\mathsf{FE.Enc}(\mathsf{PK}, \mathsf{m})$: Run $\mathsf{PKE.Enc}(\mathsf{PK}, \mathsf{m})$ to generate the ciphertext $\mathsf{CT} = (\mathsf{VK}, \mathsf{CT}_1, \sigma)$.
- $\mathsf{FE.Keygen}(\mathsf{SK}, f)$: Output $\mathsf{SK}_f = \mathcal{O}(\mathsf{G}_f)$ where the program G_f is described below.
- $\mathsf{FE.Dec}(\mathsf{SK}_f, \mathsf{CT})$ Run the program SK_f on input CT to output a string y (Fig. 3).

Program G_f

Input : ciphertext CT
Constants : SK

1. Compute $\mathsf{m} = \mathsf{PKE.Dec}(\mathsf{SK}, \mathsf{CT})$.
2. Output $\perp$ if the decryption aborts.
3. Else, output $f(m)$.

Fig. 3. Program for generating function secret key

Security Proof. We will prove this via a series of hybrid experiments where we show that every successive pair of hybrids is computationally indistinguishable and the final hybrid is independent of the challenge bit b and hence the attacker's advantage will be 0 in the final hybrid. We will show the indistinguishability of the hybrids using two different proofs in some cases to prove both Theorems 5 and 6.

- Hyb_1: This is the real world experiment with challenge bit b chosen randomly. The challenge ciphertext as $\mathsf{CT}^* = (\mathsf{VK}^*, \mathsf{CT}_1^*, \sigma^*)$.

- Hyb_2: This hybrid is identical to the previous hybrid except that now, $\mathsf{FE.Setup}(1^n)$ and the challenge ciphertext are computed differently. Instead of running the setup algorithm $\mathsf{PTBE.Setup}(1^n)$, we now run $\mathsf{PTBE.Setup\text{-}Alt}(1^n, \mathsf{VK}^*, \mathsf{m}_b^*)$ to generate $(\mathsf{PK}, \mathsf{SK}, \mathsf{SK\text{-}Alt}, \mathsf{CT}_1^*)$. The FE scheme's public key is PK, secret key is SK. Now, the challenge ciphertext is computed as follows: generate $(\mathsf{SigK}^*, \mathsf{VK}^*) \leftarrow \mathsf{OTS.Setup}(1^n)$ and compute $\sigma^* = \mathsf{OTS.Sign}(\mathsf{SigK}^*, \mathsf{CT}_1^*)$. The challenge ciphertext is $(\mathsf{VK}^*, \mathsf{CT}_1^*, \sigma^*)$. Note that the alternate secret key $\mathsf{SK\text{-}Alt}$ is not used at all.
- **For each** i **in** $\{0, 1, \ldots, q\}$, $\mathsf{Hyb}_{3,i}$: This hybrid is identical to the previous hybrid except that now, the function secret key SK_f for the ith function key query f is computed as $\mathcal{O}(\mathsf{G}_f^1)$ for the following program G_f^1 (Fig. 4).

Program G_f^1

Input : ciphertext CT
Constants : $\mathsf{SK}, \mathsf{CT}^* = (\mathsf{VK}^*, \mathsf{CT}_1^*, \sigma^*)$
1. If $\mathsf{CT} = \mathsf{CT}^*$, output y where $y = f(\mathsf{m}_0^*) = f(\mathsf{m}_1^*)$.
2. Compute $\mathsf{m} = \mathsf{PKE.Dec}(\mathsf{SK}, \mathsf{CT})$.
3. Output $\perp$ if the decryption aborts.
4. Else, output $f(m)$.

Fig. 4. Program for generating function secret key

Note that $\mathsf{Hyb}_{3,0}$ corresponds to Hyb_2.
- **For each** i **in** $\{0, 1, \ldots, q\}$, $\mathsf{Hyb}_{4,i}$: This hybrid is identical to the previous hybrid except that now, the function secret key SK_f for the ith function key query f is computed as $\mathcal{O}(\mathsf{G}_f^2)$ for the following program G_f^2 (Fig. 5).

Program G_f^2

Input : ciphertext $\mathsf{CT} = (\mathsf{VK}, \mathsf{CT}_1, \sigma)$
Constants : $\mathsf{SK}, \mathsf{CT}^* = (\mathsf{VK}^*, \mathsf{CT}_1^*, \sigma^*)$
1. If $\mathsf{CT} = \mathsf{CT}^*$, output y where $y = f(\mathsf{m}_0^*) = f(\mathsf{m}_1^*)$.
2. If $\mathsf{VK} = \mathsf{VK}^*$, output $\perp$.
3. Compute $\mathsf{m} = \mathsf{PKE.Dec}(\mathsf{SK}, \mathsf{CT})$.
4. Output $\perp$ if the decryption aborts.
5. Else, output $f(m)$.

Fig. 5. Program for generating function secret key

Note that $\mathsf{Hyb}_{4,0}$ corresponds to $\mathsf{Hyb}_{3,q}$.

- **For each** i **in** $\{0, 1, \ldots, q\}$, $\mathsf{Hyb}_{5,i}$: This hybrid is identical to the previous hybrid except that now, the function secret key SK_f for the ith function key query f is computed as $\mathcal{O}(\mathsf{G}_f^3)$ for the following program G_f^3 (Fig. 6).

Program G_f^3

Input : ciphertext $\mathsf{CT} = (\mathsf{VK}, \mathsf{CT}_1, \sigma)$
Constants : $\mathsf{SK}, \mathsf{CT}^* = (\mathsf{VK}^*, \mathsf{CT}_1^*, \sigma^*)$

1. If $\mathsf{CT} = \mathsf{CT}^*$, output y where $y = f(\mathsf{m}_0^*) = f(\mathsf{m}_1^*)$.
2. If $\mathsf{VK} = \mathsf{VK}^*$, output $\perp$.
3. Check if $\mathsf{OTS.Verify}(\mathsf{VK}, \mathsf{CT}_1, \sigma) = 1$.
4. Compute $\mathsf{m} = \mathsf{PTBE.Dec\text{-}Alt}(\mathsf{SK\text{-}Alt}, \mathsf{VK}, \mathsf{CT}_1)$.
5. Output $\perp$ if the decryption aborts or if the signature doesn't verify.
6. Else, output $f(m)$.

Fig. 6. Program for generating function secret key

Note that $\mathsf{Hyb}_{5,0}$ corresponds to $\mathsf{Hyb}_{4,q}$.

- Hyb_6: This hybrid is identical to the previous hybrid except that we now run $\mathsf{PTBE.Setup\text{-}Alt\text{-}1}\ (1^n, \mathsf{VK}^*, \mathsf{m}_b^*)$ to generate $(\mathsf{PK}, \mathsf{SK}, \mathsf{SK\text{-}Alt}, \mathsf{CT}^*)$.
- Hyb_7: This hybrid is identical to the previous hybrid except that we now run $\mathsf{PTBE.Setup\text{-}Alt\text{-}1}(1^n, \mathsf{VK}^*, \mathsf{m}_0^*)$ to generate $(\mathsf{PK}, \mathsf{SK}, \mathsf{SK\text{-}Alt}, \mathsf{CT}^*)$.

Observe that in this last hybrid, the challenge ciphertext is created independent of the bit b. Hence, the attacker's advantage in this hybrid is 0.

We refer the reader to the full version for the indistinguishability of every successive pair of hybrids.

References

[AJ15] Ananth, P., Jain, A.: Indistinguishability obfuscation from compact functional encryption. In: Gennaro, R., Robshaw, M. (eds.) CRYPTO 2015. LNCS, vol. 9215, pp. 308–326. Springer, Heidelberg (2015). https://doi.org/10.1007/978-3-662-47989-6_15

[BB04] Boneh, D., Boyen, X.: Efficient selective-ID secure identity-based encryption without random oracles. In: Cachin, C., Camenisch, J.L. (eds.) EUROCRYPT 2004. LNCS, vol. 3027, pp. 223–238. Springer, Heidelberg (2004). https://doi.org/10.1007/978-3-540-24676-3_14

[BCP14] Boyle, E., Chung, K.-M., Pass, R.: On extractability obfuscation. In: Lindell, Y. (ed.) TCC 2014. LNCS, vol. 8349, pp. 52–73. Springer, Heidelberg (2014). https://doi.org/10.1007/978-3-642-54242-8_3

[BGI+01] Barak, B., et al.: On the (Im)possibility of obfuscating programs. In: Kilian, J. (ed.) CRYPTO 2001. LNCS, vol. 2139, pp. 1–18. Springer, Heidelberg (2001). https://doi.org/10.1007/3-540-44647-8_1

[BGJS15] Badrinarayanan, S., Gupta, D., Jain, A., Sahai, A.: Multi-input functional encryption for unbounded arity functions. In: Iwata, T., Cheon, J.H. (eds.) ASIACRYPT 2015. LNCS, vol. 9452, pp. 27–51. Springer, Heidelberg (2015). https://doi.org/10.1007/978-3-662-48797-6_2

[BR94] Bellare, M., Rogaway, P.: Optimal asymmetric encryption. In: De Santis, A. (ed.) EUROCRYPT 1994. LNCS, vol. 950, pp. 92–111. Springer, Heidelberg (1995). https://doi.org/10.1007/BFb0053428

[BSW11] Boneh, D., Sahai, A., Waters, B.: Functional encryption: definitions and challenges. In: Ishai, Y. (ed.) TCC 2011. LNCS, vol. 6597, pp. 253–273. Springer, Heidelberg (2011). https://doi.org/10.1007/978-3-642-19571-6_16

[CHK04] Canetti, R., Halevi, S., Katz, J.: Chosen-ciphertext security from identity-based encryption. In: Cachin, C., Camenisch, J.L. (eds.) EUROCRYPT 2004. LNCS, vol. 3027, pp. 207–222. Springer, Heidelberg (2004). https://doi.org/10.1007/978-3-540-24676-3_13

[FO99] Fujisaki, E., Okamoto, T.: Secure integration of asymmetric and symmetric encryption schemes. In: Wiener, M. (ed.) CRYPTO 1999. LNCS, vol. 1666, pp. 537–554. Springer, Heidelberg (1999). https://doi.org/10.1007/3-540-48405-1_34

[GGG+14] Goldwasser, S., et al.: Multi-input functional encryption. In: Nguyen, P.Q., Oswald, E. (eds.) EUROCRYPT 2014. LNCS, vol. 8441, pp. 578–602. Springer, Heidelberg (2014). https://doi.org/10.1007/978-3-642-55220-5_32

[GGH+13] Garg, S., Gentry, C., Halevi, S., Raykova, M., Sahai, A., Waters, B.: Candidate indistinguishability obfuscation and functional encryption for all circuits. In: FOCS (2013)

[GKW17] Goyal, R., Koppula, V., Waters, B.: Lockable obfuscation. IACR Cryptology ePrint Archive (2017)

[Had00] Hada, S.: Zero-knowledge and code obfuscation. In: Okamoto, T. (ed.) ASIACRYPT 2000. LNCS, vol. 1976, pp. 443–457. Springer, Heidelberg (2000). https://doi.org/10.1007/3-540-44448-3_34

[HKW15] Hohenberger, S., Koppula, V., Waters, B.: Universal signature aggregators. In: Oswald, E., Fischlin, M. (eds.) EUROCRYPT 2015. LNCS, vol. 9057, pp. 3–34. Springer, Heidelberg (2015). https://doi.org/10.1007/978-3-662-46803-6_1

[HLW12] Hohenberger, S., Lewko, A., Waters, B.: Detecting dangerous queries: a new approach for chosen ciphertext security. In: Pointcheval, D., Johansson, T. (eds.) EUROCRYPT 2012. LNCS, vol. 7237, pp. 663–681. Springer, Heidelberg (2012). https://doi.org/10.1007/978-3-642-29011-4_39

[Kil06] Kiltz, E.: Chosen-ciphertext security from tag-based encryption. In: Halevi, S., Rabin, T. (eds.) TCC 2006. LNCS, vol. 3876, pp. 581–600. Springer, Heidelberg (2006). https://doi.org/10.1007/11681878_30

[Lam79] Lamport. Constructing digital signatures from a one-way function. Technical report SRI-CSL-98, SRI International Computer Science Laboratory (1979)

[MH14] Matsuda, T., Hanaoka, G.: Chosen ciphertext security via UCE. In: Krawczyk, H. (ed.) PKC 2014. LNCS, vol. 8383, pp. 56–76. Springer, Heidelberg (2014). https://doi.org/10.1007/978-3-642-54631-0_4

[MS09] Myers, S., Shelat, A.: Bit encryption is complete. In: FOCS (2009)

[NY90] Naor, M., Yung, M.: Public-key cryptosystems provably secure against chosen ciphertext attacks. In: STOC (1990)

[PW08] Peikert, C., Waters, B.: Lossy trapdoor functions and their applications. In: STOC (2008)

[Sah99] Sahai, A.: Non-malleable non-interactive zero knowledge and adaptive chosen-ciphertext security. In: FOCS (1999)

[SW05] Sahai, A., Waters, B.: Fuzzy identity-based encryption. In: Cramer, R. (ed.) EUROCRYPT 2005. LNCS, vol. 3494, pp. 457–473. Springer, Heidelberg (2005). https://doi.org/10.1007/11426639_27

[SW08] Sahai, A., Waters, B.: Slides on functional encryption, powerpoint presentation (2008)

[SW14] Sahai, A., Waters, B.: How to use indistinguishability obfuscation: deniable encryption, and more. In: Symposium on Theory of Computing, STOC 2014, New York, NY, USA, 31 May – 03 June 2014, pp. 475–484 (2014)

[Wat14] Waters, B.: A punctured programming approach to adaptively secure functional encryption. IACR Cryptology ePrint Archive 2014/588 (2014)

[WZ17] Wichs, D., Zirdelis, G.: Obfuscating compute-and-compare programs under LWE. IACR Cryptology ePrint Archive (2017)

Impossibility of Simulation Secure Functional Encryption Even with Random Oracles

Shashank Agrawal[1(✉)], Venkata Koppula[2], and Brent Waters[2]

[1] Visa Research, Palo Alto, USA
shashank.agraval@gmail.com
[2] University of Texas at Austin, Austin, USA
{kvenkata,bwaters}@cs.utexas.edu

Abstract. In this work we study the feasibility of achieving simulation security in functional encryption (FE) in the random oracle model. Our main result is negative in that we give a functionality for which it is impossible to achieve simulation security even with the aid of random oracles.

We begin by giving a formal definition of simulation security that explicitly incorporates the random oracles. Next, we show a particular functionality for which it is impossible to achieve simulation security. Here messages are interpreted as seeds to a (weak) pseudorandom function family F and private keys are ascribed to points in the domain of the function. On a message s and private key x one can learn $F(s, x)$. We show that there exists an attacker that makes a polynomial number of private key queries followed by a single ciphertext query for which there exists no simulator.

Our functionality and attacker access pattern closely matches the *standard model* impossibility result of Agrawal, Gorbunov, Vaikuntanathan and Wee (CRYPTO 2013). The crux of their argument is that no simulator can succinctly program in the outputs of an unbounded number of evaluations of a pseudorandom function family into a fixed size ciphertext. However, their argument does not apply in the random oracle setting since the oracle acts as an additional conduit of information which the simulator can program. We overcome this barrier by proposing an attacker who decrypts the challenge ciphertext with the secret keys issued earlier *without* using the random oracle, even though the decryption algorithm may require it. This involves collecting most of the useful random oracle queries in advance, without giving the simulator too many opportunities to program.

On the flip side, we demonstrate the utility of the random oracle in simulation security. Given only public key encryption and low-depth PRGs we show how to build an FE system that is simulation secure for any poly-time attacker that makes an unbounded number of message queries, but an a-priori bounded number of key queries. This bests what

B. Waters—Supported by NSF CNS-1414082, DARPA SafeWare, Microsoft Faculty Fellowship, and Packard Foundation Fellowship.

A. Beimel and S. Dziembowski (Eds.): TCC 2018, LNCS 11239, pp. 659–688, 2018.
https://doi.org/10.1007/978-3-030-03807-6_24

is possible in the standard model where it is only feasible to achieve security for an attacker that is bounded both in the number of key and message queries it makes. We achieve this by creating a system that leverages the random oracle to get one-key security and then adapt previously known techniques to boost the system to resist up to q queries.

Finally, we ask whether it is possible to achieve simulation security for an unbounded number of messages and keys, but where all key queries are made *after* the message queries. We show this too is impossible to achieve using a different twist on our first impossibility result.

1 Introduction

The traditional notion of public key encryption systems provide "all or nothing" semantics regarding encrypted data. In such a system a message m is encrypted under a public key, pk, to produce a ciphertext ct. A user that holds the corresponding secret key can decrypt ct and learn the entire message m, while any other user will not learn anything about the contents of the message. The work of Sahai and Waters [32] conceived cryptosystems that moved beyond these limited semantics to ones where a private key would give a select view of encrypted data. These efforts [13,25,32] cumulated in the concept of functional encryption. In a functional encryption system an authority will generate a pair of a public key and master key pair $(\mathsf{pk}, \mathsf{msk})$. Any user can encrypt a ciphertext ct using the public key, while the authority can use the master secret key msk to generate a secret key sk_f that is tied to the functionality f. A holder of sk_f can use it to decrypt a ciphertext ct, but instead of learning the message m, the decryptor's decryption will instead output $f(m)$.

One challenge in defining and designing functional encryption (FE) systems is in finding a definition to capture security. The earliest formal definitions of functional encryption [13,25] (back when the terminology of "predicate encryption" was used) defined security in terms of an indistinguishability game. Briefly, a system is indistinguishability secure if no poly-time attacker that receives secret keys for functions $f_1, \ldots, f_Q$ can distinguish between encryptions of m_0, m_1 so long as $f_i(m_0) = f_i(m_1)$ for $i = 1, \ldots, Q$.

Subsequent works [2,5,12,29] aimed to capture various notions of simulation-based security. To achieve simulation one must be able to show that for each attacker there exists a poly-time simulator $\mathcal{S}$ that can produce a transcript that emulates the attacker's real world view, but when only given access to what the evaluation of the secret key functions $f(\cdot)$ were on the attacker's messages. (We will return to describing simulation-based security in more detail shortly.) While these simulation definitions had the appeal of perhaps capturing a stronger notion of security than the indistinguishability-based ones, they were limited in that multiple works [2,5,12,22,29] showed that this notion is impossible to achieve in the standard model for even very basic functionalities such as identity-based encryption [11,33]. The only exception being in the restricted case where the attacker is only allowed to access an a-priori bounded number of secret keys [20].

While these results essentially put a hard stop on realizing (collusion-resistant) simulation security in the standard model, the door to leveraging the random oracle model [6] still remained wide open. Notably, Boneh, Sahai and Waters [12] building on techniques from non-committing encryption [28] showed that the random oracle could be leveraged to turn any indistinguishability secure public index FE scheme into one that was simulation secure. Recall that a public index scheme is one where an encrypted message is split into a hidden payload and a non-hidden index and the secret key operates only on the index. The set of such schemes includes identity-based encryption [11,33] and attribute-based encryption [32]. Thus, they showed that introducing a random oracle was enough to circumvent their own standard model IBE result. In this work we wish to understand what are the possibilities and limitations (if any) for using random oracles to achieve simulation security in FE systems. Our work begins with the question:

Is it possible to achieve simulation secure functional encryption for any functionality in the random oracle model?

Our main result is to show that there exist functionalities for which there cannot exist a simulation secure functional encryption system *even* in the random oracle model.

On the flip side, we demonstrate the utility of the random oracle in simulation security. Given only public key encryption and low-depth PRGs we show how to build an FE system that is simulation secure for any poly-time attacker that makes an unbounded number of message queries, but an a-priori bounded number of key queries. This beats what is possible in the standard model where it is only feasible to achieve security for an attacker that is bounded both in the number of key and message queries it makes. We achieve this by creating a system that leverages the random oracle to get one-key security and then adapt previously known techniques to boost the system to resist up to q queries.

Finally, we ask whether it is possible to achieve simulation security for an unbounded number of messages and keys, but where all key queries are made *after* the message queries. We show this too is impossible to achieve by repurposing our main impossibility result to the new setting.

1.1 Our Main Impossibility Result

We show the impossibility result for the case where messages are interpreted as keys or seeds to a (weak) Pseudo Random Function (PRF) [18] family and secret keys are points in the domain of the PRF. Agrawal, Gorbunov, Vaikuntanathan and Wee [2] showed that such a functionality could not be simulation secure in the standard model. Here we show that this limitation holds even with the introduction of random oracles.

We begin our exposition by describing the definition of simulation security in a little more depth and briefly overviewing the AGVW impossibility analysis.

Simulation Security. Simulation security for FE is defined by means of real and ideal experiments. In the real experiment, an adversary $\mathcal{A}$ gets secret keys for functions f and ciphertexts for challenge messages m of its choice. The secret key queries can either be sent before the challenge messages (also referred to as pre-challenge queries) or after the challenge messages (post challenge queries). In the ideal world, on the other hand, a simulator $\mathcal{S}$ needs to generate challenge ciphertexts and keys given only the minimal information. In particular, when $\mathcal{A}$ requests that a challenge message m be encrypted, $\mathcal{S}$ only gets $f(m)$ on all the pre-challenge functions f queried by $\mathcal{A}$ (instead of m itself), and must generate a ciphertext that $\mathcal{A}$ cannot distinguish from the one in the real world. Similarly, when $\mathcal{A}$ makes a post-challenge key query for f', $\mathcal{S}$ must generate a secret key given just f', $f'(m)$ for all challenge messages m.

An FE scheme is $(q_{\mathsf{pre}}, q_{\mathsf{chal}}, q_{\mathsf{post}})$-simulation secure if it can withstand adversaries that make at most q_{pre} pre-challenge key queries, q_{chal} challenge encryption requests, and q_{post} post-challenge key queries. Ideally, one would like to capture all polynomial-time adversaries, who can make any number of queries they want. However, even simple functionalities like identity-based encryption do not have a scheme secure against an arbitrary number of encryption requests followed by one key query, i.e., IBE does not have a $(0, \mathsf{poly}, 1)$-simulation secure scheme [5,12] in the standard model. Here poly denotes that any number of encryption requests can be made, as long as there is a polynomial bound on them.

AGVW Impossibility. A different kind of impossibility was shown by Agrawal et al. [2]. They interpret messages as seeds to a weak pseudorandom family wPRF[1] and secret keys as points in the domain of the family. When a ciphertext for s is decrypted with a secret key for x, the output is $\mathsf{wPRF}(s, x)$. They show that there does not exist a simulation-secure FE scheme for this family that can tolerate adversaries which can make an arbitrary number of pre-challenge key queries and then request for the encryption of just one message (i.e., $(\mathsf{poly}, 1, 0)$-simulation security). Intuitively, when the adversary outputs a message s in the ideal world, the simulator gets $\mathsf{wPRF}(s, x_1), \ldots, \mathsf{wPRF}(s, x_q)$ (if q is the number of post-challenge key queries), which is computationally indistinguishable from q uniformly random strings. The simulator must output a ciphertext ct now that decrypts correctly with all the keys issued before. Note that when the keys were issued, simulator had no information about s, so it must somehow *compress* q random strings into ct. However, as Agrawal et al. show, the output of a pseudorandom function family is *incompressible.* Thus, by choosing a large enough q, they arrive at the impossibility result.

Random Oracle Model. In the random oracle model though, Agrawal et al.'s impossibility argument breaks down. Informally speaking, the random oracle acts as an additional conduit of information which the simulator can program even *after* ct appears. For instance, if the decryption algorithm makes RO queries, then the simulator could program such queries when adversary tries to decrypt ct with the secret keys issued earlier. Indeed, Boneh et al. show that their $(0, \mathsf{poly}, 1)$

[1] A weak pseudorandom function family provides security only against attackers that do not get to choose the points at the which the PRF is evaluated. These points are chosen randomly by the challenger.

impossibility for IBE can be circumvented by employing RO in the encryption and decryption algorithms.

Thus we need a very different approach. We would like to build an adversary $\mathcal{A}^\star$ that "cuts off" RO in the decryption process, and is able to work without it. This involves a delicate balancing act between cutting off too early and too late. In one extreme case, if $\mathcal{A}^\star$ does not invoke RO at all and makes up its own responses, then these would not match with the actual RO responses in encryption and key generation. Thus decryption would always fail in both the real and ideal worlds, and there will be no distinction between them. On the other extreme, if $\mathcal{A}^\star$ just used the RO all the way through, it would provide the simulator enough opportunity to program in the desired information. (As a result, we will not be able to use the incompressibility of wPRF.)

At a high level, our approach is similar to the Impagliazzo-Rudich "heavy-query" algorithm [23]. First, there is an initial learning phase where $\mathcal{A}^\star$ will build a list of "high frequency" random oracle queries and responses associated with each secret key and the challenge ciphertext. Later the attacker will be able to use this list to replace the use of the actual random oracle during decryption. If some query is not found in the list, then $\mathcal{A}^\star$ will choose a random value for it on its own. Informally, we get the following result:

Theorem 1 (Main Theorem, informal). *There does not exist a* $(\mathsf{poly}, 1, 0)$*-simulation secure FE scheme for the class of (weak) pseudo-random functions in the random oracle model.*

Related Work. This bears a resemblance to the work of Canetti, Kalai and Paneth [15] who show impossibility of VBB obfuscation even with ROs. In their case they show that any obfuscated program that uses the RO can be translated into one that does not need it. They do this by collecting the frequently used RO queries and bundling this with the core obfuscated code. On one hand, these queries do not give any information about the program, but on the other, result in an obfuscation that is only approximately correct. Such imperfect correctness, however, is enough to invoke the impossibility of Bitansky and Paneth [9].

One might ask if we can show whether RO can be dispensed with in any simulation secure FE in a similar way. If we could establish this, then prior impossibility results [2,5,12] would imply RO impossibility as well. The answer to this is negative as we recall that Boneh, Sahai and Waters [12] showed specific functionalities that were impossible to simulate in the standard model, but possible to be simulation secure using random oracle. Therefore we cannot always remove the random oracle and must develop a more nuanced approach: we need to build a specific adversary for which simulation does not work.

In a recent work [27], Mahmoody et al. show that there is no fully black-box construction of indistinguishability obfuscation (iO) from any primitive implied by a random oracle in a black-box way. In light of recent FE to iO transformations [3,10], one might wonder if this rules out FE schemes in the RO model. However, these transformations are non-black box.

High Level Description of Impossibility. Recall that we want to design an adversary $\mathcal{A}^\star$ that will build a list of "high frequency" random oracle queries and responses associated with each secret key and the challenge ciphertext. It will use this list later in the decryption phase to "cut-off" the random oracle at an appropriate time.

$\mathcal{A}^\star$ starts off by querying the key-generation oracle at random points $x_1, \ldots, x_q$ in the domain of wPRF, and gets $\mathsf{sk}_1, \ldots, \mathsf{sk}_q$ in return. The RO queries made by the key-generation oracle are *hidden* from the adversary, so $\mathcal{A}^\star$ tries to find them by encrypting several randomly chosen seeds using the master public key, and then decrypting them with $\mathsf{sk}_1, \ldots, \mathsf{sk}_q$.[2] The RO queries made during the decryption process are recorded in a list Γ. The hope is that Γ will capture the RO queries that were made in generating a key sk_i.

Note that one cannot hope to capture *all* RO queries required for decryption: Suppose a polynomial number Y of high frequency queries associated with sk_i is collected, but there is an RO call that is made during key-generation which is used during $1/2Y$ fraction of the decryptions. Then it will be the case that with some non-negligible probability, Γ will fail to aid in the decryption of the challenge ciphertext with sk_i. Instead of trying to solve this issue, we make our analysis work with a decryption that might fail some of the time. For this purpose, we extend the incompressibility argument of Agrawal et al. to work even for *approximate* compression.

We are not quite done yet. Even though we have captured most of the hidden RO queries involved in key-generation that are also needed for decryption, we still need to capture those that are involved in the encryption of the challenge message, as they are also *hidden* and may be required during decryption.[3] Suppose $\mathcal{A}^\star$ outputs a randomly chosen seed $s^\star$ as the challenge message, and gets $\mathsf{ct}^\star$ in return. In order to find out RO queries associated with $\mathsf{ct}^\star$, $\mathcal{A}^\star$ cannot generate secret keys on its own (like in the pre-challenge phase when it generated ciphertexts); it must make-do with the secret keys $\mathsf{sk}_1, \ldots, \mathsf{sk}_q$ that were issued earlier. Thus, the idea is to decrypt $\mathsf{ct}^\star$ with some fraction δ of the keys using RO, recording the queries in the list Γ. It then cuts off the random oracle, and decrypts $\mathsf{ct}^\star$ with the remaining keys using the list Γ. If a query is not found in Γ, then a random value is used for it (as well as recorded in Γ for consistent responses in future). The adversary outputs 1 if a large fraction of these decryptions are correct; that is, if the decryption of $\mathsf{ct}^\star$ using sk_i outputs $\mathsf{wPRF}(s^\star, x_i)$.

In the real world, as we will see, the adversary outputs 1 with noticeable probability. On the other hand, we show that in the ideal world, the adversary outputs 1 only with negligible probability. For the adversary to output 1 in the ideal world, the simulator needs to somehow program the ciphertext and

[2] It is important that this is done before the challenge message is put out, otherwise simulator will get an opportunity to program in additional information through the random oracle.

[3] The RO queries made while setting up the FE system are also hidden from the adversary, but we ignore them here for simplicity.

the post-challenge random oracle queries so that a large number of decryptions succeed. The only opportunity a simulator has of programming post-challenge RO responses is when δ fraction of the keys are used for decrypting $\mathsf{ct}^\star$. By choosing δ appropriately, we can ensure that the simulator is not able to program the RO queries to the extent that most of the remaining decryptions succeed.

Looking Back. A simulator's success in the RO model depends on when it comes to know what to program and how much can it program. When dealing with the attacker $\mathcal{A}^\star$ described above, it gets a large amount of information, $\mathsf{wPRF}(s^\star, x_1), \ldots, \mathsf{wPRF}(s^\star, x_q)$, only in the challenge phase. Since all the key queries come before that, programming the secret keys is ruled out. If there was no random oracle, then the only possible avenue to program is the challenge ciphertext, but AGVW shows that it is not possible to compress so much information into a small ciphertext. Now with the random oracle, it might have been possible to program this information *if* there were many RO queries after the challenge phase. However, our adversary makes only a bounded number of post-challenge RO queries, and as a result, it is not possible to program all of $\{\mathsf{wPRF}(s^\star, x_i)\}$ in these RO responses.

An Alternative Approach to Proving Impossibility. Concurrent to our work, Bitansky, Lin and Paneth [7] showed an alternate approach for removing random oracles. Unlike our current impossibility, their approach requires multiple ciphertexts. We sketch the main ideas here.

This approach uses a notion of obfuscation called 'exponentially-efficient obfuscation', introduced by Lin et al. [26]. An exponentially-efficient obfuscator is allowed to run in subexponential time, and the obfuscated program is also allowed to be subexponential in the input length. For security, Lin et al. considered the $i\mathcal{O}$ equivalent, where the obfuscation of two functionally identical programs should be computationally indistinguishable. However, one can even consider simulation based notions where the output of the obfuscator can be simulated by a simulator having only black box access to the program.

In a recent work, Bitansky et al. [8] showed that IND-secure functional encryption can be used to construct exponentially-efficient indistinguishability obfuscation [26] in a black-box manner. While there exist other transformations from FE to obfuscation [3,10], the BNPW transformation is the only known black-box transformation, and this is important when studying FE or obfuscation in the random oracle model. Using the BNPW transformation, one can argue that simulation secure FE in the random oracle model implies simulation-secure exponentially-efficient obfuscation in the random oracle model. Therefore, to rule out FE in the random oracle model, it suffices to show that there exist certain functionalities for which we cannot obtain simulation-secure exponentially-efficient obfuscation in the random oracle model.

This can be achieved using the techniques of Canetti et al. [15], who showed an impossibility result for VBB obfuscation in the random oracle model. Canetti et al. showed that if there exists a VBB obfuscator in the random oracle model, then there exists an 'approximate' VBB obfuscator in the standard model. A similar argument can be used to show that if there exists simulation-secure exponentially efficient obfuscation in the random oracle model, then there exists approximately correct simulation-secure exponentially-efficient obfuscator in the standard model.

Finally, one needs to show that it is impossible to construct approximately correct simulation-secure exponentially-efficient obfuscators for certain function classes. This argument is similar to the incompressibility argument that we use. Let C be a circuit that performs PRF evaluation, and consider the obfuscation of C. A simulator must output an obfuscation given only black box access to the PRF function, which in turn is indistinguishable from a truly random function. Therefore, the simulator must output a subexponential sized string that approximately explains a truly random function, which is impossible.

1.2 A New Possibility Result in the Random Oracle Model

Now that we know that simulation security is impossible for unbounded queries even in the random oracle model, we turn to asking whether this model can be leveraged to support simulation security in any situations where it is impossible in the standard model. We already have one such example from the work of Boneh et al. [12] which gives both a standard model impossibility and a random oracle feasibility result for public index schemes. Thus, we are interested in new examples that go beyond the public index class. In this paper, we show the following possibility result:

Theorem 2 (Possibility, informal). *There exists a simulation secure FE scheme for the class of all polynomial-depth circuits in the random oracle model secure against any poly-time attacker who makes an unbounded number of messages queries, but an a-priori bounded number of key queries, based on semantically-secure public-key encryption and pseudo-random generators computable by low-depth circuits.*

Recall that such a security notion cannot be achieved even for the simple functionality of IBE in the standard model [12].

One-Bounded FE. Our starting point is a *one-bounded* simulation-secure FE scheme for all circuits, i.e., a scheme where the attacker can only make one key query, based just on the semantic security of public-key encryption. Our scheme is a variant of the Sahai-Seyalioglu [31]. Let $\mathcal{C}$ be a family of circuits wherein each circuit can be represented using t bits. Suppose U_x is a universal circuit that takes a $C \in \mathcal{C}$ as input, and outputs $C(x)$. The set-up algorithm of our FE scheme generates $2t$ key pairs of a semantically-secure public-key encryption scheme. The $2t$ public keys $(\mathsf{pk}_{1,0}, \mathsf{pk}_{1,1}), \ldots, (\mathsf{pk}_{t,0}, \mathsf{pk}_{t,1})$ form the master public key, and the $2t$ private keys $(\mathsf{sk}_{1,0}, \mathsf{sk}_{1,1}) \ldots, (\mathsf{sk}_{t,0}, \mathsf{sk}_{t,1})$ are kept secret. In order to encrypt a message x, a garbled circuit for U_x is generated. Suppose $w_{i,b}$ for $i = 1, \ldots, t$ and $b = 0, 1$ are the *wire-labels* of U_x for its t input bits. Then the $(i,b)^{th}$ component of the ciphertext consists of two parts: an encryption of a random value $r_{i,b}$ under $\mathsf{pk}_{i,b}$, and $w_{i,b}$ blinded with the hash of $r_{i,b}$. The key for a circuit C represented using bits $\beta_1, \ldots, \beta_t$ is simply the private keys corresponding to those bits, i.e., $\mathsf{sk}_{\beta_1}, \ldots, \mathsf{sk}_{\beta_t}$.

It is easy to see that the one-bounded FE scheme is correct. Specifically, the secret key for C will allow one to recover r_{i,β_i} for $i = 1, \ldots, t$. Then by running the hash function on these values, the w_{i,β_i} can be unblinded and used to evaluate the garbled circuit.

Let us now see how a simulator $\mathcal{S}$ can generate ciphertexts and a key from the right distribution in the ideal world. If the only allowed key query is made before the challenge phase for a circuit C, then $\mathcal{S}$ just runs the normal key generation algorithm, and later when adversary outputs a challenge message $x^\star$, it can generate a garbled circuit using just $C(x^\star)$.[4] When the adversary's key query is after the challenge message, however, $\mathcal{S}$ does not get any information in the challenge phase. In particular, it does not know which universal circuit to garble. Here the random oracle allows the simulator to *defer* making a decision until after the key query is made. It can set the second part of the (i,b)th ciphertext component to be a random number $z_{i,b}$ because, intuitively, adversary does not know $r_{i,b}$ (it is encrypted) so a hash of it is completely random. When adversary queries with a circuit C afterwards, simulator can program the random oracle's response on $r_{i,b}$ to be $z_{i,b} \oplus w_{i,b}$, so that decryption works out properly.

Bounded Collusion FE. Using the one-bounded scheme in a black-box way, we can design an FE scheme secure against any a-priori bounded collusions for the class $\mathsf{NC1}$, using Gorbunov et al.'s [20] transformation. While their transformation was proved secure for only one challenge message, we show that the same ideas also work for unbounded number of challenge messages. If the underlying one-bounded scheme is secure against any number of challenge messages, then so is the scheme obtained after applying their transformation.

Related Work. Sahai and Seyalioglu [31] were the first to use randomized encodings to design an FE system. Their scheme can issue one key *non-adaptively* for any function. Our one-bounded scheme can be seen as an extension of theirs to additionally support post-challenge key query. The random oracle allows a simulator to not commit to any value in the ciphertext until the function evaluation is made available.

Goldwasser et al. [19] also designed an FE system that can issue one pre-challenge key. Their scheme has succinct ciphertexts (independent of circuit size) but security is proved under stronger assumptions.

Iovino and Zebroski [24] present two results on simulation-secure FE in the public-key setting. First, they have a construction for a bounded number of challenge ciphertexts and pre-challenge key queries (and unbounded post-challenge queries), where key size grows with number of challenge ciphertexts but the ciphertext size is constant. The encryption/decryption time grows with the number of pre-challenge key queries. The second construction is for bounded key queries and challenge ciphertexts, but with constant size keys and ciphertexts.

[4] In fact, if we just want pre-challenge key query security, then there is no need for random oracle.

Here the encryption/decryption times depend on the bound on number of key queries and challenge ciphertexts. Both these results use extractability obfuscation. Our positive result presents a construction where the number of challenge ciphertexts is unbounded, but key queries are bounded. Therefore, our positive result and the results of Iovino and Zebroski are incomparable. Moreover, our construction only requires PKE and low-depth PRGs, whereas their constructions require stronger assumptions.

1.3 Another Impossibility Result

A natural question to ask is whether we can construct a simulation secure FE scheme in the random oracle model that can handle unbounded ciphertext queries, followed by an unbounded number of post-challenge key queries. We show that this is also impossible, assuming the existence of weak pseudorandom functions.

Theorem 3. *There does not exist a* $(0, \mathsf{poly}, \mathsf{poly})$*-simulation secure FE scheme for the class of (weak) pseudo-random functions in the random oracle model.*

Once again we interpret messages as seeds to a weak PRF family wPRF and secret keys as points in the domain of the PRF. A very different way to attack an FE scheme is needed though because no key query can be made before the challenge phase.

The new attacker $\mathcal{A}^\star$ starts off by outputting randomly chosen seeds $s_1, \ldots, s_k$ for wPRF, and gets ciphertexts $\mathsf{ct}_1, \ldots, \mathsf{ct}_k$ in return. The RO queries made in the encryption process are *hidden* from $\mathcal{A}^\star$, and it might need some of them later during decryption. So, it requests secret keys for randomly chosen points $x_1, \ldots, x_q$, and gets $\mathsf{sk}_1, \ldots, \mathsf{sk}_q$ in return. Then it decrypts every ct_i with sk_j and records the RO queries made in a list Γ. An important point to note here is that the simulator gets some information about the seeds chosen earlier when key-queries are made. Specifically, it gets $\mathsf{wPRF}(s_1, x_j), \ldots, \mathsf{wPRF}(s_k, x_j)$ when x_j is the query.

$\mathcal{A}^\star$ now picks a random point x^* and requests a secret key for it. The goal is to use the key obtained, say sk^*, to decrypt the challenge ciphertexts $\mathsf{ct}_1, \ldots, \mathsf{ct}_k$ later. But, in order to do so, $\mathcal{A}^\star$ also needs to find out the RO queries made during key-generation that may also be required for decryption. To solve this problem, we use the same idea as in the previous impossibility result: encrypt some random seeds on your own and decrypt them with sk^*, while adding the RO queries made to Γ.

Finally, $\mathcal{A}^\star$ decrypts $\mathsf{ct}_1, \ldots, \mathsf{ct}_k$ with sk^* *without* invoking the random oracle, using the list Γ instead. In the real world, at least a constant fraction of the decryptions succeed. The analysis is similar to that of the previous impossibility result, but with the role of ciphertext and key reversed. The ideal world analysis, on the other hand, need more care because of two reasons. First, as pointed out earlier, some information about the seeds $s_1, \ldots, s_k$ is leaked when post-challenge key queries are made. Second, the simulator needs to compress the evaluation of wPRF on seeds $s_1, \ldots, s_k$ and a common point x^*, instead of one seed and multiple points as in the $(\mathsf{poly}, 1, 0)$ impossibility. At the same time, however, the only opportunity a simulator has of programming RO responses after learning $\mathsf{wPRF}(s_1, x^*), \ldots, \mathsf{wPRF}(s_k, x^*)$ is when ciphertexts for random seeds are decrypted with sk^* with the help of RO. So, it is conceivable that one can exploit the security of wPRF to argue that it is impossible to compress $\mathsf{wPRF}(s_1, x^*), \ldots, \mathsf{wPRF}(s_k, x^*)$ into a small key and a small number of RO responses. We show that this is indeed the case in the full version [1].

1.4 Relation to De Caro et al. and Functional Encryption for Circuits with Random Oracle Gates

At the time of the initial posting of our work, De Caro et al. [16] stated (Theorem 3) that indistinguishability security for FE schemes in the random oracle model implied simulation security, resulting in an apparent discrepancy with our results. After our work was posted we contacted the authors to point out this dissonance. The authors informed us that they had earlier become aware of an issue with the theorem statement, but had not yet prepared an update to their posting. They stated that they intended to update it to a statement that indistinguishability-based definition of "functional encryption for circuits with random oracle gates" implied simulation security.

At the time, the notion of functional encryption for circuits with random oracle gates had not previously appeared in the literature and we were unable to deduce the intended definition from the phrase. Subsequently, the authors provided a revision which defined the concept and provided a transformation in the random oracle model which showed this new notion implies (regular) simulation security [17]. However, since our work shows such a notion is impossible to achieve, this must imply that this indistinguishability notion of "functional encryption for circuits with random oracle gates" was impossible to realize to begin with.

Despite sharing the term *random oracle* the new concept proposed in their revision is quite different than how the random oracle model was proposed [6]. Recall, that a cryptographic system built in the random oracle model will have the same algorithms and definitions as the standard model counterpart with the exception that each algorithm is allowed oracle access to a random function. We emphasize that the random oracle model in of itself is not impossible, it is just simply a different model.[5] Prior works would typically first establish provable security in the random oracle model and then apply the heuristic of replacing the random oracle calls with those to a hash function. It is this last step where security can actually be lost; in some cases no matter what the hash function is [14]. The concept of IND-FE in the random oracle model is not impossible

[5] We note that in practice one could actually instantiate this model with a trusted third party that dynamically builds a random table. However, this is not done since presumably one does not want to require online communication and introduce such a trusted third party.

to achieve (as far as we know), but we show that it is still insufficient to get simulation security. This impossibility holds for the random oracle model itself and is completely independent of the hash function replacement heuristic.

In the concept of functional encryption with random oracle gates as defined in the revision of [17] the random oracle is not just used as a tool to help augment functional encryption, but actually incorporated into a definition of functional encryption as the descriptions of a functionality f will depend on the random oracle. (Due to space limitations we refer the reader to [17] for a detailed description of the new definition.) As a simple argument will show, this new indistinguishability notion, unlike standard FE in the random oracle model, is impossible to begin with. So the addition of random oracle gates to FE circuits moves one to a primitive that is unachievable.

The combination of our simulation impossibility results with the implications from [17] imply this new notion of indistinguishability FE with random oracle gates is impossible to achieve. However, there is a much simpler and direct argument, which we provide in the full version of our paper [1].

1.5 Interpreting Our Impossibility Results

Impossibility results for simulation secure functional encryption in the standard model were already known before our work. If we take any FE system secure in the Random Oracle Model and then take the heuristic of replacing the oracle calls with some hash function family, then we have a standard model FE scheme. We know this new system to be impossible to be simulation secure from prior work. So a natural question to ask is what new interpretations does our result provide. We believe there are two main points here.

First, an interpretation of our result is understanding FE in idealized models. While the random oracle model is closely associated with the random oracle heuristic (i.e. replacing oracle calls with hash functions), there are different possible ways to try to "instantiate" a cryptosystem described in the random oracle model. One possibility is to replace calls to the random oracle with secure hardware tokens. Another could be a use of a blockchain.

In addition, in the interest of getting a better and deeper scientific understanding it is useful to map out cryptography in both the standard and random oracle models. There has been precedent for this in our community. For example, the Boneh et al. [12] paper which gave some examples of schemes (simulation secure FE schemes where the adversary sends unbounded challenge messages, followed by one key query) that were possible in the random oracle model, but impossible otherwise. Going further out, to best understand non-committing encryption it is useful to know both that it is impossible in the standard model and that it is possible in the RO model.

Secondly, we also posit that there may be some forms of security that lie in between simulation security and indistinguishability security, but that are hard for us to understand or formally define. Suppose there did exist an FE scheme that was simulation secure in the RO model, and one did apply the random oracle heuristic to it. It is possible that even if this new scheme is not simulation secure, the transformation could result in some gain of security. Perhaps this gain in security might even be what is right or needed for a particular application. One example is that while the Fiat-Shamir heuristic applied to zero knowledge protocol does not give a simulation secure NIZK, but might give the right form of security needed for a particular application (e.g. its use in some cryptocurrency).

2 Preliminaries

We use λ to denote the security parameter. Let $[n]$ denote the set $\{1, 2, \ldots, n\}$. If A is an algorithm, then $a \leftarrow A(\cdot)$ or $A(\cdot) \rightarrow a$ denote that a is the output of running A on the specified inputs. If $\mathcal{D}$ is a distribution, then $s \leftarrow \mathcal{D}$ denotes that s is a sample drawn according to it. Also, $x \xleftarrow{R} X$ denotes drawing a value x uniformly at random from the set X.

For two distribution ensembles $\mathcal{X} = \{\mathcal{X}_\lambda\}_{\lambda \in \mathbb{N}}$ and $\mathcal{Y} = \{\mathcal{Y}_\lambda\}_{\lambda \in \mathbb{N}}$, we use $\mathcal{X} \stackrel{c}{\approx} \mathcal{Y}$ to denote that $\mathcal{X}$ is computationally indistinguishable from $\mathcal{Y}$. Lastly, for two vectors $u = (u_1, \ldots, u_n)$ and $v = (v_1, \ldots, v_n)$, their Hamming distance $\mathsf{HD}(u, v)$ is defined to be the number of points where they don't match, i.e., the size of set $\{i \in [n] \mid u_i \neq v_i\}$.

2.1 Weak Pseudo-Random Functions

Our impossibility results rely on the existence of circuit families whose output cannot be *compressed* by a significant amount. In Sect. 4, we will show that a specific circuit family built from pseudo-random functions (PRFs) is not compressible. In fact, like Gorbunov et al. [20], a weaker type of PRF where adversary only gets evaluation at random points suffices for our purpose.

Definition 1 (Weak PRFs). *Let n, m, p be polynomials in λ. Let $\mathsf{wPRF} = \{\mathsf{wPRF}_\lambda\}_{\lambda \in \mathbb{N}}$ be a family of efficiently computable functions such that $\mathsf{wPRF}_\lambda : \{0,1\}^{n(\lambda)} \times \{0,1\}^{m(\lambda)} \rightarrow \{0,1\}^{p(\lambda)}$, where the first input is called the seed. Pick a seed $s \xleftarrow{R} \{0,1\}^{n(\lambda)}$ and $\ell + 1$ points $x_1, \ldots, x_\ell, x^\star \xleftarrow{R} \{0,1\}^{m(\lambda)}$. Let D_ℓ be the ℓ-tuple of values $(x_1, \mathsf{wPRF}_\lambda(s, x_1)), \ldots, (x_\ell, \mathsf{wPRF}_\lambda(s, x_\ell))$. Then the wPRF family is a weak pseudo-random function family if for every ℓ polynomial in λ,*

$$\{D_\ell, x^\star, \mathsf{wPRF}_\lambda(s, x^\star)\}_{\lambda \in \mathbb{N}} \quad \stackrel{c}{\approx} \quad \{D_\ell, x^\star, r\}_{\lambda \in \mathbb{N}},$$

where r is a random string of length $p(\lambda)$.

Below we present two alternate definitions of security for a weak pseudorandom family. The first one is a standard definition for PRFs/weak PRFs, while the second one is introduced for our final impossibility result. They both follow from Definition 1 above through simple hybrid arguments.

Definition 2 (Weak PRFs, many points). *Let $\mathsf{wPRF} = \{\mathsf{wPRF}_\lambda\}_{\lambda \in \mathbb{N}}$ be a family as in Definition 1. Pick $s \xleftarrow{R} \{0,1\}^{n(\lambda)}$, $x_1, \ldots, x_\ell \xleftarrow{R} \{0,1\}^{m(\lambda)}$, and*

$r_1, \ldots, r_\ell \xleftarrow{R} \{0,1\}^{p(\lambda)}$. *Then the* wPRF *family is a weak PRF family for many points if for every* ℓ *polynomial in* λ,

$$\{(x_1, \mathsf{wPRF}_\lambda(s, x_1)), \ldots, (x_\ell, \mathsf{wPRF}_\lambda(s, x_\ell))\}_{\lambda \in \mathbb{N}} \overset{c}{\approx} \{(x_1, r_1), \ldots, (x_\ell, r_\ell)_{\lambda \in \mathbb{N}}.$$

Definition 3 (Weak PRFs, many seeds with aux). *Let* $\mathsf{wPRF} = \{\mathsf{wPRF}_\lambda\}_{\lambda \in \mathbb{N}}$ *be a family as in Definition 1. Pick* k *seeds* $s_1, \ldots, s_k \xleftarrow{R} \{0,1\}^{n(\lambda)}$ *and* $\ell + 1$ *points* $x_1, \ldots, x_\ell, x^\star \xleftarrow{R} \{0,1\}^{m(\lambda)}$. *Let* $D_{k,\ell}$ *be the* $k \cdot \ell$*-tuple of values* $(x_1, \mathsf{wPRF}_\lambda(s_1, x_1)), \ldots, (x_\ell, \mathsf{wPRF}_\lambda(s_1, x_\ell)), \ldots, (x_1, \mathsf{wPRF}_\lambda(s_k, x_1)), \ldots, (x_\ell, \mathsf{wPRF}_\lambda(s_k, x_\ell))$. *Then the* wPRF *family is a weak PRF family for many seeds with auxiliary information if for every* k, ℓ *polynomial in* λ,

$$\{D_{k,\ell}, x^\star, \mathsf{wPRF}_\lambda(s_1, x^\star), \ldots, \mathsf{wPRF}_\lambda(s_k, x^\star)\}_{\lambda \in \mathbb{N}} \overset{c}{\approx} \{D_{k,\ell}, x^\star, r_1, \ldots, r_k\}_{\lambda \in \mathbb{N}},$$

where $r_1, \ldots, r_k$ *are random strings of length* $p(\lambda)$.

2.2 Randomized Encodings

We use decomposable randomized encodings [20] to simplify the description of our FE schemes. They are known to exist for all circuits due to the works of [4,34].

Definition 4 (Randomized Encodings). *Let* $\mathcal{C} = \{\mathcal{C}_\lambda\}_\lambda$ *be a family of circuits, where each circuit* $C \in \mathcal{C}_\lambda$ *takes an* $n(\lambda)$ *bit input and produces an* $m(\lambda)$ *bit output. A* decomposable randomized encoding RE *of* $\mathcal{C}$ *consists of two* PPT *algorithms:*

- $\mathsf{RE.Encode}(1^\lambda, C)$: *It takes a circuit* $C \in \mathcal{C}_\lambda$ *as input, and outputs a randomized encoding* $((w_{1,0}, w_{1,1}), \ldots, (w_{n(\lambda),0}, w_{n(\lambda),1}))$.
- $\mathsf{RE.Decode}(1^\lambda, (\tilde{w}_1, \ldots, \tilde{w}_{n(\lambda)}))$: *It takes an encoding* $(\tilde{w}_1, \ldots, \tilde{w}_{n(\lambda)})$ *and outputs* $y \in \{0,1\}^{m(\lambda)} \cup \{\bot\}$.

Correctness. Let $C \in \mathcal{C}_\lambda$ *be any circuit, and let* $((w_{1,0}, w_{1,1}), \ldots, (w_{n,0}, w_{n,1})) \leftarrow \mathsf{RE.Encode}(1^\lambda, C)$. *For any input* $x \in \{0,1\}^{n(\lambda)}$, $\mathsf{RE.Decode}(1^\lambda, (w_{1,x_1}, \ldots, w_{n(\lambda),x_{n(\lambda)}})) = C(x)$.

Security. To define the security of such a scheme, consider the following two distributions:

- $\mathsf{Real}^{\mathsf{RE}}_{\mathcal{A}}(\lambda)$. *Run* $\mathcal{A}(1^\lambda)$ *to get a* $C \in \mathcal{C}_\lambda$ *and an* $x \in \{0,1\}^{n(\lambda)}$. *Then run* RE.Encode *on input* C *to get an encoding* $((w_{1,0}, w_{1,1}), \ldots, (w_{n(\lambda),0}, w_{n(\lambda),1}))$. *Output* $\{w_{i,x_i}\}_{i \in [n(\lambda)]}$.
- $\mathsf{Ideal}^{\mathsf{RE}}_{\mathcal{S}}(\lambda)$. *Run* $\mathcal{A}(1^\lambda)$ *to get a* $C \in \mathcal{C}_\lambda$ *and an* $x \in \{0,1\}^{n(\lambda)}$. *Output* $\mathcal{S}(1^\lambda, C, C(x))$.

A randomized encoding scheme RE *is* secure *if for every* PPT *adversary* $\mathcal{A}$, *there exists a* PPT *simulator* $\mathcal{S}$ *such that*

$$\mathsf{Real}^{\mathsf{RE}}_{\mathcal{A}}(\lambda) \overset{c}{\approx} \mathsf{Ideal}^{\mathsf{RE}}_{\mathcal{S}}(\lambda).$$

3 Functional Encryption in the Random Oracle Model

A functional encryption scheme for a function space $\mathbb{F} = \{\mathbb{F}_\lambda\}_{\lambda \in \mathbb{N}}$ and a message space $\mathcal{X} = \{\mathcal{X}_\lambda\}_{\lambda \in \mathbb{N}}$ in the random oracle model consists of four PPT algorithms that have access to a random oracle $\mathcal{O} : \{0,1\}^{\ell(\lambda)} \to \{0,1\}^{m(\lambda)}$, where ℓ and m are polynomials. The algorithms are described as follows:

- $\mathsf{Setup}^{\mathcal{O}}(1^\lambda)$: It takes the security parameter (in unary representation) as input and outputs a public key pk and a master secret key msk.
- $\mathsf{KeyGen}^{\mathcal{O}}(\mathsf{msk}, f)$: It takes the master secret key msk and a circuit $f \in \mathbb{F}_\lambda$ as inputs, and outputs a secret key sk_f for the circuit.
- $\mathsf{Encrypt}^{\mathcal{O}}(\mathsf{pk}, x)$: It takes the public key pk and a value $x \in \mathcal{X}_\lambda$ as inputs, and outputs a ciphertext ct_x.
- $\mathsf{Decrypt}^{\mathcal{O}}(\mathsf{pk}, \mathsf{sk}, \mathsf{ct})$: It takes the public key pk, a secret key sk, and a ciphertext ct as inputs, and outputs a value y or $\perp$.

Correctness. The four algorithms defined above must satisfy the following correctness property. For all values of the security parameter λ, for every $f \in \mathbb{F}_\lambda$ and $x \in \mathcal{X}_\lambda$, all random oracles $\mathcal{O}$, and all $(\mathsf{pk}, \mathsf{msk})$ output by $\mathsf{Setup}^{\mathcal{O}}(1^\lambda)$,

$$\mathsf{Decrypt}^{\mathcal{O}}(\mathsf{pk}, \mathsf{KeyGen}^{\mathcal{O}}(\mathsf{msk}, f), \mathsf{Encrypt}^{\mathcal{O}}(\mathsf{pk}, x)) = f(x).$$

Without loss of generality, we can assume Decrypt to be deterministic.

One could consider weaker notions of correctness where a negligible probability of error is allowed.

Statistical Correctness. For all values of the security parameter λ, for every $f \in \mathbb{F}_\lambda$ and $x \in \mathcal{X}_\lambda$, all random oracles $\mathcal{O}$,

$$\Pr\left[\mathsf{Decrypt}^{\mathcal{O}}(\mathsf{pk}, \mathsf{sk}, \mathsf{ct}) = f(x) : \begin{array}{c} (\mathsf{pk}, \mathsf{msk}) \leftarrow \mathsf{Setup}^{\mathcal{O}}(1^\lambda) \\ \mathsf{sk} \leftarrow \mathsf{KeyGen}^{\mathcal{O}}(\mathsf{msk}, f) \\ \mathsf{ct} \leftarrow \mathsf{Encrypt}^{\mathcal{O}}(\mathsf{pk}, x) \end{array}\right] \geq 1 - \mathsf{negl}(\lambda)$$

3.1 Simulation-Based Security

Definition 5 (Experiments). *Let* $\mathsf{FE} = (\mathsf{Setup}, \mathsf{KeyGen}, \mathsf{Encrypt}, \mathsf{Decrypt})$ *be a functional encryption scheme. For any* PPT *algorithms* $\mathcal{A} = (\mathcal{A}_1, \mathcal{A}_2)$ *and* $\mathcal{S} = (\mathcal{S}_1, \mathcal{S}_2, \mathcal{S}_3, \mathcal{S}_4)$*, Fig. 1 defines two experiments* $\mathsf{Real}_{\mathcal{A}}^{\mathsf{FE}}(\lambda)$ *and* $\mathsf{Ideal}_{\mathcal{A},\mathcal{S}}^{\mathsf{FE}}(\lambda)$*. In the figure,* q_c *denotes the length of challenge message vector* $\boldsymbol{x}$ *output by* $\mathcal{A}_1$ *and* q_1 *denotes the number of key generation queries made before that.*

Definition 6 (Admissibility). *An adversary* $\mathcal{A} = (\mathcal{A}_1, \mathcal{A}_2)$ *is* $(q_{\mathsf{pre}}(\lambda), q_{\mathsf{chal}}(\lambda), q_{\mathsf{post}}(\lambda))$-admissible *if in any run of the experiments* $\mathsf{Real}_{\mathcal{A}}(1^\lambda)$ *and* $\mathsf{Ideal}_{\mathcal{A},\mathcal{S}}(1^\lambda)$*,* $\mathcal{A}_1$ *and* $\mathcal{A}_2$ *make at most* $q_{\mathsf{pre}}(\lambda)$ *and* $q_{\mathsf{post}}(\lambda)$ *key generation queries, respectively, and* $\mathcal{A}_1$ *outputs at most* $q_{\mathsf{chal}}(\lambda)$ *challenge messages.*

An adversary $\mathcal{A}$ *is* $(\mathsf{poly}, q_{\mathsf{chal}}(\lambda), q_{\mathsf{post}}(\lambda))$-admissible *if in any run of the experiments* $\mathsf{Real}_{\mathcal{A}}(1^\lambda)$ *and* $\mathsf{Ideal}_{\mathcal{A},\mathcal{S}}(1^\lambda)$*,* $\mathcal{A}_1$ *is allowed to make an unbounded*

Experiment $\mathsf{Real}^{\mathsf{FE}}_{\mathcal{A}}(\lambda)$:
1. $(\mathsf{pk}, \mathsf{msk}) \leftarrow \mathsf{Setup}^{\mathcal{O}}(1^\lambda)$
2. $(\mathbf{x}, \mathsf{st}_{\mathcal{A}}) \leftarrow \mathcal{A}_1^{\mathsf{KeyGen\text{-}RO}_1(\mathsf{msk},\cdot,\cdot)}(\mathsf{pk})$
3. $\mathsf{ct}_i \leftarrow \mathsf{Encrypt}^{\mathcal{O}}(\mathsf{mpk}, x_i)$ for $i \in [q_c]$
4. $\alpha \leftarrow \mathcal{A}_2^{\mathsf{KeyGen\text{-}RO}_2(\mathsf{msk},\cdot,\cdot)}(\{\mathsf{ct}_i\}_{i\in[q_c]}, \mathsf{st}_{\mathcal{A}})$
5. Output α

Experiment $\mathsf{Ideal}^{\mathsf{FE}}_{\mathcal{A},\mathcal{S}}(\lambda)$:
1. $(\mathsf{pk}, \mathsf{st}_1) \leftarrow \mathcal{S}_1(1^\lambda)$
2. $(\mathbf{x}, \mathsf{st}_{\mathcal{A}}) \leftarrow \mathcal{A}_1^{\mathsf{KeyGen\text{-}RO}_1(\mathsf{st}_1,\cdot,\cdot)}(\mathsf{pk})$
3. $(\{\mathsf{ct}_i\}_i, \mathsf{st}_3) \leftarrow \mathcal{S}_3(\mathsf{st}_2, \{f_j(x_i)\}_{i,j})$ where $f_1, \ldots, f_{q_1}$ are key queries made by $\mathcal{A}_1$
4. $\alpha \leftarrow \mathcal{A}_2^{\mathsf{KeyGen\text{-}RO}_2(\mathsf{st}_3,\cdot,\cdot)}(\{\mathsf{ct}_i\}_{i\in[q_c]}, \mathsf{st}_{\mathcal{A}})$
5. Output α

In the Real-world experiment, the setup algorithm, using the random oracle $\mathcal{O}$, outputs public key pk and master secret key msk. The adversary $\mathcal{A}_1$ gets pk and has oracle access to $\mathsf{KeyGen\text{-}RO}_1$. This oracle responds to random oracle queries and key generation queries. It has msk hardwired and takes two inputs inp_1 and inp_2, where inp_1 specifies whether the query is a key generation query or a random oracle query. In the former case, $\mathsf{KeyGen\text{-}RO}_1$ outputs $\mathsf{KeyGen}^{\mathcal{O}}(\mathsf{msk}, \mathsf{inp}_2)$, while in the latter case, it outputs $\mathcal{O}(\mathsf{inp}_2)$. After polynomially many oracle queries to $\mathsf{KeyGen\text{-}RO}_1$, $\mathcal{A}_1$ outputs a vector $\mathbf{x}$ of ciphertext queries and a state $\mathsf{st}_{\mathcal{A}}$. The adversary $\mathcal{A}_2$ gets encryptions of all elements in $\mathbf{x}$ (note that x_i denotes the ith entry in $\mathbf{x}$) and the state $\mathsf{st}_{\mathcal{A}}$. It also has oracle access to $\mathsf{KeyGen\text{-}RO}_2$, which is identical to $\mathsf{KeyGen\text{-}RO}_1$. After making polynomially many oracle queries, $\mathcal{A}_2$ outputs α.

In the Ideal-world experiment, the simulator $\mathcal{S}_1$ first computes the public key pk, and simulator state st_1. The adversary $\mathcal{A}_1$ gets pk and oracle access to $\mathsf{KeyGen\text{-}RO}_1$, which is simulator $\mathcal{S}_2$ in the ideal-world. The simulator $\mathcal{S}_2$ is stateful. It maintains an internal state st_2, gets $\mathcal{S}_1$'s state st_1 and takes tuple inputs $(\mathsf{inp}_1, \mathsf{inp}_2)$, which indicate whether it is a key generation query or a random oracle query. After polynomially many queries, adversary $\mathcal{A}_1$ outputs $\mathbf{x}$ and state $\mathsf{st}_{\mathcal{A}}$. The simulator $\mathcal{S}_3$ must give out encryptions of $\mathbf{x}$, using $\mathcal{S}_2's$ final state st_2 and $\{f_j(x_i)\}_{i\in[q_c],j\in[q_1]}$. The simulator outputs the ciphertexts as well as state st_3. Adversary $\mathcal{A}_2$ gets these ciphertexts, state $\mathsf{st}_{\mathcal{A}}$ and oracle access to $\mathsf{KeyGen\text{-}RO}_2$. In the ideal world, this oracle is $\mathcal{S}_4^{\mathsf{KeyIdeal}(\cdot)}(\mathsf{st}_3, \cdot, \cdot)$. Here, $\mathsf{KeyIdeal}$ takes as input a function f and outputs $(f(x_1), \ldots, f(x_{q_c}))$. Also, simulator $\mathcal{S}_4$ is stateful and has an internal state st_4. Finally, after polynomially many queries, $\mathcal{A}$ outputs α.

Fig. 1. Real and ideal experiments.

(but polynomial) number of pre-challenge key queries, $\mathcal{A}_2$ makes at most $q_{\mathsf{post}}(\lambda)$ key generation queries, and $\mathcal{A}_1$ outputs at most $q_{\mathsf{chal}}(\lambda)$ challenge messages. We can similarly define admissible adversaries where the number of challenge messages/post challenge key queries are unbounded.

On the other hand, a simulator $\mathcal{S} = (\mathcal{S}_1, \mathcal{S}_2, \mathcal{S}_3, \mathcal{S}_4)$ is admissible *if whenever $\mathcal{A}_2$ makes a key query f, $\mathcal{S}_4$ queries* $\mathsf{KeyIdeal}$ *on f only.*

Definition 7 (Simulation security). *A functional encryption scheme* $\mathsf{FE} = (\mathsf{Setup}, \mathsf{KeyGen}, \mathsf{Encrypt}, \mathsf{Decrypt})$ *is $(q_{\mathsf{pre}}(\lambda), q_{\mathsf{chal}}(\lambda), q_{\mathsf{post}}(\lambda))$-*$\mathsf{Sim}$*-secure for some polynomials q_{pre}, q_{chal}, and q_{post}, if there exists an admissible* PPT *simulator $\mathcal{S} = (\mathcal{S}_1, \mathcal{S}_2, \mathcal{S}_3, \mathcal{S}_4)$ such that for all $(q_{\mathsf{pre}}(\lambda), q_{\mathsf{chal}}(\lambda), q_{\mathsf{post}}(\lambda))$-admissible* PPT *adversaries $\mathcal{A} = (\mathcal{A}_1, \mathcal{A}_2)$,*

$$\{\mathsf{Real}^{\mathsf{FE}}_{\mathcal{A}}(\lambda)\}_{\lambda\in\mathbb{N}} \overset{c}{\approx} \{\mathsf{Ideal}^{\mathsf{FE}}_{\mathcal{A},\mathcal{S}}(\lambda)\}_{\lambda\in\mathbb{N}}.$$

We also consider adversaries that make an unbounded (but polynomial) number of pre-challenge key queries/challenge messages/post-challenge key queries.

Definition 8 (Simulation security, unbounded queries). *A functional encryption scheme* $\mathsf{FE} = (\mathsf{Setup}, \mathsf{KeyGen}, \mathsf{Encrypt}, \mathsf{Decrypt})$ *is* $(\mathsf{poly}, q_{\mathsf{chal}}(\lambda), q_{\mathsf{post}}(\lambda))$-$\mathsf{Sim}$*-secure for some polynomials* q_{chal}*, and* q_{post}*, if there exists an admissible* PPT *simulator* $\mathcal{S} = (\mathcal{S}_1, \mathcal{S}_2, \mathcal{S}_3, \mathcal{S}_4)$ *such that for all* $(\mathsf{poly}, q_{\mathsf{chal}}(\lambda), q_{\mathsf{post}}(\lambda))$*-admissible* PPT *adversaries* $\mathcal{A} = (\mathcal{A}_1, \mathcal{A}_2)$*,*

$$\{\mathsf{Real}^{\mathsf{FE}}_{\mathcal{A}}(\lambda)\}_{\lambda\in\mathbb{N}} \overset{c}{\approx} \{\mathsf{Ideal}^{\mathsf{FE}}_{\mathcal{A},\mathcal{S}}(\lambda)\}_{\lambda\in\mathbb{N}}.$$

We can similarly define simulation security when q_{chal} *and* q_{post} *are unbounded.*

Note that in the real world an adversary has explicit access to the random oracle. In the ideal world, both the key generation and random oracles are simulated by $\mathcal{S}$ throughout the experiment.

Discussion on Previous Definitions of Sim-Secure FE. There are a number of definitions of simulation secure functional encryption [2,5,12,30]. While these definitions are similar in spirit, there are minor differences. For instance, in the security game of [2,12], the adversary makes pre-challenge key queries, followed by a challenge phase (where it queries for ciphertexts), followed by a post-challenge key query phase. The definition of [5] is more general as it allows arbitrary interleaving of encryption and key-generation queries. We use the AGVW definition [2] in this work, although we believe our impossibility result can also be extended to work for the definitions in [5].

4 Hardness of Approximate Compression

In this section, we will first define the notion of approximate compression, and then show that there are certain circuit families which are hard to approximately compress. This section closely follows the work of Agrawal et al. [2], who defined the notion of (exact) compressibility of circuit evaluations, and showed that there exist certain circuit families that are (exact) incompressible.

Definition 9. *Let* ℓ, t *be polynomials and* ϵ *a non-negligible function. A class of circuits* $\mathcal{C} = \{\mathcal{C}_\lambda\}_\lambda$ *with domain* $\mathcal{D} = \{\mathcal{D}_\lambda\}_\lambda$ *and range* $\mathcal{R} = \{\mathcal{R}_\lambda\}_\lambda$ *is said to be* (ℓ, t, ϵ)*-approximately compressible if there exists a family of compression circuits* $\mathsf{Cmp} = \{\mathsf{Cmp}_\lambda\}_\lambda$*, a family of decompression circuits* $\mathsf{DeCmp} = \{\mathsf{DeCmp}_\lambda\}_\lambda$*, a polynomial* poly*, and a non-negligible function* η*, such that for all large enough* λ *the following properties hold:*

- *The circuits* Cmp_λ *and* DeCmp_λ *have size bounded by* $\mathsf{poly}(\lambda)$*.*
- *(compression) For all input* $s \in \mathcal{D}_\lambda$ *and circuits* $C_1, C_2, \ldots, C_{\ell(\lambda)} \in \mathcal{C}_\lambda$*,*

$$\left|\mathsf{Cmp}_\lambda\left(\{C_i, C_i(s)\}_{i\in[\ell(\lambda)]}\right)\right| \leq t(\lambda).$$

– *(approximate decompression) If s is chosen at random from $\mathcal{D}_\lambda$, $C_1, C_2, \ldots, C_{\ell(\lambda)}$ are chosen uniformly and independently from $\mathcal{C}_\lambda$, then*

$$\Pr\left[\mathsf{HD}\left(\mathsf{DeCmp}_\lambda\left(\{C_i\}_{i\in[\ell(\lambda)]}, \mathsf{Cmp}_\lambda\left(\{C_i, C_i(s)\}_{i\in[\ell(\lambda)]}\right)\right), (C_1(s), \ldots, C_{\ell(\lambda)}(s))\right) \leq \epsilon(\lambda)\cdot t(\lambda)\right] \geq \eta(\lambda)$$

We will now show that weak PRFs can be used to construct a class of circuits that are not approximate compressible. We will then use the more general notion of approximate incompressibility, rather than the specific case of weak PRFs, in proving our impossibility results. For simplicity of presentation, in the lemma statement below, we use specific constants which will be sufficient for our main result. However, the lemma can be easily extended to work for general ℓ, t and ϵ. We assume that the weak PRF outputs a single bit.

Lemma 1. *Let $\mathsf{wPRF} = \{\mathsf{wPRF}_\lambda\}_\lambda$ be a family of weak pseudorandom functions (for many points), where $\mathsf{wPRF}_\lambda : \{0,1\}^{n(\lambda)} \times \{0,1\}^{m(\lambda)} \to \{0,1\}$. Consider the family of circuits $\mathcal{C} = \{\mathcal{C}_\lambda\}_\lambda$, where $\mathcal{C}_\lambda = \{\mathsf{wPRF}_\lambda(\cdot, x)\}_{x\in\{0,1\}^{m(\lambda)}}$. Let $t = t(\lambda)$ be any polynomial such that $t(\lambda) \geq \lambda$ for all $\lambda \in \mathbb{N}$. Then $\mathcal{C}$ is not $(16t, t, 1/8)$ approximate compressible.*

The proof of this lemma is given in the full version of our paper [1].

5 Impossibility of Simulation Secure FE

In this section we show that there does not exist a functional encryption scheme for the family of all polynomial-sized circuits that is $(\mathsf{poly}, 1, 0)$-Sim secure in the random oracle model. Specifically, we show that a simulation secure FE scheme cannot be constructed for any family of circuits that is not approximately compressible (Definition 9). We exhibit an adversary $\mathcal{A} = (\mathcal{A}_1, \mathcal{A}_2)$ such that for *any* efficient simulator $\mathcal{S}$, the output of the real experiment, $\mathsf{Real}_{\mathcal{A}}^{\mathsf{FE}}(1^\lambda)$, is *distinguishable* from the output of the ideal experiment, $\mathsf{Ideal}_{\mathcal{A},\mathcal{S}}^{\mathsf{FE}}(1^\lambda)$ (Definition 8).

High Level Description of Adversary. Let $\mathcal{C}$ be an approximate incompressible circuit family. The adversary $\mathcal{A}_1$ first asks for secret keys for a large number of randomly chosen circuits from C, and receives $\{\mathsf{sk}_1, \ldots, \mathsf{sk}_q\}$ in return. Next, it generates encryptions of many random messages. It then decrypts each of these ciphertexts using the q secret keys. The purpose of these encryptions followed by the decryptions is to capture the random oracle queries that would have occurred while computing the q secret keys, which may also be required when these keys are used again for decryption later. Let S_{keys} denote the set of random oracle queries that occur during these decryptions.

$\mathcal{A}_1$ chooses a random message x^*, and outputs it as the challenge (along with a state that consists of its view so far). $\mathcal{A}_2$ then receives a ciphertext ct^*. It decrypts ct^* using $\mathsf{sk}_1, \ldots, \mathsf{sk}_t$, for some small t. Let S_{ct^*} denote the set of random oracle queries during these t decryptions. The purpose of these t decryptions is to capture the random oracle queries that would have occurred during the encryption of x^*, which may also be required when ct^* is decrypted again in the next step.

Finally, $\mathcal{A}_2$ decrypts ct^* using the remaining $q - t$ secret keys. An important thing to note here is that $\mathcal{A}_2$ *turns off* the random oracle, and instead uses the queries that it has already recorded. If a new random oracle query is required, then it uses a randomly chosen string. It compares the decrypted values to the correct function evaluations, and outputs 1 if most decryptions are correct.

First, we show that in the real world, $\mathcal{A}_2$ outputs 1 with probability at least 3/4. Let us focus on one of the $q - t$ decryptions, using a secret key sk_j. At a high level, this decryption can go wrong if a random oracle query is made on z, and $z \notin S_{\mathsf{keys}} \cup S_{\mathsf{ct}}$, but z was used during the computation of either sk_j or ct. We show that this event happens with low probability.

To complete the argument, we show that in the ideal world, $\mathcal{A}_2$ outputs 1 with probability around 1/2. In this world, the simulator receives q circuit evaluations on x^*, and must compress most of this information in the short challenge ciphertext and the random oracle queries made during the t post-challenge decryption operations. By choosing parameters carefully and appealing to the (approximate) incompressibility of the circuit family, we show that this is not possible.

5.1 Formal Description of Adversary

Let $\mathcal{C} = \{\mathcal{C}_\lambda\}_\lambda$ be a family of circuits such that each circuit in $\mathcal{C}_\lambda$ takes an $n(\lambda)$-bit input and is not $(16t, t, 1/8)$ approximately compressible for all polynomials t such that $t(\lambda) \geq \lambda$. Let FE be a functional encryption scheme for this family in the random oracle model. We now formally define the adversary $\mathcal{A} = (\mathcal{A}_1, \mathcal{A}_2)$.

Adversary $\mathcal{A}_1$. Let n_{key} and n_{enc} be polynomials in λ whose values will be fixed later. Let Γ be a list of (query, response) pairs that is empty at the beginning. $\mathcal{A}_1$ has four phases: setup, key query, random oracle query collection, and an output phase.

1. **Setup.** $\mathcal{A}_1$ receives the public key pk.
2. **Key query.** For $i \in [n_{\mathsf{key}}]$, it picks a circuit C_i at random from $\mathcal{C}_\lambda$, requests a secret key for C_i, and obtains sk_i in return.
3. **RO query collection 1.** $\mathcal{A}_1$ picks n_{enc} inputs $x_1, x_2, \ldots, x_{n_{\mathsf{enc}}} \xleftarrow{R} \{0,1\}^{n(\lambda)}$. For $j \in [n_{\mathsf{enc}}]$, it runs $\mathsf{Encrypt}^{\mathcal{O}}(\mathsf{pk}, x_j)$ to obtain a ciphertext ct_j. The RO queries made during the encryption process are forwarded to the random oracle.
   Now each of the ciphertexts $\mathsf{ct}_1, \ldots, \mathsf{ct}_{n_{\mathsf{enc}}}$ are decrypted with key sk_i for every $i \in [n_{\mathsf{key}}]$. If an oracle query β is made by the $\mathsf{Decrypt}$ algorithm, $\mathcal{A}_1$ queries the random oracle with the same. The response, say γ, is given to the algorithm, and (β, γ) is added to Γ (if it is not already present).
4. **Output.** $\mathcal{A}_1$ picks an input $x^* \xleftarrow{R} \{0,1\}^{n(\lambda)}$. It sets the state st to consist of pk, $C_1, \ldots, C_{n_{\mathsf{key}}}$, $\mathsf{sk}_1, \ldots, \mathsf{sk}_{n_{\mathsf{key}}}$, x^*, and Γ. Then it outputs (x^*, st).

Adversary $\mathcal{A}_2$. Let n_{eval} and n_{test} be polynomials in λ s.t. $n_{\mathsf{eval}}(\lambda) + n_{\mathsf{test}}(\lambda) = n_{\mathsf{key}}(\lambda)$ for all λ. (Their values will be fixed later.) $\mathcal{A}_2$ gets ct^* and st as input, and parses the latter to get $\mathsf{pk}, C_1, \ldots, C_{n_{\mathsf{key}}}, \mathsf{sk}_1, \ldots, \mathsf{sk}_{n_{\mathsf{key}}}, x^*$, and Γ. $\mathcal{A}_2$ has three phases: random oracle query collection, test, and an output phase.

1. **RO query collection 2.** For every $i \in [n_{\mathsf{eval}}]$, ct^* is decrypted with sk_i. If an RO query β is made by the Decrypt algorithm, $\mathcal{A}_2$ queries the random oracle with the same. The response, say γ, is given to the algorithm, and (β, γ) is added to Γ (if it is not already present).
2. **Test.** In this phase, ct^* is decrypted with rest of the keys but *without* invoking the random oracle. In order to do so, a new list Δ is initialized first, then the following steps are executed for every $n_{\mathsf{eval}} + 1 \leq i \leq n_{\mathsf{eval}} + n_{\mathsf{test}}$. The decryption algorithm is run with inputs pk, sk_i, and ct^*. When it makes an RO query β, $\mathcal{A}_2$ checks whether there is an entry of the form (β, γ) in Γ or Δ (in that order) or not. If yes, then γ is given to Decrypt and it continues to run. Otherwise, a random bit-string γ' of length $m(\lambda)$ (the output length of the random oracle) is generated, (β, γ') is added to Δ, and γ' is given to Decrypt. This process of providing responses to the RO queries of Decrypt continues till it terminates. Let out_i denote the output of Decrypt, which could be $\perp$.
3. **Output.** For every $n_{\mathsf{eval}} + 1 \leq i \leq n_{\mathsf{eval}} + n_{\mathsf{test}}$, check if out_i is equal to $C_i(x^*)$ (where x^* and C_i are part of the state transferred to $\mathcal{A}_2$). Let num be the number of keys for which this check succeeds. Output 1 if $\mathsf{num}/n_{\mathsf{test}} \geq 7/8$, else output 0.

To complete the description of $\mathcal{A}$, we need to define the polynomials n_{enc}, n_{eval} and n_{test} (recall that $n_{\mathsf{key}} = n_{\mathsf{eval}} + n_{\mathsf{test}}$). Let q_{Setup}, q_{Enc}, q_{KeyGen} and q_{Dec} be upper-bounds on the number of RO queries made by Setup, Encrypt, KeyGen and Decrypt, respectively, as a function of λ. Also, let ℓ_{ct} be an upper-bound on the length of ciphertexts generated by Encrypt. Then set

- $n_{\mathsf{enc}} = 4\lambda \cdot n_{\mathsf{key}} \cdot q_{\mathsf{KeyGen}}$,
- $n_{\mathsf{eval}} = 32\lambda\,(q_{\mathsf{Setup}} + q_{\mathsf{Enc}})$,
- $n_{\mathsf{test}} = 16(\ell_{\mathsf{ct}} + n_{\mathsf{eval}} \cdot q_{\mathsf{Dec}} \cdot m)$.

5.2 Real World Analysis

First, we will show that the adversary $\mathcal{A} = (\mathcal{A}_1, \mathcal{A}_2)$ described above outputs 1 with probability at least 3/4 in the real world experiment, as long as the scheme FE is correct. To begin with, we classify the random oracle queries made during a run of $\mathcal{A}$ into different sets as follows:

- $\mathsf{S\text{-}RO}_{C_i}$ for $i \in [n_{\mathsf{key}}]$: random oracle queries made by KeyGen while generating secret key for C_i.
- $\mathsf{S\text{-}RO}_{\mathsf{keys}} = \bigcup_{i \in [n_{\mathsf{key}}]} \mathsf{S\text{-}RO}_{C_i}$: all random oracle queries during the key query phase of $\mathcal{A}_1$.
- $\mathsf{S\text{-}RO}_{x^*}$: random oracle queries made while encrypting x^* using pk.
- $\mathsf{S\text{-}RO}_{\mathsf{Dec}\text{-}i}$ for $i \in [n_{\mathsf{test}}]$: random oracle queries made during the decryption of ct^* using $\mathsf{sk}_{n_{\mathsf{eval}}+i}$.

- $\mathsf{S\text{-}RO}_{\Gamma\text{-}b}$: random oracle queries recorded during 'RO Collection Phase b' for $b \in \{1, 2\}$. Let $\mathsf{S\text{-}RO}_{\Gamma} = \mathsf{S\text{-}RO}_{\Gamma\text{-}1} \bigcup \mathsf{S\text{-}RO}_{\Gamma\text{-}2}$.
- $\mathsf{S\text{-}RO}_{\mathsf{Setup}}$: random oracle queries made during setup phase.

Lemma 2. *For any functional encryption scheme* FE *for the circuit family* $\mathcal{C} = \{\mathcal{C}_\lambda\}_\lambda$, *the adversary* $\mathcal{A} = (\mathcal{A}_1, \mathcal{A}_2)$ *described in Sect. 5.1 outputs 1 in* $\mathsf{Real}_{\mathcal{A}}^{\mathsf{FE}}(1^\lambda)$ *with probability at least* $3/4 - \mathsf{negl}(\lambda)$.

Proof. We will use the correctness property of FE to prove this claim. Recall that, for simplicity, we assume correctness to be perfect, i.e., for all random oracles $\mathcal{O} : \{0,1\}^{\ell(\lambda)} \rightarrow \{0,1\}^{m(\lambda)}$, $x \in \{0,1\}^{n(\lambda)}$, $C \in \mathcal{C}_\lambda$

$$\Pr\left[\mathsf{Decrypt}^{\mathcal{O}}(\mathsf{pk}, \mathsf{sk}, \mathsf{ct}) = C(x) : \begin{array}{l} (\mathsf{pk}, \mathsf{msk}) \leftarrow \mathsf{Setup}^{\mathcal{O}}(1^\lambda) \\ \mathsf{sk} \leftarrow \mathsf{KeyGen}^{\mathcal{O}}(\mathsf{msk}, C) \\ \mathsf{ct} \leftarrow \mathsf{Encrypt}^{\mathcal{O}}(\mathsf{pk}, x) \end{array}\right] \geq 1 - \mathsf{negl}(\lambda)$$

In particular, we do not assume the decryption to be deterministic.

Let Bad denote the event that the adversary outputs 0 at the end of the real world experiment. This event happens if at least 1/8th fraction of the n_{test} decryptions fail in the test phase. If $\mathsf{I\text{-}Dec}_i$ is an indicator variable that takes the value 1 in case the ith decryption *fails*, then Bad happens iff $\sum_{i \in [n_{\mathsf{test}}]} \mathsf{I\text{-}Dec}_i > 1/8 \cdot n_{\mathsf{test}}$. To analyze the probability of this event, we need to consider the random oracle queries required for decryption in the test phase. In this phase, $\mathcal{A}_2$ does not query the random oracle, but instead uses the list Γ. If some query β is not present in Γ, then $\mathcal{A}_2$ tries to find it in Δ. If β is not found in Δ either, then a random value is chosen and recorded in Δ against β.

Now there are two ways in which the ith decryption can fail. The first is if there is some entry (β, γ) in Δ such that β is also among the RO queries *hidden* from the adversary (and its response is not γ), i.e., the queries made during the setup phase, key query phase or challenge ciphertext generation. The second case is when the RO query responses are consistent, but the decryption is incorrect due to 'bad' decryption coins. The second failure happens with negligible probability (due to correctness of the FE scheme). In other words, the ith decryption succeeds with overwhelming probability if all the *needed* hidden RO responses are captured in either of the two RO collection phases. This is formalized in the following observation.

Observation 1. *Let* Bad-Dec *be the following event:*

$$\begin{gathered} \exists i \in [n_{\mathsf{test}}] \ s.t. \\ (\mathsf{S\text{-}RO}_{\mathrm{Dec}\text{-}i} \bigcap (\mathsf{S\text{-}RO}_{\mathsf{Setup}} \bigcup \mathsf{S\text{-}RO}_{\mathrm{keys}} \bigcup \mathsf{S\text{-}RO}_{x^*}) \subseteq \mathsf{S\text{-}RO}_{\Gamma}) \\ \wedge \\ \mathcal{A}_2' s \text{ decryption of } \mathsf{ct}^* \text{ using } \mathsf{sk}_{n_{\mathsf{eval}}+i} \text{ does not output } C_{n_{\mathsf{eval}}+i}(x^*) \end{gathered}$$

There exists a negligible function $\mathsf{negl}(\cdot)$ *s.t.* $\Pr[\mathsf{Bad\text{-}Dec}] \leq \mathsf{negl}(\lambda)$ *where the probability is over the random coins used by setup, key generation, encryption, decryption and the adversary's choice of inputs.*

Proof. This observation follows from the statistical correctness of the scheme. Fix any index $i \in [n_{\mathsf{eval}}]$. Since $(\mathsf{S\text{-}RO}_{\mathsf{Dec}\text{-}i} \bigcap (\mathsf{S\text{-}RO}_{\mathsf{Setup}} \bigcup \mathsf{S\text{-}RO}_{\mathsf{keys}} \bigcup \mathsf{S\text{-}RO}_{x^*}) \subseteq \mathsf{S\text{-}RO}_{\Gamma})$, the oracle queries are consistent. Hence, we can use the correctness guarantee of the scheme to bound the probability of Bad-Dec.

Let $\mathsf{I\text{-}Dec\text{-}1}_i$ and $\mathsf{I\text{-}Dec\text{-}2}_i$ be indicator variables that are 1 iff $\mathsf{S\text{-}RO}_{\mathsf{Dec}\text{-}i} \bigcap (\mathsf{S\text{-}RO}_{x^*} \bigcup \mathsf{S\text{-}RO}_{\mathsf{Setup}}) \not\subseteq \mathsf{S\text{-}RO}_{\Gamma}$ and $\mathsf{S\text{-}RO}_{\mathsf{Dec}\text{-}i} \bigcap \mathsf{S\text{-}RO}_{\mathsf{keys}} \not\subseteq \mathsf{S\text{-}RO}_{\Gamma}$, respectively. Then, $\mathsf{I\text{-}Dec}_i = 1$ iff either $\mathsf{I\text{-}Dec\text{-}1}_i = 1$ or $\mathsf{I\text{-}Dec\text{-}2}_i = 1$ (or both). Let Bad-1 and Bad-2 be events that happen iff $\sum_{i\in[n_{\mathsf{test}}]} \mathsf{I\text{-}Dec\text{-}1}_i > 1/16 \cdot n_{\mathsf{test}}$ and $\sum_{i\in[n_{\mathsf{test}}]} \mathsf{I\text{-}Dec\text{-}2}_i > 1/16 \cdot n_{\mathsf{test}}$, respectively. It is easy to see that

$$\Pr[\mathsf{Bad}] \le \Pr[\mathsf{Bad\text{-}1}] + \Pr[\mathsf{Bad\text{-}2}] + \Pr[\mathsf{Bad\text{-}Dec}]$$

Below we show that $\Pr[\mathsf{Bad\text{-}1}] \le \mathsf{negl}(\lambda)$ and $\Pr[\mathsf{Bad\text{-}2}] \le 1/4$. Thus the lemma follows. ■

Claim 1. $\Pr[\mathsf{Bad\text{-}1}] \le \mathsf{negl}(\lambda)$.

Proof. Fix any random oracle $\mathcal{O}$, the randomness used in $\mathsf{Setup}^{\mathcal{O}}(1^\lambda)$, challenge message x^*, and the randomness used in $\mathsf{Encrypt}^{\mathcal{O}}(\mathsf{pk}, x^*)$. This also fixes the sets $\mathsf{S\text{-}RO}_{\mathsf{Setup}}$ and $\mathsf{S\text{-}RO}_{x^*}$. Suppose a circuit C is picked at random from $\mathcal{C}_\lambda$, and a key, sk, is generated for it by running $\mathsf{KeyGen}^{\mathcal{O}}(\mathsf{msk}, C)$. For $z \in \mathsf{S\text{-}RO}_{\mathsf{Setup}} \cup \mathsf{S\text{-}RO}_{x^*}$, let ρ_z be the probability that z is an RO query in the decryption of ct^* (the challenge ciphertext) with sk, where the probability is over the choice of C, the randomness used in KeyGen and the random coins used in decryption.

Let $X_{i,z}$ be an indicator variable that is 1 if an RO query on z is made during the ith decryption in post-challenge phase (either in the RO collection 2 or test phase). Note that the keys $\mathsf{sk}_1, \ldots, \mathsf{sk}_{n_{\mathsf{key}}}$ are generated independently by choosing circuits $C_1, \ldots, C_{n_{\mathsf{key}}}$ uniformly at random, and the random coins used in each key generation and decryption are independently chosen. Thus for any z, the variables $X_{1,z}, \ldots, X_{n_{\mathsf{key}},z}$ are independent of each other, and $\Pr[X_{i,z} = 1] = \rho_z$ for every i.

We are interested in the probability that $\sum_{i\in[n_{\mathsf{test}}]} \mathsf{I\text{-}Dec\text{-}1}_i > n_{\mathsf{test}}/16$, i.e., in at least 1/16th fraction of the decryptions in the test phase, an RO query q is made s.t. q was also an RO query in either set-up or encryption of x^*, but it was not captured in either of the collection phases. Thus, there must exist a z s.t. $z \notin \mathsf{S\text{-}RO}_{\Gamma}$ (in particular, $z \notin \mathsf{S\text{-}RO}_{\Gamma\text{-}2}$) but an RO query on z is made in at least $n_{\mathsf{test}}/16|Q|$ of the decryptions, where $Q = \mathsf{S\text{-}RO}_{\mathsf{Setup}} \cup \mathsf{S\text{-}RO}_{x^*}$. (If $Q = \phi$ then Bad-1 cannot happen, and we are done.) Therefore,

$$\Pr\left[\sum_{i\in[n_{\mathsf{test}}]} \mathsf{I\text{-}Dec\text{-}1}_i > \frac{n_{\mathsf{test}}}{16}\right] \le \sum_{z\in Q} \Pr\left[z \notin \mathsf{S\text{-}RO}_{\Gamma\text{-}2} \;\wedge\; \sum_{i\in[n_{\mathsf{test}}]} X_{i,z} > \frac{n_{\mathsf{test}}}{16|Q|}\right]$$

Based on the value of ρ_z, we can divide the rest of the analysis into two parts. Intuitively, if ρ_z is large, then the probability that z is not captured during RO collection phase is negligible. And when it is small, the probability that z causes too many decryptions to fail in the test phase is negligible. Since Q is polynomial in the security parameter, this will prove that the probability of Bad-1 is negligible as well. So now,

- If $\rho_z \geq 1/32|Q|$ then

$$\begin{aligned}\Pr[z \notin \mathsf{S\text{-}RO}_{\Gamma\text{-}2}] &= \Pr[X_{1,z} = 0 \wedge \ldots \wedge X_{n_{\mathsf{eval}},z} = 0] \\ &= \prod_{i \in [n_{\mathsf{eval}}]} \Pr[X_{i,z} = 0] \\ &= (1 - \rho_z)^{n_{\mathsf{eval}}} \leq e^{-n_{\mathsf{eval}}/32|Q|},\end{aligned}$$

  where the second equality follows from the independence of $X_{i,z}$. Recall that we set n_{eval} to be $32\lambda(q_{\mathsf{Setup}} + q_{\mathsf{Enc}})$, where q_{Setup} and q_{Enc} are upper-bounds on the number of RO queries made during Setup and Encrypt, respectively. Thus, $e^{-n_{\mathsf{eval}}/32|Q|}$ is at most $e^{-\lambda}$.
- If $\rho_z < 1/32|Q|$ then expected value of $\sum_{i \in [n_{\mathsf{test}}]} X_{i,z}$ is at most $n_{\mathsf{test}}/32|Q|$. Using Chernoff bounds we can argue that,

$$\Pr\left[\sum_{i \in [n_{\mathsf{test}}]} X_{i,z} > \frac{n_{\mathsf{test}}}{16|Q|}\right] < e^{-\frac{1}{3} \cdot \frac{n_{\mathsf{test}}}{32|Q|}}.$$

  We know that $n_{\mathsf{test}} \geq n_{\mathsf{eval}}$. Thus, $e^{-\frac{1}{3} \cdot \frac{n_{\mathsf{test}}}{32|Q|}}$ is at most $e^{-\lambda}$ as well.

Claim 2. $\Pr[\mathsf{Bad\text{-}2}] \leq 1/4$.

Proof. Fix any random oracle $\mathcal{O}$, the randomness used in $\mathsf{Setup}^{\mathcal{O}}(1^\lambda)$, the circuits $C_1, \ldots, C_{n_{\mathsf{key}}}$ chosen in the key query phase, and the randomness used in $\mathsf{KeyGen}^{\mathcal{O}}(\mathsf{msk}, C_i)$ for $i \in [n_{\mathsf{key}}]$. This, in particular, fixes secret keys $\mathsf{sk}_1, \ldots, \mathsf{sk}_{n_{\mathsf{key}}}$ and the set $\mathsf{S\text{-}RO}_{\mathsf{keys}}$. Consider the following experiment: $x \xleftarrow{\mathrm{R}} \{0,1\}^{n(\lambda)}$, $\mathsf{ct} \leftarrow \mathsf{Encrypt}^{\mathcal{O}}(\mathsf{pk}, x)$, and decrypt ct using sk_i for $i \in [n_{\mathsf{eval}} + 1, n_{\mathsf{key}}]$. Let $\hat{\rho}_z$ be the probability that at least $n_{\mathsf{test}}/16|\hat{Q}|$ of the decryptions make an RO query on z, where $\hat{Q} = \mathsf{S\text{-}RO}_{\mathsf{keys}}$.

Let $Y_{j,z}$ be an indicator variable that is 1 iff an RO query on z is made in at least $n_{\mathsf{test}}/16|\hat{Q}|$ of the decryptions of ct_j with keys $\mathsf{sk}_{n_{\mathsf{eval}}+1}, \ldots, \mathsf{sk}_{n_{\mathsf{key}}}$ in the first phase of RO query collection. Note that the ciphertexts $\mathsf{ct}_1, \ldots, \mathsf{ct}_{n_{\mathsf{enc}}}$ are generated independently by choosing $x_1, \ldots, x_{n_{\mathsf{key}}}$ uniformly at random, and the decryption coins are also chosen independently for each decryption. Thus for any z, the variables $Y_{1,z}, \ldots, Y_{n_{\mathsf{enc}},z}$ are independent of each other, and $\Pr[Y_{j,z} = 1] = \hat{\rho}_z$ for every j. In a similar way, we can also define a random variable Y_z^* that indicates whether an RO query on z is made in at least $n_{\mathsf{test}}/16|\hat{Q}|$ of the decryptions of ct^* with keys $\mathsf{sk}_{n_{\mathsf{eval}}+1}, \ldots, \mathsf{sk}_{n_{\mathsf{key}}}$ in the test phase. Y_z^* is independent of $Y_{1,z}, \ldots, Y_{n_{\mathsf{enc}},z}$ and $\Pr[Y_z^* = 1] = \hat{\rho}_z$.

In a manner similar to the previous claim, we can argue that

$$\Pr\left[\sum_{i \in [n_{\mathsf{test}}]} \mathsf{I\text{-}Dec\text{-}2}_i > \frac{n_{\mathsf{test}}}{16}\right] \leq \sum_{z \in \hat{Q}} \Pr[z \notin \mathsf{S\text{-}RO}_{\Gamma\text{-}1} \wedge Y_z^* = 1]$$

If $z \notin \text{S-RO}_{\Gamma\text{-}1}$, then none of the decryptions in the first phase of RO collection make a query on z. In particular, the variables $Y_{1,z}, \ldots, Y_{n_{\mathsf{enc}},z}$ are all zero in such a case. Therefore,

$$\begin{aligned}\Pr\left[z \notin \text{S-RO}_{\Gamma\text{-}1} \wedge Y_z^* = 1\right] &\le \Pr\left[Y_{1,z} = 0 \wedge \ldots \wedge Y_{n_{\mathsf{enc}},z} = 0 \wedge Y_z^* = 1\right] \\ &= \Pr\left[Y_z^* = 1\right] \quad \cdot \prod_{j \in [n_{\mathsf{enc}}]} \Pr\left[Y_{j,z} = 0\right] \\ &= \hat{\rho}_z (1 - \hat{\rho}_z)^{n_{\mathsf{enc}}}\end{aligned}$$

Once again we have two cases. If $\hat{\rho}_z \le 1/4|\hat{Q}|$, then $\hat{\rho}_z(1-\hat{\rho}_z)^{n_{\mathsf{enc}}}$ is at most $1/4|\hat{Q}|$ as well. Otherwise, $(1-\hat{\rho}_z)^{n_{\mathsf{enc}}} \le e^{-n_{\mathsf{enc}}/4|\hat{Q}|} \le e^{-\lambda}$ because, recall that, n_{enc} is set to be $4\lambda \cdot n_{\mathsf{key}} \cdot q_{\mathsf{KeyGen}}$, where q_{KeyGen} is an upper-bound on the number of RO queries made during KeyGen. As a result, $\sum_{z \in \hat{Q}} \hat{\rho}_z(1-\hat{\rho}_z)^{n_{\mathsf{enc}}}$ is at most $1/4$.

5.3 Ideal World Analysis

Next, we will show that any for PPT simulator, our adversary $\mathcal{A} = (\mathcal{A}_1, \mathcal{A}_2)$ outputs 1 in the ideal world with negligible probability. Let t be a polynomial in λ such that $t = \ell_{\mathsf{ct}} + n_{\mathsf{eval}} \cdot q_{\mathsf{Dec}} \cdot m$ (so that $n_{\mathsf{test}} = 16t$) where, recall that, ℓ_{ct} is the maximum length of any ciphertext generated by Encrypt. Note that $q_{\mathsf{Dec}} \cdot m$ is the maximum number of bits obtained through the random oracle during any decryption, $n_{\mathsf{eval}} \cdot q_{\mathsf{Dec}} \cdot m$ is the maximum number of bits sent to the adversary during the second RO query collection phase, and $\ell_{\mathsf{ct}} + n_{\mathsf{eval}} \cdot q_{\mathsf{Dec}} \cdot m$ is the total number of bits the adversary receives after sending the challenge message.

Lemma 3. *If $\mathcal{C} = \{\mathcal{C}_\lambda\}_\lambda$ is an $(16t, t, 1/8)$ approximately incompressible circuit family, then for any* PPT *simulator $\mathcal{S}$, the adversary $\mathcal{A} = (\mathcal{A}_1, \mathcal{A}_2)$ outputs 1 with probability at most* $\mathsf{negl}(\lambda)$.

Proof. Suppose there exists a simulator $\mathcal{S}$ such that our adversary $\mathcal{A}$ outputs 1 with a non-negligible probability η. We will use $\mathcal{S}$ to show that $\mathcal{C}$ is $(16t, t, 1/8)$ approximately compressible. In particular, we will use $\mathcal{S}$ and $\mathcal{A} = (\mathcal{A}_1, \mathcal{A}_2)$ to construct Cmp and DeCmp circuits satisfying the three properties of an approximately compressible circuit family.

Note that $\mathcal{A}_1$ picks $C_{n_{\mathsf{eval}}+1}, \ldots, C_{n_{\mathsf{eval}}+n_{\mathsf{test}}}$ and x^* uniformly at random and independent of its other choices. Let $r_{\mathcal{S}}$ and $r_{\mathcal{A}}$ denote the randomness used by the simulator $\mathcal{S}$ and adversary $\mathcal{A}$ (in choosing circuits $C_1, \ldots, C_{n_{\mathsf{eval}}}$, and in RO query collection 1 and test phases), respectively. The compression circuit takes as input $(C_1, \ldots, C_{16t}, y_1, \ldots, y_{16t})$, has a randomly chosen string for $r_{\mathcal{S}}$ and $r_{\mathcal{A}}$ hardwired, and works as follows:

- Use $\mathcal{S}$ to generate a public key pk. Give pk to $\mathcal{A}_1$.
- Use $\mathcal{S}$ to generate secrets keys $\mathsf{sk}_1, \ldots, \mathsf{sk}_{n_{\mathsf{key}}}$ for $C_1', \ldots, C_{n_{\mathsf{eval}}}', C_1, \ldots, C_{16t}$, where $C_1', \ldots, C_{n_{\mathsf{eval}}}'$ are sampled using $r_{\mathcal{A}}$. Give the secret keys to $\mathcal{A}_1$.

- Run the first phase of RO query collection. When $\mathcal{A}_1$ makes an RO query in this phase, forward it to $\mathcal{S}$. Give $\mathcal{S}$'s response back to $\mathcal{A}_1$.
- Provide $y_1, \ldots, y_{16t}$ to $\mathcal{S}$. It generates a ciphertext ct^*.
- Run the second phase of RO query collection. Respond to $\mathcal{A}_2$'s RO queries in the same way as before. Let $z_1, \ldots, z_v$ be the responses in order, where $z_i \in \{0,1\}^m$.
- Output ct^* and $z_1, \ldots, z_v$.

The decompression circuit takes $C_1, \ldots, C_{16t}$ and the compressed string $\mathsf{str\text{-}cmp}$ as inputs, which can be parsed as $\mathsf{str\text{-}cmp} = (\mathsf{ct}^*, \{z_i\})$. It also has the random value chosen before for $r_{\mathcal{S}}$ and $r_{\mathcal{A}}$ hardwired, and works as follows:

- Use $\mathcal{S}$ to generate pk and secret keys $\mathsf{sk}_1, \ldots, \mathsf{sk}_{n_{\mathsf{key}}}$ as before. Give both to $\mathcal{A}_1$.
- Run the first phase of RO query collection. Respond to $\mathcal{A}_1$'s RO queries in the same way as before. Let Γ be the list of RO queries and responses recorded in this phase.
- Run the second phase of RO query collection, where $\mathsf{sk}_1, \ldots, \mathsf{sk}_{n_{\mathsf{eval}}}$ are used to decrypt ct^*. The RO responses required in this step are available as part of the input $(z_1, \ldots, z_v)$. They are also added to Γ.
- Run the test phase with the help of Γ. Let y'_i denote the outcome of decrypting ct^* with $\mathsf{sk}_{n_{\mathsf{eval}}+i}$ for $i \in [n_{\mathsf{test}}]$.
- Output $y'_1, \ldots, y'_{16t}$.

First, note that the size of both compression and decompression circuit is bounded by a polynomial in λ. Next, the output length of the compression circuit is at most $\ell_{\mathsf{ct}} + v \cdot m$, but v is no more than $n_{\mathsf{eval}} \cdot q_{\mathsf{Dec}}$. Thus the output length is bounded by t.

Finally, we need to show that the decompression property works with probability η. When $C_1, \ldots, C_{16t}$ are chosen uniformly at random and $y_1, \ldots, y_{16t}$ is the evaluation of these circuits on a randomly chosen point, then it is easy to see that the decompression circuit emulates the ideal world experiment perfectly. We know that $\mathcal{A}_2$ outputs 1 if and only if for at least 7/8th of the decryptions, $y'_i = y_i$. Hence, if 1 is output with probability η, then the hamming distance of $\mathsf{DeCmp}(\{C_i\}, \mathsf{Cmp}(\{C_i\}, \{y_i\}))$ and $\{y_i\}$ is at most 1/8 with probability at least η.

6 Simulation Secure FE for Bounded Collusions

In this section, we will show an FE scheme that is $(q_1, \mathsf{poly}, q_2)$ simulation secure in the random oracle model, where q_1, q_2 are a-priori fixed polynomials. Since both the pre-challenge and post-challenge queries are bounded, we will simply refer to the total number of key queries. An FE scheme is q-key poly-ciphertext secure if it is $(q_1, \mathsf{poly}, q_2)$ simulation secure as in Definition 8 for all non-negative integers q_1, q_2 s.t. $q_1 + q_2 = q$. We first show a scheme that can handle 1 key query in Sect. 6.1. Then, in Sect. 6.2 (and the full version of our paper [1]), we show how to transform a 1-key poly-ciphertext scheme to one that is q-key poly-ciphertext simulation secure for an a-priori fixed q, by first building a scheme for log-depth circuits and then for all poly-size circuits. This transformation is very similar to the one showed by Gorbunov et al. [21], except that they dealt with only one ciphertext.

6.1 Simulation Secure FE for One Key Query

We will now describe our 1-key poly-ciphertext scheme. Recall that in the standard model, it is impossible to have simulation security even for IBE if the adversary is allowed to query for an unbounded number of ciphertexts, followed by one adaptive key query [5,12]. Here, we show how the random oracle can be used to bypass this impossibility result. At a high-level, the construction is similar to the Sahai-Seyalioglu [31] construction of single-key secure FE from PKE.

Let $\mathcal{C} = \{\mathcal{C}_\lambda\}_\lambda$ be a class of circuits, where each circuit $C \in \mathcal{C}_\lambda$ takes an $n(\lambda)$ bit input and produces an $m(\lambda)$ bit output, and can be represented using $t(\lambda)$ bits. For $x \in \{0,1\}^{n(\lambda)}$, let $U_x^{(\lambda)}$ be a universal circuit that takes any $C \in \mathcal{C}_\lambda$ as input and outputs $C(x)$. Let $\mathcal{U} = \{\mathcal{U}_\lambda\}_\lambda$ be a circuit family such that $\mathcal{U}_\lambda = \{U_x^{(\lambda)} \mid x \in \{0,1\}^{n(\lambda)}\}$. Our one-bounded FE scheme $\mathsf{One\text{-}FE} = (\mathsf{Setup}, \mathsf{Encrypt}, \mathsf{KeyGen}, \mathsf{Decrypt})$ uses a decomposable randomized encoding scheme $(\mathsf{RE.Encode}, \mathsf{RE.Decode})$ for $\mathcal{U}$ and a public key encryption scheme $\mathsf{PKE} = (\mathsf{Setup}_{\mathrm{PKE}}, \mathsf{Enc}_{\mathrm{PKE}}, \mathsf{Dec}_{\mathrm{PKE}})$ that can operate on messages of length λ. For simplicity of presentation, we will skip the dependence on λ.

- $\mathsf{Setup}(1^\lambda) \to (\mathsf{mpk}, \mathsf{msk})$: The setup algorithm chooses $2t$ PKE public key/secret key pairs $(\mathsf{pk}_{i,b}, \mathsf{sk}_{i,b}) \leftarrow \mathsf{Setup}_{\mathrm{PKE}}(1^\lambda)$ for $i \in [t], b \in \{0,1\}$. It sets $\mathsf{mpk} = \{\mathsf{pk}_{i,b}\}_{i\in[t],b\in\{0,1\}}$ and $\mathsf{msk} = \{\mathsf{sk}_{i,b}\}_{i\in[t],b\in\{0,1\}}$.
- $\mathsf{Enc}(\mathsf{mpk}, x) \to \mathsf{ct}$: The encryption algorithm first chooses $2t$ random strings $r_{i,b} \leftarrow \{0,1\}^\lambda$ for all $i \in [t]$, $b \in \{0,1\}$. Next, it computes a randomized encoding for the universal circuit U_x, i.e., $\{w_{i,b}\}_{i\in[t],b\in\{0,1\}} \leftarrow \mathsf{RE.Encode}(1^\lambda, U_x)$. Now, let $\mathsf{ct}_{i,b} = \mathsf{Enc}_{\mathrm{PKE}}(\mathsf{pk}_{i,b}, r_{i,b})$ and $\widetilde{\mathsf{ct}}_{i,b} = w_{i,b} \oplus \mathcal{O}(r_{i,b})$ for all $i \in [t]$, $b \in \{0,1\}$. The algorithm outputs $\mathsf{ct} = \{\mathsf{ct}_{i,b}, \widetilde{\mathsf{ct}}_{i,b}\}_{i\in[t],b\in\{0,1\}}$.
- $\mathsf{KeyGen}(\mathsf{msk}, C) \to \mathsf{sk}_C$: Let $(\beta_1, \ldots, \beta_t)$ be the bit representation of circuit C. The key generation algorithm outputs $\{\mathsf{sk}_{i,\beta_i}\}_{i\in[t]}$ as the secret key for C.
- $\mathsf{Dec}(\mathsf{mpk}, \mathsf{sk}_C, \mathsf{ct})$: Let $\mathsf{sk}_C = \{\mathsf{sk}_{i,\beta_i}\}_{i\in[t]}$ and $\mathsf{ct} = \{\mathsf{ct}_{i,b}, \widetilde{\mathsf{ct}}_{i,b}\}_{i\in[t],b\in\{0,1\}}$. The decryption algorithm first decrypts the relevant randomized encoding components, i.e., for each $i \in [t]$, it computes $r_{i,\beta_i} = \mathsf{Dec}_{\mathrm{PKE}}(\mathsf{sk}_{i,\beta_i}, \mathsf{ct}_{i,\beta_i})$ and $w_{i,\beta_i} = \widetilde{\mathsf{ct}}_{i,\beta_i} \oplus \mathcal{O}(r_{i,\beta_i})$. Finally, it outputs $\mathsf{RE.Decode}(\{w_{i,\beta_i}\}_{i\in[t]})$.

The correctness of our scheme follows directly from the correctness of the randomized encoding scheme and the public key encryption scheme.

The simulator description and proof of security is given in the full version of our paper [1].

6.2 Simulation Secure FE with Bounded Key Queries for NC1

In this section, we will show how to transform a scheme that handles one key query to one that handles a bounded number of key queries for the class of log-depth circuits. This transformation is identical to the one in [21]. However, the proof is slightly different because we handle unbounded challenge ciphertext queries.

Formal Description. Let $\mathcal{C} = \{\mathcal{C}_\lambda\}_\lambda$ be a class of circuits, where each circuit $C \in \mathcal{C}_\lambda$ takes $n(\lambda)$ bit inputs, outputs a single bit and can be represented using an $n(\lambda)$ variate polynomial of degree $D(\lambda)$ over a (large enough) field $\mathbb{F}$. Let q denote a bound on the number of secret key queries. Our FE scheme $\mathsf{FE} = (\mathsf{Setup}, \mathsf{Enc}, \mathsf{KeyGen}, \mathsf{Dec})$ uses a 1-key poly-ciphertext simulation secure FE scheme $(\mathsf{Setup}_{\mathrm{one}}, \mathsf{Encrypt}_{\mathrm{one}}, \mathsf{KeyGen}_{\mathrm{one}}, \mathsf{Decrypt}_{\mathrm{one}})$ as a building block. Our scheme is parameterized by four polynomials: N, S, v and t, whose values depend on D and q. As in GVW, we set $t(\lambda) = \Theta(q^2\lambda)$, $N(\lambda) = \Theta(N^2q^2t)$ and $v(\lambda) = \Theta(\lambda)$ and $S(\lambda) = \Theta(vq^2)$. We will skip the dependence on λ when it is clear from the context.

For any circuit $C \in \mathcal{C}_\lambda$ and set $\Delta \subset [S]$, we define a circuit $G_{C,\Delta}$ which takes $n + S$ bit inputs and works as follows:

$$G_{C,\Delta}(x_1, \ldots, x_n, y_1, \ldots, y_S) = C(x_1, \ldots, x_n) + \sum_{h \in \Delta} y_h$$

Let $\mathcal{O} = \mathcal{O}_1 \times \ldots \mathcal{O}_N$ be a hash function, where each $\mathcal{O}_i : \{0,1\}^\ell \to \{0,1\}^m$. Each of these hash functions $\mathcal{O}_i$ will be modeled as a random oracle in our security proof.

- $\mathsf{Setup}^{\mathcal{O}}(1^\lambda) \to (\mathsf{MPK}, \mathsf{MSK})$: The setup algorithm runs the one-key FE scheme's setup N times. Let $(\mathsf{mpk}_i, \mathsf{msk}_i) \leftarrow \mathsf{Setup}_{\mathrm{one}}^{\mathcal{O}_i}(1^\lambda)$. The master public key MPK is set to be $\{\mathsf{mpk}_i\}_{i \in [N]}$, and the master secret key MSK is $\{\mathsf{msk}_i\}_{i \in [N]}$.
- $\mathsf{Enc}^{\mathcal{O}}(\mathsf{MPK}, x) \to \mathsf{ct}$: Let $\mathsf{MPK} = \{\mathsf{mpk}_i\}_{i \in [N]}$ and $x = (x_1, \ldots, x_n)$. The encryption algorithm works as follows:
  - It chooses n uniformly random polynomials $\mu_1, \ldots, \mu_n$ of degree t over field $\mathbb{F}$ subject to the constraint that the constant term of μ_i is x_i.
  - It chooses S uniformly random polynomials $\zeta_1, \ldots, \zeta_S$ of degree Dt over field $\mathbb{F}$ and constant term 0.
  - It computes N ciphertexts using the $\mathsf{Encrypt}_{\mathrm{one}}$ algorithm. For $i \in [N]$, it computes $\mathsf{ct}_i \leftarrow \mathsf{Encrypt}_{\mathrm{one}}^{\mathcal{O}_i}(\mathsf{mpk}_i, (\mu_1(i), \ldots, \mu_n(i), \zeta_1(i), \ldots, \zeta_S(i)))$.

  The encryption algorithm outputs $(\mathsf{ct}_1, \ldots, \mathsf{ct}_N)$ as the final ciphertext.
- $\mathsf{KeyGen}^{\mathcal{O}}(\mathsf{MSK}, C)$: Let $\mathsf{MSK} = \{\mathsf{msk}_i\}_{i \in [N]}$. The key generation algorithm works as follows:
  - It chooses a uniformly random set $\Gamma \subset [N]$ of size $Dt + 1$.
  - It chooses a uniformly random set $\Delta \subset [S]$ of size v.
  - It uses the $\mathsf{KeyGen}_{\mathrm{one}}$ algorithm to generate $Dt + 1$ secret keys for the function $G_{C,\Delta}$. For $i \in \Gamma$, it computes $\mathsf{sk}_i \leftarrow \mathsf{KeyGen}_{\mathrm{one}}^{\mathcal{O}_i}(\mathsf{msk}_i, G_{C,\Delta})$.

The key generation algorithm outputs $(\Gamma, \Delta, \{\mathsf{sk}_i\}_{i\in\Gamma})$ as the secret key for C.

- $\mathsf{Dec}^{\mathcal{O}}(\mathsf{sk}, \mathsf{ct})$: Let $\mathsf{sk} = (\Gamma, \Delta, \{\mathsf{sk}_i\}_{i\in\Gamma})$ and $\mathsf{ct} = (\mathsf{ct}_1, \ldots, \mathsf{ct}_N)$. The decryption algorithm works as follows:
  - For each $i \in \Gamma$, let $\alpha_i = \mathsf{Decrypt}^{\mathcal{O}_i}_{\mathrm{one}}(\mathsf{sk}_i, \mathsf{ct}_i)$.
  - It computes a polynomial η of degree Dt over field $\mathbb{F}$ such that for all $i \in \Gamma$, $\eta(i) = \alpha_i$.

The decryption algorithm outputs $\eta(0^{n+S})$ as the final decryption.

Correctness. The correctness proof is identical to the one in [21]. Let μ_1, ..., μ_n, ζ_1, ..., ζ_S be the polynomials chosen during encryption, and let Γ, Δ be the sets chosen during key generation. From the correctness of the one-key FE scheme, it follows that the decryption algorithm computes $\alpha_i = C(\mu_1(i), \ldots, \mu_n(i)) + \sum_{j\in\Delta} \zeta_j(i)$ for all $i \in \Gamma$. Now, since the polynomial $\eta = C(\mu_1, \ldots, \mu_n) + \sum_{j\in\Gamma} \zeta_j$ has degree Dt and $|\Gamma| = Dt + 1$, the decryption algorithm can compute the polynomial η using the set $\{\alpha_i\}_{i\in[N]}$. Finally, note that $\eta(0^{n+S}) = C(\mu_1(0), \ldots, \mu_n(0)) + \sum_j \zeta_j(0) = C(x_1, \ldots, x_n)$.

In the full version of our paper [1], we prove security of our scheme for NC1 and describe how this scheme can be bootstrapped to all poly-size circuits.

References

1. Agrawal, S., Koppula, V., Waters, B.: Impossibility of simulation secure functional encryption even with random oracles. Cryptology ePrint Archive, Report 2016/959 (2016). https://eprint.iacr.org/2016/959
2. Agrawal, S., Gorbunov, S., Vaikuntanathan, V., Wee, H.: Functional encryption: new perspectives and lower bounds. In: Canetti, R., Garay, J.A. (eds.) CRYPTO 2013. LNCS, vol. 8043, pp. 500–518. Springer, Heidelberg (2013). https://doi.org/10.1007/978-3-642-40084-1_28
3. Ananth, P., Jain, A.: Indistinguishability obfuscation from compact functional encryption. In: Gennaro, R., Robshaw, M. (eds.) CRYPTO 2015. LNCS, vol. 9215, pp. 308–326. Springer, Heidelberg (2015). https://doi.org/10.1007/978-3-662-47989-6_15
4. Applebaum, B., Ishai, Y., Kushilevitz, E.: Computationally private randomizing polynomials and their applications. Comput. Complex. **15**(2), 115–162 (2006)
5. Bellare, M., O'Neill, A.: Semantically-secure functional encryption: possibility results, impossibility results and the quest for a general definition. In: Abdalla, M., Nita-Rotaru, C., Dahab, R. (eds.) CANS 2013. LNCS, vol. 8257, pp. 218–234. Springer, Cham (2013). https://doi.org/10.1007/978-3-319-02937-5_12
6. Bellare, M., Rogaway, P.: Random oracles are practical: a paradigm for designing efficient protocols. In: ACM Conference on Computer and Communications Security, pp. 62–73 (1993)
7. Bitansky, N., Lin, H., Paneth, O.: On removing graded encodings from functional encryption. In: Coron, J.-S., Nielsen, J.B. (eds.) EUROCRYPT 2017. LNCS, vol. 10211, pp. 3–29. Springer, Cham (2017). https://doi.org/10.1007/978-3-319-56614-6_1

8. Bitansky, N., Nishimaki, R., Passelègue, A., Wichs, D.: From cryptomania to obfustopia through secret-key functional encryption. In: Hirt, M., Smith, A. (eds.) TCC 2016. LNCS, vol. 9986, pp. 391–418. Springer, Heidelberg (2016). https://doi.org/10.1007/978-3-662-53644-5_15
9. Bitansky, N., Paneth, O.: On the impossibility of approximate obfuscation and applications to resettable cryptography. In: STOC (2013)
10. Bitansky, N., Vaikuntanathan, V.: Indistinguishability obfuscation from functional encryption. In: FOCS (2015)
11. Boneh, D., Franklin, M.: Identity-based encryption from the Weil Pairing. In: Kilian, J. (ed.) CRYPTO 2001. LNCS, vol. 2139, pp. 213–229. Springer, Heidelberg (2001). https://doi.org/10.1007/3-540-44647-8_13
12. Boneh, D., Sahai, A., Waters, B.: Functional encryption: definitions and challenges. In: Ishai, Y. (ed.) TCC 2011. LNCS, vol. 6597, pp. 253–273. Springer, Heidelberg (2011). https://doi.org/10.1007/978-3-642-19571-6_16
13. Boneh, D., Waters, B.: Conjunctive, subset, and range queries on encrypted data. In: Vadhan, S.P. (ed.) TCC 2007. LNCS, vol. 4392, pp. 535–554. Springer, Heidelberg (2007). https://doi.org/10.1007/978-3-540-70936-7_29
14. Canetti, R., Goldreich, O., Halevi, S.: The random oracle methodology, revisited. J. ACM **51**(4), 557–594 (2004)
15. Canetti, R., Kalai, Y.T., Paneth, O.: On obfuscation with random oracles. In: Dodis, Y., Nielsen, J.B. (eds.) TCC 2015. LNCS, vol. 9015, pp. 456–467. Springer, Heidelberg (2015). https://doi.org/10.1007/978-3-662-46497-7_18
16. De Caro, A., Iovino, V., Jain, A., O'Neill, A., Paneth, O., Persiano, G.: On the achievability of simulation-based security for functional encryption. In: Canetti, R., Garay, J.A. (eds.) CRYPTO 2013. LNCS, vol. 8043, pp. 519–535. Springer, Heidelberg (2013). https://doi.org/10.1007/978-3-642-40084-1_29
17. De Caro, A., Iovino, V., Jain, A., O'Neill, A., Paneth, O., Persiano, G.: On the achievability of simulation-based security for functional encryption. Cryptology ePrint Archive, Report 2013/364 (2013)
18. Goldreich, O., Goldwasser, S., Micali, S.: How to construct random functions (extended abstract). In: FOCS, pp. 464–479 (1984)
19. Goldwasser, S., Kalai, Y., Popa, R.A., Vaikuntanathan, V., Zeldovich, N.: Succinct functional encryption and applications: reusable garbled circuits and beyond. In: STOC (2013)
20. Gorbunov, S., Vaikuntanathan, V., Wee, H.: Functional encryption with bounded collusions via multi-party computation. In: Safavi-Naini, R., Canetti, R. (eds.) CRYPTO 2012. LNCS, vol. 7417, pp. 162–179. Springer, Heidelberg (2012). https://doi.org/10.1007/978-3-642-32009-5_11
21. Gorbunov, S., Vaikuntanathan, V., Wee, H.: Attribute-based encryption for circuits. In: STOC (2013)
22. Hubácek, P., Wichs, D.: On the communication complexity of secure function evaluation with long output. In: Proceedings of the 2015 Conference on Innovations in Theoretical Computer Science, ITCS 2015, Rehovot, Israel, 11–13 January 2015, pp. 163–172 (2015). https://doi.org/10.1145/2688073.2688105
23. Impagliazzo, R., Rudich, S.: Limits on the provable consequences of one-way permutations. In: Proceedings of the 21st Annual ACM Symposium on Theory of Computing, Seattle, Washington, USA, 14–17 May 1989, pp. 44–61 (1989)
24. Iovino, V., Żebroski, K.: Simulation-based secure functional encryption in the random oracle model. In: Lauter, K., Rodríguez-Henríquez, F. (eds.) LATINCRYPT 2015. LNCS, vol. 9230, pp. 21–39. Springer, Cham (2015). https://doi.org/10.1007/978-3-319-22174-8_2

25. Katz, J., Sahai, A., Waters, B.: Predicate encryption supporting disjunctions, polynomial equations, and inner products. In: Smart, N. (ed.) EUROCRYPT 2008. LNCS, vol. 4965, pp. 146–162. Springer, Heidelberg (2008). https://doi.org/10.1007/978-3-540-78967-3_9
26. Lin, H., Pass, R., Seth, K., Telang, S.: Indistinguishability obfuscation with non-trivial efficiency. In: Cheng, C.-M., Chung, K.-M., Persiano, G., Yang, B.-Y. (eds.) PKC 2016. LNCS, vol. 9615, pp. 447–462. Springer, Heidelberg (2016). https://doi.org/10.1007/978-3-662-49387-8_17
27. Mahmoody, M., Mohammed, A., Nematihaji, S., Pass, R., Shelat, A.: Lower bounds on assumptions behind indistinguishability obfuscation. In: Kushilevitz, E., Malkin, T. (eds.) TCC 2016. LNCS, vol. 9562, pp. 49–66. Springer, Heidelberg (2016). https://doi.org/10.1007/978-3-662-49096-9_3
28. Nielsen, J.B.: Separating random oracle proofs from complexity theoretic proofs: the non-committing encryption case. In: Yung, M. (ed.) CRYPTO 2002. LNCS, vol. 2442, pp. 111–126. Springer, Heidelberg (2002). https://doi.org/10.1007/3-540-45708-9_8
29. O'Neill, A.: Definitional issues in functional encryption. IACR Cryptology ePrint Archive 2010, 556 (2010). http://eprint.iacr.org/2010/556
30. O'Neill, A.: Definitional issues in functional encryption. Cryptology ePrint Archive, Report 2010/556 (2010)
31. Sahai, A., Seyalioglu, H.: Worry-free encryption: functional encryption with public keys. In: ACM CCS (2010)
32. Sahai, A., Waters, B.: Fuzzy identity-based encryption. In: Cramer, R. (ed.) EUROCRYPT 2005. LNCS, vol. 3494, pp. 457–473. Springer, Heidelberg (2005). https://doi.org/10.1007/11426639_27
33. Shamir, A.: Identity-based cryptosystems and signature schemes. In: Blakley, G.R., Chaum, D. (eds.) CRYPTO 1984. LNCS, vol. 196, pp. 47–53. Springer, Heidelberg (1985). https://doi.org/10.1007/3-540-39568-7_5
34. Yao, A.: How to generate and exchange secrets. In: FOCS, pp. 162–167 (1986)

Registration-Based Encryption: Removing Private-Key Generator from IBE

Sanjam Garg[1(✉)], Mohammad Hajiabadi[1,2], Mohammad Mahmoody[2], and Ahmadreza Rahimi[2]

[1] University of California, Berkeley, Berkeley, USA
sanjamg@berkeley.edu
[2] University of Virginia, Charlottesville, USA

Abstract. In this work, we introduce the notion of *registration-based encryption* (RBE for short) with the goal of removing the trust parties need to place in the private-key generator in an IBE scheme. In an RBE scheme, users sample their own public and secret keys. There will also be a "key curator" whose job is only to aggregate the public keys of all the registered users and update the "short" public parameter whenever a new user joins the system. Encryption can still be performed to a particular recipient using the recipient's identity and any public parameters released subsequent to the recipient's registration. Decryption requires some auxiliary information connecting users' public (and secret) keys to the public parameters. Because of this, as the public parameters get updated, a decryptor may need to obtain "a few" additional auxiliary information for decryption. More formally, if n is the total number of identities and κ is the security parameter, we require the following.

Efficiency requirements: (1) A decryptor only needs to obtain updated auxiliary information for decryption at most $O(\log n)$ times in its lifetime, (2) each of these updates are computed by the key curator in time $\text{poly}(\kappa, \log n)$, and (3) the key curator updates the public parameter upon the registration of a new party in time $\text{poly}(\kappa, \log n)$. Properties (2) and (3) require the key curator to have *random* access to its data.

Compactness requirements: (1) Public parameters are always at most $\text{poly}(\kappa, \log n)$ bit, and (2) the total size of updates a user ever needs for decryption is also at most $\text{poly}(\kappa, \log n)$ bits.

S. Garg—Research supported in part from DARPA/ARL SAFEWARE Award W911NF15C0210, AFOSR Award FA9550-15-1-0274, AFOSR YIP Award, DARPA and SPAWAR under contract N66001-15-C-4065, a Hellman Award and research grants by the Okawa Foundation, Visa Inc., and Center for Long-Term Cybersecurity (CLTC, UC Berkeley). The views expressed are those of the author and do not reflect the official policy or position of the funding agencies.

M. Hajiabadi—Supported by NSF award CCF-1350939 and AFOSR Award FA9550-15-1-0274.

M. Mahmoody—Supported by NSF CAREER award CCF-1350939, and two University of Virginia's SEAS Research Innovation Awards.

A. Rahimi—Supported by NSF award CCF-1350939.

A. Beimel and S. Dziembowski (Eds.): TCC 2018, LNCS 11239, pp. 689–718, 2018.
https://doi.org/10.1007/978-3-030-03807-6_25

We present feasibility results for constructions of RBE based on indistinguishably obfuscation. We further provide constructions of *weakly efficient* RBE, in which the registration step is done in poly(κ, n), based on CDH, Factoring or LWE assumptions. Note that registration is done only once per identity, and the more frequent operation of generating updates for a user, which can happen more times, still runs in time poly($\kappa, \log n$). We leave open the problem of obtaining standard RBE (with poly($\kappa, \log n$) registration time) from standard assumptions.

1 Introduction

Public-key encryption [10,15,21] allows Alice to send Bob private messages without any a-priori shared secrets. However, before Alice can send any messages to Bob, she must obtain Bob's public key. Enabling Alice to obtain Bob's public key often requires additional public-key infrastructure and in some cases complex certification authorities; consequently, making implementation of public-key encryption rather cumbersome.

With the goal of simplifying key-management in public-key encryption, Shamir [23] introduced the notion of identity based encryption (IBE). An IBE scheme allows Alice to encrypt her messages to Bob knowing just the identity of Bob and some additional system public parameters. In this setup, Bob can then decrypt Alice's ciphertexts using an identity-specific secret key that he obtains from the private key generator (PKG). In their celebrated work, Boneh and Franklin [3] provided the first construction of IBE using bilinear maps. A long line of subsequent research has provided many other constructions of IBE based on a variety of assumptions [9,11]. IBE serves as the basis of several real-world systems (e.g., in systems by Voltage security) to simplify key-management.

Despite its significant advantages, one important limitation of IBE schemes is the so-called *key-escrow* problem. Namely, in an IBE scheme a PKG can generate the identity-specific secret key for any identity. This allows the PKG to arbitrarily decrypt messages that are intended for specific recipients. While in certain applications it is reasonable to place trust in a PKG, doing so is not *always* acceptable. This limitation of IBE often attracts significant criticism and restricts applicability in certain scenarios. In words of Rogaway [22],

> *"But this convenience is enabled by a radical change in the trust model: Bob's secret key is no longer self-selected. It is issued by a trusted authority. That authority knows everyone's secret key in the system. IBE embeds key-escrow indeed a form of key-escrow where a single entity implicitly holds all secret keyseven ones that haven't yet been issued. [...] Descriptions of IBE don't usually emphasize the change in trust model. And the key-issuing authority seems never to be named anything like that: it's just the PKG, for Private Key Generator. This sounds more innocuous than it is, and more like an algorithm than an entity."*

With the goal of enhancing the applicability of IBE, prior works suggested ways for reducing the level of trust that parties need to place in the PKG. Boneh and Franklin [3] suggested the use of multiple PKGs, instead of just one, with the goal of making the trust de-centralized. This idea was further explored in subsequent work (e.g., see [5,19,20]). In a different approach, Goyal [16], later followed by Goyal et al. [17], studied the notion of accountable IBE, which allows users to get their decryption keys from the PKG using a secure key generation protocol. Such schemes provide safeguard against a malicious PKG who might distribute the identity-specific secret key for a particular user to unauthorized parties, as by doing so it risks the possibility of being caught in the future. Another approach to the key escrow problem, studied in [6,8,24], involves settings in which the number of identities is huge, limiting the server's ability of finding out the receiver identity when it is chosen at random; hence, guaranteeing a form of anonymity. Finally, Al-Riyami and Paterson [1] put forward the notion of "Certificateless" Public Key Cryptography which is a hybrid of IBE and public-key directories, but which, on the down side, does not let the sender use the system as a true IBE, because more information about the user needs to be read from the public-key infrastructure before a message can be encrypted to them.

None of the above approaches, however, resolve the key-escrow problem entirely, as the PKG (or a collection of several of them) can still decrypt all ciphertexts in the system. Indeed even a trusted PKG may not be able to protect ciphertexts against a subpoena requesting decryption keys. This state of affairs leads us to the main question of this work:

Can we entirely remove PKG from IBE schemes?

A New Primitive: Registration-Based Encryption (RBE). In this work, we pursue a new approach to constructing IBE schemes by introducing a new notion which we call *registration-based encryption*, and which does not suffer from the key-escrow problem. Recall that in traditional IBE schemes, the PKG plays an active role in maintaining the cryptographic secrets corresponding to the public parameters of the system, leading to the key-escrow problem. Deviating from this approach, in our RBE we replace the PKG with a much weaker entity that we call a *key curator*. A key curator does not possess any cryptographic secrets and just plays the role of *aggregating* the public keys of the users.

In more detail, in an RBE scheme each user samples its own public key and secret key and provides its identity and the chosen public key to the key curator.[1] The key curator is now tasked with the goal of curating this new user's public key in the public parameters. Towards this, the key curator updates the public parameters and publicizes the new public parameters. Thus, unlike traditional IBE schemes, the public parameters in an RBE scheme evolve as new users register in the system. For example, let $\mathsf{pp}_0, \mathsf{pp}_1, \ldots, \mathsf{pp}_n$ be the different instances of the public parameters in the system, where pp_i is the public parameter after i users have registered in the system. Just like an IBE scheme, we require that

[1] The key curator will need to verify the identity of the user requesting the registration as it is done by certification authorities in public-key infrastructure.

the size of the public parameter is always small: $|\mathsf{pp}_i| \leq \text{poly}(\kappa, \log n)$ for $i \leq n$, where κ is the security parameter and n is the number of users in the system.

In an RBE scheme, decryption by a user is performed using its secret key and some *auxiliary information* that connects its public key with system's public parameters. Note that as new users join the system and public parameters are updated, an update to the auxiliary information connecting a user's public key to the new public parameters is necessary.[2] However, it would be prohibitive to update each user's auxiliary information (needed for decryption) after each single registration. Thus, we require that the effect of registration by new users on the previously registered users is minimal. In particular, we require that a registered user needs to query the key curator for auxiliary information connecting its public key to the public parameters at most $O(\log n)$ times in its lifetime where n is the total number of registered users. Additionally, we require that the total size of the auxiliary information provided by the key curator needed for any decryption is at most $\text{poly}(\kappa, \log n)$ for security parameter κ.

Our Results. We consider two variants of RBE schemes based on the efficiency of the registration and give constructions for both of them. In particular, we construct (standard) RBE using indistinguishability obfuscation, and we construct a "weakly efficient" variant of this primitive based on more standard assumptions.

- *RBE based on IO*: First, we construct (standard) RBE schemes in which the running time of key curator for every new user registration is $\text{poly}(\kappa, \log n)$ for security parameter κ assuming the key curator has *random* access to its auxiliary information. Other than the desired efficiency itself, one motivation for such minimization in curator's complexity is that since the work done in each user registration is small, it is then more reasonable to distribute the key curator's job between the users themselves, removing the need of a dedicated key curator entirely. In such a system, a new user will only need to do a "small" amount of *public* computation to update the public parameters at the time of joining the system. Moreover, any previously registered user could obtain its updated auxiliary information needed for decryption from the public ledger as well. We obtain a feasibility result for this notion based on somewhere statistically binding hash functions [18] and indistinguishably obfuscation [2,13].
- *RBE with weakly-efficient registration*: Second, we consider a setting where the key curator is allowed to be "weakly efficient"; i.e., the running time of key curator for updating the public parameters as a single new user registers can $\text{poly}(\kappa, n)$. We call such RBE schemes weakly efficient and obtain a construction of weakly-efficient RBE based on any *hash garbling* scheme. The notion of hash garbling and its construction has been implicit in prior works [4,7,11,12], and it was shown there that hash garbling can be realized based on CDH, Factoring or LWE assumptions. In this work, we give a formal definition of this primitive (Definition 19) and use it to construct RBE.

[2] Note that since the public parameters are small, they cannot contain the public keys of all the registered parties.

Our two constructions above leave open the problem of constructing (standard) RBE with poly($\kappa, \log n$) registration time based on standard assumptions.

Communication Cost of RBE Compared with PKE and IBE. We view RBE as a hybrid between PKE and traditional IBE. PKE schemes are communication heavy for encryptors. In other words, each encryptor must obtain the public keys of each recipient that it sends encrypted messages to. In contrast, IBE schemes remove the need for the communication by the encryptors—specifically, encryptors no longer need to recover the public key of each user separately. However, the decryptor must still obtain its identity-specific secret key via communication with the PKG. Note that since this communication with PKG is only done once, the communication cost of an IBE is much smaller than the communication cost of a PKE. However, this efficiency comes at the cost of the key-escrow problem. Our RBE achieves, in large parts, the communication benefits of IBE without the key-escrow problem. More specifically, in an RBE, the encryptors do not need to recover the public key of each recipient individually. Additionally, a decryptor only needs to interact with the key curator to obtain the relevant updates at most $\log n$ times in total.

IBE was originally proposed with the goal of simplifying key management in IBE, yet the problem of key-escrow has prevented it from serving as a substitute for PKE—specifically, its applicability remains limited to specialized settings where trust is not a problem. We believe that efficient variants of our RBE constructions could indeed provide an alternative for PKE while also simplifying key management as IBE does.

1.1 Technical Overview

Here we describe the high level ideas behind our two constructions. The main challenge in realizing our RBE is to have the key curator gather together public keys of registering users in such a way that no individual's relation to the public parameter is affected too many times. Doing that is the key for having few necessary updates for decryption. We start by describing how we resolve this challenge using indistinguishability obfuscation (IO). Next, we give our ideas for realizing a (registration) weakly efficient version of this primitive based on standard assumptions such as CDH and Factoring. The IO-based construction, however, remains conceptually simpler and achieves all the desirable efficiency properties asymptotically.

Our IO based solution is inspired by prior works on using witness encryption [14], if we interpret the decryption key (i.e., the secret key together with the required auxiliary updates) as a witness that enables decryption. Additionally, both our IO-based and the hash obfuscation based solutions (and in particular their tree-based hashing of the public keys) use ideas developed recently in the context of laconic OT [7] and IBE from the CDH assumption [11]. In both of these settings, our contribution is in formalizing the subtle aspects of RBE and then realizing RBE schemes (as mentioned above) using these ideas.

High Level Description of Our IO-Based Construction of RBE. A natural first try for the solution would be for the curator to just Merkle hash together the public keys of all the users in the system (along with their corresponding identities). Here encryption could be performed by an obfuscation of the following program $\mathsf{P}[\mathsf{h},\mathsf{m}]$, with the Merkle hash root h and the encrypted message m hardwired. Given input $(\mathsf{pk},\mathsf{id},\mathsf{pth})$, the program $\mathsf{P}[\mathsf{h},\mathsf{m}]$ outputs an encryption of m under the public key pk *only if* pth is a "Merkle opening" (i.e., the right leaf to root path with siblings) for $(\mathsf{pk},\mathsf{id})$ as a pair of sibling leaves in the Merkle hash tree with root h, and it outputs $\perp$ otherwise. Decryption can proceed naturally with the right Merkle opening as auxiliary information that the key curator needs to provide for decryption. The main issue with this solution is that the Merkle hash root h changes with every new user registering in the system. Our idea for solving this problem is to maintain *multiple* Merkle hash trees such that any individual user is affected only a bounded number of times. Below, we explain this idea in more detail.

- Public parameters and auxiliary information. At a high level, in our construction, after n parties have registered, the key curator holds an auxiliary information aux_n of the following form: it consists of η *full* binary Merkle trees, $\mathsf{Tree}_1,\ldots,\mathsf{Tree}_\eta$ with corresponding depths $\mathsf{d}_1 > \cdots > \mathsf{d}_\eta$ and number of leaves $2^{\mathsf{d}_1},\ldots,2^{\mathsf{d}_\eta}$. The public parameter would be the set of the labels of the *roots* of these trees. Every leaf in either of these trees is either an identity id or its public key pk as the sibling of the leaf id, and every registered identity id appears exactly once as a leaf. Thus, half of the leaves of these trees contain the strings encoding the registered identities, and for each leaf id, the sibling leaf contains the public key pk of id. So, if there are n people registered so far in the system, then the total number of leaves in the trees is equal to $2n$. Since we stated that $\mathsf{d}_1 > \cdots > \mathsf{d}_\eta$, it means that the number of these trees η is at most $\log(n)$, simply because $(d_1,\ldots,d_\eta)$ would be the binary representation of number $2n$. This point implies that the public parameter is indeed short.
- What is needed for decryption. Even though in general it is more natural to describe encryption first, in our case it is easier to describe the information that is needed for decryption. Each identity id will hold is own secret key sk which will be necessary for decryption, but it would need more information for doing so. Indeed, if Tree is the tree hold by the curator that contains (sibling leaves) $(\mathsf{id},\mathsf{pk})$ in its leaves, then the identity id needs to know the "Merkle opening" of $(\mathsf{id},\mathsf{pk})$ to the root of Tree in order to do any decryption. Since the length of this path is at most the depth of Tree, which is at most $\log(n)$, the total size of the decryption key dk (which includes sk and the knowledge of such opening to the root of Tree) is at most $\kappa \cdot \log(n)$. This makes dk also short enough.
- How to encrypt. For simplicity, suppose there is only one tree Tree held by the key curator and that all the identities are leaves of this tree. The encryptor, knows the public parameter, which is the root rt of Tree. For any message m, the encryptor then sends the *obfuscation* of the following program P. The program P takes as input any Merkle opening that contains the path from

leaves $(\mathsf{id}, \mathsf{pk})$ to the root rt of Tree, and if such opening is given, then P outputs an encryption of m under the corresponding registered public key pk. Since id is the only identity who knows the corresponding sk to the registered pk, nobody other than id can decrypt the message m encrypted that way. When there are *multiple* trees $\mathsf{Tree}_1, \ldots, \mathsf{Tree}_\eta$ held by the key curator, the ciphertext includes η obfuscations, one for every Tree_i.

- How to register. When a new party id joins to register, we first create a single tree Tree for that party, with id, pk as its only leaves. But creating too many trees naively increases the length of the public parameter. So, to handle this issue we "merge" the trees every now and then. In particular, upon any registration, so long as there are any two trees $\mathsf{Tree}_1, \mathsf{Tree}_2$ of the *same size* held by the key curator, it "merges" them by simply hashing their roots $\mathsf{rt}_1, \mathsf{rt}_2$ into a new root rt. This way, the key curator keeps the invariance property (stated above) that the trees are always full binary trees of different sizes. After doing any such merge, the key curator sends the generated update of the form $(\mathsf{rt}_1, \mathsf{rt}, \mathsf{rt}_2)$ to all of the identities that are in *either* of the trees $\mathsf{Tree}_1, \mathsf{Tree}_2$. That is because, the identities in Tree_1 would now need to know rt_2 and the identities in Tree_2 now need the label rt_1 in order to decrypt what is encrypted for them. Alternatively, if the key curator is passive and does not send updates, the users who are in the merged tree Tree would need to pull their updates whenever they have a ciphertext that they cannot decrypt, realizing that their auxiliary information is outdated.

To prove security of the above construction, collision-resistance of the used hash function is not enough, and we rely on *somewhere statistically binding* hash functions [18] (see Definition 3).

Weakly-Efficient Construction Based on Standard Assumptions. In order to replace the use of obfuscation in the above construction, we build on the techniques by Cho, Döttling, Garg, Gupta, Miao, and Polychroniadou [7] and Döttling and Garg [11]. We abstract their idea of using hash encryption and garbled circuits as a new primitive that we call *hash garbling*. Use of this abstraction simplifies exposition. A hash garbling scheme consists of algorithms (Hash, HG, HInp).[3] Hash function is a function from $\{0,1\}^\ell$ to $\{0,1\}^\kappa$. HG takes as input a secret state stt and an arbitrary program P and outputs $\widetilde{\mathrm{P}}$. HInp takes as input a secret state stt and a value $y \in \{0,1\}^\kappa$ and outputs $\widetilde{y}$. Correctness and security require that $\widetilde{\mathrm{C}}, \widetilde{y}, x$ can be used to compute $\mathrm{C}(x)$, but also that they reveal nothing else about C.

Our construction of RBE from standard assumption is very similar to the IO-based construction except that we replace the use of IO with the less powerful primitive hash garbling. The key challenge in making this switch comes from the fact that hash garbling, unlike IO, cannot process *the entire* root to leaf Merkle opening in one shot. Thus, our construction needs to provide a sequence of hash garblings that traverse the root to leaf path step by step. Therefore, as

[3] The hash function also has a key setup function which we ignore here for the sake of simplicity.

the tree is being traversed, the hash garblings need to identify whether to go left or to go right. Note that this decision must be taken without any knowledge of what identities are included in the leaves of the left sub-tree and what identities are included in the leaves of the right sub-tree. We resolve this challenge by modifying the Merkle tree in two ways:

1. We ensure that the identities in the leave of any tree are always sorted.
2. In addition to the hashes of its two children, in the computation of the Merkle hash, we also hash the information about the largest identity that is present any leaf of the left subtree at any node. (The latter information allows us to traverse down a Merkle tree using it as a binary search tree.)

Using these enhancements over the simple Merkle trees, we can indeed substitute IO with the less powerful primitive of hash garbling, which in turn can be obtained from more standard assumptions. On the down side, this new construction needs to sort the identities for every registration, and in particular the registration cannot run in sublinear time $\mathrm{poly}(\kappa, \log n)$. We refer the reader Sect. 5 for more details on this construction.

2 Preliminaries

Notation. For a probabilistic algorithm A, by $A(x) \to y$, we denote the randomized process of running A on input x and obtaining the output y. We use PPT to denote a probabilistic polynomial-time algorithms, where running time is polynomial over the length of their main input (not the random seed). For randomized algorithms $A_1, A_2, \ldots$, by $\Pr_{A_1,A_2,\ldots}[E]$ we denote the probability of event E when the randomness is over the algorithms $A_1, A_2, \ldots$ as well. For deterministic algorithms A_1, A_2, by $A_1 \equiv A_2$, we denote that they have the same input-output functionality; namely, for all x (of the right length, if A_1, A_2 are circuits), $A_1(x) = A_2(x)$. For distribution ensembles X_n, Y_n, by $X_n \stackrel{c}{\approx} Y_n$ we mean that they are indistinguishable against $\mathrm{poly}(n)$-time algorithms. By $x||y$ we denote the concatenation of the strings x, y. By $\mathrm{negl}(\kappa)$ we denote some function that is negligible in input κ; namely for all k, $\mathrm{negl}(\kappa) \leq O(1/\kappa^k)$. U_n denotes the uniform distribution over $\{0,1\}^n$. For algorithm A, by A^B we denote an oracle access by A to oracle B. By $A^{[B]}$ we denote A accessing oracle B with read and *and write* operations. So, if A writes y at location x, reading a query x next time will return y.

Definition 1 (Public key encryption). *A public key encryption scheme consists of three PPT algorithms* (G, E, D) *as follows.*

- $\mathsf{G}(1^\kappa) \to (\mathsf{pk}, \mathsf{sk})$*: This algorithm takes a security parameter* 1^κ *as input and outputs a pair of public key* pk *secret key* sk*. Without loss of generality we assume that* $|\mathsf{pk}| = |\mathsf{sk}| = \kappa$.
- $\mathsf{E}(\mathsf{pk}, \mathsf{m}) \to \mathsf{ct}$*: takes a message* m *and a public key* pk *as input and outputs a ciphertext* ct.

- $\mathsf{D}(\mathsf{sk}, \mathsf{ct}) \to \mathsf{m}$: *takes a ciphertext* ct *and a secret key* sk *as inputs and outputs a message* m.

The completeness and security properties are defined as follows.

- **Completeness.** *The PKE scheme is complete if for every message* m:

$$\Pr_{\mathrm{G,E,D}}[\mathsf{D}(\mathsf{sk}, \mathrm{E}(\mathsf{pk}, \mathsf{m})) = \mathsf{m} : (\mathsf{sk}, \mathsf{pk}) \leftarrow \mathrm{G}] = 1.$$

- **Semantic Security.** *Any PPT adversary* Adv *wins the following game with probability* $\frac{1}{2} + \mathrm{negl}(\kappa)$:
  - *The challenger generates* $(\mathsf{pk}, \mathsf{sk}) \leftarrow \mathrm{G}(1^\kappa)$ *and sends* pk *to* Adv.
  - *The challenger chooses a random bit* b *and sends* $c \leftarrow \mathrm{E}(\mathsf{pk}, b)$ *to* Adv.
  - Adv *outputs* b' *and wins if* $b = b'$.

Definition 2 (Indistinguishability obfuscation). *A uniform PPT algorithm* Obf *is called an* indistinguishability obfuscator *for a circuit class* $\{\mathcal{C}_\kappa\}_{\kappa\in\mathbb{N}}$ *(where each* $\mathcal{C}_\kappa$ *is a set indexed by a security parameter* κ*) if the following holds:*

- **Completeness.** *For all security parameters* $\kappa \in \mathbb{N}$ *and all circuits* $\mathrm{C} \in \mathcal{C}_\kappa$, *we obtain an obfuscation with the same function:*

$$\Pr_{\mathrm{Obf}}[\mathrm{C}' \equiv \mathrm{C} : \mathrm{C}' = \mathrm{Obf}(1^\kappa, \mathrm{C})] = 1.$$

- **Security.** *For any PPT distinguisher D, there exists a negligible function* $\mathrm{negl}(\cdot)$ *such that for all* $\kappa \in \mathbb{N}$, *for all pairs of functionally equivalent circuits* $\mathrm{C}_1 \equiv \mathrm{C}_2$ *from the same family* $\mathrm{C}_1, \mathrm{C}_2 \in \mathcal{C}_\kappa$,

$$\left|\Pr_{\mathrm{Obf}}[D(1^\kappa, \mathrm{Obf}(1^\kappa, \mathrm{C}_1)) = 1)] - \Pr_{\mathrm{Obf}}[D(1^\kappa, \mathrm{Obf}(1^\kappa, \mathrm{C}_2)) = 1)]\right| \leq \mathrm{negl}(\kappa).$$

The next definition is a special case of the definition of somewhere statistically binding (SSB) hash functions introduced by Hubacek and Wichs [18] for the blockwise setting. Here we only use two-input blocks.

Definition 3 (SSB hash functions [18]**).** *A* somewhere statistically binding hash system *consists of two polynomial time algorithms* HGen, Hash.

- $\mathrm{HGen}(1^\kappa, b) \to \mathsf{hk}$. *This algorithm takes the security parameter* κ *and an index bit* $b \in \{0,1\}$, *and outputs a hash key* hk.
- $\mathrm{Hash}(\mathsf{hk}, x) \to y$. *This is a deterministic algorithm that takes as input* $x = (x_0, x_1) \in \{0,1\}^\kappa \times \{0,1\}^\kappa$ *and outputs* $y \in \{0,1\}^\kappa$.

We require the following properties for an SSB hashing scheme:

- **Index hiding.** *No* $\mathrm{poly}(\kappa)$*-time adversary can distinguish between* hk_0 *and* hk_1 *by more than* $\mathrm{negl}(\kappa)$, *where* $\mathsf{hk}_b \leftarrow \mathrm{HGen}(1^\kappa, b)$ *for* $b \in \{0,1\}$.
- **Somewhere statistically binding.** *We say that* hk *is statistically binding for index* $i \in \{0,1\}$, *if there do not exist two values* $(x_0, x_1), (x'_0, x'_1) \in \{0,1\}^\ell \times \{0,1\}^\ell$ *such that* $x_i \neq x'_i$ *and* $\mathrm{Hash}(\mathsf{hk}, x) = \mathrm{Hash}(\mathsf{hk}, x')$. *We require that for both* $i \in \{0,1\}$,

$$\Pr_{\mathrm{HGen}}[\mathsf{hk} \text{ is statistically binding for } i : \mathsf{hk} \leftarrow \mathrm{HGen}(1^\kappa, i)] \geq 1 - \mathrm{negl}(\kappa).$$

3 Formal Definition of Registration-Based Encryption

In this section, we formalize the new notion of RBE. After defining the "default" version of RBE, we define weakened forms of this primitive with a specific relaxation in the efficiency requirements. The goal of this relaxation is to base the (relaxed) RBE on more standard assumptions.

We start by defining the syntax of the default notion of RBE. We will then discuss the required compactness, completeness, and security properties.

Definition 4 (Syntax of RBE). *A* registration-based encryption *(RBE for short) scheme consists of PPT algorithms* (Gen, Reg, Enc, Upd, Dec) *working as follows. The* Reg *and* Upd *algorithms are performed by the key curator, which we call KC for short.*

- **Generating common random string.** *Some of the subroutines below will need a common random string* crs, *which could be sampled publicly using some public randomness beacon.* crs *of length* poly(κ) *is sampled at the beginning, for the security parameter* κ.
- **Key generation.** $\mathrm{Gen}(1^\kappa) \to (\mathsf{pk}, \mathsf{sk})$: *The randomized algorithm* Gen *takes as input the security parameter* 1^κ *and outputs a pair of public/secret keys* $(\mathsf{pk}, \mathsf{sk})$. *Note that these are only* public *and* secret *keys, not the* encryption *or* decryption *keys. The key generation algorithm is run by any honest party locally who wants to register itself into the system.*
- **Registration.** $\mathrm{Reg}^{[\mathsf{aux}]}(\mathsf{crs}, \mathsf{pp}, \mathsf{id}, \mathsf{pk}) \to \mathsf{pp}'$: *The deterministic*[4] *algorithm* Reg *takes as input the common random sting* crs, *current public parameter* pp, *a registering identity* id *and a public key* pk *(supposedly for the identity* id*), and it outputs* pp' *as the updated public parameters. The* Reg *algorithm uses* read and write *oracle access to* aux *which will be updated into* aux' *during the process of registration.*[5] *(The system is initialized with public parameters* pp *and auxiliary information* aux *set to* $\perp$.*)*
- **Encryption.** $\mathrm{Enc}(\mathsf{crs}, \mathsf{pp}, \mathsf{id}, \mathsf{m}) \to \mathsf{ct}$: *The randomized algorithm* Enc *takes as input the common random sting* crs, *a public parameter* pp, *a recipient identity* id *and a plaintext message* m *and outputs a ciphertext* ct.
- **Update.** $\mathrm{Upd}^{\mathsf{aux}}(\mathsf{pp}, \mathsf{id}) \to \mathsf{u}$: *The deterministic algorithm* Upd *takes as input the current information* pp *stored at the KC and an identity* id, *has* read only *oracle access to* aux *and generates an* update *information* u *that can help* id *to decrypt its messages.*[6]

---

[4] In our constructions, the algorithms Reg, Upd and Reg are deterministic, and this feature makes our KC transparent (see Remark 5), so we keep the default definition based on deterministic version of these subroutines.

[5] This is the step that needs the identity of the registering id to be verified. This verification step is similar to IBE and its details are outside scope of this work.

[6] Looking ahead, we will aim for schemes that require the identity id to launch this request as rarely as possible. However, we note that this information u does not need to be kept secret for the security of the scheme, and any user can request this update without its identity being checked.

– **Decryption.** $\mathsf{Dec}(\mathsf{sk}, \mathsf{u}, \mathsf{ct})$: *The deterministic decryption algorithm* Dec *takes as input a secret key* sk, *an update information* u, *and a ciphertext* ct, *and it outputs a message* $\mathsf{m} \in \{0,1\}^*$ *or in* $\{\perp, \texttt{GetUpd}\}$. *The special symbol* $\perp$ *indicates a syntax error, while* **GetUpd** *indicates that more recent update information (than* u*) might be needed for decryption.*

Remark 5 (Key curator is transparent). We emphasize that in the definition above the KC has no secret state. In fact, the registration and update operations are both *deterministic.* This makes KC's job fully auditable. Even the generation of the crs (that is done before KC takes control of the server's information) only needs common *random* strings (as opposed to a common *reference* string), so that can be generated using public randomness beacon as well.

We will now first describe the *completeness, compactness, efficiency* properties (under the completeness definition) and then we will describe the *security* properties. Both definitions are based on a security game that involves an "adversary" that tries to break the security, completeness, compactness, or efficiency properties by controlling how the identities (including the target/challenge identity) are registered and when the encryptions and decryptions happen.

Definition 6 (Completeness, compactness, and efficiency of RBE). *For any interactive* computationally unbounded *adversary* Adv *that still has a limited* poly(κ) *round complexity, consider the following game* $\mathit{Comp}_{\mathsf{Adv}}(\kappa)$ *between* Adv *and a challenger* Chal.

1. ***Initialization.*** Chal *sets* $\mathsf{pp} = \perp$, $\mathsf{aux} = \perp$, $\mathsf{u} = \perp$, $\mathcal{D} = \varnothing$, $\mathsf{id}^* = \perp$, $t = 0$, $\mathsf{crs} \leftarrow U_{\mathrm{poly}(\kappa)}$ *and sends the sampled* crs *to* Adv.
2. *Till* Adv *continues (which is at most* poly(κ) *steps), proceed as follows. At every iteration,* Adv *chooses exactly one of the actions below to be performed.*
   (a) ***Registering new (non-target) identity.*** Adv *sends some* $\mathsf{id} \notin \mathcal{D}$ *and* pk *to* Chal. Chal *registers* (id, pk) *by letting* $\mathsf{pp} := \mathrm{Reg}^{[\mathsf{aux}]}(\mathsf{crs}, \mathsf{pp}, \mathsf{id}, \mathsf{pk})$ *and* $\mathcal{D} := \mathcal{D} \cup \{\mathsf{id}\}$.
   (b) ***Registering the target identity.*** *If* id^* *was chosen by* Adv *already (i.e.,* $\mathsf{id}^* \neq \perp$*), skip this step. Otherwise,* Adv *sends some* $\mathsf{id}^* \notin \mathcal{D}$ *to* Chal. Chal *then samples* $(\mathsf{pk}^*, \mathsf{sk}^*) \leftarrow \mathrm{Gen}(1^\kappa)$, *makes the updates* $\mathsf{pp} := \mathrm{Reg}^{[\mathsf{aux}]}(\mathsf{crs}, \mathsf{pp}, \mathsf{id}^*, \mathsf{pk}^*)$, $\mathcal{D} := \mathcal{D} \cup \{\mathsf{id}^*\}$, *and sends* pk^* *to* Adv.
   (c) ***Encrypting for the target identity.*** *If* $\mathsf{id}^* = \perp$ *then skip this step. Otherwise,* Chal *sets* $t = t + 1$, *then* Adv *sends some* $\mathsf{m}_t \in \{0,1\}^*$ *to* Chal *who then sets* $\mathsf{m}'_t := \mathsf{m}_t$ *and sends back a corresponding ciphertext* $\mathsf{ct}_t \leftarrow \mathrm{Enc}(\mathsf{crs}, \mathsf{pp}, \mathsf{id}^*, \mathsf{m}_t)$ *to* Adv.
   (d) ***Decryption by target identity.*** Adv *sends a* $j \in [t]$ *to* Chal. Chal *then lets* $\mathsf{m}'_j = \mathrm{Dec}(\mathsf{sk}^*, \mathsf{u}, \mathsf{ct}_j)$. *If* $\mathsf{m}'_j = \texttt{GetUpd}$, *then* Chal *obtains the update* $\mathsf{u} = \mathrm{Upd}^{\mathsf{aux}}(\mathsf{pp}, \mathsf{id}^*)$ *and then lets* $\mathsf{m}'_j = \mathrm{Dec}(\mathsf{sk}^*, \mathsf{u}, \mathsf{ct}_j)$.
3. *The adversary* Adv *wins the game if there is some* $j \in [t]$ *for which* $\mathsf{m}'_j \neq \mathsf{m}_j$.

Let $n = |\mathcal{D}|$ *be the number of identities registered till a specific moment. We require the following properties to hold for any* Adv *(as specified above) and for* all *the moments (and so for all the values of* $\mathcal{D}$ *and* $n = |\mathcal{D}|$ *as well) during the game* $\mathit{Comp}_{\mathsf{Adv}}(\kappa)$.

- **Completeness.** Pr[Adv *wins in* $\mathit{Comp}_{\mathsf{Adv}}(\kappa)$] = negl($\kappa$).
- **Compactness of public parameters and updates.** $|\mathsf{pp}|, |\mathsf{u}|$ *are both* $\leq$ poly($\kappa, \log n$).
- **Efficiency of runtime of registration and update.** *The running time of each invocation of* Reg *and* Upd *algorithms is at most* poly($\kappa, \log n$). *(This implies the compactness property.)*
- **Efficiency of the number of updates.** *The* total *number of invocations of* Upd *for identity* id* *in Step 2d of the game* $\mathit{Comp}_{\mathsf{Adv}}(\kappa)$ *is at most* $O(\log n)$ *for every* n *during* $\mathit{Comp}_{\mathsf{Adv}}(\kappa)$.

Remark 7 (Other definitions based on quantifying compactness and efficiency parameters). Even though Definition 6 requires compactness and efficiency requirements using function $c(\kappa, n) \leq \text{poly}(\kappa, \log n)$, one can consider a more general definition that uses different (e.g., sublinear) functions to obtain various versions of RBE. In general, one can consider $(c_1, \ldots, c_5)$-RBE schemes where c_i's are functions of (κ, n), and that functions c_1, c_2 describe the compactness requirements (of public-key and updates), and functions c_3, c_4, c_5 describe the efficiency requirements.

The following definition instantiates the general quantified definition of Remark 7 by relaxing the efficiency of the registration and keeping the other efficiency and compactness requirements to be as needed for Definition 6.

Definition 8 (WE-RBE). *A* registration weakly efficient RBE *(or WE-RBE for short) is defined similarly to Definition 6, where the specified* poly($\kappa, \log n$) *runtime efficiency of the registration algorithm is not required anymore, but instead we require the registration time to be* poly(κ, n).

Remark 9 (Denial of service attacks using fake ciphertexts). A class of malicious adversaries that are *not* captured by Definition 6 can potentially launch a "denial of service" attack against the efficiency of the decryption procedure as follows. Specifically, such malicious completeness adversary (that can also be seen as a form of "environment") can cause an honest user to request too many updates by continually providing it with fake ciphertexts that seem to require an update for decryption. Here, we propose a generic approach for dealing with this issue. We can generalize the RBE primitive and allow the KC to have a secret state. This will take away the appealing transparency feature of the KC, but it will instead allow the KC to sign the public parameters, and those signed public parameters can then be included in the ciphertexts. Doing this will allow the decryption algorithm to detect fake ciphertexts that (maliciously) indicate that the population has grown beyond the last update, and that new update is needed for recent decryptions.

Security. For security, we require that no PPT adversary should be able to distinguish between encryptions of two messages (of equal lengths) made to a user who has registered honestly into the system, even if the adversary colludes and obtains the secret keys of all the other users. This is formalized by the adversary specifying a challenge identity and distinguishing between encryptions made to that identity. In order to prevent the adversary from winning trivially, we require that the adversary does not know any secret key for a public key registered for the challenge identity.

We present the formal definition only for the case of bit encryption, but any scheme achieving this level of security can be extended to arbitrary length messages using independent bit-by-bit encryption and a standard hybrid argument.

Definition 10 (Security of RBE). *For any interactive PPT adversary* Adv, *consider the following game* $\mathsf{Sec}_{\mathsf{Adv}}(\kappa)$ *between* Adv *and a challenger* Chal. *(Steps that are different from the completeness definition are denoted with purple stars (⋆⋆). Specifically, Steps 2c and 2d from Definition 6 are replaced by Step 3 below. Additionally, Step 3 from Definition 6 is replaced by Step 4 below.)*

1. ***Initialization.*** Chal *sets* $\mathsf{pp} = \bot$, $\mathsf{aux} = \bot$, $\mathcal{D} = \varnothing$, $\mathsf{id}^* = \bot$, $\mathsf{crs} \leftarrow U_{\mathrm{poly}(\kappa)}$ *and sends the sampled* crs *to* Adv.
2. *Till* Adv *continues (which is at most* $\mathrm{poly}(\kappa)$ *steps), proceed as follows. At every iteration,* Adv *chooses exactly one of the actions below to be performed.*
   (a) ***Registering new (non-target) identity.*** Adv *sends some* $\mathsf{id} \notin \mathcal{D}$ *and* pk *to* Chal. Chal *registers* $(\mathsf{id}, \mathsf{pk})$ *by letting* $\mathsf{pp} := \mathrm{Reg}^{[\mathsf{aux}]}(\mathsf{crs}, \mathsf{pp}, \mathsf{id}, \mathsf{pk})$ *and* $\mathcal{D} := \mathcal{D} \cup \{\mathsf{id}\}$.
   (b) ***Registering the target identity.*** *If* id^* *was chosen by* Adv *already (i.e.,* $\mathsf{id}^* \neq \bot$*), skip this step. Otherwise,* Adv *sends some* $\mathsf{id}^* \notin \mathcal{D}$ *to* Chal. Chal *then samples* $(\mathsf{pk}^*, \mathsf{sk}^*) \leftarrow \mathrm{Gen}(1^\kappa)$*, makes the updates* $\mathsf{pp} := \mathrm{Reg}^{[\mathsf{aux}]}(\mathsf{crs}, \mathsf{pp}, \mathsf{id}^*, \mathsf{pk}^*)$, $\mathcal{D} := \mathcal{D} \cup \{\mathsf{id}^*\}$, *and sends* pk^* *to* Adv.
3. (⋆⋆) **Encrypting for the target identity.** If no id^* was chosen by Adv before (i.e., $\mathsf{id}^* = \bot$) then Adv first sends some $\mathsf{id}^* \notin \mathcal{D}$ to Chal. Next, Chal generates $\mathsf{ct} \leftarrow \mathrm{Enc}(\mathsf{crs}, \mathsf{pp}, \mathsf{id}^*, b)$, where $b \leftarrow \{0,1\}$ is a random bit, lets $\mathcal{D} = \mathcal{D} \cup \{\mathsf{id}^*\}$, and sends ct to Adv.
4. (⋆⋆) The adversary Adv outputs a bit b' and wins the game if $b = b'$.

We call an RBE scheme secure if $\Pr[\mathsf{Adv}$ *wins in* $\mathsf{Sec}_{\mathsf{Adv}}(\kappa)] < \frac{1}{2} + \mathrm{negl}(\kappa)$ *for any PPT* Adv.

Equivalence to Other Definitions. One might consider a seemingly stronger security definition in which the adversary chooses its challenge identity from a *set* of previously chosen identities for which it does *not* know the keys. However, since the adversary can *guess* its own selection with probability $1/\mathrm{poly}(\kappa)$, that definition becomes equivalent to Definition 10 above. Another seemingly stronger definition would allow the adversary to register even more identities after receiving the challenge ciphertext (and before answering the challenge), however this is again an equivalent definition as the information distributed in this extra step is simulatable by the adversary and thus not helpful to her.

Choosing a Registered or an Unregistered Identity. Here we note a subtle aspect of Definition 10. If the adversary chooses Step 2b, it means that it is attacking a target identity that is registered in the system. Otherwise, the adversary shall choose the target identify in Step 3, which means that the attacked target identity is not even registered in the system. In both cases, we require that the adversary has negligible advantage in guessing the encrypted bit.

Why Not Giving Update Oracle to Adversary? In Definition 10, we did not provide explicit oracle access to Upd subroutine for the adversary. The reason is that the adversary receives the crs, chooses the identities and receives the public keys. Moreover, KC is deterministic, has no secret state, and all the inputs it receives in maintaining the auxiliary information is crs, identities, and the public-keys. Therefore, throughout the attack, the adversary knows the exact state of $(\mathsf{pp}, \mathsf{aux})$ hold by the key curator, and thus it can run the update operation itself. However, if one considers a KC with a *secret state* (perhaps for the goal of signing the public parameters as discussed in Remark 9) then the corresponding security definition shall give the adversary oracle access to the update subroutine.

Remark 11 (Unauthorized registration of an identity). A malicious KC K^*, not following the protocol as modeled in the security game of Definition 10 can generate a pair of keys $(\mathsf{pk}, \mathsf{sk})$ on its own and register pk on behalf of an identity id. By that, K^* can read messages that are subsequently encrypted to the identity id. Here we describe two approaches to tackle this problem.

1. **Bootstrapping public-key directories.** RBE schemes could be launched with respect to an external public-key directory D. Namely, only public-keys in D could be registered for matching identities. This way, a malicious key curator K^* can only register the *actual* public keys of the identities, and thus it is not able to decrypt the messages encrypted to them. Moreover, by also including (public) verification keys of the signatures by the identities in the public-key directory D, we can even prevent K^* from successfully registering any identities in the RBE scheme without having their permission (even by using their real public keys) as follows. Whenever the public parameter pp is updated, a signature of pp by the registering identity is added to the public auxiliary aux. This way, a public auditor can detect a fake registration.
2. **Proof of Knowledge.** An alternative method to prevent fake identity registrations is to use a similar approach to the one mentioned above, but replace the signature with a zero-knowledge proof of knowledge of an actual certificate from some trusted party (e.g., their driving licence information) that validates the ownership of an identity.

4 IO-Based Construction of RBE

In this section we present a formal construction of (efficient) RBE based on indistinguishability obfuscation and SSB hash functions (see Sect. 2 for formal definitions of the standard primitives used). We first describe the construction along the line of Definition 4 and then will prove its completeness, compactness, and security based on Definitions 6 and 10. We will then describe minor modifications that make the construction efficient according to Definition 8 (basically by not producing the updates in the registration).

Notation on Binary Trees. In our construction below, Tree is always a *full* binary tree (with 2^i leaves for some i), where the label of each node in Tree is calculated as the "hash" of its left and right children. We define the size of a tree Tree as the number of its *leaves*, denoted by $\mathrm{size}(\mathsf{Tree})$ (so if $\mathrm{size}(\mathsf{Tree}) = s$, the total number of nodes will be $2s-1$), and we denote the root of Tree as $\mathsf{rt}(\mathsf{Tree})$, and we use $\mathsf{d}(\mathsf{Tree})$ to refer to the depth of Tree. Since we assume that Tree is always a full tree, we always have $2^{\mathsf{d}(\mathsf{Tree})} = \mathrm{size}(\mathsf{d}(\mathsf{Tree}))$. When it is clear from the context, we use rt and d to denote the root and the depth of Tree.

Simplifying Assumption on Lengths. We note that without loss of generality, we can assume that public keys, secret keys and identities are all of the length security parameter κ.

Construction 12 (RBE from IO and SSB Hashing). *We will use an IO scheme* (Obf, Eval) *and a SSB hash function system* (Hash, HGen) *and a PKE scheme* (G, E, D)*. Using them, we show how to implement the subroutines of RBE according to Definition 4.*

- $\mathrm{Stp}(1^\kappa) \to (\mathsf{pp}_0, \mathsf{aux}_0)$. *This algorithm outputs* $\mathsf{pp}_0 = (\mathsf{hk}_1, \ldots, \mathsf{hk}_\kappa)$ *where each* hk_i *is sampled from* $\mathrm{HGen}(1^\kappa, 0)$ *and* $\mathsf{aux} = \varnothing$ *is empty.*
- $\mathrm{Reg}^{[\mathsf{aux}]}(\mathsf{pp}_n, \mathsf{id}, \mathsf{pk}) \to \mathsf{pp}_{n+1}$. *This algorithm works as follows:*
  1. *Parse* $\mathsf{aux} := ((\mathsf{Tree}_1, \ldots, \mathsf{Tree}_\eta), (\mathsf{id}_1, \ldots, \mathsf{id}_n))$ *where the trees have corresponding depths* $\mathsf{d}_1 > \mathsf{d}_2 \cdots > \mathsf{d}_\eta$*, and* $(\mathsf{id}_1, \ldots, \mathsf{id}_n)$ *is the order by which the current identities have registered.*[7]
  2. *Parse* pp_n *as a sequence* $((\mathsf{hk}_1, \ldots, \mathsf{hk}_\kappa), (\mathsf{rt}_1, \mathsf{d}_1), \ldots, (\mathsf{rt}_\eta, \mathsf{d}_\eta))$ *where* $\mathsf{rt}_i \in \{0,1\}^\kappa$ *represents the root of* Tree_i*, and* d_i *represents the depth of* Tree_i*.*
  3. *Create new tree* $\mathsf{Tree}_{\eta+1}$ *with leaves* id, pk *and set its root as* $\mathsf{rt}_{\eta+1} := \mathrm{Hash}(\mathsf{hk}_1, \mathsf{id}||\mathsf{pk})$ *and thus its depth would be* $\mathsf{d}_{\eta+1} = 1$*.*
  4. *Let* $\mathcal{T} = \{\mathsf{Tree}_1, \ldots, \mathsf{Tree}_{\eta+1}\}$*. (We will keep changing* $\mathcal{T}$ *in steps below.)*
  5. *While there are two different trees* $\mathsf{Tree}_L, \mathsf{Tree}_R \in \mathcal{T}$ *of the same depth* d *and same size* $s = 2^{\mathsf{d}}$ *(recall that our trees are always full binary trees), and roots* $\mathsf{rt}_L, \mathsf{rt}_R$*, do the following.*
     (a) *Let* Tree *be a new tree of depth* $\mathsf{d}+1$ *that contains* Tree_L *as its left subtree,* Tree_R *as its right subtree, and* $\mathsf{rt} = \mathrm{Hash}(\mathsf{hk}_{d+1}, \mathsf{rt}_L||\mathsf{rt}_R)$ *as its root.*
     (b) *Remove both of* $\mathsf{Tree}_L, \mathsf{Tree}_R$ *from* $\mathcal{T}$ *and add* Tree *to* $\mathcal{T}$ *instead.*
  6. *Let* $\mathcal{T} := (\mathsf{Tree}_1, \ldots, \mathsf{Tree}_\zeta)$ *be the final set of trees where* $\mathsf{d}'_1 > \cdots > \mathsf{d}'_\zeta$ *are their corresponding depths and* $\mathsf{rt}'_1, \ldots, \mathsf{rt}'_\zeta$ *are their corresponding roots. Set* pp_{n+1} *and* aux *as follows:*

$$\mathsf{pp}_{n+1} := ((\mathsf{hk}_1, \ldots, \mathsf{hk}_\kappa), (\mathsf{rt}'_1, \mathsf{d}'_1), \ldots, (\mathsf{rt}'_\zeta, \mathsf{d}'_\zeta)) \text{ and}$$
$$\mathsf{aux} := (\mathcal{T}, (\mathsf{id}_1, \ldots, \mathsf{id}_n, \mathsf{id}_{n+1} = \mathsf{id})).$$

[7] Keeping this list is not necessary, but simplifies the presentation of the updates.

- $\mathsf{Enc}(\mathsf{pp}, \mathsf{id}, \mathsf{m}) \to \mathsf{ct}$: *First parse* $\mathsf{pp} := ((\mathsf{hk}_1, \ldots, \mathsf{hk}_\kappa), (\mathsf{rt}_1, \mathsf{d}_1), \ldots, (\mathsf{rt}_\eta, \mathsf{d}_\eta))$. *Generate programs* $\mathrm{P}_1, \ldots, \mathrm{P}_\eta$ *where each program* P_i *works as follows:*
  Hardwired values: $\mathsf{rt}_i, \mathsf{d}_i, (\mathsf{hk}_1, \ldots, \mathsf{hk}_{\mathsf{d}_i}), \mathsf{m}, \mathsf{id}, \mathsf{r}$ *(the randomness)*
  Input: pth
  1. *Parse* $\mathsf{pth} := [(\mathsf{h}_0^0, \mathsf{h}_0^1), (\mathsf{h}_1^0, \mathsf{h}_1^1, b_1) \ldots, (\mathsf{h}_{\mathsf{d}_i-1}^0, \mathsf{h}_{\mathsf{d}_i-1}^1, b_{\mathsf{d}_i-1}), \mathsf{rt}]$.
  2. *If* $\mathsf{rt}_i \neq \mathsf{rt}$, *then output* $\perp$.
  3. *If* $\mathsf{id} \neq \mathsf{h}_0^0$, *then output* $\perp$.
  4. *If* $\mathsf{rt} = \mathrm{Hash}(\mathsf{hk}_{\mathsf{d}_i}, \mathsf{h}_{\mathsf{d}_i-1}^0 || \mathsf{h}_{\mathsf{d}_i-1}^1)$ *and* $\mathsf{h}_j^{b_j} = \mathrm{Hash}(\mathsf{hk}_j, \mathsf{h}_{j-1}^0 || \mathsf{h}_{j-1}^1)$ *for* all $j \in [\mathsf{d}_i - 1]$, *then output* $\mathrm{E}(\mathsf{h}_0^1, \mathsf{m}; \mathsf{r})$ *by using* h_0^1 *as the public key and* r *as the randomness, otherwise output* $\perp$.

  Then, output $\mathsf{ct} := (\mathsf{pp}, \mathrm{Obf}(\mathrm{P}_1), \ldots, \mathrm{Obf}(\mathrm{P}_\eta))$ *where* Obf *is* IO *obfuscation.*
- $\mathsf{Upd}^{\mathsf{aux}}(\mathsf{pp}, \mathsf{id}) \to \mathsf{u}$: *Letting* $\mathsf{aux} := (\mathsf{Tree}_1, \ldots, \mathsf{Tree}_\zeta)$ *and letting i be the index of the tree that holds* id, *return the whole Merkle opening of the path that leads to* id *in* Tree_i.
- $\mathsf{Dec}(\mathsf{sk}, \mathsf{u}, \mathsf{ct}) \to \mathsf{m}$: *Parse* $\mathsf{ct} = (\mathsf{pp}, \overline{\mathrm{P}}_1, \ldots, \overline{\mathrm{P}}_\eta)$. *Form* $\mathsf{m}_i = \mathsf{Dec}_{\mathsf{sk}}(\overline{\mathrm{P}}_i(\mathsf{u}))$ *for each program* $\overline{\mathrm{P}}_i$. *Output the first* $\mathsf{m}_i \neq \perp$.

Theorem 13. *The RBE of Construction 12 satisfies the compactness, completeness properties according to Definition 6 and security according to Definition 10.*

In the rest of this section, we prove Theorem 13. Along the way, we describe the modifications that are needed to Construction 12 to make it efficient according to Definition 8.

4.1 Proofs of Completeness, Compactness and Efficiency

Completeness is straightforward. Below we sketch why compactness holds.

Compactness of Public Parameters and Updates. The public parameter's format is of the form $\mathsf{pp} = ((\mathsf{hk}_1, \ldots \mathsf{hk}_\kappa), (\mathsf{rt}_1, \mathsf{d}_1), \ldots (\mathsf{rt}_\eta, \mathsf{d}_\eta))$ where $\mathsf{rt}_i \in \{0,1\}^\kappa$. Also, the identities are of length κ, so the depth of each tree is at most κ bits. It only remains to show that the *number* of trees at any moment is at most $\log(n)$. This is because the trees are *full* binary trees (of size 2^{d_i}) and the size of the trees are always different (otherwise, the registration step keeps merging them). Therefore, $\eta \leq \log(n)$, and so the length of the pp_n will be at most $O(\kappa^2 + \kappa \cdot \log(n))$. In fact, we can optimize this length to be at most $O(\kappa \cdot \log(n))$ by only generating the hash keys when needed (i.e., when the registered population reaches 2^k, we will generate hk_k and put it in the public parameter). Compactness of updates is trivial.

Efficiency of Runtime of Registration and Update. The efficiency of registration follows from the fact that the total number of merges is at most $\log n$. The efficiency of update runtime can also be easily guaranteed by using an appropriate data structure that maps a given identity to the leafs containing it in each tree (e.g., we can use a Trie data structure for this purpose to get such list in minimal time over the input length).

All other measures of efficiency either follows trivially, or by the $\log(n)$ upper-bound on the number of merges.

4.2 Proof of Security

We now prove the security of Construction 12. We start by giving intuition about the security proof for a simple case. We will then give a detailed proof for the general case.

Simple Case of One User. Consider the case in which only one user has registered, and that the adversary wants to distinguish between encryptions of $\mathsf{m} \in \{0,1\}$ made to that user. Let id^* be the identity of the user who has registered, and let $(\mathsf{pk}^*, \mathsf{sk}^*) \leftarrow \mathrm{G}(1^\kappa)$ be the pair of public/secret keys that the challenger Chal produced at the time of registration as per Definition 10. Since we have only one user, the public parameter is $\mathsf{pp} := \mathrm{Hash}(\mathsf{hk}, \mathsf{id}^*||\mathsf{pk}^*)$, where $\mathsf{hk} \leftarrow \mathrm{HGen}(1^\kappa, 0)$. Recall that w.l.o.g., we have $|\mathsf{id}^*| = |\mathsf{pk}^*| = |\mathsf{pp}| = \kappa$.

An encryption of a bit $\mathsf{m} \in \{0,1\}$ to identity id^* is an IO obfuscation of the circuit P in Fig. 1.

Hardwired: $\mathsf{m} \in \{0,1\}$, id^*, pp, hk and randomness r

Input: $(\mathsf{id}, \mathsf{pk})$

1. If $\mathrm{Hash}(\mathsf{hk}, \mathsf{id}||\mathsf{pk}) \neq \mathsf{pp}$, then output $\perp$ and end.
2. If $\mathsf{id} \neq \mathsf{id}^*$, then output $\perp$ and end.
3. Output $\mathrm{E}(\mathsf{pk}, \mathsf{m}; \mathsf{r})$ and end.

Fig. 1. Circuit P used for encryption of m to identity id^*

Theorem 14 (Security). *For any* id^* *we have*

$$\mathrm{Obf}(\mathrm{P}[0, \mathsf{id}^*, \mathsf{pp}, \mathsf{hk}, \mathsf{r}]) \stackrel{c}{\approx} \mathrm{Obf}(\mathrm{P}[1, \mathsf{id}^*, \mathsf{pp}, \mathsf{hk}, \mathsf{r}]), \tag{1}$$

for $(\mathsf{pk}^*, \mathsf{sk}^*) \leftarrow \mathrm{G}(1^\kappa)$, $\mathsf{hk} \leftarrow \mathrm{HGen}(1^\kappa, 0)$, $\mathsf{pp} := \mathrm{Hash}(\mathsf{hk}, \mathsf{id}^*||\mathsf{pk}^*)$, $\mathsf{r} \leftarrow \{0,1\}^*$.

Roadmap for the Proof of Theorem 14. We first alter the circuit P to obtain a circuit P_1, which works similarly except that P_1 checks whether or not its given input path is exactly $(\mathsf{id}^*, \mathsf{pk}^*)$ (i.e., the already registered identity along with its public key); if not, P_1 will return $\perp$, even if the two leaves $(\mathsf{id}, \mathsf{pk})$ correctly hashe to pp. If yes, P_1 will encrypt the hardwired bit m under the public key pk^* and the hardwired randomness r. The circuit P_1 is defined in Fig. 2.

Equipped with this new circuit P_1, first in Lemma 15 we show that under P_1 we may switch the underlying hardwired plaintext bit m from 0 to 1 while keeping the obfuscations of the resulting circuits indistinguishable. Then, in Lemma 16 we will show that for any fixed plaintext bit m, the obfuscations of P and P_1 are computationally indistinguishable. These two lemmas imply Theorem 14.

> **Hardwired:** $\mathsf{m} \in \{0,1\}$, id^*, pk^*, pp, hk and randomness r
> **Input:** $(\mathsf{id}, \mathsf{pk})$
> 1. If $(\mathsf{id}, \mathsf{pk}) \neq (\mathsf{id}^*, \mathsf{pk}^*)$, then output $\perp$ and end.
> 2. Output $\mathrm{E}(\mathsf{pk}, \mathsf{m}; \mathsf{r})$ and end.

Fig. 2. Circuit P_1

We start by defining the circuit P_1, which is a modified version of P.

We now formally show that under P_1 we may switch the underlying plaintext bit while keeping their obfuscations indistinguishable.

Lemma 15. *For any* id^* *and* hk *we have*

$$\mathrm{Obf}(\mathrm{P}_1[0, \mathsf{id}^*, \mathsf{pk}^*, \mathsf{pp}, \mathsf{hk}, \mathsf{r}]) \overset{c}{\approx} \mathrm{Obf}(\mathrm{P}_1[1, \mathsf{id}^*, \mathsf{pk}^*, \mathsf{pp}, \mathsf{hk}, \mathsf{r}]), \tag{2}$$

where $(\mathsf{pk}^*, \mathsf{sk}^*) \leftarrow \mathrm{G}(1^\kappa)$, $\mathsf{r} \leftarrow \{0,1\}^*$ *and* $\mathsf{pp} := \mathrm{Hash}(\mathsf{hk}, \mathsf{id}^* || \mathsf{pk}^*)$.

Proof. Fix id^* and hk. We slightly change the circuit P_1 into a circuit P_2, so that the circuit P_2, instead of getting m, pk^* and r hardwired into itself, it gets the resulting ciphertext c^* hardwired, and it will return this ciphertext if the check inside the program holds. This new circuit P_2 is defined in Fig. 3.

Notice that for all fixed $\mathsf{m} \in \{0,1\}$, id^*, pk^*, r and $\mathsf{pp} := \mathrm{Hash}(\mathsf{hk}, \mathsf{id}^* || \mathsf{pk}^*)$,

$$\mathrm{Obf}(\mathrm{P}_1[\mathsf{m}, \mathsf{id}^*, \mathsf{pk}^*, \mathsf{pp}, \mathsf{hk}, \mathsf{r}]) \overset{c}{\approx} \mathrm{Obf}(\mathrm{P}_2[\mathsf{id}^*, \mathsf{pp}, \mathsf{hk}, \mathsf{c}^*]), \tag{3}$$

where $\mathsf{c}^* := \mathrm{E}(\mathsf{pk}^*, \mathsf{m}; \mathsf{r})$. The reason behind Eq. 3 is that the underlying two circuits are functionally equivalent, and so their obfuscations must be computationally indistinguishable by the property of IO.

We now show that under P_2 we may switch the hardwired ciphertext from an encryption of zero to one, by relying on semantic security of the PKE. Formally,

$$\mathrm{Obf}(\mathrm{P}_2[\mathsf{id}^*, \mathsf{pp}, \mathsf{hk}, \mathsf{c}_0^*]) \overset{c}{\approx} \mathrm{Obf}(\mathrm{P}_2[\mathsf{id}^*, \mathsf{pp}, \mathsf{hk}, \mathsf{c}_1^*]), \tag{4}$$

for $(\mathsf{pk}^*, \mathsf{sk}^*) \leftarrow \mathrm{G}(1^\kappa)$, $\mathsf{c}_0^* \leftarrow \mathrm{E}(\mathsf{pk}^*, 0)$, $\mathsf{c}_1^* \leftarrow \mathrm{E}(\mathsf{pk}^*, 1)$, $\mathsf{pp} := \mathrm{Hash}(\mathsf{hk}, \mathsf{id}^* || \mathsf{pk}^*)$. Equation 4 directly follows from the semantic security of the underlying public-key encryption scheme. Finally, note that Eqs. 4 and 3 imply Eq. 2 of the lemma, and so we are done. □

We now show that for any fixed plaintext $\mathsf{m} \in \{0,1\}$, the obfuscations of the two circuits P and P_1 are computationally indistinguishable.

Lemma 16. *For fixed* $\mathsf{m} \in \{0,1\}, \mathsf{id}^* \in \{0,1\}^\kappa, \mathsf{pk}^* \in \{0,1\}^\kappa$ *and randomness* r, *it holds that*

$$\mathrm{Obf}(\mathrm{P}[\mathsf{m}, \mathsf{id}^*, \mathsf{pp}, \mathsf{hk}, \mathsf{r}]) \overset{c}{\approx} \mathrm{Obf}(\mathrm{P}_1[\mathsf{m}, \mathsf{id}^*, \mathsf{pk}^*, \mathsf{pp}, \mathsf{hk}, \mathsf{r}]), \tag{5}$$

where $\mathsf{hk} \leftarrow \mathrm{HGen}(1^\kappa, 0)$ *and* $\mathsf{pp} := \mathrm{Hash}(\mathsf{hk}, \mathsf{id}^* || \mathsf{pk}^*)$.

Hardwired: id^*, pp, hk and c^*

Input: $(\mathsf{id}, \mathsf{pk})$

1. If $(\mathsf{id}, \mathsf{pk}) \neq (\mathsf{id}^*, \mathsf{pk}^*)$, then output $\perp$ and end.
2. Output c^* and end.

Fig. 3. Circuit P_2

Proof. Let a hash key hk_1 be sampled as follows: $\mathsf{hk}_1 \leftarrow \mathrm{HGen}(1^\kappa, 1)$. We show that Eq. 5 will hold if hk is replaced with hk_1. This will complete our proof because by the index hiding property of (HGen, Hash) we know $\mathsf{hk} \stackrel{c}{\approx} \mathsf{hk}_1$. Thus, it only remains to prove

$$\mathrm{Obf}(\mathrm{P}[\mathsf{m}, \mathsf{id}^*, \mathsf{pk}^*, \mathsf{pp}, \mathsf{hk}_1, \mathsf{r}]) \stackrel{c}{\approx} \mathrm{Obf}(\mathrm{P}_1[\mathsf{m}, \mathsf{id}^*, \mathsf{pk}^*, \mathsf{pp}, \mathsf{hk}_1, \mathsf{r}]), \tag{6}$$

where $\mathsf{hk}_1 \leftarrow \mathrm{HGen}(1^\kappa, 1)$ and $\mathsf{pp} := \mathrm{Hash}(\mathsf{hk}_1, \mathsf{id}^* || \mathsf{pk}^*)$. To prove Eq. 6 we claim that the underlying two circuits are functionally equivalent; namely,

$$\mathrm{P}[\mathsf{m}, \mathsf{id}^*, \mathsf{pk}^*, \mathsf{pp}, \mathsf{hk}_1, \mathsf{r}] \equiv \mathrm{P}_1[\mathsf{m}, \mathsf{id}^*, \mathsf{pk}^*, \mathsf{pp}, \mathsf{hk}_1, \mathsf{r}]. \tag{7}$$

Note that by security definition of IO, Eq. 7 implies Eq. 6, and thus we just need to prove Eq. 7. To prove equivalence of the circuits, assume to the contrary that there exists an input $(\mathsf{id}, \mathsf{pk})$ for which we have $\mathrm{P}(\mathsf{id}, \mathsf{pk}) \neq \mathrm{P}_1(\mathsf{id}, \mathsf{pk})$. (Here for better readability we dropped the hardwired values.) By simple inspection, we can see that we have $\mathrm{P}(\mathsf{id}, \mathsf{pk}) \neq \mathrm{P}_1(\mathsf{id}, \mathsf{pk})$ iff all the following conditions hold:

1. $\mathrm{Hash}(\mathsf{hk}_1, (\mathsf{id}, \mathsf{pk})) = \mathsf{pp}$; and
2. $\mathsf{id} = \mathsf{id}^*$; and
3. $\mathsf{pk} \neq \mathsf{pk}^*$.

This, however, is a contradiction because by the somewhere statistical binding property of (HGen, Hash) and by the fact that $\mathsf{hk}_1 \leftarrow \mathrm{HGen}(1^\kappa, 1)$, Conditions 1 and 2 imply $\mathsf{pk} = \mathsf{pk}^*$, a contradiction to Condition 3. □

General Case of Multiple Users. We will prove our security for the case in which at the time of encryption, we only have one tree (of any arbitrary depth). This is without loss of generality for the following reason. Recall that for encryption, if we have m roots, we obfuscate a circuit individually for each root. Suppose at the time of encryption, we have m trees with respective roots $\mathsf{rt}_1, \ldots, \mathsf{rt}_m$. Then, between the two main hybrids which correspond to an encryption of zero and an encryption of one, we may consider m intermediate hybrids, where under the ith hybrid we encrypt 0 under the roots $\{\mathsf{rt}_1, \ldots, \mathsf{rt}_i\}$ and we encrypt 1 under the roots $\{\mathsf{rt}_{i+1}, \ldots, \mathsf{rt}_m\}$. Thus, using a hybrid argument, the result will follow.

Roadmap of the Security Proof. We will define four hybrids, where the first hybrid corresponds to an encryption of bit 0 and the last hybrid corresponds to an encryption of bit 1. We will prove that the views of the adversary in each of the two adjacent hybrids are computationally indistinguishable.

High-Level Proof Sketch. Let Tree be the underlying tree at the time of encryption. An encryption of a bit m to an identity id corresponds to an IO obfuscation of a circuit P, which takes as input a path, and which will release an encryption of m under a public key given as a leaf of the path, if the given path is "valid." As a hybrid, we will consider a circuit P_1, which does all the checks that are already performed by P, but which also does the following: if the given path is not *present* in the tree, then P_1 will return $\perp$, even if the path is valid. We will show that for any fixed bit m, if we encrypt m by obfuscating either the circuit P or P_1, the result will be indistinguishable. We will make use of the somewhere statistical binding and index hiding of the underlying hash function in order to prove this. Now under an obfuscation of P_1, one may easily switch the hardwired plaintext bit. The reason is that since under P_1, a given input path to the circuit must be present in the tree, and since the challenge identity id^* is registered only once (say under a public key pk), one may consider a related circuit which, instead of hardwiring a plaintext bit m, it hardwires into itself an encryption $c \leftarrow \mathrm{E}(\mathsf{pk}, \mathsf{m})$. The rest follows by semantic security of the PKE scheme.

We now go over the formal proof. We start by defining some notation.

Notation. Consider a path $\mathsf{pth} := [(\mathsf{id}, \mathsf{pk}), (\mathsf{h}_1^0, \mathsf{h}_1^1, b_1), \ldots, (\mathsf{h}_{t-1}^0, \mathsf{h}_{t-1}^1, b_{t-1}), \mathsf{rt}]$ where rt is the root and id and pk are the two leaves and $b_1, \ldots, b_{t-1} \in \{\mathsf{left}, \mathsf{right}\}$. For a tree Tree of depth t, we write $\mathsf{pth} \subseteq \mathsf{Tree}$ if pth is a valid path in Tree in the usual sense. The procedure $\mathrm{Valid}(\mathsf{hk}_1, \ldots, \mathsf{hk}_t, \mathsf{pth})$ checks if the given path is a 'valid path' according to the given hash keys $\mathsf{hk}_1, \ldots, \mathsf{hk}_t$ then it output $\top$, otherwise outputs $\perp$. For a path pth and integer i we write $\mathrm{Last}(\mathsf{pth}, i)$ to refer to the last i node "elements" in pth. Note that we do not consider the left-or-right bits as part of this counting. For example, letting pth be as above,

$$\mathrm{Last}(\mathsf{pth}, 5) = ((\mathsf{h}_{t-2}^0, \mathsf{h}_{t-1}^1, b_{t-2}), (\mathsf{h}_{t-1}^0, \mathsf{h}_{t-1}^1, b_{t-1}), \mathsf{rt}).$$

We also extend the notation $\subseteq$ given above to define $\mathrm{Last}(\mathsf{pth}, i) \subseteq \mathsf{Tree}$ in the straightforward way (Figs. 4 and 5).

Notation Used in Hybrids. We will write $\mathsf{id}^* \leftarrow \mathsf{Adv}(\mathsf{hk}_1, \ldots, \mathsf{hk}_\kappa)$ to mean that the adversary Adv receives $\mathsf{pp} := (\mathsf{hk}_1, \ldots, \mathsf{hk}_\kappa)$ as input, interacts with the challenger Chal as per Definition 10 and outputs id^* as the challenge identity.

- **Hybrid $\mathbf{H}_1$: Encrypt $\mathsf{m} = 0$ using** P. The ciphertext ct given to the adversary is formed as follows.
  1. For $j \in [\kappa]$ sample $\mathsf{hk}_j \leftarrow \mathrm{HGen}(1^\kappa, 0)$.
  2. $\mathsf{id}^* \leftarrow \mathsf{Adv}(\mathsf{hk}_1, \ldots, \mathsf{hk}_\kappa)$.
  3. $\mathsf{ct} \leftarrow \mathrm{Obf}(\mathrm{P}[0, \mathsf{id}^*, \mathsf{rt}, \mathsf{hk}_1, \ldots, \mathsf{hk}_t, r])$, where rt is the root of the tree, t is the depth of the tree, and $\mathsf{r} \leftarrow \{0,1\}^*$.

Hardwired: $\mathsf{m} \in \{0,1\}$, id^*, rt, $\mathsf{hk}_1, \ldots, \mathsf{hk}_t$ and randomness r
Input: $\mathsf{pth} := [(\mathsf{id}, \mathsf{pk}), (\mathsf{h}_1^0, \mathsf{h}_1^1, b_1), \ldots, (\mathsf{h}_{t-1}^0, \mathsf{h}_{t-1}^1, b_t), \mathsf{rt}']$

1. If $\mathsf{id} \neq \mathsf{id}^*$, $\mathsf{rt} \neq \mathsf{rt}'$ or $\mathrm{Valid}(\mathsf{hk}_1, \ldots, \mathsf{hk}_t, \mathsf{pth}) \neq \top$, then output $\perp$ and end.
2. Output $\mathrm{E}(\mathsf{pk}, \mathsf{m}; \mathsf{r})$.

Fig. 4. Circuit P

Circuit P_1
Hardwired: $\mathsf{m} \in \{0,1\}$, id^*, $\mathsf{pth}^*, \mathsf{rt}$, $\mathsf{hk}_1, \ldots, \mathsf{hk}_t$ and randomness r
Input: $\mathsf{pth} := [(\mathsf{id}, \mathsf{pk}), (\mathsf{h}_1^0, \mathsf{h}_1^1, b_1), \ldots, (\mathsf{h}_{t-1}^0, \mathsf{h}_{t-1}^1, b_t), \mathsf{rt}']$

1. If $\mathsf{pth} = \mathsf{pth}^*$, then output $\mathrm{E}(\mathsf{pk}, \mathsf{m}; \mathsf{r})$ and end.
2. Else, output $\perp$ and end.

Fig. 5. Circuit P_1

- **Hybrid $\mathbf{H}_2$: Encrypt $\mathsf{m} = 0$ using P_1.** The ciphertext ct given to the adversary is formed as follows.
  1. For $j \in [\kappa]$ sample $\mathsf{hk}_j \leftarrow \mathrm{HGen}(1^\kappa, 0)$.
  2. $\mathsf{id}^* \leftarrow \mathsf{Adv}^{\mathsf{Reg}_{\mathsf{sel}}, \mathsf{Reg}_{\mathsf{smp}}}(\mathsf{hk}_1, \ldots, \mathsf{hk}_\kappa)$.
  3. $\mathsf{ct} \leftarrow \mathrm{Obf}(\mathrm{P}_1[0, \mathsf{id}^*, \mathsf{pth}^*, \mathsf{rt}, \mathsf{hk}_1, \ldots, \mathsf{hk}_t, r])$, where pth^* is the path in the tree leading to the challenge node, rt is the root of pth^*, t is the depth of the tree, and $\mathsf{r} \leftarrow \{0,1\}^*$.
- **Hybrid $\mathbf{H}_3$: Encrypt $\mathsf{m} = 1$ using P_1.** The ciphertext ct given to the adversary is formed as follows.
  1. For $j \in [\kappa]$ sample $\mathsf{hk}_j \leftarrow \mathrm{HGen}(1^\kappa, 0)$.
  2. $\mathsf{id}^* \leftarrow \mathsf{Adv}(\mathsf{hk}_1, \ldots, \mathsf{hk}_\kappa)$.
  3. $\mathsf{ct} \leftarrow \mathrm{Obf}(\mathrm{P}_1[1, \mathsf{id}^*, \mathsf{pth}^*, \mathsf{rt}, \mathsf{hk}_1, \ldots, \mathsf{hk}_t, r])$, where pth^* is the path in the tree leading to the challenge node, rt is the root of pth^*, t is the depth of the tree, and $\mathsf{r} \leftarrow \{0,1\}^*$.
- **Hybrid $\mathbf{H}_4$: Encrypt $\mathsf{m} = 1$ using P.** The ciphertext ct given to the adversary is formed as follows.
  1. For $j \in [\kappa]$ sample $\mathsf{hk}_j \leftarrow \mathrm{HGen}(1^\kappa, 0)$.
  2. $\mathsf{id}^* \leftarrow \mathsf{Adv}(\mathsf{hk}_1, \ldots, \mathsf{hk}_\kappa)$.
  3. $\mathsf{ct} \leftarrow \mathrm{Obf}(\mathrm{P}[1, \mathsf{id}^*, \mathsf{rt}, \mathsf{hk}_1, \ldots, \mathsf{hk}_t, r])$, where rt is the root of the underlying tree, t is the depth of the tree, and $\mathsf{r} \leftarrow \{0,1\}^*$.

Notation. We use $\mathsf{ct}\langle \mathbf{H}_i \rangle$ to denote the value of the ciphertext ct in Hybrid $\mathbf{H}_i$.

Lemma 17. *We have,*

1. $\mathsf{ct}\langle \boldsymbol{H}_1\rangle \overset{c}{\approx} \mathsf{ct}\langle \boldsymbol{H}_2\rangle$,
2. $\mathsf{ct}\langle \boldsymbol{H}_3\rangle \overset{c}{\approx} \mathsf{ct}\langle \boldsymbol{H}_4\rangle$.

Proof. We will prove Part 1, and the proof for Part 2 will be exactly the same.

Recall that in hybrid $\mathbf{H}_1$ we encrypt $\mathsf{m} = 0$ by obfuscating P and that in hybrid $\mathbf{H}_2$ we encrypt $\mathsf{m} = 0$ by obfuscating P_1. Let t be the depth of the tree at the time of encryption.

We will define intermediate hybrids $\mathrm{P}_{2,i}$ for $i \in [2t+1]$, and we will show $\mathrm{P} \equiv \mathrm{P}_{2,1}$, $\mathrm{P}_1 \equiv \mathrm{P}_{2,2t+1}$ and for all $i \in [2t]$, $\mathrm{Obf}[\mathrm{P}_{2,i}] \overset{c}{\approx} \mathrm{Obf}[\mathrm{P}_{2,i+1}]$. These circuit programs are given in Fig. 6.

Informally, the program $\mathrm{P}_{2,i}$ works as follows: it checks whether its given path is "correct" and whether, in addition, the last i elements of the path are in accordance with the challenge path pth^* that was hardwired into the program. For example, if $i = 5$, then the root of the path and the two levels below it (five nodes in total) should match the corresponding nodes in the challenge path pth^*. If both these conditions hold, then $\mathrm{P}_{2,i}$ will encrypt the hardwired plaintext bit ($\mathsf{m} = 0$) using the public key provided in the corresponding leave of the path.

We will now define a Hybrid $\mathbf{H}_{2,i}$ below, which uses program $\mathrm{P}_{2,i}$.

- **Hybrid $\mathbf{H}_{2,i}$: Encrypt $\mathsf{m} = 0$ using $\mathrm{P}_{2,i}$.** The given ciphertext ct is as:
  1. For $j \in [\kappa]$ sample $\mathsf{hk}_j \leftarrow \mathrm{HGen}(1^\kappa, 0)$.
  2. $\mathsf{id}^* \leftarrow \mathsf{Adv}(\mathsf{hk}_1, \dots, \mathsf{hk}_\kappa)$.
  3. $\mathsf{ct} \leftarrow \mathrm{Obf}(\mathrm{P}_{2,i}[0, \mathsf{id}^*, \mathsf{pth}^*, \mathsf{rt}, \mathsf{hk}_1, \dots, \mathsf{hk}_t, r])$, where pth^* is the challenge path in the system, rt is the root of pth^*, t is the depth of the tree, and $r \leftarrow \{0,1\}^*$.

First, by inspection we can see that $\mathsf{ct}\langle \mathbf{H}_1\rangle \overset{c}{\approx} \mathsf{ct}\langle \mathbf{H}_{2,1}\rangle$ and $\mathsf{ct}\langle \mathbf{H}_2\rangle \overset{c}{\approx} \mathsf{ct}\langle \mathbf{H}_{2,2t+1}\rangle$. This is because the underlying two circuits P and $\mathrm{P}_{2,1}$ are functionally equivalent. Same holds for P_1 and $\mathrm{P}_{2,2t+1}$.

Thus, for any fixed $w \in [2t]$ we just need to prove

$$\mathsf{ct}\langle \mathbf{H}_{2,w}\rangle = \mathsf{ct}\langle \mathbf{H}_{2,w+1}\rangle. \tag{8}$$

Below, we fix $w \in [2t]$. To prove Eq. 8, we introduce two hybrids $\mathbf{H}'_{2,w}, \mathbf{H}'_{2,w+1}$ and show

$$\mathsf{ct}\langle \mathbf{H}_{2,w}\rangle \overset{c}{\approx} \mathsf{ct}\langle \mathbf{H}'_{2,w}\rangle \overset{c}{\approx} \mathsf{ct}\langle \mathbf{H}'_{2,w+1}\rangle \overset{c}{\approx} \mathsf{ct}\langle \mathbf{H}_{2,w+1}\rangle. \tag{9}$$

This will establish Eq. 8.

Informally, the hybrids $\mathbf{H}'_{2,w}$ and $\mathbf{H}'_{2,w+1}$ are defined similarly to $\mathbf{H}_{2,w}$ and $\mathbf{H}_{2,w+1}$, except that one of the many hash keys is now sampled in a different way, in order to make some binding property happen.

For $z \in \{w, w+1\}$, the hybrid $\mathbf{H}'_{2,z}$ is defined as follows.

- **Hybrid $\mathbf{H}'_{2,z}$ for $z \in \{w, w+1\}$.** The given ciphertext ct is formed as follows.

1. Let $q := t - \lfloor \frac{w}{2} \rfloor - 1$ Intuitively, q denotes the level index in the tree for which we want to use a different hash key. For all $i \in [\kappa] \setminus \{q\}$: sample $\mathsf{hk}'_i \leftarrow \mathrm{HGen}(1^\kappa, 0)$. Sample

$$\mathsf{hk}'_q \leftarrow \mathrm{HGen}(1^\kappa, v), \text{ where } v := (w+1) \bmod 2.$$

2. $\mathsf{id}_1^* \leftarrow \mathsf{Adv}(\mathsf{hk}'_1, \ldots, \mathsf{hk}'_\kappa)$.
3. $\mathsf{ct} \leftarrow \mathrm{Obf}(\mathrm{P}_{2,i}[0, \mathsf{id}_1^*, \mathsf{pth}_1^*, \mathsf{rt}_1, \mathsf{hk}'_1, \ldots, \mathsf{hk}'_t, r])$, where pth_1^* is the challenge path in the system, rt_1 is the root of pth^* and $\mathsf{r} \leftarrow \{0,1\}^*$.

Toward proving Eq. 9, first note that by the index hiding property of (HGen, Hash) we have $\mathsf{ct}\langle \mathbf{H}_{2,w} \rangle \overset{c}{\approx} \mathsf{ct}\langle \mathbf{H}'_{2,w} \rangle$ and $\mathsf{ct}\langle \mathbf{H}_{2,w+1} \rangle \overset{c}{\approx} \mathsf{ct}\langle \mathbf{H}'_{2,w+1} \rangle$. Thus, it remains to prove

$$\mathsf{ct}\langle \mathbf{H}'_{2,w} \rangle \overset{c}{\approx} \mathsf{ct}\langle \mathbf{H}'_{2,w+1} \rangle. \tag{10}$$

To prove Eq. 10, we claim that the underlying two programs are equivalent; namely,

$$\mathrm{P}_{2,w}[0, \mathsf{id}_1^*, \mathsf{pth}_1^*, \mathsf{rt}_1, \mathsf{hk}'_1, .., \mathsf{hk}'_t, r] = \mathrm{P}_{2,w+1}[0, \mathsf{id}_1^*, \mathsf{pth}_1^*, \mathsf{rt}_1, \mathsf{hk}'_1, .., \mathsf{hk}'_t, r]. \tag{11}$$

By IO security, Eq. 11 implies Eq. 10, and thus we just need to prove Eq. 11. To prove equivalence of the two circuits in Eq. 11, assume to the contrary that there exists an input pth for which we have $\mathrm{P}_{2,w}(\mathsf{pth}) \neq \mathrm{P}_{2,w+1}(\mathsf{pth})$. (Here for better readability we dropped the hardwired values.) By simple inspection we can see that we have $\mathrm{P}_{2,w}(\mathsf{pth}) \neq \mathrm{P}_{2,w+1}(\mathsf{pth})$ iff all the following conditions hold:

1. $\mathsf{Valid}(\mathsf{hk}'_1, \ldots, \mathsf{hk}'_t, \mathsf{pth}) = \top$; and
2. $\mathsf{Last}(\mathsf{pth}, w) \subseteq \mathsf{pth}_1^*$; and
3. $\mathsf{Last}(\mathsf{pth}, w+1) \not\subseteq \mathsf{pth}_1^*$.

This, however, is a contradiction because by the somewhere statistical binding property of (KGen, Hash) and by the way in which we have sampled hk'_q, Conditions 1 and 2 contradict Condition 3. □

Description of Circuit $\mathrm{P}_{2,i}$.

Hardwired: $\mathsf{m} \in \{0,1\}$, id^*, $\mathsf{pth}^*, \mathsf{rt}, \mathsf{hk}_1, \ldots, \mathsf{hk}_t$ and randomness r

Input: $\mathsf{pth} := [(\mathsf{id}, \mathsf{pk}), (\mathsf{h}_1^0, \mathsf{h}_1^1, b_1), \ldots, (\mathsf{h}_{t-1}^0, \mathsf{h}_{t-1}^1, b_t), \mathsf{rt}']$

1. If $\mathsf{id} \neq \mathsf{id}^*$ or $\mathsf{rt} \neq \mathsf{rt}'$ or $\mathrm{Valid}(\mathsf{hk}_1, \ldots, \mathsf{hk}_t, \mathsf{pth}) \neq \top$, then output $\perp$ and end.
2. If $\mathrm{Last}(\mathsf{pth}, i) \subseteq \mathsf{pth}^*$, then output $\mathrm{E}(\mathsf{pk}, \mathsf{m}; \mathsf{r})$ and end.
3. Otherwise, output $\perp$ and end.

Fig. 6. Circuit $\mathrm{P}_{2,i}$ for $i \in [\ell]$

Lemma 18. $\mathsf{ct}\langle \boldsymbol{H}_2 \rangle \overset{c}{\approx} \mathsf{ct}\langle \boldsymbol{H}_3 \rangle$.

Proof. The proof is similar to the proof of Lemma 15. □

5 Basing Weakly-Efficient RBE on Standard Assumptions

In this section, we describe our construction of RBE based on *hash garbling* and is inspired by our IO based construction from previous section. This notion and its construction has been implicit in prior works [7,11], and it was shown [4,11,12] that hash garbling can be realized based on CDH, Factoring or LWE assumptions. Specifically, implicit in these prior works are constructions of hash garbling based on hash encryption and garbled circuits. Below, we abstract out this notion and use it in our work directly. This abstract primitive significantly simplifies exposition.

Definition 19 (Hash garbling). *A* hash garbling *scheme consists of four PPT algorithms* HGen, Hash, HG, *and* HInp, *defined as follows.*

- $\mathrm{HGen}(1^\kappa, 1^\ell) \to \mathsf{hk}$. *This algorithm takes the security parameter* κ *and an output length parameter* 1^ℓ *for* $\ell \le \mathrm{poly}(\kappa)$, *and outputs a hash key* hk. *(*HGen *runs in* $\mathrm{poly}(\kappa)$ *time.)*
- $\mathrm{Hash}(\mathsf{hk}, x) = y$. *This takes* hk *and* $x \in \{0,1\}^\ell$ *and outputs* $y \in \{0,1\}^\kappa$.
- $\mathrm{HG}(\mathsf{hk}, \mathrm{C}, \mathsf{stt}) \to \widetilde{\mathrm{C}}$. *This algorithm takes a hash key* hk, *a circuit* C, *and a secret state* $\mathsf{stt} \in \{0,1\}^\kappa$ *as input and outputs a circuit* $\widetilde{\mathrm{C}}$.
- $\mathrm{HInp}(\mathsf{hk}, y, \mathsf{stt}) \to \widetilde{y}$. *This algorithm takes a hash key* hk, *a value* $y \in \{0,1\}^\kappa$, *and a secret state* stt *as input and outputs* $\widetilde{y}$.

We require the following properties for a hash garbling scheme:

- **Correctness.** *For all* κ, ℓ, $\mathsf{hk} \leftarrow \mathrm{HGen}(1^\kappa, 1^\ell)$, *circuit* C, *input* $x \in \{0,1\}^\ell$, $\mathsf{stt} \in \{0,1\}^\kappa$, $\widetilde{\mathrm{C}} \leftarrow \mathrm{HG}(\mathsf{hk}, \mathrm{C}, \mathsf{stt})$ *and* $\widetilde{y} \leftarrow \mathrm{HInp}(\mathsf{hk}, \mathrm{Hash}(\mathsf{hk}, x), \mathsf{stt})$, *then* $\widetilde{\mathrm{C}}(\widetilde{y}, x) = \mathrm{C}(x)$.
- **Security.** *There exists a PPT simulator* Sim *such that for all* κ, ℓ *(recall that* ℓ *is polynomial in* κ*) and PPT (in* κ*)* $\mathcal{A}$ *we have that*

$$(\mathsf{hk}, x, \widetilde{C}, \widetilde{y}) \overset{c}{\approx} (\mathsf{hk}, x, \mathsf{Sim}(\mathsf{hk}, x, 1^{|\mathrm{C}|}, \mathrm{C}(x))), \text{ where}$$

$\mathsf{hk} \leftarrow \mathrm{HGen}(1^\kappa, 1^\ell)$, $(\mathrm{C}, x) \leftarrow \mathcal{A}(\mathsf{hk})$, $\mathsf{stt} \leftarrow \{0,1\}^\kappa$, $\widetilde{\mathrm{C}} \leftarrow \mathrm{HG}(\mathsf{hk}, \mathrm{C}, \mathsf{stt})$ *and* $\widetilde{y} \leftarrow \mathrm{HInp}(\mathsf{hk}, \mathrm{Hash}(\mathsf{hk}, x), \mathsf{stt})$.

Notation on Binary Trees. Just like the IO construction, in our construction below, Tree is a *full* binary tree where the label of each node in Tree is calculated as the hash of its left and right children and, now additionally, with an an extra identity. Looking ahead, this identity will be the largest identity among the users registered in the left child. (Such information is useful if one wants to a binary search of an identity over this tree.) Just as in the IO-based construction, we define the size of a tree Tree as the number of its *leaves*, denoted by size(Tree), and we denote the root of Tree as rt(Tree), and use d(Tree) to refer to the depth of Tree. Again, when Tree is clear from the context, we use rt and d to denote the root and the depth of Tree.

Before describing the construction, recall that without loss of generality, we can assume that public keys, secret keys, and identities, are all of length security parameter κ.

Comparison with Construction 12 Using Signs *(=)* and *(⋆⋆)*. To help the reader familiar with Construction 12, we have denoted the steps that are identical to Construction 12 by *(=)* and the steps that are significantly *different* by *(⋆⋆)*. Other steps are close but not identical.

Construction 20 (Construction of RBE from hash garbling). *We will use a hash garbling scheme* (HGen, Hash, HG, HInp) *and a public key encryption scheme* (G, E, D). *Using them we show how to implement the subroutines of RBE according to Definition 4.*

- $\mathsf{Stp}(1^\kappa) \rightarrow (\mathsf{pp}_0)$, *where* $\mathsf{pp}_0 = \mathsf{hk}$ *is sampled from* $\mathrm{HGen}(1^\kappa, 1^{3\kappa})$.
- $\mathsf{Reg}^{[\mathsf{aux}]}(\mathsf{pp}_n, \mathsf{id}, \mathsf{pk}) \rightarrow \mathsf{pp}_{n+1}$. *This algorithm works as follows:*
  1. (=) *Parse* $\mathsf{aux}_n := (\{\mathsf{Tree}_1, \ldots, \mathsf{Tree}_\eta\}), (\mathsf{id}_1, \ldots, \mathsf{id}_n))$ *where the trees have corresponding depths* $\mathsf{d}_1 > \mathsf{d}_2 \cdots > \mathsf{d}_\eta$, *and* $(\mathsf{id}_1, \ldots, \mathsf{id}_n)$ *is the order the identities registered.*[8]
  2. *Parse* pp_n *as a sequence* $(\mathsf{hk}, (\mathsf{rt}_1, \mathsf{d}_1), \ldots, (\mathsf{rt}_\eta, \mathsf{d}_\eta))$ *where* $\mathsf{rt}_i \in \{0,1\}^\kappa$ *represents the root of tree* Tree_i *and* d_i *represents the depth of* Tree_i.
  3. *Create a new tree* $\mathsf{Tree}_{\eta+1}$ *with leaves* id, pk *and set its root as* $\mathsf{rt}_{\eta+1} \leftarrow \mathsf{Hash}(\mathsf{hk}, \mathsf{id}||\mathsf{pk}||0^\kappa)$ *and thus its depth would be* $\mathsf{d}_{\eta+1} = 1$.
  4. (=) *Let* $\mathcal{T} = \{\mathsf{Tree}_1, \ldots, \mathsf{Tree}_{\eta+1}\}$. *(We will keep changing* $\mathcal{T}$ *in step below.)*
  5. *While there are two different trees* $\mathsf{Tree}_L, \mathsf{Tree}_R \in \mathcal{T}$ *of the same depth* d *and size* $s = 2^{\mathsf{d}}$ *(recall that our trees are always full binary trees).*
     (a) *Obtain new* Tree *of depth* $d+1$ *by merging the two trees* Tree_L *and* Tree_R *as follows.*
     (b) (⋆⋆) *Let* $\mathsf{id}_1 \ldots \mathsf{id}_{n'}$ *and* $\mathsf{pk}_1 \ldots \mathsf{pk}_{n'}$ *be the identities and public keys of* n' *users in both trees* Tree_L *and* Tree_R *combined in* sorted order *according to identities.*
     (c) *For each* $i \in [n']$, *let* $h_{0,i} := \mathsf{Hash}(\mathsf{hk}, \mathsf{id}_i||\mathsf{pk}_i||0^\kappa)$.
     (d) (⋆⋆) *Next for each* $j \in \{1, \ldots \log n'\}$ *and* $k \in \{0, \ldots, (n'/2^j) - 1\}$, *let*

$$h_{j,k} = \mathsf{Hash}(\mathsf{hk}, h_{j-1,2k}||h_{j-1,2k+1}||\mathsf{id}[j,k])$$

     where $\mathsf{id}[j,k]$ *is the largest identity in the left child (which is the node with label* $h_{j-1,2k}$*); namely* $\mathsf{id}[j,k] = \mathsf{id}_{(2k+1)\cdot 2^{j-1}}$. *This completes the description of* Tree.
     (e) (=) *Remove both of* $\mathsf{Tree}_L, \mathsf{Tree}_R$ *from* $\mathcal{T}$ *and add* Tree *to* $\mathcal{T}$ *instead.*

[8] Keeping this list is not necessary, but simplifies the presentation of the updates.

6. *Let* $\mathcal{T} = \{\mathsf{Tree}_1, \ldots, \mathsf{Tree}_\zeta\}$ *where* $\mathsf{d}'_1 > \cdots > \mathsf{d}'_\zeta$ *is their corresponding depth and* $\mathsf{rt}'_1, \ldots, \mathsf{rt}'_\zeta$ *is their corresponding roots. Set* $\mathsf{pp}_{n+1}, \mathsf{aux}_{n+1}$ *as*

$$\mathsf{aux}_{n+1} = (\mathcal{T}, (\mathsf{id}_1, \ldots, \mathsf{id}_n, \mathsf{id}_{n+1} = \mathsf{id})), \mathsf{pp}_{n+1} = (\mathsf{hk}, (\mathsf{rt}'_1, \mathsf{d}'_1), \ldots, (\mathsf{rt}'_\zeta, \mathsf{d}'_\zeta)).$$

- $\mathsf{Enc}(\mathsf{pp}, \mathsf{id}, \mathsf{m}) \to \mathsf{ct}$*:*
  1. *Parse* $\mathsf{pp} := (\mathsf{hk}, (\mathsf{rt}_1, \mathsf{d}_1), \ldots, (\mathsf{rt}_\eta, \mathsf{d}_\eta))$.
  2. *For each* $i \in \{1, \ldots \eta\}$ *and* $j \in \{1, \ldots, \mathsf{d}_i\}$*, sample* $\mathsf{stt}_{i,j} \leftarrow \{0,1\}^\kappa$ *and generate* $\widetilde{\mathrm{P}}_{i,j} \leftarrow \mathrm{HG}(\mathsf{hk}, \mathrm{P}_{i,j}, \mathsf{stt}_{i,j})$*, where* $\mathrm{P}_{i,j}$ *is explained below.*
  3. *For each* $i \in [\eta]$ *obtain* $\widetilde{y}_{i,1} \leftarrow \mathrm{HInp}(\mathsf{hk}, \mathsf{rt}_i, \mathsf{stt}_{i,1})$.
  4. *Output the ciphertext* $\mathsf{ct} = (\mathsf{pp}, \{\widetilde{\mathrm{P}}_{i,j}\}_{i,j}, \{\widetilde{y}_{i,1}\}_i)$.

  The program $\mathrm{P}_{i,j}$ *works as follows:*
  Hardwired values: $\mathsf{rt}_i, \mathsf{d}_i, \mathsf{hk}, \mathsf{m}, \mathsf{id}, \mathsf{r}, \mathsf{stt}_{i,j+1}$ *(where* $\mathsf{stt}_{i,\mathsf{d}_i+1} = \perp$*)*
  Input: $a||b||\mathsf{id}^*$
  1. *If* $\mathsf{id}^* = 0^\kappa$[9] *and* $a = \mathsf{id}$ *then output* $\mathrm{E}(b, \mathsf{m}; \mathsf{r})$.
  2. *If* $\mathsf{id}^* = 0^\kappa$ *and* $a \neq \mathsf{id}$ *then output* $\perp$.
  3. *If* $\mathsf{id} > \mathsf{id}^*$ *then output* $\mathrm{HInp}(\mathsf{hk}, b, \mathsf{stt}_{i,j+1})$*, else output* $\mathrm{HInp}(\mathsf{hk}, a, \mathsf{stt}_{i,j+1})$.
- $\mathsf{Upd}^{\mathsf{aux}}(\mathsf{pp}, \mathsf{id}) \to \mathsf{u}$*: If* id *is a leaf in a tree of* aux*, say* Tree*, return the* whole *Merkle opening* pth *of leaf* id *and its sibling* pk *to the root* $\mathsf{rt}(\mathsf{Tree})$*. Otherwise, return* $\perp$.
- $\mathsf{Dec}(\mathsf{sk}, \mathsf{u}, \mathsf{ct}) \to m$*: Parse* $\mathsf{ct} = (\mathsf{pp}, \{\widetilde{\mathrm{P}}_{i,j}\}_{i,j}, \{\widetilde{y}_{i,1}\}_i)$ *and* $\mathsf{u} := (z_1 \ldots z_{\mathsf{d}_{i^*}})$*. Let* i^* *be the index of the tree that holds the corresponding identity.*[10] *Decryption proceeds as follows:*
  1. *For* $j = \{1 \ldots \mathsf{d}_{i^*} - 1\}$ *do*
     - $\widetilde{y}_{i^*,j+1} = \widetilde{\mathrm{P}}_{i^*,j}(\widetilde{y}_{i^*,j}, z_j)$.
  2. *Let* $\mathsf{ct} := \widetilde{\mathrm{P}}_{i^*,\mathsf{d}_{i^*}}(\widetilde{y}_{i^*,\mathsf{d}_{i^*}}, z_{\mathsf{d}_{i^*}})$.
  3. *Output* $\mathrm{D}(\mathsf{sk}, \mathsf{ct})$.

Theorem 21. *The RBE of Construction 20 satisfies the compactness, completeness (Definition 6), and security (Definition 10) properties.*

In the rest of this section, we prove Theorem 21. The completeness and compactness properties are proved similar to those of Construction 12. We can again verify that over the course of the system's execution, the tree that holds a user id, will not be merged with other trees more than $\log n$ times. (Each merge increases the depth of the tree by one, and the depth cannot bypass $\log n$.) We may use this fact to conclude all the efficiency features for the constructed RBE scheme.

In the rest of this section, we focus on proving security.

5.1 Proof of Security

Similar to our presentation of the proof of Construction 12, here also we first start by giving the proof for the case in which only *one* user has registered. We will then present the general proof (Fig. 7).

[9] Without loss of generality we assume that no user is assigned the identity 0^κ.

[10] Alternatively, we may perform this with respect to all values of i^*, which is up to the number of trees in the system.

Hardwired: rt, hk, $\mathsf{m} \in \{0,1\}$, id′, r and stt
Input: (id, pk, id*)

1. If $\mathsf{id}^* \neq 0^\kappa$ or $\mathsf{id} \neq \mathsf{id}'$, then output $\perp$ and end.
2. Output $\mathrm{E}(\mathsf{pk}, \mathsf{m}; \mathsf{r})$ and end.

Fig. 7. Circuit P used for encryption of m to identity id′

Theorem 22 (Security). *For any identity* id′ *we have*

$$(\mathrm{HG}(\mathsf{hk}, \mathrm{P}_0, \mathsf{stt}), \mathrm{HInp}(\mathsf{hk}, \mathsf{rt}, \mathsf{stt})) \stackrel{c}{\approx} (\mathrm{HG}(\mathsf{hk}, \mathrm{P}_1, \mathsf{stt}), \mathrm{HInp}(\mathsf{hk}, \mathsf{rt}, \mathsf{stt})) \quad (12)$$

where $\mathsf{hk} \leftarrow \mathrm{HGen}(1^\kappa, 1^{3\kappa})$, $\mathsf{stt} \leftarrow \{0,1\}^\kappa$, $(\mathsf{pk}, \mathsf{sk}) \leftarrow \mathrm{G}(1^\kappa)$, $\mathsf{rt} := \mathrm{Hash}(\mathsf{hk}, (\mathsf{id}', \mathsf{pk}, 0^\kappa))$ *and for* $\mathsf{m} \in \{0,1\}$ *the circuit program* P_m *is defined as*

$$\mathrm{P}_\mathsf{m} := \mathrm{P}[\mathsf{rt}, \mathsf{hk}, \mathsf{m}, \mathsf{id}', \mathsf{r}, \mathsf{stt}]. \quad (13)$$

Proof. For $\mathsf{m} \in \{0,1\}$ let ct_m denote the challenge ciphertext, namely

$$\mathsf{ct}_\mathsf{m} := (\mathrm{HG}(\mathsf{hk}, \mathrm{P}_0, \mathsf{stt}), \mathrm{HInp}(\mathsf{hk}, \mathsf{rt}, \mathsf{stt}))\,, \quad (14)$$

where all the variables are sampled as in the theorem. We need to show $\mathsf{ct}_0 \stackrel{c}{\approx} \mathsf{ct}_1$. By simulation security of the hash garbling scheme, for both $\mathsf{m} \in \{0,1\}$ we have

$$\mathsf{ct}_\mathsf{m} \stackrel{c}{\approx} \mathsf{Sim}(\mathsf{hk}, (\mathsf{id}', \mathsf{pk}, 0^\kappa), 1^{|\mathrm{P}_\mathsf{m}|}, \mathrm{E}(\mathsf{pk}, \mathsf{m}; \mathsf{r})). \quad (15)$$

By semantic security of the underlying public-key encryption scheme we have

$$\mathsf{Sim}(\mathsf{hk}, (\mathsf{id}', \mathsf{pk}, 0^\kappa), 1^{|\mathrm{P}_0|}, \mathrm{E}(\mathsf{pk}, 0; \mathsf{r})) \stackrel{c}{\approx} \mathsf{Sim}(\mathsf{hk}, (\mathsf{id}', \mathsf{pk}, 0^\kappa), 1^{|\mathrm{P}_1|}, \mathrm{E}(\mathsf{pk}, 1; \mathsf{r})), \quad (16)$$

and so we obtain $\mathsf{ct}_0 \stackrel{c}{\approx} \mathsf{ct}_1$. □

Proof for the General Case. As in the proof in Sect. 4.2 we may assume that at the time of encryption we have only one tree. The proof for the case of multiple trees is the same.

Proof. Suppose at the time of encryption the underlying tree with root rt has depth d. In the sequel we shall write P_j for $j \in [\mathsf{d}]$ to refer to the circuit program $\mathrm{P}_{1,j}$ described in our RBE construction. That is,

$$\mathrm{P}_1 \equiv \mathrm{P}_{1,1}[\mathsf{rt}, \mathsf{d}, \mathsf{hk}, \mathsf{m}, \mathsf{id}, \mathsf{r}, \mathsf{stt}_{1,2}], \quad (17)$$

and for $j > 1$

$$\mathrm{P}_j \equiv \mathrm{P}_{1,j}[\mathsf{rt}, \mathsf{d}, \mathsf{hk}, \mathsf{m}, \mathsf{id}, \mathsf{r}, \mathsf{stt}_{1,j+1}], \quad (18)$$

where all the variables above are as in the encryption of the construction.

For $j \in [\mathsf{d}]$ we define rt_j to be the node in the jth level of the tree (where we consider the root as level one), whose sub-tree contains the leaf with label id.[11] For example, if the path leading to id is

$$[(\mathsf{id}, \mathsf{pk}, 0^\kappa), (a_1, b_1, \mathsf{id}_1, \mathsf{left}), \ldots, (a_{\mathsf{d}-1}, b_{\mathsf{d}-1}, \mathsf{id}_{\mathsf{d}-1}, \mathsf{right}), \mathsf{rt}],$$

then $\mathsf{rt}_3 = b_{\mathsf{d}-1}$. For $j > 1$ we define

$$\widetilde{y}_j := \mathrm{HInp}(\mathsf{hk}, \mathsf{rt}_j, \mathsf{stt}_{1,j}). \tag{19}$$

We also define X_j for $j \in [t+1]$ to be the concatenate result of the node values in level j of the path leading to id. For instance, in the example above we have $X_1 = (a_{\mathsf{d}-1}, b_{\mathsf{d}-1}, \mathsf{id}_{\mathsf{d}-1})$.

Let $\mathsf{stt}_i := \mathsf{stt}_{1,i}$. Recall that P_i has stt_{i+1} hardwired, which is the state used to hash-garble P_{i+1}. Via a sequence of hybrids, we show how to replace garbled versions of P_i's, starting with $i = 1$, so that in the ith hybrid the values of $\mathsf{stt}_1, \ldots, \mathsf{stt}_i$ are never used.

- **Hybrid** 0 **(true encryption)**: The ciphertext is $\mathsf{ct}_0 := (\widetilde{\mathrm{P}}_1, \widetilde{\mathrm{P}}_2, \ldots, \widetilde{\mathrm{P}}_{\mathsf{d}}, \widetilde{y}_1)$, where all of the values are sampled as in the construction.
- **Hybrid** 1: The ciphertext is $\mathsf{ct}_1 := (\widetilde{\mathrm{P}}_{1,\mathsf{sim}}, \widetilde{\mathrm{P}}_2, \ldots, \widetilde{\mathrm{P}}_{\mathsf{d}}, \widetilde{y}_{1,\mathsf{sim}})$, where $\widetilde{\mathrm{P}}_2, \ldots, \widetilde{\mathrm{P}}_{\mathsf{d}}$ are sampled as in the construction, and where $\widetilde{\mathrm{P}}_{1,\mathsf{sim}}$ and $\widetilde{y}_{1,\mathsf{sim}}$ are sampled as follows:

$$(\widetilde{\mathrm{P}}_{1,\mathsf{sim}}, \widetilde{y}_{1,\mathsf{sim}}) \leftarrow \mathsf{Sim}(\mathsf{hk}, X_1, 1^{|\mathrm{P}_1|}, \widetilde{y}_2). \tag{20}$$

- **Hybird** $i \in [\mathsf{d}-1]$:

$$\mathsf{ct}_i := (\widetilde{\mathrm{P}}_{1,\mathsf{sim}}, \ldots, \widetilde{\mathrm{P}}_{i,\mathsf{sim}}, \widetilde{\mathrm{P}}_{i+1}, \ldots, \widetilde{\mathrm{P}}_{\mathsf{d}}, \widetilde{y}_{1,\mathsf{sim}}),$$

  where for $j \in [i]$:

$$(\widetilde{\mathrm{P}}_{j,\mathsf{sim}}, \widetilde{y}_{j,\mathsf{sim}}) \leftarrow \mathsf{Sim}(\mathsf{hk}, X_{j+1}, 1^{|\mathrm{P}_j|}, \widetilde{y}_{j+1}) \tag{21}$$

- **Hybrid** d:

$$\mathsf{ct}_{\mathsf{d}} := (\widetilde{\mathrm{P}}_{1,\mathsf{sim}}, \ldots, \widetilde{\mathrm{P}}_{\mathsf{d},\mathsf{sim}}, \widetilde{y}_{1,\mathsf{sim}})),$$

  where for $j \in [\mathsf{d}-1]$:

$$(\widetilde{\mathrm{P}}_{j,\mathsf{sim}}, \widetilde{y}_{j,\mathsf{sim}}) \leftarrow \mathsf{Sim}(\mathsf{hk}, X_{j+1}, 1^{|\mathrm{P}_j|}, \widetilde{y}_{j+1}), \tag{22}$$

  and

$$(\widetilde{\mathrm{P}}_{\mathsf{d},\mathsf{sim}}, \widetilde{y}_{\mathsf{d},\mathsf{sim}}) \leftarrow \mathsf{Sim}(\mathsf{hk}, (\mathsf{id}, \mathsf{pk}, 0^\kappa), 1^{|\mathrm{P}_{\mathsf{d}}|}, \mathrm{E}(\mathsf{pk}, \mathsf{m}; r)). \tag{23}$$

Now exactly as in the proof of Theorem 22, using the simulation security of the underlying HO scheme, we can show the indistinguishability of each two adjacent hybrids. Moreover, in the last hybrid, again using simulation security and as in the proof of Theorem 22, we may switch the underlying bit value of m. The proof is now complete. □

[11] Recall that by Definition 10 the challenge identity id must have been registered before, and exactly once.

References

1. Al-Riyami, S.S., Paterson, K.G.: Certificateless public key cryptography. In: Laih, C.-S. (ed.) ASIACRYPT 2003. LNCS, vol. 2894, pp. 452–473. Springer, Heidelberg (2003). https://doi.org/10.1007/978-3-540-40061-5_29
2. Barak, B., et al.: On the (im)possibility of obfuscating programs. In: Kilian, J. (ed.) CRYPTO 2001. LNCS, vol. 2139, pp. 1–18. Springer, Heidelberg (2001). https://doi.org/10.1007/3-540-44647-8_1
3. Boneh, D., Franklin, M.: Identity-based encryption from the Weil pairing. In: Kilian, J. (ed.) CRYPTO 2001. LNCS, vol. 2139, pp. 213–229. Springer, Heidelberg (2001). https://doi.org/10.1007/3-540-44647-8_13
4. Brakerski, Z., Lombardi, A., Segev, G., Vaikuntanathan, V.: Anonymous IBE, leakage resilience and circular security from new assumptions. In: Nielsen, J.B., Rijmen, V. (eds.) EUROCRYPT 2018, Part I. LNCS, vol. 10820, pp. 535–564. Springer, Cham (2018). https://doi.org/10.1007/978-3-319-78381-9_20
5. Chen, L., Harrison, K., Soldera, D., Smart, N.P.: Applications of multiple trust authorities in pairing based cryptosystems. In: Davida, G., Frankel, Y., Rees, O. (eds.) InfraSec 2002. LNCS, vol. 2437, pp. 260–275. Springer, Heidelberg (2002). https://doi.org/10.1007/3-540-45831-X_18
6. Cheng, Z., Comley, R., Vasiu, L.: Remove key escrow from the identity-based encryption system. In: Levy, J.-J., Mayr, E.W., Mitchell, J.C. (eds.) TCS 2004. IIFIP, vol. 155, pp. 37–50. Springer, Boston, MA (2004). https://doi.org/10.1007/1-4020-8141-3_6
7. Cho, C., Döttling, N., Garg, S., Gupta, D., Miao, P., Polychroniadou, A.: Laconic oblivious transfer and its applications. In: Katz, J., Shacham, H. (eds.) CRYPTO 2017, Part II. LNCS, vol. 10402, pp. 33–65. Springer, Cham (2017). https://doi.org/10.1007/978-3-319-63715-0_2
8. Chow, S.S.M.: Removing escrow from identity-based encryption. In: Jarecki, S., Tsudik, G. (eds.) PKC 2009. LNCS, vol. 5443, pp. 256–276. Springer, Heidelberg (2009). https://doi.org/10.1007/978-3-642-00468-1_15
9. Cocks, C.: An identity based encryption scheme based on quadratic residues. In: Honary, B. (ed.) Cryptography and Coding 2001. LNCS, vol. 2260, pp. 360–363. Springer, Heidelberg (2001). https://doi.org/10.1007/3-540-45325-3_32
10. Diffie, W., Hellman, M.E.: New directions in cryptography. IEEE Trans. Inf. Theory **22**(6), 644–654 (1976)
11. Döttling, N., Garg, S.: Identity-based encryption from the Diffie-Hellman assumption. In: Katz, J., Shacham, H. (eds.) CRYPTO 2017, Part I. LNCS, vol. 10401, pp. 537–569. Springer, Cham (2017). https://doi.org/10.1007/978-3-319-63688-7_18
12. Döttling, N., Garg, S., Hajiabadi, M., Masny, D.: New constructions of identity-based and key-dependent message secure encryption schemes. In: Abdalla, M., Dahab, R. (eds.) PKC 2018, Part I. LNCS, vol. 10769, pp. 3–31. Springer, Cham (2018). https://doi.org/10.1007/978-3-319-76578-5_1
13. Garg, S., Gentry, C., Halevi, S., Raykova, M., Sahai, A., Waters, B.: Candidate indistinguishability obfuscation and functional encryption for all circuits. In: 54th Annual Symposium on Foundations of Computer Science, Berkeley, CA, USA, 26–29 October 2013, pp. 40–49. IEEE Computer Society Press (2013)
14. Garg, S., Gentry, C., Sahai, A., Waters, B.: Witness encryption and its applications. In: Boneh, D., Roughgarden, T., Feigenbaum, J. (eds.) 45th Annual ACM Symposium on Theory of Computing, Palo Alto, CA, USA, 1–4 June 2013, pp. 467–476. ACM Press (2013)

15. Goldwasser, S., Micali, S.: Probabilistic encryption and how to play mental poker keeping secret all partial information. In: 14th Annual ACM Symposium on Theory of Computing, San Francisco, CA, USA, 5–7 May 1982, pp. 365–377. ACM Press (1982)
16. Goyal, V.: Reducing trust in the PKG in identity based cryptosystems. In: Menezes, A. (ed.) CRYPTO 2007. LNCS, vol. 4622, pp. 430–447. Springer, Heidelberg (2007). https://doi.org/10.1007/978-3-540-74143-5_24
17. Goyal, V., Lu, S., Sahai, A., Waters, B.: Black-box accountable authority identity-based encryption. In: Proceedings of the 15th ACM Conference on Computer and Communications Security, pp. 427–436. ACM (2008)
18. Hubacek, P., Wichs, D.: On the communication complexity of secure function evaluation with long output. In: Roughgarden, T. (ed.) ITCS 2015: 6th Conference on Innovations in Theoretical Computer Science, Rehovot, Israel, 11–13 January 2015, pp. 163–172. Association for Computing Machinery (2015)
19. Kate, A., Goldberg, I.: Distributed private-key generators for identity-based cryptography. In: Garay, J.A., De Prisco, R. (eds.) SCN 2010. LNCS, vol. 6280, pp. 436–453. Springer, Heidelberg (2010). https://doi.org/10.1007/978-3-642-15317-4_27
20. Paterson, K.G., Srinivasan, S.: Security and anonymity of identity-based encryption with multiple trusted authorities. In: Galbraith, S.D., Paterson, K.G. (eds.) Pairing 2008. LNCS, vol. 5209, pp. 354–375. Springer, Heidelberg (2008). https://doi.org/10.1007/978-3-540-85538-5_23
21. Rivest, R.L., Shamir, A., Adleman, L.M.: A method for obtaining digital signature and public-key cryptosystems. Commun. Assoc. Comput. Mach. **21**(2), 120–126 (1978)
22. Rogaway, P.: The moral character of cryptographic work. Cryptology ePrint Archive, Report 2015/1162 (2015). http://eprint.iacr.org/2015/1162
23. Shamir, A.: Identity-based cryptosystems and signature schemes. In: Blakley, G.R., Chaum, D. (eds.) CRYPTO 1984. LNCS, vol. 196, pp. 47–53. Springer, Heidelberg (1985). https://doi.org/10.1007/3-540-39568-7_5
24. Wei, Q., Qi, F., Tang, Z.: Remove key escrow from the BF and Gentry identity-based encryption with non-interactive key generation. Telecommun. Syst. **69**, 1–10 (2018)

Author Index

Agrawal, Shashank I-659
Agrawal, Shweta II-473
Ananth, Prabhanjan II-455
Applebaum, Benny I-152, I-317
Arkis, Barak I-317

Badrinarayanan, Saikrishna I-629
Bartusek, James II-544
Benhamouda, Fabrice I-175
Bitansky, Nir I-209
Block, Alexander R. II-36
Boneh, Dan II-699
Brakerski, Zvika I-152, II-370

Campanelli, Matteo II-66
Canetti, Ran I-476
Cash, David II-159
Chan, T.-H. Hubert II-636
Chen, Yilei II-341
Chongchitmate, Wutichai I-370
Chung, Kai-Min I-563

Damgård, Ivan II-225
Döttling, Nico II-370
Dryja, Thaddeus I-33
Dupuis, Frédéric II-282

Fehr, Serge II-282, II-315

Garg, Sanjam I-123, I-689, II-425
Gennaro, Rosario II-66
Guan, Jiaxin II-544
Guo, Yue I-563
Gupta, Divya II-36

Haitner, Iftach I-539
Hajiabadi, Mohammad I-448, I-689
Halevi, Shai II-255
Hazay, Carmit I-263

Ishai, Yuval I-123, II-255, II-699

Jost, Daniel I-345
Jutla, Charanjit S. I-235

Kazana, Tomasz II-225
Khurana, Dakshita I-286, I-629
Kiyoshima, Susumu I-67
Koppula, Venkata I-659
Kushilevitz, Eyal II-255

Lamontagne, Philippe II-282
LaVigne, Rio II-3
Libert, Benoît II-391
Lichtenberg, Amit I-476
Lin, Huijia I-175, I-209
Lin, Wei-Kai I-563
Liu, Quanquan C. I-33
Liu, Tianren I-98
Liu-Zhang, Chen-Da II-3
Lombardi, Alex II-455

Ma, Fermi II-513, II-544
Mahmoody, Mohammad I-689
Maitra, Monosij II-473
Maji, Hemanta K. II-36
Makriyannis, Nikolaos I-539
Maurer, Ueli I-345, II-3
Mennink, Bart II-192
Moran, Tal II-3
Morgan, Andrew I-507, I-597
Mularczyk, Marta II-3

Naor, Moni II-575
Narayanan, Varun I-389
Nayak, Kartik II-636
Nguyen, Hai H. II-36

Obremski, Maciej II-225
Omri, Eran I-539
Ostrovsky, Rafail I-286, I-370

Park, Sunoo I-33
Pass, Rafael I-507, I-563, I-597
Passelègue, Alain II-699
Polychroniadou, Antigoni I-175
Prabahakaran, Vinod M. I-389

Quach, Willy II-669

Rabin, Tal II-255
Rahimi, Ahmadreza I-689
Raj, Varun II-225
Ribeiro, João L. I-345
Rosulek, Mike II-98
Rotem, Lior I-421, II-575
Roy, Arnab I-235

Sahai, Amit I-629, II-699
Salvail, Louis II-282
Segev, Gil I-421, II-177, II-575
Shahaf, Ido II-177
Shi, Elaine I-563, II-636
Shirley, Morgan II-98
Siniscalchi, Luisa II-225
Srinivasan, Akshayaram I-123, I-286, II-425
Stehlé, Damien II-391

Tessaro, Stefano I-3
Thiruvengadam, Aishwarya I-3
Titiu, Radu II-391
Tsabary, Rotem I-152
Tschudi, Daniel II-3

Vaikuntanathan, Vinod II-341
Venkitasubramaniam, Muthuramakrishnan I-175, I-263

Waters, Brent I-629, I-659, II-341
Wee, Hoeteck II-341
Weiss, Mor II-603
Wichs, Daniel II-341, II-603, II-669
Wu, David J. II-699

Zhandry, Mark II-129, II-513, II-544
Zhang, Cong II-129, II-159
Zirdelis, Giorgos II-669

Printed in the United States
By Bookmasters